KU-019-356

# Social Psychology Alive

Steven J. Breckler
*American Psychological Association*

James M. Olson
*University of Western Ontario*

Elizabeth C. Wiggins
*Federal Judicial Center*

DBS Library
13/14 Aungier Street
Dublin 2
Phone: 01-4177572

THOMSON
WADSWORTH

Australia • Brazil • Canada • Mexico • Singapore • Spain
United Kingdom • United States

## Social Psychology Alive

*Steven J. Breckler, James M. Olson, Elizabeth C. Wiggins*

*The views expressed here are those of the authors and not those of the
American Psychological Association or the Federal Judicial Center.*

Publisher: *Vicki Knight*
Psychology Editor: *Marianne Taflinger*
Development Editors: *Kirk Bomont, Kristin Makarewycz*
Assistant Editor: *Jennifer Wilkinson*
Editorial Assistant: *Lucy Faridany*
Technology Project Managers: *Darin Derstine, Becky Stovall*
Marketing Manager: *Chris Caldeira*
Marketing Assistant: *Nicole Morinon*
Marketing Communications Manager: *Laurel Anderson*
Project Manager, Editorial Production: *Paul Wells*
Creative Director: *Rob Hugel*
Art Director: *Vernon Boes*

Print Buyer: *Barbara Britton*
Permissions Editor: *Sarah Harkrader*
Production Service: *The Cooper Company*
Text Designer: *The Davis Group, Inc.*
Photo Researcher: *Sabina Dowell*
Copy Editor: *Peggy Tropp*
Indexer: *Kay Banning*
Cover Designer: *Irene Morris*
Cover Image: © *Reuters/CORBIS*
Cover Printer: *Coral Graphic Services*
Compositor: *Lachina Publishing Services*
Printer: *Courier Corporation/Kendallville*

© 2006 Thomson Wadsworth, a part of The Thomson Corporation.
Thomson, the Star logo, and Wadsworth are trademarks used herein under license.

ALL RIGHTS RESERVED. No part of this work covered by the copyright hereon may
be reproduced or used in any form or by any means—graphic, electronic, or mechanical,
including photocopying, recording, taping, web distribution, information storage and
retrieval systems, or in any other manner—without the written permission of the publisher.

Printed in the United States of America
3   4   5   6   7   09   08   07   06   05

For more information about our products, contact us at:
Thomson Learning Academic Resource Center
1-800-423-0563
For permission to use material from this text or product, submit a request online at http://www.thomsonrights.com.
Any additional questions about permissions can be submitted by e-mail to thomsonrights@thomson.com.

ExamView® and ExamView Pro® are registered trademarks of FSCreations, Inc. Windows is a
registered trademark of the Microsoft Corporation used herein under license. Macintosh and
Power Macintosh are registered trademarks of Apple Computer, Inc. Used herein under license.

© 2006 Thomson Learning, Inc. All Rights Reserved. Thomson Learning WebTutor™
is a trademark of Thomson Learning, Inc.

Thomson Higher Education
10 Davis Drive
Belmont, CA 94002-3098
USA

Library of Congress Control Number: 2005927655

Student Edition: ISBN 0-534-57834-9

**DBS Library**

79945

DBS Library
13/14 Aungier Street
Dublin 2
Phone: 01-4177572

This book is due for return on or before the last date shown below.

For Ben
(SB, EW)

For Mary, Rebecca, and Sara
(JO)

# About the Authors

**Steven Breckler** was an undergraduate at UC San Diego, and completed his Ph.D. work at the Ohio State University. Following a post-doctoral year at Northwestern University, he joined the faculty of Johns Hopkins University, where he taught social psychology. In 1994, the students at Johns Hopkins selected Steve as Outstanding Teacher of the Year. Recipient of the prestigious Presidential Young Investigator Award from the National Science Foundation (NSF), Steve's research focuses primarily on the structure and function of social attitudes. In 1995, Steve was appointed Program Director for Social Psychology at NSF, where he then spent nine years helping to shape the future of social psychology through the management of a multimillion dollar funding program. In 2004, Steve was made Executive Director for Science at the American Psychological Association, where he manages the science-related programs for the world's largest professional association of psychologists. In 2003, the Society for Personality and Social Psychology honored Steve for his contributions to social psychology by giving him the Service Award on Behalf of the Discipline. In the same year, the American Psychological Association recognized Steve with a Meritorious Research Service Commendation, for his work on behalf of the entire discipline of psychology.

*Steven J. Breckler*

**James Olson** completed his undergraduate degree at Carleton University in Ottawa, Canada, and obtained his Ph.D. at the University of Waterloo. He was hired as an Assistant Professor at the University of Western Ontario in London, Canada, in 1978, where he has remained except for a year as a Visiting Professor at the University of California at Santa Barbara. Jim was promoted to Full Professor in 1990 and served as Chair of the Psychology Department from 1998 to 2003. He teaches social psychology and has twice been named Professor of the Year by the Undergraduate Psychology Club at Western Ontario. Jim has conducted research on many topics, including attitudes, social cognition, justice, and humor. He has published more than 100 articles and chapters and has edited 10 books. He is a co-organizer of the Ontario Symposium on Personality and Social Psychology, a well-known series of conferences on various topics in personality and social psychology. Jim has served as an Associate Editor of three scientific journals, including the Journal of Personality and Social Psychology (Attitudes and Social Cognition Section) from 1995 to 1998. He is a Fellow of the Canadian Psychological Association, the American Psychological Association, and the Society for Personality and Social Psychology.

*James M. Olson*

**Elizabeth Wiggins** was an undergraduate at the University of North Carolina at Chapel Hill, and received her Ph.D. from the Johns Hopkins University and her J.D. from the University of Maryland. Following a post-doctoral year at the Ohio State University, she joined the faculty at Barnard College of Columbia University, where she taught psychology and law and other courses. In 1989, Beth joined the research staff at the Federal Judicial Center and continues her career there today. The Center undertakes empirical research related to judicial processes and develops and administers educational programs for judges and other court personnel. Center projects often have policy significance and involve complex and innovative research methods, for which her social and quantitative psychology have proved invaluable. In 1998, the Judge John R. Brown Scholarship Foundation recognized her contributions to the judicial system with its Brown Award for Judicial Scholarship and Education. Beth is active in the American Psychology-Law Society, and has been a member of its Executive Committee. She recently served on a five-member international team under the auspices of the United Nations, U.S. Department of Justice, and the Council of Europe to make recommendations for restructuring the judicial and prosecutorial systems of Kosovo. Beth pursues filmmaking as a hobby, and recently co-wrote and produced the psychologically based documentary *The Building of a Sanctuary,* which was awarded a CINE Golden Eagle Award.

*Elizabeth C. Wiggins*

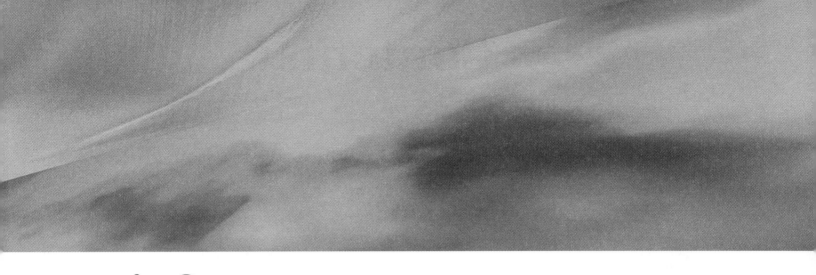

# Brief Contents

# Contents

# Social Cognition: Thinking About People

**Chapter 3**

65

# Social Perception: Perceiving the Self and Others

**Chapter 4**

111

# The Person in the Situation: Self-Concept, Gender, and Dispositions

**Chapter 5**

161

# Attitudes and Social Behavior

**Chapter 6**

197

# Attitude Change

# Conformity, Compliance, and Obedience

# Stereotypes, Prejudice, and Discrimination

## Chapter 9

343

# Group Dynamics and Intergroup Conflict

## Chapter 10

391

# Aggression and Violence

# Helpful Social Behavior

# Liking, Loving, and Close Relationships

## Chapter 13

523

# Social Psychology in Your Life

## Chapter 14

565

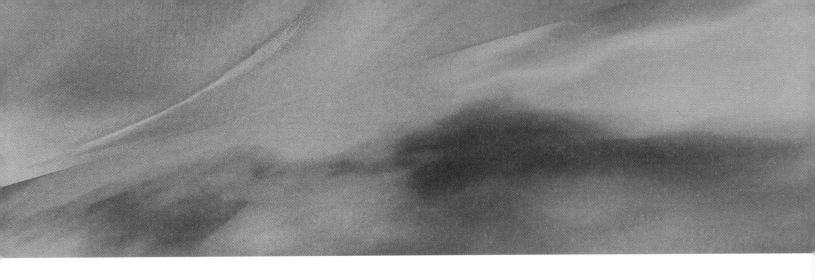

# Preface

Social psychology is a vibrant, living discipline. It addresses crucially important issues. It contains exciting, interesting studies and has ambitious, eloquent theories. It is relevant to everyday life and can help people understand themselves better. Social psychologists know that social psychology is great fun to do. We think that social psychology should also be great fun to study.

Our goal in this textbook and its supporting components is to bring social psychology *alive* for students. We want to communicate to students the enthusiasm that their professors have for the field. We want to get students excited about social psychology—to be fascinated by its experiments, to appreciate its relevance to everyday life, and to recognize that the field addresses questions we must answer to solve pressing social problems. From the inception of the *Social Psychology Alive* project, we developed the textbook, workbook, online labs, and videos in concert so that each component would work seamlessly with the other components to help students recognize social psychological phenomena in the world around them.

We believe that instructors face two key challenges in teaching social psychology. One challenge is that students resist seeing themselves as subject to the forces identified in social psychological research, perhaps especially to the power of the situation. They can understand the concepts and appreciate the cleverness of the research, but they do not really believe that they themselves would exhibit the predicted responses. A second challenge is that students often think that the findings of social psychology are obvious—the results simply confirm common sense and could have been predicted in advance. Students may recognize that the topics of research are important, but they view many results as unsurprising.

The *Social Psychology Alive* package helps instructors correct these erroneous beliefs by having students experience social psychology for themselves. The book, workbook, videos, and online labs were designed to involve the students as researchers, as participants, and as critical observers of social psychology in everyday life. For example, the workbook describes simple projects that students can do to illustrate social psychological processes (e.g., the correspondence bias, attitude change); these projects give students a sense of what it means to collect data. Social PsychologyNow is a web-based diagnostic study system that gauges each student's unique study needs and provides a personalized study plan. The online labs, integrated into Social PsychologyNow, allow students to participate in more than a dozen studies on social psychological topics (e.g., priming effects, dissonance, stereotypes); students' data are stored, enabling them to see for themselves that they responded in predicted ways. The Instructor Video (VHS or DVD) and Student CD-ROM show social psychology videos for each chapter that illustrate principles from the book in real-life settings (e.g., job interviews, video dating services); these clips show students that the findings apply to their own lives. The textbook has boxes in every chapter, labeled "Social Psychology in Your Life," describing settings and events that illustrate important findings (e.g., road rage, the shooting of Amadou Diallo), as well as a unique final chapter, also titled "Social Psychology in Your Life," that summarizes the many ways in which the field can be applied to students' lives and careers. We confront the belief that findings in social psychology are obvious in several ways. For instance, in the book, we ask students to try to predict the outcome of studies in advance. Also, when possible, we articulate competing hypotheses for an experiment. We often ask students to imagine themselves in a condition of the study and think about how they would respond. Students are also encouraged in the book and workbook to think about how contrasting principles might be applied to real-life settings, an exercise that underscores the uncertainty of social behavior.

Thus, the various elements of the *Social Psychology Alive* package get students personally involved in social psychology. Students learn that they are affected by social psychological processes and that the field has generated interesting and surprising findings. The materials demonstrate the relevance of social psychology to students' everyday lives, while providing a broad and accessible coverage of research and theory. In the following paragraphs, we identify some of the key features of the textbook and supplementary materials. We then describe the full package of ancillary materials. Taken together, the textbook and supplementary materials provide a comprehensive and absorbing introduction to social psychology.

## Relevance to Everyday Life

For social psychology to come alive, students must appreciate the relevance of social psychological knowledge to everyday life. We work toward this goal in the textbook and supplementary materials in several ways.

- **Chapter Openings**   We begin every textbook chapter by describing an event that is relevant to the topic of the chapter. We then refer back to this event at appropriate points in the chapter to provide a coherent framework for understanding the material. These events supplement our other everyday examples throughout the chapter to underscore the relevance of social psychology to real-life behavior. Most of the events used to open chapters are real, such as the events of September 11, 2001, and the tragic ending of Jim Jones's Peoples Temple; a few chapters open with hypothetical events that students are asked to imagine themselves in, such as life without advertisements and being the recipient of a substantial, unrequested favor (based on Catherine Ryan Hyde's book *Pay It Forward,* 1999).

- **Application Boxes**   A special feature in every chapter of the textbook is the series of boxes labeled "Social Psychology in Your Life." These boxes describe settings or events that illustrate important findings. Examples of topics described in these boxes include recovered memories, the false hope syndrome, advertising, corporal punishment, and jury decisions.

- **Real-Life Examples**   Throughout the text, we provide dozens of real-life examples of social psychological phenomena, both historical events (e.g., the *Columbia* disaster, the end of the Cold War, the torturing of Iraqi prisoners in Abu Ghraib prison, wrongful convictions, cults, genocide in Darfur and elsewhere) and common, everyday experiences (e.g., effects of television, friendships, comparing ourselves to others, salespersons, blood donations, the "hot hand" in sports, making attributions, priming effects, "what if" thinking after traumatic events). A continuing theme in every chapter is how theories and principles can be applied to students' own lives. The practical value of social psychological theories is emphasized.

- **Imagine Yourself**   In the textbook and supplementary materials, we often ask students to imagine how they would behave in particular situations—a strategy designed to make specific principles more personally relevant for students. We try to involve students directly in the material. Situations that students are asked to imagine are very numerous and include ones related to autobiographical memory, peer ridicule, obedience to authority, blind dates, hypocritical behavior, stereotypes, and helping behavior.

- **Cross-Cutting Contexts** Rather than having separate, individual chapters on "applied" topics such as health or law, we refer throughout the book to three cross-cutting contexts: culture, health, and law. Wherever it is appropriate, research findings are applied to these contexts, and implications for society are considered. Here are just a few examples of topics: cultural differences in identity; the strength of the correspondence bias in different cultures; attitudes research applied to HIV prevention; optimism and health; social cognition research applied to eyewitness testimony; and group polarization in juries.

- **Diversity** Instead of a separate chapter on gender, we address gender issues in every chapter. We discuss both gender differences and similarities, and present various theoretical perspectives on these findings. This integration of gender into the textbook parallels our treatment of culture. Other diversity considerations include a detailed discussion of the target's perspective in coverage of discrimination, consideration of same-sex relationships in coverage of liking and loving, and frequent discussion of the experiences of members of minority groups.

- **Applications Chapter** A unique final chapter titled "Social Psychology in Your Life" summarizes some of the many applications of social psychology to students' lives. The chapter puts the material presented in the book in the context of the students' lives, noting the discrepancy between what we know and how we sometimes behave. Finally, the chapter outlines some of the career opportunities in social psychology, explaining how social psychological knowledge can be helpful in many kinds of jobs such as business, law, government, teaching, and health, among others. The chapter concludes with a discussion of the future of social psychology, including social neuroscience, nanotechnology, and the Internet.

- **Student Workbook** A student workbook complements the relevance theme of the text by providing activities that apply the basic principles to students' lives. For instance, the workbook describes numerous simple projects that students can do to demonstrate social psychological processes. Other workbook features include Critical Thinking About Social Psychology, which reproduces newspaper and magazine articles that illustrate social psychological principles, and instructions for maintaining a *Social Psychology Alive* Journal, in which students record personal experiences related to material in the course.

## Comprehensive, Accessible Descriptions of Research

For social psychology to come alive, students must understand how theories and research develop and evolve. The *Social Psychology Alive* package is designed to provide a thorough coverage of the literature in an accessible writing style. We want students to get a clear sense of the procedures and results of individual studies and to appreciate that knowledge advances in an incremental fashion. Several features of our research coverage help to achieve this goal.

- **Mix of Research** A mix of classic and contemporary studies is presented. We provide comprehensive, up-to-date coverage of social psychology by including many contributions from the last decade, but early and influential studies are also described to provide a framework for understanding recent research. To take just one example, the coverage of cognitive dissonance theory begins with a description of Festinger and Carlsmith's (1959) famous $1/$20 experiment, and closes with descriptions of studies investigating cultural differences in how dissonance is aroused (Hoshino-Browne et al., 2002) and whether dissonance theory applies to implicit attitudes (Gawronski & Strack, 2004).

- **Accessible Writing**  Our descriptions of theories and studies are presented in a conversational writing style. Studies are described in enough detail that students get a clear idea of how participants in the research felt and how the procedures created the intended psychological conditions. Extensive use of graphs and figures makes findings easier to understand. By drawing connections between theories, experimental manipulations, and real-world variables, we help students relate social psychology to nonlaboratory settings.

- **Person in the Situation**  A distinctive chapter titled "The Person in the Situation" reviews personal characteristics that are important for understanding social behavior. The chapter begins with the *self,* describing research on self-concept, identity, and self-esteem. Gender is then discussed as a social psychological construct. Finally, a number of personality dispositions that have frequently been included in social psychological research are described, including self-monitoring, need for cognition, and dispositional optimism.

- **Know Yourself**  Throughout the textbook, features labeled "Know Yourself" provide full or condensed versions of individual differences scales for students to complete. The items, response scales, and scoring instructions are provided. The dimensions presented include self-monitoring, self-esteem, social comparison orientation, need for cognition, preference for consistency, and others. Students learn about themselves while also getting a clearer idea of what each dimension represents.

- **Online Labs**  Students have access to an online laboratory that allows them to participate in more than a dozen studies. These online experiments give students personal experience in social psychological research while expanding their knowledge of the topics addressed by the studies. Topics of the experiments include the universality of emotional expressions, evaluative conditioning as a source of attitudes, the effects of stereotypes on social perception, and cooperation/competition.

## An Engaging, Multimedia Package of Ancillary Materials

Our supplementary materials are the best and broadest in the field. These components have been developed simultaneously to create a coherent and comprehensive package. They use various media to capture students' interest and to allow them to experience social psychology themselves. We list students' ancillaries first and then instructors' ancillaries.

### Students' Ancillaries

- **Student Workbook**  Written by Elizabeth C. Wiggins and Meghan Dunn, the workbook developed for this text is unique. In addition to being a study guide, it includes exercises that students can complete to learn more about social psychological principles and their application to everyday life and world events. The exercises include simple experiments and demonstrations (Try It Yourself), readings and analytical questions about social psychology as it relates to world events (Thinking Critically About Social Psychology), instructions to students for observing social psychology in their daily lives and the world around them (*Social Psychology Alive* Journal), and Internet-based activities (On the Web). Each workbook chapter includes an introduction to the Social Psychology Labs for the corresponding textbook chapter, and concludes with questions to guide the students' study of the text (Learning Objectives) and a test (Test Yourself) comprised of multiple-choice, sentence-completion, and matching questions. Grading rubrics for the more involved activities will be available on the instructor's companion website.

  ISBN: 0-534-57835-7

- **Student Online Labs**  Developed by Stephanie Goodwin, Greg Francis, and Ian Neath of Purdue University, this unique online laboratory component gives students firsthand experience in actual social psychological experiments. Students can participate in more than a dozen studies on a variety of topics, including priming effects, mere exposure, postdecisional dissonance, and interpersonal attraction. Students are randomly assigned to participate in one condition of a study, which usually takes 10–15 minutes. They can also run through other conditions if they wish to understand the nature of the manipulations. Students' responses are saved (from their first condition only), and they can view their own responses or a summary of all responses from their class or from all classes. Full explanations and expected findings are given for each study. Students will watch as research results are compiled at the online laboratory site, and they will see how data are summarized to test hypotheses. The online laboratory will give students a sense of personal involvement in social psychology. The labs are integrated into Social PsychologyNow so it's easy for students to access them.

Online Purchase ISBN: 0-495-12955-0

Standalone ISBN: 0-495-12956-9

- **Social PsychologyNow™**  With pre- and posttests written by John Bickford of the University of Massachusetts–Amherst, this personalized study system is designed to give students maximum benefit for their study time. Social PsychologyNow helps them succeed by focusing their efforts on the concepts they're having the most difficulty mastering. It also includes an Instructor Grade Book, which assists instructors in tracking grades and monitoring student progress. Student grades can also be exported from Social PsychologyNow to a WebCT or Blackboard grade book. Whether or not instructors choose to use the grade book, students can benefit from the intelligent study system without any instructor setup or involvement.

Online Purchase ISBN: 0-495-03169-0

Standalone ISBN: 0-495-09311-4

- **WebTutor Advantage™ on WebCT® and Blackboard®**  Ready to use as soon as you log in to http://webtutor.thomsonlearning.com, WebTutor Advantage is a complete course management system and communication tool! WebTutor is preloaded with text-specific content (including practice quizzes and more) organized by chapter for convenient access. Customize this content in any way you choose—from uploading images and text to adding web links and your own practice materials. Then, manage your course by conducting virtual office hours, posting syllabi and other course materials, setting up threaded discussions, tracking student progress with quizzing material, and much more. Robust communication tools—such as a course calendar, asynchronous discussion, real-time chat, a whiteboard, and an integrated e-mail system—make it easy for you to connect with your students, and for your students to stay connected with their course.

WebTutor Advantage on WebCT ISBN: 0-534-63464-8

WebTutor Advantage on Blackboard ISBN: 0-534-63463-X

Also available with *Social Psychology Alive* in e-Book format

WebTutor Advantage Plus on WebCT ISBN: 0-495-00303-4

WebTutor Advantage Plus on Blackboard ISBN: 0-495-00304-2

- **Student CD-ROM** Developed by John Bickford of the University of Massachusetts–Amherst, a Student CD-ROM accompanies the textbook for those instructors who choose it. The CD includes videos from classic studies such as Milgram's obedience research and Bandura's bobo-doll studies. Other video segments show real-life settings that illustrate social psychological principles, such as military boot camp, job interviews, public service announcements, and video dating services. In addition, the videos present conversations with well-known researchers, including Craig Anderson, Mahzarin Banaji, Elizabeth Loftus, Claude Steele, Greg Herek, and Greg Mendoza-Denton. Each video segment on the student CD has associated multiple-choice questions and critical thinking questions for the student to answer, and the results can be e-mailed to the instructor, making it easy to assign.

ISBN: 0-534-57836-5

- **Book Companion Website**  Students will have access to a website (http://psychology .wadsworth.com/breckler1e/) that provides several additional resources. Online quizzes and flash cards will allow students to test their knowledge of textbook material (especially when combined with the guided study questions and sample test items presented in the workbook). Internet links to sites that are relevant to topics in the textbook will also be provided.

- **InfoTrac® College Edition**  For instructors who choose it, students will have access to a unique resource: Wadsworth's InfoTrac College Edition website. This website provides students with access to a variety of scholarly journals. Students enter keywords to a search engine and receive a list of relevant articles. This resource encourages students to look beyond the textbook for information and can assist them in preparing written assignments in the course.

## Instructors' Ancillaries

- **Multimedia Manager Instructor's Resource CD-ROM**  Written by Alan Swinkels, St. Edward's University, the *Instructor's Resource CD-ROM* provides a range of materials to assist instructors in the classroom. PowerPoint® summaries of principal ideas in each chapter are provided for use in lectures. PowerPoint reproductions of most figures in the textbook are also provided. The CD-ROM also includes a few sample video clips as well as a complete listing of available videos. The Multimedia Manager IRCD also contains the electronic Word files of the *Instructor's Resource Manual* and *Test Bank*.

  ISBN: 0-534-63467-2

- **Instructor's Manual**  Written by Gail Knapp, Mott Community College, the *Instructor's Resource Manual* offers a variety of information to assist lecture preparation and classroom participation. It provides detailed teaching plans for every chapter, lists ideas for classroom activities, outlines possible assignments for students, and provides information about additional resources for lecture preparation.

  ISBN: 0-534-63465-6

- **Test Bank**  Written by Eric Vanman, Georgia State University, a comprehensive *Test Bank* provides 150 multiple-choice questions for every chapter, with textbook page references for each item. Some items are also provided to test information presented in the workbook, if instructors want to require workbook activities. In addition, 10 fill-in-the-blank, 20 true/false, and 10 essay questions are presented, again with textbook page references.

  Print Test Bank ISBN: 0-534-63466-4
  Exam View ISBN: 0-534-64139-3

- **Instructor Video**  Consultant: John Bickford. This video contains all of the video that is featured on Social PsychologyNow and the Student CD-ROM. It is available in VHS or DVD format for easy in-class viewing.

  VHS ISBN: 0-495-03110-0
  DVD ISBN: 0-495-03111-9

- **JoinIn™ on TurningPoint®**  Written by John Bickford of the University of Massachusetts–Amherst, this is the easiest way to turn your lecture hall into a personal, fully interactive experience for your students. If you can use Microsoft PowerPoint®, you can use JoinIn on TurningPoint. Ask any question, collect students' responses, and immediately display the results in your PowerPoint presentation—all without switching between programs. The prebuilt content includes polls for each chapter, multiple-choice questions for each chapter, multiple-choice questions for each video in the video package, and multiple-choice questions for each lab in the online Social Psychology Labs.

  ISBN: 0-495-12957-X

# Distinctive Content

Our textbook provides comprehensive coverage of the basic content of social psychology, organized according to the major research areas in the field. The structure and order of the chapter topics are relatively traditional for an introductory social psychology textbook, although at least two chapters are unusual (The Person in the Situation, Social Psychology in Your Life). Every chapter, however, has some content that is distinctive from most textbooks in the field. We summarize some of the distinctive content in each chapter in the following paragraphs.

## Chapter 1: Introducing Social Psychology

- We describe the hindsight bias in the context of discussing the fact that social psychological findings sometimes seem to be "obvious," and offer suggestions to students about how to avoid this bias when studying social psychology.
- We compare and contrast social psychology with other disciplines (e.g., sociology, anthropology) and other areas in psychology (e.g., personality psychology, cognitive psychology).
- We provide a brief history of social psychology, including its roots in philosophy.

## Chapter 2: The Methods of Social Psychology

- In our coverage of experimental methods, we use the question "Does contact with members of a group cause more favorable attitudes toward that group?" as a recurring example when discussing many concepts, including independent variables, dependent variables, extraneous variables, random assignment, and factorial designs.
- We present a thorough discussion of ethical issues in social psychology, including deception, informed consent, debriefing, and Institutional Review Boards.
- We discuss the implications of the Internet for social psychology, as well as how technology can be made to work for social psychology.

## Chapter 3: Social Cognition

- We outline the workings of human memory as a background to social cognition, including the concepts of schemas, associative networks, automatic and controlled processes, and accessibility.
- We include a section on counterfactual thinking, describing its causes and consequences.
- We include a section on reconstructive memory, which outlines social psychological research on this topic and discusses related social issues including the validity of recovered memories of abuse and the accuracy of eyewitness testimony.

## Chapter 4: Social Perception

- We discuss developmental changes in social perception, including age-related shifts in nonverbal behavior and social comparison.
- A recurrent question we ask is whether perceptual biases identified by social psychologists, including positive self-evaluations, optimism, and perceived control, reflect adaptive or maladaptive processes; in this context, we discuss both learned helplessness and the false hope syndrome.
- In Know Yourself features, students learn about individual differences in (and their own standing on) social comparison orientation, self-handicapping, and optimism.

## Chapter 5: The Person in the Situation

- This entire chapter is distinctive; we focus on personal characteristics that have been shown to influence social behavior, including the self-concept, gender, and dispositions.

- We include a comprehensive section on identity and self-esteem, including the importance of social identity, cultural differences in self-concepts, and secure versus defensive self-esteem.
- In Know Yourself features, students learn about individual differences in (and their own standing on) self-esteem, self-monitoring, need for cognition, and dispositional optimism.

### Chapter 6: Attitudes and Social Behavior

- We discuss the measurement of attitudes, including the challenge of assessing implicit attitudes.
- We include a biological perspective on attitudes, including the effects of drugs and the role of genetic factors.
- We discuss developmental changes in attitudes, including the topic of socialization and the issue of whether people become more conservative as they grow older.

### Chapter 7: Attitude Change

- We provide a detailed consideration of propaganda, including wartime propaganda, manipulative techniques used by cults, and examples of propaganda in everyday life.
- We discuss cultural factors in attitude change, including cultural differences in dissonance arousal and in responses to persuasive messages.
- In a Know Yourself feature, students learn about individual differences in (and their own standing on) preference for consistency.

### Chapter 8: Conformity, Compliance, and Obedience

- We discuss the conformity pressure exerted on young adults to use tobacco, alcohol, and illegal drugs; we also describe prevention programs designed to teach social skills to resist this pressure.
- We discuss cultural factors in conformity and provide a Know Yourself feature that introduces students to individual differences in (and their own standing on) independent and interdependent self-construal.
- We present terror management theory as one explanation of some instances of conformity.

### Chapter 9: Stereotypes, Prejudice, and Discrimination

- We present integrated threat theory as a comprehensive model of prejudice.
- We include a detailed discussion of gender stereotypes and sexism, including Know Yourself features that introduce students to individual differences in (and their own standing on) old-fashioned versus modern sexism and ambivalent sexism.
- We discuss the topic of genocide, including conditions that may precipitate this form of mass murder.

### Chapter 10: Group Dynamics and Intergroup Conflict

- We cover the topic of leadership in detail, including how leaders emerge, the trait approach to leadership, and contingency models of leadership effectiveness.
- We discuss intergroup conflict, including conflict escalation and reduction and terrorism as a form of intergroup threat.
- We present contrasting theoretical explanations of the effects of deindividuation.

### Chapter 11: Aggression and Violence

- We use the general aggression model (GAM) as a unifying framework for the chapter.
- We present a thorough discussion of the effects of the media on aggression, including recent data on the effects of television violence, the impact of violent video games, and the effects of pornography—drawing a distinction between erotica and violent pornography.

- We discuss domestic violence, including characteristics of batterers and the effects on children of witnessing domestic violence.

### Chapter 12: Helpful Social Behavior
- We discuss whether there is an "altruistic personality" and provide a Know Yourself feature that introduces students to individual differences in (and their own standing on) interpersonal reactivity (empathy).
- We discuss cultural factors in helpful social behavior.
- We present detailed coverage of social support, including recipients' reactions to being helped, the nature of social support networks, and the relation between social support and health.

### Chapter 13: Liking, Loving, and Close Relationships
- We include an evolutionary perspective on interpersonal attraction and relationships.
- We provide a detailed discussion of attachment, including attachment theory, infant attachment, and adult attachment.
- We discuss same-sex attraction and relationships.

### Chapter 14: Social Psychology in Your Life
- This entire chapter is distinctive; we discuss the many implications of social psychology for understanding one's life.
- We discuss career opportunities in social psychology, as well as the applicability of social psychological knowledge to many occupations.
- We describe some emerging new frontiers for social psychology.

We are excited about *Social Psychology Alive.* The diverse, multimedia elements of the package give students a unique introduction to social psychology by involving them directly in the learning process. The textbook emphasizes the relevance of the discipline, the workbook complements the text with custom-made, hands-on activities, Social Psychology Online Labs give students the experience of participating as subjects in experiments (as accessed through Social PsychologyNow), and the Instructor Video was built to give you the video that you want to show and discuss in class. (The same clips are featured on Social PsychologyNow and the Student CD-ROM.) These various components combine to form an engrossing presentation of a vigorous field.

We invite feedback from students and instructors. We are eager to hear about users' experiences with all elements of the package. We have greatly enjoyed the challenge of preparing these materials and hope that you will be caught up in the fascinating science of social psychology.

# Acknowledgments

The creation of a social psychology textbook with a full range of supplementary materials is a team effort. We are extremely fortunate to have had very talented people working with us on this project. Let us acknowledge the contributions of these individuals.

John Bickford of the University of Massachusetts–Amherst played a key role in the development of the Student CD-ROM; he also created the Social PsychologyNow quizzes and the teaching tool JoinIn on TurningPoint. Stephanie Goodwin, Greg Francis, and Ian Neath, all of Purdue University, set up the online experiments in Social Psychology Labs. Gail Knapp of Mott Community College authored the *Instructor's Resource Manual.* Alan Swinkels of St. Edward's University developed the *Instructor's Resource CD-ROM.* Eric Vanman of Georgia State University wrote the *Test Bank.* Meghan Dunn of the Federal Judicial Center helped to create the *Student Workbook.*

We also thank the illustrious researchers who agreed to be interviewed for the Student CD-ROM and Instructor Video: Craig Anderson, Iowa State University; Mahzarin

Banaji, Harvard University; Sheldon Cohen, Carnegie-Mellon University; Vicki Helgeson, Carnegie-Mellon University; Greg Herek, University of California at Davis; Elizabeth Loftus, University of California at Irvine; Rodolfo Mendoza-Denton, University of California at Berkeley; Claude Steele, Stanford University; and Jeanne Tsai, Stanford University. We also want to express our appreciation to Alexandra Milgram, who graciously allowed footage of the famous studies by Stanley Milgram to be included in the video.

We are grateful to all of those who provided thoughtful reviews of the manuscript and made numerous helpful suggestions: Carolyn Adams-Price, Mississippi State University; Chris Anderson, Temple University; Nancy Ashton, Richard Stockton College; Melissa Atkins, Ohio University; Kathryn L. Baughman, George Mason University; Gordon Bear, Ramapo College; Justin Buckingham, Towson University; Mark Covey, Concordia College; Gloria Cowan, California State University, Santa Barbara; Dana S. Dunn, Moravian College; Anne Duran, California State University, Bakersfield; Steve Ellyson, Youngstown State University; Marcia Finkelstein, University of South Florida; Randy Fisher, University of Central Florida; Robin Franck, Southwestern College; R. L. Garner, Sam Houston State University; Stella Gracia-Lopez, University of Texas, San Antonio; Wayne Harrison, University of Nebraska at Omaha; Karen Huxtable-Jester, University of Texas at Dallas; Heide Island, University of Central Arkansas; Warren Jones, University of Tennessee; J. Andy Karafa, Ferris State University; Nancy Karlin, University of Northern Colorado; Tim Ketelaar, New Mexico State University; Mary Kite, Ball State University; Robin Kowalski, Clemson University; Neil Kressel, William Paterson University; Doug Krull, Northern Kentucky University; Alan Lambert, Washington University; Christopher Leone, University of North Florida; Helen Linkey, Marshall University; Stephan Mayer, Oberlin College; James McNulty, Ohio State University; Kristin Mickelson, Kent State University; Jeffrey Mio, California State University, Pomona; Matt Newman, University of Texas at Austin; Carol Oyster, University of Wisconsin, La Crosse; Jacqueline Pope-Tarrence, Western Kentucky University; Neal Roese, University of Illinois, Champaign; Brian Shrader, Emporia State University; George Schreer, Manhattanville College; Paul Silvia, University of North Carolina at Greensboro; Sam Sommers, Tufts University; Matthew Sorley, Carleton University; Jeff Stone, University of Arizona; Karen Tinsley, Guilford College; Brian Tschanz, Utah State University; Luis Vega, California State University, Bakersfield; Wayne Weiten, University of Nevada, Las Vegas; Teresa Wilcox, Texas A&M University; Bozena Zdaniuk, University of Pittsburgh.

We also appreciate the time people took to respond to a survey we sent out asking for feedback about what video content should be included in the Instructor's Video/DVD that also appears in Social PsychologyNow and the Student CD-ROM: Jeffrey Adams, Saint Michael's College; Sharon Akimoto, Carleton College; Rhianon Allen, Long Island University; Barbara Angleberger, Frederick Community College; Matthew Ansfield, Lawrence University; Jamie Arndt, University of Missouri; William Ashton, York College, CUNY; Melissa Atkins, Ohio University; Melissa Atkinson, Surry Community College; Kerri Augusto, Becker College; Brian Barry, Rochester Institute of Technology; Karen Baum, Mira Costa College; Elizabeth Bennett, Washington and Jefferson College; Michael Berg, Wheaton College; John Bickford, University of Massachusetts; Chadwick Blackwell, Mary Baldwin College; Jeffrey Blum, Los Angeles City College; Kurt Boniecki, University of Central Arkansas; Lisa Bowleg, University of Rhode Island; Steve Bradshaw, Bryan College; Linda Breytspraak, University of Missouri-Kansas City; Lisa Brown, University of Florida; Laura Browning, DePaul University; Justin Buckingham, Towson University; Ngoc Bui, University of La Verne; John Burling, University of Montevallo; Shawn Burn, Cal Poly San Luis Obispo; Thomas Cafferty, University of South Carolina; Donal Carlston, Purdue University; Kathleen Catanese, Florida State University; Sarah Cerny, Rutgers University; Andrea Chapdelaine, Albright College; Mike Chase, Quincy University; Winona Cochran, Bloomsburg University; Tamlin Conner, Boston College; Eric Cooley, Western Oregon University; Joe-Anne Corwin, Maine Maritime Academy; Mark Covey, Concordia College; Traci Craig, University of Idaho; Randy Cronk, Mt. Vernon

Nazarene University; Michael Crow, Southern Methodist University; Geraldine Curley, Bunker Hill Community College; Ken DeBono, Union College; Mike Devoley, Northern Arizona University; Dorothee Dietrich, Hamline University; Terry DiLorenzo, Stern College, Yeshiva University; Charles Dolph, Cedarville University; Barbara Dowds, Regis College; James Downing, Sul Ross State University; Kerri Dunn, Claremont McKenna College; Vera Dunwoody, Chaffey College; Valerie Eastman, Drury University; Steve Ellyson, Youngstown State University; Kim Ernst, Loyola University-New Orleans; Charles Evans, LaGrange College; J. R. Ferrari, DePaul University; Alan Ferris, Mount Marty College; Harry Fink, Los Angeles Valley College; Phillip Finney, Southeast Missouri State University; Michael Fischler, Plymouth State University; Aneka Flamm, University of Konstanz; Rita Flattley, Pima Community College, East Campus; Robin Franck, Southwestern College; Tim Franz, St. John Fisher College; Mary Louise Fraser, College of San Mateo; William Gabrenya, Florida Institute of Technology; Sam Gaertner, University of Delaware; Jesse Garcia, Morton College; Randall Garner, Sam Houston State University; Lynn Garrioch, Colby-Sawyer College; Pauline Ginsberg, Utica College; Carol Gohm, University of Mississippi; Steve Gordon, California State University Los Angeles; John Govern, Towson University; Melody Graham, Mount Mercy College; Elizabeth Gray, North Park University; Jan Griffin, USC Spartanburg; Erick Haight, North Central Michigan College; Hillary Haley, Santa Monica College; Elliott Hammer, Xavier University of Louisiana; Robert Hancock, Lincoln University; Ruth Hannon, Bridgewater State College; Judith Harackiewicz, University of Wisconsin-Madison; Lisa Harder, Grace University; Deletha Hardin, University of Tampa; Lora Harpster, Salt Lake Community College; John Harrington, University of Maine at Presque Isle; Lisa Harrison, CSU–Sacramento; Wendy Harrod, Iowa State University; Helen Harton, University of Northern Iowa; Mark Harvey, University of North Carolina at Asheville; Jacob Hautaluoma, Colorado State University; Maureen Hester, Holy Names College; Patricia Holley, St. Leo University; Misty Hook, Texas Woman's University; Mark Hoyert, Indiana University Northwest; Jean Hunt, Cumberland College; Chris Hunter, Grinnell College; Harold Hunziker Jr., Corning Community College; Sonya Lawson Hutchinson, Stillman College; Linda Isbell, University of Massachusetts-Amherst; Heide Island, University of Central Arkansas; John Iuzzini, University of Tennessee; Norine Jalbert, Western Connecticut State University; Robert Johnson, Arkansas State University; David Johnson, John Brown University; Meighan Johnson, Shorter College; Kathryn Johnson, Barat College; Lela Joscelyn, Mount Mary College; Deana Julka, University of Portland; Christine Jumpeter, SUNY–Albany; Patricia Kalata, Burlington County College; Richard Kandus, Mt. San Jacinto College; Nancy Karlin, University of Northern Colorado; Kristine Kelly, Western Illinois University; Veena Khandke, University of South Carolina-Spartanburg; Charles Kimble, University of Dayton; Ann Marie Kinnell, University of Southern Mississippi; Leslie Kirby, Vanderbilt University; Kristen Klaaren, Randolph-Macon College; Elisha Klirs, George Mason University; Gail Knapp, Mott Community College; Futoshi Kobayashi, Napa Valley College; Diane Kobrynowicz, The College of New Jersey; Kristen Koenig, Concordia College; Stuart Korshavn, St. Norbert College; Brenda Kowalewski, Weber State University; Robin Kowalski, Clemson University; Neil Kressel, William Paterson; Heather LaCost, Waubonsee Community College; Deborah Laible, Southern Methodist University; Ansley LaMar, New Jersey City University; Patricia Laser, Bucks County Community College; Beverly Lavin, Southern Connecticut State University; Mark Leary, Wake Forest University; Daniel Lehn, Coe College; Angela Lipsitz, Northern Kentucky University; John Lloyd, Coconino Community College; Margaret Lloyd, Georgia Southern University; Don Lynch, Unity College; Bruce MacDonald, Suffolk County Community College; Britton Mace, Southern Utah University; Scott Magnuson-Martinson, Normandale Community College; Deborah Mahlstedt, West Chester University; Diane Maluso, Elmira College; Kathy Manuel, Bossier Parish Community College; David Marple, Loyola Marymount University; James May, Massachusetts College of Liberal Arts; Bradley McAuliff, California State University-Northridge; Pam McAuslan, University of Michigan-Dearborn; Wanda McCarthy, Raymond Walters College–University of Cincinnati; Elaine McDuff, Truman State University; Daniel McIntosh, University of Denver; Tracy McLaughlin-Volpe, University of Vermont; Chas McMullen, Tompkins Corland Community College; Matt McMullen, Montana State University-Billings; Thomas Meriwether, Virginia Military Institute; Steven Mermini, William Paterson University; Kathy Miller, Concordia University; Dan Miller, Wayne State College; Anca Miron, University of Kansas; Joel Morgovsky, Brookdale Community College; Jennifer Ann Morrow, Old Dominion University; Jack Muller, Covenant College, William Nast, Bishop State Community College; Todd Nelson, CSU Stanislaus; Matt Newman, Bard College; Binh Nguyen, Santa Rosa Junior College; Gary Nickell, Minnesota State Moorhead; George Nielson, Dakota Wesleyan University; Virginia Norris, South Dakota State University; Sue O'Donnell, George Fox University; Karin O'Donnell, James Sprunt Community College; Sonja Olshove, Northwestern Michigan College; Julia Omarzu, Loras College; Myron Orleans, Chapman University, Irvine Campus; Wendy Ostroff, Sonoma State University; Henry Patterson, Penn State Berks–Lehigh Valley College; Kathleen Petersen, Fontbonne University; Terry Pettijohn, Mercyhurst College; Jane Pixley, Radford University; Faye Plascak-Craig, Marian College; Laura Wheeler Poms, George Mason University; Nancy Porter, Chestnut Hill College; Jack Powell, University of Hartford; Sharon Presley, California State University-Hayward; Charles Pressler, Purdue University-North Central; Dick Proctor, Andrews University; Marilyn Pugh, Texas Wesleyan University; Janice Purk, State University of West Georgia; Elizabeth Rellinger Zettler, Illinois College; Cheryl Rickabaugh, University of Redlands; Jennifer Ripley, Regent University; Pat Robertson, Whittier College; Margaret Rogers, University of Rhode Island; Tonya Rondinone, St. Joseph College; Robert Rosenwein, Lehigh University; Rosann Ross, University of Northern Colorado; Wade Rowatt, Baylor University; Thomas Rywick, SUNY Fredonia; Sherry Schnake, St. Mary of the Woods College; Patricia Schoenrad, William Jewell College; Jan Schregardus, Grace Bible College; Gretchen Sechrist, State University of New York at Buffalo; Charles Seidel, Mansfield University of Pennsylvania; Vicki Sheafer, LeTourneau University; Linda Skitka, University of Illinois at Chicago; Carol Slater, Alma College; Dani Smith, Fisk University; Vivian Smith, Lakeland Community College; Samuel Sommers, Tufts University; Sally Stabb, Texas Woman's University; Geraldine Stahly, California State University–San Bernardino; Mark Stasson, Metropolitan State University; Lee Stein, Maui Community College; Barry Stennett, Gainesville College–Ocone; Steven Stern, University of Pittsburgh at Johnstown; Lloyd Stires, Indiana University of Pennsylvania; Jeff Stone, University of Arizona; William Swart, Augustana College; Dennis Sweeney, California University of Pennsylvania; Alan Swinkels, St. Edward's University; Rowena Tan, University of Northern Iowa; John Tauer, University of St. Thomas; Susan Teague, Seton Hall University; John Teske, Elizabethtown College; James Thomas, University of Nebraska at Omaha; Inger Thompson, Glendale Community College; Todd Thorsteinson, University of Idaho; Krin Tochkov, SUNY Albany; Linda Tollefsrud, University of Wisconsin; Sue Tomlin, Rend Lake College; Beth Uhler, Miami University; Laura Valvatne, Shasta College; Eric Vanman, Georgia State University; Luis Vega, California State University-Bakersfield; Joe Ventimiglia, University of Memphis; Chris VerWys, Rensselaer Polytechnic Institute; Jennifer Waddell, Augustana College; T. Joel Wade, Bucknell University; Mary Wade, Manhattan College; Dolores Ward, Spring Hill College; David Ward, Arkansas Tech University; Rebecca Watson, Virginia Intermont College; Janet Weigel, Black Hawk College; Barbara Weimer, Mount Union College; Eric Weiser, Curry College; Carolyn Weisz, University of Puget Sound; Roger Wendt, Taylor University (online) & Norwich University (online); Sonia Werner, Bryn Athyn College of the New Church; Chris Wetzel, Rhodes College; Don Wiger, Argosy University; Edmond Willis, Central College; Betty Witcher, Peace College; Connie Wolfe, Muhlenberg College; Kevin Woller, Rogers State University; Pamela Woodman, Tabor College; Julie Woodzicka,

Washington and Lee University; Linda Woolf, Webster University; Suzette Wright, Ottawa University; Ann Marie Yaros, Matanuska-Susitna College, University of Arkansas; Jan Yoder, University of Akron; Mary Rose Zink, Wilmington College.

We also want to acknowledge the invaluable contributions of the many people at Wadsworth/Thomson who were involved in this project. The book would not have happened without Marianne Taflinger, Senior Editor, who advised and encouraged us from the beginning. Kirk Bomont, Developmental Editor, gave cogent feedback on drafts of textbook chapters, as well as helpful advice on visuals and other elements. Kristin Makarewycz, Developmental Editor, provided constructive comments on drafts of textbook and workbook chapters. Cecile Joyner was an efficient production editor. Sabina Dowell, photo researcher, found great photos while working within a tight time schedule. Darin Derstine, Technology Project Manager, was instrumental in the development of Social Psychology Labs within Social PsychologyNow and the Student CD-ROM. The Sales Representatives Advisory Board was very supportive, including Lee Sutherlin, Regional Manager; Pat Vauk, Senior Sales Representative; Tamy Ryan, Senior Sales Representative; Ron Harris, Senior Sales Representative; John Rich, Sales Representative; and Mark Francisco, Senior Sales Representative. Other people who made important contributions include Laurel Anderson, Advertising Project Manager; Vernon Boes, Art Director; Chris Caldeira, Senior Marketing Manager; Lucy Faridany, Editorial Assistant; Nicole Morinon, Marketing Assistant; Emily Smith, Production Project Manager; Becky Stovall, Video Production; Jim Strandberg, Developmental Editor; Kallie Swanson, Social PsychologyNow Project Manager; Paul Wells, Senior Production Project Manager; and Jennifer Wilkinson, Executive Ancillary Editor.

Our families know what it is for social psychology to come alive—they see it in us every day. As we worked on the book, they showed remarkable patience and understanding. As we go to press, they are also thrilled to see this book finally coming alive. It is to Ben, Mary, Rebecca, and Sara that we dedicate this first edition of *Social Psychology Alive.*

# Social Psychology Alive

© Zack Seckler/Getty Images

# Introducing Social Psychology

On September 11, 2001, terrorists attacked the United States. A well-coordinated group of men managed to commandeer four commercial aircraft. They flew two of the planes directly into the twin towers of the World Trade Center in New York City—first one, and then the other. Thousands of people were killed: the airline passengers, the people who occupied the buildings, the emergency rescue workers, and the terrorists themselves. A third plane was flown into the Pentagon building in Washington, DC, killing hundreds more. The fourth plane crashed outside of Pittsburgh, Pennsylvania, killing all aboard. Millions of people around the world witnessed these events as they were being broadcast on live television.

People responded swiftly. Emergency crews and ordinary citizens rushed to the scenes to help, often at great risk to their own lives. Government officials scrambled to contain and control the situation. Those who lived nearby were frantic in their efforts to contact friends and family who may have been injured or killed. As the days and weeks went by, people tried to cope with the trauma of the events—the loss of loved ones, the anger aroused by an unknown enemy, a nagging sense of insecurity and fear, and the need to understand why it happened. As most of the country was reeling from these tragic events, a series of anthrax-laced letters was working its way through the postal system, infecting dozens of people with a deadly disease. More deaths. More fear. Many questions.

- What could have motivated the terrorists to carry out their deadly plan? They apparently blamed the United States for its foreign policies. Whatever the motivation, it was strong enough that they were willing to die for it.

- Why did the attacks arouse a surge of patriotism and national pride? Americans rallied around the flag, exhibiting many public displays of patriotism. Political leaders, including the president and the mayor of New York, were praised for focusing on Americans' inner strengths.

- How did these events change our perceptions of the risks associated with terrorism? Many people suddenly felt vulnerable. Air traffic decreased dramatically as people stayed home rather than travel. Individuals of apparent Middle East ancestry were regarded suspiciously.

- How did people cope with the stress and trauma brought on by these events? Thousands of families were shattered by the loss of loved ones. Almost everybody felt anxious, angry, and confused.

- What role did the media play in changing our attitudes and influencing our behaviors? Coverage of the immediate events was extensive, ranging from the bravery of the firefighters to the heartbreak of families. Media stories subsequently turned to questions about who was responsible for the terrorism and what could be done to punish them.

The terrorist attack on September 11, 2001, killed thousands of people and changed how Americans see themselves and others.

© Steve Ludlum for The New York Times

*Knowing the answers to these questions would give us considerable insight into human nature. The answers might tell us how to prevent such attacks in the future, how to help victims cope more effectively if such a thing were to happen again, and how to shape social policy in a democratic society. The questions are difficult, and the answers are undoubtedly complex. But there are ways to gain insight. One way is called social psychology.*

*In this opening chapter, we introduce the field of social psychology. We begin by defining social psychology and describing a few studies that illustrate the field's breadth. Armed with these research examples, we next offer a couple of warnings about things you should keep in mind while studying the field. Notwithstanding these potential pitfalls, studying social psychology has many benefits, some of which we specify in the subsequent section. Then, to clarify the boundaries of social psychology, we explain how the field is different from other areas of psychology and from other disciplines. We next provide a brief history of social psychology. Finally, we outline the organization of the book and describe the supplementary materials that are available to enrich your understanding of the field.*

## What Is Social Psychology?

Our lives are *social:* they involve *other people.* The events of September 11, 2001, illustrated this point dramatically. We reside in societies that require us to interact many times every day with other people, including friends, teachers, partners, coworkers, and even enemies. We persuade (and are persuaded), we obey (and are obeyed), we love (and are loved)—all of these actions implicate other people. We cannot, nor would we want to, separate ourselves from the social groups to which we belong: families, neighborhoods, schools, businesses, towns, states, nations. *We are social beings.* No matter what our pursuit in life, social settings and social problems will be important.

### The Science of Social Behavior

Social psychology can be considered the science of social behavior (we give a formal definition in the next paragraph). It is a field dedicated to understanding the causes and consequences of social interactions between individuals or groups. The sorts of behaviors mentioned in the preceding paragraph—persuasion, obedience, love—are of great interest to social psychologists. In fact, entire chapters in this book are dedicated to attitude change and persuasion (Chapter 7), conformity and obedience (Chapter 8), and love and close relationships (Chapter 13). In these chapters, answers are provided to such questions as: What strategies do advertisers use to persuade viewers? When does social pressure produce conformity? How do people from different cultures think about love?

Probably the best way to get an appreciation of social psychology is via specific examples of research by social psychologists. Before we describe a few studies, however, we want to state and explain a formal definition of the field, adapted from one given by Gordon Allport (1985), which captures its pivotal elements:

> **Social psychology** is *the scientific study of how individuals' thoughts, feelings, and behaviors are influenced by other people.*

**social psychology**
*the scientific study of how individuals' thoughts, feelings, and behaviors are influenced by other people*

This definition has four key aspects, which we briefly explain in the following paragraphs, but in the reverse order of their appearance in the definition: (1) influenced by other people, (2) thoughts, feelings, and behaviors, (3) individuals' perspective, and (4) scientific study.

**Influenced by Other People.** Social psychology is the study of how other people affect us. It is *social* psychology. This "social" aspect is probably the single most important thing about social psychology and is true of all research in the field. Usually, the social component is obvious, as in research on aggression, altruism, intergroup relations, and interpersonal attraction. But sometimes the role of other people is less obvious. Have you ever had the experience of wondering what your mother, romantic partner, or close friend would think about your behavior in a particular situation? Or have you ever prepared yourself mentally for a future interaction, such as an upcoming job interview or romantic date? These are common experiences, and they show that other people can influence us without having to be physically present. Another example is worrying about terrorism: just the thought of terrorists can affect us strongly. Indeed, many people continue to experience emotional consequences of the attacks of September 11, 2001: fear, anxiety, anger, and frustration. These emotions have undoubtedly influenced many people's attitudes toward the wars in Afghanistan and Iraq.

So long as someone is being affected in any way by other people, including their imagined presence, the situation is relevant to social psychology. We will return to this "social" aspect of the field momentarily and give some examples of the broad influence of other people, including effects on how we interpret events, how we feel about ourselves, and how we behave.

**Thoughts, Feelings, and Behaviors.** Social psychologists are interested in how other people affect every aspect of individuals' lives, including thoughts (cognitions), feelings (affect), and behaviors. For example, social psychologists study how individuals process information about other people and how they store this information in memory (see Chapters 3 and 4). Social psychologists also examine people's feelings and emotions, such as their prejudice against outgroups and their affection for friends and lovers (see Chapters 9 and 13). Finally, social psychologists are, of

Social psychology focuses on how individuals are influenced by other people.

© Ed Kashi/CORBIS

course, interested in explaining social behavior. The ultimate goal of the science is to understand why various kinds of actions toward other people occur or do not occur, such as conformity, aggression, helping, and discrimination. Every chapter in this book deals with social behavior in some form.

**Individuals' Perspective.** Social psychologists take the perspective of individuals in a social setting, rather than focusing only on objective features of the situation. To understand behavior, social psychologists believe that it is necessary to look at the world through the actor's eyes. Imagine that someone tries to give you a free gift (e.g., a small flag or a flower) while you are walking in a shopping mall. On the surface, this offer is generous, and you should accept the gift and respond with thanks. But if you suspect that the person is simply buttering you up before asking for a donation to some group, you might refuse the gift and respond with annoyance. Does it matter what the other person's *real* intentions are? Probably not, if the goal is simply to understand your response: whatever *you believe* to be the other person's motive will determine how you behave. Similarly, to understand many social events, it is more important to know individual actors' subjective *perceptions* of the situation than to know the setting's objective features. Even when studying *group* processes, social psychologists adopt the perspective of individual members of the group. For instance, some groups have charismatic, powerful leaders who exert tremendous influence over members (e.g., leaders of some cults; see Chapter 7). To understand actions by these groups (e.g., mass suicides), social psychologists focus on individual members' thoughts and feelings about the leader, such as their beliefs about the leader's goals, their feelings of loyalty to him or her, and their perceptions of his or her relationship to God. Ultimately, group actions are made up of many actions by individuals.

**Scientific Study.** Finally, social psychology is a science. Social psychologists rely on direct tests of their ideas. Scientific evidence is necessary before a proposal will be taken seriously; it is not enough merely to speculate about an event and generate a plausible explanation. In Chapter 2, we discuss the scientific method and describe various methodologies used by social psychologists. For our present purposes, the important point is that, like any science, social psychology involves collecting data to test predictions. Throughout the book, you will read about experiments that have

## CONCEPT REVIEW
### How Would a Social Psychologist's Perspective on Understanding Romantic Dating Be Unique?

| Key Element of Social Psychology | Applied to Romantic Dating |
|---|---|
| Influenced by other people | Romantic dating clearly fits into the domain of social psychology because the dating individuals are influenced by one another. |
| Thoughts, feelings, and behaviors | To understand dating, social psychologists would look at each person's thoughts about the other (e.g., first impressions), feelings toward the other (e.g., emotional passion toward the other), and behaviors toward the other (e.g., telephone calls, dates, gifts). |
| Individuals' perspective | Social psychologists would focus on each person's perceptions of the other, rather than on what the individuals are "really" like; the critical factor is what each person *believes* about the other. |
| Scientific study | Social psychologists would conduct experiments to learn about the processes underlying interpersonal attraction and love. |

been conducted in the laboratory or in the field, wherein researchers have collected systematic information that bears on social behavior. Social psychology has yielded many important insights and promises to advance our understanding of social behavior further in the future.

The accompanying Concept Review table summarizes the key aspects of social psychology by asking the question "How would a social psychologist's perspective on understanding romantic dating be unique?"

## How Other People Affect Us

We have noted that the key element of social psychology is that it investigates how individuals *are influenced by other people.* One reason the field is interesting and exciting is that most individuals don't recognize just how much they are affected by others. Many of us think of ourselves as strong individualists who make our own decisions based on our central values and do not worry much about what other people think. Is this how you think of yourself? Although individuals certainly do make personal decisions, most decisions are also influenced directly or indirectly by other people. Indeed, social psychologists have shown that other people influence virtually every aspect of life, including how we interpret events, how we feel about ourselves, and how we behave.

**Other People Affect How We Interpret Events.** Have you ever read about an accident or emergency where nobody stopped to help? Perhaps a man suffered a heart attack and lay on the ground while others walked around him, or perhaps a woman was stabbed on a crowded subway car and lay bleeding even after the assailant left the scene. Did you wonder how people could be so heartless? Social psychologists also wonder why people often fail to intervene and have designed studies to explore this question. Researchers have conducted experiments in which they constructed fake emergencies and observed how people responded who did not know that the situation was staged (e.g., Latané & Darley, 1970). These studies on bystander intervention will be discussed in detail in Chapter 12. By carefully controlling the situation, including the behavior of apparent bystanders who were actually working for the experimenter, researchers determined that one important reason bystanders fail to intervene is that they rely on other people to interpret the event.

To understand this explanation, imagine that a few bystanders (each walking alone) come upon a potential emergency at about the same time, such as a man lying on the ground. They need to decide what is going on and what they should do. Is the man sick? Is he drunk? Will he be angry if they ask him questions? One source of information they might use is how *other people* in the situation are responding: Do other people seem to think that this is an emergency requiring intervention? If they are not doing anything about the event, then perhaps it is not an emergency at all. Unfortunately for the victim, all of the bystanders may be looking at one another for cues about how to respond, with the result that no one does anything! Bystanders may misinterpret the situation as a nonemergency based on the inaction of other bystanders. This analysis of emergency situations is classic social psychology, providing a compelling example of how we use other people to interpret our world.

**Other People Affect How We Feel About Ourselves.** We also rely on other people to make judgments about ourselves. Consider: Are you generous? Do you have a good sense of humor? Are you skilled at basketball? Although these questions refer to you as an individual, the answers rely partly on comparisons with other people. Deciding whether you are generous, funny, or good at basketball usually involves thinking about whether you are better or worse than other people.

Do you give more money to charities than most people of your age? Do you tell more jokes than most of your friends? Do you beat your friends when you play one-on-one basketball? Other people can have dramatic effects on how we feel about ourselves.

This process of comparing ourselves to other people to make judgments about the self is called *social comparison* (Festinger, 1954) and is discussed in detail in Chapter 4. Social comparison occurs all the time and has many implications for daily life. For example, have you ever wondered about the effects of extremely attractive men and women in the media? We are constantly exposed to very attractive and very thin models on television, in magazines, and at the movies. Do these attractive men and women affect how we feel about ourselves?

Some research in social psychology suggests that the answer to this question is *yes.* For instance, Bill Thornton and Scott Moore (1993) had male and female college undergraduates complete several questionnaires that assessed a variety of self-perceptions, including ratings of their own physical attractiveness and social skills. Some participants completed these questionnaires while seated beside a large posterboard leaning against a wall, which allegedly was from a different study that was being run in the same room at different times.

Other people can affect how bystanders interpret a potential emergency.

This posterboard displayed 24 color photographs of very physically attractive members of the same sex as the participant. Participants who were exposed to these attractive photographs rated themselves as less physically attractive and less socially competent than did participants in a control condition who were not exposed to the posterboard. Seeing very attractive people made participants feel worse about themselves. Further, these effects occurred for both men and women. This experiment is a good example of how an issue from real life (media exposure to physically attractive models) can be studied in the laboratory.

**Other People Affect How We Behave.** Other people affect not only how we interpret events and how we feel about ourselves, but also our actions. This point was demonstrated indirectly in the bystander intervention studies, because bystanders' interpretations of the situation influenced their actions: they did not intervene. But other people can also affect how we behave more directly. That is, the presence of other people can elicit very different behavior than would have occurred if individuals were alone. For example, have you ever been surprised by news reports of riots or other "mob" events? Perhaps sports fans were celebrating a victory and started smashing windows and overturning cars, or perhaps protesters were marching peacefully but began to throw stones and attack police. Did you wonder how these escalations occurred, and whether you would have responded differently in the same situation? Social psychologists have been very interested in how individuals can be transformed in group settings, including the tendency for some large groups to exhibit aggressive behavior.

One explanation for mob aggression focuses on feelings of anonymity. If people feel unidentifiable when they are immersed in a large group, they may be "released" from their normal inhibitions and do things they would not have done alone or in a smaller group. The term *deindividuation* has been used to refer to this feeling that people are unaccountable for their actions when in a large group; deindividuation will be discussed in detail in Chapter 10. The relation between group size and aggression is perhaps most clearly illustrated by an analysis of historical events conducted by Brian Mullen (1986). Mullen examined 60 newspaper reports of lynchings (mob executions) of Black men by White mobs in the southern United

© AP/Wide World Photos/The Lantern, Zach Wittig

Sometimes large groups of people exhibit aggressive, destructive behavior.

States between 1899 and 1946. The degree of viciousness or atrocity of each lynching was rated (e.g., based on whether the victim was burned or dismembered), as well as the size of the lynch mob relative to the number of victims. Results showed that as the lynchers became more numerous relative to the victims, the viciousness of the lynchings increased. That is, larger mobs were associated with more savage lynchings. Mullen hypothesized that people in the large mobs felt relatively anonymous, which led to a breakdown of normal inhibitory self-control. This study is a good example of how analyses of historical data can inform explanations of important social behaviors.

These examples of social psychological research illustrate the diverse ways individuals are affected by other people. Clearly, the field of social psychology can be applied to many settings in daily life. In a moment, we will discuss explicitly some benefits of studying social psychology, but first we need to identify some pitfalls to avoid.

## Beware!

Social psychology deals with many topics that you will recognize as having been part of your life. Forming impressions of other people, reading persuasive messages, joining groups, helping those in need, falling in love—these (and other) settings and topics will be familiar to you. This everyday familiarity of social psychological content is, on the one hand, terrific, because it means that you will learn many things that are applicable to your life (more on this point soon). But there is a downside to the familiarity of the field's subject matter: you may think you know more than you do.

**Social Psychology Is Not Just Common Sense.** Over the course of our lives, we develop considerable expertise about our own behavior: our preferences and desires, our strengths and shortcomings, and how we respond in different situations. Through our relationships with other people, we learn a lot about social interaction and what makes others tick. In a way, we are all social psychologists trying to understand and predict our world (see Chapter 4). Moreover, our beliefs and intuitions about social behavior are often correct. Because of this overlap between social psychology and intuition, students sometimes claim that social psychology is little more than common sense.

It is true that some of social psychology is common sense and consistent with folk wisdom. There is a Chinese proverb that says a courtyard shared by all will be swept by none; this insight was offered long before social psychologists suggested that group settings tend to dilute feelings of personal responsibility (see Chapter 12). Similarly, a Spanish proverb suggests that flattery makes friends, whereas truth makes enemies; it may not be surprising that social psychologists found that people like others who say nice things about them (see Chapter 13).

Does this mean that social psychology is completely common sense, just bits of wisdom already well known? Don't be fooled. Consider the case of interpersonal attraction—how and why people like or dislike one another. Which of the following two sayings is correct? Is it that *birds of a feather flock together,* or is it that *opposites attract?* That is, do we most like others who are similar to us, who think like us and look like us? Or do we prefer those who complement rather than duplicate our own interests and needs? A commonsense case could be made for either view. As you will see in Chapter 13, however, social psychological research gives us a clear-cut answer: similarity wins the day.

As another example, common sense (and a good deal of psychological theory) tells us that rewards and reinforcement are the way to change behavior. Give people money or prizes, and you can lead them to do almost anything. Social psychology, however, teaches a different lesson. It is sometimes the *absence* of an attractive reward that produces the greatest changes in attitudes and behavior. You just need to get people started in the desired direction, and a sort of social momentum will take over from there. In fact, if rewards are used too much, they can actually reduce a person's interest in an activity. Not common sense at all, but it makes good social psychological sense, as you will learn in Chapters 4 and 7.

Thus, social psychology is more than common sense or folk wisdom. But even when research findings confirm our intuitions, there is considerable value in knowing for sure. One reason is that common sense often allows competing predictions, as in the similarity and liking example given earlier. Another reason is that because intuitions are *not* always right, we must conduct research to find out which ones are valid. A final reason is that folk wisdom is often vague and simplistic; real life is usually more complicated. So even when an adage has a kernel of truth, there may be exceptions or limitations that must be identified via scientific research. For example, although people generally like others who say nice things about them, if they suspect that the flattery was not genuine but was an attempt to manipulate them, it can lead to less rather than more liking (e.g., Jones & Wortman, 1973; see Chapter 4).

"YOU'RE A WOMAN AND I'M A MAN. WHO SAYS OPPOSITES DON'T ATTRACT?"

"There's an article in that paper, all about how married couples begin to resemble one another."

Sometimes pieces of "folk wisdom" offer conflicting advice.

**Hindsight Is Not Always Golden.** Predicting future, uncertain outcomes is often difficult. Who will win an election? What decision will a jury reach? How well will you do on an upcoming exam? In advance, these kinds of outcomes can seem highly unpredictable. Once we learn about an outcome, however, it often seems that it was obvious. We may experience the feeling that "we knew it all along." Beware—this is an illusion. Things that seem obvious in hindsight may not have been easily predicted in foresight. The tendency to think that a known outcome was obvious is called the *hindsight bias,* and how and why it happens is described in Chapter 3.

We mention the hindsight bias here because it can lead you astray when you are judging the importance and value of research findings. After reading about a study and its results, you may think that the findings were obvious—anyone could have predicted that! In actuality, though, the outcome might have been quite uncertain in advance. To counteract the bias, try this: As you read about an experiment, try predicting the result before you learn it. Don't peek! Very often you will be surprised at the difficulty of predicting a result before you know it, and it will confirm that perhaps a result is not something you knew all along. Or try this: After learning about an experiment, including its result, pretend that a different result had been obtained. See if you can invent a logical explanation for the different result. Many results can be explained in retrospect, once they are known. Predicting them ahead of time is far more challenging.

Now that you know some things to avoid while studying social psychology, let's discuss the benefits of exposure to this field. We think that learning about social psychology is important for several reasons.

## Why Study Social Psychology?

The authors of this book are passionate about social psychology. We enjoy thinking about social psychological questions and conducting research on the topics covered in the book. We also delight in teaching social psychology to undergraduate and graduate students. To us, the question "Why study social psychology?" is a no-brainer—because it's interesting and useful at the same time! But we know that we may be biased (just a little), and the benefits of studying social psychology may not be so apparent to everyone. So let us articulate a few of the (many) benefits of learning about social psychology, not including our opinion that the field is truly fascinating.

**Being an Informed Citizen.** Think about the issues and problems that most concern you and your friends. Prominent among them are certain to be complex social issues and social problems. What should we, as citizens, do about gun control, the death penalty, or the legalization of abortion? How should our country fight terrorism internationally? What about post-9/11 hate crimes here at home against people who appear to be Arabs or Muslims: how can we minimize this problem? How can we stop the spread of AIDS, both within our country and around the world?

This is where social psychology comes in. Most people have their own opinions about how to deal with some of these problems. Yet, as we noted earlier, intuition and common sense can sometimes lead us astray. If we really want to develop an informed and reasoned approach to dealing with social problems, we need to understand why people behave the way they do and the likely effectiveness of different solutions. Think about a parallel example: All of us have some intuition about how to build a bridge. We know what a bridge should look like, and we know what it is supposed to do. Does that mean that we could design and build a bridge that would work? Probably not. It takes a great deal of expertise from engineering and a deep understanding of physical forces before someone can build a bridge that will carry weight and last.

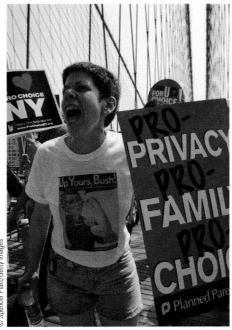

© Tim Sloan/AFP/Getty Images

© Spencer Platt/Getty Images

Social psychology can provide knowledge that might help us to deal with complex social issues.

Developing effective social policies is a lot like building a bridge. For example, we may all share the goal of stopping the spread of AIDS, but we are unlikely to agree on how best to achieve that goal. Medical science and molecular biology have taught us a great deal about the virus that causes AIDS. The reality, however, is that this disease (like many others) spreads because of human social behavior—unprotected sex and the sharing of intravenous needles. To many people, the solution may seem plain: tell people to stop doing these things. But to the knowledgeable student of social psychology, the problem is more complex and the solution less obvious. We need to understand how people judge their own susceptibility to the virus, and how those judgments influence behavior. We need to recognize that situational factors can be very powerful, and emotions can override reason. We need to know how to change attitudes effectively. In Chapter 6, we discuss the determinants of safer-sex behavior in some detail. Just as the structural engineer relies on a myriad of details to design a bridge, so the social engineer needs a broad understanding of the determinants of behavior to design a truly effective social policy. An informed citizen understands the principles of social psychology.

**Applying Social Psychological Knowledge to Everyday Life.** The principles of social psychology are relevant to understanding not only broad, complex social issues, but also more limited, everyday problems that many of us face. Elementary school teachers need to handle playground disputes and help underachieving students fulfill their true potential. Advertising and marketing executives need to design effective media campaigns. Doctors and health care providers need to get patients to comply with drug regimens and therapies. Law enforcement officials need to control crowds and obtain accurate information from eyewitnesses. Employers must make hiring decisions on the basis of limited information and must organize the workplace to maximize productivity. And all of us experience problems occasionally in our close relationships with parents, friends, siblings, bosses, employees, or romantic partners. Despite the great diversity of these problems and their settings, each has been the focus of social psychological research designed to understand and solve them. You will learn about these literatures as you read this book.

The bottom line is that social psychology is relevant. Indeed, entire scientific journals are devoted to pursuing the applications of social psychology. See if your library subscribes to the *Journal of Applied Social Psychology* or the *Journal of Social*

© Jeff Greenberg/Photo Edit

Social psychology can provide insights about our close relationships.

*Issues.* In these journals, you are sure to find applications that interest you and will be of value to you no matter what your field of study or career aspirations. But we need to be cautious. We do not want to promise more than social psychology can currently deliver. It may take dozens of studies to identify an effective strategy for solving a particular problem, and many interesting problems remain unexplored. As a science, social psychology is still in the earliest stages.

**Understanding Yourself.** Perhaps the best reason of all for studying social psychology is that you will learn some things about yourself. If you think of yourself as immune to advertising, you will learn that you may be more influenced than you believed. If you think that other people seem more poised, confident, or talented than you, you will find out that those others often harbor feelings of doubt, insecurity, and low self-esteem. If you wish you were better at handling conflict with others, you will learn some things to do and some things to avoid. If you wonder why you always seem to want what you can't have, you will discover that most people feel the same way—and you'll learn why. In sum, social psychology will help you to better understand yourself and your social world.

Thus, studying social psychology has many benefits. In part, these benefits derive from the fact that the field of social psychology is very broad. To help you understand the boundaries of social psychology, we next turn to how it connects to other fields.

## Social Psychology's Connections to Other Areas of Psychology

We have defined social psychology as the scientific study of how individuals' thoughts, feelings, and behaviors are influenced by other people. This definition encompasses a large range of settings and topics. We need to specify the boundaries of the field. Let us begin with a discussion of how social psychology overlaps with some other areas of psychology that are related but distinct.

**Personality Psychology.** The area of psychology that is perhaps most closely related to social psychology is personality psychology. Personality psychologists study traits, or *dispositions,* that help to explain human behavior. Dispositions are consistencies in thought or action that characterize an individual across time and settings and that make him or her different from other people (see Friedman & Schustack, 2003). The primary goal of personality psychologists is to identify the dispositions that are most useful for describing behavior and for differentiating between individuals. In contrast, social psychologists want to understand the impact of external, situational factors on behavior—in particular, how individuals are affected by other people. Nevertheless, social psychologists often include individual difference variables in their research, hoping they will improve the prediction of behavior above and beyond the situational factors. For instance, a social psychologist might investigate aggression by manipulating a situational factor (e.g., whether or not participants are insulted by an accomplice of the experimenter), but also include a measure of a relevant individual difference variable (e.g., self-esteem) that might further improve prediction of participants' aggressive responses. In Chapter 5, The Person in the Situation, we discuss numerous dispositional variables that have often been included in social psychological studies.

**Developmental Psychology.** Developmental psychologists study age-related changes in human abilities and behaviors, ranging from childhood to the end of the life span. Most developmental psychologists study children, often focusing on either social development (e.g., how friendships emerge, the importance of early attachments to other people) or cognitive development (e.g., how language emerges, intellectual skills). Although many social psychologists have used children as participants in research, the focus of these studies has typically been to understand a basic principle that was expected to apply to other age groups as well. Nevertheless, some research focusing specifically on developmental changes in social psychological processes will be described in various chapters of this book.

**Cognitive Psychology.** Cognitive psychologists study how the human mind works, including memory, information processing, consciousness, and decision making. This field has made important contributions to our understanding of how knowledge is organized in memory, as well as common errors in judgment and decision making. One area of social psychology overlaps substantially with cognitive psychology: *social cognition,* which is the study of how information about people is processed and stored (see Chapter 3). The "about people" (social) aspect of social cognition is critical; cognitive psychologists additionally study the processing of *non*social information. Both cognitive and social psychologists rely on experiments to test their ideas, and the two fields share some theories and models. A cognitive perspective is very common in social psychology, and the impact of information processing on social behavior will be discussed many times in this book (particularly in Chapters 3 and 4).

**Clinical and Counseling Psychology.** Clinical and counseling psychologists study people who are having difficulty coping with life's demands. Sometimes also called *abnormal psychology,* these fields focus on individuals who are suffering from some kind of psychological or emotional problem. The problems can range from relatively minor ones like mild depression or anxiety to severe ones like schizophrenia or antisocial personality disorder. In contrast, social psychologists are primarily interested in "normal" individuals' behavior in social settings. Nevertheless, there are points of contact between the fields. For example, social psychologists are interested in loneliness, shyness, relationship dissolution, and low self-esteem, all of which can lead to coping problems. Also, social psychologists have investigated whether certain styles of processing social information might predispose individuals to depression and anxiety.

---

### CONCEPT REVIEW
*Social Psychology's Connections to Other Areas of Psychology*

| Area of Psychology | Primary Focus of the Field | Related Topics in Social Psychology |
|---|---|---|
| Personality psychology | Traits that help to explain human behavior | Individual differences that affect social behavior (e.g., self-esteem) |
| Developmental psychology | Age-related changes in human abilities and behavior | Social development—how relationship skills emerge |
| Cognitive psychology | How the human mind works | Social cognition—how information about people is processed and stored |
| Clinical/counseling psychology | Psychological or mental problems affecting people's well-being | Loneliness, shyness, and other relationship problems; depression and anxiety |

---

The connections between social psychology and other areas of psychology are summarized in the accompanying Concept Review table.

## Social Psychology's Connections to Other Disciplines

It is also helpful to know how social psychology is similar to and different from a few related disciplines. These are all subjects that are taught at colleges and universities. You may have taken courses on them or even be majoring in one of them.

**Sociology.** Sociology is the discipline most closely related to social psychology. Sociology is the study of how social and cultural forces influence behavior. Sociologists focus on *groups* to understand phenomena, in contrast to social psychology's focus on the *individual.* For example, sociologists might compare the relative health standing of people from different socioeconomic levels (e.g., low vs. middle vs. upper classes) or the murder rate in states with different laws (e.g., capital punishment vs. no capital punishment). Social psychologists, on the other hand, might examine whether specific beliefs and attitudes are associated with better health, or whether individuals are more aggressive under certain social conditions. Thus, sociologists are primarily interested in large social categories and groups, rather than individuals. Another important difference between sociology and social psychology is their preferred research methodologies. Sociologists typically study existing groups and measure the relevant characteristics. Social psychologists, on the other hand, typically manipulate factors in experiments. Interestingly, there are textbooks on social psychology written by sociologists (e.g., Michener, DeLamater, & Myers, 2003), which differ quite dramatically from textbooks written by social psychologists.

**Anthropology.** Anthropology is the study of past and present cultures, particularly how cultural features influence behavior. Archaeology is one branch of anthropology, which involves the investigation of past cultures through their physical remains. But many anthropologists study modern cultures, usually comparing the features of different societies (e.g., their customs or institutions) to understand a particular outcome (e.g., divorce rate, life expectancy). Although social psychologists study some of the same outcomes as anthropologists, the two fields overlap very little in terms of theoretical perspective (cultures vs. individuals) or research approach (investigation of existing records and materials vs. experiments).

**CONCEPT REVIEW**

*Social Psychology's Differences From Other Disciplines*

| Discipline | Primary Focus of the Discipline | Differences From Social Psychology |
|---|---|---|
| Sociology | How social and cultural forces influence human behavior | Focus on groups rather than individuals; measure relevant concepts rather than manipulate in experiments |
| Anthropology | The study of past and present cultures | Focus on cultures rather than individuals; rely on existing materials rather than conducting experiments |
| Political science | The study of methods of government | Exclusive focus on the political domain; study existing systems rather than conducting experiments |

**Political Science.** Political science is the study of methods of government, including the principles and operations of political institutions. This field is more specialized than social psychology, which potentially addresses any behavior that is influenced by other people. Although the political domain is certainly of interest to social psychologists (e.g., research on voting, leadership, and justice), political scientists engage primarily in theoretical analysis of governmental systems, rather than experiments on how factors influence individuals' perceptions. Interestingly, a hybrid subdiscipline known as *political psychology* has emerged in the past 20 years in which social psychologists and political scientists sometimes work together to understand human political behavior (e.g., Ottati et al., 2002).

The differences between social psychology and other related disciplines are summarized in the accompanying Concept Review table.

## Historical Background of Social Psychology

Social psychology emerged as a field distinct from other disciplines and from other areas of psychology sometime in the middle of the 20th century, perhaps most clearly during the 1950s. Important social psychological studies had been done prior to this time, but few specialized theories had appeared, and the field's reliance on the experimental method had not solidified. Thus, "modern" social psychology has existed only 50 or 60 years. In this section, we trace some of the historical roots of modern social psychology and outline briefly some of the major early developments in the field.

### Social Psychology's Roots in Philosophy

Although we did not include philosophy in the disciplines whose connections to social psychology were described, the earliest sources of social psychology (and of psychology more generally) can be found in philosophy. In fact, several important social psychological concepts can be traced directly back to the work of philosophers.

For instance, modern social psychologists distinguish between thoughts, feelings, and behaviors—recall our definition of the field. The Greek philosopher Plato, generally considered the father of Western philosophy, suggested that people experience the world in three distinct ways: in thought, in emotion, and in action.

Thus, the triumvirate of cognitive (thoughts), affective (feelings), and behavioral aspects of experience is very old; you will see that this conceptualization continues to appear in modern social psychological theories.

As another example, social psychology is based on the fundamental point that humans are social beings. Aristotle, one of Plato's students, argued forcefully that living a good life and achieving personal happiness are both dependent on providing benefits to other people in addition to the self. Aristotle's view was that connections with others form an essential part of who we are. This idea is consistent with social psychological work on the self-concept, which has shown that our social relationships are important components of how we define ourselves (e.g., see Baumeister & Twenge, 2003).

Much attention in social psychology has been directed to *social norms,* which are perceived rules or guidelines about what behaviors are acceptable and unacceptable (see Chapter 8). The concept of social norms can be traced back to one of the great ideas of philosophy: the **social contract.** The social contract refers to the idea that, to survive and prosper, human groups had to develop some basic rules of social and moral conduct; an absence of rules would have led to societal breakdown. Thus, through the millennia, humans have evolved formalized codes and laws, which people in a society implicitly "agree" to follow (hence, the social *contract*). Modern social psychologists use the concept of norms to understand various social behaviors.

A final connection between social psychology and philosophy involves the concept of *identity.* Social psychologists have been very interested in issues related to how people see themselves (see Chapter 5). Similarly, perhaps the fundamental question in philosophy has been the essence of human existence: What is a person? What is the nature of consciousness? These questions clearly relate to self-perceptions. The issues are complex, and debate continues among philosophers. Nevertheless, social psychologists have made considerable progress in developing useful models of identity.

## Social Psychology's Early History

The field of psychology (not just social psychology) separated from philosophy and became a distinct discipline in the middle of the 19th century, when a number of European researchers began to use scientific methods (e.g., experiments) to address questions about human perception and judgment, moving away from the introspective techniques (e.g., thought and speculation) used by philosophers. The earliest publication that is widely viewed as *social* psychological appeared in 1898 in the *American Journal of Psychology* (Triplett, 1898). This experiment addressed whether the presence of an audience improves individuals' performances and is described in the accompanying box, Social Psychology in Your Life: The First Social Psychology Experiment.

In 1908, two textbooks with *social psychology* in their title appeared, one by a psychologist (McDougall, 1908) and one by a sociologist (Ross, 1908). These books were very different from one another. McDougall's text relied on the concept of *instincts* to explain much of human behavior, whereas Ross's text emphasized imitation and learning. These authors were not hesitant about proclaiming the importance of social psychology; for example, McDougall wrote on his opening page that social psychology was "the essential common foundation on which all the social sciences . . . must be built up" (p. 1). Although these textbooks ushered in the academic study of social psychology, the field was relatively undefined and did not yet have its own theoretical models.

An increasingly important view in psychology during the first few decades of the 20th century was **behaviorism,** which attempted to explain behavior purely in

**social contract**

*the idea that human societies have developed basic rules of social and moral conduct, which members of the societies implicitly agree to follow*

**behaviorism**

*an approach in psychology that assumes that behavior can be explained purely in terms of stimulus–response connections established through experience and reinforcement*

# Social Psychology in Your Life

## *The First Social Psychology Experiment*

Throughout the book, we have placed special boxes like this one to make connections between social psychology and your own life. Here, we tell you about a study that is generally regarded as the first social psychology experiment ever to be published. The issue addressed in this experiment remains relevant today: how performance is affected by the presence of other people. As you read about the study, see if you can relate the ideas to your own experiences.

Norman Triplett was a researcher at Indiana University in the late 1800s. Triplett was curious about a pattern he noticed in bicycle racing times: racing records showed faster times (about 20% faster) in multirider competitive races than in individual races against the clock. Triplett developed a variety of hypotheses that might explain this difference, including some that were based on the physics of bicycle racing. For example, in multirider races, the lead racer provides a shield against the wind for those following behind, whereas no such shelter is available when racers compete only against the clock.

Can you think of an explanation that is more social psychological in nature? Triplett could: he hypothesized that "the bodily presence of another rider is a stimulus to the racer in arousing the competitive instinct" (Triplett, 1898, p. 516). In other words, riders' competitive juices get flowing when they race against other riders. Triplett recognized that distinguishing among the competing hypotheses would require careful experimental work. Therefore, he designed a task in which children turned a crank on a fishing reel as quickly as possible. Sometimes the children did the task by themselves, and sometimes they competed against other children. The results showed clearly that the children were faster at turning the crank when they competed against other children than when they performed the task alone.

This early experiment eventually generated a fascinating line of research on how the presence of other people affects individuals' performances. This topic became known as *social facilitation* and will be discussed in detail in Chapter 10 on group dynamics. To foreshadow our later discussion a bit, can you think of any circumstances under which the presence of others is likely to make performance *worse* rather than better? It turns out that there are such conditions, which have to do primarily with the task being very complex or difficult.

**Norman Triplett was intrigued in the 1890s by records showing that bicycle racers exhibited faster times in multirider competitions than in individual races against the clock.**

© Hulton-Deutsch Collection/CORBIS

terms of stimulus–response connections established through experience and reinforcement (e.g., if a certain behavior occurs in a situation and produces a reward, the same behavior is more likely to occur again in the future in the same or similar situations). Behaviorists dismissed the importance of unobservable mental concepts like thoughts and attitudes. This view influenced some early work in social psychology, particularly theories of human aggression (e.g., Dollard et al., 1939).

In the 1930s, Adolf Hitler and the Nazi party gained influence in Germany. The spreading racism of the Nazis and the threat of impending war led many European scientists to emigrate to North America, including several psychologists who made

Kurt Lewin is often regarded as the father of modern social psychology.

**Gestalt theory**

*an approach in psychology that assumes that people's overall, subjective inter-pretations of objects are more important than the objects' physical features, and that objects are perceived in their totality, as a unit, rather than in terms of their individual features*

During the Second World War, social psychologists directed their attention to practical questions like how to motivate people at home to conserve scarce resources.

important contributions to social psychology. Perhaps the most notable example is Kurt Lewin, who is often regarded as the father of modern social psychology (for a collection of his influential articles, see Lewin, 1951). One significant characteristic of these European theorists, including Lewin, was that they were generally opposed to behaviorism, which had not achieved as much acceptance in Europe as in North America. Instead, these theorists were usually trained in **Gestalt theory,** which was based on the idea that people's overall, subjective interpretations of objects are more important than the objects' physical features. You will recognize the parallel between this approach in Gestalt theory and modern social psychology's focus on individuals' perspectives. Gestalt researchers also emphasized that objects are perceived in their totality, as a unit, rather than in terms of their individual features. For instance, we perceive an automobile as a complete, functioning unit, rather than as four tires, a hood, a steering wheel, and so on. Gestalt theorists were very interested in people's internal representations of objects—in contrast to behaviorism.

The rising influence of authoritarian dictators in such countries as Germany, the Soviet Union, and Italy in the 1930s and 1940s stimulated much interest among social psychologists in prejudice, discrimination, and totalitarianism. These topics became central issues investigated in early social psychology (e.g., Allport & Kramer, 1946; Adorno, Frenkel-Brunswik, Levinson, & Sanford, 1950).

The Second World War turned North American social psychologists' attention to practical questions relevant to the war effort, such as how to select good leaders from among army recruits, which leadership styles are most effective in small groups, how people could be encouraged to conserve essential war materials at home, and how messages could best be constructed to maintain morale. The imme-diate needs of the Allies stimulated pragmatic, problem-focused research. It became apparent that social psychology offered techniques that could yield important insights about human behavior.

## Social Psychology's Emergence as a Distinct Area of Psychology

Social psychology came out of the Second World War as a field that used experi-mental techniques to study social behavior. There were increasing numbers of social psychologists at universities, and specialized theories were beginning to appear. Social psychology was clearly emerging as a distinct area of psychology. The 1950s and 1960s were a time of excitement in social psychology, as researchers explored new topics and identified interesting phenomena.

Many researchers continued to investigate issues carrying over from the Second World War, such as conformity (e.g., Asch, 1956), obedience to authority (e.g., Mil-gram, 1963), attitude change (e.g., Hovland, Janis, & Kelley, 1953), and intergroup conflict (e.g., Sherif et al., 1961). The research programs of these and other scientists elevated social psychology to a new level of productivity as an experimental science.

The 1950s and 1960s also saw the appearance of many important theoretical models that gave social psychology a set of theories specifically related to social behavior. The names of these theories (e.g., cognitive dissonance theory, Festinger, 1957; social learning theory, Bandura, Ross, & Ross, 1963) would probably mean little to you at this point, so we will not list them here. Suffice it to say that many models from this time period will be discussed.

Most of the theories and studies described in the remaining chapters of this book have been proposed or conducted since social psychology emerged as a vibrant, unique area of psychology in the 1950s. Our goal is to give you a comprehensive and up-to-date introduction to the field, though we must of course be selective to some extent. We focus on work done in the past 20 or 30 years (and especially in the last 10), but it is important to recognize that recent advances in understanding have been possible only because of the earlier contributions of researchers and research programs we have mentioned here.

 # Organization of the Book

We have 14 chapters in this book. These chapters cover all of the classical topics or problems of social psychology, such as social cognition, attitudes, aggression, and so on. Each chapter focuses on one topic or problem and reviews the social psychological research in that area. Cross-cutting the chapters are numerous contexts or settings to which social psychology can be applied. Many contexts will be discussed in the book, but three will be especially emphasized: culture, health, and the law.

## Classical Problems of Social Psychology

Social psychology is a wonderfully—but bewilderingly—diverse field. Individuals' thoughts, feelings, and behaviors can be influenced by other people in many, many ways. Although social psychology potentially encompasses a nearly infinite number of topics, social psychologists have focused on a limited number of problems or issues in their research. We have organized this book to reflect these classical topics.

**Setting the Stage.** Chapters 1 and 2 set the stage for the remainder of the book. After the current chapter's introduction to the field, we turn in Chapter 2 to how social psychologists go about studying social behavior. We discuss the scientific method and compare different approaches to research. We summarize the things you need to know to understand and appreciate the research findings described in subsequent chapters.

**Perceiving the Social World.** Chapters 3 and 4 introduce the processes involved in making sense of the social world. In Chapter 3, we survey social cognition, which refers to how information about people is processed and stored. We discuss memory, impressions, and some common errors that people make in everyday judgments. In Chapter 4, we address more complex decisions and judgments, such as attributions, which are judgments about why an event occurred or why someone behaved in a certain way. Chapter 4 also discusses how we perceive ourselves, including judgments of our abilities and future prospects.

**The Person in the Situation.** Chapters 5 and 6 discuss some important features of individuals that are stable across settings; these enduring characteristics differentiate one person from another and must be included in any attempt to understand social behavior. In Chapter 5, we focus on the self-concept (identity), gender, and dispositions (personality traits). In Chapter 6, we focus on one of the most researched topics in social psychology: attitudes, which are good–bad evaluations of targets. We discuss where attitudes come from and how they affect behavior.

**Social Influence.** Chapters 7 and 8 address social influence: how other people can change our opinions and actions. In Chapter 7, we discuss attitude change. We articulate some of the factors that affect the success of persuasive messages, including advertisements. We also discuss the topic of propaganda. In Chapter 8, we turn our attention to conformity and obedience. This chapter is where you will learn about some of the most famous experiments in social psychology.

**Harmful Social Behavior.** Chapters 9, 10, and 11 cover some of the negative aspects of human behavior. In Chapter 9, we discuss stereotypes, prejudice, and discrimination. We consider the sources of these constructs and how they might be reduced. We also discuss sexism, which is prejudice and discrimination directed against women. In Chapter 10, we review group processes, including how groups make decisions and what kinds of leaders are most effective. We also discuss intergroup conflict, which often can be traced back to stereotypes and prejudice. In Chapter 11, we review research and theories of human aggression. We discuss conditions that elicit violence and aggression, as well as strategies for controlling harmful behavior.

**Helpful Social Behavior.** Chapters 12 and 13 address some positive aspects of human behavior. In Chapter 12, we discuss the conditions that promote helping in casual or in emergency situations. We also discuss the causes and benefits of social support. In Chapter 13, we take up the topics of liking, loving, and close relationships. From our earliest moments as infants, and continuing through to the end of our lives, the relationships and attachments we form with other people provide the foundation of social life.

**Putting It All Together.** The final chapter of most textbooks provides a summary and review of the entire book. And, in Chapter 14, we do provide a brief summary. But we do more than that. The aim of the last chapter is to show you how social psychology is relevant to your own life. By understanding social psychology, you are better informed about the determinants of behavior and can use that knowledge to help yourself and others. Chapter 14 also tells you about career opportunities in social psychology. A background in social psychology will serve you well in many fields, including marketing, advertising, government, law, health, education, and business (not to mention psychology).

## The Many Contexts of Social Psychology

One of the key features of social psychology is the diversity of contexts to which it applies. After all, social behavior occurs in almost every conceivable setting. We will discuss many contexts throughout the book, but three will appear most frequently because they are especially interesting and important: culture, health, and the law.

**The Culture Context.** Much of social psychology has been built on studies of North American college students. These studies have identified many important principles of social behavior, but there are reasons to question whether these principles always apply to other cultures. In the past two decades, social psychology has become much more international in scope, with research being conducted in many countries around the world. Some of these cross-cultural studies have identified limitations to social psychological findings from North America.

Cultures differ from one another in many ways, of course, so when a principle does not generalize to cultures outside North America, it is not always easy to know why. Also, understanding cultural differences is made more challenging by the fact that each of us is at least partly the product of our own culture, so it can be difficult to look at the world in other ways. Nevertheless, analyzing the role and influence of culture can provide significant insights into the dynamics of social behavior. The importance of studying culture is brought home by the threat of terrorism. To understand and reduce this threat, we must look at the world through the eyes of terrorists—what motivates them, how they recruit new members, and so on. Why are these young people willing to die for their cause?

© Stuart Franklin/Magnum Photos

Social psychology has become more international and cross-cultural in scope over the past two decades.

Throughout this book, we will discuss cross-cultural limits that have been identified to social psychological findings and theories. For example, we will discuss cultural differences in the favorability of self-evaluations (Chapter 4), the nature of the self-concept (Chapter 5), the ways attitudes change (Chapter 7), rates of conformity (Chapter 8), and rates and forms of aggression (Chapter 11).

These comments should not be taken to imply that every culture produces totally different patterns of social behavior. Indeed, differences between cultures are often small compared to cross-cultural similarities. Thus, studying the cultural context of social behavior also gives us a deeper appreciation for the qualities we *share* with all members of our species.

**The Health Context.** Some of the most important problems facing humans today center on health and the prevention of disease. In many chapters of this book, we illustrate how social psychology offers insight and points the way to possible solutions. For example, depression and anxiety are related to whether people think they are measuring up to important standards (Chapter 4); optimism and other dispositions are related to well-being (Chapter 5); safer sex campaigns that rely on principles of persuasion can be effective (Chapter 6); fear appeals can successfully motivate changes to unhealthy lifestyles (Chapter 7); and recovery from health-related problems is often improved by social support (Chapter 12).

**The Law Context.** As a society, we are governed and live by a system of rules and laws. You may not appreciate how your daily social behaviors are shaped and influenced by these rules and laws, but the influence is very powerful and based on principles of social psychology. From traffic regulations to criminal prosecutions, our legal institutions impose constraints and boundaries on social behavior. And those institutions themselves—police, courts, juries, judges—provide rich and important contexts for studying social behavior. For example, social psychologists have shown that eyewitness testimony is often unreliable (Chapter 3); it is usually difficult to detect whether someone is telling the truth or is lying (Chapter 4); rules and laws work, in part, because of conformity and obedience (Chapter 8); principles of group dynamics explain how and why juries make their decisions (Chapter 10); and people sometimes violate rules and legal mandates by harming one another (Chapter 11).

 ## Social Psychology Alive

Social psychology is an exciting and vibrant discipline. A rich theoretical tradition has evolved since World War II. The methods and experiments of social psychology create engaging social situations, and the problems addressed by social psychology are intrinsically interesting and relevant to people's lives. A textbook by itself can certainly provide the factual material, the theoretical models, graphs of results, and still photographs. But it takes more than that to truly appreciate and understand social psychology. You must experience experimental procedures and manipulations for yourself—you need to see social psychology in action. That's why we have developed a number of additional resources to accompany this book. Our aim is to make social psychology come *alive*.

## Social Psychology in Action

 The science of social psychology is built on a foundation of careful research. The pages of a textbook can give you an impression of these studies, but actually seeing a study in progress clarifies what they are really about. Meeting researchers and listening to them explain their studies can also be helpful. That is why we have produced *Social Psychology Alive: The Videos*. Several clips on this CD-ROM provide an inside look at actual or re-created experiments. For instance, you will see for yourself how participants behaved in Stanley Milgram's famous obedience experiments (Chapter 8) and how children responded when they observed an adult engaging in acts of aggression (Chapter 11). You will also listen to interviews with famous social psychologists talking about a variety of topics, including the unreliability of eyewitness testimony (Chapter 3), cultural influences on emotion (Chapter 4), and the devastating effects of racial stereotypes (Chapter 9). Finally, you will see real-life examples of social psychology in action, such as the challenges women face trying to juggle multiple social roles (Chapter 5), how military recruits feel after suffering through boot camp (Chapter 7), and strategies used by video dating services to match partners (Chapter 13). These video clips will help you to visualize the materials in the textbook.

## Try It Yourself

One thing we know from research in psychology and education is that active learning is often more effective than passive receipt of information. People are better able to learn and retain new knowledge when they can play with it and make connections to their own lives. We have done a variety of things to help you do that.

**Learn About Yourself.** Throughout the book, you will find commonly used scales in social psychology. These scales are presented in tables labeled Know Yourself and include all or some items from the original scale, as well as instructions for scoring your responses. For example, in Chapter 5, we discuss individual differences in *self-monitoring*. As described originally by social psychologist Mark Snyder (1974), the high self-monitor is a person who is especially sensitive to external, situational cues in interpersonal settings and who uses such cues as a guide to behavior; the low self-monitor, on the other hand, is a person who uses internal cues and personal attributes (e.g., attitudes, feelings, values) as a guide to behavior. Are you able to develop a clear sense of self-monitoring based on this conceptual description? Can you tell whether *you* are a high or low self-monitor? Perhaps. But the best way to find out is by completing items from the *Self-Monitoring Scale,* which you can do in Chapter 5 (see page 183).

**Be a Research Participant.** Another way to learn about social psychology is by experiencing the conditions and manipulations in actual experiments. Therefore, we have constructed a website, *Social Psychology Alive: Online Labs,* where you can be a participant in more than a dozen studies. These experiments relate to topics throughout the book; the titles of relevant studies are listed at the end of each chapter. For each experiment, you will be assigned to one condition and will complete the study like an actual participant. If you wish, you can subsequently run through the procedure for other conditions as well. Your data will be saved (only for the first condition you completed), and you can look at your responses when you are done. In addition, you can look at an anonymous summary of the responses of all students who have participated from your class, or a summary of all students who have participated anywhere in the country. A detailed explanation of the purpose and expected results of the study is available when you complete your participation. These online studies will give you the perspective of a research participant and make reading about social psychology experiments in the textbook more engaging.

**Do Your Own Research.** To make social psychology truly come alive, you also need to know what it is like to be a social psychologist. You need to conduct your own projects or experiments by developing the measures, collecting the data, and interpreting the results. To get you started, we have prepared a project-oriented workbook to accompany this textbook. *Social Psychology Alive: The Workbook* provides project ideas, sample stimulus materials, and help with interpreting data. A variety of possible projects are outlined, many of which can be done with the resources available to you. With the guidance and supervision of your instructor, you can personally do social psychology.

**Dig Deeper.** You will notice that, like most textbook writers, we provide many references and citations. We provide these references to give credit to the person or persons who proposed an idea or conducted a study, but also to allow you to dig a little deeper. These references generally follow the citation style of the American Psychological Association (2001), and the format we use is the same as the one you will find in scientific articles and books. All of these references are presented in alphabetical order in a list at the back of the book. If you are curious about the details of an experiment, want to get more information so you can conduct a similar study, or want to understand more fully the theoretical background to the research, the references are there to lead the way. With the citation in hand, you should be able to find the original article in your library, or have it ordered for you. Our goal is to make the social psychological literature accessible to you. For this reason, we only provide citations for articles or books that are readily found in North American college and university libraries.

There are two other ways you can dig deeper. First, at the end of each chapter, you will find sources listed under the heading *To Learn More.* These sources are ones that are particularly interesting or comprehensive for the topics in that chapter. They also should be available at most college libraries. Second, if your instructor ordered it with this book, you have access to *InfoTrac College Edition,* which is an online library of archived journal articles and periodicals dating back 22 years. You can access this information via your CD-ROM or by going directly to the website listed at the end of each chapter and using the passcode from the InfoTrac College Edition card that came with your book. To use the online library, enter a search term and see what comes up. This is an excellent way to find additional materials on specific topics in the chapters.

# Social Psychology Is All Around You

As we noted earlier, social psychology is an exciting field to study because our lives are immersed in a social world. To maximize your appreciation of social psychology, you should pay special attention to your own life. The workbook provides many connections between the ideas in the textbook and daily life, such as newspaper articles, real-life examples of social psychological principles, and suggestions about things to watch for. Here are a few specific ways you can find social psychology in your own experiences.

**Watch Television.** Television is a rich source of social psychology in action. We posed a question at the beginning of the chapter about how the media affected people's responses to the terrorism of September 11, 2001. Constant replays of the attacks probably heightened feelings of threat and fear; stories of heroism probably heightened feelings of national pride and patriotism. In many ways, reporters and commentators helped to define the events for the public.

So think about social psychology while you watch TV. Pay attention to commercials, sitcoms, the news, and (if you can) television programming in other countries and cultures. In commercials and advertisements, you will see in action the basic principles of persuasion (Chapter 7) and social influence (Chapter 8). So-called *infomercials* are especially interesting—see if you can connect this sales method to theories of persuasion. Television programs (especially dramas and situation comedies) often reflect or portray social stereotypes (Chapters 3 and 9) and close relationships (Chapter 13). The news often tells of intergroup conflict (Chapter 10) and violence (Chapter 11).

**Read the Newspaper and Magazines.** Newspapers and magazines are also brimming with rich examples of social psychology in action. Unlike television, newspaper editorials allow writers to present extended arguments. Think about the editorials you find most and least persuasive: what are the techniques used by effective writers (Chapter 7)? Study the cartoons. You will find that cartoonists often rely on basic social psychological concepts to create humor, such as the hindsight bias

Many principles of social psychology can be observed in television programs.

© AP/Wide World Photos/Nati Harnik

(Chapter 3), stereotypes (Chapters 3 and 9), social norms (Chapter 8), and close relationships (Chapter 13). You may want to develop a small portfolio of clippings from newspapers and magazines that illustrate basic social psychological principles.

**Surf the Web.** The Internet offers still another perspective on social psychology, in at least two distinct ways. First, you will find numerous websites offering links and content relating to social psychology. For instance, a good place to get started is the Social Psychology Network: http://www.socialpsychology.org. Second, many websites are little more than persuasive communications; ask yourself how the sites use basic principles of persuasion (Chapter 7) and social influence (Chapter 8). The Internet is less restricted or filtered than other mass media, so it is also easier to find examples of social extremes—portrayals of violence, racism, and stereotypes abound on the web (Chapters 9 and 11).

**Observe Others.** Part of the social psychologist's toolkit is the ability to observe the actions of others, especially in their natural environments. Watch your friends and family members as they go about their daily lives and interact with one another. Can you tell what people are thinking or feeling by simply observing their facial expressions or body language (Chapter 4)? Are people consistent in their actions and personal styles across time, places, and contexts (Chapter 5)? Do people behave differently when they are alone than when they are in groups (Chapter 10)? Why are some people attracted to one another and others not (Chapter 13)?

**Observe Yourself.** A little self-reflection and introspection will also make you a better social psychologist. Do you engage in much wishful thinking (Chapter 3)? Do you explain your own behavior in the same way you explain others' actions (Chapter 4)? Do you tend to rationalize and justify your wasted effort (Chapter 7)? Do your moods influence how helpful you are to other people (Chapter 12)?

If you want to collect some data on yourself, consider keeping a personal diary. The method is described in Chapter 13 and in the workbook. At regular times each day, write down what you are doing, how you are feeling, and what you are thinking. After several weeks, you will be surprised to see how rich and complex your social world really is.

© Louise Gubb/CORBIS SABA

You can see social psychology in action by watching other people around you.

# Chapter Summary

We end each chapter with a brief summary, which reviews the chapter's key terms and central ideas. In this chapter, we introduced **social psychology,** which is the scientific study of how individuals' thoughts, feelings, and behaviors are influenced by other people. Social psychologists take the perspective of individuals in a social setting, rather than focusing only on objective features of the situation. Other people can affect us in many ways, even without having to be physically present.

Some findings in social psychology are consistent with intuitive folk wisdom, but it is a mistake to think that social psychology is just common sense. Many findings are not common sense at all, often because folk wisdom is simplistic whereas real life is more complicated. Also, after reading about the results of a social psychology experiment, people may think that the findings were obvious, whereas the outcome was actually quite uncertain in advance. Studying social psychology has many benefits, including becoming an informed citizen, being able to apply social psychological knowledge to everyday life, and gaining a better understanding of yourself.

Social psychology's roots can be found in philosophy. For example, the concept of social norms can be traced back to the philosophical concept of the **social contract:** the idea that human societies have developed some basic rules of social and moral conduct, which members of the societies implicitly agree to follow. An influential approach in psychology during the first half of the 20th century was **behaviorism,** which attempts to explain behavior purely in terms of stimulus–response connections established through experience and reinforcement. Several influential social psychologists who came to North America in the 1930s brought with them an alternative approach: **Gestalt theory.** Gestalt theory assumes that people's overall, subjective interpretations of objects are more important than the objects' external, physical features. The Second World War turned North American social psychologists' attention to practical questions regarding the war effort. By the time the war had ended, social psychology was emerging as a distinct area of psychology.

Each chapter in this book focuses on one of the classical topics or problems of social psychology and reviews the scientific literature in that area. Cross-cutting the chapters are many contexts to which social psychology can be applied, with special emphasis on culture, health, and the law. The approach of *Social Psychology Alive* is to encourage you to experience social psychology for yourself. We have prepared many supplementary materials to help, including *Social Psychology Alive: The Videos, Social Psychology Alive: The Workbook,* and *Social Psychology Alive: Online Labs.* We want you to pay attention to things in your own life, because social psychology is all around you.

# Key Terms

**behaviorism** (18)

**Gestalt theory** (20)

**social contract** (18)

**social psychology** (5)

## Social Psychology Alive on the Web

### SOCIAL PSYCHOLOGY ALIVE: QUIZZING AND PRACTICE TESTS

You can access our website directly by going to http://psychology.wadsworth.com/breckler1e/ for online quizzes, flash cards, and Internet links.

### INFOTRAC® COLLEGE EDITION

For additional readings, explore InfoTrac College Edition, your online library of archived journal articles and periodicals dating back 22 years. If your instructor ordered InfoTrac College Edition with this book, you can access it from your CD-ROM, or go directly to http://www.infotrac-college.com/wadsworth and use the passcode from the InfoTrac College Edition card that came with your book. For this chapter, try these search terms: *social psychology, sociology, philosophy, social contract, behaviorism, Gestalt theory.*

## Social Psychology Alive: The Workbook

Chapter 1 of *Social Psychology Alive: The Workbook* provides key terms, guided study, and sample test questions. It also provides suggestions for connecting social psychology to the real world and to your life:

- Social Psychology Alive Journal: Personal Experiences

- Social Psychology Alive Journal: Events in the Media
- Proverbs, Adages, and Platitudes: Which Do Social Psychology Support?
- How Does Social Psychology Compare to Other Areas of Psychology and Other Disciplines?

## Social Psychology Alive: The Videos

To see video on the topics and experiments discussed in this chapter, you can go either to Social PsychologyNow or to the CD-ROM, if your instructor assigned either one, to the following section:

- Social Psychology: It's All Around You

## To Learn More

At the end of each chapter, we provide a few citations to books or articles that can help you learn more. These readings are good places to start if you want to gain a deeper understanding of the topics in that chapter. Here are three suggestions for Chapter 1:

- Allport, G. W. (1985). The historical background of social psychology. In G. Lindzey & E. Aronson (Eds.), *The handbook of social psychology* (3rd ed., Vol. 1, pp. 1–46). New York: Random House.

- Jones, E. E. (1998). Major developments in five decades of social psychology. In D. T. Gilbert, S. T. Fiske, & G. Lindzey (Eds.), *The handbook of social psychology* (4th ed., Vol. 1, pp. 58–95). Boston: McGraw-Hill.
- Taylor, S. E. (1998). The social being in social psychology. In D. T. Gilbert, S. T. Fiske, & G. Lindzey (Eds.), *The handbook of social psychology* (4th ed., Vol. 1, pp. 3–57). Boston: McGraw-Hill.

Courtesy of The Courtroom 21 Project, William & Mary Law School

# The Methods of Social Psychology

*It is 1961. Fred Jones works as a bank clerk in New Haven, Connecticut. As he is reading the local newspaper one Saturday morning, Mr. Jones notices the advertisement shown in Figure 2.1. It seems that a professor at nearby Yale University is offering people $4 to participate in a study of memory. Mr. Jones could use the money, so he mails in the coupon to indicate his interest. A few days later, he gets a phone call and agrees to make an appointment for the following Wednesday.*

*When he arrives at the appointed time, Mr. Jones is greeted by an experimenter dressed in a gray technician's coat. Another man—Robert Wallace—has also arrived to participate in the study. The men are paid up front for their participation, and they are free to leave at any time. The experimenter explains to both men that this is a study of the effects of punishment on learning and memory. One of the two men will be assigned the role of "teacher" and the other of "learner." The teacher will ask a series of questions, and the learner will answer. If the learner gives the correct response, the teacher is to proceed to the next question. But if the learner gives the wrong response, the teacher is instructed to administer an electric shock. What's more, for each incorrect answer given by the learner, the teacher is to administer increasingly severe and painful electric shocks.*

*As chance would have it, Mr. Jones is assigned the role of teacher and Mr. Wallace is assigned the role of learner. At first, everything is going fine. Mr. Wallace makes a few errors, and Mr. Jones delivers the electric shocks as instructed. But the learner continues to make errors, and the shocks are getting very powerful. Mr. Wallace is complaining now, and asking that the experiment stop. He says that the shocks are hurting him, and he is worried about his heart. Mr. Jones looks to the experimenter for guidance. "What should I do?" he asks. "The man wants to stop."*

*The experimenter replies coolly, "Please go on."*

*"Gee, I don't think I should," complains Mr. Jones. "He said something about his heart."*

*"The experiment requires that you continue," the experimenter responds.*

*And so Mr. Jones continues to deliver the electric shocks. Mr. Wallace continues to protest, screaming that he wants to stop. At each step, the experimenter insists that Mr. Jones continue. Eventually, he reaches the 30th shock level (a button labeled "450 volts"). Finally, the experiment is over. Mr. Jones is sweating profusely, and he has loosened his tie. He is relieved, and glad that he will soon be able to leave.*

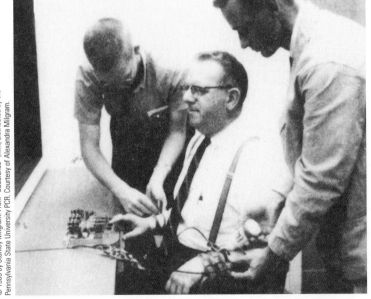

© 1965 by Stanley Milgram. From "Obedience" (film) distributed by the Pennsylvania State University PCR. Courtesy of Alexandra Milgram.

This experiment involved participants delivering electric shocks when a "learner" made mistakes on a memory task.

# The Scientific Method

The preceding story is true; only the names have been changed to protect the participants. The study actually happened, and 40 men participated in the role of teacher (the same role as Mr. Jones). The study was conducted by Stanley Milgram but had nothing to do with learning or memory: it was a social psychological investigation of obedience to authority (see Milgram, 1963, 1974). The entire scene was a setup: Mr. Wallace was an accomplice working for Milgram; the assignment of roles was rigged so Mr. Wallace would be the learner; no electric shocks were actually delivered; and all of Mr. Wallace's screams and protests were faked. The study has become a classic in social psychology, and it illustrates many of the principles and challenges of social psychological research. We will refer back to this study several times in the chapter.

We know from Chapter 1 that social psychology is a *science*—we defined the field as "the scientific study of how individuals' thoughts, feelings, and behaviors are influenced by other people." It is not simple, however, to study social behavior scientifically. Unlike physical sciences such as biology and chemistry, in which researchers often have total control over the materials they are studying, social psychologists are interested in understanding spontaneous social behavior, which is difficult to study in tightly controlled settings. Thus, social psychology is a tricky science. Social psychologists have to be very creative in using the scientific method to study how individuals are influenced by other people.

The scientific method is basically a tool (or, more correctly, a set of tools) that scientists use to find out about the world. Scientists are curious about why events occur, and the scientific method provides an objective, efficient way to answer questions. Just as early explorers used maps, telescopes, and compasses to discover things about the world, scientists use the scientific method to investigate issues in their own field. Scientists are like modern explorers trying to understand the causes of important events and phenomena. The scientific method gives them a way to collect impartial information about the world around them.

In this chapter, we discuss the research methods of social psychology. We begin by providing some general background about the scientific method. Specifically, we define *theories* and *hypotheses* and discuss issues involved in translating theories and hypotheses into testable questions. Armed with this background information, we turn to *correlational research*—studies that involve collecting two or more measures and seeing how they relate to one another. We describe three correlational methods, which differ primarily in terms of how researchers collect their data. Next, we discuss the most important method used by social psychologists: the *experiment*. In experiments, researchers *manipulate* independent variables, *measure* dependent variables, and *control* extraneous variables. We note that researchers want careful control in their experiment but also hope to be able to apply their findings to nonlaboratory settings—the sometimes competing goals of *internal validity* and *external validity*. We then differentiate between *single-factor* and *factorial* experimental designs, discuss the issue of *realism* in experiments, and consider some implications of modern technologies for research in social psychology. Finally, we raise some ethical issues that are relevant to social psychological research and explain how investigators address these issues.

---

*Public Announcement*

## WE WILL PAY YOU $4.00 FOR ONE HOUR OF YOUR TIME

### Persons Needed for a Study of Memory

\*We will pay five hundred New Haven men to help us complete a scientific study of memory and learning. The study is being done at Yale University.

\*Each person who participates will be paid $4.00 (plus 50c carfare) for approximately 1 hour's time. We need you for only one hour: there are no further obligations. You may choose the time you would like to come (evenings, weekdays, or weekends).

\*No special training, education, or experience is needed. We want:

| | | |
|---|---|---|
| Factory workers | Businessmen | Construction workers |
| City employees | Clerks | Salespeople |
| Laborers | Professional people | White-collar workers |
| Barbers | Telephone workers | Others |

All persons must be between the ages of 20 and 50. High school and college students cannot be used.

\*If you meet these qualifications, fill out the coupon below and mail it now to Professor Stanley Milgram, Department of Psychology, Yale University, New Haven. You will be notified later of the specific time and place of the study. We reserve the right to decline any application.

\*You will be paid $4.00 (plus 50c carfare) as soon as you arrive at the laboratory.

- - - - - - - - - - - - - - - - - - - - - - - -

TO:
PROF. STANLEY MILGRAM, DEPARTMENT OF PSYCHOLOGY, YALE UNIVERSITY, NEW HAVEN, CONN. I want to take part in this study of memory and learning. I am between the ages of 20 and 50. I will be paid $4.00 (plus 50c carfare) if I participate.

NAME (Please Print)......................................

ADDRESS .............................................

TELEPHONE NO................ Best time to call you .......

AGE ........OCCUPATION....................SEX......
CAN YOU COME:

WEEKDAYS........ EVENINGS....... WEEKENDS.........

**FIGURE 2.1** Newspaper advertisement for study of memory

From *Obedience to Authority: An Experimental View* by Stanley Milgram, p. 15. © 1974 Harper & Row Publishers. Reprinted by permission of Alexandra Milgram.

## Theories and Hypotheses

**theory**

*an explanation of why an event or outcome occurs; it identifies the underlying causes of an event or phenomenon*

**hypothesis**

*a specific prediction about what should occur if a theory is valid; it provides the means by which a theory can be tested*

Two key elements of the scientific method are *theories* and *hypotheses.* You can think about theories as *explanations,* and hypotheses as *predictions.* More specifically, a **theory** is a scientist's explanation of why an event or outcome occurs (see Pelham, 1999; Schmidt & Hunter, 2003); it identifies the underlying causes of something the scientist has observed. In psychology, theories typically focus on psychological processes to explain events. For instance, in attempting to explain obedience to authority, a social psychologist might propose that individuals' *fear of being punished if they do not obey* causes obedience. This simple theory explains obedience to authority in terms of an underlying psychological mechanism (fear of punishment).

Whereas theories provide a framework for understanding *why* something occurs, **hypotheses** are specific *predictions* about what should occur if a theory is valid. Hypotheses are derived from a theory and, therefore, provide a means for testing the theory. For example, if fear of punishment causes obedience to authority (theory), then increasing or decreasing individuals' fear of punishment should directly increase or decrease obedience (hypothesis). If a test of this hypothesis confirmed it, then confidence in the validity of the theory would increase. A process of evaluating theories by confirming or disconfirming hypotheses forms the core of the scientific method—a point to which we will turn momentarily.

But, first, how do scientists develop theories? What are the sources of their ideas? (See Kruglanski & Higgins, 2004, for a series of articles discussing theory construction in social psychology.) Most theories build on prior scientific work, including previous theories that have been shown to be inaccurate or limited (Cacioppo, 2004). Theories often involve applying a concept or principle from one field to another related but distinct field (Zanna, 2004). Theories also frequently rely on scientists' intuitive analyses of problems, including their personal experiences (Fiske, 2004). Some theories are the result of collaborations between scientists who have different perspectives (Levine & Moreland, 2004). In developing a theory, scientists aim for simplicity, coherence, and testability (Fiske, 2004), because these features make it more likely that the theory will generate new ideas and new discoveries (Higgins, 2004).

To make the concepts of theories and hypotheses more concrete, let's briefly consider a fascinating theory from social psychology as an example. Melvin Lerner (1977, 1980) proposed *just world theory,* in which he suggested that humans *need* to believe that the world is a fair and just place. Lerner proposed that we are all motivated to believe that people usually receive what they deserve: hard work and honesty bring rewards, whereas laziness and dishonesty do not pay. Lerner argued that if we did *not* believe that the world is largely fair, then we would fear that our *own* efforts and investments might not pay off. That is, if we believed that the world is unjust and that hardworking people do not necessarily succeed, then we would fear that our *own* hard work might be in vain! Lerner proposed that this possibility is threatening and anxiety-provoking, so we try to *protect* our belief in a just world.

What are some *hypotheses* that can be derived from just world theory? One rather straightforward hypothesis is that, when asked, most people will say that the world is generally fair. After all, if just world theory is valid, then people should report that the world is just. Lerner also derived a more indirect and interesting hypothesis from the theory's assumption that we want to *protect* our belief in a just world. Lerner made the provocative prediction that people would blame or derogate (evaluate negatively) victims who are suffering in

*Just world theory* predicts that people may blame and disparage victims.

© Tim Boyle/Getty Images

negative circumstances (e.g., unemployed people, AIDS patients), especially when their suffering is expected to continue. This prediction was based on the logic that suffering victims threaten the belief that the world is fair, *unless the victims are either responsible for their suffering or are bad people who in some sense deserve their suffering.* Therefore, if we are truly motivated to defend our belief that the world is fair, we might try to convince ourselves that people who are suffering brought it on themselves or are bad people who deserve their fate. Can you think of victims who tend to be blamed or disparaged in our society? What about people living on welfare? Or what about rape victims, who are sometimes accused of having acted in ways that somehow "invited" the rape? Lerner's hypothesis seems consistent with some people's devaluation of these victims.

Just world theory is a good example of how theories can lead to interesting, possibly unexpected predictions. Just world theory offers a novel perspective on people's beliefs about fairness and justice. As a *theory,* it explains *why* people want to believe in a just world and proposes that this need is present, at least to some extent, in everyone. It identifies psychological mechanisms that are thought to account for important social behaviors. It also provides the basis for some intriguing *hypotheses,* including the prediction that people will blame or derogate victims whose suffering is expected to continue. We will return to this prediction later in the chapter when we discuss experimental research. First, though, we continue with background information about the scientific method and discuss another important component: operational definitions.

## Translating Theoretical Ideas into Testable Questions: Operational Definitions

Theories and hypotheses in social psychology are typically expressed in *conceptual* terms: they refer to abstract ideas or concepts that cannot be observed directly. Therefore, to test theories or hypotheses, researchers must somehow translate the abstract ideas into concrete, objective measures. For instance, a researcher interested in *attitudes* cannot directly "see" participants' attitudes; this concept can only be measured indirectly. Or a researcher interested in *obedience to authority* must think of how to measure this process in a consistent, objective way across participants.

An **operational definition** of a concept is a *specific, observable response* that will be used to measure the concept (see Dooley, 2001; Pelham, 1999). For instance, people's attitudes toward religion (which are unobservable but presumably exist in people's minds) could be operationally defined by asking respondents to indicate how unfavorable or favorable they are toward religion on a scale from 0 (very unfavorable) to 10 (very favorable). Table 2.1 illustrates what the scale could look like. The concept is *attitudes toward religion;* the operational definition is *scores from 0 to 10* on a response scale.

**operational definition**
*a specific, observable response that is used to measure a concept*

---

**TABLE 2.1**
*Operational Definition of Attitudes Toward Religion*

*How unfavorable or favorable are you toward religion? Please circle the number that best represents your attitude.*

*My attitude toward religion is*

| 0 | 1 | 2 | 3 | 4 | 5 | 6 | 7 | 8 | 9 | 10 |
|---|---|---|---|---|---|---|---|---|---|----|
| Very Unfavorable | | Unfavorable | | | Neutral | | Favorable | | Very Favorable | |

As another example, obedience to authority (a process that can be displayed in many different ways) might be operationally defined as the intensity of shock participants are willing to deliver in a procedure paralleling the one in Milgram's (1963) research. The concept is *obedience to authority;* the operational definition is *severity of shock* participants will administer.

The accompanying Concept Review summarizes the meanings of theories, hypotheses, and operational definitions.

These examples of operational definitions illustrate the two most common kinds of measures in social psychology: self-report measures and behavioral measures. We briefly address the advantages and disadvantages of each kind of measure in the following paragraphs. A detailed discussion of self-report and behavioral measures in the specific context of measuring attitudes is presented in Chapter 6 (see page 205). We also provide a more general description of how to develop measures of social psychological constructs in Appendix I of this book.

**Self-Report Measures.** To measure many social psychological concepts, the easiest strategy is to ask people directly. If you want to know whether individuals believe in God, ask them. If you want to know whether people are optimistic about their future, ask them. If you want to know how often people go to the dentist, ask them. So long as a concept is something that people are *able* and *willing* to report, measuring it via self-report questions makes sense. Belief in God, optimism about the future, and visits to the dentist probably satisfy these assumptions, because people are presumably aware of these concepts and seem unlikely to be dishonest in reporting them.

Of course, even when people are able and willing to report a concept, researchers must be careful to express self-report questions clearly. It is easy to understand questions such as "How old are you?" or "What is the date of your birth?" It is harder to understand questions such as "Are you favorable to legalized abortion?" People attempting to answer this question might wonder what is meant by "legalized abortion." Does it mean in the first trimester, or anytime during a pregnancy? Does it refer to across-the-board access to abortion so long as a woman wants it, or only in special circumstances that must be approved by a physician? It can be difficult to answer a question if the meaning is not well specified.

The same question can often be asked in different ways, and subtle changes in phrasing or wording can significantly affect responses. As an illustration of this, Elizabeth Loftus and John Palmer (1974) asked people to watch a short film depicting a car accident. Everybody saw the same film, but different questions were asked to

## CONCEPT REVIEW
### Theories, Hypotheses, and Operational Definitions

| Concept | Description | Example |
|---------|-------------|---------|
| Theories | Explanations of why an outcome occurs | Individuals' fear of being punished if they do not obey causes obedience. |
| Hypotheses | Predictions about what should happen if a theory is valid | Increasing individuals' fear of being punished if they do not obey will increase obedience. |
| Operational definitions | Specific, observable responses used to measure concepts | Threatening participants with receiving electric shocks themselves if they do not obey will increase the severity of shock they administer in a procedure paralleling the one in Milgram's research. |

© Spencer Grant/Photo Edit

Observers' judgments about a car accident were affected by the questions they were asked.

different groups of viewers. One group of viewers was asked, "About how fast were the cars going when they hit each other?" On average, these viewers answered 8 miles per hour. Another group of viewers was asked a slightly different question: "About how fast were the cars going when they smashed each other?" The viewers in this group answered, on average, 10.5 miles per hour. Why did these different answers occur? It all had to do with the verb used to describe the accident: *hit* versus *smashed*. Even though all participants saw the same accident, the wording of the question influenced their answers. Similar concerns about wording are important in many occupations. For example, physicians interviewing patients must avoid leading questions if they want to diagnose problems accurately; they should ask patients to describe their symptoms, rather than inadvertently focusing patients' attention on particular sensations (e.g., "Does your stomach hurt?"). Social psychologists are very careful about how they word their questions. The answers they get may depend on it.

Sometimes the assumption that people are able and willing to report a concept is *not* valid. For instance, people may not be *aware* of some internal states, such as unconscious motives that can affect their actions (e.g., "Are you afraid of failure?") or memories that may no longer be available (e.g., "How did you feel about religion when you were a child?"). People may *believe* that they can answer these questions accurately, but their responses will probably be guesses.

Perhaps even more often than being unaware of a concept, participants in social psychological research may not *want* to report some things honestly. For instance, respondents may be motivated to create a positive impression of themselves. Responding in this manner is known as **socially desirable responding**— giving answers that portray the respondent in a favorable light. Questions like "How often do you put cans in recycling bins after finishing a drink?" and "Would you obey an order to deliver an electric shock to an unwilling recipient?" are loaded—some answers are more socially valued than others. Everyone knows that the most desirable answer to the recycling question is "always" or "every time," and the most desirable answer to the obedience question is "no." Failing to recycle and obeying questionable orders are considered undesirable in our society. So people might not answer these kinds of questions honestly.

**socially desirable responding**
*a form of responding that involves giving answers that portray the respondent in a positive light*

**Behavioral Measures.** Because people may be unable or unwilling to report some things accurately, researchers sometimes measure concepts by observing individuals' behaviors. For instance, continuing the examples of recycling and obedience, researchers interested in people's recycling behavior might give participants a canned drink while completing a questionnaire and then watch to see if they drop the can in a recycling bin on their way out of the room. For a behavioral measure of obedience, we can look again at Milgram's (1963) operational definition of obedience in terms of how severe a shock participants were willing to deliver to the learner.

One advantage of behavioral measures is that they are often **unobtrusive measures,** which means that participants do not realize that the measure is being taken. If participants are unaware that a measure is being taken, then presumably they will not try to alter their actions to create a favorable impression. For instance, participants given a canned drink and then allowed to leave would not realize that the researcher was watching to see whether they would recycle the can. Similarly, participants in Milgram's study did not realize that they were the actual focus of the research; instead, they believed that the experimenter was interested in the learner's performance, not in their own obedience to his commands.

A disadvantage of behavioral measures is that they can be difficult or time-consuming to obtain. For instance, Milgram's behavioral measure of obedience required a complex cover story and the help of an experimental accomplice. A second disadvantage is that behavioral measures are very difficult or impossible for some concepts. For instance, how could a researcher measure participants' emotional responses to a past event using behavior? Or how could a researcher measure participants' thoughts in response to a persuasive message using behavior? These limitations of behavioral measures, together with the simplicity and directness of self-report measures, explain why self-report measures are much more common in social psychological research.

No matter how a concept is operationally defined (e.g., self-report or behavioral measures), the goal is to measure the concept *accurately.* This goal is not always simple in social psychology, nor indeed in psychology generally, because many of our concepts are complex, elusive, and buried deep beneath the surface. The problem of the accuracy of psychological measures is so challenging that an entire subdiscipline within psychology—**psychometrics**—is devoted to understanding and refining methods for psychological measurement. Psychometrics tells us to focus on two properties of measures that represent accuracy: reliability and validity. We turn to these properties next.

**Reliability.** A good measure should be stable and steady. It should always give us the same answer (assuming, of course, that the concept does not change between measurements). Have you ever stood on the bathroom scale wondering if the number is really correct? You step off, let the pointer return to zero, and then step on again. Is it the same number? It will probably be very close. That's because the scale is reliable: it gives you the same answer over and over again. Perhaps you don't trust that scale, so you check out your weight on your friend's bathroom scale. Same answer again?

**Reliability** refers to the consistency or stability of scores on a measure. A reliable measure is one that produces consistent scores, free from "random" or unexplained fluctuations. We can think of consistency in at least two distinct ways. The first is consistency *over time.* In this sense, a reliable measure is one

**unobtrusive measures**

*assessments that are taken without the realization of participants, thereby minimizing socially desirable responding*

**psychometrics**

*a subdiscipline within psychology that is devoted to understanding and refining methods for psychological measurement*

**reliability**

*the extent to which a measure is free of "random" fluctuations, both over time and across judges*

© Alan Thornton/Getty Images

Scales generally provide *reliable* estimates of weight.

that produces stable scores for the same object on repeated use. Stepping off and then back on the same bathroom scale is an effort to assess consistency over time. Another form of consistency is *across judges*. In this sense, reliability occurs when an object receives similar scores from different judges. Tracking down that second scale is an effort to assess consistency across judges.

In measuring social behavior, it is quite common to have several observers record or score a person's actions (e.g., rate the aggressiveness of a child in the playground). Why? Because ensuring that there is consistency across judges (observers) for the same person shows that the scoring system is reliable. If three or four independent judges assign the same scores to an individual, then we can have confidence in the reliability of the measure. Similarly, social psychologists often videotape the behavior of research participants. This is done so that multiple observers can be used later to get repeated assessments of the same behavior, all in an effort to establish the reliability of the measure.

**Validity.**   A good measure (a good operational definition of a concept) does more than yield a reliable score. It also yields a score that truly reflects the concept it is intended to measure. This quality of measures is called **validity:** the extent to which scores on the measures really represent the underlying concept they are intended to represent. In other words, does a measure really assess what it is supposed to assess? When we step on a bathroom scale, we are pretty confident that the number it shows represents our weight and not, say, our body heat. Likewise, when we use a thermometer, we trust that the number corresponds to our body heat and not to our weight.

The validity of social psychological measures, however, is often more difficult to establish than the validity of instruments assessing physical characteristics like weight and temperature. For example, how do we know that answers to one or more self-report questions will really give us a good assessment of individuals' attitudes toward being religious? Or how can we be confident that individuals' self-reports of how many hours a week they study really give us an accurate estimate of this behavior? The most common way to demonstrate validity is by showing that scores on a measure correspond reasonably well to scores on other measures that *should* be related. These other measures presumably assess at least some aspects of the same concept, so showing that they overlap with the focal measure supports the validity of that measure.

For instance, to establish the validity of a measure of attitudes toward being religious, a researcher might try to show that scores on the scale correspond quite closely to the following additional measures: ratings of participants' religiosity by their friends; records of charitable donations by participants to religious organizations; and participants' self-reports of how often they attend a religious service. None of these additional measures is itself a perfect reflection of attitudes toward being religious, but they are all at least somewhat related; thus, if the attitude scores predict these other measures adequately, then it seems reasonable to conclude that the attitude scores are valid. To establish the validity of a self-reported estimate of time spent studying, a researcher might try to show that the self-reports of studying predict ratings of participants' studiousness by their friends, participants' academic grades, and participants' self-reports of how motivated they are to do well at school. Again, though none of these additional measures corresponds exactly with number of hours of study, they should all be at least moderately related to participants' actual studiousness and, therefore, provide appropriate checks on the validity of the self-report measure.

We have now discussed some of the key elements of the scientific method, including theories, hypotheses, operational definitions, reliability, and validity. If the scientific method produces support for a theory, then scientists begin to accept the theory as a valid basis for understanding the events to which it applies. A validated

**validity**
*the extent to which a measure really assesses what it is supposed to assess—whether scores on the measure actually reflect the assumed underlying concept*

A valid measure of *attitudes toward being religious* should predict how often a person attends a religious service.

theory is very useful, because if we understand why something occurs, we may be able to encourage it (if it is beneficial) or discourage it (if it is detrimental). For instance, if we can develop valid theories of prejudice (valid explanations of why prejudice occurs), then we should be able to design programs to reduce prejudice. Given the practical value of theories, social psychologists are constantly proposing, testing, and revising theories about important social behaviors.

Armed with this background knowledge about the scientific method, we can now turn to specific methods that are used frequently by social psychologists. We will discuss two broad categories of research: correlational research and experimental research.

## Correlational Research

**correlational research**

*studies in which investigators measure two or more concepts and see whether the concepts are associated with one another*

In **correlational research,** investigators measure two or more concepts and see whether the concepts are associated with one another—that is, whether measures of the concepts go together, or co-relate (hence, *correlational* research). This focus on whether measures are associated with one another is true of all correlational research. The various kinds of correlational studies differ primarily in *how researchers obtain the data:* by asking questions, by using historical information, or by watching behavior.

When two measures are correlated, it means that scores on the measures are systematically related: as scores on one measure change (e.g., go up), scores on the other measure also change in a consistent fashion (e.g., go down). For instance, social psychologists have found that the amount of contact people have had with members of an ethnic group is correlated with their prejudice toward that group: people who report *more contact* with members of an ethnic group also report *less prejudice* toward that group (e.g., Altemeyer, 1994; we discuss this topic in Chapter 9; see page 381).

This correlation between contact and prejudice can be used to illustrate an important limitation of correlational research: *correlations do not show that measures*

Why does contact with members of an ethnic group correlate with prejudice toward that group?

*are causally connected.* When two measures are correlated, the cause of this association cannot be known with certainty. Just because one measure correlates with another measure does not necessarily mean that the first measure causes the second, nor that the second measure necessarily causes the first. For instance, why does contact with an ethnic group correlate with prejudice? One possibility is that more frequent contact with a group causes a reduction in prejudice, perhaps because people learn that members of the ethnic group are nicer than they expected (contact reduces prejudice). But it is also possible that the *opposite* direction of cause explains the correlation: perhaps people who are prejudiced avoid contact with members of the minority group (prejudice reduces contact). It is even possible that some unidentified *third* factor causes the correlation between contact and prejudice.

The reason correlational research is ambiguous about cause is that the investigator does not (or cannot) control other factors in the environment that might partly or completely explain an obtained correlation. Instead, the researcher simply measures two or more concepts and examines their associations. *Why* associations did or did not occur is unclear.

This problem with correlational data applies to all of the methods we describe in the following sections. As you are reading examples of research for each correlational method, see if you can explain the results in different ways. You may be able to generate more than one possible interpretation.

Notwithstanding this limitation of correlational research, these methods do have some real strengths. For example, they are quite flexible and can be designed to explore many different issues (as you will see from the examples we provide). Also, obtaining correlational data is often easier than trying to set up an experiment. Finally, correlational measures are frequently obtained in naturalistic settings, as opposed to the potentially artificial settings of laboratory research.

# Surveys

The most common kind of correlational research in social psychology is the survey. A **survey** is a study in which the researcher asks questions to respondents. Survey researchers design questions to accurately assess concepts and then examine whether participants' answers to different questions are correlated.

**survey**

*a correlational study in which the researcher asks questions to respondents, either in a printed questionnaire, on a computer, over the telephone, or during an interview*

Many surveys are conducted by distributing printed questionnaires to participants. For instance, questionnaires may be distributed in a laboratory, completed by participants, and handed back to the researcher; alternatively, questionnaires can be mailed to respondents, completed at their leisure, and mailed back to the researcher. Also common are computer-based surveys, which can be completed by participants either in the laboratory or at home (e.g., on the Internet). Another common type of survey is a telephone survey. In this case, the researcher telephones participants, asks them questions over the phone, and records their answers. Finally, face-to-face interviews are also a form of survey; researchers ask questions during an interview and record participants' answers.

All of these methods are common in social psychology. We will provide just one example. Christopher Davis and his colleagues (Davis et al., 1995) were interested in *counterfactual thinking*, which refers to thoughts about how past events could have turned out differently. We will discuss counterfactual thinking in detail in Chapter 3 (see page 96). Davis et al. were interested in whether counterfactual thinking after a traumatic event correlated with emotional distress. Specifically, the researchers wondered whether people who frequently think about how a tragic event could have been avoided (one type of counterfactual thinking) would also report more emotional distress. To test this hypothesis, the researchers surveyed 93 people who had lost a loved one, either a spouse or a child, in a motor vehicle accident four to seven years previously. Names of possible participants were obtained from a list of all motor vehicle fatalities over a three-year period in Wayne County, Michigan. After agreeing to be interviewed, participants were visited in their homes by a researcher who asked them a number of questions. Some questions assessed how often participants found themselves thinking, "If only I had done something different, my child [spouse] would still be alive." Other questions concerned participants' current emotional states, such as their feelings of depression and anxiety.

Results showed that people who reported more frequent counterfactual thinking about the event also reported greater emotional distress. That is, people who frequently thought about how their loved one would still be alive if they had done something differently reported more symptoms of depression and anxiety. Based on these results, the researchers speculated that, to cope effectively with a traumatic event, people should not repeatedly chew over how the tragedy could have been avoided. This recommendation assumes that thinking about a past tragedy causes depression; can you think of an alternative interpretation of the findings? One alternative may be that depression causes people to think about unhappy events (see Chapter 3, page 105), including previous tragedies.

Before turning to the next type of correlational method, we need to discuss an issue that is specifically relevant to surveys but not to the other methods.

**Representative Samples.** Researchers who conduct surveys sometimes want to be able to generalize their results to a large population, such as all adult Americans, or all adults living in a state. For instance, political pollsters may want to use their findings to predict the outcome of a national or state election. If this ability to generalize is important, then the researcher must ensure that the sample of people who complete the survey is typical of the population. If researchers simply distribute questionnaires haphazardly to students at a college or to shoppers in a mall, they cannot assume that their findings will generalize to larger groups.

How can researchers make their findings generalizable to a large population? To achieve this goal, they must recruit a **representative sample** to complete the survey. A representative sample is a group of respondents that reflects the larger population accurately: it has ratios of various subgroups that are similar to those in the larger population. For instance, if researchers want to generalize to all adults in America, then equal numbers of men and women should complete the survey, as well as respondents from each state in approximately the same proportions as the

**representative sample**

*a group of respondents that accurately reflects a larger population from which it was drawn and to which the researcher wants to generalize the results*

states' populations. The typical way to obtain a representative sample is via **random sampling,** which refers to a recruitment process in which every person in the larger population has exactly the same probability of being in the study. For instance, random sampling of all U.S. adults would mean that every adult in the United States was equally likely to be recruited. As you can imagine, random sampling is a difficult and time-consuming procedure. Typically, social psychologists do not obtain random samples. Instead, they rely on replications of a study with different (nonrandom) samples to assess whether research findings generalize to other groups. For polling companies, however, it is usually so important to be able to generalize a survey's results to a larger population that they accept the necessary costs of time and money involved in obtaining a random sample.

**random sampling**

*a recruitment process in which every person in a particular population has exactly the same probability of being in the study; it produces a representative sample*

## Archival Research

**Archival research** refers to investigations that are based on preexisting information obtained by the researcher. Archival research is common in social psychology and can utilize a wide variety of public data. For example, historical records, newspaper articles, police reports, and past speeches by politicians have all provided data for archival research by social psychologists. You may recall that, in Chapter 1, we mentioned an archival study by Brian Mullen (1986), which showed that lynchings of Black men by White mobs between 1899 and 1946 were more vicious when the mobs were larger in number, perhaps because larger mobs provided stronger feelings of anonymity.

Researchers have been very creative in testing interesting questions using archival information. David Phillips (1977) identified 20 highly publicized suicides that occurred between 1966 and 1973 (e.g., suicides by famous actors). Phillips also obtained information about motor vehicle fatalities in the days prior to and following the appearance of these suicide stories. Across the 20 suicides, Phillips found a consistent and significant rise in motor vehicle fatalities three days after the appearance of the story. Figure 2.2 presents the results of his archival research, showing the fluctuations from the normal rate of motor vehicle fatalities in the days surrounding the publicized suicides. Phillips speculated that the suicides by well-known

**archival research**

*correlational investigations that are based on preexisting information obtained by researchers, such as historical records, newspaper articles, or other forms of public data*

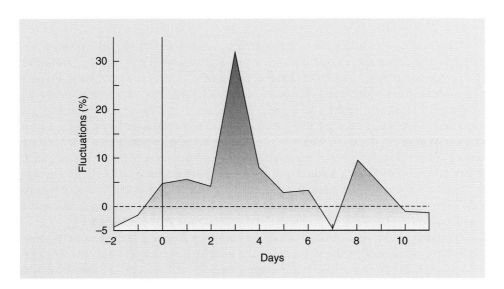

**FIGURE 2.2** Motor vehicle fatalities following publicized suicides

From D. P. Phillips, "Motor vehicle fatalities increase just after publicized suicide stories," *Science,* 196, 1464–1465, 1977. Reprinted by permission of the American Association for the Advancement of Science.

# Social Psychology in Your Life   *The Effects of Name Similarity*

Brett Pelham, Matthew Mirenberg, and John Jones (2002) reported some fascinating archival data on people's names and the places they lived. Pelham and his colleagues noted that humans generally like themselves and think positively of themselves (a point we will make several times in Chapters 3 and 4) and suggested that this liking extends to their own names. Pelham et al. further speculated that people might show enhanced liking for things that elicit connections to themselves (perhaps unconsciously), such as things that remind them of their own names. To test this idea, the researchers sifted through census data to see whether people were more likely than would be expected by chance to move to cities or states that were similar to their own names. The researchers presented a large array of relevant archival findings in their paper, but we will present only one example here.

In one set of data, the authors identified a large number of women in the United States who had moved as adults to one of four states: Florida, Georgia, Louisiana, or Virginia. The researchers looked at the first names of these women to identify possible overlap between women's names and the states to which they moved. The results showed that women named Florence were overrepresented in Florida (that is, women named Florence were more likely to move to Florida than would be expected by chance), women named Georgia were overrepresented in Georgia, women named Louise were overrepresented in Louisiana, and women named Virginia were overrepresented in Virginia. These effects were small, but statistically significant. The likelihood that women would move to states that sounded like their own name was greater than chance.

Do you think that you like things that remind you of your name? For instance, do you like actors or musicians who have the same first or last name as you? The research by Pelham et al. suggests that name similarity might even influence the places we decide to live.

individuals prompted copycat suicides using motor vehicles by depressed, vulnerable members of the public.

Another fascinating piece of archival research is described in the accompanying box, *Social Psychology in Your Life: The Effects of Name Similarity.*

## Observational Studies

**observational studies**

*correlational investigations in which researchers watch participants and code measures from the observed behavior, either "live" or from videotapes*

**Observational studies** refer to research in which the investigator watches participants and codes measures from the observed behavior. The scoring of behavior can occur either "live," while the observer is actually watching participants, or later if participants are videotaped (in which case their behavior can subsequently be evaluated and scored using the tapes). Participants in observational studies are sometimes aware that they are being observed and sometimes unaware. Also, observational studies can focus on behavior in either a naturalistic setting or a laboratory setting. These features of observational studies are interconnected. For example, if behavior is observed in a natural setting, then participants may be unaware that they are being watched, whereas laboratory settings usually require that participants know they are being observed. We will give examples of one observational study conducted in the laboratory and another conducted in a naturalistic setting.

Geraldine Downey and her colleagues (Downey, Freitas, Michaelis, & Khouri, 1998) were interested in the interaction styles of dating couples and whether certain styles were dysfunctional. Participants were 39 college-age couples who had been dating for an average of three months. Couples came to the laboratory and were asked to discuss for 20 minutes a topic that they often argued about; these discussions were videotaped. After the discussion, participants separately completed questionnaires in which they reported how angry they felt at that moment about the relationship. The videotaped discussions were later scored for the occurrence of specific interpersonal behaviors. Results revealed significant effects for the women's interaction styles but not the men's. Specifically, women who exhibited more frequent negative behaviors during the discussion (e.g., hostile voice tones, verbal put-downs, denials of responsibility for a problem, gestures that indicate disgust) tended to have male partners who reported greater anger after the discussion. Thus, a negative interpersonal style by the women during the discussion was associated with greater partner anger after the discussion. The authors speculated that the women's negative behaviors caused anger in their partners. Can you think of an alternative interpretation? Perhaps if partners started getting angry during the discussion, women responded with negative behaviors.

An interesting observational study was conducted in a parking lot by Barry Ruback and Daniel Juieng (1997). These researchers suggested that most humans are naturally territorial and want to protect their own space from intruders. The researchers further speculated that these territorial inclinations are so strong that they may even carry over into the protection of *public* space that people have occupied only temporarily. To test this idea, Ruback and Juieng went to a parking lot in front of an Atlanta shopping mall. They watched as 200 different drivers got into their cars and drove away. The researchers noted two things: how long it took the driver to completely leave the parking space and whether another car was waiting for the space. To ensure that the driver of the departing car was aware that another car was waiting, the departing driver had to have turned his head in the direction of the waiting car before opening his or her driver's side door. Using these criteria, the results were clear: drivers took *longer* to depart their space when they knew another car was waiting (an average of 39 seconds) than when no car was waiting (an average of 32 seconds). Does this surprise you? The researchers suggested that the waiting car elicited territorial feelings, and drivers unconsciously wanted to protect their territory (parking space) longer. Before you reject this interpretation, think about your own behavior in public spaces. For instance, consider escalators: when you are standing on an escalator going up or down, does it feel like you sort of "own" your step, and do you feel annoyed when other people intrude on your step?

**Participant-Observation Research.** One special kind of observational study deserves mention. Sometimes, if researchers want to observe behavior in natural settings, they must participate actively in the settings themselves. For example,

An observational study found that drivers took longer to leave their space when another car was waiting than when no car was waiting.

**participant-observation research**

*a special type of observational study in which a researcher actually joins an ongoing group to observe the members' behavior*

Robert Cialdini (2001), a well-known researcher in the area of social influence (whose work we discuss in Chapter 8), reported that he enrolled in several courses designed to train salespersons so that he could see whether specific persuasion strategies were being taught. This kind of investigation, when researchers actually join ongoing groups, is called **participant-observation research.**

Perhaps the most famous example of participant-observation research in social psychology was conducted by Leon Festinger, Henry Riecken, and Stanley Schachter (1956), who saw a newspaper article and subsequently joined a doomsday cult that had predicted the end of the world; the researchers wanted to watch as members' beliefs were (hopefully) disconfirmed. Members of the group believed that they would be picked up by an alien spaceship at midnight of December 20, prior to the destruction of the world on December 21. (This information came from the group's leader, Marion Keech, who claimed to be able to communicate with aliens from the planet Clarion.) As the hours passed after midnight on December 20, Festinger and his colleagues watched as members slowly realized they were not to be rescued. Suddenly, at about 4:30 A.M., their leader received another "message" from the aliens, which said that because of the group's unwavering faith, the world had been spared—so now they did not need to be picked up after all.

Faced with this clear disconfirmation of their initial beliefs but also a face-saving excuse from their leader, what did group members do? Festinger et al. reported that several members of the group actually became more active in their attempts to convince new people that they had saved the world. It seemed to Festinger and his colleagues that group members needed to justify the time and effort they had invested in the group, and one way to do this was to convince other people to join. This participant-observation study contributed to Festinger's development of *dissonance theory,* which we describe in Chapter 7 (see page 252).

Our discussion of correlational methods has illustrated the creative and interesting ways that social psychologists make use of surveys, archival records, and observational studies. Correlational studies are flexible and have been applied to many fascinating topics. They can provide important data on how various concepts are related. But correlational studies do not provide causal information—they do not show *why* concepts are related. To answer causal questions, researchers must use experimental research. Given that social psychologists want to understand the causes of social behavior, experiments are frequently the method of choice. So, to experiments let us turn.

  ## Experimental Research

**experimental research**

*investigations in which the researcher manipulates one concept (or more than one) and assesses the impact of the manipulation(s) on one or more other concepts*

We noted at the beginning of the chapter that theories are organized statements of the causal relations between two or more concepts. To test whether concepts are related in a causal manner (i.e., whether one concept causes another), it is necessary to use experiments. Thus, it is primarily through experimental research that social psychologists have been able to develop compelling theories about the causes of many important social behaviors. **Experimental research** refers to investigations in which the researcher manipulates one concept (or more than one) and assesses the impact of the manipulation(s) on one or more other concepts. This definition will become clearer as we explain its components.

In discussing the fundamental principles of experiments, we will use one continuing example that will hopefully illustrate both the advantages and challenges of experimentation. In the preceding section on correlational research, we stated that social psychologists have found that the amount of contact people have had with members of an ethnic group is correlated with their prejudice toward that group:

people who report *more contact* with an ethnic group also report *less prejudice* toward that group (e.g., Altemeyer, 1994). We also pointed out that it is impossible to know why this correlation occurs. Perhaps contact with a group causes a reduction in prejudice; or perhaps strong prejudice causes people to avoid members of the group.

How could this issue be tested experimentally? If social psychologists want to go beyond correlations and use experiments to assess the relation between contact and prejudice, how could they do so? We will consider how an experiment could be designed to test the hypothesis that *more contact with members of an ethnic group causes lower levels of prejudice.*

Our first task is to define three kinds of *variables* (concepts or measures that can *vary,* or take on different values) that are important in experiments: independent variables, dependent variables, and extraneous variables (see Pelham, 1999; Solso & MacLin, 2002).

## Independent, Dependent, and Extraneous Variables

The basic structure of experiments is quite simple: the researcher *manipulates* independent variables, *measures* dependent variables, and *controls* extraneous variables. This structure provides the potential for the study to yield causal information.

**Independent Variables.** Experiments are designed to test cause–effect relations; independent variables are the *causes* in these cause–effect sequences. An **independent variable** is a concept that the experimenter carefully manipulates so that participants in different conditions of the study are exposed to different levels of the independent variable.

For instance, if an experimenter wants to test whether contact with members of an ethnic group reduces prejudice, then the independent variable is *contact with group members.* The experimenter must set up the study so that participants in different conditions are given different amounts of contact with group members. One possibility would be for the experimenter to require some participants to interact with several members of an ethnic group while discussing a neutral topic, whereas other participants would not meet any members of the ethnic group during a similar discussion. In this case, there would be two levels of the independent variable: contact and no contact.

Why is the independent variable labeled the *independent* variable? Because it is independent of research participants' actions—participants have no control over what condition or group they are assigned to. It is the experimenter who manipulates the independent variable, whereas participants have nothing to do with it (they are simply exposed to one version of the independent variable). We should note that experiments often involve two (or even more) independent variables, a point that we will elaborate in the section on *factorial designs.*

**Dependent Variables.** An experiment also always involves one or more dependent variables. A **dependent variable** is a concept that is *measured* by the experimenter because it might be affected by the manipulation. Dependent variables are the *effects* in cause–effect sequences. Therefore, dependent variables must be measured *after* the independent variable has been manipulated (that is, after participants have gone through one of the conditions in the experiment), because the researcher wants to see whether the independent variable causes the dependent variable.

For example, if a researcher wants to test whether contact with members of an ethnic group reduces prejudice, then *prejudice* is the dependent variable. You might think that prejudice is a difficult thing to measure, but social psychologists have

**independent variable**

*a concept or factor that is manipulated by the researcher in an experiment; its causal impact on one or more other variables is assessed in the experiment*

**dependent variable**

*a concept that is measured by the researcher after the manipulation(s) in an experiment; it is typically expected to be affected by the manipulation(s)*

© Bill Aron/Photo Edit

*Dependent variables* are measures completed by participants after exposure to the *independent variable.*

actually developed many ways to assess prejudice (discussed in detail in Chapter 9 on Stereotypes, Prejudice, and Discrimination). One option would be for the researcher to use a self-report measure by asking participants to rate how unfavorable or favorable their feelings are toward the ethnic group on a scale from 1 (very unfavorable) to 10 (very favorable). The prediction would be that participants who were given contact with members of the ethnic group would report less prejudice (more favorable attitudes) than participants who did not have any contact with the group.

Why is the dependent variable labeled the *dependent* variable? Because it is dependent on research participants' responses. That is, participants determine their "score" on the dependent variable by completing a questionnaire or behaving in some fashion. Another way to think about this label is that the dependent variable is dependent on the independent variable (e.g., it is expected to be affected by the independent variable).

**extraneous variables**

*potential sources of error in the experiment that should be controlled; they encompass everything in the experiment except the independent and dependent variables*

**Extraneous Variables.** **Extraneous variables** refer to everything in the experimental setting other than the independent and dependent variables. Extraneous variables are potential problems, or sources of error, in the experiment, so the experimenter must *control* them by holding them constant across conditions. The experimenter does *not* want the different conditions or groups in the experiment to differ on any extraneous variables; the experimenter wants the conditions to differ *only* on the independent variable.

For instance, if an experimenter wants to test whether contact with members of an ethnic group reduces prejudice, then he or she must hold constant all aspects of the experiment except contact (all extraneous variables). Let's imagine a situation in which control did *not* occur. Imagine that participants in a condition involving contact with the ethnic group were paid $25 for participating, whereas participants in a condition with no contact were not paid anything. (Exactly *how* this circumstance could arise is not entirely clear!) Can you see why this would be a serious problem? Perhaps this difference in payment could produce differences in reported prejudice without any effects of the contact manipulation. For instance, if participants in the contact condition felt really happy about making $25, then their good mood might induce them to report less prejudice against the ethnic group than participants in the no contact (and no pay) condition. This differential payment across the two conditions would be an example of an extraneous variable that was *not* successfully controlled. Because it was not held constant across conditions, the researcher would not know whether differences in prejudice were due to the contact manipulation (the independent variable) or to the differing payments (an extraneous variable).

The key features of independent, dependent, and extraneous variables are summarized in the accompanying Concept Review.

In many fields of science, the control of extraneous variables is relatively easy. For instance, the physical sciences often allow tremendous control over the materials that are being studied (e.g., inanimate objects). But control in social psychological experiments is more challenging. Social psychologists study human social behavior; it is difficult to construct settings in which everything is carefully controlled yet participants are free to behave naturally and spontaneously. Two strategies for controlling extraneous variables are most important in social psychology; indeed, these strategies are so critical and so common that they are true of virtually every experiment conducted in the field. The strategies are *standardized procedures* and *random assignment.*

**Standardized Procedures.** Researchers will always attempt to make all conditions in the study identical except for the manipulation of the independent variable. That is, as much as possible, the procedures in the study will be standard-

## CONCEPT REVIEW
### Variables in Experiments

| Concept | Description | Action by Experimenter | Example: Experiment Testing Whether Contact Reduces Prejudice |
|---------|-------------|------------------------|----------------------------------------------------------------|
| Independent variable | The *cause* in cause–effect hypotheses; the conditions in an experiment; participants are exposed to just one level | Manipulated by the experimenter | Contact with members of the target group |
| Dependent variable | The *effect* in cause–effect hypotheses; obtained after the independent variable; participants provide the dependent variable | Measured by the experimenter | Prejudice toward members of the target group |
| Extraneous variable | Potential source of error in experiment; must be held constant across conditions | Controlled by the experimenter | Amount of payment for participation |

ized across conditions. For example, all experimental sessions will usually be conducted by the same experimenter in the same laboratory. All participants will be recruited in the same way and offered the same payment. As much as possible, participants in all conditions will be given the same explanation of the study's purpose, and will expect similar kinds of feedback after the experiment is over. The researcher will be careful to avoid running one condition only in the morning and the other condition only in the afternoon. Even though the time of day probably doesn't matter, it is safest to control this extraneous variable by running all conditions both mornings and afternoons. Standardized procedures hold constant participants' external environment, so the experimental conditions will differ only in terms of the independent variable.

**Random Assignment.** Even if participants in all conditions are treated identically except for the independent variable, one category of extraneous variables might still be a problem. Specifically, even if the environment is carefully controlled by standardizing the procedures, the *participants* in the different conditions might still vary in their personal characteristics. Let's return to our example of testing the effects of contact on prejudice. Imagine that we have two conditions: some participants are given contact with members of an ethnic group, whereas other participants do not meet anyone from the group (and payments are the same!). Imagine further that participants in both conditions report their attitudes toward the ethnic group at the end of the session, and those in the contact condition report less prejudice than those in the no-contact condition. Although this result seems to indicate that contact caused reduced prejudice, perhaps participants in the contact condition *were less prejudiced even before the study began.* How can we rule out this possibility? That is, how can we be sure that the groups were equivalent in prejudice to begin with?

Fortunately, all extraneous variables related to characteristics of the participants can be controlled with a simple methodological procedure: **random assignment.** Random assignment means that each participant in an experiment is equally likely to take part in any of the experimental conditions. For instance, any prejudiced participant in our experiment on the effects of contact on prejudice is just as likely to be assigned to the contact condition as to the no-contact condition.

**random assignment**

*a procedure by which each participant in an experiment is equally likely to take part in any of the experimental conditions; it controls extraneous variable problems arising from characteristics of the participants*

This is a very simple and elegant procedure, which effectively eliminates all extraneous variable problems coming from characteristics of the participants. If there are only two conditions, the experimenter might flip a coin, with heads meaning that the participant goes into one condition and tails meaning that the participant goes into the other condition. Alternatively, a computer program can be used to generate random numbers to assign participants to conditions.

How does random assignment eliminate this extraneous variable problem? If we use enough participants, then we should end up with approximately the same number of prejudiced people in both conditions. Therefore, if the manipulation of contact still appears to reduce prejudice, we can be more confident this was not the result of a coincidence in which unprejudiced people were more likely to participate in the contact condition. In fact, random assignment will effectively control *all* of the individual characteristics that people might carry with them into an experiment and that might influence the dependent variable.

We should note, however, that the logic of random assignment is based on the laws of chance. For instance, in the long run, a fair coin will come up heads just as often as tails. In the long run, a random number generator will come up with different numbers equally often. *In the long run.* The point is that random assignment works better with a larger number of people to assign; for example, most social psychologists try to have at least 10 or 20 participants in each condition.

**Demand Characteristics.** In social psychology experiments, the goal is to have participants respond naturally and spontaneously, rather than according to how they think the experimenter *wants* them to respond. Any cues in a study that suggest to participants how they are supposed to respond are called **demand characteristics** (labeled in this manner because the cues, or characteristics, "demand" a certain response). If demand characteristics guide participants' responses, then the experiment will not yield information about spontaneous social behavior (Orne, 1962). Therefore, researchers attempt to minimize any demand characteristics. For instance, researchers do not typically tell participants the exact purpose and predictions of the study before beginning, because participants might then try to respond in the expected manner. Standardized procedures also help to minimize demand characteristics by giving participants in all conditions the same cover story and alleged purpose of the research.

**demand characteristics**

*cues in a study that suggest to participants how they are supposed to respond*

## Internal and External Validity

When conducting research of any kind, experimental or correlational, investigators strive for accurate, valid results—results that are truly informative about the concepts being studied. This goal of obtaining accurate, valid results was elegantly summarized by Donald Campbell (1957), who distinguished between two aspects of the *validity* of research: *internal validity* and *external validity*. These kinds of validity are different from the idea of *valid measures* that we discussed earlier in the section on operational definitions of concepts.

**Internal Validity.** The reason we do experiments is to establish whether the independent variables have effects on the dependent variables. In essence, we want to know whether the experimental manipulation caused differences on the measures. If the experiment has been constructed properly, and all extraneous sources of influence have been effectively controlled, then we can be confident that any differences observed among conditions are due to the experimental manipulation. This is what is meant by **internal validity:** the extent to which the research yields clear causal information. A study with high internal validity is one in which differences on one measure were definitely caused by differences on another measure (e.g., the independent variable in an experiment).

**internal validity**

*the extent to which research yields clear causal information; it tends to be low in correlational research and high in experimental research*

Internal validity can be compromised by many things (see Aronson, Ellsworth, Carlsmith, & Gonzales, 1990). The most common threat to internal validity in research is failing to control extraneous variables. When it is impossible to standardize procedures or to randomly assign participants, a study will have low internal validity. Therefore, correlational studies, which do not control extraneous variables, are almost always low in internal validity, whereas well-conducted experiments are high in internal validity.

**External Validity.** Social psychology aspires to accomplish more than an accumulation of internally valid experiments (studies showing that one variable causes another variable in a laboratory setting). The promise and excitement of social psychology come from its potential to shed light on real-world problems: aggression, prejudice, helping, conformity, and persuasion. Social psychologists are not solely interested in understanding these problems within the confines of carefully controlled experiments. We want to know more. We want to know how these factors operate in real neighborhoods, real playgrounds, and real families. We ultimately want to understand real life. This quality is what we mean by **external validity:** the extent to which research results can be generalized beyond the current sample, setting, and other characteristics of the study.

Consider one aspect of external validity: the people to whom the results can be generalized. If the participants in an experiment consist only of college students at a single school, how far can the results be generalized? It may be safe to generalize to other college students from the same university. We may even feel confident in generalizing to students at other universities. But will the results of our experiment be valid and hold true for poorly educated people who struggled just to complete high school? These individuals are certainly an important segment of the population, yet our experiment may tell us little about them.

It is not really fair to hold a single piece of research accountable for achieving high external validity. Indeed, it is probably impossible for a single study to generalize in all the ways we might desire. Nevertheless, researchers often try to increase the external validity of their study. One way is by using a more diverse sample of participants. Another way is by making the experimental setting as similar as possible to real-life situations. The main problem with this second strategy is

**external validity**
*the extent to which research results can be generalized beyond the current sample, setting, and other characteristics of the study*

It is unclear that research results based on a sample of college students will necessarily generalize to other segments of society.

© AP/Wide World Photos

that the increased external validity often comes at a price: decreased internal validity. The more you try to model the real world and include the "noise" and complexity of daily life, the more you lose control over extraneous variables and, therefore, the internal validity of the experiment.

How does social psychology try to resolve the trade-off between internal and external validity? Most often, external validity in social psychology is achieved not within single studies, but rather by the accumulation of research: experiments that vary in who the research participants are, who the experimenters are, where and when the studies are conducted, and the kinds of materials and topics that are used. When a theory has been supported by an array of studies using different procedures, samples, and settings, its external validity can more confidently be assumed.

## Single-Factor Experiments

When we first defined independent variables, we noted that researchers manipulate one *or more* independent variables. When an experiment involves only one independent variable, it is called a **single-factor experiment** ("factor" is another word for manipulation or independent variable).

**single-factor experiment**

*an experimental study that involves only one independent variable*

Single-factor experiments are very common. Let's give a real example of a single-factor experiment in social psychology. For this experiment, we return to Melvin Lerner's (1977, 1980) *just world theory*, which we described earlier in our discussion of theories and hypotheses. Lerner theorized that humans want to believe that the world is a fair and just place, because to believe otherwise would threaten the assumption that people's own efforts will be rewarded in life. Based on this theory, Lerner derived the hypothesis that people would evaluate suffering victims negatively, especially when their suffering is expected to continue. The rationale for this hypothesis is that by evaluating victims negatively, the victims' suffering no longer seems unfair—and, thus, no longer threatens observers' belief in a just world.

*Peer discussion groups [for cancer patients] are available in many communities throughout the United States. The goal of such groups is to raise patients' quality of life. But do they?*

How could this hypothesis be tested experimentally? Lerner wanted to manipulate the extent to which a victim's suffering threatened participants' belief in a just world (independent variable) and see whether this manipulation influenced how much participants derogated the victim (dependent variable). Thus, the cause–effect sequence Lerner wanted to test was whether *threat to just world beliefs* causes *derogation of the victim.*

The experiment we will describe was conducted by Melvin Lerner and Carolyn Simmons (1966). These researchers set up a study in which female college undergraduates watched another young woman receive a series of painful electric shocks. The young woman appeared to be suffering quite severely. After participants had watched this suffering for 10 minutes, there was a pause in the experiment, and participants could no longer see the victim. At this point, the manipulation of *threat to just world beliefs* was administered. Some of the participants (high-threat condition) were told that, in a few moments, they would watch the young woman go through another set of shock trials. This condition was expected to be very threatening to participants' beliefs in a just world, because the woman's suffering was expected to continue. Other participants (low-threat condition) were told that, in a few moments, the victim was going to participate in a *reward session* that would not involve shocks—in fact, she would earn between $2 and $8 based on her memory performance. This condition was expected to be much less threatening to participants' beliefs in a just world, because the woman's suffering was over and, indeed, she was going to be compensated by earning some money.

Participants were then asked, before watching the next set of trials, to rate the victim on a variety of scales, including judgments of her likability, maturity, and admirability. Participants in the high-threat condition, who expected the victim's suffering to continue, rated her much more negatively than did participants in the low-threat condition, who expected the victim to earn money in the remaining learning trials. Thus, even though they watched the identical videotape, participants in the two conditions evaluated the victim very differently.

The researchers concluded that these results confirmed their hypothesis that people will evaluate victims negatively when the suffering is expected to continue. The researchers proposed that this effect occurs because derogating victims who are suffering makes the suffering seem less unfair. This single-factor experiment is an excellent illustration that complex concepts like "threat to beliefs in a just world" can be manipulated powerfully in a laboratory setting (for a recent review of experiments on just world theory, see Hafer & Bègue, 2005).

## Factorial Design Experiments

Many experiments in social psychology involve more than one independent variable. In studies that include two or more manipulations, the experiment's structure is called a **factorial design.** This design of experiments allows the investigator to examine the *combined* influence of more than one independent variable (see Crano & Brewer, 2002; Kirk, 2003).

An important advantage of factorial design experiments is that they allow the investigator to test for possible **interactions** between independent variables. An interaction occurs when the effect of one experimental manipulation *depends on the level of another experimental manipulation.* For instance, the effect of contact with members of an ethnic group on prejudice may depend on the *type of contact* that is involved: perhaps *cooperative contact* (e.g., working together on a project) reduces prejudice, but *competitive contact* (e.g., playing a competitive game) does not. In fact, we discuss in Chapter 9 this exact hypothesis that different kinds of contact have different effects on prejudice (see page 381). This pattern represents an interaction between the amount of contact and the type of contact.

We need to address a potentially confusing issue here. We have been stressing throughout the section on experiments that everything in the study except the manipulation (i.e., all extraneous variables) must be controlled so the researcher can be confident that the independent variable caused the results. But now we are saying that researchers often include two or more independent variables in the same study. How can they know which manipulation is causing differences between conditions? It is true that when two manipulations are operating simultaneously, it is impossible to disentangle their effects completely; nevertheless, the researcher can explore the effects of each independent variable separately *by averaging across all levels of the other independent variable.* This procedure is called looking at the *main effect* of a manipulation. For example, imagine that an experimenter tested whether humor increases the effectiveness of an advertisement (interest in buying the product) by comparing serious and funny advertisements for two different kinds of products (e.g., shampoo versus beer). The experimenter could then examine whether the funny advertisement was more effective than the serious advertisement for both kinds of products (a main effect of humor) or whether humor interacted with product type. The important point is that in factorial design experiments, the separate effects of each independent variable, as well as their combined effects, can be examined.

To get a better handle on the notion of interactions, let's consider a real example of an experiment in social psychology that used a factorial design to uncover an interaction between two independent variables. Stephen Bochner and Chet Insko (1966) were interested in the effects of *source credibility* on the effectiveness of a

**factorial design experiment**
*an experimental study that involves two or more independent variables*

**interaction**
*result showing that the effect of one experimental manipulation depends on the level of another experimental manipulation; it can only be observed in a factorial design experiment*

persuasive message. Previous researchers (e.g., Hovland & Weiss, 1951) had shown that the identical message produces more persuasion when it is believed to come from a highly credible source (e.g., an expert) than when it is believed to come from a source who is low in credibility. Bochner and Insko (1966) hypothesized that source credibility would be especially important when the position advocated in a message is relatively extreme. When an extreme view is advocated in a message, listeners are most likely to be skeptical about the information in the message. If the source is highly credible, then listeners may not reject extreme positions, whereas if the source is not credible, then an extreme message is likely to be rejected. For positions that are not extreme, however, source credibility might not matter so much. If a message advocates a position that is only slightly different from a listener's own views, the credibility of the source probably makes little difference because listeners will not be as skeptical about the information.

This reasoning suggests that source credibility might *interact* with the extremity of a message in affecting persuasion. When a message advocates a relatively extreme position, highly credible sources will be more persuasive than low-credibility sources; when a message advocates a moderate position, however, high- and low-credibility sources might not differ in persuasiveness. This hypothesis can be investigated only with a factorial design that includes two manipulations: the credibility of the source and the extremity of the message.

To test this analysis, Bochner and Insko (1966) gave participants a message that argued for a reduction in the number of hours young adults sleep. One independent variable was the credibility of the alleged author of the message. For some participants, the message was said to come from "Sir John Eccles, a Nobel prize–winning physiologist" (high credibility), whereas other participants were told that the message came from "Mr. Harry Olsen, director of the Fort Worth YMCA" (low credibility). Actually, this "low credibility" source was probably at least *somewhat* credible—it seems reasonable that someone who works at a health facility might know something about health-related issues like getting enough sleep; indeed, Bochner and Insko labeled their conditions "high credibility" and "medium credibility." Nevertheless, the Nobel prize–winning physiologist was certainly *more* credible than the YMCA director. The second independent variable was the extremity of the position argued in the message. For some participants, the message argued for a position that was only slightly discrepant from the common view that people need about 8 hours of sleep: the message argued that people need 7 hours of sleep (moderate position). For other participants, the message argued for a position that was extremely discrepant from the common view: the message argued that people need only 1 hour of sleep (extreme position).

© Bill Varie/CORBIS

The persuasive message in the experiment by Bochner and Insko (1966) argued for a reduction in the number of hours young adults sleep.

After reading the message, all participants were asked how many hours of sleep they believed were necessary for the average young adult. Figure 2.3 presents participants' answers to this question. When the message took a moderate position, the credibility of the source made no difference whatsoever: participants in the high-credibility and the low-credibility conditions both estimated that people need 7.5 hours of sleep per night. When the message took an extreme position, however, the credibility of the source made a significant difference: participants in the high-credibility condition estimated that people need 5.9 hours of sleep, whereas participants in the low-credibility condition estimated that people need 6.7 hours of sleep. Thus, the effect of source credibility on attitude change *depended* on the extremity of the position in the message: credibility made a significant difference for the extreme message but not for the moderate message. This pattern of results reflects an *interaction* between source credibility and message extremity.

Most of the experiments we describe in this textbook are factorial designs that involve more than one independent variable. And the patterns of findings often reflect interactions between independent variables. Why is this complexity common in social psychology? Because *social behavior* is complicated: people's actions often depend on a *combination* of factors.

## Making Experiments Real

The world of the experiment can be very artificial. In some fields of science, this artificiality is desired: much of physics, for example, is done in the context of a vacuum. The artificial world is created to control extraneous variables and to be sure that the only causal influences are those being manipulated by the physicist. As we noted in the opening to this chapter, however, it is not so easy to control the research environment when human social behavior is the focus. Making the experiment too artificial can produce results that are not informative about behavior in real life. This dilemma creates a special challenge for social psychology: how can we do carefully controlled experiments and still hope to generalize our results to conditions outside the research environment? Social psychologists have identified two aspects of *realism* that bear on this problem: *experimental realism* and *mundane realism* (see Aronson & Carlsmith, 1968).

**Experimental Realism.** A major goal within the world of a social psychology experiment is to engage the participants—to make the experiment real and involving for them. It is essential that participants believe that what is happening around them is real, so they will behave in natural, spontaneous ways rather than artificially. This quality is what we mean by **experimental realism:** the experimental situation feels realistic to the research participants and elicits spontaneous behavior.

Many social psychology experiments create very high levels of experimental realism. One obvious example is Milgram's (1963) research on obedience. In the Milgram study, participants really believed that the experimenter was investigating the effects of punishment on learning, that Mr. Wallace was receiving electric shocks, and that they were the ones delivering the shocks. Participants were highly engaged by the procedures and experienced strong emotions. Their responses were almost certainly spontaneous and honest.

**Mundane Realism.** Just because an experiment is high in experimental realism, however, does not mean that it looks or feels like the real world. The experimental setting in the study by Milgram (1963) did not actually resemble real-world settings: when do people ever deliver electric shocks to others? The success and importance of this experiment depended primarily on experimental realism. Yet a principal goal of research is to learn about life in the real world. We want to be able to generalize the results of experiments to settings beyond the confines of the university classroom or laboratory; this issue relates to the notion of *external validity,* which we discussed earlier.

One way to achieve the goal of generalizability is by creating experiments that look and feel like the outside world: a kind of realism that we call **mundane realism.** If you want to study how leaders emerge in groups, then set up groups that

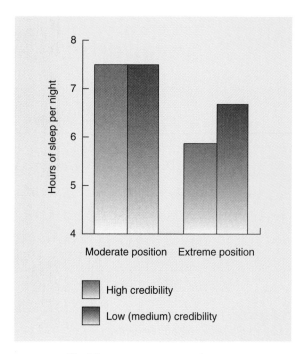

**FIGURE 2.3** Participants' estimates of number of hours of sleep needed per night

From Bochner and Insko, "Communicator discrepancy, source credibility, and attitude change," *Journal of Personality and Social Psychology*, 4, 614–621, 1966. Copyright © 1966 by the American Psychological Association.

**experimental realism**

*the extent to which the study's setting feels realistic and involving to participants and elicits spontaneous behavior*

**mundane realism**

*the extent to which the study's setting looks and feels like the outside world; it increases the external validity of research results*

Experiments conducted in field settings have high *mundane realism.*

© Fraser Hall/Robert Harding World Imagery/Getty Images

are given real tasks, and allow them to select someone to be in charge. If you want to study flirting behavior, then have participants interact with people whom they believe to be romantically unattached. If you want to study alcohol consumption, then conduct the study in a campus pub. The important point is that the context of the experiment must be similar to relevant real-life settings.

Persuasion experiments often have relatively high levels of mundane realism: participants read messages that are similar to those they encounter in real life. So long as participants consider the message to be genuine and believe the cover story of the experiment, the experimental setting parallels real-life persuasion settings. For example, Bochner and Insko's (1966) experiment examining the effects of source credibility on persuasion had a reasonably high level of mundane realism. Participants almost certainly believed that the message came either from the Nobel prize–winning physiologist or the director of the YMCA, and the message was typical of articles on social issues. These features increase our confidence that the findings will apply to real-life settings.

The connections between internal/external validity and experimental/mundane realism are summarized in the accompanying Concept Review.

**Field Experiments.** One important way to increase mundane realism and external validity is to conduct experiments outside the laboratory in natural settings, which are called **field experiments.** We mentioned in Chapter 1 a very well-known set of field experiments: Latané and Darley's (1970) studies of bystander intervention. These investigators wanted to be sure that their findings would generalize to real-world emergency settings, so they conducted several field experiments in which apparent emergencies were staged in nonlaboratory settings, and bystanders' responses were observed. These experiments provided compelling demonstrations that bystanders' interpretations of potential emergencies are influenced by the responses of other bystanders.

A high level of mundane realism is an important advantage of field experiments compared to laboratory experiments. It is reassuring when investigators can confirm their hypotheses and theories in settings where behavior is clearly natural. Field experiments also have some disadvantages, however. Most obviously, controlling extraneous variables in field settings is often difficult—for instance, unexpected interruptions are more likely than in the laboratory. Field settings also introduce

**field experiment**

*an experimental study that is conducted in a setting outside the laboratory; it tends to produce high mundane realism and external validity*

## CONCEPT REVIEW
### Internal/External Validity and Experimental/Mundane Realism

| Concept | Description | Features That Enhance It |
|---|---|---|
| Internal validity | The extent to which the research yields clear causal information | Experiment (versus correlational research); random assignment; control of extraneous variables |
| External validity | The extent to which research results can be generalized beyond the current sample, setting, and other characteristics of the study | Realistic setting; diverse sample; replications across different studies |
| Experimental realism | The extent to which the experimental setting elicits spontaneous, natural behavior | Involving procedure for participants; convincing cover story for participants; perception by participants that the study is addressing an important issue |
| Mundane realism | The extent to which the experimental setting is similar to nonlaboratory settings | Realistic setting; tasks and behaviors that occur in the real world; field experiment |

complications regarding approval and access: investigators must inform and get approval from appropriate authorities before they can conduct research in natural settings. Finally, it is more costly in terms of time and money to conduct research in the field than in the laboratory. Notwithstanding these problems, field experiments are an important tool for social psychologists to document the practical relevance of their theories.

# Social Psychology and the Internet

Ten years ago, it would have been very rare to mention the Internet in the context of research methods in social psychology. The Internet is a relatively recent phenomenon, and one that is worthy of study in its own right, but here we will briefly consider how the Internet might be used as a medium or vehicle for doing social psychological research (see Birnbaum, 2000, 2001).

**The Advantages.** An exciting aspect of the Internet is the extent of its reach throughout the world. A tremendous infrastructure of computers, cables, satellites, and software allows us to reach into millions of homes, schools, and businesses. Social psychologists used to be satisfied to draw on first-year college students as their research participants. It took great effort to reach different populations and to draw samples from other places. The Internet now makes that relatively easy. Without leaving your computer, it is possible to set up a server that presents stimulus materials, collects answers to questions, and maintains the data. And anybody, almost anywhere in the world, can participate at very negligible cost. Software designed to create web pages is very well suited for creating experiments, complete with color graphics, animation, and user input.

© Colin Young-Wolff/Photo Edit

The Internet has tremendous potential as a research tool for social psychologists, but it also has some serious limitations.

© Courtesy of the Research Center for Virtual Environments and Behavior/University of California Santa Barbara

*Immersive virtual environments technology* offers the potential of highly controlled but realistic settings for studying social behavior.

**The Disdvantages.** The Internet may sound like a social psychologist's dream come true. But we also need to recognize the downside. Perhaps most important, Internet-based methods do not currently provide a good way to conduct true experiments. A web server can certainly do random assignment of participants to conditions, but it is very difficult to control other important aspects of the research environment. How do we know who the person is on the other end? Is he sitting in a quiet room or a noisy Internet café? Is she responding alone or is she getting help from friends? Is this the first time the person has participated in your experiment, or is it the 50th?

Social psychologists are wrestling with these kinds of questions about Internet research. The potential of the Internet is almost unlimited, but the current reality is less glowing. It seems very likely, however, that the Internet will eventually become an important component of social psychological research.

## Making Technology Work for Social Psychology

Technological advancements are providing new research instruments for social psychologists. We mention two here.

**Immersive Virtual Environments Technology.** A relatively recent addition to the social psychologist's toolbox is the use of immersive virtual environments technology (e.g., Loomis, Blascovich, & Beall, 1999). This technology creates the experience of being surrounded by and immersed in a constructed environment. The computer controls the visual and auditory scene, and produces real-time feedback to give participants the sensation that they are actually there. It is only a matter of time before these synthetic environments are of such high quality that they virtually reproduce the real thing. Immersive environments offer tremendous potential for solving the problem of trade-offs between internal and external validity. Immersive environments would allow total experimental control (maximizing

© Bill Freeman/Photo Edit

Computer technology provides sophisticated ways to record daily experiences.

internal validity) while creating experiences that closely correspond to the real world (maximizing external validity).

To give you a sense of how social psychologists can utilize immersive environment technology, consider a study reported by Jeremy Bailenson, Jim Blascovich, Andrew Beall, and Jack Loomis (2003) at the University of California, Santa Barbara. Participants were confronted by the images of other people in a virtual environment. Replicating earlier social psychological experiments, these researchers found that participants maintained greater distance between themselves and the virtual other person when they approached the person from in front rather than from behind, and also when the virtual person engaged them in mutual gaze rather than looked away.

**Keeping Track of Daily Events.** Computer technology is also very useful when social psychology is taken into the real world. Later in the book, we will talk about *event sampling methods* (see Chapter 13). These methods allow researchers to record the momentary thoughts, emotions, and behaviors of people as they go about their daily lives. Our workbook suggests that you keep your own daily experiences diary. If you want to go high-tech, try using the software developed by Lisa Feldman Barrett and Daniel Barrett (2001). The Experience Sampling Program (ESP) lets you record simple ratings on a handheld computer such as a Palm Pilot. The software is available for free at http://www2.bc.edu/~barretli/esp/.

     # Ethical Issues in Social Psychology

Social psychologists conduct research on human participants with the goal of understanding social behavior. Researchers must take special care to protect the welfare of participants in their experiments. This goal is important, and it can be

**Institutional Review Board (IRB)**

*a committee that must approve all studies before they can be started; it ensures that the procedures will not cause unacceptable harm to participants*

**informed consent**

*a procedure by which participants are told beforehand what to expect in the study and are reminded that they can withdraw at any time*

**debriefing**

*a postexperimental procedure in which participants are given a full and complete description of the study's design, purpose, and expected results; if there has been any deception during the study, it must be identified and explained in the debriefing*

difficult. Researchers must carefully weigh the costs and benefits of their research, and take precautions to be sure that nobody gets hurt or otherwise experiences harm as a result of participating in a study. Think about Milgram's (1963) experiment on obedience to authority. That experiment touched off a serious debate about ethics in research, and whether the participants in such experiments suffered serious psychological harm (e.g., Baumrind, 1964; Milgram, 1964).

Three special procedures have been established to protect human participants in research. First, almost all research conducted in universities, research institutes, and companies must first be approved by an **Institutional Review Board (IRB).** An IRB is a committee given responsibility for reviewing the research protocol of an experiment or study, and making sure that the procedures will not cause unacceptable harm to the research participants. If you have participated in a psychology experiment at your school, it is almost certain that the experiment was approved by an IRB. In most research settings, two review boards are maintained. One focuses on research being conducted with human participants, and the other on research with animal participants.

The second precaution is called **informed consent,** which means that people are told beforehand that they are participating in a study. They are told what to expect and, most importantly, that their participation is voluntary and they can withdraw at any time. This does not mean that every detail of the experimental design must be revealed at the outset. Indeed, this would severely undermine the logic of many social psychology experiments. Rather, it means that people are made aware of the general nature of what they will be asked to do and are assured that they will be treated reasonably.

The third precaution is called **debriefing,** which means that a full and complete disclosure is made at the conclusion of the study. If the details of the entire experimental design and purpose of the study were not revealed beforehand, debriefing is the time to do so. The goals of a good debriefing procedure are to create a learning experience for the participants and to check for any signs of distress or harm.

In many social psychology experiments, the participants are deceived in some way. The simplest form of deception is hiding information about all of the various conditions of an experiment or not revealing the true purpose of the study. But sometimes deception is more substantial and has serious ethical considerations. Again, think about the deception involved in Milgram's obedience experiments: the entire scene was one big deception. As another example, we may wish to give people incorrect feedback about their performance on a test, and this feedback might sometimes be that the participant failed a test. Is such deception justified? Does it have any lasting consequences? Can we manage to do experiments without it? Read the *Workbook* for a more detailed discussion of these questions.

Concerns about the protection of research participants occasionally intensify. Partly as a result of medical experiments that have caused deaths, questions about informed consent and the operation of IRBs have recently become the subject of renewed, and sometimes intense, debate (e.g., National Research Council, 2003; Singer & Levine, 2003).

You will notice throughout this book that we refer to the people in studies as research participants or *participants* for short. Until recently, the terminology was a little different. In the "old days," we referred to participants as "subjects." Even though you will still find this term used occasionally, it has been properly recognized as a somewhat demeaning way to talk about people. They are not simply the objects of our research; they are individuals who deserve our respect and our appreciation for their participation.

# Chapter Summary

In this chapter, we discussed the research methods used by social psychologists to study social behavior. As in any science, social psychologists develop **theories,** which are explanations of why particular events or outcomes occur. Theories identify the underlying causes of events or phenomena. **Hypotheses** are specific predictions about what *should* occur if a theory is valid. Hypotheses are the means by which theories are tested.

It is often a challenge to translate theories and hypotheses, which are usually expressed in abstract, conceptual terms, into testable questions. **Operational definitions** are specific, observable responses that are used to measure a concept. In social psychology, researchers use both self-report measures and behavioral measures to operationally define important concepts. Self-report measures can be problematic if respondents are motivated to create a positive impression of themselves—a form of responding known as **socially desirable responding.** One strategy for reducing socially desirable responding is to use behavioral measures, which are often **unobtrusive measures**—meaning that participants do not realize that the measures are being taken.

**Psychometrics** is a subdiscipline within psychology that is devoted to understanding and refining measures for psychological measurement. This field has focused researchers' attention on the reliability and validity of measures. **Reliability** refers to the consistency or stability of scores on a measure, both over time and across judges. **Validity** refers to whether scores on a measure really represent the underlying concept they are supposed to represent.

**Correlational research** refers to studies in which investigators measure two or more concepts and see whether the concepts are associated with one another. The primary weakness of correlational research is that it cannot establish causal connections between concepts, but it is very flexible and has been used in creative ways to examine social behavior. For example, **surveys** are correlational studies in which the researcher asks questions to respondents, either in a questionnaire, on a computer, over the telephone, or during an interview. If survey researchers want to generalize their findings to larger populations, then they must recruit a **representative sample,** which is a group of respondents that accurately reflects the larger population. A common way to obtain representative samples is via **random sampling,** which means that every person in a particular population has the same probability of being in the study.

**Archival research** refers to correlational investigations that are based on preexisting information obtained by the researcher, such as historical records, newspaper articles, or other forms of public data. **Observational studies** refer to correlational investigations in which the researcher watches participants and codes measures from the observed behavior, either "live" or from videotapes. **Participant-observation research** is a special kind of observational study, in which the researcher actually joins an ongoing group to observe the members' behavior.

**Experimental research** refers to empirical investigations in which researchers manipulate one concept (or more than one) and assess the impact of the manipulation(s) on one or more other concepts. The manipulated factors in experiments are called the **independent variables.** The **dependent variables** are those concepts that are measured by the researcher and might be affected by the independent variables. **Extraneous variables** are potential sources of error in the experiment and should be controlled. One important strategy for controlling extraneous variables is *standardized procedures,* which means that participants in different conditions are treated exactly the same except for the manipulations. Another important strategy for controlling extraneous variables is **random assignment,** which means that each participant in the experiment is equally likely to take part in any of the experimental conditions. **Demand characteristics** are cues in a study that suggest to participants how they are supposed to respond; these cues must be minimized if the research is to provide information about spontaneous social behavior.

Researchers strive for both internal validity and external validity in their research. **Internal validity** refers to the extent to which the research yields clear causal information. Correlational studies tend to have low internal validity, whereas experiments tend to have high internal validity. **External validity** refers to the extent to which research results can be generalized beyond the current sample, setting, and other characteristics of the study. External validity is typically established across experiments in social psychology.

When an experiment involves only one independent variable, it is called a **single-factor experiment.** When an experiment involves two or more independent variables, it is said to have a **factorial design.** Factorial designs allow the investigator to test for possible **interactions** between independent variables, which means that the effect of one manipulation depends on the level of another manipulation. Factorial designs and interactions between variables are very common in social psychology.

Researchers also strive for realism in their experiments. **Experimental realism** refers to the extent to which the experimental setting feels realistic and involving to participants and elicits spontaneous behavior. **Mundane realism** refers to the extent to which the experimental setting looks and feels like the outside world. Mundane realism is one quality that increases the external validity of research results. **Field experiments,** which are conducted in settings outside the laboratory, tend to increase both mundane realism and external validity.

Social psychologists must take care to protect the welfare of participants in their research. One procedure that helps to achieve this goal is that all research must first be approved by an **Institutional Review Board (IRB),** which

is a committee that ensures the procedures will not cause unacceptable harm to participants. Another protective strategy is **informed consent,** whereby participants are told beforehand what to expect in the study and are reminded that they can withdraw at any time. A third protective strategy is **debriefing,** which means that a full and complete description of the study's design, purpose, and expected results are given to participants after the session is completed. If there has been any deception during the study, it must be identified and explained in the debriefing.

# Key Terms

archival research (43)

correlational research (40)

debriefing (60)

demand characteristics (50)

dependent variable (47)

experimental realism (55)

experimental research (46)

external validity (51)

extraneous variables (48)

factorial design experiment (53)

field experiment (56)

hypothesis (34)

independent variable (47)

informed consent (60)

Institutional Review Board (IRB) (60)

interaction (53)

internal validity (50)

mundane realism (55)

observational studies (44)

operational definition (35)

participant-observation research (46)

psychometrics (38)

random assignment (49)

random sampling (43)

reliability (38)

representative sample (42)

single-factor experiment (52)

socially desirable responding (37)

survey (41)

theory (34)

unobtrusive measures (38)

validity (39)

# Social Psychology Alive on the Web

## SOCIAL PSYCHOLOGY ALIVE: QUIZZING AND PRACTICE TESTS

You can access our website directly by going to http://psychology.wadsworth.com/brecklerle/ for online quizzes, flash cards, and Internet links.

## INFOTRAC® COLLEGE EDITION

For additional readings, explore InfoTrac College Edition, your online library of archived journal articles and periodicals dating back 22 years. If your instructor ordered InfoTrac College Edition with this book, you can access it from your CD-ROM, or go directly to http://www.infotrac-college.com/wadsworth and use the passcode from the InfoTrac College Edition card that came with your book. For this chapter, try these search terms: *reliability, validity, just world theory, unobtrusive measures, psychometrics, archival research, participant-observation, internal validity, external validity, experimental realism, mundane realism, Internet research, informed consent.*

## Social Psychology Alive: The Workbook

Chapter 2 of *Social Psychology Alive: The Workbook* provides key terms, guided study, and sample test questions. It also provides suggestions for connecting social psychology to the real world and to your life:

- The Rooster's Crow Raises the Sun (Or Does It?)
- What's in a Design? And Understanding the Results of Studies

- The Protection of Research Participants
- Selecting the Institutional Review Board
- Evaluating the Adequacy of Informed Consent

## Social Psychology Alive: The Videos

To see video on the topics and experiments discussed in this chapter, you may go either to Social PsychologyNow or to the CD-ROM, if your instructor assigned either one, to the section:

- Unmasking the Truth: Which Cancer Intervention Actually Works?

## To Learn More

This list contains citations to books or articles that can help you learn more. These readings are good places to start if you want to gain a deeper understanding of the topics in this chapter.

- Crano, W. D., & Brewer, M. B. (2002). *Principles and methods of social research* (2nd ed.). Mahwah, NJ: Erlbaum.

- Pelham, B. W. (1999). *Conducting experiments in psychology: Measuring the weight of smoke.* Pacific Grove, CA: Brooks/Cole.
- Birnbaum, M. H. (2001). *Introduction to behavioral research on the Internet.* Upper Saddle River, NJ: Prentice Hall.

© AP/Wide World Photos/Ted S. Warren

# Social Cognition: Thinking About People

**W**alter Gretzky, the father of hockey great Wayne Gretzky, has always considered himself to be a lucky man. But on October 13, 1991, at the age of 58, his luck almost ran out. Walter was painting, when he suddenly felt dizzy and developed a splitting headache. He wanted to go to his bedroom and lie down for a while, but a friend of his daughter's was visiting and insisted on driving him to the hospital. She almost certainly saved his life. Walter immediately underwent 5 hours of emergency surgery for a burst blood vessel on the surface of his brain. The reduced blood supply to his brain caused a stroke. Strokes are the leading cause of disability in the United States and the third leading cause of death. Approximately 700,000 Americans suffer a stroke each year.

Walter Gretzky had a long and difficult recovery period, during which he struggled to regain his physical and mental abilities. He suffered some permanent damage—for example, he lost many of his memories from the 1970s and 1980s. But he is alive and able to generate new memories with his children and grand-children.

Walter's experience shows that it is sometimes a matter of life or death to iden-tify quickly and correctly what is happening to you or to someone with you. Time is of the essence in the case of a stroke, because receiving treatment within the first three hours greatly increases the chances for a full recovery. Would you recognize the symptoms of a stroke? Common symptoms include numbness or weakness of one or both arms or legs, difficulty speaking, trouble seeing out of one or both eyes, severe headache, and nausea. The symptoms usually come on suddenly.

Why do we begin this chapter with a discussion of strokes? Labeling a set of symptoms as a stroke is one example of **catego-rization,** which is the process of recognizing and identifying some-thing. Categorization is the most basic process we use to understand and structure our world. We are constantly identifying objects around us so we can know how to behave. The example of labeling symptoms as a stroke is a particularly dramatic one, because erro-neous categorization can be fatal. The stroke example can also be an unusually difficult case of categorization, because we have so little relevant experience. Notwithstanding its drama and difficulty, identi-fying a stroke serves as a good example of how we categorize. We match features of an object (or symptoms being experienced) with our knowledge about the defining characteristics of various cate-gories. Once we have categorized the object (or symptoms), we can make more informed decisions about what to do.

For the purposes of studying social psychology, you do not need to understand all the intricacies of the human mind, but you do need to have some basic knowledge about cognitive processes. In this chapter, we discuss **social cognition,** which is the study of how information about people is processed and stored. We begin by

**categorization**

the process of recognizing and identifying something

**social cognition**

the study of how information about people is processed and stored

Walter Gretzky, father of hockey legend Wayne Gretzky, suffered a stroke at the age of 58.

© AP/Wide World Photos

*considering how the mind works—the basic elements of knowledge, the key features of memory, and the processes by which relevant knowledge is activated. We then discuss stereotypes, which are important in almost all perceptions of groups and individuals. Next, we describe some shortcuts that people use to make everyday judgments and a number of errors or biases that can occur when processing information about others. We also discuss how people think about events that could have happened but did not—called "what if" or counterfactual thinking. We close the chapter with a discussion of how motives and moods can influence social cognition. In Chapter 4, Social Perception: Perceiving the Self and Others, we go beyond this chapter's description of social cognition to discuss how people draw inferences about causes and make complex judgments about themselves and others.*

*It might be helpful at the outset to note that there are generally thought to be two basic motives that underlie human information processing. One motive is to perceive the world accurately (Heider, 1958). We are more likely to survive if we categorize objects correctly (e.g., these are the symptoms of a stroke), draw valid inferences about other people, predict others' actions accurately, and so on. A second motive is to view the self positively (Sedikides & Strube, 1997). We want to see ourselves as good, worthy people who deserve to succeed. The various concepts and processes described in this chapter all flow from these two fundamental needs.*

## How Does the Mind Work?

The human mind is a marvelous thing—it perceives, imagines, expects, remembers, infers, controls, and does other complex processes. Moreover, it often does more than one of these things simultaneously. Let's consider some of the basic aspects of the mind.

### Schemas: The Building Blocks of the Mind

All complex things are made up of simpler or more elementary things. Houses are made of bricks, bodies are made of cells, and so on. Although it is possible to break down the simpler things (bricks, cells) into even more basic elements, there are good reasons for using these particular levels of analysis for some purposes (e.g., for training bricklayers or for explaining the growth of the body to biology students). To understand the *mind* for the purposes of social psychology, we are less interested in its physical or biological elements than we are in its underlying *theoretical* elements. What are the elementary "building blocks" of the mind, beyond which we gain little by getting even simpler? For social psychologists, the building blocks of the mind are *schemas.*

**Schemas** are mental representations of objects or categories of objects (Fiske & Taylor, 1991; Hastie, 1981; Smith, 1998). You possess distinct schemas for apples, fathers, your own father, justice, robins, the moon, danger, your social psychology professor, and countless other things. Another term that is sometimes used for schemas is *concepts* (see Kunda, 1999; Medin, 1989). Schemas or concepts contain

**schemas**

*mental representations of objects or categories, which contain the central features of the object or category as well as assumptions about how the object or category works*

Your schema for apples probably includes the points that they are red and grow on trees.

the principal features of the object or category, as well as simple assumptions or "theories" about how the object or category functions. Your schema of apples probably includes that they are a type of fruit, they grow on trees, they are usually red but sometimes green or yellow, they taste sweet, and they contain vitamins. These features are held in a *probabilistic* way—they are associated with apples at various levels of certainty (e.g., all apples are fruit but only some apples are red). When you encounter an object that might be classified as an apple, you assess the similarity between the features of the object and the features in your schema of apples; if most of the features match, especially the ones that you believe characterize almost all apples, then you categorize this particular instance as an apple. This process is virtually instantaneous and effortless for familiar objects like apples.

Much of a child's early learning involves the formation of schemas. Parents teach their young children to identify types of animals, colors, foods, and flowers. This learning process may involve the presentation of explicit information about the features of schemas, such as "Fruits are almost always good to eat, and this is a type of fruit, so you can eat it." Similarly, an important goal of the educational system is to expand students' knowledge of schemas, including some very specialized schemas. For instance, introductory social psychology teaches students precise meanings of schemas (concepts) like *attitudes, dissonance,* and, of course, *schemas.*

**Categorization.** Why do humans develop schemas? The basic function of schemas is to categorize objects in ways that impose meaning and predictability. When we encounter an object, we must identify what it is (categorize it) before we can behave effectively toward it. This process occurs automatically and effortlessly with the vast majority of things we encounter every day. In the morning in our kitchen, we know without conscious thought that our bowl is a bowl and our spoon is a spoon and our cereal is cereal, and we therefore smoothly put our cereal in our bowl and eat it with our spoon. We recognize our roommate and know that he is not a threat even though he looks cranky this morning. But sometimes categorization is less clear. What was that sound I just heard downstairs? Was it the floor creaking or is someone down there? What kind of insect just buzzed by? Was it a harmless ladybug or an angry hornet? These instances illustrate that the categorization of an object has important implications for behavior. We perform these categorizations by comparing the features of the stimulus (those features that we were able to perceive) with the features of our potentially relevant schemas (e.g., ladybugs, hornets). If the fit with one of the schemas is good, we make a categorization; if the fit is poor, we continue to search for an appropriate schema.

**Going Beyond the Information Given.** How or why does categorization impose meaning on the world? The answer is that when we categorize something, we assume that it possesses the characteristics of the schema (or most of them) even if we cannot perceive those characteristics directly. Thus, we assume that this instance of fire is hot without touching it, that this apple tastes good before eating it, and that this hornet might sting us without swatting it. We are "going beyond the information given" in the sense that we are inferring other, nonvisible characteristics about the object on the basis of our categorization (Bruner, 1957). Categorization allows us to form impressions and make decisions quickly and efficiently, without having to think carefully about every object we encounter. Our world is so complex and ever-changing that we absolutely have to make simplifying assumptions in order to cope. Categorization allows us to make assumptions about objects and to direct our attention to those aspects of the environment that are most important. Sometimes we make faulty assumptions about objects based on our schemas. For example, when we categorize a person into a group (lawyer, Hispanic, or movie star) and assume that he or she possesses particular characteristics, we can make errors. Nevertheless, categorization is a necessary and effective process, especially for inanimate objects.

**Selective Information Processing.** Schemas not only impose meaning on the world, they also influence how information is processed. For instance, many researchers have shown that the schema used to categorize an object can influence what is *noticed* about the object. A classic study was conducted by Claudia Cohen (1981). Participants watched a 15-minute videotape of a woman having a birthday dinner at home with her husband. The woman ate her dinner, talked with her husband, and opened some gifts. Half of the participants were told before watching the videotape that the woman was a waitress at a local coffeeshop; the other half were told that the woman was a librarian at the city library. Thus, the schema of either waitress or librarian was activated. The videotape was specially constructed so that it included some elements that were consistent with the stereotype of waitresses and some elements that were consistent with the stereotype of librarians. For example, the woman drank beer and mentioned that she had not traveled to Europe (two elements consistent with the waitress label), and she wore glasses and listened to classical music (two elements consistent with the librarian label).

Participants' memory for information in the videotape was tested either immediately after viewing it, 4 days later, or 7 days later. Nine items in the memory test related to elements that were consistent with the stereotype of waitresses, and nine items related to elements that were consistent with the stereotype of librarians. Figure 3.1 presents the percentage of correct responses at each testing time that

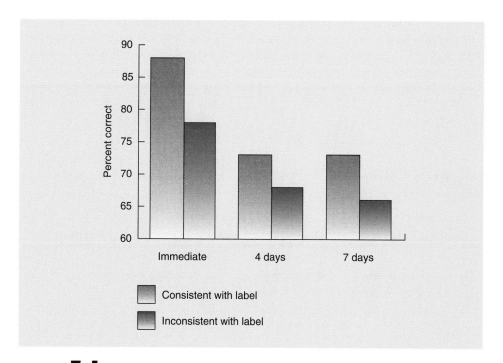

**FIGURE 3.1** Percentage correct for items consistent and inconsistent with occupation label

From C. E. Cohen, "Person categories and social perception: Testing some boundaries of the processing effects of prior knowledge," *Journal of Personality and Social Psychology,* 40, 441–452, 1981. Copyright © 1981 by the American Psychological Association. Reprinted by permission.

If a man is categorized as a *mugger*, his actions will probably be interpreted in ominous and threatening ways.

participants made for elements that were consistent and inconsistent with the occupation label they were given. Participants were more accurate in their answers about things that fit their occupation label than about things that did not fit their label at every delay interval. For example, participants who believed that the woman was a waitress were more likely to recall correctly that she drank beer than were participants who believed she was a librarian; on the other hand, participants who believed that the woman was a librarian were more likely to recall correctly that she listened to classical music than were participants who believed she was a waitress. The schema that was activated for the woman (waitress or librarian) influenced what participants noticed and recalled from the videotape, whether recall was assessed immediately or up to a week later.

Schemas also influence the *interpretation* of information. Typically, their effect will be that ambiguous information is interpreted in accordance with the schema (Fiske & Taylor, 1991; Rothbart, Evans, & Fulero, 1979). A plant's foliage and blossom might seem prettier to us if we are told it is a wildflower than if we are told it is a weed. A more ominous example might be that if a man you encounter on the street in the evening evokes the schema of "mugger," then ambiguous actions by him are likely to be interpreted in threatening ways (e.g., he is following you). Schemas lead us to assume that the object possesses particular characteristics, and anything that vaguely implies those characteristics may be taken as evidence that our assumption is accurate.

The functions and consequences of schemas are summarized in the accompanying Concept Review.

Although *ambiguous* information will usually be interpreted as consistent with a schema, anything that obviously *contradicts* our expectancies will grab our attention (Olson, Roese, & Zanna, 1996; Stangor & McMillan, 1992). How do you think you would react if you were walking through a park and saw a raccoon running toward you? You would probably be startled, to say the least, whereas similar behavior by your dog would hardly be noticed. Unexpected actions arouse our curiosity and lead to attempts to understand why the object is exhibiting characteristics that are inconsistent with its category. In the raccoon example, you might

## CONCEPT REVIEW
### Functions and Consequences of Schemas

**Definition of Schema:**

Mental representations of objects or categories of objects, which contain the central features of the object or category as well as assumptions about how the object or category works

| Function or Consequence | Description | Example |
|---|---|---|
| Function: Categorization | Identify the object | This man walking out of a hotel is probably a tourist. |
| Function: Information gain | Assume that the object probably possesses the typical characteristics of the schema | I bet he doesn't live in this city. |
| Function: Rapid, efficient decisions | Can decide quickly how to behave toward the object | I will ask him if he needs directions. |
| Consequence: Selective attention | More likely to notice information that is consistent with the schema (or that obviously contradicts it) | I see that he is carrying a camera and a map. |
| Consequence: Selective interpretation | Likely to interpret ambiguous information as consistent with the schema | He looks a bit confused, so he must be lost. |

decide that the raccoon is approaching you without fear because it is rabid, so you had better run away. The schema of *rabid animal* has been invoked to understand the raccoon, with the result that new characteristics have been attributed to it (e.g., sick, fearless, dangerous, and contagious).

## Memory: The Storage System of the Mind

It is remarkable just how much information is stored in our brain. We have knowledge about many tens of thousands of schemas (as a point of reference, most unabridged dictionaries of the English language contain several hundreds of thousands of words), and we can recollect thousands or tens of thousands of our past experiences. The storage of this information is challenging, especially storage in a way that will allow us to retrieve necessary information quickly. In this section, we will not discuss the physical structures of the brain involved in memory and cognition, such as neural structures (see Frith & Frith, 2001), but rather the way that information in memory is probably organized.

**Interconnected Schemas.** How is information organized in memory? First, given that schemas are the building blocks of the mind, memory must be a collection of interconnected schemas. Although many different models of memory have been proposed (see Carlston & Smith, 1996; Smith, 1998), we will adopt a relatively simple conceptualization for analyzing social cognition. We will assume that memory consists of a very large network of schemas that are linked together on the basis of shared meaning and/or shared experience. Thus, memory is an **associative network** of interconnected schemas. Your schemas of helpfulness and friendship, though distinct, are probably associated with one another quite strongly in memory because of their shared semantic meaning. Your schemas of baseball and hot dogs may also be associated with one another in memory, but this time because of shared experience—they have tended to occur together in your experiences.

Theorists generally assume that a particular schema is "activated" (brought into active awareness) when an object is encountered or when we consciously think of the schema. The schema of *doctor* will be activated when we see a woman in a white lab coat with a stethoscope at the hospital cafeteria. The activation of a given schema also activates (to a lesser extent) other schemas that are associated with it—schemas that are semantically similar or that have tended to occur at the same time. Activating the schema of *doctor* will also activate the schemas of *patient* and *needles*. This idea that the use (activation) of one schema increases the likelihood that other, related schemas in memory will also be used is called **spreading activation.**

**Encoding and Retrieval.** For a storage system like memory to work, material must be successfully stored and must be relatively easy to get out of storage. Cognitive psychologists label these two fundamental stages of memory *encoding* and *retrieval.* **Encoding** refers to getting information into memory, and includes attention, comprehension, and storage—the processes of perceiving information, understanding it, and recording it in memory. You are at this moment trying to encode the material in this textbook: you are paying attention to it, trying to understand it (we hope you are succeeding), and probably trying to get the material into your long-term memory (especially if you are studying for a test!). In our daily activities, many events are encoded naturally or spontaneously into memory (you can probably recall what you ate for breakfast today, even though you did not try to memorize it). We also sometimes make a conscious effort to encode information, such as when we study for a test.

**Retrieval** refers to getting information out of memory. Most theorists assume that people search memory by retrieving one schema and then proceeding to

**associative network**
*a very large system of schemas that are linked together on the basis of shared meaning or shared experience; it is one way to conceptualize the way in which information is organized in memory*

**3.1**
**ONLINE**
LAB

**spreading activation**
*the process by which the use of one schema increases the likelihood that other, related schemas in memory will also be used*

**encoding**
*the process of getting information into memory, including attention, comprehension, and storage*

**retrieval**
*the process of getting information out of memory*

schemas that are closely associated with the first one. If you are trying to remember what you gave your mother for her birthday last year, you will probably activate your schema of her, which will activate her characteristics, hobbies, and preferences (the principal features in your schema of your mother). You may also activate your schema of gift, which will activate things like books, tickets to a show, and sweaters. In either case (activating the schema of your mother or the schema of gift), you may elicit your gift from last year because it matches one of your mother's characteristics (e.g., one of her interests) or because it matches a prototypical gift (e.g., books).

## Accessibility: What's on Your Mind?

When a schema is activated, it provides expectancies about the object's probable characteristics and influences the processing of information about the object. When you categorize an animal as a dog, you expect it to be sociable and loyal, and you may interpret its behavior as reflecting these characteristics. Thus, the schema used to categorize an object is important; if two individuals categorize the same object differently (i.e., using different schemas), they may expect very different characteristics. Recall our description of the study by Cohen (1981), who provided participants with either a waitress or a librarian label for a woman; after watching a videotape, participants were more likely to recall information about the woman that was consistent with the label they had been given.

Given the significance of how an object is categorized, it is important to know the factors that influence whether a particular schema will be used. Sometimes a schema is directly activated by information, such as when participants are *told* that a woman is a librarian. But what about "spontaneous" activation without information from others? One factor is very straightforward: a schema will be activated when the object's features match the features of the schema (e.g., when you see a round, red fruit and categorize it as an apple, or when you see a man behind the wheel of a truck and categorize him as a truck driver). Another, less obvious factor that influences whether a schema will be used is its **accessibility**—the ease with which the schema comes to awareness. People are more likely to use schemas that are highly accessible to them; these schemas are "on their mind." Let's consider factors that affect the accessibility of a schema (see Higgins, 1996).

**accessibility**

*the ease with which a schema comes to awareness*

**3.2**
**ONLINE**
LAB

**priming**

*the process by which the activation of a schema increases the likelihood that the schema will be activated again in the future*

**Priming of Schemas.** Have you ever noticed that one event can get you thinking about the same thing in other situations? If you read about a car accident in the newspaper, you might find yourself driving very cautiously all day. Or if someone compliments your haircut, you might find yourself looking at everyone's hair for the rest of the day. What is going on here? The initial event (e.g., the hair compliment) activates the schema of haircut or hair, and because this schema is "on your mind," it is more accessible and more likely to be activated again. Social and cognitive psychologists have shown that when a schema has been used recently, it is more accessible, an effect that is called **priming.** In the haircut example, the compliment primed the schema of hair or haircut. Many researchers have found that priming a schema in people's minds increases the likelihood that they will use that schema in a later task.

Charles Carver and his colleagues (Carver, Ganellen, Froming, & Chambers, 1983) showed participants a videotape of a businessman asking his assistant about arrangements for a trip he was going to take. Participants were told that their memory for this videotape would be tested. Some participants saw a version of the tape in which the businessman was quite hostile and derogatory toward the assistant, whereas other participants saw a version of the tape in which the businessman was calm and relaxed toward the assistant. Carver et al. assumed that the first version of the videotape would prime (activate) the schema of "hostile" or "aggressive," whereas the second version would not (it might instead prime "polite" or "friendly"). Participants then completed a second task that they believed was unrelated to the first one. They read a paragraph describing a young man who behaved in several ways that were ambiguous with respect to hostility—he engaged in actions that could be seen as hostile or could be interpreted in other ways. For example, the young man was said to be "refusing to pay his rent until the landlord had his plumbing repaired"; this action might reflect hostility or it might reflect standing up for one's rights. After reading this paragraph, participants were asked for their impressions of the young man, including the extent to which he was hostile and unfriendly. Participants who had been exposed to the hostile videotape in the first task rated the young man in the second task as more hostile than did participants who had been exposed to the nonhostile videotape in the first task. Priming the schema of hostile increased its use in a subsequent, unrelated task (see also Martin, Seta, & Crelia, 1990; Sedikides, 1990; Skowronski, Carlston, & Isham, 1993; Srull & Wyer, 1980; Strack, Schwarz, Bless, Kubler, & Wanke, 1993).

Being pregnant, or having one's partner pregnant, makes the schemas for pregnancy and children very accessible.

A powerful example of real-world priming, which many of you will experience one day or perhaps have experienced, is when you or your partner become(s) pregnant. Suddenly, pregnant women seem to be everywhere, and small infants in baby carriages have apparently multiplied. Indeed, the world seems to be populated primarily by pregnant women, mothers, and small children. One of the authors of this text (J.O.) suffered a very embarrassing consequence of this heightened accessibility of pregnancy while his wife was pregnant. He was proctoring an exam, daydreaming at the front of the room about what it was going to be like to have a child. Near the end of the allotted time, a female student in the class, who was perhaps 25 years old, came to the front to hand in her exam. Noticing a slight roundness in her belly that looked exactly like a pregnancy of four or five months, the daydreaming professor whispered excitedly to her, "Are you pregnant?" The words were barely out of his mouth when he knew that he had made a big mistake. Let his experience be a lesson for you: do not let accessible schemas take over your life!

**Chronic Accessibility of Schemas.** For each of us, some schemas are more accessible, in general, than are other schemas. The extent to which schemas are easy to activate for an individual across time and situations is termed **chronic accessibility.** People differ in the schemas that are most chronically accessible to them. A teacher at a high school who coaches the basketball team might have "height" as a chronically accessible schema when meeting new students—she might notice the height of students immediately, and she might categorize students as potential "post players," "guards," or "forwards" based on their height. The pregnancy example given a moment ago might seem to qualify as chronic accessibility, but it is actually initiated by a specific event (one's own involvement in a pregnancy) and fades over time, so it is probably better viewed as a case of strong priming.

Tory Higgins, Gillian King, and Gregory Mavin (1982) asked university students to describe themselves, two male friends, and two female friends using a maximum

**chronic accessibility**
*the degree to which schemas are easily activated for an individual across time and situations*

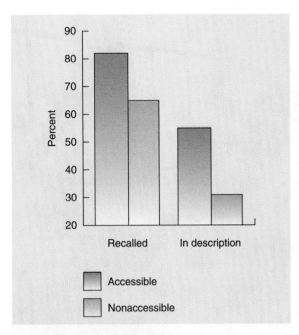

**FIGURE 3.2** Percentage of accessible and nonaccessible traits recalled or included in description

From Higgins et al., "Individual construct accessibility and subjective impressions and recall," *Journal of Personality and Social Psychology*, 43, 35–47, p. 39, 1982. Copyright © 1981 by the American Psychological Association.

of 10 traits in each description. The researchers looked for any traits (e.g., honest, intelligent, friendly) that participants used for themselves plus at least one friend or for at least three friends; these traits were considered to be chronically accessible for that participant. Two weeks later, participants were brought back for what they thought was a different experiment. They read a short essay that had been specially constructed for them (though they did not know this), which described several actions by another student; some of these actions exhibited traits that were chronically accessible for the participant, and other actions exhibited traits that were not chronically accessible for the participant. After a 10-minute delay, participants' memory for the essay was tested, and they were also asked to write a detailed description of the student. Figure 3.2 presents the percentage of the chronically accessible and nonaccessible traits that participants recalled and included in their descriptions. Results showed that participants were more likely to remember actions by the student that exhibited their own chronically accessible traits than actions that exhibited nonaccessible traits. For example, if a participant had used the trait *funny* to describe several friends at the first session, then he or she was likely to remember funny behaviors in the paragraph at the second session. Participants were also more likely to include chronically accessible traits than nonaccessible traits in their written descriptions of the student. Thus, participants' chronically accessible traits influenced both what they could remember about the student and how they described the student (see also Baldwin, Fehr, Keedian, Seidel, & Thomson, 1993; Bargh, Bond, Lombardi, & Tota, 1986).

## Cultural Differences in Accessible Schemas

Cultures differ in the schemas that are used most often to categorize both self and others. Western cultures (e.g., United States, Canada, Great Britain, Australia) emphasize in their socialization individuality, freedom, and independence, whereas Eastern cultures (e.g., China, Japan, Korea, Indonesia) emphasize in their socialization harmony, obedience, and interdependence (e.g., Hofstede, 1980; Markus & Kitayama, 1991; Triandis, 1989). This independence–interdependence (also called individualism–collectivism) difference between Western and Eastern cultures will be mentioned numerous times in this book as we discuss specific topics in social psychology. For our present purposes, we mention this point because individuals from Western and Eastern cultures are likely to differ in the schemas that are most chronically accessible to them. Americans and Canadians, for example, may be more likely than Japanese and Chinese persons to categorize people in terms of individual achievements ("he is a math wizard," "she is a natural comic"). In contrast, Japanese and Chinese persons may be more likely than Westerners to categorize people in terms of group memberships ("his family is religious," "she comes from a small town"). These differences in accessible schemas imply that people from different cultures may perceive the same event or the same person quite differently.

In a study that yielded findings consistent with this reasoning, Joseph Forgas and Michael Bond (1985) asked university students from Australia and Hong Kong to sort a set of 27 different social events (e.g., studying with another student before an exam; arriving very late to a tutorial; comparing marks with other students after they have been posted on a notice board; taking a friend of the opposite sex to the movies) into sets of events that they considered to be similar to one another. To decide which events were similar, students could use whatever aspects of the 27 events they wished. The researchers assumed that students would use their most accessible schemas to define similarity between the events. Results showed that students from Australia (but not Hong Kong) tended to organize the different events in terms of how competitive the events were. This reliance on competitiveness to classify the events is consistent with the Western emphasis on individualism. In contrast, students from Hong Kong (but not Australia) tended to group the events in terms of the number of people involved in the events. This reliance on group size is consistent with the Eastern emphasis on collectivism. Thus, different schemas appeared to be chronically accessible in the two cultures (see also Gardner, Gabriel, & Yee, 1999).

## Stereotypes: Schemas in the Social Domain

A **stereotype** is a set of characteristics that someone associates with members of a group; it is a cognitive structure containing the individual's beliefs that members of a group share particular attributes (Gardner, 1994; Hamilton & Sherman, 1994). Stereotypes are one kind of schema (defined earlier as mental representations of objects or categories of objects)—namely, schemas that represent human groups. All of us possess stereotypes of many groups, including occupations (lawyers, nurses, construction workers), racial or ethnic groups (Whites, Blacks, Hispanics), religious groups (Muslims, fundamentalists, Roman Catholics), age groups (the elderly, infants, teenagers), and many other categories (women, gay men, Democrats). Sometimes the characteristics that we associate with a group are largely positive (e.g., doctors, firefighters), but they can also be negative (e.g., telemarketers, drug addicts). Social psychologists have been most interested in the latter, negative stereotypes, especially those directed at disadvantaged groups, because researchers want to understand and reduce the prevalence of phenomena such as prejudice and discrimination (discussed in detail in Chapter 9 on Stereotypes, Prejudice, and Discrimination). Stereotypes have fundamental importance in social perception—they guide our perceptions and impressions of almost everyone we meet.

**stereotype**
*a set of characteristics that a perceiver associates with members of a group*

**Going Beyond the Information Given.** Just like other types of schemas, stereotypes reflect our attempt to categorize an object and draw inferences about it. When we learn that a woman is a lawyer, we use our lawyer categorization to infer that she is probably intelligent, persuasive, and wealthy (your stereotype of lawyers may be quite different from these features). These inferences provide us with a rapid guide for how to behave toward her. Unfortunately, the assumptions we make about members of human groups may often be oversimplified or even dead wrong.

An interesting aspect of stereotypes is that we ourselves are members of some groups about which we have stereotypes. A group to which a perceiver belongs is called his or her *ingroup*. Your ingroups probably include university students, people in your age group, your gender, and your ethnic identity (e.g., White, Black, Hispanic). An *outgroup* is a group to which a perceiver does not belong. Outgroups for you probably include professors, elderly people, the opposite sex, and ethnic groups other than your own. Stereotypes of ingroups are generally favorable, whereas stereotypes of outgroups can sometimes be unfavorable.

Stereotypes usually include information about how much variability (difference on a characteristic) exists in the group (see Hamilton & Sherman, 1994). One individual might believe that almost all nurses are outgoing, but another individual might believe that some nurses are outgoing and other nurses are shy. There is a general tendency, however, for people to overestimate the similarity within groups. This tendency to overestimate the similarity within groups is much stronger for outgroups (especially disliked and little-known outgroups) than for one's own ingroups. Whereas people often view their ingroups as being quite diverse (see Brewer, 1993; Goethals, 1986b; Judd & Park, 1988), outgroups tend to be seen as more uniform ("They're all alike!"). For example, think about how most North

**outgroup homogeneity effect**

*the tendency for people to overestimate the similarity within groups to which they do not belong*

Americans view people who live in Iran or in North Korea; people within these relatively unfamiliar countries are often seen as quite similar to one another. The exaggeration of similarity within groups to which we do not belong is called the **outgroup homogeneity effect** ("homogeneity" means similarity or uniformity).

**Selective Information Processing.** If you see a young man with a shaved head, leather clothes, several tattoos, and multiple body piercings, you may classify him as a skinhead. Once this stereotype has been activated, do you think that it will influence what else you *notice* about the man? Will you, for example, be particularly attentive for signs of aggression or hostility?

Social psychologists have argued that stereotypes can guide our attention in this manner (e.g., Plaks, Stroessner, Dweck, & Sherman, 2001). Recall the study by Cohen (1981), in which participants were more likely to recall things in a videotape that were consistent with a woman's alleged occupation (waitress or librarian). Presumably, participants were more likely to notice the occupation-consistent information while watching the video.

What about your *interpretation* of ambiguous behavior—will this be affected by stereotypic expectancies? Returning to the skinhead, will you interpret ambiguous behavior by him as aggressive and hostile? Imagine that he asks a passerby for money. Are you likely to interpret his action as threatening and intimidating, compared to how you would interpret exactly the same behavior exhibited by someone who was not a skinhead?

Again, social psychologists would answer this question affirmatively (see Kunda & Thagard, 1996); our stereotypes can change how we interpret ambiguous behavior. An interesting experimental demonstration of this effect was provided by John Darley and Paget Gross (1983), who investigated social class stereotypes. The researchers showed participants a short videotape of a 9-year-old Caucasian girl named Hannah. The videotape showed Hannah playing in her school yard and outside her home. Half of the participants saw a version of the tape that depicted Hannah in an inner-city, run-down area (the negative expectancy condition), whereas the other half of the participants saw a version of the tape that depicted Hannah in a well-to-do, suburban area (the positive expectancy condition).

Some participants were then immediately asked to rate Hannah's academic ability (the baseline condition). Other participants watched a second videotape of Hannah before rating her academic ability. On this second videotape, Hannah responded to 25 general knowledge questions (the performance condition). Her performance on these questions was inconsistent and ambiguous; she answered some items correctly, including some difficult items, but she also made some mistakes on both simple and difficult items.

How did the negative and positive expectancies influence participants' ratings of Hannah's academic abilities? Figure 3.3 presents the ratings of Hannah. Participants who believed Hannah to be from a well-to-do background (positive expectancy) consistently rated her as more skilled than did participants who believed Hannah to be from a poor background (negative expectancy). But the effect of expectancies was much stronger when participants watched Hannah answer some test items (the performance condition) than when they rated her abilities based only on the background information (the baseline condition). Among those participants who watched Hannah answer questions, those in the positive expectancy condition rated her much more positively than did those in the negative expectancy condition. Why did watching Hannah's performance increase the impact of the expectancies manipulation? The researchers suggested that partici-

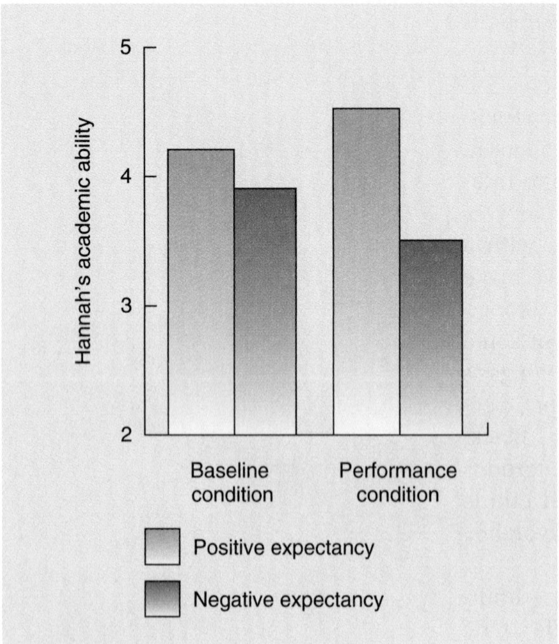

**FIGURE 3.3** Ratings of Hannah's academic ability

From Darley and Gross, "A hypothesis-confirming bias in labeling effects," *Journal of Personality and Social Psychology,* 24, 20–33, Fig. 1, p. 24, 1983. Copyright © 1983 by the American Psychological Association. Reprinted by permission.

pants' interpretations of Hannah's inconsistent performance differed based on their expectancies. If participants had positive expectancies, they probably focused on her correct answers to difficult questions when assessing her ability, whereas if participants had negative expectancies, they probably focused on her incorrect answers to easy questions when assessing her ability. Exactly the same performance was interpreted differently based on expectancies derived from social class stereotypes.

## Automatic Versus Controlled Processes

Most of us believe that we have full control over our mental processes. We can focus our attention *wherever* we wish; we can think about *whatever* we wish; and we can make judgments *whenever* we wish. We are completely in control. Right? Not always. Cognitive and social psychologists have come to realize that people do *not* have full control over all of their mental processes. Many thoughts and judgments occur whether we want them to or not. In fact, we are not even aware of some of our cognitive processes (see Nisbett & Wilson, 1977).

Theorists have proposed an important distinction based on the controllability or reflectiveness of a mental process (see Smith & DeCoster, 2000; Strack & Deutsch, 2004). An **automatic process** is a judgment or thought that we cannot control—it occurs without intention, very efficiently (demanding few cognitive resources), and sometimes beneath our awareness (Bargh, 1994; Gilbert, 1989). Thus, we cannot "turn on" and "turn off" an automatic process. It is spontaneous and not subject to intentional control; we may sometimes not even realize that it has occurred. An automatic process is also very efficient—it can occur at the same time as other processes. A **controlled process** is a judgment or thought that we command—it is intentional, requires significant cognitive resources, and occurs within our awareness. We can turn it on or off at will. Because a controlled process requires mental resources, it may not occur if we are engaged in other processes. We are consciously aware of engaging in a controlled process.

What processes occur automatically? Perhaps the clearest example of automatic processing is categorization—recognizing and identifying an object. We do not have to stop and think, "What is that rectangular piece of wood over there with four other pieces of wood going down from its corners?"; we automatically categorize the object as a table. This labeling is involuntary, immediate, and effortless. Categorization must be rapid and effortless so we can assign our limited attentional resources to more demanding tasks.

Categorization of people also occurs automatically. We perceive instantly and effortlessly various characteristics of others, including their age, sex, racial group, and physical appearance. The relevant schemas, or stereotypes, are activated automatically, whether we "want" them to be activated or not. Like other schemas, stereotypes allow us to draw inferences about individuals based on the assumption that they possess the central features of the category. In Chapter 9, we will discuss research suggesting that when people meet another individual, they cannot stop or inhibit relevant stereotypes from being activated in their minds (e.g., woman, elderly, Black), even if they reject the validity of those stereotypes. Researchers have also argued that the simple observation of an action (e.g., someone swearing at another person) leads us to label that action automatically, or spontaneously, in terms of relevant traits (e.g., as a hostile act). These "spontaneous trait inferences" occur instantly and effortlessly (see Bassili & Smith, 1986; Carlston & Skowronski, 1994; Newman, 1991; Uleman, Newman, & Moskowitz, 1996).

Of course, some cognitive processes are controlled—we can initiate them deliberately and focus them on whatever problem we need to solve. For example, thinking carefully about why someone behaved in a certain fashion is a controlled

**automatic process**

*a judgment or thought that we cannot control, which occurs without intention, very efficiently, and sometimes beneath our awareness*

**controlled process**

*a judgment or thought that we command, which is intentional, requires significant cognitive resources, and occurs within our awareness* process. Similarly, deciding how to behave toward another person is often an effortful, deliberate process. One function of controlled thinking is to correct errors from automatic processes if we suspect that errors may have occurred. For instance, we may decide that someone who acted in a hostile fashion (e.g., swore at another person) is not really hostile because he or she was responding to a prior threat. We will talk in Chapter 9 about research showing that people can consciously override the effects of stereotypes that have been elicited automatically.

## ● ● ●   Reconstructive Memory

Retrieval of information from memory can be a challenging task. We have tens of thousands of schemas stored in memory, as well as tens of thousands of recollections of our own experiences. How do we get information out of this massive storage system? Let's think of a simple example. Try to recall the last movie you saw. How did you retrieve it? We noted earlier that most social cognition theorists assume that retrieval occurs by a process of spreading activation. For instance, we begin by thinking about a schema related to our memory goal (e.g., movies), which then activates other connected schemas (comedies, dramas), which ultimately activate the information you need (the name of your most recent movie).

This example illustrates the retrieval of concrete, objective information. Sometimes, however, memory retrieval must be a "reconstructive" process. By reconstructive, we mean that cues or strategies must be used to search memory and to estimate the correct answer. **Reconstructive memory** is trying to cognitively rebuild the past based on cues and estimates. Although retrieval of things like the last movie you saw may not be susceptible to much distortion, many things in memory are less concrete and verifiable. How many soft drinks did you consume last month? How good were your study habits in high school? These sorts of questions cannot be answered solely by direct access to objective, concrete memories. They require estimations or interpretations that can be quite subjective. Therefore, the schemas, goals, and expectations that are active while you try to retrieve the information and estimate the answer can influence the outcome. John Kihlstrom (1994) captured this reconstructive aspect of memory very nicely: "memory is not so much like reading a book as it is like writing one from fragmentary notes" (p. 341).

**reconstructive memory**

*the process of trying to rebuild the past based on cues and estimates*

### Retrieval Cues

We often use a cue or clue to begin our search of memory. How many tests and exams have you written in the last year? You might attempt to answer this question by thinking about school and using this schema to search your memory. You might also count how many courses you have taken and estimate how many tests and exams were involved in each one. Or perhaps you might think specifically about tests you have written and count how many such experiences you can recollect. Because it is unlikely that you will be able to explicitly recall all of your exams in the last year, your answer will probably have to be an estimate, which will be "reconstructed" from information that you can currently retrieve. The point is that you need to begin somewhere in your search, and whatever cue you select will determine the specific information that is retrieved first. Retrieval cues increase the likelihood of some information's being retrieved and decrease the likelihood of other information's being retrieved.

Edward Hirt (1990) provided an interesting experimental example of how retrieval cues can affect reconstructive memory (see also Snyder & Uranowitz,

1978; Pyszczynski, LaPrelle, & Greenberg, 1987). Participants read a descriptive passage about a college student, Jack Whitaker, which included his grades in the first semester of a two-semester school year. Jack received a grade of 78 in chemistry, which was his middle grade out of five courses. Next, participants worked on a distracting anagrams task (forming words from scrambled letters) for 10 minutes. Participants then read a second passage about Jack, which contained information that led them to expect either improvement or decline in Jack's performance in another chemistry course taken in the second semester. Specifically, some participants were told that Jack hired a tutor for his second semester chemistry course (implying that his grade might improve), whereas others were told that Jack lost his chemistry tutor from the first semester (implying that his grade might decline). All participants then received Jack's second semester grades; we will focus here on participants who were told that Jack's grade in chemistry in the second semester was 78 (which happened to be the same as his grade in the first semester, though participants were not reminded of this). Now the interesting part: participants were asked to recall Jack's grade in chemistry in the first semester. As predicted, at least some participants used the information about the tutor, as well as Jack's second semester chemistry grade, to *reconstruct* Jack's first semester chemistry grade. Those who believed Jack hired a tutor in the second semester recalled his first semester chemistry grade as 75 (lower than 78); presumably, some of these participants guessed that the tutor produced a higher second semester grade, so Jack's first semester grade was probably lower than 78. In contrast, those who believed Jack lost his tutor recalled his first semester chemistry grade as 79 (slightly higher than 78); presumably, some of these participants guessed that the loss of the tutor reduced his grade, so Jack's first semester grade was probably higher than 78. It is remarkable that these reconstructive memory effects appeared just 15 minutes after exposure to the information about Jack's first semester grades. Over longer periods of time, reconstructive memory effects may be very powerful indeed.

## Autobiographical Memory

**Autobiographical memory** is stored information about the self—our goals, personality traits, past experiences, and other qualities. Autobiographical memory comprises our knowledge about the self, including our personal history. Because our own experiences make up so many of our memories, and because information about the self has major implications for identity and self-esteem, autobiographical memory is an important component of our memory system.

Michael Ross and his colleagues (Conway & Ross, 1984; McFarland & Ross, 1987; Ross, 1989; Wilson & Ross, 2001) have proposed a model of autobiographical memory that is based on the notion of reconstruction. Ross proposed that autobiographical memory often involves *estimating* what we were like in the past, because we may not be able to retrieve actual, concrete information. Thus, autobiographical memory is rather slippery—it involves guesswork, which can be influenced by our motives and beliefs.

Before continuing to read, look at Know Yourself 3.1: Current and Past Self. This questionnaire asks you to rate yourself on a number of characteristics at two points in time: now and when you were 16 years old. Take a look at the dimensions and rate yourself honestly in terms of how much you possess these

**autobiographical memory**

*stored information about the self, such as goals, personality traits, past experience, and other qualities*

*Autobiographical memory* includes our memories of childhood experiences.

© Jonnie Miles/Photographer's Choice/Getty Images

# Know Yourself 3.1
## *Current and Past Self*

Please rate yourself on each of the following dimensions by circling the appropriate number on the answer scale. First rate yourself as you are *now* (that is, your *current self*). Then rate yourself on the same dimensions as you were *when you were 16* (that is, a *past self*).

How much do these characteristics describe you **now**?

1. Broad-minded:

| 1 | 2 | 3 | 4 | 5 |
|---|---|---|---|---|
| Not at all | Slightly | Somewhat | Moderately | Extremely |

2. Socially skilled:

| 1 | 2 | 3 | 4 | 5 |
|---|---|---|---|---|
| Not at all | Slightly | Somewhat | Moderately | Extremely |

3. Self-confident:

| 1 | 2 | 3 | 4 | 5 |
|---|---|---|---|---|
| Not at all | Slightly | Somewhat | Moderately | Extremely |

4. Thoughtful:

| 1 | 2 | 3 | 4 | 5 |
|---|---|---|---|---|
| Not at all | Slightly | Somewhat | Moderately | Extremely |

5. Resourceful:

| 1 | 2 | 3 | 4 | 5 |
|---|---|---|---|---|
| Not at all | Slightly | Somewhat | Moderately | Extremely |

How much did these characteristics describe you **when you were 16 years old**?

1. Broad-minded:

| 1 | 2 | 3 | 4 | 5 |
|---|---|---|---|---|
| Not at all | Slightly | Somewhat | Moderately | Extremely |

2. Socially skilled:

| 1 | 2 | 3 | 4 | 5 |
|---|---|---|---|---|
| Not at all | Slightly | Somewhat | Moderately | Extremely |

3. Self-confident:

| 1 | 2 | 3 | 4 | 5 |
|---|---|---|---|---|
| Not at all | Slightly | Somewhat | Moderately | Extremely |

4. Thoughtful:

| 1 | 2 | 3 | 4 | 5 |
|---|---|---|---|---|
| Not at all | Slightly | Somewhat | Moderately | Extremely |

5. Resourceful:

| 1 | 2 | 3 | 4 | 5 |
|---|---|---|---|---|
| Not at all | Slightly | Somewhat | Moderately | Extremely |

**SCORING:** Look at your ratings on each dimension for the two time periods. Was one set of ratings consistently higher than another? Return to the text for relevant discussion.

qualities now and how much you possessed them when you were 16. After you have completed the ratings, come back to this point and continue reading.

In a series of studies, Anne Wilson and Michael Ross (2001) asked college students to rate themselves on a variety of traits like those in the Know Yourself 3.1 feature. Participants rated both their current self and the way they were at a certain point in the past (e.g., when they were 16 years old). Some participants rated the current self before the past self, whereas others rated the past self before the current self. Irrespective of the order of the two ratings, the results were clear and consistent: participants rated the current self more positively than the past self. Was this also true for you? Did you rate your current self more favorably than your 16-year-old self?

It is possible that the students in Wilson and Ross's research (and perhaps you) really did improve on these characteristics over the years, and their (or your) ratings were based on accurate, concrete memories. Wilson and Ross, however, proposed a second interpretation: their participants did not really access valid memories about themselves in the past, but instead estimated the past self based on a desire to see the current self positively. All of us want to think that we are good, worthwhile individuals. One way to feel good about ourselves is to believe that we are steadily improving over time: we are getting better and better on most qualities.

A third possible interpretation of Wilson and Ross's findings is that participants' past and present ratings were guided by their beliefs about the effects of time. For example, most of us believe that people generally improve over time on most characteristics. Thus, perhaps participants rated the past self lower than the present self because they assumed that improvement had occurred, which means that the past self must have been somewhat worse than the current self.

Which of these alternative interpretations is most plausible? In one of Wilson and Ross's (2001) studies, participants rated themselves at the beginning of the school term and then returned to the laboratory two months later. At this second session, participants rated the current self and then were asked to think back to how they were at the beginning of the term and to rate themselves again *as they were at that time.* Results showed that participants at the second session rated the past self (at the beginning of the term) less positively than the current self, whereas participants' *actual* self-ratings obtained at the beginning of the term were just as positive as the "current self" ratings at the second session. In other words, participants estimated at the second session that they had improved over the two-month period, but their original ratings indicated that they did not actually improve. This finding suggests that differences between the ratings of current and past selves do *not* necessarily reflect actual changes (improvements).

But this study did not distinguish between the second and third possibilities: perhaps participants simply wanted to see themselves favorably, or perhaps, when rating the past self, participants simply assumed that people improve over time. Therefore, in another study, Wilson and Ross (2001) asked participants to rate either themselves or an *acquaintance* (who was in the same year) on several traits; participants rated the target (self or acquaintance) both currently and when the target was 16 years old. Presumably, if people believe that everyone improves over time, then ratings of an acquaintance should show the same pattern as ratings of the self. The average ratings provided by participants are presented in Figure 3.4. These ratings revealed perceived improvement over time for the self, but *not* for the acquaintance, which suggests that the ratings of the self were caused by a desire to see the current self positively (see also Ross & Wilson,

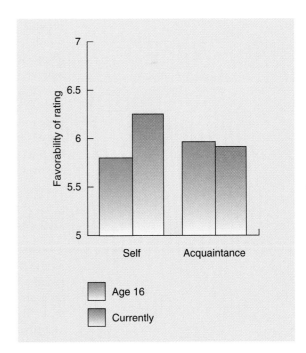

**FIGURE 3.4** Ratings of self and acquaintance currently and at age 16

From Wilson and Ross, "From chump to champ: People's appraisals of their earlier and present selves," *Journal of Personality and Social Psychology, 80,* 572–584, Table 2, p. 578, 2001. Copyright © 2001 by the American Psychological Association. Reprinted by permission.

2002). We will elaborate on this motive to see the current self positively later in this chapter.

Given that autobiographical memory is often reconstructive, an important question is whether *false* memories can be implanted in people's minds. Is it possible to make people believe that something happened to them which did not? Can people be influenced in such a way as to guide their reconstruction of the past in false directions? Think about some of your earliest memories. Are you certain that these memories are real and concrete, or could they possibly be your reconstructions based on things you have heard from your parents?

Some evidence suggests that yes, in fact, it may be possible to tamper with autobiographical memory (see Kunda, 1999; Loftus, 2004; Schacter, 1996). For example, Ira Hyman, Troy Husband, and James Billings (1995) contacted the parents of university students and obtained descriptions of a few events that had occurred in their child's life. The researchers then interviewed the students and asked them questions about these factual events and about one fictitious event that did not actually occur (fabricated by the researchers—either an eventful birthday party at age 5 or an overnight visit to the hospital at age 5). At this initial interview, no participants claimed to remember the fictitious event. The students were interviewed a second time, however, during the following week. At this second interview, they were again asked questions about both factual and fabricated events. This time, 20% of the students reported some memories of the fabricated event! Presumably, the earlier interview had put images into their minds that were now confused with real memories (see also Lindsay, Hagen, Read, Wade, & Garry, 2004).

We should not overstate the problem: human memory provides an amazing storage system for recollections of our past experiences. But human memory is *not* infallible. We often reconstruct personal memories based on information that is currently accessible to us. It is also possible for us to have seemingly real memories of events that we simply heard about or imagined occurring. Dreams can also provide fodder for erroneous memories (Bowers & Farvolden, 1996). Have you ever found yourself thinking about an event but then realized that you only dreamed about it? These points underscore that memory can be misleading—we may believe that something happened when, in fact, it did not.

A highly controversial question regarding the accuracy of autobiographical memory is whether "recovered" memories of childhood sexual abuse can be false. This emotionally charged issue has generated both vigorous debate and significant anger—but few empirical data. The conflicting perspectives on this question are outlined briefly in the accompanying box, Social Psychology in Your Life: Are Recovered Memories of Abuse Fact or Fiction?

## The Accuracy of Eyewitness Testimony

If human memory is unreliable, it may be risky to rely solely on one person's memory of a complex event to make an important decision. A domain in which exactly this circumstance can happen is legal settings. Many criminal cases are built around the testimony of an eyewitness to convict an accused person. In many trials, the eyewitness is the victim of the crime, and his or her principal role is to identify the accused person as the perpetrator of the crime. Jurors usually weigh eyewitness testimony very heavily; after all, if someone *saw* this person committing the crime (especially the victim), then he or she *must* be guilty. But how much confidence should we have in eyewitness identifications? Do errors occur?

Looking at documented cases of wrongful conviction makes the significance of erroneous eyewitness testimony very clear. There have been hundreds of examples of people who were convicted of a crime but later proven to be innocent. Legal experts have concluded that the single largest cause of these demonstrably false

# Social Psychology in Your Life

## *Are Recovered Memories of Abuse Fact or Fiction?*

Sexual abuse is a major social problem and is especially tragic when it involves children. Every year in the United States, thousands of young children are abused by a parent, other relative, or acquaintance, and the consequences of this abuse can be terrible. In addition to the immediate fear, pain, and humiliation, victims often experience long-term problems including depression, posttraumatic stress disorder, and difficulty establishing relationships with others (see Cardeña, Butler, & Spiegel, 2003; Wolfe, 1999).

In the past 20 years, increasing numbers of adults, usually women, have reported suddenly remembering childhood abuse after years of no such memory. Often, these recovered memories have appeared during psychotherapy, when therapists probed for possible abuse in the patient's past to explain her or his current difficulties. Sometimes, the memories have included bizarre elements like satanic cults and ritualistic torture. Typically, the people accused of committing these crimes have vehemently denied their guilt, claiming instead that the alleged events were somehow planted in the minds of the patients.

What should we conclude about these recovered memories? Is it possible that people can be induced to believe firmly that such violent acts occurred when they did not? Can therapists unknowingly elicit false memories of awful traumas?

Unfortunately, this question is extremely difficult to answer. For one thing, there are no objective, agreed-upon criteria for distinguishing true memories from false memories, even within more mundane domains than abuse. So unless physical evidence is available (which is unlikely for events that allegedly occurred many years ago), absolute certainty is impossible. Also, no empirical research has directly tested whether memories of sexual abuse can be implanted—nor will such research *ever* be conducted, because of the obvious ethical problems (Kunda, 1999). It is debatable whether research on less emotional issues should be generalized to the domain of recovered memories of sexual abuse (Pope, 1996). Harvard cognitive psychologist Daniel Schacter (1996) commented on the absence of relevant data: "Few times in the history of psychology or psychiatry has the ratio of data to impassioned argument been so low" (p. 277).

The stakes are very high on this issue. People accused of sexual abuse on the basis of recovered memories can go to jail—and some have. On the other side of the issue, victims of abuse worry that if recovered memories are discredited, a cloud of uncertainty will descend on *all* who claim to have been sexually abused. It is important to recognize, however, that most critics of recovered memories have limited their criticisms to allegedly forgotten memories that were drawn out in

psychotherapy. They have *not* questioned the veracity of victims' claims who have always remembered their abuse.

So what is the truth? Although not everyone agrees, many psychologists who study memory have concluded that psychotherapy can potentially generate false memories in some cases (Kunda, 1999; Schacter, 1996). For example, patients may be asked to imagine specific events and report how they would feel. This procedure may result in their subsequently perceiving their imagined experiences as real. Also, hypnosis may be employed, such as asking patients to write down whatever comes to mind while in a hypnotic trance. This procedure may result in some highly suggestible patients believing that something happened when it actually did not.

There have been a few cases in which people who were convicted of sexual assault on the basis of recovered memories have subsequently been proven innocent, or victims have recanted their testimony and sometimes even sued their therapists. Because of these cases, it is unlikely today that someone would be convicted and sentenced to prison based *solely* on the alleged victim's recovered memories, without any other corroborating evidence. Nevertheless, the issue remains highly charged and seems likely to continue to elicit spirited exchanges (e.g., Brown, 1997; de Rivera, 1997; Loftus & Ketcham, 1994; Pope, 1996).

convictions has been eyewitness error (e.g., Brandon & Davies, 1973; Huff, Rattner, & Sagarin, 1986). Not only is eyewitness testimony compelling to judges and jurors, but when an eyewitness positively identifies a suspect, the police often stop investigating all other leads (Wrightsman, 1991). The consequence is that an eyewitness identification can dramatically affect the course of the investigation and the trial. Unfortunately, eyewitnesses can sometimes be mistaken. Human memory is fallible, perhaps especially when the eyewitness was emotionally fearful or upset (e.g., was the victim of an assault).

© Jeffrey Phelps/Journal Sentinel, Milwaukee

Steven Avery served 17 years for a sexual assault that he did not commit. Mistaken eyewitness identification sent him to jail.

One factor that has dramatically increased the number of overturned convictions has been the advent of DNA testing. By matching inmates' DNA to samples obtained from the crime scene (e.g., using hairs from the scene), this form of testing can positively show that an individual is innocent. It can also sometimes positively identify someone else as the person who committed the crime.

The case of Steven Avery is typical of a wrongful conviction. This Wisconsin man was released on September 11, 2003, after serving 17 years for a sexual assault that he did not commit. DNA testing linked the assault to Gregory Allen, an inmate who is currently serving a 60-year sentence for a sexual assault committed after the one for which Avery was convicted. On what basis was Avery found guilty? The victim positively identified him as the person who assaulted her. The jury believed the victim despite 16 witnesses who testified in support of Avery's alibi. On his release, Avery was forgiving to his accuser, saying that the Sheriff's Department of Manitowoc County in Wisconsin had pressured her to identify him as the attacker—a charge the Sheriff's Department denied. Whatever the reason for the original conviction, Avery was the 137th prisoner in the United States freed on the basis of DNA evidence.

The issue of eyewitness identification has been studied systematically by social psychologists for more than 25 years, and we have learned a great deal about how false identifications can occur (see Wells, 1993, for a review). The most common experimental procedure has been to create a simulated event that is meticulously controlled by the researcher. In some studies, participants watch a film, slide show, or video, not knowing that they will later be asked to identify someone in the film. In other studies, participants are actually exposed to an unexpected, real-life event (e.g., a purse snatching) while they are waiting for the study to begin. Because participants do not know that they will later be asked to identify someone, their reactions during the event are very similar to those of real eyewitnesses of actual crimes.

What has this research found? Numerous studies have shown that people exposed to an event and later asked to identify the perpetrator often select the wrong individual (e.g., Buckhout, 1974; Cutler & Penrod, 1995). The rate of erroneous identification has ranged from less than 10% to more than 90% (Wells, 1993), depending on such factors as the duration of the event and the setting in which it occurred. Of course, even the lower end of this distribution (10% or 20%) is high enough to produce many false convictions. There appears to be an ingroup advantage (or outgroup disadvantage) in eyewitness identification: members of a particular racial group tend to be better at identifying people from their own racial group than people from other racial groups (MacLin, MacLin, & Malpass, 2001; Meissner & Brigham, 2001; Sporer, 2001; Wells & Olson, 2001), though errors can certainly occur even with ingroup targets.

Given that erroneous eyewitness identifications appear to occur frequently, an important question then becomes whether erroneous identifications differ from accurate identifications in some way that might allow us to weed out the former in real-life trials. Perhaps the most obvious candidate is the *confidence* an eyewitness expresses in his or her identification: if eyewitnesses are very confident that the accused person committed the crime, then it seems reasonable to conclude that they are probably correct. Unfortunately, research has shown that the confidence with which eyewitnesses identify the perpetrator is *not* a strong indication of their accuracy. Although there is a small correlation between confidence and accuracy (see Sporer, Penrod, Read, & Cutler, 1995), people who misidentify the perpetrator are often just as confident as people who identify the correct individual (see Brigham, 1990; Smith, Lindsay, Pryke, & Dysart, 2001; Wells, Olson, & Charman, 2002). Therefore, it is *not* the case that highly confident eyewitnesses can necessarily be trusted. Ironically, highly confident eyewitnesses *do* have more impact on jurors' decisions than do less confident eyewitnesses.

One quality that might be better than confidence is the *speed* with which eyewitnesses make their identification. In four studies that included both videotaped and "live" events, David Dunning and Scott Perretta (2002) found that eyewitnesses who identified someone as the target person in 10 seconds or less were correct almost 90% of the time (choosing from a lineup of five or six suspects), whereas eyewitnesses who took longer than 10 seconds to make their identification were correct approximately 50% of the time (see also Sporer, 1993). The authors hypothesized that eyewitnesses who made their judgment quickly were relying on automatic, unconscious processes (e.g., the feeling that the target person's face just "popped out" at them), which were likely to occur only when the match between the target and the memory was good. In contrast, eyewitnesses who made their judgment slowly were relying on controlled, conscious processes, which were more likely to lead them into making mistakes.

We have focused on the implications of unreliable memory for eyewitness identification of a perpetrator. Other aspects of eyewitness memory might also be open to distortion. For example, work by Elizabeth Loftus (1979; Loftus, Miller, & Burns, 1978) has shown that leading or suggestive questions can introduce errors into eyewitnesses' accounts of events. Participants in one study watched a slide show presentation of an accident that involved an automobile striking a pedestrian. If a false element was inserted into a question about the event, participants often later included the false element in their memories. For example, if participants were asked a question about whether something happened while the car in the slide show "was stopped at the yield sign," even though the original slides actually showed the car stopping at a stop sign, the majority of participants later believed that a yield sign had been part of the slide presentation. These findings reflect that when people cognitively reconstruct past events, they rely on cues as a starting point for retrieving memories.

*You don't just record the event and play it back the way a videotape would work—the process is much more complex.*

**Reducing Eyewitness Errors.** Despite the limitations of eyewitness testimony, eyewitnesses continue to play a key role in many trials. Psychological researchers have argued that the traditional safeguards against eyewitness errors are relatively ineffective. For instance, defense lawyers can cross-examine the witness to try to raise doubts about the identification. Also, judges usually give instructions to the jury to come to a guilty verdict only when they are convinced beyond a "reasonable doubt." Psychologists have argued that these procedures are unlikely to make jurors appropriately cautious about eyewitness identifications.

What can the legal system do to reduce both the rate of eyewitness errors and jurors' reliance on eyewitness testimony? With regard to reducing false identifications, researchers have suggested that police "lineup" procedures, in which witnesses are asked to identify the suspect from a line of individuals, need to be altered (e.g., see Wells, 1993). For instance, exposing witnesses to a **blank lineup** is a good way to assess their credibility. A blank lineup is a group (lineup) that does *not* include the suspect—everyone in the lineup is known to be innocent. If the eyewitness identifies someone in this blank lineup as the perpetrator, he or she should be dismissed. If the eyewitness states that no one in the blank lineup is the perpetrator and then identifies the true suspect in another lineup, he or she is more likely to have made an accurate identification. Another recommendation from social psychologists is that a **sequential lineup** is better than the traditional, simultaneous lineup. A sequential lineup is a procedure in which the eyewitness is presented with each person in the group (lineup) individually, rather than with the entire lineup together (simultaneously). Evidence suggests that when eyewitnesses see a traditional simultaneous lineup, they try to find the person who looks *most like* the perpetrator, which can lead to erroneous identifications; eyewitnesses may assume that the police have arrested the guilty person, who must, therefore, be in the lineup. In contrast, eyewitnesses exposed to a sequential lineup judge each person separately, which reduces errors. They tend to wait until they see someone whose face "pops out" at them—someone whose face automatically elicits recognition.

In addition to these changes to how lineups are presented, researchers have suggested that it might be possible to reduce jurors' confidence in eyewitness testimony by introducing expert psychological evidence at the trial. This expert should try to educate the jury about how reconstructive memory works, the potential inaccuracy of eyewitness identifications, and how to evaluate eyewitness testimony more effectively (see Cutler & Penrod, 1995).

**blank lineup**

*a group of individuals that does not include the suspect; everyone in the lineup is known to be innocent*

**sequential lineup**

*the procedure of showing an eyewitness each individual in the group separately rather than together in a simultaneous lineup*

Psychologists have suggested that traditional police lineup procedures need to be changed. This photo shows a portion of the actual lineup used in Steven Avery's case of erroneous identification discussed earlier (Avery is suspect number 6).

Courtesy of the Manitowoc County Sheriff's Department

# Heuristics and Biases in Everyday Judgments

All of us make many ordinary, everyday judgments quickly and without much effort. These judgments may come in response to a question from others, or simply from our own reflections: Does your neighbor have a bad temper? Which of your friends is most likely to be late for appointments? What was the breed of the dog you saw in the park last night? How old was Judy Garland in the movie *The Wizard of Oz?*

How do we make routine judgments of these kinds? It turns out that we typically use informal rules or shortcuts to come up with quick, "intuitive" answers. These informal rules or shortcuts in everyday judgments are called **heuristics.** Heuristics are "rules of thumb" or simplifying strategies for making judgments quickly. Because we cannot afford to expend large amounts of time or energy making every judgment required during the day, we rely on simple shortcuts to make reasonable guesses. Sometimes, if the decision is particularly important or if we believe we are on the wrong track, we may subsequently think more carefully and deliberatively about our initial judgment. But most of the time, we will stick with our first, intuitive judgment—and most of the time, this judgment will be reasonably accurate (see Goldstein & Gigerenzer, 2002; Kahneman, 2003). Thus, heuristics usually work well and yield fairly accurate judgments, but sometimes they can lead us astray and result in errors. The distinction we described earlier between *automatic* and *controlled* processes is similar in many respects to this distinction between heuristics and deliberative judgments.

The hypothesis that perceivers usually rely on simple rules to make judgments and engage in careful, thoughtful processing only when necessary has been called the **cognitive miser model** of information processing (see Fiske & Taylor, 1991). This perspective assumes that detailed, deliberative processing is costly or expensive in terms of psychological resources, and our resource capacity is limited. Therefore, we try to "spend" as little as possible in most cases—we are *misers* who try to protect our resources for important judgments. Heuristics are one way that we save resources.

The term *heuristics* was made famous by two cognitive psychologists, Amos Tversky and Daniel Kahneman, whose work on intuitive reasoning also captured the interest of many social psychologists. Indeed, the field of social cognition owes a great deal to Tversky and Kahneman for showing that everyday judgments are both fascinating and important to study. All psychologists were proud when Daniel Kahneman was awarded the 2002 Nobel Prize for Economics, based on the work he did with Tversky (who died in 1996; the Nobel Prize cannot be awarded posthumously).

Returning to the examples given above, your judgment of whether your neighbor has a temper will probably be based on how easily you can bring to mind times when he or she has exhibited angry behavior. If you can easily think of examples of your neighbor yelling or swearing, you will answer affirmatively that, yes, he or she does have a bad temper, whereas if you cannot think of such incidents, you will state that he or she is even-tempered. Similarly, your judgment of which of your friends is most likely to be late will probably be based on the number of such occurrences you can remember for each friend. You will choose the person who brings to mind the most examples of tardiness. A different rule will guide your judgment of the breed of the dog you saw last night. This answer will probably be based on the dog's similarity to your images (schemas) of various breeds—poodles, German shepherds, and so on. If the dog resembled a particular breed or mix of breeds, then that will be your guess. Similarly, your judgment of Judy Garland's

**heuristic**
*an informal rule or shortcut that is used to make everyday judgments*

**cognitive miser model**
*a view of information processing that assumes people usually rely on heuristics to make judgments and only engage in careful, thoughtful processing when necessary*

© Denise Applewhite, Office of Communications, Princeton University

Psychologist Daniel Kahneman was awarded the 2002 Nobel Prize for Economics based on the work he did with Amos Tversky on heuristics.

age in *The Wizard of Oz* will probably be based on the overlap between her features (e.g., height, voice) and your conceptions of various ages.

These examples illustrate the application of two heuristics that are described in the following paragraphs—the availability heuristic and the representativeness heuristic. Although we limit our consideration to these two heuristics (which are the best known and most researched heuristics), there are others that also influence everyday judgments (for additional examples, see Gilovich, Griffin, & Kahneman, 2002; Lassiter, Geers, Munhall, Ploutz-Snyder, & Breitenbecher, 2002). After describing the availability and representativeness heuristics, we discuss several other processes in social cognition that can produce errors or biases.

## The Availability Heuristic

**availability heuristic**

*the tendency to base a judgment on how easily relevant examples can be generated*

Tversky and Kahneman (1973) defined the **availability heuristic** as the tendency to base a judgment on how easily relevant examples can be generated. For instance, basing a judgment about your roommate's temper on how easy it is for you to recall temper tantrums would illustrate the availability heuristic. This heuristic makes a lot of sense. After all, it usually *is* easier to think of tantrums by an ill-tempered person than by an even-tempered person, because ill-tempered people *do* throw more tantrums (by definition)! As another example, if you were asked what percentage of municipal politicians in your city are women, it would make sense to bring to mind as many local politicians as possible and use this mental sample to make your judgment. After all, the greater the proportion of politicians in your city who are women, the easier it *should* be to think of examples.

Colin MacLeod and Lynlee Campbell (1992) provided direct evidence that people base judgments about the likelihood of future events on the ease with which they can think of examples of these events in the past. Participants read three-word descriptions of common pleasant and unpleasant events, such as "an unexpected gift," "a welcome visitor," "a painful injury," and "a disappointing vacation." As each event was presented, participants were asked to think of a specific example of that event in their own life and to immediately press a button, which allowed the computer to record how long it took them to think of the example. Participants were then asked to rate how likely it was that they would experience this event sometime in the next six months. Results showed a strong correlation between how quickly participants could think of a relevant example in their own life and their estimated likelihood that they would experience the event in the next six months: the *faster* they thought of an example, the *more likely* they judged another experience to be. The availability heuristic in action.

The availability heuristic is a sensible, useful shortcut for making many judgments. The actual frequency of an event or object *will* be related in most circumstances to the ease with which such events or objects can be brought to mind. The availability heuristic can lead to problems, however, when the examples that come to mind most easily are slanted or atypical. For instance, a recent event might have substantially increased the accessibility of a particular concept in memory. The pregnancy situation described in the earlier accessibility section illustrates this point. Being pregnant or being the partner of someone who is pregnant greatly increases the salience of pregnant women in one's environment. If someone in this condition were asked to estimate the percentage of women in the local community who are pregnant at the current time, he or she could probably think of many examples and might therefore overestimate the actual percentage.

In one of the original studies on availability, Tversky and Kahneman (1973) asked participants to read a list of 39 names: either 19 men and 20 women or 20 men and 19 women. These lists included the names of some famous people and some nonfamous people. For some participants, all of the men in the list were famous whereas the women were not; for the remaining participants, all of the women in the list were famous whereas the men were not. After reading the list, participants were asked to estimate how many men and how many women had been in the list (participants were *not* forewarned that they would be asked this question). The researchers assumed that participants would more easily recall famous names than nonfamous names. Thus, if the famous names had been men, participants were expected to be able to recall more men than women from the list, which would lead them to guess that the list contained mostly men. If the famous names had been women, however, participants were expected to be able to recall more women than men from the list, which would lead them to guess that the list contained mostly women. The results conformed exactly to these predictions. Note that the researchers deliberately constructed these lists to slant participants' recall of one of the sexes; thus, the researchers set up the situation in such a way as to make the availability heuristic misleading.

In most cases, the availability heuristic will rely on the total number of examples that can be recalled (e.g., how many men vs. women from the list are recalled). Recent research has shown, however, that people are sometimes influenced directly by the *ease* with which they can recall something, independently of the number or content of what they recall (see Haddock, Rothman, Reber, & Schwarz, 1999; Schwarz & Vaughn, 2002). For instance, Norbert Schwarz and his colleagues (Schwarz, Bless, Strack, Klumpp, Rittenauer-Schatka, & Simons, 1991) investigated the availability heuristic in the context of judgments of assertiveness. The researchers asked participants to recall and describe either 6 times they had acted assertively, 12 times they had acted assertively, 6 times they had acted unassertively, or 12 times they had acted unassertively. Pilot testing had shown that most people can think of 6 examples of their own assertive or unassertive behavior relatively easily, but it is very difficult to come up with 12 examples of either kind of behavior. The researchers therefore predicted that when participants were asked to describe 6 examples of assertive (or unassertive) behaviors, they would be able to do so relatively easily and would conclude, based on the availability heuristic, that their personality was assertive (or unassertive). In contrast, the researchers predicted that when participants were asked to describe 12 examples of assertive (or unassertive) behavior, they would find the task very difficult and show a boomerang effect, such that they would conclude that they do *not* possess that characteristic. For instance, participants asked to describe 12 examples of assertive behavior were expected to say to themselves, "I can't come up with as many examples of assertive behavior as the experimenter wants, so I guess I'm not very assertive." These inferences would be based directly on how difficult it was to recall the requested behaviors.

Figure 3.5 presents the results of the study on ratings of assertiveness of the self. As predicted, participants rated themselves as more assertive when they were asked to recall 6 examples of assertive actions than when they were asked to recall 12 examples of assertive actions, even though the latter individuals generated more total examples of assertiveness. Conversely, participants rated themselves as less assertive (more unassertive) when they were asked to recall 6 unassertive actions than when they were asked to recall 12 examples of unassertive actions. The ease of completing the task was used by participants to infer their own assertiveness.

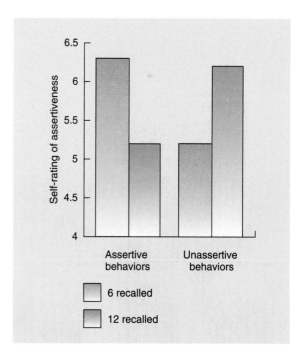

**FIGURE 3.5** Self-ratings of assertiveness after behavior recall

From Schwarz et al., "Ease of retrieval of information: Another look at the availability heuristic," *Journal of Personality and Social Psychology*, 61, 195–202, Table 1, p. 197, 1991. Copyright © 2001 by the American Psychological Association. Reprinted by permission.

## The Representativeness Heuristic

**representativeness heuristic**

*the tendency to judge the likelihood that a target belongs to a category based on how similar the target is to the typical features of the category*

Another shortcut that people use to make everyday judgments is the **representativeness heuristic** (see Kahneman & Frederick, 2002). Kahneman and Tversky (1973) defined this heuristic as the tendency to judge the likelihood that an object belongs to a certain category based on how similar the object is to the typical features of the category (how *representative* it is of the category). For instance, deciding that the dog you saw last night in the park was probably a poodle because it had curly hair that was cut in a poodle style illustrates the representativeness heuristic. This process is akin to categorization—the most basic of our cognitive processes. Thus, like the availability heuristic, this heuristic makes a lot of sense. Categorizing an object by assessing the overlap between its features and the defining features of a category is perfectly reasonable—this is precisely how we use schemas to categorize an object so we can predict its behavior (Fiske & Taylor, 1991). A small animal that looks like a cat and meows like a cat probably *is* a cat. The representativeness heuristic usually serves us well.

Problems can arise, however, when perceivers ignore everything *except* representativeness. That is, people sometimes base their judgments *only* on the overlap between an object's characteristics and the defining features of a category, even when other kinds of information could (and should) also be employed. For instance, people should pay attention to the initial, baseline probability of different categories. Imagine that you are on a bus or train and overhear a young man sitting in front of you speaking with an accent that you can identify as European—perhaps German, Swiss, Austrian, or French. He talks to his acquaintance about his love of downhill skiing and how he has skied since he was very young. What country would you guess he is from? You might think of countries known especially for downhill skiing, such as Switzerland or Austria, and guess that he is from one of these countries. But these are actually poor choices, based simply on the total populations of the four countries. Switzerland has a population of 7 million, and Austria has a population of 8 million. In contrast, Germany has a population of 82 million, and France has a population of 60 million. Although a love of skiing may be associated in our minds more closely with Switzerland and Austria than with Germany and France, the latter countries have almost 10 times as many people as the former—and, of course, there are plenty of people in Germany and France who also love skiing.

Based on the *representativeness heuristic*, you might guess that this man is from Switzerland or Austria.

In a classic demonstration of the representativeness heuristic, Kahneman and Tversky (1973) gave participants brief descriptions of individuals who were (allegedly) either engineers or lawyers and asked them to predict each stimulus person's occupation. Participants were told that each description was randomly selected from a group of 100 individuals. Some participants were told that the group was composed of 70 engineers and 30 lawyers, whereas other participants were told that the group was composed of 30 engineers and 70 lawyers. Thus, the baseline probability that a randomly selected individual would be an engineer was either 70% or 30% in the two conditions.

The brief descriptions given to participants were constructed by the researchers to be more or less representative of the stereotypes of engineers or lawyers. For instance, a stimulus person might be described as having a strong need for order and clarity, being a loner, and having hobbies that included computers and math puzzles—features chosen to resemble the stereotype of engineers. Kahneman and Tversky found that participants almost always based their predictions entirely on representativeness and not at all on the overall ratio of engineers to lawyers. That is, someone described as having a strong need for order and clarity, being a loner, and enjoying computers and math puzzles was usually classified as an engineer no matter what the baseline probabilities—it did not matter whether participants believed that engineers constituted 70% or 30% of the sample. Of course, it was reasonable for participants to base their predictions at least partly on the descriptions, but they should *also* have given some weight to the baseline probabilities of each occupation. The representativeness heuristic can lead us astray when we rely on it exclusively.

# Illusory Correlations

A correlation exists when two variables are associated with one another, such as height and weight or class attendance and exam performance. As we noted in Chapter 2, correlations do not necessarily reflect cause, although causal relations between the variables may sometimes account for some or all of the correlation (e.g., class attendance definitely improves exam performance).

An **illusory correlation** occurs when an individual believes that two variables are related to one another when, in fact, they are not (Hamilton & Gifford, 1976). For example, athletes often believe that they perform better when they follow some ritual. Basketball legend Michael Jordan wore his college shorts under his professional uniform. Would an objective test of his superstitious behavior have shown that he would have performed just as well without the college shorts? We suspect so.

**illusory correlation**
*the belief that two variables are related to one another when, in fact, they are not*

**Seeing What We Expect to See.** Why or when do illusory correlations occur? Loren Chapman and Jean Chapman (1967, 1969; see also Stroessner & Plaks, 2001) suggested that people are especially likely to notice events that confirm their expectancies, which leads them to overestimate the frequency of such confirmations. People tend to see what they expect to see.

For example, some people believe in astrology. Such individuals might read their daily horoscope every morning. Chapman and Chapman would suggest that if something happens that is congruent with the individual's horoscope for that day, he or she is more likely to notice than if nothing happens to confirm the horoscope. Therefore, those days when something confirmatory happened will be recalled better than those days when nothing happened, and the person will overestimate the accuracy of the horoscopes.

In a test of the role of expectancies in illusory correlations, Loren Chapman (1967) asked participants to read a series of word pairs (*bacon–notebook, blossoms–tiger,* etc.), which were presented several times. Some of the word pairs consisted of commonly associated words, such as *bacon–eggs* and *lion–tiger,* whereas other pairs combined unrelated words, such as *bacon–tiger* and *lion–eggs.* The commonly associated word pairs (the expected pairings) were not presented any more often than the unrelated word pairs. When participants were asked to estimate the frequency of various word pairings, however, they overestimated the frequency of the expected pairings. For example, they tended to overestimate the frequency with which bacon and eggs or lion and tiger had been paired in the trials. Chapman suggested that these illusory correlations occurred because the expected pairings were more likely to be noticed and thus were easier to retrieve from memory.

**The "Hot Hand" in Sports.** Do you think that sports athletes can get "hot" or go "cold" in their performance? Do basketball players sometimes have a "hot

Most basketball players and fans believe that players can have a "hot hand," but the data suggest otherwise.

hand" such that they just can't miss in a particular game? Do baseball players go on hitting streaks where they hit the ball well for an extended period of time? The hypothesis of the hot hand is widely accepted in sports, perhaps especially in basketball. Most basketball players and fans believe that players shoot in streaks, such that they are more likely to make a shot if they have previously made a shot than if they have previously missed a shot. Coaches also subscribe to this hypothesis, instructing teammates to get the ball to a player who has made a high percentage of shots in the game.

Thomas Gilovich, Robert Vallone, and Amos Tversky (1985; see also Gilovich, 1991) examined the validity of this hypothesis by obtaining empirical data from the National Basketball Association. Interestingly, the researchers found no evidence for a hot hand. The probability of making a shot was unrelated to whether a previous shot had been made. Figure 3.6 depicts the percentage of shots that players made, either from the floor or from the foul line, based on the outcome of their previous shot. Players made 51% of their shots from the floor after making their previous shot, compared to 54% after missing their previous shot—a tendency in the *opposite direction* of a hot hand. The most compelling test of the hot hand hypothesis is probably provided by foul shooting, because players were always shooting from the same place. But again the evidence was clearly inconsistent with the notion of a hot hand: players made 75% of their foul shots after making the previous foul shot, and 75% of their foul shots after missing the previous foul shot. No difference whatsoever.

Why do players and fans believe in the hot hand? Gilovich (1991) provided several possible reasons. Perhaps the most plausible explanation is that people notice when a player hits several shots in a row or misses several shots in a row, whereas they do not notice when hits and misses are intermixed. Thus, people's belief in the hot hand may constitute an example of seeing what we expect to see—an illusory correlation. Another possibility is that people fail to realize that occasional "runs" of consecutive hits or consecutive misses will occur even when events are truly independent—that is, people have a misperception of what "random" sequences look like. As a result, runs that are actually random may appear to many people to be more representative of nonrandom sequences, such as a series of hot and cold streaks. Thus, people's belief in the hot hand may also reflect the operation of the representativeness heuristic.

## The Hindsight Bias: I Knew It All Along

Think about a recent test that you took in a challenging course (and for which you have received your grade). How predictable in advance was your performance? If you had been asked before the test to predict your grade, what would you have said?

According to research in social and cognitive psychology, you are likely to think now that your performance was more predictable than it actually was. That is, you probably now think that if you had been asked before the test to predict the grade, you would have predicted a grade relatively close to the one you actually received. But if you had *really* been asked before the test, you would have expressed more uncertainty about how you would do.

What is different between now and before the test? *You know how you did.* This "outcome information" is very difficult to ignore and colors your judgment of what you believed before the event. This tendency for people to overestimate the predictability of known out-

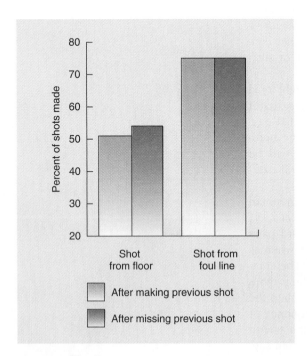

**FIGURE 3.6** Percentage of shots made after hits and misses

From Gilovich et al., "The hot hand in basketball: On the misperception of random sequences," *Cognitive Psychology*, 17, 295–314. Copyright © 1985. Reprinted by permission of Elsevier.

comes, called the **hindsight bias** (Fischhoff, 1975), has been shown to occur in both children and adults (e.g., Bernstein, Atance, Loftus, & Meltzoff, 2004). It is captured in common phrases like "I knew it all along" and "Hindsight is 20/20."

**hindsight bias**

*the tendency for people to overestimate the predictability of known outcomes*

**Armchair Quarterbacks.** A vintage example of the hindsight bias comes from sports fans, who regularly blame coaches and players for bad decisions. "That idiot coach should have changed quarterbacks," "What a stupid call to make on first down," "It was obvious that a zone defense would be murdered by the other team." Armchair quarterbacks benefit from hindsight and fail to recognize that things were not really so predictable before the event.

In a classic experimental demonstration of the hindsight bias, Baruch Fischhoff (1975) gave university students information about little-known historical events, such as a war between British soldiers and fighters from Nepal in the 19th century. Some participants (the "foresight" condition) received the background information and were asked to predict the likelihood of each of a set of possible outcomes (a British victory, a Nepalese victory, a stalemate, a peace settlement). Other participants (the "hindsight" conditions) received the background information along with a sentence allegedly presenting the actual outcome (some were told that the British won, some were told the Nepalese won, etc.). When these hindsight participants were asked to rate the pre-outcome likelihood of each of the possible outcomes, they gave higher probability ratings to the outcome that they believed had occurred than did participants in the foresight condition. For example, participants who believed the British won rated a British victory as a more likely outcome than did participants who received no outcome information. This effect occurred even though participants in the hindsight conditions were explicitly told to answer as if they did not know the actual outcome.

Harold Arkes and his colleagues (Arkes, Wortmann, Saville, & Harkness, 1981) asked physicians to read a case history and to indicate what their diagnosis would

© AP/Wide World Photos/Chris Carlson

Outcomes of events such as elections tend to look more predictable in retrospect, a phenomenon known as the *hindsight bias.*

have been. Some physicians were given only the case history with no diagnosis, whereas other physicians were told what diagnosis allegedly had been made. When asked how likely it was that they would have made a particular diagnosis based only on the case history, physicians who thought they knew the diagnosis reported a higher probability of that diagnosis than did physicians who received no diagnosis information. (For an example of the hindsight bias regarding O. J. Simpson's acquittal on murder charges, see Bryant & Brockway, 1997.)

Why does the hindsight bias occur? Several processes might contribute, but we will mention just two (see also Hawkins & Hastie, 1990; Werth, Strack, & Forster, 2002). One important cause is that people reinterpret pre-outcome information based on knowing the outcome. If you learn that a friend has dropped out of school, you might reinterpret his or her past behaviors as reflecting unhappiness or disillusionment. These reinterpretations make it seem more obvious that the decision to drop out would happen. Second, people generate explanations that would not have occurred to them if they had not known the outcome. You might think about your friend's academic history and realize that his performance has been declining since starting college. This realization might lead you to conclude that poor grades caused your friend to drop out and his decision was foreseeable. The flowchart in Figure 3.7 illustrates how the hindsight bias occurs.

The hindsight bias may have influenced people's reactions to the terrorist attacks in New York and Washington on September 11, 2001. Many commentators spoke about the "massive failure" of American intelligence in not learning about the plans in advance. Although intelligence sources may indeed have been flawed, it is also possible that the events seem more predictable in retrospect. Another domain in which the hindsight bias may occur is accusations of medical malpractice. If a patient has been seen by a physician but then suddenly deteriorates, his or her family may later look back and conclude that the correct diagnosis was obvious, whereas it may actually have been unclear. Moreover, other physicians may examine the case and also conclude that the diagnosis was more obvious than it actually was (as in Arkes et al., 1981).

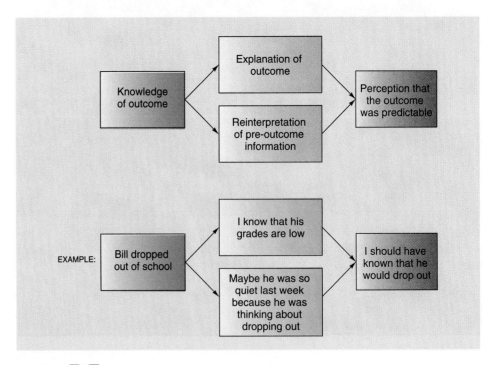

**FIGURE 3.7** Hindsight bias

# The Perseverance Effect

Another bias that shares some features with the hindsight bias can occur in social psychology experiments. Participants in social psychology studies are sometimes given false feedback about themselves, which occasionally is negative, or unfavorable, such as failure feedback on a task or test. For instance, if a researcher wants to investigate the effects of self-esteem threat on interpersonal behavior, some participants might be asked to take an alleged test of "social sensitivity" and then be given negative feedback (e.g., that their score is in the bottom 25% of university students, which indicates a lack of social sensitivity). At the end of the experiment, participants are debriefed, which includes being told that the feedback was false and did not really reflect their social sensitivity.

Does the debriefing take care of all potential problems? Unfortunately, not necessarily. Let's put ourselves in the shoes of a hypothetical male participant. During the experiment, he learns that he performed poorly on a test of social sensitivity. This outcome will probably surprise him—he has always regarded himself as sensitive to others' feelings. But when he thinks about it, he can remember that his mother told him when he was a teenager that he was insensitive to his brother's feelings. Oh, there was also the time last year when he broke up with his girlfriend, and she said he was an insensitive jerk. So maybe the feedback shouldn't be so surprising after all.

At the end of the study, the experimenter debriefs him and assures him that the feedback was unrelated to his actual social sensitivity. Let's assume that the participant accepts this information and regards the feedback as phony. What is he likely to think about his *actual* social sensitivity? Well, he can remember back when he was a teenager that his mother told him he wasn't sensitive to his brother's feelings, and last year his girlfriend told him he was an insensitive jerk. So if he performed a *real* test of social sensitivity, he would probably do poorly.

Notice what has happened here. False feedback led the participant to think of memories that he would *not* have brought to consciousness without the false feedback. When he learned that the feedback was false, he still had these memories fresh in his mind, which led him to believe that he would *really* perform in a manner similar to the false feedback.

Lee Ross, Mark Lepper, and Michael Hubbard (1975) documented exactly this effect, which they labeled the **perseverance effect.** The perseverance effect occurs when individuals continue to make self-evaluations that are consistent with information that has been discredited. Some participants in the original Ross et al. (1975) study performed a task in which they tried to identify authentic versus inauthentic suicide notes—a task they were told reflected social sensitivity. Participants received false feedback that they performed either well or poorly, but were later told that the feedback was false and randomly determined. When asked to estimate their *actual* social sensitivity, however, debriefed participants who received false negative feedback estimated lower levels of social sensitivity than did debriefed participants who received false positive feedback.

Subsequent research (e.g., Anderson, Lepper, & Ross, 1980; Lord, Lepper, & Preston, 1984) showed that in order for the perseverance effect to be avoided in research involving false negative feedback, participants must be told about the perseverance effect (how and why it occurs) and must be asked to consider the opposite outcome—to think about how they would have reacted if they had been given *positive* feedback. Presumably, this imagination task will stimulate some memories and explanations that are *in*consistent with the initial negative feedback. The implication of these findings is that when researchers give participants false negative feedback, it is their ethical responsibility to include in the debriefing an explanation of the perseverance effect and an opportunity to consider the opposite outcome.

The accompanying Concept Review summarizes the heuristics and biases we have described.

**perseverance effect**
*the tendency for people to make self-evaluations that are consistent with information that has been discredited*

## CONCEPT REVIEW
### Heuristics and Biases

| Heuristic or Bias | Description | Example |
| --- | --- | --- |
| Availability heuristic | The tendency to base a judgment on how easily relevant examples can be generated | Someone decides that the level of violence on television is very high because she can think of many examples of violence she has seen on television programs. |
| Representativeness heuristic | The tendency to judge the likelihood that a target belongs to a category based on how similar the target is to typical features of the category | Someone decides that a woman is probably Irish because she is wearing a green dress on St. Patrick's Day. |
| Illusory correlation | The belief that two variables are related to one another when, in fact, they are not | A man believes that women are worse drivers than men because he notices whenever female drivers, but not male drivers, annoy him. |
| Hindsight bias | The tendency for people to over-estimate the predictability of known outcomes | Looking back, a woman thinks that she should have been able to predict her husband's descent into alcoholism. |
| Perseverance effect | The tendency for people to make self-evaluations that are consistent with information that has been discredited | A student given false negative feedback about his performance on a difficult spelling test continues to believe that he is a poor speller even after debriefing. |

# What Might Have Been: Counterfactual Thinking

Do you ever think about how your life might have been different? Perhaps you've thought about what your life would be like if you'd gone to a different college or if you'd continued a relationship with someone who is not part of your current life. Do you ever wish that you had taken different courses in high school or college? (We hope that such a thought is not too applicable at the present moment.) Your thoughts will not always be regretful in tone—you may sometimes think about how things could have been worse. If you hadn't studied so hard, perhaps you would have failed an exam, or if you hadn't gone to your friend's party, perhaps you wouldn't have met your romantic partner.

**counterfactual thoughts**

*reflections on how past events might have turned out differently*

All of these thoughts about "what might have been" qualify as **counterfactual thoughts.** Counterfactual thoughts are reflections on how past events might have turned out differently. They are called "counterfactual" because they are counter to the facts (they imagine things that did not really happen). Counterfactual thinking is a relatively recent topic in social cognition, having received significant attention only during the past 15 to 20 years, although it has interested philosophers for much longer.

## Wishful Thinking in Everyday Life

Counterfactual thoughts are very common and may be uniquely human—the capacity to think about alternative realities is probably something that distinguishes humans from other species. Some counterfactual thoughts are playful and fanciful, such as children imagining themselves having grown up on a pirate ship;

other counterfactual thoughts are excruciatingly painful, such as parents thinking again and again how their child might still be alive if they had only taken her sooner to the hospital emergency room. The vast majority of counterfactual thoughts, however, are quite ordinary and involve thinking about how commonplace events might have been different. Counterfactual thoughts are more likely to occur when it is *easy* for the person to imagine how things could have been different— when it is easy to "undo" the event mentally (Kahneman & Miller, 1986). If a woman decides at the last minute to go to a public lecture that turns out to be dreadfully boring, she will probably think about how she could be at home relaxing, because she almost did stay home—thus, being at the lecture is easy for her to undo mentally.

Many counterfactual thoughts change something that occurred prior to an event and then imagine how the event could have turned out differently. A student might think, "If I had stayed home last night to study, I bet I would've done better on the test today." Or a woman at her place of work might think, "I wish that I'd listened to the weather this morning, because then I would've brought an umbrella and not gotten soaked by the rain at lunchtime."

Why are counterfactual thoughts important? Social psychologists have argued that counterfactual thoughts have important consequences for emotions, beliefs, and behavior (for reviews of the counterfactual literature, see Miller, Turnbull, & McFarland, 1990; Roese, 1997; Roese & Olson, 1995). These consequences depend in important ways on the *type* of counterfactual thoughts that occur.

## Upward Counterfactual Thoughts: Wanting to Improve

The most common type of counterfactual thought has been labeled **upward counterfactual thoughts.** Upward counterfactual thoughts involve reflecting on how things could have turned out *better.* Most of the examples we have given to this point have been upward counterfactual thoughts—such as the student wishing he had stayed home to study last night, and the woman wishing she had brought an umbrella to work. These alternative realities would have been preferable to what actually occurred.

Upward counterfactual thoughts are particularly likely to occur after a negative outcome (Roese & Olson, 1997; Sanna & Turley, 1996). When something bad happens, it seems almost inevitable that people will think about how the event could have been avoided, especially when it was unexpected (Shepperd & McNulty, 2002). Notice that this process can be very adaptive—people may be able to think of ways to prevent a recurrence of the negative outcome (i.e., ways to avoid a similar event in the future). When a student thinks, "I wish I had studied the textbook more instead of the lectures—I would have done better on the test," she has identified a way to improve her grade on the next exam (namely, by studying the textbook more).

Given these possible benefits of upward counterfactual thoughts, theorists have suggested that the motive or desire to improve explains why upward counterfactual thoughts occur (see Markman, Gavanski, Sherman, & McMullen, 1993; Roese, 2005; Roese & Olson, 1997). The reason we engage in upward counterfactual thinking after a negative outcome is because it helps us to avoid similar negative outcomes in the future (we want to improve).

In a study examining this possible functional benefit of upward counterfactual thinking, Suzanne Nasco and Kerry Marsh (1999) asked introductory psychology students to complete a questionnaire immediately after receiving their grade on a class test. Among other things, the questionnaire measured counterfactual thinking by asking the students to "list any things that might have occurred differently that would have resulted in a different grade on the test." The students' lists were later

**upward counterfactual thoughts**
*reflections on how past events might have turned out better*

When something bad happens, people tend to generate *upward counterfactual thoughts.*

scored for the total number of upward counterfactual thoughts that were given (thoughts about how their grade could have been better).

Approximately one month later, the day before their next test, students completed another questionnaire in which they reported how much their circumstances had changed since the first test (e.g., whether they were able to study more than last time). The next day, participants reported how much control they felt they had over their performance on the second test and then took the test.

Results showed that the number of upward counterfactual thoughts students generated after the first test predicted the extent of reported changes in circumstances prior to the second test. Students who, after the first test, generated many ways that their grade could have been better (i.e., who generated many upward counterfactual thoughts) reported, prior to the second test, that their circumstances had changed a lot. Why? Presumably, things had changed because participants had implemented some of the ideas they had generated after the first test. Upward counterfactual thinking generated ideas for improved performance, which were later implemented.

Importantly, the extent of reported changes in circumstances predicted how much control students felt they had over the second test, and perceived control predicted how well the students actually did on the second test. Thus, upward counterfactual thoughts after the first test were ultimately associated with better performance on the second test, with the improved performance apparently due to changes implemented after the first test (see also Roese, 1994).

Sometimes, upward counterfactual thoughts will not provide useful ideas for how to improve outcomes. A young man who has been paralyzed in a car accident may think repeatedly about how he could have avoided the accident, but nothing can bring back his mobility. The example given earlier of parents who lost a child is another case in which upward counterfactual thoughts (thinking about how the death could have been avoided) are unlikely to be useful. In these circumstances, ruminating about how the traumatic event could have been avoided may only rub salt in the wound (see Davis, Lehman, Wortman, Silver, & Thompson, 1995).

## Downward Counterfactual Thoughts: Wanting to Feel Better

**downward counterfactual thoughts**
*reflections on how past events might have turned out worse*

Some counterfactual thoughts involve imagining how things could have been *worse.* These reflections are called **downward counterfactual thoughts.** These kinds of thoughts usually make people feel fortunate, because their present condition is better than what it could have been. Sometimes these thoughts occur spontaneously, such as when something bad *almost* happens. Coming upon a grisly car accident scene just moments after it occurred can engender the thought "it could have been me," which is a downward counterfactual thought that causes feelings of relief. Downward counterfactual thoughts can also be generated deliberately or strategically, when people want to make themselves feel better. Someone who is not selected for a promotion might think, "Well, things could be worse—I could be unemployed," which is a downward counterfactual thought that causes feelings of satisfaction that raise the individual's injured self-image. Thus, one possible benefit of downward counterfactual thoughts is that they can make people feel better.

Whereas downward counterfactual thoughts can make people feel better (cause positive emotions), upward counterfactual thoughts can make people feel worse (cause negative emotions). We touched on this point earlier when discussing rumination about traumatic events. By thinking about how things could have been better (upward counterfactual thoughts), people make their actual situation seem worse by comparison, which can arouse dissatisfaction or unhappiness. But recall that upward counterfactual thoughts often have important benefits—they generate useful ideas for how to avoid negative outcomes. Nevertheless, upward counterfactual thoughts can make people feel bad, so the benefits come with an emotional price.

Newspaper stories after tragic events often articulate counterfactual possibilities that elicit strong emotions. For example, after the terrorism of September 11, 2001, stories appeared in the media describing many unusual cases, such as people who were called to last-minute meetings in the World Trade Center and perished in the collapse of the towers. On a happier note, one young father who worked near the top of one of the towers drove his children to preschool in the morning because his wife was sick; he was late getting to work and missed the attack. These stories derive their emotional impact from the fact that it is so easy to imagine how things could have been different.

The two categories of counterfactual thoughts are summarized in the accompanying Concept Review.

Thus, spontaneous counterfactual thoughts can influence people's emotional reactions to events in their lives. An interesting demonstration of the real-life consequences of counterfactual thinking is described in the accompanying box, Social Psychology in Your Life: Agony and Ecstasy at the Olympics.

## Hot Cognition: Adding Motives and Mood to the Cognitive Mix

To this point in the chapter, we have emphasized cognitive processes, such as categorization, retrieval cues, and counterfactual thinking, and have not paid much attention to feelings or affect. But emotions, motives, and moods are key parts of our lives. How do these "hot," emotional processes influence the "cold," cognitive processing of information about people? In this section, we take a detour from the strictly cognitive terrain to describe briefly how motives and moods can influence social cognition (see also Kruglanski, 1996; Kunda, 1990; Sorrentino & Higgins, 1986).

### CONCEPT REVIEW
#### Counterfactual Thinking

| Type of Thought | Description | Emotional Consequences | Possible Benefits | Example |
|---|---|---|---|---|
| Upward counterfactual thoughts | Thoughts about how things could have been better | Often arouse negative emotions | Provide ideas about how to avoid negative outcomes in the future | "If only I had been driving more slowly, I would have avoided the car accident." |
| Downward counterfactual thoughts | Thoughts about how things could have been worse | Often arouse positive emotions | Can be used strategically to repair self-image or improve mood | "If I lived in many other countries, I would have less freedom." |

# Social Psychology in Your Life    *Agony and Ecstasy at the Olympics*

One of the most intriguing demonstrations of how upward counterfactual thoughts can produce unhappiness and downward counterfactual thoughts can produce happiness was provided by Victoria Medvec, Scott Madey, and Thomas Gilovich (1995). These researchers obtained videotapes of all NBC television coverage of the 1992 summer Olympic games in Barcelona, Spain. The researchers selected from these tapes all coverage of silver medal winners or bronze medal winners showing the athletes either completing their event (and finishing second or third) or receiving their medals on the medal stand.

The researchers showed these selections to judges and asked the judges to rate each athlete's emotional reaction on a scale from 1 to 10, with the endpoints labeled *agony* and *ecstasy*. The judges were chosen because they stated they were uninterested in and uninformed about sports—the researchers did not want judges whose ratings might be influenced by prior knowledge about the athletes or the Olympics. Thus, all silver and bronze medalists were rated for how happy they appeared to be.

The results, depicted in Figure 3.8, revealed a fascinating difference: bronze medalists were judged to be happier than silver medalists, even though the bronze medalists had actually done worse than the silver medalists! This difference occurred both when the athletes completed their event and when they received their medal.

What was going on here? The researchers hypothesized that bronze and silver medalists generated different kinds of counterfactual thoughts. For bronze medalists, the most compelling or vivid alternative outcome was probably finishing fourth, out of the medals—a *downward* counterfactual thought. Compared to the possibility of finishing fourth, winning a bronze medal seemed great, and the athletes were ecstatic. But for silver

A study of medal winners at the 1992 summer Olympics showed that bronze medalists appeared happier than did silver medalists.

medalists, the most obvious alternative outcome was probably finishing first and winning the gold medal—an *upward* counterfactual thought. Compared to the possibility of finishing first, winning a silver medal didn't seem so great, and the athletes were disappointed.

Thus, how well the athletes did and how happy they felt were not equivalent. These data make the point that people's emotional reactions to an event depend, at least in part, on alternative possible outcomes that are conspicuous to them (for another fascinating example of how counterfactual thoughts can influence emotional responses to wins and losses, see Larsen, McGraw, Mellers, & Cacioppo, 2004).

**FIGURE 3.8** Happiness ratings of silver and bronze medalists

From Medvec et al., "When less is more: Counterfactual thinking and satisfaction among Olympic medalists," *Journal of Personality and Social Psychology, 69,* 603–610, Fig. 1, p. 605, 1995. Copyright © 1995 by the American Psychological Association. Reprinted by permission.

# Self-Serving Judgments

We noted at the beginning of the chapter that two basic goals are generally presumed to underlie social cognition: the need to perceive the world accurately and the desire to perceive the self positively. We mentioned the second goal briefly when we discussed work showing that people want to regard the "present self" as better than the "past self" (e.g., Wilson & Ross, 2001). Let us now consider three examples of how this motive to see the self positively can cause **self-serving judgments,** which are perceptions or comparisons that enhance the perceived worth of the self (Gilovich, 1991; Greenwald, Banaji, Rudman, Farnham, Nosek, & Mellott, 2002; Tesser, 2000).

**self-serving judgments**

*perceptions or comparisons that enhance the perceived worth of the self*

**Self-Serving Trait Definitions.** Imagine that you asked one of your student friends "How many hours must someone study per week for you to consider him or her studious?", and the answer was 10 hours. Imagine that you asked another student friend the same question, and the answer was 20 hours. Now the interesting part: how many hours a week would you predict these two people personally study? Research by social psychologists suggests that you probably would predict that the second person studies more than the first person, because the second person gave a more demanding definition of studiousness. You might suspect both individuals of defining studiousness based on their own study habits, so that they personally qualify as studious. (Try it for yourself: How many hours of studying do you think should qualify someone as "studious"? And how many hours per week do *you* study?)

This reasoning implies that people may define traits in ways that flatter themselves—so that they qualify for positive labels and avoid negative labels. David Dunning and his colleagues (Dunning & Cohen, 1992; Dunning, Perie, & Story, 1991) have documented this idea. In one study (Dunning & Cohen, 1992), participants attended two sessions. At the first session, they answered several questionnaires, one of which asked them to report their behavior in seven domains, including how many hours they typically spent studying in a week and how many books per month they read strictly for pleasure. At the second session 2 to 10 weeks later, participants were asked to state the level of performance that is necessary to qualify for specified traits. For example, they were asked "How many hours must a person study per week for you to consider them studious?" and "How many books must a person read per month strictly for pleasure for you to consider them well read?" Participants who studied a lot or read a lot set higher criteria for achieving the traits "studious" and "well read" than did participants who studied less or read less. In fact, participants' reports of their own behavior at the first session correlated strongly with their criteria at the second session. People set high standards for positive labels when they could personally reach them but lower standards when their own performance was lower. This tendency to define traits in a self-serving manner presumably reflected participants' desire to see themselves positively.

In another study (Dunning et al., 1991), participants were asked to indicate the extent to which a variety of characteristics were associated with their idea of being a good "leader." Participants had also rated themselves on the same characteristics in a previous experiment that they did not believe was related to the current session. People who had described themselves as task-oriented in the first experiment stated at the second session that characteristics like competitiveness and independence were crucial for being a good leader (which implied that they, personally, were good leaders), whereas people who had described themselves as relationship-oriented in the first experiment stated at the second session that characteristics like friendliness and pleasantness were crucial for being a good leader (which, again, implied that they, personally, were good leaders). These findings provide another example of a self-serving judgment that enhanced the perceived worth of the self (see also Sanitioso & Wlodarski, 2004).

### Self-Serving Perceptions of Others.

If you knew that you would have to work with another person, you would probably hope that the person would be pleasant and competent. If a friend set up a blind date for you, you would probably hope that the date would be friendly and attractive. These hopes are understandable—we don't want to work with or date someone who is unpleasant. But do you think that these hopes might lead you to perceive the individuals more positively than they really are?

Social psychologists have shown that when people believe that they will interact with or be dependent on another individual, they tend to view that individual more positively than do people who are not expecting to interact with or be dependent on the individual. In a classic experiment, Ellen Berscheid, William Graziano, Thomas Monson, and Marshall Dermer (1976) recruited participants for a dating study and showed them a videotape of three people having a discussion. One of the three persons on the tape was allegedly going to be the participant's dating partner for at least one date (and sometimes up to five dates). After watching the videotape, participants rated the three individuals. Compared to ratings by participants who were not expecting to date that individual, participants who were expecting one or more dates rated their expected partner significantly more positively. The researchers argued that participants *wanted* to see their future partner as likable and pleasant (see also Wilson, Wheatly, Kurtz, Dunn, & Gilbert, 2004).

### Self-Serving Activation of Stereotypes.

Imagine that you submit some poetry to a local poetry competition. Imagine further that the written feedback you receive from the judge of the competition is negative—the feedback states that your poems are confusing and difficult to understand. Imagine finally that you learn that the judge who was supposed to evaluate the poems, a high school English teacher, fell ill and was replaced at the last minute by one of his high school students. Do you think that you would discredit the feedback because it came from a high school student? Would you conclude that the judge was too immature to understand your poetry?

Sinclair and Kunda (2000) found that some men selectively activated a negative stereotype of women to disparage a female manager's unfavorable evaluation of them.

© Royalty-Free/CORBIS

But imagine for a moment that the same events occur except you receive *positive* feedback from the judge, who states that your poems are clear and interesting. Do you think that you would discredit this feedback because it came from a high school student? Would you even consider the questionable status of the judge?

Most of us would focus on the judge's high school status more in the first case than in the second case. We would be motivated to use our stereotype of high school students (that they are younger and more immature than adults) to discredit the negative feedback but not the positive feedback. We would use the stereotype selectively to enhance our self-worth.

Lisa Sinclair and Ziva Kunda (1999, 2000) argued precisely this point—that people can activate a stereotype strategically, based on its implications for feedback they have received. In one experiment (Sinclair & Kunda, 2000), male participants provided answers to several interpersonal skills questions (e.g., "How would you motivate your employees to complete an important project on time?"). These responses were then assessed by another participant, who was allegedly training to be a manager. This manager-in-training provided either positive or negative feedback via videotape to the participant. For half of the participants, the videotaped evaluator was a man, whereas for the remaining participants, the evaluator was a woman. All participants then rated the manager's skill at evaluating them.

The researchers predicted that participants who received negative feedback from a female evaluator would be motivated to activate a negative stereotype of women that is held by some people, which includes the invalid notion that women may not be as competent as men at assessing managerial skill (e.g., Heilman, Block, & Martell, 1995). Derogating the woman's competence at this task would negate the validity of her feedback. These participants could then attribute the negative feedback to the incompetence of the female evaluator rather than to their own poor performance. Although participants who received negative feedback from a male evaluator would also want to discredit his feedback, their stereotype of men would not allow them to do so as easily, because they see men as more competent at assessing managerial skill. In contrast, the researchers predicted that participants who received positive feedback from a female evaluator would be motivated to see her as highly competent. Figure 3.9 presents participants' mean ratings of the manager's skill at evaluating them. As predicted, participants rated the female evaluator who provided negative feedback as significantly less skilled than the male evaluator who provided negative feedback; ratings of the male and female evaluators did not differ when they provided positive feedback. Thus, it seemed that at least some participants conveniently activated their stereotype of women only when necessary to protect their self-esteem. There was self-serving activation of stereotypes.

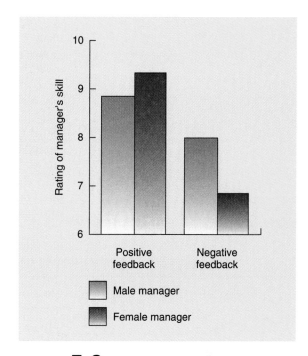

**FIGURE 3.9**  Ratings of manager's skill

From Sinclair and Kunda, "Motivated stereotyping of women: She's fine if she praised me but incompetent if she criticized me," *Personality and Social Psychology Bulletin*, 26, 1329–1342, Fig. 1, p. 1336, 2000. Reprinted by permission of Sage Publications.

## Mood and Social Cognition

Another way that social cognition can be "hot" is through mood effects. Whether we are in a happy, neutral, or negative mood can influence a variety of perceptions and judgments (see Clore, Schwarz, & Conway, 1994; Fiske & Taylor, 1991; Forgas, 1992; Schwarz & Clore, 1996). We give a few examples in this section.

**Mood and Stereotypes.**  Do you think that your mood influences your perceptions of members of minority groups? Are you less positive toward outgroups when you are angry or depressed than when you are in a good mood?

Victoria Esses, Geoffrey Haddock, and Mark Zanna (1994) investigated whether mood influenced the stereotypes that White Canadians expressed about minority groups (see also Esses & Zanna, 1995). The researchers hypothesized that negative mood would evoke more negative stereotypes of minority groups. In one experiment, participants listened to mood-inducing music for 10 minutes, either uplifting and joyous music (positive mood condition), sad and depressing music (negative music condition), or neutral and innocuous music (neutral mood condition). Participants then provided their stereotypes of several ethnic groups by listing, for each group, characteristics that they would use to describe typical members of that group. After listing characteristics for all of the groups, participants went back over their characteristics and rated each one for how positive or negative it was and for how common it was in the group. The researchers were able to use these ratings to calculate an overall score to reflect the extent to which positive or negative characteristics were ascribed to typical members of that group.

Figure 3.10 presents the average ratings by majority group members of four ethnic minority groups. In the neutral mood condition (the "baseline" condition), two of the groups—Jewish and Chinese persons—elicited relatively positive stereotypes, whereas two other groups—Pakistanis and Canadian Indians—elicited more neutral ratings. Ratings in the positive mood condition were virtually identical to ratings in the neutral mood condition for all four ethnic groups, so people did not become more positive toward minority groups when they were in a happy mood. Unfortunately, negative mood did have an effect, and it was a negative one. Participants in the negative mood condition generated significantly more negative stereotypes of the two lower-rated groups, Pakistanis and Canadian Indians, than did participants in the neutral or positive mood conditions. Negative mood did not affect the ratings of the higher-rated groups, Jewish and Chinese persons. Thus, when people were made to feel sad or depressed, their views of some minority groups became more negative. The researchers speculated that the negative mood made negative stereotype content more accessible in memory.

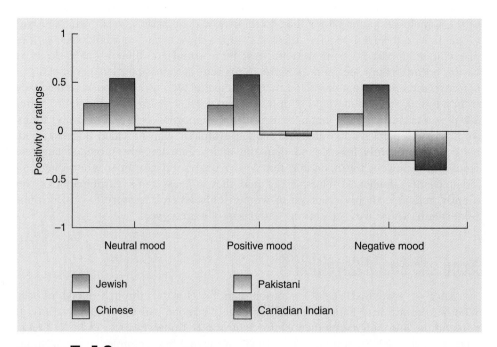

**FIGURE 3.10** Ratings of ethnic minority groups while in neutral, positive, and negative mood

From Esses et al., "The role of mood in the expression of intergroup stereotypes." In M. P. Zanna and J. M. Olson, eds., *The Psychology of Prejudice: The Ontario Symposium*, p. 86, 1994. Reprinted by permission of Lawrence Erlbaum Associates.

These findings are rather disturbing, because negative moods can occur for many different reasons. It is conceivable that anxiety about the future, sadness about the death of a loved one, or frustration from work-related problems could all potentially elicit negative stereotypes of minority groups. At a societal level, perhaps economic downturns, which produce increased unemployment and stress, will elicit more negative stereotypes and provoke racial and ethnic hostility (see Berkowitz, 1989; Hovland & Sears, 1940; Zawadzki, 1948).

**Mood-Congruent Recall.** The findings by Esses et al. (1994) suggested that negative moods can make negative stereotypes more accessible in memory. What about other kinds of information in memory? Does mood heighten the accessibility of all material that is compatible with it, such that positive mood makes positive information more accessible and negative mood makes negative information more accessible? This idea that positive feelings will activate positive memories and negative feelings will activate negative memories is called **mood-congruent recall** (Bower, 1981).

If you were asked to rate the performance of your car or your television, would your mood play a role? If you just found out that you did well on a test, would you rate your car and your television more positively than if you had not received feedback on the test? Although this may seem unlikely, evidence suggests that, in fact, you would. People do seem to give more positive evaluations of stimuli when they are in a positive mood than when they are in a neutral mood—and the positive mood does not have to be very strong! In an early, classic study of the effects of a small gift on memory, Alice Isen and her colleagues (Isen, Shalker, Clark, & Karp, 1978) approached shoppers at a mall. Some shoppers were approached by a confederate of the researchers and given a "free sample" of either a notepad or a nail clipper. The confederate told recipients that the free sample was meant to introduce potential customers to the company's product. Each sample was said to be worth 29 cents (about $1 today). Approximately 150 feet (50 m) beyond the first confederate, another (seemingly unassociated) experimenter approached the shoppers and asked whether they would be willing to complete a "consumer survey." If shoppers agreed to participate, they answered several questions about their automobile and television set, including evaluations of the performance of these products. Compared to shoppers who were *not* given a free sample, participants who received a free sample rated the performance of their automobile and television set more favorably. The small, free gift presumably induced a mildly positive mood, which made positive memories of the products more accessible in memory.

In a study that yielded a similar effect but used a different cause of moods, Joseph Forgas, George Levinger, and Stephanie Moylan (1994) asked people coming out of either a happy or a sad movie to evaluate their current (or a recent) relationship. Participants provided more favorable evaluations of their relationship after a happy movie than after a sad one. Positive feelings presumably made positive thoughts about the relationship more accessible than did negative feelings (see also Fiedler, Nickel, Muehlfriedel, & Unkelbach, 2001).

**Mood and Information Processing.** Have you noticed that when you are in a good mood, you take other people's word for things and are just generally more agreeable than usual? Positive moods seem to reduce our need for compelling evidence or arguments before we will agree to something. After learning that we did well on a test, we'll respond to a friend's request with "Yeah, sure, I'll go to that movie with you—or to another one if you'd prefer."

Several studies have supported the idea that positive moods reduce the tendency to use detailed information to make decisions (e.g., Bodenhausen, Kramer, & Susser, 1994; Sinclair, 1988), although there may be circumstances under which

**mood-congruent recall**
*the idea that positive feelings will activate positive memories and negative feelings will activate negative memories*

good moods do not lead to superficial processing (e.g., Isbell, 2004). For example, in a simulated work appraisal setting, Robert Sinclair (1988) gave participants information about the quality of several individuals' performances and then asked participants to evaluate those performances. He found that participants in a good mood relied *less* on the information about the others' behavior to make their performance appraisals than did participants in neutral or negative moods. Participants in a good mood also made less accurate appraisals overall than did participants in neutral or negative moods, presumably because the former individuals ignored (or underutilized) useful information.

If people in a good mood do not focus on detailed information to make judgments, what *do* they base their judgments on? The answer is heuristics, at least in some situations. Alice Isen and her colleagues (Isen, Means, Patrick, & Nowicky, 1982) found that participants who were in a good mood relied on the availability heuristic more than did participants who were in a neutral mood. Specifically, a good mood increased participants' tendency to base judgments of how often something occurs on the ease with which examples could be brought to mind. Good moods increased reliance on this judgmental shortcut.

**Mood as Information.** Mood can influence recall of and reliance on information, but can it also serve as a piece of information itself? If you were asked how satisfied you are with your life, would you base your answer, in part, on your current mood? It seems reasonable to conclude that you are satisfied with your life if you are currently feeling happy (the positive mood is a relevant piece of information), whereas it makes sense to conclude that you are dissatisfied with your life if you are feeling unhappy. Of course, if you were asked this question just as you came out from a really sad event, such as a funeral, you would probably not consider your current mood to be a useful piece of information about your life satisfaction, because you would realize that your mood reflected the sad setting, at least in part.

Norbert Schwarz and Gerald Clore (1983) proposed that people use their mood as a relevant piece of information for judgments of satisfaction or evaluation, but not when there is an obvious external cause of their mood. These researchers knew that the weather reliably influences people's moods—people are happier on sunny days than on rainy days. The weather is not usually recognized, however, as a determinant of mood. Schwarz and Clore conducted telephone interviews in which they asked participants how happy they were with their life. Some partici-

People report being happier with their life on a sunny day than on a rainy day, presumably because they use their mood as a source of information to infer their happiness with life.

© AP/Wide World Photos/Elaine Thompson

pants were asked on sunny days, and some were asked on rainy days. As would be expected if participants were using their mood as relevant information, participants reported greater life satisfaction on sunny days than on rainy days. But Schwarz and Clore also included another, control condition that tested whether participants would ignore their mood if they recognized the effect of the weather. These participants were first asked by the telephone interviewer what their weather was like today, which was expected to cue participants that the weather was a plausible contributing cause of their happy or sad mood. Consistent with predictions, participants who were first asked about the weather did *not* report greater satisfaction with their life on sunny days than on rainy days. This control condition indicates that the effect of mood in this study was not caused by making positive or negative information accessible, because increased accessibility of information would occur even when participants were asked about the weather. Instead, the effect of mood in this study appears to have been caused by participants' using their mood as a source of information when it was not seen to reflect an external cause like the weather (see also Bless, 2001; Clore, Wyer, Dienes, Gaspar, Gohm & Isbell, 2001; Schwarz, 1990; Schwarz & Clore, 1996).

# Chapter Summary

In this chapter, we discussed **social cognition,** which is the study of how information about people is processed and stored. The fundamental building blocks of human cognition are **schemas**—mental representations of objects or categories. Schemas contain the principal features of the object or category, as well as simple assumptions about how the object or category works. The primary function of schemas is to categorize objects in ways that impose meaning and predictability. **Categorization** is the process of recognizing and identifying something. When we categorize a target, we assume that it possesses the characteristics of the schema (or most of them) even if we cannot perceive those characteristics directly.

Memory can be viewed as an **associative network** of interconnected schemas, which means that it is a very large system of schemas that are linked together on the basis of shared meaning and/or shared experience. When one schema is used (activated), other schemas that are linked with it are more likely to be used as well, which is known as **spreading activation.** Memory consists of at least two fundamental stages: **encoding** refers to getting information into memory and includes attention, comprehension, and storage, and **retrieval** refers to getting information out of memory.

The **accessibility** of a schema is the ease with which the schema comes to awareness; more accessible schemas are more likely to be activated than are less accessible schemas. **Priming** is one process that increases the accessibility of a schema; it refers to the fact that the activation of a schema increases the likelihood of that schema's being activated again in the future. Schemas also differ in the extent to which they are easily activated for an individual across time and situations, which is termed their **chronic accessibility.**

A **stereotype** is a set of characteristics that a perceiver associates with members of a group. Stereotypes are one kind of schema—namely, schemas that represent human groups. Stereotypes usually include information about how much variability exists in the group; there is a general tendency for people to overestimate the similarity within groups to which they do not belong, which is called the **outgroup homogeneity effect.** Just like other schemas, stereotypes reflect our attempt to categorize an object (a person) and draw inferences about him or her.

Researchers have recognized that people do not have full control over all of their mental processes. An **automatic process** is a judgment or thought that we cannot control—it occurs without intention, very efficiently, and sometimes beneath our awareness. A **controlled process** is a judgment or thought that we command—it is intentional, requires significant cognitive resources, and occurs within our awareness.

Sometimes, memories cannot be retrieved directly, so retrieval must involve a "reconstructive" process. **Reconstructive memory** is trying to cognitively rebuild the past based on cues and estimates. **Autobiographical memory** refers to information in the brain that is related to the self. Autobiographical memory often involves estimating what we were like in the past.

Because human memory is fallible, eyewitnesses in trial settings sometimes make errors in identifying suspects. Experts have suggested that police lineup procedures should be changed to reduce the rate of eyewitness errors. For instance, a **blank lineup** is a good way to test the credibility of an eyewitness. A blank lineup is a group of individuals (a lineup) that does not include the suspect—everyone in the lineup is known to be innocent. If the eyewitness identifies someone in the blank lineup, he or she should be dismissed. Also, it has been found that eyewitness identification errors are reduced if the eyewitness sees each person in the group (lineup) separately, a procedure that is called a **sequential lineup.**

**Heuristics** are informal rules or shortcuts that are used to make everyday judgments. Researchers have hypothesized that people usually rely on heuristics to make judgments and will engage in careful, thoughtful processing only when necessary—a view that has been termed the **cognitive miser model** of information processing. The **availability heuristic** is the tendency to base a judgment on how easily relevant examples can be generated. The **representativeness heuristic** is the tendency to judge the likelihood that a target belongs to a certain category based on how similar the target is to the typical features of the category.

An **illusory correlation** occurs when individuals believe that two variables are related to one another when, in fact, they are not. One cause of illusory correlations is that people are more likely to notice events that confirm their expectancies than nonconfirming events.

The **hindsight bias** refers to the tendency for people to overestimate the predictability of known outcomes. The **perseverance effect** is the tendency for people to make self-evaluations that are consistent with information that has been discredited.

**Counterfactual thoughts** are reflections on how past events might have turned out differently. **Upward counterfactual thoughts** involve reflecting on how things could have turned out better, whereas **downward counterfactual thoughts** involve reflecting on how things could have been worse.

**Self-serving judgments** are perceptions or comparisons that enhance the perceived worth of the self. Researchers have identified numerous self-serving judgments, including tendencies to define trait terms in ways that flatter the self and to activate stereotypes strategically to protect the self.

Moods can influence social cognition. For example, negative moods can elicit more unfavorable stereotypes of minority groups, and positive moods can make positive information more accessible in memory. The tendency for positive or negative feelings to make similarly valenced information more accessible in memory is called **mood-congruent recall.**

# Key Terms

**accessibility** (72)

**associative network** (71)

**autobiographical memory** (79)

**automatic process** (77)

**availability heuristic** (88)

**blank lineup** (86)

**categorization** (66)

**chronic accessibility** (73)

**cognitive miser model** (87)

**controlled process** (77)

**counterfactual thoughts** (96)

**downward counterfactual thoughts** (98)

**encoding** (71)

**heuristic** (87)

**hindsight bias** (93)

**illusory correlation** (91)

**mood-congruent recall** (105)

**outgroup homogeneity effect** (76)

**perseverance effect** (95)

**priming** (72)

**reconstructive memory** (78)

**representativeness heuristic** (90)

**retrieval** (71)

**schemas** (67)

**self-serving judgments** (101)

**sequential lineup** (86)

**social cognition** (66)

**spreading activation** (71)

**stereotype** (75)

**upward counterfactual thoughts** (97)

# Social Psychology Alive on the Web

### SOCIAL PSYCHOLOGY ALIVE: ONLINE LABS

To perform the following experiments and see how you compare to other students, go to Social Psychology Lab, which can be accessed through Social PsychologyNow:

- 3.1 Lexical Decisions
- 3.2 Impression Formation

### SOCIAL PSYCHOLOGY ALIVE: QUIZZING AND PRACTICE TESTS

You can access our website directly by going to http://psychology.wadsworth.com/brecklerle/ for online quizzes, flash cards, and Internet links.

### INFOTRAC® COLLEGE EDITION

For additional readings, explore InfoTrac College Edition, your online library of archived journal articles and periodicals dating back 22 years. If your instructor ordered InfoTrac College Edition with this book, you can access it from your CD-ROM, or go directly to http://www.infotrac-college.com/wadsworth and use the passcode from the InfoTrac College Edition card that came with your book. For this chapter, try these search terms: *social cognition, schema, accessibility, priming, stereotype, reconstructive memory, availability heuristic, representativeness heuristic, illusory correlation, hindsight bias, counterfactual thinking, mood-congruent recall.*

# Social Psychology Alive: The Workbook

To apply what you've learned in this chapter to what happens in the real world, go to Chapter 3 of *Social Psychology Alive: The Workbook*:

- The Sports Illustrated Jinx: Does Appearance on the Cover Doom the Featured Athlete to a Terrible Fate?
- Spreading Activation of Schemas in Memory
- Priming Effects in Impression Formation

- Try These Experiments!
- Eyewitness Testimony and Reconstructive Memory
- Is It a Hot Hand or an Illusory Correlation?
- The Perseverance Effect: Implications for the Ethical Treatment of Research Participants
- Have You and Your Friends Experienced These Social Cognition Phenomena?

# Social Psychology Alive: The Videos

To see video on the topics and experiments discussed in this chapter, you can go either to Social PsychologyNow or to the CD-ROM, if your instructor assigned either one, to the following section:

- Reconstructive Memory: Recalling What Never Happened

# To Learn More

This list contains citations to books or articles that can help you learn more. These readings are good places to start if you want to gain a deeper understanding of the topics in this chapter.

- Gilovich, T. (1991). *How we know what isn't so: The fallibility of human reason in everyday life.* New York: Free Press.

- Kunda, Z. (1999). *Social cognition: Making sense of people.* Cambridge, MA: MIT Press.
- Roese, N. J. (2005). *If only: How to turn regret into opportunity.* New York: Broadway Books.

© AP/Wide World Photos/Kevork Djansezian

# Social Perception: Perceiving the Self and Others

I n Catherine Ryan Hyde's novel Pay It Forward (1999), an investigative reporter by the name of Chris Chandler stumbles onto a plan that was initiated by a 12-year-old boy, Trevor McKinney, for his social studies class. The plan was designed to make the world a better place, and it involved doing favors for other people. Trevor (played by Haley Joel Osment in a movie version of the book) decided to do an unrequested and substantial favor for three different people and to ask in return only that they do a similar unrequested favor for three other people (that they pay it forward). If everyone followed through on these commitments, there would soon be large numbers of people doing favors for others.

The event that initially alerted Chris to the plan occurred while he was standing in an intersection looking under his car's hood at the engine of his old, stalled vehicle. A complete stranger came up to him, helped him push his car out of the intersection, and said that they should trade cars. Chris eventually drove away in a nice two-year-old silver Acura, but not before feeling very confused about what was going on.

Imagine yourself in Chris's position. How would you respond if a stranger tried to give you his car when yours stalled? Wouldn't you wonder why he was doing this? You might even suspect that it was a trick—perhaps "his" car was stolen, or perhaps he was trying to make you feel indebted to him for some reason. Ultimately, your actions would depend on your conclusion about the cause of his apparent generosity. If you decided that the gift was sincere, you might eventually drive off in the car, but if you remained suspicious that all was not well, you would probably decline the offer and pursue more traditional ways of dealing with a stalled car (such as phoning for a tow truck).

How would you respond if a stranger offered to trade cars when yours stalled?

© Lucinda Dowell Photographs

*In this chapter, we discuss these sorts of judgments about the causes of behavior, as well as other inferences that are made in daily life. The topics covered in this chapter extend the basic processes described in the previous chapter on Social Cognition to more complex judgments. We discuss perceptions of other people (e.g., judgments about what caused them to act in a certain way), perceptions of ourselves (e.g., our motivation to see ourselves as better than other people), and other people's perceptions of us (e.g., whether they can detect when we are lying). Taken together, these topics provide a broad overview of social psychological research on social perception and self-perception.*

## What We See in Others: Social Perception

The most important things in our lives are other people. Our family, friends, children, and colleagues give our lives meaning, security, and happiness—and bring us our most intense pain as well. For us to cope effectively in a social world, it is essential that we predict other people's actions reasonably well. Such knowledge will help us control our environment. Perhaps a few hermits and religious isolates do not need to deal with other people, but for the rest of us, predicting the actions of those we meet is an important goal. How can we predict what people will do? First, we need to understand *why* they acted as they did in the present and the past—we need to figure out what their present or previous actions tell us about their personality, attitudes, and other personal characteristics. It is also important to have a good understanding of how various external or situational forces influence people's behavior (e.g., money, situational norms, laws). These judgments about personal qualities and external forces fall into the domain of *attribution theories*.

## Attribution Theories: Explaining Social Behavior

Judgments about why an event occurred or why someone behaved in a certain way are called **attributions.** Thus, attributions are causal judgments. As illustrated in the *Pay It Forward* example given above, the causal judgments we make about another person's behavior influence how we behave toward him or her (e.g., whether we accept a gift automobile from him). More mundane examples of actions that require causal analysis are abundant. If your housemate gets angry with you one afternoon for not keeping the kitchen clean, you must decide whether he or she is in a bad mood (and will get over it) or whether the state of the kitchen really does upset him or her (in which case you will have to be cleaner). If someone you are attracted to is very friendly to you late in the evening at the college pub, you must decide whether he or she likes you (in which case you will definitely ask for a date) or is being so friendly because he or she has consumed several alcoholic drinks (in which case you will be more cautious in your approach). Judgments about the causes of people's actions and outcomes are made constantly and have important implications for our own behavior.

Many social psychologists have studied how people make attributions for others' behavior. Indeed, interest in the attribution process in the 1970s was one of the first steps toward a "cognitive" perspective in social psychology, which is now probably the dominant approach in the field. Attribution theories are models that attempt to delineate the processes underlying judgments of cause.

**attributions**

*causal judgments about why an event or behavior occurred*

**intuitive scientists**

*untrained scientists who try to make causal judgments in a rational, scientific manner*

**The Intuitive Scientist.** One of the best-known attribution theories was proposed by Harold Kelley (1967, 1973), who suggested that people often make causal judgments in a relatively scientific manner—as if they were **intuitive scientists** (i.e., untrained or lay scientists). How do scientists test their ideas? They make repeated observations (e.g., across many trials or across many participants) and determine whether certain events or responses reliably occur under certain conditions. For example, a medical scientist might recruit a large number of patients with a particular medical problem and test whether giving them Medicine A improves their condition, whereas Medicine B does not.

Building on earlier work by Fritz Heider (1958), Kelley suggested that people behave as intuitive scientists in testing everyday causal questions. For example, imagine that you went to a friend's place and found him or her crying in front of the television as a videotape of the movie *Million Dollar Baby* (a drama about a female boxer released in 2004, starring Hilary Swank and Clint Eastwood) came to an end. Imagine also that you had never seen *Million Dollar Baby*, so you did not have a personal opinion about whether it was a sad movie. What attribution would you make for your friend's behavior? Two obvious possibilities would be that the movie is really sad (an *external* attribution) or that your friend is a sentimental person who cries very easily at movies (an *internal* attribution). How would you decide which of these possibilities was more plausible? Kelley suggested that you would think back over how your friend has behaved during other movies in the past and how other people you know have responded to *Million Dollar Baby*. Thus, for example, if you could think of several occasions when your friend cried at movies, you would be more likely to conclude that (s)he cried this time because (s)he is sentimental. If you knew several other people who had seen *Million Dollar Baby* and also happened to know that none of them cried (we will finesse the issue of how you could know this if you hadn't been there watching the movie!), you would again be inclined to conclude that your friend cried because (s)he is sentimental. On the other hand, if you had never seen your friend cry at any movie before, and if several people had told you they cried at the end of *Million Dollar Baby*, you would probably conclude that your friend cried because the movie is sad. Notice how rational this process is—you are systematically testing whether crying was associated with your friend or with *Million Dollar Baby*.

Hilary Swank and Clint Eastwood played the lead roles in the 2004 movie *Million Dollar Baby.*

Kelley suggested that we use this kind of reasoning when we have multiple observations of several individuals across several settings. He proposed that we think back over all our relevant observations and try to figure out whether the behavior was associated with a particular person, with a particular situation (or object), or with some combination of persons and situations. Kelley labeled this theory the **covariation model of attribution,** because it assumes that people try to determine whether a behavior *covaried* (correlated, was associated) with a person, a situation, or some combination of persons and situations. Many researchers have obtained evidence that is consistent with Kelley's covariation model (e.g., Hazlewood & Olson, 1986; Hewstone & Jaspars, 1983; McArthur, 1972). Thus, ordinary people sometimes test causal questions in a relatively scientific manner (but for limitations, see Cheng & Novick, 1992; Forsterling, 2001; Hilton & Slugoski, 1986; Johnson, Boyd, & Magnani, 1994; Smith, 1994).

**covariation model of attribution**

*an attribution theory proposing that we make causal judgments by determining whether a particular behavior correlated with a person, a situation, or some combination of persons and situations*

**The False Consensus Effect.** What would happen if you had seen *Million Dollar Baby* before you found your friend crying at the end of the movie? Would your own reaction to the movie influence how you interpreted your friend's reaction? Research on the attribution process suggests that the answer to this question is yes. When individuals have personal experience with a situation, they usually assume that most other people would respond similarly to themselves, and they draw conclusions about the cause of behavior based on this assumption. For example, if you did *not* cry while watching the movie, you would probably decide that your friend cried because (s)he is sentimental. If you *did* cry at the end of the movie, however, you would probably decide that your friend cried because the movie is sad (unless you view yourself as a sentimental softie!). These inferences reflect an assumption that most people would respond to the movie the same way that you did.

There is, in fact, a general tendency for individuals to assume that other people share their attitudes and behaviors to a greater extent than is actually the case; this tendency is called the **false consensus effect.** Perceivers overestimate the "consensus" (agreement) that exists for their attitudes and actions (for reviews, see Kreuger, 1988; Marks & Miller, 1987).

**false consensus effect**

*the tendency to assume that other people share our own attitudes and behaviors to a greater extent than is actually the case*

Imagine yourself in the following situation: You arrive at an experiment and learn that the purpose of the study is to investigate how people respond to different types of messages. If you are willing, your task will be to wear a "sandwich board" sign and walk around the campus for 30 minutes keeping track of how people respond to you. The message board that you will be wearing says "Repent" on the front and on the back. The experimenter states that if you do not want to do this task, you can decline and still receive your experimental credit. What would you do? Would you agree to wear the sign or decline to wear it?

Now answer another question: What percentage of students at your college do you think would make the *same* decision as you? Lee Ross, David Greene, and Pamela House (1977) did exactly what you have just imagined. They asked college students to walk around the campus wearing unusual messages on sandwich boards (either "Repent" or "Eat at Joe's"). After making their decision, participants were asked to predict what percentage of other participants would agree to wear the sign.

Table 4.1 (p. 116) presents the results of Ross et al.'s (1977) experiment. Exactly 50% of the participants agreed to wear the "Repent" sign (and 50% refused), whereas 70% of the participants agreed to wear the "Eat at Joe's" sign (and 30% refused). With the one exception of participants who agreed to wear the "Eat at Joe's" sign, all groups overestimated the number of participants who would do whatever they had done themselves. For example, participants who agreed to wear the "Repent" sign predicted, on average, that 63% of other people would also agree, whereas participants who refused to wear the "Repent" sign predicted that 77% of other

Would you agree to wear a sign like this for an experimenter?

## TABLE 4.1
### Predictions for Other Participants' Decisions About Wearing a Sign

| Participant's Own Decision | Predictions for What Other Participants Will Decide | |
|---|---|---|
| | Will Agree to Wear Sign | Will Refuse to Wear Sign |
| **"Repent"** | | |
| Agreed to Wear Sign (50%) | 63% | 37% |
| Refused to Wear Sign (50%) | 23% | 77% |
| **"Eat at Joe's"** | | |
| Agreed to Wear Sign (70%) | 61% | 39% |
| Refused to Wear Sign (30%) | 43% | 57% |

Adapted from Ross et al., 1977 (Study 4, p. 292)

people would similarly refuse. These overestimates are examples of the false consensus effect.

Why does the false consensus effect occur? There are probably several reasons (see Dawes, 1989; Gilovich, 1991; Kunda, 1999; Nickerson, 2001). One reason for the bias is that we tend to interact mainly with other people who agree with us. Think about your friends. Most of them are probably quite similar to you in terms of interests, attitudes, and values. Indeed, as we will see in Chapter 13 on Liking, Loving, and Close Relationships, attitude similarity is a strong predictor of liking and friendship. The people you interact with the most, therefore, are not representative of the general population—they are more similar to you than is the average person. But we do not always recognize this fact, so we tend to overestimate the degree of agreement that exists in the general population for our attitudes and behaviors. A second reason is a motivational one—we *want* to believe that others agree with us. We are motivated to believe that our opinions are accurate and our actions are appropriate (e.g., Festinger, 1957). If lots of other people agree with us, it seems likely that our attitudes and actions are good ones. Therefore, people may overestimate consensus because it makes them feel good about their attitudes and behaviors (Sherman, Presson, & Chassin, 1984). Consistent with this second, motivational explanation of the false consensus effect is evidence that people sometimes *under*estimate consensus when it makes them look good. For example, people who report that they would perform altruistic acts such as stopping to help a stranded motorist tend to underestimate how many other people would behave in the same way, perhaps because this perception of uniqueness makes them feel good about themselves (see Goethals, 1986a; Kernis, 1984; Tesser, 1988).

**Discounting and Augmentation.** The covariation model of attribution assumes that people have multiple observations of the target person (e.g., how your friend has reacted to other movies). But, of course, we often encounter complete strangers in our daily lives, and we certainly do make attributions about their behavior. How do we make judgments about why a stranger acted in a particular way? Kelley (1973) suggested that when we make attributions about a person based on just one observation, we rely on our knowledge of "plausible causes" in the situation. That is, we use our general knowledge to infer one or more causes that might explain the behavior and then simply look to see whether those plausible causes were, in fact, present.

Imagine that you are walking home one winter day and come upon a car in the ditch at the side of the road. Your general knowledge of why cars leave the road will probably identify at least two plausible causes: bad driving (e.g., the driver was inattentive) and bad conditions (e.g., the road was slippery). You cannot "see" the driver's skill or attentiveness, so you instead look at the road to see if it is covered with ice. If you see a patch of ice, you will probably conclude that the car left the road because of bad conditions, whereas if there is no ice, you will probably conclude that the car left the road because of bad driving.

Many everyday attribution situations conform to the car example just given—there is a plausible *internal* or dispositional cause, which is often nonobservable (e.g., poor driving skills), and one or more plausible *external* or situational causes, which are normally observable (e.g., bad road conditions). Therefore, the attribution process based on a single observation frequently involves looking to see whether a plausible external cause is present. If an external cause *is* present, then the behavior is attributed, at least partly, to that cause, but if there is *no* external cause present, then the behavior is attributed to an internal cause.

The sequence of looking for an external cause and, if one is present, reducing the perceived importance of internal causes, is an example of the **discounting principle.** The discounting principle states that the perceived role of one cause will be diminished if other plausible causes are also present. Usually, discounting involves reducing the perceived role of an *internal* cause because an *external* cause is known to be present (e.g., inferring that a traffic accident was *not* caused by poor driving skills, because you can see that the road is icy). There are many, many examples of discounting in everyday life. When an attractive young woman or man marries a wealthy older man or woman, observers discount the importance of love (an internal factor causing marriage) and attribute the younger person's behavior to the external force of money. When a student does well on a test that yielded a class average of 85%, observers reduce the perceived role of intelligence (an internal factor causing good test performance) and attribute his or her high score, at least partly, to the external factor of an easy test. Numerous researchers have obtained empirical evidence of discounting effects (see Hansen & Hall, 1985; Hull & West, 1982; Morris & Larrick, 1995).

The discounting principle implies that internal factors will be downplayed when plausible external causes are present. The flip side of the discounting principle is the **augmentation principle.** The augmentation principle applies to situations in which there are factors present that should have worked *against* the behavior (rather than factors that might have *caused* the behavior). The augmentation principle states that the perceived role of a cause will be *increased* when other causes are present that would work against the behavior. For example, behavior sometimes occurs despite the presence of difficult, inhibitory external circumstances. In such cases, observers attribute the behavior to especially strong internal causes (see Mills & Jellison, 1967; Trope, Cohen, & Maoz, 1988). If a student does very well on a test that yielded a class average of 45%, observers "augment" the role of intelligence and conclude that he or she is *extremely* smart. If a climber successfully reaches the top of Mount Everest, observers conclude that he or she is an *extremely* talented or determined climber. The flowchart in Figure 4.1 (p. 118) illustrates the processes underlying the discounting and augmentation principles.

**discounting principle**

*a rule of attribution which states that the perceived role of a cause will be discounted (reduced) if other plausible causes are also present*

**augmentation principle**

*a rule of attribution which states that the perceived role of a cause will be augmented (increased) if other factors are present that would work against the behavior*

© Jimmy Chin/Outdoor Collection/Aurora

Reaching the top of Mount Everest is extremely difficult, so anyone who does so will be seen as an extremely talented climber—an inference that reflects the *augmentation principle.*

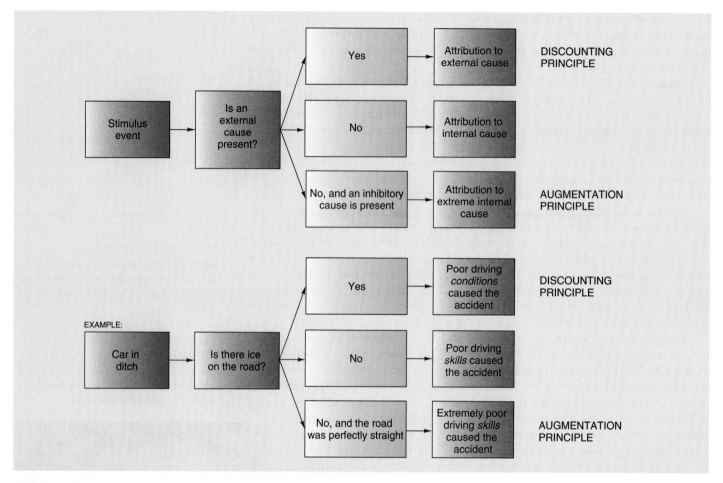

**FIGURE 4.1** Processes underlying the discounting and augmentation principles

## The Correspondence Bias: A Fundamental Attribution Error

The intuitive scientist perspective on attribution emphasizes the relatively rational processes involved in deciding why someone behaved in a particular way. In the present section, we discuss an important error that is very common in our perceptions of others—so common that it has been called the *fundamental attribution error* (Ross, 1977). We will refer to it as the **correspondence bias,** which is the label preferred by the researcher who initially identified it, Edward (Ned) Jones (e.g., Jones, 1979, 1990; Jones & Harris, 1967; Snyder & Jones, 1974).

If we asked you to describe one of your close friends, how would you do so? A major part of your description would probably involve personality traits—things like funny, honest, and reliable (Park, 1986). You could likely generate a large number of relevant traits for almost everyone you know well (Ross & Nisbett, 1991) and even for celebrities and public figures you have never met personally but have seen in the media. All of us believe that other people possess many stable personality traits (Kunda & Nisbett, 1986). Of course, people *do* possess some personality traits, as we will discuss in Chapter 5 on The Person in the Situation. But we tend to rely *too much* on personality to explain other people's actions. When someone is late, we tend to assume that he or she is a tardy person, rather than late on this one occasion. When someone does well on a test, we tend to assume that he or she is intelligent, rather than wondering whether the test was easy. When someone is friendly to us, we tend to assume that he or she is a friendly person and not just conforming to a norm of politeness.

**correspondence bias**

*the tendency to assume that people's actions and words reflect their personality, their attitudes, or some other internal factor, rather than external or situational factors*

The overreliance on personality traits to understand behavior is an example of the correspondence bias. The correspondence bias is "the tendency to see behavior as caused by a stable personal disposition of the actor when it can just as easily be explained as a natural response to situational pressures" (Jones, 1990, p. 138). In other words, the correspondence bias is the tendency to assume that people's actions and words reflect their personality, their attitudes, or some other internal factor, rather than external or situational factors. The correspondence bias can involve both overestimating the role of personality factors and underestimating the role of situational factors.

**A Laboratory Demonstration of the Correspondence Bias.** Imagine that you participated in an experiment where you and another student played a simulated quiz-show game. The experimenter flipped a coin, and the other student was assigned to be the "questioner" and you were assigned to be the "contestant." The experimenter then told the questioner to think of 10 questions to ask you, which should be "challenging but not impossible." How do you think you would do in answering these questions? How many of your answers would you expect to be correct? Imagine that you were able to answer just 4 of the 10 questions correctly. Would you feel smart or stupid? Would you think that you were less intelligent than the questioner?

But now think about the reverse role assignment. If you were the one who thought of 10 questions for the other participant, how many do you think he or she would get correct? Would you feel smarter than the other participant if he or she got just 4 of the 10 questions correct?

Lee Ross, Teresa Amabile, and Julia Steinmetz (1977) conducted a study that used this exact procedure. Pairs of student participants came to the lab and were randomly assigned to be either the "questioner" or the "contestant" in a simulated quiz-show game. Because the participants were *randomly assigned* to the two roles, the groups of questioners and contestants were presumably comparable in intelligence. There was also a group of uninvolved observers who watched the questioners and contestants on videotape. Questioners thought of 10 questions that would be "challenging but not impossible." The contestants were able to answer an average of only 4 of the 10 questions correctly. When later asked to estimate the intelligence of the questioner and the contestant, contestants and uninvolved observers both estimated that the questioner was more intelligent than the contestant (see Figure 4.2). Interestingly, questioners did not show this bias, perhaps recognizing that everyone has some relatively obscure knowledge and they appeared intelligent only because they were given the questioner role.

The contestants and observers did not seem to recognize that the apparent knowledge difference between the questioner and the contestant occurred only because of the role assignments: if the contestant had been assigned to the role of questioner, he or she would have appeared more intelligent than the other participant. Why is this an example of the correspondence bias? Because people saw the poor performance of the contestant as being caused by the internal characteristic of low intelligence (compared to the questioner) when it could just as easily be explained by the external factor of being assigned to the role of contestant.

**Causes of the Correspondence Bias.** Why is the correspondence bias common in our perceptions of other people? There are probably several processes or mechanisms

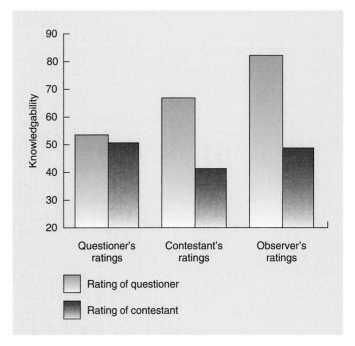

**FIGURE 4.2** Ratings of questioner's and contestant's general knowledge

From Ross et al., "Social roles, social control, and biases in social-perception processes," *Journal of Personality and Social Psychology*, 35, 485–494, Table 1, p. 489, 1977. Copyright © 1977 by the American Psychological Association.

that contribute to our tendency to see others' behavior as caused by stable internal characteristics even when there are plausible external explanations (see Fiske & Taylor, 1991; Gilbert & Malone, 1995; Jones, 1990; Ross & Nisbett, 1991). First, we may simply *overlook* or be unaware of situational factors that influence other people's behavior. Situational factors guiding behavior are often subtle or nonobvious. For example, many behaviors are guided by norms that specify how to behave in a particular situation: people listen quietly in class because students are supposed to be attentive, people line up in an orderly way at the cash register because that is how they are supposed to act in a store, and so on. We are not generally aware of these external norms even though they guide everyone's behavior, so we may not consider them when trying to determine why someone behaved in a particular fashion.

A second cause of the correspondence bias is that we simply underestimate the *power* of situational factors. Even when we notice external factors (which, as just noted, will *not* always be the case), we might still underestimate their strength (Trope, 1986). For example, contestants and observers in the quiz-show experiment by Ross et al. (1977) clearly underestimated the ability of people to come up with challenging questions if assigned to the role of questioner.

A third factor contributing to the correspondence bias is that the process of taking situational factors into account requires cognitive resources, which may not always be available. Daniel Gilbert and his colleagues (Gilbert & Malone, 1995; Gilbert, Pelham, & Krull, 1988) hypothesized that when perceivers observe another individual's actions, they first assume that the behavior reflected the individual's dispositions, but then adjust this initial assumption, if necessary, based on situational information about possible external causes of the behavior. For example, seeing a man yell at his neighbor will initially create the impression of hostility or aggressiveness, but perceivers might subsequently adjust this impression based on situational information; if they know, for instance, that the neighbor stole tomatoes from the man's garden, they will probably adjust their initial inference of a hostile disposition and instead attribute the man's behavior to his neighbor's provocation. How can this two-stage model of the attribution process explain the correspondence bias? It turns out that the initial step of assuming that a behavior reflected an internal disposition is relatively *automatic* and spontaneous (e.g., see Winter & Uleman, 1984). The second step of using situational information to adjust the initial impression, however, is not automatic and in fact requires significant cognitive resources (e.g., thinking about the possible role of situational factors). Because the second step requires deliberative thought, it is much more susceptible to disruption than is the first step (see Gilbert et al., 1988). For example, distraction or multitasking can interfere with the second step, which will leave perceivers with their initial impression that the target's behavior reflected an internal disposition—i.e., the correspondence bias. From this perspective, the correspondence bias is not inevitable in social perception, but instead will occur mainly when perceivers lack either the motivation or the cognitive resources necessary to use situational information to adjust initial, automatic, dispositional inferences.

**Culture and the Correspondence Bias.** A fourth possible cause of the correspondence bias is cultural influences. Specifically, the emphasis in Western cultures on individualism and personal accomplishments may account, in part, for the frequent appearance of the correspondence bias in research conducted in North America. Western cultures preach that anyone can be successful if they try hard enough, and values like personal freedom and liberty are held very high in Western cultures. It is possible that this emphasis on individualism causes people from Western cultures to focus on internal, personal variables like personality traits, attitudes, and values when explaining behavior.

But what about cultures in which there is less emphasis on individuality and more emphasis on such things as group harmony, social obligations, and conformity to tradition (collectivism)? Perhaps members of these cultures will be *less* likely to explain behavior in terms of personal, internal characteristics (i.e., they will be less likely to exhibit the correspondence bias). We will discuss the individualism versus collectivism dimension in more detail later in this chapter. For our present purposes, it is necessary only to note that several researchers have compared individualist North American and collectivist Asian participants in experiments investigating the correspondence bias (e.g., Choi & Nisbett, 1998; Krull, Loy, Lin, Wang, Chen, & Zhao, 1999; Masuda & Kitayama, 2004; Miller, 1984; Miyamoto & Kitayama, 2002; Morris & Peng, 1994; Norenzayan, Choi, & Nisbett, 2002). Although the findings have not been perfectly consistent, most researchers have found that Asian participants exhibited a significantly weaker correspondence bias than did North American participants. The bias did not usually disappear altogether in Asian participants, but these individuals were consistently less likely to make internal attributions than were North Americans. These findings suggest that cultural factors do contribute to the correspondence bias, but do not explain it entirely (see also Peng & Knowles, 2003).

The various causes of the correspondence bias are summarized in the accompanying Concept Review.

A fascinating real-life illustration of cultural differences in the correspondence bias has been documented in newspaper reports of murders. For a description of this phenomenon, see Social Psychology in Your Life: Cultural Differences in the Correspondence Bias (p. 122).

**The Appeal of Social Psychology?** It is probably accurate to say that the correspondence bias contributes to the appeal of social psychology. By this we mean that the correspondence bias helps to explain why so many findings in social psychology are surprising (see Gilbert & Malone, 1995; Jones, 1990; Ross, 1977). People often overlook the situational forces that influence behavior and instead interpret others' behavior in terms of internal, dispositional factors. For example, one of the most famous research programs in social psychology is Stanley Milgram's (1963,

## CONCEPT REVIEW
### Causes of the Correspondence Bias

| Cause | Example |
| --- | --- |
| We are unaware of subtle external factors that influence behavior. | We conclude that a student who failed a test lacks ability because we are unaware that she felt sick during the exam. |
| We underestimate the power of external factors on behavior. | We conclude that a man who put money into a Salvation Army kettle is generous because we do not believe that seeing a previous person donate could have influenced him. |
| We do not have the cognitive resources necessary to take situational factors into account when explaining behavior. | We conclude that a student who slipped and fell at the other end of the cafeteria is uncoordinated because we are distracted by a conversation with a friend and do not bother to look for possible external causes like a wet floor. |
| Western culture emphasizes the importance of personal, internal causes of behavior. | We conclude that a successful businessman is hardworking because we believe that individuals in our society can accomplish anything if they work hard enough. |

# Social Psychology in Your Life    *Cultural Differences in the Correspondence Bias*

Comparisons of actual newspaper articles have revealed fascinating cultural differences in the causal explanations for behavior offered by reporters: North American reporters exhibit the correspondence bias (the tendency to attribute others' actions to internal causes) more than do Asian reporters. For example, Michael Morris and Kaiping Peng (1994) examined newspaper articles about two U.S. murders, one committed by a Chinese man in Iowa and one committed by an American man in Michigan. The newspaper articles appeared either in the *New York Times,* an English-language paper, or in *World Journal,* a Chinese-language paper based in New York. A total of 22 articles in the two newspapers dealing with the murders were examined. Analysis of the

articles showed that the English-language reporters focused on internal characteristics of the murderers (e.g., "very bad temper," "martial arts enthusiast," and "darkly disturbed man who drove himself to success and destruction"), whereas the Chinese-language reporters stressed external factors that precipitated the murders (e.g., "did not get along with his advisor," "isolation from Chinese community," and "gunman had recently been fired").

In another survey of newspaper articles on a very different topic, Fiona Lee, Mark Hallahan, and Thaddeus Herzog (1996) examined sports coverage of soccer games. The newspaper reports appeared in one of three U.S. newspapers (e.g., *Los Angeles Times*) or in an English-

language Hong Kong newspaper (*South China Morning Post*). A total of 39 articles about soccer, all written by local reporters, were compared. Analysis of the articles showed that the American reporters tended to focus on internal explanations of events in the soccer games (e.g., "The more talented team was victorious"; "He was ejected from the game because he didn't control his hot temper"). In contrast, Hong Kong reporters tended to focus on external explanations of events in the games (e.g., "The winning team defeated an exhausted opponent at the end of a long road trip"; "He was ejected from the game because he retaliated when an opposing player insulted him").

1974) research on obedience, which showed that ordinary people will follow the orders of an experimenter to deliver intense shock to another person (this research is discussed in Chapter 8 on Conformity, Compliance, and Obedience). Why did this research have such an impact? Because people were surprised that the situational pressure provided by the authority of an experimenter was sufficient to produce such obedience. In other words, people were surprised by the influence of an external factor (authority) on behavior. Another research program that generated a lot of attention was conducted by Bibb Latané and John Darley (1970) on bystander intervention; these studies showed that people who witness an emergency situation often fail to help because of situational factors such as the presence of other bystanders (this research is discussed in Chapter 12 on Helpful Social Behavior). This research was interesting to nonpsychologists because they were surprised by the failure of bystanders to intervene; the situational forces inhibiting assistance seemed relatively weak on the surface, yet exerted strong effects on behavior.

## Beyond Words: Understanding Nonverbal Behavior

**nonverbal behavior**

*actions and cues that communicate meaning in ways other than by words*

One important determinant of how we interpret other people's words and actions (and, therefore, one determinant of the impressions we form) is their **nonverbal behavior**—actions and cues that communicate meaning in ways other than direct verbal statements. Do you pay attention to the little signs people exhibit in their eyes, voice, or hands that suggest their mood? Do you watch for clues that your romantic partner is happy, unhappy, or bored with you? Nonverbal behavior comprises everything other than the words themselves. Thus, nonverbal behavior includes a multitude of cues such as facial expressions, vocal qualities like pitch and intensity, interpersonal space, eye gaze, and gestures (see DePaulo & Friedman, 1998). We comment below on a few interesting questions about nonverbal behavior that have been investigated by social psychologists. We will also return to research on nonverbal behavior later in the chapter (in the section on What Others See in Us) when we discuss whether other people can tell when you are lying.

We often infer how people are feeling based on their nonverbal actions.

**It's Not Only What You Say, It's Also How You Say It.** Words are important. When we say "I love you" to our partner, parents, or children, it communicates something meaningful and important. But there is another aspect of interpersonal communication that often matters just as much, and sometimes more, than the words themselves: *how* the words are expressed.

Consider the following situation: You overhear someone saying "What a *nice* haircut!" to another person in a mocking tone with a quick laugh at the end. How would you interpret the speaker's meaning? Would you rely on the words themselves, which are positive, or the tone of the words, which is negative? Research evidence suggests that when verbal and nonverbal cues directly conflict like this, observers rely more on the nonverbal cues in interpreting the message's meaning (e.g., Argyle, Alkema, & Gilmour, 1971; Mehrabian, 1972). Thus, the haircut comment would be interpreted as a statement that was meant to be sarcastic and negative.

Typically, nonverbal cues do not directly conflict with verbal content, but instead provide additional information. Researchers have found that nonverbal information does enhance our understanding of interactions. For example, Dane Archer and Robin Akert (1977) showed participants brief videotapes of two or three people talking or interacting and then asked participants questions that were not specifically answered in the videotapes (thus, participants had to infer the answers from things in the videotapes). The videotapes were genuine, spontaneous interactions among two or three individuals, which lasted between 30 and 60 seconds. For example, one scene depicted two women playing with a 7-month-old baby, and participants were later asked to predict which of the women was the baby's mother. Another scene involved two men discussing a game of basketball they had played, and participants were later asked to predict which of the men had won the game. Participants who simply read a written transcript of the verbal communications did not differ from chance in answering the questions correctly, whereas participants who watched the videotapes performed much better (about 50% better). Thus, nonverbal information was helpful to participants and improved their comprehension of the social interactions.

Nonverbal cues are particularly useful in judging the emotion of speakers—how other people are feeling. The most obvious nonverbal cues for inferring emotions are facial expressions, such as smiling and frowning. But other cues like a quivering voice, shaking hands, and frequent shifting of body posture reflect such emotions as nervousness and embarrassment. One of the reasons nonverbal cues are seen as informative about true feelings is that they are not completely under voluntary control. Even when people try to mask their feelings, nonverbal cues can "leak" their emotions (e.g., Ekman & Friesen, 1969a). If someone is very upset but denying it ("I'm not upset"), their voice may quiver or their hands may shake no matter what they do to try to hide their feelings. Nonverbal cues are usually taken as a more accurate sign of underlying emotions than are words themselves.

**Developmental Changes in the Weighting of Verbal and Nonverbal Cues.** We have noted that when verbal and nonverbal cues directly conflict, such as in a sarcastic compliment ("What a *nice* haircut!") or an unsuccessful attempt to mask one's feelings ("I'm not upset"), perceivers rely on the nonverbal cues to interpret the speaker's meaning or emotional state. This use of nonverbal cues to qualify verbal meaning requires a relatively sophisticated understanding of how emotions are expressed nonverbally. Research with children indicates that very young children do not possess such understanding.

Bruce Morton and Sandra Trehub (2001) asked children between the ages of 4 and 10, as well as college students, to judge whether a speaker was feeling happy or sad. Participants listened to 40 utterances in which the speaker stated something happy (e.g., "My soccer team just won the championship") or sad (e.g., "I lost my sticker collection") in a tone of voice that was either happy or sad. Twenty of the utterances presented consistent verbal and nonverbal cues, and 20 presented inconsistent cues (e.g., happy content expressed in a sad voice). Figure 4.3 summarizes the results. On the utterances that involved conflicting cues, more than 80% of the youngest children (ages 4 and 5) relied on the verbal content to judge the speaker's emotion (e.g., judging someone who expressed happy content in a sad voice to be feeling happy). This tendency fell to approximately 40% by the time children were 9 or 10 years old. In contrast, 100% of the adults relied exclusively on the nonverbal cues in making their judgments. Presumably, children must learn such things as the difficulty of hiding emotions before they can judge the appropriate weight to give to verbal content and nonverbal cues in spoken communication. Interpretation of nonverbal cues is a skill that slowly develops over children's early years.

**Facial Expressions.** Charles Darwin proposed in 1872 that facial expressions in humans are biologically based and universal. Darwin believed that facial expressions evolved from more primitive behaviors (e.g., the expression for disgust is a simplified derivative of vomiting or spitting) and all humans expressed their emotions similarly (although, of course, people might attempt to hide their emotions). Darwin believed that the ability to recognize emotions in others' faces was adaptive; for example, if someone shows a fear or anger expression, other people can infer that a threat is present and either address the threat or escape (see Hansen & Hansen, 1988).

If facial expressions are biologically based and have evolved from primitive behaviors, then people from different cultures should be able to recognize facial expressions from other cultures relatively accurately. This hypothesis has, in fact, been tested many times. For example, Paul Ekman and a large number of collabora-

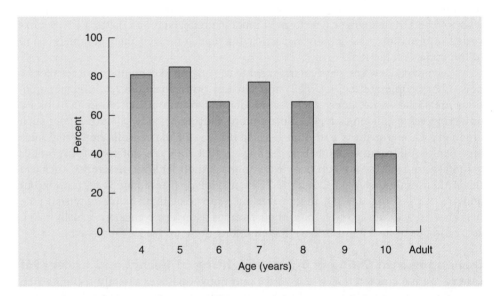

**FIGURE 4.3** Percent of respondents at each age who relied on verbal content (words) to judge emotion

From Morton and Trehub, "Children's understanding of emotion in speech," *Child Development*, 72, 834–843, Table 2, p. 837, 2001. Reprinted by permission of Blackwell Publishing.

tors (Ekman et al., 1987) conducted a cross-cultural study involving 10 countries, in which college-age participants were shown 18 facial photographs of Caucasian men and women expressing one of six emotions. For each photograph, participants were asked to select which emotion was being expressed. Although there were some variations across cultures, all of the emotions were correctly identified by the majority of participants from every culture. Considering the limitations of these two-dimensional photographs (e.g., real-life emotional expressions change dynamically over time and are three-dimensional), the level of accuracy was quite remarkable. Some researchers have criticized this study (e.g., see Russell, 1994), but evidence for the universality of emotion recognition is accumulating. After a comprehensive review of 87 articles, Hillary Elfenbein and Nalini Ambady (2002) concluded that cross-cultural recognition accuracy was substantially above chance on every one of seven basic emotions: anger, contempt, disgust, fear, happiness, sadness, and surprise. Some emotions have been recognized in research better than others (e.g., across studies, happiness and anger have been the best-recognized emotions), but all have shown substantial cross-cultural generalizability. This pattern of findings supports Darwin's argument that facial expressions of certain fundamental emotions are biologically based and mostly similar in all cultures (see also Elfenbein & Ambady, 2003; Rozin, Lowery, Imada, & Haidt, 1999).

**4.1**
**ONLINE**
LAB

## Gender and Cultural Differences in Nonverbal Behavior

Although facial expressions and other nonverbal behaviors have been shown to be similar across many groups, there are also differences in the ways that people express emotions and communicate nonverbally. We will discuss two sources of differences: gender and culture.

**Gender Differences in Nonverbal Behavior.** Do you think that men and women differ in their nonverbal behavior? A common stereotype is that women are more emotional and are allowed to express more emotion (men should be "stoic" and unemotional); do you think that this stereotype occurs in real life?

Researchers have identified a number of interesting gender differences in nonverbal behavior. First, women are better judges than men of *other people's* emotions (e.g., Hall, 1984). This tendency for women to identify emotions in others more accurately than men may reflect that women are more oriented toward interpersonal harmony than men; alternatively, it may be that women must be more vigilant about others' emotions because they are less physically powerful and therefore more vulnerable than men (Deaux & LaFrance, 1998). Second, whereas women are better judges of emotions than are men, women's own facial expressions of emotion are generally easier to judge than are men's expressions (Hall, 1984; DePaulo & Friedman, 1998). This difference may reflect the stereotype that it is more socially acceptable for women to express their emotions than it is for men (Mayo & Henley, 1981).

Women gaze at other people more than men, smile more often than men, and are gazed at by other people more than men (Hall, 1984; LaFrance, Hecht, & Paluck, 2003). Women also approach other people more closely than do men and are approached by other people more closely than men (Hall, 1984). These various tendencies reflect women's greater expressions of behaviors that reflect intimacy and liking (Mehrabian, 1972; Mayo & Henley, 1981). Women may express greater nonverbal intimacy than men because women are more concerned about interpersonal relationships, or because men are not supposed to show their feelings.

**Cultural Differences in Nonverbal Behavior.** There are also many cultural differences in nonverbal behavior. In particular, cultures differ in their **display rules**—norms for how and when emotions should be expressed (Ekman &

**display rules**

*norms in a culture for how and when emotions should be expressed*

*Culture seems to shape how we express our emotions on our faces as well as how we talk about our emotions when we're in the throes of an emotional event.*

In Japan, it is considered inappropriate to show strong negative emotions—one of the *display rules* in that culture.

Friesen, 1969b). For example, it is considered inappropriate in Japan to show strong emotions, especially strong negative emotions (Leathers, 1997), whereas North American culture allows freer expression of emotional states.

Cultures also differ in nonverbal gestures and greetings (see Archer, 1997; Axtell, 1991; Leathers, 1997). For example, in North America, it is traditional to shake hands when greeting others, whereas people in Japan bow to one another, and people in eastern Europe often exchange kisses on the cheek. Hand signals are almost always culture-specific, such as the North American "thumbs up" sign, which is obscene in some Middle Eastern countries. It is acceptable in North America to point and wave at other people from a distance, whereas these actions are considered impolite in many Asian countries.

Finally, there are substantial differences in how close or far apart individuals stand in different cultures. Have you ever felt "crowded" by someone who talked to you while standing nose to nose? In North America, people have a relatively large "personal space" zone (Hall, 1984), which is not supposed to be entered except by individuals who have an intimate relationship (e.g., family members) or who don't know any better (e.g., children). In some Middle Eastern cultures, in contrast, people stand very closely to one another even during casual conversation. There is also more touching by Middle Eastern acquaintances than by acquaintances in North America. These differences can create considerable discomfort when two people from cultures with different norms for personal space and touching interact.

## ● ● ●    What We See in Ourselves: Self-Perception

Do you have a clear conception of who you are? Can you describe your strengths and weaknesses, your important attitudes and values, your goals and dreams? These are questions about self-perception. We will discuss issues related specifically to *identity* in Chapter 5, but first we want to consider more generally how people make judgments about their abilities, ambitions, and attitudes. What kind of information do we seek to assess our strengths and weaknesses? In this section, we discuss the important role of comparisons to other people in judgments about the self. We also propose that people sometimes make judgments about themselves in a detached, logical manner that closely parallels how they make judgments about other people.

### The Looking Glass Self

**looking glass self**

*the tendency to internalize other people's judgments about us into our self-concept*

We rely on other people for much of our self-concept. It may seem ironic that judgments about the self rely heavily on other people, but it is true nonetheless. We rely on others in at least two ways. First, other people sometimes *tell us* about ourselves. Our mother will say "You are such a thoughtful child"; our teacher will say "You are a good speller"; a friend will say "You are so funny!" These judgments by other people may be internalized into the self-concept, especially if they come from more than one person. This idea that other people's judgments about us will be integrated into our self-concept was labeled the **looking glass self** (we see ourselves as others see us) in an early, influential book by Charles Cooley (1902). A classic example of the looking glass self is children's internalization of their parents' labels.

In a well-known study of the looking glass self, Richard Miller, Philip Brickman, and Diana Bolen (1975) tried to teach children in the fifth grade not to litter and to clean up after others. Some children were repeatedly told that they were neat and tidy people (the labeling condition), whereas others were told that they *should* be neat and tidy (the persuasion condition). Results showed that children in the labeling condition changed their behavior more than children in the persuasion condition. The authors hypothesized that children in the labeling condition internalized the labels, at least to some extent.

Social psychologists have also shown that individuals' self-judgments (estimates of the extent to which various traits describe them) are made *more quickly* after they have thought about other people's impressions of them (e.g., Lord, Desforges, Chacon, Pere, & Clubb, 1992; Tschanz & Rhodewalt, 2001). Presumably, respondents in these studies used others' impressions to make the self-judgments, because the impressions formed part of their self-concept (see also Jussim, Soffin, Brown, Ley, & Kohlhepp, 1992).

## Social Comparison

A second way that other people are involved in judgments about the self is that we often compare ourselves to other people. Let's consider an example of self-assessment borrowed from the book *Pay It Forward*. Think about your own generosity or helpfulness toward others. Do you consider yourself to be generous? What is the degree of your generosity? Now an important question: *how* did you come to the conclusion that you are generous or not?

If you're like most people judging themselves, you probably tried to think of examples of generous behavior that you have performed. Then you probably compared your own generous behavior to the amount of generous behavior that you have seen your friends and acquaintances exhibit (or perhaps the amount of generosity that you believe the average person your age exhibits). If you estimated that you have exhibited more generosity than most of your acquaintances, then you judged yourself to be high in generosity, whereas if you estimated that your acquaintances' generous behavior has exceeded your own, then you judged yourself to be low in generosity. The important point is that it was necessary to compare yourself to other people in order to make a judgment about the self.

This process of explicitly comparing ourselves to other people in order to judge the self is called **social comparison.** The term was coined by Leon Festinger (1954), who proposed that we often rely on comparisons with other people to assess our abilities and our attitudes. Festinger hypothesized that, if possible, we test our abilities or beliefs in an objective, physical way. We can test our ability to dunk a basketball by trying to dunk a basketball, or test our cooking skills by attempting to make a gourmet meal, or test whether our prediction for an event is accurate by waiting to see if it comes true. But often we cannot test our abilities or beliefs in a direct, physical manner. In these cases, we compare our performance or belief to the performances or beliefs of others. To assess our generosity, we must compare the frequency of our generous behavior to the frequency of generous behavior by others, as in the example above; to assess the validity of our belief in an afterlife, we must compare our belief to the beliefs of others to see whether others agree with us (see Suls, Martin, & Wheeler, 2002).

**social comparison**

*the process of comparing ourselves to others in order to judge the self*

**Social Comparison With Similar Others: Wanting to Assess Oneself Accurately.** Festinger's theory of social comparison was based on the assumption that people are motivated to make *accurate* judgments about their abilities and opinions. He assumed that we want to know our true strengths and weaknesses and

We would not compare ourselves to Andy Roddick to judge our ability at tennis.

the actual validity of our attitudes and opinions. This desire to make accurate judgments about the self is highly adaptive, because an inaccurate view of the self might lead to serious problems (Buunk, 1995; Sedikides & Strube, 1997; Wheeler, Martin, & Suls, 1997). If we assess our abilities too optimistically, we might get ourselves into situations that are above our heads (e.g., taking a course in mathematics that is too difficult for us). If we assess our abilities too harshly, we might avoid challenging ourselves in productive ways (e.g., deciding not to attend college).

The goal of assessing our abilities accurately is usually best achieved by comparing ourselves with other people who are *similar* to us on dimensions that are relevant to performance (Goethals & Darley, 1977; Goethals & Klein, 2000; Smith & Arnkelsson, 2000). If you wanted to assess your level of ability in tennis, to whom would you compare yourself? Comparing yourself to a 5-year-old child would not be informative, because you are older, stronger, and more experienced at tennis. Comparing yourself to Andy Roddick or Serena Williams would also not be informative, because they have tremendous natural ability and have played much more than you. You would probably choose one or more persons who are about the same age as you and have played about the same amount of tennis as you. These characteristics of age and experience affect tennis performance and need to be taken into account when assessing natural ability. If you are better than these similar persons, then you probably have a natural talent for tennis, whereas if you are worse than these similar persons, then you probably lack natural ability at tennis.

The flowchart in Figure 4.4 depicts how social comparisons are used to make judgments about the self.

**Upward Social Comparison: Wanting to Improve.** Having an accurate view of our strengths and weaknesses is probably beneficial in most cases. But performance is not static: we can become better at many things, even when our ability is low. If we want to improve ourselves, one excellent source of information is other people (Collins, 1996; Taylor, Wayment, & Carrillo, 1996; Wood, 1989).

What kind of social comparisons will be stimulated by the desire to improve? Let's imagine that you wanted to improve your study habits; whom would you choose for social comparison in this case? The most likely choice would be some-

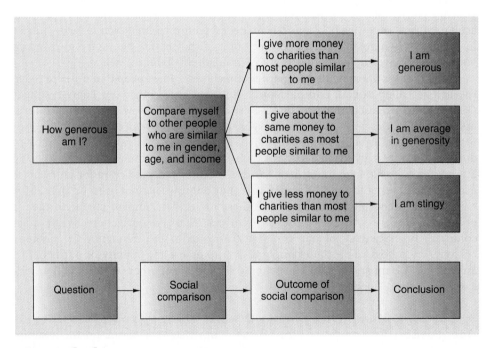

**FIGURE 4.4** Social comparison processes

one who has *better* study habits than you—someone who studies more effectively and gets better grades. You would be able to copy this person's behavior and discuss strategies for improving your habits, whereas someone who has worse study habits would not provide useful ideas. "Latrell is much more focused than I am when he studies; I need to change my habits so I'm more like Latrell." This kind of social comparison is labeled **upward social comparison.** Upward social comparison involves comparing yourself to someone who is better off than you are (better performance, better outcomes) and can provide useful ideas for how to improve. The link between upward social comparison and the desire to improve parallels our discussion of upward counterfactual thoughts in Chapter 3 (see Olson, Buhrmann, & Roese, 2000).

**upward social comparison**
*social comparison with people who are better off or more skilled than we are*

### Downward Social Comparison: Wanting to Feel Better.

The desire to assess one's abilities accurately and the desire to improve are two important motives that occur in many settings in everyday life. There is at least one additional motivation, however, that also occurs frequently: the desire to feel good (or to feel better). We like to feel good about ourselves, and this motive can be particularly strong if something bad has happened, such as if we have performed poorly or experienced an unfavorable outcome (Helgeson & Mickelson, 1995; Taylor & Brown, 1988; Taylor & Lobel, 1989; Wills, 1981).

What kind of social comparisons will be stimulated by the desire to feel good about oneself? Let's imagine that you wanted to feel good about your performance on an exam. Whom would you seek out? The most likely choice would be someone you think probably did *worse* than you on the test (Wood, Michela, & Giordano, 2000). Exposure to people whose performances or outcomes are less positive than our own makes our situation seem better in contrast. "I didn't do great, but at least I did better than my friends in the class." This kind of social comparison is labeled **downward social comparison.** Again, this link between downward social comparison and feeling good parallels our discussion of downward counterfactual thoughts in Chapter 3.

**downward social comparison**
*social comparison with people who are worse off or less skilled than we are*

Bram Buunk, Frans Oldersma, and Carsten de Dreu (2001) recruited undergraduate students who were involved in a dating relationship. Some participants were asked to list as many ways as possible that they or their partners were *better* than other partners (downward social comparison condition). Other participants were asked to list as many ways as possible that they or their partners were *good* partners (positive features condition). All participants then completed a measure of relationship satisfaction. Participants who were asked to generate downward social comparisons reported significantly greater satisfaction with their relationship than did participants who were asked to generate positive features of their relationship. These results provide direct support for the hypothesized link between downward social comparison and feeling good.

### Diverse Consequences of Upward Social Comparisons.

When we compare ourselves to people who are better off or who perform better than we do, we may feel bad (see Thornton & Moore, 1993). Although upward comparisons often provide useful information, we can also experience negative affect because our circumstances or our performances seem worse in contrast to those of someone more accomplished. These upward comparisons can make us feel depressed or inadequate because others are more successful than we are.

On the other hand, upward comparisons can make us angry and resentful, if we think that we *should* be doing as well as other people who are better off. When we feel that we *deserve* better outcomes than we are receiving, we experience **relative deprivation,** which is a feeling of anger or resentment about one's outcomes based on comparisons with others. For example, if workers in another company are making more money for doing the same job we do, we may feel unfairly treated.

**relative deprivation**
*a feeling of anger or resentment about our outcomes based on comparisons with better-off others*

The emotion of relative deprivation can lead to actions intended to improve our status, such as complaining to our boss or looking for another job (see Crosby, 1976; Walker & Smith, 2002).

There are also some conditions, however, under which upward social comparisons may not elicit negative affect at all, but instead might produce hope or optimism about the future (see Collins, 2000; Gardner, Gabriel, & Hochschild, 2002; Lockwood & Kunda, 1997; Mussweiler, 2003; Mussweiler & Strack, 2000; Smith, 2000). Cancer patients, for example, have been shown to prefer comparisons with other patients who are doing well (e.g., Taylor & Lobel, 1989; Wood & Van der Zee, 1997), presumably because such persons give them hope for improvement.

Another interesting circumstance is when someone who is close to us does extremely well. How do you think you would feel if a close friend of yours achieved success and fame? Would you be jealous, or would you feel proud that you were friends with a famous person? Abraham Tesser and his colleagues (Beach & Tesser, 2000; Tesser, 1988; Tesser, Millar, & Moore, 1988), in their *self-evaluation maintenance* model, have argued that it might depend on whether your friend was successful in a domain that you also were pursuing or in a domain very different from your own pursuits. Imagine that your occupational goal is to establish your own software company in the computer field. If your friend achieves success and fame in the software field, it might make you feel like a failure in comparison, and you might be jealous. But if your friend achieves success and fame in another field, such as music, you might be happy about his or her success and feel proud of your friendship. Robert Cialdini and his colleagues (Cialdini, Borden, Thorne, Walker, Freeman, & Sloan, 1976) labeled this latter process "basking in the reflected glory" of the other person.

**social comparison orientation**

*a disposition that represents how often people engage in social comparison*

**Individual Differences in the Tendency to Engage in Social Comparison.** All of us compare ourselves to other people at least occasionally. But some of us engage in social comparison more often than others and are more affected by social comparison information than others. What about you? Do you frequently seek out other people to assess your own abilities and beliefs? When you are trying to make a decision, do you talk to other people about their relevant experiences? Does information about how other people are doing have a strong impact on your feelings about yourself? Frederick Gibbons and Bram Buunk (1999) developed a scale to measure individuals' tendencies to engage in social comparison, a dimension they labeled **social comparison orientation.** This scale is reproduced in Know Yourself 4.1: Social Comparison Orientation. Answer the items and see whether you score high or low on this characteristic. Does your score correspond to your intuition about how often you compare yourself to other people?

Gibbons and Buunk (1999) showed that students who scored high on this scale were more interested in learning about how other students performed on a test than were students who scored low. In another study, the researchers showed that downward social comparison information suggesting that participants' romantic relationship was better than most made discontented individuals feel better about their relationship, but only if they scored high on social comparison orientation. Thus, this scale appears to predict relevant social comparison outcomes.

## Developmental Changes Across the Life Span in Social Comparison

Besides individual differences in social comparison (measured by the social comparison orientation scale), there are age-related differences in this behavior. That is, patterns of social comparison vary across the life span.

# Know Yourself 4.1
## *Social Comparison Orientation*

Please indicate the extent to which you agree or disagree with each of the following statements by circling the appropriate number on the answer scale.

1. I often compare how my loved ones (boy- or girlfriend, family members, etc.) are doing with how others are doing.

   | 1 | 2 | 3 | 4 | 5 |
   |---|---|---|---|---|
   | I disagree strongly | | | | I agree strongly |

2. I always pay a lot of attention to how I do things compared with how others do things.

   | 1 | 2 | 3 | 4 | 5 |
   |---|---|---|---|---|
   | I disagree strongly | | | | I agree strongly |

3. If I want to find out how well I have done something, I compare what I have done with how others have done.

   | 1 | 2 | 3 | 4 | 5 |
   |---|---|---|---|---|
   | I disagree strongly | | | | I agree strongly |

4. I often compare how I am doing socially (e.g., social skills, popularity) with other people.

   | 1 | 2 | 3 | 4 | 5 |
   |---|---|---|---|---|
   | I disagree strongly | | | | I agree strongly |

5. I am not the type of person who compares often with others.

   | 1 | 2 | 3 | 4 | 5 |
   |---|---|---|---|---|
   | I disagree strongly | | | | I agree strongly |

6. I often compare myself with others with respect to what I have accomplished in life.

   | 1 | 2 | 3 | 4 | 5 |
   |---|---|---|---|---|
   | I disagree strongly | | | | I agree strongly |

7. I often like to talk with others about mutual opinions and experiences.

   | 1 | 2 | 3 | 4 | 5 |
   |---|---|---|---|---|
   | I disagree strongly | | | | I agree strongly |

8. I often try to find out what others think who face similar problems as I face.

   | 1 | 2 | 3 | 4 | 5 |
   |---|---|---|---|---|
   | I disagree strongly | | | | I agree strongly |

9. I always like to know what others in a similar situation would do.

   | 1 | 2 | 3 | 4 | 5 |
   |---|---|---|---|---|
   | I disagree strongly | | | | I agree strongly |

10. If I want to learn more about something, I try to find out what others think about it.

   | 1 | 2 | 3 | 4 | 5 |
   |---|---|---|---|---|
   | I disagree strongly | | | | I agree strongly |

11. I *never* consider my situation in life relative to that of other people.

   | 1 | 2 | 3 | 4 | 5 |
   |---|---|---|---|---|
   | I disagree strongly | | | | I agree strongly |

**SCORING:** All items except 5 and 11 are scored using the answer scales as presented (1-2-3-4-5); items 5 and 11 are reverse-scored (that is, 5-4-3-2-1). Add up all of the items for your overall social comparison orientation. Possible scores range from 11 to 55, and higher scores represent more frequent social comparison.

Jerry Suls (1986) proposed that young children (ages 3–5 years) engage in very little social comparison, because they do not grasp the idea of comparing themselves to other people. Instead, young children focus on personal improvement—temporal changes in their own behavior from past to present. Social comparisons are rare in the preschool years.

When children enter school and are exposed to many peers, social comparisons begin to emerge, but the early comparisons are unsystematic and are aimed at gathering information about *how to perform tasks,* rather than at evaluating their own ability (Pomerantz, Ruble, Frey, & Greulich, 1995). These children (ages 5–8 years) are trying to learn how to do things, and this focus predominates over judging how well they are doing compared to other children. As children progress through elementary and into high school, however, social comparisons slowly increase and become more evaluative in nature: *how am I doing relative to others?* Older children recognize that other people provide standards against which their own performance can be judged (Butler, 1989; Ruble & Frey, 1991). Thus, "mature" social comparisons become common during the high school years (corresponding to the time of greatest peer pressure for conformity to peer standards).

In the adult years, social comparisons are made for all of the reasons previously discussed: to assess the self, to improve the self, and to self-enhance. Adults show considerable flexibility in the use of social comparison and engage in it frequently and spontaneously (see Mussweiler, Rüter, & Epstude, 2004).

Finally, in old age, people decrease the frequency of social comparisons, perhaps because self-assessment is less important to them. Instead, older people make more temporal comparisons between their current status and how they used to be (Suls, 1986; Wilson & Ross, 2000). Recognizing that one's life is drawing to a close may reduce the urgency of evaluating oneself compared to others.

## Self-Perception Theory

We asked you earlier in this chapter to think about how generous you are. We speculated that you would make this judgment by thinking about your generous behavior in the past and comparing your actions to the rate of generous behaviors you have seen exhibited by other people. Our point was to illustrate the importance of social comparison in judgments about the self. But this process of using our own behavior to infer generosity also illustrates another important theory in social psychology: **self-perception theory.**

**self-perception theory**

*a theory proposing that we often judge our own internal states by reviewing our past behavior and inferring internal states consistent with our behavior unless there were clear external causes of our behavior*

Darryl Bem (1967, 1972) developed self-perception theory to describe how we make judgments about our internal states, such as our attitudes, emotions, and personality traits. He proposed that we often judge our own internal states in a manner exactly parallel to how we judge other people's internal states: we review our behavior and the situation in which it occurred and infer an internal state consistent with the behavior unless there were clear external causes of our behavior. This idea seems relatively straightforward for many internal states, such as personality traits like generosity. After all, we cannot "feel" our generosity, so we have to examine our behavior and infer our level of generosity using some sort of criteria.

But Bem (1972) proposed a more controversial hypothesis, which was that we use this same process for internal states that are normally thought to include an affective component that people can access directly. For instance, Bem proposed that we use self-perception logic to infer many of our likes and dislikes. The notion that we need to infer from our behavior how much we like or dislike something strikes most people as implausible. Most of us believe that we can "feel" our likes and dislikes, and we make judgments about these internal states by accessing them directly. We judge our liking for apple pie by thinking about apple pie and appraising how this image makes us feel (good or bad).

Think about some of your own likes and dislikes—can you directly "sense" them? Do you like or dislike puppies? Worms? Chocolate? Speaking in front of an audience? We suspect that you believe you can access these feelings directly. These targets elicit clear and strong affective reactions from most people. But let's think of some other examples. Do you like or dislike brown bread? Biographical books? Genetically engineered foods? We suspect that your likes and dislikes for these targets may be more difficult to "feel."

What was different about the second set of examples? These examples probably involved targets toward which you have weaker or more ambiguous feelings. You may not yet have developed clear feelings toward genetically engineered food. Your feelings may be neutral toward brown bread, which is a target that does not evoke strong feelings either way in many people. And your feelings about biographies may include both positive and negative elements, because you have enjoyed some biographies but found others boring. Consequently, liking for these targets cannot simply be "felt"; we must estimate our liking for them in some other manner. Perhaps self-perception theory describes how.

Can you "feel" your liking for these puppies?

### Inferring Our Own Attitudes From Our Behavior.

Bem (1967) originally proposed that we infer *all* our internal states from our behavior. This provocative proposal was subsequently revised, however, to the hypothesis that self-perception occurs for internal states that are *weak or ambiguous*. When we do not have a clearly defined evaluation of a target, we infer our attitude (or like/dislike) from our past actions toward the target. Eventually, our attitude becomes strong and clear enough for us to be able to access it directly without self-perception.

A clever study by Shelly Chaiken and Mark Baldwin (1981) provided empirical evidence that self-perception occurs for ambiguous attitudes but not for well-defined attitudes. Participants had previously completed a questionnaire that assessed their feelings and beliefs about the environment (feelings and beliefs about acting in a pro-ecology way, such as recycling and minimizing energy use). Some participants were identified as having "well-defined" views, because they had feelings and beliefs that either consistently supported or consistently opposed behaving in a pro-ecology manner. Other participants were identified as having "poorly defined" views, because their feelings and beliefs were inconsistent; for instance, some of these individuals had positive beliefs about the benefits of behaving in a pro-ecology way but reported that they disliked doing things like recycling and turning down the thermostat at night.

Chaiken and Baldwin gave participants a questionnaire to complete that required them to review their past behaviors in the environmental domain (e.g., recycling, conserving energy). The questionnaire was intentionally constructed, however, to produce a *biased* review of past behavior: one version of the questionnaire forced participants to focus on their pro-environmental actions, whereas the second version emphasized anti-environmental actions. The authors hypothesized that if participants used a self-perception process to infer their environmental attitude, then the questionnaire that highlighted pro-environmental actions would lead them to report that their attitude was pro-environment, whereas the questionnaire that highlighted anti-environmental actions would lead them to report that their attitude was anti-environment (or, at least, less pro-environment). After completing one of the two questionnaires, participants reported their attitude toward environmental issues.

Figure 4.5 presents the mean ratings of environmental attitudes by participants with poorly defined and well-defined views after completing one of the questionnaires. The figure shows that the questionnaire

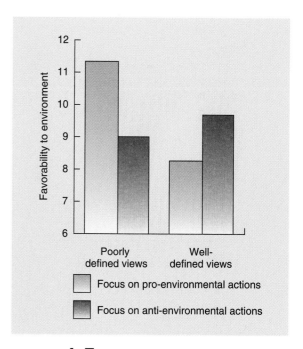

**FIGURE 4.5** Favorability of reported attitudes toward the environment

From Chaiken and Baldwin, "Affective-cognitive consistency and the effect of salient behavioral information on the self-perception of attitudes," *Journal of Personality and Social Psychology*, 41, 1–12, Table 1, p. 6, 1981. Copyright © 1981 by the American Psychological Association. Reprinted by permission.

that focused attention on pro-environmental actions led to more pro-environmental attitudes than the questionnaire that focused attention on anti-environmental actions, but *only* for participants who had *poorly* defined attitudes. Participants who had well-defined views were not significantly influenced by the biased review of past behaviors. Chaiken and Baldwin hypothesized that participants with well-defined views were able to access their attitude directly and did not need to use their past behaviors to make the judgment, whereas participants with poorly defined views had to rely on their past behaviors to infer their attitude (and the questionnaire led them to review their past behaviors in a biased way).

**The Overjustification Effect.** One of the most interesting applications of self-perception theory has been to understanding the effects of rewards on liking for an activity or task. Sometimes people perform activities because they must do so (e.g., schoolwork, job responsibilities). At other times, however, they engage in activities for *intrinsic* reasons—because they enjoy the activities or find them fulfilling in some way. Let's begin our discussion of this topic with a thought experiment. If you saw a boy who lives next door to you playing the piano as you walked by his house in the evening, would you think that he enjoys playing the piano? Why? What if you learned that his parents had told him that he could watch his favorite television show later in the evening if he played the piano for an hour? Would you then conclude that he enjoys the piano?

Now think about yourself. If you pick up a friend's book that he or she recommended and spend a couple of hours reading it, what is the best explanation for your behavior? If someone asked you, "Did you read the book because you wanted to read it?" what would you say? But what if the book was not your friend's, but one that you were assigned to read for an English course? Now how would you answer the question about why you were reading it?

Both of these examples illustrate that when there is a good external reason for a behavior (e.g., to be able to watch a favorite television show, or to prepare for an English test), we tend to downplay internal causes (e.g., enjoyment). The **overjustification effect** occurs when people decide that they performed a potentially enjoyable task for external reasons rather than because they enjoyed it. A reward (or threat) provides sufficient justification for performing the task, so the individual infers that he or she did not really enjoy the task. The overjustification effect is an example of the *discounting principle* that we discussed earlier.

Mark Lepper, David Greene, and Richard Nisbett (1973) conducted a well-known experiment with children in a nursery school in the San Francisco area. All of the children (ages 3 to 5) were given an opportunity to draw some pictures using a really attractive set of marker pens. Before using the pens, children in one condition were told that they would be given a "Good Player Award" if they drew some pictures for the experimenter with the pens. These children were shown the award in advance so it would be salient in their minds (it was a 3-by-5-inch certificate with a gold star, spaces to write the child's name and school, and a red ribbon). Children in a second group were not told about the Good Player Award in advance, but were unexpectedly given the award after using the marker pens. Children in a third condition were not told about the award and did not receive one unexpectedly after using the pens.

Between one and two weeks after the children drew pictures for the experimenter, the marker pens were placed on a table in the nursery school for one hour on three different days and left for the children to use or not. Observers recorded how long each child played with the pens during the free-play periods. Figure 4.6 presents the percentage of

**overjustification effect**

*an inference that we performed a potentially enjoyable activity for external reasons (e.g., for a reward) rather than because we enjoyed it*

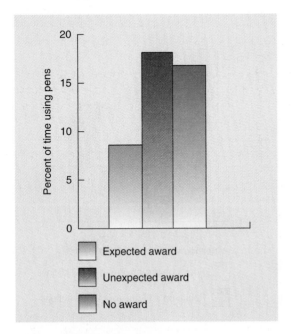

**FIGURE 4.6** Percent of free-play time spent drawing with pens

From Lepper et al., "Undermining children's interest with extrinsic rewards: A test of the 'overjustification effect,'" *Journal of Personality and Social Psychology*, 28, 129–137, Table 1, p. 134, 1973. Copyright © 1973 by the American Psychological Association. Reprinted by permission.

their free-play time that children spent drawing with the pens. Children who were promised a Good Player Award in advance if they used the pens subsequently spent less of their free time using the pens than did children who received an unexpected award or who did not hear anything about an award.

What was going on in the minds of the children? Lepper et al. suggested that the children who were promised the award concluded that they were using the pens *in order to get the reward,* so the pens were not "toys" that were fun to use. The extrinsic reward of the Good Player Award was enough to produce an overjustification effect: the children believed that the pens were simply a way of getting the award, which reduced their perception of being intrinsically motivated to use the pens.

These findings are disturbing for parents and teachers who use rewards or other external incentives to encourage their children and students to engage in important activities such as reading or playing a musical instrument. The goal of parents and educators should be to produce intrinsic motivation in their children and students, because liking for a task enhances persistence and improves performance (e.g., see Deci & Flaste, 1995; Harackiewicz & Elliot, 1998; Losier & Koestner, 1999; Vallerand, 1997). If offering rewards to encourage the activity, or forcing the activity via some other external pressure, leads people to conclude that the activity is not enjoyable, then the rewards or pressure may be counterproductive in the long run (see Lepper & Greene, 1978).

Are rewards or other incentives always a bad idea when the activity is one for which we want intrinsic motivation to develop? No, not necessarily. It turns out that if the reward is given only when performance is good, then the reward may not have a negative effect. Rewards given for good performance show recipients that they are skilled at an activity, which can actually increase personal motivation (Tang & Hall, 1995). Think about times that you have been given a reward or recognition because you did something extremely well—it made you feel good about yourself and the activity, didn't it? On the other hand, if rewards are given simply because the activity was undertaken, the rewards will not show recipients that they performed well, but instead will be seen as "controlling," which will serve to reduce perceived enjoyment (Deci & Flaste, 1995; Deci & Ryan, 1985). Parents should *not* say "Play the piano for one hour, and you can watch television" and then let the child plunk away randomly on the keys for an hour. Instead, parents should say "If you can play all of your songs at least once without any mistakes, you can watch television" and then comment on the child's good performance when the reward criterion is reached. Thus, rewards are not necessarily bad, even when the activity for which they are given is enjoyable. Nevertheless, rewards should be used cautiously and given only for good performance. If there is no need of reward to encourage the activity in the first place (e.g., if a child is certain to read a colorful book without any pressure), then it is probably best to avoid rewards altogether.

There is also evidence that verbal praise (one form of reward) should be used carefully. When children are successful, it may be best to praise their effort ("You worked so hard!") rather than their ability ("You're so smart!"), because when children believe that success depends on effort, they are more likely to persist in the future if they fail (e.g., Mueller & Dweck, 1998). The goal of praise should be to produce feelings of competence and confidence that success is possible with good effort (see Henderlong & Lepper, 2002).

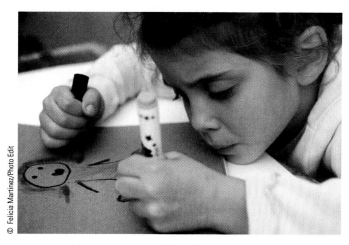

Lepper, Greene, and Nisbett (1973) found that giving children a reward for drawing with pens reduced the children's interest in using the pens during a subsequent free-play period.

© Felicia Martinez/Photo Edit

# Self-Serving Judgments

In Chapter 3, we defined *self-serving judgments* as perceptions or comparisons that enhance the perceived worth of the self. We all want to believe that we are good people, and this desire colors many of our judgments (Gilovich, 1991; Tesser, 2000). Research described in Chapter 3 showed that people define traits in ways that allow themselves to qualify for desirable labels. Earlier in this chapter, we described downward social comparison, which is often motivated by self-enhancement and makes people feel good about themselves. In the present section, we provide additional examples of self-serving judgments about the self.

**I'm Better Than Average: Unrealistic Self-Evaluation.** How do you think you compare to the average person on such dimensions as honesty, friendliness, and compassion? Would you say that you are above average? But perhaps we should restrict our comparisons to similar others, because you are, after all, a college student, which suggests that you may well be more talented than the average person in our society. Okay, let's think only about other college students. How would you compare yourself to other college students in terms of honesty, friendliness, and compassion? Would you say that you are above average?

If you are like most other people, you would rate yourself as above average on all of these dimensions. Almost all of us think that we are above average in our group, which, of course, is statistically impossible. Somebody must be below average! The range of traits on which self-serving evaluations have been obtained is very wide. Researchers have found that most of us rate ourselves as more honest, more fair, more loyal, more considerate, less lazy, less deceitful, more polite, and more capable than the average person (e.g., Alicke, 1985; Allison, Messick, & Goethals, 1989; Brown, 1986; Dunning, 1993; Dunning, Meyerowitz, & Holzberg, 1989; Goethals, Messick, & Allison, 1991; Kreuger, 1998; Van Lange & Sedikides, 1998). We also perceive ourselves as less persuasible than average by negative media communications such as advertising and political appeals, though we consider ourselves just as responsive as other people to positive communications such as health information (e.g., Brosius & Engel, 1996; Duck, Hogg, & Terry, 1998; Hoorens & Ruiter, 1996). Tom Gilovich (1991, p. 77) described a particularly interesting survey of 1 million high school seniors, which found that 70% of the respondents thought they were above average in leadership ability, and only 2% thought they were below average. On the dimension of ability to get along with others, 100% of the high school respondents thought they were above average, 60% thought they were in the top 10%, and 25% thought they were in the top 1%!

Let's take a final example. How do you honestly think you compare to other students in how much you engage in self-enhancing evaluations? Do you think that you engage in this bias less than the average student at your college? Most of us would probably answer this question affirmatively, providing an ironic illustration of the strength of the bias. In fact, Emily Pronin, Daniel Lin, and Lee Ross (2002) coined the term the **bias blind spot** to refer to the tendency for people to think that biases and errors in judgments are more common in others than in themselves (we have a "blind spot" when it comes to our own biases). In one study, Pronin et al. described eight different cognitive and motivational biases to participants, including the correspondence bias and self-enhancing evaluations, and found that respondents reported greater tendencies toward bias by others than by the self on all eight biases.

If we exaggerate the extent to which we are better than others, is it because we have inflated views of our own characteristics, or are we too critical of other people? Nicholas Epley and David Dunning (2000) explored this question by comparing people's responses with actual data. For example, participants in one study

**bias blind spot**

*the tendency to think that biases and errors in judgments are more common in others than in ourselves*

were given $5.00 for taking part in the experiment and were then asked how much of this $5.00 they would have been willing to donate to one of three charities (e.g., the American Red Cross) if they had been given this opportunity. Participants also predicted how much the average student at their college would give in such a situation. Participants' mean estimates were $2.44 for themselves and $1.83 for the average student. To assess the accuracy of these predictions, Epley and Dunning also ran a group of participants who were actually given the opportunity to donate money to the charities. The average actual donation was $1.53. These data suggest that the original participants had inflated views of their own generosity and more accurate views of other people (though still somewhat inflated).

Monica Biernat and her colleagues (Biernat, Vescio, & Green, 1996) conducted an interesting survey of women in sororities at the University of Florida and men in fraternities at the University of Kansas. Many college students have a stereotype of people who join sororities and fraternities, which includes both positive traits (e.g., well-dressed, outgoing) and negative traits (e.g., conceited, conforming). The researchers asked sorority/fraternity members to rate (1) their own sorority/fraternity, (2) sororities/fraternities in general, and (3) students at their own college on a series of traits and attributes. Figure 4.7 presents some of the ratings provided by women in sororities at the University of Florida, and Figure 4.8 (p. 138) presents some of the ratings provided by men in fraternities at the University of Kansas. The ratings provide a clear demonstration of self-enhancement. For *positive* traits in the stereotype of sororities and fraternities, respondents indicated that their own group *did* possess these traits, as did sororities/fraternities in general, compared to other college students. For example, sorority members reported that women in their own sorority and members of sororities in general were more popular than typical students at the University of Florida (71% and 67% versus 37%). But for *negative* traits in the stereotype of sororities and fraternities, respondents indicated that their own group did *not* possess these traits, even though sororities or fraternities in general

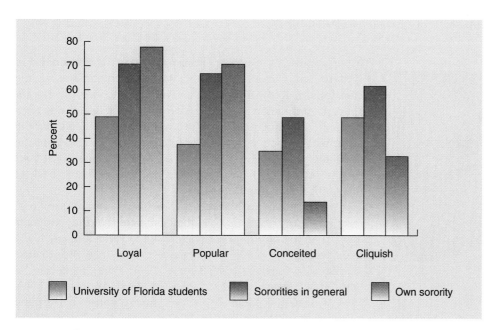

**FIGURE 4.7** Percent of students judged by sorority members to possess positive and negative traits

From Biernat et al., "Selective self-stereotyping," *Journal of Personality and Social Psychology,* 71, 1194–1209, Table 1, p. 1198, 1996. Copyright © 1996 by the American Psychological Association. Reprinted by permission.

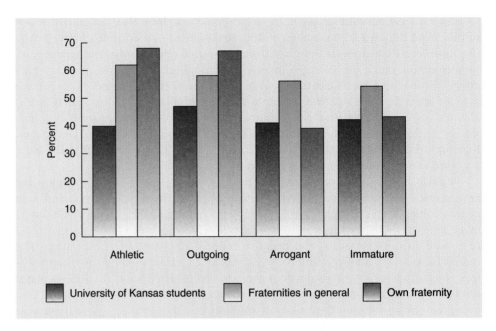

**FIGURE 4.8** Percent of students judged by fraternity members to possess positive and negative traits

From Biernat et al., "Selective self-stereotyping," *Journal of Personality and Social Psychology,* 71, 1194–1209, Table 2, p. 1201, 1996. Copyright © 1996 by the American Psychological Association. Reprinted by permission.

did possess them compared to other college students. For example, fraternity members reported that men in their own fraternity and typical students at the University of Kansas were less arrogant than members of fraternities in general (39% and 41% versus 56%). Thus, respondents accepted positive but rejected negative elements of the stereotype of their group.

Most of us believe that we are more likely than average to experience positive events in our lives, an optimism that may often be unrealistic.

**My Future Is Better Than Average: Unrealistic Optimism.** Before continuing to read, try answering the questions in Know Yourself 4.2: The Likelihood of Events for Yourself and Other Students. For each event listed, choose a percent between 0 and 100 to represent the likelihood that the event will happen to you and another percent to represent the likelihood that the event will happen to other students at your college. After you have completed the ratings, come back to this point and continue reading.

When people are asked to answer these sorts of questions, most show an optimistic bias: they estimate that they are *more* likely than average to experience *positive* events and *less* likely than average to experience *negative* events (e.g., Brinthaupt, Moreland, & Levine, 1991; Harris, 1996; Price, Pentecost, & Voth, 2002; Regan, Snyder, & Kassin, 1995; Weinstein, 1980, 1984; Weinstein & Klein, 1996). Did your responses correspond to this pattern? The optimistic bias appears to occur mainly in overestimating our chances of *common* positive events and underestimating our chances of *rare* negative events (see Kruger & Burrus, 2004).

Tara MacDonald and Michael Ross (1999) asked students involved in a dating relationship to predict whether their relationship would be together at several points in the future,

# Know Yourself 4.2
## *The Likelihood of Events for Yourself and Other Students*

What do you think is the likelihood that each of the following events will happen to you, and what is the likelihood that they will happen to other students at your college? Choose a percent between 0% and 100% to show the probability that the events will happen to you or to other students, where 0% would mean no chance at all, 50% would mean an equal chance that it will happen or it won't happen, and 100% would mean a sure thing.

|  | YOURSELF | OTHER STUDENTS |
|---|---|---|
| 1. Having a heart attack | _____ | _____ |
| 2. Being happy with your romantic or marital partner in later life | _____ | _____ |
| 3. Being physically healthy in middle age | _____ | _____ |
| 4. Being refused a bank loan | _____ | _____ |
| 5. Having a mentally gifted child | _____ | _____ |
| 6. Being killed in a car accident | _____ | _____ |
| 7. Becoming alcoholic | _____ | _____ |
| 8. Developing arthritis | _____ | _____ |
| 9. Having your work recognized with an award | _____ | _____ |
| 10. Becoming actively involved in a charitable organization | _____ | _____ |

**SCORING:** Compare the likelihood ratings you gave to yourself and other students for positive events (2, 3, 5, 9, and 10). Did you tend to give yourself higher probabilities? Now compare the likelihood ratings you gave to yourself and other students for negative events (1, 4, 6, 7, and 8). Did you tend to give yourself lower probabilities? Return to the text for relevant discussion.

including six months and one year later (see Figure 4.9, p. 140). Participants estimated a likelihood of 83% that they would be together in six months and 68% that they would be together in one year. The researchers also interviewed participants' roommates and parents, who provided lower estimates of the likelihood that participants' relationships would survive (approximately 10–20% lower). The researchers subsequently contacted the participants six months and one year later, and found that the *actual* survival rates for the relationships were 61% at six months and 48% at one year. Thus, the students were more unrealistically optimistic about the stability of their relationship than were their roommates or their parents.

Why are we unrealistically optimistic about our future? One possible factor is a motivational one: we *want* our futures to be rosy and are threatened by the possibility of negative life events (Sherman & Cohen, 2002; Sherman, Nelson, & Steele, 2000). Therefore, we convince ourselves that good things are in store for us. A second possibility is we think that we *deserve* positive outcomes, because we are, after all, good people (this possibility draws a connection between unrealistic self-evaluation and unrealistic optimism). Most of us believe that the world is, in general, a fair and just place, where good things happen to good people and bad things happen to bad people (see Lerner, 1980; Montada & Lerner, 1998). Because we are good people, good things will happen to us. A third possibility is that we are aware of factors that might reduce our own risk for certain problems (e.g., we do not smoke, we exercise at least occasionally), but we do not realize that many other people also possess these risk-reducing features (Weinstein, 1980). Predictions for our own outcomes relative to others' outcomes, therefore, tend to be too optimistic.

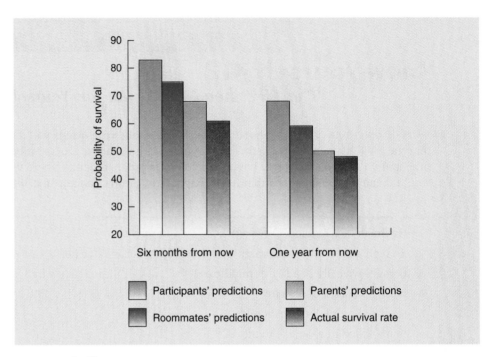

**FIGURE 4.9** Predicted likelihood of survival of relationship in six months and one year

From MacDonald and Ross, "Assessing the accuracy of predictions about dating relationships: How and why do lovers' predictions differ from those made by observers?" *Personality and Social Psychology Bulletin*, 25, 1417–1429, Table 2, p. 1422, 1999. Reprinted by permission of Sage Publications.

**Are Unrealistic Self-Evaluation and Unrealistic Optimism Adaptive or Maladaptive?** Accurate perceptions of the self would seem to be adaptive. Accurate perceptions should facilitate successful prediction of our own outcomes and of others' behavior toward us. The more accurately we see ourselves, the more effectively we should be able to deal with the world. Also, if we are too optimistic about the future, we may fail to perform preventive health behaviors. From this perspective, unrealistically positive self-evaluations and unrealistically optimistic predictions for the future would be expected to be maladaptive (see Radcliffe & Klein, 2002).

What do you think? Do you think that it is a bad thing for people to have an overly positive view of themselves? Can you see any potential benefits of self-enhancement?

Some theorists have proposed that self-enhancement can be adaptive. Shelley Taylor and Jonathon Brown (1988, 1994) argued that self-enhancement is associated with mental well-being. These researchers proposed that "positive illusions" about the self are associated with contentment, high self-esteem, creativity, high effort and persistence at tasks, and coping effectively with stressful events (see also Oettingen & Mayer, 2002). Many findings are consistent with this view. Sandra Murray and John Holmes (1997) found that people in a dating relationship who were very optimistic about the stability of the relationship and who idealized their partner (i.e., who rated their partner more positively than they rated the typical partner) were more likely to remain in that relationship than less optimistic individuals. Perhaps the positive impressions of their partner protected against conflicts and doubts that damaged other relationships. Studies have also linked self-enhancement to better coping with serious illness (e.g., Helgeson & Taylor, 1993) and to success in achievement settings (see Sternberg & Kolligan, 1990).

Other researchers have argued that self-enhancement is not always, or even not usually, adaptive. Instead, these theorists have argued that excessive self-enhancers will be seen as arrogant and selfish (Colvin & Block, 1994; Colvin, Block, & Funder, 1995; Paulhus, 1998). Why would self-enhancement lead to negative impressions of the individual? One possibility is that the negative impressions are caused by unrelenting self-promotion (e.g., bragging), which becomes tiresome over time. It has also been suggested that narcissism (excessive self-admiration) interferes with the establishment of meaningful social relationships with others; people who are overly fond of themselves may fail to make others feel valued and respected.

Nevertheless, greater self-enhancement has been shown to be associated with numerous positive states, including higher self-esteem, lower depression, and greater perceived purpose in life (e.g., Taylor, Kemeny, Reed, Bower, & Gruenewald, 2000; Taylor, Lerner, Sherman, Sage, & McDowell, 2003a). There is even evidence that self-serving tendencies are positively correlated with some biological signs of well-being, including lower cardiovascular responses to stress, more rapid cardiovascular recovery from stress, and lower baseline levels of cortisol—a steroid hormone associated with high chronic levels of stress (Taylor, Lerner, Sherman, Sage, & McDowell, 2003b). It seems likely that at least moderate self-enhancement is beneficial without having negative consequences such as being seen as arrogant and self-absorbed. One situation where self-enhancement may be particularly valuable is when individuals face extreme stress. Extremely adverse situations may simply overwhelm anyone who does not have a strongly positive self-concept. George Bonanno and his colleagues (Bonanno, Field, Kovacevic, & Kaltman, 2002) obtained some evidence consistent with this idea. These researchers interviewed two groups of individuals who had experienced extreme stress: civilians who had lived through four years of civil war in Bosnia, and individuals who had lost a spouse prematurely (between the ages of 21 and 55). All participants completed measures that assessed self-enhancement, and all were interviewed by a mental health professional who rated their adjustment to the stressful events. Results showed that individuals who exhibited high self-enhancement were rated as better adjusted than individuals who exhibited less self-enhancement. Very positive self-views may have served as a buffer against the potential negative impact of adverse life events. But even this study revealed a downside of self-enhancement: participants in the loss-of-spouse sample were videotaped responding to some questions, and when these videotapes were shown to untrained observers, highly self-enhancing participants were rated more negatively on such traits as self-centered, friendly, and honest than were less self-enhancing participants. Thus, extreme self-enhancement had both positive and negative correlates.

## Cultural Differences in Self-Serving Judgments

All of the research on self-serving judgments that we have described to this point was based on North American samples. There are reasons to believe, however, that the tendency toward self-enhancement may differ across cultures.

**Individualist Versus Collectivist Cultures.** Most social psychologists interested in cultural differences have compared two types of societies: individualist and collectivist (see Fiske, Kitayama, Markus, & Nisbett, 1998; Hui, 1988; Oyserman, Coon, & Kemmelmeier, 2002; Sorrentino, Cohen, Olson, & Zanna, 2005; Triandis, 1995). Individualist cultures include most Western European (e.g., United Kingdom, Germany) and North American countries (e.g., United States, Canada), whereas collectivist cultures include most East Asian (e.g., China, Japan) and African countries (e.g., Nigeria, Egypt). These two groups of societies have different views of the "self," as well as different views of what is good and what is healthy for people in society. In Chapter 5, The Person in the Situation, we will discuss cultural differences in identity and the self-concept. In the current section, we consider the implications of this dimension for self-serving judgments.

First, we need to describe the individualism–collectivism dimension in a little more detail (see Fiske et al., 1998; Markus & Kitayama, 1991). Let's begin with individualism: what are some of the key beliefs and attitudes in these societies? In **individualist cultures,** people are seen as free, independent beings who possess stable abilities, traits, and attitudes. "Healthy individuals" are considered to be those who have a strong sense of identity, who feel good about themselves, and who have achieved individual success (e.g., personal wealth, fame). Personal identity is defined largely in terms of how people are unique and different from others.

In **collectivist cultures,** however, people are seen as part of a social fabric that joins individuals together. Group needs are emphasized above individual needs. People are seen as *interdependent* rather than independent. "Healthy individuals" are considered to be those who understand their connections to others, who feel good about their social roles, and who contribute effectively to harmonious group functioning. Group achievements are valued above individual achievements. Personal identity is defined largely in terms of people's social roles and relationships.

**individualist cultures**

*cultures in which people are seen as independent beings who possess stable abilities, traits, and attitudes*

**collectivist cultures**

*cultures in which people are seen as interdependent beings who should contribute to harmonious group functioning*

*Interviewer: "I see that you designed a computer program for academic advising. Can you tell me what you did to develop that program?"*

*Job candidate: "Not really so much. I could see that much of advising is based on rules, so I only needed to write a program simple enough for advisors to use. It was not that hard."*

**Cultural Differences in Unrealistic Self-Evaluation.** Steve Heine and Darrin Lehman (1997b) proposed that data showing excessively positive self-evaluation by North American students reflected the fact that Western society "encourages people to think positively about themselves as a means to approach the culturally defined ideals of independence and autonomy" (p. 1269). They argued that, in contrast, people from collectivist cultures are encouraged to gain a sense of belongingness, which is not achieved by perceiving the self as better than other people.

To test the prediction that unrealistic self-evaluation is absent or weaker in collectivist cultures, Heine and Lehman (1997b) collected data from college students in Canada and Japan. On one task, participants were asked to estimate the percentage of the population of the same age and gender as themselves who were better than they on 10 desirable traits, 5 of which were selected to be "independent" or "individualistic" in nature (attractive, interesting, independent, confident, and intelligent) and 5 of which were selected to be "interdependent" or "collectivistic" in nature (cooperative, loyal, considerate, hardworking, and dependable). Participants were also asked to identify the member of their own family to whom they "felt closest." They then estimated the percentage of the population of the same age and gender as their family member who were better than this family member on each of the 10 traits. These judgments about a family member were included as another test of self-enhancement, because believing that one's family members are better than average should make people feel good about themselves as well.

The researchers calculated the percentages of the matched population that participants believed were better than they (or their family member) on the 5 independent traits and on the 5 interdependent traits. Estimates would be expected to hover around 50% if people were making unbiased judgments. Estimates substantially smaller than 50% would suggest unrealistically positive self-evaluations—relatively few people are better than you (or your family member).

Figure 4.10 presents the average estimates for Canadian and Japanese participants on the four principal measures. Notice that the Canadian respondents showed biased self-evaluations on *all* of the judgments: both self and family member on both independent and interdependent traits, with an average of approxi-

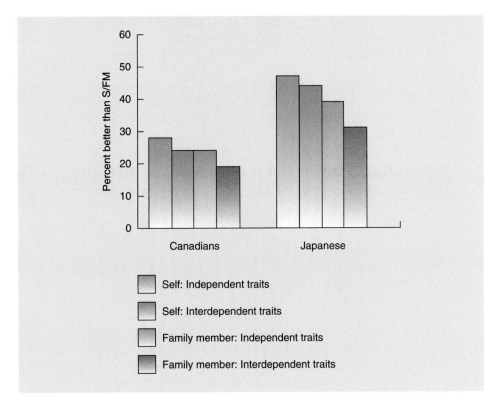

**FIGURE 4.10** Estimated percent of matched population who are better than self or family member

From Heine and Lehman, "The cultural construction of self-enhancement: An examination of group-serving biases," *Journal of Personality and Social Psychology*, 72, 1268–1283, Table 1, p. 1272, 1997. Copyright © 1997 by the American Psychological Association. Reprinted by permission.

mately 25% of the population estimated to be better than the self or family member. In contrast, Japanese respondents gave higher (more modest) estimates on all of the items, with an average of approximately 40% of the population estimated to be better than the self or family member. For judgments about the self, Japanese participants showed almost no unrealistic self-evaluation at all, with their estimates coming quite close to 50%. For judgments about their family member, Japanese participants did show some positive enhancement, but less than was exhibited by Canadian respondents. It is interesting that even on *interdependent* traits, Japanese respondents showed less self-evaluative bias than Canadian respondents. Given that interdependent traits are highly valued in collectivist cultures, a positive bias by Japanese respondents might be expected, but this did not occur.

A different pattern of findings was obtained, however, by Constantine Sedikides, Lowell Gaertner, and Yoshiyasu Toguchi (2003). These researchers asked American and Japanese college students to rate themselves on a number of desirable personality traits, compared to the typical member of their group. Some traits were individualistic (e.g., independent, original) and others were collectivistic (e.g., respectful, good listener). Figure 4.11 (p. 144) depicts the findings. Both cultural groups self-enhanced (rated themselves as significantly higher than the average member of their group) on both kinds of traits. American students self-enhanced more than Japanese students on the individualistic traits, whereas Japanese students self-enhanced more than American students on the collectivistic traits. Thus, both American and Japanese respondents showed self-enhancement, especially on the traits that were most valued in their culture.

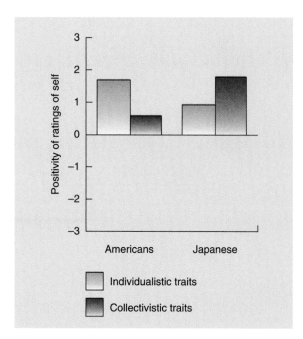

**FIGURE 4.11** Ratings of self versus typical group member on desirable personality traits

From Sedikides et al., "Pancultural self-enhancement," *Journal of Personality and Social Psychology,* 84, 60–79, Table 3, p. 66, 2003. Copyright © 2003 by the American Psychological Association. Reprinted by permission.

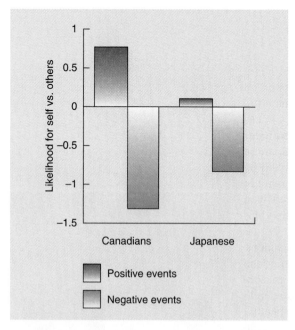

**FIGURE 4.12** Predicted likelihood of positive and negative events for self versus others

From Heine and Lehman, "Cultural variation in unrealistic optimism: Does the West feel more invulnerable than the East?" *Journal of Personality and Social Psychology,* 68, 595–607, Table 1, p. 599, 1995. Copyright © 1995 by the American Psychological Association. Reprinted by permission.

What are we to conclude from these conflicting results? Clearly, the issue is not settled. On balance, however, it seems likely that members of collectivist cultures engage in *less* unrealistic self-evaluation than do members of individualist cultures, but they still self-enhance to some degree (see also Kitayama & Uchida, 2003). Also, there may be some collectivist cultures whose self-evaluations are very similar to those in individualist cultures (e.g., see Kurman, 2001).

**Cultural Differences in Unrealistic Optimism.** Heine and Lehman (1995) also suggested that members of collectivist cultures might not show unrealistic optimism about their future, because they do not want to isolate themselves from others in their culture by perceiving themselves and their futures much more favorably than average.

To test this reasoning, Heine and Lehman (1995) recruited Canadian and Japanese college students and asked them to estimate the likelihood that they would experience a variety of positive and negative life events. They were specifically asked, "Compared to other university students of the same sex as you, what do you think are the chances that the following events will happen to you?" Possible answers ranged from –3 (much below average) to 0 (average for other university students of your sex) to +3 (much above average). The events that people estimated included 5 positive events, such as "You will live past the age of 80" and "Sometime in the future you will own your own home," and 10 negative events, such as "Sometime in the future you will become an alcoholic" and "You will have a heart attack before the age of 50."

For the positive events, positive scores reflected optimism (more likely to happen to self), whereas for the negative events, negative scores reflected optimism (less likely to happen to self). Answers close to 0 constituted unbiased estimates. Figure 4.12 presents the mean likelihood ratings for Canadian and Japanese respondents. The results showed that Canadian participants were unrealistically optimistic about both positive and negative events. Japanese participants, on the other hand, showed no optimistic bias for positive events, and a weaker optimistic bias for negative events than did Canadian respondents. Thus, participants from a collectivist culture showed less unrealistic optimism than did participants from an individualist culture, as the researchers had predicted.

These and other data (see also Chang & Asakawa, 2003; Chang, Asakawa, & Sanna, 2001) have indicated that members of collectivist cultures exhibit weaker optimistic biases than do members of individualist cultures. These differences are consistent with the reduced tendency for unrealistic self-evaluation outlined in the previous section. Presumably, the interdependent self that is fostered in collectivist cultures minimizes perceived differences between the self and others, even in predictions for the future (see also Cohen & Hoshino-Browne, 2005).

# I Think I Can: Self-Efficacy in Everyday Life

Have you ever had the sinking feeling that you would probably *not* be able to do something that you were supposed to do (or something that you wanted to do)? Perhaps you avoided your text-book readings for a course until the day before the exam and then realized that there was no way you'd be able to read all of the chapters carefully. Or perhaps, in a moment of enthusiasm on New Year's Eve, you publicly resolved that you would start exercising regularly, but the next morning you were not at all confident that your exercise commitment would last very long. Each of these situations involves the belief that you are not capable of performing particular behaviors (reading all chapters carefully, exercising regularly). Now an important question: How would your belief affect your actual behavior? Would you try even harder to succeed? Or, instead, would you give up quickly and stop trying?

Members of *collectivist cultures,* such as these Chinese students, tend to show less positive self-evaluations and less optimism about their future than do members of *individualist cultures,* such as American students.

Albert Bandura (1977, 1991) proposed that feelings of **self-efficacy** are very important determinants of whether people achieve goals that they have set for themselves. Self-efficacy refers to the belief that you are capable of performing a particular behavior that is required for a particular goal. Bandura argued that when people doubt that they can perform a behavior, they are less likely to attempt it and are less likely to persist in the face of obstacles or failure. Bandura, therefore, would predict that you would quickly give up in the situations described above. You would try to read some of the text-book chapters carefully but quit when you began to feel confused; you would exercise once or twice but then stop as soon as you found it slightly inconvenient to continue. Note that these decisions to stop would occur in response to events that virtually everyone would experience in the situations. *Everyone* feels confused when initially trying to read a large number of chapters; exercise will *inevitably* be inconvenient sometimes. Thus, the lack of self-efficacy almost guarantees that the goal will not be achieved.

**self-efficacy**
*the belief that we are capable of performing a particular behavior that is required for a certain goal*

High self-efficacy, relative to low, has been shown in many studies to predict both undertaking a behavior and continuing a behavior despite negative feedback (see Bandura, 1986; Mischel, Cantor, & Feldman, 1996). If you are confident that you will be able to perform the necessary things to do well in a math course, such as reading and understanding the textbook, completing assignments successfully, and solving questions on exams, then you are more likely to enroll in the course and more likely to stay in the course even if an early test goes poorly than if you lack such confidence. When we have high self-efficacy, we interpret problems and failures as temporary and correctable—after all, we believe that we are capable of performing the necessary behaviors. This perception that failure can be overcome is associated with increased effort and persistence (e.g., Dweck, 1986; Dweck & Leggett, 1988; Oettingen & Mayer, 2002).

The concept of self-efficacy has also been applied to understanding why some people cope with adversity better than do others. When people feel confident that they can perform actions that are necessary for coping, they show better adjustment to such stressors as the pain of rheumatoid arthritis, coping with abortion, and adjusting to new parenthood (e.g., Cozzarelli, 1993; Cutrona & Troutman, 1986; Major, Cozzarelli, Sciacchitano, Cooper, Testa, & Mueller, 1990; Schiaffino & Revenson, 1992).

**Illusions of Control?** Self-efficacy is a form of control: people believe that they can perform an action successfully. In general, people are motivated to believe that they have control over their environment. What about you? Do you feel that you have control over your outcomes in most situations? An absence of control would clearly be undesirable, because then you might not be able to obtain necessary resources and avoid negative events.

**illusion of control**

*the tendency to overestimate our control of situations and events*

Given that we want to see ourselves as having control, it may not be surprising to learn that we often think we have *more* control than we really do. There is a general tendency for people to overestimate their control of situations and events. This **illusion of control** has been documented by several researchers (see Crocker, 1981; Langer, 1975; Taylor & Brown, 1988). A good example of the illusion of control is superstitious beliefs. Many people believe that certain rituals are associated with better outcomes (e.g., wearing your "lucky socks" when you play baseball). In reality, these superstitious beliefs are fallacious (except, perhaps, your lucky socks) and reflect, at least in part, our desire to perceive ourselves as in control.

We noted earlier that theorists have argued about whether self-enhancement is associated with better or worse functioning (e.g., Colvin & Block, 1994; Taylor & Brown, 1988). Illusions of control are another form of self-enhancing response that could potentially have either adaptive or maladaptive consequences. Perceived control might be adaptive because believing that one has control will encourage persistence at an activity: we may try again if we did not initially succeed. Indeed, when people believe that they have no control over events in their life, they often show symptoms of **learned helplessness**—a state of apathy, in which people simply give up trying to achieve their goals because they believe they lack control (Seligman, 1975). Learned helplessness is one possible cause of depression (Abramson, Metalsky, & Alloy, 1989).

**learned helplessness**

*a state of apathy in which we simply give up trying to achieve our goals*

On the other hand, it is probably maladaptive to keep attempting behaviors that are completely beyond our control. Believing that we have control when we do not may lead to repeated failure. Social psychologists Janet Polivy and Peter Herman (2002) coined the term **false hope syndrome** to refer to cases in which individuals repeatedly try and fail to achieve a goal (e.g., losing weight, stopping smoking) because they have unrealistic expectations about their likelihood of success. This syndrome is described in the accompanying box, Social Psychology in Your Life: The False Hope Syndrome.

**false hope syndrome**

*the tendency to try repeatedly but unsuccessfully to achieve a goal because of unrealistic expectations about the likelihood of success*

## Self-Perception in the Health Domain: Self-Discrepancy Theory

Do you ever think about characteristics that you *wish* you had? Perhaps you wish that you were more extraverted, or that you were better in math, or that you could sing. We already know from Chapter 3 that these thoughts qualify as *counterfactual thoughts* because they refer to how things could have been different. In the present context, these thoughts are important because they refer to an alternative conception of yourself: the way that you would ideally like to be. How does it make you feel when you think about the features that you would like to possess but do not?

Let's take another perspective on the self. Are there qualities that you think you *ought* to possess but do not? These characteristics are things that you *should* do or be. Perhaps you think that you should be less selfish, or that you should work harder, or that you should exercise more often. These features represent yet another alternative conception of yourself: the way you think you ought to be. How does it make you feel when you think about the features that you ought to possess but do not? Are these feelings different from the ones you imagined in the preceding paragraph?

**actual self**

*a conception of the self describing our perception of how we really are*

**ideal self**

*a conception of the self describing our perception of how we would ideally like to be*

**Actual, Ideal, and Ought Selves.** Psychologists have recognized for a long time that people have multiple conceptions of themselves (e.g., Cooley, 1902; James, 1890). The most frequently discussed self-conceptions have been the **actual self,** how people believe they really are, and the **ideal self,** how people would ideally like themselves to be (e.g., Colby, 1968; Rogers, 1961). Theorists have predicted that when the actual and ideal selves differ substantially, people will have low self-esteem.

# Social Psychology in Your Life    *The False Hope Syndrome*

Do you make New Year's resolutions? Most adults do. How successful have you been in keeping your resolutions? If you're like most people, you haven't done very well. In fact, you may have failed numerous times with the same resolution. James Prochaska, Carlo DiClemente, and John Norcross (1992) reported that, on average, people make the same pledge for five or more years before they manage to keep their resolution for six months. Also, approximately 60% of those who break their resolution will make the same one again the next year.

Why do we so often fail to keep our resolutions? Janet Polivy and Peter Herman (2002) suggested that most of us have unrealistic expectations about our ability to change our behavior (in general, not only at New Year's), which produce what they termed the *false hope syndrome*. This syndrome involves exaggerated feelings of control and overconfidence about our ability to change our behavior successfully. We often begin with an unrealistic goal (e.g., "I will exercise for two hours every day!"). We also underestimate how difficult it will be to change our behavior (e.g., "I'll have no trouble stopping smoking!"). Finally, we tend to expect dramatic, rapid results (e.g., "I'll probably lose about 10 pounds a week!"). Given these erroneous expectations, it is not surprising that we usually fail. When the new behavior proves to be

more difficult than we anticipated, and when visible results turn out to be slow, we often abandon our attempt to change.

But why doesn't the false hope syndrome disappear? Why do we *keep* trying again and again to achieve the same goals? Why don't we learn from our failures and direct our energies elsewhere? Polivy and Herman argued that we often explain our failures in ways that maintain false hope for the future. For instance, we often blame ourselves for not trying hard enough (e.g., "If only I try a bit harder next time, I'm sure I'll succeed"). We may also blame external circumstances for our failure and decide that these circumstance are unlikely to occur again (e.g., "I won't be as busy next year as I have been this year, so I'll have more time to exercise"). Thus, we remain hopeful—often unrealistically hopeful—that we'll succeed in our next attempt. We convince ourselves that *this* diet will be easier to follow than the Atkins diet, or *this* method for quitting smoking will be more effective than going cold turkey, or *this* kind of exercise will be less boring than using a stationary bicycle. Unfortunately, the new strategy is often no easier, no more effective, or

People often make the same resolution year after year to change their behavior despite previous failures, which might reflect the false hope syndrome.

no less boring than the last one, and we fail again.

Polivy and Herman (2002) did not argue that we should give up attempting self-improvement. Rather, they suggested that we adopt realistic goals (thereby avoiding overly ambitious plans) and recognize that success will be difficult. If we understand that changing our behavior will be challenging and results may be slow, we are less likely to become discouraged quickly and more likely to structure our environment to encourage our new lifestyle (e.g., by convincing another person to join us or help us). The key is to recognize false hopes and work to replace them with realistic determination.

---

Tory Higgins (1987, 1989) agreed that the actual and ideal selves are important, but added another self-conception to the mix: the **ought self,** how people think they ought to be (see also Ausubel, 1955; Schafer, 1967). The ought self is similar to the notion of a conscience. Higgins integrated these ideas in his **self-discrepancy theory,** which hypothesized that perceived discrepancies between the actual self and either the ideal self or the ought self have important (and different) consequences.

Before we discuss the consequences of self-discrepancies, let's describe how the different selves can be measured. In one procedure, participants are asked to list up to 10 attributes that they think they *actually* possess, up to 10 attributes that they would like *ideally* to possess, and up to 10 attributes that they believe they *should* or *ought* to possess. Participants are told that they can use the same or

**ought self**

*a conception of ourself describing our perception of how we think we should or ought to be*

**self-discrepancy theory**

*a theory proposing that perceived differences between the actual self and the ideal self produce depression, and perceived differences between the actual self and the ought self produce anxiety*

different attributes in more than one category. The researcher then compares participants' responses to the different selves. If attributes listed for the actual self and the ideal or ought self are similar, then discrepancy scores are low. If attributes listed for the actual self are opposite from attributes listed for the ideal or ought self, then discrepancy scores are high. The scores can be conceptualized as representing the extent to which people believe that they have failed to measure up to what they would ideally like to be or to how they think they ought to be.

**Implications for Depression and Anxiety.** We asked you to reflect on how you feel when you think about characteristics that you would like to possess but do not and when you think about characteristics that you ought to possess but do not. Did you imagine that the feelings were different? In self-discrepancy theory, Higgins predicted that the two kinds of discrepancies have very different emotional consequences, and empirical tests have supported his predictions (e.g., Higgins, Bond, Klein, & Strauman, 1986; Higgins, Klein, & Strauman, 1985).

Higgins proposed that when we fail to achieve our ideals (the things we want to be), we experience negative emotion along a *dejection* dimension. He suggested that this situation is psychologically experienced as the absence of positive things: we do not possess things that we want to possess. We therefore feel unhappy, disappointed, sad, and depressed (negative dejection emotions). In contrast, Higgins proposed that when we fail to live up to our ought self (the things we should be, our conscience), we experience negative emotion along an *agitation* dimension. He suggested that this situation is psychologically experienced as the presence of negative things: we believe that we have behaved inappropriately and are worried that we may be punished or criticized. We therefore feel anxious, guilty, nervous, and ashamed (negative agitation emotions). Thus, discrepancy between the actual and ideal selves is expected to produce depression, whereas discrepancy between the actual and ought selves is expected to produce anxiety. The key elements of self-discrepancy theory are summarized in the accompanying Concept Review.

The most common psychological complaints reported to clinical psychologists and psychiatrists are depression and anxiety. Depression and anxiety are extremely common problems, which are experienced by most of us sometime during our lifetime. Higgins's work on self-discrepancy theory links a particular pattern of self-perceptions to each of these two states. He proposed that failure to reach our ideals can lead to depression, whereas failure to live up to our obligations can lead to anxiety. This reasoning provides possible clues to clinical psychologists about where they might focus their treatment of these common problems.

## CONCEPT REVIEW
### Self-Discrepancy Theory

| Concept | Description | Example | Consequences of Discrepancies |
|---|---|---|---|
| Actual self | How we believe we actually are | I am intelligent. | |
| Ideal self | How we would ideally like to be | I would like to be a good singer. | |
| Ought self | How we think we should or ought to be | I should attend a religious service at least once a week. | |
| Discrepancy between actual and ideal selves | Failing to achieve our ideals | I will never be a good singer. | Depression and sadness |
| Discrepancy between actual and ought selves | Failing to fulfill our obligations | I almost never attend a religious service. | Anxiety and guilt |

 # What Others See in Us

Do you often think about the fact that other people make judgments about *you*? Do you wonder what sort of impression you make on people you meet for the first time? Do you sometimes try to *create* a certain impression?

In this section, we consider some of these issues. We describe how people present themselves publicly, especially to achieve the goals of appearing likable and competent. We discuss a potentially maladaptive strategy that people sometimes use to give themselves an excuse for failure. We also address the issue of whether people can tell when someone is lying.

## All the World's a Stage: Managing Others' Impressions

Professional actors deliberately portray roles they are given. They make themselves appear angry, happy, or depressed, depending on the character and the setting they are depicting. There is skill and artistry in the acting trade.

Does your life sometimes feel like it is on a stage? Are you an actor portraying your life in a certain manner? Or, instead, is your public life always fully spontaneous and "honest"? Sociologists and social psychologists have suggested that most of us fall in between these extremes: we do not always monitor our behavior and try to make a particular impression, but neither do we always behave in an open, unrestrained fashion. We are selective actors; when it is important, we adopt deliberate guises to achieve particular goals.

This deliberate control of our public behavior to create a certain impression is called **self-presentation** and also **impression management**: we "present" the self to others, and our goal is to "manage" their impression of us (Baumeister, 1982, 1998; Leary, 1995; Schlenker, 1980). We engage in self-presentation in many different settings with many different people.

How can a researcher show that someone is engaging in self-presentation? People are unlikely to admit that they are trying to manage someone's impression of them, so evidence must be obtained in an indirect way. The most common strategy for testing self-presentation predictions has been to compare situations in which people's behavior is public with situations in which their behavior is private. If public behavior differs from private behavior, then individuals are modifying their actions because someone can observe them, which constitutes self-presentation (Baumeister, 1982; Leary, 1995). For example, Kay Satow (1975) showed that public donations to charities were larger than private donations, presumably because people were trying to appear generous in the public condition (see also Olson, Hafer, Couzens, & Kramins, 2000).

Think about your own public behavior. Do you ever act differently when other people can see you? Do you express somewhat different attitudes to different people? If so (and almost all of us do), then your public behavior sometimes reflects impression management.

**Self-Presentation Goals.** Think about the times that you have tried to make a certain impression on someone. What were your goals? Can you think of an occasion when you wanted to appear dangerous or strong so others would be afraid of you (e.g., to intimidate members of an opposing sports team)? Can you think of another time when you wanted someone to think you were moral and virtuous (e.g., to impress your imam, priest, or rabbi)?

Although appearing dangerous or virtuous can serve as self-presentation goals in some circumstances, Ned Jones and Thane Pittman (1982) proposed that two other goals are more common. Indeed, Jones and Pittman argued that these two

**self-presentation**
*the deliberate control of our public behavior to create a certain impression*

**impression management**
*self-presentation*

goals are operative almost *all* of the time—they are so basic that they are virtually "automatic" parts of our public personae. The two self-presentation goals are to appear *likable* and to appear *competent*.

**ingratiation**

*behavior designed to make someone like us*

**Ingratiation** is behavior that is designed to make someone like you. What actions are common examples of ingratiation? Flattery is one; friendliness is another; giving gifts and doing favors are still others. Jones and Pittman suggested that we almost always want to appear likable, so our public behavior follows certain rules without our even thinking about it. For example, we are polite to everyone, unless there is preexisting dislike or a conflict of interest between us and another person. Our public face is almost always happy, friendly, and relaxed; we want to appear well-adjusted and comfortable with ourselves and others (even when we may not *feel* comfortable).

Ingratiation has some risks, because other people may know that we want them to like us. Excessive flattery and syrupy friendliness can elicit suspicion, which can actually lead to less rather than more liking (Jones & Wortman, 1973). When you walk into a store and a salesperson walks up and greets you warmly, do you believe that he or she really likes you a lot? Probably not. This risk of appearing false is particularly great when we are highly dependent on someone, because the person will be more aware that we might be trying to evoke liking. Imagine that you have a part-time job at a grocery store. It is more important for you to get your boss to like you than it is to get a coworker to like you. Unfortunately, flattering your boss is more likely to be suspected than flattering your coworker. Ironically, then, when ingratiation is most important (because we are highly dependent on someone), it is most likely to arouse suspicion. Fortunately, most people like being flattered or receiving gifts, so they are often quite willing to overlook the possibility that our friendly behavior is based on ulterior motives (see Vonk, 2002).

**self-promotion**

*behavior designed to make someone respect us*

**Self-promotion** is behavior that is designed to make someone respect you. What actions exemplify self-promotion? Bragging is an obvious example, but it can elicit negative reactions. What can you do besides boasting if you want to look competent? *Performing well* is a good start! Showing effort also engenders respect, and self-confidence is helpful as well. Jones and Pittman proposed that, similar to likability, we virtually always want to be seen as competent. As a result, we automatically try to appear intelligent, motivated, and competent.

Job interviews are a wonderful place to investigate self-promotion, because candidates are trying very hard to look competent. Researchers who have studied job interviews have found that self-promotion strategies generally do increase the perceived competence of the candidate (e.g., Kacmar, Delery, & Ferris, 1992; Stevens & Kristof, 1995). Self-promotion can also have the unintended effect, however, of reducing liking, especially for female candidates (Rudman, 1998). Why would women be particularly vulnerable to this unintended effect of reduced liking? Perhaps because frankly stating one's accomplishments is inconsistent with the stereotypical expectation that women will be modest (Miller, Cooke, Tsang, & Morgan, 1992).

Candidates in job interviews try to appear competent, which is a form of *self-presentation* known as *self-promotion*.

## Self-Handicapping: Setting Yourself Up for Failure

Imagine that you report for an experiment and learn that you will be taking a test of analogical reasoning, which involves selecting the correct answer for questions like "Puppy is to dog as _____ is to cow," with the possible answers being *meat, milk, calf,* and *bull* (the correct answer is *calf*). For almost all of the items, however, you cannot identify any response that makes sense, so you end up just guessing. You give your response sheet to the experimenter and wait for the bad news while he scores it in another room. To your considerable surprise, when the experimenter returns, he congratulates you on your outstanding performance and says that your score is one of the best he has seen. You can only conclude that you were lucky enough to guess right on a lot of the items.

Now comes the interesting part. The experimenter says that you will be taking another test of analogical reasoning, because he is studying the effects of drugs on performance. You will therefore ingest a drug and take another test. The experimenter says he does not care which specific drug you take, so you can select between two drugs: *pandocrin* and *actavil.* One of the drugs is expected to improve performance on analogical reasoning, and the other is expected to impair or worsen performance. You can choose whichever one you like.

Which drug would you choose? The one that is expected to improve your performance or the one that is expected to worsen your performance? Why?

When Steven Berglas and Ned Jones (1978) conducted a study that used a similar procedure, most participants chose the drug that was expected to *hurt* their performance—the drug that would actually increase their chances of performing *poorly.* Why did this pattern occur? The authors suggested that participants were worried that they would not perform well on the next test (because they were just lucky on the first test) and wanted to give themselves an *excuse* for doing badly. By taking the performance-impairing drug, participants could blame their poor performance on the drug rather than on their lack of analogical reasoning skill.

This tendency to seek or create inhibitory factors that interfere with performance and thus provide an explanation for potential failure has been termed **self-handicapping** (Higgins, Snyder, & Berglas, 1990; Jones & Berglas, 1978). This strategy involves deliberately doing something that can hurt performance so that failure will not imply low ability. Self-handicapping is often employed in the service of protecting the public appearance of competence and represents a clear example of self-presentation (Arkin & Baumgardner, 1985; Rhodewalt, 1990).

Can you think of methods of self-handicapping that you have used or that you have seen others use? One technique is simply not preparing—not studying for a test or not practicing a task. If people know that Rachel was out late at a movie and did not study before a math test, they will not necessarily infer from poor performance that she is poor at math (although they might draw *other* negative inferences about her, such as being unmotivated—see Luginbuhl & Palmer, 1991; Rhodewalt, Sanbonmatsu, Tschanz, Feick, & Waller, 1995). Another possibility is taking on an obstacle that must be overcome. If a boy is worried that he might lose a one-on-one game of basketball to a girl, he might say "I'll play you with one hand held behind my back!" If he loses this game, it does not mean that the girl is better at basketball—after all, he had one hand behind his back. And if he happens to win, he will look *really* good. A third possible self-handicapping strategy is to simply *claim* that you did not prepare, or that you are sick, or that you have been under a lot of stress. These claimed impediments provide you with an excuse that, depending on the situation, can be effective in protecting your public image of competence (e.g., Leary & Shepperd, 1986; Smith, Snyder, & Perkins, 1983). The first two methods of self-handicapping (not preparing and taking on an obstacle) have been termed *behavioral* self-handicapping, because they involve actually creating impediments to performance, whereas the third method has been called *self-reported* self-handicapping, because it involves simply claiming that an impediment was present (Arkin & Baumgardner, 1985; Leary & Shepperd, 1986).

**self-handicapping**

*the tendency to seek, create, or claim inhibitory factors that interfere with performance and thus provide an explanation for potential failure*

© Royalty-Free/CORBIS

Drinking heavily the night before an exam might reflect *self-handicapping.*

It may seem as though self-handicapping has no downside. If people fail, it doesn't reflect badly on them, and if they succeed, they look great. But behavioral self-handicapping does have a downside, a *big* downside: it increases the actual likelihood of poor performance (e.g., Rhodewalt & Fairfield, 1991; Tice & Baumeister, 1990). By failing to study for a test, for example, individuals might directly cause their own failure, which might *not* have occurred if they had studied; thus, the individuals generated an excuse for failure, but no excuse would have been necessary if the excuse hadn't been generated! (Whew. Did you follow that?) To put it another way, if people think that they might need an excuse for failure and take steps to create such an excuse, they might *cause* the very failure that they fear.

Researchers have uncovered a gender difference in self-handicapping: men are more likely to *behaviorally* self-handicap (i.e., take on actual impediments) than are women (see Hirt, Deppe, & Gordon, 1991; Hirt, McCrea, & Kimble, 2000; Janes, 2003). The two sexes engage in *self-reported* self-handicapping about equally. Why do men engage in behavioral self-handicapping more than women? One possibility is that men are more threatened by potential failure than are women, which makes them more willing to risk damaging their own performance. A second possibility is that women know that self-handicapping is ineffective for them because observers tend to attribute women's failures to lack of ability even when external impediments are present (e.g., Dweck, Goetz, & Strauss, 1980; Hirt et al., 1991). If self-handicapping is unlikely to work for women in the first place, then there is little reason to absorb the real costs of taking on an impediment.

**Individual Differences in the Tendency to Engage in Self-Handicapping.** In addition to a gender difference in self-handicapping, there are differences between individuals in their general tendency to engage in this behavior. That is, some people self-handicap more often than do other people. Edward Jones and Frederick Rhodewalt (1982) developed the **self-handicapping scale** to measure this tendency. Sample items from the scale are presented in Know Yourself 4.3: The Self-Handicapping Scale. Answer the items to see whether you tend to score high or low on this dimension.

Researchers have found that scores on this scale predict whether people will actually engage in self-handicapping behavior in experimental settings (for a review, see Rhodewalt, 1990). High scorers are more likely than low scorers to take on handicaps that provide excuses for poor performance.

**self-handicapping scale**

*a scale that measures how often people engage in self-handicapping behavior*

## Return to the Correspondence Bias

No discussion of "what others see in us" would be complete without consideration of the correspondence bias. Recall from earlier in the chapter that the correspondence bias refers to the tendency to explain other people's actions using internal concepts, such as personality traits and attitudes, more than we should. We tend to see other people's behavior as reflecting stable, internal characteristics.

Guess what? Other people are committing the correspondence bias with *you* as the target. Your friends and acquaintances are forming (or have formed) clear and confident impressions of your personality. Some of these impressions are undoubtedly accurate: we do differ in shyness, self-esteem, and other characteristics (see Chapter 5). But you would probably be surprised by some people's impressions of you. In fact, it is quite likely that different people have opposing impressions of you, which means that someone *must* be wrong. You are probably seen as friendly by some people but aloof by others, helpful by some people but selfish by others, and mature by some people but self-centered by others. Where do these competing impressions come from? Perceivers are willing to draw inferences about personality traits based on very little evidence, so small snippets of behavior will suffice to

# Know Yourself 4.3
## *The Self-Handicapping Scale*

Please indicate the extent to which you agree or disagree with each of the following statements by circling the appropriate number on the answer scale.

1. When I do something wrong, my first impulse is to blame the circumstances.

| 0 | 1 | 2 | 3 | 4 | 5 |
|---|---|---|---|---|---|
| Disagree very much | Disagree pretty much | Disagree a little | Agree a little | Agree pretty much | Agree very much |

2. I tend to put things off to the last moment.

| 0 | 1 | 2 | 3 | 4 | 5 |
|---|---|---|---|---|---|
| Disagree very much | Disagree pretty much | Disagree a little | Agree a little | Agree pretty much | Agree very much |

3. I always try to do my best, no matter what.

| 0 | 1 | 2 | 3 | 4 | 5 |
|---|---|---|---|---|---|
| Disagree very much | Disagree pretty much | Disagree a little | Agree a little | Agree pretty much | Agree very much |

4. I tend to get very anxious before an exam or "performance."

| 0 | 1 | 2 | 3 | 4 | 5 |
|---|---|---|---|---|---|
| Disagree very much | Disagree pretty much | Disagree a little | Agree a little | Agree pretty much | Agree very much |

5. I would rather be respected for doing my best than admired for my potential.

| 0 | 1 | 2 | 3 | 4 | 5 |
|---|---|---|---|---|---|
| Disagree very much | Disagree pretty much | Disagree a little | Agree a little | Agree pretty much | Agree very much |

6. I sometimes enjoy being mildly ill for a day or two because it takes off the pressure.

| 0 | 1 | 2 | 3 | 4 | 5 |
|---|---|---|---|---|---|
| Disagree very much | Disagree pretty much | Disagree a little | Agree a little | Agree pretty much | Agree very much |

7. I would rather not take any drug that interfered with my ability to think clearly and do the right thing.

| 0 | 1 | 2 | 3 | 4 | 5 |
|---|---|---|---|---|---|
| Disagree very much | Disagree pretty much | Disagree a little | Agree a little | Agree pretty much | Agree very much |

8. I admit that I am tempted to rationalize when I don't live up to others' expectations.

| 0 | 1 | 2 | 3 | 4 | 5 |
|---|---|---|---|---|---|
| Disagree very much | Disagree pretty much | Disagree a little | Agree a little | Agree pretty much | Agree very much |

9. When something important is coming up, like an exam or a job interview, I try to get as much sleep as possible the night before.

| 0 | 1 | 2 | 3 | 4 | 5 |
|---|---|---|---|---|---|
| Disagree very much | Disagree pretty much | Disagree a little | Agree a little | Agree pretty much | Agree very much |

10. I often think that I have more than my share of bad luck in sports, card games, and other measures of talent.

| 0 | 1 | 2 | 3 | 4 | 5 |
|---|---|---|---|---|---|
| Disagree very much | Disagree pretty much | Disagree a little | Agree a little | Agree pretty much | Agree very much |

**SCORING:** Items 1, 2, 4, 6, 8, and 10 are scored using the answer scales as provided (0-1-2-3-4-5); Items 3, 5, 7, and 9 are reverse-scored (that is, 5-4-3-2-1-0). Add up all of the items for your self-handicapping score. Possible scores range from 0 to 50, and higher scores represent stronger tendencies to engage in self-handicapping.

Sample items from Jones and Rhodewalt. "Self-handicapping scale," 1982 (unpublished). Department of Psychology, Princeton University, and Department of Psychology, University of Utah. Reprinted by permission of the authors.

form an impression. If different people are exposed to different snippets, they may come to differing conclusions about your personality. Also, people tend to see you in one particular situation: your siblings see you mainly at home, your teachers see you mainly at school, and your friends see you mainly in social settings. Do your siblings, teachers, and friends have the same impressions of you? Unlikely.

What can you do about people forming quick or erroneous impressions of your personality? Probably very little. For people who are important to you, you might monitor whether they have drawn a trait inference that you think is wrong. In such cases, calm discussion of their impression might be warranted. You might also want to keep in mind, however, the evidence presented earlier on self-serving tendencies in self-perception: your own view of your qualities might be enhanced to some extent by rose-colored glasses.

**The Actor–Observer Difference.** Other people tend to attribute your behavior to your internal dispositions and traits, and, in return, you tend to attribute their behavior to their internal dispositions and traits; these patterns constitute the correspondence bias. But how do people view the causes of their *own* behavior? Does the correspondence bias occur for self-attributions? No. To explain their own behavior, people tend to focus on *external* factors. This pattern of differences in attributions has been called the **actor–observer difference:** actors tend to make external attributions for their own behavior, whereas observers tend to make internal attributions for the same actions (Jones & Nisbett, 1972).

Why does the actor–observer difference occur? The "observer" part of the phenomenon reflects the correspondence bias, which we have already said occurs for several reasons (e.g., the situational factors guiding other people's behavior are often subtle or nonobvious). Where does the "actor" part come from? Why do we attribute our own behavior more externally than do observers? Think about yourself: why might you give greater weight than observers to environmental causes for your own behavior? Social psychologists have suggested one important reason is that we have a lot of knowledge about our own behavior in the past. We know that we have been outgoing in one social situation but reserved in another, that we have been kind and generous toward one person but more selfish toward another, and that we have been happy and contented sometimes but unhappy and depressed at other times. Knowing these variations across time and settings makes clear to us that we are *not* as consistent or stable as implied by a trait attribution. A second reason for viewing our behavior as externally caused is that we *want* to view ourselves as flexible—we want to believe that we can respond appropriately to different situational contexts (Sande, Goethals, & Radloff, 1988). If we possess strong, stable personality traits, we may not have the capacity to respond flexibly to environmental demands. A third reason is that our visual focus while we behave is on the environment, whereas the visual focus of observers is on us (on our behavior); consequently, the environment is more salient to us, whereas we (as persons) are more salient to observers. Thus, there are informational, motivational, and perceptual reasons for actors' tendency to focus on external causes of their own behavior.

## Do Others Know When You Are Lying? Detecting Deceit

Are you a good liar? Can people tell when you are lying? Imagine the following situation (perhaps this imagination task will ring true for some of you): You are back in junior high school, and your parents have a rule that there must be adult supervision at parties in order for you to go. There is a *really* awesome party happening this weekend, and a boy or girl that you *really* want to date has already told you that he or she is going. Unfortunately, you know that there won't be any adults there. You decide that you won't tell your parents about the lack of adult supervi-

**actor–observer difference**

*a pattern of differences in attributions in which actors tend to make external attributions for their own behavior, whereas observers tend to make internal attributions for the same actions*

sion. After all, you know that you'll behave yourself. (Right.) So later that evening, you mention that there is a party you want to go to on Friday night. Your parents ask if there will be any parents there. You say, "Yes, I think so." They say, "You *think* so?" Oops. You say, "I meant that, yes, the guy hosting the party said that his parents would be at home." Your parents look at you suspiciously.

How would this scenario go for you? Are you good at convincing your parents that you are telling the truth when you are actually stretching it a bit? What might give you away? Quivering voice? Inability to look them in the eye?

Now put yourself in the other role—figuring out whether someone else is lying. Have you ever given someone a present and then wondered whether they really liked it? Perhaps you bought a friend a sweater that had an unusual design. Your friend opened the gift and said, "Oh wow, this is really nice. Thanks so much." What kind of nonverbal signs would lead you to suspect that perhaps she or he didn't really like it?

Most people think that they can recognize some of the signs of lying. In comedy films and television programs, characters will often be portrayed in a way that lets the audience know they are lying (e.g., a quivering voice and unsteady hands). In the 2000 movie *Meet the Parents*, Ben Stiller played a character who was attached to a polygraph (lie detector) and interrogated by his potential father-in-law (played by Robert De Niro). Stiller's character had to respond to many tough questions, and his facial and nonverbal reactions were quite hilarious.

© Lucinda Dowell Photographs

Can your parents tell when you are lying?

Is there truth to people's intuitions about signs of deceit? Do liars exhibit any reliable signs of lying? The answer is both yes and no. The answer is yes in the sense that there are several nonverbal signs that occur significantly more often in liars than in truth-tellers. But the answer is no in the sense that no nonverbal cue *always* appears, and some effective liars exhibit no nonverbal signs at all (for reviews, see DePaulo & Friedman, 1998; DePaulo, Lindsay, Malone, Muhlenbruck, Charlton, & Cooper, 2003). In other words, although there are some signs that are more likely to be exhibited by liars than by people telling the truth, no single cue is a failsafe "lie detector," and some people have such good control of their nonverbal expressions that they show none of the signs of lying.

What are some of the nonverbal behaviors that are correlated with lying? One source of useful information is the speaker's voice. It turns out that when people are lying, their voice goes up in pitch (it becomes higher or squeakier). Of course, you must know what the speaker normally sounds like to be able to detect a heightened pitch. Also, people tend to stutter or stammer more when they are lying, and there are more hesitations in their speech (perhaps because they are trying to think of what to say). All these voice cues are probably consistent with most people's stereotype of liars. A second source of information is the eyes. One eye cue might surprise you: liars blink more frequently than do truth-tellers. Liars also tend to have larger eye pupils (their pupils dilate), but this cue is almost impossible to see during normal conversation. A third source of information is body movements. Liars shift their posture more frequently than do truth-tellers; they also move their hands more often. These cues probably fit most people's stereotype of liars as being uncomfortable and moving restlessly while they speak.

Thus, some nonverbal cues are correlated with lying. But none of them is a perfect predictor—they are simply more *likely* when people are lying than when they are telling the truth. How good are we at using these cues to *detect* deceit? Bella DePaulo and Howard Freidman (1998) summarized the existing literature in the following way: "People's success at detecting lies is generally unimpressive. Although accuracy is almost always better than chance, it is almost never very much greater" (p. 20). Most people are not particularly good at identifying liars. Correct identification of liars usually exceeds chance rates, but rarely goes higher than 70% accuracy when 50% represents a chance rate. There is some evidence that training people to detect lying by giving them feedback on their accuracy can improve their performance to some extent (e.g., Zuckerman, Koestner, & Alton, 1984). In addition, people engaged in professions that require them to be sensitive to deception, such as U.S. Secret Service agents, have occasionally been found to be slightly better than average in detecting deceit (e.g., Ekman & O'Sullivan, 1991).

Why are most of us only mediocre at detecting lying? One reason is that many liars do not exhibit very much in the way of telltale signs—they are good liars who can fool just about everyone (see Frank & Ekman, 2004). Another reason is that no single cue is a highly accurate indicator of lying, so people must rely on multiple cues, which is difficult even for experts. A third reason is that people believe that some cues indicate lying when, in fact, those cues are useless—our stereotypes of liars are not entirely accurate. For example, Miron Zuckerman, Bella DePaulo, and Robert Rosenthal (1981) concluded after reviewing the literature that most people have misconceptions about the informativeness of facial expressions in general, and smiling in particular. People believe that liars exhibit facial expressions that give them away, and also that liars tend not to smile; both of these beliefs are fallacies. Attending to facial cues does not improve the accuracy of detection of deceit, and liars smile just as often as truth-tellers.

Returning to the question that we used as the title of this section, "Do others know when you are lying?" the answer is probably a qualified "yes." Most of us do exhibit some nonverbal cues that can inform someone who knows us well to suspect our sincerity. So, in the long run, honesty is undoubtedly the best policy.

This chapter describes social and self-perception—how we make judgments about others and ourselves. Causal judgments about why an event occurred or why someone behaved in a particular way are called **attributions.** Attribution theories are models that attempt to delineate the processes underlying causal judgments. One of the best-known attribution theories portrays people as **intuitive scientists**—untrained scientists who try to make causal judgments in a rational, scientific manner. This theory is labeled the **covariation model of attribution,** because it assumes that people try to determine whether a particular kind of behavior covaried (correlated) with a person, a situation, or some combination of persons and situations.

People tend to assume that other people share their attitudes and behaviors to a greater extent than is actually the case. This tendency is called the **false consensus effect.**

When individuals make causal judgments about a person based on just one observation, they rely on their knowledge of plausible causes in the situation. Perceivers look to see whether plausible external causes are present and make their causal judgments based on this information. The **discounting principle** states that the perceived role of a cause will be discounted (reduced) if other plausible causes are also present. The **augmentation principle** states that the perceived role of a cause will be augmented (increased) if other factors are present that would work against the behavior.

The **correspondence bias** is the tendency to see other people's behavior as caused by internal factors, such as their personality traits and attitudes, even when plausible external causes are present. The correspondence bias is so common that it has been called the *fundamental attribution error.*

**Nonverbal behavior** refers to actions and cues that communicate meaning in ways other than direct verbal statements, such as facial expressions, voice cues, interpersonal space, eye gaze, and hand gestures. Nonverbal cues are particularly useful in judging the emotions of speakers.

Researchers have identified numerous gender differences and cultural differences in nonverbal behavior. For example, women are better judges than men of other people's emotions. One important difference between cultures is in their **display rules,** which are their norms for how and when emotions should be expressed.

We rely on other people for many judgments about ourselves. For example, we may internalize other people's judgments about us into our self-concept, a process that has been called the **looking glass self.** We also explicitly compare ourselves to other people in order to make judgments about ourselves, a process labeled **social comparison.** One reason we engage in social comparison is to improve ourselves. This motive is usually best served by **upward social comparison**—comparisons with people who are better off or more skilled than we are. Yet another motive for social comparison is to feel good about ourselves. This motive is usually best served by **downward social comparison**—comparisons with people who are worse off than we are. Upward social comparison can have diverse emotional consequences: sometimes it produces hope for the future, but sometimes it causes **relative deprivation,** which is a feeling of anger or resentment about one's outcomes based on comparisons with better-off others. Some people engage in social comparison more often than do other people; this dimension has been labeled **social comparison orientation.**

**Self-perception theory** proposes that we often judge our own internal states by reviewing our past behavior and the situation in which it occurred and inferring internal states consistent with the behavior unless there were clear external causes of our behavior. The **overjustification effect** occurs when people decide that they performed a potentially enjoyable activity for external reasons rather than because they enjoyed it, which can occur when people are offered a reward for engaging in the activity.

Most people think that they are above average on many dimensions, including honesty, fairness, and ability to get along with others. An example of this unrealistically positive self-evaluation is the **bias blind spot,** which refers to the tendency for people to think that biases and errors in judgments are more common in others than in themselves.

A distinction between individualist and collectivist cultures may have implications for positive illusions about the self. In **individualist cultures,** people are seen as free, independent beings who possess stable abilities, traits, and attitudes. In **collectivist cultures,** people are seen as part of a social fabric—as *inter*dependent rather than independent.

**Self-efficacy** refers to the belief that you are capable of performing a particular behavior that is required for a certain goal. High self-efficacy has been shown to increase the likelihood that people will undertake a behavior and continue it despite negative feedback. People tend to have **illusions of control**—they overestimate their control of situations and events. This bias may often be adaptive, because when people believe that they have no control over events in their life, they may show symptoms of **learned helplessness,** which is a state of apathy wherein people simply give up trying to achieve their goals. On the other hand, excessive perceptions of control can also cause problems;

for example, overconfidence can lead to the **false hope syndrome,** in which individuals repeatedly try (unsuccessfully) to achieve a goal despite previous failures.

The **actual self** is how people believe they really are. The **ideal self** is how people would ideally like themselves to be. The **ought self** is how people think they should or ought to be. **Self-discrepancy theory** hypothesizes that perceived differences between the actual and ideal selves produce depression, and perceived differences between the actual and ought selves produce anxiety.

**Self-presentation** refers to the deliberate control of our public behavior to create a certain impression. This kind of behavior is also called **impression management.** Two very common self-presentation goals are to appear likable and to appear competent. Behavior that is designed to make someone like you is called **ingratiation;** behavior that is designed to make someone think you are competent is called **self-promotion. Self-handicapping** occurs when people create or claim an impediment to their own performance, which gives them an excuse for failure (e.g., not studying for a test). The **self-handicapping scale** measures individuals' tendencies to engage frequently in self-handicapping.

The **actor–observer difference** refers to the differing patterns of attribution for one's own versus others' behavior. Actors tend to make external attributions for their own behavior, whereas observers tend to make internal attributions for actors' behavior (this latter tendency constitutes the correspondence bias).

# Key Terms

# Social Psychology Alive on the Web

## ▶ SOCIAL PSYCHOLOGY ALIVE: ONLINE LABS

To perform the following experiment and see how you compare to other students, go to Social Psychology Lab, which can be accessed through Social PsychologyNow.

- 4.1 Facial Expressions

## SOCIAL PSCYHOLOGY ALIVE: QUIZZING AND PRACTICE TESTS

You can access our website directly by going to http://psychology.wadsworth.com/breckler1e/ for online quizzes, flash cards, and Internet links.

## ☞ INFOTRAC® COLLEGE EDITION

For additional readings, explore InfoTrac College Edition, your online library of archived journal articles and periodicals dating back 22 years. If your instructor ordered InfoTrac College Edition with this book, you can access it from your CD-ROM, or go directly to http://www.infotrac-college.com/wadsworth and use the passcode from the InfoTrac College Edition card that came with your book. For this chapter, try these search terms: *attribution, discounting, correspondence bias, nonverbal behavior, social comparison, self-perception, unrealistic optimism, individualism–collectivism, self-efficacy, self-discrepancy theory, self-presentation, self-handicapping.*

## Social Psychology Alive: The Workbook

To apply what you've learned in this chapter to what happens in the real world, go to Chapter 4 of *Social Psychology Alive: The Workbook:*

- The Intuitive Scientist
- "We just didn't bring our 'A' game today"
- Are Facial Expressions Universal?
- The Alex Trebek Effect: Replicating the Quiz Show Study

- Encouraging Children to Read: Can You Design a Better Program?
- Unrealistic Optimism
- School Spirit
- Measuring Our Different Selves
- Can People Reliably Detect When a Person Is Lying?

## Social Psychology Alive: The Videos

To see video on the topics and experiments discussed in this chapter, you can go either to Social PsychologyNow or to the CD-ROM, if your instructor assigned either one, to the following section:

- We Don't Feel the Same Way: Cultural Influences on Emotion
- Getting the Job: Self-Presentation in the Job Interview

## To Learn More

This list contains citations to books or articles that can help you learn more. These readings are good places to start if you want to gain a deeper understanding of the topics in this chapter.

- Leary, M. R. (1995). *Self-presentation: Impression management and interpersonal behavior.* Madison, WI: Brown & Benchmark.

- Ross, L., & Nisbett, R. E. (1991). *The person and the situation: Perspectives of social psychology.* New York: McGraw-Hill.
- Suls, J. M., & Wheeler, L. (Eds.). (2000). *Handbook of social comparison: Theory and research.* New York: Kluwer Academic/Plenum Press.

© Vera Atchou/Getty Images

# The Person in the Situation: Self-Concept, Gender, and Dispositions

A'tasha and Courtney are two college sophomores taking the same course in Greek Mythology, who do not know one another. They both earned a "B" average in their first year. The course is an elective for both women, and, after the first four weeks, they are enjoying the course. The professor is a good lecturer, and the textbook is interesting to read. Everything is going smoothly—until the first exam.

The first test in the course consists of multiple-choice and short-answer questions, many of which seem very difficult to A'tasha and Courtney. Both women leave the exam uncertain about their performance. At class the following week, the professor returns the exams, and the news isn't good: both women learn that their mark was 55%.

A'tasha responds to this outcome with disappointment mixed with determination. She feels that the exam was difficult and did not allow her to show her knowledge, but is confident she can prepare better now that she knows the professor's exam style. She is resolved to do better on the next test and prove to herself—and the professor— that she is a strong student in this subject. She does not doubt for a moment that she is capable of much better performance.

Courtney, on the other hand, feels very discouraged by her mark. She blames herself for her poor performance and wonders whether she lacks natural ability in this subject. She hopes that she will do better on the next test but does not feel confident that such will be the case. She wonders whether she should have taken a different course.

A'tasha and Courtney responded very differently to the same circumstance of a poor exam mark. A'tasha was disappointed by her grade, attributed it to a difficult exam, and was determined to improve. Courtney was discouraged by her mark, blamed herself for it, and was not confident that she could do much better. How can we understand the differing responses of these two women?

Social psychologists typically focus on external, situational factors to understand social behavior (see Ross & Nisbett, 1991). Indeed, we noted in the preceding chapter that social psychological findings are often surprising to nonpsychologists precisely because the findings demonstrate the powerful effects of the situation on human behavior (e.g., Milgram's work on obedience). But social psychologists also recognize that behavior reflects the person in the situation. That is, individuals' personal characteristics affect how social events unfold.

Clearly, the critical difference between A'tasha and Courtney was an internal, personal characteristic that influenced how they interpreted and responded to the same situational event. Psychologists define **dispositions** (also called individual difference variables or personality traits) as consistencies across time and

Individual students may respond very differently to the same exam result.

**dispositions**

*individuals' consistencies across time and settings in a specific type of feeling, thought, and/or action, which make individuals different from other people*

*settings in a specific type of feeling, thought, and/or action, which make individuals different from other people (Friedman & Schustack, 2003; Snyder & Cantor, 1998). Dispositions reflect stable differences in a particular domain between persons (e.g., friendliness, generosity, athleticism).*

*What disposition might help us to understand the differing responses of A'tasha and Courtney? Perhaps the most-studied disposition in social psychology is **self-esteem,** which refers to people's judgments of their own worthiness. People with high self-esteem think positively about themselves and consider themselves to be worthwhile individuals, whereas people with low self-esteem evaluate themselves negatively and are less confident about their self-worth. Later in this chapter, we will describe some of the many implications of self-esteem.*

*A'tasha has high self-esteem, whereas Courtney has low self-esteem. This difference was associated with divergent patterns of emotional reactions, causal attributions, and expectations for the future. A'tasha was disappointed, deflected blame from herself, and remained confident of her own abilities, whereas Courtney was discouraged, blamed herself, and was uncertain about her ability to improve her grade. Looking at the disposition of self-esteem rendered the two different responses to the same situational event understandable.*

*In their research, social psychologists frequently measure individual difference variables that, together with situational factors, might influence behavior. These personal characteristics are diverse, ranging from demographic variables like gender to psychological dispositions like self-esteem. The purpose of this chapter is to describe some of the personal characteristics that have been studied most often by social psychologists (see Judge, Erez, Bono, & Thorsen, 2002). We begin with variables related to the self-concept, including identity and self-esteem. We then turn to the issue of gender, discussing some of the characteristics on which women and men are either similar or different. The third section describes several interactions between "person" factors and "situation" factors, representing the most common perspective on individual difference variables in social psychology. Finally, we discuss the interesting issue of how personal dispositions are related to health. The goal of the chapter is to introduce you to how social psychologists investigate the person in the situation.*

**self-esteem**

*a disposition that represents people's judgments of their own worthiness*

## Self-Concept and Identity

Our self-concepts represent the most fundamental aspect of our makeup. How we identify ourselves, the values we endorse most strongly, and how we feel about ourselves are important characteristics that influence many of our feelings and actions. In this section, we describe how social psychologists have studied the self-concept.

## Who Am I? The Self in Me

**self-concept**

*all information about the self in memory*

**identity**

*the characteristics that individuals think define them and make up their most important qualities*

The **self-concept** refers to all information about the self in memory (Baumeister, 1998). The self-concept contains memories of one's past behavior, beliefs about one's current qualities, expectations for one's future, and many other self-oriented bits of knowledge. A closely related but narrower construct is **identity,** which refers to those characteristics that individuals think define them and make up their most important qualities. If someone asked you to describe who you are, your answer would constitute your identity. You might identify yourself as a college student, an honest person, a cousin of someone famous, or a redhead; your identity consists of whatever characteristics you see as highly self-descriptive.

**Attitudes, Gender, and Dispositions.** What are some of the specific contents of your identity? Your attitudes and values are certainly important. You might identify yourself as conservative or liberal, as supporting or opposing the death penalty, and as religious or nonreligious. In Chapter 6, we will describe social psychological research on attitudes. Another key element of your identity is probably your gender; people frequently identify themselves as a woman or a man (Deaux & LaFrance, 1998). We discuss some research on gender later in this chapter. Finally, your dispositions, or traits, are also probably central to your identity. You may describe yourself as shy or outgoing, as optimistic or pessimistic, and as competitive or cooperative. We will discuss several dispositions that have been studied by social psychologists later in this chapter.

But where do these elements of identity come from? How do we come to see ourselves in a particular way? We discussed some important processes in Chapter 4 on Social Perception: Perceiving the Self and Others. For example, *social comparison* is one way that we evaluate and define ourselves: we compare ourselves to other people and assess whether we are strong or weak in a certain ability, and whether our attitudes are shared or unusual. We observe that we do better than most other kids at school and decide that we are intelligent. We notice that we are shorter than most of our friends and label ourselves as short.

A second process is *self-perception:* we infer our attitudes and feelings directly from our own experiences and behavior. For instance, we know that we love chocolate because we have tasted it. We label ourselves as athletic if we participate suc-

**5.1**
ONLINE
LAB

**5.2**
ONLINE
LAB

Individuals' *identity* refers to the characteristics that they think describe their most important qualities, such as their religious and ethnic affiliations.

© Richard T. Nowitz/CORBIS

cessfully in many sports. We decide that we are generous because we often donate to charities. Once we have applied a label to ourselves via self-perception, we can access the label directly and do not have to repeat the inference process.

### Priming and Situational Distinctiveness.

Although it is true that everyone has certain traits and characteristics that are central to his or her identity, there is also some variability over time and across situations in how people see themselves. For instance, a young woman might think of herself as a student while on her way to college but as a dancer while on her way to dance classes. People juggle numerous identities, which can sometimes even conflict with one another (e.g., the challenge of integrating professional careers and parenthood). Changes over time and settings reflect, in part, that only limited portions of the self-concept can be accessible at any specific moment.

The aspects of identity that are in conscious awareness at a given point in time make up what is called the **spontaneous self-concept** (McGuire & Padawer-Singer, 1976). The spontaneous self-concept changes in response to personal and situational factors. For example, the accessibility of a particular feature of the self will depend on how recently it has been activated. If someone spends a weekend at a dog show, the feature *pet owner* will be more accessible to him or her during the following week than if the dog show had been held several months ago. This example shows how recent activation can increase the likelihood of subsequent activation, which is called *priming,* as we discussed in Chapter 3 (see p. 72).

Another variable that influences the spontaneous self-concept is the distinctiveness of a feature in a particular setting. Which of the following situations would make you more conscious of your gender? In one situation, you are discussing a topic in class with a group of three other individuals of your own sex. In the second situation, you are discussing a topic in class with a group of three individuals of the opposite sex.

William McGuire and his colleagues (e.g., McGuire, McGuire, & Winton, 1979; McGuire & Padawer-Singer, 1976) hypothesized that people are more aware of a specific characteristic when it makes them distinctive from other people in the situation. Any feature that distinguishes individuals from others in the setting is expected to become more accessible. Thus, in the question just posed, McGuire would predict that you will be more aware of your gender when you are the only member of your sex than when you are in a group of same-sex individuals. Is this consistent with your own intuition?

McGuire conducted several interesting studies to test his hypothesis. McGuire et al. (1979) interviewed 560 schoolchildren (grades 1, 3, 7, or 11) and asked them to "Tell us about yourself" for 5 minutes. The boys and girls talked spontaneously into a tape recorder, and their self-descriptions were later scored for whether or not the child mentioned his or her sex. Information was also obtained about the sex composition of the child's home—how many males and females lived with the child (parents, siblings, or others). Figure 5.1 (p. 166) provides the percentages of children who mentioned their own gender, broken down by sex composition at home. The figure shows that *boys* were much more likely to mention their sex when *females* were in the majority at home than when males were equal or in the majority at home. *Girls* were much more likely to mention their sex when *males* were in the majority at home than when females were equal or in the majority at home.

In another study, William McGuire and Alice Padawer-Singer (1976) interviewed 252 boys and girls in grade 6 and used the same "Tell us about yourself" method to elicit their

**spontaneous self-concept**
*the aspects of identity that are in conscious awareness at a given point in time*

© MediaImages/Getty Images

A woman's spontaneous self-concept is more likely to include her sex when she is the only woman in a group.

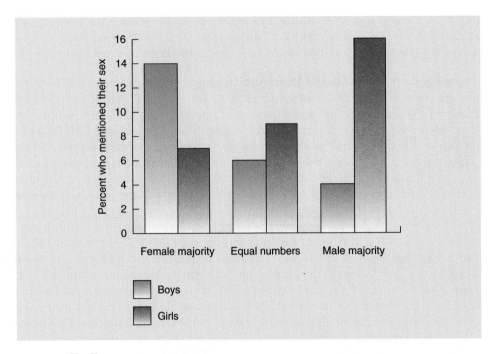

**FIGURE 5.1** Percent of schoolchildren who mentioned their sex in spontaneous self-description

From McGuire et al., "Effects of household sex composition on the salience of one's gender in the spontaneous self-concept," *Journal of Experimental Social Psychology*, 15, 77–90, Table 2, p. 86, 1979. Reprinted by permission of Elsevier.

spontaneous self-concepts, except this time participants were given 7 minutes to provide their answers in writing. Participants were then given another sheet of paper and were asked to "Describe what you look like." The researchers then looked to see whether students were more likely on these two tasks to mention characteristics on which they were relatively unusual. This hypothesis was confirmed for several features. For example, most of the children (70%) were born in the city where their school was located. Only 6% of these children (born in the same city) spontaneously mentioned their place of birth in their self-description, whereas 22% of the children who were born elsewhere mentioned their birthplace (e.g., "I was born in Texas"). Mention of physical characteristics was also influenced by the distinctiveness of the feature. Most children in the sample had brown or black hair (88%) and most had brown eyes (70%). When asked to describe their appearance, only 54% of the children with brown or black hair mentioned their hair color, whereas 79% of the children with red or blonde hair mentioned their hair color. Only 56% of the children with brown eyes mentioned their eye color, whereas 77% of the children with blue or green eyes mentioned their eye color.

These studies suggest that situational factors can make features more prominent, which increases the likelihood that those features will be activated and become part of the spontaneous self-concept. In different situations or at different times, we may see ourselves quite differently. Sometimes our height or weight may seem most important, and other times we will be conscious of our sex or age. Even personality characteristics like helpfulness or assertiveness can become more accessible when the features differentiate us from others. If we are the only person in our class who volunteers to stay late to help the teacher clean up the classroom, we may feel quite helpful or unselfish. If we are the only person in our class to tell the teacher that a test was unfair when we know our friends agree with us, we will feel quite assertive. The spontaneous self-concept is fluid.

# Is It Me or We?

Our identity consists of the characteristics that we believe define us and describe our most important qualities. These qualities can include our personal traits, attitudes, abilities, and physical characteristics. But our identity can also include *group memberships*—we see ourselves as a student, a basketball fan, an African American, a young person, a woman. These groups define some of our most valued characteristics (see Ashmore, Deaux, & McLaughlin-Volpe, 2004). In a very real sense, *me* is often *we*.

*". . . I get stressed and it's sometimes really hard to balance everything. When I'm an employee, I'm an employee, and I concentrate on that. When I'm a mom, I'm a mom, and when I'm a wife, I'm a wife."*

In the following paragraphs, we describe a theory that assumes group memberships are central to our identities, called *social identity theory*. We then turn to a theory that hypothesizes that individuals need to feel both similar to other people and different from other people, called *optimal distinctiveness theory*. Both theories address the role of group memberships in the self-concept.

**Social Identity Theory.    Social identity theory** was proposed by Henri Tajfel (1970, 1978; Tajfel & Turner, 1986), who hypothesized that an important component of individuals' identity comes from their group memberships. Tajfel assumed that we want to maintain a positive identity, including a positive group (social) identity. How can a positive social identity be achieved? Tajfel suggested that we achieve this goal by judging our groups to be superior to other groups. Just as social comparison makes us feel good when we outperform another individual, so, too, comparisons between our group and other groups make us feel good when our group outperforms the other groups.

**social identity theory**

*a model hypothesizing that people want to have positive appraisals of groups to which they belong*

The most provocative finding from research on social identity theory has been that when people are given an opportunity to distribute resources between members of their ingroup and members of an outgroup, they systematically favor their ingroup (see Bourhis, 1994; Taylor & Moghaddam, 1994). Tajfel interpreted these data as reflecting people's desire to make their group superior to the outgroup—to *create* a positive social identity.

For example, one of the earliest studies of social identity theory (Tajfel, 1970) involved British teenage boys, who began the study by completing a dot estimation task in which they guessed how many dots were flashed briefly on a screen. Participants were told that some people consistently overestimate the number of dots and some people consistently underestimate the number of dots. Half of the participants (randomly selected) were told at the completion of the dot estimation task that they were a consistent overestimator, and half were told that they were a consistent underestimator. The boys then learned that they would perform a completely different kind of judgment task, which would require them to divide rewards between other participants. The boys were told that their decisions would have no effect on their own reward, and they would not know the individual identities of the other participants but would know only whether the others were overestimators or underestimators. Participants then made a series of decisions about allocating rewards to other boys. Results showed that when participants made an allocation decision that involved an ingroup member and an outgroup member, they consistently favored the ingroup member. For example, when a partici-

An important part of our identity comes from the groups to which we belong.

pant who believed himself to be an overestimator was asked to divide resources between another overestimator and an underestimator, the participant tended to give more reward to the overestimator.

These kinds of studies use a method called the **minimal group paradigm,** because the "groups" that are created are trivial and meaningless (they are "minimal" groups). In the overestimator–underestimator study, for example, participants did not even know who the other ingroup members were. Also, the basis for the discrimination, overestimating versus underestimating, was pretty ridiculous—why did the boys care whether another person was similar or different on this dimension anyway? Research since this early study has shown that ingroup bias occurs even when groups are formed randomly—by the flip of a coin! Tajfel argued that if ingroup bias occurs in these trivial situations, then strong bias probably occurs when groups are formed on the basis of characteristics that people truly value (e.g., religion, nationality).

**Optimal Distinctiveness Theory.** In social identity theory, Tajfel (1970, 1978) hypothesized that people want to create a *distinctive* group identity, and one that is also *positive*. That is, people want their ingroup to be both different from and better than other groups. The distinctiveness element, however, was not pursued in depth in social identity theory.

Other theorists have argued that although distinctiveness is an important goal in social identity, it coexists with a need to belong to groups (e.g., Brewer, 1991; Pickett, Gardner, & Knowles, 2004; Snyder & Fromkin, 1980; Vignoles, Chryssochoou, & Breakwell, 2000). These theorists have suggested that people want a *balance* between similarity and distinctiveness—that is, people want to feel similar to other members of their group, but not *too* similar, because they also want to feel like an individual with a distinct identity. This struggle for a balance or equilibrium between similarity and distinctiveness is the focus of **optimal distinctiveness theory** (Brewer, 1991). Marilyn Brewer hypothesized that people are constantly adjusting their perceived similarity or perceived distinctiveness in order to maintain the optimal level. If people are exposed to a situation that makes them feel indistinguishable from other people, they will want to reestablish their unique identity. If people are exposed to a situation that makes them feel very different from other people, they will want to reestablish their group belongingness.

An interesting example of the push-and-pull between the competing motives for similarity and distinctiveness was documented in a study by Hazel Markus and

**minimal group paradigm**

*a procedure in which participants are divided into groups based on trivial features or information*

**optimal distinctiveness theory**

*a model hypothesizing that people want to maintain a balance between similarity to other people and individuality from other people*

If people feel too similar to other members of their group, they will be motivated to establish their unique or distinctive characteristics.

Ziva Kunda (1986). Female students at the University of Michigan were shown 18 different sets of three items each and were asked to identify from each set the one they liked the best. For example, they were shown three cartoons and asked to select their favorite; they were shown three greeting cards and asked to select their favorite; and they were shown three colors and asked to select their favorite. Participants completed this task together with three other alleged participants, who were actually confederates of the experimenter. The real participant always answered first, followed by the three confederates. In the *unique condition,* the confederates all disagreed with the participant on 15 of the 18 trials and agreed with each other. For example, if the participant selected option A, the three confederates might all select option C. On the remaining 3 trials (included to increase the plausibility of the confederates' responses), one of the confederates agreed with the participant but the other two confederates disagreed. In the *similar condition,* all three confederates agreed with the real participant on 15 of the 18 trials. On the remaining 3 trials (again included for plausibility reasons), none of the confederates agreed with the participant.

Immediately after completing this task, participants rated their own similarity to several groups; we will focus here on participants' ratings of *ingroups*—that is, groups to which they belonged (e.g., women, Michigan students, Americans). The authors predicted that participants in the unique condition would be feeling very dissimilar from other people and would want to emphasize their similarity to their ingroups, whereas participants in the similar condition would be feeling nearly identical to other people and would want to downplay their similarity to their ingroups. As predicted, the unique condition produced higher ratings of similarity to ingroups than did the similar condition. These data indicate that people try to balance the needs to be similar to others and to have a unique identity (see also Hornsey & Jetten, 2004). The flowchart in Figure 5.2 diagrams the hypothesized processes in each condition.

## Cultural Differences in Identity

Almost all of the research on identity we have described to this point was based on North American or Western European samples. This fact raises questions about

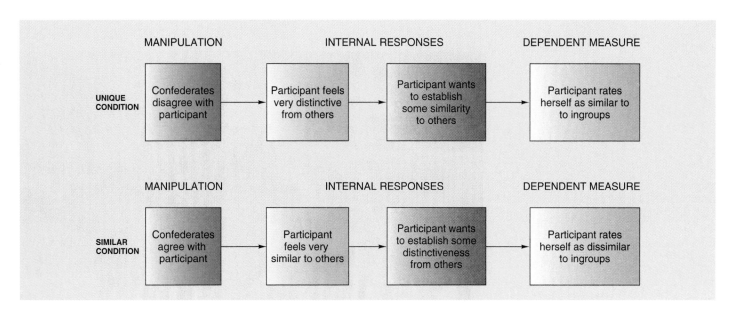

**FIGURE 5.2**  Conditions in experiment by Markus and Kunda (1986)

whether the principles we have delineated, such as optimal distinctiveness, may reflect specific aspects of Western cultures—and, perhaps, be limited to those cultures. In this section, we consider how other cultures might differ from the American and European findings for identity (see also Kashima, Kokubo, Kashima, Boxall, Yamaguchi, & Macrae, 2004, for data on cultural differences in identity between people who live in large urban areas and people who live in smaller, regional cities).

**Independent Versus Interdependent Selves.** In Chapter 4, we described the dimension that has been used most often to distinguish between cultures: the individualist–collectivist dimension (Fiske, Kitayama, Markus, & Nisbett, 1998; Triandis, 1995). Individualist cultures, such as North America and Western Europe, conceptualize people as possessing stable abilities, traits, and attitudes. Collectivist cultures, such as most East Asian countries, conceptualize people as fitting into social roles and following important communal norms.

It seems obvious that these different perspectives should affect members' personal identities. Perhaps most fundamental is the relative emphasis on an independent self versus an interdependent self. In individualist cultures, the self is seen as independent from other people, whereas in collectivist cultures, the self is seen as interdependent with other people.

**Is It Me or We?** In our previous discussion of *me* versus *we,* we described optimal distinctiveness theory, which hypothesizes that people want to achieve a moderate degree of differentiation from others. Too much similarity to other people threatens our sense of uniqueness, whereas too much difference from other people threatens our sense of belonging. Researchers have shown that individuals prefer to maintain a moderate or intermediate level of distinctiveness from other people— enough uniqueness to have their own identity but not so much that they feel disconnected.

Is it possible that the greater emphasis on interdependence and social relationships in collectivist cultures reduces the importance of personal distinctiveness? Do people in collectivist cultures have a lower level of optimal distinctiveness, compared to the level desired in individualist cultures?

Harry Triandis was one of the first social psychologists to study cross-cultural differences and has made important contributions to the literature on individualism versus collectivism (e.g., Triandis, 1995). In a 1990 paper, Triandis and his colleagues investigated whether the self-concepts of members of collectivist cultures

People from China define themselves in terms of social groups more than do people from North America.

© Chuck Nacke/Woodfin Camp

are more interpersonal (*we* rather than *me*) than the self-concepts of members of individualist cultures (Triandis, McCusker, & Hui, 1990). On one task, the researchers asked participants from several different cultures to give 20 completions to the statement, "I am . . ." (Kuhn & McPartland, 1954). The percentage of these statements that referred to social groups was calculated for each respondent. For example, social group completions might include "I am a daughter," "I am a Roman Catholic," or "I am the captain of my hockey team," whereas nonsocial completions might include "I am honest," "I am interested in astronomy," or "I am a fast runner." Respondents from Illinois gave an average of only 19% social group completions; similarly, respondents from Greece, another individualist culture, gave an average of only 15% social group completions. In contrast, participants from collectivist cultures listed more social groups in their answers. For example, respondents from Hawaii who were of Japanese origin gave an average of 28% social group completions, and respondents from the People's Republic of China gave an average of 52% social group completions. These data indicate that people from collectivist cultures define themselves in terms of their relationships to others more than do people from individualist cultures.

Is it possible, then, that optimal distinctiveness theory does not apply to individuals from collectivist cultures? Some theorists warn us against drawing such a conclusion. Vivian Vignoles and her colleagues (Vignoles et al., 2000) argued that people in collectivist cultures *do* want to feel distinctive from other people, but the *way they define their distinctiveness* is different. These theorists argued that people in collectivist cultures define themselves in terms of social relationships, rather than individual achievements. That is, people in collectivist cultures want to feel distinctive, but they accomplish this goal by thinking about their unique pattern of social relationships. Whereas people in individualist cultures tend to define themselves in terms of intrinsic qualities of the individual, such as traits, abilities, opinions, and physical characteristics (e.g., "I am reliable, I am good at math, I weigh 120 pounds"), people in collectivist cultures tend to define themselves in terms of interpersonal characteristics, such as social relationships and group memberships (e.g., "I am Joan's father, I am a member of the Book Club, I am a teacher of elementary school students"). To be sure, saying "I am Joan's father" does convey distinctive information—most people have only one father. But the information is social in nature. Thus, it may be that members of collectivist cultures do value distinctiveness, but the distinctiveness they want is a unique pattern of social roles and relationships, rather than a unique set of traits and opinions.

## Self-Esteem: Liking for the Self

Do you know someone who is always hard on himself or herself? These individuals don't give themselves a break and criticize themselves frequently. They often take negative feedback to heart and are devastated by it, even when the feedback is presented constructively. Individuals who are hard on themselves in this manner have very low *self-esteem*—the disposition we used to understand the example given at the beginning of the chapter. Self-esteem refers to an individual's evaluation (good–bad judgment) of himself or herself. Self-esteem can be conceptualized as an *attitude* toward the self—a judgment that the self is worthy or unworthy.

Most people have reasonably high self-esteem—most have positive views of themselves, a point we have made several times in previous chapters. Humans appear to be motivated to strive for high self-esteem (e.g., Crocker & Park, 2004; Sheldon, Elliot, Kim, & Kasser, 2001), and most people rate themselves as above average on most positive traits. Nevertheless, there are some people who have negative self-views.

Self-esteem is usually assessed with a self-report scale. In Know Yourself 5.1: Self-Esteem Scale, you can measure your own self-esteem using a well-known scale

# Know Yourself 5.1
## *Self-Esteem Scale*

Please indicate the extent to which you agree or disagree with each of the following statements by circling the appropriate number on the answer scale.

1. On the whole, I am satisfied with myself.

| 1 | 2 | 3 | 4 |
|---|---|---|---|
| Strongly agree | Agree | Disagree | Strongly disagree |

2. At times, I think I am no good at all.

| 1 | 2 | 3 | 4 |
|---|---|---|---|
| Strongly agree | Agree | Disagree | Strongly disagree |

3. I feel that I have a number of good qualities.

| 1 | 2 | 3 | 4 |
|---|---|---|---|
| Strongly agree | Agree | Disagree | Strongly disagree |

4. I am able to do things as well as most other people.

| 1 | 2 | 3 | 4 |
|---|---|---|---|
| Strongly agree | Agree | Disagree | Strongly disagree |

5. I feel that I do not have much to be proud of.

| 1 | 2 | 3 | 4 |
|---|---|---|---|
| Strongly agree | Agree | Disagree | Strongly disagree |

6. I certainly feel useless at times.

| 1 | 2 | 3 | 4 |
|---|---|---|---|
| Strongly agree | Agree | Disagree | Strongly disagree |

7. I feel that I'm a person of worth, at least on an equal plane with others.

| 1 | 2 | 3 | 4 |
|---|---|---|---|
| Strongly agree | Agree | Disagree | Strongly disagree |

8. I wish I could have more respect for myself.

| 1 | 2 | 3 | 4 |
|---|---|---|---|
| Strongly agree | Agree | Disagree | Strongly disagree |

9. All in all, I am inclined to think I am a failure.

| 1 | 2 | 3 | 4 |
|---|---|---|---|
| Strongly agree | Agree | Disagree | Strongly disagree |

10. I take a positive attitude toward myself.

| 1 | 2 | 3 | 4 |
|---|---|---|---|
| Strongly agree | Agree | Disagree | Strongly disagree |

**SCORING:** Items 2, 5, 6, 8, and 9 are scored using the answer scales as presented (1-2-3-4); Items 1, 3, 4, 6, and 10 are reverse-scored (that is, 4-3-2-1). Add up all of the items for your overall self-esteem score. Possible scores range from 10 to 40, and higher scores represent higher self-esteem.

Sample items from Morris Rosenberg, *Society and the Adolescent Self-Image,* Revised Edition (Middletown, CT: Wesleyan University Press, 1989).

developed by Morris Rosenberg (1979). A recent series of studies (Robins, Hendin, & Trzesniewski, 2001) tested the validity of the Rosenberg Self-Esteem Scale and found that it successfully predicted numerous relevant variables, including friends' ratings of the target's behavior. Moreover, the scale predicted well for both men and women, for different ethnic groups, and for different age samples.

**Sources of Self-Esteem.** Where do people's positive or negative evaluations of themselves come from? Why do some people consider themselves worthy and some consider themselves unworthy?

Personal experiences are one obvious source of attitudes toward the self. To the extent that people experience many positive outcomes (e.g., success, praise) across varied situations, they are likely to develop favorable beliefs about themselves and positive feelings about their personal worthiness, whereas to the extent that they experience many negative outcomes (e.g., failure, criticism), they are likely to develop unfavorable beliefs about themselves and negative feelings about their personal worthiness. In children's early years, parents are an important source of these positive or negative experiences. Many parenting books emphasize the importance of unconditional love for the child, so that he or she develops a stable sense of being cared for and respected. Recall also the concept of the *looking glass self* in Chapter 4 (see p. 126), which refers to the idea that people may internalize others' views of them—such as children internalizing their parents' labels.

Personal experiences of successful or unsuccessful social relationships are very important for self-esteem: friendships and social acceptance produce self-confidence and high self-esteem, whereas loneliness and social rejection produce self-doubts and low self-esteem (see Leary & Baumeister, 2000). Academic achievement at school also affects people's sense of self-worth: consistent success or consistent failure at school can strongly affect individuals' self-esteem (see Crocker, Sommers, & Luhtanen, 2002).

Experiences of success at school can contribute to high self-esteem.

Social comparison is also involved in the development of self-esteem. People compare themselves to others on performance, traits, and attitudes, and the results of these comparisons influence judgments of self-worth (e.g., Alicke, 2000; Smith, 2000). When social comparisons show that the self is better in performances or virtues than other people, self-esteem is raised. In contrast, when social comparisons show that the self falls below others, self-esteem suffers. These same principles apply to comparisons of one's ingroups, as we noted in the earlier section on social identity theory. People want a positive social identity, which serves as one aspect of the self-concept and self-esteem. When comparisons show that one's ingroups are better or more virtuous than other groups, a positive social identity is established, which raises self-esteem; when comparisons show that one's ingroups fall below other groups in performances or virtues, a negative social identity is implied, which lowers self-esteem.

Of course, the factors discussed above—personal experiences, social comparisons, and group comparisons—do not occur in an entirely unbiased fashion. Most people want to view themselves positively and, therefore, engage in various self-serving judgments (see Chapters 3 and 4). For example, most of us tend to focus on our positive accomplishments and downplay our failures (see Mezulis, Abramson, Hyde, & Hankin, 2004). We also interpret traits in ways that are favorable to ourselves, and we harbor overly optimistic views of our own future. We also make social comparisons in a selective way, especially when something bad has happened: we make *downward* comparisons (that is, we compare ourselves with someone who is worse off than we are), so we feel better (Wills, 1981). Finally, we may help to create a positive social identity for ourselves by treating ingroup members more favorably than outgroup members (as in the previously described *minimal group studies*). In sum, we exhibit numerous biases that provide most of us with a reasonably high level of self-esteem.

**Correlates of Self-Esteem.** What are the correlates of high or low self-esteem? How does this dimension relate to other aspects of people's lives? It turns out to have wide-ranging associations.

First, people with high self-esteem have clearer and more certain views of themselves than do people with low self-esteem (Baumgardner, 1990; Campbell, 1990). Self-esteem is also correlated with expectancies for success: although low self-esteem individuals *want* to succeed just as much as people with high self-esteem, those with low self-esteem do not really *expect* to succeed, whereas people with high self-esteem anticipate success. Because of these differences in expectancies, people with high self-esteem approach situations hoping to demonstrate their skill and garner praise, whereas people with low self-esteem approach situations simply hoping to avoid failure and escape without looking bad (see Baumeister, 1998).

Perhaps the most consistent findings in the self-esteem literature have concerned the issue of self-serving judgments. People with high self-esteem exhibit more self-enhancement in a variety of ways (see Blaine & Crocker, 1993, for a review). Compared to people with low self-esteem, people with high self-esteem are more likely (1) to attribute success to internal factors, (2) to attribute failure to external factors, (3) to recall information about personal successes better than information about personal failures, and (4) to exaggerate their control over situations. Thus, people with high self-esteem process information in ways that magnify their virtues. Note, however, that the direction of causality in these findings is unclear. Does high self-esteem lead to more self-enhancement, or does self-enhancement lead to higher self-esteem? Perhaps both directions occur.

People with high self-esteem also tend to be happier than people with low self-esteem. Self-esteem correlates negatively with depression and anxiety, and positively with life satisfaction (Baumeister, 1998; Leary & Kowalski, 1995; Sedikides, Rudich, Gregg, Kumashiro, & Rusbult, 2004; Tennen & Affleck, 1993).

What about personal relationships? Here, again, high self-esteem is associated with greater satisfaction. People with high self-esteem have more stable dating relationships and report happier marriages than do people with low self-esteem (Fincham & Bradbury, 1993; Hendrick, Hendrick, & Adler, 1988). The former individuals also rate their romantic partners more positively, focusing on their partner's virtues rather than deficiencies (Murray, Holmes, & Griffin, 1996a, 1996b). People with high self-esteem also seem to use their romantic relationships as a way to cope with threats to their sense of self-worth. Sandra Murray and her colleagues (Murray, Holmes, MacDonald, & Ellsworth, 1998) gave people negative feedback about either their considerateness in their romantic relationship or their intellectual abilities. In subsequent ratings of their partner, high self-esteem individuals responded to these threats by becoming more confident about their partner's commitment to the relationship and by rating their partner more positively, whereas low self-esteem individuals responded to the threats with greater doubts about their partner's commitment to the relationship and by rating their partner more negatively. These correlates of high self-esteem are summarized in the accompanying Concept Review.

All of this sounds pretty good for high self-esteem, doesn't it? High self-esteem appears to be a terrific quality to possess. The world would be a better place if we could raise every child to have high self-esteem. But wait a minute—do these conclusions fit comfortably with your own experiences? Do you think that the world would be better off if everyone had high self-esteem? Have you always found peo-

## CONCEPT REVIEW
### Correlates of High Self-Esteem (Relative to Low Self-Esteem)

*Definition of High Self-Esteem:* Favorable evaluation of the self

Clear and certain views of the self

Expect to succeed

Approach situations hoping to demonstrate skill

High self-enhancement and self-serving judgments
- Attribute success internally
- Attribute failure externally
- Recall information about personal successes
- Exaggerate personal control over situations

High happiness:
- Low depression
- Low anxiety
- High satisfaction with life

Stable dating relationships

Happy marriages

Rate romantic partners positively

Use relationships as a way to cope with threats

---

ple with high self-esteem to be the most admirable and thoughtful individuals? What about that conceited jerk back in high school who treated everyone like dirt? Or what about that arrogant teacher who was so obnoxious about his knowledge and training?

These hypothetical examples of conceited individuals illustrate the point that high self-esteem may be a mixed bag (see Crocker & Park, 2004; Kernis & Paradise, 2002; Kernis & Waschull, 1995). Yes, some people with high self-esteem are self-confident, well-adjusted, and optimistic without being nasty or arrogant. But other people with high self-esteem are not so pleasant: they brag, make other people feel inferior, and are hostile if they don't get their own way. How can we distinguish between these two conflicting types of high self-esteem?

One dimension that might help is **narcissism,** which refers to an *excessive* love for the self. People who are high in narcissism have inflated views of their self-worth, which are not connected to reality. Narcissism can be measured by a self-report scale developed by Robert Raskin (Raskin & Hall, 1979; Raskin & Terry, 1988), which contains 40 items that are answered either *true* or *false*. People who score high on this scale answer *true* to items like "I am going to be a great person" and "If I ruled the world, it would be a much better place." It turns out that narcissism correlates with self-esteem, but only moderately, which means that people with high self-esteem are *not* always high in narcissism (Sedikides et al., 2004). Perhaps well-adjusted individuals are high in self-esteem and low in narcissism, whereas obnoxious, conceited people are high in both self-esteem and narcissism.

Some data consistent with the view that narcissists can be hostile was obtained by Brad Bushman and Roy Baumeister (1998). Participants in this study received from another person a negative, critical evaluation of an essay they had written. Later, participants had the opportunity to make the critic listen to loud, unpleasant noise while trying to perform a competitive task. Participants who were high in narcissism made the critic listen to louder and longer bursts of noise than did participants who were low in narcissism. In contrast, self-esteem was unrelated to aggression. The authors suggested that narcissists are defensive about criticism that threatens their ego and respond with aggression. This process of self-threat leading to aggression by narcissists was termed **threatened egotism** (Baumeister, Smart, & Boden, 1996; see also Morf & Rhodewalt, 1993; Twenge & Campbell, 2003). Although it might be desirable to have more people who have high self-esteem without being arrogant, more narcissists would not make the world a better place.

**narcissism**

*a disposition that represents the extent to which people have excessive love for themselves*

**threatened egotism**

*a hostile, aggressive response to criticism from others, which has been linked to narcissism*

Narcissists have excessively positive views of themselves and may respond in a hostile way to criticism.

**secure high self-esteem**

*a positive self-view that is confidently held*

**defensive high self-esteem**

*a positive self-view that is fragile and vulnerable to threat*

**Secure and Defensive High Self-Esteem.** Another perspective on this issue of the good and bad sides of high self-esteem was provided by Christian Jordan, Steve Spencer, Mark Zanna, and their colleagues (Jordan, Spencer, & Zanna, 2003; Jordan, Spencer, Zanna, Hoshino-Browne, & Correll, 2003). These researchers distinguished between people who have **secure high self-esteem** and those who have **defensive high self-esteem** (see also Kernis & Paradise, 2002). Both of these groups report positive self-evaluations on self-report measures of self-esteem such as Rosenberg's (1979) scale. However, people with *secure* high self-esteem possess positive self-views that are *confidently* held; these individuals feel good about themselves and do not need constant reassurance from others to maintain their high self-esteem. In contrast, people with *defensive* high self-esteem possess positive self-views that are *fragile* and vulnerable to threat; these individuals harbor subconscious self-doubts and insecurities, which can lead them to react very negatively to criticism. People with defensive high self-esteem need repeated positive feedback from others to maintain their uncertain feelings of self-worth. This unending need for praise can be associated with boastful, arrogant behavior, as well as hostility and aggression toward anyone who questions the perceiver's self-worth (threatened egotism).

How can secure and defensive high self-esteem be distinguished empirically? Jordan and his colleagues proposed that a measure of an individual's automatic, spontaneous self-evaluation was necessary. Recall our discussion of *automatic processes* in Chapter 3 (see p. 77); these processes cannot be controlled deliberately. In the domain of self-esteem, automatic (also called *implicit*) self-evaluations refer to people's uncontrolled, spontaneous feelings about the self (positive or negative). People may not be aware of their automatic, implicit self-evaluations. Therefore, whereas explicit self-evaluations are conscious and can be measured with self-report scales, implicit self-evaluations are often unconscious and can only be measured by indirect means. The technique used by Jordan and his colleagues to assess implicit self-evaluations was a reaction-time task that we will describe in detail in the next chapter (the *Implicit Association Test*); for our present purposes, we need only know that this task assesses the extent to which people automatically associate positive or negative feelings with a target—in this case, the target was the self (see also Pelham, Koole, Hardin, Hetts, Seah, & Dettart, 2005).

In a series of studies, Jordan and his colleagues showed that people who scored high on a self-report scale of self-esteem but who exhibited negative self-evaluation on an implicit measure of self-esteem (i.e., those with *defensive high self-esteem*) behaved more self-protectively in several contexts than did people who scored high on a self-report scale of self-esteem and who exhibited positive self-evaluation on an implicit measure of self-esteem (i.e., those with *secure high self-esteem*). The researchers also found that people with defensive high self-esteem scored higher on a *narcissism* scale than did people with secure high self-esteem; thus, narcissists may be insecure about themselves on a subconscious level.

These findings suggest that secure high self-esteem is generally a good thing, whereas defensive high self-esteem has some undesirable correlates. Thus, encouraging positive *automatic* or *implicit* self-regard might be beneficial, if it would increase the number of individuals with secure high self-esteem. How this goal can best be reached, however, is a question that awaits further research.

# Gender and Social Behavior

Another "person" factor that social psychologists often study is gender. How important is this characteristic for understanding social behavior? For example, does gender influence people's social lives, such as dictating the settings they enter or the roles they adopt? Do women and men differ reliably across time and settings in their feelings, thoughts, and actions? Are women and men mostly similar or mostly different on important dispositions and abilities?

Let's begin with some self-analysis. How central is your gender identity in your self-concept? For example, if you were asked to define yourself, how early would your gender as a man or a woman be mentioned? Now think about your personality traits. Do you suppose that your dispositions and abilities reflect your gender? More broadly, do you think that any particular traits occur much more often in one gender than the other?

In the following sections, we discuss some of the most interesting findings by social psychologists regarding gender similarities and differences. We consider both the nature and the possible causes of gender differences.

## Gender Similarities and Differences

The issue of similarities and differences between women and men is both fascinating and complex. Gender plays a huge role in our lives, affecting our identity, our relationships with others, and our views of the world. Any differences between women and men could reflect both biological factors (e.g., differences in hormones, or different evolutionary pressures on women and men) and socialization factors (e.g., different gender roles or institutional forces).

**The Importance of Gender in Everyday Life.** There is no doubt that, right from birth, our lives are affected by our sex. Boys and girls are almost always treated differently, encouraged to pursue divergent interests, and socialized differently by parents, peers, and societal institutions. Think about your own daily experiences and how they are affected by your gender. It is typical for women and men to wear different clothes, to have mostly same-sex friends, to use separate bathrooms, to watch different television shows, to play sports separately, and so on—gender is an enormously influential "gate" to specific environments and activities.

The significance of gender in our society is humorously illustrated in parents' reactions to misperceptions of their baby's sex. An infant girl whose hair has not started to grow may elicit "What a cute little boy!" from observers, with an immediate correction from the parents, "Oh no, she is a girl." Why should this sort of mistake bother parents? Why do they care whether their child's sex is perceived accurately by strangers? The fact is that gender is a fundamental element of our conceptions of people. Indeed, there is evidence that gender is the characteristic that is used *more often than any other characteristic* to spontaneously categorize people we encounter (Fiske, Haslam, & Fiske, 1991; Stangor, Lynch, Duan, & Glass, 1992). Gender seems more basic even than age, occupation, or ethnic category. Thus, more than anything else, we categorize people as men and women, boys and girls.

It is also the case that most people *believe* that there are at least some gender differences in personality. These expectations constitute *gender stereotypes:* beliefs about the characteristics that are associated with men and women. For example, men are often believed to be more aggressive than women, whereas women are often believed to be more emotional than men (e.g., Bergen & Williams, 1991). As we will note below, there may be some truth in these beliefs, but gender stereotypes often exaggerate any real differences (see Martin, 1987). We will talk about gender stereotypes in detail in Chapter 9 when we discuss sexism.

Our lives are affected by our gender right from the beginning.

There is also considerable evidence that people's *identity* as a man or a woman is important to them. Children learn that they are male or female at an early age and incorporate this feature as a central aspect of their identity (Deaux & LaFrance, 1998; Martin, Ruble, & Szkrybalo, 2002). People also come to view many of their other characteristics as related to their gender (Spence, 1993). The extent to which individuals view themselves in ways that are consistent with sex-role stereotypes can be measured using Sandra Bem's Sex Role Inventory (see Bem, 1981, 1984).

**Gender Similarities and Differences in Dispositions.** Given the importance of gender as a gate to environments and activities in everyday life, it may be surprising that empirical data have shown that men and women do *not* differ significantly on most dispositions that have been investigated by social psychologists. For example, approximately equal proportions of men and women have high (or low) self-esteem; similar proportions of men and women are extraverted (or introverted); and men and women are equally intelligent (though men tend to score higher than women on visual-spatial tasks, and women tend to score higher than men on verbal tasks; see Halpern, 1992, 2004; Silverman, Choi, Mackewn, Fisher, Moro, & Olshansky, 2000; Weiss, Kemmier, Deisenhammer, Fleischhacker, & Delazer, 2003). Thus, although men and women experience different patterns of daily experiences (e.g., interacting with mostly same-sex friends), these experiences do not produce reliable gender differences on most personality traits. Presumably, the general absence of gender differences reflects that the settings encountered by women and men produce approximately equal rates of success and failure, provide similar numbers of interpersonal interactions, and involve comparable opportunities for intellectual growth (see Friedman & Schustack, 2003).

As mentioned, many people believe that women and men differ in some traits (gender stereotypes). For instance, men are often thought to be more dominant than women, who, in contrast, are thought to be more nurturing than men. Empirical investigations of these expected gender differences, using participants' self-ratings, have often supported parts of the stereotypes, but the differences tend to be small (e.g., Martin, 1987; White, 2003). In an illustrative study, Yoshihisa Kashima and his colleagues (Kashima, Yamaguchi, Kim, Choi, Gelfand, & Yuki, 1995) used a 12-item questionnaire in several countries to assess the extent to which respondents felt compassion toward other people and reported experiencing their feelings. Items included "I feel like doing something for people in trouble because I can almost feel their pain," "I often do what I feel like doing without paying attention to others' feelings" (reverse scored), and "I am not too concerned about other people's worries" (reverse scored). Kashima et al. found that women scored significantly higher on these items than did men in Australia, the United States, and Japan. Thus, women reported feeling closer to other people than did men—a difference that is consistent with the gender stereotype of women as more nurturing than men.

**Gender Differences in Homicidal Aggression.** Perhaps the clearest difference between men and women is in violent physical aggression. Men commit between 70% and 90% of murders around the world (see Archer, 1994; Daly & Wilson, 1988; Knight, Fabes, & Higgins, 1996). This is not to say that women are never aggressive—in fact, women engage in some kinds of aggressive behaviors almost as often as men, including verbal insults and slapping (see Bjorkvist, Osterman, & Lagerspetz, 1994; Ramirez, 1993). But in terms of homicidal aggression, men—particularly, young men between the ages of 18 and 30—are much more likely than women to be perpetrators. The greater physical strength of men may explain part of this pattern; a man is more likely to cause serious injury or death when he strikes another person with a fist or weapon than is a woman. But more than just strength is at play. Men consider violence to be a more acceptable response to

Men commit the vast majority of homicides.

many kinds of provocations than do women, including insults to their reputation, masculinity, or "honor" (especially when they come from certain cultural backgrounds; see Cohen & Nisbett, 1997). Men also have higher levels of certain hormones that have been implicated in physical aggression, especially testosterone. We will return to some of these determinants of aggression in Chapter 11.

**Gender Similarities and Differences in Romantic Attraction.** Another area that has revealed gender differences is romantic attraction. Let's begin, however, with some noteworthy *similarities* in this realm: when asked to describe the ideal mate, women and men across many cultures agree that three extremely important characteristics are honesty, kindness, and intelligence (see Berscheid & Reis, 1998; Buss, 1989). Thus, everybody wants a truthful, generous, and smart mate.

But women and men disagree about the importance of some other qualities. In particular, women place more weight than men on the status and material wealth of possible mates, whereas men place more weight than women on the physical attractiveness of possible mates (e.g., Buss, 1999; Feingold, 1992a; Kenrick, Ackerman, & Ledlow, 2003; Townsend & Wasserman, 1998). For example, women rate male targets who are ambitious and well-educated more highly as mates than targets who do not possess these qualities, whereas men are less influenced by information about the ambitiousness or education of possible female mates. In contrast, men rate female targets who are youthful and physically attractive more positively as mates than older and less attractive targets, whereas women are less influenced by the age and physical attractiveness of potential male mates. These differences have been found in many different cultures, so they appear to be relatively universal. We will offer possible explanations of these findings shortly.

We discuss a final interesting difference between the sexes in Social Psychology in Your Life: Gender Differences in Responses to Threats (p. 180). The box describes a recent hypothesis that women and men have fundamentally different automatic responses to threats and stress.

## Causes of Gender Differences

Although women and men are similar on most qualities, we have identified a few areas where, on average, they differ, including nurturance, homicidal aggression, and romantic attraction. An important question—and a politically charged one (e.g., see Brescoll & LaFrance, 2004)—is *why* these sex differences occur. This

# Social Psychology in Your Life

## *Gender Differences in Responses to Threats*

It has long been assumed that all humans have a natural reaction to threat that can be characterized as a *fight-or-flight* response (Cannon, 1932). This response begins when the perception of a threat stimulates the release of adrenalin into the blood, which provides a surge of energy and strength. The surge of energy can be used either to confront the threat directly (fight) or to flee the threat (flight). The fight response will occur when the individual either has no escape or thinks that the threat (e.g., a predator) can be overcome physically; the flight response will occur when escape is possible and direct confrontation is judged likely to be either unsuccessful or extremely costly. For example, seeing a bear while strolling through the woods will cause a rush of fear and adrenalin that will facilitate a hasty retreat from the situation. Presumably, the fight-or-flight response evolved because it increased humans' survival rates by helping them to overcome or escape from dangerous situations.

Shelley Taylor and her colleagues (Taylor, Klein, Lewis, Gruenewald, Gurung, & Updegraff, 2000) made the interesting proposal that the fight-or-flight response is how men react to threat, but not how women react. These researchers noted

that most prior research testing the fight-or-flight response focused on men, and the relatively few studies that included women yielded inconsistent findings. They suggested that the inconsistent results occurred because women's reactions to threat are fundamentally different from men's. Throughout human history, women have been primarily responsible for the care of infants and children. Being pregnant or being burdened with infants and children would greatly interfere with women's capacity to fight, as well as reducing their chances of successful escape from the situation. Therefore, a fight-or-flight response to threat might not have been adaptive for ancestral women.

Instead, Taylor and her colleagues proposed that women show a *tend-and-befriend* response to threat. The *tend* component refers to looking after offspring. For many kinds of threats, it was probably adaptive for women to focus on their children—for example, to hide from the threat by quieting their children and blending into the environment. The *befriend* component refers to affiliating with others when threatened. It was also probably adaptive in response to many threats for women to seek other humans who could provide resources and protec-

Women may show a tend-and-befriend response to threats.

tion for them and their offspring. As a result, gathering into groups may have become a natural response of women to threats.

Taylor and her colleagues proposed that both men and women experience arousal when threatened, but the consequences of this arousal and the hormones that are released differ between the sexes. They suggested that men's fight-or-flight responses to threat are guided by male androgen hormones, especially testosterone, which are present only in low levels in women. In contrast, they suggested that women's tend-and-befriend responses to threat are guided by the female hormones of estrogen and oxytocin, which are largely absent in men.

issue is very complex, because gender differences reflect many factors, including social, biological, political, and institutional processes. Although it is an oversimplification, we will focus on two broad categories of variables that may contribute to gender differences: biological processes and social processes.

Some researchers have identified possible *biological* sources of gender differences, arguing that genetic and physiological differences between the sexes are important. For example, there is evidence that hormonal differences between women and men (e.g., levels of estrogen and androgen) may contribute to the sexes' differential performance on specific kinds of ability tests, such as women's superiority on verbal measures and men's superiority on spatial measures (see Duff & Hampson, 2000, 2001; Hampson, 2002).

Another biological perspective on gender differences comes from evolutionary theory (see Buss, 1996; Buss & Kenrick, 1998; Gangestad & Simpson, 2000; Geary,

1999; Kenrick et al., 2003). This perspective assumes that, in our distant ancestral past, men and women faced different reproductive pressures, which led to the evolution of certain gender differences. For example, the **parental investment hypothesis** (Trivers, 1972) contends that having children is more costly for women than for men (women must *invest* more to be a *parent,* hence *parental investment* hypothesis). Women carry the fetus during pregnancy and typically nurse the baby for some time after birth; women also provide most of the postnatal care and socialization of infants and young children. These high costs of parenting make women more selective than men about potential sexual mates; the costs also induce women to focus especially on characteristics that suggest a man will be able and willing to provide support and protection for the mother and child. These pressures may explain the findings described earlier that women put more emphasis on status and wealth cues in rating the attractiveness of potential mates than do men: mates who are high in status and wealth should be able to provide excellent support for mother and child. In contrast, because men invest less in becoming a parent, they are less selective about potential sexual mates and emphasize characteristics that imply reproductive fertility, such as youth and physical attractiveness.

Other researchers have identified *social,* or *cultural,* sources of gender differences, noting that men and women are socialized to behave differently, to want different things, and to expect different actions from other men and women (e.g., Deaux & LaFrance, 1998; Eagly, 1987). We observed earlier that gender has profound effects on the daily experiences of men and women. The cultural perspective argues that these different experiences, which are assumed to result mainly from society's gender stereotypes, produce some differences between men and women (see Abele, 2003). For example, women may be more nurturing than men because, from infancy, girls are socialized more than boys to be compassionate and supportive; these gender-based socialization practices lead to differences in adult personalities.

Socialization explanations for gender differences in romantic attraction have also been proposed (e.g., Caporael & Brewer, 1995; Eagly, 1995). For example, theorists have noted that everyone, at least in Western cultures, is bombarded with messages in the media that emphasize the importance of women's physical beauty; these messages may convince both women and men that beauty is important in determining the worth of women. Also, women's socialization toward domestic

**parental investment hypothesis**
*the idea that having children is more costly for women than for men, which has led to the evolution of some differences between the sexes in the characteristics they seek in mates*

Both biological and social factors probably contribute to sex differences in dispositions and behavior.

© David Alan Harvey/Magnum Photos

roles may lead them to assume that they should rely on men for financial support; this belief might explain the greater weight put on resources by women than by men in evaluating possible mates.

There seems little doubt that biological, social, and other processes all play some role in gender differences. Wendy Wood and Alice Eagly (2002; Eagly & Wood, 1999) argued that women and men have been assigned different social roles throughout history based, in part, on biological demands: women must bear children and care for infants, and men can use their superior speed and strength for certain kinds of hunting and fighting. These biological facts have encouraged the evolution of numerous differences between the two sexes across all cultures. But most roles assigned to women and men within specific cultures do not follow directly from biological characteristics. Indeed, Wood and Eagly (2002) noted that there are substantial differences between cultures in some of the specific roles and duties assigned to women and men. They concluded from these cultural differences that women and men both "appear to possess sufficient psychological flexibility to accommodate to a wide range of socioeconomic roles" (p. 718). In sum, although biology places a few inevitable constraints on gender roles, many differences between men and women reflect gender-specific socialization.

## Interactions Between Persons and Situations

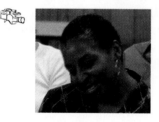

Social psychologists focus on situational factors that influence behavior. When social psychologists include "person" variables in their studies, they typically conceptualize the dispositions' effects in terms of *interactions between persons and situations*. This interactionist approach to understanding social behavior assumes that situational factors can have different effects on people with dissimilar personal characteristics—that is, dissimilar people can act differently in the same situation.

In the current section, we present four examples of this interactionist perspective on social behavior. Although there are dozens of individual difference variables that have been studied by social psychologists, we will focus on these four variables in depth.

*So, if she's friendly with her peers but not with her professors, we know a little bit about her psychology . . .*

## Self-Monitoring

**self-monitoring**

*a disposition that represents the extent to which people rely on external or internal cues to guide their behavior*

Mark Snyder (1974, 1987; Snyder & Gangestad, 1986) developed a scale to measure the dimension of **self-monitoring.** Self-monitoring refers to the extent to which people rely on external or internal cues to guide their behavior. People who are high self-monitors pay attention to external cues, such as group norms or what other people want, in deciding how to behave. High self-monitors shape their behavior to fit the external guidelines: they conform to group norms and rules, or they tailor their words to avoid offending someone who disagrees with them. In contrast, low self-monitors are largely insensitive to external cues, instead deciding how to behave based on internal states like attitudes and values (Kardes, Sanbonmatsu, Voss, & Fazio, 1986; Snyder & Swann, 1976). Low self-monitors are less likely to follow group norms or to tailor their public behavior: they "say what they believe" without much regard for the consequences. As is the case with most dispositional variables, there is no "good" or "bad" level of self-monitoring.

# Know Yourself 5.2
## *Self-Monitoring Scale*

Please indicate whether each of the following sentences is more true or more false about you.

1. I find it hard to imitate the behavior of other people.
   True          False

2. I can only argue for ideas that I already believe.
   True          False

3. I would probably make a good actor.
   True          False

4. In different situations and with different people, I often act like very different persons.
   True          False

5. I am not particularly good at making people like me.
   True          False

6. I'm not always the person I appear to be.
   True          False

7. I would not change my opinions (or the way I do things) in order to please someone or win their favor.
   True          False

8. At a party, I let others keep the jokes and stories going.
   True          False

9. I can look anyone in the eye and tell a lie with a straight face (if for a good cause).
   True          False

10. I may deceive people by being friendly when I really dislike them.
    True          False

**SCORING:** One point is assigned for answering *True* to Items 3, 4, 6, 9, or 10; one point is assigned for answering *False* to Items 1, 2, 5, 7, or 8. Possible scores range from 0 to 10, and higher scores indicate that the respondent is a high self-monitor.

Sample items from Snyder and Gangestad, "On the nature of self-monitoring: Matters of assessment, matters of validity," *Journal of Personality and Social Psychology,* 51, 125–139, 1986. Copyright © 1986 by the American Psychological Association. Reprinted by permission.

Self-monitoring can be measured with an 18-item, self-report questionnaire in which respondents answer either *true* or *false* to each item. Sample items are presented in Know Yourself 5.2: Self-Monitoring Scale. How would you answer these items?

Scores on the self-monitoring scale have been shown to predict how numerous situational factors influence behavior. For example, one application has been to the area of interpersonal attraction. Imagine yourself in the following situation: You have an opportunity to go on a date with one of two individuals. One possible dating partner is someone who is very attractive physically but has a number of undesirable personal characteristics: he or she is reserved toward strangers, is more concerned about himself/herself than other people, and has a tendency toward moodiness. The second possible dating partner is someone who is physically unattractive

© Simon Marcus/CORBIS

High self-monitors are more concerned about the physical attractiveness of their date than are low self-monitors.

**need for cognition**

*a disposition that represents how much people enjoy and engage in thinking*

but has highly positive personal characteristics: he or she is outgoing, listens well to other people, and values a sense of humor. Which of these two persons would you choose for a date?

Mark Snyder, Ellen Berscheid, and Peter Glick (1985) conducted a study in which male participants were given exactly this choice: they could date either a physically attractive woman who had the undesirable characteristics noted above or a physically unattractive woman who had the desirable characteristics noted above. Participants also completed the self-monitoring scale. The findings were dramatic: low self-monitors chose the partner with the desirable personal characteristics 81% of the time, whereas high self-monitors chose the partner who was physically attractive 69% of the time. Why did this division along self-monitoring lines occur? The authors speculated that because low self-monitors behave on the basis of internal cues like attitudes and beliefs, they focus on the internal characteristics of other people as well (see also Jamieson, Lydon, & Zanna, 1987). High self-monitors, on the other hand, are more concerned about external cues, such as physical attractiveness. High self-monitors also care more about making a good impression on other people than do low self-monitors, and an attractive partner enhances one's public image (see also Glick, DeMorest, & Hotze, 1988; Sharp & Getz, 1996).

This example of research on self-monitoring illustrates nicely how dispositions can interact with other factors to predict behavior. The physical attractiveness of a potential date influenced choices by high but not low self-monitors, whereas the personality characteristics of a potential date influenced choices by low but not high self-monitors.

## Need for Cognition

Some people engage in and enjoy thinking more than other people do. John Cacioppo and Richard Petty (1982) suggested that such differences in cognitive activity appear in numerous aspects of social life; they labeled this variable the **need for cognition.** People who are high in the need for cognition enjoy challenging cognitive tasks and are likely to think and reflect frequently about their world, whereas people who are low in need for cognition do not enjoy thinking as much and are less likely to engage in reflection and analysis.

The need for cognition can be measured with an 18-item self-report scale (Cacioppo, Petty, & Kao, 1984). Respondents indicate the extent to which each statement is characteristic of them on a 5-point scale from *extremely uncharacteristic* (1) to *extremely characteristic* (5). Sample items are presented in Know Yourself 5.3: Need for Cognition Scale. See how you would respond to these items.

Numerous studies have shown that people who are high in need for cognition generate more thoughts in a variety of situations and recall more of the information they encounter than do people who are low in need for cognition (for a review, see Cacioppo, Petty, Feinstein, & Jarvis, 1996). We will describe one example of research on the need for cognition.

If both high and low need for cognition individuals are exposed to a convincing message, do you think they will differ in how persuaded they are? Or might they differ in the *persistence* of any persuasion? Haugtvedt and Petty (1992) tested these questions by having participants watch a number of television advertisements. After each advertisement, participants answered several questions, including their evaluations of the advertised product. The focus of the study was one specific advertisement, which was presented 6th out of 12 advertisements and promoted a telephone answering machine. The advertisement had been created by the researchers and was designed to be quite convincing; it described many features of the answering machine including remote message retrieval, call screening, voice-activated recording,

# Know Yourself 5.3
## *Need for Cognition Scale*

Please indicate to what extent each statement is uncharacteristic or characteristic of *you* by circling the appropriate number on the answer scale.

1. Thinking is not my idea of fun.

| 1 | 2 | 3 | 4 | 5 |
|---|---|---|---|---|
| Extremely uncharacteristic | | | | Extremely characteristic |

2. I prefer to think about small, daily projects to long-term ones.

| 1 | 2 | 3 | 4 | 5 |
|---|---|---|---|---|
| Extremely uncharacteristic | | | | Extremely characteristic |

3. I really enjoy a task that involves coming up with new solutions to problems.

| 1 | 2 | 3 | 4 | 5 |
|---|---|---|---|---|
| Extremely uncharacteristic | | | | Extremely characteristic |

4. Learning new ways to think doesn't excite me very much.

| 1 | 2 | 3 | 4 | 5 |
|---|---|---|---|---|
| Extremely uncharacteristic | | | | Extremely characteristic |

5. I prefer my life to be filled with puzzles that I must solve.

| 1 | 2 | 3 | 4 | 5 |
|---|---|---|---|---|
| Extremely uncharacteristic | | | | Extremely characteristic |

6. I usually end up deliberating about issues even when they do not affect me personally.

| 1 | 2 | 3 | 4 | 5 |
|---|---|---|---|---|
| Extremely uncharacteristic | | | | Extremely characteristic |

7. I like to have the responsibility of handling a situation that requires a lot of thinking.

| 1 | 2 | 3 | 4 | 5 |
|---|---|---|---|---|
| Extremely uncharacteristic | | | | Extremely characteristic |

8. I feel relief rather than satisfaction after completing a task that required a lot of effort.

| 1 | 2 | 3 | 4 | 5 |
|---|---|---|---|---|
| Extremely uncharacteristic | | | | Extremely characteristic |

9. I find satisfaction in deliberating hard for long hours.

| 1 | 2 | 3 | 4 | 5 |
|---|---|---|---|---|
| Extremely uncharacteristic | | | | Extremely characteristic |

10. I think only as hard as I have to.

| 1 | 2 | 3 | 4 | 5 |
|---|---|---|---|---|
| Extremely uncharacteristic | | | | Extremely characteristic |

**SCORING:** Items 3, 5, 6, 7, and 9 are scored using the answer scales as presented (1-2-3-4-5); Items 1, 2, 4, 8, and 10 are reverse-scored (that is, 5-4-3-2-1). Add up all of the items for your overall need for cognition score. Possible scores range from 10 to 50, and higher scores represent stronger need for cognition.

Sample items from Cacioppo et al., "The efficient assessment of need for cognition," *Journal of Personality Assessment*, 48, 306–307, 1984. Reprinted by permission of Lawrence Erlbaum Associates, Inc.

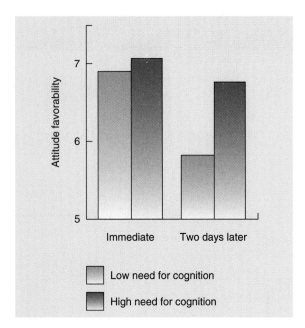

**FIGURE 5.3** Favorability of attitudes of low and high need for cognition participants toward telephone answering machine immediately and two days after advertisement

From Haugtvedt and Petty, "Personality and persuasion: Need for cognition moderates the persistence and resistance of attitude changes," *Journal of Personality and Social Psychology*, 63, 308–319, Fig. 1, p. 313, 1992. Copyright © 1992 by the American Psychological Association. Reprinted by permission.

**achievement motivation**

*a disposition that represents the extent to which people are positively or negatively aroused by performance settings*

**Thematic Apperception Test (TAT)**

*a procedure that involves showing participants drawings of ambiguous scenes and asking them to write stories about what is happening, which are then scored for the presence of particular themes*

automatic save, fast forward/rewind, a 3-year warranty, and other features. After watching and evaluating the 12 advertisements, participants were dismissed. Two days later, participants returned to the laboratory expecting to view additional ads. Instead, they were asked to evaluate some of the products they had seen advertised two days earlier, including the focal telephone answering machine.

The participants' ratings of the answering machine on the two days are presented in Figure 5.3. As the figure shows, high and low need for cognition participants did not differ in their initial responses to the advertisement: both groups were quite favorable toward the answering machine. But when attitudes were reassessed two days later, the attitudes of people high in need for cognition showed more persistence than did the attitudes of people low in need for cognition (whose attitudes declined in favorability). Why did this effect occur? The authors speculated that participants who were high in need for cognition thought more about the advertisement while watching it than did participants who were low in need for cognition; consequently, the former individuals were able to recall more positive information about the answering machine at the second session than were the latter individuals. Consistent with this reasoning, when participants were asked at the end of the second session to list any thoughts they had about the answering machine, those who were high in need for cognition listed more positive thoughts than did those who were low in need for cognition. These results show that people who are high and low in the need for cognition may respond differently to the same external stimulus (e.g., an advertisement).

## Achievement Motivation

**Achievement motivation** refers to the extent to which people are attracted to performance settings, rather than being frightened by such settings (Atkinson, 1964; McClelland, Atkinson, Clark, & Lowell, 1953). Two groups of individuals have been distinguished. People who are *success-oriented* are positively motivated by opportunities to perform: they approach challenges and thrive in testing situations. People who are *failure-threatened,* on the other hand, are negatively motivated by performance settings: they avoid challenges and can "choke" in testing situations. Thus, success-oriented individuals are generally expected to perform better than failure-threatened individuals in achievement settings.

Do you know people who are extreme in one of these two categories? Do you have a friend who is really "juiced" by challenging situations and who doesn't seem afraid of failing at all? Isn't it amazing what these sorts of people will attempt? Do you know someone else who seems afraid to try any sort of challenge because he or she is worried about disaster? These kinds of people may not achieve their potential because they are afraid to test themselves.

Most of us are more "mixed" in our motivations—we feel both positively and negatively motivated in achievement settings. We like to succeed but also feel somewhat anxious about failure. Our reactions to achievement settings will therefore be conflicted; if we feel confident about success, then our positive motivation will probably predominate, whereas if we feel unsure of ourselves in the setting, our negative motivation may predominate.

Achievement motivation is usually measured using the **Thematic Apperception Test** (Murray, 1943), or **TAT.** The TAT involves showing participants drawings of an ambiguous scene (e.g., two people working in a laboratory on a piece of equipment; or several young people sitting in a lounge talking) and asking them to write a story about what is happening. They are asked to describe what led up to the current scene, what the characters are doing and thinking, and what will happen in the future. These stories are expected to reflect the storytellers' underlying motivations (see Smith, 1992). To score achievement motivation, the stories are examined by trained judges who look for the presence of achievement "themes," such as someone thinking about going to college and facing new challenges. Judges also score whether the story reflects a positive outlook (e.g., excitement about the opportunity to succeed at college) or more neutral or negative reactions. Typically, researchers will ask participants to write stories for several pictures, and achievement scores will be averaged across the stories (or summed across the stories if everyone writes the same number of stories). An example of a picture used to elicit stories is presented in Figure 5.4.

Consider a question about performance settings: Do you think that easy, moderate, or difficult tasks will arouse the strongest achievement motives in people? Which level of difficulty is the most "motivating"? Do you enjoy easy, moderate, or difficult tasks the most? One of the originators of the concept of achievement motivation, John Atkinson, argued that tasks that are believed to be of *moderate* or *intermediate* difficulty are most motivating (Atkinson, 1964). His rationale was that tasks that are believed to be very easy pose little challenge, and tasks that are believed to be very difficult provide little opportunity for success. Tasks that are perceived to be of intermediate difficulty, on the other hand, provide a reasonable chance of either success or failure, and the outcome is seen as highly informative about the performer's level of ability. Therefore, tasks of intermediate difficulty were hypothesized to arouse the most positive motivation (excitement) in success-oriented individuals and to arouse the most negative motivation (fear) in failure-threatened individuals.

Based on this reasoning, researchers have predicted that success-oriented individuals will perform better on moderately difficult achievement tasks than will failure-threatened individuals, but this performance difference will be smaller on easy and difficult tasks. For example, Stuart Karabenick and Zakhour Youssef (1968) recruited participants for an experiment using a *paired associates learning task.* This task required participants to learn a set of 15 pairs of words (e.g., *butterfly–automobile; elevator–coffee*). After one initial exposure to all 15 pairs of words, test trials began, which involved presenting one word and asking participants to recall the other word that had been paired with it. If the answer was incorrect, the participant was told the correct word. This procedure was continued for 10 trials (thus, participants were tested for recall of all 15 pairs of words 10 times).

Now for the interesting part: before beginning, participants were told that some of the pairs of words were more difficult to learn than other pairs, and the difficulty of each pair would be indicated by the *color* of the words. For instance, some participants were told that 5 *easy* pairs would be presented in *red,* 5 *intermediate* pairs would be presented in *green,* and 5 *difficult* pairs would be presented in *yellow* (other people were given different color codes). In fact, all 15 word pairs were intermediate in difficulty, but the color was used to manipulate participants' *perceptions* of difficulty. It was expected that participants' achievement motives (which were measured in an initial session two weeks before the memory test) would be aroused most strongly while they were trying to learn pairs that were allegedly intermediate in difficulty.

Figure 5.5 (p. 188) presents the memory performances by success-oriented and failure-threatened participants for each category of word pairs. The figure shows that success-oriented participants performed better than failure-threatened participants only on word pairs that were believed to be intermediate in difficulty. Presumably, these word pairs aroused the most excitement in success-oriented participants and the most fear in failure-threatened participants. On the allegedly easy and difficult pairs, the positive or negative motivations were presumably not aroused as strongly, so performance differences did not occur. These findings represent an

© Harvard University Press

**FIGURE 5.4** Sample picture used to elicit story in Thematic Apperception Test (TAT)

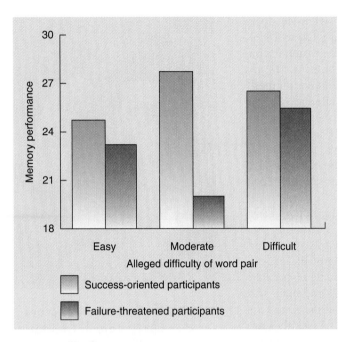

**FIGURE 5.5** Memory scores on allegedly easy, moderate, and difficult word pairs by success-oriented and failure-threatened participants

From Karabenick and Youssef, "Performance as a function of achievement motive level and perceived difficulty," *Journal of Personality and Social Psychology*, 10, 414–419, Table 1, p. 416, 1968. Copyright © 1968 by the American Psychological Association. Reprinted by permission.

**uncertainty orientation**

*a disposition that represents the extent to which people want to learn new things about themselves and their environment*

interaction of personal and situational factors: the personal characteristic of achievement motivation influenced how individuals responded to items that were believed to be intermediate in difficulty.

## Uncertainty Orientation

Richard Sorrentino and his colleagues (Sorrentino & Roney, 2000; Sorrentino, Short, & Raynor, 1984) have identified the trait of **uncertainty orientation,** an individual difference variable that reflects people's interest in learning new things about themselves and their environment. Similar to research on achievement motivation, research on uncertainty orientation has focused on two groups of people—this time, people who are oriented either toward uncertainty or toward certainty. People who are *uncertainty-oriented* want to learn new things about themselves and are attracted by novelty and unpredictability. People who are *certainty-oriented* want to maintain their current conceptualizations of themselves and the environment and are attracted by familiarity and predictability.

Uncertainty orientation is another variable that can be measured using the TAT. Specifically, respondents generate TAT stories, which are scored for the presence of "themes" related to uncertainty. For example, a story in which a character wonders what will happen in the future and looks forward to a new environment would generate a high uncertainty score. In contrast, a story in which the character focuses on the past and thinks only about events that have already taken place would generate a low uncertainty score. Again, participants are normally asked to write several stories, and their uncertainty scores are averaged or summed across all stories.

Sorrentino and his colleagues have conducted a diverse research program over the past 20 years investigating the implications of uncertainty orientation (for a review, see Sorrentino & Roney, 2000). These researchers have identified numerous situational factors that interact with uncertainty orientation to predict behavior. We will describe one example here.

Richard Sorrentino and Erin Hewitt (1984) showed that uncertainty-oriented and certainty-oriented individuals responded very differently to an opportunity to learn about themselves. These researchers had participants complete a task that allegedly measured a new aspect of their mental abilities. They were given feedback that was somewhat unclear and uncertain. Some participants were told that their performance showed that they were *not low* in this ability, but it was unclear whether they were *average* or *high* in the ability. Other participants were informed that their performance showed that they were *not high* in this ability, but it was unclear whether they were *low* or *average.*

All participants then learned that they would be performing another test of this same mental ability, but this time they would have some input into the makeup of the test. They were informed that there were two different sets of test items from which they could choose. One set of test items was very good at distinguishing between *low* and *average* ability, whereas the other set of test items was very good at distinguishing between *average* and *high* ability. Participants were instructed that they could select items from either set for their next test.

Participants who were uncertainty-oriented (UOs) chose items that would clarify their uncertainty. UOs who had been told that they did not have low ability (but did not know whether they were average or high in ability) selected most of their items from the set that was good at distinguishing between average and high ability; UOs who had been told that they did not have high ability (but did not know whether they were low or average in ability) selected most items from the set that was good at distinguishing between low and average ability. Obviously, these uncertainty-oriented participants wanted to zero in on their actual level of ability, so they could find out exactly where they stood.

On the other hand, certainty-oriented participants (COs) *avoided* the most diagnostic items. If they knew they were not low in ability (but did not know whether they were average or high), COs chose most of their items from the set that was good at distinguishing between low and average ability, which would not clarify their own ability. If they knew they were not high in ability (but did not know whether they were low or average), COs chose most of their items from the set that was good at distinguishing between average and high ability—again, selecting items that would not clarify their own ability. Obviously, these certainty-oriented participants simply did not want to learn anything new about this aspect of their mental abilities. The personal disposition of uncertainty orientation predicted how individuals behaved in the same situation. The flowchart in Figure 5.6 depicts the hypothesized responses of uncertainty-oriented and certainty-oriented participants.

## Dispositions and Health

Some of the most interesting research in the area of individual differences has addressed the issue of health, specifically the connections between dispositions and well-being. Are people with particular traits more likely to be in good health? In some studies, "good health" has been defined in terms of objective health outcomes (e.g., physical symptoms, behavioral recovery, admission to hospital); in other studies, it has been defined in terms of subjective judgments (e.g., distress, happiness, satisfaction with life).

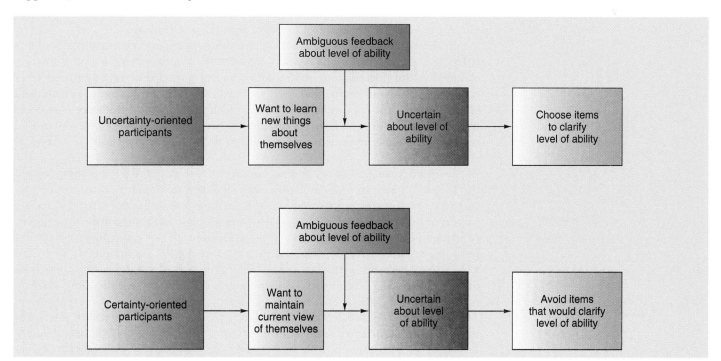

**FIGURE 5.6.** Hypothesized responses of uncertainty-oriented and certainty-oriented participants in experiment by Sorrentino and Hewitt (1984)

You may have heard of Norman Cousins, who wrote a book titled *Anatomy of an Illness,* which was published in 1979 and received wide popular acclaim. Cousins wrote about his personal battle with an inflammatory illness of the spine and joints. In particular, the book focused on Cousins's use of humor and laughter to fight the disease. He deliberately sought out humor and comedy to maintain his spirits; he also believed that laughter directly reduced his pain. Cousins's book stimulated considerable interest in the role of humor and optimism in health.

How accurate is this view of fighting disease? Can an individual's emotional state or outlook play a role in his or her health outcomes? We need to be careful not to "blame the victim" by concluding that people who do not recover from illnesses are somehow responsible for their negative outcome because they were not optimistic enough in their outlook (see Martin, 2001). On the other hand, if emotional states can enhance people's health, we may be able to work to improve our own and others' well-being. In the following sections, we discuss three individual differences that seem to be related to well-being (see also Kling, Ryff, Love, & Essex, 2003): optimism, intelligence, and the Type A coronary-prone behavior pattern. Keep in mind that data involving personal dispositions are correlational, so we must be careful about drawing causal conclusions.

## Dispositional Optimism

**dispositional optimism**

*a disposition that represents the extent to which people have positive, confident expectations about their own future outcomes*

**Life Orientation Test (LOT)**

*a measure of dispositional optimism*

In 1985, Michael Scheier and Charles Carver published a paper that introduced an 8-item scale to measure **dispositional optimism,** which they defined as the tendency to have positive, confident expectations about one's own future outcomes. Scheier and Carver labeled their scale the **Life Orientation Test (LOT).** People who are optimistic generally expect things to go well, whereas people who are pessimistic generally expect things to go poorly. Note that optimists do not necessarily believe that they have *personal control* over their outcomes (i.e., they do not necessarily have high self-efficacy; see Chapter 4)—they are simply optimistic that things will go well, for whatever reason (e.g., they might believe they are "lucky people").

Are you generally an optimist or a pessimist? In Know Yourself 5.4: Life Orientation Test, you can measure your own dispositional optimism.

In their initial research, Scheier and Carver (1985) surveyed college students twice, the second time four weeks after the first. A measure of optimism was obtained at the first session, and at both sessions participants reported their level of several common symptoms, such as dizziness, muscle soreness, fatigue, and blurred vision. The researchers found that optimistic respondents were less likely to show an increase in reported symptoms between sessions than were pessimistic respondents. Thus, optimism was associated with fewer newly reported physical complaints.

In another study, Scheier and his colleagues (Scheier et al., 1989) administered the LOT to 51 men on the day before they underwent coronary artery bypass surgery. The men were interviewed two more times: one week and six months after surgery. Findings showed that men who scored high on optimism before surgery recovered faster, as indicated by such behaviors as walking, returning to work, and resuming vigorous exercise, than did men who scored low on optimism. Also, men who scored high on optimism before surgery reported greater satisfaction with their recovery and less distress about their condition six months after surgery, compared to men who scored low on optimism.

Other researchers have also found that optimism is associated with lower distress after surgery or stressful life events (e.g., Carver et al., 1993; Kaiser, Major, & McCoy, 2004; Litt, Tennen, Affleck, & Klock, 1992), although it is important to note that the correlations between optimism and healthy outcomes are sometimes small and occasionally absent altogether (see Salovey, Rothman, & Rodin, 1998). Notwithstanding the occasional null result, the findings for optimism are impressive.

# Know Yourself 5.4
## *Life Orientation Test (LOT)*

Please indicate the extent to which you agree or disagree with each of the following statements by circling the appropriate number on the answer scale.

1. In uncertain times, I usually expect the best.

| 0 | 1 | 2 | 3 | 4 |
|---|---|---|---|---|
| Strongly disagree | Disagree | Neutral | Agree | Strongly agree |

2. If something can go wrong for me, it will.

| 0 | 1 | 2 | 3 | 4 |
|---|---|---|---|---|
| Strongly disagree | Disagree | Neutral | Agree | Strongly agree |

3. I always look on the bright side of things.

| 0 | 1 | 2 | 3 | 4 |
|---|---|---|---|---|
| Strongly disagree | Disagree | Neutral | Agree | Strongly agree |

4. I'm always optimistic about my future.

| 0 | 1 | 2 | 3 | 4 |
|---|---|---|---|---|
| Strongly disagree | Disagree | Neutral | Agree | Strongly agree |

5. I hardly ever expect things to go my way.

| 0 | 1 | 2 | 3 | 4 |
|---|---|---|---|---|
| Strongly disagree | Disagree | Neutral | Agree | Strongly agree |

6. Things never work out the way I want them to.

| 0 | 1 | 2 | 3 | 4 |
|---|---|---|---|---|
| Strongly disagree | Disagree | Neutral | Agree | Strongly agree |

7. I'm a believer in the idea that "every cloud has a silver lining."

| 0 | 1 | 2 | 3 | 4 |
|---|---|---|---|---|
| Strongly disagree | Disagree | Neutral | Agree | Strongly agree |

8. I rarely count on good things happening to me.

| 0 | 1 | 2 | 3 | 4 |
|---|---|---|---|---|
| Strongly disagree | Disagree | Neutral | Agree | Strongly agree |

**SCORING:** Items 1, 3, 4, and 7 are scored using the answer scales as presented (0-1-2-3-4); Items 2, 5, 6, and 8 are reverse-scored (that is, 4-3-2-1-0). Add up all of the items for your overall dispositional optimism score. Possible scores range from 0 to 32, and higher total scores represent stronger optimism.

Sample items from Scheier and Carver, "Optimism, coping and health: Assessment and implications of generalized outcome expectancies," *Health Psychology*, 4, 219–247. Copyright © 1985 by the American Psychological Association. Reprinted by permission.

Why might a confident outlook predict heightened well-being? One possibility is that optimists may be more likely to engage in healthy behaviors than pessimists (e.g., Shepperd, Maroto, & Pbert, 1996), such as lowering their intake of saturated fats, perhaps because they expect those behaviors to be effective (after all, they *are* optimistic). Second, optimists avoid dwelling on negative affect (e.g., Scheier et al., 1989), which can reduce the sense of well-being directly.

But what about the research on *unrealistic optimism* we described in Chapter 4 (see page 138)? Recall that most people predict that they are less likely than average to experience negative life events and more likely than average to experience positive life events (e.g., Weinstein & Klein, 1996). There is some evidence that unrealistic

People who are optimistic about the future may recover from surgery more quickly than people who are pessimistic.

optimism is associated with fewer health-protective behaviors, perhaps because unrealistically optimistic individuals do not feel vulnerable to health threats (e.g., Perloff, 1983; Tennen & Affleck, 1987).

Are people who score high on dispositional optimism also more unrealistically optimistic about specific negative and positive events? At least concerning heart disease, the answer appears to be no! Nathan Radcliffe and William Klein (2002) studied 146 middle-aged adults, who completed the LOT as a measure of dispositional optimism. Respondents also provided detailed personal information (e.g., family history, blood pressure, cholesterol level) that allowed the researchers to calculate their actual risk of suffering a fatal heart attack, based on data from large-scale studies of heart disease. Respondents were also asked to estimate the likelihood that they would have a fatal heart attack. It was then possible to calculate objectively the degree to which respondents were unrealistically optimistic—the extent to which their estimates were lower than their actual risk. Results showed that participants who were high in dispositional optimism were *not* more unrealistic about their vulnerability to heart disease than were pessimistic participants. In fact, optimistic respondents had more knowledge about heart disease than did pessimistic respondents. Thus, being optimistic and being unrealistic were not the same.

These findings are interesting because they suggest that optimism as measured by the LOT does not involve "sticking one's head in the sand" like an ostrich and simply denying real risks or refusing to obtain information about risks. Instead, dispositional optimism seems to be an outlook or approach to life that tries to focus on the positive aspects of events, including positive ways of dealing with real risks.

## Intelligence

On June 1, 1932, almost every child attending school in Scotland who was born in 1921 (then either 10 or 11 years old) took an intelligence test. This process was repeated in 1947, testing all children attending school in Scotland who were born in 1936. These two huge samples of boys and girls have been followed into adulthood, completing several surveys since the initial interviews. The resulting data have allowed researchers to examine the long-term health implications of intelligence scores. Follow-up studies have examined rates of illness and death from various causes, including cancer and cardiovascular disease.

These studies have consistently shown that intelligence (measured in childhood) is positively correlated with subsequent health (freedom from illness) and longevity (life span). For example, Lawrence Whalley and Ian Deary (2001) traced the records of 2,185 men and women in 1997 who had taken the intelligence test as children living in 1932 in the city of Aberdeen, Scotland. Of this total, 1,101 were alive and 1,084 were dead at age 76. Intelligence scores as children predicted survival: every 15-point increase in IQ scores was associated with a 20% increase in survival rate.

Specific illnesses that have been shown to be predictable from childhood intelligence scores include lung cancer, stomach cancer, and heart disease (e.g., Deary, Whiteman, Starr, Whalley, & Fox, 2004). One possible explanation of these findings is that higher intelligence is associated with higher socioeconomic status (SES). That is, individuals who are highly intelligent also tend to be wealthier, which might improve their health through better nutrition, better access to health services, and so on. However, SES cannot entirely explain the findings, because the correlation between intelligence scores and longevity remains significant even when individuals who are equal in SES are examined.

What other factors might explain the correlations between childhood intelligence scores and length of life? Linda Gottfredson and Ian Deary (2004) suggested that intelligence may increase people's skill at maintaining their own health. For example, intelligent people may recognize possible risks quickly and thereby avoid accidental injuries. Intelligent people may also understand the significant health implications of lifestyle choices such as smoking or eating fatty foods. Finally, intelligent people may be good at implementing and maintaining complex treatment programs, such as remembering to take medications at specific times and monitoring their physical status (e.g., blood sugar levels for diabetics).

## "Type A" Coronary-Prone Behavior Pattern

The **"Type A" coronary-prone behavior pattern** refers to a constellation of characteristics that has been linked with heart disease (e.g., Chesney & Rosenman, 1985; Friedman & Rosenman, 1974; Glass, 1977). It represents a hard-driving, competitive style, as reflected in impatience, time urgency, competitiveness, ambitiousness, anger, and hostility.

The Type A pattern is usually assessed by interviewing individuals and posing a set of standard questions. The questions mostly concern competitive situations, such as whether the person always plays games to win. The individual's verbal and nonverbal responses are used to decide whether he or she meets the criteria for classification as Type A. For example, if someone answers the question about playing to win affirmatively, and if his or her response is immediate and forceful, then classification as a Type A person is more likely. In general, nonverbal cues indicating tension, aggressiveness, time urgency, and anger increase the likelihood of a Type A label. Self-report measures have also been developed to assess the Type A pattern (e.g., Krantz, Glass, & Snyder, 1974), but the interview procedure is generally regarded as the most valid diagnostic method (see Matthews, 1982, 1988).

The assumption underlying research on the Type A pattern has been that the emotional volatility of these individuals (due to impatience, competitiveness, hostility, etc.) produces frequent states of arousal and stress, which increase blood pressure, stimulate the release of stress hormones, and generally hasten the onset of cardiopulmonary problems. Type A individuals respond to many situations more intensely than the average person. All of us can think of times when we have felt stressed and under pressure; we know that the pounding heart, aching gut, and suppressed emotions cannot be healthy. This stress is experienced quite frequently by individuals who are Type A.

To make matters even worse, Type A individuals also tend to have unhealthy lifestyles (e.g., to smoke and drink more than average) and to ignore physical warning signals they may experience (e.g., Carver, Coleman, & Glass, 1976; Matthews, 1982). Obviously, these lifestyle issues can amplify the physical vulnerability of those with a Type A disposition.

The Type A pattern is a very broad one, incorporating emotions, behaviors, and personality. Some researchers have argued that only certain portions of the behavior pattern are unhealthy, whereas other portions may be innocuous (Booth-Kewley & Friedman, 1987; Salovey et al., 1998). There is some evidence that the major risk factor in the Type A pattern is the tendency toward anger and hostility. The emotional reactivity of angry and hostile people may increase their susceptibility to heart disease; there may not be serious negative health implications of ambitiousness or competitiveness per se (Barefoot, 1992; Friedman, 1992; Smith, 1992). Future research will explore further whether anger and hostility are the key negative aspects of the broader concept of the Type A behavior pattern.

**"Type A" coronary-prone behavior pattern**
*a constellation of characteristics, including impatience, anger, and hostility, that has been linked to heart disease*

People who fit the "Type A" coronary-prone behavior pattern experience anger more often than most people.

# Chapter Summary

**Dispositions** refer to individuals' consistencies across time and settings in a specific type of feeling, thought, and/or action, which make individuals different from other people. For example, **self-esteem** represents people's judgments of their own worthiness; people with high self-esteem think positively about themselves, but people with low self-esteem evaluate themselves negatively.

The **self-concept** refers to all information about the self in memory. **Identity** is a narrower construct, which refers to the characteristics that individuals think define them and make up their most important qualities. The **spontaneous self-concept** refers to those aspects of the identity that are in conscious awareness at a given point in time. Aspects of the self that have been recently activated and aspects that make the self distinctive from others in the situation are especially likely to be part of the spontaneous self-concept.

Identity consists of both personal qualities and group memberships. **Social identity theory** proposes that people want to maintain a positive social (group) identity, which can be achieved via the perception that groups to which they belong are superior to other groups. Several **minimal group studies,** which assign participants to arbitrary and meaningless groups, have shown that participants generally treat ingroup members more favorably than outgroup members.

**Optimal distinctiveness theory** proposes that individuals want a balance between similarity to other people and separateness from other people; they want enough individuality to have their own identity but not so much that they feel disconnected from others. People from collectivist cultures are more likely to define themselves in terms of their social relationships than are people from individualist cultures.

Individuals' levels of self-esteem predict a variety of psychological processes. For example, higher self-esteem is associated with greater optimism about the future, more self-serving judgments, greater reported happiness, and more confidence in one's relationships. But high self-esteem can have negative associations: some people with high self-esteem are also high in **narcissism,** which refers to an excessive love for the self. People who are high in narcissism have been shown to respond with greater aggression to personal threat than people who are low in narcissism—a response that has been labeled **threatened egotism.** A distinction can also be made between **secure high self-esteem,** which refers to a positive self-view that is confidently held, and **defensive high self-esteem,** which refers to a positive self-view that is fragile and vulnerable to threat. People with defensive high self-esteem need repeated praise from others, which can be associated with boastful, arrogant behavior and hostility toward anyone who questions their self-worth.

Gender is another "person" factor that affects many aspects of our daily lives. Although women and men do not differ on most dispositions, there are gender differences in some traits, as well as in homicidal aggression, romantic attraction, and behavioral responses to threat. The differences between women and men probably reflect a combination of biological and social processes. An example of a biological process is the **parental investment hypothesis,** which contends that having children is more costly for women than for men; these differential costs are hypothesized to have led to the evolution of some differences between the sexes in the characteristics they seek in mates.

Social psychologists often conceptualize social behavior in terms of *interactions between persons and situations;* this perspective assumes that situational factors can have different effects on people with dissimilar personal characteristics. Illustrative dimensions discussed in the chapter include **self-monitoring,** which refers to the extent to which people rely on external or internal cues to guide their behavior; **need for cognition,** which refers to how much people enjoy and engage in thinking; **achievement motivation,** which differentiates between people who are positively aroused by performance settings (labeled *success-oriented* individuals) and people who are negatively aroused by performance settings (labeled *failure-threatened* individuals); and **uncertainty orientation,** which distinguishes between people who want to learn new things about themselves and the environment (labeled *uncertainty-oriented* individuals) and people who want to maintain their current conceptualizations of themselves and are attracted by familiarity and predictability (labeled *certainty-oriented* individuals). To assess both achievement motivation and uncertainty orientation, researchers typically use the **Thematic Apperception Test,** or **TAT.** The TAT involves showing participants drawings of ambiguous scenes and asking them to write stories about what is happening; trained judges score the stories for the presence of certain themes, such as achievement or uncertainty.

Several dispositions have been shown to be related to health and well-being. For instance, **dispositional optimism,** which is the tendency to have positive, confident expectations about one's own future outcomes, has been found to predict both physical and psychological well-being. Dispositional optimism is usually measured using the **Life Orientation Test** (or **LOT**). The **"Type A" coronary-prone behavior pattern** refers to a constellation of characteristics, including impatience, anger, and hostility, that has been linked to heart disease.

# Key Terms

# Social Psychology Alive on the Web

## SOCIAL PSYCHOLOGY ALIVE: ONLINE LABS

To perform the following experiments and see how you compare to other students, go to Social Psychology Lab, which can be accessed through Social PsychologyNow.

- 5.1 Personality Test
- 5.2 Self-Description

## SOCIAL PSYCHOLOGY ALIVE: QUIZZING AND PRACTICE TESTS

You can access our website directly by going to http://psychology.wadsworth.com/brecklerle/ for online quizzes, flash cards, and Internet links.

## INFOTRAC® COLLEGE EDITION

For additional readings, explore InfoTrac College Edition, your online library of archived journal articles and periodicals dating back 22 years. If your instructor ordered InfoTrac College Edition with this book, you can access it from your CD-ROM, or go directly to http://www.infotrac-college.com/wadsworth and use the passcode from the InfoTrac College Edition card that came with your book. For this chapter, try these search terms: self-concept, identity, social identity theory, self-esteem, narcissism, self-monitoring, need for cognition, achievement motivation, optimism, Type A.

# Social Psychology Alive: The Workbook

To apply what you've learned in this chapter to what happens in the real world, go to Chapter 5 of *Social Psychology Alive: The Workbook*:

- Did Martha Get Shafted?
- Who Am I?
- Self-Monitoring and Finding Mr. or Ms. Right

- Assessing Your Personality: Are You a Thrill-Seeker?
- Does Your Life Orientation Affect Your Health?
- Assessing Your Personality: Are You a Type A Personality?
- The Barnum Effect
- Processing Information About Oneself

# Social Psychology Alive: The Videos

To see video on the topics and experiments discussed in this chapter, you may go either to Social PsychologyNow or to the CD-ROM, if your instructor assigned either one, to the following section:

- Which Is the Real Me? Being One Woman With Many Hats
- It's Not All About You: Knowing When to Blame Your Circumstances

# To Learn More

This list contains citations to books or articles that can help you learn more. These readings are good places to start if you want to gain a deeper understanding of the topics in this chapter.

- Baumeister, R. F. (Ed.). (1993). *Self-esteem: The puzzle of low self-regard.* New York: Plenum.

- Hunter, A. E., & Forden, C. (Eds.). (2002). *Readings in the psychology of gender: Exploring our differences and our commonalities.* Needham Heights, MA: Allyn & Bacon.
- Salovey, P., & Rothman, A. J. (Eds.). (2003). *Social psychology of health.* New York: Psychology Press.

RATHER GO NAKED THAN WEAR FUR

WE'D RATHER GO NAKED THAN WEAR FUR

SEARS SUPPORT THE TORTURE OF INNOCENT ANIMA

WEAR YOUR OWN

© AP/Wide World Photos/Chuck Stoody

# Attitudes and Social Behavior

P hillip occasionally drives his car after drinking alcohol. He doesn't drink very much, but when he does, he never really thinks about the possibility that he shouldn't drive—the idea of taking a taxi just doesn't occur to him.

Phillip also smokes cigarettes. He smokes about a pack a day and feels free to smoke wherever he wants. He often smokes in the presence of nonsmokers, although he'll extinguish his cigarette if someone asks him to. He smoked throughout his wife's pregnancies.

Phillip never wears a seatbelt while driving. It doesn't feel comfortable, so he doesn't use it. He also never makes his children buckle up in the car.

What is your impression of Phillip? Is he someone to be admired or to be condemned? Do you think that he is a responsible person? What other characteristics do you think he might possess?

Our description of Phillip is based on a real person. If you thought that Phillip sounded a bit old-fashioned, you were right—he lived from 1910 to 1985. He was caring, funny, and kind. He was a good father and a good husband. But he also sometimes drove after drinking, smoked wherever he wished, and never used seatbelts even after they became standard equipment in the early 1960s.

Do you want to know something else? Your grandfathers were probably a lot like Phillip. Phillip reflected the attitudes of his times, and it is a testament to how much attitudes have changed that Phillip now sounds rather irresponsible. In the 1950s and 1960s people routinely drove their cars after drinking, smokers thought it was their right to smoke anywhere, and almost no one used seatbelts. But today? Driving after drinking is evaluated negatively by most people, and the concept of designated drivers has caught on. Nonsmokers insist on their right to healthy air,

Today, attitudes toward smoking require that smokers indulge their habit outside of buildings.

*and most smokers agree that they should not smoke around nonsmokers. Most people use seatbelts consistently and feel vulnerable if they are not buckled up. The different prevailing attitudes of the two time periods help us to understand the different patterns of behavior.*

*Attitudes may be the most studied topic in social psychology. Back in 1935, Gordon Allport stated that attitudes were the most indispensable concept in social psychology. Many social psychologists would argue that this statement is still true today (e.g., Eagly & Chaiken, 1993; Oskamp, 1991). Literally thousands of experiments have been conducted exploring various aspects of attitudes.*

*This chapter describes some of the social psychological research and theory on attitudes, particularly attitude formation and the relation between attitudes and behavior. (In Chapter 7, we discuss attitude change.) We begin the current chapter by defining attitudes and considering why humans have evolved to possess attitudes. We then describe how attitudes are measured by social psychologists. Next, we address how attitudes form, and we identify some developmental trends in attitudes across the life span. We then turn to the effects of attitudes on behavior, addressing both* how *attitudes affect behavior and* when *they do so. We close the chapter with a discussion of culture and attitudes.*

## ● ● ●   What Are Attitudes?

Jeff Keller is president of the company Attitude Is Everything, Inc. He says that success "is a matter of having a positive attitude." He sells lots of materials that encourage people to "build a positive attitude" (e.g., motivational music, with titles like "Born for Greatness" and "Bitter or Better?").

What does Jeff Keller mean by the term *attitude*? He means a general perspective on life, an outlook that can be positive (leading to success) or negative (leading to failure). The "attitude" he prescribes corresponds reasonably closely to the dimension of *dispositional optimism* that we discussed in Chapter 5 (see page 190).

Social psychologists do *not* use the term *attitude* to refer to a general perspective, outlook, or approach to life. Social psychologists have a much more specific meaning for the term.

## Attitudes: Evaluations of Targets

An **attitude** is *an individual's evaluation of a target* (Eagly & Chaiken, 1993; Wood, 2000; Zanna & Rempel, 1988). The target can be an object, an issue, a person, a group, a behavior, or any other identifiable aspect of the environment (e.g., a color, an emotion). By calling it an *evaluation,* theorists mean that an attitude is a *good–bad* judgment: it represents the individual's overall assessment of whether a particular target is positive or negative. As we mentioned in Chapter 2 (see page 35), attitudes cannot be seen directly, so researchers must infer attitudes from individuals' observable responses.

**attitude**

*an individual's evaluation of a target along a good–bad dimension*

Attitudes *always* have a target—they are directed *at* something. People have attitudes toward many, many targets, ranging from broad *ideologies or values* (e.g., democracy, education) to *controversial issues* (e.g., stem cell research, the conflict in the Middle East) to *individual people* (e.g., your mother, Jennifer Lopez) to *groups* (e.g., computer programmers, college students) to *objects* (e.g., cars, ice cream) to *behaviors* (e.g., exercising, drinking coffee). Obviously, the concept of attitude is very broad; there is an almost infinite number of targets toward which someone might have an attitude (e.g., green bicycles, china teapots, paper clips). Although it is true that people can have an attitude toward almost anything, social psychologists have been interested mainly in attitudes that are directed at important targets, such as controversial issues, ethnic groups, and consequential behaviors.

Think about some of your own attitudes. Which ones do you think are most important in your daily life? Your attitudes toward individual people? Your attitudes toward foods? Your attitudes toward broad goals like getting an education and staying healthy? Your attitudes toward specific activities like watching television and studying? Your attitudes toward social and ethnic groups? You can probably think of examples of attitudes from each of these categories that influence your behavior in everyday settings. By understanding where these attitudes come from and how they affect us, you can gain insight into the causes of your daily actions.

## Three Parts of Attitudes

Cockroaches . . . big cockroaches crawling on your floor. How would you feel about this situation? Probably not too good. Let's analyze your reaction in terms of attitudes. What is your attitude toward cockroaches? How do you evaluate this species of insects? Almost certainly, you will say that your attitude is negative. But *why* is it negative? What things about cockroaches make your evaluation negative? It turns out that attitudes can come from emotional reactions, cognitive information, and past behavior.

One aspect of your negative reaction to cockroaches is probably based on the fact that cockroaches (or even *thoughts* of cockroaches) make you feel rather sick. Cockroaches are disgusting. These are your affective or emotional reactions to cockroaches.

Another aspect of your evaluation is probably based on information you have about cockroaches. You know that they are likely to infest dirty or old buildings, and you believe that they can spread disease. You know that cockroaches crawl around at night, which makes them seem secretive and frightening. You also know that they are hard to get rid of—they can be a very persistent pest. These are some of the cognitive elements contributing to your negative attitude.

A third part of your reaction to cockroaches may be based on your past behavior toward them. You may be able to remember recoiling from a cockroach (or a similar large beetle) and expressing disgust or even screaming involuntarily. You might also have killed a cockroach in the past by stepping on it or by spraying pesticide in the cracks where the insects can live. If you are asked whether you like or dislike cockroaches and think about having killed them in the past, you are likely to decide that you dislike them.

In trying to decompose attitudes into their components, social psychologists have identified the three elements just described: affect, cognition, and past behavior (e.g., Breckler, 1984; Crites, Fabrigar, & Petty, 1994; Rosenberg & Hovland, 1960; Zanna & Rempel, 1988). Theorists have proposed that whether an individual evaluates a target positively or negatively will depend on three things: (1) how the object makes the person feel, (2) the person's beliefs about the object, and (3) the person's

Most people have a negative attitude toward cockroaches.

© Anthony Bannister; Gallo Images/CORBIS

previous actions toward the object. Targets that arouse negative feelings and emotions (e.g., snakes, hypodermic needles) are more likely to generate unfavorable attitudes than are targets that arouse positive feelings and emotions (e.g., puppies, chocolate). Targets that are known or believed to possess negative characteristics (e.g., criminals, cholesterol) are more likely to generate unfavorable attitudes than are targets that are known or believed to possess positive characteristics (e.g., medical doctors, healthy foods). Targets toward which someone has behaved negatively in the past (e.g., enemies, weeds) are more likely to be seen as disliked than are targets toward which someone has behaved positively in the past (e.g., friends, kittens). When we discuss attitude formation later in this chapter, we organize the material in terms of affective, cognitive, and behavioral sources of attitudes.

It might be helpful at this point to acknowledge a potentially confusing issue in the attitudes literature: the *two-way* relation between attitudes and behavior. We have just noted that *previous behavior* toward a target may contribute to an individual's *current attitude* toward the target. Thinking about the fact that she or he has killed cockroaches in the past might actually strengthen a person's negative attitude toward them ("I must really hate cockroaches because I have killed them in the past"). But don't *current attitudes* also cause *future behavior?* Our opening example of Phillip's behavior was explained by stating that attitudes in his time were different from prevailing attitudes today, an explanation that implies that attitudes cause behavior. Doesn't the fact that someone is negative toward cockroaches increase the likelihood that she or he will kill them in the future?

The answer is that *both* directions of influence can occur, which can be confusing for students learning about attitudes. Past behaviors influence current attitudes, and current attitudes influence future behavior. If people have behaved positively toward something in the past, they are more likely to judge that they like it, whereas if they have behaved negatively toward something, they are more likely to judge that they dislike it. But people also will behave in the future in ways that reflect their current attitudes: they will approach things they like and avoid things they don't like. We will talk about each of these directions of influence in this chapter.

Let's now return to the idea that attitudes can have three components or sources: feelings, beliefs, and past behavior. Steven Breckler and Elizabeth Wiggins (1989) found that attitudes toward certain targets depend mostly on people's feelings toward those targets, whereas attitudes toward other targets depend mostly on people's knowledge and beliefs (see also Esses & Maio, 2002; Haddock & Zanna, 1998; Trafimow & Sheeran, 1998). For instance, attitudes toward blood donation tend to rely heavily on people's feelings (e.g., their level of fear at the thought of giving blood), whereas attitudes toward controversial social issues are heavily reliant on people's beliefs (e.g., their agreement with arguments supporting each side of the issue). Which of these sources is most important for attitudes toward cockroaches, do you think? It seems likely that emotions and feelings usually dominate.

Often, people's feelings, beliefs, and past actions toward a target are reasonably consistent with one another—either mostly positive or mostly negative. Think about your attitude toward a close friend: you probably feel affection for this person, believe that he or she possesses many desirable characteristics, and have behaved in friendly, positive ways toward him or her in the past. Your attitude toward garbage is also probably based on relatively uniform components, but this time negative ones: you have negative feelings about the unpleasant smell of garbage, you believe that garbage can grow unhealthy bacteria, and your principal action toward garbage in the past has been to dispose of it.

But now think about your attitude toward chocolate cake. Is it also based on uniformly positive or uniformly negative elements? If you are like most people, you may *feel* positively toward chocolate cake (e.g., you love the taste) but *believe* that chocolate cake has some negative characteristics (e.g., it is high in calories and

Many people have an *ambivalent attitude* toward chocolate cake, which means that it contains both positive and negative elements.

generally not a healthy thing to eat). Your attitude toward many individuals and social groups may similarly include a mix of positive and negative feelings and beliefs: you believe that many rock musicians are talented but egotistical; Susan's jokes make you laugh but she can also be immature; you respect Juan but know that he can be selfish. When, as in these examples, attitudes contain conflicting elements (both positive and negative), they are called **ambivalent attitudes** (Kaplan, 1972; Katz & Hass, 1988; Thompson, Zanna, & Griffin, 1995).

**ambivalent attitudes**

*evaluations of targets that include both positive and negative elements*

We will talk a bit more about ambivalence in the next section on how to measure attitudes. For now, let's just consider briefly why ambivalence is an important concept. The key implication of ambivalence is for the consistency of behavior. What kind of behavior do you think an ambivalent attitude will produce? If an individual has both positive and negative feelings/thoughts about another person, will the individual's behavior be constant (the same) or variable (changing) toward the other? If you said variable, you predicted what has been found by social psychologists (e.g., Armitage & Conner, 2000; Lavine, Thomsen, Zanna, & Borgida, 1998). Ambivalent attitudes can lead to different behavior over time because either the positive or the negative elements about the target may come to mind at a particular point, and whichever type of element is dominant will drive behavior. In contrast, attitudes that are low in ambivalence (all positive or all negative elements) will not produce such variable responses. A good example of this latter case is your attitude toward cockroaches: it is probably low in ambivalence (all of the elements are negative), and your behavior toward cockroaches will probably be negative every time you encounter them!

## Explicit Versus Implicit Attitudes

**explicit attitudes**

*evaluations that people can report consciously*

**Explicit attitudes** are those that people can report consciously. Most of the examples we have given so far represent explicit attitudes. You are aware that you dislike cockroaches and that you like puppies, and you can report these attitudes confidently on a self-report scale. Explicit attitudes have been the focus of the vast majority of social psychological research on attitudes, so the remainder of this chapter will deal mainly with explicit attitudes.

**implicit attitudes**

*automatic evaluative responses to a target, which may occur without awareness*

Recently, however, researchers have identified another, more subtle effect of attitudes on cognition and behavior, which has led to the term *implicit* attitudes. An **implicit attitude** is an individual's automatic evaluative response to a target, which can occur without awareness (Blair, 2001; Dasgupta & Greenwald, 2001; Greenwald & Banaji, 1995; Wilson, Lindsey, & Schooler, 2000). An implicit attitude is a spontaneous, immediate, good–bad response to the target that cannot be consciously controlled. It reflects how the individual evaluates the target at a subconscious level. Recall our discussion of *automatic processes* in Chapter 3 (page 77), which cannot be controlled. Implicit attitudes are automatic.

Typically, implicit attitudes conform to explicit attitudes; that is, our spontaneous, automatic response to a target typically parallels our conscious evaluation of the target. Cockroaches elicit an *implicit* negative response that is consistent with our *explicit* negative attitude. Thus, the distinction between explicit and implicit attitudes will not always be important.

Inconsistency between explicit and implicit attitudes can occur, however. An individual might consciously support an issue or policy (e.g., busing children to integrated schools) but feel anxious about it at a subconscious level (e.g., be worried about its implications for his or her own children). Or someone might express liking for an individual whom he or she subconsciously envies. Because implicit attitudes are automatic and subconscious, people may not realize that their implicit and explicit attitudes toward a target differ. Later in this chapter, we will discuss at least one way that implicit attitudes might affect behavior without an individual's awareness.

# Why Do We Evaluate?

Why have humans evolved to form attitudes? What useful functions are served by storing thousands of evaluations of different targets in our brains? Although social psychologists have proposed numerous functions of attitudes, two in particular have been emphasized in research and theory. Let's begin our consideration of this "why" question by putting ourselves in the role of a master designer.

Imagine that you are a brilliant scientist who is developing a robot that must be able to survive on its own in the world. The robot must be able to learn and perform some simple tasks and respond adaptively to the demands of the environment. The robot must be able to seek help when necessary and recognize dangerous situations that should be avoided.

Besides the ability to move and manipulate objects, what senses and abilities would you need to give your robot? What kinds of skills would be essential for it to cope effectively in a changing environment?

Sight and hearing are probably two critical senses; if the robot were unable to visually scan the environment or to hear auditory stimuli, it would be severely limited. Another necessity would be some sort of memory system, whereby the robot could recognize objects that it had encountered before. But would a simple memory system be enough? Recognition, per se, is not very informative unless the memory system also triggers some sort of *evaluation* of the object. The robot would need to be able to recall how the object had behaved in the past and to predict whether it is likely to be helpful or harmful in the present situation. A rapid appraisal of the object's implications for the robot (i.e., a rapid good–bad judgment) would be extremely useful. This evaluative judgment would then allow the robot to approach, or to flee from, the object.

## Assessing Objects

Just like our hypothetical robot, humans benefit from quick assessments of the positive or negative implications of objects that they encounter in the environment. In humans, *attitudes* provide these rapid evaluations of objects, people, and issues; this has been termed the **object appraisal function** of attitudes (Fazio, 2000; Smith, Bruner, & White, 1956). These attitudes give the individual a quick assessment (*appraisal*) of whether targets are likely to be helpful or hurtful. Almost all attitudes serve this function at least to some extent, because attitudes always provide a summary good–bad judgment of a target. Object appraisal is the most basic function of attitudes and probably the principal reason why humans have evolved to form attitudes. In our distant evolutionary past, ancestors who formed and stored evaluations of objects in their brains were more likely to survive than would-be ancestors who did not form attitudes; for instance, the former individuals avoided objects that aroused negative evaluations (e.g., sabre-toothed tigers) while their less evaluative peers occasionally suffered nasty outcomes.

You might be thinking that this object appraisal function should generalize beyond humans. Wouldn't other animals also benefit from forming positive or negative evaluations of objects and basing their actions on those evaluations? Yes, absolutely. Think about dogs: do you believe that they have attitudes? When a dog wags its tail and runs toward its owner, or when it bares its teeth and snarls at a threatening stranger, or when it jumps up and down with excitement while its food dish is being prepared—these seem to be clear behavioral manifestations of attitudes. So dogs probably do possess attitudes. If so, dogs undoubtedly experience attitudes differently than do humans, because we have a complex cognitive component of attitudes that is presumably missing in dogs. But the fundamental goal of object appraisal can be served by simple, affective responses that do not rely on

**object appraisal function**
*a function of attitudes in which attitudes provide rapid evaluative judgments of targets, facilitating approach or avoidance*

Teenagers' attitudes toward clothing sometimes serve a *value-expressive function.*

**value-expressive function**

*a function of attitudes in which attitudes communicate individuals' identity and beliefs*

complex cognition. If they exist, dogs' attitudes must be based more on affect than on cognition, but they are attitudes nonetheless, and they serve an object appraisal function.

## Expressing Values

Dogs do not wear certain clothes to express their identity (but don't they look cute in sweaters?). Dogs also do not adopt certain attitudes to express their values (except maybe their hopeful expressions at the dinner table, reflecting their devotion to food). Indeed, dogs probably do not even *have* "identities" or "values." But humans do. And humans use their attitudes to express their identity and their values a lot. Teenagers wear certain clothing or pierce certain body parts to fit into a desired group. Religious partisans adopt specific positions on issues to show their support for their faith. Parents express contempt for cheaters to communicate the importance of honesty to their children.

These attitudes serve, at least in part, *symbolic* functions for the holders—symbolizing support for and commitment to particular people, groups, institutions, values, or movements. These symbolic attitudes have a **value-expressive function** (Herek, 1986; Katz, 1960; Maio & Olson, 2000b), which means that they allow people to convey an identity that connects them to some groups and makes them distinct from other groups (Brewer, 1991). For example, teenagers may embrace a particular musical style (e.g., heavy metal) because they want to associate themselves with a peer group and dissociate themselves from their parents.

## Testing the Functions of Attitudes

Although social psychologists have talked about the functions of attitudes for a long time (e.g., Katz, 1960; Smith et al., 1956), there was for many years little research on this topic. The main reason for the lack of research was the perceived difficulty of measuring attitude functions: how can an investigator determine whether a particular attitude fulfills an object appraisal or a value-expressive function?

Over the past 15 years, however, there has been an increase in research on the functions of attitudes (e.g., see the book by Maio & Olson, 2000a, in which numerous researchers describe their work in this area). Researchers have developed several novel and creative ways of investigating the functions fulfilled by attitudes (e.g., DeBono & Packer, 1991; Herek & Capitanio, 1998; Murray, Haddock, & Zanna, 1996).

For example, Sharon Shavitt (1990) had the clever idea that attitudes toward a particular object may fulfill the *same* function for almost everyone. Let's think about two examples of the attitudes she studied: attitudes toward *coffee* and attitudes toward *perfume.* Shavitt proposed that one of these attitudes typically fulfills an object appraisal function, and the other typically fulfills a value-expressive function. Can you guess which is which? Object appraisal attitudes give the individual a quick evaluation of the target, whereas value-expressive attitudes tell other people about the individual's identity or values. Shavitt hypothesized that attitudes toward coffee typically fulfill an object appraisal function: people either like or dislike the taste of coffee (as well as its dose of caffeine). Shavitt hypothesized that attitudes toward perfume, on the other hand, often fulfill a value-expressive function: many people purchase a particular brand of perfume because it projects a desired image or because it is promoted by a beautiful model or movie star with whom they identify.

In one study, Shavitt (1990) asked participants to write down thoughts about their attitudes toward a particular target (e.g., coffee, perfume) and to explain why they felt that way. These thoughts were later examined by judges who recorded how often the participants mentioned specific themes. The results were consistent with Shavitt's predictions. When participants described an object appraisal attitude (e.g., their attitude toward coffee), they were likely to mention positive or negative features of the object. In contrast, when participants described a value-expressive attitude (e.g., their attitude toward perfume), they were likely to mention their values, their identity, and what the object communicated to others.

In a second study, Shavitt (1990) tested the implications of attitude functions for the effectiveness of persuasive messages—in this case, advertisements. If attitudes toward coffee give people a quick evaluation of this target, how do you think an advertisement should be constructed to promote a new brand of coffee effectively? Shavitt proposed that the most effective strategy would be to focus on the positive features of the coffee and the rewards it will bring. But if attitudes toward perfume reflect individuals' identities and desired images, how should an advertisement for a new brand of perfume be constructed? Shavitt proposed that the most effective strategy would be to focus on the desirable impression the perfume will make on others.

To test these predictions, Shavitt created two different versions of advertisements for a fictitious brand of coffee and a fictitious brand of perfume. One version of the advertisements stressed the rewards provided by the product, such as "The delicious, hearty flavor and aroma of Sterling Blend coffee come from a blend of the freshest coffee beans," or "The fresh, floral scent of Cadeau perfume comes from a balanced blend of oils and essences." The second version of the advertisements emphasized how the product created a particular image in others' minds, such as "The coffee you drink can reveal your rare, discriminating taste," or "Cadeau perfume is the sophisticated scent that tells people that you are *not* one of the crowd." Participants read one of these advertisements and were asked how much they wanted to try the product (coffee or perfume). The coffee ad focusing on *rewards* generated more interest than did the coffee ad focusing on *image*. In contrast, the perfume ad focusing on *image* generated more interest than did the perfume ad focusing on *rewards*. Thus, the advertisements were more effective when they were consistent with the function fulfilled by the attitude: object appraisal attitudes responded to information about rewards, whereas value-expressive attitudes responded to information about image. These findings show that the function an attitude fulfills has important implications for other psychological processes.

 ## Measuring Attitudes

Social psychologists who want to study attitudes must measure them accurately. In Chapter 2, we introduced the concepts of *validity* and *reliability* (see pages 38–39), both of which are necessary for accurate measurement. Validity refers to whether a measure actually assesses what it is supposed to assess, and reliability refers to whether participants' scores on the measure are stable and free from "random" fluctuations. In striving for these goals of validity and reliability, attitude researchers have developed numerous measurement techniques. We briefly describe some of the most common methods in this section.

# Self-Report Measures of Attitudes

An attitude is an individual's evaluation of a target: his or her judgment of an object, issue, or person on a "good–bad" dimension. Because people are usually aware of their attitudes (or, at least, their *explicit* attitudes), it would seem sensible to ask them directly to report their evaluations. And, indeed, most attitude measurement techniques are *self-report* in nature. Items are administered either in a paper-and-pencil questionnaire or on a computer. Respondents indicate their attitudes by circling a number or word on a response scale (or typing a number or word on the computer) or by placing an *X* along a response dimension. In this section, we describe four common self-report techniques and then discuss some limitations to self-report measures. You can find a more general description of how to develop self-report measures of social psychological constructs in Appendix I of this book.

**Likert-type Scales.** Over the past 70 years, researchers have probably used **Likert-type scales** more than any other technique to measure attitudes. This method evolved from early work by Rensis Likert (1932), who made many contributions to survey methodology. In a Likert-type attitude scale, respondents read a number of statements, each of which expresses a clear position (pro or con) on an issue or a clear attitude (favorable or unfavorable) toward a target. Respondents are asked to indicate their agreement or disagreement with each item. For example, if a researcher wanted to measure participants' attitudes toward capital punishment, he or she might ask them to indicate their agreement or disagreement with such statements as "The death penalty is an effective deterrent to murder," "Murderers deserve to lose their own life," "The death penalty is cruel and unusual punishment," and "Society should never commit murder to punish murder." The first two statements express a clear pro–capital punishment attitude, whereas the last two statements express a clear anti–capital punishment attitude. Respondents would indicate their agreement with each statement by circling one of five possible responses: *Disagree Strongly, Disagree, Undecided, Agree,* or *Agree Strongly.* Participants' attitudes would be calculated by scoring responses to each question from 1 to 5, with higher numbers always reflecting the same direction of attitude (e.g., with higher numbers always reflecting a pro–capital punishment response) and then summing all of the items. For example, the statement "Murderers deserve to lose their own life" could be scored such that *Agree Strongly* would get a score of 5 and *Disagree Strongly* would get a score of 1; the statement "Society should never commit murder to punish murder" would then be scored such that *Disagree Strongly* would get a score of 5 and *Agree Strongly* would get a score of 1. (For both items, the response *Undecided* would get a score of 3.) Participants' total scores across all items would represent their attitude score.

Typically, researchers constructing a Likert-type scale conduct analyses to ensure that all of the items are valid reflections of the target attitude. For example, the correlations between participants' responses to each individual item and their total scores (based on all items) may be calculated, and any items that do not correlate significantly with total scores are dropped from the scale. Some advantages of Likert-type scales for measuring attitudes are that they are relatively easy for researchers to construct, are clear and simple for respondents to complete, and have been shown to produce reliable scores.

**Thurstone Scales.** A more complex technique is a **Thurstone scale,** based on some very early work on measuring attitudes (Thurstone, 1928). A Thurstone scale contains numerous statements on an issue, including some that are clearly favorable and some that are clearly unfavorable, such as "Murderers deserve to lose their own life" (pro–capital punishment) and "Society should never commit murder

---

**Likert-type scale**

*an attitude measurement technique that requires respondents to indicate the extent of their agreement or disagreement with several statements on an issue*

**Thurstone scale**

*an attitude measurement technique that requires respondents to place a check mark beside statements with which they agree*

to punish murder" (anti–capital punishment). But, unlike a Likert-type scale, a Thurstone scale must also include some items that are more neutral on the issue, such as "Capital punishment is a very complicated issue" and "The death penalty may be justifiable in some cases, but very few." All items in a Thurstone scale must have been tested earlier with pilot participants, who would have rated each item for how much it supports or opposes the issue. Based on this pilot work, the final Thurstone scale is administered by giving participants all of the items in a random order and asking them simply to put a check mark beside any statement with which they agree. (Thus, Thurstone scales do not ask for a rating of the *extent* of agreement or disagreement with each statement, but only whether or not the respondent agrees.) Participants' attitude scores are calculated based on those items with which they agreed (i.e., those items they placed a check mark beside). The ratings obtained from the previous pilot participants are used to give each item a "scale value." Participants' attitude scores reflect the average scale value of the statements with which they agreed. More information about the details of how to score Thurstone scales is provided in Chapter 6 of the Student Workbook.

Advantages of Thurstone scales include that they are simple for participants to answer and include items that represent all possible positions on the issue. Disadvantages include that they are more difficult to construct than other methods yet do not appear to be more valid or reliable than simpler methods such as Likert-type scales or semantic differential scales.

**Semantic Differential Scales.** A simple but effective method for measuring attitudes is a **semantic differential scale** (Osgood, Suci, & Tannenbaum, 1957). This procedure asks respondents to rate an attitude object on several evaluative dimensions. The target of the attitude is written at the top of the page, and several rating scales are presented below the target. For example, "Capital Punishment" is written at the top, with such dimensions as "good–bad," "favorable–unfavorable," "support–oppose," and "fair–unfair" written below it. The opposing adjectives appear at each end of a 5-point response scale, and the respondent is instructed to put an *X* or a check mark somewhere on the scale to indicate his or her evaluation. Participants' attitudes are calculated by summing their ratings across all of the evaluative dimensions, with responses for each dimension scored so that high scores always reflect the same direction of attitude. For example, the items might be scored so that high scores reflect pro–capital punishment responses: if respondents put an *X* immediately beside the adjective "good" or "fair," they are given a score of 5, but if they put an *X* immediately beside the adjectives "bad" or "unfair," they receive a score of 1 (an *X* in the middle of either scale gets a score of 3). The total scores across all items represent participants' attitude scores.

Some advantages of semantic differential scales are that they are easy for researchers to construct and straightforward for respondents to complete. Also, a semantic differential scale assesses evaluations very directly, because participants rate the attitude object on dimensions that are explicitly evaluative (including the fundamental dimension underlying attitudes, the *good–bad* dimension).

In Know Yourself 6.1: Attitudes Toward Watching Television (p. 208), you can measure your favorability toward watching television using the two most common kinds of scales in social psychology. The first set of items constitutes a Likert-type scale, and the second set of items constitutes a semantic differential scale.

**Opinion Surveys.** A final type of self-report measure is one that you are probably familiar with: the opinion survey. Opinion surveys are designed to assess public opinion about an issue, event, or group. Sometimes, the survey researcher wants to be able to generalize the findings to a larger population (e.g., all adults in the United States), in which case the sample must be representative of that population. But on other occasions, survey researchers simply want a "snippet" of public

**semantic differential scale**
*an attitude measurement technique that requires respondents to rate a target on several evaluative dimensions (such as good–bad and favorable–unfavorable)*

# Know Yourself 6.1
## *Attitudes Toward Watching Television*

**LIKERT-TYPE SCALE:**

Please indicate the extent to which you agree or disagree with each of the following statements by circling the appropriate number on the answer scale.

1. Many programs that I watch on television are educational and informative.

| 1 | 2 | 3 | 4 | 5 |
|---|---|---|---|---|
| Disagree strongly | Disagree | Undecided | Agree | Agree strongly |

2. Watching television is a big waste of time.

| 1 | 2 | 3 | 4 | 5 |
|---|---|---|---|---|
| Disagree strongly | Disagree | Undecided | Agree | Agree strongly |

3. I enjoy watching television.

| 1 | 2 | 3 | 4 | 5 |
|---|---|---|---|---|
| Disagree strongly | Disagree | Undecided | Agree | Agree strongly |

4. Society would be better off if people watched less television.

| 1 | 2 | 3 | 4 | 5 |
|---|---|---|---|---|
| Disagree strongly | Disagree | Undecided | Agree | Agree strongly |

5. Television portrays too much violence and aggression.

| 1 | 2 | 3 | 4 | 5 |
|---|---|---|---|---|
| Disagree strongly | Disagree | Undecided | Agree | Agree strongly |

6. Watching television is a good way to relax.

| 1 | 2 | 3 | 4 | 5 |
|---|---|---|---|---|
| Disagree strongly | Disagree | Undecided | Agree | Agree strongly |

**SCORING:** Items 1, 3, and 6 are scored using the answer scales as presented (1-2-3-4-5); Items 2, 4, and 5 are reverse-scored (that is, 5-4-3-2-1). Add up all of the items for your overall attitude score. Possible scores range from 6 to 30, and higher scores represent more favorable attitudes toward television.

**SEMANTIC DIFFERENTIAL SCALE:**

Please put an *X* or a check mark on each of the following scales to indicate how you evaluate *watching television*.

### Watching Television:

| | | | | | | |
|---|---|---|---|---|---|---|
| Bad | _____ : | _____ : | _____ : | _____ : | _____ | Good |
| Worthless | _____ : | _____ : | _____ : | _____ : | _____ | Valuable |
| Unpleasant | _____ : | _____ : | _____ : | _____ : | _____ | Pleasant |
| Boring | _____ : | _____ : | _____ : | _____ : | _____ | Interesting |
| Unfavorable | _____ : | _____ : | _____ : | _____ : | _____ | Favorable |
| Harmful | _____ : | _____ : | _____ : | _____ : | _____ | Beneficial |

**SCORING:** Score all items 1-2-3-4-5 from left to right. Add up all of the items for your overall attitude score. Possible scores range from 6 to 30, and higher scores represent more favorable attitudes toward television.

opinion and will not present their findings as necessarily applicable to larger populations. Most opinion surveys contain just one or two items on a particular issue, and responses are often limited to "yes" or "no." For example, an opinion survey on gun control might ask respondents, "Do you support compulsory gun registration for all gun owners?" and/or "Do you believe that everyone has the right to own a gun?" with possible responses being *yes* or *no* (and perhaps also *undecided*). Opinion surveys are very useful for gathering information about public opinion, but social psychologists rarely use them. Empirical research on attitudes generally requires the more elaborate techniques described earlier.

The accompanying Concept Review summarizes the key features of the four self-report measures of attitudes.

**Problems With Self-Report Measures.** All of the self-report techniques we have described rest on at least two assumptions: (1) people know what their attitudes are, and (2) they will report those attitudes honestly. Sometimes these assumptions are doubtful. If researchers are interested in *implicit attitudes,* for example, then they cannot use self-report measures. Recall that an implicit attitude is an individual's automatic evaluative response to a target, which can occur without his or her awareness. By definition, people do not have direct access to their implicit attitudes. To deal with this problem, researchers have developed specific techniques to measure implicit attitudes, which we describe in the next section.

The second assumption underlying self-report measures—that people will report their attitudes honestly—is also questionable in some cases. For instance, often one position on an issue is more socially desirable than other positions (recall our discussion of *socially desirable responding* in Chapter 2; see page 37). In the domain of ethnic attitudes, for example, the socially desirable position is to express positive attitudes toward all ethnic groups. Other topics that can be influenced by

---

## CONCEPT REVIEW
### *Self-Report Measures of Attitudes*

| Measurement Technique | Key Features | Advantages and Disadvantages |
|---|---|---|
| Likert-type scale | Respondent rates agreement or disagreement with attitude statements | Relatively easy to construct |
| | All statements are clearly favorable or clearly unfavorable | Clear and simple to answer |
| | Researcher must identify nonvalid items and eliminate them | Reliable scores |
| Thurstone scale | Respondent indicates agreement with items | More complex to construct |
| | Items include favorable, neutral, and unfavorable statements | Clear and simple to answer |
| | Score is based on those items with which respondent agreed | Neutral items are included |
| Semantic differential scale | Respondent rates attitude object on evaluative dimensions | Very simple to construct |
| | All dimensions reflect the good–bad dimension | Clear and simple to answer |
| | Score is sum of the respondent's ratings | Very direct measure of evaluations |
| Opinion survey | Respondent answers just one or two items on each issue | Very simple to construct |
| | Responses are usually yes, undecided, or no | Useful for gathering information about public opinion |
| | Researchers sometimes obtain a representative sample | Usually not detailed enough for use in psychological research |

social desirability include attitudes toward illegal activities (e.g., illicit drug use, cheating on taxes), attitudes toward harmful behaviors (e.g., aggression, gossiping), and attitudes toward helpful but costly or time-consuming actions (e.g., donating money to charities, volunteering). Given that people want to appear likable, moral, and competent, they may be tempted to shift their answers on attitude scales in the direction of the socially desirable position. Simply put, people may lie a little bit to make themselves look better, which will reduce the accuracy of the measure of attitudes. Partly to inhibit socially desirable responding, some researchers have developed alternative measures of attitudes (e.g., Vargas, von Hippel, & Petty, 2004). In the next section, we describe several alternative strategies that employ nonverbal responses.

Another problem with self-report techniques is that they typically do not yield a clear and easy way to measure the *ambivalence* of an individual's attitude. Recall that an ambivalent attitude includes both positive and negative elements, such as positive feelings but negative beliefs (e.g., someone who loves the taste of banana cream pie but knows it is high in fat and calories). The techniques we have described yield a single, overall score to represent the attitude. Semantic differential scales explicitly require respondents to indicate their evaluations along scales like *good–bad* and *favorable–unfavorable*. Someone whose attitude has both good *and* bad elements cannot express such ambivalence on these sorts of scales.

To measure ambivalence, some researchers have asked respondents to rate the target on *both* positive scales *and* negative scales separately (e.g., Maio, Esses, & Bell, 2000; Priester & Petty, 1996; Thompson et al., 1995). For instance, participants might rate the target on a scale from *not at all good* to *extremely good* and on another scale from *not at all bad* to *extremely bad*. In this way, participants can indicate that they have mixed reactions to the target.

## Nonverbal Measures of Attitudes

In response to the first two problems with self-report measures mentioned above, social psychologists have developed several nonverbal measures of attitudes. These methods do not rely on participants' ability or willingness to report their attitudes. Also, nonverbal measures may provide better assessments of people's unconscious, affective responses to objects than self-report measures (which reflect people's conscious, often primarily cognitive, evaluations). On the negative side, these measures are often difficult to obtain and may not be as sensitive for assessing explicit attitudes as self-report measures. Nonverbal measures include behavioral measures, physiological measures, and implicit measures.

**Behavioral Measures.** Some researchers have used participants' overt behavior to infer their attitude toward an object. For instance, Steven Breckler (1984) used people's willingness to approach a live snake as a behavioral measure of their attitudes. He assumed that people who were unwilling to come close to a snake possessed more negative attitudes than did people who would come right up to a snake (an assumption that was supported by self-report measures that were also obtained).

Douglas Hazlewood and James Olson (1986) required participants to go into a room where another person (the target) was waiting and conduct a brief interview with that individual. Participants had been given information about the target person that was expected to produce positive or negative attitudes. Results showed that participants in the negative attitude condition sat further away from the individual and smiled less often than did participants in the positive attitude condition.

One advantage of behavioral measures of attitudes is that they are usually *unobtrusive measures:* participants usually do not realize that their attitudes are being assessed. By being unobtrusive, behavioral measures reduce problems of self-presentation and social desirability (see Word, Zanna, & Cooper, 1974). Unfortunately, it is often difficult to design a behavioral measure of an attitude. For example, how could attitudes toward nuclear power plants be inferred from behavior? Also, using behavior to measure attitudes assumes that there is a strong, inevitable link between attitudes and actions. As we will see in the section on "When Do Attitudes Predict Behavior?" there are conditions under which attitudes do not predict behavior very well.

**Physiological Measures.** Is it possible that there are objective, physiological reactions that reveal positive or negative evaluations? One category of physiological reactions that has received attention is symptoms of arousal, such as heart rate and blood pressure. Some researchers have found that exposure to negative or disliked objects increases arousal as measured by these symptoms (e.g., Clore & Gormly, 1974; Rankin & Campbell, 1955). These findings make sense if exposure to a negative object is conceptualized as a threat: arousal would prepare the individual for possible "fight or flight." Other researchers, however, have obtained nonsignificant results for arousal symptoms as measures of attitudes (see Zanna, Detweiler, & Olson, 1984). It appears that although heart rate and blood pressure may sometimes indicate the *intensity* of people's feelings about a target, arousal symptoms are poor at distinguishing between positive and negative evaluations (Guglielmi, 1999). That is, strong feelings of liking and strong feelings of disliking may produce similar levels of physiological arousal—a very serious limitation to the usefulness of these measures as indicators of attitudes!

Another category of physiological responses that has been explored as a measure of attitudes is muscle movements in the face, especially in the eye and cheek regions. These movements can be monitored by putting electrodes at certain places on the face—a procedure known as **facial electromyography** (or **facial EMG**). Facial EMG can record very small muscle contractions. Work by John Cacioppo and his colleagues has shown that specific patterns of facial muscle contractions are associated with positive versus negative emotional responses to a stimulus (e.g., Cacioppo, Bush, & Tassinary, 1992; Cacioppo, Martzke, Petty, & Tassinary, 1988; Cacioppo, Petty, Losch, & Kim, 1986). There is also some evidence that the magnitude of people's eye-blink response to a puff of air directed at their eye while they are looking at a target object (e.g., a White face or a Black face) reveals their affective response (e.g., Amodio, Harmon-Jones, & Devine, 2003). Although these findings are interesting and provocative, there are several challenges to using physiological measures of attitudes. First, obtaining physiological measures is a complex and time-consuming procedure. Second, facial EMG appears to be quite sensitive to emotional reactions, but less sensitive to evaluations that lack a strong affective component (e.g., attitudes that are based primarily on cognitive beliefs, such as attitudes toward many consumer products). Third, it is possible for people to deliberately alter or inhibit some of their facial responses, thereby making facial EMG less accurate.

**Implicit Measures.** Implicit attitudes are people's automatic evaluative responses to a target. Implicit attitudes cannot be measured by simply asking people about them, because the responses can occur without awareness (e.g., people's spontaneous, uncontrollable responses to spiders). To measure implicit attitudes, therefore, researchers have designed procedures that assess the extent to which people have an automatic positive or negative response to an object.

How can automatic responses be measured? Researchers have proposed that *reaction times* provide a way (e.g., Cunningham, Preacher, & Banaji, 2001; Fazio, Jackson, Dunton,

**facial electromyography (facial EMG)**

*a procedure for measuring muscle contractions in the face that may be sensitive to positive versus negative responses to a stimulus*

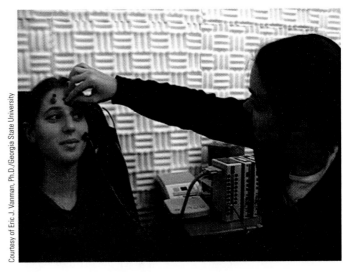

*Facial EMG records muscle contractions in the face that are associated with positive or negative reactions to a stimulus.*

**Implicit Association Test (IAT)**

*a reaction time procedure that provides a measure of implicit attitudes; participants sort targets into a "good" category or a "bad" category, and the speed at which the sorting is completed is taken as a measurement of implicit attitude toward the object*

*"I might report having a feeling of a certain kind. I might say 'I really like X.' But the implicit attitude need not always fit with that. In other words, it's something that resides a little bit below the surface of conscious awareness."*

& Williams, 1995; Kawakami & Dovidio, 2001). The most common reaction time procedure for measuring implicit attitudes is the **Implicit Association Test,** or **IAT** (Greenwald, McGhee, & Schwartz, 1998). In essence, this procedure requires participants to complete two sorting tasks as quickly as possible. On one sorting task, the target of the attitude (e.g., elderly persons, automobiles) must be sorted into the same category as some "good" objects (e.g., words with positive meanings, such as *good, beautiful,* and *honest*). On the second sorting task, the target must be sorted into the same category as some "bad" objects (e.g., words with negative meanings, such as *bad, ugly,* and *dishonest*). We need not go into the details of the methodology here. The basic idea is that if participants complete the task in which the target is associated with "good" things *more quickly* than the task in which the target is associated with "bad" things, they are assumed to have a *positive* implicit attitude toward the target. If, on the other hand, they complete the task in which the target of the attitude is associated with "bad" things *more quickly* than the task where the target of the attitude is associated with "good" things, they are assumed to have a *negative* implicit attitude toward the target.

Although the IAT can be time-consuming to administer and has been the target of some criticism (e.g., Brendl, Markman, & Messner, 2001; Govan & Williams, 2004; Olson & Fazio, 2004), it and other implicit measures of attitudes have been shown to predict individuals' responses, especially spontaneous, nonverbal reactions to targets, such as eye contact, speech hesitations, and smiling (e.g., Dovidio, Kawakami, Johnson, Johnson, & Howard, 1997; Fazio et al., 1995; McConnell & Leibold, 2001; Neumann, Hülsenbeck, & Seibt, 2004). Because these measures are presumed to reflect people's automatic evaluations, they would not be used to measure explicit attitudes.

The key features of different nonverbal measures of attitudes are summarized in the accompany Concept Review.

## CONCEPT REVIEW
### *Nonverbal Measures of Attitudes*

| Measurement Technique | Key Features | Advantages and Disadvantages |
|---|---|---|
| Behavioral measures | Observe respondent's actions toward attitude object | Unobtrusive (respondent unaware) |
| | Favorable actions (e.g., approach object, smile at object) are assumed to reflect favorable attitudes | Not possible for all attitude objects |
| | | Assumes inevitable link between attitudes and behavior |
| Physiological measures | Assess respondent's physiological reactions to object | Time-consuming to obtain |
| | Examples include arousal symptoms and facial EMG | May reflect intensity but not direction of attitude |
| | | May not be very sensitive |
| Implicit measures | Respondent's reaction times are used to infer automatic responses | Respondent cannot easily distort answers |
| | Example is the Implicit Association Test (IAT) | Shown to predict spontaneous, nonverbal reactions to attitude object |
| | Implicit attitudes are assumed to influence the speed with which the attitude object can be paired with good or bad things | Time-consuming to obtain |

# How Do Attitudes Form?

When we discussed the structure of your attitude toward cockroaches, we suggested that it contained three components: an affective component (e.g., feelings of disgust, fear), a cognitive component (e.g., beliefs about cockroaches, such as their potential to spread disease), and a behavioral component (e.g., a history of killing them). These three sources can each contribute to the development of an evaluative response, so if we want to understand how attitudes form, we need to discuss each source separately.

## Affective Sources of Attitudes

Humans are emotional animals. We like to feel good and do not like to feel bad. It is not surprising, therefore, that *affect*—feelings and emotions—influences our attitudes. Think about a food that you dislike because of its taste or smell: it is difficult to evaluate such foods positively even if we know that they are good for us. Now think about a location that is always associated with positive feelings, such as an amusement park: it is difficult to evaluate such places negatively even if we know that they are expensive.

When an object or event consistently produces positive feelings or pleasurable biological responses, we will form a favorable attitude toward it. Watermelon tastes sweet, massages feel good, and water quenches our thirst, so we develop positive attitudes toward watermelon, massages, and drinking water. When an object or event consistently produces unpleasant feelings or aversive biological responses, we will form an unfavorable attitude toward it. Punches to the body cause pain, spoiled milk smells bad, and getting a cold makes us feel lousy, so we develop negative attitudes toward punches, spoiled milk, and colds.

We develop negative attitudes toward colds because they make us feel sick.

**Evaluative Conditioning.** The examples we just gave represent straightforward effects of feelings and emotions on attitudes: when an object or event directly causes positive or negative affect, our attitudes are influenced in the corresponding positive or negative direction. But there is another way that feelings can be linked to targets and thus influence attitudes, in which the target is not the direct cause of the feelings.

Have you ever noticed that things that coincide with a pleasant event can evoke happy feelings? Perhaps you have special feelings for the song that was playing when you first met your romantic partner. Perhaps you think fondly of the restaurant where you were eating when a good friend gave you a surprise gift. In contrast, have you noticed that things that coincide with an unpleasant event sometimes evoke negative feelings? Perhaps you harbor negative feelings for the city you were visiting when you lost your wallet. Perhaps you dislike a television show that you were watching when you received a phone call delivering bad news.

In these examples, an object that had no causal role in the outcome nevertheless comes to evoke positive or negative feelings simply by its association with the affect-arousing event. This process is called **evaluative conditioning** and is a common source of feelings toward objects, settings, and people (for a review, see De Houwer, Thomas, & Baeyens, 2001). A famous example of research on conditioning is Ivan Pavlov's (1927) work with dogs, in which he showed that if a bell was rung together with the presentation of meat powder several times, then simply ringing the bell would cause the dogs to salivate in anticipation (a conditioned response to the bell).

Humans are very easily conditioned (e.g., see Blair & Shimp, 1992; Van Reekum, Van den Berg, & Frijda, 1999; Walther, 2002; Zanna, Kiesler, & Pilkonis, 1970). Many of your attitudes probably reflect, in part, conditioned positive or negative

**evaluative conditioning**

*a process by which objects come to evoke positive or negative affect simply by their association with affect-inducing events*

6.1
**ONLINE**
LAB

feelings. One interesting experiment that documented evaluative conditioning in humans was conducted by John Cacioppo, Beverly Marshall-Goodell, Louis Tassinary, and Richard Petty (1992). These researchers asked participants to read a series of 6-letter words (e.g., reason, finger, winter) and 6-letter nonwords (e.g., petory, triwen, begrid), which were projected onto a screen in front of participants for 7 seconds. Now for the interesting part: mild electric shocks were delivered to the leg of participants in association with either the words or the nonwords. (Participants selected the level of shock in pretesting so that it was "annoying but not painful.") For some participants, a shock was delivered with every real word but with none of the nonwords. For other participants, a shock was delivered with every nonword but with none of the real words. After the exposure trials were completed, participants were asked to rate each of the words and nonwords for how unpleasant it was on a scale from 1 ("very pleasant") to 9 ("very unpleasant"). Figure 6.1 presents the results. As you can see from the figure, nonwords were rated as much more unpleasant when they were associated with shock than when they were not. The same effect occurred for real words: they were rated as more unpleasant when they were associated with shock than when they were not. Thus, participants' ratings of the nonwords and words were influenced by the electric shocks, consistent with an evaluative conditioning perspective. You might also have noticed in the figure that the effect of shock on participants' ratings was stronger for nonwords than for words. The authors speculated that conditioning was stronger for nonwords because participants had never seen them before, whereas they had a long history of exposure to the real words, which interfered to some extent with the conditioning.

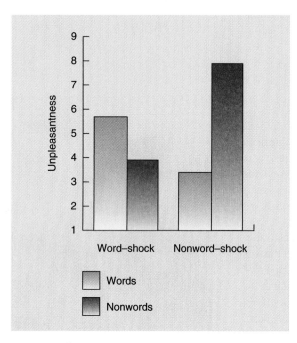

**FIGURE 6.1** Unpleasantness ratings of words and nonwords

From Cacioppo et al., "Microexpressive facial actions as a function of affective stimuli: Replication and extension," *Personality and Social Psychology Bulletin, 28,* 207–233, Fig. 1, p. 218, 1992. Reprinted by permission of Sage Publications.

**mere exposure effect**

*the tendency for repeated contact with an object, even without reinforcement, to increase liking for the object*

**Mere Exposure Effect.** "Familiarity breeds contempt." Do you agree with this well-known saying? Do you think that becoming more familiar with an object or a person leads to unfavorable (or, at least, less favorable) attitudes? Perhaps boredom sets in, or perhaps we learn things about people that reflect negatively on them. For instance, we get tired of songs that have been played too much on the radio, and friendships can wane over time as an acquaintance's habits become increasingly annoying (we will skirt the issue of whether *we* become increasingly annoying to others).

But what about the feelings of comfort and ease that develop when we know someone well? And can't you think of examples of highly familiar things that are very dear to you, such as a childhood toy or a longtime pet? Also, strange or new situations are often intimidating until we become familiar with them. These examples seem inconsistent with the "familiarity breeds contempt" saying.

Robert Zajonc (1968) argued that exposure to an object generally leads to a *more favorable* attitude toward it, especially for relatively novel objects. He proposed that the more often we are exposed to something, even without reinforcement, the more we will tend to like it. Zajonc labeled this effect the **mere exposure effect** and suggested that the well-known phrase about familiarity should be changed to "familiarity breeds *content*."

Why does the mere exposure effect occur? One possibility is that we are uncertain about how to respond to novel objects, and this uncertainty is unpleasant. When we come to know the object better, there is less uncertainty about how to respond to it. Another possibility is that when we are familiar with an object, we can perceive and categorize it more quickly and easily than unfamiliar objects. This ease of recognition is pleasing, so we come to feel good about familiar things. Through mere exposure, positive affect can be linked with an object, which will increase the favorability of the person's attitude toward the object.

Zajonc tested his hypothesis in several experiments, which yielded supportive results. In one study, he showed participants photographs of human faces and asked them how much they thought they would like each person. Some of the faces were shown numerous times before being rated, whereas others were seen only once or twice before rating. The results showed that participants gave more favorable ratings to faces that they had seen more often (see also Bornstein, 1989; Bornstein & D'Agostino, 1992; Murphy, Monahan, & Zajonc, 1995).

6.2
ONLINE
LAB

An interesting phenomenon that might reflect the mere exposure effect is the finding that people tend to like the letters that appear in their own name more than do people whose names do not include those letters (Hoorens & Nuttin, 1993; Nuttin, 1987). For example, people named Paul will tend to rate the letters *a, l, p,* and *u* more favorably than people whose names do not include these letters. The effect is especially strong for people's first and last initials. One explanation for this finding is that people are more familiar with the letters in their own name. (Another possibility is that the letters of one's own name are linked to one's identity, and people like the letters because they view themselves positively—recall the discussions of *self-serving judgments* in Chapters 3 and 4, pages 101 and 136; see Jones, Pelham, & Mirenberg, 2002.)

What about the possible negative effects of repeated exposure mentioned at the beginning of this section? It is true that repeated exposure to a stimulus can sometimes lead to boredom or satiation, such as hearing a song on the radio too many times. Consumer and marketing psychologists have commented on the problem of "wear-out," which occurs when advertising exposure of a product goes beyond the limit and begins to cause a reduction in attitude favorability. But these effects are the exception rather than the rule and occur only after many, many exposures. For most targets, our attitude becomes more positive as we are exposed to it more frequently.

Mere exposure is a phenomenon that is easy to find in everyday life outside the laboratory. One interesting study that tested the effect in a classroom setting is described in Social Psychology in Your Life: Familiarity Effects in the Classroom (p. 216).

Can you think of other examples of the mere exposure effect in real life? Have you ever noticed that something that seemed strange at first eventually became familiar and likable? In Table 6.1, we provide a few examples of everyday experiences

## TABLE 6.1
### *Some Everyday Examples of the Mere Exposure Effect*

You do not really like a new song that you hear for the first time, but after a number of exposures, you come to love the song.

Wine usually tastes awful to people when they first try it as children or teenagers, but many people develop a liking for wine over time.

New fashions can look ridiculous when you see them for the first time, but soon they evoke more positive reactions.

You don't like your new hairstyle at all, but as you get used to it, you begin to like it.

You are introduced to someone at work with the first name of Lydellium; you think the name is really strange, but as you hear the name used occasionally over the next few weeks, you come to think of it as quite natural.

New foods often taste strange at first, but people can come to love unusual foods eventually.

Brand names that are very familiar (e.g., Kleenex, Xerox, Maytag) are usually perceived as trustworthy and high in quality.

Your new neighbor looks rather weird to you the first time you see him, but after you've seen him working in his yard several times, he looks more normal to you.

Abstract art often seems jarring or unattractive when viewed for the first time, but is appreciated more after several viewings.

A foreign language can sound bizarre and undecipherable when you first visit a country, but as your visit continues, the language comes to sound more structured and attractive.

# Social Psychology in Your Life    *Familiarity Effects in the Classroom*

Do you think that you would like a person better if you'd seen him or her several times before? In a test of this idea in a natural social setting, Richard Moreland and Scott Beach (1992) hired four young women to serve as confederates in a study. The women were rated as equally attractive by undergraduate students in a pretest. The women posed as students and attended an undergraduate course on personality psychology—a large class consisting of 191 students. The lectures took place in a 200-seat classroom that was fan-shaped, narrower at the front than the back, and sloping upward from the front to the back. Anyone seated in the front rows was visible to the rest of the class.

On the days that they attended, the women entered the hall a few minutes before the class was to begin, walked slowly down the stairs to a front row, and sat where they could be seen by everyone. During the class, they listened and took notes quietly. At the end of the class, they rose, walked slowly up the stairs to the back of the hall, and left without speaking to any other students. A total of 40 class sessions were held during the term, with a typical attendance rate by the real students of about 75%. One of the target women attended 15 lectures in the course, another attended 10 lectures,

another attended 5 lectures, and another did not attend any lectures at all. Only one target woman attended any particular lecture.

After the term ended, students in the course were shown photos of each of the four women's faces and were asked to rate her on 10 scales that reflected liking and attraction (e.g., ranging from cold to warm, unattractive to attractive, and dishonest to honest). The results are presented in Figure 6.2. The results were simple and clear: the more often the woman had attended the

class, the more positively she was rated. Even though no one in the class had even spoken to any of the women, visual exposure led to more liking.

After making the liking ratings, students in the class were also asked whether they had ever seen each target woman. Only about 10% of the students

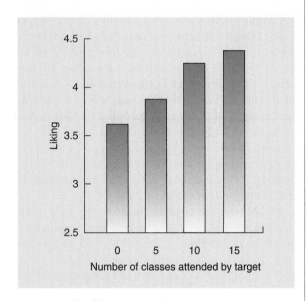

**FIGURE 6.2** Liking for target women based on their class attendance

From Moreland and Beach, "Exposure effects in the classroom: The development of affinity among students," *Journal of Experimental Social Psychology*, 28, 255–276, Table 2, p. 262, 1992. Reprinted by permission of Elsevier.

reported recognizing any of the women, and this rate was similar for all four targets. Thus, the effects of exposure on liking occurred even though most participants could not actually recall seeing the women who attended most often.

that show the mere exposure effect. Perhaps you will recognize your own experiences in some of these examples. Politicians certainly seem to believe in the mere exposure effect: they do everything they can to put their names and photos everywhere, especially during election campaigns.

## Cognitive Sources of Attitudes

What is your attitude toward taking vitamin supplements? Are you favorable or unfavorable? Now consider: *why* are you favorable or unfavorable toward taking vitamin supplements?

Most people would answer this question by referring to their beliefs about the health consequences of taking vitamin supplements. If they believe that vitamin supplements strengthen the body and increase resistance to disease, they will be favorable to vitamin supplements. If, on the other hand, they believe that vitamin supplements do not improve health and might even produce toxic levels of some vitamins, they will be unfavorable to vitamin supplements.

As these comments indicate, your attitude toward vitamin supplements probably depends to a significant degree on your analysis of the rational arguments for and against taking supplements. If you think that vitamin supplements have more positive consequences than negative consequences, you are likely to be favorable toward them, whereas if you think that vitamin supplements have more negative consequences than positive ones, you are likely to be unfavorable toward them.

This influence of cognitive information occurs in many attitudes. Your attitudes toward people you know are influenced by your beliefs about their positive and negative characteristics. If you think that Ronnelle is friendly and honest, your attitude toward her will be favorable; if you think that she is conceited and a troublemaker, your attitude toward her will be negative. Your attitudes toward consumer products are influenced by your perceptions of their quality and performance. If you believe that your refrigerator has been reliable and economical, your attitude toward it will be positive; if you know that it has been unreliable and required expensive repairs, your attitude toward it will be negative.

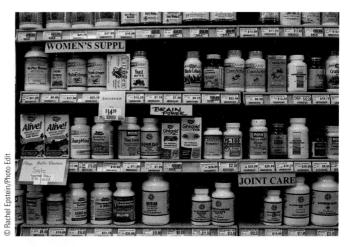

What is your attitude toward taking vitamin supplements?

This idea that our beliefs about an object, person, or issue influence our attitude toward it may seem a bit obvious, but the idea is important nonetheless. We tend to evaluate objects, people, and policies positively when we believe that they possess mostly positive characteristics, and we tend to evaluate them negatively when we believe that they possess mostly negative characteristics.

This link between beliefs and attitudes has been documented in many studies (see Ajzen & Fishbein, 1980; Doll & Orth, 1993; Eagly & Chaiken, 1993; Sheppard, Hartwick, & Warshaw, 1988). For example, William Fisher, Jeffrey Fisher, and Barbara Rye (1995) measured participants' attitudes toward several "safer sex behaviors," such as *using condoms during intercourse* and *discussing contraception with partners.* Participants were asked to rate these behaviors on good–bad evaluative scales. The researchers also measured participants' beliefs about the consequences of the various behaviors. For example, they measured whether participants believed that using condoms would effectively protect against AIDS and other sexually transmitted diseases. Results showed that participants' attitudes toward these safer sex behaviors were strongly correlated with their beliefs about the positive and negative consequences of the behaviors. For example, participants who knew that condoms provide effective protection against sexually transmitted diseases expressed more favorable evaluations of using condoms than participants who were uncertain of the effectiveness of condoms for avoiding STDs. Thus, participants' attitudes were directly and logically related to their beliefs.

## Behavioral Sources of Attitudes

In Chapter 4, we discussed several processes involved in making judgments about ourselves. One of the theories described was *self-perception theory* by Daryl Bem (1967, 1972). Self-perception theory is based on the intriguing hypothesis that if we cannot directly "feel" our internal states, we may *infer* them from our actions. For example, if we are asked about our attitude toward seatbelts, and our attitude is weak or ambiguous, we may think about how we have behaved with regard to seatbelts in the past. If our behavior has been predominantly positive (e.g., we have typically used seatbelts in cars and taxis), we will infer that we are favorable toward using seatbelts; if our behavior has been more negative (e.g., we have often failed to use seatbelts in cars and taxis), we will infer that our attitude toward using seatbelts is unfavorable.

Thus, attitudes can be based on behavioral information—specifically, information about our own past behavior toward the target (see Albarracín & Wyer, 2000; Olson, 1992). This process is unlikely to occur when we have strong and well-developed attitudes (Chaiken & Baldwin, 1981; Holland, Verplanken, & van Knippenberg, 2002). For example, we do not need to review how we have acted toward ice cream before we can report our evaluation: we *know* we love it! We also do not need to review our past actions toward mosquitoes before we can report our evaluation: we *know* we hate them!

Can you think of an attitude domain in which you might use your own behavior to infer your evaluation? What about an activity that you perform only occasionally? For example, if asked the question "Do you like hiking?" you might reply by referring to your behavior: "Yeah, I guess so—I go hiking several times a year" or "No, not really—I haven't gone hiking for a couple of years." Some people, of course, know that they love or hate hiking, but others may gauge their attitudes toward the activity by reflecting on their actions.

## Physiological Processes and Attitudes

We have addressed three sources of attitudes that have been studied by attitude theorists: affective, cognitive, and behavioral sources. There is another domain, however, that also has implications for attitudes: physiological or biological processes. The topic of the biology of attitudes has historically received little attention from social psychologists, but it has been the focus of more research recently.

It may seem implausible to you that biological processes are important for understanding people's attitudes. After all, don't attitudes have to be learned? We are not born liking or disliking objects and issues. If attitudes are learned, doesn't this mean that they must be environmentally caused?

But let's think about this for a moment. Have you ever been intoxicated with alcohol? If so, did this drug affect your behavior—for example, did you do anything that you wouldn't normally have done? Humorous examples of this phenomenon might include dancing more energetically than usual at the bar or singing on the way home on the bus with your friends. More ominous examples might include getting involved in a violent confrontation in the bar or having unprotected sex—actions that can kill.

How does alcohol affect behavior? For one thing, alcohol changes how people feel about various actions (i.e., it changes their attitudes toward the actions, at least temporarily); it also impairs their ability to think rationally about the consequences of different actions. The fact that alcohol has these effects underscores that humans are biological beings, whose cognitive and emotional systems are influenced by chemicals in the blood and brain. These effects of alcohol and other drugs show that physiological processes have important implications for attitudes.

**Alcohol Myopia.** The effect of alcohol on information processing has been termed **alcohol myopia** (Steele & Josephs, 1990). Alcohol myopia refers to the fact that intoxication reduces cognitive capacity, which results in a narrowing of attention (hence, *myopia*). When individuals are intoxicated, their ability to pay attention to multiple cues is impaired. As a result, only the most obvious and strongest cues, external or internal, will be perceived, which will increase the impact of these cues compared to times when the individual is sober. For instance, if the obvious external cues are consistent with aggressive behavior (e.g., someone insults and shoves another person), then aggression is more likely when an individual is intoxicated

**alcohol myopia**

*the tendency for intoxication to reduce cognitive capacity, which results in a narrowing of attention*

than when he or she is sober. If the strongest external and internal cues are consistent with having sex (e.g., the individual is alone with the potential partner and is sexually aroused), then unprotected sexual behavior is more likely when an individual is intoxicated than when he or she is sober.

Several interesting studies by Tara MacDonald, Mark Zanna, and Geoff Fong (1995, 1996) at the University of Waterloo tested whether alcohol intoxication influenced university students' willingness either to drive while intoxicated or to have unprotected sexual intercourse. In one experiment, male students were randomly assigned to either a *sober* or *intoxicated* condition (women were not included because of concerns about possible negative health effects of consuming alcohol while pregnant). In the sober condition, participants viewed a videotape and answered some questions without having consumed any alcohol. In the intoxicated condition,

*Alcohol myopia* results in a narrowing of attention.

participants consumed three alcoholic drinks, spaced 20 minutes apart, and then viewed the same videotape and answered the same questions. The 10-minute videotape portrayed two undergraduates, Mike and Rebecca, in a situation in which sexual intercourse without using a condom was possible. The videotape showed the two individuals talking in a hallway after writing an exam, where Mike asked Rebecca out on a date. The next scene showed the couple at the campus bar, where they were drinking and dancing, including a slow dance during which they kissed. In the next scene, the couple was kissing passionately on a couch at Rebecca's apartment, and Rebecca suggested they move to her bedroom. Mike awkwardly stated that he didn't have any condoms, but Rebecca said that she was on the pill. The two then discussed that they were "clean" and did not "sleep around." Mike then asked Rebecca what she wanted to do. She kissed him and replied, "I don't know. What do *you* want to do?" The video then ended with a freeze frame.

Participants had been instructed to imagine themselves in the role of Mike as they watched the video. Do you think that this procedure was involving and engaging for participants? That is, did it create *experimental realism* (see Chapter 2, page 55)? Because the video was very well done, an acceptable level of experimental realism was probably achieved.

When the video ended, participants completed a questionnaire that assessed their willingness to have unprotected sexual intercourse if they were in Mike's position. Results showed that intoxicated participants expressed greater willingness to have unprotected sex with Rebecca than did sober participants. Intoxicated participants also expressed stronger agreement with a number of questionable "justifications" for having unprotected sex, such as "Rebecca looks totally healthy, so it's unlikely that she has AIDS or other sexually transmitted diseases." Thus, intoxication increased the likelihood that participants would act in a risky fashion when the most obvious cues supported such behavior. Other studies by the same researchers showed that intoxicated participants expressed greater willingness to drive after drinking than did sober participants.

These studies have an important message: we must realize that we are, quite literally, *different people* when we are intoxicated—with different attitudes and different behavioral inclinations. We must either avoid becoming heavily intoxicated or arrange to have someone else help us when we are impaired (e.g., by serving as a designated driver).

**Attitude Heritability.** Many characteristics are inherited from our parents (who may have inherited them from their parents). Obvious examples include hair color, eye color, and height. The physical characteristics shared by almost all humans, such as having two eyes, two ears, and two legs, are also inherited. Interest in the genetic determination of things other than physical characteristics has greatly increased in the past 20 or 30 years, with important discoveries identifying genetic "markers" for a number of illnesses or conditions (e.g., breast cancer, muscular dystrophy).

What about attitudes? Is it possible that we inherit some of our attitudes from our parents? For instance, if someone has a positive attitude toward sports, could the person have inherited this attitude from his or her parents? The answer is almost certainly no if, by inherited, we mean that a particular gene caused the attitude (e.g., a gene caused the person to be favorable toward sports). But the answer is very possibly yes if we mean that biological characteristics (e.g., strength, coordination) inherited from the parents made it more *likely* that he or she would develop a favorable attitude toward sports.

Think about yourself. What are some important features or abilities that you think you probably inherited from your parents? Such features or abilities might include your height, facial features, intelligence, shyness, or musical ability. (We should note that not all scientists would agree that such things as intelligence, shyness, or musical ability are highly heritable.) Now think about whether the features or abilities that you inherited might have influenced your attitudes. Is it possible that some of your attitudes were shaped by your inherited features or abilities?

Let's consider some feasible hypothetical examples. Javier inherited unusual physical strength and coordination from his parents. These abilities made him successful in various sports. Because of this success, he developed positive attitudes toward athletic activities.

Rolanda inherited high intellectual abilities from her parents. Because she was so intelligent, she did extremely well at school and also became an excellent chess player. These achievements fostered positive attitudes toward education and intellectual pursuits.

John inherited from his parents an inner-ear structure that was very sensitive to changes in balance. As a result, he felt nauseated quite easily. This tendency toward nausea made him dislike roller coasters, boats, and airplane rides.

Do you think that characteristics you inherited from your parents affected any of your attitudes?

© Jose Luis Pelaez, Inc./CORBIS

Sara inherited an outgoing, extraverted disposition from her parents. This sociability meant that she felt very comfortable in social surroundings and interpersonal interactions. Her extraversion fostered positive attitudes toward parties, group activities, and other social settings.

Do these examples clarify how people's inherited abilities and characteristics might predispose them to having certain kinds of experiences, such as success at sports or success at school, which then foster certain attitudes? Although the experiences (e.g., success at sports) are the specific events that cause the attitudes (e.g., positive attitudes toward sports), the experiences occur partly *because of the inherited characteristics* (e.g., natural athletic ability). Thus, the final attitudes reflect a combination of biology and experience. The flowchart in Figure 6.3 depicts the hypothesized process.

James Olson, Anthony Vernon, Julie Harris, and Kerry Jang (2001) distributed an attitude survey that measured attitudes toward 30 different targets to a total of 336 pairs of same-sex twins: 195 pairs of identical twins (who share all of their genes) and 141 pairs of fraternal twins (who share some but not all genes). Research using samples of twins is based on the idea that by comparing the responses of identical and fraternal twins, it is possible to estimate the extent to which differences between the respondents can be attributed to genetic factors. Specifically, if identical twins report more similar attitudes to one another than do fraternal twins, then a genetic component in attitudes is indicated. The researchers found that almost all of the attitudes (26 of 30) showed at least some genetic component, supporting the hypothesis that many attitude differences between individuals are partly due to genetic differences (see also Abrahamson, Baker, & Caspi, 2002; Eaves, Eysenck, & Martin, 1989; Waller, Kojetin, Bouchard, Lykken, & Tellegen, 1990; Zuckerman, 1995). The five attitudes that yielded the highest genetic influence were attitudes toward reading books, abortion on demand, playing organized sports, roller-coaster rides, and the death penalty for murder.

Researchers do not yet understand why particular attitudes have a large genetic component (e.g., attitudes toward the death penalty) and why other particular attitudes have little or no genetic component (e.g., attitudes toward capitalism). Research to date has focused on identifying *which* attitudes are heritable, rather than *why* they are heritable. One goal of future research will be to understand the mechanisms that make some attitudes more heritable than others.

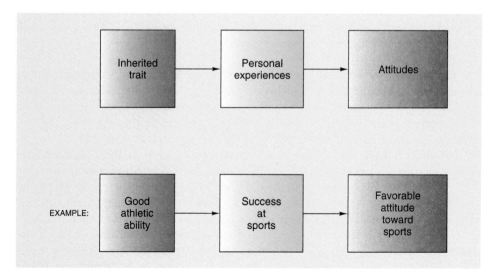

**FIGURE 6.3** How attitudes could be partly inherited

Abraham Tesser (1993; Crelia & Tesser, 1996) proposed that attitudes with a substantial biological component might be more important to people than attitudes with very little biological component. To test this hypothesis, he measured the speed with which people could report their attitudes; he assumed that important attitudes can be reported more quickly than unimportant attitudes. Tesser compared the response speeds for attitudes shown in previous studies to be highly heritable (e.g., attitudes toward the death penalty and attitudes toward the use of birth control) with the response speeds for attitudes shown in previous studies to be very low in heritability (e.g., attitudes toward capitalism and attitudes toward social support for immigrants). As predicted, people could report the highly heritable attitudes more quickly than the attitudes with little heritable component. In another study, Tesser showed that people were more attracted to someone else who was similar to them on highly heritable attitudes than to someone who was similar to them on low heritability attitudes. Again, this finding supports the idea that people care more about highly heritable attitudes than attitudes low in heritability.

# Attitudes Across the Life Span

Have your attitudes changed as you have gotten older? Have you found yourself becoming more like your parents? Less like them? Can you see a consistent trend in yourself toward becoming either more liberal or more conservative on social and economic issues? What have been the sources of important changes in your opinions: Friends? The media? Thinking about the issues yourself?

In this section, we discuss a few developmental issues in the area of attitudes. We consider some of the early experiences that can influence attitudes and address the issue of whether people become more conservative as they grow older.

## The Effects of Early Experiences on Attitudes

Personal experience is necessary before attitudes will form. Infants are born with no attitudes except a few that are closely related to survival, such as an aversion to pain and an attraction to the human face. Other attitudes require input from experience before they develop.

During our formative years, we are influenced by many people. In the earliest years of childhood, parents and family are extremely influential. As we approach adolescence, our peer groups become increasingly important.

**socialization**

*the process by which infants are molded into acceptable members of their society*

**Parental Socialization.** **Socialization** is "the process by which an infant becomes an acceptable member of his or her society—one who behaves appropriately, knows the language, possesses the requisite skills, and holds the prevailing beliefs and attitudes" (Harris, 1995, pp. 461–462). For the first few years of life, the family is the most important source of socialization, especially parents.

Researchers have shown that parents exert influence over their children in a variety of ways. Parents express opinions and values that children may internalize. Can you think of times when your parents expressed a value such as honesty and tried to explain why it was important? Parents also model behavior, which children may imitate. Can you think of times when you imitated your parents' actions, such as treating toys as if they were your children? Parents also provide much of the information that young children obtain about the world. Can you think of topics that you first learned about primarily from your parents, such as religious issues and educational values? Given these various modes of influence, it is not terribly surprising that children express attitudes that are similar to those of their parents on a variety of issues, including gender roles, cigarette smoking, political views, and values (e.g., Chassin, Presson, & Sherman, 1984; Cunningham, 2001; Jessop, 1982; Rohan & Zanna, 1996; Ruble & Goodnow, 1998).

There is also evidence that parenting styles influence children's values in adulthood. Tim Kasser, Richard Koestner, and Natasha Lekes (2002) reported data from 79 individuals whose values were measured at age 31 and whose parents had been interviewed 26 years earlier (when the participants were 5 years old). Based on the early interviews, parents were classified in terms of restrictiveness (e.g., their use of physical punishment, their demands for sexual modesty) and in terms of coldness (e.g., their avoidance of physical affection, their limited use of praise). Results showed that *nonrestrictive* parenting was associated with greater emphasis at age 31 on imaginativeness and independence, whereas *restrictive* parenting was associated with greater emphasis at age 31 on obedience and politeness. Results also showed that a *warm* parenting style was associated with greater emphasis at age 31 on freedom and personal responsibility, whereas a *cold* parenting style was associated with greater emphasis at age 31 on safety issues such as family and national security. These findings suggest that nonrestrictive and warm parenting styles, which give children autonomy and acceptance, are more likely to instill adult values that encourage independence and caring relationships with others (see also Kasser, Ryan, Zax, & Sameroff, 1995; Williams, Cox, Hedberg, & Deci, 2000).

One rather surprising domain in which researchers have *not* always found strong correlations between children's and parents' attitudes is racial attitudes. Frances Aboud and Anna-Beth Doyle (1996), for example, found no relation between the racial attitudes of third-grade children and their mothers in Montreal. Tamara Towles-Schwen and Russell Fazio (2001) found no relation between White college students' implicit attitudes toward Blacks and their reports of their parents' racial attitudes. Instead, these latter researchers found that implicit attitudes toward Blacks were correlated with positive interactions with Blacks in high school, suggesting the importance of personal experiences.

**Reference Groups.** Parents do not always rule our world. Developmental psychologists have found that as children's exposure to people outside the family increases, parental influence is gradually overtaken by peer influence, most notably in the form of reference groups. In fact, some theorists have argued that, in the long run, peer groups are more important agents of socialization than are parents. For example, Judith Harris (1995, 1998) has argued that parents do not socialize children—*children* socialize children. She believes that children's experiences outside the home, in the company of their peers, are very influential in determining attitudes, beliefs, and personality traits.

A **reference group** is a group that serves as a standard of comparison for an individual, whether in terms of attitudes, values, or behavior. Individuals try to conform to the norms and values of their main reference groups. A reference group can be any collective that an individual recognizes: a group of friends, people who prefer a certain musical style, a club, a gang, a political party, or any other identifiable group. The most obvious ways that people conform to reference groups is by joining them, if possible (e.g., a friendship group or a club), or by copying their appearance and behavior. Thus, adolescents may adopt the dress and language of goths, rappers, preppies, or skaters—sometimes to the horror of their parents.

Theodore Newcomb (1943) conducted a famous early study of reference groups by following an entire class of students at Bennington College (an all-women school at that time) through their four years at the university. The prevailing values at the college were very liberal, whereas most of the students came from wealthy, conservative backgrounds. Newcomb found that most students became increasingly liberal over their four-year period at the college. He also found that

**reference group**
*a collection of people that serves as a standard of comparison for an individual, whether in terms of attitudes, values, or behavior*

students who expressed liberal views tended to be more popular on campus than those who expressed conservative views, and the latter students (those who expressed conservative views) tended to identify strongly with their family. These data show the power of reference groups.

Newcomb and his colleagues followed up his original survey approximately 25 and 50 years later and compared the Bennington College graduates with a comparable group of women from similar socioeconomic backgrounds who did not attend the college (Alwin, Cohen, & Newcomb, 1991a; Newcomb, 1963; Newcomb, Koeing, Flacks, & Warwick, 1967). These researchers found that the Bennington graduates expressed more liberal attitudes and married men with more liberal attitudes than the comparison group. It appears that their experiences at Bennington College had a long-lasting impact on the women's attitudes and lives.

**Jeer Pressure.** Think back to when you were in high school (which may not be very long ago!). What do you remember as your *greatest fear* at that time in your life? What possible event caused you to lose the most sleep? Being a victim of crime? Global nuclear war? Having a car accident? Failing at school? Coming down with a serious illness?

Based on a survey of high school students conducted by Jeremy Shapiro, Roy Baumeister, and Jane Kessler (1991), there is a good chance that you chose "none of the above" for your greatest fear. Instead, the most common answer given by high school students asked to identify their greatest fear was *being ridiculed*. Does this surprise you? This finding shows how important it is to teenagers to be accepted by their peer group.

*Ridicule* is derogatory humor directed at an individual concerning some aspect of his or her behavior or appearance. It occurs in many forms: laughing at someone's looks or clothes, mocking someone's values, insulting someone's family, or otherwise humiliating someone, usually in public. Ridicule is very common in our society, but its frequency and emotional impact are greatest during adolescence and the teenage years, when the desire to belong and to be popular is at its peak. Being the target of ridicule is extremely painful, as most of us know from personal experience. Being a constant target of ridicule can lead to withdrawal, depression, and even suicide. It can also lead to violence, in which the target of ridicule exacts revenge on his or her tormentors by fighting or, in extreme cases, shooting them in the school or schoolyard.

Why do people ridicule others? One reason is that, by mocking another person, the individual doing the ridiculing feels superior and may be seen as clever by people in his or her clique who witness it. But the more common reason is, quite simply, to gain or establish control. Peer pressure involving ridicule can be a powerful way to enforce conformity to group norms. Ridicule can be an effective tool for influencing others—both the target of the ridicule and observers. Research on the intentional use of embarrassment (which is often milder than true ridicule) has shown that more than 90% of people who use embarrassment to establish control say that they successfully achieved their goals (Sharkey, 1992).

**jeer pressure**

*the conformity pressure that is produced by seeing someone ridiculed by another person*

Leslie Janes (Janes & Olson, 2000) coined the term **jeer pressure** to refer to the conformity pressure that is produced by seeing someone ridiculed by another person. People do not have to be the direct target of ridicule to feel jeer pressure; even observers of the ridicule will conform to norms so that they will not be ridiculed too. Think of a group of teenagers sitting outside a high school. If one of the individuals ridicules a student walking by who isn't wearing the newest fashions, other members of the group are unlikely to say anything that will draw notice to themselves—instead, they will quietly conform to the clique's norms. Similarly, other bystanders are unlikely to intervene, opting instead to try to sneak away without being ridiculed as well.

Janes and Olson (2000) showed that jeer pressure can make people express public attitudes and opinions that conform to other people's views. (We discuss conformity in greater detail in Chapter 8.) In one study, university students watched a videotape showing two men changing a tire on a bicycle. In the process of changing the tire, one of the men made a number of mistakes, such as pinching his finger in a pump. In one version of the videotape, the second man ridiculed the mistakes (e.g., "I guess that's why they call it a *foot* pump!") and made other, generally derogatory but potentially humorous comments (e.g., "If a loser like him can fix a tire, so can you"). In another version of the videotape, the man who made the mistakes expressed the same derogatory comments, but this time *directed at himself* (e.g., "If a loser like me can fix a tire, so can you"). This self-ridicule condition was not expected to create jeer pressure, because making fun of oneself is not threatening to others. Finally, in a third version of the videotape, no ridicule or derogatory comments occurred. After watching the videotape, participants were asked to evaluate it on a number of dimensions, such as clarity, enjoyability, and overall educational value. They recorded their ratings on sheets that already included the alleged answers of two previous participants. These "previous ratings" were actually made by the experimenter and were designed to be inaccurate (e.g., these answers rated the tape as low in clarity and high in enjoyability, whereas actual pilot testing had shown that students rated all three versions of the tape as high in clarity and low in enjoyability). Participants who had observed one person ridiculing someone else on the videotape conformed more closely to the ratings of the alleged previous subjects than did participants who had observed self-ridicule or no ridicule at all. Thus, observing an individual being ridiculed by another individual led to conforming responses on the questionnaire—jeer pressure altered the public expressions of attitudes.

© Michael Newman/Photo Edit

*Jeer pressure* is pressure to conform that is produced by seeing someone ridiculed.

## Aging and Attitudes: Do We Become More Conservative As We Grow Older?

A widely held public opinion is that older people tend to be more conservative than younger people. For example, it is commonly believed that older people are more likely to identify with conservative political parties. Older people are often also thought to be more conservative (right-wing) on moral and religious issues. Although some evidence has supported age-related party affiliations (e.g., Crittenden, 1962), recent surveys have yielded divergent findings. During the 1980s, for example, the proportion of young people supporting the Republican party in the United States increased (Axelrod, 1986). Similarly, the gap between older and younger respondents on issues of morality declined during the 1980s, as young people became more conservative (Oskamp, 1991).

An alternative perspective on aging and attitudes is that particular experiences of a generation influence the attitudes of that generation. For instance, living through the Great Depression in the 1930s or the Second World War in the 1940s was thought to give all members of that generation a particular perspective on many issues. There is some evidence that people who were active in the protest movements of the 1960s were significantly influenced by their experiences (Jennings, 1987). There is also evidence that adults tend to be most familiar with the political events that occurred when they were first entering active political involvement, which means that people from the same generation are most familiar with the same political events (Schuman & Rieger, 1992). But, on balance, the evidence for "generational effects" is weak, which may not be surprising given the huge differences in the specific experiences of individuals who lived through the same generation (Holsti & Rosenau, 1980; Kinder, 1998). The study by Newcomb (1963) described earlier supports the idea that exposure to a particular reference group (e.g., the liberal atmosphere at Bennington College) can affect attitudes across the life span. Given that different members of a single generation will have many different reference groups, strong generational effects seem unlikely.

So what is the answer to the question with which we titled this section? The evidence seems most supportive of a negative answer: older people are not consistently more conservative than younger people. Does this challenge your impressions of your grandparents? In Chapter 7, we will again consider age-related differences, but this time in attitudinal rigidity—whether older people's attitudes are more resistant to change. The answer may surprise you.

## How Do Attitudes Affect Behavior?

One reason that social psychologists are interested in attitudes is that attitudes are presumed to influence behavior. We opened the chapter with a description of Phillip, whose actions seem surprising or inappropriate when viewed in the context of today's attitudes and beliefs. We suggested, however, that Phillip's behavior was quite understandable given the prevalent attitudes of his time. Our comments assumed that attitudes are an important cause of people's behavior—an assumption that has motivated much of the research in this chapter.

Let us mention once again the potentially confusing two-way relationship between attitudes and behavior. We discussed earlier how someone might use his or her past behavior to infer an attitude (e.g., "I guess I don't like peanut butter, because I almost never eat it"). This reasoning reveals that past behavior can influence judgments about current attitudes. But current attitudes can also affect future behavior—the focus of the present section. For instance, someone's current attitude toward peanut butter can influence how often he or she eats it in the future.

But *how* do current attitudes affect future behavior? What are the psychological mechanisms that might explain the effects of attitudes on actions? We describe in this section two principal mechanisms: *rational choice* and *selective perception*. Rational choice refers to making deliberate, reasoned decisions based on our attitudes. Selective perception refers to a more subtle process: the biasing effect of our attitudes on how we interpret and understand the world.

### Rational Choice

One source of attitudes (the *cognitive component*) is information—beliefs about the target. You believe that apples are healthful and taste good. You believe that cars made by Mercedes-Benz are high in quality but very expensive. You believe that cockroaches are dirty and hide in dark corners. These pieces of information about the targets can guide your behavior in a rational manner. You will eat apples regularly. You will pass on buying a Mercedes-Benz until you've made your first million (just a matter of time, right?). If you find cockroaches in your apartment, you will try to kill them and to spray pesticide into dark corners.

These examples illustrate that attitudes guide many of our rational choices. Behavior is often (though not always) voluntary and deliberate, based on our knowledge about the options. When we go to the grocery store, we are free to buy whatever kind of food we want, so we choose to buy things that we believe taste good and are nutritious. Our actions are often sensible and logical.

**The Theory of Reasoned Action.** This idea that behavior is often rational forms the core of Martin Fishbein and Icek Ajzen's (1975) **theory of reasoned action.** This model views humans as rational decision makers who behave on the basis of logical beliefs (hence its name, *reasoned action*). The theory is one of the most influential models in the history of research on attitudes.

Figure 6.4 presents the key concepts in the theory of reasoned action. Let's work backwards from behavior in the model. Fishbein and Ajzen proposed that the most immediate cause of a behavior is a **behavioral intention,** which refers to the individual's plan to perform or not perform the action. When you took a can of ginger ale from the refrigerator last night and drank it, you *intended* to do so—your behavior of drinking ginger ale was preceded by the behavioral intention to drink ginger ale ("I think I'll have a ginger ale now"). Most of our actions are based on intentions in this manner, because most of our actions are voluntary (we can either do them or not do them).

The idea that behavior normally follows from intentions is not really very useful for understanding *why* people do things; stating that people do things "because they intend to do them" seems rather circular. To understand behavior better, it is necessary to look at the factors that cause intentions. Fishbein and Ajzen proposed that behavioral intentions are caused by two variables: the individual's attitude toward the behavior and the individual's subjective norm concerning the behavior.

In their model, an attitude is an individual's overall evaluation (good–bad judgment) of a particular behavior, which is based on the individual's beliefs about the *consequences* of the behavior. Their model parallels the perspective we presented earlier when discussing cognitive sources of attitudes: attitudes represent the overall

**theory of reasoned action**
*a model of behavior that views humans as rational decision makers who behave on the basis of logical beliefs*

**behavioral intention**
*an individual's plan to perform or not perform an action*

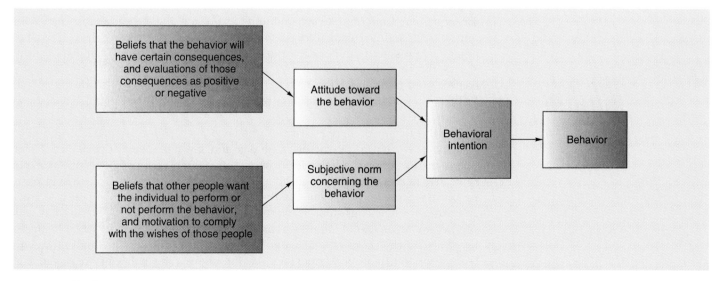

**FIGURE 6.4** The theory of reasoned action

Adapted from Ajzen & Fishbein, 1980, p. 8.

## TABLE **6.2**
### *Attitudes Toward Doing Volunteer Work in the Theory of Reasoned Action: Attitudes Are Based on the Individual's Beliefs About the Consequences of the Behavior*

| Belief About a Consequence of Doing Volunteer Work | Evaluation of the Consequence |
| --- | --- |
| Helps others | Very good |
| Makes me feel good about myself | Good |
| Introduces me to new people | Very good |
| Takes time away from other activities | Bad |
| Gives me useful skills and experiences | Good |
| Sometimes makes me tired | Bad |
| Provides a good example to others | Good |
| Overall Attitude Toward Doing Volunteer Work = Positive | |

**subjective norm**

*an individual's feelings of social pressure to perform or not perform an action*

favorability of someone's beliefs. Table 6.2 provides a set of illustrative beliefs that might underlie someone's attitude toward *doing volunteer work*. This hypothetical individual has seven beliefs about the consequences of doing volunteer work, which include "helps others," "makes me feel good about myself," and "takes time away from other activities." Most of these consequences are evaluated positively by the individual. As a result, his or her overall attitude toward doing volunteer work is also positive.

What are **subjective norms?** Let's begin with the more general concept of *norms,* which are cultural standards that define proper behavior (e.g., we should wait our turn when there is a lineup at the grocery store, we should tell the truth); people feel social pressure to follow norms (see Chapter 8). In the theory of reasoned action, *subjective norms* are individuals' feelings of social pressure to perform or not perform an action. They are based on individuals' beliefs that other people want them to perform the action or do not want them to perform the action, as well as their motivation to do what these other people want. A husband might feel social pressure from his wife and children to stop smoking; he knows that they want him to stop, and he generally tries to comply with his family's wishes. A woman might feel pressure from her doctor to perform regular breast self-examinations; she knows that her doctor wants her to do these examinations regularly, and she doesn't want to disappoint him or her. In both of these cases, the individuals will feel some social pressure to act in a particular way, either to stop a behavior or to perform a behavior.

In the theory of reasoned action, behavioral intentions depend on attitudes and subjective norms. Favorable attitudes and favorable subjective norms foster intentions to perform a behavior, whereas unfavorable attitudes and unfavorable subjective norms foster intentions to avoid performing it. If attitudes and subjective norms are consistent with one another, then behavioral intentions will be strong and actions will be consistent. If, on the other hand, attitudes and subjective norms conflict, then behavioral intentions may be uncertain and actions may be inconsistent. A man who wants to smoke but knows that his family wants him to stop will feel very conflicted about smoking. His intentions (and behavior) may vacillate depending on whether he thinks about his personal preferences or his family's wishes. (This example might remind you of the concept of *ambivalent attitudes,* which contain both positive and negative elements about a target and can lead to inconsistent behavior.)

© Erik S. Lesser/Getty Images

Research has shown that people are more likely to donate blood when they have a positive attitude toward this behavior and when their subjective norms support this behavior.

The theory of reasoned action has been tested and supported in many different domains, including voting behavior, donating blood, consumer purchases, eating at fast-food restaurants, and participating in political protest marches (see Ajzen & Fishbein, 1980; Brindberg & Durand, 1983; Eagly & Chaiken, 1993; Kelly & Breinlinger, 1995). These tests of the theory have shown that attitudes and subjective norms predict behavioral intentions, and behavioral intentions predict behavior. People make rational choices in deciding how to behave, and their choices are based on both attitudes and social pressure.

For example, Kevin McCaul, Katherine O'Neill, and Russell Glasgow (1988) measured participants' beliefs, attitudes, subjective norms, and behavioral intentions regarding flossing one's teeth every day. Participants also maintained a record of their actual behavior over a one-week period. Attitudes were measured by asking participants to rate "flossing my teeth every day" on several evaluative scales, such as good–bad and beneficial–harmful. Beliefs were measured by asking participants whether they thought that flossing their teeth every day would have various consequences, such as preventing gum disease, preventing tooth decay, and making their teeth feel clean. Subjective norms were measured by asking participants whether people who were important to the participants wanted them to floss their teeth every day. The beliefs underlying subjective norms were measured by asking participants whether certain specific individuals (e.g., their parents, dentist, partner) wanted them to floss their teeth every day, as well as their motivation to do what these individuals wanted them to do. Finally, behavioral intentions were measured by asking participants to rate how likely it was that they would floss their teeth every day over the next week.

Figure 6.5 (p. 230) presents the correlations from the McCaul et al. (1988) study, which supported every component of the theory of reasoned action. First, participants' beliefs that tooth-flossing will have positive or negative consequences correlated strongly with their attitudes toward tooth-flossing, $r = .52$ (correlations of .5 or more indicate strong relationships). Thus, participants with positive beliefs about tooth-flossing tended to have favorable attitudes toward tooth-flossing. Second, beliefs that other people want them to floss or not correlated quite highly with subjective norms

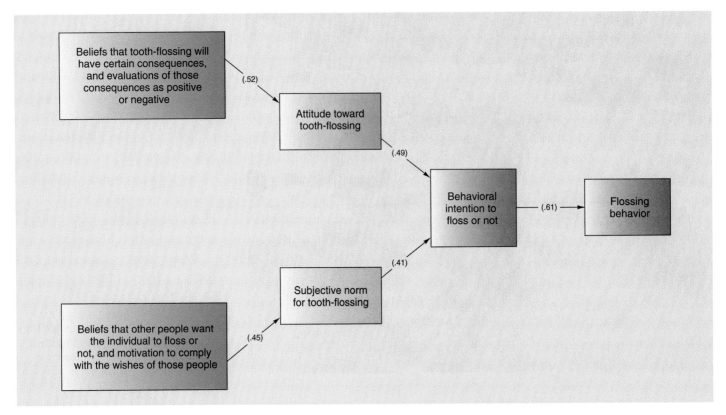

**FIGURE 6.5** Correlations between components of the theory of reasoned action for tooth-flossing

Adapted from McCaul, O'Neill, & Glasgow, 1988, Figure 2, p. 121.

for tooth-flossing, $r = .45$ (correlations between .4 and .5 indicate moderately strong relationships). Thus, participants who believed that others wanted them to floss felt social pressure to floss. Third, attitudes and subjective norms both correlated quite highly with behavioral intentions to floss or not, $r = .49$ and $r = .41$. Thus, participants who were favorable toward flossing and who felt social pressure to floss were likely to intend to floss. And finally, behavioral intentions correlated very strongly with actual flossing behavior, $r = .61$. Thus, participants who intended to floss generally did floss. In sum, these correlations supported the view that tooth-flossing is a behavior that is based on individuals' reasoned decisions, as predicted by the theory of reasoned action.

**Attitudes and Behavior in the Health Domain: The IMB Model.** A second model that analyzes behavior in terms of rational choices is the **IMB model of AIDS-preventive behavior** (Fisher & Fisher, 1992). Jeffrey Fisher and William Fisher, who are at the University of Connecticut and the University of Western Ontario, respectively, proposed the IMB model (the letters stand for Information, Motivation, and Behavioral skills), which is based partly on the theory of reasoned action. These researchers wanted to identify the most important determinants of "safer sex behaviors," such as using a condom during intercourse and refusing to have unsafe sex.

Figure 6.6 presents the key concepts in the IMB model. The authors proposed that three major elements contribute to safer sex behaviors. *Information* refers to basic knowledge about sexually transmitted diseases, contraception, and protective methods. For example, unless people have a general understanding of AIDS, how it

**IMB model of AIDS-preventive behavior**

*a theory postulating that information, motivation, and behavioral skills guide individuals' protective actions in the sexual domain*

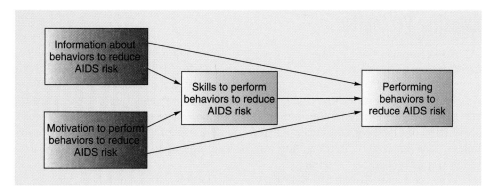

**FIGURE 6.6** The IMB model of AIDS-preventive behaviors

Adapted from Fisher, Fisher, Misovich, Kimble, & Malloy, 1996.

is transmitted, and how it can be prevented, they cannot engage in protective behaviors. *Motivation* encompasses the concepts of attitudes and subjective norms from the theory of reasoned action. Fisher and Fisher proposed that both favorable attitudes toward safer sex behaviors and perceived pressure from others to perform these behaviors would increase individuals' motivation to engage in the preventive behaviors. Finally, *behavioral skills* refer to the ability to perform safer sex behaviors effectively. For example, people must be able to use condoms correctly and be able to discuss and negotiate safer sex with their partner (e.g., to raise the issue and to discuss it openly) in order for unsafe sex to be avoided.

Like the theory of reasoned action, the IMB model conceptualizes behavior as involving deliberate choices among options. Ultimately, individuals must decide themselves whether to engage in risky sexual behaviors or instead to behave safely. Their choices will depend on the information they possess, their motivation to perform risky or safer behaviors, and their skill at performing preventive behaviors correctly.

A fascinating test of the IMB model was conducted by the Fishers and their colleagues (Fisher, Fisher, Misovich, Kimble, & Malloy, 1996). These researchers developed an educational program that was designed to improve every component of the theoretical model. A slide show provided basic information about AIDS and about contraceptive methods. A small group discussion was designed to make participants' attitudes toward safer sex behaviors more favorable. Videos of using condoms and live portrayals of negotiating safer sex with a partner were designed to improve participants' behavioral skills. The educational program consisted of three 2-hour sessions that were held one week apart. The program was offered on some floors, but not all, of several dormitories at the University of Connecticut. More than 500 students completed the program.

Two months later, these students were contacted and compared to other students who lived on floors of the dormitories where the program was not available. Results showed that students who completed the program were more likely to have protected themselves by using condoms during sexual intercourse than were students who did not participate in the program. Thus, a critical risk-reducing behavior was more common after the educational program (see also Jemmott, Jemmott, & Fong, 1992).

Think for a moment about your own actions in the domain of sexual behavior. Have you ever behaved in a risky manner, such as not using a condom during intercourse? If the answer is yes, does the IMB model help you to understand your actions? Do you think you fell short in terms of information, motivation, or behavioral skills?

# Selective Perception

Attitudes can guide behavior in a second, more subtle way than rational choice. Attitudes are a lens through which we view the world. Attitudes can influence what we notice, how we interpret information, and what we remember (e.g., Eagly & Chaiken, 1998; Eagly, Chen, Chaiken, & Shaw-Barnes, 1999; Fazio, 1990; Fazio & Williams, 1986; Frey, 1986; Kennamer, 1990; Schuette & Fazio, 1995). Attitudes can also affect the counterfactual thoughts we generate about past events (e.g., Crawford & McCrea, 2004). By changing our perceptions of the world around us, attitudes can influence our actions.

Have you ever listened to political commentators after a candidates' debate? If so, you may have noticed that commentators from different political leanings gave very different evaluations of the debate. After a presidential debate, for example, Democratic commentators may compliment the Democratic candidate's performance and criticize the Republican candidate, whereas Republican commentators may compliment the Republican candidate's performance and criticize the Democratic candidate. Such differences can leave viewers wondering, "Did these people watch the same debate?"

We tend to be suspicious of political commentators, because their allegiances might cause them to be untruthful about how they actually think the candidates performed. But sometimes the differences of opinion are real—commentators from the different parties truly believe that their own candidate was more effective. How do these contrasting perceptions of the same event occur?

**Biasing Effect of Attitudes.**  The bottom line is that people often see what they *expect* to see and what they *want* to see, based on their attitudes. You may recall from Chapter 3 (see page 69) that *schemas,* or *concepts,* can produce selective information processing, such that information that is consistent with an activated schema is more likely to be noticed and recalled. Claudia Cohen's (1981) experiment, in which participants watched a videotape of a woman and tended to recall information consistent with her alleged occupation (waitress or librarian), illustrated this phenomenon. We also discussed in Chapter 3 how *stereotypes* (which are a type of schema—namely, schemas representing human groups) can guide interpretation (see page 76). If a young man is categorized as a skinhead, the negative stereotype of skinheads will lead people to interpret ambiguous actions as hostile. These processes reflect that people often see what they expect to see (recall also *illusory correlations* from Chapter 3, see page 91, which occur when someone believes that two things are correlated when, in fact, they are independent).

In the same fashion, *attitudes* can influence what we notice and how we interpret things. If we have a positive attitude toward a coworker, we will be predisposed to notice positive things about him or her and to interpret ambiguous information positively; exactly the opposite will occur if we have a negative attitude toward the coworker. These biases reflect the tendency to see what we *expect* to see. Thus, attitudes can influence how we see the world. Our perceptions of the coworker would have been different if we did not have our existing attitude toward him or her. Given that our impressions affect how we behave, attitudes can influence behavior by changing our perceptions.

Note that this biasing effect of attitudes can occur for both *explicit* and *implicit* attitudes (see Strack & Deutsch, 2004). Even when individuals are unaware that they have an automatic positive or negative evaluative response to an object, the implicit attitude may affect their perceptions of the object. For instance, if someone has an implicit negative response to members of a minority group, this automatic evaluative response may lead him or her to interpret actions by members of the group as negative, which, in turn, may cause him or her to behave negatively toward members of the group. Thus, selective perception represents one way that implicit attitudes can subtly affect behavior without the individual's awareness.

We also tend to see what we *want* to see, based on our attitudes. For instance, we are generally motivated to interpret information as *supporting* our attitudes. After all, we want to believe that our attitudes are correct, and information that supports our views implies that we are correct. Also, some attitudes express important aspects of our identity (recall the *value-expressive function* of attitudes), so information that supports our attitudes can serve to validate our identity.

Charles Lord, Lee Ross, and Mark Lepper (1979) conducted a well-known study that showed selective perception of information based on participants' attitudes toward the death penalty. Participants were selected because they had previously expressed either clearly favorable or clearly unfavorable attitudes toward capital punishment. When they came to the experimental session, they were given two articles to read and evaluate, each of which described a study that had investigated whether the death penalty deters people from committing murder. These two articles had actually been constructed by the experimenter to present opposing views of capital punishment. One study (article) concluded that capital punishment does reduce the murder rate (it is an effective deterrent), whereas the other study concluded that the murder rate was unaffected by capital punishment (it does not have any deterrent effect). Participants were asked to evaluate and comment on each article and then to report their current attitude on this issue.

What should have happened in this study if people processed the articles objectively? All participants were given mixed information, some supporting and some opposing capital punishment. The most sensible outcome, therefore, would seem to be to become *less extreme* on the issue—less certain about which side is correct. After all, the contradictory research findings showed that it is unclear whether or not the death penalty is effective as a deterrent. If people processed the material in an unbiased manner, pro–capital punishment participants should have become less pro, and anti–capital punishment participants should have become less anti.

But what actually happened? Pro–capital punishment participants became *more pro,* and anti–capital punishment participants became *more anti.* People became *more extreme* after reading the mixed information on the issue! Why? It turns out that participants evaluated the study that supported their own view more positively than the study that opposed their view (see also Edwards & Smith, 1996). They thought that the study supporting their view was methodologically strong, whereas they saw problems in the study opposing their view. Table 6.3 (p. 234) presents a few examples of actual comments that participants wrote about each study.

Although the information given to participants was mixed, it did not *seem* mixed to participants themselves. In their eyes, the evidence consisted of one strong study supporting their view and one weak study opposing their view. Obviously, then, their own view was correct! These findings illustrate rather dramatically how people's attitudes can influence the interpretation of attitude-relevant information. If the researchers had followed the participants and watched their behavior with regard to the death penalty (e.g., how strongly the participants argued for their own position with other people), those who originally favored the death penalty would presumably have argued for it even more strongly, whereas those who originally opposed the death penalty would have argued against it even more strongly. By changing perceptions of information, attitudes can ultimately change our behavior.

Why do people process information in this biased, defensive manner? In an interesting set of studies, David Sherman, Geoffrey Cohen, and their colleagues (Cohen, Aronson, & Steele, 2000; Sherman & Cohen, 2002; Sherman, Nelson, & Steele, 2000) provided evidence that the biasing effect of attitudes represents a *self-serving* process. These researchers suggested that because people want to believe that their attitudes are correct, it is threatening to the self-concept to admit that

**TABLE 6.3**
*Selected Comments by Pro— and Anti—Capital Punishment Participants on Pro—*
*and Anti—Capital Punishment Studies*

| | Comments On | |
|---|---|---|
| **Participant's Attitude** | **Pro—Capital Punishment Study** | **Anti—Capital Punishment Study** |
| Pro—capital punishment | "The experiment was well thought out, the data collected was valid, and they were able to come up with responses to all criticisms." | "There were too many flaws in the picking of the states and too many variables involved in the experiment as a whole to change my opinion." |
| Pro—capital punishment | "It seems that the researchers studied a carefully selected group of states and that they were careful in interpreting their results." | "The research didn't cover a long enough period to prove that capital punishment is not a deterrent to murder." |
| Anti—capital punishment | "The study was taken only 1 year before and 1 year after capital punishment was reinstated. To be a more effective study, they should have taken data from at least 10 years before and as many years as possible after." | "The states were chosen at random, so the results show the average effect capital punishment has across the nation. The fact that 8 out of 10 states show a rise in murders stands as good evidence." |
| Anti—capital punishment | "I don't feel such a straightforward conclusion can be made from the data collected." | "There aren't as many uncontrolled variables in this experiment as in the other one, so I'm still willing to believe the conclusion made." |

Adapted from Lord, Ross, & Lepper, 1979, Table 2, page 2103.

attitude-inconsistent information might be valid. Therefore, people process information in a way that protects their attitudes ("I must be right"). But how will people respond to mixed information if they are made more confident about their self-worth? Will people who have affirmed their self-worth show less bias in evaluating information? The answer appears to be yes. Cohen et al. (2000) presented a debate on the issue of abortion to people who strongly supported one or the other side on this issue. When participants were simply exposed to this debate without an opportunity to affirm their self-worth, they showed the same bias as in Lord et al. (1979): participants evaluated the information supporting their own side as much more reasonable and intelligent than the information supporting the opposite side. But when participants were given an opportunity to write about a value that was important to them and that had proved meaningful in their life (e.g., family, sense of humor), the biasing effect of attitudes was significantly reduced. Presumably, these latter participants were less biased because they were confident about their self-worth, so admitting the validity of attitude-inconsistent information was not as threatening.

**Perceiving Media Coverage.** One of the most long-standing, bitter, and complex political issues of our generation has been the situation in the Middle East. Many people have very strong views and high emotional involvement in this issue. Based on the notion of selective perception, it might be expected that individuals on different sides of the Israeli–Palestinian conflict would interpret similar information differently. In fact, this pattern has been documented in several studies of people's perceptions of the media (Giner-Sorolla & Chaiken, 1994; Perloff, 1989; Vallone, Ross, & Lepper, 1985).

For instance, Roger Giner-Sorolla and Shelly Chaiken (1994) asked participants to watch a videotape compiled from national news broadcasts (CBS and NBC evening reports) on two consecutive evenings, which included 11 minutes of coverage of the Middle East. The coverage reported the killings of an Israeli settler and two Palestinian men in a confrontation in the West Bank, along with the reactions of Israeli settlers and Palestinian militants. Coverage also included scenes from the funeral of the settler and scenes of the Israeli Army destroying Arab homes in retaliation.

Participants' attitudes on the Middle East conflict were measured in a pretest, and approximately equal numbers of pro-Israeli, pro-Palestinian, and neutral individuals were brought to the laboratory. After watching the videotape, participants answered several questions about the news coverage, including a key question about whether the coverage was biased toward one side or the other. The results showed that participants' perceptions of the coverage were strongly correlated with their personal views on the issue. Pro-Israeli respondents judged the news coverage to be biased against the Israeli side and in favor of the Palestinian side. Pro-Palestinian respondents, on the other hand, judged the news coverage to be biased against the Palestinian side and in favor of the Israeli side. Neutral respondents fell in between the two groups of partisans. Thus, participants who had strong initial attitudes regarded the media coverage as unfair to their own side. This phenomenon of both sides viewing the media as biased against them was labeled the **hostile media phenomenon** by Vallone et al. (1985; see also Matheson & Durson, 2001).

**hostile media phenomenon**

*the tendency for people who feel strongly about an issue to believe that the media coverage of the issue is biased against their side*

Why did these perceptions of "hostile media" occur? One possibility is that individuals with strong attitudes believed that most of the evidence presented in the news reports should have favored their own side, because, after all, their side was right and occupied the higher moral ground. Thus, to be "fair" in these partisans' eyes, the news coverage should have presented more evidence for their own side than for the other side. But the impartial news reporters presented an equal, balanced account of both sides—which did not satisfy *either* group of partisans. Each group saw the coverage as biased because the weight of the information did not favor their own side of the conflict.

A story in the *New York Times* on April 14, 2002, suggests that the tendency for pro-Israeli and pro-Palestinian individuals to see the American media as biased has not changed much since Giner-Sorolla and Chaiken's study in 1994. The newspaper story reported that more and more people are subscribing to specialized Middle Eastern television stations, specifically either the Israeli Network or Al Jazeera, an Arab channel that broadcasts from Qatar. These channels provide very different coverage of the Israeli–Palestinian conflict, strongly emphasizing one side or the other. Thus, people are able to watch coverage that suits their bias. In explaining why they subscribed to one of these channels, the comments of people on the different sides are instructive. An Arab man was quoted as saying, "The American media is totally, totally biased toward Israel." In direct contradiction, an Israeli man was quoted as saying, "I do see the bias [in the American media]—they're not exactly Jew-lovers."

Together with the capital punishment results described earlier, these differences in perceptions of the media illustrate how individuals' attitudes can affect their perception of information. Exactly the same material can be seen very differently by participants with opposing attitudes. By altering our perceptions of events and information that we encounter, attitudes can change our behavior. For example, if people believe that the American media are biased, they may subscribe to a specialized channel—an action that is likely

People on both sides of the Middle East conflict believe that the mass media are hostile toward their own side.

to widen the breach between the two sides. Individuals with different attitudes behave differently, in part, because they view the same events, people, and information differently.

## ● ● ● When Do Attitudes Predict Behavior?

In our discussion of *how* attitudes influence behavior, we identified rational choice and selective perception as the two principal mechanisms. The first of these processes is relatively direct and presumably occurs at a conscious level (e.g., buying apples because we think they are good for us), whereas the second is more subtle and spontaneous—in fact, we may not even be aware of it (e.g., changing how we interpret media coverage).

In this section, we examine the related question of *when* attitudes predict behavior. Our goal here is to specify some of the conditions under which attitudes predict behavior strongly. Let's begin our discussion by generating some nonlaboratory examples of attitude-based actions. If we asked you to think of some instances of behavior by other people that obviously reflected their attitudes (rather than external factors, such as following a rule or earning money), what actions would come to your mind?

Here are two examples. One is the behavior of social activists, such as environmental activists who use their bodies to block lumber trucks from entering a tree-cutting area, or antiabortion advocates who picket abortion clinics. These behaviors seem attitude-driven because they are both unusual and costly (e.g., potentially injurious, time-consuming); observers assume, therefore, that the individuals must feel very strongly about the issue. A second domain of behavior that is commonly presumed to reflect attitudes is leisure activities, such as tennis, reading, or fishing. We believe that most people are basically free to do whatever they want during their time off, so they probably have positive attitudes toward their hobbies and leisure activities. If someone goes fishing regularly, we assume that he or she must like fishing.

These examples of attitude-driven behavior domains (activism, leisure) can be used to illustrate some important principles about *when* attitudes will predict behavior. In particular, they highlight the fact that certain kinds of attitudes and certain kinds of behavior are especially likely to yield high attitude–behavior correlations. We elaborate on these points below.

### When the Attitude Is Strong

Strong attitudes predict behavior better than weak attitudes. The activism example illustrates this idea nicely. Activists care a lot about the issue and usually possess relatively extreme attitudes (they are *extremely* pro or *extremely* anti). When people are willing to risk physical injury by blocking trucks or engaging in some other form of protest, it is abundantly clear that their attitudes are strong.

What do social psychologists mean, exactly, by a *strong* attitude? The concept of attitude strength actually incorporates several qualities (see Bassili, 1996; Bizer & Krosnick, 2001; Petty & Krosnick, 1995; Visser & Mirabile, 2004). We just mentioned the feature of *extremity:* people with strong attitudes often endorse extreme positions near the end of the scale. A second feature that reflects the strength of the attitude is *importance:* the individual says that the attitude is very important to him or her. A third quality of strong attitudes is *accessibility,* which is a characteristic that we discussed in Chapter 3 (see page 72). Accessibility refers to how easy it is to activate a schema or attitude (Bassili, 1996; Higgins, 1996). Highly accessible

## CONCEPT REVIEW
### Aspects of Attitude Strength

| Feature | Explanation | Feature of Strong Attitudes |
|---|---|---|
| Extremity | Extreme attitudes are very unfavorable or very favorable. | Strong attitudes tend to be extreme. |
| Importance | Important attitudes are ones that the individual cares about. | Strong attitudes tend to be very important. |
| Accessibility | Accessible attitudes are ones that can be activated quickly and easily. | Strong attitudes tend to be highly accessible. |
| Direct experience | Attitudes based on direct experience come from personal contact with the attitude object. | Strong attitudes tend to be based on direct experience. |

attitudes come to mind quickly and spontaneously when we encounter or think about the target. Finally, a fourth feature of strong attitudes is that they are often based on *direct experience* with the attitude object, rather than on indirect information obtained from other people. For example, if a perceiver's attitude toward a young man is based on actual interactions with him, it is likely to be stronger and more confidently held than if it is based on information about him provided by an acquaintance of the perceiver. These aspects of attitude strength are summarized in the accompanying Concept Review.

Findings in numerous studies have supported the idea that extreme, important, accessible, and direct-experience attitudes predict behavior better than do moderate, unimportant, less accessible, and indirect-experience attitudes (Bassili, 1996; Doll & Ajzen, 1992; Fazio, 1990; Fazio & Zanna, 1981; Houston & Fazio, 1989; Kraus, 1995). Each of these findings can be interpreted as showing that when an attitude is strong, it predicts behavior better than when it is weak.

For example, Russell Fazio and Carol Williams (1986) telephoned people during the 1984 U.S. presidential campaign and asked them to evaluate the candidates, Ronald Reagan and Walter Mondale. The interviewer measured both the content of participants' attitudes (for or against each candidate) and the *speed* with which they provided the evaluations. This reaction time measure was assumed to reflect the *accessibility* of participants' attitudes. A follow-up telephone interview was conducted *after* the election, and participants were asked to report their voting behavior. The researchers then divided the sample into two groups: those who reported their attitude toward Ronald Reagan in the first interview relatively quickly (high accessibility group) and those who were relatively slow to respond in the first interview (low accessibility group). The correlation between participants' attitudes toward Reagan in the first interview (positive or negative) and their voting behavior was strong in both groups, but it was significantly stronger in the high accessibility group ($r = .82$) than in the low accessibility group ($r = .60$). If people were pro-Reagan, they were more likely to vote for him if they had provided their evaluation quickly than if they had been slow; if people were anti-Reagan, they were more likely to vote against him if they had provided their evaluation quickly than if they had been slow. Thus, highly accessible attitudes predicted behavior better than attitudes low in accessibility.

# When the Behavior Is Controllable

If someone held a gun to your head and said that you had to write a letter to the local newspaper stating that automobiles should be banned, would you comply? Of course you would. Would your letter reflect your actual attitude toward automobiles? No, it would not. Does the fact that you behaved inconsistently with your attitude pose problems for social psychologists who argue that attitudes predict behavior? Again, no. You had *no choice* but to comply with the demand to write the letter.

Attitudes are assumed to guide behavior when the individual has the freedom to behave in whatever way he or she chooses. The example of leisure activities given earlier illustrates this point. Behavior must be voluntary, or controllable, in order for the individual's personal preferences to play a role. If the person is not allowed to choose how to behave, then his or her attitudes are irrelevant (he or she doesn't have any choice!). In contrast, if the person is free to decide how to behave, then his or her attitudes will presumably guide behavior, at least in part. For instance, people are generally free to engage in whatever leisure activities they most enjoy.

It turns out that many domains of behavior are *not* completely controllable. People quite often lack—or *believe* that they lack—behavioral control, thus perceiving that they are not free to behave as they choose. Under these conditions, attitudes may not predict behavior, because individuals do not feel completely free to choose their actions. In fact, Icek Ajzen, who developed the theory of reasoned action together with Martin Fishbein (Fishbein & Ajzen, 1975), thought that perceptions of control are so important that he proposed a revised model labeled the *theory of planned behavior* (Ajzen, 1985, 1991). The theory of planned behavior retained the constructs of attitudes and subjective norms as predictors of behavioral intentions, but added the construct of *perceived behavioral control* as a third predictor of intentions. Ajzen hypothesized that people will intend to perform a particular behavior when they have a favorable attitude toward the behavior, when they feel social pressure to perform the behavior, and when they perceive that they have control over the behavior (e.g., are capable of performing it). If perceived behavioral control is low, then favorable attitudes and subjective norms may not be enough to produce intentions to perform the behavior.

What are some everyday examples of situations in which people lack or believe that they lack control, which can lead to attitude-inconsistent behavior?

1. *External threat.* Sometimes there are strong external threats or pressures that force us to behave in a certain way whether we want to or not. As a teenager, did you avoid doing some things that you wanted to do (e.g., skipping class on a nice day, drinking alcohol at a party) because you were afraid of the punishment you'd receive if your parents found out? If so, these cases represented acting in ways that were inconsistent with your attitudes because threat of punishment took away your freedom to do what you wanted.

2. *Lack of alternatives.* Sometimes a lack of alternative choices can take away our behavioral freedom. Have you ever hung around with someone you didn't really like because he or she was the only person available? Or, if you live in a small city or town, you may have only one local newspaper. Everyone in the town must read that newspaper or none at all (at least for local news). Someone might have a negative attitude toward the local paper but read it anyway, because there is no other way to keep up to date on local events.

3. *Biological needs or addictions.* Sometimes biological needs force us to do things we do not really want to do. Can you remember when you were a child and your parents tried to get you to eat healthy foods that you did not like? Did your parents try the old trick of not giving you any options for eating? You had to eat the fish or nothing at all. For most kids, hunger eventually motivates

the attitude-inconsistent behavior of eating the disliked food. Another example of biological pressure is addiction—smokers might desperately want to quit smoking but not even try because they believe they are so addicted that stopping is impossible. A perceived lack of control "forces" them to smoke despite a desire to stop.

4. *Lack of time.* Let's close with a factor that is common for college students. Most college students report favorable attitudes toward exercising regularly. Yet most college students do not engage in regular exercise. Why? One common reason given by students is that they simply "do not have the time" to exercise. College students are busy at school and sometimes at a part-time job as well. Although they wish they could exercise, they often feel that it is simply impossible given their busy schedule. This belief may well be true for some students, but other students might be able to incorporate exercise into their schedule if they really tried. Unfortunately, if individuals *believe* that they do not have the time to exercise, they may not even try to do so, irrespective of their favorable attitudes. The lack of perceived behavioral control will mean that their favorable attitudes are irrelevant and do not predict behavior.

## When the Measures Match

Some famous early studies on attitudes appeared to show that attitudes do not predict behavior very well (for a review, see Wicker, 1969). For instance, Richard LaPiere (1934) took a well-dressed Chinese couple on a tour of the United States, visiting more than 250 restaurants and hotels. Sometimes the Chinese couple went into the establishment alone, and sometimes LaPiere accompanied them. At the time the study was conducted, anti-Chinese sentiment was quite common in the United States. Nevertheless, only one of the 250+ establishments refused to serve the Chinese couple. After the tour was completed, LaPiere sent a letter to each establishment asking whether they served members of the Chinese race. Approximately 50% of the establishments replied. Surprisingly, more than 90% of those who replied said they would not serve Chinese guests. Thus, most of the responders expressed negative attitudes toward Chinese guests even though LaPiere had already found that their establishment would serve his Chinese couple. These results certainly seem to imply that attitudes do not predict behavior strongly.

There was a consistent problem in many of these early studies, however, including LaPiere's work. Most of the studies involved correlating a measure of a broad attitude (e.g., attitudes toward members of the Chinese race) with a measure of a single, specific behavior (e.g., serving a specific Chinese couple). It is inappropriate to use a general attitude to predict a specific behavior. The two measures do not *match*—one is general (broad) and one is specific (narrow). When the measures do match, attitudes will predict behavior strongly.

An example will illustrate this point. Imagine that you are doing a research project on the relation between attitudes and behavior. You interview two individuals, Daesha and Robert, and ask them to report their attitudes toward "living a healthy lifestyle" on a scale from 1 to 10. They report somewhat different attitudes: Daesha states that she is very favorable toward living a healthy lifestyle (9 on the 10-point scale), and Robert states that he is moderately favorable (7 on the 10-point scale). To measure a behavior that should be related to this attitude, you ask Daesha and Robert whether they exercise regularly, with possible answers being "always," "usually," "sometimes," and "never." Surprisingly, Daesha reports that she "usually" exercises regularly, whereas Robert reports that he "always" exercises regularly.

But notice that a relatively general attitude (toward "living a healthy lifestyle") is being used to predict a narrower, more specific behavioral measure (the regularity of

**TABLE 6.4**
*Living a Healthy Lifestyle: Daesha Versus Robert*

| Healthy Behaviors | Always, Usually, Sometimes, or Never? | |
| --- | --- | --- |
| | Daesha | Robert |
| Exercising regularly | Usually | Always |
| Eating healthy foods | Always | Usually |
| Not smoking | Always | Always |
| Avoiding too much alcohol | Always | Usually |
| Getting enough sleep | Usually | Sometimes |
| Using suncreen | Always | Always |
| Seeing a doctor annually | Usually | Never |
| Wearing a seatbelt | Always | Always |

exercise). Table 6.4 lists a number of behaviors that all represent "living a healthy lifestyle." Healthy behaviors can include exercising regularly, eating healthy foods, not smoking, avoiding too much alcohol, getting enough sleep, and so on. The table shows that although Daesha reports exercising less regularly than Robert, she performs most of the other healthy behaviors *more* regularly than Robert. For example, she "always" eats healthy foods and avoids excess alcohol, whereas Robert only "usually" eats healthy foods and avoids excess alcohol. A measure of healthy living that included *all* of these domains would show that Daesha lives a healthier lifestyle, overall, than does Robert, consistent with Daesha's more favorable attitude. Thus, to test whether a broad, general attitude (e.g., toward living a healthy lifestyle) predicts behavior, the behavior measure must also be broad and general, sampling from most or all of the relevant specific behaviors (e.g., exercising, eating healthy foods, not smoking, etc.).

A classic and compelling empirical demonstration of the idea that broad attitudes predict broad measures of behavior was conducted by Russell Weigel and Lee Newman (1976). These researchers studied a group of residents of a small town in New England, assessing their attitudes and behaviors relating to environmental issues. First, participants completed a measure of attitudes toward a variety of topics, including their attitudes toward protecting the environment. Over the next six months, several measures of pro-environmental behaviors were obtained in unobtrusive ways (i.e., without the participants knowing that the measures were part of

© AP/Wide World Photos/The Morning Call, Betty E. Cauler

Exercising regularly is only one aspect of living a healthy lifestyle.

a study). The first behavioral measures were taken three months after participants' attitudes were assessed. An alleged member of an environmental protection organization (actually an experimental assistant) came to the door of each resident and asked him or her to sign three petitions on environmental issues. One petition opposed offshore drilling along the New England coast, one opposed construction of nuclear power plants, and one proposed tougher laws for cars' exhaust systems. Participants could sign each petition and were also asked whether they would be willing to circulate the petitions to family or friends. Six weeks later, another set of behavioral measures was obtained. Participants were contacted by a different individual and asked to participate in a roadside litter pickup program in the town. Three possible times were specified, and participants were encouraged to bring a friend or family member to the pickup as well. The behavioral measures were whether individuals attended at least one of the sessions and whether they brought another person to one of the sessions. Finally, two months after the litter pickup request, participants were contacted by yet another person, who asked them to participate in a test program for recycling newspapers and glass (the study was conducted before such programs were common). Residents were asked to put out recyclable materials on the same day each week. A behavioral measure was then obtained for each of eight weeks, reflecting whether or not participants put out any materials that week.

Weigel and Newman computed the correlations between participants' attitudes toward protecting the environment and various measures of behavior. Table 6.5 presents the correlations from the study. The first column of 14 correlations shows how well the measure of attitudes toward protecting the environment (a broad, general attitude) predicted each of the specific, *single* behavior items. As expected when a general attitude is used to predict a specific behavior, these correlations were not very large, with an average $r = .32$ (correlations of .3 indicate relatively weak relationships). The second column of three correlations shows how well the measure of attitudes toward protecting the environment predicted each of the three *categories* of behavior (petitions, litter pickup, and recycling); these categories represented somewhat broader and more general measures of behavior. As expected, these correlations were larger than those in the first column, with an average $r = .42$. Finally, the third column of just one correlation shows how well the measure of attitudes toward protecting the environment predicted a measure of behavior

## TABLE **6.5**

*Correlations Between Attitudes Toward Protecting the Environment and Various Behavioral Measures*

| Single Behaviors | $r^a$ | Categories of Behavior | $r^b$ | Behavioral Index | $r^b$ |
|---|---|---|---|---|---|
| Offshore oil | .41** | | | | |
| Nuclear power | .36* | Petitioning behavior | .50** | | |
| Auto exhaust | .39** | scale (0–4) | | | |
| Circulate petitions | .27 | | | | |
| Individual participation | .34* | Litter pickup | .36* | | |
| Recruit friend | .22 | scale (0–2) | | | |
| Week 1 | .34* | | | Comprehensive behavioral index | .62*** |
| Week 2 | .57*** | | | | |
| Week 3 | .34* | | | | |
| Week 4 | .33* | Recycling behavior | .39** | | |
| Week 5 | .12 | scale (0–8) | | | |
| Week 6 | .20 | | | | |
| Week 7 | .20 | | | | |
| Week 8 | .34* | | | | |

Note: $N = 44$

a. Point-biserial correlations are reported in this column.

b. Pearson product-moment correlations are reported in this column.

  $*p < .05$

 $**p < .01$

$***p < .001$

From Weigel and Newman, "Increasing attitude-behavior consistency by broadening the scope of the behavioral measure," *Journal of Personality and Social Psychology*, 33, 793–802, Table 1, p. 799, 1976. Copyright © 1976 by the American Psychological Association. Reprinted by permission.

that combined *all* of the single behaviors together. This last correlation was between a general measure of attitudes and a general measure of behavior, and it was very strong, $r = .62$. Thus, as the measures of behavior became broader and more inclusive, they correlated more strongly with the measure of broad attitudes toward protecting the environment.

We have explained that a measure of a broad, general attitude will predict a broad, general measure of behavior that samples across most or all of the relevant domains. The reverse is also true: a measure of a narrow, specific attitude will predict a narrow measure of behavior that is limited to one domain. For instance, if a researcher measured individuals' attitudes toward *using sunscreen,* these attitudes should predict the extent to which the individuals actually use sunscreen over a certain period of time. Returning to our earlier example, if a researcher wanted to predict whether Daesha and Robert exercise regularly, then he or she should measure their attitudes toward *exercising regularly* (rather than their attitudes toward living a healthy lifestyle).

This matching effect of measures of attitudes and behavior is called the **compatibility principle.** The compatibility principle refers to the fact that measures of attitudes and measures of behavior must be matched in terms of generality (both should be general or both should be specific). Reviews of the literature have shown that, across many studies, when attitudes and behavior are measured at similar levels of generality, they correlate strongly, whereas mismatched or incompatible measures of attitudes and behavior yield much lower correlations (e.g., Ajzen & Fishbein, 1977; Eagly & Chaiken, 1993, 1998; Kim & Hunter, 1993; Kraus, 1995).

**compatibility principle**

*a theory stating that a measure of attitudes will correlate highly with a measure of behavior only when the two measures are matched in terms of being general/broad or specific/narrow*

  ## Culture and Attitudes

**culture**

*the set of values, beliefs, and behaviors shared by a group of people and communicated from one generation to the next*

David Matsumoto (1996) defined **culture** as "the set of attitudes, values, beliefs, and behaviors shared by a group of people . . . [and] communicated from one generation to the next" (p. 32). Recall that we defined socialization earlier in this chapter as the process by which individuals are made into acceptable members of their

Cultures communicate core beliefs about what is good and moral.

society, which includes holding the prevailing beliefs and attitudes (Harris, 1995). These two definitions underscore how central attitudes are to the concept of culture. Social psychologists assume that when people from different cultures respond differently to the same event, it is *because* their perceptions and reactions are guided by different attitudes, values, and norms.

Culture-specific attitudes and values occur because cultures communicate several "core ideas" to their members, such as what is good and what is moral (Fiske, Kitayama, Markus, & Nisbett, 1998; Kitayama & Markus, 1994). These core ideas and beliefs help to shape the customs, norms, and institutions of the culture (e.g., family structures, the educational system), which then socialize individuals to adopt the prescribed attitudes and values.

The best-known analysis and comparison of cultures was conducted by Geert Hofstede (1980, 2001), who assessed the work-related values of IBM marketing managers in 40 countries around the world. He proposed that the different countries could be characterized in terms of several underlying dimensions of culture. The dimension that has received the most attention (and which we discussed in Chapters 4 and 5) is *individualism* versus *collectivism*. Individualist cultures emphasize individual identity and achievement, whereas collectivist cultures emphasize group harmony and tradition. North American and European countries tend to be individualistic, whereas East Asian and African countries tend to be collectivistic.

Another interesting dimension identified by Hofstede was **power distance,** which refers to the extent to which a culture accepts unequal power distribution among individuals and institutions. Cultures that are high in power distance accept and support unequal power distribution, where some individuals have much more influence than others. In contrast, cultures that are low in power distance prefer equal distributions of influence, where everyone has the same opportunity to affect decisions. East Asian and eastern European countries tend to be high in power distance, whereas North American and especially western European countries tend to be low in power distance. Does it surprise you that North America is characterized as preferring equal rather than unequal power, given the wide disparity in wealth that exists in North American society? The dimension of power distance refers to the distribution of *influence,* such as the ability to "have one's say," rather than to the distribution of income. North Americans value democracy and individual freedom very highly—principles that are based on the idea that everyone should be treated equally under the law. North Americans also pride themselves on living in the "land of opportunity," where people can achieve whatever they like if only they work hard enough. Whether these perceptions are true or not is arguable, but North Americans do fall more toward the low than the high end of the power distance dimension.

Many researchers have investigated cultural differences in specific attitudes and values (e.g., see Hofstede, 1991, 2001; Schwartz & Bardi, 1997; Schwartz & Sagiv, 1995; Smith & Bond, 1994; Triandis, 1994, 1995). In one interesting study, Jennifer Aaker, Verónica Benet-Martínez, and Jordi Garolera (2001) surveyed American, Japanese, and Spanish adults, who were asked to report their perceptions of several *commercial brand names* that were well known in their country (e.g., Americans rated Marlboro cigarettes, Coca-Cola, Levi's jeans, etc.). The researchers found that Americans responded positively to brand names that evoked perceptions of "ruggedness" (e.g., masculine, outdoorsy, tough); Japanese participants responded positively to brand names that evoked perceptions of "peacefulness" (e.g., mild-mannered, shy, naive); and Spanish participants responded positively to brand names that evoked perceptions of "passion" (e.g., intense, passionate, spiritual). The authors proposed that these differences in preferences for brand names reflected cultural differences in attitudes and values: Americans appreciate rugged independence, Japanese individuals cherish peaceful harmony, and Spaniards value passionate emotions.

**power distance**
*the extent to which a culture accepts an unequal distribution of influence within the society*

## Cross-Cultural Commonalities in Attitudes: We Are More Alike Than Different

We have focused on differences between cultures in attitudes and values, but it is important to recognize that there are many cross-cultural similarities as well. Although cultures differ in the average ratings or rankings of some goals, all cultures place positive worth on most of the same goals. For example, although East Asians tend to place greater value on interpersonal harmony than do North Americans, both cultures consider harmony to be a desirable goal. Although North Americans tend to value freedom more than do East Asians, both cultures consider freedom to be desirable. For the most part, cultures differ in the *degree* to which they endorse particular goals or in how their values are *expressed*, not in whether the goals are worthwhile (see Schwartz, 1992, 1996). This point about cross-cultural similarity is particularly true when relatively specific attitudes and values are considered, such as honesty, reliability, compassion, and peace. Thus, we should keep in mind that humans around the world are much more alike than they are different.

Also, even when cultures yield average differences in an attitude or in the importance rating of a value, there is almost always substantial overlap in the ratings across cultures (Fiske et al., 1998; Triandis, 1994). For instance, although the average rating of the importance of freedom by American respondents is higher than the average rating of the importance of freedom by Japanese respondents, there are many individual Japanese who consider freedom to be more important than do many individual Americans. Overlapping distributions mean that cultures differ on average, but individuals from the two cultures do not necessarily differ.

In conclusion, cultures vary in several important ways, such as their perception of the individual as independent or interdependent and their acceptance of power differences between people. These differences affect the attitudes and norms that develop in the culture, as well as the psychological makeup of its members. Nevertheless, people from all cultures share many fundamental beliefs, including the desirability of such values as honesty and compassion.

# Chapter Summary

An **attitude** is an individual's evaluation of a target along a good–bad dimension. Attitudes are always directed *at* something—they have a target. Sometimes attitudes contain both positive and negative elements, in which case they are labeled **ambivalent attitudes. Explicit attitudes** are those that people can report consciously. **Implicit attitudes** are individuals' automatic evaluative responses to a target, which can occur without awareness.

Attitudes serve at least two important functions for the individual. First, an attitude provides a rapid evaluation of an object, person, or issue, which allows the individual to decide whether to approach or avoid it. This function is called the **object appraisal function** of attitudes. Second, some attitudes communicate the individual's identity and values, which is called the **value-expressive function.**

The most common techniques for measuring attitudes use self-report approaches. **Likert-type scales** require respondents to indicate the extent of their agreement or disagreement with several statements on an issue. **Thurstone scales** require respondents to place a check mark beside statements with which they agree. **Semantic differential scales** require respondents to rate an attitude object on evaluative dimensions, such as good–bad and favorable–unfavorable. Nonverbal measures of attitudes have also been developed. For instance, **facial electromyography (facial EMG)** records muscle contractions in the face that may be sensitive to positive versus negative responses to a stimulus. Reaction time procedures have been used to measure implicit attitudes, including the **Implicit Association Test (IAT).**

One possible source of attitudes is affect. Affect can become linked to objects through a process of **evaluative conditioning,** whereby objects that had no causal role in producing positive or negative affect nevertheless come to evoke affect simply by being associated with the affect-arousing events. Another source of affect is the familiarity of an object. The **mere exposure effect** is that repeated exposure to an object, even without reinforcement, will increase liking for the object. Attitudes can also be influenced by physiological and biological processes. For example, alcohol intoxication reduces cognitive capacity, which results in a narrowing of attention—an effect that has been labeled **alcohol myopia.**

**Socialization** is the process by which infants are molded into acceptable members of their society. A **reference group** is a group that serves as a standard of comparison for an individual. Ridicule is derogatory humor directed at an individual concerning some aspect of his or her behavior or appearance. Ridicule produces **jeer pressure,** which is conformity pressure that is caused by seeing someone ridiculed by another person.

Attitudes influence behavior in two primary ways: rational choice and selective perception. The **theory of reasoned action** epitomizes the rational choice perspective; it views humans as rational decision makers who behave on the basis of logical beliefs. According to this theory, the most immediate cause of a behavior is a **behavioral intention,** which refers to the individual's plan to perform or not perform the action. Two concepts are assumed to cause behavioral intentions: attitudes toward the behavior and subjective norms concerning the behavior. **Subjective norms** are individuals' feelings of social pressure to perform or not perform an action, which are based on their beliefs about how significant others want them to behave. Another model that focuses on rational choice is the **IMB model of AIDS-preventive behavior.** This model proposes that three major elements contribute to safer sex behaviors: information, motivation, and behavioral skills.

Selective perception refers to the biasing effect of our attitudes on how we interpret and understand the world. One example of selective perception is the **hostile media phenomenon,** which refers to the tendency for people who feel strongly about an issue to believe that the media coverage of the issue is biased against their own side.

Attitudes predict behavior best under certain conditions. One condition of attitude–behavior consistency is the **compatibility principle,** which refers to the fact that measures of attitudes and measures of behavior must be matched in terms of generality: both must be broad and general or both must be narrow and specific.

**Culture** can be defined as the set of values, beliefs, and behaviors shared by a group of people and communicated from one generation to the next. One dimension along which cultures differ is **power distance,** which refers to the extent to which a culture accepts unequal distribution of influence among individuals and institutions.

# Key Terms

alcohol myopia (218)

ambivalent attitudes (202)

attitude (199)

behavioral intention (227)

compatibility principle (242)

culture (242)

evaluative conditioning (213)

explicit attitudes (202)

facial electromyography (facial EMG) (211)

hostile media phenomenon (235)

IMB model of AIDS-preventive behavior (230)

Implicit Association Test (IAT) (212)

implicit attitudes (202)

jeer pressure (224)

Likert-type scale (206)

mere exposure effect (214)

object appraisal function (203)

power distance (243)

reference group (223)

semantic differential scale (207)

socialization (222)

subjective norm (228)

theory of reasoned action (228)

Thurstone scale (206)

value-expressive function (204)

# Social Psychology Alive on the Web

### ▶ SOCIAL PSYCHOLOGY ALIVE: ONLINE LABS

To perform the following experiments and see how you compare to other students, go to Social Psychology Lab, which can be accessed through Social PsychologyNow.

- 6.1 Word Evaluation
- 6.2 Shape Judgment

### SOCIAL PSYCHOLOGY ALIVE: QUIZZING AND PRACTICE TESTS

You can access our website directly by going to http://psychology.wadsworth.com/breckler1e/ for online quizzes, flash cards, and Internet links.

### INFOTRAC® COLLEGE EDITION

For additional readings, explore InfoTrac College Edition, your online library of archived journal articles and periodicals dating back 22 years. If your instructor ordered InfoTrac College Edition with this book, you can access it from your CD-ROM, or go directly to http://www.infotrac-college.com/wadsworth and use the passcode from the InfoTrac College Edition card that came with your book. For this chapter, try these search terms: *attitudes, ambivalent attitudes, implicit attitudes, attitude functions, Likert scale, semantic differential, Implicit Association Test, mere exposure, reference groups, theory of reasoned action, hostile media phenomenon, compatibility principle.*

## Social Psychology Alive: The Workbook

To apply what you've learned in this chapter to what happens in the real world, go to Chapter 6 of *Social Psychology Alive: The Workbook*:

- *Lockhart v. McCree:* Social Science Evidence and the Supreme Court
- Caffeine and Patriotism: Demonstrating the Function of Attitudes
- Measuring Attitudes Using a Single-Item Scale and a Likert Scale
- Measuring Attitudes: Do Semantic Differentials Measure Affect or Cognition?

- Implicit Intergroup Bias and the Implicit Association Test
- Evaluative Conditioning
- What's in a Name? Demonstrate the Mere Exposure Effect
- Do Attitudes Predict Behavior? The Theory of Reasoned Action
- Do Attitudes Predict Behavior? The Compatibility Principle

## Social Psychology Alive: The Videos

To see video on the topics and experiments discussed in this chapter, you can go either to Social PsychologyNow or to the CD-ROM, if your instructor assigned either one, to the following section:

- Reading the Unconscious Mind: The Implicit Association Test

## To Learn More

This list contains citations to books or articles that can help you learn more. These readings are good places to start if you want to gain a deeper understanding of the topics in this chapter.

- Eagly, A. H., & Chaiken, S. (1993). *The psychology of attitudes*. Fort Worth, TX: Harcourt Brace Jovanovich.

- Perloff, R. M. (2003). *The dynamics of persuasion: Communication and attitudes in the 21st Century* (2nd ed.). Mahwah, NJ: Erlbaum.
- Oskamp, S. (1991). *Attitudes and opinions* (2nd ed.). Englewood Cliffs, NJ: Prentice Hall.

© AP/Wide World Photos/Koji Sasahara

# Attitude Change

*Imagine how different your life would be if there were no advertisements. Newspapers would certainly be shorter without their ads for grocery stores, movie theaters, department stores, and other products. You would check your e-mail and not be inundated with spam messages selling everything from mortgages to get-rich-quick schemes to alleged wonder drugs. When you watched television, you would not be forced to view approximately 20 commercials per hour. When you rented a movie on videotape, you would not have to fast-forward through a series of "coming soon" theatrical trailers. You would not see billboards on signs or buildings. You would not get phone calls in the evening from marketing companies offering you a deal on rug cleaning or some other service.*

*Sounds rather appealing, doesn't it? Unfortunately, the truth is that we cannot escape from advertisements in our society—they are everywhere. It has been estimated that the average American is exposed to more than 200 advertisements per day (Pratkanis & Aronson, 2000), which would come to a total of more than 73,000 per year! Although many of us complain about the glut of ads, we're generally pretty apathetic about our level of exposure. Young people, in particular, even seem comfortable with the surplus of advertising. One of the authors of this book has a 17-year-old daughter who says she loves to read ads, especially in magazines for young women. He recently looked at one of her magazines—an issue of* Elle*—and counted the number of pages that were dedicated to advertisements. The count showed that 322 of the 398 pages in the magazine were taken up either by explicit advertisements (211 pages) or by "articles" that consisted only of photographs of models wearing clothes, with the prices and store locations listed at the bottom of the page (111 pages). The first real article in the magazine (with any written content) began on page 115!*

*Advertisements are designed to create positive attitudes toward a product, with the ultimate goal being to induce people to buy that product. They are the most*

© Cosmo Condina/Photographer's Choice/Getty Images

Imagine how different life would be if there were no advertisements.

*common and visible form of persuasive communication that we encounter in our daily lives. But ads are certainly not the only example of attempts to change attitudes and behavior. Interpersonal influence is another important category: your friends may try to convince you to come with them to a movie; your doctor may suggest that you exercise more often; your romantic partner may argue with you about the pros and cons of downloading music from the Internet. Of course, you also initiate attempts to persuade others, including your friends, family, and romantic partner. Institutions in society are another source of persuasion attempts, including schools (e.g., sex education classes), religious institutions (e.g., sermons), and the military (e.g., basic training).*

*The goal of the present chapter is to describe research in social psychology that has investigated attitude change. We already know from Chapter 6 that attitudes are an important determinant of behavior. We discussed attitude formation in Chapter 6 but did not consider how attitudes, once formed, can change. In this chapter, we tackle this topic. As the chapter outline suggests, there are numerous ways that attitudes can change, including rationalization, persuasion, and propaganda. Rationalization constitutes a form of self-persuasion, whereby people convince themselves that their decisions or actions are justified. Persuasion refers to attitude change that results from an influential communication initiated by someone else. Sometimes persuasion occurs because information in the message convinces the individual that the recommendation is a good one. But sometimes persuasion occurs simply because the individual assumes that the recommendation is probably valid, without considering arguments for or against it. Propaganda is a persuasion attempt that is ideologically motivated and often intentionally misleading. Sometimes propaganda can convince people to make huge changes to their attitudes and behavior, as when individuals join a cult.*

*We begin this chapter with perhaps the most famous theory in social psychology, cognitive dissonance theory, which addresses how attitude change can occur through a process of rationalization. We then turn to attitude change resulting from persuasive communications and describe several different perspectives on this phenomenon. We also discuss age and cultural differences in attitude change, as well as the effectiveness of fear appeals in changing health-related attitudes. We then describe the psychology of propaganda. We close the chapter with a discussion of how people can resist attempts to change their attitudes.*

## ● ● ● Rationalizing Our Own Behavior: Dissonance Theory

Would you be willing to eat a grasshopper? That's right, eat a grasshopper—fried. These insects can, in fact, be eaten safely, although they do not appear on most people's food lists.

Would you be willing to eat a grasshopper?

Imagine that you were asked to eat a grasshopper for a researcher who said he was investigating whether grasshoppers could serve as a suitable survival food for soldiers in extreme circumstances. If given a choice, do you think that you would agree to eat one? Now imagine that you *did* eat one; would you feel a need to *rationalize* your behavior—to justify the behavior to yourself?

Phillip Zimbardo and his colleagues (Zimbardo, Weisenberg, & Firestone, 1965) conducted a classic study in which young men were asked to eat a fried grasshopper. For half of the participants, the experimenter was extremely polite and pleasant prior to asking them to eat a grasshopper, whereas for the remaining participants, the experimenter acted like an arrogant, cold, and thoroughly unpleasant person before he asked them to eat a grasshopper. It turned out that about 50% of the participants in each of these two conditions actually ate a grasshopper, so the likable and unlikable experimenters were about equally successful in getting participants to comply with their request. Now for the interesting part: after they ate the grasshopper, participants were asked to evaluate the insect as a food source. Who do you think gave more favorable ratings of grasshoppers—participants who ate the grasshopper for the pleasant or the unpleasant experimenter?

Results showed that the *unpleasant* experimenter produced more favorable ratings than the pleasant experimenter. Those participants who ate a grasshopper for the rude and unlikable experimenter said grasshoppers were a more feasible food source than did participants who ate a grasshopper for the polite and likable experimenter. Does this result surprise you? We will return to the study shortly and give the authors' explanation.

The grasshopper experiment is one of the many colorful studies that have tested one of the most colorful and famous theories in social psychology: cognitive dissonance theory. Dissonance theory has achieved fame not only among social psychologists but also in the general public, where terms like *dissonance* appear in normal conversation. Dissonance theory has achieved a level of public recognition that rivals such famous psychological models as reinforcement theory and Freudian psychoanalysis. Within social psychology, dissonance theory has had a fascinating history, which has included periods of intense interest, periods of virtual neglect, heated disagreements between researchers, and numerous proposed alternative explanations for findings.

## Feeling Bad About Irrational Behavior: The Arousal of Dissonance

Leon Festinger proposed **cognitive dissonance theory** in 1957. Festinger was interested in the consequences of the "fit" or consistency between different *cognitions* in people's minds. He defined a cognition as a belief or piece of knowledge, such as "My name is Kierstin," "Apples are red," "It snowed last night," and "I brush my teeth twice a day." People have thousands of cognitions stored in their memories, but will be aware of only a small number at any one time. Most cognitions are irrelevant to one another. The cognitions "Apples are red" and "It snowed last night" have no implications for each other. But some cognitions are logically connected, either positively or negatively. **Consonant cognitions** are *consistent* with one another; they imply that the other is valid or good. The two cognitions "I brush my teeth twice a day" and "Toothbrushing prevents cavities" support one another. **Dissonant cognitions,** on the other hand, are *inconsistent* with one another; they imply that the other is wrong or bad. The two cognitions "I smoke" and "Smoking causes cancer" are logically discrepant.

Festinger hypothesized that awareness of consonant cognitions makes us feel good, whereas awareness of dissonant cognitions makes us feel bad. The fact that he named his theory *dissonance theory* shows that he was particularly interested in the latter case, involving inconsistent cognitions. Festinger proposed that the unpleasant

**cognitive dissonance theory**

*a model proposed by Leon Festinger, which states that awareness of consonant cognitions makes us feel good, whereas awareness of dissonant cognitions makes us feel bad. Further, the unpleasant feelings produced by dissonant cognitions motivate us to do something to change our state.*

**consonant cognitions**

*beliefs that are consistent or compatible with one another*

**dissonant cognitions**

*beliefs that are inconsistent or logically discrepant with one another*

© Catherine Karnow/Woodfin Camp

feelings produced by dissonant cognitions motivate people to do something to change their state. His research was designed to investigate these attempts to deal with dissonance.

Our example of dissonant cognitions about smoking illustrates an important feature of research on dissonance theory. Although it is theoretically possible to experience dissonance between many different kinds of cognitions, Festinger focused on inconsistencies that involved cognitions about one's own *behavior.* Specifically, he focused on dissonance between knowing that you behave or have behaved in a certain way (e.g., "I smoke"; "I hurt Jermaine's feelings") and another piece of knowledge implying that your behavior was wrong or illogical or otherwise inappropriate (e.g., "Smoking causes cancer"; "I like Jermaine"). Researchers since Festinger have maintained this focus on cognitions about behavior. Thus, for the purposes of research by social psychologists, dissonance can be defined as the state of feeling bad or conflicted about one's own irrational behavior.

Let's generate a few examples of dissonance in everyday life. Someone who pays a substantial registration fee for a workshop on using computers and then finds the workshop useless will feel dissonance between the cognitions "I paid $100 to take this course" and "This course didn't teach me anything." A student who performs poorly on an important test may feel dissonance between the cognitions "I did badly on this test" and "I expected to do well on the test." Someone who buys a stylish jacket at a Nike store and then remembers that Nike has been accused of employing children in their factories in the Third World will feel dissonance between the cognitions "I bought a jacket at a Nike store" and "Nike might engage in unethical business practices." Can you generate some examples of times when you have experienced dissonance? We all occasionally behave in ways that might be considered irrational or unproductive, so we all know how dissonance feels.

Festinger also proposed that the *importance* of the cognitions influences the amount of dissonance. Dissonance between very important cognitions causes more intense negative feelings than does dissonance between less important cognitions. Spending $1,000 on a useless workshop will arouse more dissonance than spending $100 on the workshop. Thinking that you chose the wrong college will arouse more dissonance than thinking that you chose the wrong shirt to wear today. Hurting the feelings of your best friend will arouse more dissonance than hurting the feelings of a stranger.

## Making Irrational Behavior Rational: The Reduction of Dissonance

We don't like the feeling of dissonance. Festinger described dissonance as a state of "aversive arousal" and said that we are motivated to reduce it. How can this goal be accomplished? How can we reduce cognitive dissonance?

If dissonance represents feeling bad about one's own irrational behavior, then reducing dissonance must somehow involve making the irrational behavior seem rational (or, at least, making it seem *less* irrational). In other words, dissonance reduction must involve *rationalization:* convincing ourselves that our current or past behavior made sense after all. Dissonance theory, then, is a motivational model focusing on self-persuasion.

The specific ways that dissonance can be reduced are best understood in the context of an example, such as dissonance between the two cognitions "I smoke" and "Smoking causes cancer." Festinger hypothesized that one way to reduce dissonance is to change one of the dissonant cognitions directly. The individual might stop smoking, in which case the cognition "I smoke" becomes "I do not smoke," which is consonant with the cognition "Smoking causes cancer." Or the individual might decide that the research on smoking is not definitive or that smoking is unlikely to affect him or her personally, in which case the cognition "Smoking causes cancer" becomes "Smoking will not cause cancer in me," which is more con-sonant with the cognition "I smoke." As you will see when we review the empirical research on dissonance, the dissonance-reduction strategy of changing one of the dissonant cognitions is the strategy that has been studied most often.

Directly reducing dissonance may not always be possible, however. Changing one's behavior can be challenging, and many cognitions are based on strong evi-dence that we cannot easily distort or deny (e.g., the link between smoking and cancer). If changing one of the dissonant cognitions is difficult, then another way that people can reduce dissonance is by adding consonant cognitions. These cogni-tions support the person's behavior and make it seem more reasonable. For exam-ple, a smoker might think "Smoking is enjoyable" or "Smoking keeps my weight down," which are consonant with the cognition "I smoke." In this way, the behavior of smoking appears more rational or justified. Adding consonant cognitions is a common way to deal with dissonance in everyday life—people often rationalize undesirable behavior by arguing that it has some positive benefits. For instance, politicians from tobacco-producing states or provinces may oppose legislation that would restrict smoking by saying that the tobacco industry has economic benefits for their constituents. The flowchart in Figure 7.1 illustrates the application of dis-sonance theory to smoking behavior.

Festinger proposed that there is one other way to reduce dissonance besides changing one of the dissonant cognitions or adding consonant cognitions. Recall that dissonance between important cognitions is more intense than dissonance between unimportant cognitions. Dissonance can be reduced, therefore, by reducing the importance of one of the dissonant cognitions and/or increasing the importance of one of the consonant cognitions. A smoker might accept the link between smoking and cancer but decide that he or she doesn't really want to live forever anyway—he or she wants to "live fast and die young!" (This philosophy tends to lose its appeal as one grows older.) Or a smoker might accept the smoking–cancer link but decide that the pleasure of smoking more than compensates for its risks. These rationaliza-tions involve reducing the importance of the cognition "Smoking causes cancer" or increasing the importance of the cognition "Smoking is enjoyable."

## Early Research on Dissonance Theory

We mentioned earlier that dissonance theory has had a colorful history. We can summarize here only a small part of the literature—published experiments on dis-sonance theory number in the hundreds, probably even the thousands. Several

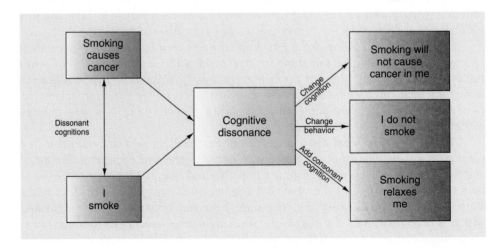

**FIGURE 7.1** Arousal and reduction of dissonance related to smoking

phases of research on dissonance can be identified. The first phase followed the publication of the theory by Festinger in 1957 and lasted for about 10 years. The theory had an immediate impact on the field, because the counterintuitive nature of some of the findings captured researchers' interest. The second phase of dissonance research began in the late 1960s and continued for 10 or 15 years. This phase saw the appearance of several alternative interpretations of dissonance findings, as well as responses to those alternatives from dissonance loyalists. The third phase of dissonance research, which lasted from approximately 1980 to the early 1990s, was one of relative neglect. During this time, dissonance slipped into the background of social psychology, which was then focusing its attention on attribution processes and social cognition. Finally, beginning in the mid-1990s and continuing to the present time, there has been a renewed interest in dissonance. These recent studies have identified new applications of dissonance theory.

We begin our review of dissonance research by describing three major domains of the theory, which were identified during the first phase of research. These domains have been studied using different *experimental paradigms,* or research methodologies. Each of the three paradigms—induced compliance, effort justification, and free choice—explored one important application of dissonance theory. Table 7.1 summarizes the key features of these three paradigms, which are described in more detail in the following paragraphs.

### Induced Compliance: Dissonance From Counterattitudinal Behavior.

To capture dissonance in an experiment, a researcher must elicit behavior from participants that they will perceive as irrational or otherwise inappropriate. This is not easy to do. One category of behavior that usually fits this requirement is *counterattitudinal behavior*—behavior that is counter to, or inconsistent with, an individual's attitudes, values, or beliefs. Most of us feel bad when we do something that conflicts with our attitudes, such as accidentally hurting the feelings of someone we like or pretending to agree with someone on an issue simply because we don't want to argue.

Dissonance researchers have taken advantage of this type of behavior in the **induced compliance paradigm.** This paradigm investigates dissonance that results from counterattitudinal behavior. Participants are *induced* to *comply* with the experimenter's request that they behave in a way that is known to be inconsistent with their attitudes. Most often, the paradigm involves either getting people to say something they know is untrue or asking them to generate arguments against a position

**induced compliance paradigm**
*a research methodology used to test dissonance theory that arouses dissonance by getting people to engage in counterattitudinal behavior. In this paradigm, participants are induced to comply with an experimenter's request that they behave in a way that is inconsistent with their attitudes.*

---

## TABLE 7.1
### Three Research Paradigms Used to Test Dissonance Theory

| Research Paradigm | Nature of Behavior That Arouses Dissonance | Examples |
| --- | --- | --- |
| Induced compliance paradigm | Counterattitudinal behavior | Knowingly lie to another person<br>Write an essay supporting a position that is discrepant with one's attitude<br>Eat a disgusting food |
| Effort justification paradigm | Wasted effort or money | Endure a severe initiation to join a group that turns out to be boring<br>Pay for admission to a movie that turns out to be unenjoyable |
| Free choice paradigm | Making a decision | Choose between two or more alternatives (chosen option will usually have some negative features, and rejected options will usually have some positive features) |

Leon Festinger (in photo) conducted a famous experiment with J. Merrill Carlsmith (1959), in which participants completed two boring tasks and were then induced to tell someone else that the tasks were fun.

they personally support. The dissonance is created between the two cognitions "I believe X" and "I knowingly stated that I do not believe X" (or "I argued against X").

In one of the earliest dissonance experiments, Leon Festinger and J. Merrill Carlsmith (1959) made participants work for an hour on two very boring tasks: turning pegs on a board and placing spools on and off another board. After completing these tasks, participants were told that the purpose of the study was to investigate the effects of expectancies on task performance, and they had been in a control condition where no pretask expectancies were created. But there was another condition, participants were told, in which people were being given positive expectancies about the enjoyability of the tasks. These positive expectancies were being created by having an experimental confederate sit beside subjects in the waiting room, pretend that he or she has just completed the study, and tell them that the tasks would be fun and exciting. The experimenter then made an unexpected request of the current participant: the usual confederate was unavailable, and there was someone in the waiting room who was supposed to be in the positive expectancies condition. Would they be willing to go into the waiting room and tell the person that the tasks were fun and exciting? (Participants were also told that if they agreed to do this task, the experimenter would keep their name on file as a possible replacement for the confederate in the future.) Almost all participants agreed to tell this lie and then went into the next room and told the waiting subject (who was actually a confederate of the experimenter) that the study was fun and exciting.

Participants were thereby induced to behave in a counterattitudinal fashion. The cognitions "The tasks were boring" and "I told someone that the tasks were fun" were expected to produce dissonance. How could this dissonance be reduced? It would be difficult for participants to convince themselves that they didn't tell another person that the tasks were fun—this behavior had just occurred. But dissonance could be reduced by changing the cognition "The tasks were boring" by deciding that maybe the tasks weren't so bad after all. If the tasks were somewhat enjoyable, then telling someone that they were fun is less discrepant.

Another manipulation in the experiment was expected to influence the *amount* of dissonance people would feel. Participants were told that they would be *paid* for serving as the confederate, but the amounts they would be paid differed. Some participants were told that they would be paid $20 for telling the lie—a huge amount in the 1950s when the study was conducted. Other participants were told that they would be paid only $1 for serving as the confederate. Participants who were paid $20 were expected to feel less dissonance than those who were paid $1. Why? Because those paid $20 would have a strong, consonant cognition to support their behavior: "I was paid a lot of money to say the tasks were fun." Thus, individuals paid $20 were not expected to have to convince themselves that the tasks were fun, whereas those paid $1 were expected to reduce dissonance by evaluating the tasks more positively.

After telling the lie, participants were told that the experiment was over and were asked to visit a secretary in the psychology department, who would give them a questionnaire that was being completed by all participants in all experiments. This questionnaire asked participants to rate how interesting and enjoyable the tasks in their experiment had been. Figure 7.2 presents the results for the $1 and $20 conditions, as well as for a control condition in which participants completed the tasks but did not tell anyone that the tasks were fun (this condition presumably showed how interesting or enjoyable the tasks really were). As predicted, participants in the $1 condition rated the tasks as more enjoyable than did control participants; telling the lie appeared to arouse dissonance, which was reduced by deciding that the tasks were somewhat enjoyable. Also as predicted, participants in the $20 condition did not differ from control participants; the large payment appeared to serve as a strong consonant cognition for telling the lie, which meant that participants did not have to reevaluate the tasks.

The Festinger and Carlsmith (1959) experiment was the first of many to document dissonance using an induced compliance paradigm. Another common procedure was to ask participants to write a counterattitudinal essay arguing against their own view (e.g., asking college undergraduates to write an essay supporting tuition increases for college students). If participants were given a choice and willingly agreed to write such an essay (rather than simply being instructed to write it or being highly paid to write it), they tended to move their own attitude in the direction of their essay (e.g., Cohen, 1962; Stone, 1999; Zanna & Cooper, 1974). Presumably, participants in these studies reduced dissonance between "I believe X" and "I willingly wrote an essay arguing against X" by altering their initial cognition to be something closer to "I am against X."

Now let's return to the grasshopper experiment with which we opened our discussion of dissonance theory. Recall that Zimbardo et al. (1965) found that people who ate a grasshopper for a rude and unlikable experimenter rated grasshoppers more favorably as a food source than did people who ate a grasshopper for a polite and likable experimenter. How do these data support dissonance theory?

First, eating the grasshopper was counterattitudinal behavior: it seems safe to say that none of the participants came to the study with a favorable attitude toward eating insects of any kind. Thus, the study utilized an induced compliance paradigm to create dissonance between the cognitions "Eating grasshoppers is gross" and "I ate a grasshopper." But those participants who ate a grasshopper for a likable experimenter at least had the cognition "I helped a nice person," which was consonant with their behavior. The experimenter's pleasant personality served as a justification or reason for the participant's decision to eat a grasshopper. Those participants who ate a grasshopper for an unlikable experimenter, however, had no such cognition; indeed, they may have been thinking "Why am I helping this obnoxious person?" To reduce their dissonance, they were forced to change their evaluation of eating grasshoppers to "Eating grasshoppers isn't so bad." (Steak sauce, anyone?)

### Effort Justification: Dissonance From Wasted Effort.

How do you feel when you have worked hard on something but then received little in return? Have you studied hard for a test but nevertheless done poorly? Have you spent a lot of money on something that you subsequently used very little? Have you put a lot into a dating relationship but eventually realized that the other person wasn't reciprocating? Suspecting that we have wasted time, effort, or money on something is upsetting. "I worked hard" and "I gained nothing" are highly dissonant cognitions. Dissonance theory predicts that people who suspect they have wasted effort will be motivated to change one of the dissonant cognitions or to add consonant cognitions. For example, individuals might change the cognition about effort, deciding that they didn't really exert too much effort after all. Alternatively, individuals might change the cognition about having gained nothing, deciding instead that their payoff was worthwhile. Finally, individuals might add consonant cognitions, deciding that they learned an important lesson or benefited in some other way from the experience.

Recognizing that wasted effort was a form of dissonance that could be experimentally manipulated, dissonance researchers designed the **effort justification paradigm.** The effort justification paradigm involved leading participants to suspect that effort they had invested may have been worthless. The prediction was that participants would reduce dissonance by convincing themselves that the goal was actually worthwhile.

Elliot Aronson and Judson Mills (1959) published the first study using the effort justification paradigm. Female college students were asked whether they wanted to

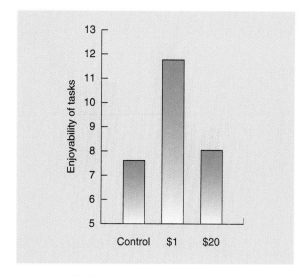

**FIGURE 7.2** Ratings of enjoyability of tasks

Adapted from Festinger and Carlsmith, "Cognitive consequences of forced compliance," *Journal of Abnormal and Social Psychology,* 58, 203–210, 1959. Copyright © 1959 by the American Psychological Association.

**effort justification paradigm**

*a research methodology used to test dissonance theory that arouses dissonance by getting people to invest time or energy to achieve a goal that may not be worthwhile*

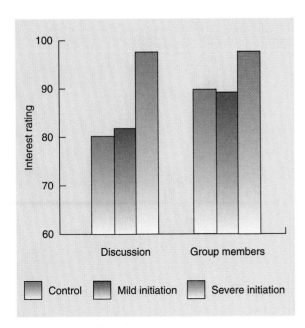

**FIGURE 7.3** Interest ratings of discussion and group members

From Aronson and Mills, "The effect of severity of initiation on liking for a group," *Journal of Abnormal and Social Psychology*, 59, 177–181, 1959. Copyright © 1959 by the American Psychological Association. Reprinted by permission.

join a "sexual discussion group"—an opportunity that interested many of them. Those who applied for the group were told that they had to undergo a "screening test" to ensure that they would be able to participate fully in the group. Some participants were then put through a "severe" test that required them to read out loud a list of obscene words and detailed descriptions of sexual activity. Other participants were put through only a "mild" test that required them to read out loud more ordinary words like *petting* and *prostitute.* After completing either the severe or the mild screening test, participants were told that they would join the group next week, but they would listen to the first week's discussion over headphones. Participants then listened to a tape recording of a discussion that had been created to be hideously boring. Aronson and Mills described the discussion by saying that it concerned "secondary sex behavior in the lower animals. [The people on the tape] inadvertently contradicted themselves and one another, mumbled several non sequiturs, started sentences that they never finished, hemmed, hawed, and in general conducted one of the most worthless and uninteresting discussions imaginable" (p. 179).

After listening to the tape, participants were asked to rate how interesting they found the discussion and the group members. Aronson and Mills predicted that participants who went through the severe screening test would experience dissonance between the cognitions "I went through an embarrassing test to join this group" and "This group is boring." To reduce their dissonance, these participants were expected to change the cognition "This group is boring" to "This group is somewhat interesting." Figure 7.3 presents the mean ratings of the discussion and of the group members by participants in the mild and severe screening test conditions, as well as ratings by participants in a control condition who simply listened to the taped discussion without going through any screening test (this condition presumably showed how boring the discussion really was). As predicted, participants in the severe test condition rated both the discussion and the group members as more interesting than did participants in the control condition. Thus, it appears that the severe test aroused dissonance, which was reduced by perceiving the discussion as more interesting than it really was. Participants in the mild test condition did not differ from control participants in their ratings of the discussion or group members. It appears that the mild test was not effortful or embarrassing enough to arouse dissonance when the discussion group turned out to be boring.

Has it occurred to you that these findings suggest that a severe "initiation" to join a group might, paradoxically, increase recruits' evaluations of the group? If individuals willingly go through a painful or embarrassing initiation to join a sports

*How can some people such as these coal miners persist with an occupation that entails strenuous work, hazardous conditions, and often low pay?*

team, a fraternity, or some other group, they will be motivated to justify their suffering by perceiving the group as attractive and worthwhile. So a painful initiation might actually increase the commitment of new members to the group, which may explain why some groups have such procedures. Similarly, if someone spends a lot of money to join a golf club or to undergo prolonged psychotherapy, he or she will be motivated to see the golf club as prestigious or the psychotherapy as helpful. We are motivated to come to like or value things we have invested time and effort to attain (see also Axsom & Cooper, 1985; Cooper, 1980).

It may interest you to know that feelings of dissonance from potentially wasted effort are quite common among research scientists, including social psychologists (even dissonance researchers!). Many scientific activities are time-consuming and expensive but can sometimes bear little fruit. A series of experiments can yield null results; a long and detailed grant proposal seeking financial support for research can be turned down; a paper submitted for publication can be rejected from one journal after another. Each of these experiences is very frustrating. How do scientists deal with their dissonance? It is difficult for them to change the dissonant cognitions directly—the effort that has been invested and the lack of output are both quite obvious and undeniable. Instead, scientists often add consonant cognitions: they rationalize that the effort was worthwhile because it "clarified their thinking" or "forced them to move in new research directions" or "motivated them to establish connections with other researchers." All of these observations may be true, of course, but they also constitute consonant cognitions that help to alleviate feelings of dissonance. No one is immune to dissonance, not even social psychologists who know what it is.

Enduring a difficult or embarrassing initiation can motivate people to believe that the group is worthwhile.

**Free Choice: Dissonance From Making a Decision.** Decisions always involve choosing one option from various alternatives: deciding which automobile to buy, deciding whom to ask out on a date, or deciding how to solve a problem. Thus, decisions always involve a *chosen option* and at least one *rejected option*. Festinger (1957) hypothesized that after making a decision, people almost always experience some dissonance; this kind of dissonance has (logically) been labeled *postdecisional dissonance.*

Why do people experience dissonance after most decisions? Because the chosen option will usually have some negative features, and the rejected option will usually have some positive features. Imagine that you are choosing between two cars: car A performs better and is more attractive than car B, but car A is also more expensive and less fuel efficient than car B. If you choose car A, its costliness will arouse dissonance, and the fuel efficiency of car B will also arouse dissonance. If you choose car B, its low attractiveness will arouse dissonance, and the better performance of car A will also arouse dissonance. So no matter which car you choose, there will be some dissonant cognitions. (Of course, there will also be some consonant cognitions, such as the performance and attractiveness of car A if you choose it, so you will probably focus on these qualities after making your decision.)

The **free choice paradigm** is used to study postdecisional dissonance in the lab. It involves asking participants to make a choice between two or more alternatives. Participants' evaluations of the alternatives are assessed before making the decision and then again after the decision. Dissonance theory predicts that thinking about the negative features of the chosen alternative or the positive features of the rejected alternative will arouse dissonance after the decision is made. People will reduce this dissonance by focusing on the positive features of the chosen alternative and the negative features of the rejected alternative. As a result, after making a decision, people will tend to evaluate the chosen alternative even more positively and the rejected alternative even more negatively than before making the decision.

Jack Brehm (1956) published the first study employing the free choice paradigm to study postdecisional dissonance.

**free choice paradigm**

*a research methodology used to test dissonance theory that arouses dissonance by getting people to choose between two or more alternatives*

Deciding which appliance to buy can arouse *postdecisional dissonance.*

7.1
ONLINE
LAB

College women were asked to rate a number of consumer items, including a toaster, an electric coffeepot, and a silk-screen print, on evaluation scales. They were then given the opportunity to choose one of two items as a gift for taking part in the study. Some participants were given a difficult choice: they had to select between two items that they had rated very closely on the evaluation scales. Other participants were given an easy choice: they had rated one of the items much more favorably than the other. Difficult choices (between alternatives that were equally attractive) were expected to cause more postdecisional dissonance than easy choices.

After making their choice, all participants were asked to rate the items again on the same evaluation scales. Brehm could then examine whether participants had changed their ratings from before the decision to after the decision. Figure 7.4 presents the mean changes in ratings in the difficult (high dissonance) and easy (low dissonance) conditions. As predicted, participants in the high dissonance condition increased their rating of the chosen item and decreased their rating of the rejected item, whereas participants in the low dissonance condition did not show much change in ratings of either the chosen or the rejected item. The difficult condition aroused more postdecisional dissonance, which was reduced by exaggerating the difference between the chosen and rejected items. This tendency to rate the chosen item more favorably and the rejected item less favorably after a decision has been termed *spreading of the alternatives*—that is, the evaluations of the chosen and rejected items are spread further apart (see also Johnson & Rusbult, 1989; Shultz, Leveille, & Lepper, 1999; Zanna & Sande, 1987).

## Alternative Interpretations of Dissonance Findings

Despite the supportive experiments in the first phase of dissonance research, alternative interpretations of dissonance findings began to appear about a decade after Festinger's (1957) book was published. We describe three alternative interpretations here. The key points of these alternatives, and of dissonance theory itself, are summarized in Table 7.2.

**Self-Perception Theory.** The first serious attack on dissonance theory came from Daryl Bem (1967, 1972) when he proposed *self-perception theory*. We discussed this theory in Chapter 4 (see pages 132–135) and again briefly in Chapter 6 (see pages 217–218). Bem hypothesized that people sometimes infer their internal states, such as attitudes and emotions, from their behavior and the situation in which the behavior occurred. For instance, individuals might infer that their attitude toward golfing is unfavorable because they have rarely golfed despite having had opportunities to do so. Using behavior to infer internal states is presumed to occur mainly when the internal states are weak or ambiguous.

How does self-perception theory offer an alternative interpretation of dissonance findings? Let's focus on just one of the dissonance paradigms: induced compliance. Recall that Festinger and Carlsmith (1959) induced participants to tell another person that some boring tasks were interesting. So long as they were not paid much for telling this lie (the $1 condition), participants subsequently reported that the tasks were somewhat interesting. According to the original researchers, this relatively favorable evaluation of the tasks reflected that participants felt dissonance between the cognitions "the tasks were boring" and "I told someone that the tasks were interesting"; participants reduced dissonance by changing one of the dissonant cognitions (from "the tasks were boring" to "the tasks were somewhat interest-

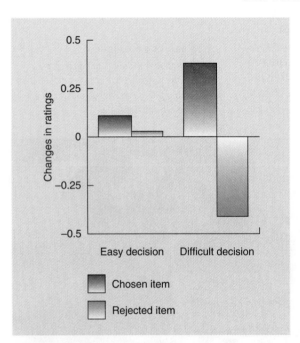

**FIGURE 7.4** Changes in ratings of chosen and rejected items after decision

From Brehm, "Post-decision changes in desirability of alternatives," *Journal of Abnormal and Social Psychology*, 52, 384–389, Table 1, 1956.

## TABLE 7.2
### Key Points of Dissonance Theory and Alternative Interpretations

| Theory | Key Points/Assumptions |
|---|---|
| Dissonance theory | Recognition that their actions have been irrational or erroneous makes people feel unpleasant arousal, which motivates them to change a dissonant cognition or to add consonant cognitions. |
| Self-perception theory | People logically infer their attitudes from their behavior and the circumstances in which the behavior occurred, without the occurrence of any arousal. |
| Impression management theory | People in dissonance experiments want to appear consistent to the researcher and therefore lie about their attitudes: they falsely report attitudes that are relatively consistent with their behavior in the study. |
| Self-affirmation theory | Recognition that their actions have been irrational or erroneous threatens people's positive self-views, which causes unpleasant arousal; people can reduce this arousal by doing anything that reaffirms their value and worth as individuals. |

ing") so that it would be more consonant with "I told someone that the tasks were interesting."

Bem (1967) suggested, however, that participants in the $1 condition (high dissonance) in Festinger and Carlsmith's (1959) study rated the tasks as somewhat interesting *because they inferred this attitude from the fact that they told someone the tasks were interesting without much justification for doing so.* From this perspective, participants were not upset by their lie or motivated to distort their evaluation of the tasks; rather, they simply inferred in a logical manner that the tasks must have been interesting because they willingly told someone the tasks were interesting. Participants in the $20 condition did not infer that they liked the tasks because the large payment provided a very plausible explanation of their behavior.

Does this interpretation make sense to you? Do you think that participants were unaware of how interesting or boring the tasks were? Imagine yourself turning pegs for an hour. Would you know that you were bored? Dissonance researchers thought so. They responded to Bem's critique by arguing that participants knew perfectly well that the tasks were boring and felt bad after telling the lie; this aversive arousal motivated the favorable evaluation of the tasks in order to reduce the arousal.

This last comment highlights an important difference between dissonance and self-perception theories: the role of unpleasant arousal. Dissonance theorists hypothesized that aversive arousal motivated the attitude change, whereas self-perception theorists hypothesized that there was no arousal at all. Several experiments were conducted over the next few years to investigate the role of aversive arousal. These experiments consistently supported dissonance theory and thereby cast doubt on a self-perception interpretation of dissonance findings. For example, researchers found that if participants in high dissonance conditions were given alcohol or a tranquilizer, either of which reduces arousal, they did not exhibit the usual attitude change (e.g., Cooper, Zanna, & Taves, 1978; Steele, Southwick, & Critchlow, 1981). These findings indicated that aversive arousal is necessary for attitude change to occur (see also Croyle & Cooper, 1982; Fazio, Zanna, & Cooper, 1977; Zanna & Cooper, 1974).

Although it has not fared well as an alternative to dissonance theory, self-perception theory made important contributions to the study of other phenomena in social psychology. For example, we discussed in Chapter 4 the usefulness of self-perception theory for understanding the effects of rewards, especially the *overjustification effect* (the finding that giving people a reward for an enjoyable activity can reduce their intrinsic interest in the activity; see page 134).

**impression management theory**

*an alternative to dissonance theory that argues that participants in dissonance experiments want to appear consistent to the experimenter and therefore lie about their attitudes*

**Impression Management Theory.** A second alternative interpretation of dissonance findings made the provocative proposal that participants in dissonance experiments were often simply *faking* attitude change. **Impression management theory** (Tedeschi, Schlenker, & Bonoma, 1971) proposed that participants in dissonance studies did not want to appear inconsistent to the experimenter and therefore *falsely* reported attitudes that were relatively consistent with the counterattitudinal behavior that they had exhibited. These researchers argued that participants were just trying to manage the experimenter's impression of them, and the reported attitudes were not genuine.

Imagine yourself in an induced compliance experiment in which you voluntarily agreed to write an essay arguing in favor of tuition increases for college students. After writing this essay, the experimenter asked you to report your own attitude toward tuition increases. Would you feel that you'd look stupid or weak to the experimenter if you admitted that you were actually against tuition increases? If so, perhaps you would decide to lie about your attitude—to state that you think that tuition increases are a good idea.

There is no doubt that research participants want experimenters to view them positively. Recall from Chapter 4 our discussion of *self-presentation goals* (see page 149). Common self-presentation goals include being seen as likable and competent: we want others to think of us as nice and talented people. It is also true that some dissonance experiments have elicited counterattitudinal behavior under very public conditions that probably aroused the motive to report an attitude consistent with the behavior even if that attitude was not truthful.

But it is unlikely that impression management theory can explain all dissonance findings. For one thing, participants in some studies reported attitudes that were consistent with their counterattitudinal behavior even though the person who took the attitude measure was not the person who observed the counterattitudinal behavior (e.g., Linder, Cooper, & Jones, 1967); there should have been no need to lie about one's attitude to someone who didn't even observe the counterattitudinal behavior. Also, attitudes consistent with counterattitudinal behavior have been obtained even when the counterattitudinal behavior occurred in very private settings that virtually eliminated any impression management motives (e.g., Harmon-Jones, Brehm, Greenberg, Simon, & Nelson, 1996). These findings indicate that, although impression management motives do influence public behavior, the attitude change that occurs in dissonance-arousing situations is almost certainly real.

**self-affirmation theory**

*an alternative to dissonance theory that argues that people are threatened by behavior that challenges their self-worth and can deal with this threat by reaffirming an important value*

**Self-Affirmation Theory.** Perhaps the most compelling alternative to dissonance theory was proposed by Claude Steele (1988; Steele & Liu, 1981), building on earlier work by Elliot Aronson (1968). **Self-affirmation theory** argues that people want to view themselves as moral, capable individuals. Extrapolating from this idea that people want to see themselves positively, Steele and his colleagues argued that counterattitudinal or irrational behavior threatens participants' views of themselves as honest and intelligent. That is, counterattitudinal behavior is upsetting because it *threatens self-worth*—it implies that participants are dishonest or foolish. For instance, self-affirmation researchers proposed that people in the Festinger and Carlsmith (1959) study were not upset about the inconsistency between "The tasks were boring" and "I told someone that the tasks were fun," but instead were disturbed by the inconsistency between "I am an honest person" and "I lied to someone." The flowchart in Figure 7.5 depicts the self-affirmation reinterpretation of Festinger and Carlsmith's experiment.

Self-affirmation theorists predicted that people can deal with threats to their self-worth in ways other than changing their attitudes. After all, if people are upset by counterattitudinal behavior because it implies they are dishonest, then they should be able to make themselves feel better by doing something honest or good even without changing their attitudes. Prior to Steele's research, however, dissonance researchers did not provide such alternatives in their experiments.

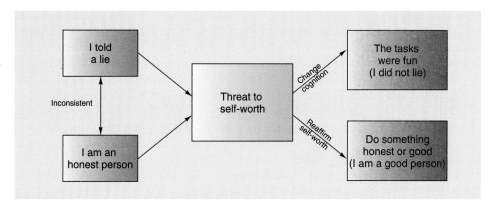

**FIGURE 7.5** Self-affirmation theory reinterpretation of Festinger and Carlsmith (1959) experiment

In several studies, Steele and his colleagues showed that giving people an opportunity to demonstrate their self-worth after counterattitudinal behavior reduces or eliminates attitude change (Steele, 1988; Steele & Liu, 1981, 1983; Steele, Spencer, & Lynch, 1993). For example, in one study (Steele & Liu, 1981), college students were asked to write an essay arguing against government funding of facilities for the disabled—a position that was counterattitudinal for the participants. Prior to writing the essay, some participants were told that they would later be asked to help a blind student, whereas other participants were not told about such an opportunity. After writing the essay, participants' attitudes toward the issue of government funding for the handicapped were measured. Those participants who did *not* expect to help a blind student reported more negative attitudes toward government assistance for the disabled (consistent with their essay) than did participants who expected to help a blind student. The researchers proposed that the latter participants knew that they would soon be able to demonstrate their positive worth by helping the blind student and, therefore, were not disturbed by their counterattitudinal essay.

**Summary.** What should we conclude about the various alternative interpretations that have been proposed for dissonance theory? Perhaps the most sensible conclusion at the present time is that each alternative has a "kernel of truth," but none provides a complete account of all dissonance findings. Self-perception theory, impression management theory, and self-affirmation theory all describe psychological processes that occur under certain conditions. Each perspective can account for some dissonance findings and has implications for some nondissonance settings as well. But the full range of experimental paradigms used by dissonance researchers is still explained most simply by dissonance theory itself. It is a testament to the creativity of Leon Festinger both that his model has generated so much attention and that it remains a viable theory today.

## Recent Research on Dissonance Theory

We close our discussion of dissonance theory with a brief consideration of trends in recent research. There has been renewed interest in dissonance theory over the past decade (e.g., see Harmon-Jones & Mills, 1999; Olson & Stone, in press), including investigations of how people learn to

© Peter Byron/Photo Edit

*Self-affirmation theory* predicts that helping a blind person can reduce dissonance caused by a prior, unrelated behavior.

experience dissonance (Cooper, 1998) and attempts to integrate dissonance and self-affirmation theories (e.g., Blanton, Cooper, Skurnik, & Aronson, 1997; Stone, Wiegand, Cooper, & Aronson, 1997). Researchers have also proposed sophisticated, formal models that aim to specify the psychological mechanisms that underlie dissonance effects (e.g., Harmon-Jones & Harmon-Jones, 2002; Shultz & Lepper, 1996; Stone, 2001, 2003; Stone & Cooper, 2001, 2003; Van Overwalle & Jordens, 2002).

One issue that has received attention is whether the arousal of dissonance requires that bad consequences result from the individual's actions. Some theorists have proposed that people will not feel upset about behaving in a counterattitudinal way unless something negative happens, such as the behavior hurts another person (Cooper & Fazio, 1984). Recent research has indicated, however, that negative consequences are *not* necessary for dissonance to occur (e.g., Harmon-Jones et al., 1996). In fact, researchers have identified a new paradigm for studying dissonance in which the individual's behavior has no aversive consequences whatsoever.

**The Hypocrisy Paradigm.** Earlier, we described three paradigms—induced compliance, effort justification, and free choice—that have been used to study dissonance experimentally. More recent research by Elliot Aronson and his students (e.g., Aronson, Fried, & Stone, 1991; Dickerson, Thibodeau, Aronson, & Miller, 1992) has added a fourth paradigm, which they labeled the **hypocrisy paradigm.** Imagine that you arrive for an experiment and are asked to prepare and deliver a speech promoting the conservation of water. You are told that this speech might be included in a videotape being developed for viewing by high school students (to increase their awareness of the problem). The experimenter gives you a sheet with some relevant information on it about the world's dwindling water resources, and you spend a few minutes organizing your thoughts. The experimenter then videotapes you while you explain why it is important to conserve water. Now the interesting part. After giving this little speech, you are asked to complete a questionnaire about your own behavior related to water conservation. In answering these questions, you realize that you often take longer showers than necessary, sometimes turn on the dishwasher before it is completely full, and occasionally let the water hose run when washing your car. How do you think these realizations would make you feel?

Aronson and his students hypothesized that this situation arouses dissonance. The situation makes people aware that they have sometimes failed to perform the behaviors they just recommended on the videotape. This realization arouses dissonance between the cognitions "I publicly recommended water conservation" and "I sometimes fail to conserve water."

This is an interesting form of dissonance because the public behavior that provokes it is completely *pro*attitudinal—the individual recommends a socially beneficial behavior such as conserving water. Yet privately knowing that he or she has not always performed the behavior makes the individual feel hypocritical (because people should "practice what they preach"). Aronson and his colleagues predicted that dissonance aroused by hypocrisy would motivate individuals to change their behavior to be more consistent with what they publicly promoted. Thus, the hypocrisy paradigm was expected to elicit more socially beneficial behavior.

In one experiment using the hypocrisy paradigm, Jeff Stone, Elliot Aronson, and their colleagues (Stone, Aronson, Crain, Winslow, & Fried, 1994) recruited college students who had been sexually active in the previous three months and asked them to prepare a speech about the importance of safer sexual behaviors, such as always using a condom during sex. Participants were told that these speeches would be shown to high school students to promote the safer behaviors. Participants were given some information to help them prepare the speech, which they wrote and then delivered in front of a camera. After the speech was videotaped,

**hypocrisy paradigm**

*a research methodology used to test dissonance theory that arouses dissonance by having people publicly promote a socially desirable behavior and then be made aware that they have not always exhibited the behavior themselves in the past*

participants completed a questionnaire that was designed to make them aware of their own failures to practice safer sex behaviors. For example, the questionnaire listed 10 common reasons why people do not use condoms, and participants were asked whether any of these reasons applied to their own past failures to use condoms; they were also encouraged to generate additional reasons why they had failed to use condoms in the past.

Participants were then told that the experiment was finished and were given four $1 bills as payment for their participation. The experimenter then explained that when the campus health center heard that this study was focused on safer sex behaviors, it made available a supply of condoms at a price of 10 cents each. The experimenter pointed to a table in the room where a clear plastic container was filled with 140 condoms in individual packages. A bowl of loose change was beside the container, as well as an envelope with numerous $1 bills. The experimenter said that if the participant wanted to buy any condoms, he or she could put a bill in the envelope and take the necessary change from the bowl. The experimenter then left the room, and the participant was able to purchase condoms privately and anonymously if he or she wished before leaving the room.

After delivering a speech advocating safer sex behaviors and then being reminded of past personal failures to use condoms, 83% of participants purchased at least one condom. Thus, most individuals in this condition apparently wanted to make their future sexual behavior safer. In three control conditions in which participants (1) delivered a similar speech but were not reminded of past failures, (2) were reminded of past failures but did not deliver a speech, or (3) were simply given the opportunity to purchase condoms (without delivering a speech or being reminded of past failures), less than 50% of participants purchased at least one condom. These findings are presented in Figure 7.6. The results showed that the feeling of hypocrisy created by the *combination* of delivering the speech *and* being reminded of past failures was necessary to arouse dissonance; the dissonance then motivated people to make their sexual behavior safer in the future (see also Son Hing, Li, & Zanna, 2002).

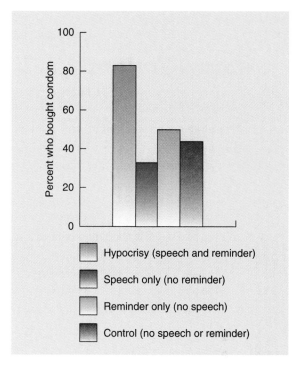

**FIGURE 7.6** Percentage of participants who bought condom

From Stone et al., "Inducing hypocrisy as a means of encouraging young adults to use condoms," *Personality and Social Psychology Bulletin*, 20, 116–128, Fig. 1, p. 121, 1994. Reprinted by permission of Sage Publications.

**Individual Differences in Preferences for Consistency.** Are some people more sensitive to dissonance than others? Robert Cialdini, Melanie Trost, and Jason Newsom (1995) thought so and developed a scale to measure such differences. They labeled the dimension **preference for consistency (PFC)** and hypothesized that scores on the scale revealed the extent to which people desired predictability and compatibility within their own responses and within others' responses. For instance, people who score high in PFC are presumed to want their actions and attitudes to be consistent with one another (as assumed by dissonance theory), whereas people who score low in PFC are presumed to be less concerned about such consistency (in contrast to the assumptions of dissonance theory).

Know Yourself 7.1: Preference for Consistency (p. 266), presents the nine items from the brief form of the PFC scale (Cialdini et al., 1995). Answer the items and see whether you score high or low on this dimension.

Cialdini and his colleagues hypothesized that typical findings in dissonance experiments would be stronger for people who are high in the preference for consistency than for those who are low in this disposition. In a test of this hypothesis, students were asked to write an essay in favor of a tuition increase—a position that was assumed to be counterattitudinal for all participants. Those in the choice (high dissonance) condition were asked whether they would be willing to write this

**preference for consistency (PFC)**

*a disposition that represents the extent to which people desire predictability and compatibility within their own responses and within others' responses*

# Know Yourself 7.1
## *Preference for Consistency*

Please indicate the extent to which you agree or disagree with each of the following statements by circling the appropriate number on the answer scale.

1. It is important to me that those who know me can predict what I will do.

| 1 | 2 | 3 | 4 | 5 | 6 | 7 | 8 | 9 |
|---|---|---|---|---|---|---|---|---|
| Strongly disagree | Disagree | Somewhat disagree | Slightly disagree | Neither agree nor disagree | Slightly agree | Somewhat agree | Agree | Strongly agree |

2. I want to be described by others as a stable, predictable person.

| 1 | 2 | 3 | 4 | 5 | 6 | 7 | 8 | 9 |
|---|---|---|---|---|---|---|---|---|
| Strongly disagree | Disagree | Somewhat disagree | Slightly disagree | Neither agree nor disagree | Slightly agree | Somewhat agree | Agree | Strongly agree |

3. The appearance of consistency is an important part of the image I present to the world.

| 1 | 2 | 3 | 4 | 5 | 6 | 7 | 8 | 9 |
|---|---|---|---|---|---|---|---|---|
| Strongly disagree | Disagree | Somewhat disagree | Slightly disagree | Neither agree nor disagree | Slightly agree | Somewhat agree | Agree | Strongly agree |

4. An important requirement for any friend of mine is personal consistency.

| 1 | 2 | 3 | 4 | 5 | 6 | 7 | 8 | 9 |
|---|---|---|---|---|---|---|---|---|
| Strongly disagree | Disagree | Somewhat disagree | Slightly disagree | Neither agree nor disagree | Slightly agree | Somewhat agree | Agree | Strongly agree |

5. I typically prefer to do things the same way.

| 1 | 2 | 3 | 4 | 5 | 6 | 7 | 8 | 9 |
|---|---|---|---|---|---|---|---|---|
| Strongly disagree | Disagree | Somewhat disagree | Slightly disagree | Neither agree nor disagree | Slightly agree | Somewhat agree | Agree | Strongly agree |

6. I want my close friends to be predictable.

| 1 | 2 | 3 | 4 | 5 | 6 | 7 | 8 | 9 |
|---|---|---|---|---|---|---|---|---|
| Strongly disagree | Disagree | Somewhat disagree | Slightly disagree | Neither agree nor disagree | Slightly agree | Somewhat agree | Agree | Strongly agree |

7. It is important to me that others view me as a stable person.

| 1 | 2 | 3 | 4 | 5 | 6 | 7 | 8 | 9 |
|---|---|---|---|---|---|---|---|---|
| Strongly disagree | Disagree | Somewhat disagree | Slightly disagree | Neither agree nor disagree | Slightly agree | Somewhat agree | Agree | Strongly agree |

8. I make an effort to appear consistent to others.

| 1 | 2 | 3 | 4 | 5 | 6 | 7 | 8 | 9 |
|---|---|---|---|---|---|---|---|---|
| Strongly disagree | Disagree | Somewhat disagree | Slightly disagree | Neither agree nor disagree | Slightly agree | Somewhat agree | Agree | Strongly agree |

9. It doesn't bother me much if my actions are inconsistent.

| 1 | 2 | 3 | 4 | 5 | 6 | 7 | 8 | 9 |
|---|---|---|---|---|---|---|---|---|
| Strongly disagree | Disagree | Somewhat disagree | Slightly disagree | Neither agree nor disagree | Slightly agree | Somewhat agree | Agree | Strongly agree |

**SCORING:** Items 1–8 are scored using the answer scales as presented (1-2-3-4-5-6-7-8-9), but Item 9 is scored in the reverse direction (that is, 9-8-7-6-5-4-3-2-1). Add up all of the items for your overall preference for consistency score. Possible scores range from 9 to 81, and higher scores represent stronger preferences for consistency.

Sample items from Cialdini et al., "Preference for consistency: The development of a valid measure and the discovery of surprising behavioral implications," *Journal of Personality and Social Psychology*, 69, 318–328, 1995. Copyright © 1995 by the American Psychological Association. Reprinted by permission.

essay, whereas those in the no choice (low dissonance) condition were simply told to write the essay. After preparing the essay, participants reported their own attitudes toward a tuition increase. As predicted by Cialdini and his colleagues, participants who were high in the preference for consistency reported more favorable attitudes toward a tuition increase in the choice condition than in the no choice condition, whereas participants who were low in the preference for consistency reported equivalent attitudes in the two conditions. Thus, using an induced compliance paradigm, dissonance theory was supported only for high PFC individuals.

This individual differences perspective on dissonance theory opens up many possibilities for future research. It will be interesting to see whether other dissonance paradigms also work better for people who are high rather than low in preferences for consistency.

**Dissonance and Explicit Versus Implicit Attitudes.** In Chapter 6, we distinguished between *explicit attitudes* and *implicit attitudes* (see page 202). Explicit attitudes refer to people's *conscious* evaluations of a target, whereas implicit attitudes refer to people's *automatic* evaluative responses to a target, which can occur without awareness. All of the research on dissonance theory that we have described thus far used explicit measures of attitudes.

Bertram Gawronski and Fritz Strack (2004) hypothesized that dissonance might *not* affect implicit attitudes. Why? Dissonance arousal and reduction rely on conscious mental inferences. For instance, counterattitudinal behavior is assumed to motivate attitude change when people consciously recognize that their behavior has been inconsistent with their attitude. Awareness of this inconsistency causes people to alter their conscious attitudes. But perhaps implicit attitudes, which are spontaneous and automatic, are not directly affected by conscious inferences.

Gawronski and Strack (2004) tested this reasoning by asking German college students to write an essay in favor of banning alcoholic beverages in their country (a counterattitudinal position). Some participants (high dissonance condition) were asked whether they would be willing to write the essay, whereas others (low dissonance condition) were simply told to write the essay. After generating the message, participants' explicit attitudes were assessed using self-report items, and their implicit attitudes were assessed using the Implicit Association Test (see page 212). Results showed that, consistent with dissonance theory, participants in the high dissonance condition reported more favorable explicit attitudes toward banning alcoholic beverages than did participants in the low dissonance condition. The two groups did not differ, however, in their implicit attitudes toward alcoholic beverages. Thus, dissonance changed explicit, but not implicit, attitudes. An interesting question for future research will be whether people's implicit attitudes might, over time, become consistent with their new explicit attitudes.

In closing, dissonance theory has stimulated a great deal of research and has provided a useful analysis of how everyday actions can change attitudes. The theory continues to inspire innovative experiments and seems likely to remain a vibrant theory in social psychology for many years to come.

## Information-Based Persuasion: Cognitive Response Theory

As noted at the beginning of this chapter, attitude change can occur in many ways. Dissonance theory deals with one way—namely, self-persuasion: we sometimes change our attitudes to rationalize our own behavior so that we feel better about it. Another way that attitudes change—perhaps the most common way—is as a result of *persuasive communications,* which are attempts (oral, written, face-to-face, media-based) by an individual or group to convince another person or persons to adopt a particular position. Many theories of attitude change in social psychology are designed to understand the factors that influence the success or failure of persuasive communications. Persuasive communications can be aimed at any kind of attitude—political views, evaluations of people, food preferences, or other targets (see Perloff, 2003; Seiter & Gass, 2004).

What are some common examples of persuasive communications? Let's begin by thinking about persuasive communications that you are exposed to regularly. Advertising is one category of such messages, with ads intended to make you more favorable toward a product. Education is another domain in which persuasive communications are frequent; for instance, your professors (and textbook authors) try to persuade you that their science is important. Family and friends also direct persuasive communications at you: your family tries to convince you to work hard at school, and your friends try to convince you to play hard after school.

What about persuasive communications that you initiate? What are some examples of your attempts to influence other people's opinions? You almost certainly generate many persuasive communications, even if you don't recognize them as such: you try to convince your housemate that she should take a course in psychology; you try to convince a friend to go to a movie with you; you try to convince an acquaintance that someone he currently dislikes is actually very nice. Often these communications are designed to change people's behavior toward you, such as going to a movie with you or helping you in some way.

Many (but *not* all) persuasive communications rely on *information* to convince the recipient to adopt the advocated position. Information-based messages consist of arguments about an issue and/or evidence supporting a position; they try to use reason or logic to make their case.

The social psychology theory that focuses most directly on information-based persuasion is **cognitive response theory** (Eagly & Chaiken, 1984; Greenwald, 1968; Petty & Cacioppo, 1981). Cognitive response theory assumes that the effectiveness of a message in causing attitude change is determined by the thoughts evoked by the message. The thoughts can be about the communicator, the issue, or the message. If the message elicits mostly positive thoughts (called *proarguments* in the theory), then the individual will be inclined to adopt the position advocated in the message. If the message elicits mostly negative thoughts (called *counterarguments* in the theory), then the individual will be inclined to reject the position advocated in the message. In both cases, the cognitive responses (or thoughts) are assumed to cause the acceptance or rejection of the advocated position. For instance, if a message evokes thoughts about how intelligent the communicator is and how convincing the arguments are, then the recipient is likely to adopt the recommended position. If, on the other hand, a message evokes thoughts about how biased the communicator is and how weak the arguments are, then the recipient is likely to reject the recommended position.

Think about your own reactions to persuasive communications, such as advertisements, in-class discussions about politics, or arguments about the best movie of the year. Sometimes you probably find yourself thinking, "This is a great feature to have in this product," or "What an interesting argument—I never thought of that before," or "This person is really smart." These kinds of thoughts are normally associated with being persuaded by the ad, discussion, or argument. But other times you probably find yourself thinking, "This is a useless product," or "What a stupid argument," or "What a loser this guy is." These kinds of thoughts are normally associated with rejecting the recommendations of the ad, discussion, or argument. We should all keep in mind that when we try to persuade others, they are silently generating thoughts about us and our message—and those thoughts may not always be flattering!

**cognitive response theory**

*a model of persuasion that assumes that the impact of a message on attitudes depends on the thoughts evoked by the message*

## Strong Arguments, Strong Attitudes

What factors determine whether a message will elicit positive or negative thoughts? Once again, think about your own reactions to persuasive communications. What features characterize successful communications? Humorous? Eye-grabbing? Interesting?

All of these factors probably have some impact, as do characteristics of the recipient such as mood and amount of knowledge about the issue. But perhaps the most important factor is a simple and straightforward one: the *strength of the arguments* in the message. When a message contains strong arguments, it usually elicits positive thoughts about the communicator, the issue, and the message. By definition, strong arguments provide compelling reasons for adopting the advocated position. Thus, strong arguments tend to produce correspondingly strong attitudes that are consistent with the recommended position. In contrast, weak arguments provide poor support for the advocated position and usually elicit negative thoughts. Weak arguments do not typically move the recipient's attitude in the direction of the message. The flowchart in Figure 7.7 depicts these effects of strong and weak arguments.

John Cacioppo and Richard Petty (1985) conducted a study that illustrated nicely the importance of the strength of the arguments in a message. College students listened to a message arguing that seniors at their college should have a new requirement that they must pass a comprehensive examination in their major area before they can graduate. Needless to say, almost all students opposed this idea. Two messages were used, one containing strong arguments and the other containing weak arguments. An example of a strong argument was "Graduates from colleges with comprehensive exams are recruited more heavily by employers." An example of a weak argument was "Comprehensive exams maintain a tradition dating back to the ancient Greeks." A second independent variable was also manipulated in the experiment: participants heard the message either once or three times.

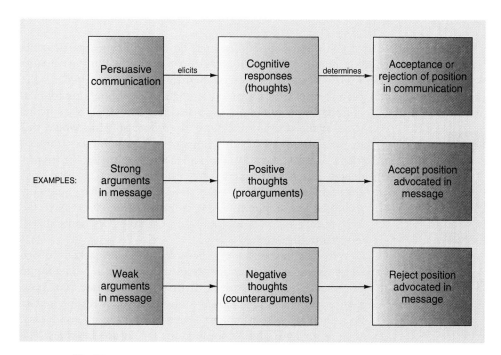

**FIGURE 7.7** Cognitive response theory and persuasive communications

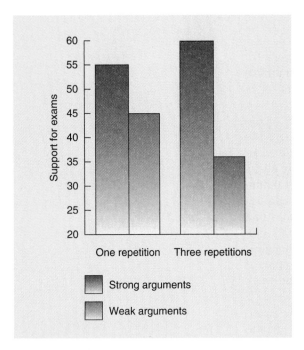

**FIGURE 7.8** Favorability of attitudes toward comprehensive exams: Repetition

From Petty and Cacioppo, "The elaboration likelihood model of persuasion," in L. Berkowitz, ed., *Advances in Experimental Social Psychology* (Vol. 19, pp. 123–205), p. 142, 1986. Reprinted by permission of Elsevier.

The researchers hypothesized that repeating the message three times should heighten the impact of argument strength because participants would have three chances to think about how convincing or how stupid the arguments were.

After hearing the strong or weak message once or three times, participants were asked to report their own attitude toward instituting comprehensive exams for seniors. In addition, their memory for the message was tested. Figure 7.8 presents the attitude findings from the experiment. When participants heard the message just once, the strong arguments produced more positive attitudes toward comprehensive exams than did the weak message, as would be expected. When participants heard the message three times, this difference was exaggerated: the strong message produced even more positive attitudes, and the weak message produced even more negative attitudes. Thus, the impact of the message in this study depended on its quality, as well as participants' opportunities to consider it carefully.

The researchers also analyzed participants' memory for the message. The memory data showed that repeated exposure improved recall of the arguments, whether strong or weak. Participants who heard the strong message three times recalled more strong arguments than did those who heard the strong message just once; participants who heard the weak message three times recalled more weak arguments than did those who heard the weak message just once. Thus, participants were paying attention to the message, and repeated exposure allowed them to analyze the message more thoroughly. Have you ever noticed that many commercials are shown more than once during the same TV show? These repetitions reflect the assumption by many advertisers that repeated exposure will enhance the impact of positive information about their products.

## Are You Listening?

The experiment we just described manipulated how many times participants heard the message. This manipulation influenced how carefully the participants were able to process the message. The more opportunities they had to hear the message, the greater was the impact of argument strength. What about a manipulation that went in the opposite direction, in which participants were *inhibited* from processing the message? How would this manipulation affect the impact of argument strength? Richard Petty, Gary Wells, and Timothy Brock (1976) predicted that if participants were inhibited from paying close attention to a message, then the strength of the arguments would be less important. After all, unless recipients have the opportunity to process a message carefully, its content will make little difference.

To test this reasoning, Petty et al. (1976) asked college students to listen to a message arguing for a reduction in tuition—a position that most participants supported. The message contained either strong arguments for a tuition reduction, such as reducing students' debt load, or weak arguments, such as giving students more money for leisure activities. The researchers also asked participants to complete a second task while listening to the message. This second task required participants to record on a sheet the quadrant in which *X*s appeared on a screen in front of them (e.g., upper left quad-

If you want to convince someone of a position for which you have only weak arguments, it might be a good idea to present the arguments while the person is being distracted by something else, such as a newspaper.

rant, lower right quadrant, etc.). For some participants (the *low distrac-tion* condition), the Xs appeared at 15-second intervals—a frequency that was not disruptive to listening to the message. But for other par-ticipants (the *high distraction* condition), the Xs appeared at 5-second intervals—a frequency that was very disruptive to processing the mes-sage. After hearing the message once while performing this low or high distraction task, participants reported their own attitude toward a tuition reduction. They were also asked to write down any thoughts that had occurred to them during the message.

Figure 7.9 presents the results on the attitude measure. In the low distraction condition, participants who heard a strong message were more favorable toward reducing tuition than were participants who heard a weak message, as expected. But in the high distraction condition, the impact of argument strength was greatly reduced: the strong message was only slightly more persuasive than the weak mes-sage. If you compare the two strong argument bars, you will see that the strong message was somewhat less persuasive when participants were more distracted, which makes sense because distracted partici-pants were not able to think about the arguments.

But the most interesting result was for weak arguments: notice that the weak message was actually somewhat *more persuasive* in the high distraction condition than in the low distraction condition. When participants were distracted from a weak message, its impact actually increased. Why did this effect occur? Examination of the thoughts that participants generated gives us a clue. Recall that participants were asked to write down any thoughts that had occurred to them while they listened to the message. The researchers coded each thought as favorable (a *proargument*) or unfavorable (a *counterargument*). For the weak message, the high distraction condition yielded fewer counterarguments than did the low distraction condition. Thus, the weak message was more persuasive in the high distraction condition than in the low distraction condition because partici-pants had fewer chances to generate criticisms of the arguments. In a sense, partici-pants were less able to determine just how bad the arguments were.

This finding has an interesting implication. If you want to convince people of something but do not have any strong arguments, then it might be a good idea to talk to them while the television is blaring or some other distraction is interfering with their ability to counterargue your reasoning!

Advertisers use a number of strategies to promote products. One general approach to advertising, which is consistent with the predictions of cognitive response theory, is known as the **hard sell.** It is described in Social Psychology in Your Life: Adver-tising the Old-Fashioned Way: The Hard Sell (p. 272).

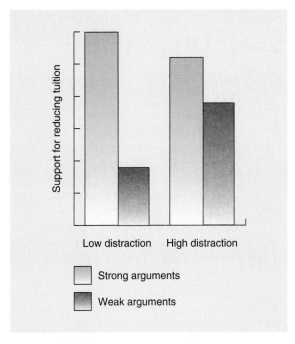

**FIGURE 7.9** Favorability of attitudes toward reducing tuition

From Petty et al., "Distraction can enhance or reduce yielding to propaganda: Thought disruption versus effort justification," *Journal of Personality and Social Psychology*, 34, 874–888, 1976. Copyright © 1976 by the American Psychological Association.

**hard sell**

*an advertising strategy that relies on presenting information about the positive features of a product*

# If You Say So: Heuristic Persuasion

Most people would use the term *persuasion* in a manner consistent with the preceding section: it is the result of reasoned thinking and occurs when people are convinced by strong arguments in a message. But there is another way that persua-sion can occur, which is very different from the information-based process. This second mode of persuasion has been labeled **heuristic persuasion** by Shelly Chaiken (1980, 1987).

Heuristic persuasion is so named because it focuses on attitude change that results from the use of *heuristics,* which are simple rules, shortcuts, or assumptions that individuals have been taught or have learned from experience. In Chapter 3, we

**heuristic persuasion**

*attitude change resulting from cues that indicate that the position advocated in a message is valid*

# Social Psychology in Your Life  *Advertising the Old-Fashioned Way: The Hard Sell*

When advertisers talk about the hard sell as one possible technique for promoting a product, they are referring to the use of information about the quality of a product to market it. The positive characteristics of the product are front and center: the message attempts to convince the recipients that the product is a good one. The appeal is rational and logical, rather than emotional or symbolic. The hard sell relies on information about the product, and it adopts a model of persuasion very much like cognitive response theory. The hard sell assumes that people process advertisements carefully and can be convinced by information to purchase or use the product.

Some types of products are more easily promoted with a hard sell than others. First, products whose performance can be objectively specified—such as stereo equipment, computers, appliances, and automobiles—lend themselves well to the hard sell. These products can be promoted by comparing their performance to that of other brands and highlighting their advantages. A written mode of communication, such as newspaper ads, is often an effective way to present this information. Second, products that are strictly functional and do not have any status or symbolic value—such as garden tools, insect repellants, air conditioners, and surge protectors—also lend themselves well to the hard sell. Let's face it, we don't buy a spade or an insect repellant to make an impression on other people. With these kinds of products, people are simply looking for ones that work effectively, so the only relevant consideration is information about their features

(Shavitt, 1990). An example of a magazine advertisement that uses the hard sell is presented in Figure 7.10. Allergy medications are purchased for a specific purpose—to relieve congestion. The way to convince people to buy the product is to tell them why and how it works. This ad presents information about the speed and duration of relief as well as a toll-free number and a website where additional information can be found.

Public information campaigns, such as mass media campaigns to promote a healthy lifestyle, also frequently use the hard sell (Mendelsohn, 1973). These campaigns present information explaining the benefits of adopting a certain lifestyle: "You'll feel better if you exercise regularly"; "You'll save money if you stop smoking." The assumption is that people will change their lifestyle if they can be convinced that there will be important benefits. Another important component is often to provide specific advice about how to undertake new behaviors, such as how to exercise without injury or whom to contact for help in stopping smoking (Backer, Rogers, & Sopory, 1992; Leventhal & Cameron, 1994; Olson & Zanna, 1987).

Political advertisements also frequently adopt the hard sell. Think about the political campaign ads you have seen. The most common strategy in political ads seems to be to describe the candidate's positions on important issues and to extol his or her integrity and honesty. Negative ads about opponents are also quite common, which usually ascribe negative qualities to those individuals (they are "weak on crime," "intolerant of diversity," or

*Courtesy of The Advertising Archives*

**FIGURE 7.10** Magazine advertisement that uses the hard sell

"puppets of the big corporations"). Both types of political ads are based on the assumption that *information* about the candidates will alter voters' attitudes.

Information-based campaigns can be very successful, as some researchers have documented. Mass media campaigns designed to increase public knowledge about heart disease, to enhance public awareness of crime prevention, or to sell political candidates have all been shown to have statistically significant effects on public opinion and relevant behavior (e.g., Kinder, 1998; Meyer, Nash, McAlister, Maccoby, & Farquhar, 1980; O'Keefe, 1985).

discussed the *availability heuristic* (see page 88) and the *representativeness heuristic* (see page 90). People often use heuristics to help them make decisions and judgments. With respect to attitude change, this perspective recognizes that people do not always exert a lot of effort to judge the validity of a persuasive message, but may instead base their agreement or disagreement on rather superficial cues, or informal rules, that are assumed to be instructive about the message's validity. These cues or heuristics can include things like "Experts are reliable sources of information," "People I like usually have correct opinions," and "Mom always knows best." People can use these rules to decide whether a particular message or recommendation is likely to be valid. For instance, the heuristic "Mom always knows best" implies that any communication from Mom should be accepted as accurate.

Do you think that *you* sometimes use heuristics to decide whether a persuasive communication is valid, rather than analyzing the arguments carefully? You may doubt that you accept or reject recommendations based on simple cues or clues. But let's think of some possible examples. You visit your family doctor because you have a persistent cough, and she or he tells you to take a certain medicine and reduce your physical activity for a week or two. Would you try to analyze the validity of these instructions? Most of us accept our doctor's recommendations without debate, because we assume that he or she is the expert. We may even think it would be inappropriate to question his or her instructions. The relevant heuristic here is "Experts are reliable sources of information."

Or imagine that you are watching television, and a story comes on about legal fees. One of the people interviewed is a lawyer, who presents some arguments in favor of increasing legal fees. How would you respond to this interview? Most of us are automatically suspicious of arguments that are delivered by someone who stands to gain or lose from an issue, because we believe that people often argue in self-serving ways even if evidence for their position is lacking. The relevant heuristic here is "People who argue for something that will benefit them personally are not reliable sources of information." Thus, you may simply ignore the interview with the lawyer or reject his or her arguments without careful thought.

As a third example, imagine that you open the local newspaper and see an unusually long and detailed editorial with the title "Using Cell Phones While Driving Should Be Banned." You don't really feel like reading the editorial carefully, so you just skim it and turn to the next page. Would seeing this article influence your attitude toward this issue? Most of us assume that long and detailed messages are probably based on lots of good evidence. After all, don't long messages require more arguments and more substance than short messages? The relevant heuristic here is "Long messages are valid." Thus, you might not read the editorial carefully, but nevertheless assume that it is probably accurate. Simply seeing the long editorial might make you more favorable toward banning the use of cell phones while driving.

## Says Who?

Does it matter *who* says something? Are messages from some sources more likely to elicit agreement than identical messages from other sources? The answer to this question is *yes*. Source characteristics can serve as heuristic cues that lead people to agree with a message. As an example of heuristic persuasion, we gave the case of obeying without question our doctor's orders. This example illustrates one of the most researched heuristic cues: the credibility or expertise of the source of the message (see Benoit & Strathman, 2004). The prediction is that people may agree with a message based simply on the credibility of the source rather than on the strength of the arguments. Using this rule probably makes sense in many cases, but it can also lead people to ignore the quality of the message, which may have negative consequences.

In an experiment by Richard Petty, John Cacioppo, and Rachel Goldman (1981), college students listened to a message arguing that graduating seniors should be required to pass a comprehensive examination—a position that was counterattitudinal

Expert, authoritative sources can produce agreement through *heuristic persuasion,* based on the idea that experts are reliable sources of information.

© Bob Daemmrich/Stock Boston

for almost all students (this topic was also used in a previously described study). The message contained either 8 strong arguments or 8 weak arguments. Also, the message was said to have been prepared either by "The Carnegie Commission on Higher Education, chaired by a Princeton University professor" (high credibility condition) or by "a local high school class" (low credibility condition). We want to focus here on a subset of the conditions in the experiment, in which participants were told that *comprehensive exams would not be instituted for at least a decade*—which meant that the participants would not be affected themselves. These conditions were expected to reduce the threat of the message, because the issue of comprehensive exams would not be personally relevant to the participants. The researchers predicted that these "low relevance" participants would not really care about the issue and, therefore, would use the heuristic cue of source credibility to judge the message, rather than the strength of the arguments. After listening to the message, participants reported their attitude toward the idea of comprehensive exams for seniors.

Figure 7.11 presents the relevant attitude data. As predicted, participants in these low relevance conditions were more favorable toward comprehensive exams when the message came from the Carnegie Commission on Higher Education (the two left-hand bars) than when it came from a local high school class (the two right-hand bars). In contrast, the manipulation of argument strength had less effect on attitudes: strong arguments produced only slightly more favorable attitudes than did weak arguments. Thus, it didn't matter very much whether the message was strong or weak—what mattered was whether the source was credible or not (see also Chaiken & Maheswaran, 1994; Kumkale & Albarracín, 2004; Wood & Kallgren, 1988).

Credibility is not the only characteristic of the source that influences agreement. We are also more likely to agree with likable people, with attractive people, and with famous people, compared to unlikable, unattractive, and unknown people (e.g., Chaiken, 1980; Petty, Cacioppo, & Schumann, 1983; Shavitt, Swan, Lowery, & Wanke, 1994; Wegener & Petty, 1997). Why? The heuristic model of persuasion explains these effects in terms of our assumptions

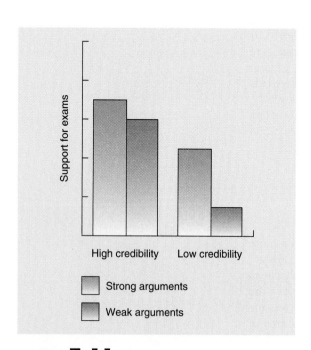

**FIGURE 7.11** Favorability of attitudes toward comprehensive exams: Source credibility

From Petty et al., "Personal involvement as a determinant of argument-based persuasion," *Journal of Personality and Social Psychology,* 41, 847–855, 1981. Copyright © 1981 by the American Psychological Association.

(heuristics) that likable, attractive, and famous people are usually reliable sources of information.

Earlier, we described the *hard sell* approach to advertising, which is consistent with the predictions of cognitive response theory. A second general approach to advertising, which is consistent with the concept of heuristic persuasion, is known as the **soft sell.** It is described in Social Psychology in Your Life: Advertising by Association: The Soft Sell (p. 276).

**soft sell**

*an advertising strategy that relies on the use of images, emotions, symbols, or values to promote a product*

# ● ● ● Two Models of Persuasive Messages

We have described two ways that persuasive communications can produce agreement. One way is via strong arguments that elicit positive thoughts from the recipient. The other way is via superficial cues or heuristics that the recipient assumes indicate that the message is valid, such as an expert source. The first way is described by cognitive response theory, and the second way has been called heuristic persuasion.

Can these different perspectives on persuasive communications be integrated in a single theoretical model? In fact, attitudes researchers have proposed two theories that encompass both ways that messages can elicit agreement: the **systematic-heuristic model** (Chaiken, 1980, 1987) and the **elaboration likelihood model** (Petty & Cacioppo, 1981, 1986; Petty, Rucker, Bizer, & Cacioppo, 2004). These theories are similar, though not identical (see Eagly & Chaiken, 1993). They were developed independently by the researchers and appeared at nearly the same time in the published literature. This is an interesting case of different researchers coming to the same conclusions about how to make sense of a diverse set of findings.

**systematic-heuristic model**

*a theory of attitude change that distinguishes between two types of processing that can occur in response to a persuasive message—systematic processing and heuristic processing*

**elaboration likelihood model**

*a theory of attitude change that specifies the conditions under which people will think carefully about the content of a persuasive message. It distinguishes between two types of processing—the central route to persuasion and the peripheral route to persuasion.*

## Two Types of Processing or Two Routes to Persuasion

The systematic-heuristic model of persuasion is designed to explain the effectiveness of persuasive messages. The model distinguishes between two types of processing that can occur when people encounter a persuasive communication. **Systematic processing** occurs when people think earnestly about the message; it involves a thoughtful analysis of the relevant information. **Heuristic processing** occurs when people rely on cues (heuristics) to make judgments about the message, without thinking carefully about the arguments that are presented.

Similarly, the elaboration likelihood model of persuasion is designed to explain the effectiveness of persuasive messages and distinguishes between two "routes to persuasion," which correspond closely to the types of processing identified in the systematic-heuristic model. The **central route to persuasion** occurs when attitude change results from a careful analysis of the information in a persuasive communication; it parallels systematic processing. The **peripheral route to persuasion** occurs when attitude change results from noncognitive factors; it parallels heuristic processing, although it also encompasses other affective processes like evaluative conditioning and mere exposure (see Chapter 6). This model was called the *elaboration likelihood model* because it specifies the conditions under which people are *likely* to *elaborate* on a message (i.e., to think about the message's arguments).

Each theory hypothesizes that the effectiveness of messages depends on different factors in the two types of processing or routes to persuasion. When recipients of a message are processing systematically (which activates the central route to persuasion), the main determinant of attitude change is the strength of the arguments.

**systematic processing**

*careful, deliberative analysis of the arguments in a message*

**heuristic processing**

*superficial analysis of a message that focuses on cues indicating the validity or invalidity of the advocated position*

**central route to persuasion**

*persuasion that occurs when attitude change results from a careful analysis of the information in a persuasive communication*

**peripheral route to persuasion**

*persuasion that occurs when attitude change results from noncognitive factors; it encompasses evaluative conditioning and mere exposure*

# Social Psychology in Your Life

## Advertising by Association: The Soft Sell

We previously described the hard sell, which involves promoting a product by stressing its positive characteristics and performance. Advertisers do not always try to sell products in this manner, however. In fact, they probably use the soft sell just as often as the hard sell. What is the soft sell? It refers to the use of images, emotions, symbols, or values to sell a product. The advertiser tries to associate the product with positive feelings or images, in the hope that consumers will come to like the product. The soft sell relies, in many cases, on heuristic cues implying that the product is a good one without necessarily providing relevant information.

Examples of the soft sell are easy to find. Many advertisements try to arouse positive emotions or moods, which will then be associated with the product in consumers' minds: humorous ads use jokes or slapstick to evoke positive affect; sentimental ads use babies or puppies to arouse warm feelings and happy memories; and many ads use cheerful or lively music to elicit good moods. These ads often have little information about the product—the goal of the ad is simply to make viewers feel good.

Other advertisements try to link a product with success, attractiveness, or high status without providing specific facts. For instance, beer ads show attractive young people having lots of fun at a party; car ads portray the handsome drivers as popular and successful; and

clothing ads show beautiful models in prestigious settings. These images are intended to evoke impressions of happiness, attractiveness, prosperity, and status, which consumers will subconsciously associate with the product. An example of a magazine advertisement that uses the soft sell is presented in Figure 7.12. This advertisement for sunglasses simply shows a beautiful young woman wearing the glasses—no information whatsoever is presented about the features or effectiveness of the sunglasses. The image *is* the message.

Soft sell advertisements sometimes use heuristics about the source to influence consumers. Recall that likable, credible, and famous people often elicit stronger agreement than unqualified or unknown people, even when the message is identical. Advertisers recognize this fact and hire likable celebrities, known experts, and famous athletes to promote their products. They hope that the positive evaluation of the celebrity endorser will serve as a heuristic cue to accept his or her recommendation.

What do you think of the soft sell? Do these factors affect you? Are you more likely to buy a product if you find its ads funny? Do cute babies give you a warm glow that generalizes to the product? Do your emotional responses influence your response to messages (see DeSteno, Petty, Rucker, Wegener, & Braverman, 2004)? Are you more likely to try something if it is endorsed by Shaquille O'Neal

Courtesy of The Advertising Archives

**FIGURE 7.12** Magazine advertisement that uses the soft sell

or Mandy Moore than if it is endorsed by someone you don't know? Most of us probably think we are relatively immune to these effects, but research suggests that the techniques can be effective. For example, celebrity endorsements, humorous content, and physically attractive sources have all been shown empirically to elicit more favorable attitudes toward advertised products, at least in some circumstances (e.g., Atkin & Block, 1983; Duncan & Nelson, 1985; Petty & Cacioppo, 1983; Wilcox, Murphy, & Sheldon, 1985).

---

**peripheral cues**

*simple features or heuristics that are assumed to indicate that a message is valid*

Strong arguments elicit agreement, whereas weak arguments elicit disagreement. On the other hand, when recipients of a message are processing heuristically (which activates the peripheral route to persuasion), the main determinant of attitude change is the presence of simple features or heuristics (labeled **peripheral cues** in the elaboration likelihood model) that the recipient assumes indicate that the message is valid, such as a famous source or a long message. If such cues are present, the recipient agrees with the message, but if such cues are absent, the recipient rejects the message.

## CONCEPT REVIEW
### Two Models of Persuasive Messages

| Theory | Key Processes | Nature of Processing | Determinants of Persuasion |
|---|---|---|---|
| Systematic-heuristic model | Systematic processing | Rational, information-based | Argument strength |
| | Heuristic processing | Superficial, simple cues | Heuristic cues |
| Elaboration likelihood model | Central route to persuasion | Rational, information-based | Argument strength |
| | Peripheral route to persuasion | Superficial, noncognitive | Peripheral cues |

The Concept Review above summarizes the key features of the systematic-heuristic and elaboration likelihood models.

Do you think that persuasion that results from one type of processing will be more enduring than persuasion that results from the other type of processing? Will someone's endorsement of a position be more stable if it resulted from thinking about the arguments (systematic processing; the central route) or if it resulted from adopting a position because of the source or the length of the message (heuristic processing; the peripheral route)? If you said that systematic processing will produce more enduring attitude change than heuristic processing, your prediction matches that of the original theorists (see Chaiken, 1987; Petty & Cacioppo, 1986). Why would this difference in stability occur? When we think carefully about the arguments on an issue and decide that they are compelling, we can use those arguments to resist subsequent attacks on our new position. But if we simply adopt a position because the source is famous or the message is long, we do not have any arguments that we can use to resist new persuasive attacks; thus, our new attitude is less likely to survive over time.

## Motivation and Ability

The key contribution of the systematic-heuristic and elaboration likelihood models was that they specified *when* each kind of persuasion is likely to occur. Both models predict that the recipient's *motivation* and *ability* jointly determine which route is activated.

These predictions are based on the idea that the process of thinking carefully about a message and analyzing the strength of the arguments is effortful and potentially difficult. Therefore, people will engage in this kind of demanding thought only when it is necessary (recall the *cognitive miser model* of information processing in Chapter 3; see page 87). Why tire yourself out thinking about issues that won't affect you? Why bother analyzing a message carefully that addresses a problem you will never have? In these sorts of situations, people will opt for the easier route of looking for heuristics that give them clues about the message's validity.

Each model predicts that systematic processing (the central route) can occur *only* when the individual (1) is *motivated* to exert the necessary effort *and* (2) has the *ability* to process the message carefully (e.g., can pay attention and understand the arguments). If either motivation *or* ability is missing, then the only way that persuasion can occur is via the peripheral route (heuristic processing).

Thus, both motivation and ability are necessary for systematic processing to occur. When are these conditions likely to be present? Researchers have identified several variables that affect either recipients' motivation or their ability to process a message carefully. We will discuss two of these factors: personal relevance and message complexity.

**Personal Relevance.** The most-studied factor affecting people's motivation to process a message carefully has been personal relevance: whether or not the topic or issue will affect someone directly. If the topic of a persuasive communication has implications for someone's personal outcomes, then it is high in personal relevance, and the individual is likely to be motivated to process the message carefully. If a persuasive communication addresses something that will not affect the recipient, then it is low in personal relevance, and the individual will probably not be motivated to think about the arguments carefully.

Imagine that you are looking to buy a new car and have definitely narrowed your choice to a Ford Focus or a Toyota Echo. If you are sitting in your doctor's office and see a magazine story on the Ford Focus, you will be very motivated to read it carefully because it might give you information that is important for your decision. But if you see a magazine story on the GM Cobalt, you will be less likely to read it carefully, because it does not have personal implications for you. In the former case, when the message is high in personal relevance, your response to the article (e.g., your evaluation of the Ford Focus) will be based on the strength of the arguments. In the latter case, when the message is low in personal relevance, your response to the article (e.g., your evaluation of the GM Cobalt) may be based on heuristic cues like the expertise of the author or the attractiveness of the models in the photographs.

Researchers testing the heuristic-systematic or elaboration likelihood models have conducted experiments in which they manipulated the personal relevance of a persuasive message for participants. The prediction of the researchers was that when a message was high in personal relevance, persuasion would depend on the strength of the arguments, whereas when a message was low in personal relevance, persuasion would depend on the presence of heuristic cues like source expertise.

In fact, the experiment by Richard Petty and his colleagues (1981) that we described earlier for the heuristic model of persuasion actually tested the larger, integrative theories. Recall that participants heard a message arguing that graduating seniors should be required to pass a comprehensive examination. The message contained either strong arguments or weak arguments, and was allegedly prepared either by a Princeton University professor (a high credibility source) or by a local high school class (a low credibility source). When participants were told that the comprehensive examinations would not be instituted for at least 10 years (the low personal relevance conditions; Figure 7.11), participants were somewhat more persuaded by strong arguments than by weak arguments, but the credibility of the source made even more difference: the message from the high credibility source produced much more favorable attitudes toward comprehensive exams than did the message from the low credibility source. We have reproduced these low relevance data again in Figure 7.13 (the four bars on the left half of the figure). But we also have included in Figure 7.13 the attitude findings for another set of conditions, in which participants were told that comprehensive exams were being considered for possible adoption *at their own college in the coming year*. This information meant that the exams could affect the participants directly, which made the topic high in personal relevance. Figure 7.13 shows that in these high personal relevance conditions (the four bars on the right half of the figure), the expertise of the source made almost no difference whatsoever; all that mattered was the strength of the arguments. When participants were motivated to process the message carefully, they were persuaded by strong arguments and rejected weak arguments, irrespective of the source of the arguments. These findings suggest that the high personal relevance conditions elicited systematic processing (or activated the central route to persuasion). In contrast, the low personal relevance conditions elicited heuristic processing (or activated the peripheral route to persuasion).

**Message Complexity.** The personal relevance of a topic influences whether people will be *motivated* to process a persuasive communication carefully. Other

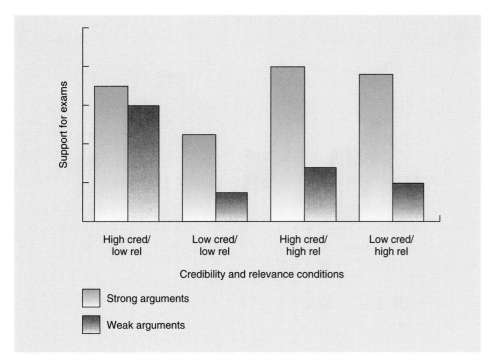

**FIGURE 7.13** Favorability of attitudes toward comprehensive exams: Low and high relevance conditions

From Petty et al., "Personal involvement as a determinant of argument-based persuasion," *Journal of Personality and Social Psychology*, 41, 847–855, 1981. Copyright © 1981 by the American Psychological Association.

factors influence whether people will be *able* to process a message carefully. For example, people who are being distracted from a message cannot pay close attention to its content. But perhaps the clearest example of a factor that influences the ability to process carefully is the complexity or comprehensibility of the message (Cooper, Bennett, & Sukel, 1996; Hafer, Reynolds, & Obertynski, 1996).

Carolyn Hafer and her students (1996) conducted an interesting experiment in St. Catharines, Ontario, Canada, that tested college students' responses to a persuasive message on *plea bargaining*. Plea bargaining occurs when a person accused of a crime agrees to plead guilty in return for getting a reduced charge or a shorter sentence. At the time the study was conducted, there had recently been a highly criticized case of plea bargaining in St. Catharines, which allowed one person who was involved in the murder of two local teenage girls to get off with a relatively short sentence in return for pleading guilty and testifying against the other person who was involved. Almost everyone in St. Catharines thought that this arrangement was too lenient on the person who was allowed to plea bargain; thus, almost everyone had a negative attitude toward plea bargaining.

Participants listened to a taped message that argued in favor of plea bargaining. The credibility of the source was manipulated: some participants were told that the speaker was His Honor Judge William Grovestead, a summa cum laude graduate of Harvard Law School, who had been sitting on the bench for 15 years and was an expert on plea bargaining, whereas other participants were told that the speaker was William Grovestead, a second-year law student at Rockway University, who had recently become interested in plea bargaining. The strength of the arguments was also manipulated: the message contained either five strong arguments or five weak arguments supporting plea bargaining. Finally, and most importantly for our current focus, the complexity or comprehensibility of the message was manipulated: the arguments were stated either in clear and straightforward language (e.g., "Plea bargaining may make a charge more appropriate to the circumstances of a

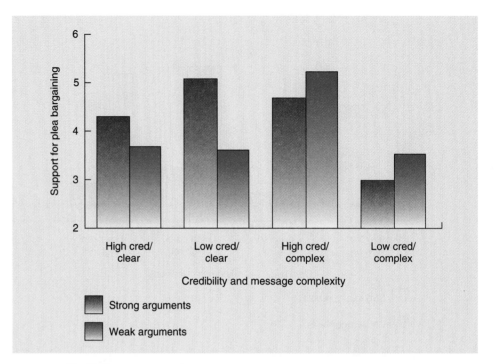

**FIGURE 7.14** Favorability of attitudes toward plea bargaining

From Hafer et al., "Message comprehensibility and persuasion: Effects of complex language in counterattitudinal appeals to laypeople," *Social Cognition*, 14, 317–337, 1996. Reprinted by permission of Guilford Publications.

crime") or in complex and difficult-to-understand language (e.g., "Plea bargaining can acquire a conviction by obtaining a guilty plea in a weak case that may otherwise yield an acquittal, should the case be held over for trial").

The researchers predicted that even though the message would be high in relevance to everyone because of the well-publicized local trial, participants who listened to the complex message would not be *able* to understand what the speaker was saying; thus, the strength of the arguments would not matter, and the only factor that would influence persuasion would be the expertise of the source (a heuristic cue). In contrast, participants who listened to the simpler and clearer version of the message *would* be able to understand the arguments, so strong arguments would produce more persuasion than weak arguments, and the expertise of the source would be relatively unimportant. These patterns were exactly what the results showed (see Figure 7.14). When participants were unable to process the message carefully because it was complex (the four bars on the right side of the figure), they were more favorable toward plea bargaining when the source was Judge Grovestead than when the source was student Grovestead, but the strength of the arguments did not affect persuasion. When participants listened to the easy-to-understand message (the four left-most bars), they were more favorable toward plea bargaining when the arguments were strong than when the arguments were weak, and the credibility of the source did not affect persuasion.

## Attitude Change: Age and Cultural Differences

Most empirical studies of persuasion have been conducted with college students as participants, which raises questions about the generalizability of the findings to nonstudent samples (e.g., see Sorrentino & Roney, 2000). Most attitude change studies have also been conducted in North America, so the findings might differ in other cultures. In this section, we consider some possible differences in attitude change processes based on age or culture.

## Age and Attitude Change

How do you think age might be related to attitude change? Do you think that people's openness to persuasion changes across their life span? If so, how? Are older adults less open to new ideas and new attitudes? Is it possible that very elderly adults might actually be more susceptible to persuasion than younger adults? If you look within your family—siblings, parents, and grandparents—do you see any connection between age and persuasibility?

A number of hypotheses have been proposed concerning the relation between age and attitude change (see Alwin, Cohen, & Newcomb, 1991b; Sears, 1981; Tyler & Schuller, 1991; Visser & Krosnick, 1998). These hypotheses are portrayed graphically in Figure 7.15. One possibility is the *null hypothesis,* which is that there is no relation between age and susceptibility to attitude change—that is, people of different ages are all about equally influenced by new information and experiences (panel A in the figure). A second possibility is that there is a linear negative relation between age and openness to persuasion—

Do you think that age is related to openness to attitude change?

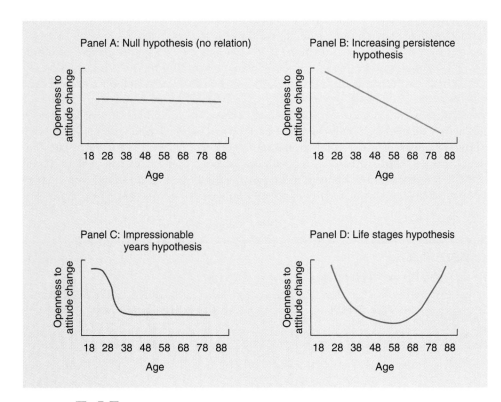

**FIGURE 7.15** Possible relations between age and openness to attitude change

From Visser and Krosnick, "Development of attitude strength over the life cycle: Surge and decline," *Journal of Personality and Social Psychology,* 75, 1389–1410, Fig. 1, p. 1390, 1998. Copyright © 1998 by the American Psychological Association. Reprinted by permission.

that is, people become steadily more resistant to influence as they grow older, because their attitudes become more entrenched; this has been called the *increasing persistence hypothesis* (panel B in the figure). A third hypothesis is that people exhibit a lot of attitude change while they are crystalizing their views as young adults (e.g., 18–25 years of age), but then become resistant to persuasion and continue to be resistant throughout their lives; this has been called the *impressionable years hypothesis* (panel C in the figure). Finally, a fourth hypothesis is that people are most susceptible to persuasion at two stages of life: their young adult years (when they are crystalizing their views) and their elderly years (when they experience significant role changes such as retirement and when their cognitive skills may decline); this has been called the *life stages hypothesis* (panel D in the figure).

Researchers have examined the relation between aging and attitude change in different ways, and the findings have depended on which technique was used. For example, Jon Krosnick and Duane Alwin (1989) examined the *stability* of attitude responses in two representative U.S. national samples of 1,132 and 1,320 adults of varying ages who were interviewed three times at two-year intervals, either in 1956, 1958, and 1960, or in 1972, 1974, and 1976. The participants reported their attitudes on a variety of issues, such as racial integration in schools, federally guaranteed employment for all U.S. citizens, the police, and their political party affiliation. The authors calculated how stable the reported attitudes were—that is, how much participants' answers to items changed over the three measurements. Table 7.3 presents the mean "stability coefficients" for each age group in the surveys, from ages 18 to 83. The table shows that the youngest respondents (18–25) exhibited the lowest stability, and the second-youngest group (26–33) exhibited the second-lowest stability. Subsequent age groups showed consistently high stability. This pattern of results is most consistent with the *impressionable years hypothesis:* younger adults were less stable while they developed their views on issues, but once their attitudes had formed, people showed more stability for the rest of their lives.

Penny Visser and Jon Krosnick (1998) tested directly whether people of different ages would change their attitudes when presented with new information. In one study, participants of varying ages were asked in a telephone interview whether they supported or opposed certain policies; after expressing support or opposition, participants were asked whether they would change their mind if they learned a related fact. For example, participants were asked whether they supported or opposed preferential admission to colleges and universities for Black students. Those who expressed support were asked, "Would you still feel that way even if it means fewer opportunities for qualified Whites, or would you change your mind?" Those who initially expressed opposition were asked, "Would you still

**TABLE 7.3**
*Stability of Attitudes by Age Group*

| Age Group | Stability Coefficient |
|---|---|
| 18–25 | .85 |
| 26–33 | .88 |
| 34–41 | .94 |
| 42–49 | .93 |
| 50–57 | .90 |
| 58–65 | .93 |
| 66–83 | .92 |

Possible scores range from 0 to 1, with higher values reflecting more stability.
Adapted from Krosnick & Alwin, 1989, Table 1, p. 420.

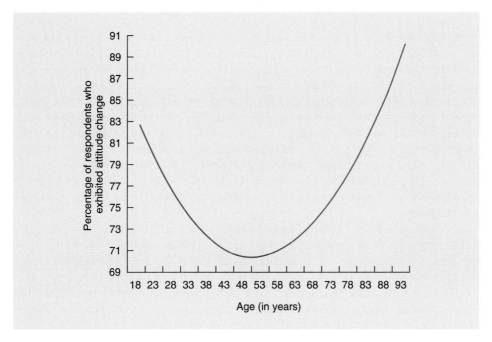

**FIGURE 7.16** Relation between age and attitude change

From Visser and Krosnick, "Development of attitude strength over the life cycle: Surge and decline," *Journal of Personality and Social Psychology*, 75, 1389–1410, Fig. 3, p. 1395, 1998. Copyright © 1998 by the American Psychological Association. Reprinted by permission.

feel that way even if it means that hardly any Blacks would be able to go to the best colleges and universities, or would you change your mind?" The interviewer recorded whether participants said they would change their mind or not.

The researchers calculated how many participants in each age group exhibited attitude change based on the new information. Figure 7.16 presents the relation that emerged between age and attitude change. (Notice that the majority of people at all ages said they would change their mind, which is rather surprising given that little "new information" was presented.) These data are most consistent with the *life stages hypothesis,* because attitude change was greatest at the youngest and oldest ages, with the middle years showing less change.

So what should we conclude about aging and attitude change? Visser and Krosnick's (1998) experiment was the most direct test to date, but the attacks on people's opinions in this research were mild (simply asking people, "Would you change your mind if . . . ?"). We need more studies using other techniques of persuasion, such as the presentation of strong arguments or the use of heuristic cues like source credibility, before we can come to a firm conclusion. It is also possible that, ultimately, we will learn that different attitude domains (e.g., attitudes toward ethnic groups vs. consumer products vs. social issues) exhibit different patterns of relations between aging and attitude change. Clearly, the issue is not yet settled.

## Culture and Attitude Change

In Chapters 4 and 5, we noted that the *self* is viewed as independent and autonomous in *individualist cultures* (e.g., Western Europe and North America) but as interdependent and role-based in *collectivist cultures* (e.g., East Asian countries). Are these cultural differences relevant to any processes involved in attitude change? In this section, we discuss two possible cultural differences: in dissonance arousal and in responses to persuasive messages.

**Cultural Differences in Dissonance Arousal.** Dissonance theory suggests that people feel bad when they behave in ways that are inconsistent with their attitudes and, as a result, may change their attitudes to be more consistent with their actions. For example, asking people to tell someone else that a boring task is interesting causes them to rate the task as more enjoyable (e.g., Festinger & Carlsmith, 1959), or inducing people to write a counterattitudinal essay sways them to become more favorable to the position they argued in the essay (e.g., Cohen, 1962). These effects are presumed to reflect that people believe that they *should* behave in ways that are consistent with their attitudes and values.

But do the assumptions underlying dissonance theory generalize to collectivist cultures? Do people who have an interdependent self feel the same need to behave in ways that are consistent with their attitudes? Some evidence suggests that they might not.

Yoshihisa Kashima, Michael Siegal, Kenichiro Tanaka, and Emiko Kashima (1992) found that participants from Japan, a collectivist culture, were less likely than participants from Australia, an individualist culture, to believe that other people's behavior normally reflects their attitudes. Why would a collectivist perspective lead to the expectation that people's behavior will sometimes conflict with their personal attitudes? One possibility is that collectivists believe the self must be responsive to social settings and relationships—people *should* adapt their behavior based on whom they are interacting with (see also Suh, 2002; Triandis, 1989).

If consistency between attitudes and behavior is less important to people from collectivist cultures, then perhaps they will experience less dissonance arousal following one of the standard dissonance manipulations. Steve Heine and Darrin Lehman (1997a) tested this prediction in a study of postdecisional dissonance using the free choice paradigm. Canadian and Japanese participants were given a choice between one of two music CDs as payment for their participation. The two CDs (along with eight others) had been evaluated previously by the participant and were always approximately equal in attractiveness. Shortly after their selection of one CD, participants reevaluated all 10 CDs that they had rated earlier (including the chosen and rejected CDs). Dissonance theory predicts that after making a decision, people are motivated to evaluate the chosen alternative more positively and the rejected alternative more negatively (e.g., Brehm, 1956; Zanna & Sande, 1987). Heine and Lehman found that Canadian participants exhibited this "spreading of alternatives," with the chosen CD going up in attractiveness and the rejected CD going down in attractiveness. Japanese participants, however, did not show significant changes in their evaluations of either CD. The authors concluded that dissonance theory might not generalize to collectivist cultures.

Etsuko Hoshino-Browne, Adam Zanna, Steve Spencer, and Mark Zanna (2004), however, challenged the conclusion that people from collectivist cultures do not experience dissonance. These researchers suggested instead that *different kinds of events cause dissonance* in collectivist cultures. They proposed that people in all cultures experience dissonance when their culturally valued self-views are threatened by their own behavior. In North America, the culturally valued self-view is an *independent* self, which is threatened when behavior is inconsistent with personal attitudes or goals. But in collectivist cultures, the culturally valued self-view is an *interdependent* self. When will an interdependent self be threatened? Hoshino-Browne et al. had the clever idea that asking collectivist participants to make a decision that has implications *for someone else* might arouse postdecisional dissonance. After all, people from collectivist cultures define the self in terms of relations with other people, so they might feel threatened when someone else is disappointed with a decision they made.

Hoshino-Browne and her colleagues (2004) included as participants both European-Canadians born in Canada and Asian-Canadians born in Asia who identified strongly with their Asian culture. Participants were told that they were helping a Chinese restaurant develop a special lunch menu. Some participants rated how much they would like each of 10 Chinese dishes. They were then told that they would receive a gift certificate for one of two dishes and made a choice between two of the dishes that were approximately equally attractive. Other participants were asked to rate how much *a close friend* would like each of the 10 dishes. They were then told that their friend would receive a gift certificate for one of two dishes and made a choice between two equally attractive dishes *for their friend*. All participants subsequently rerated the 10 dishes for how much they or their friend would like them, including the chosen and rejected dishes.

Figure 7.17 shows how much participants exhibited attitude change (a "spreading of alternatives," presumably to reduce dissonance) after their decision—that is, the extent to which they rated the chosen dish more positively and/or the rejected dish less positively after the decision. European-Canadians showed more attitude change (spreading of alternatives) after making a choice for themselves than after making a choice for a close friend. Asian-Canadians, however, showed more attitude change after making a choice for a close friend than after making a choice for themselves. In fact, the Asian-Canadians did not show any dissonance reduction at all when choosing for themselves—a finding that replicated the results for Japanese participants by Heine and Lehman (1997a). Asian-Canadians apparently experienced postdecisional dissonance only when their decision had implications for another person.

These data suggest that dissonance arousal does occur in people from collectivist cultures, but the types of behavior that produce it are different in collectivist and individualist cultures (see also Kitayama, Snibbe, Markus, & Suzuki, 2004). In collectivist cultures, actions may have to relate to other people in order to threaten the individual's "interdependent" self.

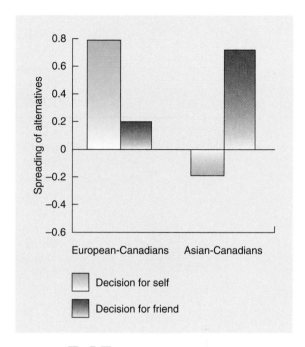

**FIGURE 7.17** Attitude change after decision by European-Canadians and Asian-Canadians

From Hoshino-Browne, et al., "Investigating attitudes cross-culturally: A case of cognitive dissonance among East Asians and North Americans," in Haddock and Maio, eds., *Contemporary Perspectives on the Psychology of Attitudes* (pp. 375–398), Fig. 4, 2002. Reprinted by permission of the Taylor & Francis Group.

**Cultural Differences in Responses to Persuasive Messages.** As we noted in the earlier section on cognitive response theory, persuasive messages often rely on information. Information-based communications are effective when they present strong evidence or compelling arguments that there will be positive consequences associated with accepting the recommendations in the message (e.g., positive consequences will be associated with abolishing the death penalty, or with buying this product). But is it possible that people in different cultures will find different evidence or arguments compelling? Will people in individualist versus collectivist cultures respond favorably to different kinds of information?

Sang-pil Han and Sharon Shavitt (1994) predicted that people from individualist cultures would respond most favorably to messages describing positive *personal* consequences of the recommendations, because such appeals are consistent with the "independent self" that is encouraged in these cultures. In contrast, Han and Shavitt predicted that people from collectivist cultures would respond most favorably to messages describing positive *interpersonal* consequences of the recommendations, because such appeals are consistent with the "interdependent self" that is encouraged in these cultures.

To test this reasoning, the researchers looked at magazine advertisements in the United States (an individualist culture) and Korea (a collectivist culture). They sampled a total of 100 ads from each of two American and two Korean magazines (*Newsweek, Redbook, Wolgan Chosun,* and *Yosong Donga*). They then showed these ads to bilingual judges, who scored each ad for individualism and collectivism. An ad received a high score for individualism when it appealed to independence (e.g.,

"She's got a style all her own"), personal benefits (e.g., "A quick return for your investment"), or personal goals (e.g., "Make your way through the crowd"). An ad received a high score for collectivism when it appealed to family or group cohesiveness (e.g., "We have a way of bringing people closer together"), interdependent relationships (e.g., "Successful partnerships"), or group goals (e.g., "The dream of prosperity for all of us").

Results showed that, overall, the ads were rated as more individualistic than collectivistic, which probably reflected that everyone buys products for personal benefits, at least in part. However, American ads were rated as significantly more individualistic than were Korean ads, whereas Korean ads were rated as significantly more collectivistic than were American ads. Thus, the nature of the advertisements in each country reflected, to some extent, the individualism–collectivism of the culture.

Han and Shavitt (1994) followed up their survey of American and Korean magazines with a controlled experiment that tested the same reasoning. The researchers created two versions of advertisements for four products (chewing gum, running shoes, detergents, and clothes irons). All of the ads contained a headline and illustrations. One version presented an "individualistic" headline (e.g., "Treat yourself to a breath freshening experience") and a picture of an individual using the product, whereas the second version presented a "collectivistic" headline (e.g., "Share the Freedent breath freshening experience") and a picture of a group of people. Participants from the United States and Korea rated each ad for how persuasive it was and how much they would like to try the product. Americans rated the individualistic versions of the ads more favorably than the collectivistic versions, whereas Koreans showed the opposite pattern—more favorable ratings of the collectivistic versions of the ads. These data show that cultural differences can occur in responses to persuasive messages.

In summary, social psychologists have found that both age and cultural factors are related to attitude change. The precise patterns of some of these relations (e.g., age-related differences in persuasion) are not completely clear, but as more data are collected, firmer conclusions will be possible. In the meantime, the important point is that researchers cannot assume that findings obtained with North American college students will generalize to all other samples.

## Persuasion in the Health Domain: Fear Appeals

Have you ever looked at the warnings that are printed on cigarette packages? If you are a smoker, you will certainly have seen them, but if you are a nonsmoker, you might not know much about them. The warnings consist of statements that smoking can cause serious health problems, such as heart disease and lung cancer. For example, warnings in the United States include "SURGEON GENERAL'S WARNING: Smoking Causes Lung Cancer, Heart Disease, Emphysema, and May Complicate Pregnancy" and "SURGEON GENERAL'S WARNING: Cigarette Smoke Contains Carbon Monoxide." What do you think of this idea to have warning messages on cigarette packages? Are they likely to have any impact? Will they persuade young people (or old people) to stop smoking?

In Canada, the required warnings are much more dramatic than in the United States. Beginning in 2000, tobacco companies were required to put explicit, full color, and sometimes graphic photos on their cigarette packages—things like a cancerous lung or a damaged heart—along with appropriate text (e.g., "Warning: CIGARETTES CAUSE LUNG CANCER. Every cigarette you smoke increases your chances

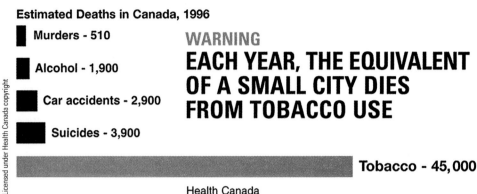

Licensed under Health Canada copyright

**Estimated Deaths in Canada, 1996**

Murders - 510

Alcohol - 1,900

Car accidents - 2,900

Suicides - 3,900

Tobacco - 45,000

**WARNING**

# EACH YEAR, THE EQUIVALENT OF A SMALL CITY DIES FROM TOBACCO USE

Health Canada

Do fear-provoking images on cigarette packages convince smokers to quit?

of getting lung cancer"). Another photo shows a curled, limp cigarette, along with a warning that smoking can cause impotence. The photos and statements completely fill the top half of both the front and the back of the package. Inside the cigarette package, another written message is presented, which often contains tips about how to quit. In 2001, the Canadian Cancer Society conducted a national survey of smokers to assess the impact of the new, vivid warnings. The survey showed that 90% of Canadian smokers had noticed the new warnings (what on earth were the other 10% doing?), 44% said that the warnings increased their motivation to quit smoking, 43% said that they were more concerned about the health effects of smoking because of the warnings, and among those people who had attempted to quit smoking, 38% said that the warnings were a motivating factor. These data indicate that the warnings were having considerable impact on smokers.

Questions about effective persuasion concerning health issues are very important. How can the government motivate healthy lifestyles, both to improve the quality of people's lives and to save money on health care? How can spouses or parents convince a family member to stop smoking or avoid drug use? How can doctors motivate their patients to stay on a medication or perform simple self-examinations? Answers to these questions are, quite literally, life-and-death.

In most cases, health campaigns seem designed to threaten people with the dire consequences of performing, or of failing to perform, certain actions (Salovey & Wegener, 2002). Antidrug campaigns illustrate "your brain on drugs" as an egg sizzling loudly in a frying pan. Pro-exercise campaigns identify obesity and heart disease as consequences of inactivity. Anti–drunk-driving campaigns show home videos of young children or young families who were subsequently killed by a drunk driver. Clearly, one goal of these messages is to arouse the emotion of fear in listeners.

## Effectiveness of Fear Appeals

Is arousing fear an effective way to change your attitudes and behavior? Are you more likely to follow the recommendations of a message when it has frightened you about what might happen if you don't?

Social psychologists have been interested in the effectiveness of fear appeals for many decades. The results of early studies were inconsistent (see Janis & Feshbach, 1953; McGuire, 1969), but there is now little doubt that the arousal of fear generally *increases* the impact of messages on attitudes and behavioral intentions (see Cho & Witte, 2004; Das, de Wit, & Stroebe, 2003; Eagly & Chaiken, 1993; Perloff, 2003). The usual explanation of this finding is that fear is an aversive state, which people want to reduce; people accept the recommendations of the message because doing so reduces their fear (this is called a "drive reduction" hypothesis).

Does this conclusion surprise you? Some social commentators argue that fear is a poor way to motivate people, because it is a "negative" and "extrinsic" motivator that will not have lasting effects. These observers suggest that because fear is unpleasant, people either will try to escape or will be so distracted that they won't listen to the message. But the empirical data indicate that fear does *not* typically reduce attention or comprehension of information related to the fear; if anything, fear tends to increase attention (e.g., Baron, Logan, Lilly, Inman, & Brennan, 1994; Gleicher & Petty, 1992; Salovey, Rothman, & Rodin, 1998).

## Protection Motivation Theory

What kinds of health problems (or other threats) arouse the most fear? Think about your own reactions to information about illnesses such as cancer, heart disease, mental illness, and Alzheimer's disease: what specific aspects of these problems are fear-arousing? For instance, why are people more afraid of cancer than colds? Why are North Americans more afraid of heart disease than leprosy?

Ronald Rogers and his colleagues (Maddux & Rogers, 1983; Rogers, 1983) suggested that two specific beliefs arouse threat: (1) the problem is *severe,* and (2) you are *susceptible* to the problem. For instance, cancer is more fear-provoking than colds because cancer is more severe: cancer can kill you, but colds only make you uncomfortable. Heart disease is more fear-arousing in our culture than leprosy not because it is necessarily more severe, but rather because we feel susceptible to heart disease but not to leprosy: we can easily imagine how we might develop heart disease, but cannot easily imagine how we would get leprosy.

Rogers proposed that these perceptions of severity and susceptibility are threatening and arouse fear (see Das et al., 2003). But two additional factors are necessary before the fear will translate into attitude and behavior change. In order for a message about a health problem to actually change listeners' behavior, they must also believe (3) the *recommendations will be effective* in avoiding the problem, and (4) they are *personally capable* of performing the recommended behaviors. If the recommendations will not necessarily reduce listeners' risk, or if they feel incapable of doing the recommended behaviors, then they will not change their lifestyle. For instance, people who feel threatened by heart disease won't start exercising as a solution unless they believe that exercise will definitely reduce their risk. If it might not work, why bother? Also, people who feel threatened by lung cancer won't try to quit smoking as a solution unless they believe that they are personally capable of quitting successfully. If they're just going to fail, what's the point?

**protection motivation theory**

*a model that articulates how threatening messages can influence attitudes and behavior*

Rogers (1983) combined these four principles into **protection motivation theory,** which is a model that articulates how threatening messages can influence attitudes and behavior. Rogers proposed that people will change attitudes and behavior only when they are *motivated* to *protect* themselves (hence, *protection motivation* theory), which will occur only when all four beliefs are present.

Table 7.4 provides an analysis of how, based on protection motivation theory, a message could be designed to convince college students *to reduce their unprotected exposure to the sun and their visits to tanning salons* (see also Witte, Meyer, & Martell, 2001). First, they must believe that the problem is severe. Skin cancer is definitely severe. Even leathery, wrinkled skin at an early age is pretty severe to young people concerned about their appearance. Second, they must believe that they are personally susceptible to the problem. This goal might be accomplished by explaining that even a small number of serious sunburns dramatically increases the probabil-

**TABLE 7.4**

*Using Protection Motivation Theory to Create*
*a Message About Sun Exposure*

| Belief That Must Be Created | Possible Arguments |
| --- | --- |
| 1. The problem is severe. | Exposure to the sun can cause skin cancer, which can disfigure and even kill. |
| | Exposure to the sun causes the skin to become leathery and wrinkled at an early age. |
| 2. They are susceptible to the problem. | Suffering just a few serious sunburns greatly increases the probability of skin cancer. |
| | People with all hair colors and skin shades can develop skin cancer from too much sun. |
| 3. The recommended behaviors will be effective in avoiding the problem. | Statistics show that smaller numbers of sunburns over one's lifetime are associated with lower rates of skin cancer. |
| | Applying sunscreen virtually eliminates harmful rays from the sun. |
| 4. They are capable of performing the recommended behaviors. | If someone wants a tanned appearance, it can be safely achieved with skin-darkening creams. |
| | Applying sunscreen is simple and can even be fun when members of a couple apply it to one another. |

ity of eventually developing skin cancer. Perceived susceptibility might also be increased by stating that people with all hair colors and skin shades, even those with dark hair and skin, can develop skin cancer from too much sun exposure. Third, they must be convinced that staying out of the sun and using sunscreen when exposure is unavoidable will significantly reduce their chances of developing a problem. Statistics about relative risk, focusing on how the probability of skin cancer decreases with decreased exposure, might achieve this goal. Also, explaining that applying sunscreen virtually eliminates harmful rays will increase perceived effectiveness. Finally, they must believe that they are capable of performing the recommended actions. Some people will argue, for example, that they simply must look good and, therefore, cannot give up the sun. Perhaps these individuals could be told that they can use products to darken their skin without sun exposure and still achieve the "golden" look they desire. They can also be told that applying sunscreen is simple—and can even be *fun* when members of a couple apply it to one another!

Tests of protection motivation theory have been largely supportive (see Aspinwall, Kemeny, Taylor, Schneider, & Dudley, 1991; Das et al., 2003; Rogers & Mewborn, 1976; Sturges & Rogers, 1996; van der Velde & van der Pligt, 1991; Witte & Allen, 2000). Fear appeals seem to be most effective when they successfully create the four beliefs identified by the theory.

## ● ● ● Propaganda

We have discussed a variety of ways that attitudes can change. For the most part, our examples have focused on "legitimate" persuasion: attitude change that occurs in normal, familiar sorts of situations, such as postdecisional dissonance, interpersonal influence, and persuasive messages in the media (although some of our examples have admittedly been unusual, such as the grasshopper-eating study). Our goal has been to understand rationalization and persuasion in everyday life.

But some kinds of influence go beyond the usual limits. The person or group doing the persuading may have selfish motives that are kept secret, or may intentionally distort the facts to achieve persuasion. These examples move into the domain of propaganda.

## What Is Propaganda?

**propaganda**

*a persuasive attempt that is motivated by an ideology, or set of values, and that is deliberately biased in its presentation of information*

**Propaganda** is a persuasive attempt (or a campaign of many persuasive attempts) that is motivated by a specific ideology, or set of values, and that is deliberately biased in its presentation of the issues. The source of the propaganda has a value-based agenda (e.g., a religious view, a political position, or some other value system) and is willing to distort the facts to convince others to adopt the same view. Anthony Pratkanis and Elliot Aronson (2000) described propaganda as attempted influence through "the use of images, slogans, and symbols that play on our prejudices and emotions . . . with the ultimate goal of having the recipient of the appeal come to 'voluntarily' accept this position as if it were his or her own" (p. 11). A key element of propaganda, then, is that the source does not present a balanced treatment of the issues and allow listeners to weigh the arguments for each side in a rational manner; instead, the propagandist presents only his or her desired side and usually appeals to emotions rather than to reason.

Of course, judgments about whether a person or group has "a value-based agenda" and is "willing to distort the facts" are subjective. Are political campaigns value-based, and do political candidates knowingly distort the facts? What about advertising: is the goal of profit an ideology? And do advertisers care if consumers are fooled into buying something they don't want or don't need? What about established, organized religions: are they deliberately selective in presenting religious information to members?

Rather than classifying persuasive attempts as either propaganda or nonpropaganda, it makes sense to think about them as being *more* or *less* "propagandistic"—a dimension from *not at all* to *extremely* propagandistic. An example of a persuasive attempt that is not at all propagandistic would be a two-sided, argument-based message that is presented without extrinsic pressure (e.g., an article in *Consumer Reports* outlining the strengths and weaknesses of a product, or a lecture in a class presenting supportive and nonsupportive evidence for a scientific theory). An example of a persuasive attempt that is somewhat propagandistic would be an emotional appeal that is unabashedly one-sided (e.g., an advertisement for a charity that is designed to arouse guilt, or a "soft sell" advertisement that uses images to sell a product). An example of a persuasive attempt that is extremely propagandistic would be a deliberately deceptive presentation that promotes an ideology (e.g., a regimented program of indoctrination in a cult, or an advertisement in a political campaign that knowingly distorts the facts to arouse fear about an opponent).

Propaganda, then, is a matter of degree. In the following sections, we describe examples of propaganda, beginning with some extreme or obvious cases and then moving to some everyday and more subtle cases.

# War and Propaganda

One event that is a reliable cause of unambiguous propaganda is war. The saying "All is fair in love and war" seems to be embraced by all governments during wartime. There is usually deliberate manipulation of the media at home, as well as distribution of propagandistic materials in enemy territories. For example, during World War II, allied military sources strictly controlled all information about the war that was given to the media; the information was manipulated to maintain morale and support for the war effort. The allies also sent radio broadcasts and dropped leaflets into enemy areas, which were designed to lower morale and to encourage resistance.

More recently, in the war in Iraq to depose Saddam Hussein, media correspondents were "embedded" into military units and actually accompanied soldiers into battle areas. The reporters were strictly controlled, however, in terms of the information they could convey to viewers. For example, one correspondent, Geraldo Rivera, was thrown out of Iraq after he used a stick to draw a rough map in the sand to show on camera the movements of his unit.

Prisoners of war have sometimes been exposed to "indoctrination" procedures, designed either to create total obedience or to generate sympathy toward the captors' cause. For instance, Nazi treatment of Jewish prisoners and, to a lesser extent, allied military prisoners was brutal, with physical punishment and executions used frequently and openly to produce terror and obedience. There was little attempt by the Nazis to change their POWs' attitudes—many of them regarded their prisoners as subhuman (Welch, 1983). In the Korean War, however, Chinese captors exposed American POWs to more humane, but nevertheless manipulative, propaganda techniques (see Lifton, 1961). The Chinese did not try to convince American soldiers that Communism was the best thing for the United States, but they did try to convince them that Communism was right for China. The Chinese captors (1) made prisoners listen to repeated information sessions, (2) spread rumors about American actions in the war, and (3) carefully rewarded any positive comments about the Communist system. The result of these techniques was that when the soldiers

© AP/Wide World Photos/Dusan Vranic

During wartime, governments and military authorities exert tight control over information provided to the media.

returned to the United States after the war, some expressed sympathy for Communism in China. The American military became very concerned about the "brainwashing" that had been performed, although further investigation showed that very few soldiers were strongly affected. Nevertheless, military leaders suggested to politicians that the U.S. education system should promote patriotism more passionately.

## Cults and Propaganda

**destructive cult**

*a rigidly structured group, led by a charismatic leader, that recruits and retains members using manipulative, deceptive techniques*

Another source of unambiguous propaganda is cults. Although the term *cult* is familiar to most people, we need to provide a specific definition. We adopt the perspective of Frank MacHovec (1989), who defined a **destructive cult** as "a rigidly structured group . . . under a charismatic leader, which isolates itself from established societal traditions, values, and norms, recruits members deceptively without informed consent, and retains them by . . . manipulative techniques which deny freedom of choice" (p. 10). Thus, cults normally revolve around a persuasive, magnetic figure who preaches that contact with the rest of society must be minimized, often describing people outside the cult as evil and dangerous. Perhaps most important, cults use techniques for recruitment and retention that are knowingly designed to induce people to join and stay even if they don't really want to.

What are some well-known cults in North America? One example is the Unification Church, whose members are also known as "Moonies" (see Clay, 1987; Hassan, 1988; Swenson, 1987). The Unification Church is led by Sun Myung Moon, who was born in Korea in 1920. Moon established the church in 1954, claiming that Jesus came to him in a vision when he was 16 years old and told him that he was the second Messiah, who would form the nucleus of God's family on earth. In 1957, Moon published *The Divine Principle,* which became the bible of his movement. In 1972, with the church well established in South Korea, Moon moved to the United States, where he purchased a $625,000 estate in northern New York. The Unification Church invested in many businesses, including hotels, newspapers, and fish-processing plants. It also expanded to other countries, including Canada, Nigeria, Japan, and Uruguay. In 1982, Moon was convicted of conspiracy, obstruction of justice, and perjury relating to his failure to pay taxes on interest income from a $1.6 million bank account. He spent 13 months in prison—a sentence that his followers declared was the result of religious prejudice.

The church's income is currently in the hundreds of millions of dollars annually. Estimated membership is approximately 2 million worldwide. Members receive only food and shelter—all earned income goes to the church. Much of the money earned by the church is tax-free because of the organization's religious status. Members live in communal groups, segregated by sex. Marriage is allowed only by the personal decision of Moon, who matches partners. In one particularly extraordinary marriage ceremony in 1997, Moon officiated at the simultaneous weddings of 28,000 couples at the RFK Stadium in Washington, DC.

Another cult in North America ended in tragedy. This cult formed in California in the 1990s around the leadership of a man in his early 60s, Marshall Applewhite. The group called itself Heaven's Gate and had some bizarre beliefs. For example, Applewhite, along with several other male members of the cult, had been castrated in pursuit of "androgenous immortality." Also, group members believed that the passage of the Hale-Bopp comet near the earth in 1997 was a sign that they should leave their bodies (their "earthly containers") and join a spaceship of aliens hiding behind the comet. When their spirits left their bodies, they would be picked up by the aliens and transported to heaven. How could they leave their bodies? In March 1997, when the comet was closest to earth, 39 members of the cult committed mass suicide in Rancho Sante Fe, California (near San Diego). In groups of three or four, members sedated themselves with barbituates mixed in pudding or applesauce, washed down with vodka. Other members then placed plastic bags over the heads of the sedated individuals, causing death by suffocation.

How do cults obtain such obedience and sacrifice? How do they convince people to change their lifestyle completely, or even to end their lives? We describe in the following paragraphs some of the techniques used by cults (see Baron, 2000; Clay, 1987; Galanter, 1989; Hassan, 1988; Pratkanis & Aronson, 2000; Swenson, 1987). These techniques are neither unusual nor extremely powerful individually; indeed, the techniques are used routinely by salespersons, advertisers, and religious and nonreligious groups that we would not consider cults. But cults use the techniques simultaneously, deliberately, and forcefully, which can be very powerful.

**Selective Targeting of Potential Recruits.** In seeking potential recruits, cults target young people between the ages of 18 and 30, especially those with a strong social conscience who are looking for a "cause" to follow. Cults will focus on people who have experienced a recent trauma or loss, such as the death of a loved one, the breakup of a relationship, or a significant failure at school or work. People who have suffered a recent loss are emotionally vulnerable and may be easier to manipulate than people who feel satisfied with their current lifestyle.

**Isolation of Recruits Away From Noncult Influences.** Cults try to bring recruits to locations that are removed from their familiar surroundings. For instance, young people will be invited to attend a "weekend retreat," where they can learn more about the group. These retreats give the cult complete control over the recruits' environment, allowing extensive socialization procedures and significant interpersonal pressure to be applied. If someone does join a cult, he or she is almost always forced to move into a cult-controlled environment (e.g., a commune) and to sever all contact with noncult friends and family.

**Sleep Deprivation.** At weekend retreats, cults often deprive potential recruits of sleep for 36 or 48 hours. The resulting fatigue induces both mental confusion and emotional vulnerability. Cults do not want recruits thinking carefully and logically about whether or not to join; they want recruits to accept the cult's messages uncritically. Fatigue and stress can reduce the attentional capacity of recruits, causing them to overlook the negative consequences of joining the cult and to be swept away by the emotion of the moment (see Baron, 2000).

**Love Bombing.** A powerful technique that cults use is to shower potential recruits with "love": physical affection (e.g., hugs, hand-holding), flattery (e.g., "You're so talented"), and unconditional caring and security (e.g., "You will always be loved and protected in our group"). These sorts of words and actions can affect young people very strongly, especially those who have experienced a recent breakup or who have suffered from long-term loneliness. Many cults also adopt a "buddy system" at recruitment meetings, whereby one member of the cult is assigned to each recruit. This buddy tries to establish an emotional bond with the recruit, in the hopes of creating greater commitment to the cult.

**Repetition.** Recruits are exposed to long, repetitive lectures that regurgitate the doctrine of the cult (undiluted propaganda). These lectures often contain little substance, but lots of catchwords and clichés. When information is heard

Cults use a variety of persuasion techniques to recruit and retain members.

many times, it begins to sound plausible and to develop an aura of legitimacy. Increasing familiarity with the material can produce a more positive attitude toward it (recall the *mere exposure effect* from Chapter 6).

**Foot-in-the-Door Technique.** The foot-in-the-door technique refers to the fact that if you can get someone to agree to a small request, he or she is more likely to also agree to a much larger, related request (we will describe research documenting this technique in Chapter 8). Cults take advantage of this technique by initially requesting only small things from potential recruits: come to the meeting, introduce yourself to others, listen to the lecture. Gradually, the requests get larger: talk about your past experiences, make a donation to the group. Eventually, the requests become extreme: quit your job and join the group! Recruits would never have agreed to the extreme requests at the beginning of the process, but each of their small actions increases the likelihood of subsequent compliance with larger requests.

**Denial of Privacy.** During weekend retreats, potential recruits are never left alone. They are kept involved in group activities or discussions with at least one member of the cult (often the "buddy" we mentioned earlier). The cult does not want people to be able to sit and think quietly about the situation. Instead, the cult wants constant social pressure on the recruit to join.

**Reciprocity.** There is a norm in our society that when someone does a favor for you, you should repay that favor in kind. This *norm of reciprocity* will be discussed in Chapter 8. Cults take advantage of this norm to pressure potential recruits to join. Recruits are subtly reminded that they are guests of the cult, are receiving free food and accommodation, and have been treated well by everyone. The idealistic, vulnerable young people who are brought to retreats have a strong conscience and do not want to appear to be ungrateful guests. How can they repay all the favors done for them? Easy: join the group.

**Fear Mongering.** In their lectures and discussions, cults often appeal to fears about the future, such as nuclear war, financial collapse, or the dissolution of society into anarchy. The government is said to be corrupt and evil; powerful members of society are labeled selfish and dangerous; and the future is portrayed as bleak and ominous. In the context of this apocalyptic outlook, the cult provides stability, security, and even a possible solution to society's problems. Joining the cult therefore becomes a way for the recruit to reduce the fear that has been aroused.

**Summary.** We have described nine techniques that are used by many cults to recruit and retain members. The simultaneous application of these strategies can be very effective, especially when the potential recruits' environment is completely controlled by the cult, as at weekend retreats. There is nothing magical in these techniques—their effects can all be understood from a social psychological perspective. The use of the techniques by cults is unethical, however, because cults use the techniques deliberately to overwhelm freedom of choice—to confuse and pressure vulnerable young people into joining the cult whether they really want to or not. Members who are "true believers" rationalize these strategies by saying that the end justifies the means: by joining the movement, people will be better off even if they might not have joined without the pressure. For the leader and others who benefit personally from the members, the motivation may be darker: greed.

## Everyday Propaganda

Wartime propaganda and cult propaganda are pretty extreme. But other, more mundane examples of influence attempts that are moderately propagandistic are all around us. Let's consider some of these "everyday" examples of propaganda (see also Levine, 2003; Pratkanis & Aronson, 2000).

**Advertising.** Advertisements are openly one-sided. They rarely present the weaknesses of a product alongside its strengths. They often appeal to emotions and symbols, rather than to reason (e.g., advertisements that use the soft sell). Advertisements also reflect an ideology—namely, materialism. Although companies do not usually design their ads to promote materialism per se, there are implicit messages that spending is good and the way to be happy is to get or consume more things.

*Interest groups are like any other entity with an agenda that includes changing your attitude, in that they all have a varied bag of tricks to use in their efforts to persuade you.*

Advertisements also communicate other, unintended messages. Clothing designers have used skinny models so exclusively that women have developed unrealistic beliefs about their ideal weight. The nearly complete absence of anyone over 50 in advertisements contributes to our culture's negative stereotypes of aging and the elderly. Racial minorities are also underrepresented in advertisements, which implicitly endorses the existing hierarchical status structure in society.

**Television and Movies.** Directors and producers of television shows and movies sometimes create products that are propagandistic. War movies may portray historical events in a one-sided and emotional way. Televised sporting events like the Super Bowl may open with patriotic music and images (e.g., featuring the American flag). News stories about an international event sometimes take a narrow view of the history of a conflict or issue.

Like advertisements, television shows and movies can communicate unintended messages. The professional and domestic roles of men and women in television programming generally conform to stereotypic divisions of labor, thereby reinforcing the stereotypes. Music videos often portray women as sexual objects, who use their physical beauty to attract and control men. The focus on negative events in news programs can lead viewers to overestimate the dangers they face in daily life, causing both unnecessary fear and withdrawal from the community.

**Education.** You may be wondering how education can be propagandistic. After all, isn't "education" by definition open-minded and information-based? Maybe not. (For an interesting discussion of this issue, see "Education or Propaganda?" in Pratkanis & Aronson, 2000, pp. 261–268.) Judgments of whether a topic belongs in the classroom often depend on whom you ask. For instance, fundamentalist Christians and left-wing liberals will probably differ in their judgments about whether the theory of evolution or the Ten Commandments are (1) "facts" that must be presented or (2) "ideologically based ideas" that should be excluded from the curriculum.

It is undeniable that the education system shapes and strengthens students' values. In North America, for example, the school system deliberately advocates values such as democracy, religious tolerance, and individualism. Social institutions such as marriage, the family, and the legal system are also actively promoted. And the field of science is generally presented as objective and trustworthy—judgments with which your text's authors largely concur, but we also know that personal biases can and do affect scientists' work and conclusions.

Unintentional effects on beliefs and values also come from the school system. For instance, educators do not intend

Is education a form of propaganda?

© Will & Deni McIntyre/CORBIS

to contribute to a fear of other cultures or religions because of limited knowledge. Nor do they intend to confirm sex role stereotypes by failing to teach about the role of women in history. Yet decisions about the curriculum can have these sorts of indirect effects.

**Religious Institutions.** Most of us accept the principle of religious freedom. People should be able to practice religion (or not) in their own way. But do our organized religions really encourage choice and freedom? Most practicing people are raised in their parents' places of worship and are never exposed to other religious views. Within religious organizations themselves, classes and sermons are exclusively based on the ideology and values of that particular church, temple, or mosque. Should this be considered propaganda? On the one hand, information presented by religions is one-sided. On the other hand, everyone *knows* that religions teach within the framework of their beliefs, and no one expects religious institutions to talk about alternative views. Clearly, this issue is difficult to settle.

Religious training does not only affect religious beliefs, of course. Different religions also influence attitudes and values regarding the roles of women and men, the morality of birth control, whether homosexuality is accepted or denounced, and the value of diversity. These broader effects are less obvious but no less important.

**Summary.** The "everyday" sources of propaganda that we have discussed may not present biased views *intentionally*. For instance, news coverage may reflect a reporter's values without his or her awareness. Advertisers may not realize that they are causing eating disorders in young women. Educators may not recognize that they are teaching more than the designated curriculum in their classes. Therefore, these examples do *not* represent the more extreme forms of propaganda, in which a communicator deliberately omits relevant information or intentionally misrepresents the facts. Nevertheless, these forms of influence rest on ideological foundations and do not always involve an objective presentation of the facts. It is useful for us to recognize how our social institutions shape our perceptions of the world.

     # Resisting Persuasion

The preceding section on propaganda may have given you the impression that attitude change is simple. All someone has to do is employ a few tricks or apply a little pressure, and persuasion is guaranteed. You might think that a recipe of repetition, reciprocity, and rationalization will cook up a large serving of successful influence.

But if your experiences are anything like ours, you know that attitude change is *not* such an easy thing to achieve. Other people seem strangely resistant to our ideas and arguments. (What's the matter with them, anyway?) Although attitude change sometimes occurs, significant forces seem to be acting against persuasion in most people.

Why do people resist attempts to persuade them? In this section, we outline two important sources of resistance. One way that people resist messages is by generating counterarguments; researchers have tested procedures that use the elicitation of counterarguments to produce resistance to persuasion. We then discuss an important motivational process that contributes to resistance. We close by considering the implications of these two factors for protecting yourself against persuasive influence.

An interesting observation about resistance to influence was made by Zakary Tormala and Richard Petty (2002). These researchers showed that if people successfully resisted an attempt to persuade them, they became even more certain about their initial attitude. That is, if people maintained their attitude in the face of a message arguing for a discrepant position, their confidence in the initial position increased. Thus, successful resistance can produce increased confidence, which should then further increase subsequent resistance. Resistance can be a self-strengthening process.

## Inoculation Against Persuasion

A marvelous advance in medical treatment occurred when scientists realized that humans could be inoculated against some diseases. For example, many people around the world were immunized as children to protect against measles, mumps, rubella, and polio viruses, among other things. How do these injections work? What is the biological basis of the protection provided by inoculations?

The serum injected into people contains a weakened, modified, or dead sample of the virus. For instance, the flu shot that is made available each year contains dead or degraded samples of the flu viruses that are expected to be most prevalent that year. The body reacts to these modified viruses as if they were living, invading microorganisms and builds up antibodies against them. As a result, if live cases of the virus are encountered later during the flu season, the body has already produced the antibodies necessary to kill the invading organisms, and the individual does not come down with a full-blown case of the flu.

In his **inoculation theory,** William McGuire (1964, 1972; McGuire & Papageorgis, 1961) suggested that the process of medical inoculation could be used as an analogy for understanding resistance to argument-based persuasion. He proposed that a key ingredient of resistance to persuasion is counterarguing—coming up with logical responses to refute arguments that have been offered. Just as an antibody fights off a virus, a counterargument fights off a persuasive attack. For example, McGuire suggested that when people have thought about both sides of an issue and decided which side is more persuasive, they will be more resistant to influence than someone who has considered only one side of the issue, because they will have counterarguments ready to refute persuasive attempts. For instance, someone who has thought about the pros and cons of joining a campus fraternity or sorority and decided not to join will be more resistant to a pro-fraternity or pro-sorority message than will someone who is also opposed to joining but has not thought carefully about possible arguments in favor of joining.

You may have noticed that McGuire's reasoning about the importance of counterarguments is very compatible with cognitive response theory, which we described earlier in this chapter. According to cognitive response theory, people will not be influenced by a persuasive message if it produces mostly unfavorable thoughts, termed counterarguments (as opposed to favorable thoughts about the message, termed proarguments). Reviews of research on cognitive response theory (e.g., Eagly & Chaiken, 1984; Greenwald, 1968) cite McGuire's experiments on inoculation as important early examples of relevant research, which served as precursors to many later studies.

McGuire utilized a clever procedure to test his ideas about inoculation. His research focused on attitudes and beliefs that are shared widely in society and that are rarely challenged, which he called **cultural truisms** (things that are assumed to be *true* in a *culture*). Examples of cultural truisms that he studied were "Mental illness is not contagious" and "Toothbrushing after every meal is a good idea." Before we continue, think about your own view on these issues. Do they seem obviously true? Can you think of arguments against them?

William McGuire and Demetrios Papageorgis (1961) wanted to demonstrate that these truisms, despite being widely accepted, were highly susceptible to attack because people had never thought about them carefully. Sure enough, the researchers were able to generate persuasive messages that produced dramatic changes in agreement with the truisms. For example, a message suggesting that too

**inoculation theory**

*a model of building resistance to persuasion by exposing people to arguments against their attitude position and giving them counterarguments that refute the attack. It is based on the process of medical inoculation.*

**cultural truisms**

*attitudes and beliefs that are widely shared and rarely challenged in a society*

much toothbrushing wears down the enamel of the teeth, or that one person's mental illness can create an unstable environment that causes another person to develop psychological problems, proved to be very convincing to participants. On a scale from 1 to 15, where 15 reflected complete agreement with the truism and 1 reflected complete rejection of the truism, McGuire and Papageorgis found that participants who had *not* been exposed to any attack on the cultural truisms gave a mean response of 12.62, whereas those who had been exposed to a persuasive message arguing against the truism gave a mean response of only 6.64—a huge decline in agreement.

Can "inoculation" protect against this kind of attack? McGuire and Papageorgis (1961) included a condition in their experiment in which participants were inoculated against the upcoming persuasive message by exposing them to what was termed a **refutational defense.** The refutational defense consisted of giving participants two arguments *against* the cultural truism, along with counterarguments that *refuted* these attacks. For example, participants might be exposed to the argument "Too much toothbrushing wears down the enamel of the teeth," along with the counterargument "Soft brushes clean the teeth without producing any wear." Participants who were exposed to a refutational defense later gave a mean response of 10.33 after an attack on the truism, which represented a much smaller decline in agreement than was found for participants who were exposed to the persuasive message without any inoculation.

A final condition in the McGuire and Papageorgis (1961) study gave participants a **supportive defense** prior to a persuasive message. The supportive defense consisted of several points in favor of the truism, without any exposure to arguments against the truism or counterarguments refuting the attacks. For example, participants might be told "Brushing your teeth after every meal keeps your breath fresh"; this argument supports toothbrushing but does not address the argument that too much brushing can wear down the enamel. It turned out that this supportive defense did *not* increase resistance to persuasion: participants in this condition gave a mean rating of 7.39 after being exposed to the attack, which reflected a large decline in agreement (in fact, this group did not differ significantly from the condition in which participants did not get any defense at all before being exposed to the message). These data indicate that only a refutational defense will increase resistance to persuasion: participants must think specifically about criticisms of the truism along with counterarguments to those criticisms. It should be noted, however, that a few studies since McGuire and Papageorgis have found that a supportive defense can provide some protection against persuasion (e.g., Adams & Beatty, 1977; Bernard, Maio, & Olson, 2003; Pfau et al., 1997; Syzbillo & Heslin, 1973; for a review, see Pfau & Szabo, 2004).

What implications do these findings have for resistance to persuasion? First, they help us to understand why people may often withstand our attempts to influence them. For many or even most issues, people are aware that two sides exist and have done at least some thinking about both sides. As a result, they have counterarguments ready to use against our reasoning. By thinking about both sides, people have "inoculated" themselves against persuasion for most issues. Second, the findings highlight a strategy for how to increase our own or other people's resistance to persuasive attacks. Thinking carefully about or discussing both sides of an issue, including counterarguments against each side, increases the ability to resist subsequent influence attempts. For educators and parents, the findings imply that children should be exposed to two-sided discussions of issues, so the children will not be caught unprepared by a persuasive attack. Discussing why some people believe that racial discrimination is okay, together with counterarguments to that view, will strengthen children's resistance to subsequent attempts to induce a racist view. Although it is tempting to ignore positions that we find repugnant, it may be a mistake to do so. Paradoxically, by discussing those positions with our children,

**refutational defense**

*exposing people to arguments against their attitudinal position along with counterarguments that refute the attack*

**supportive defense**

*exposing people to arguments that are consistent with their attitude position*

we may actually reduce the likelihood that they will later adopt them (see also Maio & Olson, 1998; Maio, Olson, Allen, & Bernard, 2001).

# Reactance Theory

Imagine yourself in the following situation. You are engaged to be married and are trying to decide with your fiancé where to hold the ceremony and reception. You have been considering several, quite different options: an outdoor ceremony at your parents' home, with a relaxed and informal reception afterwards; a church ceremony, followed by a more formal reception in a room next to the chapel; and a legal ceremony at a reception hall, with a party-oriented reception afterwards. Each option has advantages and disadvantages. You are torn between them, but really want to make the right decision.

Suddenly the phone rings. It is the minister from your church, who tells you that the time you were considering for your wedding has just been taken by someone else. So if you want a church ceremony and reception, it will have to be at a different time or on a different day.

How would you feel? What effect would this news have on your interest in each of the options? If you are like most people, the church option would suddenly appear more attractive. Perversely, now that you can't have it, you'd really want it. If only you'd made your decision earlier! If only the minister had phoned before giving the time to someone else! If only! (These thoughts are, of course, *counterfactual thoughts,* as discussed in Chapter 3, pages 96–99.)

The feeling that occurs when people lose an option or a freedom is called *reactance,* and the theory that addresses the causes and consequences of this state is **reactance theory.** Jack Brehm (1966, 1972), who proposed the theory, hypothesized that when an individual's perceived freedoms are threatened, those freedoms become more attractive, and the individual may try to retain or regain the freedom. If your parents tell you that you cannot go to a party, this will make you *really* want to go, and you may even risk being grounded by going to the party despite your parents' orders. If you go to a store to buy an advertised item on sale, but the item is sold out, you will *really* want the item and may buy it at another store even though it is not on sale.

"The grass is always greener on the other side of the fence." "Everybody wants what they can't have." These clichés capture the feeling and effects of reactance: when something is denied to us, we want it even more.

What does this theory have to do with resistance to *persuasion?* Although the examples we have given so far have all involved restrictions on people's freedoms to *do* something (to hold a wedding at the church, to go to a party, to buy an item), the theory also applies to threats on people's freedoms to *believe* something. If someone tries to pressure you into supporting a cause, you may resent the pressure and resist the influence attempt. If your professor tells you that you *must* believe that Theory X is true, you may think to yourself, "Oh yeah? I'm never going to believe that stupid theory!" (We recommend that you keep this thought to yourself.)

Several researchers have investigated people's responses to heavy-handed attempts to change their attitudes. Reactance theory predicts that people will resist overt pressure to adopt a certain view, because the pressure threatens their freedom to hold a different view. Thus, obvious and forceful attempts to influence someone may be less successful than more subtle attempts based on persuasion rather than coercion. In one study, Stephen Worchel and Jack Brehm (1970) gave participants a message that took the position that the Communist Party should be treated the same as all other political parties in the United States. For some participants, the message included heavy-handed statements like "You cannot believe otherwise" and "You have no choice but to believe this." For other participants, the

**reactance theory**

*a model of how people respond to threats on their freedoms*

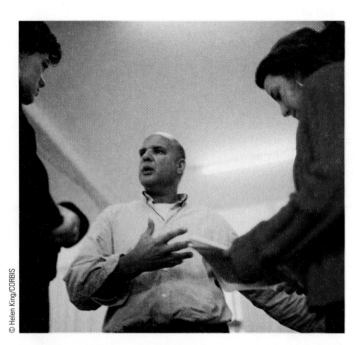

*Reactance* motivates people to resist overt pressure to adopt a certain view.

message did not include these statements. Results showed that participants were *less* persuaded by the message with the explicit demands than by the low-key message. Telling people that they *had* to believe something actually decreased their agreement with the message (see also Heller, Pallak, & Picek, 1973; Sensenig & Brehm, 1968).

Reactance theory helps us to understand why attitude change is often difficult in real life. In many persuasion settings, the individuals being influenced probably feel at least some reactance, because they recognize that the source of the message wants them to adopt a particular position. Even when heavy-handed tactics are not used, targets of influence attempts may feel some pressure to adopt the recommended position. Because this pressure threatens their freedom to believe otherwise, they might resist the influence attempt and not change their attitude.

## A Final Comment: Preparing Yourself to Resist Persuasion

We have discussed two factors that work against persuasion: counterarguing and reactance. Counterarguing is cognitive and argument-based, whereas reactance is affective and motivation-based. Taken together, they can produce considerable resistance to influence.

What advice about preparing yourself to resist persuasion can we derive from these two factors? One key ingredient of both counterarguing and reactance is the *recognition of persuasive intent.* Before individuals can actively counterargue a message, and before they can experience reactance, they must recognize that someone is trying to change their attitude. After all, counterarguing requires that individuals think carefully about what is being said and generate responses to the arguments. Similarly, reactance requires that individuals realize that their freedom to hold a particular attitude is being threatened. Neither of these processes can occur if individuals fail to recognize that they are the target of attempted influence.

Our recommendation? Be on the lookout for attempted persuasion and influence. Recognize that advertisers are trying to get you to buy their products. Think about the intentions of people who are "discussing" a topic with you—are they trying to change your attitude? Don't forget that movie reviewers, newspaper editors, and politicians are trying to persuade you. Realize that peers who are pressuring you to try drugs or to drink alcohol may have selfish motives, not friendly ones, and are trying to change both your attitudes and your behavior. Be suspicious of groups that preach fear and offer simple solutions. Remind yourself that salespersons want to sell things. In sum, be aware of the fact that you live in a complex social world where attempted interpersonal influence goes on all the time.

**Resisting Illegitimate Authority-Based Appeals.** In an interesting set of studies, Brad Sagarin, Robert Cialdini, William Rice, and Sherman Serna (2002) developed and tested a "treatment" that was designed to make college students better able to identify and resist deceptive advertisements. In particular, the treatment focused on appeals that used illegitimate authority figures. *Illegitimate* was defined as using sources who had no real expertise related to the product. For instance, illegitimate advertisements used in the study included ones in which famous celebrities promoted something about which they had no expertise (e.g., Ivana Trump promoting the National Fluid Milk Processor Promotion Board) and ones in which actors portrayed the role of an expert (e.g., a model dressed as a stockbroker promoting the *Wall Street Journal*). Some participants in this research read a six-page discussion of legitimate and illegitimate uses of authorities in advertisements, which included several sample magazine ads. Compared to control participants who did not read these materials, participants who completed the treatment subsequently rated illegitimate magazine ads as less persuasive and legitimate magazine ads as more persuasive. Thus, it proved possible to sensitize people to illegitimate uses of authority. These findings are encouraging for attempts to educate consumers about deceptive advertising. It may be possible to teach people to be skeptical about advertisers who use manipulative techniques in their appeals.

# Chapter Summary

This chapter described research and theory on the many ways that attitudes can change. One way that attitudes can change is through rationalization—convincing ourselves that our decisions or actions are justified. This process of rationalization is described by **cognitive dissonance theory.** Dissonance theory deals with the consequences of being aware of **dissonant cognitions,** which are beliefs that are inconsistent with one another, such as "I smoke" and "Smoking causes cancer." In contrast, **consonant cognitions** support one another, such as "I eat apples" and "Apples are good for me." Dissonance theory proposes that the awareness of dissonant cognitions produces an unpleasant state of arousal, which people are motivated to reduce. Dissonance can be reduced by changing one of the dissonant cognitions, adding consonant cognitions, or changing the importance of one or more of the relevant cognitions.

Dissonance theory has been tested in several different experimental *paradigms,* or research methodologies. The **induced compliance paradigm** investigates dissonance that results from counterattitudinal behavior. It involves inducing participants to behave in a way that is inconsistent with their attitudes. To reduce dissonance, participants often change their attitude in the direction of their behavior. The **effort justification paradigm** investigates dissonance that results from wasted effort. It involves leading participants to incur some costs for a goal that might not be worthwhile. To reduce dissonance, participants often increase the perceived value of the goal. The **free choice paradigm** investigates dissonance that results from making a decision or choice, which is termed *postdecisional dissonance.* It involves asking participants to choose between two or more alternatives. To reduce dissonance, participants often increase

the perceived attractiveness of the chosen alternative and decrease the perceived attractiveness of the rejected alternative—a pattern of reevaluation that is termed *spreading of the alternatives.*

Several alternative interpretations of dissonance findings have been proposed. *Self-perception theory* proposes that people change their attitudes after counterattitudinal behavior because they logically infer their attitudes from their behavior. **Impression management theory** proposes that people in dissonance experiments may not change their attitudes at all, but simply *report* new attitudes so they will not appear inconsistent to the experimenter. **Self-affirmation theory** proposes that counterattitudinal behavior induces attitude change because it threatens people's sense of self-worth, and they can reduce the threat by reaffirming an important value.

Recent research on dissonance has produced the **hypocrisy paradigm,** in which participants deliver a speech arguing for a prosocial behavior and are then made aware that they have not always exhibited the behavior themselves in the past. Individual differences in sensitivity to dissonance have also been investigated. People differ in their **preference for consistency (PFC),** which refers to their desire for predictability and consistency within their own responses and within others' responses. People who are high in PFC exhibit dissonance effects more strongly than people who are low in PFC.

Another way that attitudes can change is via *persuasive communications,* which are attempts by individuals or groups to convince another person or persons to adopt a particular position. **Cognitive response theory** suggests that an information-based message is effective at changing attitudes when it elicits mostly positive thoughts (termed *proarguments* in the theory), but does not change attitudes when it elicits mostly negative thoughts (termed *counterarguments* in the theory). In the domain of advertising, some advertisers use information about the quality and features of their product to generate strong rational arguments in favor of buying it; this strategy is called the **hard sell.**

A persuasive communication can also produce attitude change by **heuristic persuasion,** which results from the use of *heuristics:* simple rules or assumptions such as "Experts are reliable sources of information." In the domain of advertising, some advertisers use emotions, symbols, or images to sell a product; this strategy is called the **soft sell.**

Two theories of persuasive communications can encompass attitude change resulting from both strong arguments and the use of heuristics. One is the **systematic-heuristic model.** This model distinguishes between **systematic processing,** which occurs when people think carefully about the arguments in a message, and **heuristic processing,** which occurs when people rely on heuristics to make judgments about the message. The second theory, the **elaboration likelihood model,** distinguishes between the **central route to persuasion** and the **peripheral route to persuasion.** The central route occurs when attitude change results from a careful analysis of the information in the message; the peripheral route occurs when attitude change results from the use of heuristics or other noncognitive factors (which are termed **peripheral cues** in the model).

In the health domain, persuasive messages often try to arouse fear. **Protection motivation theory** provides an analysis of how threatening messages produce attitude change. It predicts that attitude and behavior change is more likely when recipients of a message are convinced that (1) the problem is serious, (2) they are personally susceptible to the problem, (3) the recommended behaviors will be effective in avoiding the problem, and (4) they are personally capable of performing the recommended behaviors.

**Propaganda** is a persuasive attempt that is motivated by an ideology, or set of values, and is deliberately biased in its presentation of information. Propaganda is employed by **destructive cults,** which can be defined as groups led by a charismatic leader that isolate themselves from the rest of society and use deceptive techniques to recruit and retain members. It is also possible to consider messages from many "legitimate" sources to be somewhat propagandistic.

Persuasive attempts often fail—people resist persuasion. **Inoculation theory** uses the process of medical inoculation as an analogy for understanding resistance to argument-based persuasion. Research has focused on **cultural truisms,** which are beliefs that are widely shared and rarely questioned in a culture. Researchers have found that a **refutational defense,** which involves giving people arguments against the truism and counterarguments that refute these attacks, increases resistance to influence. Another, less effective form of inoculation is a **supportive defense,** which involves giving people only points in favor of the truism, without any exposure to attacks.

**Reactance theory** predicts that when people believe that one of their freedoms is threatened or restricted, they experience a state called *reactance,* which motivates them to restore that freedom. The threatened freedom becomes more attractive, and the individual may try to regain the freedom directly.

# Key Terms

**central route to persuasion** (275)

**cognitive dissonance theory** (252)

**cognitive response theory** (268)

**consonant cognitions** (252)

**cultural truisms** (297)

**destructive cult** (292)

**dissonant cognitions** (252)

**effort justification paradigm** (257)

**elaboration likelihood model** (275)

**free choice paradigm** (259)

**hard sell** (271)

**heuristic persuasion** (271)

**heuristic processing** (275)

**hypocrisy paradigm** (264)

**impression management theory** (262)

**induced compliance paradigm** (255)

**inoculation theory** (297)

**peripheral cues** (276)

**peripheral route to persuasion** (275)

**preference for consistency (PFC)** (265)

**propaganda** (290)

**protection motivation theory** (288)

**reactance theory** (299)

**refutational defense** (298)

**self-affirmation theory** (262)

**soft sell** (275)

**supportive defense** (298)

**systematic processing** (275)

**systematic-heuristic model** (275)

## Social Psychology Alive on the Web

### SOCIAL PSYCHOLOGY ALIVE: ONLINE LABS

To perform the following experiment and see how you compare to other students, go to Social Psychology Lab, which can be accessed through Social PsychologyNow.

- 7.1 Travel Planner

### SOCIAL PSYCHOLOGY ALIVE: QUIZZING AND PRACTICE TESTS

You can access our website directly by going to http://psychology.wadsworth.com/brecklerle/ for online quizzes, flash cards, and Internet links.

### INFOTRAC® COLLEGE EDITION

For additional readings, explore InfoTrac College Edition, your online library of archived journal articles and periodicals dating back 22 years. If your instructor ordered InfoTrac College Edition with this book, you can access it from your CD-ROM, or go directly to http://www.infotrac-college.com/wadsworth and use the passcode from the InfoTrac College Edition card that came with your book. For this chapter, try these search terms: *dissonance, rationalization, induced compliance, effort justification, impression management, self-affirmation, hypocrisy, systematic processing, heuristic processing, elaboration likelihood model, fear appeals, protection motivation, propaganda, inoculation theory, reactance theory.*

## Social Psychology Alive: The Workbook

To apply what you've learned in this chapter to what happens in the real world, go to Chapter 7 of *Social Psychology Alive: The Workbook:*

- Does Hazing Enhance the Attractiveness and Worth of Fraternities and Sororities to Their Members?
- Postdecisional Dissonance: How to Make a Candy Bar Taste Better

- Making Choices
- Advertising in Daily Life
- Need for Cognition and Persuasive Communications
- How to Persuade People Not to Smoke
- What Is a Cult?

## Social Psychology Alive: The Videos

To see video on the topics and experiments discussed in this chapter, you can go either to Social PsychologyNow or to the CD-ROM, if your instructor assigned either one, to the following sections:

- When Trauma Makes the Heart Grow Fonder: Cognitive Dissonance and the Justification of Effort
- Moving the Masses: Public Service Announcements

## To Learn More

This list contains citations to books or articles that can help you learn more. These readings are good places to start if you want to gain a deeper understanding of the topics in this chapter.

- Seiter, J. S., & Gass, R. H. (Eds.). (2004). *Perspectives on persuasion, social influence, and compliance gaining.* Boston: Pearson Education.

- Levine, R. (2003). *The power of persuasion: How we are bought and sold.* Hoboken, NJ: Wiley.
- Pratkanis, A., & Aronson, E. (2000). *Age of propaganda: The everyday use and abuse of persuasion* (rev. ed.). New York: Freeman.

©Leif Skoogfors/CORBIS

# Conformity, Compliance, and Obedience

eep in the tropical jungle of Guyana—a small country in the north-eastern corner of South America—about 1,000 members of the Peoples Temple established what they intended to be a utopian settlement. The Reverend Jim Jones was their leader; most members of the community called him father. The Peoples Temple began in Indianapolis in the 1950s, then moved to California in 1965. Its beliefs were similar to those of many other Christian gospel congregations. The members included both Black and White Americans who were attracted by Jones's mix of Christianity, racial equality, socialism, and activism. They were normal, hardworking people, who wanted to make the world a better place. Those in Guyana had followed Jones from two primary congregations in the United States, one in Ukiah, California, and one in San Francisco, giving up everything and moving their entire families to South America. Members fervently believed that their community could serve as an example for others to copy.

On November 17, 1978, California congressman Leo Ryan visited Jonestown on a fact-finding mission. There had been rumors that some people wanted to leave Jonestown but were being held against their will. Ryan was allowed to talk to some members and to tour the compound. The next day, Ryan returned to a nearby airport together with 16 people who wanted to leave. Just as they were boarding the plane, a truck carrying Peoples Temple guards pulled up, and the guards opened fire on Ryan and his party. Five people were killed, including Ryan. The guards returned to Jonestown and informed Jones of the events.

Jim Jones gathered the entire community together. Unaware of the shooting, most people expected him to talk about how well the congressman's visit had gone. Instead, Jones declared that the end had come for the people of Jonestown. He said that outside events had forced the community into a situation in which "revolu-

More than 900 people obeyed Jim Jones's command that they poison themselves and their children.

© AP/Wide World Photos

*tionary suicide" was the best option. With little dissension or resistance, most of his followers then drank down a cyanide-laced punch. Parents gave the drink to their children first, and then consumed the poison themselves. That day, 914 people died, including 276 children.*

*What could possibly account for this behavior? Why would so many people willingly give up their lives and the lives of their children for the man they knew as* father? *Were they all suffering from some deep psychological problems? No. They were ordinary people. They were devoted members of their church. They were victims of powerful pressures for conformity, compliance, and obedience (Osherow, 1999). Before you write off the Jonestown massacre as an oddity, consider that you, too, are subject to the very same forces. These social pressures are with you every day, and they influence much of what you do.*

## ● ● ● Defining Conformity, Compliance, and Obedience

In this chapter, we review social psychological research on three specific kinds of *social influence* (i.e., influence from other people): conformity, compliance, and obedience. These terms all refer to *changes in behavior caused by other people,* but they differ in their breadth. Let us first define each term and then explain the differences between them. **Conformity** is the most general concept and refers to any change in behavior caused by another person or group; the individual acted in some way because of influence from others. Note that conformity is limited to changes in *behavior* caused by other people; it does not refer to effects of other people on internal concepts like attitudes and beliefs. **Compliance** refers to a change in behavior that is *requested* by another person or group; the individual acted in some way because others asked him or her to do so (but it was possible to refuse or decline). **Obedience** refers to a change in behavior that is *ordered* by another person or group; the individual acted in some way because others commanded him or her to do so (failing to obey was not presented as an option, though it may have been considered by the individual).

Conformity encompasses compliance and obedience, because it refers to *any* behavior that occurs as a result of others' influence—no matter what the nature of that influence. For example, there may not have been any request or order given to the individual; the behavior might have occurred because the person copied, learned from, wanted to impress, or was in some other way influenced by another person. Compliance and obedience refer to behavior that resulted specifically from requests or orders. Even though the concept of conformity technically encompasses these other concepts, we will limit discussion in the section on conformity to studies focused on behavior that was *not* specifically requested or ordered by others (because, after all, requests or orders would move the behavior into the more specific literatures on compliance or obedience). We will particularly emphasize in the conformity section studies that involve people behaving in ways that are similar to how others are behaving (*doing as others do*) without any preceding request or order.

Why would this kind of *conformity*—doing as others do without any request—occur? For one thing, when you find yourself in a new or unusual situation, it is

**conformity**

*any change in behavior caused by another person or group*

**compliance**

*a change in behavior that is requested by another person or group*

**obedience**

*a change in behavior that is ordered by another person or group*

Panhandlers try to get you to comply with their request for money.

natural—even sensible—to look to others in deciding what to do. Other people may have more experience, more information, or better skills than you do. Going along with others may be the best way to do the right thing or to avoid appearing foolish, especially when the situation is ambiguous and you are uncertain about your own judgment and experience. But suppose the other people around you are doing things that just don't make sense. Would you go along then? Would you try to "fit in" with the crowd? Research on conformity provides some surprising answers—people often go along with the incorrect responses of others, even when reality is as plain as it can be.

What about *compliance,* which refers to actions caused by a request? Even in everyday and familiar situations, we are susceptible to the requests of others. Indeed, some people we encounter are compliance professionals—getting us to do things, to buy things, and to say things that we would not otherwise have done or bought or said. If a salesperson has ever convinced you to spend more money than you intended, if you have given in to a panhandler's request, or if you have agreed to accompany a friend to an event that you would really rather have avoided, then you know what it means to feel compliance pressure. Research on compliance has identified some fascinating strategies that are effective in eliciting compliance with requests.

*Obedience* refers to a more extreme form of social influence, when another person simply tells someone to do something. Obedience commands start early in childhood, when we are socialized to follow the orders of parents and teachers. By the time we are adults, most of us have learned to be relatively obedient—to follow the orders of police, government officials, higher-ranking military officers, the boss, and, indeed, most people who wear a uniform or hold a position of authority. But how far does this go? We know that members of the Peoples Temple followed orders to poison their children and then themselves. Would you obey the orders of an authority even if that meant causing harm to another person? The answer may surprise you—research on obedience to authority has shown that people are remarkably susceptible to this form of social influence.

The three varieties of social influence we describe in this chapter are not the only ways we are influenced by others (e.g., see Nail, MacDonald, & Levy, 2000).

Indeed, virtually all of social psychology deals with social influence in some fashion (how individuals' thoughts, feelings, and behaviors are influenced by other people). For instance, in Chapter 7, we looked at how other people can affect attitudes and beliefs through such mechanisms as advertising, persuasive appeals, and propaganda. In Chapter 10, we will see how the dynamics of social groups shape our identity and influence our judgments. In the present chapter, you can anticipate learning about some of the best-known—and most disturbing—results of social psychological research.

We normally obey the commands of police officers.

## Why Do We Conform?

Conforming behaviors occur for two principal reasons, which are captured by the terms *informational influence* and *normative influence* (coined by Deutsch & Gerard, 1955).

**Informational influence** occurs when people are influenced by others because of a desire to be correct and to obtain valid information. This kind of influence reflects that people often rely on others as a source of information—they trust others' judgments to be useful in a particular context. Perhaps the other people are more knowledgeable, or perhaps the judgment is ambiguous and the person is unsure about the correct answer.

**Normative influence,** on the other hand, occurs when people are influenced by others to gain rewards or to avoid punishment. They might not necessarily think that others' judgments or behaviors are correct; they might simply want to be liked or to avoid conflict. One example of normative influence can be law: people sometimes obey laws simply to avoid being punished, such as driving at the speed limit when they would actually like to go faster. Another example is when teenagers conform in words, deeds, or appearance to popular peers whom they hope to befriend.

Informational and normative influence can occur simultaneously. For instance, an individual might believe that another person's judgment is correct and also hope to be rewarded by that person for agreeing with him or her. Indeed, we often want to please other people (normative influence) whose judgments we respect (informational influence).

We will mention the distinction between informational and normative influence several times in the chapter as we discuss conformity, compliance, and obedience. We will also return to the distinction for a more thorough analysis in the final section, where we discuss general mechanisms underlying the three topics described in the chapter.

**informational influence**

*influence from other people that is motivated by a desire to be correct and to obtain accurate information*

**normative influence**

*influence from other people that is motivated by a desire to gain rewards or avoid punishment*

# ● ● ● Conformity: Doing As Others Do

We often find ourselves going along with the behavior of others—doing as others do. This behavioral conformity can occur without our even realizing that we are doing it. Sometimes we go along with others because we do not understand what is happening or we are unsure what to do. But sometimes we go along when we know we shouldn't. Two famous early series of experiments in social psychology looked at these different kinds of conformity: Muzafer Sherif's (1935, 1936, 1937) work on the *autokinetic effect* and Solomon Asch's (1951, 1952, 1956) work on judgments of line lengths. These studies provide a nice package, because Sherif investigated conformity in situations where the correct judgment was ambiguous, whereas Asch investigated conformity in situations where the correct judgment was obvious.

**social norm**

*a rule or guideline in a group or culture about what behaviors are proper and improper*

## Sherif's Autokinetic Effect Studies

Muzafer Sherif (1935, 1936, 1937) conceptualized his research on conformity as addressing the development of *social norms.* A **social norm** is a rule or guideline about what behaviors are proper and improper. Norms can be formal, such as laws and contracts, or informal, such as customs and traditions within small groups (families, peer groups, etc.). Typically, the reward for following a norm is social acceptance or approval, whereas the punishment for breaking a norm is social rejection or disapproval. Social norms govern the way

The norm in the United Kingdom is for people to drive on the left-hand side of the road.

we dress, the way we speak, and the way we behave. An example of a formal norm is the law in North America to drive on the right-hand side of the road. Violating this norm is usually met with swift punishment, not to mention dirty looks and gestures from other drivers. But in other parts of the world, the norm is exactly the opposite—driving on the left-hand rather than right-hand side of the road keeps you out of trouble. Examples of more informal norms are everywhere. In some business communities, the expected business attire for men includes a suit and tie (think of Wall Street), whereas in other places, every day is "casual Friday" (think of the Silicon Valley). In some families, children are allowed significant input into decisions, whereas in other families, parents are the sole decision makers. The social norms on some college campuses promote serious studying and on others promote intense socializing.

Social norms are one source of conformity (they represent influence from other people and guide behavior). Sherif wanted to study the development and influence of social norms. He did so by setting up a novel situation in which most of the research participants had little or no prior experience. Under these conditions, he expected norms to emerge.

**autokinetic effect**

*in a darkened room, a stationary point of light will appear to move periodically*

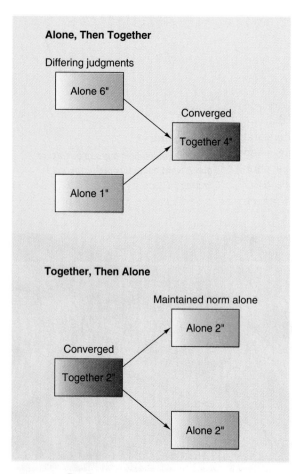

**FIGURE 8.1** Conditions in Sherif's (1936) second study of social norms

**The Autokinetic Effect.** Imagine that you are sitting in a completely darkened room. The only visible thing is a tiny point of light projected on the wall 16 feet in front of you. If you watch that point of light, it will appear to move, and it may even seem to be periodically jumping about in different directions. The light is not really moving; it is an illusion. This is known as the **autokinetic effect**, and it occurs partly because no other visual frame of reference is available to locate the light and partly because of occasional rapid movements of your eye.

In his first study, Sherif (1935) asked 19 men, participating individually, to report how far (in inches) the light appeared to move. Other than the experimenter, no one except the person making the judgment was in the room. Over the course of 100 judgments, each man settled on a relatively stable distance, but these average estimates of movement ranged widely, from a low of 0.4 inches for one man to a high of 9.6 inches for another. Thus, a relatively wide range of perceived movement occurred from person to person—just the results Sherif needed to study the formation and influence of a group norm.

In a second study, Sherif (1936) assembled people in groups of two or three (see Figure 8.1). The task was the same as before: to announce out loud the distance of perceived motion of what was really a stationary point of light. Judgments were recorded in four sessions on four different days. For half of the participants, the first session involved making judgments alone, and then being joined by the other participants in the following three sessions. When they started alone, a wide range of perceived movement was observed, as expected from the first study (averages from less than 1 inch to more than 9 inches). But when the participants began making their judgments in groups of two or three, judgments of perceived movement began to converge. By the end of three sessions together, judgments of the two or three people in a group were very similar (typically differing by less than 1 inch), although the different groups tended to converge on different norms. For instance, one two-person group converged on a norm of about 1 inch, whereas another converged on a norm of about 5 inches.

The other half of the participants made their judgments in the group situation from the very beginning. These groups converged very rapidly on their own group norms. It was in these groups that a very interesting result was obtained. During the last (fourth) session, the participants in these groups were broken up and made their judgments alone. Yet the group norm carried on: the judgments now being made individually were nearly identical to the standard that had been established for the group. The flowchart in Figure 8.1 depicts the two conditions in this experiment.

Having observed the development and subsequent impact of a group norm, Sherif (1937) wanted to know if such "standards" could be arbitrarily established by experimental assistants (confederates). In one of the best-known autokinetic experiments, participants were assembled in groups of two. But only one member of each pair was naïve about the procedure; the other member was planted by the experimenter and was instructed to vary his judgments around a particular standard. In all, seven different pairs of people were tested, with the arbitrary standard (introduced by the confederate) ranging from 2 to 8 inches. For the first 50 judgment trials, the two participants in each pair made their judgments together (sometimes the naïve participant responded first, sometimes the confederate responded first). For the second set of 50 judgment trials, however, the naïve participant was tested alone. The results are shown in Figure 8.2. The blue line represents the naïve participant's responses during the first 50 trials, when the confederate was present and gave responses that remained consistently around a standard of between 2 to 8 inches; the purple line represents the naïve participant's responses during the second set of 50 trials, when the confederate was no longer present. The figure shows that the naïve participant's individual responses in the second set of trials remained very close to the standard established during the first 50 trials. Thus, the arbitrary standard introduced by the confederate clearly established a group norm, and that norm then carried over to influence the naïve participant's judgments when alone.

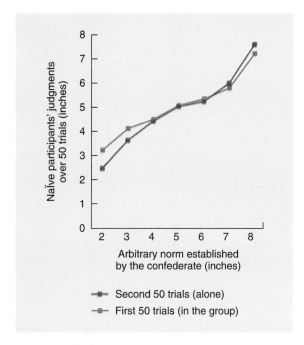

**FIGURE 8.2** Naïve participants' judgments of movement on the first 50 trials and the second 50 trials

Adapted from Sherif, 1937, An experimental approach to the study of attitudes, *Sociometry*, 1, 90–98.

**Multigenerational Norms.** Taken together, Sherif's early experiments (1935, 1936, 1937) showed that group norms are spontaneously established and carry over into individual judgments. Of course, in everyday life, many norms have been around for a long time. We do not typically know how a particular norm got started, nor for how many generations the norm has been passed along. For example, the norm that servers in restaurants should be given tips has been common in our society for many years. MacNeil and Sherif (1976) showed that the transmission of a norm from generation to generation is something that can be modeled in the laboratory. These researchers established an arbitrary group norm in a four-person group; three members of the group were planted by the experimenter. The three experimental confederates established an arbitrary group norm of about 12 inches over a series of 30 judgment trials. After a brief rest, one of the three confederates left the group and was replaced by a new naïve participant. The new group then provided 30 more sets of judgments, with the same arbitrary group norm being continued by the two remaining confederates. This process was then repeated, until all of the confederates had finally been replaced with naïve participants by the fourth generation. In the fifth generation, the original naïve participant was replaced with a new one. The study continued for 11 generations, each one involving the replacement of the oldest group member with a new member. After 11 generations, responses were beginning to drift from the initial group norm of 12 inches, but not far—the original standard was still evident. Norms can persist long after their original instigators are gone.

## Asch's Length Judgment Studies

If you imagined yourself as one of the "naïve" participants in Sherif's autokinetic experiments, you could probably see yourself going along with the others. After all, the judgment was an ambiguous one. But now imagine yourself participating in a very different experiment. In this study, social norms about the range of appropriate responses (as in Sherif's studies) are not really relevant, because the task is simple and clear-cut.

When you arrive at the laboratory, seven other students (just like you) are waiting to begin. The group is seated and told that this is an experiment involving the discrimination of lengths of lines. On each trial, you are shown one "standard" line, and three "comparison" lines. Your task is simply to indicate which of the three comparison lines matches the standard line in length. You can try the judgment out for yourself by using the set of lines shown in Figure 8.3. Unlike the Sherif experiments, this judgment is not ambiguous at all. One of the comparison lines is *exactly* the same length as the standard, and the two other comparison lines differ from the standard by at least ³/₄″. The lines are printed in a dark black ink, and each is ³/₈″ wide. There is a single correct answer (in this case, comparison line #3). The task is so easy that students rarely make an error when they make the judgments alone.

As the experiment begins, you learn that each member of the group is to announce his or her judgment out loud so the entire group can hear. You happen to be seated in the second row of chairs, and six students announce their judgments before it is your turn. At first, everything proceeds smoothly. For the first two comparison trials, everyone else sees the lines the same way you do. But then something strange happens for the third set of lines. The six students who go before you all announce the wrong answer. Instead of selecting the line that matches exactly, they *all* select a line ³/₄″ longer than the standard line. You can't believe it. You rub your eyes. You wonder if you have missed something, or has the entire group gone crazy? What would you do in this circumstance? Would you give the correct answer even though it goes against what everyone else has said, or would you conform to the others' response? Whatever your decision, the same

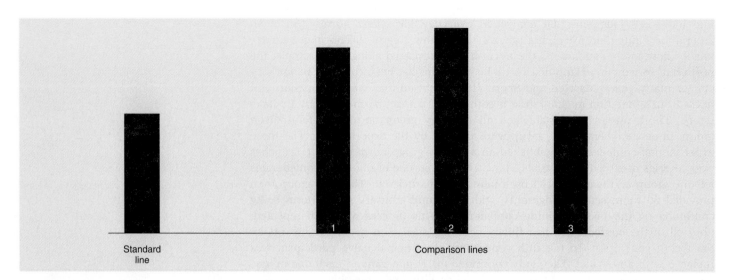

Standard
line

Comparison lines

**FIGURE 8.3** Sample stimulus trial from Asch's length judgment studies

From Asch, S.E. (1951). "Effects of group pressure upon the modification and distortion of judgments," in H. Guetzkow, ed., *Groups, Leadership and Men* (pp. 177–190). Reprinted by permission of Carnegie Press.

dilemma occurs on the fourth set of lines: everyone who goes before you selects the comparison line that is 1″ shorter than the standard. Would you give the correct answer, or conform?

Solomon Asch (1951, 1952, 1956) did a series of experiments just like this. In his studies, seven members of each group were confederates of the experimenter, instructed to give the wrong answer on designated trials. Only one participant (to whom we will refer as the "critical participant") was naïve about the experimental situation. In total, the experiment included 12 trials on which the other students (the confederates) unanimously selected the wrong comparison line. In the face of this pressure, only 23% (28 out of 123) of the critical participants always gave the correct answer and went against the group on all 12 trials. These students remained completely independent.

The remaining 77% of the critical participants went along with the group on at least one of the 12 trials. Across the 12 trials, 45% of the critical participants gave between 1 and 6 wrong answers, and 32% gave between 7 and 12 wrong answers. So, at one extreme, a substantial number of critical participants (23%) remained completely independent, but at the other extreme, an even larger number of critical participants (32%) yielded to group pressure many times by giving 7 or more wrong answers.

**The Crutchfield Apparatus.** Asch's procedure was very effective at generating conformity pressure. Being confronted by seven other people who disagree with your judgment in a face-to-face setting creates powerful social influence. But Asch's procedure also required many experimental confederates and involved elaborate stage-setting. The confederates needed to be carefully trained, and, like any theater production, their acting potentially differed from session to session. Also, there was the possibility that the confederates would act differently depending on how the critical participant responded.

To improve efficiency, flexibility, and control, Richard Crutchfield (1955) developed a clever procedure for studying conformity. Rather than using confederates, the **Crutchfield apparatus** simulates the responses of other people. When participants arrive for the experiment (usually in groups of five), they are seated in separate cubicles. Each cubicle contains an electrical panel with five rows of 11 lights and one row of 11 switches. The experimenter explains that each of the five participants controls one row of lights. Participants are told that they will answer questions projected on the wall facing the cubicles, so everyone can see the question at the same time. They are also told that, as each person indicates his or her response (by throwing one of the 11 switches), a corresponding light will be illuminated on the panel in all cubicles. Thus, each participant believes that he or she will learn about the responses of others and that his or her own responses will be publicly known.

In reality, the experimenter controls all of the lights and is able to simulate patterns involving a wrong but unanimous majority. The procedure is very efficient, because no confederates are needed and all five participants can be treated as "critical participants." The procedure also affords a high degree of experimental control. On any given judgment trial, each person can be instructed to respond in any of the possible serial positions (first, second, third, fourth, or fifth). Also, by controlling the lights, the experimenter can create any pattern of responses among the "other participants."

Crutchfield (1955) used his apparatus to reproduce the original Asch (1951) experiment involving judgments of line lengths with a unanimous majority of other respondents providing the wrong answer. Crutchfield's findings were very similar to those of Asch. In addition to line length judgments, Crutchfield employed a variety of other tasks, involving perceptual judgments, attitudes and opinions, personal preferences, and assessments of factual material. On virtually all of these tasks, participants showed some conformity to the judgments of others.

**Crutchfield apparatus**

*a machine that consists of an electrical panel with several rows of lights; it allows the efficient study of conformity by simulating the responses of numerous hypothetical participants*

The only exception was for judgments that involved selecting which of two drawings was preferred. In this case of expressing personal preferences, there was little
or no effect of group pressure.

**Nature of the Task.** The *amount* of conformity found in Asch-type experiments, or using the Crutchfield apparatus, depends on features of the judgment task
(Allen, 1965). One feature is the ambiguity of the task: conformity is more likely
when tasks are ambiguous. For example, in a study by Crutchfield (1955), participants were required to solve a number series that, in fact, had no solution. The
other (simulated) participants unanimously provided the same incorrect answer,
and 79% of the participants went along with it. This context is quite similar to
Sherif's studies using the autokinetic effect.

Conformity is also influenced by the *difficulty* of the task. Can you guess the
nature of this effect? Do you think that people are more likely to conform to others' responses when a task is difficult or when it is easy? Reasons can be generated
for either prediction. On the one hand, difficult tasks might increase conformity
because people are less certain of their own answer. On the other hand, difficult
tasks might reduce conformity because it is okay to differ from others when a task
is difficult. Imagine that you were asked a difficult trivia question: would you be
more strongly influenced by others' responses than on an easier question? If you
think that you would be more influenced on difficult questions, your intuition
matches the findings in social psychological experiments (e.g., Baron, Vandello, &
Brunsman, 1996; Coleman, Blake, & Mouton, 1958). For example, in an experiment
using Asch's procedures, Morton Deutsch and Harold Gerard (1955) had participants make line length judgments in two series. For one series, the lines were in
plain view—a relatively easy task. But for the other series, a more difficult judgment was required. Here, the lines were removed before participants made their
judgments, forcing people to rely on their memory of the lines. More conformity
was found when judgments were based on memory than when the lines were in
plain sight.

Why do ambiguous and difficult tasks produce more conformity than clear and
easy tasks? To answer this question, let's return to the distinction between informational and normative influence. On ambiguous or difficult tasks (e.g., Sherif's studies), other people's responses exert both *informational* and *normative* influence,
whereas on clear and easy tasks (e.g., Asch's studies), only *normative* influence
occurs. Put another way, on ambiguous or difficult tasks, the individual not only
feels some normative pressure to go along with others' judgments (which is also
true on clear and easy tasks), but the individual also uses the others' judgments as
a source of information about the correct answer (which is not true on clear and
easy tasks). The additional impact of informational influence increases the overall
rate of conformity on ambiguous and difficult tasks.

**Individual Differences.** Not everyone conforms. Remember that 23% of the
critical participants in Asch's (1956) experiment *never* yielded to the group pressure. Is there something consistently different in the personality traits or other
characteristics of people who stay independent compared to people who consistently yield? Researchers investigating individual differences in conformity on various tasks (not only line judgments) have found that people who remain independent are somewhat higher in their motivation to achieve (McClelland, Atkinson,
Clark, & Lowell, 1953) and in their leadership ability (Crutchfield, 1955) than people who conform. Also, compared to conformers, people who remain independent
tend to be less concerned about obtaining the approval of others (Strickland &
Crowne, 1962), less authoritarian (Petersen & Dietz, 2000), and less conscientious
(Roccas, Sagiv, Schwartz, & Knafo, 2002). Finally, there is evidence that individuals

**8.1**
**ONLINE**
**LAB**

with high self-esteem are less likely to conform than individuals with low self-esteem (Santee & Maslach, 1982; Singh & Prasad, 1973; Stang, 1972), especially when high self-esteem is based on intrinsic qualities like honesty or generosity, as opposed to extrinsic things like achievements (see Arndt, Schimel, Greenberg, & Pyszczynski, 2002).

What profile emerges from these various characteristics? Perhaps most clearly, it seems that a strong sense of self is associated with remaining independent, as reflected in such qualities as high self-esteem, high motivation to achieve, high leadership ability, and minimal concern about others' approval. These individuals seem to be more confident about their own judgments and, therefore, less influenced by others' judgments. We should bear in mind, however, that these qualities do not predict conformity perfectly; in fact, individual differences correlate relatively weakly with conformity and are only part of the puzzle of why and when people conform.

Age differences in conformity have also been explored. When attention is limited to children and teenagers, researchers have found that conformity to same-age peers increases during elementary school, peaks around grade 9, and then declines up to the university years (e.g., Berndt, 1979). Presumably, grade 9 is about the time when adolescents are most concerned about being popular and not being ridiculed (see Janes & Olson, 2000). When attention is limited to adults between the ages of 18 and 85, there is a general tendency for conformity to decrease as age increases (e.g., Pasupathi, 1999). As adults grow older, it seems that they gradually feel less pressure to agree with others, although some degree of conformity pressure remains throughout the life span.

Older adults tend to be less conforming than younger adults.

**Effects of Group Size.** Do larger unanimous majorities produce greater conformity in settings like those in Asch's experiments? That is, does conformity increase as the size of the unanimous group grows? This issue was one of the first things investigated by Asch (1951), who found that conformity did increase as the size of the group grew from one to three. Unanimous groups numbering more than three, however, did not produce further increases in conformity.

In a later experiment, Harold Gerard, Roland Wilhelmy, and Edward Conolley (1968) found that conformity continued to increase when the size of the majority grew beyond three. These researchers' results, presented in Figure 8.4, show that conformity rose rapidly as the group size grew from one to five, but additional increases in size had no impact on conformity (indeed, there was a downward turn for groups of six). Taken together, the studies on group size indicate that increases in the group beyond four or five have relatively little effect on conformity.

We should note, however, that these laboratory studies did not extend to very large groups, such as mobs or crowds. It seems likely that very large groups do, indeed, exert more conformity pressure than small groups. For example, members of the Peoples Temple in Guyana faced the weight of the entire congregation when ordered to drink poison by Jim Jones. A group of many hundreds, all pressing for obedience to their revered leader, must have generated enormous pressure to conform.

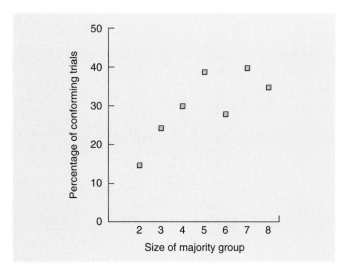

**FIGURE 8.4** Percentage of conforming trials as the size of the group increases

From Gerard et al., "Conformity and group size," *Journal of Personality and Social Psychology*, 8(1), 79–82, 1968. Copyright © 1968 by the American Psychological Association.

**How to Make Conformity Disappear.** If we want to understand what is going on in the conformity situation developed by Asch, one useful strategy is to find out what makes conformity *disappear.* Two rather different methods have been found to reduce very substantially the level of conformity exhibited in the original Asch studies. Learning about these two methods provides insight into why people often yield to a unanimous but obviously wrong majority.

In a variation on the original experiment, Asch (1956) made one change. Instead of having the "critical participants" announce their judgments out loud (public responses), he had them silently record their judgments in writing (private responses). The other alleged participants (the confederates) still announced their answers out loud; this procedure was justified by leading the critical participant to believe that he or she had arrived late and, therefore, would have to provide answers in a different manner than the other participants. This shift to private, confidential judgments by the critical participant produced a dramatic reduction in conformity. Deutsch and Gerard (1955) also found a substantial reduction in conformity when judgments were anonymous rather than face-to-face with the opposing majority. In a similar vein, more recent research has shown that individuals are more likely to conform to other people's judgments when they must communicate their judgments to those people than when they do not have to communicate their judgments (Pennington & Schlenker, 1999; Quinn & Schlenker, 2002). Taken together, these results suggest that participants in the original conformity experiments did not privately accept the incorrect judgments of the majority, but instead conformed publicly because of normative pressure.

In another variation on the original experiment, Asch (1951) broke up the unanimity of the group facing the critical participant. In this variation, one of the experimental confederates deviated from the other confederates by announcing the correct answer. The presence of just one "partner"—someone else who called it the same way as the critical participant—virtually *eliminated* yielding to the majority. Thus, a little social support was all that participants needed to stand up against the majority in this context (Allen, 1975). Again, these results show that conforming participants in the original experiments were simply conforming in public and would have given the correct answer if there had been any crack in the wall of pressure against them.

## Cultural Differences in Conformity

Most conformity experiments using the procedures of Sherif and Asch have been conducted in the United States. But a number of conformity experiments have been done in other parts of the world, including Western and Northern Europe, Japan, South America, and Africa. Do these different cultures produce different rates of conformity?

**Individualism Versus Collectivism.** We have discussed the dimension of individualism versus collectivism in earlier chapters (Hofstede, 2001; Markus, Kitayama, & Heiman, 1996; Triandis, 1995). It seems plausible to predict that people from individualist cultures (e.g., North America and Western Europe) will conform less than people from collectivist cultures (e.g., Asia, South America). After all, individualism implies a strong personal identity based on one's unique features (an *independent* self), whereas collectivism implies commonality and interconnections with others (an *interdependent* self). Also, compared to people in individualist cultures, people in collectivist cultures are more concerned about their relationships with others, value tradition more highly, and define themselves more in terms of their social roles. All of these factors should increase conformity in collectivist cultures compared to individualist cultures. These comments also recall our discussion of individual differences in conformity, where we noted that a strong sense of self was associated with low rates of conformity.

By the mid-1990s, more than 100 conformity experiments had been conducted around the world using a line judgment task, either in the face-to-face procedure employed by Asch or in the Crutchfield apparatus. Rod Bond and Peter Smith (1996) reviewed 133 of these experiments. When they compared experiments done in different cultures, they confirmed that conformity was indeed higher in collectivist than in individualist countries. In fact, culture predicted participants' conformity even more strongly than did other influential factors, such as size of the group. These results show that people's socialization into either individualist or collectivist cultures has important effects on their tendency to go along with others when the answer is clearly wrong.

**Individual Differences in Independent Versus Interdependent Self-Concepts.** People from individualist cultures tend to have independent self-concepts, whereas those from collectivist cultures tend to have interdependent self-concepts. Nevertheless, people vary in their self-concepts even within the same culture. For example, some people in a collectivist culture have relatively independent self-concepts compared to others in their culture. Given the results of Bond and Smith (1996), it seems relatively straightforward to predict that people whose self-concepts are independent will conform less than people whose self-concepts are interdependent.

Theodore Singelis (1994) developed a scale to measure the extent to which individuals' self-concepts are independent or interdependent. Sample items from this scale are presented in Know Yourself 8.1: Self-Construal Scale (p. 318). You can answer these items to find out whether your own self-concept is primarily independent or interdependent. Although we are unaware of any direct tests of correlations between scores on this scale and conformity, this hypothesis would be interesting to pursue.

**Cultural Changes Over Time.** There is another interesting way to look at the effects of culture on conformity. Within the United States, the earliest and best-known conformity experiments were conducted in the 1950s—an era in U.S. history marked by strong normative pressures to conform (e.g., in response to anti-Communist fears elicited by Senator Joseph McCarthy). But in the 1960s and 1970s, college students were more likely to express their independence and to challenge the status quo (e.g., the hippie and counterculture movements), and the 1980s and 1990s have been characterized as the "me generation," which suggests less concern about others. Can differences in the rates of conformity in social psychology experiments be observed over these time periods?

In their review of experiments using a line judgment task, Rod Bond and Peter Smith (1996) identified 97 studies that were conducted in the United States and looked at changes over time between 1950 and the early 1990s. As predicted, there was a decline in overall rates of conformity in these studies from the earliest to the most recent experiments. Thus, broad changes in the culture of the United States were mirrored in social psychological research.

# Gender Differences in Conformity

Do you think that women and men differ in their conformity to others' opinions and perceptions? If there is a gender difference, why does it occur?

Reviewers of the conformity literature have concluded that there is a small overall gender difference in conformity, such that women conform slightly more than do men (e.g., Bond & Smith, 1996; Eagly & Carli, 1981). Our choices of words,

# Know Yourself 8.1
### Self-Construal Scale

Please indicate the extent to which you agree or disagree with each of the following statements by circling the appropriate number on the answer scale.

1. It is important for me to maintain harmony within my group.

| 1 | 2 | 3 | 4 | 5 | 6 | 7 |
|---|---|---|---|---|---|---|
| Strongly disagree | Disagree | Slightly disagree | Neutral | Slightly agree | Agree | Strongly agree |

2. I am comfortable with being singled out for praise or rewards.

| 1 | 2 | 3 | 4 | 5 | 6 | 7 |
|---|---|---|---|---|---|---|
| Strongly disagree | Disagree | Slightly disagree | Neutral | Slightly agree | Agree | Strongly agree |

3. My happiness depends on the happiness of those around me.

| 1 | 2 | 3 | 4 | 5 | 6 | 7 |
|---|---|---|---|---|---|---|
| Strongly disagree | Disagree | Slightly disagree | Neutral | Slightly agree | Agree | Strongly agree |

4. I am the same person at home that I am at school.

| 1 | 2 | 3 | 4 | 5 | 6 | 7 |
|---|---|---|---|---|---|---|
| Strongly disagree | Disagree | Slightly disagree | Neutral | Slightly agree | Agree | Strongly agree |

5. I often have the feeling that my relationships with others are more important than my own accomplishments.

| 1 | 2 | 3 | 4 | 5 | 6 | 7 |
|---|---|---|---|---|---|---|
| Strongly disagree | Disagree | Slightly disagree | Neutral | Slightly agree | Agree | Strongly agree |

6. Being able to take care of myself is a primary concern for me.

| 1 | 2 | 3 | 4 | 5 | 6 | 7 |
|---|---|---|---|---|---|---|
| Strongly disagree | Disagree | Slightly disagree | Neutral | Slightly agree | Agree | Strongly agree |

7. I should take into consideration my parents' advice when making education/career plans.

| 1 | 2 | 3 | 4 | 5 | 6 | 7 |
|---|---|---|---|---|---|---|
| Strongly disagree | Disagree | Slightly disagree | Neutral | Slightly agree | Agree | Strongly agree |

8. I feel comfortable using someone's first name soon after I meet them, even when they are much older than I am.

| 1 | 2 | 3 | 4 | 5 | 6 | 7 |
|---|---|---|---|---|---|---|
| Strongly disagree | Disagree | Slightly disagree | Neutral | Slightly agree | Agree | Strongly agree |

9. It is important to me to respect decisions made by the group.

| 1 | 2 | 3 | 4 | 5 | 6 | 7 |
|---|---|---|---|---|---|---|
| Strongly disagree | Disagree | Slightly disagree | Neutral | Slightly agree | Agree | Strongly agree |

10. I enjoy being unique and different from others in many respects.

| 1 | 2 | 3 | 4 | 5 | 6 | 7 |
|---|---|---|---|---|---|---|
| Strongly disagree | Disagree | Slightly dsagree | Neutral | Slightly agree | Agree | Strongly agree |

11. I will stay in a group if they need me, even when I'm not happy with the group.

| 1 | 2 | 3 | 4 | 5 | 6 | 7 |
|---|---|---|---|---|---|---|
| Strongly disagree | Disagree | Slightly disagree | Neutral | Slightly agree | Agree | Strongly agree |

12. My personal identity, independent of others, is very important to me.

| 1 | 2 | 3 | 4 | 5 | 6 | 7 |
|---|---|---|---|---|---|---|
| Strongly disagree | Disagree | Slightly disagree | Neutral | Slightly agree | Agree | Strongly agree |

**SCORING:** Add up the numbers you circled on all of the odd-numbered questions (1, 3, 5, 7, 9, and 11). This score represents the extent to which your self-concept is *interdependent:* scores can range from 6 to 42, and higher scores reflect a more interdependent self-construal. Also add up the numbers you circled on the even-numbered questions (2, 4, 6, 8, 10, and 12). This score represents the extent to which your self-concept is *independent;* scores can range from 6 to 42, and higher scores reflect a more independent self-construal. You can compare your scores for the interdependent and independent items to see whether you have predominantly one kind of self-construal.

Sample items from Singelis, T. M., "The measurement of independent and interdependent self-construals," *Personality and Social Psychology Bulletin*, 20, 580–591, Table 1, p. 585. Reprinted by permission of Sage Publications, Inc.

"small" and "slightly," are deliberate—the effect is not large, and many men conform more than many women (the distributions overlap). Various reasons have been offered for the gender difference. One suggestion is that most conformity researchers have been men, who may have been unconsciously biased toward finding greater independence among men than women (e.g., Eagly & Carli, 1981). Another suggestion is that the topics in conformity studies have typically been "masculine," with the result that women were less confident in their judgments than men and, therefore, more susceptible to social influence (e.g., Sistrunk & McDavid, 1971). A third suggestion is that women are more concerned about harmony in social relationships than are men, which makes them less willing to disagree with others (e.g., Eagly, 1978).

All of these possibilities are plausible, but another important qualification is that the gender difference in conformity appears only when participants' responses are public—that is, only when their responses will be communicated to other members of the group (e.g., Eagly & Chrvala, 1986; Eagly, Wood, & Fishbaugh, 1981). When responses are *private,* women do *not* conform more than men, but when responses are *public,* a gender difference often appears. This pattern of greater conformity in public suggests that women may be somewhat more susceptible to *normative influence* than men. Why would a gender difference in susceptibility to normative influence exist? Perhaps women's historically disadvantaged status has required them to be careful about deviating from others' judgments—they have to pick and choose when to disagree (see Wood & Eagly, 2002). On average, women are physically smaller than men and often fill less powerful social roles—both of which make deviating from a group relatively risky. These power differentials may explain, at least in part, the gender difference in conformity.

# ● ● ●   Compliance: Doing As Others Want

Sometimes our behavior is influenced by direct requests from other people, a type of conformity called *compliance.* Others may ask us to lend them our lecture notes, go to a movie with them, give them money, or do some other favor for them. The requesters typically imply that we can refuse if we want to, though they would appreciate our compliance. Social psychologists have been interested in identifying factors that increase or decrease compliance with these sorts of requests and have documented an array of techniques that can be effective in getting people to act in the desired way (see Cialdini, 2001; Cialdini & Goldstein, 2004; Cialdini & Trost, 1998; Pratkanis & Aronson, 2001). We discuss six compliance techniques in this section. Some of the techniques rely on basic processes we have described in previous chapters (e.g., self-perception, dissonance, heuristics); others rely on social norms implying that compliance is the "proper" response. You may recognize some or all of these techniques, because they probably have been used by others to gain your compliance (and maybe even by you to gain others' compliance).

## The Foot-in-the-Door Technique

We mentioned the **foot-in-the-door technique** in our discussion of how cults recruit new members in Chapter 7 (see page 294). This technique refers to the fact that if you can get someone to agree to a small request, then he or she is more likely to also agree to a much larger, related request. Jonathan Freedman and Scott Fraser (1966) conducted the first demonstration of this technique. These researchers went door-to-door to homeowners and asked if the residents would be

**foot-in-the-door technique**

*a strategy to increase compliance, based on the fact that agreement with a small request increases the likelihood of agreement with a subsequent larger request*

Complying with a small request, such as signing a petition, increases the chances that someone will also comply with a larger request.

willing to have a large "Drive Carefully" sign installed in their front yards. The residents were shown a picture of another home with a poorly lettered sign obstructing much of the home's front. This was the large request—the one to which compliance was ultimately sought. When the large request was made without any prior contact, only 16% of homeowners agreed. But other residents were first contacted and asked a much smaller request, such as signing a petition or posting a small sign in their windows. When the larger request was then made two weeks later, more than 55% of the residents agreed to it. Thus, the initial contact and small request (the foot in the door) dramatically increased compliance. The foot-in-the-door effect has been replicated many times and in many contexts (see Burger, 1999), including the Internet (Guéguen & Jacob, 2001). It is probably one of the most common compliance techniques in everyday life.

Why does the foot-in-the-door technique work? What psychological mechanisms explain why agreement to a small request increases the likelihood of subsequent agreement to a larger request? Researchers have focused on two, related processes: self-perception and consistency.

**Self-Perception Processes.** We introduced *self-perception theory* in Chapter 4 (see page 132) and referred to it again briefly in Chapters 6 and 7. Daryl Bem (1972) hypothesized that people sometimes infer their internal states, such as attitudes and emotions, from their behavior and the situation in which the behavior occurred. How does self-perception relate to the foot-in-the-door technique? When people agree to an initial, small request, they may engage in a self-perception process whereby they label themselves as "helpful," because they willingly complied with the request. Therefore, when the second request is made, these individuals are more likely to agree because, after all, *they are helpful people*—a label that might not have existed, or not have been as prominent in their minds, if they had not agreed to the first request. Thus, the initial request stimulated a self-perception of helpfulness, which subsequently increased compliance with the second request (Beaman, Cole, Preston, Klentz, & Steblay, 1983; Burger, 1999; Dolinski, 2000; but see Gorassini & Olson, 1995).

**Consistency Processes.** A second process potentially involved in the foot-in-the-door technique is a desire for consistency. In the preceding chapter, we described *dissonance theory* (see page 251). Leon Festinger (1957) hypothesized that people want their attitudes and behaviors to be consistent with one another and are distressed by inconsistencies. We also mentioned impression management theory (see page 262), which postulates that people want to *appear* consistent to others and are embarrassed by public inconsistencies. Both of these motivations (to *be* consistent and to *appear* consistent) could contribute to the foot-in-the-door technique. After agreeing to an initial request, even a small one, people may feel that refusing a second, related request would be (or would appear) inconsistent (see Burger, 1999; Greenwald, Carnot, Beach, & Young, 1987).

**Individual Differences in Preferences for Consistency (PFC).** In Chapter 7, we presented the *preference for consistency scale,* developed by Robert Cialdini, Melanie Trost, and Jason Newsom (1995), in Know Yourself 7.1 (see page 266). People who score high on this scale agree with statements such as "I want to be described by others as a stable, predictable person" and "I make an effort to appear consistent to others." We also mentioned in Chapter 7 that people who score high in PFC exhibit stronger dissonance effects than do people who score low in PFC.

If the foot-in-the-door technique is caused, at least in part, by a desire for consistency, then people who score high in PFC may be more susceptible to the technique than people who score low in PFC. In fact, this is exactly what Cialdini et al. (1995) found in an experiment using the foot-in-the-door technique (see also Guadagno, Asher, Demaine, & Cialdini, 2001).

The role of desire for consistency in making people susceptible to the foot-in-the-door technique was also supported in a study of age-related changes. Nancy Eisenberg, Robert Cialdini, Heather McCreath, and Rita Shell (1987) tried a foot-in-the-door procedure with groups of kindergarten, second-grade, and fifth-grade children. The kindergartners were immune to the technique, but the fifth graders were just as susceptible as adults. The second graders were somewhere in between—beginning to show signs of susceptibility, but less susceptible than the fifth graders. Additional data collected by Eisenberg et al. showed that the procedure was not effective until grade 5 because it was only then that children understood that people possess traits that are stable over time. How can a child desire consistency if he or she does not even recognize that traits are stable? Also, just as Cialdini et al. (1995) found with college students, Eisenberg et al. found that the second and fifth graders who were most susceptible were those who expressed a stronger preference for personal consistency.

# The Door-in-the-Face Technique

Robert Cialdini and his coworkers (Cialdini, Vincent, Lewis, Catalan, Wheeler, & Darby, 1975) wondered if the *opposite* of the foot-in-the-door technique might also, ironically, increase compliance with a second request. The **door-in-the-face technique** begins by making a very *large* request—one that is sure to be *turned down.* Once denied, the request is then followed by a *smaller* request—the one to which compliance is ultimately sought. The expectation is that these individuals, who have turned down one request, will be more likely to agree to a second request (we will explain why later!).

For example, in one study (Cialdini et al., 1975, Experiment 1), students were approached on a college campus and asked if they would be willing to accompany a group of juvenile delinquents on a two-hour trip to the zoo. For some students, this was the only request they received; as expected, most people declined (only 16% agreed). For other students, this request had been preceded

**door-in-the-face technique**
*a strategy to increase compliance, based on the fact that refusal of a large request increases the likelihood of agreement with a subsequent smaller request*

*"Excuse me, sir, would you be willing to volunteer four hours of your time at a homeless shelter next Saturday afternoon?"*

by an even *larger* request: would they be willing to serve as a counselor to juvenile delinquents for at least two years? *Nobody* agreed to this initial large request. Yet when the large request was followed by the smaller request, fully 50% of the students agreed to accompany the group on a two-hour trip to the zoo. Thus, refusing a large request increased compliance with a smaller (but, in this case, still quite substantial) request.

How does the door-in-the-face technique work? It cannot be via self-perception or consistency processes (which contribute to the foot-in-the-door technique), because these processes would operate to make people who decline the first request *less* likely to agree to the second request as well. What, then, causes greater compliance after a refusal? Cialdini and his colleagues (1975) proposed that a critical factor is the **norm of reciprocity.** Before we explain how this norm may account for the door-in-the-face technique, we need to define the norm itself: the norm of reciprocity is that we should reciprocate (give back in return) favors done for us. For example, if someone invites us to dinner, lends us money, or helps us in some other way, we should return the favor. You may have had the experience of receiving a birthday gift from someone and thinking, "Oops, I didn't give *him* (or her) a gift on his (or her) birthday." Did you feel guilty? If so, the norm of reciprocity may explain why: you know that if you received a gift, then you should have given a gift. The norm of reciprocity is very strong in North America and appears to exist to some extent in most cultures around the world (Gouldner, 1960).

How does the norm of reciprocity explain the door-in-the-face technique? Cialdini et al. (1975) suggested that when someone presents a second, smaller request following the refusal of a larger request, this second request may be seen as a *concession* on his or her part—a compromise in response to the initial refusal: "Well, then, would you at least be willing to . . . ?" Admittedly, this notion of a concession by the requester is rather illogical, because the target did not *ask* him or her to make the first request! Nevertheless, the target is susceptible to seeing the second request as a compromise on the requester's part. Therefore, given that the requester has made a concession by lowering the demand, the least the target can do is make a concession in return (reciprocity); the most obvious concession would be to agree to the smaller request, which produces the door-in-the-face effect.

To get the door-in-the-face technique to work, the initial request must be large enough that most people will decline it, but it cannot be so outrageous that people consider it illegitimate (Schwarzwald, Raz, & Zvibel, 1979). If the initial request is illegitimate, then the requester will simply be ignored or dismissed. Also, the second request must be relatively close in time to the declined request, presumably because a long delay eliminates the perception that the two requests are connected—which is necessary if the second request is to be interpreted as a concession or compromise (Cann, Sherman, & Elkes, 1975).

## The Free-Gift Technique

It is possible to take advantage of the norm of reciprocity in a more straightforward way than the door-in-the-face technique. Specifically, *giving a small gift* to someone, or *doing a small favor* for someone, will make him or her feel indebted, which should increase willingness to comply with a subsequent request. A real-life example of this **free-gift technique** procedure comes from charities, which often mail small unsolicited gifts to potential donors, such as address labels, greeting cards, or calendars. The cover letter usually says

**norm of reciprocity**

*the principle that we should give back in return any favors that are done for us*

**free-gift technique**

*a strategy to increase compliance, based on the fact that giving someone a small gift increases the likelihood of agreement with a subsequent request*

Giving someone a small, free gift makes it more likely that her or she will then reciprocate by donating some money in return.

that the gift is unconditional, but "a donation would certainly be appreciated." Recipients often feel enough pressure to reciprocate that they make a donation they would not have made if the gift had not been received. "Free gift," indeed.

Most of us can probably think of times when we have done a favor for someone we will need in the near future. Buying a drink for a friend before asking him or her to help you move might be an example. An experiment reported by Dennis Regan (1971) illustrated how the free-gift technique can be used to gain compliance. The real participants in this study were college students paired with another student, who was actually an accomplice of the experimenter. In the "favor" condition of the experiment, the confederate went to get a soda and returned with an extra one for the unsuspecting student. In the "no favor" condition, the confederate left the room for the same amount of time but returned with nothing. When the main part of the study was over, the confederate asked the naïve student to purchase some raffle tickets. Presumably feeling a need to return the earlier favor of a free soda, students in the favor condition responded by purchasing nearly twice as many raffle tickets as did students in the no favor condition (for a related compliance technique, see Horvitz & Pratkanis, 2002).

## The Low-Ball Technique

Imagine yourself in the showroom of a car dealership. You have just made the deal of your life: a great car, all the features you want, and at a bargain price. As the paperwork is being prepared, you are imagining yourself driving home in that new car. Then the salesperson returns with some bad news. It seems the manager will not allow the deal to go through, because the dealership would be losing just too much money. You were so close to having that car. But, for another $1000, the car can still be yours! You decide to go through with it—what's another thousand dollars? If you have fallen for this trick of the compliance trade, you have been the victim of the **low-ball technique**. The salesperson may never have intended to sell the car for the lower price and probably did not go to see the manager while you sat and waited.

The low-ball technique involves offering something at a given price and then raising the price after the individual agrees to the purchase. In an experimental demonstration of low-balling, college students were called on the telephone to be scheduled for participation in a psychology experiment (Cialdini, Cacioppo, Bassett, & Miller, 1978). Students in the control condition were told, right up front, that the experiment would need to be scheduled for 7:00 A.M. Even for that early time of day, 31% made the appointment and 24% actually showed up. In the low-ball condition, students were asked if they would agree to participate, but they were not told at what time. Only after they agreed were they told the time of day. Among these students, 56% made the appointment and 53% showed up at the designated time and place.

Why does the low-ball technique work? One process may be a desire for consistency, such that people want to act consistently with their initial decision, or perhaps fear that they would look inconsistent if they did not carry through with the decision. Another, probably stronger component may be *postdecisional dissonance* produced by the commitment. We explained in Chapter 7 that postdecisional dissonance leads to more favorable evaluations of the chosen alternative (see page 259). To continue with the car example of the low-ball technique, when people decide to buy a particular car and

**low-ball technique**

*a strategy to increase compliance, in which something is offered at a given price, but then, after agreement, the price is increased*

The *low-ball technique* involves offering something at a given price and then raising the price after the individual agrees to the purchase.

Stores often try to utilize the *scarcity technique.*

**scarcity technique**

*a strategy to increase the attractiveness of a product by making it appear rare or temporary*

then go through the process of negotiating a price with the salesperson, they have made a private and public commitment to the car (see Burger & Cornelius, 2003). To justify this choice and commitment to themselves, people are likely to enhance their evaluation of the car. Thus, when the salesperson returns with the bad news, the purchaser now has an even more favorable attitude toward the car than he or she did before the negotiations. Hence, he or she is more likely to follow through on the purchase at the higher price.

The effectiveness of the low-ball technique is not limited to car sales and appointments for experiments. Among other applications, modified low-ball techniques have been shown to be successful in raising money for a museum (Brownstein & Katzev, 1985) and in getting people to abstain from smoking (Joule, 1987).

## The Scarcity Technique

Scarcity is a quality that sells products. An artist's works become more valuable posthumously, because no additional works will be forthcoming; parents climb all over one another trying to buy one of the few remaining samples of the latest rage for their children; and drivers line up at gas stations for blocks when there is fear of gas shortages. We discussed in the context of *reactance theory* in Chapter 7 (see page 299) that people often want what they can't have. So if people think they may not be able to get something, then, masochistically, they really want that thing! Robert Cialdini (2001) summed up this effect of scarcity very clearly: "opportunities seem more valuable to us when they are less available" (p. 205).

The **scarcity technique** relies on these positive connotations of scarcity. In fact, this technique is one of the favorite methods used by retail stores to boost sales. How many times have you heard advertising appeals like these: *Hurry, a limited time offer! Only five left at this price! This sale will not be repeated!* The implications are clear: if you don't act now, you will miss a fantastic opportunity. Manufacturers sometimes deliberately produce products in limited numbers or offer them for a limited time to inflate the price and increase demand (e.g., some Disney videos). Making a product appear to be a scarce commodity increases its perceived value.

A simple demonstration of the scarcity technique was reported by Stephen Worchel, Jerry Lee, and Akanbi Adewole (1975). People were given a chocolate chip cookie and asked to taste it and then rate it on several scales. In one condition, the cookie was taken from a jar containing 10 cookies. In another condition, the jar contained only 2 cookies, creating an experimental version of a scarce resource. Even though the cookies were all identical, they were rated as more desirable when they were taken from the 2-cookie jar than from the 10-cookie jar.

## The Liking Technique

We are more likely to comply with the requests of people we like than with the requests of people we dislike (Cialdini, 2001). This **liking technique** may not strike you as an earth-shattering revelation, but some of its implications may surprise you. Liking can be based on a variety of qualities and still exert an impact on compliance: we are more likely to be influenced by people who are physically attractive, people whom we know, people who are similar to us, and people who are trustworthy. In short, just about any source of likability or attractiveness increases a requester's success.

**liking technique**

*a strategy to increase compliance, based on the fact that people are more likely to assist others they find appealing than others they do not find appealing*

*Why* does likability increase compliance effectiveness? There are probably two main processes involved. First, we want to please and make happy people whom we like. It is rewarding to us to please them (and painful to us to displease them), so we are more likely to help them when requested to do so. Second, there is a *heuristic* that often contributes to this effect; we discussed heuristics in Chapter 3 (see page 87) and Chapter 7 (see page 271). Heuristics are simple, informal rules or shortcuts that we use to make judgments under some conditions, primarily when the decision is not terribly important. One heuristic that most of us follow is "I help people I like."

You have surely experienced the influence of this liking technique: when a friend asks a favor or when an outgoing and attractive salesperson makes a pitch, it is hard to resist. It is easier to say *no* to a stranger or to resist the suggestions of an unfriendly, dislikable salesperson. The positive effect of liking lies at the heart of several compliance-producing techniques. For example, we are more likely to comply with the request of someone who has just flattered us than of someone who has not (Drachman, DeCarufel, & Insko, 1978), even if the flattery is as simple as the other person remembering our name (Howard, Gengler, & Jain, 1995).

Liking can even come from rather fleeting and arbitrary sources and still be influential. Dariusz Dolinski, Magdalena Nawrat, and Izabela Rudak (2001) showed that very brief conversations between a confederate and a participant can increase compliance with a subsequent request. For example, in one experiment, a female college student approached other students individually in their dormitories and asked whether they would help out collecting money, books, and toys for children in an orphanage. Some participants were simply asked this request directly (after an opening "Hi!"); among this group, only 28% agreed. Other participants were exposed to a brief conversation prior to the request. Specifically, the woman asked them, "Hi! Is this session [examination period] going to be hard for you? How many exams are you taking? So, how are you feeling before the session?" Among participants exposed to this minimal conversation, 68% agreed to help out with the collections. The researchers suggested that this kind of conversation is characteristic of encounters with friends and acquaintances, so it serves as a heuristic to elicit responses like those directed to friends and acquaintances (see also Burger, Soroka, Gonzago, Murphy, & Somervell, 2001).

In another set of studies, Jerry Burger and his colleagues (Burger, Messian, Patel, del Prado, & Anderson, 2004) showed that college students were more likely to comply with another student's request (either for feedback on an essay or for money for a charity) when they shared a birthday, or a first name, or a "fingerprint type" with the student than when they did not have these coincidental similarities. In each study, the shared feature approximately doubled the rate of compliance or the size of donations. Taken together, these studies suggest that relatively minor manipulations of liking can have very substantial effects on compliance.

We have described six techniques that increase the likelihood that people will comply with another person's request. These techniques are used systematically by compliance professionals (salespersons, advertisers, real estate agents, etc.) and haphazardly by most of the rest of us. By studying the techniques—summarized in the Concept Review on page 326—we can arm ourselves against unwanted influence by watching for telltale signs of the techniques.

One unfortunate consequence of conformity and compliance pressure can be unhealthy behaviors, including alcohol, drug, and tobacco use. Exposure to these behaviors is an inevitable part of young people's lives, and the extent to which the exposure has a negative impact depends, at least in part, on the individuals' ability to resist compliance pressure. We discuss this issue in Social Psychology in Your Life: Alcohol, Drug, and Tobacco Use (p. 327).

## CONCEPT REVIEW
### Compliance Techniques

| Technique | Description | Example |
|---|---|---|
| Foot-in-the-door technique | Agreeing to a small request increases the likelihood of agreeing to a second, larger request. | A struggling student asks a more talented classmate to explain something from the class, and then asks if the classmate would be willing to study together regularly. |
| Door-in-the-face technique | Refusing a large request increases the likelihood of agreeing to a second, smaller request. | Someone asks to borrow $100, then reduces the request to $20 after the first request is refused. |
| Free-gift technique | Receiving a small gift increases the likelihood of agreeing to a subsequent request. | A charity send free address labels to potential donors with a request for a contribution. |
| Low-ball technique | Agreeing to purchase something at a given price increases the likelihood of agreeing to purchase it at higher price. | A car salesperson offers a car at a good price but is then "forced" by the "manager" to raise the price after the customer has agreed to the initial offer. |
| Scarcity technique | Making a product appear rare or temporary increases its attractiveness. | A store advertises a "limited time offer" for a product. |
| Liking technique | People are more likely to help others whom they like. | A salesperson flatters a customer to appear likable. |

  # Obedience: Doing As Others Command

*Obedience* refers to conformity that results from another person's command or order (i.e., failing to obey was not presented as an option). We are taught from an early age to obey the commands of our parents. We learn quickly that disobedience can be costly—the withdrawal of rewards, or even punishment. By the age of 3 or 4, most children also know that police officers and doctors have special authority status, and it is best to obey their instructions. By the time we enter formal schooling environments (at the ripe old of age of 5 or 6), most of us already know that the teacher is in command and obedience is expected.

**norm of obedience to authority**

*the principle that we should obey legitimate authorities*

The **norm of obedience to authority** refers to people's knowledge that legitimate authorities should be obeyed. This norm is powerful enough in our society that just the trappings of authority can be sufficient to produce obedience. For instance, when passersby on a street were randomly approached and instructed to give a dime to a stranger, obedience was much greater when the individual was wearing the uniform of a security guard than when the same individual was wearing street clothes (Bickman, 1974).

It is easy to see how the trappings of authority can be used to extract obedience to small demands. It is also understandable that real authority typically elicits obedience. After all, people typically occupy positions of authority for a reason. Police officers are authorized by society to keep the peace, doctors have special knowledge and skills to treat disease, and teachers are assigned the responsibility of guiding and training our children. An authority structure is especially important in the military, where soldiers are thoroughly trained to obey the orders of a superior officer.

# Social Psychology in Your Life    *Alcohol, Drug, and Tobacco Use*

Do you smoke cigarettes? Do you drink alcohol? Have you ever tried marijuana? What about your friends? Do any of them have a substance abuse problem?

Chances are good that by late adolescence, most people have used alcohol, tobacco, or marijuana. Think about the social conditions that foster these behaviors among young people. Very often, they involve social influence processes, such as conformity pressure and compliance techniques (Cohen & Fromme, 2002). People may go along with others to fit in, to be cool—because others are doing it. When the basic mechanisms of social influence are understood, it is not so surprising or puzzling that many young adults use or experiment with alcohol, drugs, or tobacco.

How, then, can we prevent people from getting involved with these substances? Historically, most prevention campaigns have used a combination of information and fear to curb substance abuse. As we discussed in the preceding chapter, fear appeals can be effective if they convince listeners that they are personally susceptible to a problem. But it is often difficult to convince young people that they may develop substance abuse problems. Also, information and fear campaigns do not teach people any skills for resisting conformity and compliance pressure. Such skills might be important when young people encounter pressure in daily activities and at social events.

Some recent prevention programs have made specific attempts to address influence resistance skills. A good example is Project ALERT (Ellickson & Bell, 1990), a middle school program that uses what we know about social norms and peer influence to prevent adolescent drug use. ALERT consists of 11 lessons in grade 7 and 3 lessons in grade 8. Teachers follow a curriculum to achieve several goals. One important goal is to change students' beliefs about drug and smoking norms. It turns out that most children overestimate the number of their peers who have used drugs and cigarettes, and overestimate the number who are favorable toward drug use and smoking. By providing accurate information, the program helps students realize that there is substantial social support for *not* using drugs and cigarettes. A second goal of the ALERT program is to provide specific skills to help young people resist conformity pressure. For example, students are helped to identify pro-drug pressures from peers, the media, and even parents (e.g., who might model cigarette or alcohol use). Students also discuss and rehearse ways to respond to these pressures. Small group activities are an important component of this program, as opposed to lectures.

A large-scale evaluation of Project ALERT was reported by Phyllis Ellickson, Daniel McCaffrey, Bonnie Ghosh-Dastidar, and Douglas Longshore (2003). Forty-eight clusters of middle schools and high schools in South Dakota were assigned randomly to the ALERT program or a control condition. More than 4,000 students

Conformity pressure sometimes induces young adults to smoke.

in Grade 7 participated in the study. Before the program began, the experimental and control students were equivalent in alcohol, cigarette, and marijuana usage.

Eighteen months later, the students were surveyed again. The results were dramatic: students who had participated in the ALERT program reported substantially less substance use. Specifically, ALERT participants were significantly less likely to have used cigarettes, to have used marijuana, and to have *misused* alcohol (e.g., getting sick, binge drinking). The reductions in these outcome measures ranged from 19% to 39%, which represent major reductions. The focus on providing social skills for resisting influence appeared to work; presumably, when students subsequently encountered conformity pressure, they were better able to withstand it.

---

So it is a good thing that we usually comply with the requests and obey the commands of legitimate authorities. Much of our social structure depends on respect and influence being given to authority figures. At the same time, however, our willingness to obey authorities may create a vulnerability to *destructive* social influence. What if a person of authority commands you to do something that conflicts with other important and valued goals? Suppose, for example, that an authority insists that you cause harm to another person. Would you obey? The norm of obedience to authority would press you to obey. But at the same time, you are not the kind of person who would deliberately cause harm to another, which would push you away from obedience. Which force would win in the end? When Stanley Milgram put this question to experimental test, the results were both surprising and disturbing.

## Milgram's Obedience Studies

We described one of Milgram's obedience studies briefly in the opening of Chapter 2 on research methods. But it is necessary to go over the procedure more thoroughly here, especially because your professor may not have assigned Chapter 2 (or you may not recall the details!).

**The Basic Procedure.** Milgram (1963) devised a laboratory situation for studying obedience to authority. The goal of Milgram's obedience research was to create a setting that would be involving and realistic for the participants, but that would also permit a high degree of experimental control. Participants were recruited through advertisements in the local newspaper. When they arrived at the laboratory (at Yale University), they were greeted by an experimenter and by one other person who also arrived as a participant. In fact, the other "participant" was really the experimenter's accomplice (confederate). The experimenter explained that this was an investigation of memory and learning. One of the two participants would be assigned the role of "learner" and the other the role of "teacher." The two then drew slips of paper from a hat to determine who would be the learner and who would be the teacher. The drawing was rigged so that the naïve participant was always the teacher and the confederate was always the learner.

The experimenter went on to explain that this particular study was looking at the role of punishment in the learning process. The teacher would administer a memory test to the learner. Whenever the learner made a mistake, the teacher was to administer an electric shock. The learner was then strapped into a chair next to a wall, and electrodes were attached to his wrist.

The teacher was then taken to a different room and seated in front of a shock-generating machine. This machine was an instrument panel consisting of 30 switches in a horizontal row (see Figure 8.5). The switch at the far left was labeled "15 volts," and each successive switch was labeled in 15-volt increments, reaching "450 volts" at the far right. Verbal designations were also attached to sets of four switches—from left to right: Slight Shock, Moderate Shock, Strong Shock, Very Strong Shock, Intense Shock, Extreme Intensity Shock, and Danger: Severe Shock. The last two switches were simply labeled "XXX."

The teacher was given a "sample" shock from the 45-volt switch, which was enough to give a bit of a jolt. The teacher was instructed to administer an electric shock each time the learner made a mistake on the memory test. The key instruction was that the teacher was to move one level higher after each mistake. If the teacher expressed concern or wanted to stop at any point, the experimenter responded with a series of planned prods. The first prod was "Please continue" or "Please go on." The second prod was "The experiment requires that you continue." The third prod was "It is absolutely essential that you continue." The fourth prod was "You have no other choice, you *must* go on." These prods were always given in sequence, and only until the teacher obeyed. If the teacher still refused to go on after the fourth prod, the study was halted.

Several additional features of the laboratory setup should be mentioned. The experimenter was carefully trained to play the role of an authority. He was dressed in a gray coat, and maintained a stern (but

**FIGURE 8.5** The "shock machine" in Milgram's obedience studies

© 1965 by Stanley Milgram. From *Obedience* (film). Courtesy of Alexandra Milgram.

not mean) appearance throughout the procedure. The learner was also specially trained for the role; he was a mild-mannered and likable 47-year-old accountant (see page 32 in Chapter 2 for a photo of the learner). The study was clearly connected with Yale University—an institution generally held in very high regard. The "teachers" (the only naïve participants in the study) were recruited from the community. There were 40 of them, all male, between the ages of 20 and 50. They represented a variety of occupations and educational levels. They were paid $4.00 for their participation, but they were told that payment was solely for coming to the laboratory, and that the money was theirs to keep no matter what happened during the study.

The responses of the learner were all programmed. He gave wrong answers about 75% of the time. When the 300-volt shock level was reached, the teacher could hear a pounding on the wall, presumably from the learner banging on the wall next to his chair. The same thing happened after the 315-volt shock. After that point, the learner no longer responded to the test questions and no sounds were heard from him. The experimenter told the teacher that no answer was to be considered a wrong answer, and prodded him to continue. Although the teachers never knew it, keep in mind that the "learner" never received an electric shock. It was all an elaborate show.

**What Would You Do?** That is the basic procedure of Milgram's (1963) initial study. Imagine yourself as the teacher. How far would you go? Would you administer even a single shock? Would you go all the way to the end (30 switches)? When Milgram asked students and colleagues to predict what 100 hypothetical "teachers" would do, they agreed that only a very small percentage would go all the way to the end. They guessed that very few teachers would even go beyond the "Very Strong Shock" level (195–240 volts; switches 13–16). When Milgram (1974) asked 31 college students to predict their *own* behavior in such a study, not a single one predicted obedience to the end (to the 450-volt level). In fact, the highest prediction was to switch 14 (210 volts). On average, these students predicted that they would stop after switch 9 or 10.

**The First Study.** When Milgram (1963) did his first study, just as it has been described here, he found that 26 of the 40 teachers, or 65%, were completely obedient—they continued to press the electric shock switches all the way to the end (switch 30; 450 volts). The first point at which *any* teacher refused to go on was at switch 20 (300 volts; the last of the "Intense Shock" switches). On average, these participants playing the role of teacher gave a maximum shock corresponding to switch 27.

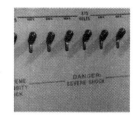

*"[Scream of agony] Let me out of here! Let me out of here! My heart's bothering me! Let me out, I tell you! Let me out! Let me out! Let me out of here! Let me out! Let me out! Let me out!"*

**Variations on the Theme.** The results of the first obedience study were surprising, to say the least. Nobody, including Milgram, expected to find obedience to that extent. The results prompted Milgram to conduct a number of variations on the original study (reported in Milgram, 1974). In the first variation (the second obedience study), more extensive vocal feedback was programmed from the learner. Remember that the original study involved pounding on the wall by the learner starting at the 300-volt shock level. In this variation, the teacher could hear protests from the learner starting at a much earlier stage. At first, the learner could be heard exclaiming in pain. The protests got louder, and at 150 volts (switch 10), the learner yelled that he wanted to stop and that his heart was bothering him. The protests grew in their intensity at each succeeding shock level. Of the 40 new "teachers" who participated in Study 2, 25 of them (62.5%) were completely obedient (going all the way to shock level 30). On average, they gave a maximum shock corresponding to switch 25.

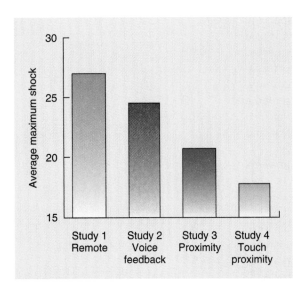

**FIGURE 8.6** Average maximum shock delivered by "teachers" in Milgram's first four obedience studies

From S. Milgram, *Obedience to Authority: An Experimental View,* p. 36. Copyright © 1974 by Stanley Milgrim. Reprinted by permission of HarperCollins Publishers.

Lyrics from Peter Gabriel's song "We Do What We're Told (Milgram's 37)."

In a third study, the learner was moved into closer proximity of the teacher. Instead of being seated in an adjacent room, the learner was seated in the same room. Forty more "teachers" participated; 16 of them (40%) were fully obedient. The average maximum shock in this study was switch 21. In a fourth study, the teacher was required to hold the learner's hand down on a plate to receive the electric shock. Forty more "teachers" were tested; 12 of them (30%) went all the way to shock level 30, with an average maximum shock of switch 18.

The results of the first four studies are graphed in Figure 8.6, which shows how the average maximum shock decreased across the studies. Even though obedience was still very high in the fourth study, it was clearly decreasing as the learner was brought into closer and closer proximity of the teacher (Milgram, 1974). Milgram continued to explore variations on the basic theme. He moved the laboratory away from Yale University, he changed the personnel who played the roles of learner and experimenter, and he had women participate as teachers. Still, the average maximum shock rarely went lower than switch number 20.

In another variation of the study (Milgram, 1974), the naïve participant acted as one of the "teachers," but was not responsible for actually pressing the shock-generating switch. Instead, another teacher (actually the experimenter's confederate) was assigned the job of pressing the switches. The naïve teachers were in a position to halt the procedure by refusing to go on at any point. Although they were not pressing the switches themselves, they would be passively permitting a peer to cause harm by simply continuing to participate as an assistant. And that's precisely what happened. Out of 40 teachers, 37 of them permitted the other teacher to continue all the way to switch number 30. Being one step removed from the act itself, almost all of the naïve teachers were willing to serve as accessories to the act. This result was so disturbing that it moved singer/songwriter Peter Gabriel to record "We Do What We're Told" (subtitled "Milgram's 37").

**What Makes Obedience Go Away?** The results of the obedience studies were very troubling. It is hard to believe that people would obey authority to the extent of causing physical harm to another person for no good reason. Is it possible that people are naturally aggressive, and that the teachers were just taking the opportunity to unleash their aggressive urges? As it turns out, this is probably not a valid explanation for the results. When Milgram (1974) allowed the teachers to *select their own shock level* (rather than prodding them to continue up the scale), remarkably little "aggression" was observed. Only 1 teacher (out of 40) ever pushed switch number 30. Almost all of them stayed below switch number 10, and on average they gave a maximum shock corresponding to switch number 6. So, clearly, people would prefer *not* to administer intense shocks to another person.

What, then, can be done to liberate people from the destructive influence of the authority? In one variation on the basic procedure (Milgram, 1974), two experimenters were in charge. Both had all the trappings of authority, and both proceeded in complete agreement until the teacher got to switch number 10. At that point, one of the experimenters delivered the standard prod for the teacher to continue. But the other experimenter instructed the teacher to stop. Of the 20 teachers in this study, 1 had stopped just before the disagreement (at switch 9), 18 refused to continue precisely at the point of the experimenters' disagreement (switch 10), and the 1 remaining teacher refused to continue after switch 11. At last, a procedure was identified that effectively halted teachers along the escalating scale of switches. In an important sense, however, this was still a case of obedience to authority—only now, teachers were able to choose which of two equal authorities they would obey. Their choice was the authority who commanded them to stop.

# The Legacy of the Obedience Studies

Milgram's studies have had a profound influence. Within the field of social psychology, they stirred an intense debate about research ethics, and led ultimately to the enactment of federal regulations regarding the treatment of human participants in research. Beyond the field of social psychology, the studies became widely known and widely cited—perhaps more than any other program of research in psychology (Miller, 1986). The research has been extended in many directions (Miller, 1986), and it has been used to help understand crimes of obedience (e.g., Kelman & Hamilton, 1989).

**Beyond the Original Obedience Studies.** Several studies have replicated or extended the basic obedience study (e.g., Blass, 1991; Miller, 1986). Studies have been conducted with participants in other countries, with children, and with other procedural variations. The same basic result is consistently obtained: many people readily accept the influence of an authority, even when that means causing potential harm to another person. One interesting application of this concept has been to the nurse–physician relationship. Several studies have shown that nurses will often carry out the orders of a physician even when there is good reason to believe that potential harm could come to the patient (Hofling, Brotzman, Dalrymple, Graves, & Pierce, 1966; Krackow & Blass, 1995).

**Obedience in Society: How Far Can We Generalize?** In Milgram's (1963) original paper, he motivated the study of obedience to authority by noting how obedience pressures could be implicated in the atrocities committed by German soldiers under the Nazi regime. In the very first paragraph of his paper, Milgram noted the following:

> Gas chambers were built, death camps were guarded, daily quotas of corpses were produced with the same efficiency as the manufacture of appliances. These inhumane policies may have originated in the mind of a single person, but they could only be carried out on a massive scale if a very large number of persons obeyed orders. (p. 371)

The experimental analysis of obedience has been used to understand other tragic events and crimes, including the My Lai massacre, the Watergate scandal, and the Iran–Contra affair (see Kelman & Hamilton, 1989). Are such extensions and applications valid? After all, the laboratory version of obedience developed by Milgram is a far cry from the settings and the social conditions that were operating at the time of such historical incidents. Indeed, critics of Milgram's approach (e.g., Baumrind, 1964) have argued that there is only a very weak parallel, at best. In reply, Milgram (1964) pointed out that the events of the Holocaust provided the *incentive* to begin a formal analysis of obedience to authority; the intent was not, nor could it be, to re-create those events in the laboratory.

Yet sometimes events in the news remind us of Milgram's findings. The obedience observed in Jonestown in 1978, when more than 900 average citizens committed suicide by drinking poison, was shocking. How did Jim Jones exert such influence? Many followers regarded him as a prophet whose authority was indisputable. Notwithstanding these beliefs, it remains difficult to comprehend why there was almost no discussion of, or resistance to, his order.

American soldiers humiliated and tortured Iraqi prisoners at the Abu Ghraib Prison in Iraq.

More recently, in 2004 during the Iraq war, photos became public of American military guards humiliating and torturing Iraqi prisoners at Abu Ghraib Prison in Baghdad. People around the world were appalled by the photos—how could these young men and women have engaged in such practices? Abuse of prisoners is something done by other, immoral armies, not the United States military. But there was no possible denial—the photos were unambiguous. Why did these actions occur? Were the individuals in the photos simply following orders from higher up? Some of the soldiers claimed that, indeed, they were just following orders. Other guards indicated that they believed the end justified the means: the goal of obtaining information from the prisoners (a goal that was certainly shared by commanding officers) justified extreme actions, including humiliation, sleep deprivation, and torture. Whatever the precise causes (which probably differed across soldiers), it is clear that the setting in the prison elicited harmful, degrading actions from ordinary young American men and women.

Thus, Milgram's research probably does inform us about destructive obedience in our society. His studies documented that people are more obedient to authority than most of us realize. At the same time, his research identified some of the factors that influence obedience, including the proximity of the victim, the actions of other people in the setting, and situational cues in the immediate environment (e.g., the labels on the shock generator). His participants were not blindly obedient—their actions were affected by relevant factors around them (although the overall level of obedience was higher than we might wish).

One perspective on Milgram's research that is not always recognized is that participants were placed in a situation that involved a slow escalation of aggression, which made it difficult for them to stop at any particular point. If a teacher had delivered a shock of 150 volts, why would a shock of 165 volts be immoral? And if the teacher had delivered a shock of 165 volts, why would a shock of 180 volts be immoral? And so on, up the scale on the shock generator, until teachers found themselves administering intense shocks. Thus, participants became slowly committed to their role in the study, once they began administering shock after the learner's first error. This escalating commitment made a later decision to disobey very difficult. Perhaps Milgram's studies offer a warning that resistance to unethical commands must begin immediately, before people commit themselves in any way to their role in the setting.

**The Question of Research Ethics.** A serious criticism leveled against Milgram's obedience studies was that they involved the unethical treatment of human participants in psychological research (Baumrind, 1964; Kelman, 1967). The concern was that naïve participants were brought into a situation that could cause them serious emotional harm, without being informed at the outset of what they might experience. Milgram (1964) defended the research, and pointed out that the vast majority of participants indicated afterwards that they were glad to have been in the study. A follow-up interview, conducted one year after the study, suggested that none of the participants had suffered any psychological harm.

Some researchers have used active role-playing as a way of reducing ethical concerns about research on obedience (e.g., Meeus & Raaijmakers, 1995). In role-playing studies, participants are placed in a full physical replication of the original obedience studies, but they know that shocks are not being administered and the setting is staged. They are instructed to act as they would if the situation were real. These role-playing studies have produced results that are quite similar to the original studies.

The debate about ethics stimulated by Milgram's research ultimately contributed to the enactment of federal regulations governing the treatment of human participants in research. These regulations require institutions receiving federal research grants to establish Institutional Review Boards (IRBs) to review all institutional research involving human participants (see Chapter 2, page 59). The purpose of the review is to determine that risks to participants are minimized and are reasonable in relation to any anticipated benefits, that selection of participants is equitable, that truly informed consent is obtained, and that adequate provisions are made to protect the safety and privacy of participants and to maintain the confidentiality of data (Wiggins, 2000).

In the next, concluding section of the chapter, we turn from the specifics of conformity, compliance, and obedience to a broader perspective, identifying some of the underlying processes common to all of these behaviors. Researchers are interested in these general mechanisms in order to develop models of conformity that have the widest possible application.

# General Mechanisms Underlying Conformity, Compliance, and Obedience

Research on social influence has produced a remarkable array of results. Social psychologists now know some of the factors that produce conformity to others' actions, can identify numerous techniques that are effective in getting people to comply with requests, and understand something about humans' vulnerability to authority. But are there general processes or motivations that apply to all of these domains? In the following pages, we describe three perspectives that have some applicability to conformity, compliance, and obedience.

## Informational and Normative Influence: Accuracy and Social Motivation

The first perspective comes from the distinction we introduced at the beginning of the chapter between informational influence and normative influence. These two types of influence represent different underlying motivations.

**Accuracy Motivation.** People are motivated to have a correct understanding of events in the world, to make accurate decisions, and generally to be competent in dealing with their environments. One important way that people achieve these accuracy goals is by observing, copying, or interrogating others. For example, by engaging in social comparison, people can evaluate their beliefs and modify them, if necessary, to be more similar to others' beliefs. By watching and imitating experts, people can benefit from their experience and knowledge. When people encounter ambiguous tasks like the one in Sherif's studies, they can look to others for guidance about the appropriate response.

All of these examples refer to *informational influence* from other people. That is, people are an important source of information about the world, and it often makes sense to conform to their actions or attitudes.

**Social Motivation.** Part of being human is a desire to establish and maintain social relationships. Indeed, to survive and thrive, humans *need* other people; we are inherently social creatures. This need for affiliation and interpersonal relationships underlies, at least in part, conformity, compliance, and obedience. Even when

Ostracism from a group is an extremely painful experience.

the nature of a relationship with another person is minimal, such as the relationships between participants in a study (e.g., between the various group members in Asch's experiments), people try to be agreeable and to make others like them. You may recall from our discussion of *impression management* in Chapter 4 that one *self-presentation goal* that is almost always active in people's minds is to appear likable, even to strangers (see pages 149–150). Conforming to others' opinions and judgments is one way to get them to like us.

These examples refer to *normative influence* from others. That is, people want to be liked and respected by others, and conformity sometimes represents individuals' attempts to maintain positive relationships or avoid unpleasant interactions.

The connections between informational/normative influence and accuracy/social motivation are summarized in the accompanying Concept Review.

The importance of social attachments and positive interpersonal relationships is made very clear by the devastating psychological effects of *ostracism*—the exclusion of someone from a group (Gruter & Masters, 1986). Ostracism has been shown to produce a range of negative reactions, including depression, anxiety, and feelings of helplessness (e.g., Leary, 1990; Sommer, Williams, Ciarocco, & Baumeister, 2001). Ostracism, or the threat of ostracism, also increases individuals' conformity to the norms of the group: people try to show their loyalty to the group by conforming to the actions and attitudes of group members, hoping to avoid exclusion (e.g., Baumeister & Leary, 1995; Leary & Baumeister, 2000; Rudman & Fairchild, 2004; Williams, Cheung, & Choi, 2000).

More subtle evidence suggesting that it can be painful to disagree with others was reported by John Bassili (2003). Bassili summarized the results of four attitude surveys that were conducted over the telephone. Respondents were asked to state their position on a variety of social issues, such as "Do you think that large companies should have quotas to ensure a fixed percentage of women are hired, or should women get no special treatment?" and "Do you think that it should be against the law to write or speak in a way that promotes hatred toward a particular racial or religious group?" Participants' responses were recorded, as well as the *speed* of each response (reaction time). Bassili found that people who held the *more* common view answered significantly more quickly, on average, than did people who held the *less* common view on 20 of the 36 items, whereas the reverse was true (significantly faster responses by people who held the *less* common view) on only 2 of the

## CONCEPT REVIEW
### *Informational/Normative Influence and Accuracy/Social Motivation*

| Concept | Description | Interconnections |
|---|---|---|
| Informational influence | Influence from other people that derives from their serving as sources of information | Often caused by accuracy motivation |
| Normative influence | Influence from other people that derives from perceptions of what behavior is considered proper and improper | Often caused by social motivation |
| Accuracy motivation | The desire to make accurate judgments and decisions | One important source of informational influence |
| Social motivation | The desire to establish and maintain social relationships | One important source of normative influence |

36 items (the other 14 items showed no significant differences in either direction). For instance, on the quota question, 39% of respondents thought that quotas were a good idea, whereas 58% supported no quotas (3% had no opinion). The average response times for these groups were 5.19 seconds for the quota position (the less common view) and 4.56 seconds for the no quota position (the more common view). Similarly, response times for the hatred question differed for respondents holding different positions. In this case, 30% thought that it should *not* be against the law to promote hatred, whereas 69% thought that it should be against the law. Respondents who expressed the first position (less common view) took an average of 5.27 seconds, whereas respondents who expressed the second position (more common view) took an average of 3.27 seconds.

Why do people who hold less common views on an issue answer questions about that issue more slowly than people who hold the more common view? Bassili (2003) suggested that there is implicit pressure to conform to the more common positions in society, and people who hold less common positions feel hesitant about reporting their opinion. The possible negative responses of others inhibit those with less common views from expressing their attitudes (see also Christensen, Rothgerber, Wood, & Matz, 2004).

## Terror Management Theory

A second perspective on conformity comes from a theory with the intriguing name of **terror management theory,** which was developed primarily by Jeff Greenberg, Sheldon Solomon, and Tom Pyszczynski (Greenberg, Solomon, & Pyszczynski, 1997; Solomon, Greenberg, & Pyszczynski, 1991). Building on work in cultural anthropology (e.g., Becker, 1962), these theorists suggested that humans face a unique problem among animal species: we know that we are mortal—that, one day, we will die. This awareness of our mortality is hypothesized to be deeply threatening; in fact, it is hypothesized to arouse potentially paralyzing terror. This hypothesis may strike you as implausible, because you do not feel terror about your own mortality. But terror management theorists would say that your lack of terror is the result of protective strategies that you have been taught during socialization or have developed on your own.

How do humans control the terror caused by knowing that we will die? Terror management theorists propose that humans embrace *cultural worldviews*—cultural conceptions of reality. For instance, people take comfort in cultural belief systems (norms, religious teachings, etc.) that impose stability on the world and give meaning to their existence. Importantly, cultural worldviews also provide a sense of immortality. Some people derive from their cultural worldview a belief in *literal* immortality—they will live on after death (e.g., religious beliefs in heaven, reincarnation, afterlife, etc.); such beliefs obviously help to reduce terror about one's own physical mortality. But even without believing in literal immortality, a cultural worldview can give people a feeling of *symbolic* immortality because they know that things like their children, their valued achievements, and important social institutions will live on after their own death. This symbolic immortality is hypothesized to reduce the threat of one's own physical demise.

Terror management theory has been applied to many different topics in social psychology, including research on self-esteem, aggression, attitudes, and prejudice. The fundamental point the theory makes in each of these domains is that belief in a cultural worldview can serve the function of managing death-related anxiety. For example, prejudice and aggression against members of outgroups may protect individuals from a fear of death by confirming their own group's values and ideology. If prejudice and aggression against outgroup members do serve this function, then prejudice and aggression may be more extreme when individuals have been

**terror management theory**

*a model hypothesizing that recognition of their own mortality raises anxiety in humans, which they can reduce by affirming and conforming to their cultural worldview*

© AP/Wide World Photos/Doug Kanter

*Terror management theory* hypothesizes that thinking about our mortality arouses anxiety.

*reminded* of their own mortality—and exactly this effect has been documented in research (e.g., Greenberg, Pyszczynski, Solomon, Rosenblatt, Veeder, Kirkland, et al., 1990; Harmon-Jones, Greenberg, Solomon, & Simon, 1996).

What relevance does terror management theory have to understanding conformity? This theory hypothesizes that conformity to social values and cultural worldviews can serve to protect people from death anxiety. By conforming to a group's norms and beliefs, people show others (and perhaps convince themselves) that this cultural worldview is valid. Validating one's cultural worldview allows people to be more confident that it will live on past their own death. Thus, conformity to a group's norms and beliefs can, indirectly, provide a sense of symbolic immortality. Presumably, conformity can be in the form of copying other group members' behaviors, complying with requests from group members, or obeying the commands of group leaders.

If conformity to one's cultural worldview protects against fear of mortality, then making people aware of their mortality should heighten their commitment to, and endorsement of, cultural values. This effect has been documented in several studies. For example, Jeff Greenberg and his colleagues (Greenberg, Pyszczynski, Solomon, Simon, & Breus, 1994) induced some participants to think about their own death by answering two questions: "Please briefly describe the emotions that the thought of your own death arouses in you" and "Jot down, as specifically as you can, what you think will happen to you physically as you die and once you are physically dead." After answering these questions, participants were given two essays about the United States allegedly written by different foreign students. One essay was pro-American, focusing on freedom, opportunities, and safety, whereas the other was anti-American, focusing on economic inequities, materialism, and lack of sympathy for people. Participants then rated the authors of the essays (e.g., intelligence) and indicated their agreement with the arguments in the essay. Participants who had been induced to think about their own death rated the pro-American author much more positively than the anti-American author and agreed much more with the content of the pro-American essay than the anti-American essay; in contrast, participants in a control condition who were not induced to think about their own death were only slightly more positive about the pro-American author and essay. Presumably, when their own mortality was salient, participants wanted to reaffirm the values of American society, because this cultural worldview gave their lives meaning and provided symbolic immortality (see also Landau, Solomon, Greenberg, Cohen, Pyszczynski, Arndt, et al., 2004).

Terror management theory provides a unique perspective on conformity. It views conformity as one means to achieve a goal that people may not recognize in themselves—namely, to control the anxiety created by awareness of their own mortality. The theory does not claim that fear of death is the only cause of conformity—people may conform for other reasons as well (e.g., relying on others to make an accurate decision). Nevertheless, this approach renders understandable some instances of conformity that would otherwise seem difficult to explain.

## Social Impact Theory

Perhaps the broadest and most comprehensive attempt to explain social influence has been **social impact theory** (Latané, 1981; Tanford & Penrod, 1984). This theory conceives of social influence as being the result of *social forces* (pressures from other people) that operate on a target. The theory uses the metaphor of *physical* forces, such as light or sound, that can affect an object. The overall influence of a set of social forces depends on the forces' strength, immediacy, and number. *Strength* refers to the *intensity* of each social force, which reflects things like status, power, or credibility. Your boss can exert more influence on you than can a coworker because your boss has more power over you. *Immediacy* refers to the *closeness* of each social force, which can reflect either physical or psychological proximity. Someone standing right next to you can exert more influence than someone communicating by e-mail, because face-to-face interaction is more immediate. *Number* refers simply to the *quantity* of social forces present. Five friends trying to get you to do something can produce more influence than one friend, because there are more sources of pressure.

A schematic version of this view of social influence is shown in Figure 8.7. The amount of influence bearing on a target is a function of the strength of each source

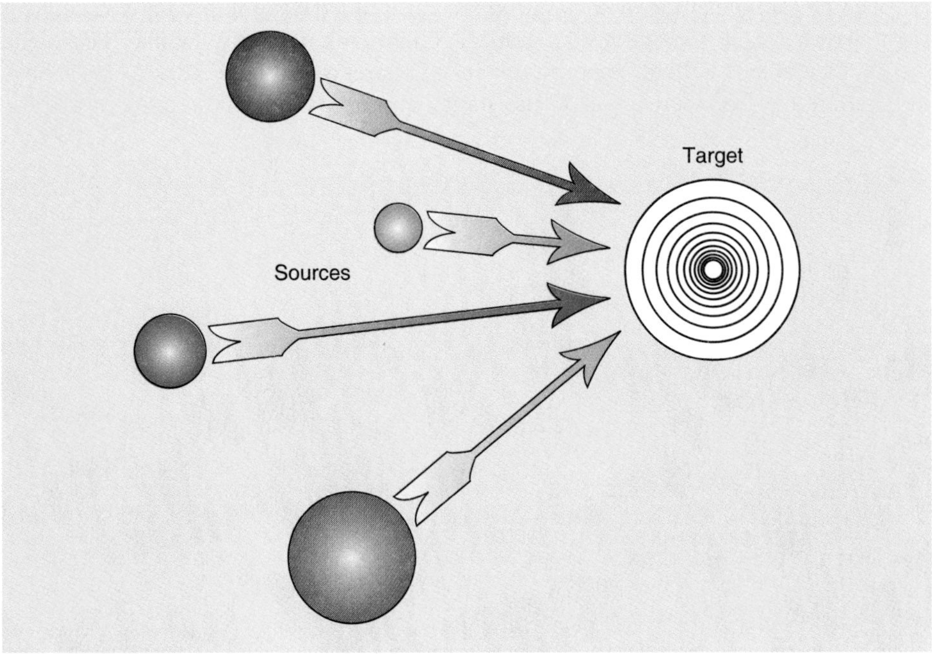

**social impact theory**
*a model that conceives of influence from other people as being the result of social forces acting on individuals, much as physical forces can affect an object*

**FIGURE 8.7** A pictorial representation of social impact theory, showing the influence of strength, immediacy, and number of sources on a target

Adapted from Latané, 1981, "The psychology of social impact," *American Psychologist*, 36, 343–356.

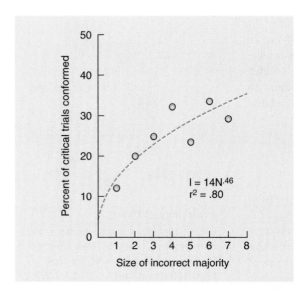

**FIGURE 8.8** Fitting the psychosocial law equation from social impact theory to the data of Gerard, Wilhelmy, and Conolley (1968)

Adapted from Latané, 1981, "The psychology of social impact," *American Psychologist*, 36, 343–356.

**psychosocial law**

*a principle in social impact theory that specifies the nature of the relation between the size of a group and its social influence. The principle predicts that as the number of social forces increases, overall social influence also increases, but at a declining rate.*

(depicted by the size of each source's circle), the immediacy of each source (depicted by the distance between each source and the target), and the total number of sources (Latané, 1981).

Mathematical models are quite rare in social psychology, because the concepts and principles in the field are usually difficult to express in quantitative terms (see Fiske, 2004). Because social impact theory views social forces as akin to physical forces, it offers formulas that specify quite precisely the relationships between (1) the strength, immediacy, and number of social forces and (2) overall social influence. These formulas can capture important features of social influence.

For example, one principle of social impact theory deals specifically with the relation between the *number* of social forces and overall social influence. The principle is called the **psychosocial law** (Latané, 1981) and expresses the relation in terms of a mathematical equation. For our purposes, the important point about the equation is that it predicts that as the *number* of social forces increases, overall social influence also increases *but at a declining rate.* That is, each additional source of influence will have a diminishing impact on overall social influence. For example, increasing the number of sources from 5 to 6 will have less impact than increasing the number from 2 to 3.

This reasoning may sound familiar to you, because it is exactly what Harold Gerard, Roland Wilhelmy, and Edward Conolley (1968) found when they investigated the effects of group size on conformity in the Asch line judgment task. We talked earlier about this experiment (see page 315), which showed that conformity increased as the size of the incorrect majority increased, but only up to a certain point. A graphical version of the findings is reproduced in Figure 8.8. In the graph, the actual results of the 1968 experiment are depicted as open circles. The dashed curve is the predicted function generated by the equation from the psychosocial law; the curve does a good job of capturing the pattern of results (Latané, 1981).

Another simple study of social influence also illustrates the predictive accuracy of the psychosocial law. Stanley Milgram, Leonard Bickman, and Leonard Berkowitz (1969) conducted a field experiment in the streets of New York City. These researchers had between 1 and 15 assistants stop on a sidewalk and begin looking

The act of looking up is contagious.

up at the sixth floor of a building. Unknown to naïve passersby, their responses were being recorded—in particular, whether they looked up as well. When even 1 confederate was looking up, 42% of the passersby also looked up. When the group of confederates was 15, 86% of the passersby looked up. But once again, with each added group member, the size of the increase in conformity diminished. These results are shown in Figure 8.9, where again the original results are depicted as open circles and the dashed curve represents the predicted function generated by the psychosocial law equation, which does an excellent job of capturing the observed data (Latané, 1981).

Social impact theory has been used to describe many of the conformity and compliance effects discussed in this chapter. Equations from the theory predict results from a range of experiments quite well. The major shortcoming is that the theory, and others like it (e.g., Tanford & Penrod, 1984), do not really *explain* what is happening inside the minds and bodies of the people who are being influenced. The equations provide a good *description* of social influence effects, but they do not tell us much about *why* social influence occurs.

It remains for future theorists to understand why the equations from social impact theory work so well and to translate them into psychological processes. Perhaps the other general mechanisms we have described—informational versus normative influence and terror management theory—will provide some of the conceptual basis for an integrative model.

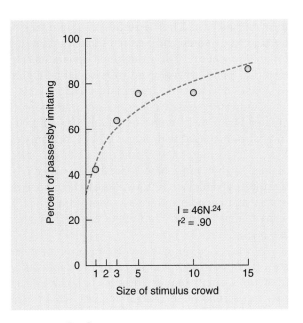

$$I = 46N^{.24}$$
$$r^2 = .90$$

**FIGURE 8.9** Fitting the psychosocial law equation from social impact theory to the data of Milgram, Bickman, and Berkowitz (1969)

Adapted from Latané, 1981, "The psychology of social impact," *American Psychologist*, 36, 343–356.

# Chapter Summary

In this chapter, we reviewed social psychological research on three kinds of social influence. **Conformity** refers to *any* change in behavior caused by another person or group. **Compliance** refers to a change in behavior that is *requested* by another person or group. **Obedience** refers to a change in behavior that is *ordered* by another person or group. Conformity is the most general of these concepts and, in fact, encompasses compliance and obedience.

Conforming behaviors happen for two principal reasons. **Informational influence** occurs when people are influenced by others because of a desire to be correct and to obtain valuable information. **Normative influence** occurs when people are influenced by others to gain rewards or avoid punishment. These kinds of influence can occur simultaneously.

People sometimes go along with the behavior of others because of **social norms**—socially defined standards of proper and improper behavior. In a series of studies, Muzafer Sherif used the **autokinetic effect** to study the emergence of norms. The autokinetic effect refers to the fact that in a darkened room, a stationary point of light will appear to move. When asked to estimate the amount of movement of the light—an ambiguous task—people are influenced by the responses of others, and norms that emerge in groups are maintained when members respond individually.

Solomon Asch studied conformity on a task in which the correct answer was obvious. Participants often conformed on a line judgment task when several experimental confederates had unanimously given the same, clearly incorrect answer. The **Crutchfield apparatus** was developed to study conformity more efficiently than using Asch's original procedure. The Crutchfield apparatus consists of an electrical panel with several rows of lights; it simulates the responses of numerous hypothetical participants.

Conformity researchers found that conformity was greater when tasks were ambiguous and difficult. Conformity also increased with larger groups, but only up to about four or five members. Studies in different cultures have yielded higher rates of conformity in collectivist cultures than in individualist cultures. Researchers have also uncovered a small gender difference, with women tending to conform somewhat more than men, but only when responses are public.

A variety of compliance techniques have been identified. The **foot-in-the-door technique** reflects that agreement to a small request results in higher rates of agreement to a subsequent, larger request. This technique may rely on self-perception processes and/or a desire for consistency. The **door-in-the-face technique** reflects that refusal of a very large request results in higher rates of agreement to a subsequent, smaller request. This technique probably relies on the **norm of reciprocity,** which is that we should reciprocate favors done for us. In the door-in-the-face circumstance, the presentation of a smaller request after refusal of the first request may be seen as a concession, which should then be reciprocated by agreeing to it. The **free-gift technique** also relies on the norm of reciprocity; it involves giving someone a small gift in order to increase the likelihood that he or she will comply with a subsequent request. The **low-ball technique** occurs when something is offered at a given price but then, after agreement, the price is increased. Even though the modified deal is less attractive, people have committed themselves to the course of action and may have engaged in postdecisional dissonance reduction. The **scarcity technique** involves making a product appear scarce or temporary to increase its attractiveness. Reactance may contribute to the effectiveness of this technique. The **liking technique** reflects the fact that we are more likely to comply with the requests of people we like than with the requests of people we dislike. This technique may rely on the fact that we want to please people we like and on the heuristic that we help people we like.

The **norm of obedience to authority** refers to people's knowledge that legitimate authorities should be obeyed. A series of studies by Stanley Milgram showed how powerful this norm is in our society. On the insistence of a person of authority (an experimenter in a white lab coat), participants were willing to administer what they believed to be painful electric shocks to an innocent victim. The rate of obedience was influenced systematically by cues in the setting (e.g., the proximity of the victim), but the overall level of obedience was unexpectedly high. These studies raised considerable awareness about people's susceptibility to authoritative commands. They also raised concerns about the ethics of psychological research and ultimately contributed to the enactment of federal regulations concerning the treatment of human participants in research.

Several general mechanisms may apply across the domains of conformity, compliance, and obedience. Informational influence, which reflects a motive to make accurate judgments, and normative influence, which reflects a motive to maintain social relationships, can be applied to all of the topics in this chapter. **Terror management theory** hypothesizes that recognition of their own mortality raises anxiety in humans, which they can reduce by conforming to the values and standards of their group—that is, their cultural worldview. **Social impact theory** conceives of social influence as being the result of social forces acting on individuals, much as physical forces can affect an object. The theory provides mathematical models of conformity and compliance. For example, the **psychosocial law** specifies the nature of the relation between the size of a group and its social influence; the principle predicts that as the number of social forces increases, overall social influence also increases, but at a declining rate. The theory has been well supported but does not really explain what is happening inside the minds of the people who are being influenced.

# Key Terms

**autokinetic effect** (310)

**compliance** (307)

**conformity** (307)

**Crutchfield apparatus** (313)

**door-in-the-face technique** (321)

**foot-in-the-door technique** (319)

**free-gift technique** (322)

**informational influence** (309)

**liking technique** (324)

**low-ball technique** (323)

**norm of obedience to authority**
   (326)

**norm of reciprocity** (322)

**normative influence** (309)

**obedience** (307)

**psychosocial law** (338)

**scarcity technique** (324)

**social impact theory** (337)

**social norm** (309)

**terror management theory** (335)

# Social Psychology Alive on the Web

## SOCIAL PSYCHOLOGY ALIVE: ONLINE LABS

To perform the following experiment and see how you compare to other students, go to Social Psychology Lab, which can be accessed through Social PsychologyNow.

- 8.1 Judging Groups

## SOCIAL PSYCHOLOGY ALIVE: QUIZZING AND PRACTICE TESTS

You can access our website directly by going to http://psychology.wadsworth.com/breckler1e/ for online quizzes, flash cards, and Internet links.

## WEBSITES OF INTEREST

- A website featuring the work of Stanley Milgram is available at http://www.stanleymilgram.com.
- A website with information about the Jonestown massacre is http://www.crimelibrary.com/notorious_murders/mass/jonestown. A more recent set of concerns was raised in a story covered by CNN at http://www.cnn.com/US/9811/18/jonestown.anniv.01 A Jonestown Memorial Fund is described at http://www.jones-town.org.
- A website with information about Project ALERT is at http://www.projectalert.com.

## INFOTRAC® COLLEGE EDITION

For additional readings, explore InfoTrac College Edition, your online library of archived journal articles and periodicals dating back 22 years. If your instructor ordered InfoTrac College Edition with this book, you can access it from your CD-ROM, or go directly to http://www.infotrac-college.com/wadsworth and use the passcode from the InfoTrac College Edition card that came with your book. For this chapter, try these search terms: *conformity, compliance, obedience, informational influence, normative influence, social norms, foot-in-the-door, door-in-the-face, low-ball, terror management, social impact theory.*

# Social Psychology Alive: The Workbook

To apply what you've learned in this chapter to the real world, go to Chapter 8 of *Social Psychology Alive: The Workbook:*

- Can a Strategy Based on Social Norms Reduce College Drinking?
- Design Your Own Persuasion Campaign
- Studying Conformity With the Crutchfield Apparatus: A Computerized Demonstration
- Are You Inclined to Comply With Others? Test Your Need for Consistency!
- Social Norms and Suicide Bombings
- The Conformity and Obedience Experiments and Research Ethics
- Reacting to Requests and Demands

# Social Psychology Alive: The Videos

To see video on the topics and experiments discussed in this chapter, you can go either to Social PsychologyNow or to the CD-ROM, if your instructor assigned either one, to the following sections:

- Just Following Orders: Obedience to Authority
- Getting What You Want: Two Compliance Strategies in Action

# To Learn More

This list contains citations to books or articles that can help you learn more. These readings are good places to start if you want to gain a deeper understanding of the topics in this chapter.

- Cialdini, R. B. (2001). *Influence: Science and practice* (4th ed.). Boston: Allyn & Bacon.
- Turner, J. C. (1991). *Social influence.* Pacific Grove, CA: Brooks/Cole.
- Milgram, S. (1974). *Obedience to authority.* New York: Harper & Row.

© Nathan Benn/CORBIS

# Stereotypes, Prejudice, and Discrimination

In the year 2000, the FBI recorded a total of 28 anti-Muslim hate crimes in the United States. In the four months following September 11, 2001, the FBI recorded more than 400 anti-Muslim hate crimes across the country: more than 10 times the number in just one-third of the time. Some of these hate crimes were deadly. Abdo Ali Ahmed was a 51-year-old owner of a convenience store, which was located across the street from his modest home in Reedley, California. On September 27, 2001, he found a threatening note on his car's windshield: "We're going to kill all you [expletive] Arabs." Two days later, while working in his store, he was shot three times at close range, near an American flag that was draped in the window. Abdo crawled from his store to a bar next door. His wife was called and came immediately; Abdo died in her arms while waiting for an ambulance to arrive. Witnesses said that a group of four teenagers was responsible for the shooting. Abdo had lived in the United States for 35 years and had eight children. The owner of the bar next to the store said that Abdo put the American flag in his window because "He wanted people to know he supported the U.S.A."

Abdo Ali Ahmed was murdered on September 27, 2001, because he was an Arab.

© AP Photo/Fresno Bee, Mark Crosse

The terrible tragedy of September 11, 2001, brought on a wave of backlash hate crimes against Muslims and Arabs in the United States (as well as people thought to be Muslims or Arabs, such as Sikhs, who wear turbans). Of course, these victims of hate crimes had nothing whatsoever to do with the terrorism. Nevertheless, some people appeared to generalize anger at Al Qaeda to hatred of all Muslims.

This sort of animosity based simply on belonging to a group is called **prejudice.** Prejudice can be formally defined as a negative attitude toward members of a group, which is often very strongly held. The term derives from the fact that the perceiver "prejudges" the targets (hence, prejudice), disliking them based only on their group membership. Although it is possible to be positively prejudiced toward a group (e.g., to prejudge members of one's own ethnic group favorably), social psychologists have been interested in understanding negative prejudice. In this chapter, we will use the term prejudice to refer specifically to a negative attitude toward members of a group.

One possible consequence of prejudice is negative, harmful behavior (e.g., aggression) toward people based on their group membership. **Discrimination** is the term used to refer to such actions. Whereas prejudice is an attitude, discrimination is a behavior. Again, although positive discrimination can occur (sometimes called reverse discrimination), such as giving favored treatment to members of one's own ethnic group, social psychologists have focused on harmful behavior toward members of a group, and, in this chapter, we will use the term in this specific manner. Negative treatment can range from relatively mundane actions such as avoiding or not speaking to members of a group all the way to horrible actions such as attempting to systematically eliminate an ethnic group through banishment or murder (an action referred to as **genocide**). We opened the chapter with an example of extreme discrimination: the murder of a Muslim man for ethnic reasons. Social psycholo-

**prejudice**

a negative attitude toward members of a group, which is often very strongly held

**discrimination**

negative, harmful behavior toward people based on their group membership

**genocide**

an attempt to systematically eliminate an ethnic group through banishment or murder

gists have devoted much time and energy to trying to understand why people treat others badly based simply on group membership.

An important concept in this chapter will be stereotypes, *which we defined in Chapter 3 as individuals' beliefs that members of a group share particular attributes (see page 75). Unlike prejudice and discrimination— terms that social psychologists use to refer specifically to* negative *attitudes or actions—stereotypes can be either positive or negative. Stereotypes of some groups are largely positive (e.g., scientists), whereas stereotypes of other groups are largely negative (e.g., criminals). Negative stereotypes can provide the basis for prejudice and discrimination.*

*In this chapter, we discuss social psychological theory and research on stereotypes, prejudice, and discrimination (see also Brewer & Brown, 1998; Fiske, 1998; Jones, 1997; Nelson, 2002; Zanna & Olson, 1994). We address both the causes and consequences of these concepts. We begin by considering the magnitude of prejudice and discrimination today. We then turn to the* sources *of prejudice, focusing primarily on racial and ethnic prejudice. These sources of prejudice include stereotypes (a cognitive concept) and several emotional factors. We then discuss prejudice and discrimination directed against women, which is called* sexism. *Next, we take the perspective of people who are victims of prejudice and discrimination, describing two programs of research that have examined victimization from the inside. We then briefly discuss genocide. Our final section describes various strategies that have been proposed to reduce prejudice and discrimination.*

## ● ● ● Prejudice and Discrimination Today

Before we begin our analysis of the causes and consequences of prejudice and discrimination, let's consider how widespread these problems are today. On the one hand, it is quite easy for us to look around the world and find recent examples of ethnic conflict and religious hatred. The Middle East, Bosnia, Rwanda, Northern Ireland, the Phillippines, Afghanistan, Somalia—the list goes on and on. Groups seem unable or unwilling to find peaceful solutions to longstanding disagreements. The high frequency of conflict and war around the globe is discouraging to say the least. On the other hand, racial and religious confrontations in North America seem rarer than 20 or 30 years ago. Indeed, most people in the United States claim to have relatively favorable attitudes toward most minority groups. These considerations are encouraging, but should we believe what we are told? Do you think that prejudice and discrimination are declining?

It is probably true that blatant, overt discrimination is less common today than 20 or 30 years ago (see Schuman, Steeh, Bobo, & Krysan, 1997), although it certainly still exists (e.g., see Bushman & Bonacci, 2004; Mellor, 2003). Discrimination has been made illegal, and equal access has become mandatory policy for employers in the public and private sectors. Social norms now censure prejudice, and people are less likely to express negative feelings publicly. But some groups are still victims of hate crimes, including Muslim Americans (as noted in the opening story) and people who are gay or lesbian. Also, some people have become more sophisticated at hiding their prejudice; they may feel negatively toward minority groups but try to avoid displaying discrimination.

Further, some people may even be fooling themselves into thinking they are unprejudiced when, in fact, they remain biased against members of disadvantaged groups. Can you think of a time when you heard someone say something that revealed an unrecognized prejudice toward a group? One of the authors of this book recalls an event related to actress Margot Kidder, who is best known for playing Lois Lane opposite Christopher Reeves's Superman in four movies between 1978 and 1987. Kidder suffers from bipolar disorder (a mental illness, usually treatable with medication, that is characterized by alternating periods of extreme highs and extreme lows) and, in 1996, was found wandering confused and lost in Los Angeles. Shortly after this event, Kidder came up in a conversation at a party, and several people laughed out loud at the mention of her name. They did not seem to recognize the demeaning stereotype of mental illness their laughter revealed. The concept of *implicit attitudes* was introduced in Chapter 6 (see page 202) and defined as individuals' automatic—and often unconscious—evaluations of a target. Some people possess unfavorable implicit attitudes toward disadvantaged groups but are not consciously aware of these negative automatic responses.

John Dovidio and Samuel Gaertner (1998, 2000; Gaertner & Dovidio, 1986) have argued that "old-fashioned," blatant racial discrimination has been replaced by more subtle and ambiguous discrimination (see also Katz & Hass, 1988; McConahay, 1986; Sears & Henry, 2003). Dovidio and Gaertner proposed that many White Americans have *ambivalent,* or conflicted, feelings toward minorities such as African and Hispanic Americans; Whites often support equal opportunities and regard themselves as unprejudiced and nondiscriminatory, but simultaneously harbor some negative beliefs and hostile feelings toward Blacks and Hispanics. Dovidio and Gaertner labeled this "new" or "modern" kind of prejudice **aversive racism,** because the White Americans who hold these views do not consider themselves to be prejudiced and would find any accusation of being prejudiced aversive (unpleasant or upsetting). Nevertheless, aversive racists are hypothesized to exhibit discrimination under some circumstances. Specifically, Dovidio and Gaertner predicted that many White Americans would exhibit discrimination toward African and Hispanic Americans when the circumstances made negative treatment justifiable, thereby providing an excuse (perhaps even to themselves) for discrimination.

For example, Dovidio and Gaertner (2000) reported data from two different samples of White Americans, one obtained in 1989 and the other in 1999. The

**aversive racism**

*a "modern" kind of prejudice held by people who do not consider themselves prejudiced and who would find any accusation of being prejudiced aversive, but who nevertheless harbor some negative beliefs and hostile feelings toward members of minority groups*

*Aversive racists* consider themselves unprejudiced but harbor some negative beliefs or feelings toward minority groups such as African Americans.

© Mike Powell/Getty Images

researchers predicted that the more recent sample would report less *blatant preju-dice* toward African Americans than the earlier sample, but there would be little change over the 10-year period in *discriminatory behavior* when the circumstances provided an excuse. Participants reported their explicit attitudes toward Blacks by indicating the extent of their agreement with such statements as "I would mind it if a Black family with about the same income and education as my own would move next door to my home." In a second, separate session, participants were asked to evaluate a male candidate for a peer counseling program at their college. The candidate was either White or Black and possessed either strong, ambiguous, or weak qualifications. Participants made a yes/no decision about whether the applicant should be recommended for the counseling position. The researchers predicted that when the applicant's qualifications were clear (either strong or weak), participants would assess White and Black applicants similarly, but when the qualifications were ambiguous, participants would assess the White applicant more positively than the Black applicant.

The items assessing explicit attitudes toward Blacks revealed less prejudice in 1999 than in 1989. Thus, as predicted, blatant prejudice declined over the 10-year period. What about participants' yes/no decisions for the job applicants? Figure 9.1 presents the percentages of participants who decided that the White or Black applicant *should* be recommended for the position. When the applicant's qualifications were strong, participants at both time periods recommended him whether he was White or Black. When the applicant's qualifications were weak, participants at both time periods did not recommend him whether he was White or Black. But now for the critical results: When the applicant's qualifications were ambiguous, participants recommended the White applicant more often than the Black applicant, and the effect in 1999 (77% vs. 40%) was just as strong as, or even a bit stronger than, the effect in 1989 (75% vs. 50%). Thus, although the more recent sample reported less blatant, overt prejudice, this sample evaluated the Black applicant with ambiguous qualifications just as negatively as the previous sample. Discrimination continued to occur when the circumstances masked it (see also Fiske, 2002).

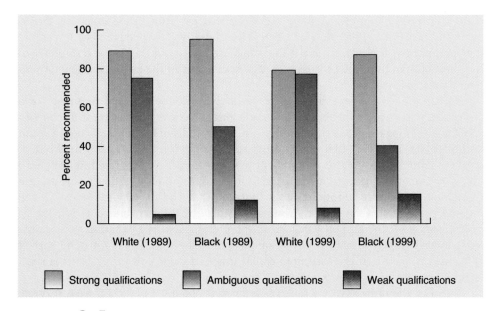

**FIGURE 9.1** Percentage of White and Black applicants recommended for peer counseling position in 1989 and 1999

From Dovidio & Gaertner, "Aversive racism and selection decisions: 1989 and 1999," *Psychological Science*, 11, 315–319, Table 1, p. 317, 2000. Reprinted by permission of Blackwell Publishing.

These and other data suggest that some White Americans continue to harbor prejudice against minority groups, but either lie about it when reporting their attitudes or perhaps even deny it to themselves. Because many people may be unwilling to admit, or be unaware of, negative feelings toward racial or ethnic groups (see Crandall & Eshleman, 2003), direct questions such as "How favorable is your attitude toward African Americans?" may be an ineffective way to assess prejudice.

To address this problem, some researchers have used indirect measures of racial attitudes. For example, the *Implicit Association Test (IAT)*, which we described in Chapter 6 (see page 212), has been used to assess respondents' automatic, implicit attitudes toward minority groups (e.g., McConnell & Leibold, 2001). Facial EMG, which we also described in Chapter 6 (see page 211), has been used as a physiological measure of prejudice (Vanman, Saltz, Nathan, & Warren, 2004). Another indirect measure of racial attitudes was designed by Donald Saucier and Carol Miller (2003); this scale asks respondents to rate how well arguments support positive or negative conclusions about African Americans. The assumption underlying the scale is that prejudiced individuals will be more inclined to downgrade arguments supporting *positive* conclusions about Blacks and praise arguments supporting *negative* conclusions about Blacks, compared to unprejudiced individuals. Saucier and Miller labeled their scale the **Racial Arguments Scale (RAS)** and showed that people who scored high on the RAS exhibited more negative behavior toward Blacks than did people who scored low. Importantly, RAS scores improved prediction of behavior even when scores on two existing measures of prejudice were also included—that is, the RAS significantly improved prediction above and beyond existing measures of prejudice. The RAS provides a promising method for obtaining prejudice scores that are less contaminated by social desirability.

**Racial Arguments Scale (RAS)**

*an indirect measure of prejudice in which respondents rate how well arguments support positive or negative conclusions about an outgroup*

 ## Stereotypes: Cognitive Sources of Prejudice and Discrimination

One major contribution of social psychology to understanding prejudice has been to identify common cognitive processes that can establish or maintain prejudice (e.g., see Fiske, 1998; Kunda, 1999). This cognitive perspective does not imply that prejudice is acceptable, but it does suggest that prejudice is the byproduct of "normal" human thinking processes. The key element in the cognitive view of prejudice is *stereotypes*.

As mentioned earlier, stereotypes are individuals' beliefs that members of a group share particular attributes. Someone might believe that doctors are intelligent and compassionate, the elderly are knowledgeable but frail, or Roman Catholics are religious and family-oriented. Stereotypes qualify as one kind of *schema*—namely, schemas that represent human groups. We explained in Chapter 3 that schemas serve important functions for us: they allow us to sort objects into categories, to make assumptions about those objects, and thereby to impose meaning and predictability on our environment. We called this process *going beyond the information given*. When you categorize a plant as poison ivy, what do you "gain"? Most importantly, you gain information that the plant will cause an itchy rash if you touch it, based on the assumption that this particular poison ivy plant is similar to other poison ivy plants.

In much the same way, we make assumptions about people when we categorize them into groups based on stereotypes. When you categorize a person as a policewoman, what do you gain? You can probably assume such things as she wants to uphold the law, she is armed, and she will help you if asked to do so. These assumptions can be made quickly and effortlessly and will provide a solid basis for behavioral decisions. Thus, stereotypes "efficiently" provide us with information about target persons that can guide behavior; they allow us to make rapid inferences about target persons (Bodenhausen, 1988; Gilbert & Hixon, 1991; Pratto & Bargh, 1991).

## Two Costs of Stereotypes: Oversimplification and Negativity

Unfortunately, although they simplify our judgments, stereotypes also have some big costs associated with using them: oversimplification and excessive negativity. First, we may assume *too much* uniformity or similarity within groups of people, especially with respect to large collections such as ethnic groups, nationalities, genders, and occupations. Recall our discussion of the *outgroup homogeneity effect* in Chapter 3 (see page 76); this term refers to the tendency for perceivers to overestimate the similarity within groups to which they do not belong. Think about your own perceptions of some nationalities—say, Iranians or North Koreans. Do you tend to think of people in these countries as all being quite similar to one another?

The reality is that, in contrast to categories of inanimate objects and plants, categories of humans tend not to be uniform or predictable. Poison ivy plants *always* cause an itchy rash when touched; apples *always* grow on trees; fire is *always* hot. In contrast, lawyers are *not* always wealthy; women are *not* always emotional; skinheads are *not* always violent. Stereotypes of large groups are oversimplified and, when applied to a particular individual, often inaccurate. Some stereotypes may have a kernel of truth, but none will apply to everyone in the group. Thus, when we rely on stereotypes to categorize and draw inferences about targets, we frequently make assumptions about them that are wrong.

A second cost of stereotypes is that they are often unfavorable in tone. Although some stereotypes consist mainly of positive characteristics (e.g., the common stereotypes of doctors, college students, and astronauts), other stereotypes contain negative traits (e.g., some people's stereotypes of racial minorities, car salesmen, or communists). Why are stereotypes often unfavorable? One reason is that stereotypes may refer to groups that are believed to be competing with the perceiver's group for desired resources (we elaborate the role of competition in prejudice later). If perceptions of minority groups are tinged by perceived competition, they may become negative. There is also some evidence that being in a bad mood leads perceivers to interpret their stereotypes of minority groups more negatively (e.g., Esses & Zanna, 1995). For example, believing that immigrants are close-knit might normally be seen as neutral or even positive (e.g., family-loving), but when a perceiver is in a bad mood, he or she might interpret "close-knit immigrants" as cliquish or secretive—negative characteristics. Negative emotions, then, can both elicit and intensify unfavorable stereotypes.

Another reason that stereotypes are often negative is that people may be unfamiliar with members of the targeted group and feel anxious or uncomfortable when interacting with them; people may label their anxiety as dislike for the group. Thus, unfamiliarity and anxiety may spill over into mistrust and hostility (see Plant, 2004; Plant & Devine, 2003; Stephan & Stephan, 1985). Anxiety about interacting with members of the outgroup will also lead people to avoid such interactions altogether.

## Stereotypes Distort Information Processing

The fact that stereotypes are oversimplified and excessively negative might not be so problematic if we processed information in an unbiased way. For example, imagine that someone initially assumes, erroneously, that a young woman, Juanita, is conceited simply because she is from a wealthy family (whereas she is actually quite modest); this erroneous view will be corrected if the perceiver remains open

When a person is categorized as a policewoman, several assumptions about her can be made quickly and effortlessly.

to new information (so long as he or she continues to interact with Juanita, which might *not* be the case when stereotype-based expectations are negative). Unfortunately, as discussed in Chapter 3, humans are *not* open and unbiased processors of information related to stereotypes. Stereotypes (like other schemas) guide attention and interpretation in such a way as to increase the probability that perceivers' expectancies will be *confirmed.* The perceiver in our example is quite likely to decide that Jaunita is, indeed, conceited.

**Stereotypes Guide Attention.**    Stereotypes can distort information processing in several ways. One way is by affecting what perceivers *notice* about members of the stereotyped group. Generally, perceivers are sensitive to, and looking for, information that *confirms* the stereotype. In our example, the perceiver is likely to notice anything boastful Juanita says about herself, because the perceiver will be expecting such comments. (As we noted in our discussion of schemas in Chapter 3, very unexpected information can also grab our attention under certain conditions; see Olson, Roese, & Zanna, 1996; Plaks, Stroessner, Dweck, & Sherman, 2001.)

Social psychologists have conducted experiments demonstrating that stereotypes can bias attention. For example, using a simulated courtroom setting, Galen Bodenhausen (1988) gave participants information about a legal case involving a 24-year-old man accused of criminal assault. The information provided to participants was mixed: some supported a guilty verdict and some supported an innocent verdict. For example, the victim and the defendant were observed quarreling in a bar earlier in the evening (evidence supporting a guilty verdict), but no eyewitnesses could positively identify the attacker (evidence supporting an innocent verdict). Before reading the case materials, some participants learned that the defendant was Robert Johnson of Dayton, Ohio, whereas other participants learned that the defendant was Carlos Ramirez of Albuquerque, New Mexico. A common, harmful stereotype of Hispanic American men is that they are aggressive (e.g., Marin, 1984); therefore, Bodenhausen thought that participants who believed the defendant was Hispanic might pay more attention to evidence suggesting aggression than participants who believed the defendant was White.

Consistent with Bodenhausen's predictions, participants who believed the defendant was Carlos Ramirez recalled a higher percentage of the evidence that supported a guilty verdict than did participants who believed the defendant was Robert Johnson. Also, participants in the Ramirez condition gave more extreme judgments of guilt than did participants in the Johnson condition. It appears that the stereotype of Hispanic men increased participants' attention to the evidence supporting a guilty verdict. This study has disturbing implications for our legal system, because a member of a minority group was judged more harshly than a member of the majority group, based on exactly the same information (only the name was changed).

**Stereotypes Guide Interpretation.**    Stereotypes also distort information processing by affecting how perceivers *interpret* the behavior of people in the group (e.g., Sekaquaptewa & Espinoza, 2004). Actions that are ambiguous will tend to be interpreted as consistent with expectations. Consequently, behaviors that do not necessarily support the stereotype will strengthen it. In our Juanita example, the perceiver may interpret neutral or ambiguous comments by Juanita as conceited.

An example of how stereotypes can affect the interpretation of ambiguous behavior in a racial context was provided by Andrew Sagar and Janet Schofield (1980). These researchers showed sixth-grade boys drawings of Black and White models engaged in potentially aggressive behaviors (e.g., one child taking a pencil away from another child without asking permission). The authors hypothesized that exactly the same actions would be rated as more aggressive when performed by a Black model than by a White model because a common, damaging stereotype of Blacks is that they can be aggressive or hostile. As predicted, actions were rated

© David Young-Wolff/Photo Edit

In an experiment by Bodenhausen (1988), a defendant in a criminal case was more likely to be judged guilty when his name was Carlos Ramirez than when his name was Robert Johnson.

as more threatening and less playful when they were performed by a Black model than when they were performed by a White model (see also Duncan, 1976). Sagar and Schofield included both African American and White participants in their study. Unexpectedly, the bias toward interpreting the behavior as more aggressive when performed by a Black model than when performed by a White model was equally strong for both African American and White participants. The researchers concluded from this finding that the differential interpretations reflected knowledge of a cultural stereotype rather than personal prejudice.

Joshua Correll, Bernadette Park, Charles Judd, and Bernd Wittenbrink (2002) conducted a fascinating, and disturbing, set of studies utilizing a video game procedure that required White participants to decide as quickly as possible whether a male target person was armed or unarmed. Sometimes the target person's skin color was black, and sometimes it was white. A photo of a target person was presented on a video screen, and participants were instructed to push one button (labeled *shoot*) if he was armed, but another button (labeled *don't shoot*) if he was unarmed. Participants earned points if they responded correctly and lost points if they responded incorrectly. They were told that the participants who scored highest in the game would receive monetary prizes. On a given trial, participants had to respond very quickly (in less than 1 second) to earn any points with a correct response; this rule was necessary to keep participants from responding slowly to avoid errors, and also to make the situation more comparable to real-life decisions faced by police officers, who must decide quickly whether a suspect is armed or unarmed.

Figure 9.2 presents samples of the photos used in the experiments. Each target appeared in each of the backgrounds for some participants. The armed targets held either a silver snub-nosed revolver or a black pistol; the unarmed targets held either an aluminum can, silver camera, black cell phone, or black wallet.

**9.1**
**ONLINE**
**LAB**

Courtesy of Joshua Correll/University of Colorado at Boulder

**FIGURE 9.2** Target and background example scenes from video game

Correll, Park, Judd, & Wittenbrink, 2002

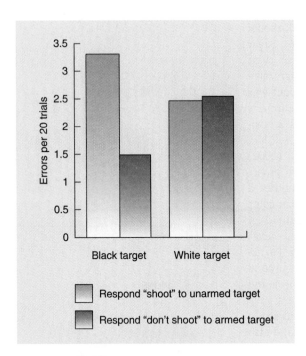

**FIGURE 9.3** Mean numbers of errors in responses to unarmed and armed Black and White targets

From Correll et al., "The police officer's dilemma: Using ethnicity to disambiguate potentially threatening individuals," *Journal of Personality and Social Psychology*, 83, 1314–1329, Table 1, p. 1317, 2002. Copyright © 2002 by the American Psychological Association. Reprinted by permission.

Across three experiments with White participants, the researchers found that participants were *faster* to judge correctly that Black targets were armed than to judge correctly that White targets were armed. The harmful stereotype of young Black men as aggressive or dangerous appeared to prime participants to identify a Black target as armed more quickly than a White target. In contrast, participants were *slower* to judge correctly that Black targets were unarmed than to judge correctly that White targets were unarmed. The stereotype of Black men interfered with participants' ability to identify a Black target as unarmed, compared to a White target.

There was another disturbing aspect of Correll and his colleagues' results: errors. Figure 9.3 presents the mean number of errors per 20 trials in responding to Black and White armed and unarmed targets from one of the experiments (the other studies yielded similar patterns of errors). When confronted with an unarmed target, the White participants were more likely to erroneously push the *shoot* button when the target was Black than when the target was White. In contrast, when confronted with an armed target, participants were more likely to erroneously push the *don't shoot* button when the target was White than when the target was Black. If these errors are applied to the context of real-life behavior, they lead to the prediction that unarmed Black men are more likely to be shot in error by police officers than are unarmed White men (see also Greenwald, Oakes, & Hoffman, 2003; Payne, 2001; Payne, Lambert, & Jacoby, 2002).

One final result from these studies is important to mention. In a fourth experiment, Correll et al. recruited *both* African American and White participants from the community (at bus stations, malls, and food courts in Denver). Exactly the same pattern of biased responding in the video game was obtained in this study, and the pattern was equally strong for Black and White participants. That is, even African American participants erroneously interpreted unarmed Black targets as armed more often than unarmed White targets (recall that Sagar & Schofield, 1980, also found identical effects with White and Black participants).

The occurrence of the bias within African American participants suggests that the impact of targets' skin color on judgments of whether they were armed or unarmed reflected knowledge of a cultural stereotype rather than personal prejudice. In other words, the errors probably occurred because stereotypes distorted how the situation was interpreted, not because all participants disliked, or were prejudiced toward, Black targets (see also Judd, Blair, & Chapleau, 2004; Payne et al., 2002). These conclusions are reminiscent of some famous studies conducted many years earlier, in which Kenneth Clark and Mamie Clark (1947) asked Black and White children to choose dolls to play with. Some dolls had black skin and some had white skin. Both Black and White children tended to choose white dolls as toys. Some commentators interpreted these findings as indicating "self-hatred" among Blacks, but another interpretation is that Black children were aware of the cultural stereotype that white skin is more valued than black skin and were conforming to this stereotype (a pattern of responding that declined when school integration and the black pride movement weakened the cultural stereotype; e.g., Hraba & Grant, 1970).

The laboratory data collected by Correll and his colleagues (2002) examining the effects of race on misperceptions of weapons are worrisome, because real-life police officers must make similar decisions under conditions that can be stressful and threatening. For example, when police officers confront a suspect, they must make rapid decisions about whether the suspect is armed and whether his or her

# Social Psychology in Your Life    *The Shooting of Amadou Diallo*

In 1999, Amadou Diallo was a 22-year-old young Black man living in New York City. He was born in the West African country of Liberia and lived at various times in Guinea, Thailand, and Singapore. His father, Saikou Diallo, was a businessman who traveled extensively. Amadou moved to New York in 1996, where he hoped eventually to go to school to obtain computer training. He first got a job as a delivery man, and later worked as a street peddler selling gloves, socks, and videotapes on 14th Street in Manhattan. He worked 12 hours a day, 6 days a week, and was saving money for his return to school.

Amadou was a practicing Muslim who often studied the Koran. He was a quiet, polite young man who shared a small apartment in the South Bronx with two other men. He loved to read and was also an avid sports fan. His favorite North American sport was basketball, and his favorite player was Michael Jordan.

On February 4, 1999, just after midnight, Amadou came home from work, but decided to go back out to get something to eat. After eating nearby, he returned to his apartment building. As he entered the vestibule of his building, a group of four White plainclothes police officers called out to him from the street and ordered him not to move. Amadou turned toward them and reached into his pants pocket. All four police officers immediately opened fire, shooting a total of 41 bullets at Amadou.

Amadou was hit by 19 bullets and died instantly. It turned out that he was unarmed and was reaching into his pocket to get his wallet. He had no criminal record.

The four police officers were from the Street Crimes Unit of the NYPD and were looking for a serial rape suspect. They claimed that Amadou resembled the suspect they were seeking and said they believed he was reaching for a gun when he put his hand into his pocket.

The shooting of Amadou Diallo outraged many people and galvanized the African American community into action to protest how police officers treat members of minority groups. Three days after the shooting, hundreds of people attended a rally outside Amadou's apartment building, and several other protests followed, involving numerous celebrities including former New York mayor David Dinkins and actress Susan Sarandon. Singer Bruce Springsteen wrote a song titled "American Skin: 41 Shots," which questioned why so many shots were fired and implied that Amadou's black skin was the reason he was killed.

Under intense pressure, authorities eventually brought charges of second-degree murder against the four police officers. In the highly publicized trial, all four officers were ultimately acquitted of all criminal charges. Their actions were judged to have been a tragic but justifiable mistake.

Why was Amadou Diallo shot that night? Did the fact that he was Black contribute to the policemen's decisions to open fire? Would they have given a White man the benefit of the doubt and waited until they saw what was in his hand? Did they view Amadou as suspicious because their stereotypes of Blacks were negative?

We cannot know with certainty why Amadou Diallo was shot. Research by social psychologists, however, such as the study we described by Correll and his colleagues (2002), shows that erroneous judgments about unarmed Black targets are more likely than parallel errors about White targets. Perhaps teaching police officers about this unconscious bias would motivate them to confirm that *any* suspect is armed before opening fire.

Amadou Diallo was shot 41 times by White police officers on February 4, 1999.

actions are threatening. Perhaps tragic errors occur more often when the suspect is Black rather than White. It is impossible to be certain, of course, that distorted interpretations caused any specific incident, but the findings in social psychological research are disturbing. One possible real-world example of these processes is described in the accompanying box, Social Psychology in Your Life: The Shooting of Amadou Diallo.

## The Potential Vicious Cycle of Stereotypes

Imagine that, as part of a group assignment in an abnormal psychology course, you must interview a hospitalized male paranoid schizophrenic patient at a psychiatric institution. Think about how you would feel just before meeting the patient. Think about how close you would sit to him, whether you would smile a lot or remain serious, and how personal your questions would be.

For many of us, our stereotypes of paranoid schizophrenic patients would probably influence our behavior in this meeting. We would feel nervous before meeting the patient; we would not sit close to him during the interview; and we would avoid personal questions. These effects are understandable. Our stereotypes provide a guide for how to behave toward other people, and our stereotype of paranoid schizophrenic patients includes such things as unpredictable, strange, hostile, and maybe even dangerous.

But let's consider a further issue: Do you think that the *patient's* behavior might be influenced by *your* behavior? That is, might he behave in certain ways because of how you behave toward him? If he notices that you are nervous and that you are staying a safe distance from him, he might infer that you do not like him and act differently than he would have acted if you had been more relaxed and friendly. The irony is that his behavior might be affected in such a way as to *confirm* what you expected: he might act in a hostile fashion and thereby confirm your suspicion that he is unpredictable and dangerous. This process is depicted in Figure 9.4.

**Self-Fulfilling Prophesies.**   This sequence of events, where (1) a perceiver's stereotype or expectancy about a target influences the perceiver's behavior toward the target, and (2) the perceiver's behavior toward the target then elicits the expected behavior from the target (i.e., the target's behavior confirms the perceiver's stereotype or expectancy), is called a **self-fulfilling prophesy.** In essence, the perceiver has acted in such a way as to make his or her own prophesy come true (Rosenthal, 2003).

Many fascinating studies in social psychology have demonstrated that stereotypes can influence the perceiver's behavior (see Wheeler & Petty, 2001, for a review) and the perceiver's behavior, in turn, can elicit the expected behavior from the target: a self-fulfilling prophesy in the domain of stereotypes. For example, in a famous set of studies on this topic, Carl Word, Mark Zanna, and Joel Cooper (1974)

**self-fulfilling prophesy**

*a process in which a perceiver's expectancy about a target person influences the perceiver's behavior toward the target person in such a way as to elicit the expected actions from the target person*

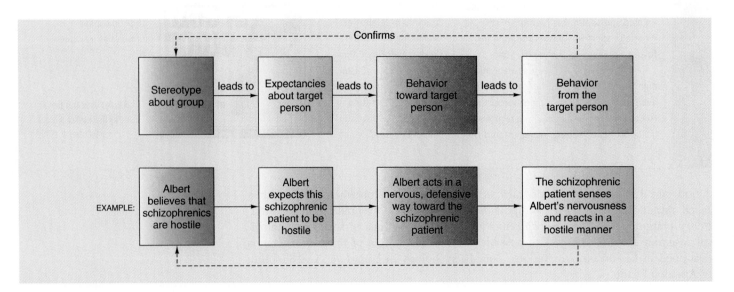

**FIGURE** **9.4** Self-fulfilling prophesy

White interviewers might treat Black and White job applicants differently.

recruited Princeton University students to serve as interviewers of applicants for a job. All participants (interviewers) were White. The researchers gave the interviewers a set of questions they could ask the applicants and told them to ask as few or as many of the questions as they wished. Unbeknownst to the interviewers, the job applicants were actually accomplices of the experimenter who had been trained to respond consistently to the interviewer's questions. Some of the job applicants were White Americans and some were Black Americans. The job interviews were videotaped, and the interviewers' behaviors were subsequently coded. It turned out that the White interviewers treated White and Black applicants differently. For instance, the interviews with White applicants lasted longer than the interviews with Black applicants. Also, the interviewers exhibited more nonverbal behaviors that Mehrabian (1968) has labeled "immediacy" (e.g., eye contact, forward body lean) while interviewing the White applicants than while interviewing the Black applicants. Thus, the White applicants were exposed to more favorable and intimate nonverbal behaviors than were the Black applicants.

Given that White and Black job applicants were treated differently, an important question is whether such treatment would actually influence the performance of real applicants. Word et al. (1974) tested this question in a second experiment. This time, the participants (all White) served as job applicants, and the interviewers were accomplices of the experimenter. The interviewers were White and were trained to treat job applicants either in the manner that White applicants had been treated in the first experiment (longer interview, more eye contact, and forward body lean) or in the manner that Black applicants had been treated in the first experiment (shorter interview, less eye contact, and backward body lean). The job applicants were videotaped, and their performance was subsequently evaluated by judges who did not know which condition each applicant was in. These judges rated the performances of applicants who received longer interviews and more intimate nonverbal behavior as significantly better than the performances of applicants who received shorter interviews and less intimate nonverbal behavior. Thus, the differential treatment of White and Black applicants in the first experiment was shown to be enough to create differences in the actual performance of the applicants in the second experiment.

These data suggest that stereotypes can produce expectancies about a target individual, which can then alter the perceiver's actions in ways that elicit the expected behavior from the target (see also Chen & Bargh, 1997; Olson et al., 1996). Given that stereotypes of minority groups can be unfavorable, self-fulfilling prophesies may often be damaging and harmful. For instance, expecting members of a group to be unfriendly might actually produce unfriendly actions from them (caused by the perceiver's own behavior toward the group members). Negative stereotypes can produce vicious cycles that perpetuate prejudice and discrimination against disadvantaged groups.

We should not exaggerate the inevitability of self-fulfilling prophesies. If targets are *aware* of someone's expectancy for them, they may work to *disprove* it, especially when it is negative (see Hilton & Darley, 1991; Miller & Turnbull, 1986; Neuberg, 1994; Stukas & Snyder, 2002). But in many cases, targets are unaware that perceivers have strong expectancies for them, which makes self-fulfilling prophesies more likely. Also, targets may sometimes behave consistently with a negative stereotype simply to maintain a smooth interaction (see Snyder & Haugen, 1995). Finally, as we will discuss in detail shortly (in the section on *stereotype threat*), even when individuals are aware that someone expects them to do poorly, their attempt to disconfirm that expectancy can sometimes actually hurt their performance—in colloquial terms, people sometimes "choke" when trying to disprove a negative stereotype about their group.

## Do Stereotypes Influence Our Perceptions If We Disagree With Them?

All of us are aware of stereotypes that we don't personally endorse. We know that some people possess negative stereotypes about groups that we admire. Examples of groups targeted by negative stereotypes include African Americans, elderly persons, immigrants, Jews, Muslims, gays and lesbians, overweight persons, and recipients of social assistance. What is your view of these groups? Whether your own views are positive or negative, you can probably identify some of the characteristics that are part of the negative stereotypes.

Let's use recipients of social assistance as an example. Negative beliefs about recipients of social assistance can include that they are lazy, unintelligent, and dishonest (trying to cheat the system). The trait of laziness may be the most common belief: "If they really wanted a job, they could get off social assistance." What do you think of this belief? Do you endorse it or reject it?

When people agree with a stereotype, it may not be surprising that it influences what they notice and how they interpret behavior, as we have described in previous sections. But what happens when someone *knows* a stereotype but does *not* endorse it? If someone is aware that recipients of social assistance are often viewed as lazy, but does not agree with this generalization, can the simple knowledge of the stereotype somehow influence his or her perceptions? In other words, can stereotypes influence our perceptions even if we disagree with them?

**subliminal priming procedure**

*a method of activating a schema or stereotype by flashing words or pictures very briefly on a computer screen in front of a participant*

Some social psychological research has suggested an affirmative answer to this question. For example, Patricia Devine (1989) used a **subliminal priming procedure** to activate the stereotype of African Americans in some of her White participants. A subliminal priming procedure involves flashing a word or picture very briefly (sometimes as little as 1/100th of a second) on a computer screen in front of the participant. At these fast exposure speeds, participants can only see a flash of light and cannot even say whether the presentation was a word. Nevertheless, it turns out that participants do perceive such stimuli subconsciously, and concepts related to the words or pictures become activated in memory (see Bargh & Pietromonaco, 1982).

Half of Devine's participants were exposed to extremely brief presentations of words that were related to the stereotype of African Americans, such as Negroes, ghetto, blues, and Black. The remaining participants were exposed to extremely brief presentations of neutral words that were unrelated to the African American stereotype. Devine assumed that a common stereotype of African American men includes the trait of *hostility;* she also assumed that only some of her White participants would agree with this stereotype, but almost all of them would be aware of it.

All participants then completed a task in which they were given a written description of a young man (whose race was unspecified, so he was probably assumed to be White) who engaged in several actions that were ambiguous with respect to hostility; his actions could be viewed as assertive (positive) or hostile (negative). Participants rated the hostility of the young man.

Participants for whom the stereotype of African Americans had been activated rated the man as more hostile than did participants for whom the stereotype had not been activated. Thus, activating the stereotype increased the likelihood that ambiguous actions would be interpreted as hostile, presumably because hostility was part of the stereotype. It is important to note that none of the words used to prime the African American stereotype (e.g., Negroes, ghetto) was directly related to hostility. Hostility was activated indirectly, via the stereotype.

Devine also measured participants' levels of reported prejudice against African Americans, and it is here that she addressed the issue of whether stereotypes influence perceptions even in people who do not endorse them. Surprisingly, she found that, for both prejudiced and unprejudiced participants, exposure to words related to the stereotype of African Americans increased the perceived hostility of ambiguous behavior. Even people who did not consciously endorse the stereotype of African Americans (unprejudiced participants) showed an effect of the priming manipulation. Given that, in real life, encountering a Black person will almost certainly activate the stereotype of African Americans, Devine's findings imply that there might be a general bias to interpret Blacks' actions as hostile, which will serve to reinforce the stereotype.

**Implicit Intergroup Bias.** This notion that stereotypes can automatically influence judgments without the perceiver's awareness has been termed **implicit intergroup bias** (see Blair, 2001). It is *implicit* because it is not deliberate and may be unrecognized by the perceiver. It is *intergroup bias* because it reflects distorted, usually unfavorable judgments about members of an outgroup. Researchers have documented implicit intergroup bias against several groups, including women, African Americans, and the elderly (e.g., Banaji & Greenwald, 1994; Cunningham, Nezlek, & Banaji, 2004; Greenwald, McGhee, & Schwartz, 1998; Levy, 1996; Wittenbrink, Judd, & Park, 2001). Implicit intergroup bias is similar to negative implicit attitudes toward a group, which are spontaneous negative feelings toward members of a group, of which the perceiver may be unaware.

Devine's (1989) findings suggest that everyone may show some implicit intergroup bias, even those who disagree with a common stereotype. Of course, this does not mean that discrimination will necessarily follow. Although the stereotype of a group might be elicited automatically, actual behavior remains primarily under conscious control, so people who disagree with a stereotype are unlikely to knowingly discriminate against members of the group.

Further, there is recent evidence that implicit intergroup bias may *not* be inevitable, but instead can be reduced by deliberate attempts to be open-minded (for a review, see Blair, 2002). For example, Brian Lowery, Curtis Hardin, and Stacey Sinclair (2001) found that instructing participants to be "as unprejudiced as possible" significantly reduced implicit

**implicit intergroup bias**

*distorted judgments about members of a group based on a stereotype, which can occur without the person's awareness*

*Implicit intergroup bias* has been documented in perceivers' judgments about the elderly.

intergroup bias against African Americans on a subsequent task (see also Barden, Maddux, Petty, & Brewer, 2004; Maddux, Barden, Brewer, & Petty, 2005). In contrast to Devine's (1989) findings, other researchers have found that implicit intergroup bias is more likely to occur in prejudiced people than in unprejudiced people (e.g., Fazio, Jackson, Dunton, & Williams, 1995; Lepore & Brown, 1997; Wittenbrink, Judd, & Park, 1997). Therefore, individuals who do not endorse a stereotype may not show effects, or only very weak effects, without their awareness. These findings are comforting for people who reject negative stereotypes of minority groups and do not want their own judgments to be unknowingly affected by the stereotypes. Some research also suggests that unprejudiced individuals actually seek out information to *disconfirm* common stereotypes (e.g., Wyer, 2004). Further, there is evidence that people who exhibit weak or no implicit intergroup bias also tend to behave in other positive ways toward the target group (e.g., Dovidio, Kawakami, & Gaertner, 2002; Hugenberg & Bodenhausen, 2003, 2004).

Can you think of strategies that might *counteract* the implicit effect of stereotypes on individuals' judgments even for people who agree with a stereotype? One possibility might be to instruct them to think about members of the group who do *not* fit the stereotype. For instance, to counter implicit bias against elderly people, individuals could be asked to visualize elderly persons who remained vigorous and productive late in life, such as Mother Theresa and Nelson Mandela. Thinking about vigorous elderly people might weaken the stereotype of the elderly and neutralize its implicit effect. In fact, Nilanjana Dasgupta and Anthony Greenwald (2001) showed exactly this effect. These researchers asked some participants to think of admired and active elderly people, such as Mother Theresa. These participants showed less evidence of implicit intergroup bias against the elderly on a subsequent task.

In a similar study focusing on gender rather than age stereotypes, Irene Blair, Jennifer Ma, and Alison Lenton (2001) asked some participants to "take a few minutes to imagine what a strong woman is like, why she is considered strong, what she is capable of doing, and what kinds of hobbies and activities she enjoys." Participants who performed this mental imagery task showed less evidence of implicit intergroup bias against women on subsequent tasks than participants who did not perform the imagery task. There is also evidence that exposing women to role models of independent, successful women reduces their automatic gender bias (Dasgupta & Asgari, 2004). These findings offer hope that getting people to think about counterstereotypic examples might reduce the implicit effects of stereotypes.

One possible limitation to this strategy of asking people to imagine counterstereotypic examples is that extremely discrepant cases may be dismissed as exceptions or as subtypes of the category (e.g., an extremely assertive woman might be labeled a feminist who is not representative of most women). Therefore, the most effective counterstereotypic examples may be individuals who are only moderately discrepant from the stereotype on a dimension and who are otherwise quite prototypical (Kunda, 1999; Kunda & Oleson, 1997). For instance, a moderately assertive woman may be more likely than an extremely assertive woman to provoke stereotype change of women as unassertive, especially if she seems feminine in most other ways (e.g., wears makeup, is warm and caring, etc.).

## Emotional Sources of Prejudice and Discrimination

We have focused so far in this chapter on stereotypes as a cause of prejudice, but negative attitudes toward specific groups sometimes spring from other, noncognitive sources. Theorists have identified several emotional or motivational processes that can contribute to prejudice and discrimination. For example, prejudice some-times results from negative emotions such as frustration, anger, and hostility. Prej-udice may also sometimes satisfy basic motives such as the need to evaluate the self positively. In this section, we discuss four theoretical models of prejudice that revolve around emotional or motivational factors.

## Frustration and Prejudice: Scapegoat Theory

One of the oldest explanations of prejudice is that people become frustrated during difficult economic times and vent their frustration on weak, scapegoat tar-gets (Allport, 1954; Berkowitz, 1962). From this perspective, prejudice involves the dominant group's "lashing out" at subordinate groups because of frustration and dis-appointment. Members of the disadvantaged group serve merely as scapegoats: they had little or no direct role in causing the frustration, but provide a convenient target of blame. Hence, this perspective on prejudice is known as **scapegoat theory.**

In Chapter 11, we discuss the role of frustration in aggression more generally, but at this point we limit our attention to how frustration can lead to prejudice and discrimination. In one of the most famous investigations of scapegoat theory, Carl Hovland and Robert Sears (1940) examined the correlation between the number of lynchings of Black Americans in the Deep South of the United States between 1882 and 1930 and the price of cotton over the same period. The researchers hypothe-sized that Black men became the targets of angry, frustrated White Americans when cotton prices were low. Consistent with this reasoning, Hovland and Sears found a significant negative correlation between cotton prices and lynchings: as prices went down, lynchings went up.

Another example of a group that was targeted during times of economic diffi-culty was Jews in Nazi Germany in the late 1930s. Hitler roused anger against Jews in the Third Reich by blaming them for the economic problems in Germany—the country had been slow to come out of the worldwide depression. Jews were an identifiable group who were already disliked by many Germans, and when Hitler initiated his campaign of misinformation, some Germans latched onto his message. The accusations from Hitler provided an excuse for some Germans to vent their frustrations by aggressing viciously against Jewish men, women, and children.

**scapegoat theory**
*a theory proposing that prejudice occurs because members of dominant groups use discrimination against members of weak target groups to vent their frustration and disappointment*

© Time Life Pictures/Getty Images

In Nazi Germany, Jews were wrongly blamed for the country's economic problems. In this photo, Jewish citizens are being rounded up and taken to trains for transportation to concentration camps.

# Perceived Competition and Prejudice: Realistic Group Conflict Theory

**realistic group conflict theory**

*a theory proposing that when groups in society are perceived to be competing with one another for resources, intergroup hostility can be aroused, which leads to prejudice*

Another perspective on prejudice, which shares some elements with the frustration model, focuses on perceived competition between groups for scarce resources. When groups in society are believed to be competing with one another for such things as jobs, housing, political power, and health care, hostility can be aroused. This competitive hostility can lead, in turn, to prejudice. The effects of perceived competition have been articulated in a theory called **realistic group conflict theory** (Campbell, 1965; Pettigrew, 1978).

Many incidents in history illustrate this consequence of perceived competition, including wars over disputed claims for land (e.g., the conflict between India and Pakistan over Kashmir) and legal battles over natural resources (e.g., lawsuits initiated by Native Americans for the rights to land, mining, and fishing resources). But perhaps the clearest example is prejudice against immigrants (see Verkuyten, 2004; Zárate, Garcia, Garza, & Hitlan, 2004). In many countries, immigrants have been perceived to be competing directly with current residents for jobs and social benefits. Immigrants are accused of taking jobs away from native-born workers. There have been demonstrations in Great Britain, Germany, France, and many other countries where protesters (often composed of right-wing groups like skinheads and associated "hooligans," to use the British term) have denounced immigration and promoted hatred of immigrants. Social psychologist Victoria Esses has studied attitudes toward immigrants for many years and has concluded that perceived competition from immigrants for jobs, health care, and other resources leads people to oppose open, lenient immigration policies (e.g., see Esses, Dovidio, Jackson, & Armstrong, 2001).

A famous demonstration of the effects of competition was provided by Muzafer Sherif and his colleagues (Sherif, Harvey, White, Hood, & Sherif, 1961) in a study of 11-year-old boys at a summer camp (known as the *Robber's Cave experiment*). Two groups of boys at a camp learned that they would be competing in sporting events for several days, and the winning team would receive some very nice prizes. Almost immediately, the two groups expressed substantial hostility and prejudice toward one another and engaged in "discriminatory" behavior such as stealing things from members of the other group. As predicted by realistic group conflict theory, introducing competition between the groups elicited strong dislike and derogation of the outgroup (see also Judd & Park, 1988).

Sometimes groups perceive not only competition for scarce resources from members of outgroups, but also threats to important values. People may believe that members of another group (e.g., Mexican immigrants to California or Texas) bring with them a set of values and customs that threaten the status quo. This cultural threat can produce intergroup anxiety, resentment, and prejudice (Stephan & Stephan, 1985; Zárate et al., 2004). The competition is not economic, but rather symbolic.

David DeSteno and his colleagues (DeSteno, Dasgupta, Bartlett, & Cajdric, 2004) have proposed that the emotion of anger can itself create prejudice against outgroups. The researchers noted that anger is often aroused by intergroup conflict and competition. Because intergroup conflict is associated with anger (i.e., it can cause anger), some people might assume that when they feel angry, there may be an intergroup conflict that is making them feel this way. In two experiments, DeSteno et al. (2004) induced some participants to feel angry by writing about an event that had made them very angry in the past, whereas other participants were induced to feel sad by writing about an event that had made them very sad in the past. Participants' implicit attitudes toward members of an outgroup were then measured. The angry participants showed more negative outgroup evaluations than did the sad participants, confirming the predicted effect of the emotion of anger.

# Self-Enhancement Motivation: Social Identity Theory

The frustration and competition perspectives articulated to this point focus on how negative affect (frustration, hostility, anger) can generate prejudice. A third affect-related factor in prejudice involves a potential *positive* emotional benefit of derogating outgroups: feeling good about the self, or self-enhancement.

We have noted many times in this book that people want to see themselves favorably (see, in particular, the sections on *self-serving judgments* in Chapters 3 and 4). One way to judge the self positively is in relative terms: "I am better than you." If another person is evaluated negatively, then the perceiver will probably conclude that he or she is better than the other. Feeling superior to another person can be gratifying, because it indirectly confirms one's own worth.

Self-enhancement does not happen only at the individual level ("I am better than you"); it also happens at the group level ("My group is better than your group"). We described *social identity theory* in Chapter 5 (see page 167). According to this theory (Tajfel, 1978; Tajfel & Turner, 1986), one important component of people's identity is their group memberships. Just as we strive for a positive personal identity, we also strive for a positive social (group) identity. Deciding that our ingroup is better than an outgroup is one way to enhance our self-esteem (see Aberson, Healy, & Romero, 2000; Fein & Spencer, 1997; Rubin & Hewstone, 1998). Recall our discussion of the *minimal group paradigm* in Chapter 5 (see page 168), which involves assigning individuals to groups on the basis of a trivial feature (e.g., whether they allegedly overestimate or underestimate the number of dots shown on a screen). Even when groups are formed in these meaningless, arbitrary ways, people show ingroup favoritism: they give members of their ingroup more resources than members of an outgroup.

These findings imply that a positive social identity makes us feel good. Consistent with this reasoning, researchers have found that when people's ingroup performs better than an outgroup, they report higher self-esteem and more positive judgments of their own abilities. A somewhat lighthearted demonstration of this effect was provided by Edward Hirt, Dolf Zillman, Grant Erickson, and Chris Kennedy (1992), who had students at Indiana University watch a live basketball game involving the Hoosiers (IU's team). After the game (in an allegedly unrelated study), participants reported their self-esteem and estimated their own future performance on a number of tasks (e.g., an anagrams task involving 5-letter scrambled words, a motor skills task involving throwing velcro-covered balls onto a felt dart board, and a social skills task involving asking members of the opposite sex to go to a concert). When the Hoosiers won the game, participants reported higher self-esteem and made more optimistic predictions about their own future performance than when the Hoosiers lost the game. Thus, when their ingroup (college team) proved to be superior to an outgroup (another college team), people felt better about themselves.

Past studies indicate that derogating members of an outgroup can enhance self-esteem. Perhaps prejudice can be motivated, therefore, by a desire for self-enhancement. Some people who are highly prejudiced may be trying to make themselves feel good in comparison. A context that seems analogous to prejudice is peer ridicule among high school students. Groups of teenagers often engage in merciless ridicule of other teens. Why does this happen? Do they realize how painful it is to the target? Perhaps their motivation is to make themselves feel superior.

The film *The Eye of the Storm* (1971) showed how teacher Jane Elliott decided to give her grade 3, all-White class a firsthand experience of prejudice. She divided the class into two groups based on eye color. She then declared that children with blue eyes were superior to children with brown eyes. For an entire day, she made blue-eyed children feel good about themselves and brown-eyed children feel disadvantaged. Then on the next day, she declared that she was wrong the day before, and it

*"I watched what had been marvelous, cooperative, wonderful, thoughtful children turn into nasty, vicious, discriminating little third graders in the space of fifteen minutes."*

was actually brown-eyed children who were superior to blue-eyed children. After this second day of making one group feel superior to the other, things returned to normal on the third day. One of the most interesting observations made by Ms. Elliott in the film was that, each day, the children in the "superior" group changed dramatically from their normal personalities, becoming arrogant, insulting, and condescending to children in the "inferior" group. She noted that it was as if the children really *wanted* to feel and act in this superior manner, and her eye-color rules "released" this inherent tendency. Perhaps the children's behavior reflected a basic human desire for a positive social identity.

## A Unifying Model: Integrated Threat Theory

**integrated threat theory**

*a theory proposing that prejudice results from four types of threats: realistic threats, symbolic threats, threats stemming from intergroup anxiety, and threats arising from negative stereotypes*

A relatively recent addition to theories of prejudice was proposed by Walter Stephan and Cookie Stephan (2000), a model they labeled **integrated threat theory.** These researchers suggested that negative attitudes toward an outgroup can result from four different kinds of threats: realistic threats, symbolic threats, threats stemming from intergroup anxiety, and threats arising from negative stereotypes. This model unifies several other perspectives on prejudice. Stephan and Stephan chose the term *threats* to refer to the fact that prejudiced people expect members of the disliked outgroup to behave in ways that are detrimental to ingroup members. These "detrimental" actions may include (but are not limited to) taking jobs away from ingroup members, challenging the ingroup's fundamental values, or simply making ingroup members feel uncomfortable during interactions.

How do Stephan and Stephan define each type of threat? *Realistic threats* are those emphasized by realistic group conflict theory—that is, competition for jobs, political power, or other scarce resources. The outgroup is perceived to pose a significant threat to the material well-being of the ingroup. *Symbolic threats* refer to perceived threats to the ingroup's important attitudes, beliefs, and values. In this case, the values of the outgroup are thought to be different from those of the ingroup; given that the ingroup believes in the moral correctness of its own views, the outgroup may be seen as threatening the moral fiber of the community. Threats from *intergroup anxiety* arise when people feel uncertain and anxious about interacting with members of the outgroup. A lack of familiarity with the outgroup and its customs can create awkwardness and discomfort before and during interactions. Finally, threats from *negative stereotypes* occur when people believe that members of the outgroup possess undesirable characteristics (e.g., aggressiveness, untrustworthiness) that may lead to detrimental actions toward the ingroup.

Think about your own attitudes toward outgroups. Are there any outgroups that make you feel uncomfortable? Immigrants, gays and lesbians, ethnic minorities—do you feel threatened by any of these groups? Perhaps you can recognize some of the elements of integrated threat theory in your own feelings, such as perceived competition for resources or discomfort during interactions.

Integrated threat theory hypothesizes that these four threats arouse aversive feelings toward the outgroup, such as anxiety, frustration, hostility, and anger, thus leading to negative intergroup attitudes (prejudice). One compelling aspect of the theory is that it can be applied equally well to understanding either the attitudes of the majority group toward minority groups or the attitudes of minority groups toward the majority group. For instance, Walter Stephan and his colleagues (Stephan, Boniecki, Ybarra, Bettencourt, Ervin, Jackson, et al., 2002) recruited 559 White Americans and 452 African Americans from six colleges across the United States. Participants completed measures of each type of perceived threat (realistic,

## CONCEPT REVIEW
### Emotional Sources of Prejudice and Discrimination

| Emotional Source | Relevant Theory | Description | Example |
|---|---|---|---|
| Frustration | Scapegoat theory | People vent their frustrations from daily life by lashing out against members of a weak minority group | Gay bashing: Looking for gay men to beat up simply because it gets rid of feelings of frustration and stress |
| Perceived competition | Realistic group conflict theory | People dislike members of a group who are thought to be competing for scarce resources such as jobs or land | Disliking immigrants because they are believed to take jobs away from native-born workers |
| Self-enhancement | Social identity theory | People form negative impressions of members of an outgroup in order to make their own group seem superior | Laughing at the unusual customs or beliefs of a minority religious group in order to make the majority religious view seem superior |
| Threats | Integrated threat theory | People dislike members of a group who are competing for scarce resources, hold different attitudes and values, arouse anxiety, or are believed to possess undesirable characteristics | Avoiding contact with disabled people because interactions are awkward and anxiety-provoking |

symbolic, intergroup anxiety, and negative stereotypes), as well as attitudes toward the outgroup. Results for both groups supported the usefulness of three threats for predicting prejudice: realistic, symbolic, and intergroup anxiety. These three variables predicted White Americans' degree of prejudice toward African Americans, as well as African Americans' degree of prejudice toward White Americans. The fourth type of threat in the theory (negative stereotypes) appeared to influence respondents' prejudice indirectly—namely, by increasing the other three threats. For instance, more negative stereotypes of the outgroup were associated with greater perceived symbolic threat to the ingroup's values. The authors suggested that the integrated threat theory should perhaps be revised to limit the principal threat variables to realistic, symbolic, and intergroup anxiety. It will be interesting to see how future tests of this theory turn out in the coming years.

The various emotional sources of prejudice and discrimination are summarized in the accompanying Concept Review.

# Sexism: Prejudice and Discrimination Against Women

To this point, we have focused on minority groups (e.g., African Americans, Hispanic Americans, gays and lesbians, immigrants) in our discussion of prejudice and discrimination. But there is another group in society that, historically, has been a target of discrimination. This group is different from the others we have discussed in that it is not a "minority" group at all—in fact, its members constitute approximately half of the humans on the planet. We refer, of course, to women.

In most societies around the world, men have occupied and continue to occupy the principal positions of power, wealth, and status. Although women have made gains over the past few decades, they remain underrepresented in positions of influence in most countries and badly disadvantaged in others. Women are subjected to prejudice, as well as both intentional and unintentional discrimination. Prejudice and discrimination directed against women because of their gender is called **sexism.**

**sexism**

*prejudice and discrimination directed against women because of their gender*

Because women constitute approximately 50% of the population, virtually everyone has extensive experience with and exposure to women—a factor that makes this group distinct from other targets of discrimination. Also, almost all men (the dominant group in most societies) love and care about many women, including their mothers, wives, daughters, and female friends. So the problem is not so much that men dislike women, but rather that men do not always treat women as their equals. This unequal treatment has significant, detrimental effects on the lives of many women. In the current section, we discuss some of the causes and consequences of sexism.

## Sexism Today

In today's North American society, most men consider themselves to be fair-minded and unbiased toward women. But are these self-perceptions accurate? Do you think most men's true beliefs about women are egalitarian, or are most men instead chauvinistic? Perhaps sexist attitudes and actions have simply become more subtle and elusive—paralleling our earlier discussion of racial prejudice.

Janet Swim and her colleagues (Swim, Aikin, Hall, & Hunter, 1995) have argued that, indeed, sexism has become more sophisticated than it used to be. *Old-fashioned sexism* refers to beliefs that women are inherently inferior to men, as well as endorsement of traditional gender roles; *modern sexism* reflects perceptions that women are no longer disadvantaged, together with antagonism toward women's demands for special treatment. These researchers developed sexism scales to measure both old-fashioned and modern sexism.

The accompanying Know Yourself 9.1: Old-Fashioned and Modern Sexism Scales presents sample items from Swim et al.'s (1995) two scales. How would you answer these items?

Swim et al. (1995) found that, as predicted, men's scores on the modern sexism scale were higher than their scores on the old-fashioned sexism scale, and men's scores on both scales were higher than women's scores.

Another perspective on modern sexism was provided by Peter Glick and Susan Fiske (1996), who suggested that men often hold *ambivalent* attitudes toward women. Recall from Chapter 6 that ambivalent attitudes contain both positive and negative elements (see page 302). Glick and Fiske argued that many men have mixed responses to women. On the one hand, these men have positive (if somewhat paternalistic) attitudes toward women in the sense that they like women and want to "protect" the women in their lives. On the other hand, these men have negative, hostile attitudes toward women who violate the traditional stereotype, such as femi-

© Digital Vision/Getty Images

*Sexism* is prejudice or discrimination directed against women because of their gender.

# Know Yourself 9.1
## *Old-Fashioned and Modern Sexism Scales*

*Please indicate the extent to which you agree or disagree with each of the following statements by circling the appropriate number on the answer scale.*

### OLD-FASHIONED SEXISM SCALE

1. Women are generally not as smart as men.

| 1 | 2 | 3 | 4 | 5 |
|---|---|---|---|---|
| Strongly Disagree | | Undecided | | Strongly Agree |

2. I would be equally comfortable having a woman as a boss as a man.

| 1 | 2 | 3 | 4 | 5 |
|---|---|---|---|---|
| Strongly Disagree | | Undecided | | Strongly Agree |

3. It is more important to encourage boys than to encourage girls to participate in athletics.

| 1 | 2 | 3 | 4 | 5 |
|---|---|---|---|---|
| Strongly Disagree | | Undecided | | Strongly Agree |

4. When both parents are employed and their child gets sick at school, the school should call the mother rather than the father.

| 1 | 2 | 3 | 4 | 5 |
|---|---|---|---|---|
| Strongly Disagree | | Undecided | | Strongly Agree |

5. Women are just as capable of thinking logically as men.

| 1 | 2 | 3 | 4 | 5 |
|---|---|---|---|---|
| Strongly Disagree | | Undecided | | Strongly Agree |

### MODERN SEXISM SCALE

1. Discrimination against women is no longer a problem in the United States.

| 1 | 2 | 3 | 4 | 5 |
|---|---|---|---|---|
| Strongly Disagree | | Undecided | | Strongly Agree |

2. Women often miss out on good jobs due to sexual discrimination.

| 1 | 2 | 3 | 4 | 5 |
|---|---|---|---|---|
| Strongly Disagree | | Undecided | | Strongly Agree |

3. It is rare to see women treated in a sexist manner on television.

| 1 | 2 | 3 | 4 | 5 |
|---|---|---|---|---|
| Strongly Disagree | | Undecided | | Strongly Agree |

4. Over the past few years, the government and news media have been showing more concern about the treatment of women than is warranted by women's actual experiences.

| 1 | 2 | 3 | 4 | 5 |
|---|---|---|---|---|
| Strongly Disagree | | Undecided | | Strongly Agree |

5. It is easy to understand the anger of women's groups in America.

| 1 | 2 | 3 | 4 | 5 |
|---|---|---|---|---|
| Strongly Disagree | | Undecided | | Strongly Agree |

**SCORING:** For each scale (old-fashioned sexism and modern sexism), score Items 1, 3, and 4 using the answer scales as presented (1-2-3-4-5); Items 2 and 5 in each scale are reverse-scored (that is, 5-4-3-2-1). Add up the five items in each scale to get your overall old-fashioned sexism or modern sexism score. Possible scores on each scale range from 5 to 25, and higher scores represent greater sexism.

Sample items from Swim et al., "Sexism and racism: Old-fashioned and modern prejudices," *Journal of Personality and Social Psychology*, 68, 199–214, 1995. Copyright © 1995 by the American Psychological Association. Reprinted by permission.

**ambivalent sexism inventory**

*a measure of stereotyped attitudes toward women, which is composed of two dimensions, one positive and one negative: benevolent sexism and hostile sexism*

**benevolent sexism**

*positive but paternalistic attitudes toward women*

**hostile sexism**

*negative attitudes toward women who violate the traditional stereotype of women*

nists. Glick and Fiske developed a measure that they labeled the **ambivalent sexism inventory,** which included items to assess these two dimensions of sexism, which were labeled **benevolent sexism** and **hostile sexism.** Sample items for each dimension are presented in Know Yourself 9.2: Ambivalent Sexism Inventory. See how you would answer these items.

Glick and a large number of collaborators (Glick, Fiske, Mladinic, Saiz, Abrams, Masser, et al., 2000) administered the ambivalent sexism inventory to large samples in 19 countries around the world, including the United States, Australia, Colombia, Cuba, Nigeria, Chile, Turkey, Japan, and Botswana. The researchers were then able to calculate the average benevolent sexism and average hostile sexism scores in each country. They also obtained from the United Nations two measures of gender equality in each country, based on such things as women's participation in the economy and politics. Results showed that the levels of both benevolent sexism and hostile sexism in a country were negatively correlated with the measures of gender equality in that country. Countries where respondents exhibited more sexism (whether benevolent or hostile) tended to give women less access to economic and political arenas. Even measured at national levels, sexist attitudes were associated with gender discrimination and inequality. (You might be interested to know where the United States ranked on these indices. Of the 19 countries, the United States was the sixth least sexist country on benevolent sexism and the fourth least sexist country on hostile sexism. It ranked fourth best on the two measures of gender equality.)

## Gender Stereotypes

In Chapter 5, we defined *gender stereotypes* as beliefs about the characteristics that are associated with men and women (see page 177). We noted that although there are some characteristics on which men and women actually differ significantly (e.g., aggressiveness, romantic attraction), many people *believe* that the sexes differ on an even wider variety of characteristics.

The traditional view of men is that they are strong, aggressive, dominant, independent, and mathematical, whereas the traditional view of women is that they are warm, compassionate, indecisive, emotional, and verbally skilled (e.g., see Bergen & Williams, 1991). You might note that the characteristics believed to be associated with women are not necessarily negative; for example, it is presumably good to be warm and compassionate. In fact, women are often evaluated more positively than men, whose stereotype has been characterized as "bad but bold" (Glick, Lameiras, Fiske, Eckes, Masser, Volpato, et al., 2004). Characteristics that are associated with women, however, are not ones that would lead to positions of power and status, especially compared to the characteristics believed to be associated with men. Women are perceived as warmer than men, but also as less competent than men (Fiske, Cuddy, Glick, & Xu, 2002). Thus, gender stereotypes mirror the division of roles between men and women in society and can make it difficult for women to achieve positions of power and status (e.g., see Eagly & Karau, 2002).

**Origins of Gender Stereotypes.**   Where do gender stereotypes come from? Why do people believe that men and women differ on various traits? Think about your own beliefs about the characteristics of men and women: where did your beliefs come from?

One important factor is parental socialization: boys and girls are often raised differently. Boys are typically encouraged to be assertive, to engage in independent exploration, and to be physically active; girls are typically encouraged to be compassionate, to engage in quiet play, and to be polite. These parenting patterns teach boys to be self-confident and girls to be nurturant and also lead children to expect similar characteristics in other boys and girls.

# Know Yourself 9.2
## *Ambivalent Sexism Inventory*

*Please indicate the extent to which you agree or disagree with each of the following statements by circling the appropriate number on the answer scale.*

### BENEVOLENT SEXISM SCALE

1. Women should be cherished and protected by men.

| 0 | 1 | 2 | 3 | 4 | 5 |
|---|---|---|---|---|---|
| Disagree Strongly | Disagree Somewhat | Disagree Slightly | Agree Slightly | Agree Somewhat | Agree Strongly |

2. Men are complete without women.

| 0 | 1 | 2 | 3 | 4 | 5 |
|---|---|---|---|---|---|
| Disagree Strongly | Disagree Somewhat | Disagree Slightly | Agree Slightly | Agree Somewhat | Agree Strongly |

3. Women, compared to men, tend to have a superior moral sensibility.

| 0 | 1 | 2 | 3 | 4 | 5 |
|---|---|---|---|---|---|
| Disagree Strongly | Disagree Somewhat | Disagree Slightly | Agree Slightly | Agree Somewhat | Agree Strongly |

4. Men should be willing to sacrifice their own well-being in order to provide financially for the women in their lives.

| 0 | 1 | 2 | 3 | 4 | 5 |
|---|---|---|---|---|---|
| Disagree Strongly | Disagree Somewhat | Disagree Slightly | Agree Slightly | Agree Somewhat | Agree Strongly |

5. Many women have a quality of purity that few men possess.

| 0 | 1 | 2 | 3 | 4 | 5 |
|---|---|---|---|---|---|
| Disagree Strongly | Disagree Somewhat | Disagree Slightly | Agree Slightly | Agree Somewhat | Agree Strongly |

6. A good woman should be set on a pedestal by her man.

| 0 | 1 | 2 | 3 | 4 | 5 |
|---|---|---|---|---|---|
| Disagree Strongly | Disagree Somewhat | Disagree Slightly | Agree Slightly | Agree Somewhat | Agree Strongly |

### HOSTILE SEXISM SCALE

1. Women exaggerate problems they have at work.

| 0 | 1 | 2 | 3 | 4 | 5 |
|---|---|---|---|---|---|
| Disagree Strongly | Disagree Somewhat | Disagree Slightly | Agree Slightly | Agree Somewhat | Agree Strongly |

2. Feminists are making entirely reasonable demands of men.

| 0 | 1 | 2 | 3 | 4 | 5 |
|---|---|---|---|---|---|
| Disagree Strongly | Disagree Somewhat | Disagree Slightly | Agree Slightly | Agree Somewhat | Agree Strongly |

3. Once a woman gets a man to commit to her, she usually tries to put him on a tight leash.

| 0 | 1 | 2 | 3 | 4 | 5 |
|---|---|---|---|---|---|
| Disagree Strongly | Disagree Somewhat | Disagree Slightly | Agree Slightly | Agree Somewhat | Agree Strongly |

4. Most women interpret innocent remarks or acts as being sexist.

| 0 | 1 | 2 | 3 | 4 | 5 |
|---|---|---|---|---|---|
| Disagree Strongly | Disagree Somewhat | Disagree Slightly | Agree Slightly | Agree Somewhat | Agree Strongly |

5. Many women are actually seeking special favors, such as hiring policies that favor them over men, under the guise of asking for "equality."

| 0 | 1 | 2 | 3 | 4 | 5 |
|---|---|---|---|---|---|
| Disagree Strongly | Disagree Somewhat | Disagree Slightly | Agree Slightly | Agree Somewhat | Agree Strongly |

6. Women seek to gain power by getting control over men.

| 0 | 1 | 2 | 3 | 4 | 5 |
|---|---|---|---|---|---|
| Disagree Strongly | Disagree Somewhat | Disagree Slightly | Agree Slightly | Agree Somewhat | Agree Strongly |

**SCORING:** For each scale (benevolent sexism and hostile sexism), score Items 1, 3, 4, 5, and 6 using the answer scales as presented (0-1-2-3-4-5); Item 2 in each scale is reverse-scored (that is, 5-4-3-2-1-0). Add up the six items in each scale to get your overall benevolent sexism or hostile sexism score. Possible scores on each scale range from 0 to 30, and higher scores represent greater sexism.

Sample items from Glick and Fiske, "The ambivalent sexism inventory: Differentiating hostile and benevolent sexism," *Journal of Personality and Social Psychology, 70*, 491–512, 1996. Copyright © 1995 by Peter Glick and Susan T. Fiske. Reprinted by permission.

Religious institutions also contribute to gender stereotypes. In many religions, men and women are treated differently and/or assigned different roles in the church. For instance, women are required to pray separately from men in some religions, such as Islam. Positions of power in most religions are dominated by men. For example, women cannot become priests in the Roman Catholic church. These traditions teach young people that men and women differ in significant ways and are best suited to specific roles in society. There is some evidence that stronger religious beliefs are correlated with greater endorsement of stereotypical gender roles (Morgan, 1987).

Another source of gender stereotypes is the mass media. Men and women are portrayed in stereotypical ways in many television shows and movies. Some counter-stereotypic portrayals occur, of course, but most characters fall into typical gender roles. For example, sitcoms usually portray women as very concerned about their physical appearance and as highly emotional. Music videos often portray women as sex objects. These characterizations may serve to influence young viewers' beliefs about gender traits and roles.

It is also likely that distorted interpretations and self-fulfilling prophesies serve to strengthen gender stereotypes. For instance, people may interpret a man's request for help as assertive, but a woman's request for help as submissive. In terms of self-fulfilling prophesies, people's actions may elicit stereotype-consistent behavior. For instance, if parents expect their sons to be independent and decisive, they may act toward their sons in ways that evoke independent and decisive behavior (e.g., insisting they make a speedy decision). In contrast, if parents expect their daughters to be nurturant and compassionate, they may act toward their daughters in ways that evoke such behaviors (e.g., sending them to visit a sick relative).

**Accuracy of Gender Stereotypes.**   The *accuracy* of gender stereotypes is a complex issue. We have mentioned several origins of stereotypes that may not have a basis in reality (e.g., media portrayals of men and women). But some researchers have argued that there is a substantial "kernel of truth" in gender stereotypes (and in other domains of interpersonal perception as well; see Jussim, 1991). What should we conclude about the accuracy of gender stereotypes?

Sex differences that parallel the content of gender stereotypes, including aggressiveness and concern for others' feelings, have been documented in research actually comparing men and women. Also, Janet Swim (1994) asked men and women to estimate the sizes of the gender differences on numerous characteristics that had yielded reliable male–female differences in past research. She found that perceivers were generally quite good at judging the sizes of gender differences, which suggests that gender stereotypes have a factual basis.

But there is also evidence that gender stereotypes considerably exaggerate any real gender differences (e.g., Diekman, Eagly, & Kulesa, 2002). Carol Martin (1987) conducted an interesting study at the University of British Columbia in Vancouver, Canada. She asked men and women to indicate whether various characteristics were self-descriptive and also to estimate the percentage of men and women who possess the same characteristics. Martin used the self-ratings of men and women as a rough estimate of *actual* sex differences. These responses produced a few substantial differences between the sexes (e.g., on self-ratings of egotistical, cynical, and whiney) and a few smaller differences. She used the estimated percentages of each gender to assess *perceived* sex differences (i.e., stereotypes). These estimates of men and women as groups revealed many more significant differences than did the self-ratings. Indeed, participants judged that men and women as groups differed on virtually every trait that was measured. On 34 of 40 traits, perceived sex differences (based on ratings of the groups) were significantly larger than actual sex differences (based on self-ratings; see also Allen, 1995). Some traits were believed to differ substantially between the genders but were not actually endorsed differentially by men and women, including independent, helpful, and kind.

These findings show that, like other stereotypes, gender stereotypes are certainly oversimplifications—in this case, oversimplifications of men and women. Although the two genders may differ, on average, on a few characteristics, these differences are probably smaller than most of us believe. Also, differences *within* each sex (comparing different men or different women) are always larger than average differences *between* the two sexes. And most of us believe that men and women differ on some traits where there are no real differences at all. Thus, when gender stereotypes are used to form impressions of a particular target, they will often be inaccurate.

Of course, even if gender stereotypes have a kernel of truth, this does not mean that gender differences are inevitable. For example, even if men and women actually differ at the present time in how aggressive they are (on average), it is possible that socialization that treated boys and girls the same would reduce or eliminate this difference. We must distinguish between *current* gender differences (which do exist on some characteristics) and *inevitable* or *biological* sex differences (which may be very few in number). In Chapter 5, we discussed possible biological and social sources of gender differences (e.g., see Buss & Kenrick, 1998; Wood & Eagly, 2002) and suggested that both kinds of factors play some role. Future researchers will have to disentangle the contributions of biology and socialization.

In conclusion, gender stereotypes may be accurate in some respects, but they exaggerate gender differences and include features that reflect, in whole or in part, the different cultural roles assigned to men and women (see Abele, 2003; Diekman & Eagly, 2000; Eagly & Wood, 1999). These observations imply that societies should not limit individuals' goals and opportunities on the basis of their gender.

## Prejudice Against Overweight Women

Obesity is a devastating stigma in our culture. People who are overweight are the targets of widespread prejudice and discrimination, ranging from schoolyard ridicule to denial of employment. A negative, damaging stereotype of overweight individuals is common in our society. Compared to normal weight persons, obese individuals are perceived as less attractive, less intelligent, less popular, less athletic, and less successful (e.g., Crandall, 1994; Harris, Harris, & Bochner, 1982; Hebl & Heatherton, 1997).

One reason that obese individuals are evaluated negatively is that they are often seen as personally responsible for being overweight—their weight is believed to reflect poor eating habits and a lack of willpower. Tragically, obese individuals often agree with these perceptions and, therefore, blame themselves for being ridiculed and rejected.

Although both overweight women and overweight men are subject to prejudice and negative treatment, the impact of being overweight is greater on women, because physical appearance is more highly valued for women than men in our culture (Crocker, Cornwell, & Major, 1993; Roehling, 1999). Consistent with this reasoning, researchers have found that although being overweight is associated with lower self-esteem in both women and men, the connection is stronger among women (Miller & Downey, 1999).

How bad is discrimination against overweight women? Michelle Hebl and Laura Mannix (2003) found that if a man was simply sitting beside an overweight woman, even when the two were strangers, he was judged more negatively than if he was sitting beside a normal weight woman. In perhaps the most disturbing

© Stephen Ferry/Getty Images

Prejudice and discrimination directed against people who are overweight is common in our society.

demonstration of discrimination against overweight women, Christian Crandall (1995) found that females who were heavier than average were less likely to receive financial support from their parents for college education than were normal weight females; no such effect was found for males. Data also showed that there was no association between weight and family income or between weight and academic credentials (e.g., high school GPA) among women, so it appears that the financial support statistics occurred because parents were discriminating against their own heavyweight daughters.

**Fear of Obesity Among Normal Weight Women.** Given the profound negative consequences of obesity for women, it may not be surprising that even normal weight women tend to be very concerned about their weight. Patricia Pliner, Shelly Chaiken, and Gordon Flett (1990) surveyed 639 visitors to a museum in Toronto, Canada. The sample included women and men of various ages from 10 to 79 years. The researchers found that women reported more anxiety about their eating habits, less satisfaction with their physical appearance, and more concern about their body weight than did men. Moreover, these sex differences occurred across the entire life span. Figure 9.5 presents the mean responses of men and women at each age group on a measure of **appearance self-esteem,** which assessed respondents' satisfaction with their looks. Higher bars represent greater satisfaction with one's physical appearance. The figure shows that women were less satisfied than men at every age in the sample.

Why are so many women dissatisfied with their body shapes and sizes? One reason is that they are constantly exposed to unrealistic standards of thinness. In the mass media, female models, actors, and even reporters tend to be physically attractive and very thin. Magazine advertisements, for example, show so-called supermodels who are starvation-skinny. The term "heroin chic" has been used to describe models who are so thin and wasted that they appear to be heroin addicts, yet are presented as beautiful and sexy. Researchers have found that exposure to

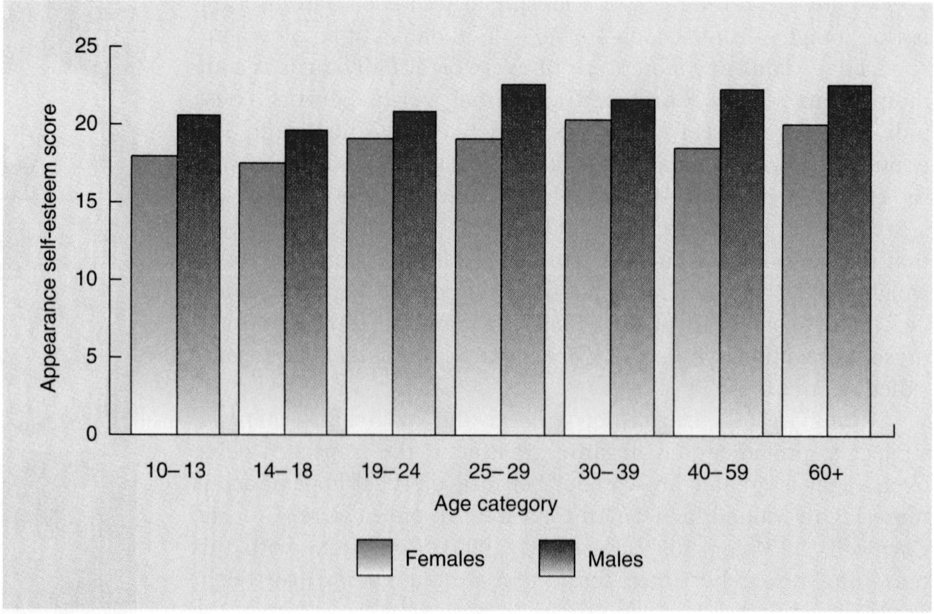

**appearance self-esteem**

*an individual's satisfaction with his or her physical looks*

**FIGURE 9.5** Mean appearance self-esteem for females and males at each age group

From Pliner et al., "Gender differences in concern with body weight and physical appearance over the lifespan," *Personality and Social Psychology Bulletin*, 16, 263–273, Table 1, p. 268, 1990. Reprinted by permission of Sage Publications.

thin media images can have negative effects on women's self-concepts and eating patterns (e.g., Mills, Polivy, Herman, & Tiggemann, 2002; Stice & Shaw, 1994).

Fear of gaining weight can affect even athletic women. Heather Hausenblas and Albert Carron (1999) reviewed 92 studies examining eating disorders among athletes and found that female athletes experienced more problems with anorexia nervosa (starvation brought on by an intense fear of gaining weight) and bulimia (binge eating followed by purging) than did female nonathletes. Eating disorders were especially common in what the authors called *aesthetic sports,* which involved subjective evaluations that might be based on appearance, such as gymnastics, figure skating, dance, and diving.

Women are frequently exposed to unrealistic standards of thinness in the media.

# The Victim's Perspective: Prejudice and Discrimination From the Inside

To this point, we have focused on the causes of prejudice, discrimination, and sexism, trying to understand why people sometimes develop negative attitudes and behave in discriminatory ways toward members of other groups. But what about the people who are the *victims* of prejudice and discrimination? What are their lives like?

Think about your own experiences. Are you a member of any minority or disadvantaged groups? Some of you belong to ethnic or religious minority groups. Many of you are women, who can face significant discrimination, as noted in the preceding section. But even those of you who are not members of groups that are typically considered to be disadvantaged (e.g., Caucasian males) may be able to think of times when your group membership hurt you or was held against you. College students might be denied rental housing; men are sometimes viewed suspiciously as babysitters or child care workers; varsity athletes might have to contend with a stereotype that they are not academically competent; and so on. Can you think of instances when you were judged in a biased way because you belonged to a certain group? How did this experience make you feel? What would it be like to be greeted with hostility or suspicion frequently throughout your life?

Social psychologists have directed less attention to the experiences of disadvantaged group members than to the causes of prejudice, largely because a long-term goal of research has been to *reduce* prejudice and discrimination. Thus, we have focused on the people who *are* prejudiced rather than the *targets* of prejudice. But in the last 10 or 20 years, some researchers have started to explore the psychology of victimization (e.g., see Swim & Stangor, 1998).

Before turning to this research, we should note that the most significant consequence of being a member of a severely disadvantaged group (e.g., an ethnic minority group) is probably not psychological but rather material: one's life is more difficult economically and occupationally than the lives of members of advantaged groups. Members of disadvantaged groups are more likely to live in poverty, to be the victims of violence, and to be denied opportunities than are members of majority or dominant groups in society. The term *disadvantaged* can be taken quite literally: the lives of these individuals are objectively more difficult than the lives of members of advantaged groups.

But prejudice and discrimination also have psychological consequences. For example, being the victim of discrimination is stressful; many researchers have found that experiences of discrimination are associated with higher levels of emotional anguish (e.g., Branscombe, Schmitt, & Harvey, 1999; Williams & Williams-Morris, 2000). Moreover, Frederick Gibbons, Meg Gerrard, and their colleagues (Gibbons, Gerrard, Cleveland, Wills, & Brody, 2004) found that experiences of discrimination led not only to emotional distress (e.g., feelings of worthlessness and anxiety), but also to greater use of alcohol and illegal drugs. The researchers argued that discrimination increased individuals' substance use because the alcohol and drugs were being used to reduce the emotional distress caused by discrimination.

Clearly, it is important to study how prejudice and discrimination affect their victims. In this section, we consider two lines of social psychological research that have focused specifically on members of minority or subordinate groups: research on the *personal–group discrimination discrepancy* and research on *stereotype threat*.

## The Personal–Group Discrimination Discrepancy

Return again to your own experiences of discrimination, when membership in a group has hurt you. Thinking about whatever group this may be, how would you answer the following question: Have you experienced more, less, or about the same amount of discrimination as the average member of your group? For example, if you are a woman, have you experienced more, less, or about the same amount of gender discrimination as the average woman? If you are African American, have you experienced more, less, or about the same amount of racial discrimination as the average African American? If your discrimination experiences have been based on being a college student, have you experienced more, less, or about the same amount of discrimination against students as the average college student?

Social psychologists studying members of disadvantaged groups have uncovered an interesting pattern in people's judgments of their own experiences of discrimination relative to the average member of their group: respondents consistently report that they have personally experienced *less* discrimination than the average member of their group. In other words, people who belong to groups that are targets of discrimination report that their own experiences have been less frequent or less serious than the experiences of the "typical" member of their group. This tendency for most people to report less personal discrimination than the typical member of their group cannot be accurate, because it is statistically impossible for *most people* to be less than *average.*

**personal–group discrimination discrepancy**

*the tendency for people to report that they as individuals have experienced less negative treatment based on their group membership than the average member of their group*

This phenomenon has been labeled the **personal–group discrimination discrepancy,** because personal discrimination is seen as discrepant from group discrimination: people report less personal discrimination than discrimination aimed at their group. Did your own answer follow this pattern? If so, your judgment is consistent with findings that have been obtained with *many* different disadvantaged groups. For example, in a study of inner-city African American men in Miami, participants reported that their personal experiences of racial discrimination had been less frequent than the experiences of the typical African American man (Taylor, Wright, & Porter, 1993). Similarly, Faye Crosby (1984) found that working women in the United States reported having personally experienced less gender discrimination in their workplace than the average woman. Researchers have also found the personal–group discrimination discrepancy in surveys of immigrant women in Montreal (Taylor, Wright, Moghaddam, & Lalonde, 1990), single mothers receiving government assistance (Olson, Roese, Meen, & Robertson, 1995), Chinese and Pakistani residents of Toronto (Dion & Kawakami, 1996), and other disadvantaged groups (for reviews, see Olson & Hafer, 1996; Taylor et al., 1993).

Why does this bias occur? Why do people consistently report less-than-average discrimination directed against themselves? Faye Crosby (1984) argued that motivational factors are important. She suggested that members of disadvantaged groups want to see themselves as experiencing relatively little discrimination because this allows them to feel that they have more control over their lives. Being a victim of discrimination means that your life is affected by others who dislike or have negative expectations for you, which might induce feelings of helplessness. In contrast, believing that discrimination does not occur much in one's own life maintains a perception of control. People want to distance themselves from being a victim of discrimination (see also Hodson & Esses, 2002; Quinn & Olson, 2003).

Another motivational factor may be that denying personal discrimination gives members of minority groups an excuse for not doing anything about prejudice against their group. People who exhibit bigotry often belong to powerful or dominant groups in society, so taking action against bigots can be dangerous or costly. If members of minority groups see themselves as relatively untouched by discrimination, they can rationalize (to themselves and to other people) their own inaction.

People may also avoid saying that they have personally experienced discrimination because such claims are seen by others as whiney or complaining (see Kaiser & Miller, 2001). There are social costs associated with claiming discrimination, and these costs may cause members of minority groups to publicly minimize their own experiences of discrimination (Sechrist, Swim, & Stangor, 2004). Unfortunately, this avoidance may prevent people who really do experience discrimination from confronting the obstacles they face in their daily lives.

In addition to being motivated to *understate* discrimination directed against themselves *personally* for the reasons discussed above, members of disadvantaged groups might also be motivated to *exaggerate* discrimination at the *group* level (i.e., exaggerate how much discrimination the "typical" member of their group experiences). Such exaggeration could contribute to the personal–group discrimination discrepancy. Why might people exaggerate discrimination against their group? If one's group is the target of a lot of discrimination, then it deserves special programs such as affirmative action or social assistance. Thus, by exaggerating group-level discrimination, individuals may be hoping to provide a justification for these programs, which might benefit them personally.

Cognitive factors may also contribute to the personal–group discrimination discrepancy. For example, people may compare the discriminatory events in their own lives (a small sample) with all the discriminatory events they have heard about from other people and in the news. Their personal experiences with discrimination may seem quite minimal in comparison to the breadth of events involving others.

**stereotype threat**

*the pressure experienced by individuals who fear that if they perform poorly on a task, their performance will appear to confirm an unfavorable belief about their group*

## Stereotype Threat

A second line of research on the effects of being a victim of prejudice has focused on the impact of negative social stereotypes on performance. In 1995, Claude Steele and Joshua Aronson published an important paper on **stereotype threat.** Stereotype threat occurs when individuals believe that if they perform poorly, their performance will appear to confirm an unfavorable stereotype about their group. Stereotype threat puts pressure on people to do as well as possible in order to discredit the negative stereotype. Unfortunately, this added pressure can itself cause poor performance—people can "choke" under the pressure.

For example, African Americans know that some observers hold a negative, harmful stereotype that Blacks perform relatively poorly on academic tasks. Thus, whenever African Americans work on explicitly intellectual tasks, they may worry that if they perform poorly, they will confirm this stereotype in the eyes of some prejudiced people. They may feel that they "represent" their group and, therefore, must perform well to disconfirm the stereotype. This pressure—or stereotype threat—can impair performance. White Americans may not face this kind of pressure when performing academic tasks.

Steele and Aronson (1995) documented this phenomenon with African American students at Stanford University—an elite institution where it might be expected that all students would be confident about their academic abilities. Steele and Aronson recruited African American and White students and administered a difficult test constructed from items from the verbal section of the Graduate Record Examination (GRE). Half of the participants (both White and Black) took the test

African Americans can experience *stereotype threat* when they write an academic exam.

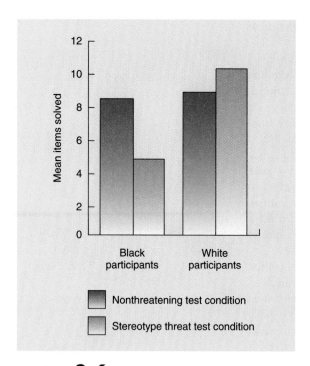

**FIGURE 9.6**

Performance by Black and White participants in nonthreatening and stereotype threat test conditions

From Steele and Aronson, "Stereotype threat and the intellectual test performance of African Americans," *Journal of Personality and Social Psychology,* 69, 797–811, Fig. 2, p. 802, 1995. Copyright © 1995 by the American Psychological Association. Reprinted by permission.

under conditions that were expected to elicit stereotype threat among the Black students. These individuals were told that the study was investigating "various personal factors involved in performance on problems requiring reading and verbal reasoning abilities" and that they would receive feedback on their own abilities after the test. The remaining participants completed the test under more relaxed and nonevaluative conditions; they were not told that the test assessed verbal abilities and did not expect feedback on their own abilities after the test.

Figure 9.6 presents the performance data in each condition for Black and White students. As predicted, Black participants performed just as well as White students in the relaxed condition, but Black participants performed significantly worse than White students in the stereotype threat condition. Note also that the performance of White participants was not affected by the threat manipulation, whereas the performance of Black participants declined in the stereotype threat condition compared to the relaxed condition.

These data show that stereotype threat can impair the performance of African American students. As if dealing with objective disadvantage were not enough, African Americans must also carry the weight of representing their group when they perform academic tasks. The added pressure of this responsibility may interfere with clear thinking; thus, their performance can deteriorate. Unfortunately, this pressure-induced decrement in performance might be interpreted by prejudiced observers as evidence that the negative stereotype is accurate.

African Americans are not the only target of negative stereotypes regarding performance on academic or other tasks. For example, Jean-Claude Croizet and Theresa Claire (1998) reported that, in France, some people hold a negative stereotype of individuals from low socioeconomic status (SES) backgrounds, who are believed to lack intellectual ability. (This damaging stereotype is endorsed by some people in other countries as well.) These researchers tested whether stereotype threat might occur among low-SES college students by administering a difficult test under conditions that were expected either to elicit stereotype threat or to be nonthreatening. As predicted, participants from low-SES backgrounds performed worse under the threatening than nonthreatening conditions, whereas participants from high-SES backgrounds were not affected by the manipulation of stereotype threat.

Another stereotype that some people hold is that women are less skilled at mathematics than are men. Steven Spencer, Claude Steele, and Diane Quinn (1999) tested whether women might, under certain conditions, experience stereotype threat on tests of mathematics, which would impair their performance. These researchers recruited men and women at the University of Michigan, all of whom were skilled at math: all participants had taken at least one semester of calculus, had received at least a B in the course, and had previously scored in the top 15% of their age group on the math subsection of the Scholastic Aptitude Test. Further, all participants had completed a survey in which they indicated agreement with the following two statements: "I am good at math" and "It is important to me that I am good at math."

Participants completed a difficult test taken from the advanced GRE for mathematics. Half of the participants were administered the test under conditions that were expected to arouse stereotype threat among women: they were told that this test had shown significant gender differences in performance in the past. The remaining participants were administered the test under conditions that were expected to prevent stereotype threat: they were told that this test had never shown gender differences in the past.

Figure 9.7 presents the mean performance scores for women and men in the nonthreatening and threatening conditions. As predicted, women performed just as well as men in the nonthreatening condition. In contrast, women in the stereotype threat condition performed significantly worse than did men in this condition (and also significantly worse than did women in the nonthreatening condition).

These data are striking in that the affected women were highly talented at mathematics; it may seem surprising that people who are good at something can be so negatively affected (see also Sekaquaptewa & Thompson, 2003). In fact, however, it turns out that people for whom a domain of ability is important (and who therefore care about how they perform in that domain) are *more* susceptible to stereotype threat than people who are less invested in the domain (Stone, 2002; Stone, Lynch, Sjomeling, & Darley, 1999). For instance, women who care about their mathematics ability are more susceptible to stereotype threat on math tests than are those who do not; similarly, African Americans who care about academic achievement are more susceptible to stereotype threat on academic tasks than are those who do not. Presumably, people who do not care about their performance in a particular domain will not experience additional pressure from stereotype threat—after all, they *don't care* about this domain. Of course, people who do care about the domain must also be aware of a negative stereotype of their group in order for stereotype threat to occur (Brown & Pinel, 2003). There is also evidence that people who identify strongly with their group will be more affected by stereotype threat than people who identify only weakly with their group (Schmader, 2002).

Joshua Aronson and his colleagues (Aronson, Lustina, Good, Keough, Steele, & Brown, 1999) showed that stereotype threat can even affect the performance of members of typically "advantaged" groups under the appropriate circumstances. These researchers administered a difficult mathematics test to White male Stanford University students who were selected to be strong in mathematics (similar to the selection criteria for participants in Spencer et al.'s 1999 experiment). Note that the common stereotype of White males is that they are *good* at math.

Half of the participants were told that the experiment was designed to investigate the phenomenal math achievement of Asian students and to try to understand the "growing gap in academic performance between Asian and White students." This alleged purpose was expected to induce stereotype threat in these White males, who would fear confirming the relatively inferior performance by Whites compared to Asians. The remaining participants did not hear anything about Asian students prior to taking the test.

Men in the stereotype threat condition performed significantly worse (an average of 6.55 correct answers out of 18 questions) than did men in the nonthreatening condition (an average of 9.58 correct answers). Thus, stereotype threat was documented for White men in mathematics when an allegedly even more talented group was highlighted as a possible comparison.

What mechanisms explain stereotype threat? How does the pressure of stereotype threat impair performance? One clearly important factor is emotional arousal: when people perform a test under conditions that create stereotype threat, they exhibit more numerous nonverbal signs of anxiety (Bosson, Haymovitz, & Pinel, 2004), as well as higher levels of sympathetic arousal (e.g., heart rate, blood pressure; O'Brien & Crandall, 2003). Other emotions may also occur: people report feeling disappointed and sad, perhaps because conditions producing stereotype threat accentuate a negative stereotype of their group (Keller & Dauenheimer, 2003). Stereotype threat also appears to reduce people's mental capacity—their ability to

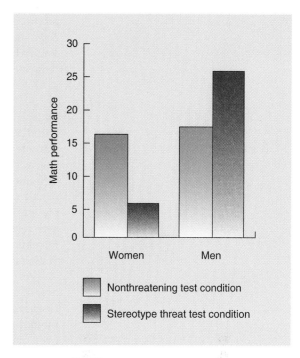

**FIGURE 9.7**  Performance by women and men in nonthreatening and stereotype threat test conditions

From Spencer et al., "Stereotype threat and women's math performance," *Journal of Experimental Social Psychology*, 35, 4–28, Fig. 2, p. 13, 1999. Reprinted by permission of Elsevier.

retain information in memory (Croizet, Després, Gauzins, Huguet, Leyens, & Méot, 2004; Schmader & Johns, 2003). This reduction in memory capacity probably occurs because feelings of anxiety and disappointment are distracting. Obviously, reduced memory capacity will hurt performance on difficult tests. The processes involved in stereotype threat are illustrated in Figure 9.8.

Are there ways to reduce the impact of stereotype threat on vulnerable populations? Thomas Ford and his colleagues (Ford, Ferguson, Brooks, & Hagadone, 2004) found that people who use humor to cope with stress are better able to deal with stereotype threat. Why does humor help? Ford et al. found that using humor to deal with stress was associated with lower levels of anxiety, resulting in better performance. There is also evidence that exposure to a role model who violates the negative stereotype alleviates the negative effects of stereotype threat. For example, in one study, reading about four individual women who had succeeded in architecture, law, medicine, and invention significantly improved women's performance on a difficult math test under conditions of stereotype threat (McIntyre, Paulson, & Lord, 2003; see also Marx & Roman, 2002).

An interesting strategy for reducing the impact of stereotype threat was proposed by Joshua Aronson, Carrie Fried, and Catherine Good (2002). These researchers hypothesized that students, particularly African American students, might benefit from perceiving intelligence as something that can grow and change over time, rather than as a stable, unchangeable quality. If intelligence is viewed as a flexible capacity that can be increased, then performance on a given intellectual task is less threatening and anxiety-provoking. Students who consider intelligence to be changeable might be less worried that poor performance on a particular test will confirm the negative stereotype of their group.

To test this reasoning, Black and White students at Stanford University were recruited early in a school term to take part in a "pen pal" program with children, in which they wrote several letters to children who were experiencing problems at school. In the experimental condition, participants were given materials that portrayed intelligence as something that can be increased via mental exercise (much

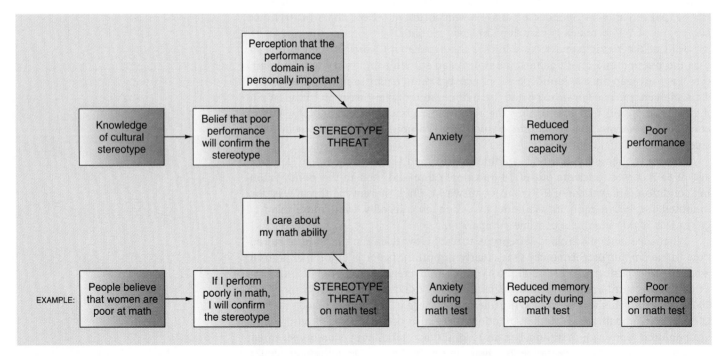

**FIGURE 9.8**  Processes involved in stereotype threat

as a muscle can be strengthened with physical exercise) and were encouraged to convince their younger pen pal that academic performance is changeable. In fact, the "pen pal" cover story was fictitious; the purpose of writing the letters was simply to convince the college students (or, more correctly, to help them convince themselves) that intelligence is something that can be increased.

The academic performance of the experimental participants at the end of the school term was compared to the performance of students in a control condition. Results showed that African American students who had participated in the experimental condition earlier in the term obtained significantly higher grade point averages than did African American students in the control condition. A similar pattern was obtained for White students, with grade point averages somewhat higher in the experimental condition, but the effect was not statistically significant. These data suggest that the negative impact of stereotype threat on academic performance might be reduced by changing students' conceptions of intelligence. Even members of an advantaged group showed some benefit, but the findings for African Americans were more noteworthy because members of disadvantaged groups are the ones most often affected by stereotype threat. Future research will be needed to investigate whether this strategy has widespread applicability for reducing the negative effects of stereotype threat on the academic performance of various groups.

## Genocide

We have discussed many negative consequences of prejudice, including distorted information processing, interpersonal aggression, job discrimination, and stereotype threat. But the worst consequence of prejudice is undoubtedly *genocide,* which we defined at the beginning of the chapter as an attempt to systematically eliminate an ethnic group through banishment or murder. Human history is unfortunately filled with instances of genocide, including many in the last century.

The most infamous case of genocide is probably the Holocaust, committed by the Nazis during the Second World War. The Holocaust involved the murder of about 6 million Jews in Germany and other Nazi-occupied countries. The slaughter was terrible. For instance, out of about 600,000 Jews in Hungary at the beginning of the war, approximately 450,000 (75%) were murdered.

The Second World War may seem a distant event. We can find several instances of genocide in the past 15 years. In 1994, approximately 800,000 people were murdered in Rwanda in only 100 days (a killing rate 5 times higher than the Nazis' slaughter of Jews; see Prunier, 1995). The genocide was committed by extremist members of the majority ethnic group in Rwanda, the Hutus, who targeted members of the minority ethnic group, the Tutsis, as well as moderate Hutus. Roving gangs armed with machetes brutally massacred men, women, and children. One of the many troubling aspects of this tragedy was that it occurred despite the presence of United Nations peacekeeping troops.

"... The SS people walked up and down, and [indicated] with thumb up to go right, and thumb down to go left. I was chosen to the right, some of my friends to the left. The right was chosen to work; the left was chosen to go to the gas chambers."

Between 1992 and 1995, civil war in Bosnia and Herzegovina (one of several independent states that emerged from the former Yugoslavia in Europe) killed up to 250,000 people. Tens of thousands of these deaths were murders of civilians. For instance, Radislav Drstic, a Bosnian Serb general, was convicted in 1999 of murdering up to 8,000 Bosnian Muslims in Srebrencia in 1995. This civil war in Bosnia and Herzegovina was not the end of ethnic conflict in the region. In 1998–1999, between

5,000 and 10,000 ethnic Albanians were murdered in Kosovo (a province in Serbia, another state that emerged from Yugoslavia) by Serbian forces, and about 500,000 ethnic Albanians were displaced. Slobodan Milosevic, the president of Serbia at the time, was arrested in 2001 and charged with committing crimes against humanity during the Kosovo conflict.

In the most recent case of apparent genocide, up to 100,000 Black Sudanese civilians were killed in 2003–2004 in the Darfur region of Sudan by Arab Sudanese militias. There had been conflict for many years between the nomadic Arabs and the Black farmers. In addition to the killings, more than 1 million Black Sudanese were displaced and faced starvation in refugee camps. International relief efforts were hampered by interference from Sudanese authorities.

Some flagrant cases of mass murder were based on politics and education more than ethnicity, including brutal purges by Joseph Stalin in the U.S.S.R. in the 1930s and 1940s and by Mao Zedong in China in the 1950s, 1960s, and 1970s. For instance, it is estimated that during the so-called Cultural Revolution in China between 1966 and 1976, several million Chinese citizens were killed, including most of the country's intellectual elite. The Chinese Communists also supported Pol Pot and his Khmer Rouge in Cambodia, who conducted an equally bloody purge between 1975 and 1978. The Khmer Rouge murdered about 1.7 million Cambodians (more than 20% of the population), including virtually every influential thinker and known opponent to the Pol Pot regime.

## Causes of Genocide

Genocide is such an extreme event that it almost defies explanation. How can anyone deliberately and systematically slaughter defenseless civilians? It is, of course, impossible to conduct experimental research on extreme harmdoing, for ethical reasons. But theorists can apply findings from research on less extreme aggression to try to understand genocide. Also, social scientists have sought to identify common elements in historical cases of genocide; these theorists have included social psychologists (e.g., Baumeister, 1997; Staub, 1989, 1999; Staub, Pearlman, & Miller, 2003; Waller, 2002) and political scientists (e.g., Adelman, 2000, 2004). We summarize a few insights from this literature in the following paragraphs.

Genocide is almost always preceded by what Ervin Staub (1989, 1999) calls *difficult life conditions*. These conditions may consist of serious economic problems, major political changes or turmoil, and intense conflict between groups in a society. Difficult life conditions create both material and psychological deprivation; that is, people in the society are suffering in terms of basic physical needs (e.g., food, housing) and basic psychological needs (e.g., security, positive identity, sense of control). For instance, the political breakup of Yugoslavia after the 1980 death of its longtime Communist dictator, Marshall Tito, led to extreme instability. The new independent republics that emerged from Yugoslavia faced severe economic hardship, including high levels of unemployment. These conditions aggravated preexisting tensions and conflict among the numerous ethnic groups in the region and undoubtedly contributed to the murders in Bosnia and Kosovo.

A second prerequisite for genocide appears to be the *dehumanization or devaluation of the outgroup* (Bar-Tal, 1990; Opotow, 2001; Staub, 1989; Waller, 2002). There is often a long history of hostility between the groups, but difficult life conditions intensify the antagonism and derogation. Members of the outgroup may be seen as subhuman and, therefore, not deserving of the usual rights and protections given to members of society. For example, in Rwanda, the majority Hutus had long disliked the Tutsis, who held many positions of influence. Mistrust and derogation of the Tutsis increased prior to the genocide because of rumors and propaganda spread by extremist factions within Hutu society.

A third element in many cases of genocide is *excessive respect for authority* (Baumeister, 1997; Staub, 1989; Waller, 2002). If people in a dominant group are overly trusting of authorities' claims and interpretations of events, they may accept exaggerated accusations without supportive evidence. Obedient individuals may also carry out harmful acts when ordered to do so, even if they have personal doubts about the morality of their behavior. Highly respectful cultures also look to their leaders for direction, which gives autocratic rulers like Adolf Hitler, Mao Zedong, and Pol Pot even more power. Respect for authority was very high in most of the countries mentioned earlier as cases of genocide, including Germany, China, Serbia, and Cambodia.

Between 1975 and 1978, Pol Pot and the Khmer Rouge murdered approximately 1.7 million Cambodians, more than 20% of the country's population.

Genocide does not appear suddenly, without warning; there is always *a gradual escalation of aggression and violence.* This escalation means that people slowly become committed to harming the outgroup (Baumeister, 1997; Staub, 1999). Gangs of thugs might begin by threatening or beating up victims; as observers see aggression occurring without punitive consequences, they become more likely to copy such behavior. What begins as isolated scare tactics and intimidation can transform into widespread violence and murder. Nazi Germany provided a clear example of this escalation. Anti-Semitic acts gradually increased after Hitler's rise to power in 1933. As it became clear that authorities would accept lawless behavior toward Jews, groups of Nazi sympathizers became more aggressive. On the night of November 9, 1938, a coordinated set of attacks took place against Jewish homes, businesses, and synagogues—an event that became known as *Kristallnacht,* or the Night of Broken Glass. About 100 Jews were killed, and thousands of Jewish businesses were destroyed. This event signaled to all Germans that Jewish citizens were legitimate targets of violence.

Finally, genocide cannot occur without *passive bystanders.* Therefore, to understand incidents of mass murder, it is necessary to understand why people who could have intervened did not do so (Adelman, 2004; Baumeister, 1997; Staub, 1989, 1999). One important influence is, of course, fear of the aggressors. It can be dangerous to try to intervene in genocide, as many moderate Hutus learned in Rwanda—sometimes paying with their lives. Another factor is bureaucratic red tape and slow decision making. For example, a U.N. peacekeeping force in Rwanda when the violence began was directly prohibited by the United Nations from intervening because such action would violate the force's mandate, which was simply to observe; by the time the Security Council realized the foolishness of its policy, the slaughter was over. A third factor contributing to passivity is simple imitation: if other people do not intervene, then they must support the violence. As a result, bystanders who do not support the violence tolerate it because they assume everyone else supports it.

These five factors do not "explain" genocide. Nothing can provide compelling reasons for mass murder. Moreover, there have been countless cases of difficult life conditions that did not lead to genocide despite the presence of other factors such as dehumanization and excessive respect for authority. Nevertheless, the factors seem to have been present in many cases of genocide, which suggests they may be precipitating conditions. Other triggers are probably also necessary, and the specific causes of genocide undoubtedly differ from incident to incident. Although we are unlikely to develop a checklist that can predict genocide before it occurs, there is reason to hope that understanding the causes of this extreme form of harmdoing might suggest strategies for defusing potential hotspots. Along these lines, some of the social psychologists cited in this section (e.g., Ervin Staub, Daniel Bar-Tal) have worked with governments and humanitarian organizations to increase communication and decrease hostility in longstanding conflicts such as in the Middle East and in the former Yugoslavia.

# Reducing Prejudice and Discrimination

If you were put in charge of a government agency whose goal was to reduce prejudice and discrimination, what would you do? Where do you think the limited money and resources could best be directed to improve relations between ethnic, racial, and religious groups? Should we focus on majority group members and try to change their attitudes? Should we emphasize educational programs for children in the school system? Should we introduce social programs designed to give minority groups more access to resources? What about the problems of negative stereotypes about women, the elderly, gays and lesbians, and other groups: how can we discredit these beliefs and promote greater understanding and tolerance?

Thinking about these issues brings home the fact that the problems of prejudice and discrimination are extremely complex and challenging. There is likely no single "best" way to attack the problems. Prejudice and discrimination have multiple causes; thus, multifaceted programs will be necessary to have a significant impact. But social psychologists have been at the forefront of designing and testing techniques to reduce prejudice and discrimination. Some of these techniques can be quite effective, and a broad-based approach utilizing numerous strategies might be highly successful. In the following paragraphs, we describe some of the research that has investigated how to reduce prejudice and discrimination and discuss the implications of these studies for real-life programs.

## Dissonance and Prejudice Reduction

In Chapter 7, we discussed a variety of ways that attitudes can be changed. Some of these techniques can be applied to prejudice, which is a negative intergroup attitude. One theory we described was Festinger's (1957) *dissonance theory* (see pages 251–267). Dissonance theory proposes that people want their attitudes, beliefs, and behaviors to be consistent with one another; if they become aware of inconsistencies, they feel bad and are motivated to restore consistency. Research derived from dissonance theory has documented that if people are induced to behave in a counterattitudinal fashion, they often change their attitudes to be more consistent with the behavior. For instance, if college students write an essay arguing in favor of increasing tuition (a position that almost all students oppose), they subsequently become more favorable toward increasing tuition.

Michael Leippe and Donna Eisenstadt (1994) adapted the essay-writing technique to attack racial attitudes. White students at Adelphi University were asked to write an essay arguing in favor of doubling the percentage of the college's scholarship funds that would be specifically directed to Black students only. Half of the participants were simply told to write this essay (*low-choice* condition), and half were asked whether they would be willing to write the essay—instructions designed to make them feel that their essay writing was voluntary (*high-choice* condition). In addition, half of the participants signed their essay and recorded their phone number on a consent form (*public* condition), and half prepared the essay privately and never recorded their name or phone number on any of their materials (*private* condition). The researchers predicted that either high choice or high publicity would arouse dissonance, which participants would reduce by changing their racial attitudes to be more favorable toward Blacks. Racial attitudes were measured in an allegedly different study that followed the essay-writing task. Participants answered 10 items measuring pro-Black attitudes (e.g., "Too many Blacks still lose out on jobs and promotions because of their skin color").

Figure 9.9 presents the attitudes reported by participants in each condition who complied with the request to write a pro-Black essay; higher bars reflect more favorable attitudes toward Blacks. As predicted, the results showed that participants who wrote an essay under *either* high-choice *or* high-publicity conditions (the low-choice/public condition, high-choice/private condition, and high-choice/public condition) reported more favorable attitudes than did participants in the low-choice/private condition. Thus, performing a behavior that communicated a positive racial attitude significantly improved racial attitudes when the behavior was either voluntary or public (or both).

The procedure in the public conditions of Leippe and Eisenstadt's study might remind you of the *hypocrisy paradigm* we discussed in Chapter 7 (see page 264). In the hypocrisy paradigm, individuals are asked to make a public statement supporting a socially desirable position (e.g., conserving water) and are then reminded of their own past failures to behave consistently with this position. After this public commitment, participants tend to behave more in line with their stated position (e.g., Stone, Aronson, Crain, Winslow, & Fried, 1994).

It turns out that the hypocrisy paradigm has been used to attack prejudice. Leanne Son Hing, Winnie Li, and Mark Zanna (2002) recruited a sample of college students who, in a previous study, had exhibited a negative implicit attitude toward Asians. Half of these students were asked to make a public statement supporting nonprejudicial behavior toward Asians and were then induced to think about their own past actions toward Asians that had been negative or prejudiced. In a subsequent survey, these students responded in a pro-Asian manner: they expressed stronger opposition to reducing the budget of the Asian Students Association at their college than did participants who had not experienced the hypocrisy induction.

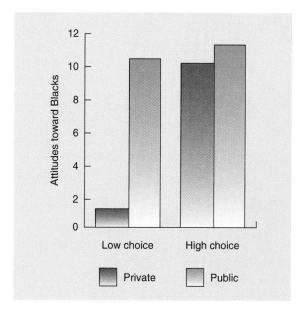

**FIGURE 9.9** Attitudes toward Blacks following pro-Black essay in each condition

From Leippe and Eisenstadt, "Generalization of dissonance reduction: Decreasing prejudice through induced compliance," *Journal of Personality and Social Psychology*, 67, 395–413, Table 1, p. 401, 1995. Copyright © 1994 by the American Psychological Association. Reprinted by permission.

## The Contact Hypothesis and Prejudice Reduction

One straightforward idea for making people less prejudiced is to show them by direct exposure that members of the targeted group deserve decent treatment. This approach is based on the **contact hypothesis,** which predicts that contact between members of different groups will produce more positive intergroup attitudes (Allport, 1954; Pettigrew, 1986). You may recall the *mere exposure effect* discussed in Chapter 6 (see page 214), which refers to the tendency for attitudes toward an object to become more favorable as people are repeatedly exposed to it (Zajonc, 1968). The contact hypothesis is compatible with this positive effect of familiarity.

Many researchers have reported correlational data showing that greater contact is associated with more favorable intergroup attitudes. For instance, Whitely (1990) found that increased contact with gays and lesbians was associated with more favorable attitudes toward these groups among heterosexuals. Altemeyer (1994) found that prejudiced individuals reported having had relatively little contact in childhood with members of outgroups. A problem with correlational data, however, is that they cannot distinguish whether contact is producing positive attitudes or whether positive attitudes are encouraging more contact (see Islam & Hewstone, 1993). It is quite possible that both directions are operating.

A real-world test of the contact hypothesis was provided by the decision to desegregate classrooms in the United States in the 1950s and 1960s. This decision

**contact hypothesis**

*the idea that exposure to members of an outgroup will produce more favorable attitudes toward that group* was based, in part, on the assumption that contact between racial groups would reduce prejudice. Early evaluations of the effects of desegregation were decidedly mixed, however, with evidence suggesting that the attitudes of some White children toward minority groups actually became more *negative* after desegregation (see Stephan, 1986). Why would contact with children of different racial groups fail to produce more favorable attitudes?

If contact is to have a positive effect, the interactions between the individuals should be positive, or at least neutral. But simply throwing racial groups together in a school setting does not ensure that contact between the children will be positive—indeed, hostility, suspicion, and rejection can intensify negative attitudes within each group. How can contact be structured in order for exposure to have positive effects?

Researchers and educators have come to realize that several prerequisites must be met if contact is to have a positive effect on intergroup attitudes (Brewer & Miller, 1984; Pettigrew, 1998; Pettigrew & Tropp, 2000; Stephan, 1986). In other words, certain *kinds* of contact can be beneficial. What are these prerequisites? We will mention four.

First, the groups must be approximately *equal in status* before contact will be conducive to positive attitudes (Amir, 1969; Stephan, 1986). When one group is lower in status than the other, resentment can arise within both groups. Real-life desegregation has often involved busing inner-city African American children to suburban, predominantly White schools; the Black and White children are unlikely to have equal status in this situation.

Second, the groups must be involved in *cooperative behavior* together (Bettencourt, Brewer, Croak, & Miller, 1992; Sherif et al., 1961). There must be shared activities between the groups, and the groups must have interdependent goals, such that each group relies on the other to some extent. Competition between groups, on the other hand, is harmful to intergroup attitudes (as we noted in the section on realistic group conflict theory). Again, real-life desegregation often fails to meet this prerequisite, because students from different groups do not need to cooperate to fulfill school assignments; indeed, students might feel that they are *competing* with students in other racial groups for attention of the teacher, grades, and so on.

A third requirement for intergroup contact to be beneficial is *support from legitimate authorities,* such as teachers, parents, and school board trustees (Allport, 1954; Stephan, 1986). If desegregation is not supported by the teacher and by the students' parents at home, then it is unlikely to have much benefit. Children often adopt their parents' attitudes on important issues, and if the parents oppose intergroup contact, children may be resistant and resentful themselves.

Finally, contact must be reasonably *intimate* or *personally important* if it is to improve intergroup attitudes (Amir, 1969; Pettigrew, 1998; van Dick et al., 2004). It is not enough for children to be in the same class or to see one another in the schoolyard. Children must talk to one another, play together, form intergroup friendships, and come to know one another reasonably well before attitudes are likely to change substantially. The contact should be significant enough to be personally meaningful to the individuals.

How or why does intergroup contact produce more favorable attitudes toward an outgroup (assuming that the contact is equal status, cooperative, supported by authorities, and intimate)? A key element appears to be anxiety reduction (see Paolini, Hewstone, Cairns, & Voci, 2004; Plant & Devine, 2003). When people have had little exposure to members of an outgroup, they may feel anxious about interacting with those individuals. Such anxiety will cause them to avoid possible interactions (Plant, 2004; Stephan & Stephan, 1989). In contrast, having some positive experiences with members of an outgroup reduces anxiety and encourages additional interactions. For instance, White children who are initially anxious about playing with Black children because they lack interracial exposure will become more comfortable after experiencing some positive intergroup interactions. The reduction in anxiety will be associated with more favorable attitudes toward, and more frequent interactions with, Black children. Emotional reactions to members of outgroups are strong determinants of our behavior (see Esses & Dovidio, 2002), so it is essential that people overcome their anxiety about intergroup interactions. Positive intergroup contact may be the best avenue for achieving this goal.

Positive intergroup contact can also reduce other factors besides anxiety that lead to prejudice. For instance, when people work together cooperatively, negative stereotypes may be disconfirmed. People learn that members of the outgroup are not aggressive, arrogant, or whatever negative characteristics had previously been attributed to them. Positive contact also shows that the values and attitudes of the two groups are more similar than previously thought, which will reduce the perceived symbolic threat from the outgroup.

Social psychologist Elliot Aronson developed a teaching method he called the **jigsaw classroom** that can be used in classrooms to bring about positive interracial contact. This method is described in Social Psychology in Your Life: The Jigsaw Classroom (p. 384).

## Categorization Processes and Prejudice Reduction

Victims of prejudice are categorized by bigots as belonging to a disliked group that is distinct from the bigot's ingroup. Such categorization is necessary before the bigot's negative stereotype can be applied to the target. Perhaps we can alter the categorization process somehow to reduce prejudice. Several theorists have offered possible strategies.

One proposed approach is to discourage any categorization at all: we should judge other people as individual persons rather than as members of groups. For instance, an individual should be perceived as Lekisha Johnson, rather than as an African American woman. This approach has been called *personalization* (versus *categorization*) or, in the context of racial prejudice, the **color-blind approach** (Brewer & Brown, 1998; Brewer & Miller, 1984; Jones, 1997; Nelson, 2002). Although this idea has some merit, categorization is a process that is automatic, at least in part, and therefore virtually impossible to eliminate. Comparisons of the color-blind approach with alternative strategies have not always supported its effectiveness (e.g., Richeson & Nussbaum, 2004).

A second strategy is to encourage "higher-level," or *superordinate,* categorizations that encompass both the perceiver and the target (Brewer & Brown, 1998; Dovidio, ten Vergert, Stewart, Gaertner, Johnson, Esses, et al., 2004; Gaertner, Dovidio, Anastasio, Bachman, & Rust, 1993). For example, rather than categorizing individuals as Black or White Americans, members of both groups should be seen simply as Americans. The rationale is that emphasizing shared memberships (or common identities) will reduce prejudice based on subcategories because outgroup members will be seen as part of the self. There is some evidence that this approach can reduce bias against outgroups (e.g., Gaertner et al., 1993; Galinsky & Moskowitz, 2000).

A third idea has produced the most encouraging results. This approach involves accepting group categorizations as inevitable but encouraging *mutual respect* for different groups. This perspective is known as **multiculturalism:** different cultural groups within a society will each maintain their own identity while simultaneously respecting other groups. This idea sounds wonderful, but is it possible to achieve? Some research suggests that it might be.

For instance, Christopher Wolsko and his colleagues (Wolsko, Park, Judd, & Wittenbrink, 2000) gave White participants either a message advocating a multicultural approach to improving intergroup relations (e.g., we need to appreciate our diversity and recognize and accept each group's positive and negative qualities), a message advocating a color-blind approach to improving intergroup relations (e.g.,

**jigsaw classroom**
*a method of teaching designed to foster positive interracial contact, which involves forming small, culturally diverse groups of students who are each given one part of the material to be learned*

**color-blind approach**
*the hypothesis that to reduce prejudice, people should be encouraged to categorize other people as individual persons rather than as members of groups*

**multiculturalism**
*the hypothesis that to reduce prejudice, different cultural groups within a society should each maintain their own identity while simultaneously respecting all other groups*

Multiculturalism means that ethnic groups within a society maintain their cultural traditions and respect other ethnic groups.

# Social Psychology in Your Life    *The Jigsaw Classroom*

In typical classrooms in elementary schools, students compete with one another for their teacher's attention, as well as for grades. This competitive atmosphere does not encourage positive relationships with other students, perhaps especially not with students who are perceived to belong to an outgroup, such as a different racial or ethnic group.

To address this problem, Elliot Aronson designed the jigsaw classroom (Aronson, 1990; Aronson, Stephan, Sikes, Blaney, & Snapp, 1978). The jigsaw classroom is structured in such a way as to induce children to cooperate. It is designed for use in elementary schools, with the goal of promoting positive intergroup attitudes among the children. It makes all students equal in status and dependent on one another for learning.

In the jigsaw method, children work in small groups (five or six students), each of which is composed of children from different ethnic groups. When the group works on an assignment, each child is given one part of the relevant information. For example, if the group is studying whales, one child will receive information from the teacher about what whales eat, another will receive information about where whales are found, another will receive information about the different species of whales, and so on. This feature explains why Aronson named his method the *jigsaw classroom:* each child is given one part of the total information, just as a jigsaw puzzle is composed of numerous parts that fit together to form the whole.

Each child will eventually present his or her information to the full group, and after all of the presentations, a test will be given to everyone in the group to assess their knowledge about the various topics. Importantly, students in the group will be able to obtain information about a topic *only* from the child in their group assigned to that topic, not from the teacher or children in other groups. Therefore, all children are dependent on all of the other children in their group for a full understanding of the topic.

After children receive their initial information, those who are assigned the same topic meet together to discuss the material and prepare their presentation. For instance, the children assigned to what whales eat (one from each group) meet together to go over the information and make sure they understand it. These meetings allow students who might have initial difficulty with the material to improve their comprehension. The students also prepare and rehearse their presentation.

When all of the children are ready to present their information, they return to their groups. Each child gives his or her presentation, and then the other children in the group ask questions, discuss the material, and identify the key details. Children become quite expert at interviewing other children and drawing out from each presenter the most important information.

The jigsaw classroom gives each member in the group an essential part to play in learning about a topic. It encourages listening, cooperative discussion, and engagement with the other children in the group. Given that each group includes members from different ethnic or racial groups, the jigsaw method facilitates cooperative intergroup contact.

Note that the jigsaw classroom creates all of the prerequisites for intergroup contact to be beneficial: (1) the children have equal status; (2) members of the groups must cooperate with one another; (3) the intergroup contact is supported and encouraged by the teacher, who is the primary legitimate authority in the setting; and (4) the interactions between children will be relatively intimate, in that they must talk together for extended periods of time.

Several investigators have tested the effectiveness of the jigsaw method versus traditional classroom procedures. Consistently, the jigsaw classroom has been shown to produce more positive intergroup attitudes than traditional classrooms (Aronson, 1990; Aronson et al., 1978; Desforges et al., 1991). Interestingly, the jigsaw classroom has also been shown to produce equal or better performance on tests of knowledge. These findings indicate that the jigsaw classroom deserves widespread implementation.

**In a jigsaw classroom, children work together in small groups to learn about a topic.**

© Bob Daemmrich/Photo Edit

we must recognize that all men and women are created equal, and we are, first and foremost, a nation of individuals), or no message. On subsequent measures, participants in both message conditions reported more favorable attitudes toward African Americans than did participants in the control condition. Interestingly, participants in the multicultural message condition were more willing to assign characteristics to African Americans as a group than were participants in either the color-blind message or no message conditions, but these characteristics were both positive (e.g., humorous) and negative (e.g., superstitious) in valence. Thus, the multicultural perspective seemed to increase participants' willingness to stereotype, but on both favorable and unfavorable features, and the overall effect on attitudes was positive. The authors suggested that the multicultural perspective was ultimately more likely to succeed than the color-blind approach because the maintenance of ethnic and cultural identity is important for psychological well-being and therefore should be encouraged within a cooperative, diverse society (see also Richeson & Nussbaum, 2004; Rudman, Ashmore, & Gary, 2001).

## Antidiscrimination Legislation

We have discussed several techniques that could be used to reduce prejudice. What about the undesirable behavioral consequences of prejudice, namely, *discrimination*? Can we influence people's behavior directly? Is it a good idea to do so?

In fact, most societies do try to influence discrimination directly: they declare it illegal. In the United States, Canada, and many other countries around the world, antidiscrimination legislation makes it illegal for employers, landlords, and other authorities to base decisions on individuals' race, religion, sex, age, physical mobility, sexual orientation, or other irrelevant features. These laws make no attempt to outlaw prejudice—it is impossible to prohibit feelings and attitudes. But it *is* possible to control the behavioral manifestations of prejudice by making discrimination illegal.

As a student of social psychology, do you think antidiscrimination legislation is a good idea? Will it have a positive or negative effect on public attitudes? Might the short-term and long-term effects differ?

Most social psychologists believe that antidiscrimination legislation will have largely positive effects, especially over the long term. Although the most important benefit of antidiscrimination legislation is to directly improve the lives of minority group members by reducing damaging behavior toward them, there may be other positive effects as well. In particular, there are reasons to believe that antidiscrimination legislation will reduce prejudice over time (i.e., change intergroup attitudes in a favorable direction).

Both dissonance theory and self-perception theory predict that people may change their attitudes to be consistent with their behavior (see Chapters 4 and 7). Dissonance theory states that people feel bad when their attitudes and behaviors are inconsistent; self-perception theory states that people infer their attitudes from their behaviors. Thus, if prejudiced people treat minority group members in a nondiscriminatory fashion, both theories would predict that those individuals might shift their attitudes toward being unprejudiced. The effects of dissonance and self-perception are limited, however, to conditions in which people perceive their behavior to be voluntary. When antidiscrimination legislation is first passed, prejudiced people probably know that they are changing their behavior because of the law, not voluntarily; attitude change is unlikely at this time. But over time, nondiscriminatory behavior may become more of a habit, and people may forget that the law was the original reason for their current behavior. When the salience of the law fades, people are likely to consider their behavior to be voluntary, at which point both dissonance and self-perception processes will operate to make attitudes consistent with behavior.

**Same-Sex Marriage Laws.** On November 2, 2004, George W. Bush was reelected U.S. president. On the same day, 11 states voted on constitutional amendments to ban same-sex marriages. All 11 anti-same-sex-marriage amendments were supported, most by very large margins, including amendments proposed in some states that are not usually regarded as very conservative, including Michigan and Oregon.

These anti-same-sex-marriage votes represented, in part, a backlash against the Massachusetts Supreme Judicial Court, which in May 2004 granted gays and lesbians the right to marry in that state—the first such decision in the United States (in 2000, Vermont recognized same-sex unions as having the same legal rights as heterosexual unions, but did not go so far as to allow same-sex couples to be married). Some other countries have been moving toward recognizing same-sex marriages; for instance, federal legislation was introduced in Canada in 2004 to grant legal status to same-sex marriages.

Same-sex marriage is a controversial issue. Many people feel passionately about one side or the other. Banning same-sex marriage is probably not seen as an act of "discrimination" by many who support the ban. Nevertheless, this decision means that some people will be denied, on the basis of their sexual orientation, a fundamental right that is available to others—namely, to have their relationship with their partner recognized as a legal union.

Would making same-sex marriage *legal* influence attitudes toward gays and lesbians? Although the societal debate that would precede such a law would be difficult and potentially divisive, recognizing same-sex marriages would likely reduce prejudice against gays and lesbians over time. For one thing, same-sex marriages would become more common, so mere exposure would presumably work to make attitudes toward these unions more favorable. Also, as explained earlier, dissonance and self-perception processes seem likely to improve attitudes over time. Finally, such a law would establish a social norm that same-sex relationships deserve the same respect and protections as heterosexual relationships.

These arguments are consistent with comments from Howard Dean, the former governor of Vermont, who was quoted in the *Boston Globe* on May 17, 2004 (shortly after the decision of the Massachusetts Judicial Supreme Court), regarding

*"We also see very large numbers of people giving ratings of zero to lesbians and gay men, meaning that they have very hostile feelings."*

his state's move in 2000 to grant legal rights to same-sex couples: "Just as the civil rights movement and subsequent integration began the process of removing painful stereotypes held by whites about African Americans, so does the open declaration and subsequent demand for equal rights begin to remove stereotypes about the gay, lesbian, bisexual, and transgendered community."

**Norms Against Discrimination.** Laws have an educative function: they can be used to teach important values and principles. That is, laws help to establish *norms* in society, which are rules or guidelines about what behaviors are acceptable and unacceptable. Norms influence people in two ways: they can be internalized, such that people accept that the norms define "good" behavior, and they also put external pressure on people to conform, because failure to follow norms might result in punishment or rejection. Because most of us consider discrimination to be a bad thing, it is important to show that discrimination will not be tolerated. Antidiscrimination legislation does that. For instance, as mentioned earlier, if same-sex marriages were declared legal, a norm would be established that same-sex relationships deserve the same respect and rights as heterosexual relationships.

There is also evidence that social norms coming from interpersonal sources (rather than from laws) are influential in the area of stereotypes and prejudice. Researchers have shown that having someone verbally express an antiracist view inhibits others from expressing prejudiced views, presumably because a social norm against showing prejudice is invoked by the first person's comments (e.g., Blanchard, Lilly, & Vaughn, 1991). This effect occurs in both prejudiced and unprejudiced individuals, because no one wants to be rejected. But people who are low in prejudice also experience *guilt* when they become aware that they have acted in a manner that might be seen as prejudiced. This guilt motivates unprejudiced persons to change their behavior to be more nondiscriminatory (Monteith, 1993, 1996).

# Outlook for the Future

So what is the outlook for the future, given these various perspectives on reducing prejudice and discrimination? Can effective programs be developed to ameliorate these important social problems? We think that the answer to this question is *yes*.

Encouraging contact between groups is probably the most important step, particularly among children in the school system. It is very difficult, though not impossible, to change the attitudes of highly prejudiced adults (Cook, 1969, 1990), so children should probably be our focus. As well as fostering equal-status contact (e.g., in a jigsaw classroom), schools should teach norms of multicultural tolerance. Engendering a positive attitude toward diversity is important.

At the societal level, legislation against discrimination minimizes the impact of prejudice, establishes a norm of tolerance, and probably influences attitudes in a desirable direction over time. Public education campaigns might also be beneficial. Procedures that elicit dissonance (e.g., by inducing feelings of hypocrisy) can be effective, although they may be difficult to apply to large numbers of individuals.

Prejudice underlies many of the problems we face in our world. Negative attitudes toward members of particular groups are a fundamental cause of human conflict and misery, ranging from interpersonal hostility to war and genocide. Social psychology has important things to contribute to the fight against prejudice, such as Elliot Aronson's idea of the jigsaw classroom. We need to convince politicians and lawmakers to give more of these ideas a try.

# Chapter Summary

**Prejudice** is a negative attitude toward members of a group, which is often very strongly held. **Discrimination** is negative, harmful behavior toward people based on their group membership. Perhaps the most extreme form of discrimination is **genocide,** which is an attempt to systematically eliminate an ethnic group through banishment or murder.

Blatant prejudice is probably less common today than it was 20 or 30 years ago, but discrimination based on racial, ethnic, or other group membership still occurs, especially when the circumstances provide an excuse for negative treatment. The term **aversive racism** has been used to refer to people who do not consider themselves prejudiced and who would find any accusation of being prejudiced aversive, but who nevertheless harbor some negative beliefs and hostile feelings toward members of minority groups. Because people often do not want to admit prejudicial attitudes, the **Racial Arguments Scale (RAS)** was developed to provide a less obvious assessment of racial attitudes; respondents are asked to rate how well arguments support positive or negative conclusions about an outgroup.

Stereotypes are individuals' beliefs that members of a group share particular attributes. Stereotypes are almost always oversimplified and often excessively negative. Unfavorable stereotypes can lead to prejudice and discrimination. Stereotypes distort information processing about members of the target group. Stereotypes can also create vicious cycles by leading people to behave toward members of a group in ways that actually elicit the expected actions from those members; this process is called a **self-fulfilling prophesy.**

Stereotypes can influence perceivers' judgments without their awareness—effects that are called **implicit intergroup biases.** Researchers have documented implicit intergroup biases for numerous target groups; these studies have often used **subliminal priming procedures,** which involve flashing words or pictures very briefly on a computer screen in front of the participant.

Several emotional sources of prejudice and discrimination have been proposed. The **scapegoat theory** of prejudice proposes that members of the dominant group use discrimination against members of weak target groups to vent their frustration and disappointment. The disadvantaged targets may have had little or no role in causing the frustration, but provide a convenient target of blame. **Realistic group conflict theory** proposes that when groups in society are perceived to be competing with one another for resources, intergroup hostility can be aroused, which leads to prejudice. Social identity theory proposes that prejudice can make people feel good about themselves because they see their own group as better than the derogated outgroup. **Integrated threat theory** unifies several other theories by proposing that prejudice toward an outgroup results from four types of perceived threats: realistic threats, symbolic threats, threats stemming from intergroup anxiety, and threats arising from negative stereotypes.

Prejudice and discrimination directed against women because of their gender is called **sexism.** A measure of sexism is the **ambivalent sexism inventory.** This scale includes items to assess two dimensions of sexism: **benevolent sexism,** which involves positive but paternalistic attitudes toward women (e.g., women are good but need protection), and **hostile sexism,** which involves negative attitudes toward women who violate the traditional stereotype (e.g., feminists).

Gender stereotypes are beliefs about the characteristics that are associated with men and women. Gender stereotypes are probably accurate in some respects and may even reflect some inevitable, biological differences between the sexes, but they also exaggerate sex differences and contain some differences that are not inevitable but instead are caused by the different social roles assigned to women and men.

People who are overweight are the targets of prejudice and discrimination in our society. Obesity is a particularly devastating stigma for women, because physical appearance is more highly valued for women than for men in our culture. Therefore, women tend to be very concerned about their weight. Measures of **appearance self-esteem,** which assess respondents' satisfaction with their physical looks, show that women are less satisfied with their appearance than men at all age levels.

The **personal–group discrimination discrepancy** refers to the tendency for people to report that they as individuals have experienced *less* negative treatment than the average member of their group. For instance, most women report that they have experienced less discrimination based on their gender than has the typical woman.

**Stereotype threat** occurs when individuals believe that if they perform poorly on a task, their performance will appear to confirm an unfavorable belief or stereotype about their group. Stereotype threat puts pressure on people to do as well as possible in order to discredit the negative stereotype, and this pressure can itself lead to poor performance. Stereotype threat impairs performance by arousing anxiety and reducing memory capacity.

One idea for reducing prejudice is through direct contact with members of the disliked group. This idea is based on the **contact hypothesis,** which predicts that exposure to members of an outgroup will produce more favorable attitudes toward that group. It turns out that intergroup contact must meet several prerequisites in order to produce positive attitudes, including equal status and cooperative behavior. A teaching method that encourages positive interracial contact among elementary school children is the **jigsaw classroom.** In this method, small, culturally diverse groups of students are formed, and each student receives one part of the material to be learned. Members of a group share their information with other members, and the children discuss the information together before being tested on their knowledge.

Another idea for reducing prejudice is the **color-blind approach,** which suggests that we should categorize other people as individual persons rather than as members of groups. A contrasting perspective is **multiculturalism,** which proposes that different cultural groups within a society should each maintain their own identity while simultaneously respecting all other groups.

# Key Terms

ambivalent sexism inventory (366)

appearance self-esteem (370)

aversive racism (346)

benevolent sexism (366)

color-blind approach (383)

contact hypothesis (381)

discrimination (344)

genocide (344)

hostile sexism (366)

implicit intergroup bias (357)

integrated threat theory (362)

jigsaw classroom (383)

multiculturalism (383)

personal–group discrimination discrepancy (372)

prejudice (344)

Racial Arguments Scale (RAS) (348)

realistic group conflict theory (360)

scapegoat theory (359)

self-fulfilling prophesy (354)

sexism (364)

stereotype threat (373)

subliminal priming procedure (356)

# Social Psychology Alive on the Web

## SOCIAL PSYCHOLOGY ALIVE: ONLINE LABS

To perform the following experiment and see how you compare to other students, go to Social Psychology Lab, which can be accessed through Social PsychologyNow:

- 9.1 Don't Shoot

## SOCIAL PSYCHOLOGY ALIVE: QUIZZING AND PRACTICE TESTS

You can access our website directly by going to http:// psychology.wadsworth.com/brecklerle/ for online quizzes, flash cards, and Internet links.

## INFOTRAC® COLLEGE EDITION

For additional readings, explore InfoTrac College Edition, your online library of archived journal articles and periodicals dating back 22 years. If your instructor ordered InfoTrac College Edition with this book, you can access it from your CD-ROM, or go directly to http://www.infotrac-college.com/ wadsworth and use the passcode from the InfoTrac College Edition card that came with your book. For this chapter, try these search terms: *prejudice, discrimination, stereotypes, aversive racism, self-fulfilling prophesy, realistic group conflict, sexism, gender stereotypes, stereotype threat, contact hypothesis, jigsaw classroom, multiculturalism.*

# Social Psychology Alive: The Workbook

To apply what you've learned in this chapter to what happens in the real world, go to Chapter 9 of *Social Psychology Alive: The Workbook*:

- The Death Penalty and Aversive Racism
- Understanding How Stereotypes Can Be Self-Fulfilling: The Use of a Positive Test Strategy
- Don't Shoot!

- Sexism and Music
- Thin Is In
- Math Is (NOT) Just for Boys
- The Pernicious Effects of Prejudice
- Multiculturalism Versus Color Blindness on the College Campus

# Social Psychology Alive: The Videos

To see video on the topics and experiments discussed in this chapter, you may go either to Social PsychologyNow or to the CD-ROM, if your instructor assigned either one, to the following section:

- Prized Eyes: Stereotypes and Prejudice Then and Now
- Genocide: Mike Jacob's Story
- Sexual Stigma: Hating People for the People They Love

# To Learn More

This list contains citations to books or articles that can help you learn more. These readings are good places to start if you want to gain a deeper understanding of the topics in this chapter.

- Whitely, B. E., Jr., & Kite, M. (2006). *Psychology of prejudice and discrimination.* Belmont, CA: Wadsworth.

- Oskamp, S. (Ed.). (2000). *Reducing prejudice and discrimination.* Mahwah, NJ: Erlbaum.
- Swim, J. K., & Stangor, C. (Eds.). (1998). *Prejudice: The target's perspective.* New York: Academic Press.

© Clive Mason/Getty Images.

# Group Dynamics and Intergroup Conflict

The African National Congress (ANC) is the ruling political party in the country of South Africa, having received about 70% of the votes in the most recent election in 2004. It is a group with a long and interesting history, which is tied closely to the emergence of South Africa from the shadow of apartheid—the discriminatory system of segregation based on race that created different social structures for Whites and Blacks in the country.

The ANC was formed in 1912 at a meeting of Black tribal chiefs, lawyers, and religious leaders, with the goal of promoting the interests of Blacks in the newly formed Union of South Africa. The early leaders of the ANC were conservative in their approach, calling for nonconfrontational, passive strategies, such as meeting with White leaders to try to convince them to make changes. These techniques were not very effective, however, as the White South African government passed a series of laws over the years that progressively stripped Blacks of their rights.

In the early 1940s, several bright young Black lawyers joined the ANC, including Nelson Mandela and Oliver Tambo. These new members argued for more aggressive tactics and formed the ANC Youth League to push for change. An event that gave strong impetus to the call for new strategies occurred in 1948, when the National Party was voted into power by the White electorate and introduced the system of apartheid to make segregation the official law of the land.

Members of the ANC began more militant actions. In 1952, Nelson Mandela took charge of a "defiance campaign," which involved civil disobedience such as walking through "Whites only" entrances and breaking curfews that existed for Blacks. Tension in the country grew as police responded to peaceful protests with violence, including the Sharpeville Massacre in 1960, where police fired into an unarmed crowd and killed 69 people.

© Alexander Joe/AFP/Getty Images

Nelson Mandela and the ANC led South Africa out of the shadow of apartheid.

In response to this violence, the ANC decided in 1961 to form a military wing, which began a campaign of sabotage against government installations that resulted in more than 200 attacks in 18 months. The commander of the ANC's military unit was Nelson Mandela. The White government promptly outlawed the ANC and arrested many of its leaders, including Mandela. Mandela was sentenced to jail in 1962, where he remained until 1990.

During the 1960s and 1970s, the ANC was forced underground, where it organized protests, initiated strikes, and appealed for international support against apartheid. In 1976, a series of protests by students across the country resulted in more than 1,000 deaths, most of the victims killed by police. The disturbances peaked in the Soweto Riots in 1976, during which the police opened fire on unarmed schoolchildren. These events prompted an outcry in the international community; in response, the South African government introduced some minor, cosmetic reforms to apartheid.

In 1985, the ANC instructed its supporters to make the country "ungovernable." This call resulted in many battles between young people and the police and much damage to government property. The government declared a state of emergency in 1986, which lasted until 1990. Thousands of people died in violent confrontations. International pressure on South Africa grew, and the White leaders slowly realized that they could not stop the inevitable collapse of apartheid.

In 1990, the South African government repealed its ban on the ANC and released most of the imprisoned leaders, including Nelson Mandela. Mandela was elected president of the ANC in 1991 and began extended negotiations with the White government. Eventually, a one-person, one-vote election was held in 1994, in which Mandela was elected president of South Africa and the ANC won the majority of seats in the parliament. Mandela retired in 1999, at age 80, and was replaced by Thabo Mbeki; the ANC won reelection in both 1999 and 2004.

The ANC has been a very successful group, in the sense that it has fulfilled its core purpose of giving Blacks a democratic voice in the country. Within the party, Nelson Mandela has been an extremely effective leader, whose eloquence and intelligence have won support from around the world. In the remainder of this chapter, we will use the ANC or Nelson Mandela to illustrate a number of issues in the study of how groups operate.

The topic of this chapter is the social psychological study of groups and group processes, *an area of research often called **group dynamics**. Groups play a huge role in our lives: many of our daily activities occur in face-to-face groups (e.g., family, friends) and, more broadly, our ability to live a free and prosperous life depends on large groups such as nations. There are also new kinds of groups emerging today: the advent of the Internet has made it easy for people to communicate and form virtual groups. Indeed, the Internet can be considered an incubator of groups, some dangerous and some worthwhile. It is possible to find websites and chat groups that

**group dynamics**

*the social psychological study of groups and group processes promote hatred and racism, but it is also possible to find ones that encourage helpfulness and positive thinking. This is an exciting (and scary) time to be studying groups.*

*We begin our coverage of group dynamics by defining what social psychologists mean by a group. Then we turn our attention to individuals within groups: how does the presence of other people affect individuals' performances and actions? We also discuss how individuals' performances combine to determine group productivity. Moving to a group level of analysis, we discuss how groups make decisions; we describe conditions that can lead to poor decision making and how to avoid these conditions. Next, we turn to the issue of leadership and discuss both how leaders are chosen and which kinds of leaders are most effective in different groups. We close the chapter with our broadest level of analysis: how do groups interact with other groups? This discussion of intergroup conflict identifies factors that heighten intergroup tensions and ways that such tensions can be reduced or managed.*

**group**

*two or more persons who are interacting with one another and/or influencing one another*

*A necessary place to begin our discussion of group dynamics is by defining what social psychologists mean by the term* **group.** *The most common definition of a group in social psychology is* two or more people who are interacting and/or influencing one another. *This definition highlights two points. First, an obvious requirement for a group is that there must be at least two people (!), and of course most groups are larger than two. Second, the members of a group must be interacting with one another in some way, or at least influencing one another (Burn, 2004; Levine & Moreland, 1994). For example, if passengers on a plane have no interaction and pay no attention to one another, then they do not constitute a group in the sense that social psychologists use the term. On the other hand, if the passengers talk to one another, feel some bond with one another, or otherwise influence one another, then they might constitute a meaningful group. These observations suggest that, instead of drawing a hard line between "groups" and "nongroups," it may be sensible to think about collections of individuals as ranging along a continuum from little or no "group character" to a great deal of "group character." Passengers on a plane usually have little or no group character, but occasionally they have a lot of group character—such as the passengers on United Flight 93 who rose up against the terrorist hijackers on September 11, 2001, forcing the plane to crash in Pennsylvania before reaching its intended target.*

*Social psychologists have directed most of their attention to groups of two different sizes. First, researchers interested in such topics as group productivity and group decision making have focused on* small groups—*usually between 3 and 7 members, though potentially up to groups of 20 (Cartwright & Zander, 1968; Kerr, Aronoff, & Messe, 2000; Levine & Moreland, 1998). This size has made it possible for researchers to create small groups in the laboratory and to examine the processes underlying performance and judgment. Most of the groups within which our daily activities occur are small in size, such as our family, coworkers, and leisure groups, so this is a critical size to understand. Second, researchers interested in such topics as intergroup conflict and international relations have focused on* large collectives (more than 20 members), *such as nations, religions, and ethnic groups (Brown, 1988; Taylor & Moghaddam, 1994). These researchers cannot create collectives in the laboratory, but instead have investigated how individuals perceive large collectives. For example, individual participants may be asked to report their impressions of large groups or their recommendations about how their ingroup should behave toward particular outgroups. It is important to understand collectives because they are the basis for many critical decisions, such as whether to make peace or war.*

Most of the groups within which our daily activities occur are small in size.

## Individual Performance and Behavior in Group Settings

We begin our discussion of group dynamics at an individual level of analysis. That is, before getting into how groups operate as a unit, we need to consider how individuals change when they experience certain aspects of group settings, such as the presence of other people or the anonymity created by being in a group. We also need to consider how performances by individuals combine to determine group productivity.

## Social Facilitation: The Effects of an Audience

Imagine playing a familiar electronic game—one that you play very well—by yourself, with no one watching. Now imagine playing the same game in front of an audience of three or four friends. In which circumstance do you think you would perform better? Would you excel, or would you choke, in front of the audience?

Now imagine a different scenario. Imagine playing a *new* electronic game that you have never played before, which requires some unusual manipulations of the controller or keyboard, by yourself with no one watching. Now imagine playing the same novel game in front of three or four friends. Which performance do you think would be better in this case?

These hypothetical scenarios capture one of the oldest questions in social psychology: the effects of the presence of other people on an individual's performance. You may recall our description, in the section on the history of social psychology in Chapter 1 (see Social Psychology in Your Life: The First Social Psychology Experiment), of the first publication of a social psychology experiment by Norman Triplett (1898). Triplett conducted a study in which children were asked to wind a fishing reel either alone or with another child doing the same task and found that the children performed better when another child was also present. Triplett concluded that people perform better in the presence of others—an effect that became known as **social facilitation.**

**social facilitation**

*the effects of the presence of other people on individual performance, which will usually be improved performance on simple tasks and impaired performance on complex tasks*

**dominant response**

*the action that is most likely to occur in a situation or on a task when the individual is alone*

But it turned out that subsequent studies specifically testing the effects of an audience on individuals' performance yielded inconsistent findings. Participants in some studies did better when an audience was present than when one was not (e.g., Travis, 1925), whereas participants in other studies did better when alone than when an audience was present (e.g., Pessin, 1933). These contradictory findings slowly eroded interest in the issue, and researchers turned to other questions.

In 1965, however, Robert Zajonc rekindled interest in social facilitation (this is the same researcher who identified the *mere exposure effect* described in Chapter 6, see page 214). Zajonc observed that most studies that had shown an *improvement* in performance in front of an audience utilized relatively *simple* tasks, whereas most studies that had shown a *decrease* in performance in front of an audience utilized relatively *complex* tasks. Zajonc hypothesized that the presence of other people increases the probability of the **dominant responses** on a task. The dominant responses on a task are the ones that are most likely to occur when the person is alone. When a task is simple or is something that people have done many times (e.g., driving a car), the dominant responses will be correct ones or well-practiced ones (e.g., stepping on the gas, steering the car). When a task is complex or novel, however (e.g., someone attempting to juggle three balls for the first time), the dominant responses are more likely to be incorrect ones (e.g., tossing the balls badly, failing to catch a ball). Zajonc predicted that these tendencies will be *heightened* by the presence of an audience.

Consistent with Zajonc's hypothesis, research has shown that performance on simple, well-learned tasks typically improves in front of an audience, whereas performance on complex, novel tasks typically worsens in front of an audience (see Baron, Moore, & Sanders, 1978; Bond & Titus, 1983; Geen & Gange, 1977). Why do audiences increase the likelihood of dominant responses? Zajonc proposed that the presence of other people is physiologically arousing (e.g., causing faster heart rate), perhaps because the individual is anxious about performing well in front of others (Cottrell, Wack, Sekerak, & Rittle, 1968; Sanna, 1992). Zajonc knew that previous research by cognitive psychologists had shown that physiological arousal restricts individuals' range of attention: people can focus only on a few cues in the setting (Easterbrook, 1959). Zajonc suggested that when a task is simple, this narrowed focus of attention actually improves performance because it blocks out distractions, but when a task is complex, the narrowed focus of attention makes it difficult for the individual to attend to all of the cues necessary for good performance.

An interesting study of social facilitation was conducted by Jim Blascovich, Wendy Mendes, Sarah Hunter, and Kristen Salomon (1999). Participants were presented with two-digit numbers on a computer screen (25, 97, 34, 81, etc.) and had to push one of two response keys. The participants had to figure out that they were supposed to push one key when the number was smaller than 68 and the other key when the number was larger than 68. They were not told about the number 68 in advance, so they had to discover this "rule" by trial and error (correct/incorrect feedback was given on each trial). Participants performed the task either alone or in front of two other students (one male and one female). When participants were allowed to *practice* this task for 25 trials before being tested (which made it an *easy* task because they had already figured out that 68 was the critical number), they performed better in front of an audience than alone. When participants were required to do this task without any practice, however (which made it a *difficult* task because they had not yet figured out the critical number), they performed significantly worse in front of an audience than alone. Thus, the presence of other people improved performance on a simple task but worsened performance on a difficult task.

Let's return to the question about whether you would perform better on a familiar electronic game alone or in front of an audience. Because this game is familiar to you, the dominant responses during the game should be the correct ones. Zajonc would predict, therefore, that an audience would *improve* your performance. But what about a new and challenging electronic game? In this case, the game is novel and relatively difficult, so the dominant responses are probably incorrect. Zajonc would predict, therefore, that an audience would *harm* your performance. Do these predictions match your own intuitions? The flowchart in Figure 10.1 depicts the processes involved in social facilitation.

It is interesting to think about the implications of research on social facilitation for where students should study. Will students learn material better if they study alone in their room or in the presence of other people in the library? If the material is very simple or already very familiar, then students may be better off studying in the library, because the presence of others should narrow their focus of attention and block out distractions. On the other hand, if the material is very complex or unfamiliar, then the narrowed focus of attention in the library might cause students to overlook aspects of the material, so they may be better off studying alone.

## Social Loafing: Goofing Off When Others Can Do the Work

The social facilitation literature focuses on tasks that are performed individually, such as winding a fishing reel or figuring out which response key to push when a number is presented. What about tasks that involve *group* performance and where individual contributions are not identifiable? What happens when we are a small (and often invisible) part of a collective effort? From one perspective, it seems possible that being part of a group will increase our effort by motivating us—we'll give our all for the team! But from another perspective, it seems possible that we might slack off and let others do the work—why kill ourselves when no one will be able to identify our contribution anyway? If you have participated in group projects for courses, where all students in the group receive the same grade, you may have found that some group members did not really put in a full effort.

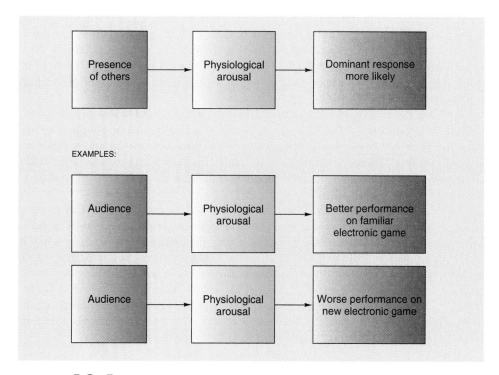

**FIGURE 10.1** Social facilitation

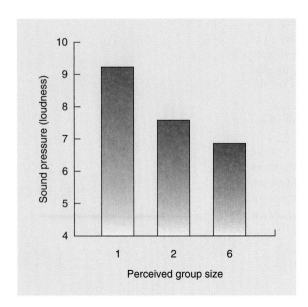

**FIGURE 10.2** Loudness of cheering as a function of perceived group size

From Latane et al., "Many hands make light the work: The causes and consequences of social loafing," *Journal of Personality and Social Psychology*, 37, 822–832, Fig. 2, p. 827, 1979. Copyright © 1979 by the American Psychological Association. Reprinted by permission.

**social loafing**

*the reduction of effort that people often exhibit when working in a group where individual contributions are unidentifiable*

Bibb Latané, Kipling Williams, and Stephen Harkins (1979) coined the term **social loafing** to capture the idea that people may slack off in groups. In contrast to social facilitation, which is assumed to involve arousal (caused by the presence of others), social loafing is assumed to involve relaxation or reduced motivation (caused by believing that one's personal contribution is unidentifiable). To test whether social loafing occurs, Latané and his colleagues asked college students to cheer as loudly as possible while blindfolded and wearing headphones to mask the sounds. The researchers led participants to believe on some trials that they were cheering alone, but on other trials that they were cheering together with one or five other participants. In actuality, participants always responded alone, and their individual cheers were recorded. Figure 10.2 presents the results of the study. Participants cheered the loudest when they thought they were performing alone (perceived group size of 1), whereas they cheered only 82% as intensely when they believed one other person was also cheering (perceived group size of 2) and only 74% as intensely when they believed five others were also cheering (perceived group size of 6).

Many studies have investigated social loafing (for a review, see Karau & Williams, 1993), and the effect is a reliable one: the larger the group, the less effort individuals tend to exert on joint tasks. One necessary component for social loafing is individual anonymity; if people believe that their own performance within the group will be identifiable, social loafing disappears (e.g., Williams, Harkins, & Latané, 1981). In the next section of the chapter, we discuss another phenomenon that reflects, at least in part, being anonymous and unidentifiable in groups: *deindividuation*.

Do you think that social loafing is more likely in some groups than in others? It turns out that one factor influencing social loafing is the importance of the group to members. People are less likely to loaf when the group is important or meaningful to them than when the group is relatively unimportant (e.g., Brickner, Harkins, & Ostrom, 1986). These findings suggest that in real-life groups whose members consider the group's goals to be worthwhile and believe the group is making a valuable contribution, social loafing is less likely. For instance, members of the ANC in South Africa probably did not exhibit social loafing even when their individual actions were unidentifiable.

Another factor that influences social loafing is the cohesiveness or attractiveness of the group itself. When the group is composed of friends or people who are attractive for other reasons, an individual's motivation is increased and social loafing declines (e.g., Hardy & Latané, 1988). Again, these data suggest that in real-life groups where people value their membership (such as the ANC), social loafing is less likely.

Is social loafing *intentional*? That is, do people *deliberately* slack off in groups, or is the reduction in effort unconscious and unintentional? The answer is *both*. Sometimes, people *know* that they are not giving maximum effort, such as when a lazy student does as little work as possible in a group project. But sometimes people do not realize that their effort has been affected, such as in the study described earlier that used a cheering task (Latané et al., 1979). It seems unlikely that participants in this study deliberately cheered less loudly when they believed others were also cheering; instead, the belief that others were cheering probably unconsciously reduced participants' motivation to yell as loudly as possible.

**Gender and Cultural Differences in Social Loafing.** There are also some interesting data on *who* is most likely to exhibit social loafing. One relevant characteristic is gender: men are more likely to do it than women. In fact, studies using groups composed *only* of women have generally found no evidence of social loafing at all (see Karau & Williams, 1993). Although various possible explanations for this gender difference probably occur to our female readers, most theorists suspect that the difference occurs because women are more group-oriented and more concerned about collective outcomes than are men, who tend to be more individualistic in their orientation. Women's focus on group outcomes motivates them to exert maximum effort even when their individual contributions are not identifiable.

*Social loafing* occurs when people do not exert maximal effort because individual contributions are not identifiable.

If this reasoning about gender differences in social loafing is correct, then social loafing might also be expected in individualistic cultures such as the United States more than in collectivistic cultures such as China. After all, people who have been socialized in a culture that emphasizes independence and individual achievements (individualistic cultures) may be less concerned about group outcomes than people who have been socialized in a culture that emphasizes interdependence and group achievements (collectivistic cultures). At least one study has produced exactly this pattern of findings: Christopher Earley (1989) found significant social loafing in a sample of participants from the United States, but no evidence of social loafing in a sample of participants from China. Thus, social loafing is at least partly a reflection of Western values and culture.

## Deindividuation: Immersion in a Group

Feelings of anonymity contribute to social loafing, as we have noted. But anonymity can have other consequences as well. In particular, social psychologists have proposed that being a member of a group can sometimes produce a state of **deindividuation** (Festinger, Pepitone, & Newcomb, 1952), which refers to a loss of personal identity and a sense of immersion in a group: people feel relatively anonymous and can be caught up in the actions of those around them. Wearing clothes that make identification difficult (e.g., the same uniform as other people in a setting, or a costume that conceals one's identity) can heighten deindividuation. Numerous studies have shown that when people are deindividuated, they are more likely to engage in socially undesirable behavior (e.g., Prentice-Dunn & Rogers, 1989; Zimbardo, 1969).

**deindividuation**

*a psychological state in which people lose their sense of personal identity and feel immersed in a group*

Theorists have proposed different psychological processes through which deindividuation affects behavior (see Mullen, Migdal, & Rozell, 2003). One perspective is that deindividuation weakens people's inhibitions against performing harmful or socially disapproved actions. A second perspective is that deindividuation heightens people's responsiveness to external cues, which may be either negative or positive. A third perspective is that deindividuation increases people's adherence to norms that emerge in a group. We discuss each of these perspectives in the following paragraphs.

Some theorists have argued that deindividuation weakens people's inhibitions against acting in ways that violate norms, such as selfish or aggressive behavior. From this perspective, deindividuation is hypothesized to "release" people from their normal ethical constraints. For example, the concept of deindividuation has been used to explain negative, antinormative actions such as theft, vandalism, and interpersonal violence (e.g., Mullen, 1986; Silke, 2003a). If deindividuation dissolves inhibitions, then an interesting legal issue is whether a state of deindividuation

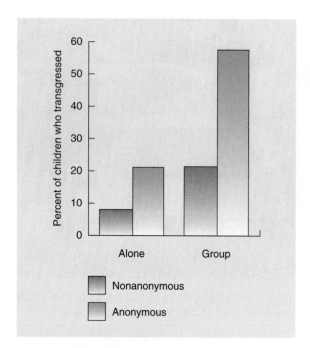

**FIGURE 10.3** Percent of children who transgressed (took more than one candy bar or both candy and money)

From Diener et al., "Effects of deindividuation variables on stealing among Halloween trick-or-treaters," *Journal of Personality and Social Psychology*, 33, 178–183, Table 1, p. 181, 1976. Copyright © 1976 by the American Psychological Association. Reprinted by permission.

could be considered an extenuating circumstance (i.e., an excuse) for criminal actions committed while part of a large group of people (e.g., "He couldn't help himself—being immersed in the group swept away his inhibitions!"). Although it may sound implausible to posit deindividuation as an excuse, this strategy has already been used successfully by some lawyers (see Colman, 1991).

An illustrative study of deindividuation, investigating relatively mild antinormative behavior, was conducted by Ed Diener, Scott Fraser, Arthur Beaman, and Roger Kelem (1976). These researchers observed the actions of costumed children on Halloween in 27 different homes in the Seattle area. Inside the front door of each home was a table with a large bowl full of bite-sized candy bars and a smaller bowl full of coins (pennies and nickels). When children came to the door, a woman greeted them and invited them inside. Half of the children were randomly assigned to the *nonanonymous condition:* the woman asked them their names and where they lived. The remaining children were not asked their names or addresses (*anonymous condition*). It was also noted whether the children were alone or in a group of between 2 and 6 children. After the children entered the home, the woman said that she needed to return to her work in another room. She instructed the children to take *one* of the candy bars, and then exited the room. There was an unobtrusive observer positioned behind a backdrop who recorded the behavior of the children.

Figure 10.3 presents the percentage of children who took more than one candy bar or who took money as well as candy from the table. These data show that children were more likely to break the rules when they were anonymous rather than nonanonymous and when they were in a group rather than alone. The authors concluded that anonymity produced deindividuation in the children, especially when they were in a group, which reduced their inhibitions and led them to behave more greedily or selfishly than they normally would have.

Prisons can induce deindividuation. Typically, both prisoners and guards wear uniforms, and names are often replaced with impersonal numbers. If guards feel unaccountable when interacting with prisoners, they may act maliciously. Philip Zimbardo (1972) conducted a study at Stanford University, where college men

*Guard: "What is happening to Prisoner 189?"*

*Prisoners (in unison): "Prisoner 189 is being punished, Mr. Correctional Officer!"*

*Guard: "Say it five times—make sure you remember it!"*

volunteered to take part in a simulated prison. The volunteers were randomly assigned to the roles of guards or prisoners and received uniforms appropriate to their roles; the guards also were given mirrored sunglasses to increase their sense of anonymity. All participants were given a list of rules to be followed by the prisoners, and the guards were told to enforce these rules. Zimbardo planned to continue the simulation for two weeks. Interactions between the guards and prisoners became so aggressive and insulting, however, that the simulation was terminated after just six days. Zimbardo reported that the guards had resorted to several control tactics that were degrading or cruel, which they justified by arguing that the prisoners would not otherwise obey the rules. This study suggests that deindividuation in a prison setting can produce unacceptable behavior by guards. These findings may remind you of the actions of the American military guards who humiliated and tortured Iraqi prisoners at the Abu Ghraib prison in Baghdad, which we mentioned briefly in Chapter 8 in the section on obedience. Perhaps deindividuation contributed to the Abu Ghraib events.

A different perspective on deindividuation was proposed by Kenneth Gergen and his colleagues (Gergen, Gergen, & Barton, 1973). These researchers suggested that deindividuation increases people's responsiveness to external cues, such as noticeable features of the setting, and these cues might sometimes be *prosocial* in nature. A study that supported this perspective was conducted by Robert Johnson and Leslie Downing (1979). Female participants wore either cloaks like those of the Ku Klux Klan (negative cue) or nursing uniforms (positive cue). In addition, some participants remained highly identifiable despite the clothing because they wore large name tags, whereas others did not have name tags and were expected to feel deindividuated because of the similarity of their cloaks or uniforms. All participants were asked to make recommendations about the intensity of electric shocks that should be administered to a "learner" in a verbal learning task. Compared to the identifiable condition, deindividuation (no name tags) led to *more* aggression in the KKK cloak condition but to *less* aggression in the nursing uniform condition. Thus, deindividuated participants responded either more negatively or more positively than identifiable participants, depending on the situational cues.

Does *deindividuation* increase aggressive behavior by prison guards?

A third perspective on deindividuation was presented by Tom Postmes and Russell Spears (1998). These researchers reviewed 60 studies that investigated deindividuation and agreed with past theorists that this state was reliably associated with increases in undesirable behavior, especially for larger groups. They hypothesized, however, that the effects were not due to people being "released" from normal constraints when in large groups. Instead, they suggested that large groups (and the anonymity they provide) serve to *increase people's adherence to emerging norms in that group,* which are sometimes aggressive or self-serving. For example, a political protest rally might turn into a riot; this occurs not because people become "uninhibited" and therefore ignore social norms, but rather because a new norm of *aggression against authority* develops in the group. People feel part of the group and adopt its central norms, including the idea that it is okay to attack police or to damage property to make a political statement. Or consider the worst kind of mob violence—lynch mobs in the southern United States in the 1800s and early 1900s (Mullen, 1986). Groups of White men would search for a Black man accused of some act; if found, he might be hanged immediately without any opportunity to defend himself. Did this behavior reflect disinhibition from social constraints or did it reflect the emergence of a norm within the mob that it was appropriate to punish the Black man? Perhaps both processes operated to some extent.

Postmes, Spears, and their colleagues have also speculated that a state of deindividuation can occur during Internet communication (e.g., Postmes, Spears, Sakhel, & de Groot, 2001; Spears, Lea, Corneliussen, Postmes, & ter Haar, 2002). They propose that the anonymity of computer-mediated communication elicits a sense of immersion into online groups, a diminishment of personal identity, and a willingness to follow unconventional norms within those virtual groups. For instance, think about Internet chat rooms. The anonymity provided by chat rooms can produce a willingness to be more candid than during face-to-face interactions. Contributors to a chat room may conform to group norms that they would not obey off-line. For instance, expressing racist beliefs or explicitly describing sexual fantasies may be normative in an online group, and people who would not admit to such things in daily life may conform to the group norm.

It remains for future researchers to resolve questions about the psychological processes involved in deindividuation. Whether feelings of anonymity produced by being in a group release individuals from inhibitions, increase responsiveness to external cues, or increase adherence to emerging group norms must be disentangled in empirical research. Everyone agrees that deindividuation occurs, but there is disagreement about its mechanisms.

## Individual Performance and Group Productivity

An individual level of analysis is useful for one final issue: how do the performances of individual members of a group combine to determine overall group productivity? For example, are groups inevitably more *productive* than individuals—that is, do they generate a higher quantity and/or quality of whatever it is they make (their "commodity")? What about productivity *per person*? This refers to *efficiency*—for example, do groups produce more than the total sum of a similar number of people working individually?

**Types of Tasks.** Empirical research on individual performance and group productivity has shown that answers to these questions depend on the characteristics of the task being performed (see Shaw, 1976). Some kinds of tasks tend to be associated with greater group productivity than individual productivity, but others tend to show the reverse effect.

Researchers interested in group productivity (e.g., Shaw, 1976; Steiner, 1972) commonly distinguish at least three different kinds of tasks. **Additive tasks** are ones in which everyone does the same thing and the group output reflects the total of all individuals' contributions (they are *added* together). Examples include assembly-type tasks (e.g., putting together a product), some manual tasks (e.g., a team pulling a rope as hard as possible in a tug-of-war game), and tasks in which the goal is to come up with as many ideas or examples as possible (e.g., to list as many breeds of dogs as possible).

**Conjunctive tasks** are ones in which the performance of the group depends on the *least* talented member. The entire group can do only as well as its worst member. Examples include challenging physical tasks (e.g., mountain climbing, where a team can go only as fast as the slowest climber), many kinds of teaching/learning tasks (e.g., a teacher explaining a math concept to a class, where he or she must ensure that everyone understands before moving to another topic), and some study groups (where, as in the classroom, the weakest student can slow everybody else down).

**Disjunctive tasks** are ones in which the performance of the group depends on the *most* talented member. The entire group will do as well as its best member. Examples include tasks that involve a single correct answer (e.g., solving a math problem), creativity-based tasks (e.g., generating the most creative architectural design for a building), and many decision-making tasks in which discussion of diverse ideas increases the quality of the final decision (e.g., military officials discussing options for a battle or war).

Can you deduce from these definitions how groups will fare relative to individuals on each of these kinds of tasks? Let's begin with additive tasks. If individual contributions can be added together, then it will generally be the case that groups will be more productive than individuals. If one person can assemble 10 "widgets" per hour, then a group of three people will certainly assemble *more* than 10 widgets per hour. But this does not mean that the group will necessarily be more *efficient*

**additive tasks**

*activities in which the group output reflects the total of all individual members' contributions*

**conjunctive tasks**

*activities in which the performance of the group depends on the least talented member*

**disjunctive tasks**

*activities in which the performance of the group depends on the most talented member*

than individuals. What previously described phenomenon is relevant to this kind of task? *Social loafing* might occur: people might reduce their effort when in a group if their unique contribution will not be clear. Thus, for example, if one person can assemble 10 widgets per hour working alone, a group of three people may assemble 25 widgets per hour—less efficient than summing the productivity of three people working alone. On additive tasks, then, groups will usually outperform individuals but they will usually be less efficient than individuals.

What about conjunctive tasks? If the group's performance depends on its least talented member, then it will generally be the case that groups will perform *more poorly* than individuals. After all, the entire group is slowed to the rate of its worst member. For instance, if a group of mountain climbers scales a peak in 12 hours, it is likely that most of the individual climbers could have reached the peak in less than 12 hours—they would have performed better than the group (assuming that climbing the mountain alone is possible). This tendency for groups to perform worse than individuals on conjunctive tasks poses a challenge to teachers. How can the needs of weak students be balanced with the needs of strong students to be stimulated to achieve their potential? Many teachers try to deal with this issue by combining group instruction with individual study (e.g., the brightest students can work on their own with enriched material).

Disjunctive tasks are the mirror image of conjunctive tasks: the group's performance depends on its most talented member, as when a problem must be solved or a creative plan must be developed. As a result, groups will usually perform *better* than individuals. A group is more likely to solve a difficult math question or a challenging puzzle than an individual, because the group can rely on its smartest member. Also, members can help one another with comments and suggestions, which might generate a solution that could not have come from any single member (not even from the most talented member alone). Thus, a group is often capable of making better plans or decisions than individuals because it can use all of its members' resources and ideas. Also, if a group integrates its members' personal answers to a problem in order to produce an overall judgment, the group's answer will balance the various biases of the individual members and will probably be quite accurate (see Gigone & Hastie, 1997; Yaniv, 2004).

The three types of tasks are summarized in the accompanying Concept Review. In the next section of the chapter, we move to a group level of analysis. As we will see, groups do not always live up to the potential for high-quality decision making implied in our discussion of disjunctive tasks.

---

## CONCEPT REVIEW
### Types of Tasks

| Type of Task | Description | Group Versus Individual Performance | Example |
|---|---|---|---|
| Additive | Everyone performs the same task, and group output is simply the total of the individual outputs | Groups are more productive, but less efficient, than individuals | Assembly-type tasks |
| Conjunctive | Performance of the group depends on the least talented member | Groups usually perform worse than individuals | Climbing a mountain |
| Disjunctive | Performance of the group depends on the most talented member | Groups usually perform better than individuals | Solving a difficult math problem |

## ● ● ● Decision Making in Groups

One of the most important functions fulfilled by groups is decision making. Most of the critical decisions made in all societies occur at the level of groups: political groups make decisions about international affairs, Supreme Court justices make decisions about legal principles, military groups make decisions about troop deployment and battlefield strategy, and so on. Many of the decisions that affect each of us in our daily lives are also made by groups: families decide where to go on vacation, work groups decide how to divide the responsibilities on a new project, friendship groups decide who will serve as the designated driver prior to going to a bar, and so on. Group decisions are a pervasive part of life, so it is important for social psychologists to understand how groups make decisions.

In this section, we discuss three issues related to group decision making. First, we describe how bad decisions can result from a desire to avoid disagreement in a group. Second, we discuss how majority ideas tend to intensify in a group. Third, we consider how one or a few people can sometimes make a big difference in a group.

## Groupthink: Bad Decisions Because of Pressure to Agree

We noted at the end of the preceding section that groups have the potential to make better decisions than individuals. Groups have access to more information than a single person. Groups also provide multiple perspectives on an issue, which should help to identify problems with proposed solutions. The phrase "Two heads are better than one" seems to capture accurately the potential for groups to make good decisions.

But groups do *not* always make good choices. In fact, sometimes they make *terrible* decisions, such as when the directors of a drug company decide to introduce a new product despite safety concerns or when a group of generals makes a military decision that proves disastrous. What happened in these cases? Why didn't the decision-making group assess the options better and make a sounder judgment?

There are many reasons for bad decisions, of course. Sometimes, the correct course of action is highly uncertain and/or all of the options involve risks, as when a financial management company is trying to decide how to invest its clients' money. At other times, groups lack the necessary expertise to make informed judgments, as when a volunteer organization mismanages its budget because of a lack of relevant experience. These examples do not represent failures of the group to process information—the decision was either very difficult (for anyone), or the group lacked relevant knowledge (and had little chance from the start of making a well-informed choice).

Bad decisions can also result, however, from poor group functioning, as when the group engages in biased or faulty reasoning based on the information available to them. These cases are interesting because they were *unnecessary*—they could have been prevented if the group had operated more effectively. In this section, we describe one common source of error in group decision making.

**groupthink**

*a way of thinking that can occur in decision-making groups when pressure to agree leads to inadequate appraisal of options and poor decisions*

Irving Janis (1972, 1982) coined the term **groupthink** to refer to a way of thinking that can occur in decision-making groups, when pressure to agree leads to biased appraisal of options and poor decisions. The fundamental idea of groupthink is that when members of a group are highly motivated to agree with the leader and with one another, they do not express their reservations openly and do not criticize one another. Because many or all of the members are engaging in the same self-censorship, everybody believes that everyone else in the group strongly supports the decision. The result can be poor decisions that are not based on a thorough analysis of the options.

Janis hypothesized that groupthink is most likely to occur in certain kinds of groups. One important condition is that the group is highly cohesive. **Group cohesiveness** refers to the strength of the forces acting on group members to stay in the group (Festinger, 1950; Mullen & Cooper, 1994; Shaw, 1976). In highly cohesive groups, members are strongly motivated to remain: they like the other members, membership is prestigious, and/or they receive tangible benefits from being in the group. Thus, members of highly cohesive groups do not want to be ostracized or excluded from the group, which leads them to conform and to avoid criticizing other members' ideas. (We should note that group cohesiveness can have positive consequences as well. For example, members of highly cohesive groups are willing to work hard and make sacrifices for the group. Also, cohesiveness can help groups survive difficult events. Notwithstanding these potential benefits, group cohesiveness can have a stifling effect on discussion.) A second important factor contributing to groupthink is a *directive leader.* Directive leaders openly express their own opinions—often before any discussion has occurred—and control subsequent conversation in the group. When a leader is highly directive, group members know exactly where he or she stands, which puts pressure on them to agree. Also, because directive leaders control the group's discussion, it can be difficult for members to raise questions or concerns. A third factor that makes groups vulnerable to groupthink is high stress. Stress can arise for several reasons, including when a group faces external threat or when there is severe time pressure to make a decision. Whatever its cause, stress makes members feel even more pressure to follow the leader's opinion and to avoid rocking the boat. Stress intensifies the effects of group cohesiveness and directive leadership on the tendency for group members to keep their reservations to themselves.

**Symptoms of Groupthink.** If we see a group making bad decisions, how can we tell if groupthink is responsible? Janis identified eight *symptoms* of groupthink, which are described in Table 10.1 (p. 406). These symptoms are thought to occur in most cases of groupthink, although some will not apply to particular cases. All of the symptoms reflect group members' desires to agree and to maintain a positive group feeling. The symptoms cause faulty assumptions, inadequate assessment of possible options, a willingness to take excessive risks, and, ultimately, poor decisions. The groupthink process is depicted in the flowchart in Figure 10.4.

Groupthink may help us to understand why some tragic events occurred. For instance, on February 1, 2003, the space shuttle *Columbia* reentered the earth's

**group cohesiveness**

*the combined strength of all forces acting on members of a group to remain in the group*

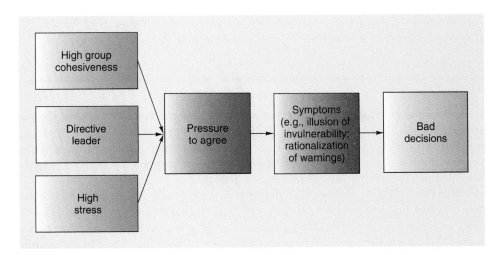

**FIGURE 10.4** Groupthink process

---

**TABLE 10.1**
*Symptoms of Groupthink*

---

1. *An illusion of invulnerability:* If a group feels invincible, it tends to make decisions that are very risky; there is no need for caution because the group cannot lose. This symptom is interconnected with some of the other symptoms such as rationalizing warnings.

2. *Rationalization of warnings:* An essential element of good decision-making is to assess carefully any possible problems with an option. If warning signals are discounted or rationalized as being harmless, then risky and low-quality decisions may occur. Rationalization of warnings is related to the illusion of invulnerability: rationalization can result in perceived invulnerability, and perceived invulnerability can encourage rationalization.

3. *An unquestioned belief in the inherent morality of the group:* Most of us believe that we are moral and ethical people. When a group assumes that it is inherently moral, it can fail to recognize that self-interest might be coloring its perspective. This failure may lead the group to ignore ethical aspects of its decisions, which can result in decisions that appear to others to be selfish or corrupt.

4. *Stereotyped views of enemy leaders:* Negative stereotypes about an outgroup are often believed to apply especially well to the leaders of that outgroup. When a group views enemy leaders as evil, it will be unwilling to negotiate with those leaders, increasing the chance of aggression. When a group views enemy leaders as weak and stupid, it may underestimate those leaders and make decisions that are risky or foolish. This symptom can contribute to an illusion of invulnerability—the first symptom above.

5. *Pressure on group members who challenge the consensus:* Highly cohesive groups usually want agreement and harmony. Therefore, it is upsetting when someone in the group criticizes assumptions or tentative decisions. Social pressure from other group members may be directed at these individuals, which will communicate that dissent is inconsistent with being a loyal member of the group. This social pressure can result in the exclusion of important information from discussion.

6. *Self-censorship of misgivings, questions, and counterarguments:* Because group members want agreement and know that dissent is inconsistent with being a loyal member of the group, they often engage in self-censorship by not expressing their doubts about ideas or assumptions. Like social pressure on people who raise questions, self-censorship can result in the exclusion of important information from the discussion.

7. *An illusion of unanimity:* Members of the group will often believe that everyone agrees with a tentative decision (partly because of social pressure on critics and self-censorship). This illusion that unanimity exists will further inhibit discussion. Perceived unanimity can lead to risky decisions and a failure to consider ethical aspects of the decision.

8. *Emergence of self-appointed mindguards:* Janis suggested that in highly cohesive groups, one or more members sometimes act as *mindguards*—people who protect the "mind" of the leader by shielding him or her from criticisms, doubts, and so on (a mental version of *bodyguards,* who protect the leader's physical well-being). These mindguards are self-appointed: they decide themselves that their actions are necessary for the peace of mind of the leader and the harmony of the group. Mindguards sometimes intercept people who might want to criticize a tentative decision and deny them access to the group.

Adapted from Janis, 1972, pp. 197–198

---

atmosphere after a successful 16-day mission. The on-board astronauts were in continuous communication with NASA flight controllers in Houston, and everything seemed to be going routinely. Suddenly, with no more than 1 or 2 seconds of warning, the shuttle exploded over Texas, killing all seven crew members. This tragedy horrified the nation and put NASA's shuttle program on hold.

Was the *Columbia* explosion an example of groupthink? Based on the information that became public after the tragedy, communication researchers Claire Ferraris and Rodney Carveth (2003) concluded that groupthink was at least partly responsible (for a similar analysis of the relevance of groupthink to the 1986 explosion of the space shuttle *Challenger,* see Griffin, 1997). NASA employees wanted so much to believe that things were okay that they did not do their jobs—they did not conduct a careful review and discussion of the available information.

For example, an investigation board studied the accident and concluded that the cause of the explosion was damage to the left wing of the shuttle, which was struck by a piece of foam insulation that came off about 80 seconds after launch. This piece of debris hit some heat-resistant tiles on the front of the wing that were designed to protect against the extremely high temperatures generated on reentry. The damaged tiles allowed superheated gases to enter the wing, causing the explosion. It turns out that a previous shuttle flight, the *Atlantis* in 2000, was known to have sustained damage to one of its wings, which allowed molten plasma to enter the wing on reentry, though without catastrophic consequences. Thus, NASA knew that wing damage was possible. Even more disturbing, at least one expert raised alarms during the *Columbia*'s flight about possible damage sustained during the launch. After reviewing videotapes of the foam hitting the shuttle, Rodney Rocha, a structural engineer, urged NASA managers to obtain photographs of the shuttle's wings using spy satellites to assess whether damage had occurred. His suggestion was not pursued by the flight officials.

Did *groupthink* contribute to the explosion of the space shuttle *Columbia* on February 1, 2003?

Which of the specific symptoms of groupthink listed in Table 10.1 were present in the *Columbia* tragedy? It is possible to find some evidence of almost all of them (see Ferraris & Carveth, 2003). The members of the mission management team appeared to view the space shuttle fleet as relatively invulnerable (#1). The team engaged in numerous rationalizations of warnings, including the dismissal of questions that were raised about the foam insulation that broke off 80 seconds into the flight (#2). The general culture within NASA encouraged isolation from outsiders who might disagree (possibly reflecting #8), while putting strong pressure on both employees and independent contractors to avoid rocking the boat (#5). For example, NASA programs depended heavily on successful completion of missions—within the original budget and on time. Cost overruns, delays, and cancellations were viewed as threats to the very existence of the agency. This time pressure caused a lot of stress among members of the mission management team, who desperately wanted things to run smoothly. Also, contractors received bonuses for on-time launches—a policy that would obviously spur them to keep any worries to themselves. After the event, some members of the mission management team admitted publicly that they had engaged in self-censorship during meetings (#6), which led them to think that everyone else unanimously believed that there were no serious risks in the flight (#7). There was also a tendency for members of NASA to view themselves as inherently moral (#3): officials of the agency did not appear to think carefully about their responsibility for the very lives of the astronauts. Were the risks to the astronauts, given previous problems with wing damage, really justified by the benefits of the flight? If they had discussed the ethical implications of their judgments, they might have made more cautious decisions.

**Avoiding Groupthink.** Janis (1972, 1982) identified several decision-making strategies that could be implemented in cohesive groups to reduce the likelihood of groupthink. Three recommendations, which address different elements of groupthink, seem particularly important.

1.  The leader should be nondirective and allow other group members to express their opinions before stating his or her view. One cause of groupthink is that members do not want to challenge or upset the leader. When leaders begin

meetings by announcing their position or preference, pressure on other group members to agree is immediately introduced. To avoid groupthink, leaders should remain quiet and neutral early in the discussion, allowing other group members to express their opinions freely.

2. A norm of openness and candor should be established in the group (a norm that may have to originate from the leader). A major cause of groupthink is that members seek consensus and are loath to criticize or raise questions. But if the leader makes it clear that frank discussion is desirable and that all suggestions must be evaluated thoroughly, members will be more willing to raise questions about proposed ideas. Of course, instituting this norm will not have much impact if people who do criticize are then condemned by the leader or other members. But if members are rewarded for raising questions, the likelihood of groupthink can be greatly reduced. Janis suggested that it might even be possible to designate one member at each meeting (a different member each time) as the *devil's advocate,* whose specific role is to question everything.

3. People from outside the group should be included in the decision-making process. Highly cohesive groups often insulate themselves from outsiders. They want consensus, so the prospect of a different opinion is unattractive. But to make good decisions, it is important that groups seek out all possible views and involve as many relevant experts as possible in the decision-making process. Thus, outside experts should be invited to meetings of the group to share their ideas.

**Empirical Tests of Groupthink Predictions.** Janis (1972, 1982) used the concept of groupthink to understand several historical examples of bad decisions (similar to Ferraris & Carveth's 2003 analysis of the *Columbia* disaster). Case studies of this kind are interesting but do not test the model directly. Although there has not been a lot of empirical research on groupthink, some studies have been conducted (for reviews, see Esser, 1998; Mullen, Anthony, Salas, & Driskell, 1994; Park, 1990). Researchers have primarily investigated two predictions from Janis's model, relating to the effects of group cohesiveness and leadership styles. These issues have usually been explored by creating groups in the laboratory, manipulating cohesiveness and/or leadership style, and observing the decision-making process.

With regard to group cohesiveness, Janis predicted that highly cohesive groups are more likely to show evidence of groupthink than are less cohesive groups. Empirical support for this prediction, however, has been very limited. Researchers (e.g., Moorhead & Montanari, 1986; Turner, Pratkanis, Probasco, & Leve, 1992) have found that highly cohesive groups discourage dissent and produce more confident decisions, but also that members of cohesive groups report *less* self-censorship. In terms of the *quality* of decisions and solutions, most experimental tests of group cohesiveness have yielded null results (see Esser, 1998). One possible explanation of these null results is that the manipulations of group cohesiveness have been too weak: manipulations have included comparing groups of friends to groups of strangers (e.g., Flowers, 1977) and giving participants false information indicating that they are very similar to one another or very different from one another (e.g., Callaway & Esser, 1984). Research on this issue illustrates the ambiguities of null results: should scientists conclude that the model is wrong, or are the existing studies flawed? At any rate, it is possible that stronger manipulations in the future will produce different results, but current evidence does not support Janis's predictions for group cohesiveness.

DoD photo by Tech. Sgt. Andy Dunaway, U.S. Air Force

To avoid *groupthink,* decision-making groups should involve outside experts in their decisions.

Empirical tests of the effects of leadership style have been more supportive of Janis's reasoning (Esser, 1998). Matie Flowers (1977) trained a confederate to lead a group in a highly directive or nondirective way and found that groups with directive leaders used less information and produced fewer possible solutions than did groups with nondirective leaders. Carrie Leana (1985) identified directive or nondirective leaders based on group members' ratings of the leader's style in previous decisions; she found that groups with directive leaders produced fewer possible solutions and more frequent acquiescence to the leader's preferred position than did groups with nondirective leaders. In general, the evidence supports the hypothesis that an open leadership style is likely to produce a better and more broadly based decision than a directive leadership style (but see Peterson, 1997, for a different perspective).

Other research relevant to groupthink has found that more information is considered by a group when there is a norm of critical thinking than when there is a norm of consensus seeking (Postmes, Spears, & Cihangir, 2001). Finally, individual differences may exist in how people respond to directive versus nondirective leaders (Hodson & Sorrentino, 1997); some people actually prefer and respond more positively to directive than nondirective leaders.

## Group Polarization: Moving Toward the Majority View

One of the authors of this book recently participated in an interesting meeting of the psychology department's appointments committee, which is responsible for hiring new professors. The committee had to make a difficult decision, because it could approve job offers to only two of three highly qualified candidates who had all impressed the department during their interviews. The candidates came from different areas of psychology, so it was not obvious how to compare them. The meeting began with some preliminary comments from the department chairperson, and then each member expressed his or her own initial views on who should receive the two job offers. No candidate was selected by all of the members, but two candidates were named more often than the third. Next, the chair invited discussion of the candidates, and the committee members talked for almost an hour about the candidates. After this discussion, the chair called a vote on who should receive the two offers.

Can you predict the outcome of this process? Do you think that the candidate who received the fewest initial nominations was selected or not? On the one hand, it is plausible to speculate that people who *did* initially name this least-preferred candidate might feel threatened by their minority status in the committee and argue forcefully in favor of this individual, resulting in his or her ultimately being chosen to receive an offer. On the other hand, it is plausible that people who initially named the least-preferred candidate might feel foolish or intimidated and keep their mouths shut during the discussion, resulting in the candidate's not receiving an offer.

What actually happened? At the end of the discussion, the two candidates who had initially been named by the most committee members were selected *unanimously* to receive the job offers. Not a single committee member included the initially least-preferred candidate in his or her set of two choices.

This outcome is a classic example of group polarization. Perhaps someday, after reading and studying the following material, you might also recognize group polarization in your own experiences of group decision making.

**Group polarization** refers to the tendency for group discussion to strengthen the initial leanings of the members in a group. Whatever position or option is initially (prediscussion) preferred by the majority of group members will tend to become even more widely preferred after group discussion (e.g., support for the

**group polarization**
*the tendency for group discussion to strengthen the initial leanings of the members in a group*

two initially preferred candidates in the appointments committee meeting became unanimous after discussion).

Let's do an exercise to illustrate group polarization. Consider the following two situations and think about what you would recommend in each case:

1.   The coach of a low-ranked basketball team in a tournament is scheduled to play one of the top-ranked teams. She thinks that her team might be able to surprise the other team by using an unusual defensive strategy, but she knows it is risky and might backfire. Would you encourage her to try the risky defense or would you recommend a more cautious approach?

2.   The father of a young family is able to provide adequately for his family but does not have much money for luxuries. He hears from an acquaintance that a company is developing a new product that might greatly increase the value of its stock, although there is some risk that the product will fail. The young man is thinking about cashing in his life insurance policy to purchase stocks in the company. Would you encourage him to buy stocks or to be more cautious?

It turns out that most college students would encourage the coach to use the risky defense but discourage the father from buying the risky stocks (Myers & Lamm, 1976; Stoner, 1968; Wallach, Kogan, & Bem, 1962). How did your inclinations match these tendencies? But now the important question: what happens when college students discuss these situations in a group and *then* indicate what the individuals should do? Group polarization is what happens: after discussion, even more students recommend that the coach *should* try the risky defense, and even more students recommend that the father should *not* buy the risky stocks. The positions that most people initially preferred tend to become even more widely endorsed after group discussion.

The group polarization effect has been obtained in many studies examining a wide variety of discussion topics (e.g., Blascovitch, Ginsburg, & Veach, 1975; Brauer, Judd, & Gliner, 1995; Knox & Safford, 1976; Madsen, 1978; Whyte, 1993). The effect has been found when groups discuss political attitudes, public sex education, racetrack betting, investment decisions, and many other topics. In each case, whatever inclination existed in the group prior to discussion was even more popular after discussion.

Research on group polarization in the past decade has taken the effect in new directions. For example, Markus Brauer, Charles Judd, and Vincent Jacquelin (2001) tested whether groups would show polarization of *stereotypes*. If most members of a group believe that another target group is characterized by certain traits, will discussion make the stereotype more widely held and perhaps stronger? To test this question, Brauer et al. created a stereotype in the laboratory. All participants were given fictitious information about a group of adolescent boys that emphasized negative qualities, including selfishness and violence. Some participants then engaged in discussion with other participants about their impressions of the group of boys before reporting their stereotypes, whereas other participants reported their stereotypes without engaging in any discussion. Figure 10.5 presents the mean ratings of selfishness and violence by participants who did and did not engage in group discussion. The results showed that participants who first discussed their impressions with other participants reported stronger stereotypes—higher ratings of selfishness and violence—than did participants who rated the group without engaging in any discussion.

The implications of this study are somewhat worrisome. It suggests that if people share a common stereotype, then discussing it

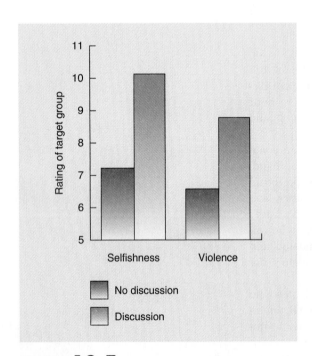

**FIGURE 10.5** Ratings of target group on selfishness and violence

From Brauer et al., "The communication of social stereotypes: The effects of group discussion and information distribution on stereotypic appraisals," *Journal of Personality and Social Psychology, 81,* 463–475, Table 3, p. 470, 2001. Copyright © 2001 by the American Psychological Association. Reprinted by permission.

among themselves will tend to reinforce it. Perhaps this process contributes to the strong stereotypes that sometimes exist within groups (e.g., within families, peer groups, or cultural groups). Thus, group polarization may contribute to intergroup hostility (see also Myers & Bishop, 1970).

There are other settings where group polarization might also be problematic. For instance, in penitentiaries, antisocial attitudes may be intensified by interactions and conversations among prisoners. On the Internet, people expressing their opinions on racist or sexually exploitative websites might strengthen each others' attitudes and cause their dysfunctional views to become more common.

**Causes of Group Polarization.** Why does the group polarization effect occur? Two principal explanations have been offered for the phenomenon (see Eagly & Chaiken, 1993; Isenberg, 1986). The first explanation focuses on the arguments that are presented during group discussion. People usually argue in favor of their own view on an issue. This means that the majority of arguments offered during a discussion are likely to support whatever view was predominant before the discussion began. Because most arguments offered during the discussion favor the predominant view, members of the group are most likely to be persuaded in that direction, which results in group polarization (Vinokur & Burnstein, 1974).

The second explanation, which is *not* incompatible with the first, focuses on people's desire to appear knowledgeable and intelligent. Group discussion lets everyone know each other's positions; members learn which view is endorsed by the majority. There is then social pressure to move in the direction of the preferred view, because members do not want to appear ill-informed or unyielding (Sanders & Baron, 1977).

Notice that these two causes of group polarization parallel the concepts of *informational influence* and *normative influence* introduced in our discussion of conformity in Chapter 8 (see pages 308–309). Group discussion leads to polarized judgments because members of the group use other members' arguments as a source of information (informational influence) and because they feel social pressure to move toward the dominant view (normative influence).

Jury decision making is one of the most interesting applications of the concept of group polarization. This topic is described in Social Psychology in Your Life: Group Polarization in the Courtroom (p. 412).

# Minority Influence: The Power of the Few

Group polarization reflects the impact of the majority on group decisions. The initially preferred position (the *majority* position) tends to become more strongly supported after discussion. This effect constitutes the norm in social influence: more often than not, groups will exhibit polarization toward the dominant view during discussion and decision making. This effect probably reflects that most arguments will favor the majority view and that people feel social pressure to agree with the majority.

But the majority does not *always* carry the day—the minority view in a group can sometimes be profoundly influential. For example, the ANC was for many years a low-power, minority view in South Africa. Although Blacks outnumbered Whites, the use of militant tactics was not broadly supported within the Black community until the 1970s. Moreover, the ANC maintained its influence even when membership was illegal from 1962 to 1990. How did this low-power group achieve such influence? Social psychologists have conducted studies that may help to answer this question. In this section, we begin by discussing the qualities that can make a minority group influential, then turn to the question of whether exposure to a minority view stimulates creative thinking, and close with a discussion of how social impact theory conceptualizes minority influence.

# Social Psychology in Your Life    *Group Polarization in the Courtroom*

Juries are a crucial element of justice systems around the world. Juries make decisions about the guilt or innocence of defendants—a responsibility that is enormously important. How do juries go about reaching their decisions? Through discussion: the members discuss the details of the case. Social psychologists have observed that, like any other group discussions, jury deliberations are likely to produce group polarization (see Hans & Vidmar, 1986; Hastie, Penrod, & Pennington, 1983). That is, the predominant leaning toward a guilty or innocent verdict among jurors prior to discussion predicts the final outcome quite well, because discussion tends to favor the initially preferred decision.

Specifically, researchers have found that the results of an initial, predeliberation vote among the jurors predicts the final outcome: If most jurors are leaning toward conviction, then the unanimous decision is likely to be guilty, whereas if most jurors are leaning toward acquittal, then the unanimous decision is likely to be not guilty. This group polarization effect has been found among simulated juries created in the laboratory (e.g.,

Davis, Kerr, Atkin, Holt, & Meek, 1975), as well as in real juries. Harry Kalven and Hans Zeisel (1966) surveyed people who had served on actual juries and found that the final verdict was almost always consistent with the majority view in an initial vote held before discussion began. Thus, jury deliberations typically led the group to a final decision that corresponded to the prediscussion tendency.

One important qualification to the group polarization effect in juries is that it occurs more strongly for verdicts of *innocent* than for verdicts of *guilty* (Kalven & Zeisel, 1966; MacCoun & Kerr, 1988). That is, when most jurors initially lean toward acquittal, the final verdict is very likely to be acquittal, whereas when most jurors initially lean toward conviction, the final verdict is less predictable (though still more likely to be guilty than innocent).

Why would an initial leaning toward guilty be less influential on the final verdict than an initial leaning toward innocent? Robert MacCoun and Norbert Kerr (1988) argued that jurors take to heart the principle of *beyond reasonable doubt:* they know that they should con-

vict only if they are certain that the defendant is guilty beyond reasonable doubt. This principle leads jurors to require more evidence to convict than to acquit. Therefore, even when a guilty verdict is initially preferred by most jurors, acquittal might nevertheless prevail because all that must happen is that some doubt be introduced into the minds of the jurors who hold the majority view.

In juries, group polarization is greater for verdicts of innocent than for verdicts of guilty.

© Joan Marcus

**Confidence and Persistence.** Perhaps the best-known researcher on minority influence is French social psychologist Serge Moscovici, who wrote extensively on this issue (e.g., Moscovici, 1980; Moscovici & Doise, 1994). Moscovici argued that minorities can be successful in their influence only if they are firm and resolute in their position. That is, members of a minority subgroup must show that they are confident in their view and will not yield to majority pressure. Members of the ANC illustrated the kind of determination necessary for minority influence; nothing could silence their call for justice in South Africa. Even being sent to prison failed to intimidate people like Nelson Mandela. Confidence within a minority raises questions in the minds of people who hold the majority view: "Why are these people so confident? Could their views be correct?" Members of a minority must persist in their position unwaveringly and also remain consistent among themselves. Evidence of either waffling on the issue or divisions within the minority subgroup greatly reduces its impact on the majority.

At the same time as remaining resolute, minorities should try to avoid appearing too rigid, extremist, or impervious to information (Papastamou & Mugny,

1990). Instead, they must seem reasonable and logical, *but also resolute in their opinion on this issue.* One way for a minority to achieve these appearances is by agreeing with the majority on other issues. Such agreement gives the members of the minority more credibility when they disagree, because they have shown that they do not always hold deviant views. When members of a minority disagree with the majority on virtually everything, their views are likely to be dismissed.

These points do not mean that minority influence is either easy or painless. People who take unpopular positions in any group usually face conformity pressure and may be rejected (Bassili, 2003; Evans, 2001; Levine, 1989; Schachter, 1951). Serving as a voice of dissent is usually thankless, and always difficult. Nevertheless, perhaps our discussion of minority influence will help you to remain resolute in the future when you are certain that you hold a correct, but unpopular, view on an important issue.

**Unique Effects of Minority Influence?** Moscovici and other researchers interested in minority influence (e.g., Nemeth, 1987) have argued that minorities have a special kind of influence on others in the group. These researchers have suggested that exposure to a minority view stimulates *divergent thinking*—novel, creative thoughts that consider alternative approaches to a problem. Because a minority voice underscores the fact that different views on the issue are possible, people in the majority are provoked to think carefully and to consider new perspectives (see Martin, Hewstone, & Martin, 2003). Even if the minority does not convince the majority to change its decision on a specific issue, it may elicit delayed effects on other judgments or tasks.

These effects of minorities are believed to differ from those of majorities, which are characterized as eliciting *convergent thinking*—standard or typical approaches to a problem. When exposed to a majority, people are pressured to conform with the majority view, as well as to suppress counterarguments.

Charlene Nemeth has reported data showing that exposure to a minority view increases people's subsequent willingness to take an unpopular position themselves. In one study (Nemeth & Chiles, 1988), participants took part in a color-judging task, in which they had to identify slides as blue or green. Some participants were exposed to confederates who gave unusual color judgments (e.g., calling a blue slide green), whereas other participants were not exposed to these minority judgments. All participants then took part in a conformity study utilizing Solomon Asch's (1956) line-judging task (see page 312). Asch's task required participants to identify which of several lines on a card matched the length of a line on a second card. The correct answer was always obvious, but before giving their responses, participants heard a set of confederates unanimously give erroneous line judgments on some trials. Asch found that participants often conformed with the confederates by giving the wrong answer. In the study by Nemeth and Chiles (1988), participants who had been exposed to a minority view in the color-judging task were much less likely to conform on the line-judging task than were participants who had not been exposed to a minority view in the first task. Seeing someone express a minority judgment on a previous task increased participants' willingness to disagree with the majority on the line-judging task.

**Social Impact Theory.** Not all social psychologists agree that minority influence is qualitatively different from majority influence. In Chapter 8, we described *social impact theory* (see pages 337–339), which asserts that social influence is the result of psychological "forces" acting on an individual (Latané, 1981; Wolf, 1987). This theory interprets "social pressure" quite literally: people experience psychological forces pressing on them, just as they experience physical forces such as sound and weight.

Factors assumed to influence the social pressure felt by an individual include the number, strength, and closeness (immediacy) of sources of influence. When many people exert strong pressure in close proximity to the target, such as when several members of a family urge the father to stop smoking, successful social influence is more likely. Social impact theorists do not distinguish between majority and minority sources of influence; they hypothesize that both majorities and minorities exert their influence through similar processes. If minorities sometimes appear to have unusual impact, it may be because the strength or closeness of their influence is heightened in some way. For instance, the fact that minority views are often unexpected may increase their psychological strength. Similarly, minorities that are firm and resolute may be more influential than timid minorities because confidence translates into stronger social pressure.

Researchers will undoubtedly continue to debate the parallels between minority and majority influence. We suspect that the underlying processes of influence are similar, but minorities are likely to have some unique effects on subsequent tasks, such as increasing willingness to express dissent.

In the following section, we turn from research on groups as a whole to investigations of one specific member of the group: the leader. How leaders emerge in groups and why some leaders are more effective than others are important questions if we want to understand the functioning and performance of groups.

# ● ● ● Leadership

The most important individual in a group is usually the leader. (Our earlier discussion of the role of the leader in creating groupthink illustrates this point.) The leader typically guides the group toward its goals, serves as a representative of the group, and tries to maintain morale. We will articulate some of the leader's functions shortly. Given the importance of this individual, it is not surprising that both social and industrial-organizational psychologists have been very interested in leadership. Two fundamental questions have received the most attention from researchers: "Who is *selected* (or emerges) as the leader of a group?" and "Who makes an *effective* (or successful) leader?"

The issues of emergence and effectiveness have been examined from three different perspectives on leadership: trait, situational, and interactionist approaches. Trait approaches focus on the characteristics of people who become leaders; situational approaches focus on external factors that influence the selection and effectiveness of leaders; and interactionist approaches investigate the combined effects of traits and situational factors. We discuss each of these approaches separately. But first, we need to define some relevant terms.

## Definitions of Leader and Leadership Effectiveness

Think about groups to which you belong, such as your family, sports teams, friendship groups, work groups, religious groups, recreational clubs, or other groups. Can you identify a primary "leader" in all of these groups? If not, why not?

When you think carefully about various groups, it is surprising how complicated the issue of leadership becomes. Leaders can do *many* different things for their group, and leaders can become leaders in *many* different ways. Moreover, some groups have *several* leaders, whereas others have *no* clear leader. Sometimes, members in the same group even disagree about who should be considered the leader of their group.

**Defining a Leader.** So how can we define or identify a leader? There are numerous possibilities, but we will mention only three (see Burn, 2004; Chemers &

Ayman, 1993; Hollander, 1985; Levine & Moreland, 1998; Shaw, 1976). (1) In some groups, the leader is the person who holds a formal position of authority, perhaps involving an election. These kinds of leaders are relatively easy to identify; examples include the president or prime minister of a government, the chairperson of a committee, and the judge in a courtroom. (2) If there is no formal leadership position, another way to define a leader is to say that he or she is the person who is so named by most members. Thus, we might ask members of a friendship group to identify the leader of their clique; there might be disagreement among members, but the leader would be defined as the person who received the most "votes." (3) A third way to define the leader is in terms of his or her *impact* on the group. For instance, the leader could be considered the person who exerts the most influence on members of the group, or who can best motivate members to work hard or to behave in a certain way. From this perspective, members of a group might not even realize who the true leader is; for example, there might be an "official" leader who fills a position of authority (e.g., the coach of a hockey team), but the "real" leader might be someone who inspires the other members to work hard (e.g., a star player). This third approach is exemplified by the concept of **transformational leaders.** Transformational leaders are leaders who *transform* the members of their group—these individuals stimulate fundamental changes in how members view themselves and the group (Bass & Avolio, 1993; House & Shamir, 1993; Ross & Offermann, 1997). Obviously, transformational leaders have a large impact on their group. For example, Mother Teresa radically changed how the nuns in her order saw themselves and their mission on earth. Traditionally, her order had emphasized prayer and contemplation, but Mother Teresa transformed the group into a problem-focused organization dedicated to helping the poor in the Calcutta slums. She inspired her followers by example and elicited great loyalty.

Nelson Mandela qualified as a leader on all of these criteria at some point in his life. He served as president of the ANC and then president of South Africa, both important, formal positions of authority. Informally, he was viewed by most Black South Africans as their symbolic leader while he was imprisoned. And he certainly had a large impact on his group—he played a large role in the transformation of South Africa from an apartheid regime to a true democracy.

### Functions Fulfilled by Leaders.

Part of the difficulty in defining leadership comes from the fact that leaders can fulfill so many different functions for their groups. In specific groups, certain functions will be most important, but across groups there is an amazing diversity of things that leaders do (see Cartwright & Zander, 1968; Hollander, 1985; Vroom & Yetton, 1973). Table 10.2 (p. 416) describes 10 possible functions of leaders, and this list does *not* constitute an exhaustive catalogue of the possibilities.

Some theorists have suggested that the various functions fulfilled by leaders fall into two major categories: task achievement and group maintenance (Bales & Slater, 1955; Hollander, 1985). The **task achievement function** involves all of the things necessary for group productivity, such as providing expert advice or training, planning how to achieve the goals of the group, distributing tasks to members, developing policies, monitoring and evaluating performance, and so on. The **group maintenance function** involves all of the things related to morale in the group, such as motivating members to remain committed, resolving disputes between members, and providing counseling to troubled members. In some groups, different individuals may emerge to fulfill these two functions; the two leaders are referred to as the **task leader** and the **socioemotional leader.**

© Raghu Rai/Magnum Photos

Mother Teresa was a *transformational leader.*

**transformational leaders**
*individuals who produce fundamental changes in how members of a group view themselves and the group*

**task achievement function**
*aspects of leadership that relate to group productivity*

**group maintenance function**
*aspects of leadership that relate to morale in the group*

**task leader**
*an individual who takes charge of issues related to productivity in a group*

**socioemotional leader**
*an individual who takes charge of issues related to morale in a group*

**TABLE 10.2**

*Functions Potentially Fulfilled by Leaders*

| Leader Function | Definition | Example |
|---|---|---|
| Expert | Teaches skills to members | Dance instructor demonstrates movements to students |
| Planner | Plans how to achieve group goals | Military officer plans attack |
| Executive | Assigns tasks to members | Head chef assigns food preparation duties to kitchen staff in restaurant |
| Policy maker | Develops policies to guide group | Retail store manager implements new commission-based salary for salespersons |
| Performance appraiser | Evaluates members' performance | Supervisor provides formal evaluation of subordinate's job performance |
| External representative | Represents group to outside groups and individuals | Political leader visits foreign country |
| Motivator | Motivates members to perform and remain in group | Football coach gives emotional pregame pep talk to players |
| Arbitrator | Resolves conflicts between members | Parent intervenes between fighting children and suggests solution |
| Exemplar | Sets example and inspires members | Religious leader lives exemplary life |
| Counselor | Helps members deal with personal problems | College residence adviser (RA) counsels students on how to cope with first-year stressors |

Sometimes the most important functions fulfilled by groups' leaders change over time. For example, when the ANC was formed in South Africa in 1912, the most important functions of the leaders were probably to attract new members and to establish the credibility of the group. But later, when apartheid became official, the ANC needed leaders who would confront White politicians and argue persuasively for justice. These shifting functions help to explain why the ANC leadership changed over the years from being relatively conservative to more militant.

**Defining Leadership Effectiveness.** The wide range of functions potentially fulfilled by leaders complicates any attempt to define and measure leadership *effectiveness.* How can we assess the effectiveness of leaders when they fill such different roles in different groups? One leader might be an effective planner, whereas another might be an effective motivator. How can we compare these two individuals?

Just as there are different ways to define or identify a leader, there are different ways to define or measure leadership effectiveness (see Chemers & Ayman, 1993; Forsyth, 1999; Hollander, 1985). A common approach, especially in research in industrial-organizational psychology, has been to define an effective leader as one whose group is highly *productive.* When groups produce an output that can be quantified (e.g., counting the number of products assembled), this definition makes particular sense.

A second approach has been to define an effective leader as one whose group members are very *satisfied.* If the members of the group are happy, isn't that enough to consider the leader effective? This definition is particularly appropriate for groups whose primary purpose is socializing (e.g., friendship groups, social clubs).

A third approach to leadership effectiveness has been to define an effective leader as someone who has a large *impact* on the group. If a leader moves the group significantly toward its goals, then he or she is effective. But what if a leader has a large impact on a group but moves it in his or her own directions rather than toward the group's original goals? Adolph Hitler had a large impact on Germany, but he moved the country in a despicable direction that was abhorred by many Germans. Should we consider him to have been an effective or ineffective leader? Some theorists have argued that leader effectiveness should be defined in terms of achieving only the group's goals (which would assess Hitler as ineffective), whereas others have argued that any kind of impact, even the achievement of selfish goals, should be considered equally influential (which would assess Hitler as more effective).

Finally, a straightforward way of defining leadership effectiveness—and the most common method in social psychological research—has been in terms of *group members' ratings of the leader's effectiveness*. This allows members to focus on whatever aspect of leadership they personally consider to be important (productivity, morale, etc.) when evaluating the leader.

Having clarified what we mean by leaders, functions of leaders, and leadership effectiveness, we can now turn to the three approaches mentioned earlier that have been taken by social psychologists interested in leadership. We begin with the trait approach.

## Great Person Theory: Trait Approaches to Leadership

Much of the research on leadership has taken an individual difference perspective, trying to identify the personal characteristics that predict being chosen as a leader or being a successful leader. This **trait approach to leadership** has been called **Great Person theory:** great leaders are assumed to possess rare qualities that make them effective. When most of us think of famous leaders, such as Nelson Mandela, Martin Luther King, Jr., or Winston Churchill, we presume that they achieved their positions of influence because they were special in some way—charismatic, intelligent, decisive. This is the trait approach.

Most studies in this tradition have used correlational designs, in which people who achieve leadership positions (in naturally occurring or laboratory-created groups) are compared to people who do not. Researchers have measured a variety of personal characteristics that might predict leadership: physical features (e.g., height, gender), abilities (e.g., intelligence, task expertise), and personality traits (e.g., extraversion, need for achievement).

These studies have produced some interesting findings. For instance, people who emerge as leaders tend to be somewhat *taller* than nonleaders, at least among men (e.g., Stodgill, 1974). Does this surprise you? A more reassuring result is that leaders tend to be more capable or intelligent than nonleaders (e.g., Lord, DeVader, & Alliger, 1986).

There is also some evidence that these characteristics (height and intelligence) predict not only leader *emergence* but also leader *effectiveness*. For instance, Stewart McCann (1992) calculated the correlations between several characteristics of past American presidents and their ratings of effectiveness by historians. Presidents who were tall and intelligent tended to receive higher ratings of effectiveness than did shorter and less intelligent presidents (see also Simonton, 1987). The result for intelligence makes sense, but what processes might explain the effect of height on presidential greatness? One possibility is that tall people are more physically intimidating and therefore more likely to influence others successfully. Another possibility

**trait approach to leadership**
*the perspective that people become leaders, or perform well as leaders, because of their individual characteristics, such as intelligence and charisma*

**Great Person theory**
*the hypothesis that exceptional leaders possess extraordinary qualities and skills—consistent with the trait approach to leadership*

What made Martin Luther King, Jr., a great leader?

is that a height stereotype exists, such that tall individuals are viewed as more talented or more forceful than short individuals, and this stereotype results in tall individuals having more influence.

**Gender and Leadership.** Leaders are also more likely to be male than female. Alice Eagly and Steven Karau (1991) examined a total of 110 comparisons of men and women in groups that were initially leaderless but that required members to rate the leadership abilities of each other or to elect a leader. Men received higher ratings or were elected as leader in 74 of the 110 comparisons (67%). A small number (15) of the comparisons involved ratings of *social* leadership skills, such as empathy or likability; in these comparisons, women almost always received higher ratings than men (87%). Eagly and Karau suggested that men are more likely to emerge as the task leader of a group, whereas women are more likely to emerge as the socioemotional leader of a group.

Why do these gender differences occur? Why are men more likely to emerge as task leaders—which is probably the most common type of leader—than women? Eagly and Karau (1991, 2002) speculated that the findings reflected the operation of gender stereotypes, which characterize men as *agentic* (e.g., assertive, controlling) and women as *communal* (e.g., sympathetic, helpful). Perhaps men are more likely to *seek* positions as task leaders than are women, because the positions are consistent with their gender role; or perhaps group members are more likely to *select* men than women as task leaders, because they think that men will be more skilled or more comfortable in the role. Or perhaps both of these processes contribute.

Gender also influences the perceived effectiveness of leaders. Alice Eagly, Steven Karau, and Mona Makhijani (1995) reviewed all prior studies that compared the effectiveness of male versus female leaders. Measures of *effectiveness* in these studies included group productivity, members' ratings of the leader's effectiveness, and frequency counts of "effective leader behaviors" by trained judges (usually scored from videotapes of the group). When the results of all studies were combined, leaders performed better when the role demands of the leadership position matched their gender. That is, men tended to perform better (had more productive groups, were rated as a more effective leader, etc.) than women when the leader's role called for traditionally masculine strengths (e.g., it required the ability to direct and control people), whereas the reverse direction tended to occur when the

When the leader's role in a group calls for such things as directing and controlling members, a female leader may be evaluated more negatively than a male leader.

© Bruce Ayres/Getty Images

leader's role called for traditionally feminine strengths (e.g., it required the ability to cooperate and get along with other people). This pattern is consistent with the finding mentioned previously that men are more likely to be chosen as task leaders, whereas women are more likely to be chosen as socioemotional leaders. Again, given that positions requiring task leadership are probably more common than positions requiring socioemotional leadership, these biases in evaluations favor men in most cases (see also Eagly & Karau, 2002; Ridgeway, 2001; Sczesny & Kuhnen, 2004).

We have noted that leaders are evaluated more favorably when their role demands match their gender; it may not be surprising, therefore, that men and women adopt different styles when they do become leaders (Carli, 2001; Rudman & Glick, 2001). Alice Eagly and Blair Johnson (1990) concluded on the basis of a literature review that men are more likely than women to adopt a controlling, autocratic leadership style, whereas women are more likely than men to adopt an open, democratic leadership style. The autocratic style chosen by men fits the stereotype that men are dominant and controlling, and the democratic style chosen by women fits the stereotype that women are nurturant and cooperative (see Atwater, Carey, & Waldman, 2001; Eagly, Makhijani, & Klonsky, 1992; Foels, Driskell, Mullen, & Salas, 2000; Rudman & Kilianski, 2000).

It is interesting to think about the implications of autocratic versus democratic leadership styles for the probability that a group will be affected by groupthink. Controlling, autocratic leaders often make their own positions known at the outset, which increases the chances of groupthink, especially if the group is high in cohesiveness. Democratic leaders, on the other hand, allow greater input from group members, which should help to protect against groupthink. If these inferences are valid, then groups led by men are more likely to exhibit groupthink than groups led by women, because men are more likely than women to adopt an autocratic style. To our knowledge, this prediction has not been directly tested in existing studies of groupthink.

**Personality and Leadership.** Researchers have also identified a number of personality dimensions that are associated with emerging as the leader of a group. Timothy Judge and his colleagues (Judge, Bono, Ilies, & Gerhardt, 2002) reviewed more than 70 studies that had investigated personality predictors of leader *emergence*. Across this large set of studies, the researchers found that people who become leaders tend to be more *extraverted* (outgoing), more *conscientious* (reliable), and more *open to new experiences* (flexible) than those who do not become leaders. Judge and his colleagues also identified about 15 studies that specifically assessed leadership *effectiveness* and found that the same dimensions (extraversion, conscientiousness, and openness) predicted effectiveness significantly across the set of studies.

In Know Yourself 10.1: Extraversion, Conscientiousness, and Openness (p. 420), we reproduce a very brief measure of these three dimensions (Gosling, Rentfrow, & Swann, 2003). Each of the dimensions has been shown to relate to leadership, but even as a package, they explain only a part of why people become leaders. See how you would answer the items.

In another investigation of personality and leadership, Richard Sorrentino and Nigel Field (1986) tested whether the variables of achievement motivation and affiliation motivation were related to leadership. We explained in Chapter 5 (see page 186) that *achievement motivation* reflects the extent to which people are attracted to, rather than frightened by, performance settings. People who are high in achievement motivation enjoy performance tasks and thrive on challenges, whereas people who are low in achievement motivation avoid performance settings and tend to choke in challenging situations. The dimension of *affiliation motivation* reflects the extent to which people approach or avoid *social* settings. People who are high in

# Know Yourself 10.1
## *Extraversion, Conscientiousness, and Openness*

Here are a number of personality traits that may or may not apply to you. Please circle a number on each scale to indicate the extent to which you see yourself in that way.

1. I see myself as extraverted.

| 1 | 2 | 3 | 4 | 5 | 6 | 7 |
|---|---|---|---|---|---|---|
| Disagree strongly | Disagree moderately | Disagree a little | Neither agree nor disagree | Agree a little | Agree moderately | Agree strongly |

2. I see myself as dependable.

| 1 | 2 | 3 | 4 | 5 | 6 | 7 |
|---|---|---|---|---|---|---|
| Disagree strongly | Disagree moderately | Disagree a little | Neither agree nor disagree | Agree a little | Agree moderately | Agree strongly |

3. I see myself as open to new experiences.

| 1 | 2 | 3 | 4 | 5 | 6 | 7 |
|---|---|---|---|---|---|---|
| Disagree strongly | Disagree moderately | Disagree a little | Neither agree nor disagree | Agree a little | Agree moderately | Agree strongly |

4. I see myself as reserved.

| 1 | 2 | 3 | 4 | 5 | 6 | 7 |
|---|---|---|---|---|---|---|
| Disagree strongly | Disagree moderately | Disagree a little | Neither agree nor disagree | Agree a little | Agree moderately | Agree strongly |

5. I see myself as disorganized.

| 1 | 2 | 3 | 4 | 5 | 6 | 7 |
|---|---|---|---|---|---|---|
| Disagree strongly | Disagree moderately | Disagree a little | Neither agree nor disagree | Agree a little | Agree moderately | Agree strongly |

6. I see myself as conventional.

| 1 | 2 | 3 | 4 | 5 | 6 | 7 |
|---|---|---|---|---|---|---|
| Disagree strongly | Disagree moderately | Disagree a little | Neither agree nor disagree | Agree a little | Agree moderately | Agree strongly |

7. I see myself as enthusiastic.

| 1 | 2 | 3 | 4 | 5 | 6 | 7 |
|---|---|---|---|---|---|---|
| Disagree strongly | Disagree moderately | Disagree a little | Neither agree nor disagree | Agree a little | Agree moderately | Agree strongly |

8. I see myself as self-disciplined.

| 1 | 2 | 3 | 4 | 5 | 6 | 7 |
|---|---|---|---|---|---|---|
| Disagree strongly | Disagree moderately | Disagree a little | Neither agree nor disagree | Agree a little | Agree moderately | Agree strongly |

9. I see myself as complex.

| 1 | 2 | 3 | 4 | 5 | 6 | 7 |
|---|---|---|---|---|---|---|
| Disagree strongly | Disagree moderately | Disagree a little | Neither agree nor disagree | Agree a little | Agree moderately | Agree strongly |

10. I see myself as quiet.

| 1 | 2 | 3 | 4 | 5 | 6 | 7 |
|---|---|---|---|---|---|---|
| Disagree strongly | Disagree moderately | Disagree a little | Neither agree nor disagree | Agree a little | Agree moderately | Agree strongly |

11. I see myself as careless.

| 1 | 2 | 3 | 4 | 5 | 6 | 7 |
|---|---|---|---|---|---|---|
| Disagree strongly | Disagree moderately | Disagree a little | Neither agree nor disagree | Agree a little | Agree moderately | Agree strongly |

12.  I see myself as uncreative.

| 1 | 2 | 3 | 4 | 5 | 6 | 7 |
|---|---|---|---|---|---|---|
| Disagree strongly | Disagree moderately | Disagree a little | Neither agree nor disagree | Agree a little | Agree moderately | Agree strongly |

**SCORING:**

1.  *Extraversion:* Items 1 and 7 are scored using the answer scales as presented (1-2-3-4-5-6-7); Items 4 and 10 are reverse-scored (that is, 7-6-5-4-3-2-1). Add up your score on all four items for your total extraversion score. Possible scores range from 4 to 28, and higher scores reflect greater extraversion.
2.  *Conscientiousness:* Items 2 and 8 are scored using the answer scales as presented; Items 5 and 11 are reverse-scored. Add up your score on all four items for your total conscientiousness score. Possible scores range from 4 to 28, and higher scores reflect greater conscientiousness.
3.  *Openness to new experiences:* Items 3 and 9 are scored using the answer scales as presented; Items 6 and 12 are reverse-scored. Add up your score on all four items for your total openness score. Possible scores range from 4 to 28, and higher scores reflect greater openness to new experiences.

From Gosling et al., " A very brief measure of the Big-Five personality domains," *Journal of Research in Personality*, 37, 504–528, 2003. Reprinted by permission of Elsevier.

affiliation motivation are comfortable in social settings and seek them out, whereas people who are low in affiliation motivation are uncomfortable in social settings and try to avoid them.

How might these dimensions predict who will emerge as a leader? Sorrentino and Field hypothesized that high levels of achievement motivation and high levels of affiliation motivation would both be associated with becoming a leader, because leaders should want to perform well and should enjoy interacting with others. To test these hypotheses, introductory psychology students completed measures of achievement and affiliation motivation early in a school term. Based on students' scores, the researchers constructed 12 groups of four members each: one member was high in both achievement and affiliation motivation, one member was low in both motivations, one member was high in achievement but low in affiliation motivation, and one member was high in affiliation but low in achievement motivation. Each group came into the lab on five separate occasions. At each session, the group worked for between 1 and 2 hours on an involving, complex problem-solving task. For instance, at one session, group members had to rank-order a list of materials in terms of their importance for survival in the Arctic. At another session, group members had to try to break a computer code. After the final problem-solving task in the fifth session, group members rated one another on a variety of leadership skills and nominated two members as leaders of the group.

Figure 10.6 presents the mean ratings received by each personality type on two leadership dimensions: how motivated they were to help the group reach its goal, and how much they contributed to attaining the group's goal. The figure shows that participants who were high in both achievement and affiliation motivation tended to receive the highest ratings, and participants who were low in both achievement and affiliation motivation tended to receive the lowest ratings. Participants' nominations for leaders were also informative:

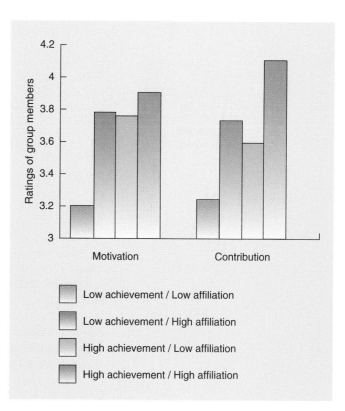

**FIGURE 10.6** Ratings of motivation and contribution of group members

From Sorrentino and Field, "Emergent leadership over time: The functional value of positive motivation," *Journal of Personality and Social Psychology*, 50, 1091–1099, Table 1, p. 1094, 1986. Copyright © 1986 by the American Psychological Association. Reprinted by permission.

the individual who was high in both achievement and affiliation motivation was nominated as one of the two leaders by 34 of the 36 other participants. Thus, the high-high person was almost always seen as a leader by the other members of the group.

**Talent or Talk?** What do you think are the implications of the findings we have described so far for the importance of *talent* in leadership emergence? Do people who emerge as leaders deserve to do so because of relevant skills and knowledge, or do leaders instead emerge on the basis of characteristics that shouldn't matter? Some of the findings seem to support a talent interpretation (e.g., intelligence, achievement motivation, affiliation motivation), whereas others suggest that irrelevant factors play a role (e.g., height, gender).

One specific aspect of this talent question has been investigated directly in some interesting research by social psychologists. The issue involves the relative importance of the *quality* versus the *quantity* of contributions to a group. Does it matter for leadership emergence whether someone makes good rather than poor suggestions? You have probably been in a group in which one individual dominated the conversation but rarely said anything helpful. These sorts of people don't become leaders, do they? Surely the quality of contributions is more important than the quantity?

Maybe not. In a classic study, Richard Sorrentino and Robert Boutillier (1975) directly investigated the importance of quality and quantity of contributions to a group. Their research is noteworthy because it was an *experimental* test of a factor that might affect leader emergence. All of the studies we have described to this point have involved *measuring* existing traits—a correlational approach; Sorrentino and Boutillier *manipulated* the quality and quantity of individuals' contributions to a group.

Male participants came to the laboratory in groups of three, together with a fourth male who was actually a confederate of the experimenter. Participants were taken to separate rooms and told that they would perform a problem-solving task as a group; the rooms had audio connections that allowed participants to speak to one another. The goal of the group was to maximize the number of points they earned on a task. Each trial of the task required the group to select one response from among several alternatives; based on information they had been given, as well as the payoffs on preceding trials, it was possible for the group to decode a pattern that could guide their choices.

The confederate followed a script that varied his contributions to fit one of four patterns. The *high-quality* scripts involved offering the correct answer on 11 of the 15 trials and the incorrect answer on 4 trials; the *low-quality* scripts involved offering 4 correct and 11 incorrect answers on the 15 trials. The *high-quantity* scripts involved many comments in addition to the offered answers; the *low-quantity* scripts involved very few comments in addition to the offered answers. The entire session lasted approximately one hour.

After completion of all 15 trials, participants rated one another's leadership abilities. Figure 10.7 presents the mean rating in each condition of the confederate's overall leadership skills (combining separate ratings of his task and socioemotional leadership skills). The figure shows that the *number* of the confederate's comments had a large impact on ratings of his leadership skills (the two right-hand bars are higher than the two left-hand bars), whereas the *correctness* of the confederate's comments had less impact. Statistical analyses revealed a significant effect of the quantity manipulation but no effect of the quality manipulation. In terms of perceived leadership ability, it appeared to matter *how much* the confederate talked, rather than the *quality* of what he said.

Were participants in this study illogical or deficient in their evaluations? The authors speculated that the finding may not be absurd at all. Perhaps people who

**10.1**
**ONLINE**
**LAB**

participate a lot in group discussions are seen as being highly *motivated* to belong to the group. Even if their contributions are not always stellar, these individuals are seen as trying their best. Such motivation is believed to be necessary to lead a group. In contrast, individuals who speak infrequently, even if their comments are almost always good ones, are seen as low in motivation to belong to the group—they are not exerting a lot of effort on behalf of the group. Such individuals are not regarded as appropriate leaders (see also Anderson, John, Keltner, & Kring, 2001; Mullen, Salas, & Driskell, 1989). Thus, relying on quantity of participation as a basis for judgments of leadership potential may be at least somewhat rational.

So what should we conclude about the trait approach to leadership? For example, do these findings help us to understand Nelson Mandela's effectiveness as a leader? Does he possess characteristics identified in social psychological research? The answer is that he probably does possess a rare combination of qualities. There is no doubt that he is highly intelligent. He is also friendly and extraverted, with strong social skills. Although we cannot know for sure, he is probably high in both achievement motivation and affiliation motivation. One important element of his character that is not reflected in research on leadership is a strong sense of justice and fairness. This concern for justice may have provided the motivation for Mandela's efforts, while the other characteristics made him effective in achieving his goals.

# Being in the Right Place at the Right Time: Situational Approaches to Leadership

We have described evidence showing that certain characteristics increase the likelihood that an individual will emerge as the leader of a group. It is important, however, to avoid overstating this point with regard to everyday groups. In fact, most people are perfectly capable of serving as the leader of small groups—and most of us *are* the leader of one or more groups in our lives (family, friends, clubs, work groups, committees, etc.). Leaders of most groups do not need great oratorical skills or exceptional ambition; they simply need the commitment to do the necessary work and the goodwill of other members in the group. From this admittedly unromantic perspective, it becomes clear that leadership can be mundane or routine.

Indeed, it can sometimes be difficult to find *anyone* to serve as the leader of a group. For instance, university clubs often have subcommittees that are given specific responsibilities, such as organizing social events, maintaining membership lists, or advertising the club's events. Finding people who are willing to lead (chair) these subcommittees can be difficult; there tend to be a lot of lowered heads and averted gazes when the president of the club calls for volunteers on election night.

Emerging as leader, then, sometimes reflects being in the right place at the right time (or, depending on one's perspective, being in the wrong place at the wrong time). Traits and skills may be largely irrelevant—it was the leader's turn, or the leader was the only one willing to take on the position, or the leader happened to walk into the room exactly when the group was searching for a nominee! This perspective is known as the **situational approach to leadership:** external, situational factors can influence the selection of the leader.

What are some of these situational factors that affect leadership emergence? Believe it or not, one factor can be the seating arrangements at an initial group meeting. In a classic study (Howells & Becker, 1962), participants were required to

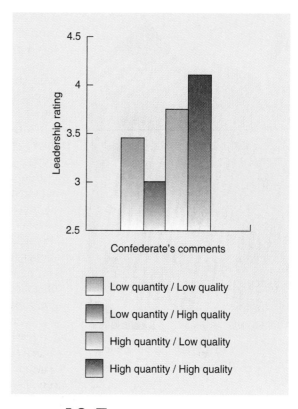

**FIGURE 10.7** Ratings of leadership ability of confederate

From Sorrentino and Boutillier, "The effect of quantity and quality of verbal interaction on rating of leadership ability," *Journal of Experimental Social Psychology*, 11, 403–411, Table 1, p. 408, 1975. Reprinted by permission of Elsevier.

**situational approach to leadership**

*the perspective that external, situational factors, such as seating arrangements, can influence who will become leader of a group*

External threats often prompt people to support their leaders.

**interactionist approach to leadership**

*the perspective that certain kinds of people are likely to emerge as leaders (or to be effective leaders) under one set of conditions, whereas other kinds of people are likely to emerge as leaders (or to be effective leaders) under a different set of conditions*

**contingency model of leadership effectiveness**

*a theory that predicts that task-oriented leaders will be more successful than relationship-oriented leaders in groups where the situation is either very favorable or very unfavorable for the leader, whereas relationship-oriented leaders will be more successful than task-oriented leaders in groups where the situation is mixed for the leader*

work together in groups of five on several tasks at a rectangular table, with two individuals on one side and three individuals on the other side of the table. When later asked to identify the leader of the group, participants were significantly more likely to select someone on the 2-person side than on the 3-person side. Why? The authors suggested that communication tends to go back and forth across a table; thus, participants on the 2-person side would be directing comments to more people (3 rather than 2), which would facilitate the perception that they were the leader.

Another situational factor that can affect leadership emergence is external threat. When a group perceives external threat, its members look for strong leadership to deal with the threat. The anxiety aroused by the threat motivates members to find an authority figure to guide them through the problem. After the attacks of September 11, 2001, many Americans rallied around President Bush and supported his decisions to fight terrorism, such as the war in Afghanistan and the war to remove Saddam Hussein in Iraq. If there is no existing leader in a group, external threat increases the probability that a leader (any leader) will emerge (e.g., Altemeyer, 1988; Worchel, Andreoli, & Folger, 1977).

As a final example of the situational approach to leadership, consider the role of seniority in many organizations. People who have belonged to groups the longest are often seen as the ones who should serve as leaders, irrespective of their standing on relevant skills like intelligence or motivation. Seniority frequently seems to be the "default" basis for selecting leaders. Thus, when a group has a lot of turnover, the probability increases that a particular individual will eventually serve as leader. Chet Insko and his colleagues (Insko et al., 1980) conducted an interesting study that explored the role of seniority. Participants in the study were assigned to four-person groups that worked on making simple products (folding paper into particular shapes). Over the course of 5 hours, members were removed from groups and replaced with a new member. This renewal continued for a total of 9 "generations." Almost without exception, groups developed a seniority rule for assuming the role of leader: the longest-serving group member became leader when the current leader was removed from the group. Why was seniority used to select leaders? The authors argued that this rule made sense for several reasons. First, more senior members were more experienced in making the product; second, newer members tended to be unfamiliar to other members and therefore seemed risky as choices for leader; and third, seniority was unambiguous and provided a simple rule for the orderly succession of leadership. These points may often apply to real-life groups as well, so perhaps it makes sense that groups rely, at least in part, on seniority in selecting leaders.

## Person and Situation: Interactionist Approaches to Leadership

Social psychologists usually take an integrative approach to understanding social behavior: dispositions and situational factors combine to influence actions (e.g., see the section on Interactions Between Persons and Situations in Chapter 5, pages 182–189). In the current context, the **interactionist approach to leadership** predicts that certain kinds of people are likely to emerge as leaders (or to be effective leaders) under one set of conditions, whereas other kinds of people are likely to emerge as leaders (or to be effective leaders) under a different set of conditions. Many individuals can become leaders (or can be effective leaders) if the appropriate situational factors are present.

The best-known interactionist approach to leadership is Fred Fiedler's (1967, 1978) **contingency model of leadership effectiveness.** Although the details of this theory have been only partially supported, it remains a useful way of viewing the topic of leadership. Fiedler selected the name *contingency model* because the theory assumes that the effectiveness of a particular style of leadership is *contingent* (depends) on situational factors.

Fiedler distinguished between two major categories of leadership styles: task-oriented leaders and relationship-oriented leaders (these styles correspond quite closely to our earlier distinction between *task leader* and *socioemotional leader*). Task-oriented leaders are primarily concerned with the performance and success of their group; they want group members to be productive. Relationship-oriented leaders, on the other hand, are primarily concerned with interpersonal relationships and morale in the group; they want group members to be happy.

The way that Fiedler proposed measuring this leadership style is interesting. His technique involves asking respondents to think of their *least-preferred coworker*—that is, the person whom they *disliked* working with the most in all of their work experiences. Respondents are then asked to rate this incompetent or disagreeable coworker on a number of personality dimensions. Of course, most people rate this person quite negatively, but some rate him or her *more* negatively than do others. Fiedler assumed that those individuals who give extremely negative ratings to their least-preferred coworker are task-oriented, because they cannot see anything positive in a person who was difficult to work with. In contrast, he assumed that those individuals who give less negative ratings to their least-preferred coworker are relationship-oriented, because they seem to find even this disagreeable person tolerable (they must like everybody!).

The key aspect of Fiedler's model is the prediction that task-oriented leaders will be more effective than relationship-oriented leaders in some situations, whereas the reverse will be true in other situations. When the group situation is *favorable* for the leader (e.g., the leader has a lot of power and group members like the leader), Fielder predicted that task-oriented leaders will do better because they continue to push group members even when things are going well, whereas relationship-oriented leaders tend to relax in this situation. When the group situation is *mixed* for the leader (e.g., the leader has little power but group members like the leader), relationship-oriented leaders are hypothesized to do better because they are more skillful at maintaining the morale and motivation of group members in this mixed situation. Finally, when the group situation is *unfavorable* for the leader (e.g., the leader has little power and group members dislike the leader), task-oriented leaders are once again hypothesized to do better because they keep trying to push group members even under terrible circumstances, whereas relationship-oriented leaders tend to withdraw or give up when they are disliked and have no power.

Researchers have tested the contingency model of leadership effectiveness by creating groups in the laboratory that possess either favorable, mixed, or unfavorable conditions for the leader (for reviews of such studies, see Chemers, 2000; Northouse, 1997; Peters, Hartke, & Pohlmann, 1985; Strube & Garcia, 1981). For instance, some leaders are given substantial power to control the members' rewards and punishments, whereas other leaders have little power to influence members' outcomes. Groups are assigned either a task-oriented or a relationship-oriented leader (based on the leader's ratings of his or her least-preferred coworker). These studies have provided some support for the predictions outlined above, but the results have been inconsistent. For example, a study may confirm one or two predictions from the theory but fail to support another. The amount of research on Fiedler's model has gradually declined in the face of these weakly supportive data.

If we focus on the interactionist approach to leadership more generally, rather than Fiedler's specific theory, the conclusion that different styles of leadership are more effective in different conditions seems justifiable (see Chemers, 2000; Peterson, 1997; Van Vugt, Jepson, Hart, & De Cremer, 2004). Unfortunately, broad models that can integrate all of the findings are not yet available. Nevertheless, the interactionist perspective is a good place for us to conclude our consideration of leadership, because it makes the point that, given the appropriate situation, most

## CONCEPT REVIEW
### Approaches to Leadership

| Approach | Description | Examples of Variables |
| --- | --- | --- |
| Trait approach | Goal is to identify the personal characteristics that predict being chosen a leader or being a successful leader | Height, intelligence, extraversion |
| Situational approach | Goal is to identify external, situational factors that influence being chosen a leader | Seating position, external threat, seniority |
| Interactionist approach | Goal is to understand how dispositional and situational factors combine to influence who is chosen a leader or who makes an effective leader | Contingency model, style × situation analyses |

of us can be effective leaders. Although many of the great leaders in history probably possessed rare combinations of characteristics like exceptional intelligence, charisma, and ambition, the average individual can do just fine in many everyday groups. The three general approaches to leadership are summarized in the accompanying Concept Review.

# Intergroup Conflict

To this point, we have presented individual-level and group-level analyses—that is, we have discussed psychological processes that occur *within* a particular group (productivity, decision making, and leadership). It is also important, however, to understand how different groups relate to one another—*inter*group processes. The significance of intergroup issues is perhaps most obvious in international relations, including war and peace. But everyday life also involves many intergroup perceptions and interactions; for instance, all of us have stereotypes of various ethnic, occupational, and gender groups, and all of us interact with people who belong to social and demographic groups different from our own. In the following paragraphs, we discuss some social psychological research that has explored intergroup processes (see also Brewer & Brown, 1998; Deutsch & Coleman, 2000; Taylor & Moghaddam, 1994; Worchel & Austin, 1986). Because of the particular significance of *negative* relations between groups, we focus on intergroup *conflict*. We separately discuss factors that *escalate* conflict and factors that *reduce* conflict.

## Development and Escalation of Intergroup Conflict

A few points that we made in earlier chapters are relevant to our present consideration of how intergroup conflict can develop. First, memberships in groups constitute an important part of people's identities (Ashmore, Deaux, & McLaughlin-Volpe, 2004). If you were asked to describe yourself, some of your answers would probably involve groups, such as "I am an African American," "I am a student at the University of Illinois," or "I am a psychology major." Recall from Chapters 5 and 9 our discussions of *social identity theory* (see page 167 and page 361). This theory (Tajfel, 1970, 1978) postulates that we want to maintain a positive identity, including a positive view of the groups to which we belong. To achieve this positive social identity, we sometimes belittle members of outgroups and/or give preferential treatment to members of our ingroups. For instance, we might express negative comments about students at other universities, or we might vote for another psychology major in an election for student government. These actions sometimes reflect an active attempt to make our own groups seem better than other groups. People who identify strongly with an ingroup are especially likely to want to heighten the status of that group relative to other groups (e.g., Stürmer & Simon, 2004; Van Vugt & Hart, 2004).

If people want to view their own groups as better than other groups, it may not be surprising that negative stereotypes about outgroups often develop. Unfortunately, although they may serve our need for a positive social identity, negative stereotypes also engender mistrust, hostility, and discrimination between groups. They elicit, in other words, prejudice and intergroup conflict.

Another relevant concept was introduced in Chapter 3 on Social Cognition. In our discussion of stereotypes, we noted that people tend to see members of a group as similar to one another (to see them as a relatively uniform group). Individuals exhibit this tendency toward perceiving group uniformity even for groups to which they belong (ingroups), but the effect tends to be stronger in perceptions of outgroups ("They're all alike!"). The exaggeration of similarity within outgroups is called the *outgroup homogeneity effect,* as we noted in Chapter 3 (see pages 75–76).

A final aspect of intergroup situations that increases the likelihood of conflict can be illustrated with a thought experiment. Imagine that you are playing a game of chess or checkers with another student. How competitive would you be? Now imagine that the student you are playing attends another college and is wearing a sweatshirt from the school. How competitive would you be in this case? If you think that you might be more competitive in the second situation, where group identities are emphasized, than in the first situation, where only individual identities are clear, your intuition matches the results of social psychological research.

Chester Insko, John Schopler, and their colleagues at the University of North Carolina (e.g., Insko, Thibaut, Moehle, Wilson, Diamond, Gilmore, et al., 1990; Schopler, Insko, Graetz, Drigotas, Smith, & Dahl, 1993) conducted numerous experiments in which participants played games against other participants. Sometimes the players were on their own, playing as an individual against another individual. Other participants played on behalf of a group, representing a three-person team that had been randomly formed at the beginning of the session. Participants played games in which they could employ either a strategy of cooperation or a strategy of competition. When participants represented a group, they were significantly more competitive and less cooperative than when they played as individuals. Thus, when a situation was perceived as involving intergroup behavior, it elicited greater competitiveness than when it involved only interpersonal behavior (for a review, see Wildschut, Pinter, Vevea, Insko, & Schopler, 2003). The researchers argued that intergroup situations elicit greater greed and greater fear of being exploited than do interpersonal situations (see also Winquist & Larson, 2004).

The factors we have discussed (social identity theory, negative stereotypes about outgroups, the outgroup homogeneity effect, and the tendency for intergroup situations to elicit competition) suggest that intergroup contexts may be predisposed to degenerate into conflict. Conflict is not inevitable, of course, but it may often occur. Next, we consider three factors that can escalate a minor conflict into a major one: threats, self-presentation goals, and dehumanization.

**Threats.** Can you think of a recent occasion when you used a threat to try to influence another person? Perhaps you threatened a roommate by saying that you would move out

Courtesy of James Olson

When intergroup identities are obvious, people tend to be more competitive.

of the apartment if she didn't start keeping the kitchen and bathroom clean. Or perhaps, as a babysitter, you threatened a child by saying that you would tell his parents that he had been bad if he did not go to bed immediately. Or perhaps you threatened an acquaintance that you'd "get" him somehow if he didn't stop spreading a rumor about you.

Almost all of us use threats occasionally. How effective are threats at inducing compliance? Do they have any "side effects"? Let's consider this issue by looking at the opposite side of the coin: can you think of times when you were threatened by someone who wanted to influence you? Perhaps your parents threatened to ground you if you disobeyed them in some way. Perhaps a friend threatened to drive off without you if you did not arrive at her apartment on time. Perhaps a supervisor threatened to fire you if you did not perform better. How did these threats make you feel? Were they effective at influencing your behavior?

When people think about being the *target* of a threat, they almost always recognize the problems with using threats to influence behavior. Most of us feel very angry when others threaten us, even if we understand why they are doing so. We feel like they are taking away our freedom to make up our own mind, or they are acting as if they control us. In fact, threats often make us want to do exactly the *opposite* of what the other person is telling us to do, so he or she won't threaten us again in the future. Recall *reactance theory* from the section on resisting persuasion in Chapter 7 (see page 299). Reactance theory (Brehm, 1966, 1972) hypothesizes that people are motivated to protect their behavioral freedoms. When a freedom is threatened, it becomes even more attractive to the individual, who may, as a result, defy the threat and engage in the prohibited behavior. But even if the threat is severe enough to make us change our behavior, it leaves us feeling unhappy and upset. Threats can leave seeds of discontent and smoldering anger. None of us likes to be controlled by threats.

Despite the strong intuition that it is unproductive for other people to threaten us, we are much less likely to recognize that our own use of threats against others may be equally harmful (see Kemmelmeier & Winter, 2000). Think again about a time that you threatened another person. Didn't it seem obvious to you that the threat was necessary and justified, even fair? Anyone else would have done the same thing. The other person should have understood this point, right? In reality, however, most people respond to our threats in exactly the same way we respond to others' threats—badly.

There have been some fascinating studies in social psychology documenting the destructive effects of threats. Using threats can escalate a conflict between individuals or groups. In one of the earliest studies of threat, Morton Deutsch and Robert Krauss (1960) assigned participants to play the roles of managers of competing trucking companies. Their job was to move trucks back forth from one location to another on a game map as quickly as possible; the more trips they made, the more profit they would reap. Both companies had a possible shortcut that would increase their profits, but there was a problem: the shortcut included a *one-lane* section. In this one-lane section, trucks could not pass one another, so if two trucks from the competing companies met, they would be stuck unless one backed up to allow the other to pass. If the companies cooperated, however, they could take turns using the shortcut and increase both companies' profits.

The crucial manipulation in the study was that Deutsch and Krauss gave some participants a "threat" that they could use. Specifically, some participants were given a gate they could place on the one-way section that would stop all trucks from using the road. Players could use this gate as a threat to try to force the other company to obey commands. Sometimes neither company had a gate, sometimes only one company had a gate (the *unilateral threat condition*), and sometimes both companies had a gate (the *bilateral threat condition*).

How did the presence of threats influence outcomes? Companies made significantly *less* money when one company had a gate (the unilateral threat condition) than when there were no gates. Further, companies made even *less* money when both companies had a gate (the bilateral threat condition) than when only one company had a gate. Thus, gates reduced companies' profits, and the more gates there were, the less profit was earned. The presence of threats somehow changed the dynamics of the game, such that cooperation was less likely, and profits were therefore reduced.

These findings are not surprising when we think again about how we feel when someone else threatens us. Threats make us angry, and anger rarely encourages cooperation. So when threats are used in a conflict, the two parties generally stop communicating and try to intimidate one another instead of finding a constructive solution.

What are the practical implications of these findings? In the context of international relations, they suggest that the use of threats by one country toward another (e.g., the threat of invasion, or the threat of nuclear weapons) may escalate hostility and conflict. Although threats may effectively influence behavior (e.g., a country may conform to demands in the face of a nuclear threat), they may also heighten negative feelings and perceptions. Thus, if it is possible to exert influence without threats, such a strategy seems preferable in most cases.

© Reuters/CORBIS

The use of threats heightens hostility and conflict.

Although threats are often counterproductive, they may sometimes be necessary to *begin* a process of negotiation, especially if the dominant side has no intention of cooperating or compromising with the less powerful side. For example, the ANC did not elicit much attention from the White South African government until they threatened disruptions with their defiance campaign in the 1950s and their acts of sabotage against government installations in the 1960s. In this case, threats communicated to the government that the ANC was not going to submit to apartheid.

**Self-Presentation Goals.** Intergroup relations are influenced by self-presentation goals, just like interpersonal relations. You may recall from Chapter 4 on Social Perception our discussion of how people try to control others' impressions of them. We focused in that discussion on two goals of self-presentation that are virtually always present in interpersonal settings: to appear likable and to appear competent.

Appearing competent is probably also a goal in most intergroup situations, but appearing likable to other groups is not necessarily seen as important. For example, two ethnic groups that are in conflict may not care whether the other group likes them. Instead, another self-presentation goal of many groups is to appear *powerful* or *strong*. The impression of strength is important because other groups will be more likely to follow a powerful group's recommendations. Indeed, the importance of appearing strong is one reason why threats tend to arouse resistance and resentment. Groups that have been threatened by another group do not want to appear weak. If a group timidly bows to the pressure of a threat from another group, it may be seen as easy to push around, which will encourage the other group (and anyone else who witnesses the timid submission) to use threats again in the future. This reasoning helps us to understand why groups sometimes behave in ways that seem counterproductive during a conflict. Groups are concerned about their "image" or "reputation" (see Brown, 1968).

**Dehumanizing the Enemy.** Threats and the desire to appear strong can escalate intergroup conflict, as we have noted. But these factors seem insufficient to account for many of the extreme historical cases of intergroup violence, such as genocide, which we discussed in Chapter 9 (see pages 377–380). As we noted in our earlier discussion, one of the prerequisites for extreme harmdoing seems to be a

In the 18th and 19th centuries, slavery was rationalized by some Whites through a process of *dehumanization*.

**dehumanization**

*the process of perceiving members of a group as subhuman or inferior to members of one's own group; it allows people to inflict pain and suffering on the group without worrying about the morality of their behavior*

perception that the target group is subhuman or inferior to the perpetrating group (e.g., see Bar-Tal, 1990; Staub, 1989; Waller, 2002). This process of **dehumanization** allows people to inflict pain and suffering on members of the target group without worrying about the morality of their behavior. By viewing the target group as subhuman, the perpetrating group sees the normal rules of justice and fairness as irrelevant (Opotow, 1994, 2001; Opotow & Weiss, 2000). Treatment of members of the target group can then be similar to the treatment of animals, who are not normally seen as possessing the same rights as humans. For instance, this perception characterized many White plantation owners' views of Black slaves in the 1700s and 1800s. Blacks stolen violently from Africa were seen as very different from White Americans—as not having the same feelings and needs as Whites. Apparently, it did not occur to egotistical slaveholders that they were destroying personal and family lives with their actions.

Another perception that leads to detrimental behavior is seeing a target group as evil or malevolent. Evil people *deserve* to be treated badly (see Hafer & Olson, 2003). Many historical cases of genocide were preceded by propaganda campaigns depicting the target group as treacherous, immoral, and corrupt. For example, Adolf Hitler blamed an evil "Jewish conspiracy" for many of Germany's problems in the 1930s. His paranoid speeches fed a preexisting anti-Semitism among the German population. Hitler characterized the Jewish minority as untrustworthy and dangerous. His message that the Jews were villainous eventually persuaded the majority of Germans either to support or to passively tolerate his murderous campaign (Bar-On, 2001).

**Cultural Differences in Conflict Escalation.** There is some evidence that members of collectivistic cultures, such as China and Japan, approach situations of interpersonal and intergroup conflict with a more cooperative, open-minded attitude than do members of individualistic cultures, such as the United States and western Europe, which may reduce the likelihood of a conflict's escalating in collectivistic cultures. For example, Kimberly Wade-Benzoni and her colleagues (Wade-Benzoni, Okumura, Brett, Moore, Tenbrunsel, & Bazerman, 2002) found that Japanese participants were more likely to deal with a conflict by cooperating with other people in the dispute and by dividing resources equally among all claimants than were American participants. In a similar vein, Michele Gelfand and her colleagues (Gelfand, Higgins, Nishii, Raver, Dominguez, Murakami, et al., 2002) found that Japanese participants did not see their own behavior in a dispute as fairer than the behavior of other disputants, whereas American participants showed a strong tendency to consider their own behavior in the conflict to be fairer than opponents' actions. Perceiving one's own behavior as fairer than opponents' actions is likely to escalate a situation of minor conflict into one of high conflict and mistrust. Thus, the individualistic perspective that is predominant in North America and western Europe may increase the likelihood of severe intergroup conflict compared to the collectivistic perspective (see also Carnevale & Leung, 2001; Mayer, 2000).

**terrorism**

*actual or threatened violence against civilians for alleged political purposes*

**Terrorism.** Terrorism represents perhaps the ultimate escalation tactic in a conflict. **Terrorism** can be defined as actual or threatened violence against civilians for alleged political purposes (McCauley & Segal, 1987). It can take the form of a suicide car bomb in a marketplace, a random shooting spree at a train station, an airplane crashed into a skyscraper, or a variety of other murderous actions targeting innocent people.

One important observation about terrorism is that its psychological impact far exceeds its material or physical impact (see Silke, 2003b). Terrorist actions that kill only a handful of people and damage limited property can nevertheless receive worldwide media coverage, cause widespread fear, and stimulate hugely expensive government self-protection programs. The number of people killed by terrorism each year is dwarfed by the number of victims of road accidents, mishaps in the workplace, and various diseases. Yet terrorism probably causes more anxiety than any of these other threats.

Another point about terrorism is that it often reflects a desire to create fear and confusion, rather than to resolve an issue or conflict. Terrorists typically do not want to negotiate; their goal is often to bring anarchy to a society—the breakdown of social control. Further, terrorist organizations are highly secretive, so it is hard for authorities to communicate with them unless they have a political wing. These features of terrorism make it extremely difficult to control or eliminate.

So what can governments do to reduce the terrorist threat facing them? One response that is often taken is military action against the terrorists or supporters of the terrorists. For example, the war in Afghanistan can be seen as a response to the events of September 11, 2001. The long-term effectiveness of military responses to terrorism has been questioned, however, by some social scientists (e.g., see Plous & Zimbardo, 2004). Perhaps the major problem with military action is that civilians will almost inevitably be killed in addition to terrorists, and these deaths of non-combatants may reinforce impressions that the country battling terrorism is selfish and aggressive, making it easier for terrorists to recruit new members.

Improving vigilance and security within one's own country can offer some protection but does not address the underlying problem. International actions are also required. Scott Plous and Philip Zimbardo (2004) suggested that increasing foreign aid to countries that are working actively to fight terrorism might be effective. This tack makes terrorism more difficult to practice. A related strategy is to work for broad international consensus on issues of human rights, so alliances can be built that will cooperate in the long-term battle against terrorism.

Fathali Moghaddam (2005) argued that, in the long run, the only way to combat terrorism effectively is to address the social problems that motivate terrorist actions. People join terrorist organizations, in part, because they feel frustrated by their inability to produce change through legitimate channels. Moghaddam argued that we must reduce this sense of hopelessness by nourishing democracy around the world. For example, we should support governments that work to improve the educational, professional, and political opportunities available to their citizens. These kinds of reforms may forestall the emergence of the next generation of terrorists.

## Reduction of Intergroup Conflict

It is not inevitable that conflict will spiral out of control. Sometimes, groups find solutions to disagreements and evolve strategies for cooperative behavior. Several factors increase the likelihood that intergroup conflict will be reduced.

**Communication.** Perhaps the most important factor in the reduction of conflict is communication. If the opposing groups do not exchange information and suggestions, it is very unlikely that a resolution satisfactory to both sides will be found. In contrast, open and continued communication between antagonistic groups greatly increases the chances of reducing the intensity of the conflict.

The importance of communication was documented in a couple of studies by Morton Deutsch and Robert Krauss, which used the trucking game they previously developed. In one study (Deutsch & Krauss, 1962), participants were forced to communicate on every trial. This procedure reduced the negative impact of threats, but only when just one company had a gate. If both companies had gates (threats), not even forced communication was enough to avoid conflict and poor outcomes.

The researchers suggested that communication did not have stronger positive effects because participants were not necessarily exchanging positive, constructive information. Indeed, they reported that many participants in the study used the mandatory communication as an opportunity to deliver a verbal threat! In a subsequent study using the trucking game (Krauss & Deutsch, 1966), the researchers explicitly tutored some participants in how to communicate fair proposals. These participants were instructed to take the other player's perspective and to work for a strategy that was fair to both sides. The remaining participants did not receive this tutoring about constructive communication. Results showed that the tutored participants obtained significantly better outcomes than did the nontutored participants even when both players had gates (threats). Thus, when communication was molded to be constructive in nature, it helped to reduce conflict and encourage cooperation.

How, exactly, does communication serve to reduce conflict? Dean Pruitt (1998) suggested that communication can have a variety of positive effects (see also Kerr & Kaufman-Gilliland, 1994; Orbell, van de Kragt, & Dawes, 1988; Tyler & Blader, 2000). For one thing, communication usually leads the opposing sides to generate ideas and strategies for how to cooperate. Without communication, each side is likely to focus instead on strategies for exploiting its opponent. Second, while discussing ideas for cooperation, group members may make public statements that commit them to cooperate. This commitment increases the chances that people will actually follow through with cooperative behavior. Third, communication can increase people's confidence that the *other* side will cooperate. In other words, communication tends to increase trust between the opponents. Finally, communication often makes connections or similarities between the opponents more apparent. For instance, the groups might recognize that they share a common identity (e.g., as humans), or they might realize that they both want the same goal (e.g., an equitable solution).

For all of these reasons, communication is a key element in conflict reduction. We will return to the importance of communication in Chapter 12 (Helpful Social Behavior) when we talk about cooperation. Communication played a role in the eventual success of the ANC in establishing a true democracy in South Africa. After Nelson Mandela and other leaders were released from prison in 1990, they began a long process of communication and negotiation with the White government. These discussions eventually produced an agreement to hold a one-person, one-vote election in 1994.

**Trust.** We just mentioned trust as one of the possible, positive consequences of communication. Trust means that individuals or groups think that another person or group has good intentions and will not take advantage of them. Trust turns out to be a critical factor influencing cooperation (see Webb & Worchel, 1986). For example, organizational researchers have found that cooperative behaviors are more common in companies in which employees trust one another and management (e.g., Kramer, 1999; Zaheer, McEvily, & Perrone, 1998). When individuals or groups do not trust one another, they are unwilling to act in ways that leave themselves vulnerable. Cooperation usually requires putting oneself in a position where exploitation is possible (e.g., allowing the other person or group to use shared resources), so a lack of trust reduces the chances of cooperation.

Recall also that intergroup settings tend to elicit more competitiveness than interpersonal settings (Insko et al., 1990; Schopler et al., 1993), and one cause of this effect is that groups fear being exploited by other groups more than individuals fear being exploited by other individuals. This reasoning suggests that groups will generally be trusted less than individuals, which has indeed been found (Insko & Schopler, 1998). Thus, intergroup settings elicit not only competitiveness, but also distrust.

There is an unfortunate asymmetry in the ease of creating versus destroying trust. It can take a long time for secure trust to develop between two groups. In contrast, trust can be dissolved very quickly—often a single action is sufficient to eliminate trust. For instance, friendly neighbors can quickly become enemies if one family calls the police to complain about noise at a party hosted by the other family. This asymmetry (with trust being harder to create than to destroy) means that intergroup relations are often characterized by a lack of trust, especially when groups have a long history of interaction.

Can conflict ever be reduced if groups do not trust one another? Daniel Bar-Tal (2000) argued that long-standing intergroup disputes, such as the Arab–Israeli conflict in the Middle East, create a **conflictive ethos,** which is an atmosphere of distrust and hatred. To reduce conflict significantly, an **ethos of peace** must develop, which is an atmosphere of acceptance and cooperation. But how can this atmosphere be created between opponents in an intractable conflict? A few procedures make groups more willing to cooperate in the absence of trust (Deutsch, 1973; Pruitt, 1998). One strategy is to make a decision reversible (rather than final and unchangeable), which allows each side to withdraw if the other fails to cooperate. For example, a decision to share important resources might be made contingent on certain conditions, with the understanding that the decision will be reversed if the conditions are not met. A second strategy is to divide a significant cooperative move into many smaller and less risky moves, which allows each side to minimize its losses if the other side fails to cooperate. For instance, a loan of $10 million might be broken down into 10 loans of $1 million made over a period of time. A third procedure is to find an external group or authority who will supervise the planned cooperation, preferably a well-respected and powerful neutral party. For example, the United Nations might be recruited to supervise the return of territory from one side to the other. If these strategies can be used to elicit initial cooperation, then a broader process of reconciliation can begin.

**Unilateral Conciliatory Initiatives.** Imagine that you are the representative of a group that has a substantial history of suspicion and conflict with another group. For instance, imagine that you work for a large company and represent a group of employees who have had bitter negotiations with management in the past. Your group does not trust management's motives, and management appears to believe that your group is a bunch of lazy and greedy workers. Over the last few years, management has taken several actions and instituted some rules that have annoyed your group, such as installing cameras to monitor workers, refusing to allow workers to take personal phone calls at work, and threatening layoffs if profits don't increase. Your group has also engaged in some confrontational behavior, such as a work slowdown for several weeks, letter campaigns complaining about the company to local politicians, and even threats of an illegal walkout. Simply put, things can't get much worse in terms of intergroup relations.

Can you think of anything that might quickly and significantly change the nature of the relationship between your group and management? Is there something that could happen that would be a very positive influence? Sale of the company might work, but it could also result in layoffs or cutbacks. Increased demand for the product or new contracts with other businesses would undoubtedly make the company more secure, but would it necessarily improve labor–management relations?

What if management suddenly announced that it was discontinuing one of its actions or rules that have annoyed members of your group? For instance, without any explicit request from your group, management quietly removed all cameras from the building. This action was not accompanied by any new demands on your group; it was a unilateral move by management.

Social psychologists studying intergroup relations have proposed that unilateral actions of this sort can be very effective in reducing intergroup conflict and tension. The term used to refer to these actions is **unilateral conciliatory initiatives** (Osgood, 1962; Pruitt, 1998). One side undertakes the action (hence, *initiative*) without any explicit demands for similar concessions from the other side (hence, *unilateral*), and the action represents a significant concession, thereby implying a sincere

**conflictive ethos**
*an atmosphere of distrust and hatred that can develop in long-standing disputes*

**ethos of peace**
*an atmosphere of acceptance and cooperation, which can facilitate the resolution of disputes*

**unilateral conciliatory initiatives**
*actions to reduce conflict that one group takes without any request from the opponent and without any explicit demands for concessions from the opponent*

motive for reconciliation (hence, *conciliatory*). Because the action is spontaneous and no demands are attached, the opposing group is likely to believe that it represents a real attempt to ease tensions. You may recall our discussion of the *norm of reciprocity* in Chapter 8 (see page 322)—favors should be returned in kind—which is a strong norm in most cultures around the world. Given the norm of reciprocity, the opposing group is likely to feel that it should respond to a unilateral conciliatory initiative with a concession of its own. As a result, one or two concessions by one side can trigger a dramatic de-escalation of tension and suspicion—the opposite of a vicious cycle.

There are some famous examples of the effectiveness of unilateral conciliatory initiatives in international relations. For instance, the United States and the former Soviet Union greatly reduced international tensions near the end of the so-called Cold War when each side made unilateral reductions in nuclear armaments. In the 1980s, Soviet President Mikhail Gorbachev and U.S. President Ronald Reagan independently announced significant reductions in their nuclear arsenals. These announcements consistently led the other side to make a reciprocal concession. A collective determination to reduce the threat of war produced enormous changes in the relationship between these superpowers.

It takes courage and determination to perform a unilateral conciliatory initiative. The side that takes the action puts itself at risk of exploitation; indeed, it is this vulnerability that makes the action effective at reducing tension. These actions may be most effective when the initiator is equal or greater in power than the opponent. If the side that initiates the action is more powerful, then the action is very likely to be seen as genuine, whereas a concession by a weak opponent may be seen as an act of desperation that does not call for a reciprocal concession (Lindskold & Aronoff, 1980).

Our international examples throughout this section of the chapter underscore the importance of knowledge about intergroup conflict—how it develops and how it can be reduced. There is more than just group productivity or employee satisfaction involved; the very survival of our species may hang in the balance. Concepts like unilateral conciliatory initiatives might literally save our lives if we can effectively communicate our knowledge to relevant leaders. If you wonder sometimes about the importance of social psychology, think back to this topic of intergroup conflict and reflect on the nuclear capabilities of many countries.

In the 1980s, Ronald Reagan and Mikhail Gorbachev each performed *unilateral conciliatory initiatives,* which helped to end the Cold War.

# Chapter Summary

**Group dynamics** is the social psychological study of groups and group processes. By **group,** social psychologists mean two or more persons who are interacting with one another and/or influencing one another. Social psychologists have focused on groups of two different sizes: small groups range from 2 to 20 members, and large collectives consist of groups larger than 20.

**Social facilitation** refers to the effects of the presence of other people on individual performance. When a task is simple or well-learned, the presence of other people tends to produce better performance. When a task is difficult or novel, the presence of other people tends to produce worse performance. These two findings reflect that the presence of other people is arousing, which increases the probability of the **dominant responses** (the responses that are most likely to occur when the person is alone).

**Social loafing** refers to the reduction in effort that people often exhibit when working in a group where individual contributions are unidentifiable. Social loafing tends to increase with larger groups and with increased anonymity.

**Deindividuation** refers to a psychological state in which people lose their sense of personal identity and feel immersed in a group. Large groups and clothing that reduces identifiability can produce deindividuation. Deindividuation tends to increase socially undesirable behavior, but it is unclear whether this finding reflects that being in a group releases people from inhibitions, increases their responsiveness to external cues, or increases adherence to emerging group norms.

The relative productivity of individuals versus groups depends on the type of task. **Additive tasks** are ones in which the group output reflects the total of all individuals' contributions. On additive tasks, groups will usually be more productive than individuals, but less efficient because of social loafing. **Conjunctive tasks** are ones in which the performance of the group depends on the least talented member. On conjunctive tasks, groups will usually be less productive than individuals. **Disjunctive tasks** are ones in which the performance of the group depends on the most talented member. On disjunctive tasks, groups will usually be more productive than individuals.

Groups often must make decisions. **Groupthink** refers to a way of thinking that can occur in decision-making groups when pressure to agree leads to biased appraisal of options and poor decisions. Groupthink is hypothesized to occur mainly in groups that are high in **group cohesiveness,** which refers to the combined intensity of all forces acting on group members to stay in a group. Groupthink produces a number of symptoms that involve illusions, rationalizations, and excessive risk taking.

Another phenomenon that occurs in group decision making is **group polarization.** Group polarization refers to the tendency for group discussion to strengthen the initial leanings of the members in a group. It may happen because most arguments presented during group discussion support the initially preferred side or because people feel pressure to adopt the predominant view. Group polarization has been shown to occur in juries, but the effect is stronger for initial leanings toward acquittal than for initial leanings toward conviction.

Although majorities usually prevail in group discussion, minorities sometimes exert considerable influence. Minorities are more likely to be influential if they are firm and resolute in their position. Some theorists have argued that the nature of minority influence is qualitatively different from the nature of majority influence. For example, minorities may stimulate *divergent thinking,* which consists of novel and creative thoughts, whereas majorities may stimulate *convergent thinking,* which consists of typical or standard approaches to a problem.

Research on leadership has focused on two issues: "Who becomes a leader?" (leadership emergence) and "Who makes a good leader?" (leadership effectiveness). Leaders can fulfill many functions in a group, which fall into two major categories. The **task achievement function** involves all of the things necessary for group productivity. The **group maintenance function** involves all of the things related to morale in the group. In some groups, different individuals may fulfill these two categories of functions; the two leaders are labeled the **task leader** and the **socioemotional leader.**

The **trait approach to leadership,** also called **Great Person theory,** tries to identify the personal characteristics that are associated with being chosen as a leader or with being a successful leader, such as intelligence and charisma. Characteristics that have been shown to predict leadership include intelligence, extraversion, conscientiousness, openness to new experiences, achievement motivation, and affiliation motivation. The **situational approach to leadership** tries to identify external, situational factors that can influence leadership emergence, such as physical seating arrangements. The **interactionist approach to leadership** predicts that certain kinds of people are likely to emerge as leaders (or to be effective leaders) under one set of conditions, whereas other kinds of people are likely to emerge as leaders (or to be effective leaders) under a different set of conditions. For example, the **contingency model of leadership effectiveness** predicts that task-oriented leaders will be more effective than relationship-oriented leaders in groups where the situation is either very favorable or very unfavorable for the leader, whereas relationship-oriented leaders will be more effective than task-oriented leaders when the situation is mixed for the leader.

Intergroup relations are often negative. Several factors serve to predispose intergroup situations to degenerate into conflict. For example, simply perceiving a situation as involving inter*group* behavior elicits greater competitiveness than situations involving only inter*personal* behavior. The use of threats tends to escalate conflict between groups. Extreme forms of intergroup violence, such as genocide, may be facilitated by perceptions that the target group is subhuman or inferior. This **dehumanization** of members of the target group allows people to inflict pain and suffering without worrying about the morality of their behavior. **Terrorism** refers to actual or threatened violence against civilians for alleged political purposes. Terrorism often has more psychological impact than material or physical impact. Unfortunately, it is very difficult to control or eliminate terrorism.

To reduce intergroup conflict, communication and trust are very important. Long-standing disputes create a **conflictive ethos,** which is an atmosphere of distrust and hatred. Reducing conflict requires developing an **ethos of peace,** which is an atmosphere of acceptance and cooperation. **Unilateral conciliatory initiatives** occur when one group takes a step to reduce conflict without any explicit demands for concessions by the other side. Because the action is spontaneous and no demands are attached, the opposing group is likely to believe that it represents a sincere attempt to reduce tension, which can significantly ease intergroup conflict.

# Key Terms

**additive tasks** (402)

**conflictive ethos** (433)

**conjunctive tasks** (402)

**contingency model of leadership effectiveness** (424)

**dehumanization** (430)

**deindividuation** (399)

**disjunctive tasks** (402)

**dominant response** (396)

**ethos of peace** (433)

**Great Person theory** (417)

**group** (394)

**group cohesiveness** (405)

**group dynamics** (393)

**group maintenance function** (415)

**group polarization** (409)

**groupthink** (404)

**interactionist approach to leadership** (424)

**situational approach to leadership** (423)

**social facilitation** (395)

**social loafing** (398)

**socioemotional leader** (415)

**task achievement function** (415)

**task leader** (415)

**terrorism** (430)

**trait approach to leadership** (417)

**transformational leaders** (415)

**unilateral conciliatory initiatives** (433)

# Social Psychology Alive on the Web

## SOCIAL PSYCHOLOGY ALIVE: ONLINE LABS

To perform the following experiment and see how you compare to other students, go to Social Psychology Lab, which can be accessed through Social PsychologyNow.

- 10.1 Judging Leadership

## SOCIAL PSYCHOLOGY ALIVE: QUIZZING AND PRACTICE TESTS

You can access our website directly by going to http://psychology.wadsworth.com/brecklerle/ for online quizzes, flash cards, and Internet links.

## INFOTRAC® COLLEGE EDITION

For additional readings, explore InfoTrac College Edition, your online library of archived journal articles and periodicals dating back 22 years. If your instructor ordered InfoTrac College Edition with this book, you can access it from your CD-ROM, or go directly to www.infotrac-college.com/wadsworth and use the passcode from the InfoTrac College Edition card that came with your book. For this chapter, try these search terms: *groups, social facilitation, social loafing, deindividuation, group productivity, groupthink, group cohesiveness, group polarization, minority influence, leader, leadership, conflict, dehumanization, terrorism.*

## Social Psychology Alive: The Workbook

To apply what you've learned in this chapter to what happens in the real world, go to Chapter 10 of *Social Psychology Alive: The Workbook*:

- How Do You Define a Group and Its Leader?
- Can You Demonstrate These Trademarks of Group Behavior?
  Experiment A: Social Facilitation: Will They Excel or Choke?
  Experiment B: Groupthink: Let's All Follow the Leader

- Masks and the Mob
- Decisions About the War in Iraq and Groupthink
- Is Your Group Susceptible to Groupthink?
- Preparing Yourself to Be a Jury Foreperson
- What Do You Prefer in a Leader?
- Judging Leadership
- So You Want to Be a Diplomat: Preparing for Your State Department Job
- Taking Steps to Promote Tolerance

## Social Psychology Alive: The Videos

To see video on the topics and experiments discussed in this chapter, you can go either to Social PsychologyNow or to the CD-ROM, if your instructor assigned either one, to the following section:

- Imprisoned in a Role: The Stanford Prison Study

## To Learn More

This list contains citations to books or articles that can help you learn more. These readings are good places to start if you want to gain a deeper understanding of the topics in this chapter.

- Burn, S. M. (2004). *Groups: Theory and practice.* Belmont, CA: Thomson/Wadsworth.

- Forsyth, D. R. (2006). *Group dynamics* (4th ed.). Belmont, CA: Thomson Learning/Wadsworth.
- Chemers, M. M., & Ayman, R. (Eds.). (1993). *Leadership theory and research: Perspectives and directions.* San Diego, CA: Academic Press.

©Jose Luis Quintana/Reuters/CORBIS

# Aggression and Violence

O n October 26, 2002, 18-year-old Daniel Fears got into an argument in front of his house in Sallisaw, Oklahoma, with a neighbor who criticized his reckless driving after Fears almost ran over some neighborhood children. Fears went into his house, retrieved his father's shotgun, came back out, and shot the neighbor who had confronted him. He also shot the neighbor's 2-year-old daughter and some other neighbors who happened to be standing nearby. He then jumped into his car and went on a shooting rampage, taking random shots at people as he drove through several small towns. In the end, two people were dead, many others were injured, and Daniel Fears was in jail facing multiple murder charges (see Figure 11.1). Although this case did not remain long in the national focus, it is instructive for us because it highlights several of the social psychological principles that apply to aggressive actions.

Speculation immediately focused on the coincidence that Fears's shooting spree followed shortly after the notorious sniper shootings that terrorized the communities surrounding Washington, DC, in the fall of 2002. Much had been written about the murderous actions of John Allen Muhammad and Lee Boyd Malvo. Was Fears's behavior a case of copycat killing—was he modeling his actions on those of Muhammad and Malvo, who had been featured incessantly on television and in the print media for the previous three weeks?

Most people who were familiar with the case dismissed this explanation. Fears's own attorney said that the 18-year-old suffered from depression and "just flipped out."

Of course, Fears was provoked, in a way, by the neighbor's criticism. Nobody likes to be criticized, and perhaps his anger got so intense that an act of retaliation was inevitable. He certainly overreacted, but many of us have responded to criticism with some form of aggression.

Perhaps the event tells us something about the culture of the American South, which may have created a predisposition for Fears to respond to criticism with aggression. He may have felt that he had to defend his "reputation" in the face of the neighbor's criticism.

Whatever the specific cause(s) of Fears's actions, he showed that people are capable of extreme forms of aggression. Understanding the nature of human aggression, especially knowing the factors that increase or decrease it, is one of social psychology's most important challenges.

In this chapter, we describe social psychological research on aggression and violence. We begin by defining aggression and distinguishing among different varieties of aggressive behavior. With this necessary background about the concept of aggression, we turn to theories of aggression—models that attempt to explain why aggression occurs. There are numerous theories that present quite different approaches to aggression (as implied by our brief analysis of the Fears shootings), as well as a recent theory that combines several prior models to provide a relatively comprehensive analysis. We then turn to the effects on aggression of several factors, including personality traits, alcohol, and heat. Next, we discuss the social

## Okla. teen accused of shooting 10 after being scolded

SALLISAW, Okla. — A teenager apparently upset by complaints about his driving shot four neighbors, including a 2-year-old girl, then went on a 20-mile shooting spree, apparently targeting people at random, police said. Two of the victims died.

Daniel Fears, 18, was arrested after losing control of his pickup truck and crashing near a police roadblock, authorities said. As police cars surrounded him, he threw out a 20-gauge shotgun and surrendered, said Oklahoma State Bureau of Investigation spokeswoman Kym Koch.

Authorities hadn't determined a motive for the Saturday rampage in which 10 people were shot, but police said they believed Fears became angry when a neighbor scolded him for driving recklessly in the middle-class neighborhood.

**FIGURE 11.1**

Newspaper report of shootings by Daniel Fears

From *The Baltimore Sun*, Oct. 28, 2002, Section A, p. 2. Reprinted by permission.

*context of aggression by focusing on the role of cultural factors, as well as aggression on the playground, in close relationships, and in groups. We then discuss effects of the media, including violence on television, violent video games, and pornography. We close the chapter by discussing how aggression in society might be controlled and reduced.*

In 2002, Daniel Fears went on a shooting spree during which he killed two people and injured many others.

# ● ● ●  Definition and Varieties of Aggression

The first thing we need to do is define what we mean by the term *aggression.* In everyday conversation, the term has many meanings. For example, people may talk about someone having an *aggressive attitude* or a musician *playing a piece aggressively.* Although these are legitimate uses of the term, they differ from the meaning intended by social psychologists. First, when social psychologists talk about aggression, they refer specifically to observable behavior. Although thoughts and attitudes can lead to aggression, they are not themselves a form of aggression. Second, harm or potential harm is involved in all cases of aggression—but not all harmdoing should be labeled aggression. Consider the physician or dentist whose intent is to help, but whose behavior can cause pain. Or consider a salesperson who knowingly sells us something at a higher price than we would have paid elsewhere (and therefore causes financial harm). Do we want to label these behaviors as true aggression?

In wrestling with these kinds of ambiguities, Leonard Berkowitz (1993) summed up the social psychological definition of **aggression** as "any form of behavior that is intended to injure someone physically or psychologically" (p. 3). Notice that the inclusion of *intent* to harm would make the physician's behavior something other than aggression and the emphasis on *injury* (physical or psychological) would make the salesperson's behavior something other than aggression.

When aggression is intended to cause *extreme* injury—such as death—we call it **violence.** Notice that violence is always a form of aggression, but not all aggression is violence because it is not always aimed at causing extreme injury (Anderson & Bushman, 2002a). For instance, shooting or stabbing someone is aggressive and violent; insulting or pushing someone is aggressive but not violent.

Several types or varieties of aggression need to be identified before we turn to theoretical models of the causes of aggression.

## Hostile and Instrumental Aggression

When we think about some of the most common kinds of aggression (e.g., insults, pushes), they often involve negative emotional states such as anger, frustration, or hatred. Aggression that results from these sorts of negative emotions has been called **hostile aggression** (Buss, 1961). Hostile aggression is often impulsive rather than planned, and the primary goal is to hurt the target.

But people also commit aggressive acts in order to achieve more distant goals than simply hurting the target. For example, when a parent spanks a child, the motivation may be to teach the child to control some undesired behavior. When a robber knocks someone to the ground, the robber's ultimate goal is to grab a purse or wallet. Admittedly, in both of these cases, there is the intent to inflict some pain or arouse some fear, but the principal underlying motive is a more distant goal—to teach a lesson or to obtain something of value. Aggression that is motivated by goals other than harming the target has been called **instrumental aggression**

**aggression**

*behavior that is intended to injure someone physically or psychologically*

**violence**

*aggression that is intended to cause extreme injury*

**hostile aggression**

*harmdoing that arises out of negative emotions such as anger, frustration, or hatred*

**instrumental aggression**

*harmdoing that is motivated by goals other than hurting the target, such as obtaining something of value*

(Buss, 1961). Instrumental aggression is often premeditated or planned rather than impulsive.

You may be tempted to think of hostile aggression and instrumental aggression as an *either/or* dichotomy—that aggressive behavior is either hostile or instrumental. Such an assumption would be a mistake, however, because aggression is more complicated than that. People's motives for aggression are often multifaceted. Brad Bushman and Craig Anderson (2001a) gave a compelling example to make this point. In April of 1999, Eric Harris and Dylan Klebold perpetrated the Columbine High School massacre, murdering a total of eight people. These two teenagers carefully planned their actions—they did research, they mapped out their steps, they even rehearsed the scenario. These facts would seem to make their actions consistent with instrumental aggression. In the aftermath of Columbine, however, it became clear that Harris and Klebold were also very angry young men. They nurtured a great deal of hostility, often aimed at the athletes at their school who had been known to anger and provoke them. These facts make their actions consistent with hostile aggression. This episode illustrates that aggressive behavior can be caused by several factors simultaneously (see also Aronson, 2000). In fact, most acts of aggression reflect some mixture of anger and a desire to achieve more distant goals.

Therefore, the distinction between hostile and instrumental aggression is only occasionally useful for precisely classifying a particular aggressive act (Bushman & Anderson, 2001a). Nevertheless, the distinction is often helpful in thinking about why aggression occurs.

Earlier, we gave as an example of instrumental aggression a parent's decision to spank a child. Presumably, spanking is intended to teach the child a lesson and to modify the child's behavior in some way. Does spanking actually work? Is it effective in achieving the parent's distant goals? The accompanying box, Social Psychology in Your Life: Is Corporal Punishment Effective? discusses this issue.

## Relational Aggression

Aggression starts early in social life. By the time children reach school age, they have developed a fairly diverse repertoire of aggressive behaviors, including nonphysical aggression. For example, even at preschool age, especially among girls, we can observe some forms of psychological harmdoing (Crick, Casas, & Mosher, 1997; Underwood, 2003). Whereas boys tend to exhibit physical aggression, girls are more likely to rely on **relational aggression** (Crick & Grotpeter, 1995). Relational aggression is behavior that is intended to damage another person's peer relationships. Have you seen people use social exclusion or rumor spreading as a means of inflicting harm on others? This is relational aggression: it may leave no physical damage, but it can inflict very significant psychological damage. The Concept Review on page 444 summarizes the types of aggression we have described.

Nicki Crick and her colleagues have uncovered a great deal of evidence of relational aggression. In one study (Crick et al., 1997), the aggressive behaviors of preschoolers were recorded by having teachers monitor the social behaviors of their students, and by having the students themselves describe their interactions with one another. For example, the teachers were asked to rate students on items such as these:

- Tries to get others to dislike a peer
- Verbally threatens to keep a peer out of the play group if the peer doesn't do what the child asks

In addition to the teachers' ratings, the children were asked to indicate which of their peers engaged in relational aggression. This was done by showing each

**relational aggression**

*behavior that is intended to damage another person's peer relationships*

# Social Psychology in Your Life    *Is Corporal Punishment Effective?*

An important practical question that has been put to psychological science is whether or not the spanking of children is effective as a method of discipline (Gershoff, 2002; Kazdin & Benjet, 2003). First, it is important to be clear about what we mean by *spanking* and *corporal punishment.* Spanking typically refers to the hitting of a child with an open hand, usually on the extremities such as the buttocks. The intent of spanking is to punish by producing some pain, but without causing physical injury such as bruising. Corporal punishment is the more general term used in reference to "the use of physical force with the intention of causing a child to experience pain but not injury for the purpose of correction or control of the child's behavior" (Straus, 1994, p. 4). Corporal punishment encompasses both spanking and the use of objects (paddles, belts, etc). Both of these concepts differ from *physical abuse,* which is the intentional infliction of injury.

Elizabeth Thompson Gershoff (2002) reviewed the literature on corporal punishment. She found that spanking a child is an effective way of achieving immediate compliance. But this was really the only "positive" effect of corporal punishment. The evidence indicates that such punishment does not produce long-term compliance, which would reflect the child's acceptance of the moral lesson presumably being taught by corporal punishment. Indeed, the use of corporal punishment is associated with a variety of negative effects in children: greater aggression, higher degrees of delinquent and antisocial behavior, lower quality of the parent–child relationship, lower mental health, and an increased chance of physical abuse.

A word of caution: these findings are, for the most part, correlational. So we don't know whether the relationship between corporal punishment and children's aggression means that the punishment causes increased aggression, or a child's aggressive behavior elicits corporal punishment, or both; it is also possible that some third variable is influencing both the use of corporal punishment and aggressive behavior in children. Still, the array of associations found between the use of corporal punishment and negative outcomes (some of which extend into adulthood) is a chilling cause for concern.

The American Academy of Pediatrics and the American Psychological Association caution parents not to hit their children. In addition to the evidence just cited, there are other good theoretical reasons why corporal punishment should be avoided. For example, we will soon be describing research on the modeling of aggression: children imitate adults, including their aggressive behavior. What are children being taught when their parents hit them? They may imitate this behavior by hitting other people to teach them a lesson. The best parenting advice provided by the research suggests that nonphysical methods—timeouts, suspension of privileges, grounding—are more effective forms of punishment in producing long-term changes in behavior (Kazdin & Benjet, 2003).

© BananaStock/PictureQuest

Spanking tends to produce short-term, but not long-term, compliance.

child pictures of his or her peers, and asking him or her to point to the pictures that corresponded to:

- Kids who say they won't invite someone to their birthday party if they can't have their own way
- Kids who tell other kids that they can't play with the group unless they do what the group wants them to do

To complement these measures, other assessments were designed to reflect overt, physical aggression. For example, the teachers were asked to rate students on such items as:

- Hurts other children by pinching them
- Pushes or shoves other children

## CONCEPT REVIEW
### Types of Aggression

| Type | Description | Examples |
|------|-------------|----------|
| Aggression (all) | Behavior that is intended to hurt someone physically or psychologically | Punch, insult |
| Hostile aggression | Aggression that results from negative emotional states such as anger, frustration, or hatred | Road rage, jealousy-induced assault |
| Instrumental aggression | Aggression that is motivated by goals other than harming the target | Armed robbery, parental spanking |
| Relational aggression | Behavior that is intended to damage another person's peer relationships | False gossip, ridicule |

Similarly, the children picked out their peers to identify:

- Kids who push or shove other kids
- Kids who throw things at other kids when they don't get their way

In the teachers' assessments, the boys were judged as engaging in more overt (physical) aggression than were the girls. In contrast, the girls were judged as relying on more relational aggression than were the boys. When the children were grouped based on the teacher ratings, 12% of the boys but only 3% of the girls were categorized as physically aggressive. However, when it came to relational aggression, the teachers indicated that 26% of the girls but none of the boys could be described as relationally aggressive. Thus, even at 4 to 5 years of age, children showed important gender differences in their forms of aggressive actions.

It is interesting and important to note that this straightforward pattern of results was not observed in the preschoolers' own ratings. At this young age, children had not yet developed a reliable sense of assigning aggressive inclinations to their peers. It does not take long, however, for children to sort these things out. By the time they reach grade school, teachers and students show a good degree of consensus on which children and peers rely more on physical versus relational aggression (Crick, 1996; Crick & Grotpeter, 1995; Grotpeter & Crick, 1996). And the evidence bears out that girls more than boys generally rely on social forms of aggression (Galen & Underwood, 1997).

One result of using social exclusion or spreading rumors about others is the possibility that others will come to dislike you. Even among preschoolers, Nicki Crick and her colleagues (1997) found signs of social maladjustment among girls who used relational aggression. Some evidence suggests that this relationship continues into young adulthood: Nicole Werner and Nicki Crick (1999) found that relational aggression among college students was associated with peer rejection and antisocial personality.

But we should not be too quick to draw a final conclusion. It appears that aggressive behavior can sometimes be associated with *popularity*. Amanda Rose, Lance Swenson, and Erika Waller (2004) recently found that among older (seventh- and ninth-grade) youths, both overt and relational aggression were positively related to popularity. It seems that aggression can sometimes be "cool" and lead to increased rather than decreased peer acceptance. This is reminiscent of

© Peter Marlow/Magnum Photos

Boys engage in more physical aggression than do girls.

our observation in Chapter 6 that people who use *ridicule* to control others may be seen as clever (see page 224). More research is needed to untangle the complex relationship between aggression and popularity.

## Theories of Aggression

Having defined and clarified relevant terms, we can now turn to the question of when and why people engage in aggressive (and sometimes violent) behavior. We begin with a general framework that integrates several previous models, each of which is then reviewed separately. We conclude by returning to the general framework and elaborating its key features.

## General Aggression Model (GAM)

A broad framework for answering the question of why people behave aggressively was developed by social psychologist Craig Anderson and his colleagues (Anderson, 1997; Anderson & Bushman, 2002a; Anderson, Deuser, & DeNeve, 1995; Bartholow, Anderson, Carnagey, & Benjamin, 2005; Lindsay & Anderson, 2000). Anderson brought together decades of social psychological thinking about aggression in what he called the **general aggression model (GAM).** A simplified version of the GAM is shown in Figure 11.2.

**general aggression model (GAM)**

*a broad theory that conceptualizes aggression as the result of a chain of psychological processes, including situational events, aggressive thoughts and feelings, and interpretations of the situation*

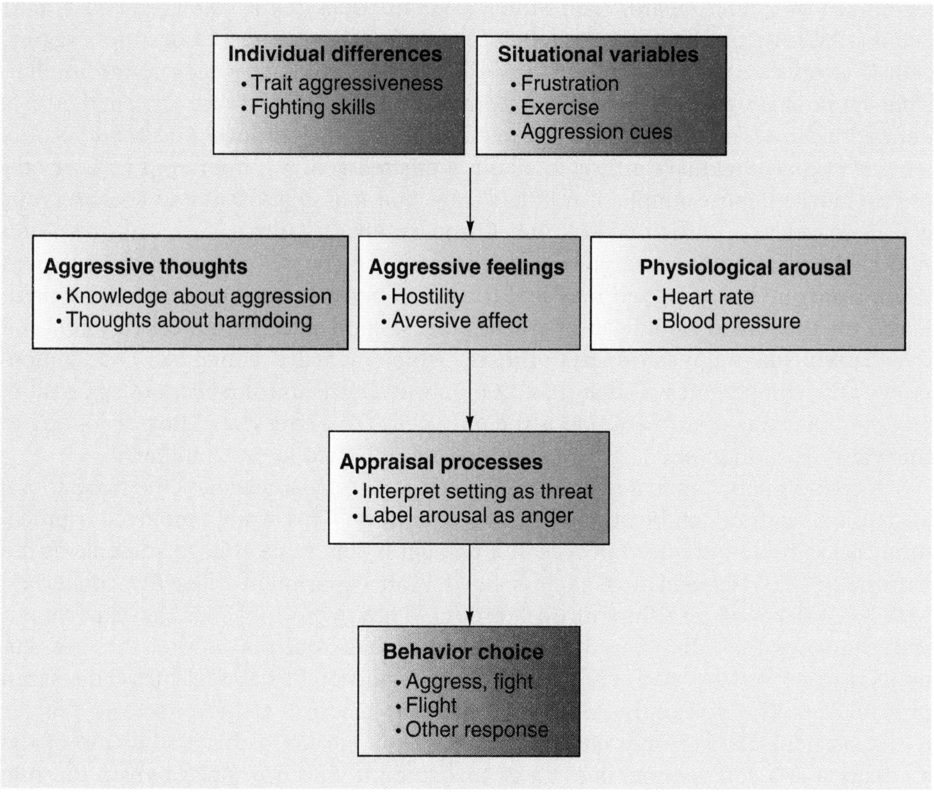

**FIGURE 11.2** Simplified version of the general aggression model

From Anderson, "Effects of violent movies and trait hostility on hostile feelings and aggressive thought," *Aggressive Behavior,* 23, 161–178, 1997. Reprinted by permission of Wiley-Liss, Inc., a subsidiary of John Wiley & Sons, Inc.

The fundamental idea is that aggressive behavior is the result of a chain of psychological processes. People respond to situational events (e.g., someone insults them or frustrates them) by generating some or all of the following: aggressive thoughts, aggressive feelings, and physiological arousal. Some people are more likely than others to respond to situational events with aggressive thoughts and feelings; this idea is reflected in the category of *individual differences* in the model. The aggressive thoughts, feelings, and arousal within the person increase the probability of aggressive behavior, but the individual must first interpret the situation as one in which aggression is appropriate (e.g., he has been insulted, feels angry, and must defend his honor). How do people decide whether aggression is appropriate? The GAM uses the term *appraisal processes* to represent this decision. For instance, if the individual appraises (or interprets) the setting as one involving danger or threat, the interpretation may lead directly to aggressive behavior.

We will elaborate each of these steps in a later section. One of the nice features of the GAM is that it pulls together four rich theoretical traditions in the study of aggression, which we review in the following sections:

- Frustration and aggression
- Excitation transfer
- Social learning theory
- Cognitive neoassociation model

## Frustration and Aggression

One of the earliest efforts to develop a general theory of human aggression was developed by John Dollard, Neal Miller, Leonard Doob, O. H. Mowrer, and Robert Sears (1939). At the heart of their theory was a rather simple conjecture: "aggression is always a consequence of frustration" (p. 1). Although it may sound implausible to propose that all aggression comes from just one cause, these theorists defined frustration broadly enough to encompass many settings. *Frustration* occurs whenever an individual's efforts to obtain a desired goal are interfered with or otherwise blocked. For example, if traffic is slow, you may feel frustrated because your goal is to get to a particular location. If you receive a failing mark on a test, you may feel frustrated because your goal is to pass the course. If you experience pain when someone hits you, you may feel frustrated because your goal is to avoid pain. Based on this broad definition of frustration, Dollard and his coworkers proposed the **frustration–aggression hypothesis,** which actually contained two components. One component was that frustration always leads to some form of aggression, and the other was that frustration is the only cause of aggression. Thus, according to this view, frustration and aggression are inextricably tied to one another.

An experiment conducted by Russell Geen (1968) illustrates how the frustration-aggression relation can be studied in the laboratory. This study employed a procedure that is frequently used in research on aggression. Male college students at the University of Wisconsin arrived in pairs for an experiment allegedly concerned with the effects of punishment on learning. They were told that the experiment would involve the administration of electric shocks, and that one of the two students at each session would act as the teacher and one as the learner. This setup probably reminds you of the Milgram obedience experiments described in Chapter 8, but participants were not *ordered* to administer shocks in this study. One of the students was a confederate, and it was this student who was always given the role of learner.

Prior to this alleged learning task, the real participant was assigned to one of four experimental conditions. In one condition, frustration was induced by having the participant work on a jigsaw puzzle that was described as being a test of intelli-

**frustration–aggression hypothesis**

*the twin propositions that frustration always leads to some form of aggression and frustration is the only cause of aggression*

gence. Unknown to the participant, the puzzle had no solution! Certainly a frustrating experience. Participants in a second condition worked on a jigsaw puzzle that was solvable. As they worked on the puzzle, however, the confederate interfered and prevented them from finishing. In a third condition, the confederate allowed the participant to finish his puzzle but insulted his intelligence by suggesting that his puzzle was not very difficult. Rather than inducing frustration, this condition was expected to induce *anger.* A fourth, control condition was included in which participants simply completed a solvable puzzle while seated alone.

Following the puzzle procedure, participants were given an opportunity to engage in aggression against the confederate. The participant played the role of teacher in a series of learning trials. Every time the learner (actually the confederate) made a mistake on the learning task, the teacher could "punish" him by delivering an electric shock. Thus, the participant was provided with an opportunity to inflict harm. Using this procedure, the extent of aggression could be indexed in different ways, such as by counting the number of electric shocks given or by gauging the intensity of the shocks selected. In reality, this was all a setup—no electric shocks were actually delivered. But the participant didn't know that. As far as he was concerned, depressing the shock button was causing another person some degree of harm.

What happened? Figure 11.3 presents the number of shocks delivered in each condition. Participants in the two frustration conditions delivered many more shocks than did participants in the control condition. As a result of being frustrated, these "teachers" took the opportunity to harm the "learner." Notice that *both* frustration conditions produced equally high levels of aggression. Whether the frustration was caused by task difficulty or by interference from a person, the frustration caused an increase in aggression. One other result was important: participants in the insult condition showed even higher levels of aggression—they delivered the most electric shocks of all. These participants, who were presumably angered rather than frustrated, seized the opportunity to be aggressive toward the person who had provoked them.

The Geen (1968) experiment highlights a problem with the original frustration–aggression hypothesis. Specifically, the results showed that factors other than frustration—in this case, anger—can also cause aggression. Indeed, ever since its introduction, the hypothesis that frustration is the *only* cause of aggression has been the target of criticism. In response to data like those collected by Geen, researchers investigating the frustration–aggression link (e.g., Berkowitz, 1989) have modified their claims by proposing that frustration *sometimes* causes aggression and aggression is *sometimes* caused by frustration. As the qualifications "sometimes" imply, factors other than frustration are recognized as possible causes of aggression. This more defensible position is sometimes called the *revised frustration–aggression hypothesis.*

**Displaced Aggression.** Two final aspects of the frustration–aggression hypothesis deserve brief mention. Dollard and his colleagues initially assumed that frustration-induced aggression would always be directed at the person who caused the frustration. It was soon recognized, however, that even when frustration does lead to aggression, people may not direct their aggression toward the actual source. For one thing, it may be unwise or dangerous to do so. If the person who blocks you from obtaining a desired goal is stronger or more powerful than you, then you might be smart to inhibit your

Being unable to complete a jigsaw puzzle is frustrating.

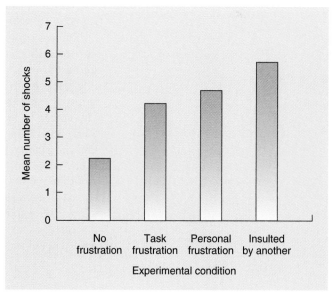

**FIGURE 11.3** Number of shocks delivered in each condition

From Geen, "Effects of frustration, attack, and prior training in aggressiveness upon aggressive behavior," *Journal of Personality and Social Psychology, 9,* 316–321, 1968. Copyright © 1968 by the American Psychological Association. Reprinted by permission.

**displaced aggression**

*harmdoing that is directed at someone or something that was not the actual source of frustration*

aggression. Or if that person has left the scene, it may not even be possible to retaliate against him or her. Under these circumstances, people may direct their aggression elsewhere. This phenomenon is known as **displaced aggression.** For example, if you experience frustration at work because your boss gives you a poor performance evaluation or treats you badly in some other way, you may exhibit aggression against a subordinate or even against members of your own family later after you return home. The idea of displaced aggression has been supported in many studies (for a review, see Marcus-Newhall, Pedersen, Carlson, & Miller, 2000).

Although displaced aggression can occur without the unfortunate target having done anything to provoke it (e.g., someone comes home from a frustrating day at work and kicks a sleeping dog), it often occurs in response to a minor triggering frustration. For example, someone who experiences frustration at work but cannot retaliate against the boss may later hit a family member who is slightly annoying at the dinner table. This kind of aggression, called *triggered displaced aggression,* may often be far more intense than would be expected from the relatively minor trigger. These reactions illustrate the proverbial phrase "the straw that broke the camel's back": a small triggering event (one more piece of straw; a minor frustration) elicits a large response (a broken back; extreme aggression). Norman Miller, William Pedersen, and their colleagues have developed a model of triggered displaced aggression that specifies the conditions under which it is most likely to occur (see Miller, Pedersen, Earleywine, & Pollock, 2003; Pedersen, Gonzales, & Miller, 2000; Vasquez, Denson, Pedersen, Stenstrom, & Miller, 2005).

**catharsis**

*the idea that aggressive behavior releases people's pent-up frustration and reduces the likelihood of subsequent aggression*

**Catharsis.** A second interesting aspect of Dollard et al.'s thinking has not been so well supported. Specifically, aggression was assumed to relieve frustration and, therefore, to reduce any further aggression. This effect was called **catharsis.** Perhaps the best way to think about catharsis is by drawing an analogy to hydraulics: frustration causes pressure to build up inside you. As the pressure builds, there is an increasing need to release it. We often speak of people whose anger "boils over." One outlet for all this pressure may be aggressive behavior. And once you do it, the pressure is reduced. Your impulse to be aggressive is relieved or even eliminated. In short, catharsis implies that aggressive behavior reduces the likelihood of additional aggression.

This is a provocative idea, and some early experiments seemed to confirm the idea of catharsis (e.g., Doob & Wood, 1972). Most experiments, however, have *not* found the effect to be reliable (see Baron & Richardson, 1994). In fact, the *opposite* effect has more often been obtained. That is, when people are provided an opportunity for aggression (or observe aggression) against a source of frustration, it usually serves to heighten, rather than lessen, subsequent aggression (e.g., Bushman, 2002; Bushman, Baumeister, & Stack, 1999). Why might a heightening effect occur? One possibility is that any aggression in a situation makes subsequent aggression seem more appropriate: a norm is established that aggression is permissible. Another possibility is that the initial act of aggression leads people to see themselves as aggressive, and this self-perception increases the likelihood of subsequent aggressive responses. Whatever the cause of a heightening effect, catharsis does *not* appear to occur: engaging in aggressive behavior does not reliably reduce the probability of subsequent aggression.

## Excitation Transfer

A theoretical perspective known as *excitation transfer* begins with an assumption that aversive arousal leads to aggression. This assumption was actually borrowed from research on the frustration–aggression hypothesis, which assumed that aggressive behavior is preceded by frustration—a form of emotional arousal. For example, in a paper discussing the revised frustration–aggression hypothesis, Leonard Berkowitz (1989) described frustration as producing a state of aversive and uncomfortable arousal, which presumably explains why frustration can lead to aggression. A variety of early experiments had confirmed that physiological arousal (e.g., blood pressure, heart rate) increases when people are frustrated or angered (e.g., Gambaro & Rabin, 1969; Hokanson & Shetler, 1961; Kahn, 1966). If aversive arousal causes or heightens aggression, then the passage of time (cooling off), listening to soothing music, or otherwise distracting oneself with pleasant things may reduce aggression by reducing aversive arousal. Consistent with this reasoning, Vladimir Konečni (1975a, 1975b) showed that aggressive behavior was reduced by having insulted or angered participants engage in activities known to reduce aversive arousal, such as those just mentioned. These data support the idea that aversive arousal increases aggressive behavior.

Can arousal from exercise increase aggression?

If aversive arousal leads to aggression, then an interesting question is whether arousal from sources *other than* frustration or anger can also produce (or increase) aggression. Many situations that do not involve frustration or anger can cause a person to become aroused, including exercise, viewing sporting events, and exposure to sexually themed material. Can these sources of arousal cause an increase in aggressive behavior, even though the arousal itself did not come from being angered or provoked? The answer to this question appears to be *yes*.

In one classic experiment, Dolf Zillmann, Aaron Katcher, and Barry Milavsky (1972) led participants to believe that they were interacting with another person in a study of the effects of punishment on learning. In one condition, the "partner" delivered a series of moderately painful electric shocks to the participant, based on the participant's responses to attitude questions. These shocks were expected to anger the participant and to motivate an aggressive retaliation. In the other condition, the "partner" was much less provocative and delivered only a few mild electric shocks in response to the participant's attitude expressions.

Following one of these two conditions, participants completed a second, allegedly unrelated experiment having to do with motor behavior. Some participants sat quietly at a table performing a nonstrenuous task (threading small discs with off-center holes). Other participants spent the same amount of time pedaling a stationary bicycle. Measures of physiological arousal (heart rate, blood pressure, and skin temperature) confirmed that participants in the bicycle-pedaling condition experienced much greater arousal than did those in the disc-threading condition.

All participants then had an opportunity to retaliate against the "partner" by delivering electric shocks in a teacher–learner procedure (similar to the one used by Geen, 1968). That is, the participant played the role of teacher and the "partner" played the role of learner. Alleged responses of the learner were preprogrammed so that errors were deliberately made, and the teacher's job was to select an intensity of electric shock as punishment.

To summarize, participants were exposed initially to a procedure that either elicited anger or did not, which was followed by either vigorous or quiet motor activity. Of the resulting four conditions, only one produced a high level of aggression: when participants *both* were angered *and* spent the intervening time on the exercise bicycle. Presumably, the arousal produced by riding the bicycle was labeled as anger or became attached to participant's anger, resulting in more aggressive behavior. Figure 11.4 summarizes the results in

|  | Arousal | No arousal |
|---|---|---|
| **Anger** | Aggression | No aggression |
| **No anger** | No aggression | No aggression |

**FIGURE 11.4** Diagram of conditions in Zillmann, Katcher, and Milavsky experiment, 1972

**excitation transfer**

*the idea that physiological arousal from sources other than frustration or anger can be linked to anger-related thoughts and cognitions, thereby increasing aggression*

each of the four conditions. Zillmann and his colleagues referred to the effect in the *Anger + Arousal* condition as **excitation transfer:** unrelated physiological arousal can be linked to anger-related thoughts and cognitions, and ultimately increase anger-related aggression. In the condition where participants were angered but then spent some time quietly performing a nonstrenuous task, anger-induced arousal presumably dissipated over time.

One of the interesting things about excitation transfer is that it can increase aggressive behavior even when people are no longer consciously aware of a state of arousal. Dolf Zillmann and Jennings Bryant (1974) found that the transfer of excitation increased aggression after participants had left the arousing setting and their physiological arousal had partly dissipated. These findings imply that an arousing event (e.g., a raucous sports game or a boisterous concert) may cause people to respond to insults or other provocation with greater intensity of aggression even after they have left the arousing setting.

## Social Learning Theory

**social learning theory**

*an approach proposing that humans learn many kinds of responses, including aggressive ones, by observing others; observation shows people both how to perform a behavior and whether that behavior will be rewarded or punished*

The perspectives on aggression we have described (frustration–aggression and excitation transfer) assume that physiological arousal is a key cause of aggression. But how do people *learn* to be aggressive in the first place? Where do they acquire knowledge about how to hit, push, or insult others? **Social learning theory** (Bandura, 1973; Bandura & Walters, 1963) proposes that humans learn many kinds of responses, including aggressive ones, by observing other people (who may *not* be *intentionally* demonstrating the responses). For example, children may watch other children and adults during their daily activities. Watching other people both shows us how to perform a behavior and teaches us whether that behavior will be rewarded or punished (based on whether the people we watch are rewarded or punished). A social learning perspective on aggression posits that people often learn aggressive behaviors by observing others being rewarded (or, at least, not being punished) for aggressive actions, then imitate or model those responses. Individuals' personal experiences of rewards or punishments following their own aggression then further shape their behavior. This perspective raises obvious concerns about depictions of violence in the mass media, because children (and adults) can presumably learn aggressive behavior from the media.

Let us describe one of the classic experimental demonstrations of social learning. This study used Bobo dolls, which are inflatable dolls with a weighted, rounded bottom, so they always bounce back if you try to knock them over. They are typically painted with a smiling clown's face. Albert Bandura, Dorothea Ross, and Sheila Ross (1963) gave nursery school children the opportunity to play with a Bobo doll. The children, who ranged in age from 3 to 5 years, were first divided into three experimental groups and one control group. One experimental group observed an adult model acting very aggressively toward a Bobo doll. The model punched the doll, sat on it and punched it in the nose, hit it on the head with a mallet, tossed it in the air and kicked it around the room, all the while saying things like "Sock him in the nose," "Hit him down," "Throw him in the air," "Kick him," and "Pow." This kind of behavior is far more aggressive than what children would ordinarily or spontaneously do, but provided a number of very specific things for the children to learn. A second experimental group saw the same adult model perform the same actions, but in a film rather than live. The third experimental group watched a cartoon version of aggressive behavior, in which a cartoon cat was shown being aggressive with the Bobo doll. The control group of children did not see any aggressive models.

After witnessing these aggressive acts (in the experimental conditions), the child was led to another room. The room was filled with highly attractive toys—a

© Thomson Higher Education

After watching an adult aggress against a Bobo doll, children were likely to engage in imitative aggression against a similar doll.

young child's dream! The child definitely wanted to play with some of those toys. But it was not to be. The experimenter explained that these were her very best toys, and that she did not let just anyone play with them. No, these toys were being reserved for some *other* children. Talk about frustrating. Indeed, this was the point. To provide some instigation for aggression, the children were deliberately frustrated by being denied access to these wonderful toys.

The child was then led to yet another room containing a variety of less dazzling, everyday toys. These toys included nonaggressive toys, such as a tea set, crayons, dolls, cars, and trucks. But also available in the room was a small Bobo doll, a mallet, and other aggressive toys such as dart guns and a suspended tether ball with a face painted on it. The child was given 20 minutes of free play time, during which observations were made of aggressive behavior. Figure 11.5 presents the average levels of imitative aggression exhibited by children in each group. Children in the control group engaged in very few of the aggressive actions that had been specifically modeled by the adult, confirming that children of this age are unlikely to spontaneously engage in aggressive actions against a Bobo doll. This is not to say that aggression was absent in the control group; in fact, children in the control group were just as likely as children in the experimental groups to engage in aggression that had not been modeled by the adult, such

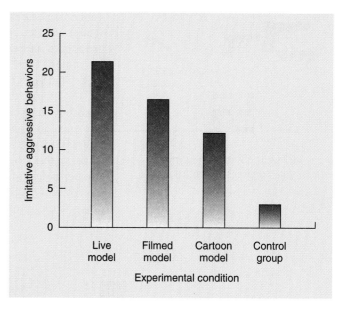

**FIGURE 11.5**  Number of acts of imitative aggression in each condition

From Bandura et al., "Imitation of film-mediated aggressive models," *Journal of Abnormal and Social Psychology*, 66, 3–11, 1963. Copyright © 1963 by the American Psychological Association. Reprinted by permission.

as gun play. However, children in the experimental groups were far more likely to also exhibit imitative aggression—striking the Bobo doll, kicking it, tossing it in the air, and so on. Thus, these children had learned a specific way to act aggressively when frustrated.

Social learning theory identifies the learning processes involved in aggressive behavior. It does not dispute the role of frustration or aversive arousal in the *instigation* of aggression; instead, it focuses on how people learn specific patterns of aggressive responding, which will be exhibited when they are angry or frustrated. We will return to this theory when we discuss the effects of media violence on aggression.

One of the important lessons of the social learning approach is that people acquire knowledge about aggressive behavior. The next perspective builds on this point.

## Cognitive Neoassociation Model

Over time, people pick up knowledge about aggression and aggressive behavior, which gets stored and organized in memory. For example, by watching others and by acquiring information in the environment, people learn that certain situations and feelings are associated with aggressive responding. You will recall from Chapter 3 (Social Cognition) that human memory is organized around *schemas* and *associative networks* that connect those schemas. Once a schema becomes *activated* in memory, it tends to bring to mind other schemas through a process of *spreading activation.*

These basic features of social cognition were used by Leonard Berkowitz (1990; Berkowitz & Heimer, 1989) to develop a **cognitive neoassociation model of aggression.** The idea is that aggression results from a process of spreading activation. Initially, an unpleasant event arouses negative affect (negative emotion). This negative affect then simultaneously activates two distinct schemas, or response

**cognitive neoassociation model of aggression**

*a theory of harmdoing proposing that aversive events activate the schemas for fight and flight, which elicit the emotions of anger and fear; whether people respond with aggression or escape depends on the pattern of cues in the situation*

Many different objects and symbols can serve as aggression-related cues.

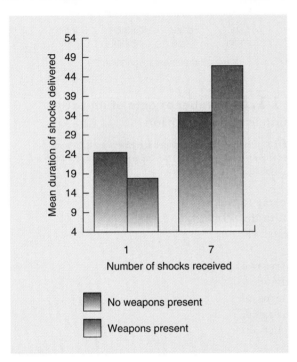

**FIGURE 11.6** Duration of shocks delivered in each condition

From Berkowitz and LePage, "Weapons as aggression-eliciting stimuli," *Journal of Personality and Social Psychology*, 7, 202–207, 1967. Copyright © 1967 by the American Psychological Association. Reprinted by permission.

11.1
ONLINE
LAB

tendencies. One is the tendency to *fight*—the type of responses we associate with aggression or harmdoing. The other is the tendency toward *flight*—the type of responses we associate with escape or avoidance. Through a process of spreading activation, these two schemas further activate *anger* (the emotion associated with fight) and *fear* (the emotion associated with flight).

If an unpleasant event causes you to simultaneously experience anger and fear, how do you decide to act on one versus the other? How does frustration or provocation or any other unpleasant event ultimately lead to the choice between aggression versus running away? The answer is that it depends on the pattern of cues in the situation. If other events or cues in the situation produce relatively greater activation of schemas related to anger, then aggression is more likely to be the result. If other cues are more likely to activate schemas related to fear, then flight is the more probable response.

What sorts of cues will activate anger and aggression? Unfortunately, aggression-related cues are very common. Guns, knives, aggressive song lyrics, violent movies, insulting phrases, and hostile symbols are readily associated in North American culture with anger and aggression. According to the cognitive neoassociation model of aggression, the presence of such cues in the environment will lead to more aggressive behavior in response to aversive arousal. Most of the research on this hypothesis has supported it.

A classic experiment was conducted by Leonard Berkowitz and Anthony LePage (1967). Student participants at the University of Wisconsin received either 1 or 7 electric shocks from a partner (actually a confederate of the experimenter). The students were then given an opportunity to return electric shocks back to their partner, presumably as a method for evaluating his performance; the duration of these shocks (how long the shock lever was held down) was recorded. In some conditions, the table at which the participant was seated was empty except for the shock button. In other conditions, however, a 12-gauge shotgun and a .38-caliber revolver were lying on the table near the shock button—they were described as belonging to the participant's partner (this cover story might not work today). As shown in Figure 11.6, the participants clearly retaliated with shocks of greater duration when they had earlier received 7 rather than 1 shock themselves. In addition, however, the extent of retaliation to 7 shocks was significantly greater when weapons were present than when they were absent.

Some researchers (e.g., Page & Scheidt, 1971) suggested that this "weapons effect" was the result of *demand characteristics,* which we defined in Chapter 2 as cues in a study that suggest to participants how they are supposed to respond (see page 50). The idea is that participants guessed that the guns were supposed to make them more aggressive, so they responded to confirm this hypothesis. Subsequent studies have produced evidence arguing against the role of demand characteristics, however. The basic effect has been found numerous times in different settings with different aggression cues (e.g., Bartholow et al., 2005; Leyens & Parke, 1975; Turner, Layton, & Simons, 1975) and has been confirmed in comprehensive reviews of the literature (e.g., Bettencourt & Kernahan, 1997). Thus, the conclusion that aggressive cues, such as weapons, can increase aggressiveness seems valid.

## GAM Again

This brings us back to the *general aggression model (GAM)* with which we began our discussion of theories of aggression (see Figure 11.2). How do the specific theories fit into this general model? The category of *situational variables* in the GAM encompasses elements of several specific theories, including frustration (from the frustration–aggression hypothesis), exercise (from excitation transfer), and aggression cues (from the cognitive neoassociation model). These sources of arousal and cognition initiate a process that can lead to aggression. The category of *individual differences* in the GAM is relatively distinct from the specific theories we have covered, but the next section, Influences on Aggression, will discuss some of these variables.

The three categories of *aggressive thoughts, aggressive feelings,* and *physiological arousal* in the GAM capture elements of each of the specific theories. For example, frustration is a form of emotional arousal, and the excitation transfer perspective assumes that arousal from any source can heighten aggressive responding. Social learning theory and the cognitive neoassociation model emphasize the importance of knowledge and thoughts about aggression.

The category of *appraisal processes* in the GAM is probably most closely connected to the cognitive neoassociation model of aggression, which posits that when anger schemas are activated, the response tendency to *fight* will guide behavior. The excitation transfer perspective is also related to the category of *appraisal processes,* because it assumes that arousal from any source can be (mis)interpreted as anger.

Finally, the category of *behavioral choice* in the GAM encompasses elements of social learning theory and the cognitive neoassociation model. Social learning theory addresses how people learn aggressive responses, and the cognitive neoassociation model posits that either *fight* or *flight* responses can occur depending on the strength of the activation of anger versus fear schemas.

The GAM provides a useful framework for future research on aggression. Each step in the model identifies important aspects of the transition from negative events to aggressive behavior. In the following sections, we describe additional research on factors that influence aggression. Although these studies were not specifically guided by the GAM, they can be seen as relevant to one or more of the categories in the model. The various theories of aggression are summarized in the accompanying Concept Review.

## CONCEPT REVIEW
### Theories of Aggression

| Theory | Description/Key Features | Limitations/Outlook |
|---|---|---|
| General aggression model (GAM) | Aggressive behavior is the result of a chain of processes; this model integrates the other theories | A recent model that provides a useful framework for future research |
| Frustration–aggression hypothesis | Interference with obtaining desired goals causes aggression | Factors other than frustration cause aggression; catharsis does not occur |
| Excitation transfer model | Arousal from any source can produce or increase aggression | Does not address the most common causes of aggression |
| Social learning theory | Individuals learn aggressive responses by observing other people | Focuses on how aggression is learned rather than when aggression will occur |
| Cognitive neoassociation model | Unpleasant events arouse negative emotions, which cause aggression if aggression cues in the situation activate *fight* and *anger* schemas | Applies recent work in social cognition to aggression |

# Influences on Aggression

Most of the current research on aggression is aimed at understanding its determinants—factors that cause an increase or decrease in aggressive behavior. In this section, we discuss several of these influences.

## Individual Differences

Have you ever noticed that some people are more aggressive than others? They may be defensive and argumentative, especially when criticized. Or they may just seem more likely than most people to respond to unpleasant events with aggression rather than walking away or some other less confrontational response. The GAM includes a category of influences on aggression labeled *individual differences* (see Figure 11.2). Why are some people more aggressive? We mention two relevant dimensions here.

**Narcissism.** In Chapter 5, The Person in the Situation, we discussed the dimension of *narcissism,* which refers to an excessive love for the self (see page 175). People who are high in narcissism have inflated views of their self-worth, which are not connected to reality. We noted in Chapter 5 that narcissistic individuals tend to be defensive about criticism that threatens their high ego. Therefore, when criticized, narcissistic individuals often respond with hostility and aggression—a response labeled *threatened egotism* (see Baumeister, Smart, & Boden, 1996; Baumeister, Bushman, & Campbell, 2000; Bushman & Baumeister, 1998; Twenge & Campbell, 2003). Thus, one cause of individual differences in aggression is narcissism.

**trait aggressiveness**

*a disposition that represents how likely people are to respond to provocations with aggression*

**Aggression Questionnaire (AQ)**

*a scale that measures individual differences in trait aggressiveness*

**Trait Aggressiveness.** Arnold Buss and Mark Perry (1992) observed that some people are more likely to respond to any provocation with aggression than are other individuals. They labeled this dimension **trait aggressiveness** and developed the **Aggression Questionnaire (AQ)** to measure it. The AQ consists of four related dimensions: physical aggression, verbal aggression, anger, and hostility. Selected items from the scale are reproduced in Know Yourself 11.1: Trait Aggressiveness. People who score high on this scale are hypothesized to be more aggressive. Do you consider yourself to be an aggressive person? Answer the items in the Know Yourself feature to see whether the descriptions tend to be characteristic or uncharacteristic of you. Buss and Perry (1992) presented evidence showing that scores on the AQ correlated with ratings of participants' aggressiveness obtained from acquaintances (that is, high scorers were rated as more aggressive by acquaintances than were low scorers).

Brad Bushman (1996) wondered whether people who score high on the AQ also possess more elaborate schemas related to aggression. This idea was based on the cognitive neoassociation model of aggression described earlier. To test the hypothesis, Bushman selected 160 students to participate in his study: 80 had scored very high on the AQ and 80 had scored very low. Bushman asked these students to examine pairs of words and to evaluate how "similar, associated, or related" each word pair was. The words were drawn from two sets: a set of 10 aggressive words (blood, butcher, choke, fight, gun, hatchet, hurt, kill, knife, wound) and a set of 10 ambiguous words (alley, animal, bottle, drugs, movie, night, police, red, rock, stick). The ambiguous words were selected so they could be interpreted as reflecting aggressiveness but would not necessarily be so interpreted. When the words were paired in all possible combinations, they fell into three word-pair categories: aggressive–aggressive, aggressive–ambiguous, and ambiguous–ambiguous.

# Know Yourself 11.1
## *Trait Aggressiveness*

Please indicate for each of the following items how *characteristic* or *uncharacteristic* it is of *you* by circling the appropriate number on the answer scale.

1. Once in a while, I cannot control my urge to strike another person.

| 1 | 2 | 3 | 4 | 5 |
|---|---|---|---|---|
| Extremely uncharacteristic | | | | Extremely characteristic |

2. When people annoy me, I may tell them what I think of them.

| 1 | 2 | 3 | 4 | 5 |
|---|---|---|---|---|
| Extremely uncharacteristic | | | | Extremely characteristic |

3. I have trouble controlling my temper.

| 1 | 2 | 3 | 4 | 5 |
|---|---|---|---|---|
| Extremely uncharacteristic | | | | Extremely characteristic |

4. I wonder why sometimes I feel so bitter about things.

| 1 | 2 | 3 | 4 | 5 |
|---|---|---|---|---|
| Extremely uncharacteristic | | | | Extremely characteristic |

5. If somebody hits me, I hit back.

| 1 | 2 | 3 | 4 | 5 |
|---|---|---|---|---|
| Extremely uncharacteristic | | | | Extremely characteristic |

6. I can't help getting into arguments when people disagree with me.

| 1 | 2 | 3 | 4 | 5 |
|---|---|---|---|---|
| Extremely uncharacteristic | | | | Extremely characteristic |

7. Sometimes I fly off the handle for no good reason.

| 1 | 2 | 3 | 4 | 5 |
|---|---|---|---|---|
| Extremely uncharacteristic | | | | Extremely characteristic |

8. When people are especially nice, I wonder what they want.

| 1 | 2 | 3 | 4 | 5 |
|---|---|---|---|---|
| Extremely uncharacteristic | | | | Extremely characteristic |

**SCORING:** Add up all of the circled numbers for your overall trait aggressiveness score. Possible scores range from 8 to 40, and higher scores represent more trait aggressiveness.

Sample items from Buss and Perry, "The aggressional questionnaire," *Journal of Personality and Social Psychology*, 63, 452–459, 1992. Copyright © 1992 by the American Psychological Association. Reprinted by permission.

Most of the students judged the aggressive–aggressive word pairs (e.g., fight–gun) to be very similar and related to each other. Even for these word pairs, however, the students who scored high on the AQ tended to rate them as *more* similar than did the students who scored low on the AQ. A more interesting difference occurred for the aggressive–ambiguous word pairs, such as blood–animal, hurt–rock, or knife–stick. If people who score high on the AQ tend to have well-developed schemas related to aggression, then they should more readily perceive aggressive connections between these pairs. As predicted, students who had high scores on the AQ, compared to those with low scores, rated the aggressive–ambiguous word pairs as

Alcohol intoxication tends to increase aggressive behavior.

significantly more similar to one another. Thus, people who scored high on a measure of trait aggressiveness seemed to possess relatively elaborate schemas of aggression. The two groups of participants did not differ in their ratings of the similarity of ambiguous–ambiguous word pairs.

## Alcohol

We often hear of aggressive behavior in the context of drunken brawls, barroom fights, and other settings in which people have consumed alcohol. The research evidence confirms that alcohol does indeed increase aggression (Bushman & Cooper, 1990). The typical study in this area uses a procedure originally developed by Stuart Taylor (1967). Participants are asked to consume a beverage that may or may not contain alcohol. In the alcohol conditions, participants drink a mixture containing about 2/5 vodka and 3/5 ginger ale, and they end up consuming about 1.5 ounces of vodka for every 40 pounds of body weight (Gantner & Taylor, 1992). In the control or placebo conditions, the cocktail consists entirely of ginger ale. However, even in the placebo conditions, the researcher might place a small amount of vodka around the rim of the glass so that participants cannot easily guess that they have been assigned to the placebo condition.

From that point forward, the typical experiment looks like those we described earlier. The participants are angered or provoked, and then provided an opportunity to retaliate (e.g., by administering electric shocks). Across dozens of experiments like this, it is clear that the consumption of alcohol causes an increase in aggressive behavior.

Why does alcohol increase aggression? First, alcohol is a depressant, which affects the brain in such a way that normal inhibitions against aggression are often reduced (Graham, 1980). Second, alcohol has indirect effects on aggression by causing changes in thought, perception, and interpretation. You may recall from Chapter 6 (Attitudes and Social Behavior) our discussion of the concept of *alcohol myopia* (Steele & Josephs, 1990; see page 218). Alcohol intoxication reduces cognitive capacity and produces a narrowing of attention. Fewer environmental cues than normal can be monitored when an individual is intoxicated. As a result, the most obvious external cues have more impact on behavior than usual; if these cues are consistent with aggressive behavior, then aggression is more likely by an intoxicated than by a sober person. Think about the places where people drink: these settings are often loud, crowded, or competitive. By causing a person to focus in on these particular aspects of the environment, alcohol can have the effect of increasing the tendency to respond aggressively.

## Heat

Another factor known to affect aggression is temperature. Both anecdotal stories and empirical research tell us that aggressive behavior is more likely to occur when it is hot. For example, crime statistics show that deadly assault is more frequent in hot years than in relatively cooler years (Anderson, Bushman, & Groom, 1997). Generally, field studies show that heat increases aggression, and many laboratory experiments show the same (see Anderson, 1989). Some experiments in this area have shown that people became increasingly aggressive as the temperature of the room went up—but only to a certain point (Baron, 1979). Once the heat became excessive, aggression actually went down. Perhaps people simply wanted to escape the extreme heat, or perhaps their energy was sapped by the highest temperatures.

Why do increases in heat, at least to a certain point, cause increases in aggression? One possibility is that heat makes people uncomfortable and angry, thereby causing aversive arousal that contributes to aggressive behavior, consistent with an excitation transfer effect. Another possibility is that heat activates cognitive schemas of aggression or violence (perhaps because of physical discomfort), which might increase aggressive responding. An experiment by Craig Anderson and his colleagues (Anderson et al., 1995) provided some support for both of these possible explanations. Participants who had been randomly assigned to sit in a hot room showed significant increases in both aversive arousal and aggressive thoughts compared to participants who had been randomly assigned to sit in a room with a comfortable temperature.

## ● ● ●  The Social Context of Aggression

The causes and characteristics of aggression change across different social settings. In this section, we consider a few contextual aspects of aggression. We begin by discussing the influence of *culture* on aggression: some cultures condone or permit aggression as an acceptable way to handle conflict more than do other cultures. We then discuss some of the particular social contexts in which aggression appears: on the playground, in close relationships, and in groups.

## Culture and Aggression

Social learning theory teaches us that people must *learn* to be aggressive. Our aggressive behaviors are shaped by the environment, especially what we observe in others. If people are immersed from an early age in a culture that encourages and supports aggressive behavior, then we should not be surprised to find that the people of that culture display a propensity for violence.

If social and cultural environments play a role in shaping aggressive behavior, then we should find considerable variability in the violence of different cultures and countries. Consistent with this reasoning, Dane Archer and Rosemary Gartner examined a variety of violence-related crimes in 110 countries over the period from 1900 to 1970. Archer and Gartner (1984) looked at the statistics on such crimes as homicide, rape, and assault. When they compared countries, they found that some exhibited a greater propensity for violence than others. For example, of all the industrial nations around the world, the United States had the highest rate of homicides during this period. Why? The researchers suggested that it was because of the ease with which firearms can be obtained in the United States.

Of course, the United States is itself a quilt of varying norms, customs, traditions, and subcultures. And regional differences in violence do exist within the United States. Perhaps the most important of these regional differences is that the homicide rate is greater in southern parts of the country than in northern parts. This finding is one of those results for which a multitude of explanations could be developed. Try to explain this effect yourself. Perhaps it is due to differences in climate. We know that the American South is warmer than the North, and we have already reviewed evidence showing a relationship between heat and aggression. Or perhaps it has something to do with the deeper poverty of the South: poor economic conditions create a breeding ground for frustration and violence. And it may have occurred to you that the southern history of slavery and racial conflict might still be exerting a residual effect.

These are all reasonable explanations, and each probably contributes at least in part to the observed regional differences in homicide rates. But social psychologists Richard Nisbett and Dov Cohen (1996) suggested that another factor was important. These researchers proposed that the people of the southern United States belong to a **culture of honor**—a culture in which White non-Hispanic men, in particular, are taught from an early age to defend their honor and their reputation for strength and toughness. According to this view, when a southern man is insulted, thus threatening his reputation, the proper response is one of dominance, violence, or aggression.

Nisbett and Cohen marshaled considerable evidence for this interpretation. They linked the culture of honor with a regional history of people deriving their livelihood from the herding of animals. Unlike the North, much of the southern United States was settled chiefly by immigrant herders from Ireland, Scotland, and Wales. Nevertheless, not all parts of the southern United States have roots in a herding economy; in support of Nisbett and Cohen's analysis, homicide rates within the southern United States are substantially higher in the *herding* regions (the hills and dry plains) than in the *farming* regions.

The relationship between insults and aggression in the southern culture of honor has also been studied in the laboratory. Cohen and Nisbett and their colleagues Brian Bowdle and Norbert Schwarz (1996) observed White male students at the University of Michigan who had been raised in the South or the North of the United States. Students were considered to be of southern origin if they had spent six or more years living in such states as West Virginia, Virginia, North Carolina, South Carolina, Georgia, Florida, Kentucky, Tennessee, Alabama, Mississippi, Arkansas, Oklahoma, Louisiana, or Texas. The basic procedure was to deliver an insult to the experimental participant and then measure an aggression-related outcome. The procedure involved asking participants to complete a short questionnaire and then take it to a table at the end of a long and narrow hallway. Cohen et al. (1996) described what happened next:

> As the participant walked down the hall, a confederate of the experimenter walked out of a door marked "Photo Lab" and began working at a file cabinet in the hall. The confederate had to push the file drawer in to allow the participant to pass by him and drop his paper off at the table. As the participant returned seconds later and walked back down the hall toward the experimental room, the confederate (who had re-opened the file drawer) slammed it shut on seeing the participant approach and bumped into the participant with his shoulder, calling the participant an "asshole." (p. 948)

In one of the experiments, the aggression-related outcome focused on changes in participants' hormone levels. The researchers measured cortisol levels, which is a hormone associated with stress and arousal. They also measured testosterone levels, which is a hormone associated with aggressive and dominant behavior. Both hormones can be assessed from a small sample of saliva, and saliva samples were taken prior to the insult and again right afterwards. Figure 11.7 compares the testosterone results for southern and northern participants who had either been insulted or assigned to a no-insult control condition (the results for cortisol were similar). It is clear that the southern and northern participants responded to the insult in different ways. The southern participants showed elevated testosterone levels, indicating a readiness to respond with aggression.

**culture of honor**

*a social network in which men are taught from an early age to defend their reputation for strength by responding to insults or threats with aggression*

**FIGURE 11.7** Changes in testosterone levels for southern and northern participants in each condition

From Cohen et al., "Insult, aggression, and southern culture of honor: An 'experimental ethnography,'" *Journal of Personality and Social Psychology*, 70, 945–960, 1996. Copyright © 1996 by the American Psychological Association. Reprinted by permission.

# Social Psychology in Your Life    *Aggression on the Highway*

A new form of aggressive behavior has been recognized in the past two decades: road rage. The American Automobile Association (1997) estimated that more than 10,000 incidents of aggression on the highways occurred in the United States between 1990 and 1996. These incidents resulted in more than 200 deaths and more than 12,000 injuries.

It is easy to understand how the highway can be a breeding ground for aggression. Traffic jams produce frustration, and the discomfort of sitting for long periods in a car (especially in hot weather) can produce aversive arousal. Combine these factors with even a small provocation by another driver, and aggression will be elicited from some people.

The response to road rage in most parts of the country has been legislation and public information campaigns (American Automobile Association, 1999). Another possible approach is to focus on characteristics of high-anger drivers, with the goal of developing interventions that might curtail their aggressive driving. Jerry Deffenbacher and his colleagues

have shown that when high-anger drivers recognize their problem and indicate a desire to control it, interventions can be effective in reducing their risky behaviors (e.g., Deffenbacher, Filetti, Richards, Lynch, & Oetting, 2003; Deffenbacher, Huff, Lynch, Oetting, & Salvatore, 2000). These interventions teach high-anger drivers to recognize potentially frustrating and confrontational situations and to reinterpret them as noncompetitive. One specific strategy is to teach *empathy:* the angry driver is told to put himself or herself in the other driver's place. This new perspective often reduces hostility. A key to successful treatment, however, is the admission of a problem. Some angry drivers refuse to acknowledge their problem, and psychological interventions are ineffective for them.

What can you do for yourself? Try to avoid being an angry driver.

Don't let another driver's provocation be interpreted as a cause for retaliation. The American Automobile Association recommends that you avoid offending others in your driving habits and do not get engaged in an escalation of hostility. Try putting yourself in the other driver's place, and try deliberate relaxation techniques such as deep breathing and counting to 10. Everyone loses when aggression appears on the highway.

© Anthony Redpath/CORBIS

Road rage has been associated with many deaths and injuries.

These findings indicate that cultural factors affect how people respond to provocations. Norms about appropriate responses to insults and threats can influence the aggressiveness of people's actions. In the accompanying box, Social Psychology in Your Life: Aggression on the Highway, we discuss another form of aggression that is common in our culture—road rage.

## Aggression on the Playground

One of the most active areas of research on aggression focuses on children and the development of aggressive behavior (Coie & Dodge, 1998). In this section, we briefly summarize some of this interesting and important developmental work.

Anger emerges as a distinct emotional response within the first six months of life (Stenberg & Campos, 1990). Between the ages of 1 and 2 years, children begin to target aggressive behavior at others. Presumably because of socialization pressures, physical aggression tends to decline and be replaced by verbal aggression as children approach their schooling years. Still, some children continue to engage in physical aggression to control their peers.

Earlier in the chapter, we noted that relational aggression is sometimes associated with peer rejection and sometimes with peer acceptance. The complexity of this relationship emerges even at young ages. When John Coie and Janis Kupersmidt (1983) assembled small groups of previously unacquainted fourth-grade boys, the ones who were rejected by the others were also the ones who most often started fights and engaged in both physical and verbal aggression. Kenneth Dodge (1983) similarly found that second-grade boys rejected peers who engaged in verbal aggression and hitting during the initial periods of becoming acquainted. It seems fairly clear that, at least during the early years of grade school, aggression is not a good way to make new friends.

Two additional observations, however, complicate the issue (Coie & Dodge, 1998). The first is that aggressive behavior is sometimes viewed as appropriate and justified. For example, children view aggression positively when their peers use it to stand up for themselves. Children who use aggression in this way tend to be liked by their peers (Lancelotta & Vaughn, 1989).

The second observation is that there are subgroups among aggressive children, some of whom are not rejected by their peers. Karen Bierman and her colleagues (Bierman, Smoot, & Aumiller, 1993) were able to classify grade-school-age boys into four distinct groups that represented the crossing of two dimensions: boys were classified as either aggressive or not aggressive on the one hand, and as rejected or not rejected by their peers on the other hand. This resulted in the four combinations shown in Figure 11.8. The two subgroups of aggressive boys were equally aggressive, whether they were rejected by their peers or not. The primary thing that distinguished the *rejected* aggressive boys was that they engaged in additional antisocial actions: they were also more argumentative and disruptive than their nonrejected counterparts.

As children get older, they typically learn to use behaviors other than aggression as means for resolving conflict and achieving goals. Yet some children and adolescents continue to engage in physical and verbal aggression, and often target their aggressive behavior toward specific individuals. In the research literature, an everyday term is used to describe such children and adolescents: *school bullies* (Perry, Williard, & Perry, 1990). School bullies tend to fall into the category of rejected and aggressive. Because they are rejected by many of their peers, their main source of affiliation is among themselves (Coie & Dodge, 1998). This fact is a serious problem, because bullies find themselves in a social environment that reinforces and encourages their antisocial behavior: their friends all do it, and their victims tend to avoid rather than confront their aggression. School bullies are at high risk of school failure, which in turn makes the rest of their life more difficult.

Understanding the development of aggression in children is essential if we hope to intervene to teach adaptive social skills. Such interventions will be an important topic in future research.

**FIGURE 11.8** Combinations of rejected or not rejected aggressive or not aggressive boys

From Bierman et al., "Characteristics of aggressive-rejected, aggressive (nonrejected), and rejected (nonaggressive) boys," *Child Development*, 64, 139–151, 1993. Reprinted by permission of Blackwell Publishing.

## Aggression in Close Relationships

When we think about our close relationships—the ones with parents, children, siblings, and lovers—we prefer to focus on the positive and fulfilling aspects of those relationships. Yet even in the closest of relationships, violent aggression sometimes enters the scene. It has been estimated that 25% or more of intimate couples have experienced at least one episode of physical aggression within the relationship (Straus & Gelles, 1990). In fact, women are more likely to be physically abused by current or former male partners than by strangers (Koss, Goodman, Browne, Fitzgerald, Keita, & Russo, 1994). Homicide is the fourth leading cause of death among children and youth in the United States, and most homicides of infants are committed by their parents or caretakers (Finkelhor, 1997). These are sobering statistics and emphasize a need to focus on and understand violence in the context of close relationships.

Most of the research on aggression in close relationships has focused on heterosexual married couples. In this context, it is important to distinguish between psychological aggression and physical aggression. Examples of psychological aggression against a partner include public humiliation, threats of harm, or destruction of a partner's possessions. Physical aggression includes pushing, hitting, burning, kicking, using a weapon, or otherwise causing direct physical harm to a partner. In one longitudinal study of early marriages, Christopher Murphy and K. Daniel O'Leary (1989) found that psychological aggression is a good predictor of later physical aggression. In another large-scale study involving more than 10,000 couples, Helen Pan, Peter Neidig, and K. Daniel O'Leary (1994) found that women were more likely to be the victims of physical aggression when their husbands suffered from an alcohol or drug problem, depression, low income, or the stress of marital discord. Perhaps not surprisingly, incidents of aggression early in a marriage are very predictive of a marriage breaking apart (Rogge & Bradbury, 1999).

School bullies tend to be rejected by most of their peers.

**Batterers.** We have noted that husbands sometimes engage in psychological and physical aggression against their wives. What kind of men direct aggressive behavior toward female partners? Work in clinical psychology suggests that subgroups of batterers share certain characteristics. In particular, research by Amy Holtzworth-Munroe and her colleagues has shown that violent husbands generally fall into one of three subgroups (Holtzworth-Munroe, 2000; Holtzworth-Munroe & Stuart, 1994; Holtzworth-Munroe, Stuart, & Hutchinson, 1997; see also Waltz, Babcock, Jacobson, & Gottman, 2000):

*Family-only:* These are the least violent men, and they rarely exhibit aggressive behavior outside the home. Their aggression can typically be traced to stress, poor relationship skills, and perhaps exposure to marital violence when they were children. Family-only aggressors tend to regret their actions, and interventions can produce a positive change in behavior.

*Dysphoric/borderline:* These are relatively more violent men, who sometimes engage in severe physical abuse. Although focused mainly on their wives, these men occasionally exhibit aggressive behavior outside the home. But more important, these men exhibit signs of psychological distress: depression, anxiety, fear of rejection, extreme mood swings, and poor relationships skills. Dysphoric/borderline aggressors often have a history of being abused by their own parents, and it is much more difficult to bring about a positive change in behavior.

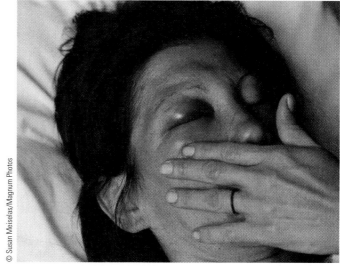

Women are more likely to be physically abused by current or former male partners than by strangers.

*Generally violent/antisocial:* These are violent men who do not discriminate in their aggression—it just happens that their wives are more often available as targets. Substance abuse, criminal behavior, and other signs of antisocial personality characteristics are common among these men. They harbor hostile attitudes toward women and generally consider violence to be an acceptable way of interacting with others. They are extremely resistant to interventions designed to reduce their violence against their wives.

These distinctions among batterers are important, because husbands who engage in family-only aggression are most amenable to interventions that can curb their violence and allow them to develop a healthier marital relationship (Holtzworth-Munroe, 2000). Thus, the limited resources available for interventions should probably be directed primarily at these husbands. Law enforcement may be the only way to deal with the more violent batterers. The distinctions also illustrate the idea from the *general aggression model* that there are individual differences in people's tendencies to have aggressive thoughts and feelings.

**Effects on Children.** Domestic violence is often witnessed by children. As we noted above, one characteristic of many men who abuse their wives is that they once witnessed their own parents' violence. Many (but not all) children who are exposed to violence between their parents show adverse consequences in their own psychological adjustment, interactions with peers, and progress in school (Kitzmann, Gaylord, Holt, & Kenny, 2003). Consistent with social learning accounts of aggressive behavior, surveys and longitudinal studies have found that children who are exposed to domestic violence between their parents are at increased risk, as adults, of either perpetrating or being the victim of violence in their own close relationships (e.g., Ehrensaft, Cohen, Brown, Smailes, Chen, & Johnson, 2003; Kwong, Bartholomew, Henderson, & Trinke, 2003). It is not a cliché to say that interventions are needed to break the cycle of violence that is passed on from one generation to the next.

## Aggression in Groups

To this point, the type of aggression we have focused on has been that of individuals aggressing against other individuals. Sometimes, however, people behave aggressively in the context of a social group. Riots, lynchings, and the behavior of unruly crowds at sporting events are often cited as examples of *mob violence*. A **mob** is "a crowd acting under strong emotional conditions that often lead to violence or illegal acts" (Staub & Rosenthal, 1994, p. 281). Mob violence can reflect organized leadership, such as the planned actions of the Ku Klux Klan, but more often it is relatively unorganized and even spontaneous, such as violence that occurs at sporting events or inner-city riots.

We have discussed in previous chapters two social psychological processes that might contribute to mob violence. One is *deindividuation*, which we defined in Chapter 10 as a loss of personal identity and a sense of immersion in a group (see page 399). Deindividuation tends to occur in large groups and may reduce individuals' sense of responsibility for their actions, which can then decrease their inhibitions against committing violence. A second process is *conformity pressure*, which can lead individuals to copy the behavior of others even when the action runs contrary to what those individuals would ordinarily do when alone (see Chapter 8, Conformity, Compliance, and Obedience).

Several laboratory studies have provided experimental evidence that deindividuation can increase aggressive behavior. For instance, Steven Prentice-Dunn and Ronald Rogers (1980; Rogers & Prentice-Dunn, 1981) developed a laboratory proce-

**mob**

*a crowd acting under strong emotional conditions that often lead to violence or illegal acts*

© AP/Wide World Photos/CP, Ryan Remiorz

Mob violence is often unplanned and unorganized.

dure that either induced deindividuation or emphasized participants' personal identities. Participants arrived for the experiment in small groups of four or five. Unknown to the participants, one member of the group was always an accomplice who worked for the experimenter. As is frequently done in laboratory experiments on aggression, the situation was set up so that the naïve participants believed that they could administer electric shocks to a victim.

Some participants were randomly assigned to a condition that fostered a sense of deindividuation: these participants were never addressed by name, were told that their individual levels of electric shocks would not be known to the experimenter, believed that they would never meet the recipient (victim) of the shocks, and heard the experimenter accept full responsibility for the victim's well-being. Participants in the identity-enhancing condition, in contrast, wore name tags, were addressed by their first names, were led to believe that their individual choices of electric shocks would be known to the experimenter, anticipated meeting the victim afterwards, and were given personal responsibility for any harm done to the victim.

All participants then completed a procedure that allowed them to administer electric shocks to the experimental accomplice. Participants exhibited significantly more aggression (administered more electric shock) when they were in a state of deindividuation than when their personal identity was emphasized. Presumably, deindividuation weakened participants' restraints against aggression.

Although mob violence occurs, it is important to remember that people often gather in large groups or crowds without engaging in aggressive or violent acts. Just as people seldom act aggressively when alone, groups seldom engage in violence without some kind of instigating event (Staub & Rosenthal, 1994). What kind of events can precipitate mob violence? Typically, they are events that make people *angry*. Most of the riots that have occurred in North American cities can be traced to specific events that instilled anger among the participants (Downes,

1968). For example, an occurrence (or perceived occurrence) of police brutality can spark a riot (Stark, 1972), such as occurred in 1992 after the acquittal of police officers involved in the beating of Rodney King in Los Angeles in 1991. A combination of anger and deindividuation produced by a large group can be a recipe for aggressive behavior. These kinds of events illustrate that people may respond to situational variables with aggressive thoughts and feelings, as predicted by the *general aggression model*.

## ● ● ● Media Effects on Aggression

To this point, we have focused on *person-to-person* ways of transmitting aggression, such as interpersonal frustration, modeling effects, and cultural learning. The *mass media,* including television, movies, and the Internet, have the potential to magnify these person-to-person processes many times over. For example, millions of viewers watch particular episodes of a television show, and most of us surf the Internet at least occasionally. This enormous exposure explains why social psychologists have been very interested in studying the possible effects of the mass media on aggression. The media fit into the category of *situational variables* in the GAM: television programs or video games can elicit aggressive thoughts, feelings, and arousal within individuals, which may eventually lead to aggressive behavior.

The primary reason social psychologists are concerned about possible effects of the media is that violence is so common in television, movies, and video games. Think about your own exposure to media violence: viewing television programs with frequent episodes of aggression, listening to popular music with violent lyrics, watching aggressive sports, and playing video games with violent content. In North America, at least, it is very difficult to avoid exposure to media violence. Have you ever noticed yourself acting differently because of violence you saw on television? Some defenders of the television and movie industries have suggested that violent programs actually provide safe and harmless outlets for aggressive impulses.

The question of whether the media cause or encourage aggressive behavior is at the center of a great societal debate. Some of the person-to-person processes we have covered in the chapter raise serious questions about possible negative effects of media violence. But these studies were not designed to investigate the media directly. In the following paragraphs, we turn to research that has specifically investigated the effects of the mass media on aggressive behavior.

### Television Violence

One of the best examples of social psychological research on the effects of exposure to violent television programming was reported recently by a research team at the University of Michigan led by L. Rowell Huesmann (Huesmann, Moise-Titus, Podolski, & Eron, 2003). This study actually started in the late 1970s, with a sample of more than 500 8- or 9-year-old children in the Chicago area who were followed over a period of three years (Huesmann & Eron, 1986). The children were observed and tested to determine the amount of their exposure to TV violence, the degree to which they identified with aggressive television characters, and the extent of their aggressive behavior with peers. Results from this initial wave of observation showed that the more aggressive children were also the ones who watched more television, indicated a preference for violent shows, and more strongly identified with the aggressive characters in those shows. It was the combination of heavy exposure to television violence and identification with aggressive characters that particularly predicted aggressive behavior.

You may be thinking that childhood aggression is just a normal part of growing up. We have already noted that many children hit and push each other on the playground, but this is hardly the kind of aggression we worry about among adult members of society. Hold that thought. Fast-forward 15 years, when the original sample of children studied by Huesmann and Eron are in their early 20s. It is the 1990s, and the children are now young adults: they have jobs and spouses, and some have already been convicted of violent crimes.

Huesmann and his colleagues were able to locate and reinterview nearly 400 of the participants from the earlier study. The measures of aggression used in the follow-up study reflected the kinds of aggression we *do* worry about among adult members of society: indirect aggression such as stealing things or getting others to dislike a person; verbal aggression such as calling a person names or mocking another's abilities; physical aggression such as hitting, kicking, or shoving people; spousal abuse; and criminal violence. Now 15 years later, the earlier results were confirmed. The most aggressive adults were the ones who, as children, had watched more violence on television and had identified more strongly with the aggressive characters. This was true for both the men and the women, and was independent of socioeconomic status, intellectual ability, and other demographic variables (Huesmann et al., 2003).

What are the processes through which exposure to violent television programming might increase aggressive behavior? Several of the factors discussed previously in the chapter could be involved. Perhaps most directly, violence on television presents models of aggressive behavior, who teach viewers how to aggress and typically show that aggression has positive consequences. Violent programming can also prime hostile and aggressive thoughts, as well as elicit aggressive feelings (e.g., anger at the "bad guys" and satisfaction when they are shot). Frequent violence on television might also desensitize viewers to aggression, making violent behavior seem more normal and acceptable.

The findings of Huesmann and his colleagues (2003) are sobering. Long-term exposure to television violence is correlated with aggressive behavior within viewers who identify strongly with violent characters. Of course, these data are correlational, so we cannot be certain about cause and effect (e.g., aggressive people may be

Children who watch a lot of violent television programming tend to be more aggressive than children who watch less violent television programming.

attracted to aggressive television). But numerous experimental studies have also been conducted, and they have generally shown a significant effect of exposure to violent television programs on aggression (for summaries, see Geen, 1998; Paik & Comstock, 1994; Wood, Wong, & Chachere, 1991). Many of these experimental studies were admittedly artificial (and therefore lacked mundane realism—see page 355), but when combined with the field studies make for a convincing indictment of violent television programming (Anderson et al., 2003; Anderson & Bushman, 2002b; Bushman & Anderson, 2001b; Johnson, Cohen, Smailes, Kasen, & Brook, 2002).

It is interesting to consider the "size" of the effect of viewing television violence on aggressive behavior. Just how "big" or "significant" is television's impact on aggression? Brad Bushman and Craig Anderson (2001b) compared the size of television's effect on aggression to other effects that help us to interpret the importance of the findings. Figure 11.9 presents the relative sizes of several effects. The first column represents the effect of smoking on lung cancer; the second column represents the effect of viewing violent television programs on aggression; the third column represents the effect of playing violent video games on aggression (which we discuss in the next section); and the fourth column represents the effect of calcium intake on bone mass. You can see from the figure that the effect of violent television on aggressive behavior is not as strong as the effect of smoking on lung cancer, but it is larger than the effect of calcium intake on bone mass—a finding that is considered well proven by medical researchers.

In summary, it seems that a specific mixture of variables involving violent television is predictive of adult aggressive behavior. Not everyone is negatively affected by television violence. But elevated adult aggression is found among men and women who, as children, (1) *watched a lot of violent television,* and (2) *identified strongly with aggressive characters featured on television.* These results make good social psychological sense. Watching a lot of violent television programs provides repeated opportunities to learn aggressive behaviors. Identifying strongly with aggressive television characters motivates viewers to copy the characters' behavior.

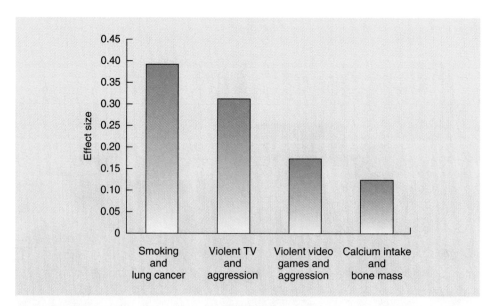

**FIGURE 11.9** Comparisons of the effect of television violence on aggression with other effects

From Bushman and Anderson, "Media violence and the American public: Scientific facts versus media misinformation," *American Psychologist,* 56, 477–489, 2001. Copyright © 2001 by the American Psychological Association. Reprinted by permission.

After all, violence seemed to work on television, so it might be effective in dealing with one's own problems as well. This hypothesized process through which violent television can influence behavior is depicted in the flowchart in Figure 11.10.

## Violent Video Games

The advent of violent video games in the past 15 years has added a new wrinkle to media aggression. Unlike television, video games are highly *interactive*—players make rapid-fire decisions to behave aggressively in the games. The immediate satisfaction of seeing an enemy destroyed might be a strong reinforcement for aggression. Also, playing violent video games seems likely to elicit aggressive thoughts and emotions, which might influence subsequent behavior. On the other hand, the violence in video games is less realistic than the violence on television (e.g., the characters are animated), which might reduce its impact.

The first video games came out in the late 1970s, but violent games became common only in the 1990s with titles like Mortal Kombat and Street Fighter. More recent games have become increasingly graphic in their portrayal of violence (e.g., Grand Theft Auto, Halo 2). Statistics indicate that the majority of regular video game players identify *violent* games as their favorites. Many parents and educators have expressed concern about aggressive video games, particularly after events of schoolyard violence such as the Columbine shootings in 1999—Eric Harris and Dylan Klebold enjoyed playing Doom, a highly graphic shooting game. In 2000, the mayor of Indianapolis introduced a law banning children under 18 from playing violent arcade video games unless accompanied by an adult (Halladay & Wolf, 2000).

Despite the fact that violent video games have been around only 10 or 15 years, numerous studies have examined the connections between playing these games and aggression. Most studies have been correlational (that is, they simply measured violent video game use and aggression), but some have been experimental (that is, participants were randomly assigned to play violent or nonviolent video games and then given an opportunity to engage in aggression). The measures of aggression have ranged from aggression against inanimate objects (e.g., a Bobo doll) to aggression against another person (e.g., delivering electric shock to someone).

Playing violent video games may increase subsequent aggression.

Researchers who have reviewed this literature, however, have made different judgments about the evidence. Mark Griffiths (1999) concluded that all of the published studies on violent video games to that date had enough methodological problems to prevent any clear conclusion. Lillian Bensley and Juliet Van Eenwyk (2001) similarly argued that "current research evidence is not supportive of a

*"[People who play a lot of violent video games] will start making more aggressive decisions about how they'll respond to ambiguous or threat situations, conflict situations, than they would have if they had not spent so many hours basically practicing how to be an aggressive person."*

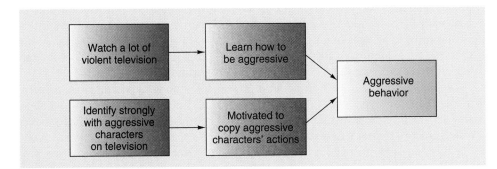

**FIGURE 11.10** Hypothesized effects of television violence on behavior

major concern that violent video games lead to real-life violence" (p. 256). But Craig Anderson and Brad Bushman (2001) came to another conclusion based on a statistical analysis of 33 investigations of the effects of playing violent video games on aggressive behavior by children and young adults. Across the set of studies, there was a small but statistically significant effect, such that playing violent video games increased aggression. The size of this effect is depicted in Figure 11.9 relative to some other findings, including the effect of violent television on aggressive behavior. The figure shows that the impact of video games is smaller than the impact of violent television (see also Sherry, 2001), but nevertheless larger than such widely accepted findings as the impact of calcium intake on bone mass.

The most consistent evidence that playing violent video games can increase aggressive behavior has been obtained in studies that used young children (ages 10 and under) and that measured aggression by observing the children at play (Bensley & Van Eenwyk, 2001; Griffiths, 1999). For example, A. Roland Irwin and Alan Gross (1995) randomly assigned 60 7- or 8-year-old boys to play either an aggressive martial arts video game or a nonaggressive but equally arousing motorcycle race video game. After playing the game, the boys interacted with another child in a setting where a variety of toys were available. During this free play period, the boys who had played the martial arts game exhibited more physical aggression toward toys (e.g., punching or kicking a toy) and more verbal aggression toward the other child (e.g., threats or insults) than did the boys who had played the racing game.

If we accept the evidence that violent video games can have undesirable effects, what should we do about it? For instance, should violent video games be banned or legally restricted? Should we instead leave the issue to parents, who should monitor their children's leisure activities (but who do *not* always do so)? These are difficult questions that relate more to social policy than social psychological research. Reactance theory (described in Chapter 7, see page 299) implies that banning or censoring a product may backfire—people seem to want products even more when they are restricted. Anderson and Bushman (2001) made an interesting suggestion at the end of their review of research on violent video games; they speculated that video games could potentially be developed that would teach and reinforce *nonviolent* solutions to social conflicts. Although some video games already exist that allow "prosocial" actions (e.g., The Sims), few games specifically reward positive, nonviolent responses by the characters. Given that video games appear capable of teaching antisocial responses, perhaps they could be designed to teach prosocial responses instead.

## Pornography

A final question about the effects of the media on aggression relates to sexually explicit materials. The term *pornography* is often used in a general way to refer to sexual materials, such as sexually explicit videotapes, men's magazines, and Internet websites with sexual content. Critics sometimes claim that pornography increases aggressive behavior, especially sexual aggression such as rape. A close look at the literature indicates that the picture is rather complicated.

The first thing we need to do is differentiate among types of pornography. William Fisher and Azy Barak (2001) suggested that three types of sexually explicit materials should be distinguished, although the boundaries between the categories are not precise. **Erotica** is sexually explicit material that depicts nonviolent, consensual sexual activity (e.g., a couple engaging in consensual sexual intercourse). **Degrading pornography** is sexually explicit material that debases or dehumanizes people, usually women (e.g., a woman having serial sexual intercourse with several

**erotica**

*sexually explicit material that depicts nonviolent, consensual sexual activity*

**degrading pornography**

*sexually explicit material that debases or dehumanizes people, usually women*

men). **Violent pornography** is sexually explicit material that depicts aggressive, hostile sexual activity (e.g., rape). The effects of these three kinds of materials on viewers' attitudes and actions probably differ.

It appears that *erotica* has few, if any, negative effects. When sought out and viewed by couples, erotica results in a short-term increase in their typical sexual activity (see Fisher, 1986). Experiments in which participants have been given an opportunity for aggression after viewing erotica (e.g., after viewing photographs of nudes) have generally found that erotica *reduced* aggression (see Allen, D'Alessio, & Brezgel, 1995). Thus, the portrayal of nonviolent, consensual sexual activity seems to have positive, not negative, effects on aggressiveness.

The effects of degrading or violent pornography are less clear. Depending on whom you talk to, you might be convinced that degrading pornography causes unfavorable attitudes toward women and violent pornography causes aggression against women, or you might be convinced that it is unclear from current research how these stimuli affect attitudes and behavior in natural settings. Before we elaborate on this controversy, we want to describe a couple of illustrative studies.

In one of the best-known experiments on the effects of pornography, Ed Donnerstein (1980) assigned male participants randomly to view one of three films. One group of men watched a mild and neutral control film—it had nothing to do with either sex or violence. A second group watched an explicit depiction of heterosexual sex—it was highly erotic, but did not contain any suggestion of aggression, force, or violence between the depicted couple. A third group of men watched a film that was both sexually explicit and aggressive—it portrayed a violent rape.

After viewing one of the films, participants were provided an opportunity to deliver electric shocks to another person. Half of the time, this other person was a woman, and half of the time, it was a man. Results showed an increase in aggression (as measured by the number and intensity of electric shocks) when participants had viewed the violent rape and then had an opportunity to be aggressive toward a woman. The nonviolent, erotic film did not produce any more (nor less) aggression than did the neutral film, and the violent rape film caused an increase in aggression only when the target of that aggression was female and not male.

Not surprisingly, Donnerstein's results received a lot of attention and raised concerns about the negative impact of violent pornography—which is widely available in adult video stores (and now on the Internet). But some researchers expressed doubts about the conclusion that violent pornography causes aggression. For example, William Fisher and Guy Grenier (1994) asked male participants to write a short essay, which was then evaluated very unfavorably by a female coparticipant (actually an accomplice of the experimenter). After receiving this negative evaluation, the male participants were asked whether they would be willing to rate some pretest materials for a study on pornography. All participants agreed, at which point they watched a videotape that depicted a violent rape. After viewing this violent pornography, participants served as the "teacher" in a memory task over an intercom, on which the female coparticipant (who had evaluated their essay negatively) was the "learner" in a different room. She made numerous errors on the memory task; participants indicated verbally to her on each trial whether her response was correct or incorrect. After the memory task was completed, participants were told that, if they wished, they could provide an overall evaluation to the woman in one of two ways: they could speak with her over the intercom to give their overall evaluation of her performance, or they could deliver between 1 and 10 electric shocks to the woman to indicate their evaluation (with 1 or few shocks meaning a good performance, and many shocks meaning a poor performance). [A plausible cover story was given for this shock option.] But participants were also given a third option: because the woman already knew how many mistakes she had made, the participant could simply leave the laboratory immediately if he wished. Only 14% of the

**violent pornography**
*sexually explicit material that depicts aggressive, hostile sexual activity*

men chose to deliver any electric shocks to the woman. The remaining 86% did not engage in any aggression, deciding instead either to leave the experiment (64%) or to provide a verbal evaluation (21%). The authors concluded that exposure to pornography does not motivate men to be aggressive against women—at least, it doesn't motivate them enough to want to remain in an experiment to shock someone who frustrated them.

So what are we to conclude about the effects of violent pornography? Some researchers (e.g., Fisher & Barak, 2001; Fisher & Grenier, 1994) argue that existing data are insufficient to conclude that pornography increases aggression or rape. In this regard, these authors point to police data showing that the incidence of forcible rape in the United States decreased between the years of 1995 and 1999—a period when pornographic materials of all sorts were becoming much more widely available over the Internet. Other researchers (e.g., Malamuth, Addison, & Koss, 2000; Seto, Maric, & Barbaree, 2001) argue that violent pornography is harmful for some men who view it. Specifically, these researchers believe that men who are already predisposed to engage in sexual aggression may be negatively influenced by watching violent pornography, such that they are even more likely to behave violently. These researchers agree that violent pornography has little or no behavioral effect on most people (though it may affect attitudes toward sexuality and women), but they link it to aggression by a few high-risk individuals. Malamuth et al. (2000) suggested that men with a predisposition toward sexual aggression interpret the same pornography differently than do nonaggressive men. For example, men with a controlling, hostile approach to sexuality may be more likely than nonaggressive men to pick out images in violent pornography that reinforce links between power, sex, and aggression.

The issue of the effects of violent pornography on aggression will undoubtedly receive more attention from researchers over the next decade. This is an important social question that needs to be answered. Even if it can be indisputably established that certain kinds of pornography have negative effects on some individuals, however, the solution will remain uncertain. Introducing legislation to make depictions of certain sexual acts among adults illegal would be both difficult to define precisely and difficult to enforce. Education about the negative effects of violent pornography is an appealing approach, but would such efforts reach the relatively few individuals who are most at risk?

## ● ● ● Controlling Aggression and Violence

Social psychologists have learned a great deal about the causes and consequences of human aggressive behavior. What ideas does this knowledge provide about how aggression and violence might be controlled?

The distinction between hostile and instrumental aggression may be relevant to the issue of controlling aggression. To reduce aggression that results primarily from negative emotional arousal (hostile aggression), one approach might be to teach people how to *control* their negative emotions, such as anger, so aggressive behavior does not necessarily follow from arousal. To reduce aggression that is designed to obtain a desired goal (instrumental aggression), the most direct approach is probably to teach people alternative, nonaggressive strategies. Finally, another, more general approach to reducing aggression would be to reduce aversive environments that cause pain and frustration. We consider each of these ideas in the following paragraphs.

## Controlling Anger

One approach to reducing aggressive behavior, which is compatible with the *general aggression model,* focuses on controlling anger. The GAM emphasizes the role of aggression-related feelings, thoughts, and arousal. According to the model, anger, frustration, or similar emotions *combine* with aggression- or violence-related thoughts to create a tendency to act aggressively. If the aggression-related thoughts can be short-circuited, then aggressive behavior should be less likely.

For example, one approach is to teach people how to control their anger by changing their thoughts (Novaco, 1975). Jerry Deffenbacher and his colleagues at Colorado State University, whose work with angry drivers is described in Social Psychology in Your Life: Aggression on the Highway (page 459), developed an intervention for general anger reduction along these lines (Deffenbacher, Thwaites, Wallace, & Oetting, 1994). College students who identified themselves as having problems with anger and who desired some help with anger management were recruited into the study. The intervention consisted of **cognitive-relaxation coping skills training,** or **CRCS** for short. In this training, people are first taught a series of relaxation skills—how to keep themselves calm and tension-free. Next, they are introduced to the idea of **cognitive restructuring,** learning to reduce their anger by recognizing and modifying their thoughts and attributions. For example, they are taught to think about the fact that another person who has provoked them probably did not *intend* to do so. The final step is to imagine or visualize situations that arouse anger, and then to use the relaxation and cognitive restructuring skills to reduce that anger.

The CRCS intervention has been shown to be effective in producing a reduction in anger, both in the short term and over the long term (Deffenbacher, Oetting, Huff, & Thwaites, 1995). It has also been shown to work well with adolescents (Deffenbacher, Lynch, Oetting, & Kemper, 1996). Thus, this intervention has considerable promise and may eventually be used more widely in the educational system.

**cognitive-relaxation coping skills training (CRCS)**
*an intervention program designed to reduce anger, which involves teaching people a set of relaxation techniques and ways to modify their anger-related thoughts*

**cognitive restructuring**
*recognizing and modifying anger-related thoughts and attributions; it forms part of CRCS training*

## Teaching Alternatives to Aggression

Reducing aggression that results primarily from trying to obtain a desired goal (instrumental aggression) is challenging, because this kind of aggression is seen as *necessary* for achieving the goal. For example, when a parent punishes a child for disobedience, or when a schoolyard bully takes a desired toy away from another child, the aggression is seen as the means to an end.

The best approach to reducing instrumental aggression is probably to convince people that nonaggressive strategies are more successful in the long run. For example, parents can be informed that corporal punishment is ineffective (see Social Psychology in Your Life: Is Corporal Punishment Effective?, page 443) and can be taught how to use timeouts and grounding (these techniques also model nonviolence in parents' own actions). Aggressive schoolchildren can be taught that bullying makes them unpopular and can be shown how to reduce conflict in other ways.

Programs that teach children effective, nonaggressive approaches to problem solving have been developed for use in elementary schools (e.g., Eargle, Guerra, & Tolan, 1994). One important skill these programs try to teach is *communication—* children are taught to *talk* about problems and conflicts with peers instead of reacting aggressively. Another important goal of these school programs is to teach *empathy—*putting oneself in the shoes of another and imagining how that person feels. As we noted in our discussion of road rage, empathy often reduces aggressive behavior (e.g., Richardson, Hammock, Smith, & Gardner, 1994). More generally, improving children's social skills and problem-solving strategies can reduce their reliance on aggressive tactics to achieve goals.

# Reducing Aversive Environments

Many aggressive acts occur because people find themselves in aversive environments. Hot, crowded settings elicit discomfort; a slap from another person elicits pain; poverty is associated with hunger. These states of discomfort, pain, and hunger can lead to aggression, as predicted by the *frustration–aggression hypothesis,* the *excitation transfer effect,* and the integrative *GAM.* If it were possible to reduce the number of aversive environments in society, the amount of aggression would be reduced as well.

How could aversive environments be reduced? Some strategies are difficult to implement but would have substantial impact. For example, poverty is strongly linked with aggression and violence, so ensuring that more people have enough to eat, a decent place to live, and reasonable prospects for employment would certainly help. Of course, these actions are political, not psychological, but it is important to recognize that social policies can significantly affect the amount of societal violence.

Physical discomfort and pain also cause aggression, so actions that reduce pain and suffering would reduce aggression as well. Even small actions to reduce others' discomfort can have great effect when done many times over by large numbers of people. For example, such actions could include municipalities' providing air-conditioned shelters during the summer for those who need them, police officers' minimizing the use of aggressive tactics with suspects or protesters, and even personal decisions by individuals to refrain from criticizing others. Trying to minimize others' discomfort is actually a big part of living and working successfully in families and social groups. Actions that make the world a less hostile place for others have the added benefit of reducing the amount of aggression that might affect us personally.

Aversive environments increase aggressive behavior.

© Janet Jarman/CORBIS

# Chapter Summary

**Aggression** is behavior that is intended to injure someone physically or psychologically. When aggression is intended to cause *extreme* injury, we call it **violence.** Aggression can take many forms. **Hostile aggression** is harmdoing that arises out of negative emotions like anger, frustration, or hatred. In contrast, **instrumental aggression** refers to harmdoing that is motivated by a more distant goal, such as teaching someone a lesson or obtaining something of value. One example of instrumental aggression is corporal punishment, which refers to the use of physical force (including spanking) with the intention of causing a child to experience pain but not injury for the purpose of correction or control of the child's behavior. **Relational aggression** is behavior that is intended to damage another person's peer relationships.

Social psychologists have conducted a great deal of research investigating the causes of aggression and violence. A general framework for research on aggression is provided by the **general aggression model** (or **GAM**), which conceptualizes aggression as the result of a chain of psychological processes. People respond to situational events by generating aggressive thoughts, aggressive feelings, and/or physiological arousal; in turn, these states initiate appraisal (interpretation) processes that can lead to aggressive behavior.

The **frustration–aggression hypothesis** proposes that frustration always leads to some form of aggression and that frustration is the only cause of aggression. Although studies have shown that frustration can indeed cause aggression, other factors such as anger also play a role. **Displaced aggression** occurs when people cannot be aggressive toward the actual source of their frustration, so they direct aggression elsewhere. The **catharsis** effect proposes that aggressive behavior releases people's pent-up frustration and reduces the likelihood of subsequent aggression. Researchers have found, however, that catharsis does not typically occur; in fact, the opposite is typically true.

Aggressive behavior is often preceded by some form of emotional and physiological arousal. This arousal can even come from sources unrelated to aggression, such as exercise. Researchers have shown that arousal from any source can be linked to anger-related thoughts and can ultimately cause an increase in aggressive behavior—an effect that has been called **excitation transfer.**

**Social learning theory** proposes that humans learn many kinds of responses, including aggressive ones, by observing other people. Watching other people shows us both how to perform a behavior and whether that behavior will be rewarded or punished. The **cognitive neoassociation model of aggression** is based on the idea that aversive or unpleasant events activate the schemas for *fight* and *flight,* which themselves elicit the emotions of anger and fear. Whether people respond with aggression or escape depends on the pattern of cues in the situation. This hypothesis has been supported in studies showing the *weapons effect:* participants are more likely to behave aggressively when aggressive cues (e.g., weapons) are present in the environment.

Not everyone is equally aggressive. Individuals who are high in *narcissism* have inflated views of their self-worth and often respond to criticism with hostility and aggression—a response that has been labeled *threatened egotism.* Also, some people are more likely to respond to any provocation with aggression than are other people—an individual difference that has been termed **trait aggressiveness.** The **Aggression Questionnaire (AQ)** measures trait aggressiveness. People who score high on the AQ have elaborate schemas related to aggression.

Alcohol typically causes an increase in aggressive behavior. This conclusion comes from studies that compared conditions in which alcohol was consumed with placebo conditions in which participants believed they were given alcohol but actually received nonalcoholic fluids. Alcohol's effects may be a consequence of *alcohol myopia,* which is the tendency for alcohol to narrow intoxicated individuals' range of attention to the most obvious cues in the setting. Heat also tends to increase aggressive behavior. Heat may create aversive arousal that increases aggressive behavior and may activate aggression-related cognitions.

Cultural factors also influence aggression. It has been proposed that many people in the southern United States were raised in a **culture of honor**—a culture in which men are taught from an early age to defend their honor and their reputation for strength and toughness. Within this culture, when a man is insulted or his reputation threatened, the proper response is one of dominance, violence, or aggression.

Children often engage in aggression. Once at school, physical aggression tends to be replaced by verbal aggression, but some children remain physically aggressive. Some, but not all, of these aggressive children are rejected by their peers. One group of aggressive and rejected individuals consists of *school bullies*, who often target their aggressive behavior toward specific individuals.

Violence also occurs in close relationships. Some men are physically abusive to their female partners. These batterers fall into three subgroups: those who are aggressive primarily at home (*family-only*), those who exhibit signs of psychological distress (*dysphoric/borderline*), and those who are generally violent (*generally violent/antisocial*). Children who witness domestic violence are very often adversely affected.

A **mob** is a crowd acting under strong emotional conditions that often lead to violence or illegal acts. Mob violence may be caused by *deindividuation,* which is a loss of personal identity and a sense of immersion in a group, or by *conformity pressure,* which can lead individuals to copy the behavior of others even when the action runs contrary to how they would normally behave.

Longitudinal research on the relation between television viewing and aggressive behavior has found that children who (1) watched a lot of violent television and (2) identified strongly with aggressive characters featured on television were more likely to exhibit aggressive behavior as adults than were children who did not meet these criteria. These correlational findings are supported by experiments that have demonstrated a significant effect of viewing television violence on aggressive behavior. There is also evidence that playing violent video games is associated with a significant increase in aggression, especially among young children.

**Erotica** is sexually explicit material that depicts nonviolent, consensual sexual activity. This kind of material generally reduces aggressive responding. **Degrading pornography** is sexually explicit material that debases or dehumanizes people, usually women. **Violent pornography** is sexually explicit material that depicts aggressive, hostile sexual activity. Some, but not all, researchers have argued that violent pornography makes men who were already predisposed to engage in sexual aggression more likely to behave violently.

Ideas for controlling aggression include controlling anger, teaching alternatives to aggression, and reducing aversive environments. With regard to anger control, **cognitive-relaxation coping skills training (CRCS)** involves teaching people a series of relaxation skills and introducing them to the idea of **cognitive restructuring,** which involves modifying their thoughts to reduce anger.

# Key Terms

**aggression** (441)

**Aggression Questionnaire (AQ)** (454)

**catharsis** (448)

**cognitive neoassociation model of aggression** (451)

**cognitive restructuring** (471)

**cognitive-relaxation coping skills training (CRCS)** (471)

**culture of honor** (458)

**degrading pornography** (468)

**displaced aggression** (448)

**erotica** (468)

**excitation transfer** (450)

**frustration–aggression hypothesis** (446)

**general aggression model (GAM)** (445)

**hostile aggression** (441)

**instrumental aggression** (441)

**mob** (462)

**relational aggression** (442)

**social learning theory** (450)

**trait aggressiveness** (454)

**violence** (441)

**violent pornography** (469)

# Social Psychology Alive on the Web

## SOCIAL PSYCHOLOGY ALIVE: ONLINE LABS

To perform the following experiment and see how you compare to other students, go to Social Psychology Lab, which can be accessed through Social PsychologyNow.

- 11.1 Sentencing

## SOCIAL PSYCHOLOGY ALIVE: QUIZZING AND PRACTICE TESTS

You can access our website directly by going to http:// psychology.wadsworth.com/brecklerle/ for online quizzes, flash cards, and Internet links.

## INFOTRAC® COLLEGE EDITION

For additional readings, explore InfoTrac College Edition, your online library of archived journal articles and periodicals dating back 22 years. If your instructor ordered InfoTrac College Edition with this book, you can access it from your CD-ROM, or go directly to http://www.infotrac-college.com/ wadsworth and use the passcode from the InfoTrac College Edition card that came with your book. For this chapter, try these search terms: *aggression, violence, relational aggression, frustration, excitation transfer, social learning, domestic violence, mob, erotica, pornography.*

# Social Psychology Alive: The Workbook

To apply what you've learned in this chapter to the real world, go to Chapter 11 of *Social Psychology Alive: The Workbook:*

- Venting Your Rage
- Girls and Aggression

- Violence and the Media
- Violent Video Games and Aggressive Behavior
- Sentencing
- School Violence

# Social Psychology Alive: The Videos

To see video on the topics and experiments discussed in this chapter, you can go either to Social PsychologyNow or to the CD-ROM, if your instructor assigned either one, to the following section:

- Teach Me a Lesson: Learning to Be Violent

# To Learn More

This list contains citations to books or articles that can help you learn more. These readings are good places to start if you want to gain a deeper understanding of the topics in this chapter.

- Baron, R. A., & Richardson, D. (1994). *Human aggression.* New York: Plenum Press.

- Berkowitz, L. (1993). *Aggression: Its causes, consequences, and control.* New York: McGraw-Hill.
- Underwood, M. K. (2003). *Social aggression among girls.* New York: Guilford Press.

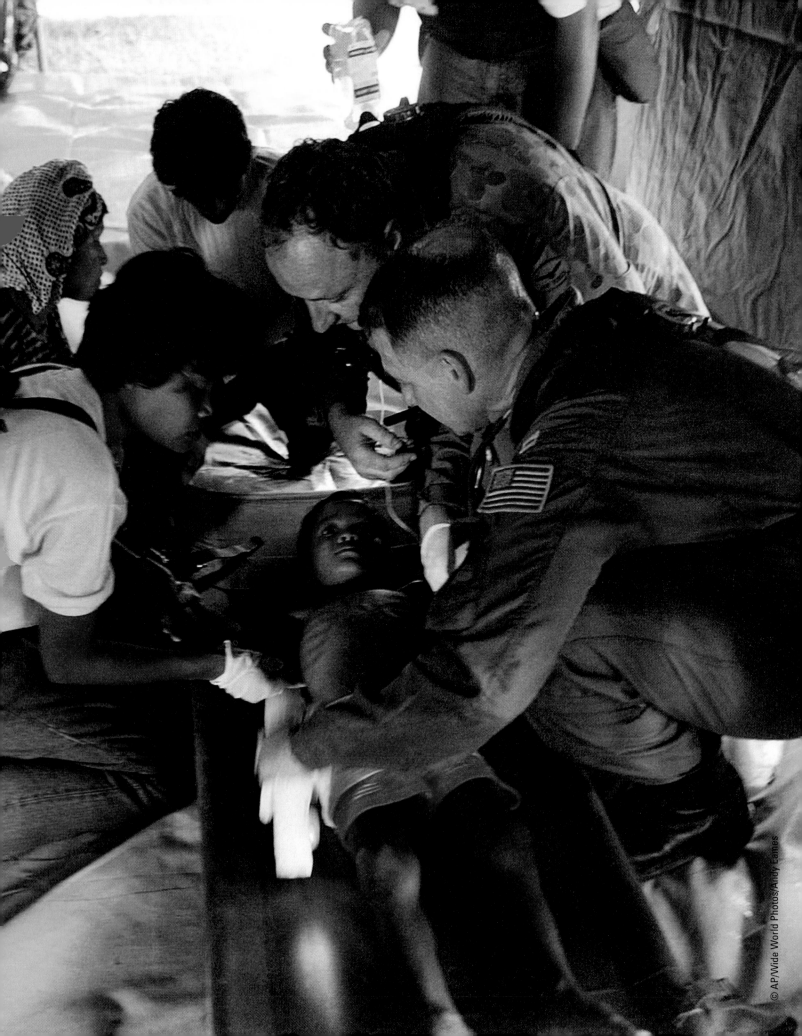

© AP/Wide World Photos/Andy Eames

# Helpful Social Behavior

When the massive waves, or tsunami, *hit the beaches of Indonesia and other countries along the Indian Ocean on December 26, 2004, they were up to 30 feet tall and traveling between 30 and 60 miles per hour—much too fast to outrun. The source of the waves was a violent earthquake, measuring 9.0 on the Richter scale (the most powerful earthquake in the world in 40 years), which occurred off the west coast of Sumatra, one of the islands comprising Indonesia in the Indian Ocean. The displacement of the ocean floor triggered immense ripples in the water that moved along the entire depth of the ocean, releasing unimaginable amounts of energy. In the open seas, the surface waves traveled up to 600 miles per hour, faster than most jet planes. Although there is a warning system for tsunamis in the Pacific Ocean, one does not exist for tsunamis in the Indian Ocean. Therefore, areas that were not breached for several hours nevertheless received no warning of the impending devastation. Most of the damage from the tsunami was caused not by the initial wave front, but instead by the huge mass of water that came in behind. The depth of the water along the flooded areas rose very suddenly, and the sheer weight of the water pulverized objects in its path, reducing buildings to their foundations and crushing vehicles, homes, and people. Many people who were not killed instantly were swept out to sea when the surge of water receded.*

*The extent of the devastation did not become clear immediately. Initial estimates of a few thousand casualties rose dramatically over the following weeks, reaching almost 250,000 deaths by the end of April, 2005, four months after the event. In Indonesia alone, 165,000 lives were lost. Other countries badly hurt by the tsunami included Sri Lanka with 31,000 deaths, India with 16,000 deaths, and Thailand with 5,400 deaths. The number of people left homeless and destitute*

The tsunami on December 26, 2004, caused enormous damage along the coastlines of the Indian Ocean, including this town of Banda Aceh, Indonesia.

© AP/Wide World Photos/Achmad Ibrahim

*by the tsunami was also in the hundreds of thousands, and these numbers included untold children left orphaned by the deaths of both parents.*

*Perhaps just as extraordinary as the tsunami was the helping response from the rest of the world to victims of the event. In the weeks following December 26, 2004, governments from around the world pledged billions of dollars to the relief effort and provided human assistance to distribute the aid and reconstruct damaged infrastructure. Also amazing was the response of individuals and small groups to the emergency. Individual donors made special contributions to agencies despite recent holiday spending; schoolchildren collected money in tin cans for victims; churches, synagogues, and mosques held auctions to raise funds; retail businesses held special sales with the profits going to tsunami survivors; and sports teams played fundraising games to raise money. People recognized that the tragedy exceeded most others in recent history and required a vast response from those able to help. One remarkable—and very modern—aspect of the helping response was the role of websites and online groups. Many sites provided ways for aid groups to obtain funds. For example, on February 15, 2005, CNN's website provided links to the websites of 78 relief agencies collecting money for tsunami victims, including agencies with Christian, Jewish, Islamic, and nonreligious affiliations. Online donations were in the hundreds of millions of dollars. The tragedy of December 26 was terrible, but the helping response from the rest of the world was inspiring. We will return to this event at several points in the chapter to illustrate theoretical concepts.*

*The purpose of this chapter is to describe social psychological research on helpful behavior. We begin by defining relevant terms, including* helping *and* prosocial behavior. *Armed with this background information, we consider a debate in social psychology about the motivation that underlies helping behavior: Are helpers sometimes motivated purely by a concern for others' welfare, or do helpers always provide assistance in order to make themselves feel good? This debate about* altruism *versus* egoism *is difficult to resolve, and many researchers have therefore turned to the more straightforward task of identifying factors that influence helping, such as norms, guilt, and modeling. We describe some of these factors. Next, we discuss volunteerism—a type of helping behavior that is usually not a response to a specific event or request but rather a commitment to provide assistance to a worthwhile organization. We then consider a specific form of helping behavior that has received a lot of attention in the popular press: bystander intervention in emergencies. We identify the psychological processes that are involved in the decision to provide emergency helping. After a brief discussion of cultural differences in helping behavior, we shift gears and consider the* recipients *of help: Are they typically thankful to receive assistance, or do they sometimes experience negative emotions? Then we discuss another form of prosocial behavior besides helping:* cooperation *in settings known as* social dilemmas, *in which actions that seem beneficial in the short term can be disastrous in the long run. Finally, we close the chapter with a discussion of* social support, *which is a form of helping behavior that is typically substantial in nature and directed at family members or close friends. It turns out that this form of support has considerable impact on recipients' physical and mental well-being.*

 ## Helping Behavior

**helping**

*behavior that is intended to assist another person*

Helpful social behavior, or **helping,** can be defined as behavior intended to assist another person; the recipient may or may not have requested assistance, but the helper perceives that aid is needed. You are being helpful when you provide directions to a lost driver, hold the door open for a stranger, pick up packages that have been dropped, or let someone in a hurry cut before you in line. These forms of helping are not very costly, and most of us give and receive such benefits every day. Helping in these ways is so common that we often take them for granted as just a basic element of social life. But other forms of helping can be more costly. People may go out of their way to return a lost wallet, offer assistance after an accident, or help to free a stranger's car stuck in the snow. Not everyone does these things, but they occur frequently. Some forms of helping are less tangible than holding open a door or pushing a car out of the snow. Often we are needed—or we need others—to provide moral support, some encouraging words, or a shoulder to cry on. This kind of emotional helping and social support is common among families and friends, and it contributes in important ways to a happy and healthy life.

**prosocial behavior**

*any action that provides benefit to others*

A broader category of behavior is **prosocial behavior,** which can be defined as any action that provides benefit to other people (Batson, 1998). Prosocial behavior encompasses helping, but it also includes actions that are not necessarily intended to assist others, such as following the rules in a game, being honest, and cooperating with others in social situations.

## Types of Helping

As our examples in the preceding paragraphs illustrate, there are many different ways in which a person can help others. Because of this diversity, it is useful to identify some basic categories of helping behaviors. Anne McGuire (1994) asked college students to describe instances of helping that they had personally experienced, either as the helper or as the recipient, and involving either friends or strangers. The students described nearly 1,500 examples of such help. These helping behaviors varied in terms of their relative frequencies, costs, benefits, causes, and consequences. McGuire proposed that the behaviors fell into four major categories. As shown in Table 12.1, these categories consisted of casual helping, emergency helping, substantial personal helping, and emotional helping. Casual helping and emergency helping typically involve strangers, whereas substantial personal helping and emotional helping typically involve family or friends. Casual helping and emotional helping can be relatively simple to perform, whereas substantial personal helping and emergency helping are potentially more difficult. Each of these categories of helping has different causes and consequences, and we will refer back to them at various points in the chapter.

In a similar effort to understand the basic dimensions of helping, Philip Pearce and Paul Amato (1980) looked at the similarities and differences among 62 helping situations. This analysis identified three major dimensions along which helping behaviors vary. The first dimension is the degree to which helping is planned or formal versus spontaneous or informal. As an example, chaperoning juvenile delin-

## TABLE **12.1**
### *Four Basic Categories of Helping Behaviors*

| Category | Examples |
|---|---|
| Casual helping | Giving someone a snack |
| | Answering a short question |
| | Lending a pen |
| Emergency helping | Offering assistance or calling for help after an accident or injury |
| | Returning a wallet or money |
| | Taking someone to the hospital in an emergency |
| Substantial personal helping | Giving a ride longer than 20 miles |
| | Doing laundry for someone |
| | Sending homemade food |
| Emotional helping | Giving moral support; being supportive |
| | "Being there" for someone; providing security and loyalty |
| | Comforting someone |

Adapted from McGuire, 1994, "Helping behaviors in the natural environment: Dimensions and correlates of helping." *Personality and Social Psychology Bulletin*, 20; 45—56.

quents on a trip to the zoo is usually planned well in advance, whereas giving the correct directions to a stranger on the street is usually done spontaneously. The second dimension of helping situations involves the seriousness of the problem. Giving someone change to make a phone call is not a very serious situation, whereas giving help to a heart attack victim is quite serious. The third dimension found by Pearce and Amato involves a distinction between "giving what you have" and "doing what you can." When you donate money to a charity or share food with friends, you are providing help by *giving what you have.* When you break up a fight or pick up a dropped package for someone, you are providing help by *doing what you can.*

Can you envision how these dimensions might relate to the categories of helping identified by McGuire (1994)? Casual helping is typically unplanned and not serious; it can involve either giving what you have (e.g., giving money to a street musician) or doing what you can (e.g., opening a door for another person). Like casual helping, emergency helping is also usually unplanned, but it is serious and always involves doing what you can (e.g., contacting the police after an accident). Substantial personal helping is typically planned; it is often serious and can involve either giving what you have (e.g., donating a significant sum of money) or doing what you can (e.g., providing long-term social support to a sick relative). Finally, emotional helping is usually planned and involves doing what you can; it can be either serious (e.g., comforting a friend who has lost a family member) or not serious (e.g., expressing encouragement to someone who will soon write an exam). Thinking about the intersection of these two categorization schemes underscores just how diverse helping behaviors can be.

Courtesy of James Olson

When you help a neighbor shovel her driveway, you are providing help by *doing what you can.*

## Altruism Versus Egoism

Social psychologists have been very interested in the question of *why* individuals help others (e.g., Batson, 1991; Schroeder, Penner, Dovidio, & Piliavin, 1995). What motivates individuals to offer assistance to people whom they often don't even know? After all, most types of helping impose some cost on the helper, such as time, money, or even physical danger. Yet despite these costs, helping behaviors happen frequently. Two basic explanations have been proposed to account for helping behaviors.

**Help Others and Help Yourself.** Think back to some instances in which you have helped another person. Perhaps you provided local directions, gave some change to a homeless person, held the door open for someone in a wheelchair, or donated money to a charity. You certainly provided a benefit to another person. But didn't you also feel pretty good about yourself? And those pats on the back or looks of approval from others didn't hurt either. Maybe the reward was just an internal one—wouldn't Mom be proud of me? These points illustrate that one consequence of helping others is that it makes *you* feel good too. And what about those times when you chose *not* to help another in need? You passed by a motorist in distress, avoided eye contact with a panhandler, or didn't offer directions to a stranger who was clearly lost. Did you feel a twinge of guilt? Perhaps you tried to rationalize it, but those looks of disapproval from others hurt. It does not take long for us to learn that helping is associated with rewards and other positive outcomes, and that not helping is associated with punishments and other negative outcomes. In the end, perhaps our prosocial actions are really driven by a self-centered desire to obtain rewards and avoid punishments. This is an **egoistic motivation** for helping. The outcome of helping may indeed provide some benefit to another, but the helper's true motivation—the end goal—is to gain some benefit for the self.

**egoistic motivation**

*a motive for helping in order to obtain rewards or avoid punishments*

**altruistic motivation**

*a motive for helping purely for the sake of providing benefit to another person*

**Helping Others for Others' Sake.** Yet surely there are times when the intent of the helper is to benefit another without regard for personal rewards or punishments. An **altruistic motivation** for helping is when the helper's end goal is simply to provide some benefit to another. The helper may gain some benefit along the way, but that is not the reason for helping. Try to think of instances of pure altruism—helping that is motivated only out of a concern for another's welfare. Suppose a man discovers that his 5-year-old daughter is trapped inside a burning building. Without concern for his own life, the man rushes in to save his daughter. Does this count as altruism? Certainly the man is concerned more about the welfare of another person than about himself. And it is doubtful that he is motivated by a desire for public recognition or social approval. Or consider a woman who offers to donate one of her kidneys to a sister who will surely die without the transplant. The operation is painful and dangerous. It is hard to imagine anything other than an altruistic motivation.

The distinction between egoistic and altruistic motivations for helping, however, is not clear-cut. The problem is that we cannot directly observe the reason for people's helping; we must somehow infer the underlying motivation or internal state of the helper. This has proven to be extremely difficult. Consider, for example, an anonymous donor who gave a large sum of money to help victims of the tsunami, but who refused to be identified or otherwise given credit. Is this altruism or egoism? Perhaps the donor was acting on the pure desire to help others, with no concern about gaining social approval or self-satisfaction, which would be an altruistic motivation. But it is also possible that the donor was acting on the need to feel useful, or to compensate for the guilt of having refused an earlier request for assistance, which would be egoistic reasons for helping. We could ask the donor directly, but he or she may be reluctant or unable to reveal the true reason. And it is quite possible that both motivations contribute simultaneously—a mixture of altruism and egoism.

**The Evolution of Altruism?** Perhaps a more basic question relevant to the issue of altruism versus egoism is: why would people *ever* be altruistic? It hardly seems to be in one's self-interest to make a large sacrifice in favor of another person. There is plenty to be lost when a father risks his own life to save his daughter or when a sister donates her kidney. In both cases, we can list many reasons for not helping. What, then, would motivate a person to be altruistic? One explanation is an evolutionary one, based on the principle of **inclusive fitness** (Hamilton, 1964). This principle refers to the idea that some social behaviors have been selected during the course of evolution because they increase the survival of our *genes*—not necessarily within us, but within other relatives (Kenrick, Li, & Butner, 2003). For example, by saving his daughter, the father is improving the odds that some of his own genes will survive—whether or not he survives. In early human history, people lived in small hunter–gatherer bands, in which members were highly interdependent and often related. Therefore, altruism toward any member of the band could potentially benefit one's own genes as well.

Inclusive fitness may explain why people are willing to sacrifice their own personal resources (including their lives) in favor of offspring and other close genetic relatives (Dawkins, 1976; Kenrick et al., 2003). When Eugene Burnstein, Christian Crandall, and Shinobu Kitayama (1994) asked college students whom they would most likely help in a number of everyday and life-and-death situations, the students said they would rather help a brother (close kin) than a nephew or a cousin (more distant kin). Similarly, Gregory Webster (2003) found that students said they would distribute more money from a lottery win to close relatives than to more distant relatives (see also Neyer & Lang, 2003).

If altruism toward kin can have survival benefits for people's genes, then some sort of motivational or emotional state presumably evolved in humans to induce them to behave altruistically toward kin. Martin Hoffman (1981) suggested that the state of *empathy* provides a motivational mechanism for altruistic behavior.

Imagine that you have just observed a friend accidentally touch the red-hot element of a stove. "Ouch! That hurts!" you exclaim. You can almost feel the pain yourself. The ability to comprehend how another person experiences a situation is known as **empathy** (Davis, 1996). You may recall from Chapter 11, Aggression and Violence, that empathy reduces the likelihood of aggressive behavior (e.g., it can reduce road rage; see page 459). Empathy for someone in need increases the likelihood that an individual will be helpful to that person (e.g., Levy, Freitas, & Salovey, 2002; Schlenker & Britt, 2001).

We are more likely to feel empathy with others who are similar to us, because their similarity makes it is easier to imagine what they are feeling. Empathy is also easier with familiar others, because our knowledge of them makes it easier to put ourselves in their shoes. These factors will work to make us especially empathic with kin, who tend to be similar and well known to us. Thus, by evolving the capacity for empathy, humans evolved a motivation that induced helpful behavior selectively directed toward genetic relatives.

**Empathy–Altruism Hypothesis.** Some social psychologists have suggested that the helping triggered by empathy is often altruistic—it is not motivated out of a concern for one's own well-being. According to this **empathy–altruism hypothesis**, feelings of empathy for a person can lead to behavior that is truly aimed at helping that person, such as an adult's altruism toward a child in need (Batson, 1991, 1998).

On the other hand, the empathy–helping relationship can be interpreted as yet another version of egoistic motivation. The *real* reason you help is to escape your own distress. Suppose you see that another person is in need of help—he or she has just dropped a bag of groceries, and canned goods are rolling in every direction. How would that make you feel? If you empathize, it should cause you to experience some distress yourself—almost as if it were you who had dropped the

The principle of *inclusive fitness* provides one explanation for why people behave altruistically toward close genetic relatives.

**inclusive fitness**
*the principle that some social behaviors have been selected during the course of evolution because they increase the survival of our genes*

**empathy**
*the ability to comprehend how another person is experiencing a situation*

**empathy–altruism hypothesis**
*the idea that feelings of empathy for a person can lead to behavior that is motivated solely by wanting to help that person*

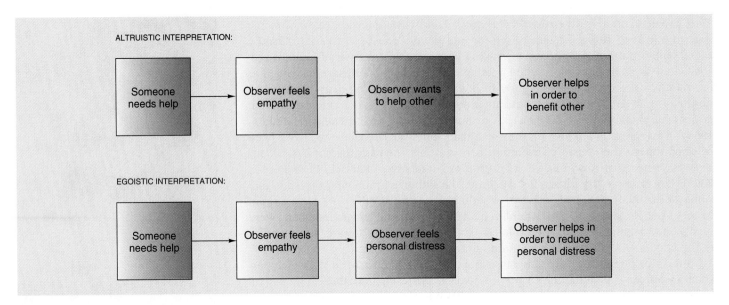

ALTRUISTIC INTERPRETATION:

Someone needs help → Observer feels empathy → Observer wants to help other → Observer helps in order to benefit other

EGOISTIC INTERPRETATION:

Someone needs help → Observer feels empathy → Observer feels personal distress → Observer helps in order to reduce personal distress

**FIGURE 12.1** Altruistic and egoistic interpretations of how empathy leads to helping

bag. This is not a pleasant feeling, and most people would want to make themselves feel better. How? By helping to pick up the cans. The victim will be grateful, and others will see you as a kind and generous person. And in the process, you will have shed your own distress. These two competing interpretations of the effects of empathy are depicted in the flowchart in Figure 12.1.

How can the empathy–altruism hypothesis be tested against an egoistic interpretation of empathy? This has proven to be difficult, and it has led to heated debate in the research literature. Let's look at a couple of examples of how this debate has developed. If you are interested in learning more, social psychologist Mark Davis (1996) provides a very nice summary of this research controversy.

Suppose you find that a person is in need of help. You empathize—you feel his/her pain. You could help, but doing so will cause some distress or discomfort for yourself. Daniel Batson and his coworkers (Batson, Duncan, Ackerman, Buckley, & Birch, 1981) created a laboratory version of this situation. Female students at the University of Kansas arrived at the laboratory for what they thought was a study of task performance under stressful conditions. The students were told that they would be paired with another female student, and that one of them would be randomly selected to perform a task under aversive conditions while the other would observe. The aversive conditions involved performing a memory task while receiving electric shocks at random intervals. In fact, there was no second student. Under the guise of showing up late, the participants were told that the "other student" had been led to another room, but that she could be observed through a closed-circuit television monitor. What the real participants actually saw on the monitor was a prerecorded video.

A drawing was then held, which was rigged so that the real participant always drew the role of observer and the other student—her name was Elaine—always drew the role of worker. It became clear during the course of observation that Elaine (actually a videotaped actor) was quite distressed upon receiving the first few shocks. When the experimenter (appearing as part of the videotaped act) expressed concern, Elaine explained that a childhood experience—being thrown by a horse onto an electric fence—had made her especially sensitive to electric shock. The experimenter offered to end the study, but Elaine said that she wanted to go on. Then the experimenter proposed that the observer might be willing to change places with her.

That was fine with Elaine, so the experimenter went to ask the real participant if she would be willing to trade places and receive the electric shocks in Elaine's place.

Unknown to the participants in the experiment, they had been randomly assigned to one of four conditions. Two conditions were designed to create high empathy for Elaine, whereas two created low empathy. In the high empathy conditions, the student learned that she and Elaine were very similar in their attitudes and values (on the basis of a survey completed earlier in the semester). In the low empathy conditions, the student learned that she and Elaine were very different in their attitudes and values. The empathy–altruism hypothesis predicts that the high empathy conditions should arouse altruistic motivation, whereas the low empathy conditions should arouse egoistic motivation.

A second manipulation was designed to make it either easy or difficult for the participants to avoid watching Elaine continue to receive the shocks. In the easy escape conditions, the participant was told that if she did not trade places, she would *not* continue to observe Elaine receive the remaining shocks—these instructions provided an easy escape from the distress of watching Elaine suffer. In the difficult escape conditions, however, the participant was told that if she did not trade places, she would continue to observe Elaine receiving the shocks.

Participants then had to decide whether or not to help by trading places. When it was difficult to escape, the choice was expected to be to help whether participants were egoistically or altruistically motivated. After all, if they were egoistically motivated, then helping was the best way to reduce their own distress, since they would otherwise be forced to watch Elaine receive more shocks. And if they were altruistically motivated, then helping was the only way to reduce Elaine's distress. Either way, helping was likely to occur. The more interesting circumstances were when escape was easy. If participants were egoistically motivated, then choosing not to help (escaping) was the best way to minimize their own distress—they wouldn't have to observe Elaine anymore and they wouldn't have to receive the shocks themselves. But if they were altruistically motivated, then helping was still the only way to reduce Elaine's distress.

The results of the study are presented in Figure 12.2. The only condition in which low helping rates occurred was when low empathy had been induced and escape from watching Elaine's suffering was easy. In both of the high empathy conditions, in which altruistic motivation was presumably aroused, more than 80% of the participants offered to trade places with Elaine, irrespective of how easy it was for them to escape. In the low empathy conditions, helping depended on ease of escape. When escape was difficult, more than 60% of the participants offered to trade places, but presumably for egoistic reasons. When escape was easy, on the other hand, only 18% offered to help.

The results from this experiment are consistent with the empathy–altruism hypothesis, and similar patterns of results have been obtained in other experiments reported by Batson and his colleagues (e.g., Batson, O'Quin, Fultz, Vanderplas, & Isen, 1983; for reviews, see Batson, 1991, 1998; Davis, 1996). These studies call our attention especially to the combination of high empathy and easy escape. It is this combination of factors that is hypothesized to reflect altruistic motivation when people help.

But Robert Cialdini and his colleagues (Cialdini, Schaller, Houlihan, Arps, Fultz, & Beaman, 1987) have challenged this interpretation. In particular, they suggest that the combination of high empathy and a suffering victim causes observers to feel sadness, even when escape is easy. People don't like to feel sad and will often help a victim in distress in an effort to make themselves feel better (Baumann, Cialdini, & Kenrick, 1981)—an egoistic rather than altruistic motivation for helping.

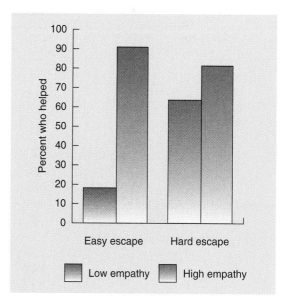

**FIGURE 12.2** Percent who helped in each condition

From Batson et al., "Is empathic emotion a source of altruistic motivation?" *Journal of Personality and Social Psychology,* 40, 290–302, Table 2, p. 296, 1981. Copyright © 1981 by the American Psychological Association. Reprinted by permission.

Cialdini and his coworkers conducted their own version of the experiment done by Batson and his coworkers, but with some additional conditions and measures. Cialdini and his colleagues found two results that point to egoistic helping under conditions of high empathy and easy escape. First, the amount of helping was directly related to the extent of the observer's reported sadness: the more sadness reported by the observer, the more likely it was that help was offered. Second, when the observers were led to believe that helping would not relieve their sadness, they no longer offered to help. Thus, even under conditions designed to bring out altruistic helping, it is difficult to rule out egoistic concerns entirely.

**An Unresolved Debate.** Researchers continue to address this matter of egoistic versus altruistic motivations for helping. On one side of the debate are those who believe that helping is almost always the result of egoistic motivations (e.g., Maner, Luce, Neuberg, Cialdini, Brown, & Sagarin, 2002). On the other side are those who believe that empathy elicits pure altruism in some circumstances (e.g., Batson, Chang, Orr, & Rowland, 2002; Batson, et al., 2003). The jury is still out on this one. Perhaps it doesn't matter whether people help because they want to make themselves feel better or because they care only about the other person, so long as they help. After all, no matter why it occurs, helping is a good thing. It may be more important simply to identify the factors that influence whether people help or not. Many social psychologists have taken this perspective, not worrying about the underlying motivation behind helping but simply focusing on situational and personal variables that predict helping. In the next section, we review some of these factors.

## Factors Influencing Helping

In the following paragraphs, we discuss six factors that influence helping behavior. The research we describe has focused on low-cost helping to strangers, mainly because this kind of helping can be studied in a controlled fashion relatively easily (e.g., by staging an event that may elicit helping). This kind of helping falls into the category of *casual helping* identified by McGuire (1994). In terms of Pearce and Amato's (1980) dimensions underlying helping, most of these studies focused on helping that is spontaneous and not very serious. We should note, however, that the principles we discuss in this section probably apply to any kind of helping, including actions that fall into McGuire's categories of substantial personal helping and emotional helping.

**Social Norms.** One explanation for helping behavior, perhaps especially low-cost helping, is that it is prescribed by *social norms,* which are culturally defined rules or guidelines about what behaviors are proper and improper (see Chapter 8, page 309). For example, the **norm of social responsibility** dictates that we should help those who need help (Berkowitz, 1972). It is easy to demonstrate this norm. Try it for yourself: simply approach a stranger in a public place and ask if he/she would tell you the time of day. In all likelihood, you will receive the help you request. Bibb Latané and John Darley (1970) had their students at Columbia University walk the streets of New York City making simple requests of passersby. More than 80% agreed to tell a student what time it was or how to get to Times Square. Even the more intrusive request of change for a quarter was granted by 73% of the strangers. Although these figures may not surprise you, such high rates of compliance show that people generally accept the norm that they should be helpful when it is simple to do so. Fewer people were willing to reveal their names (39%) or to give the student a dime (34%). But when Latané and Darley's students tacked on an explanation for wanting a dime—"I need to make a telephone call" or "My wallet

**norm of social responsibility**

*the rule or guideline that we should help those who need help, if possible*

has been stolen"—they doubled their chances of getting the money. Help is given to those who appear to have a need.

It seems likely that media coverage following the tsunami on December 26, 2004, as well as the helpful responses of governments and organizations, made some people think about the norm of social responsibility. Awareness of the norm may then have motivated some people to make a contribution.

Another social norm is the *norm of reciprocity*, which we defined in Chapter 8 as the principle that we should give back in return any favors that are done for us (see page 322; Gouldner, 1960). This norm instructs us to help those who have helped us in the past and can be utilized to increase our chances of receiving help. When Latané and Darley's (1970) students volunteered their names before asking for a dime, they improved their success from 34% to 50%. A one-for-one trade of the same "commodity" works even better—when the students gave their own name, they were able to get 59% of the strangers to reciprocate by revealing their names.

Shalom Schwartz (1977) pointed out that social norms will guide helping only to the extent that those norms have been internalized and incorporated as part of individuals' own values. Schwartz referred to these as **personal norms**—expectations for oneself in particular situations. If you have internalized the norm of social responsibility, and you see it as appropriate or fitting in a particular helping situation, then you are likely to help. On the other hand, if you have not adopted this norm as an important personal value, or you don't see it as applying in the situation, then you are less likely to help. Schwartz's model explains why broad social norms fail to predict helping for some people (see Batson, 1998).

The *norm of social responsibility* tells us to help those who need help.

**personal norms**

*guidelines that have been internalized to become expectations for oneself in particular situations*

**Modeling Helpful Behavior.** Observing the actions of a helpful model increases individuals' helpfulness (e.g., Sarason, Sarason, Pierce, Shearin, & Sayers, 1991). A classic demonstration of this effect was reported by James Bryan and Mary Ann Test (1967). On two consecutive Saturday afternoons, a broken-down car was planted on a busy road in Los Angeles. It was a Ford Mustang, with a flat left-rear tire and an inflated spare leaning against it. Any passerby could easily see the flat tire and a woman standing by the car waiting for some help. An experimenter watched from nearby, counting the number of cars that passed and the number of motorists who stopped to offer assistance. In the model condition, an Oldsmobile had been planted about ¼ mile before the Mustang. Any passerby could see that the Oldsmobile was raised by a jack under the left-rear bumper while a woman was watching a man changing the flat tire. In the control condition, there was no Oldsmobile. In each condition, the experimenters waited for 2,000 would-be helpers to pass by. How often did the woman receive help with her Mustang? In the control condition, 35 motorists stopped to offer assistance. In the model condition, 58 stopped—a significant increase.

The effect of models can be seen in the influence of parents on their children's helpfulness. Paul Mussen and Nancy Eisenberg-Berg (1977) reported that children whose parents modeled helping were themselves more helpful than children whose parents did not model helping. Presumably, modeling helpful behavior teaches children how to be helpful and shows them that helping brings positive consequences for the helper and the recipient (Batson, 1998; Grusec, 1991).

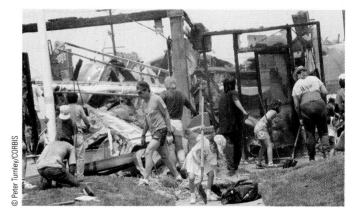

The children of parents who model helpful behavior tend to become more helpful themselves.

Modeling probably also played a role in responses to the 2004 tsunami. People saw that others were responding generously, including others who were similar to them. These models then led observers to act similarly.

**Blaming the Victim.** How would you respond if someone came up to you in a bar and asked you for some money to make a phone call, explaining that his wallet had been stolen a few minutes ago? What if he asked you for money to make a phone call and explained that he had spent his last money on a beer a few minutes ago?

This example illustrates the point that people are more receptive to the requests of victims who did not get themselves into trouble in the first place. If victims brought about their own problems, then observers tend to blame them and are less likely to offer help. For example, Greg Schmidt and Bernard Weiner (1988) asked college students to indicate their willingness to lend their notes from a previous class to another student who needed the notes either because of eye problems that had made it difficult for him to see or because he had gone to the beach instead of class. Participants also reported the extent to which they felt sympathy and anger about the request. Results showed that participants reported more willingness to lend the notes for medical reasons than for a deliberate decision to skip class, and this greater likelihood of helping was associated with reports of more sympathy and less anger. Thus, when the victim was blameworthy, participants were less willing to help.

This mention of blaming the victim may remind you of our brief discussion of Melvin Lerner's **just world theory** in Chapter 2 (see page 34), where we used the model to illustrate some characteristics of theories and hypotheses. Lerner (1980) hypothesized that humans *need* to believe that the world is a fair and just place, where individuals receive approximately what they deserve: good people tend to get rewarded, and bad people tend to suffer. When observers see individuals who are suffering innocently—through no fault of their own—their belief in a just world is threatened. One straightforward way to deal with this threat is to help the victim(s) directly, which can restore justice to the situation (see Haynes & Olson, in press). Responses from around the world to victims of the tsunami in December 2004 probably reflected, in part, people's recognition that the situation was terribly unjust. The victims were blameless, and helping them restored at least some justice to the situation. Thus, the belief in a just world can motivate helping.

But the belief in a just world can sometimes interfere with helping. When victims cannot easily be helped, especially when their suffering is also expected to continue, the situation is very threatening to the belief in a just world (see Hafer, 2000; Hafer & Bègue, 2005). In this circumstance, people may protect their belief by convincing themselves either that the victims did something to cause their own suffering or that the victims are "bad people" who, in some sense, *deserve* to suffer. By blaming the victims for their plight or devaluing their worthiness, people can maintain their belief in a just world and rationalize their own inaction. Indeed, people sometimes *look* for reasons to blame victims so they do not have to offer help.

**Good Mood.** Have you ever noticed that when you feel good, you are a little more helpful or kindly to others? It's as if the warm glow of positive feelings causes you to be more helpful. Alice Isen and Paula Levin (1972) conducted two simple but well-known experiments to confirm this intuition. In one experiment, cookies were distributed to students who were studying in the library. A control group of other students who were studying in the same library did not receive the cookies. A few minutes later, the experimenter approached each student and asked if he would be willing to help out by serving as a confederate in an experiment. The students who had received a cookie were more likely to volunteer and to offer more of their time than the students who had not received a cookie. In a second experiment, good mood was induced by having shoppers in a mall find an unexpected dime in the

**just world theory**

*a model proposing that humans need to believe that the world is a fair place where people generally get what they deserve*

coin return slot of a public telephone. A control group of shoppers had used the same phone, but did not find the unexpected money. After a shopper left the phone, the experimenter followed alongside and then dropped a manila folder full of papers. Almost 90% of the shoppers who had found the unexpected dime stopped to help the experimenter pick up the papers. In contrast, only 1 out of 25 shoppers in the control group offered such help. The effects of a good mood on helping have been replicated many times (e.g., Carlson, Charlin, & Miller, 1988; Cunningham, Shaffer, Barbee, Wolff, & Kelly, 1990), and seem to last for about 10 minutes after the positive mood has been induced (Isen, Clark, & Schwartz, 1976).

**Guilt.** To this point, we have considered only instances in which another's misfortune was not a result of the *helper's* actions—the helper did not cause the other person to need help. But sometimes we are the cause of another person's need for help—you bump into somebody and cause the person to drop a package, you spill coffee on a stranger, or you accidentally let a door slam in someone's face. It's embarrassing and it can make you feel guilty. But will it increase your chances of offering to help? The answer is yes (e.g., Carlsmith & Gross, 1969; Cunningham, Steinberg, & Grev, 1980). Moreover, people will not only try to rectify the victim's misfortune, but they will also be more helpful to others whom they did not affect.

In a classic study of guilt and helping, Vladimir Konečni (1972) utilized pedestrians on the streets of Toronto, Canada. To get a sense of the baseline rate of helping, an experimenter walked toward pedestrians and, at a distance of about 4 yards, dropped some computer key-punched cards. As he knelt down to pick them up, he said to the passerby, "Please don't step on them." Even though they were not directly asked to help, 16% nevertheless offered to assist. In a guilt-inducing condition, the experimenter approached from behind and, at the moment he caught up, brushed the pedestrian's arm and then dropped the computer cards. As before, the experimenter knelt down to pick up the cards. Under these conditions, in which the pedestrian was made to feel partly responsible for the mishap, 39% offered to assist. A third condition showed that the guilt generalized to helping others. In this condition, the experimenter was carrying some books when he absentmindedly bumped into the pedestrian, causing the books to fall. The experimenter quickly picked them up, muttering "They are not mine, and you have to do this." About 60 yards down the walkway, another experimenter staged the same card-dropping accident used in the baseline condition. Now 42% of the pedestrians who had been made to feel guilty a minute or two earlier offered to help.

**Individual Differences in Helping: The Altruistic Personality.** Some people just seem to have a helpful personality. You know the type: always willing to lend a helping hand, frequently expressing concern about the welfare of others, and constantly being kind to strangers. Other people prefer to mind their own business and do not typically show much empathy or concern about others' needs. These observations suggest that people differ in their basic predispositions to be helpful. This view was explored by Samuel and Pearl Oliner (1988), who tried to understand why, in Nazi Europe, some ordinary men and women were willing to risk their own lives to rescue Jews. Trying to distinguish between *rescuers* and *nonrescuers* during the Holocaust, the Oliners suggested that rescuers' actions were determined by "their own personal qualities . . . it was the values learned from their parents which prompted and sustained their involvement" (p. 142). (Recall our earlier discussion of parental modeling.) Through the course of extensive interviews, the Oliners concluded that rescuers differed from nonrescuers in their relationships with their parents. Rescuers consistently reported a warm and stable relationship with their parents—a kind of relationship that has been labeled a *secure attachment* (see Chapter 13 on close relationships). Nonrescuers, on the other hand, tended to report less positive relationships with their parents.

**Interpersonal Reactivity Index (IRI)**

*a measure reflecting the extent to which people feel empathy in response to others' experiences*

Experimental research on personality and helping has focused primarily on individual differences in *empathy,* the ability to imagine what another person is experiencing. The **Interpersonal Reactivity Index** (**IRI**), developed by Mark Davis (1983, 1996), was designed to measure such differences. The IRI has four parts or subscales:

- *Perspective Taking* measures the extent to which a person routinely takes the point of view of others.
- *Empathic Concern* measures the tendency of a person to experience sympathy or compassion for others.
- *Personal Distress* reflects the degree to which a person experiences distress or discomfort in response to another's extreme distress.
- *Fantasy* reflects a tendency to imagine oneself in hypothetical situations.

Selected items from the scale are reproduced in Know Yourself 12.1: Interpersonal Reactivity Index. People who score high on this scale are hypothesized to be more empathic. Answer the items in the Know Yourself feature to see whether they tend to describe you well or not.

Research has examined whether high scores on these scales are related to helping. For example, Gustavo Carlo, Nancy Eisenberg, and their coworkers (Carlo, Eisenberg, Troyer, Switzer, & Speer, 1991) gave college students the option of changing places with another student (a confederate of the experimenter) who was very upset performing an unpleasant task. Some participants were told that they would have to watch the other student complete additional trials on the task if they did not switch places (difficult escape), whereas other participants were told that they would not have to watch additional trials (easy escape). Recall from our previous discussion of the empathy–altruism hypothesis that empathy would be expected to predict helping best when escape is easy (because most people will help when escape is difficult, irrespective of their empathy). As predicted, Carlo, Eisenberg, and their colleagues found that individual differences in altruistic personality traits (including the IRI scales of Perspective Taking, Empathic Concern, and Personal Distress) predicted helping significantly when the escape from watching the clearly distressed victim was easy. Empathic individuals were helpful even when they did not "have" to be (i.e., even when escape was easy).

The same group of researchers (Eisenberg et al., 2002) reported the results of a longitudinal study of 32 individuals who were first interviewed when they were 4 or 5 years old and then interviewed again 11 times over the next 20 years. At the very first session, the children were observed in free play interactions with other children, and their behavior was coded for the frequency of several helpful acts toward other children, such as sharing toys and offering comfort. At later sessions, a variety of self-report measures of empathy and altruism were obtained. We can mention only a few of the findings here. In general, the researchers found that participants' scores on measures of altruistic personality traits were relatively stable over time: individuals who scored high in empathy and altruism in early sessions also tended to score high in later sessions. Perhaps the most remarkable finding was that individual differences in altruistic personality traits measured at ages 24 or 25 (including the IRI scales of Perspective Taking and Empathic Concern) were significantly correlated with the frequency with which those individuals had shared toys with other children during free play 20 years earlier. Sharing behavior at an early age was predictive of altruistic traits in young adulthood.

It would be interesting to investigate whether people who responded to the 2004 tsunami by making a donation or organizing a money-raising event would score highly on the IRI. Perhaps being able to empathize with (imagine themselves in the situation of) victims of the tragedy motivated them to help. The Concept Review on page 492 summarizes the factors that influence helping.

# Know Yourself 12.1
## *Interpersonal Reactivity Index*

For each of the following items, please indicate how well it describes you by circling the appropriate number on the answer scale.

1.  I try to look at everybody's side of a disagreement before I make a decision.

    | 1 | 2 | 3 | 4 | 5 |
    |---|---|---|---|---|
    | Does not describe me well | | | | Describes me very well |

2.  I often have tender, concerned feelings for people less fortunate than me.

    | 1 | 2 | 3 | 4 | 5 |
    |---|---|---|---|---|
    | Does not describe me well | | | | Describes me very well |

3.  In emergency situations, I feel apprehensive and ill at ease.

    | 1 | 2 | 3 | 4 | 5 |
    |---|---|---|---|---|
    | Does not describe me well | | | | Describes me very well |

4.  I daydream and fantasize, with some regularity, about things that might happen to me.

    | 1 | 2 | 3 | 4 | 5 |
    |---|---|---|---|---|
    | Does not describe me well | | | | Describes me very well |

5.  I sometimes try to understand my friends better by imagining how things look from their perspective.

    | 1 | 2 | 3 | 4 | 5 |
    |---|---|---|---|---|
    | Does not describe me well | | | | Describes me very well |

6.  When I see someone being taken advantage of, I feel kind of protective toward them.

    | 1 | 2 | 3 | 4 | 5 |
    |---|---|---|---|---|
    | Does not describe me well | | | | Describes me very well |

7.  I sometimes feel helpless when I am in the middle of a very emotional situation.

    | 1 | 2 | 3 | 4 | 5 |
    |---|---|---|---|---|
    | Does not describe me well | | | | Describes me very well |

8.  I really get involved with the feelings of the characters in a novel.

    | 1 | 2 | 3 | 4 | 5 |
    |---|---|---|---|---|
    | Does not describe me well | | | | Describes me very well |

9.  Before criticizing somebody, I try to imagine how I would feel if I were in their place.

    | 1 | 2 | 3 | 4 | 5 |
    |---|---|---|---|---|
    | Does not describe me well | | | | Describes me very well |

10. I would describe myself as a pretty soft-hearted person.

    | 1 | 2 | 3 | 4 | 5 |
    |---|---|---|---|---|
    | Does not describe me well | | | | Describes me very well |

11. Being in a tense emotional situation scares me.

    | 1 | 2 | 3 | 4 | 5 |
    |---|---|---|---|---|
    | Does not describe me well | | | | Describes me very well |

12. When I watch a good movie, I can very easily put myself in the place of a leading character.

    | 1 | 2 | 3 | 4 | 5 |
    |---|---|---|---|---|
    | Does not describe me well | | | | Describes me very well |

**SCORING:**

1.  *Perspective Taking:* Add up the circled numbers for Items 1, 5, and 9 for your overall perspective-taking score. Possible scores range from 3 to 15, and higher scores reflect a stronger tendency to take other people's perspectives.
2.  *Empathic Concern:* Add up the circled numbers for Items 2, 6, and 10 for your overall empathic concern score. Possible scores range from 3 to 15, and higher scores reflect more empathic concern.
3.  *Personal Distress:* Add up the circled numbers for Items 3, 7, and 11 for your overall personal distress score. Possible scores range from 3 to 15, and higher scores reflect a stronger tendency to feel distressed in emotional settings.
4.  *Fantasy:* Add up the circled numbers for Items 4, 8, and 12 for your overall fantasy score. Possible scores range from 3 to 15, and higher scores reflect a greater tendency to imagine oneself in hypothetical situations.
5.  *Total Interpersonal Reactivity:* Add up the scores for all four subscales for your overall interpersonal reactivity score. Possible scores range from 12 to 60, and higher scores reflect a stronger reactivity to the experiences of others.

Sample items from Davis, "Measuring individual differences in empathy: Evidence for a multidimensional approach," *Journal of Personality and Social Psychology, 44,* 113–126, 1983.

## CONCEPT REVIEW
### Factors Influencing Helping

| Factor | Description | Example |
| --- | --- | --- |
| Social norms | Culturally defined guidelines about proper and improper behavior | Norm of social responsibility: we should help those who need help |
| Models | Helpful actions by other people | Observe someone helping to change a flat tire |
| Blame | Victim's responsibility for getting into the situation | Help victims only when they did not get themselves into trouble in the first place |
| Good mood | Positive emotions from any cause | Find an unexpected dime in the coin return slot of a public telephone |
| Guilt | Feeling partly responsible for the victim's situation | Bump into someone, who drops what he or she is carrying |
| Individual differences | Ability to experience empathy and visualize oneself in the victim's place | Scores on the Interpersonal Reactivity Index (IRI) |

## Volunteerism

**volunteerism**

*unpaid helping behavior that is given willingly to a worthwhile cause or organization*

The studies reviewed in the preceding section focused largely on helpful actions toward individuals who need assistance at a particular time. But there is another category of helping behavior that is not in response to a specific need or request for help. This kind of helping usually involves deliberation and forethought, extends over time, can be substantial in size, and often benefits strangers. We refer here to **volunteerism**—unpaid helping behavior given willingly to a worthwhile cause or service organization. Volunteerism falls into the category of *substantial personal helping* in McGuire's categorization scheme. Surveys suggest that approximately half of the adults in the United States engage in some form of volunteerism (Penner & Finkelstein, 1998).

Do you volunteer your time to a worthwhile cause? If so, what is your motivation? Do you volunteer because you enjoy it, or are you motivated by wanting to help others? Social psychologists have directed less attention to volunteerism than to other forms of helping behavior, but researchers have begun to investigate what motivates individuals to be volunteers and what kinds of experiences as volunteers keep them involved.

Allen Omoto and Mark Snyder (1995) surveyed volunteers at AIDS organizations across the United States. The researchers proposed five distinct reasons (motives) why people might volunteer their time and developed a scale to measure these motives. They conceptualized two of the motives (values and community concern) as primarily other-oriented, or "humanitarian," motives and three (understanding, personal development, and esteem enhancement) as primarily self-oriented, or "egoistic," motives. Each hypothesized motive is listed below with two sample items from the scale:

- *Values.* Because I enjoy helping other people. Because of my personal values, convictions, and beliefs.

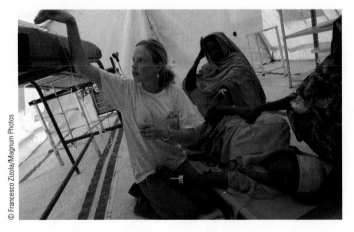

What motivates people to become volunteers?

© Francesco Zizola/Magnum Photos

- *Community Concern.* Because of my concern and worry about the gay community. To help members of the gay community.
- *Understanding.* To understand AIDS and what it does to people. To learn more about how to prevent AIDS.
- *Personal Development.* To challenge myself and test my skills. To meet new people and make new friends.
- *Esteem Enhancement.* To feel better about myself. To feel needed.

Omoto and Snyder (1995) used their measures of these motives, as well as participants' reports of personal experiences as a volunteer, to predict how long the participants had served as AIDS volunteers. The results were interesting. First, satisfaction with one's experiences as a volunteer predicted tenure: participants who had served the longest reported being very satisfied with their experiences as a volunteer (e.g., their experiences had been interesting, and they looked forward to their volunteer work). Second, Omoto and Snyder found that the relatively self-oriented, egoistic motives for being a volunteer were associated with longer tenure. That is, participants who joined the organization to gain understanding about AIDS, to develop themselves personally, or to enhance their esteem tended to be long-serving volunteers. In contrast, joining because of one's values or because of concern about the gay community did not predict length of service as a volunteer.

Louis Penner and Marcia Finkelstein (1998), however, reported a somewhat different pattern of findings in another sample of volunteers at AIDS organizations. Penner and Finkelstein replicated the finding that satisfaction with one's experiences as a volunteer was important. But in terms of the motives identified by Omoto and Snyder (1995), Penner and Finkelstein found that the only significant predictor of participants' length of service was the other-oriented motive of values: people who joined because they enjoy helping other people tended to be long-serving volunteers. Penner and Finkelstein also included a measure of individual differences in empathy, which included items from the Perspective Taking, Empathic Concern, and Personal Distress subscales of the Interpersonal Reactivity Index described in the preceding section. High scores on this measure of empathy were associated with longer service as a volunteer. Thus, Penner and Finkelstein's findings suggest that humanitarian motives and an empathic personality describe long-serving volunteers (see also Simon, Stürmer, & Steffens, 2000).

Mark Davis, Jennifer Hall, and Marnee Meyer (2003) surveyed volunteers in nine different organizations, only one of which was AIDS related. These researchers obtained additional evidence that satisfaction with one's experiences as a volunteer predicts helping: the extent to which participants were satisfied with their volunteer experiences strongly predicted the amount of time they donated per week. Also, the researchers found that the extent to which participants felt that their motives for joining the group had been fulfilled—whether those motives were other-oriented or self-oriented—predicted their satisfaction with their experiences. Thus, it appears that either humanitarian or egoistic motives can increase volunteerism, so long as individuals feel that their motives are being met by the volunteer experience.

In an interesting extension of work on the motives underlying volunteering, Marc Kiviniemi, Mark Snyder, and Allen Omoto (2002) found that respondents who had only one principal motive for becoming a volunteer (e.g., personal development) reported less stress and more satisfaction with their volunteer activities than did respondents who had two or more important motives for becoming a volunteer (e.g., personal development and community concern). Why might this effect of multiple motives occur? It is possible that conflict between the different motives, with each being satisfied by different experiences, causes stress and dissatisfaction (see also Grube & Piliavin, 2000). So perhaps it is advantageous to have just one overriding reason for volunteering, because roles and activities in the charitable organization can then be chosen to satisfy the single central motive.

# Emergency Helping

On February 12, 1993, two 10-year-old boys, Robert Thompson and Jon Venables, kidnapped and murdered 2-year-old James Bulger in Liverpool, England. The case was shocking and tragic in many respects, including the ages of those involved. But in terms of a social psychological analysis of helping in emergency settings, one important part of this incident was that several adults saw the three boys together and wondered whether something was wrong, but did not pursue their suspicions. Thompson and Venables, who were troubled boys with a history of theft and truancy, saw Bulger at a shopping mall and decided to kidnap him "just for the hell of it." They took him by the hand and led him out of the mall (security cameras at the mall videotaped them leaving, which led to their arrests after Bulger's body was found). It seems that their initial intentions were to beat up Bulger and leave him lost. They first took the boy to an isolated area beside a canal, where they picked him up and dropped him on his head, which caused a big bruise and cut on his forehead. They then walked around aimlessly for about two hours with the little boy, trying to decide what to do and where to leave him. It was during this period that they were seen by several adults. Most of these adults assumed that the boys were brothers and the older boys were trying to deal with an uncooperative younger brother. One elderly woman noticed that Bulger was crying and injured; she approached the boys and asked them what the problem was. The boys said they had just found Bulger lost at the bottom of the hill. The woman suggested the boys take Bulger to the police station down the road, but then did nothing as the boys went off in the opposite direction. Later, another woman who was walking a dog saw the bruise on Bulger's head and said she would accompany the boys to the police station, but when another adult who was present refused to watch her dog, she didn't argue when the boys said they knew the way and walked off. Eventually, the boys took Bulger to another isolated location next to railroad tracks, where they beat him severely and left him dying. His body was found two days later.

Why didn't the adults investigate more carefully when they were suspicious about the boys? There was no physical intimidation involved—the 10-year-olds were children themselves. Primarily, it seems that the witnesses were uncertain about the seriousness of the situation. Some assumed that the boys were related; others probably didn't want to get involved and convinced themselves that nothing was wrong. The two women who directly confronted the boys had no particular reason to doubt their story about having found the 2-year-old, although the subsequent actions of the boys (heading off in the wrong direction) should perhaps have

Why didn't the adults who saw 2-year-old James Bulger in the company of Robert Thompson and Jon Venables investigate the situation more thoroughly?

© MER/CORBIS SYGMA
© MER/CORBIS SYGMA

triggered deeper suspicion and additional actions. The end result is that we are left with a terrible tragedy that took one boy's life and brought enormous pain to several families.

Social psychologists have been interested in the processes involved in deciding to intervene in a potential emergency. McGuire (1994) included *emergency helping* as one of her four major categories of helping behavior. You may have read about cases of bystander apathy, where someone was assaulted on a subway or sidewalk, or someone collapsed in a public place, and bystanders did nothing to intervene or help the victim. What goes through the minds of bystanders in these kinds of situations?

**The Decision Tree.** Bibb Latané and John Darley (1970) conducted one of the most famous series of studies in social psychology to investigate the dynamics of bystander intervention in emergencies. Their research was guided by a theoretical analysis that specified a series of decisions that must be made before a bystander will intervene in an emergency. This **decision tree** is presented in Figure 12.3. Latané and Darley proposed that in order for intervention to occur, five separate things must happen: the bystander must (1) notice the event, (2) interpret the event as an emergency, (3) accept personal responsibility for helping, (4) decide on an appropriate form of assistance, and (5) implement the action. If *any* of these steps does not occur, then the bystander will not intervene. For example, someone might notice an event and interpret it as an emergency, but if he or she does not assume responsibility for helping, intervention will not happen.

In the following paragraphs, we discuss each step in the decision tree. We also describe some fascinating experiments that have illuminated the psychological processes that underlie the first three steps. We conclude by identifying some techniques that people can use to improve the odds that they will receive help in an emergency.

**Notice the Event.** Before intervention in an emergency can occur, one requirement is that people must notice the event. This point may seem obvious, but the real world is full of distractions and complications that can interfere with attention to emergencies. John Darley and Daniel Batson (1973) used a simple manipulation to interfere with participants' awareness of events around them: time pressure.

Participants in this experiment were students attending the Princeton Theological Seminary. The students were told that they would be delivering a talk on one of two topics in another building. For half of the students, the assigned topic was the parable of the Good Samaritan (see sidebar). For the other half of the students, the assigned topic was unrelated to the theme of helping. The students were given directions to the other building and then were exposed to the manipulation of time pressure: some of the students were told that they really had to hurry, because they were already late (high hurry condition); other students were told that they should not delay, because they had just enough time to make it (intermediate hurry condition); a third group was told that there was no rush, because they had lots of time to get there (low hurry condition).

On their way to the other building, the students passed by a "victim" who was sitting slumped in a doorway, in obvious need of assistance (he was actually an actor playing the

**decision tree**

*a set of five steps that must be completed before an individual will intervene in an emergency situation*

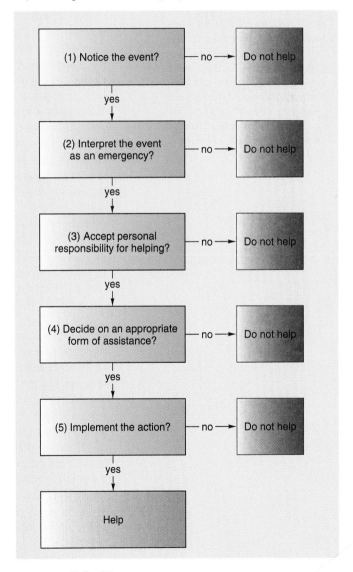

**FIGURE 12.3** The decision tree leading to bystander intervention in emergencies

Data from Latané and Darley, *The unresponsive bystander: Why does*
© 1970. Adapted by permission of Pearson Education, Inc., Upper ╴

*"And who is my neighbor?" Jesus replied, "A man was going down from Jerusalem to Jericho, and he fell among robbers, who stripped him and beat him, and departed, leaving him half dead. Now by chance a priest was going down the road; and when he saw him he passed by on the other side. So likewise a Levite, when he came to the place and saw him, passed by on the other side. But a Samaritan, as he journeyed, came to where he was; and when he saw him, he had compassion, and went to him and bound his wounds, pouring on oil and wine; then he set him on his own beast and brought him to an inn, and took care of him. And the next day he took out two dennarii and gave them to the innkeeper, saying 'Take care of him; and whatever more you spend, I will repay you when I come back.' Which of these three, do you think, proved neighbor to him who fell among the robbers?" He said, "The one who showed mercy on him." And Jesus said to him, "Go and do likewise."*
*[Luke 10:29–37 RSV]*

part). The manipulation of time pressure exerted a strong effect on whether participants stopped to help the victim: the percentage of students who helped was 63% in the low hurry condition, 45% in the intermediate hurry condition, and only 10% in the high hurry condition. Participants in the high hurry condition typically claimed that they did not see the victim in the doorway. Thus, even the first step of noticing the event can sometimes derail helping.

Interestingly, the topic of participants' talk (Good Samaritan or unrelated to helping) had no effect on helping. It may seem ironic that *seminary* students on their way to give a talk about the *Good Samaritan parable* helped only 10% of the time when they were in a rush, but these findings underscore the importance of situational factors such as time pressure.

**Interpret the Event as an Emergency.**   Before bystanders will intervene in an event, they must interpret it as an emergency—as a situation that calls for action of some kind. We mentioned earlier that it seems likely this step played a role in the James Bulger case. Many real-life events are ambiguous. Is this man sick or drunk? Did that person call "help" or simply cough? Are those boys fighting or just fooling around? The response that will be made in each of these cases depends on observers' interpretations.

Latané and Darley (1968) illustrated the importance of how events are interpreted in a clever study. College students attending Columbia University were invited to a discussion of problems in the lives of students at an urban university. When they arrived for the discussion, they were directed to a waiting room to complete a preliminary questionnaire. Some of the students were seated alone, whereas others were seated with two other students. Soon after they were seated, a clearly visible stream of white smoke began entering the room through a vent. The smoke continued to come into the room throughout the session, eventually becoming thick enough to partially obscure participants' vision.

When the students were waiting alone, about 75% of them got up to report the problem within 2 minutes—they interpreted the situation as one that might be dangerous. But when the students were working in groups of three, only 38% of the groups reported the smoke. In a third condition, two of the three students were actually confederates of the experimenter and only one person in each group was a real participant. The confederates were instructed to remain passive and indifferent. Only 10% of the real participants in these groups reported the smoke.

What was going through participants' minds? Those who did not report the smoke typically said that they assumed the smoke was not dangerous or was part of the experiment. But why was this conclusion more frequent in the second and third conditions, where multiple bystanders were present? Latané and Darley suggested that participants in these conditions were looking at the other participants to decide whether or not the situation was serious. When they saw other people doing nothing (e.g., the two passive confederates in the third condition), they concluded that the situation must not be an emergency. Or, at least, they were uncertain enough about the situation that they did not want to possibly make a fool of themselves by getting up and investigating the smoke. In the single-participant condition, people did not have these other bystanders affecting how they interpreted the situation, so they were more likely to decide that they should do something.

It is noteworthy that this experiment investigated a situation in which participants *themselves* may have been in danger, yet bystander apathy still occurred. Inaction was more "dangerous" than action, because failing to respond to a real fire has far worse consequences than responding when there is no real fire. In real-life emergencies, it is often dangerous for bystanders to intervene, and their inaction may sometimes be "rational" in the sense that they could be hurt. But in this smoke study, inaction was potentially dangerous, yet participants often failed to act when other bystanders were present.

## Accept Personal Responsibility for Helping.

The third step in the decision tree is that the bystander must accept personal responsibility for intervening. For example, if someone witnesses a fight at a sports event where many police are present, he or she is unlikely to feel responsible for breaking up the fight.

Darley and Latané (1968) demonstrated the importance of perceived responsibility in another study. Male students at New York University believed they were having a discussion with either one, two, or five other students. In fact, the "discussion" was all prerecorded, and only one naïve student participated at a time. When the naïve student arrived for the study, he was seated in a small room off a corridor containing a number of other small rooms. Once seated, the student was fitted with headphones and listened to the remaining instructions. He was told that he would be participating in a discussion with one, two, or five other students, and that all the students would take turns talking for 2 minutes about themselves and their personal problems. It was explained that the headphones and the separate cubicles would help protect everyone's anonymity. The experimenter would *not* be listening, and only the *speaker's* microphone would be turned on at any given time. During one of the other student's second turn speaking (actually a prerecording), he could be heard having a seizure. He said that he was having a problem, and that he could really use some help. The experimenter waited in the corridor to observe how long it took the naïve student to come out of the room to look for help (recall that only the speaker's microphone was allegedly turned on).

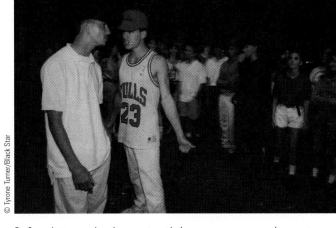

Before intervening in a potential emergency, people must accept personal responsibility to help.

When the group size was believed to be two—just the student and the seizure victim—every single student got up to help within 3 minutes. When the group size appeared to be three—the student, the victim, and one other—85% of the students responded within 3 minutes. But when the group size appeared to be six—the student, the victim, and four others—only 62% of the students ever responded to the victim's plea for help. Thus, the greater the number of perceived bystanders, the less likely a participant was to come to the victim's aid.

What explains the reduced helping in the (apparently) larger groups? Personal responsibility is probably the critical factor. Participants who believed that other bystanders were present felt less personal responsibility for helping the victim, because others could help just as well. Their *interpretation* of the event seems unlikely to have been affected by the other alleged bystanders, because they were always by themselves in a room. Rather, their beliefs about how many other bystanders were present influenced whether they felt responsible for helping the victim.

Another experiment, by Bibb Latané and Judith Rodin (1969), probably influenced both participants' interpretation of the situation and their sense of responsibility for helping. Imagine that you have just arrived for a marketing research study, and you are seated alone in a small room to complete a questionnaire. The marketing representative tells you that she will be working in the office next door. The two rooms are separated by a collapsible divider. As you are working, you can hear the woman climbing on a chair, probably trying to reach something on a bookcase. Then you suddenly hear a loud crash and a scream. "Oh, my god, my foot...I...I...can't move it!" The woman moans in obvious pain. "Oh, my ankle! I can't get this thing off me!" What would you do? Would you get up to check on her?

When Latané and Rodin conducted this experiment with students at Columbia University, 70% offered to help, usually by getting up from their seat and opening the room divider. But that was when the students were alone. Other students were brought together in pairs—two strangers seated at the same table working on their questionnaires. In only 40% of the two-stranger groups did either member of the pair come to her assistance. It was even worse when the experimenter planted a confederate to sit in the room with an unknowing student. The confederate was instructed to be passive: during the emergency he looked up, shrugged his shoulders, and then went back to work on his questionnaire. In these cases, fewer than 10% of the naïve participants went to check on the woman.

In this experiment, bystanders presumably had dual effects. When the other bystander did not immediately assist the woman, participants were more likely to think, "she's probably fine" (benign interpretation of the event) and "it's not my responsibility anyway" (denial of personal responsibility). Each of these inferences would reduce the likelihood that individuals would intervene.

**bystander effect**

*the likelihood that an individual will intervene in an emergency goes down as the number of bystanders increases*

This inhibitory effect of bystanders on the likelihood of an individual's helping is called the **bystander effect.** The bystander effect can be defined as follows: The likelihood that an individual will intervene in an emergency goes down as the number of bystanders increases. For example (these figures are hypothetical), individual bystanders may intervene 75% of the time in a particular emergency situation when alone, whereas these same individuals may intervene only 50% of the time when two other bystanders are also present and only 30% of the time when five other bystanders are also present. The bystander effect does not necessarily mean that victims are less likely to receive help when many bystanders are present than when only one is present. Instead, the effect refers to the probability that a *specific person* will intervene; the probability goes down as the number of bystanders increases. The bystander effect can be caused by the impact of bystanders on how events are interpreted, on feelings of responsibility to help, or both.

*Fifty women were harassed and groped in broad daylight in the midst of crowds in Central Park. Not only were the women's cries for help ignored, bystanders videotaped the assaults.*

It is possible that even *thinking about being in a group* may have a diffusing effect on perceived responsibility for helping. Stephen Garcia, Kim Weaver, Gordon Moskowitz, and John Darley (2002) used a priming procedure to get participants to visualize being with a group: participants were asked to imagine that they had won a dinner for themselves and some of their friends at their favorite restaurant. Some participants were asked to imagine that they had won dinner for themselves and 30 of their friends; others were asked to imagine that they had won dinner for themselves and 10 friends; and others were asked to imagine that they had won dinner for themselves and 1 friend. All participants then answered a question about this imaginary dinner that was intended simply to justify the imagination task. Next, the critical question (allegedly unconnected to the imagination task) was posed: participants were asked to estimate how much of their salary they expected to give to charities after they were well established in a career. Participants who had imagined a dinner with 30 friends estimated giving a smaller percentage of their salary to charity than did participants who had imagined a dinner with 10 friends, who in turn estimated giving a smaller percentage of their salary to charity than did participants who had imagined a dinner with 1 friend. A follow-up study showed that the same imagination task influenced participants' willingness to volunteer extra time for research. The researchers labeled these findings the *implicit bystander effect,* because simply thinking about being in a group produced an effect parallel to the original bystander effect.

The *bystander effect* (both original and implicit) suggests that living in large cities may foster bystander apathy. For example, residents of large cities may generally feel less responsible for the well-being of strangers than residents of small cities, because most settings in the large city have many people present. Interpreting events as nonemergencies may also be more common in large cities, with their relatively dense populations. The accompanying box, Social Psychology in Your Life: Choosing Where to Live, describes research on the relation between population density and helping.

**Decide on an Appropriate Form of Assistance.** Even when bystanders have noticed and interpreted an event as an emergency and accepted personal responsibility for helping, they must still decide how to intervene. Sometimes this step will stymie potential helpers: how can they effectively assist? For example, bystanders may sometimes lack the ability to help, such as when they do not know how to administer CPR to an apparent heart attack victim. Or people may be unsure why someone has lost consciousness: did the person choke, or have a heart attack, or what? People may also lack the necessary tools to help, such as when they see a boat in difficulty on the water; if they lack a means of offering help (e.g., their own boat), they may remain indecisive. It is true that in virtually every circumstance, people could, at the very least, *seek help* by dialing 911 or looking for other helpers, but if a bystander is trying to think of more immediate assistance, he or she may remain inactive.

**Implement the Decision to Help.** Finally, even when bystanders have noticed and interpreted an event as an emergency, accepted personal responsibility for helping, and decided how to help, they may not implement that decision

© AP/Wide World Photos/The York Dispatch, Jason Plotkin

People are more likely to intervene in an emergency when they possess relevant skills, such as knowing how to administer CPR to a heart-attack victim.

# Social Psychology in Your Life    *Choosing Where to Live*

Some social critics contend that big cities bring out the worst in human nature. Diffusion of responsibility, lack of respect for others, crime, and violence are all part of life in big cities like New York, Chicago, or Los Angeles. People also try to protect their privacy in big cities—don't bother me and I won't bother you. It is no coincidence—the critics suggest—that cases involving bystander apathy happen most often in big cities. Stanley Milgram (1970) proposed that the high population density of large urban centers necessarily creates a diffusion of social responsibility.

Robert Levine, Todd Martinez, Gary Brase, and Kerry Sorenson (1994) set out to study helping in 36 U.S. cities. In every city, they staged a number of different helping opportunities: a pen was dropped on the sidewalk, pedestrians were asked to make change for a quarter, actors played the part of a blind person needing help across the street, and so on. In addition, per capita contributions to the United Way were calculated for each city. All of these results were assembled to calculate an overall helping index. The results are presented in Table 12.2.

Results confirmed what Milgram and others have suggested: people are indeed more helpful in cities with lower population densities. For example, large cities (more than 2 million people) accounted for just 4 of the top 18 ranks, but 8 of the bottom 18 rankings. You are more likely to receive help in Rochester, NY, or East Lansing, MI, than you are in Los Angeles, CA, or New York, NY. Paul Amato (1983) found similar results across 55 communities in Australia. It seems that characteristics of large cities—especially their high population densities—set the stage for less helping (Steblay, 1987).

### TABLE 12.2
**Ranking of 36 U.S. Cities on Helping Measures**

| City | Helping Score | Rank | Size of Population |
|---|---|---|---|
| Rochester, NY | 10.81 | 1 | M |
| Houston, TX | 10.74 | 2 | L |
| Nashville, TN | 10.69 | 3 | M |
| Memphis, TN | 10.66 | 4 | M |
| Knoxville, TN | 10.62 | 5 | S |
| Louisville, KY | 10.58 | 6 | S |
| St. Louis, MO | 10.58 | 7 | L |
| Detroit, MI | 10.55 | 8 | L |
| East Lansing, MI | 10.54 | 9 | S |
| Chattanooga, TN | 10.54 | 10 | S |
| Indianapolis, IN | 10.46 | 11 | M |
| Columbus, OH | 10.42 | 12 | M |
| Canton, OH | 10.35 | 13 | S |
| Kansas City, MO | 10.33 | 14 | M |
| Worcester, MA | 10.24 | 15 | S |
| Santa Barbara, CA | 10.17 | 16 | S |
| Dallas, TX | 10.13 | 17 | L |
| San Jose, CA | 10.11 | 18 | M |
| San Diego, CA | 10.05 | 19 | L |
| Springfield, MA | 9.92 | 20 | S |
| Atlanta, GA | 9.90 | 21 | L |
| Bakersfield, CA | 9.75 | 22 | S |
| Buffalo, NY | 9.71 | 23 | M |
| San Francisco, CA | 9.66 | 24 | L |
| Youngstown, OH | 9.56 | 25 | S |
| Sacramento, CA | 9.56 | 26 | M |
| Salt Lake City, UT | 9.51 | 27 | M |
| Boston, MA | 9.50 | 28 | L |
| Providence, RI | 9.50 | 29 | S |
| Chicago, IL | 9.49 | 30 | L |
| Shreveport, LA | 9.44 | 31 | S |
| Philadelphia, PA | 9.38 | 32 | L |
| Fresno, CA | 9.34 | 33 | S |
| Los Angeles, CA | 9.26 | 34 | L |
| New York, NY | 9.03 | 35 | L |
| Paterson, NJ | 8.92 | 36 | M |

Size of population: S = small (350,000–650,000), M = medium (950,000–1,450,000), L = large
(> 2,000,000). Based on 1989 statistics.

From Levine, Martinez, Brase, & Sorenson, 1994, "Helping in 34 U.S. cities." *Journal of Personality and Social Psychology, 67,* 69–82.

for a number of reasons. Perhaps the most common cause of hesitation in real-life emergencies is perceived danger—the costs of helping are potentially too high. For example, people are hesitant to intervene in cases of assault or robbery because they may be injured. Indeed, police recommend against intervening in dangerous situations. People may also fear "becoming involved" because, in the future, the perpetrator may seek them out or they may have to go to court to testify. Another reason people may not implement a decision to help is potential embarrassment. We have been socialized to respect others' privacy and do not want to offer help that will be rejected by the victim or criticized by other bystanders. Thus, even when we think a person needs help and we know how to help, we may waver for fear of a negative response from the victim or others in the situation.

**Improving the Odds.** Armed with this knowledge about intervention in emergencies, there are things you can do to improve the chances that you will get help when you need it. Ambiguity or uncertainty should probably be your chief concern: people are less likely to help when they are uncertain that an emergency is happening. Lack of perceived personal responsibility is also an important culprit: diffusion of responsibility in a crowded situation means that individuals are less likely to step forward with assistance than if they were alone. Sometimes, others' initial reactions to an emergency are to experience fear or guilt, which will focus their attention inward on themselves or motivate them to leave the situation. Getting people to focus attention on you and *your* distress is likely to increase their empathy and helping.

Knowing these facts, Robert Cialdini (2001) suggested a very simple and straightforward way to help yourself in an emergency: "You, sir, in the blue jacket, I need your help. Call an ambulance" (p. 118). These two sentences (or something similar) are short, simple, and to the point. They clarify the situation ("I need your help"), assign personal responsibility to an individual, and identify a specific action that will assist you. You should say similar things to several bystanders if possible.

Fortunately, bystanders often do complete the five steps necessary to intervene in an emergency. Bystander apathy may be more common than we would like, but we should not downplay the heroics of some bystanders. Events like the terrorist attacks of September 11, 2001, and the tsunami of December 26, 2004, elicit remarkable acts of courage and selflessness.

# Cultural Differences in Helping

Given the previously described evidence that factors such as social norms and modeling influence helping behavior, it seems very likely that the culture into which people are socialized will affect their helping response in different settings. Yet, surprisingly little research has examined cross-cultural differences in helping behavior (Moghaddam, Taylor, & Wright, 1993).

In one investigation designed to understand how culture might influence the *development* of helping behavior, Beatrice and John Whiting (Whiting, Whiting, & Longabaugh, 1975) studied the social and family settings of children living in six locations, all small farming communities but in different cultures:

- Nyansongo, Kenya
- Juxtlahuaca, Mexico
- Tarong, Philippines
- Taira, Japan
- Khalapur, India
- Orchard Town, United States

In each locale, the researchers observed the structure of household chores, the division of family and work responsibilities, and the helping behavior of children. Examples of helpful behavior included direct help when needed (e.g., giving food to another, scratching another's insect bite), providing social support (e.g., consoling a crying baby, praising another's help), and maintaining positive relationships (e.g., greeting others in a friendly way, holding another's hand).

When children are socialized to take some responsibility for family life, they may become more helpful in other ways as well.

One important difference between these cultures was the extent to which children were socialized to be nurturant and responsible. Most notably in Kenya, Mexico, and the Philippines, children were expected to help with the household chores, the farming work of the family, and caring for younger siblings. In short, children in these cultures were socialized to take responsibility for family life. It was in these same cultures that the children scored highest in helpful behaviors. Compare that to socialization practices in the United States, where children were more likely to be competitive in school and where they were typically assigned very few family responsibilities. The Orchard Town children scored the lowest in helpful behaviors. Although considerable variability was found within each culture, it was clear that children's orientation toward others versus themselves was affected by their socialization.

We have discussed in previous chapters the dimension of individualism–collectivism (see Sorrentino, Cohen, Olson, & Zanna, 2005; Triandis, 1995). Could this difference between cultures influence people's willingness to help others? Joan Miller, David Bersoff, and Robin Harwood (1990) compared the views of children and adults living in the United States with those living in India concerning perceived responsibilities for helping others. Participants were asked whether there was a moral obligation to help people in various situations, or whether helping was instead a matter of choice. In both the United States and India, people were seen as having a moral responsibility to help their children and generally to help others in life-threatening situations. However, when it came to less serious situations and giving help to friends or strangers, the Americans regarded helping as a matter of personal choice, not moral obligation. The Indians saw things differently. Hindu culture places greater emphasis on interdependence, social duty, and mutual aid. The Indians viewed helping as a moral responsibility even when the need was less serious or when strangers were involved.

There is also evidence that, when they do give help, people from individualist cultures think it is fine to discuss one's helpfulness publicly, whereas people from collectivist cultures consider it inappropriate to tell others (Fu, Lee, Cameron, & Xu, 2001). This difference probably reflects, in part, the stronger expectations for helpfulness that exist in collectivist cultures, where helping is not really something to brag about—it is simply expected. The findings may also reflect a greater emphasis on modesty in collectivist cultures compared to individualist cultures.

## The Recipient's Reaction to Help

To this point in the chapter, we have focused on the *helper*—the motives that underlie helping, the factors that encourage people to help, and so on. But there is another side to helping—the person being helped. When someone suffers a heart attack, receiving help can mean the difference between life and death. But sometimes people do not like to be on the receiving end of help. In this section, we look at the recipient's view of helping: what it feels like to need help, and what it might say about our ability. Help can be a positive and supportive thing. But needing help, especially from strangers, can sometimes threaten our self-esteem.

Have you ever refused an offer of help? Perhaps you were carrying a load of heavy packages, and a stranger asked if you needed some help. You feel the strain building in your muscles and wonder if you really can make it out the door by yourself. "No, thanks, I can handle it," you reply. Or have you ever been lost in an unfamiliar part of town? You had no idea where you were, yet you continued to drive past gas stations where help was readily available.

Why do we sometimes resist seeking help, or even refuse an offer of help? And why does receiving help sometimes make us feel worse rather than better? Social psychological research has identified several possible reasons (Fisher, Nadler, & Whitcher-Alagna, 1982; Nadler & Fisher, 1986).

**Norm of Reciprocity.** One view is that the acceptance of aid puts you in another's debt. We have previously discussed the norm of reciprocity, which states that when someone helps you, you should help him/her in return. When the help is minor and casual, it is possible that a simple "Thank you" will suffice. But the debt is greater when someone goes out of his or her way to help. People do not generally like to be in such social debt and may be reluctant to request or accept help if they have doubts about their ability to reciprocate.

Martin Greenberg and Solomon Shapiro (1971) provided a nice illustration of this principle in a well-known early study. Students at the University of Pittsburgh participated in what they thought was a study of physical disability and work performance. Upon arrival, the student was joined by another student who was actually a confederate working for the experimenter. It was explained to the students that they would each be playing the role of a disabled worker who is trying to meet a production quota. One student—always the naïve participant—was assigned the role of a worker with a *motor* disability. This was simulated by placing the student's preferred arm in a sling. The other student—always the confederate—was assigned the role of a worker with a *visual* disability, which was simulated by wearing an eye patch and a pair of sunglasses. The students were told that they would be working on two tasks. The first task would be to construct paper boxes from sheets of paper—a task deliberately chosen because of its difficulty for the student with a simulated motor disability. The second task would be to check sheets of paper for typographical errors and to circle each error with a red pen, which was chosen because of its potential difficulty for the student with a simulated visual disability. The students were told that a quota would be set for each task, and that money could be earned by meeting and exceeding the quota. The students were also told that if one finished early, the other could ask for help:

> If either of you needs help from the other in order to meet your quota, feel free to request such assistance. Of course, neither of you is obliged to help the other. If you would like to help the other person you must first wait until he asks for assistance. Keep in mind the fact that you are not in competition with each other and that both of you can earn 50 cents and more. (p. 294)

Before they went to work on their quotas, the students were given a practice period on each of the tasks. As expected, the naïve student—who had a simulated motor disability—had a difficult time with the box-making task and was not able to finish during the allotted practice period. The other student—the confederate—was able to finish the box-making task well before the practice time was up. Practice on the typographical error task was next. The naïve student was always able to finish well within the allotted practice time. Here is where the experimental manipulation was introduced. In the reciprocation condition, the confederate was not able to complete the second task before the end of the practice time. In the no-reciprocation condition, however, the confederate finished the second task at just about the same time as the naïve participant. What were Greenberg and Shapiro trying to do? The naïve student always knew he or she would have difficulty with the box-making task, and that the other student—who could do it easily—would be a good source of help. In the reciprocation condition, an opportunity for reciprocation had been created: the naïve student was in a position to offer help on the typographical error task. In the no-reciprocation condition, however, the opportunity for reciprocation was not there, because the other student (the confederate) appeared to be good at both tasks. How often would students in the two conditions ask the other student for help?

The results were very clear. When the students perceived that they would later have an opportunity to reciprocate, 71% asked for assistance in meeting their box-making quota on the first task. But when the students perceived no such opportunity for reciprocation, only 37% requested help. Knowing that they would be able to repay the favor on the second task, students in the reciprocation condition were more favorable toward receiving help.

**Threat to Self-Esteem.** We all need help from time to time, and often we are glad to accept help when it is offered. But what does it say about you when you need help? It may signify nothing more than one of those everyday situations in which all of us, at one time or another, could use a little help. Sometimes we get lost and could use some directions. The need for such help does not mean that you are unintelligent or less capable than anyone else. But in other settings, finding yourself in need of help could suggest that you are not a very capable person—especially when you discover that nobody else seems to need help. Have you ever found yourself trying to learn a new subject, and you just couldn't get it? At first, you make the attribution that it is a very difficult subject, or the teacher is lousy. But then you discover that all of your friends—people who are very similar to you in other respects—are having an easier time with the subject. Now needing help seems to expose a weakness. It makes you look less intelligent and less capable than you thought. It can be a threat to your self-esteem.

Arie Nadler, Jeffrey Fisher, and Siegfried Streufert (1976) demonstrated one case in which receiving help actually hurts. Students played a game in which they could win money if they performed well. Although they played the game in an isolated cubicle, the students were told that they had been matched with a "pair-mate" with whom they would interact later. The pair-mate was actually fictitious and simply provided a way to create threat to the real participant's self-esteem. The experiment was arranged so that, at one point, the student learned that he and his pair-mate were either very similar in their attitudes, values, and interests or very dissimilar.

When the game began, the students discovered that it was extremely challenging and would be difficult to win. As the student proceeded through the game, his earnings dwindled and he was very close to being eliminated. His pair-mate was doing much better and was in a position to share some of his earnings to help keep

Sometimes receiving help can threaten the recipient's self-esteem.

the real participant in the game. In one condition of the experiment, the pair-mate did come through with some assistance by delivering a donation to the real student. In another condition, no such donation was made. So here we have four conditions in which a student either received helped or not from another student who was portrayed as either very similar or very dissimilar. Nadler et al. (1976) reasoned that receiving help from someone who was very similar and who appeared to be performing much better on the same task would pose a threat to one's self-esteem: it would make a person feel less worthy and less intelligent. And that is exactly what they found. Students in this combination of conditions described themselves as feeling sadder, less confident, less intelligent, and less able, even though their actual performance was exactly the same as that of participants who did not receive help or who received help from a dissimilar other. This deflating effect was especially true among the students who had rated themselves earlier in the semester as having high self-esteem. The more positively participants thought of

©LWA-Dann Tardif/CORBIS

themselves, the more they were threatened by another person who was similar to them, outperformed them, and then helped them. It actually hurt these participants' self-esteem to receive assistance from such a person.

**The Helper's Reason for Helping.** We have identified two conditions under which people may not respond positively to help from others: when they cannot reciprocate the help and when the help threatens their self-esteem. Daniel Ames, Francis Flynn, and Elke Weber (2004) proposed that a third determinant of people's reactions to help is their perceptions of why the helper decided to help—his or her *reason for helping*. Think about occasions when someone has helped you. Did you wonder why they did so?

Ames and his colleagues suggested that when people receive help, they try to figure out why the help was offered because this information tells them how the helper feels about them: does he or she care about me? If people decide that the helper cares about them, then they feel positively about the help, want to interact with the helper again in the future, and want to reciprocate the helping. But if people decide that the helper was guided by considerations other than caring, then they feel less positively and are less motivated to interact again in the future and to reciprocate the help.

The researchers suggested that when recipients of help think about why they received help, they typically contemplate three main reasons: because of liking/caring, because of a cost–benefit calculation, or because of role demands (see also Morris, Podolny, & Ariel, 2000). The *liking/caring* explanation indicates that the helper is helping "from the heart" and is not necessarily expecting anything in return. Paradoxically, this absence of reciprocation pressure makes recipients more likely to want to reciprocate! The *cost–benefit* explanation indicates that the helper deliberately weighed potential rewards for himself or herself against potential costs of helping. This "cold, calculating" decision to help implies that the helper does not necessarily like the recipient and is probably expecting something in return. The *role demands* explanation indicates that the helper felt it was his or her obligation, or duty, to help, such as when a police officer gives help or when a coworker's job responsibilities include assisting on a particular task. This reason for helping implies that the helper does not necessarily like the recipient and may even feel superior in the sense that he or she "is responsible" for the welfare of the recipient.

Ames and his colleagues (2004) conducted several studies in which participants either read descriptions of hypothetical situations in which they might receive help, or described actual experiences of receiving help, and then reported how they would or did feel in the situation. Results supported the prediction that helping motivated by caring produces the most positive responses from the recipient. The researchers suggested that recipients' perceptions of the reasons for the helping influence their judgments about the nature of their relationship with the helper: the caring explanation implies a close, affectionate relationship, whereas the cost–benefit and role demands explanations imply a more formal, businesslike relationship.

**Individual Differences in Gratitude.** Michael McCullough, Robert Emmons, and their colleagues have taken a very different approach to understanding recipients' reactions to helping: these researchers have conceptualized **dispositional gratitude** as an individual difference variable, with some people being more inclined toward feeling thankful for receiving help than other people (McCullough, Emmons, & Tsang, 2002; McCullough, Kilpatrick, Emmons, & Larson, 2001). At one end of this dimension are people who always seem grateful for any help they receive. These individuals are likely to thank others explicitly and to recognize help they received. At the other end of the dimension are people who might informally be labeled "ingrates." These individuals never thank anyone for help and do not seem even to know that their success is partly due to others' efforts.

**dispositional gratitude**
*an individual differences variable reflecting the extent to which people feel thankful for receiving help from others*

Some people are more dispositionally grateful for receiving help than are other people.

McCullough et al. (2002) developed a 6-item scale to measure dispositional gratitude, which is reproduced in Know Yourself 12.2 Dispositional Gratitude. Answer the items to see how you score on this dimension.

McCullough et al. (2002) found that scores on the measure of dispositional gratitude were correlated with measures of happiness, life satisfaction, and optimism, such that grateful people tended to be happier, more satisfied with life, and more optimistic than ungrateful people. In contrast, ungrateful people reported more anxiety and depression than did grateful individuals. Of course, these are correlational data, so we cannot know whether being grateful makes people happier, whether being happy makes people feel grateful, or whether some third factor influences both happiness and gratitude. Nevertheless, it seems clear that feeling grateful is associated with other positive states.

Scores on the gratitude scale also correlated with the Perspective Taking and Empathic Concern subscales of the Interpersonal Reactivity Index: grateful individuals tended to take other people's perspectives more (to be more empathic) than ungrateful individuals. Finally, McCullough et al. (2002) obtained from participants the names of people who knew them well; these individuals were subsequently contacted and asked to rate the participant on a variety of measures, including helpful behavior (e.g., how often the target person goes out of his or her way to do favors for others; how often the target person volunteers time to help others). Higher scores on the measure of dispositional gratitude were associated with higher scores on the peer ratings of helpful behaviors. Thus, people who were grateful for help they received also tended to be more helpful to others. This finding might serve as a lesson for all of us: perhaps we should make more effort to feel thankful for the help we receive from others—we might even become more helpful ourselves. The various factors influencing how the recipients of help react to the assistance are summarized in the accompanying Concept Review.

## CONCEPT REVIEW
### Factors Influencing How Recipients of Help React to the Assistance

| Factor | Relevant Question | Answer | Recipient's Response to Help |
|---|---|---|---|
| Reciprocity norm | Can the recipient return the favor? | Yes | Positive |
| | | No | Negative |
| Self-esteem threat | Does the help imply that the recipient lacks ability? | Yes | Negative |
| | | No | Positive |
| Reason for helping | Why did the helper offer help to the recipient? | Liking/caring | Positive |
| | | Cost–benefit | Negative |
| | | Role demands | Negative |
| Dispositional gratitude | How does the recipient score on dispositional gratitude? | High | Positive |
| | | Low | Negative |

# Know Yourself 12.2
## *Dispositional Gratitude*

Please indicate how much you agree or disagree with each of the following items by circling the appropriate number on the answer scale.

1. I have so much in life to be thankful for.

| 1 | 2 | 3 | 4 | 5 | 6 | 7 |
|---|---|---|---|---|---|---|
| Strongly disagree | Disagree | Slightly disagree | Neutral | Slightly agree | Agree | Strongly agree |

2. If I had to list everything that I felt grateful for, it would be a very long list.

| 1 | 2 | 3 | 4 | 5 | 6 | 7 |
|---|---|---|---|---|---|---|
| Strongly disagree | Disagree | Slightly disagree | Neutral | Slightly agree | Agree | Strongly agree |

3. When I look at the world, I don't see much to be grateful for.

| 1 | 2 | 3 | 4 | 5 | 6 | 7 |
|---|---|---|---|---|---|---|
| Strongly disagree | Disagree | Slightly disagree | Neutral | Slightly agree | Agree | Strongly agree |

4. I am grateful to a wide variety of people.

| 1 | 2 | 3 | 4 | 5 | 6 | 7 |
|---|---|---|---|---|---|---|
| Strongly disagree | Disagree | Slightly disagree | Neutral | Slightly agree | Agree | Strongly agree |

5. As I get older, I find myself more able to appreciate the people, events, and situations that have been part of my life history.

| 1 | 2 | 3 | 4 | 5 | 6 | 7 |
|---|---|---|---|---|---|---|
| Strongly disagree | Disagree | Slightly disagree | Neutral | Slightly agree | Agree | Strongly agree |

6. Long amounts of time can go by before I feel grateful to something or someone.

| 1 | 2 | 3 | 4 | 5 | 6 | 7 |
|---|---|---|---|---|---|---|
| Strongly disagree | Disagree | Slightly disagree | Neutral | Slightly agree | Agree | Strongly agree |

**SCORING:** Items 1, 2, 4, and 5 are scored in the way they appear (1-2-3-4-5-6-7), but Items 3 and 6 are scored in the reverse direction (7-6-5-4-3-2-1). Add up your scores across all of the items for your total dispositional gratitude score. Possible scores range from 6 to 42, and higher scores reflect more dispositional gratitude.

Sample items from McCullough et al., "The grateful disposition: A conceptual and empirical topography," *Journal of Personality and Social Psychology*, 82, 112–127, 2002. Copyright © 2002 by the American Psychological Association. Reprinted by permission.

 # Social Dilemmas: Cooperating for the Common Good

Self-interest, or egoistic motivation, is a powerful force. In some facets of life, being concerned primarily for one's own well-being seems natural and even makes sense: it is a competitive, dog-eat-dog world, so looking out for number one may be the key to survival.

But there are also situations in which a narrow focus on one's own short-term rewards can be counterproductive. In these situations, individual, competitive motives conflict with group, cooperative motives. These settings also tend to contrast short-term against long-term considerations. The term used to refer to these situations is *social dilemmas*. Some of the greatest threats to human survival will require cooperation and sacrifice of immediate personal gain if we are to defeat them. Perhaps nowhere is this more evident than in the erosion of natural resources and the environment; we must all conserve, thereby giving up some individual gain, in order for the world to remain healthy.

The behavior we discuss in this section is **cooperation:** collaborative behavior with other people that takes into account both one's own interests and the interests of the others. Cooperation is one form of *prosocial behavior*—behavior that provides benefit to others. Cooperation is not precisely *helping behavior* (behavior intended to assist another person); for example, it does not fit into any of McGuire's (1994) four categories of helping behavior (see Table 12.1). Rather, it is joint behavior that balances self- and other interests and often takes a long-term perspective.

**cooperation**

*collaborative behavior with other people that takes into account both one's own outcomes and the outcomes of the others*

## Definition of Social Dilemmas

A **social dilemma** is a situation in which individual interests conflict with interests of the group. All social dilemmas are characterized by two features: (1) selfish choices produce better immediate outcomes for the individual than do cooperative choices, but (2) long-term outcomes for everyone will suffer if everyone behaves selfishly (Schroeder, 1995). These characteristics make choices between selfishness and cooperation very difficult. For example, when a stock of resources is fixed, taking as much as possible may often appear to be the best way to come out ahead. But at what cost? Your own immediate personal outcomes may be maximized, but if everybody makes the same selfish decisions, the pool of resources will soon be depleted. Cooperation may entail giving up some of your own potential benefit so that, in the long run, everyone comes out ahead. The nature of this dilemma was nicely illustrated in a story about farmers, cattle, and an open pasture recounted by Garrett Hardin (1968).

**social dilemma**

*a situation in which selfish choices produce better immediate outcomes for the individual than do cooperative choices, but long-term outcomes for everyone will suffer if everyone behaves selfishly*

**Tragedy of the Commons.** Hardin (1968) described how shared but fixed resources can quickly become depleted if everyone seeks to maximize their own outcomes—a **tragedy of the commons**. Imagine a common pasture—open and free to all—that is capable of sustaining 100 cows. Ten farmers each have 10 cows grazing in that pasture. Because the number of cows equals exactly the capacity of the pasture, the collective benefit is maximized. But individual farmers are also seeking to maximize their own personal benefits. "What harm would it do," thinks a farmer, "if I add one more cow?" That farmer's benefit will increase by almost 10%. The cost of one more cow would be very small—the pasture will be stressed a small amount, and so the productivity of each cow will be slightly diminished. But the cost would be spread over 100 other cows and 9 other farmers, and so the cost to any single cow or farmer will be very small. Adding one more cow may therefore seem to be the rational and sensible thing to do. Of course, the other farmers might get the same idea—all being rational, sensible, and seeking to maximize their own gains. Soon, the pasture contains 110 cows. Again, at this point, farmers may decide that one more cow added by them wouldn't hurt much, and soon 120 cows are in the pasture. If all of the farmers continue to pursue their selfish interests, the pasture's resources will be fully depleted and no longer capable of sustaining even a single cow. In the end, every farmer loses—a tragedy born out of each individual's seeking to maximize his or her own outcomes.

Hardin (1968) cites several examples of the tragedy of the commons. Overgrazing of common pastures is a real problem. The world's oceans are also treated as a

**tragedy of the commons**

*the depletion of a communal resource, such as a shared cow pasture for a group of farmers, because each individual pursues selfish interests*

commons, and the result has been overharvesting of fish and whales to the point of driving many species to extinction. Environmental pollution is another example: the garbage, sewage, and carbon monoxide contributed by one person is hardly enough to cause noticeable harm to the environment, but the sum of many small individual contributions can add up to irreparable harm to all. In every case, the short-term pursuit of self-interest and maximization of self-benefits creates a long-term cumulative and collective loss.

**The Prisoner's Dilemma.** One variation of the commons problem that social psychologists have utilized in the laboratory is the **prisoner's dilemma game** (Rapoport & Chammah, 1965). This game also forces a choice between selfishness and cooperation. Imagine that two partners in crime are being held in separate cells at police headquarters. They stand accused of a series of robberies, but a confession is needed to make the most serious charges stick. Without the confession, enough evidence is available to convict them only of minor crimes, and each would receive a 1-year sentence. The prosecutor promises to recommend less than the maximum 10-year sentence if a confession is made. If both confess, they both receive 8-year sentences. If only one confesses, that one gets just 3 months, and the other gets 10 years. The main catch is that each prisoner must make a decision independently and without communicating with the other. All of the possible outcomes are summarized in the **payoff matrix** shown in Table 12.3 (Luce & Raiffa, 1957). The "cooperative" choice for each suspect is to *not confess*—it will produce the best collective outcomes. But there is a strong temptation to act selfishly, or *confess*. In fact, confessing is the rational thing to do. If you think that your partner will make the cooperative choice (not confess), then you come out ahead by confessing (3 months vs. 1 year). If you think that your partner will confess, then you still come out ahead by confessing (8 years vs. 10 years). But notice that if both make this same "rational" choice to confess, then both end up worse off (8 years) than if the two had cooperated by not confessing (1 year).

The hypothetical dilemma of the two prisoners lacks one important quality of real-life social dilemmas: repeated "trials" over time. If a prisoner needs to make a one-time decision to confess or not confess, it is indeed rational to be selfish by confessing. But in almost all social dilemmas, there will be a continuing relationship between the people involved, and early decisions will exert strong effects on

The *tragedy of the commons* can be illustrated with cases of shared pastures being overgrazed.

**prisoner's dilemma game**

*a simulated social dilemma that requires participants to make choices between acting selfishly and cooperatively when selfishness looks better initially but can damage long-term joint outcomes of the players*

**payoff matrix**

*a table representing the outcomes for each player in a prisoner's dilemma game based on the players' combined choices*

## TABLE 12.3
### A Payoff Matrix for the Prisoner's Dilemma Game

| | Prisoner 2's Decision: | |
| --- | --- | --- |
| | **Not Confess** (Cooperative response) | **Confess** (Selfish response) |
| **Prisoner 1's Decision:** | | |
| **Not Confess** (Cooperative response) | Both prisoners get a 1-year sentence | Prisoner 1 gets a 10-year sentence; Prisoner 2 gets a 3-month sentence |
| **Confess (Selfish response)** | Prisoner 1 gets a 3-month sentence; Prisoner 2 gets a 10-year sentence | Both prisoners get an 8-year sentence |

After Luce & Raiffa, 1957, *Games and decisions: Introduction and critical survey*, New York: Wiley.

**12.1**
**ONLINE**
**LAB**

later decisions. For example, to return to the tragedy of the commons, if farmers learn that one of the other farmers has added a cow, then they may be more likely to add a cow themselves. So a situation that could have remained cooperative is rendered selfish and competitive by the actions of one person.

In fact, when researchers use the prisoner's dilemma game to study behavior in social dilemmas, they require participants to play many trials of the game. Hence, participants never actually hear the hypothetical story of the two prisoners, nor is the game labeled "the prisoner's dilemma game." Instead, the game is described simply as a multitrial game in which participants select one of two possible responses on each trial, and their payoffs on each trial are determined by the combined choices. Participants are also typically given a copy of a payoff matrix (like the one in Table 12.3, but with the labels Person 1, Person 2, Response A, and Response B, and with the payoffs expressed in points rather than prison sentences).

## Decision Making in Social Dilemmas

How do people in social dilemmas decide whether to act selfishly or cooperatively? J. Mark Weber, Shirli Kopelman, and David Messick (2004) proposed that people are guided primarily by their perceptions of what behavior is *appropriate* in the situation: "What does a person like me do in a situation like this?" Based on features of the situation itself, social norms, personal experiences in similar situations, and dispositional traits related to cooperativeness, people might judge a particular social dilemma to be a setting in which either selfish or cooperative responses are appropriate. This perception of appropriate behavior will guide the individuals' actual responses.

What does the word *appropriate* mean in this model? Responses that are judged "appropriate" in a setting might be those that are considered morally right, or those that are expected to produce the best outcomes, or those that are believed to be typical for this setting. The specific meaning of appropriate varies across individuals and even across situations for the same person. This model of decision making is appealing because it integrates research on many factors that have been shown to affect cooperative behavior in social dilemmas. In the following paragraphs, we review some of the literature on social dilemmas, using the appropriateness model as an integrative framework.

**Situational Labels.** There is a lot of evidence that the way individuals *label* a social dilemma influences their behavior. In a simple but compelling demonstration of this idea, Varda Liberman, Steven Samuels, and Lee Ross (2004) had college students play a 7-trial version of the prisoners' dilemma game. For some participants, the game was called the Community Game (cooperative label), whereas for others it was called the Wall Street Game (selfish label). This simple manipulation of the game's name exerted a huge impact on cooperation. Those participants who were playing the Community Game made the cooperative choice on 66% of the trials, whereas those who were playing the Wall Street Game made the cooperative choice on 31% of the trials. Why did the labels exert such a strong effect? Presumably, the label of the game influenced participants' perceptions of what responses were appropriate, including how other players were likely to respond and whether selfish responses were ethical or unethical.

**Priming.** It is possible to affect participants' responses in social dilemmas more subtly than with overt situational labels. Specifically, *priming* the schema of cooperation or competition can influence reactions. For example, Aaron Kay and Lee Ross (2003) required participants to rearrange five-word sequences into proper sentences using four of the five words. A total of 24 sequences were provided, and 16 of the sequences created four-word sentences related either to cooperation (e.g., "helped friend computer she her" could be rearranged into "she helped her friend") or competition (e.g., "today is tournament often the" could be rearranged into "today is the tournament"). Participants then read about a multitrial prisoner's dilemma game and were asked how they would respond in such a game. Those participants who had their schema of *cooperation* primed reported that they would behave more cooperatively than did those participants who had their schema of *competition* primed. Presumably, the priming manipulation influenced how participants thought about the game, which affected whether cooperative or selfish responses were considered appropriate.

In another study of priming effects, Arjaan Wit and Norbert Kerr (2002) gave participants the opportunity to divide some money among several "bank accounts," including a private account for themselves and a group account that would be divided among all six participants who were taking part at the session. Before making this division, participants were exposed to a manipulation designed to make either an individual or a collective perspective salient (prominent). Specifically, some participants were told that each of the six participants would individually throw dice to determine the percentage of money in the bank accounts they would receive (individual perspective), whereas other participants were told that the experimenter would throw dice one time to determine the percentage of money in each account all six participants would receive (collective perspective). This simple procedure had a significant impact on how much participants assigned to their own private account: the individual perspective led participants to put more money into their private account than did the collective perspective. Presumably, making a collective perspective salient increased the perceived appropriateness of sharing responses (see also De Cremer & van Dijk, 2002; Kramer & Brewer, 1984).

**Social Norms.** Earlier in the chapter, the concept of social norms was used to explain why people might engage in helpful behavior. For example, the norm of social responsibility dictates that we should help others who are in need. Similarly, there is evidence that cooperation in social dilemmas is influenced by norms. In one experiment, Harvey Hornstein and his colleagues (Hornstein, LaKind, Frankel, & Manne, 1975) made a cooperative norm especially salient by having students listen to a (fictitious) news story about a man who donated his kidney to a total stranger. Other groups of students listened to a news story featuring antisocial behavior, and still others heard no news story at all; the norm of social responsibility was not expected to be activated in these conditions. The students then played a prisoner's dilemma game in which they had to choose between a cooperative and a selfish strategy. The students were more likely to choose the cooperative strategy, and to assume that their partner would also do so, after hearing the story that involved helpful behavior than in the other two conditions.

Making people aware of social norms may be a good way to increase cooperative strategies involving the environment. Joseph Hopper and Joyce McCarl Nielsen (1991) found that Denver, Colorado, residents were more likely to participate in a community recycling program when they perceived that their own neighborhood had a norm for recycling. Why do norms affect cooperative behavior? Norms represent shared views of what is appropriate behavior in the situation, including what is fair or unfair for those involved (see Schroeder, Steel, Woodell, & Bembenek, 2003).

**Actions of Similar Models.** People's behavior in social dilemmas is also influenced by the actions of other people, especially those who are similar in important ways. This

When people believe that their neighborhood has a norm for recycling, they are more likely to recycle themselves.

point was demonstrated in a study by Craig Parks, Larry Sanna, and Susan Berel (2001). College students played a multitrial prisoner's dilemma game, but before actually starting were given information about how three (fictitious) previous participants had behaved. Additional background information about these alleged previous participants made them seem either very similar or very dissimilar to a typical college student. Participants' own responses on the subsequent social dilemma task were significantly affected by the alleged actions of similar others: participants cooperated more when similar models were believed to have cooperated than when similar models were believed to have responded selfishly. The alleged responses of very dissimilar models had no impact on participants' responses on the task. These findings suggest that the actions of similar others influenced perceptions of appropriate behavior in the social dilemma.

**Communication.** Communication in social dilemmas tends to increase cooperative responses. In the original scenario of two criminal suspects facing the dilemma of whether or not to confess, part of their difficulty is that they are not allowed to talk to one another. Communication might allow the prisoners to express their intentions to cooperate. This idea was put to experimental test by Robyn Dawes, Jeanne McTavish, and Harriet Shaklee (1977). A variation of the prisoner's dilemma was created so that students in small groups had to make a choice between a cooperative and a competitive response. The game was set up so that the payoff for a particular student would be very high if he or she chose a selfish response and most of the others chose a cooperative strategy. The greater the number of selfish responses, however, the lower the payoff—and if numerous students chose the selfish option, the payoff actually turned negative! In this case, the cooperative strategy clearly maximized the collective payoff.

In one condition of the experiment, the students were not permitted to talk with one another before making their individual decisions; 70% of these students responded selfishly. In another condition, the students were given 10 minutes to discuss their dilemma before making their decisions; the selfish response rate was cut to 28% here. A little bit of communication went a long way to enhancing cooperation and maximizing the collective outcome, presumably because people discussed the benefits of cooperation and were convinced that it was the appropriate response (see also Kerr & Kaufman-Gilliland, 1994; Tazelaar, Van Lange, & Ouwerkerk, 2004). This effect of communication may remind you of our discussion of intergroup conflict in Chapter 10, where we suggested that communication between groups may be the most important factor in the reduction of conflict.

**Individual Differences in Cooperativeness: Social Value Orientation.** Earlier in the chapter, we talked about the altruistic personality—people who are especially helpful toward others. Researchers interested specifically in social dilemmas have identified an individual difference variable that predicts people's responses in such settings. The variable is known as **social value orientation,** and three major orientations are normally distinguished. *Individualists* are primarily concerned with maximizing their own outcomes. *Competitors* are primarily concerned with maximizing their own outcomes relative to others' outcomes. *Prosocials* are primarily concerned with maximizing the total outcomes of everyone in the setting.

Social value orientation is typically assessed by asking people to select which of three hypothetical distributions of money or points they would prefer (Van Lange & Kuhlman, 1994). For example, they might be asked to choose among the following three options: Option A pays 600 points to the self and 300 points to an unknown other, Option B pays 500 points to the self and 100 points to the other, and Option C pays 500 points to the self and 500 points to the other. Option A is the individualistic choice, because it maximizes personal points. Option B is the

**social value orientation**

*a disposition that reflects individual differences in cooperativeness in social dilemmas; three orientations are typically distinguished: individualists, competitors, and prosocials*

competitive choice, because it maximizes the difference between the points assigned to the self and the other. Option C is the prosocial choice, because it maximizes the total points for self and other combined (see Steinel & De Dreu, 2004). In similar fashion, participants are asked to choose one of three alternatives on nine different items. If they make a particular type of choice (e.g., competitive) on at least six of the nine items, then they are considered to have a specific social value orientation (e.g., competitor). If they do not choose one type of option on at least six items, then they are assumed to have mixed motives and are not included in tests of social value orientation.

Researchers have found that people with a prosocial value orientation cooperate more often in social dilemmas than do individualists or competitors (e.g., Kramer, McClintock, & Messick, 1986; Roch & Samuelson, 1997; Smeesters, Warlop, Van Avermaet, Corneille, & Yzerbyt, 2003; Utz, 2004). Prosocials also expect other people to cooperate, respond positively to others' cooperation, and remain optimistic about future cooperation (e.g., Liebrand, Jansen, Rijken, & Suhre, 1986; Parks & Rumble, 2001; Parks, Sanna, & Posey, 2003). In research on the related topic of negotiation, researchers have found that prosocial negotiators are less contentious and engage in more problem solving than individualistic or competitive negotiators (see De Dreu, Weingart, & Kwon, 2000).

How does social value orientation influence people's behavior? Prosocials consider cooperation in social dilemmas to be the appropriate behavior, whereas competitors and individualists consider self-interested actions to be appropriate (Weber et al., 2004). Specifically, prosocials consider cooperation to be morally correct and also the most rational choice in terms of maximizing personal outcomes in the long run. Competitors and individualists often consider cooperative responses to be "weak" and expect selfish responses to maximize personal outcomes in the long run (Liebrand et al., 1986).

The factors we have discussed that influence cooperation in social dilemmas are summarized in the accompanying Concept Review.

## CONCEPT REVIEW
### Factors Influencing Cooperation in Social Dilemmas

| Factor | Description | Example of Relevant Manipulation or Measure |
|---|---|---|
| Labels | Cooperative versus competitive labels increase or decrease cooperation | Use Community Game versus Wall Street Game as label for the prisoner's dilemma game |
| Priming | Activating the schema of cooperation or competition increases or decreases cooperation | Have participants rearrange sentences relating to cooperation or competition |
| Social norms | Cooperative norms will increase cooperation when they are salient | Have participants read an article about an organ donor |
| Models | Actions of similar others can increase or decrease cooperation | Tell participants about the responses of previous participants who were similar to typical students |
| Communication | Allowing people to communicate can increase cooperation | Give participants 10 minutes to converse before choosing responses |
| Individual differences | Social value orientation influences cooperation | Measure whether participants are individualists, competitors, or prosocials |

## Social Support

> I get by with a little help from my friends.
>
> —*John Lennon and Paul McCartney (1967)*

## Social Support Networks

Two of the four categories of helping behaviors we described at the beginning of this chapter (McGuire, 1994; see Table 12.1) have received relatively little discussion so far (except for the section on volunteerism): substantial personal helping and emotional helping. One difference between these two categories and casual or emergency helping is who does them—strangers versus acquaintances. Whereas casual and emergency helping are typically done by strangers, substantial personal helping and emotional helping are typically done by friends and family members. Thus, the availability and quality of this kind of helping depend considerably on a **social support network:** people who can be called upon for help and who will provide it when needed, such as family members, friends, neighbors, and other acquaintances.

**social support network**

*people who can be called upon for help and who will provide help when needed, such as family, friends, and neighbors*

Social support has received less attention as a research topic from social psychologists than have casual and emergency helping, although clinical psychologists have studied this topic for several decades. Recently, however, social psychologists have become more actively involved in research on social support and have generated interesting findings from a variety of theoretical perspectives (e.g., Abend & Williamson, 2002; Feeney & Collins, 2001; Neff & Karney, 2005; Neyer & Lang, 2003; Simpson, Rholes, Oriña, & Grich, 2002; Taylor, Sherman, Kim, Jarcho, Takegi, & Dunagan, 2004). In this section, we review some of this work, as well as some important findings by clinical psychologists.

**Perceived Availability of Social Support Versus Actual Receipt of Social Support.** An interesting distinction must be made in the domain of social support, which reflects that social support networks serve at least two functions (Stroebe & Stroebe, 1996). Specifically, it is important to distinguish between the *perceived availability* of social support and the *actual receipt* of social support. On the one hand, people may believe that family and friends are available should they ever be needed; this *perceived availability* of social support presumably gives people confidence that they can deal with stress and a feeling that others care for them. On the other hand, people must truly receive social support when they need it; this *actual receipt* of social support encompasses helping with physical tasks, expressing emotional support, and providing information that helps individuals cope with their situation.

It turns out that the benefits of a social support network have been easier to document for one kind of social support than for the other. Which kind would you expect to be associated more strongly with positive outcomes, the perceived availability of social support or the actual receipt of social support? Perhaps surprisingly, data suggest that *perceiving* help is nearby is more consistently connected to well-being than is actually *receiving* help when needed (Wethington & Kessler, 1986). We will discuss this interesting result shortly.

A *social support network* consists of people who can be called on for help when it is needed, such as family members and friends.

**Measuring the Perceived Availability of Social Support.** To measure people's perceptions that others are available if needed, Irwin Sarason and his coworkers (Sarason, Levine, Basham, & Sarason, 1983) developed a Social Support Questionnaire (SSQ). This scale consists of 27 items that ask respondents to list all of the people on whom they can rely in a variety of circumstances, and to rate how satisfied they are with these social supports. Respondents who nominate many people providing support and who report high satisfaction receive higher scores on the SSQ. Here are some sample items:

- Whom can you really count on to listen to you when you need to talk?
- Whom could you really count on to help you out in a crisis situation, even though they would have to go out of their way to do so?
- Whom can you really count on to be dependable when you need help?
- With whom can you totally be yourself?
- Who do you feel really appreciates you as a person?

**Measuring the Actual Receipt of Social Support.** To measure how much social support people have actually received, Manuel Barrera, Irwin Sandler, and Thomas Ramsay (1981) developed the Inventory of Socially Supportive Behaviors (ISSB). This scale consists of 40 instances of helping that people might have received. Each item is rated for its frequency of occurrence during the past month, on a scale from 1 (not at all) to 5 (about every day). Respondents who report more frequent occurrence of the social support behaviors receive higher scores on the ISSB. Here are some sample items:

- Expressed interest and concern in your well-being
- Joked and kidded to try to cheer you up
- Told you that you are OK just the way you are
- Gave you some information on how to do something
- Was right there with you (physically) in a stressful situation

**Social Support and the Reciprocity Norm.** One interesting aspect of social support networks is that they provide help without the pressure of immediate reciprocation (although social support in close relationships may be most beneficial when each partner supports the other; see Gleason, Iida, Bolger, & Shrout, 2003). The terminally ill and the very old depend heavily on their social support networks even though they are the least able members of the network to ever reciprocate for the physical, financial, and emotional support they receive. Of course, these individuals often have a history of providing support to others in the past.

Toni Antonucci and James Jackson (1990) proposed the metaphor of a social support network being like a *bank*. You make deposits when you are able, and you take withdrawals when you need them. There is no expectation of one-to-one reciprocation between members of a social support network. Rather, it is a collective bank to which its members contribute and from which its members are entitled to draw. It is not coincidental that a person's social support network is primarily comprised of others with whom close interpersonal relationships are enjoyed— relatives, spouses, children, parents, and close friends. In Chapter 13, we will learn that close relationships often move beyond a one-for-one exchange of benefits to something more like a communal sharing of benefits (Clark & Mills, 1979). In communal relationships, the receipt of a benefit creates no specific obligation to return that benefit: from each according to their ability, and to each according to their need.

# Social Support and Health

Research on the effects of social support has focused on its potential health benefits, both physical and mental. Why or how might social support be beneficial to well-being? There are at least four ways that social support might improve recipients' mental or physical health (Schaefer, Coyne, & Lazarus, 1981; Wills, 1991):

- *Informational support* provides advice, instructions, directions, and generally useful information about health-related topics. Examples include giving advice about helpful exercise routines and finding out where to obtain needed medication.

- *Instrumental support* is the provision of physical assistance or material resources that provide aid. These resources could include providing physical care during an illness, lending money, or providing other services and resources that may be needed by someone in distress.

- *Companionship support* provides company to the person in need, creating a sense of belonging. Sitting with or reading to a sick friend, going shopping, or having lunch together are examples of companionship support.

- *Emotional support* is the giving of acceptance and reassurance, providing a source of intimacy and confidence. Expressing love, comforting when sad, and discussing fears are examples of emotional support.

### Health Consequences of the Perceived Availability of Social Support.

The evidence is quite clear and consistent that perceiving a wide social support network has positive effects on health and well-being. For example, perceiving that a wide social support network is available if necessary has been shown to improve recovery from physical illness, to reduce the negative impact of stressful events,

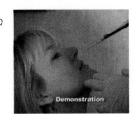

*The purpose of the study is to make the guests sick. A cold virus is placed into the nose, and the volunteers are sequestered at a local motel for six days, where they're tested daily to see just how sick they get.*

and to protect against depression (e.g., Cortina, 2004; Cross & Vick, 2001; House, Landis, & Umberson, 1988; Katz, Monnier, Libet, Shaw, & Beach, 2000; Lindorff, 2000; McCaskill & Lakey, 2000). Believing that they can call on a social support network increases individuals' feelings of control: if necessary, they can face problems together with friends and family (Cohen, 2004).

In one well-known early study, Lisa Berkman and S. Leonard Syme (1979) surveyed almost 5,000 adults living in Alameda County, California, in 1965. The adults ranged in age from 30 to 69. For the following nine years (through 1974), the sample was followed and deaths were recorded. Throughout the period of study, the residents who had reported relatively poor social networks in 1965 were twice as likely to die as those who had reported relatively good social networks (the quality of social networks was defined in terms of the number and extent of social relationships, including marriage, family and friends, church membership, and other group affiliations).

Heart disease is one aspect of physical health that seems clearly influenced by the perceived availability of social support. Between 1974 and 1989, more than 1,300 patients at Duke Medical Center were enrolled in a study of coronary artery disease and social support (Williams et al., 1992). The patients all had significant coronary artery disease, and records were kept of those who died as a result of their heart problems. A simple measure of social support availability was obtained: the patients were asked whether or not they were married or had a close confidant on whom they could rely. During one five-year period, the unmarried patients who did not have a close confidant were more than three times as likely to die as were the married patients or those who did have a confidant. Even when a variety of other socioeconomic factors were taken into account (e.g., income, number of dependents, education), the most important predictor of mortality was the presence versus absence of a spouse or confidant (see also King, Reis, Porter, & Norsen, 1993).

## Health Consequences of the Actual Receipt of Social Support.

In contrast to clear evidence showing that the perceived availability of social support is beneficial to people's health, it has proven more difficult to connect the *actual receipt* of social support with positive outcomes. Indeed, several studies have found that people receiving more social support reported *worse* symptoms and problems (e.g., Barrera, 1981; Bolger, Zuckerman, & Kessler, 2000; Neuling & Winefield, 1988). How is this possible when the receipt of social support should presumably make people feel better, not worse? One reason may be that the data have often been correlational. People may have received a lot of social support *because their health was bad,* rather than the social support actually being harmful (Stroebe & Stroebe, 1996). But this criticism does not apply to all of the studies that have failed to show positive effects of actual receipt of social support.

For example, Niall Bolger and his colleagues (Bolger, Foster, Vinokur, & Ng, 1996) interviewed 102 breast cancer patients in Detroit, Michigan, at two different times: the women were visited in their homes at 4 months and 10 months after diagnosis. At each session, the women were asked about physical impairments and emotional distress (anxiety, depression). In addition, at each session, the spouse or "significant other" (often the patient's daughter) reported the amount of social support he or she was currently providing to the patient. This was done by rating how much he or she was doing such things as:

- Providing encouragement and reassurance when she needs it
- Providing her with direct help (doing things for her, giving her things she needs)
- Listening to her when she needs to talk about things that are important to her
- Saying things that raise her self-confidence
- Giving her useful information or advice when she needs it

Because well-being and social support were each measured twice, the researchers could examine how the two concepts changed and influenced one another over time. The results showed that physical limitations caused by the breast cancer led to increased social support, as would be expected. However, social support did not appear to improve physical recovery or to reduce distress over time: support had no effect. Even more troubling was the finding that patients who experienced a lot of emotional distress subsequently received *less* social support from their support person; in other words, social support appeared to be *eroded* by the patient's distress. The researchers suggested that support givers may have seen emotional distress as something the patient should be able to control, so they reduced support because they felt unappreciated or because it was simply unpleasant being around the patient.

How should we interpret the apparent lack of benefit of actually received social support? Some researchers have suggested that the null results might reflect imperfect measures. For example, Brian Lakey, Catherine Lutz, and their colleagues have identified characteristics of respondents that can color judgments of received support (Lakey, Adams, Neely, Rhodes, Lutz, & Sielky, 2002; Lutz & Lakey, 2001). Other researchers have suggested that social support may affect well-being for some individuals, but not for others. For example, Patricia Frazier, Andrew Tix, and Cecil Barnett (2003) found that unsupportive behaviors (e.g., criticizing, refusing to discuss problems) from spouses of kidney transplant patients were associated with more distress only when the marital relationship was unsatisfying to begin with (see also Feeney & Collins, 2003).

Niall Bolger, Adam Zuckerman, and Ronald Kessler (2000) made perhaps the most interesting proposal about this issue. These researchers proposed that when people recognize that they have received social support, this recognition can have an emotional cost. Recall our discussion earlier in the chapter that receiving help may sometimes threaten self-esteem (Nadler et al., 1976). Such a reduction in self-esteem might counteract any benefit from the social support. To test this idea, Bolger and his colleagues studied 68 heterosexual couples in which one person was preparing to write the New York State Bar Examination to become a lawyer—a stressful event. Participants completed a brief questionnaire each day for 5 weeks, indicating their emotional feelings and social support (the person preparing for the bar exam reported any social support he or she had received, and the other member of the dyad reported any social support he or she had provided).

Results showed that when the person preparing for the exam reported receiving social support, he or she tended to report *more distress* on the following day. Thus, knowing that they had received social support appeared to make people feel worse, perhaps because the support threatened their self-esteem. Also, many acts of social support reported by the support giver were *not* reported by the recipient, suggesting that people do not always recognize everything that is done for them. The researchers labeled these unrecognized acts of support "invisible" social support. The most interesting finding of all was that "invisible" acts of support were associated with the recipient reporting *less distress* on the following day! In other words, acts of social support that were reported by the giver but *not* recognized as such by the recipient tended to have a positive impact. The researchers suggested that when it is "invisible," social support does not threaten self-esteem.

In closing, perhaps the actual receipt of social support does have beneficial effects on health in some circumstances (e.g., when the support is unrecognized) or for some people (e.g., in certain kinds of relationships). It may seem strange that received social support can have *negative* effects on well-being, but the data suggest that this can sometimes be the case. It will be interesting to see whether future research identifies more clearly the conditions under which received support is either beneficial or harmful.

# Chapter Summary

**Helping** is behavior that is intended to assist another person. It is one type of **prosocial behavior,** which is any action that provides benefit to other people. Helping behavior falls into a number of distinct categories, including casual helping, emergency helping, substantial personal helping, and emotional helping.

People often help because of an **egoistic motivation**—a desire to obtain rewards or to avoid punishments. It is also possible that people sometimes help out of an **altruistic motivation**—purely for the sake of providing benefit to another, without regard for self-gain. One explanation why humans have evolved to be altruistic is based on the principle of **inclusive fitness,** which is the idea that some social behaviors have been selected during the course of evolution because they increase the survival of our genes. **Empathy** is the ability to comprehend how another person is experiencing a situation. The **empathy–altruism hypothesis** proposes that feelings of empathy for a person can lead to behavior that is motivated solely by wanting to help that person.

Social norms are culturally defined rules or guidelines about what behaviors are proper and improper. Several norms are relevant to helping behavior. For example, the **norm of social responsibility** dictates that we should help those who need help, if possible. The norm of reciprocity states that we should return favors to others who have helped us. These norms will guide behavior only when they have become **personal norms** for the individual—when they have been internalized to become expectations for oneself in particular situations.

Seeing another person model helpful behavior increases helping. On the other hand, perceiving the victim as responsible for his or her own problems reduces helping. Such victim blaming may help to protect people's belief in a just world even when they see others suffering; this belief is hypothesized to be important in **just world theory.** Good mood and feelings of guilt are two other factors that have been shown to increase helping.

Some people are more helpful than others. One variable that predicts helpful behavior is individual differences in empathy, which can be measured by the **Interpersonal Reactivity Index (IRI).** The IRI has four parts, which assess different aspects of empathy: perspective taking, empathic concern, personal distress, and fantasy.

**Volunteerism** is unpaid helping behavior that is given willingly to a worthwhile cause or service organization. Several motives for engaging in volunteer behavior have been identified. One important predictor of continuing volunteerism is satisfaction with one's volunteer experiences.

Social psychologists interested in emergency helping have suggested that a series of decisions must be made before a bystander will intervene in an emergency. This **decision tree** consists of the following steps: the bystander must (1) notice the event, (2) interpret the event as an emergency, (3) accept personal responsibility for intervening, (4) decide on an appropriate form of assistance, and (5) implement the action. If any of the steps does not occur, the bystander will not intervene. The presence of multiple bystanders can reduce the chances that the event will be interpreted as an emergency, because bystanders may use the inaction of other bystanders to conclude that the event is not serious. The presence of multiple bystanders can also reduce the chances that bystanders will accept personal responsibility for intervening, because they will feel that others could help just as well. These inhibitory effects of bystanders on interpretations and responsibility produce the **bystander effect:** the likelihood that an individual will intervene in an emergency goes down as the number of bystanders increases.

Cross-cultural research has shown that children who are socialized in homes and cultures that emphasize shared responsibility and interdependence are more likely to engage in helpful behavior. There is also some evidence that people from collectivist cultures regard more kinds of helping to be social obligations than do people from individualist cultures.

People who receive help sometimes respond negatively. One reason may be that they do not want to feel obligated to reciprocate the help. Another possibility is that receiving help threatens their self-esteem. Finally, the helper's reason for helping can affect the recipient's reaction: when helping is done because of liking/caring, recipients typically respond positively, whereas when helping is done because of a cost–benefit analysis or because of role demands, recipients may respond negatively.

**Dispositional gratitude** refers to the extent to which people feel thankful for receiving help from others. People who are high on this dimension are more likely than people low on the dimension to recognize help they received, to feel grateful for help, and to be helpful themselves.

**Cooperation** is collaborative behavior with other people that takes into account both one's own outcomes and the outcomes of the others. Cooperative behavior is essential in settings known as **social dilemmas,** which are situations in which selfish choices produce better immediate outcomes for the individual than do cooperative choices, but long-term outcomes for everyone will suffer if everyone behaves selfishly. One example of a social dilemma is the **tragedy of the commons**—the depletion of a communal resource, such as a shared cow pasture for a group of farmers, because each individual pursues selfish interests. A simulated social dilemma is created in the **prisoner's dilemma game,** in which participants make choices between acting selfishly and acting cooperatively when selfishness looks better initially but can damage long-term joint outcomes of the players. Each prisoner's dilemma game has a **payoff matrix** associated with it, which specifies the outcomes for each player based on their combined choices.

People's actions in social dilemmas depend on their perceptions of what behavior is appropriate in the situation. These perceptions of appropriate behavior can be influenced by labels, priming, social norms, actions of other people, and communication with other individuals. There are also individual differences in people's cooperativeness in social dilemmas, which have been labeled **social value orientation.** Three social value orientations are typically distinguished: *individualists* are primarily concerned with maximizing their own outcomes, *competitors* are primarily concerned with maximizing their outcomes relative to others' outcomes, and *prosocials* are primarily concerned with maximizing the total outcomes of everyone in the setting.

**Social support networks** are people who can be called upon for help and who will provide help when needed, such as family, friends, and neighbors. Some kinds of helping behavior, such as substantial personal helping and emotional helping, are provided mainly by individuals' social support networks. It is important to distinguish between the *perceived availability* of social support and the *actual receipt* of social support. Many studies have found that perceiving a wide network of support that can be called upon if necessary is associated with positive health outcomes, including longevity and recovery from coronary artery disease. It has been more difficult to show positive health benefits of actually receiving social support, perhaps because receiving support threatens recipients' self-esteem. It has been suggested that unrecognized social support, called *invisible* social support, may have beneficial health effects.

# Key Terms

**altruistic motivation** (482)

**bystander effect** (498)

**cooperation** (508)

**decision tree** (495)

**dispositional gratitude** (505)

**egoistic motivation** (482)

**empathy** (483)

**empathy–altruism hypothesis** (483)

**helping** (480)

**inclusive fitness** (483)

**Interpersonal Reactivity Index (IRI)** (490)

**just world theory** (488)

**norm of social responsibility** (486)

**payoff matrix** (509)

**personal norms** (487)

**prisoner's dilemma game** (509)

**prosocial behavior** (480)

**social dilemma** (508)

**social support network** (514)

**social value orientation** (512)

**tragedy of the commons** (508)

**volunteerism** (492)

# Social Psychology Alive on the Web

## SOCIAL PSYCHOLOGY ALIVE: ONLINE LABS

To perform the following experiment and see how you compare to other students, go to Social Psychology Lab, which can be accessed through Social PsychologyNow.

- 12.1 Prisoner's Dilemma

## SOCIAL PSYCHOLOGY ALIVE: QUIZZING AND PRACTICE TESTS

You can access our website directly by going to http://psychology.wadsworth.com/breckler1e/ for online quizzes, flash cards, and Internet links.

## INFOTRAC® COLLEGE EDITION

For additional readings, explore InfoTrac College Edition, your online library of archived journal articles and periodicals dating back 22 years. If your instructor ordered InfoTrac College Edition with this book, you can access it from your CD-ROM, or go directly to www.infotrac-college.com/wadsworth and use the passcode from the InfoTrac College Edition card that came with your book. For this chapter, try these search terms: *helping, prosocial behavior, altruism, empathy, bystander intervention, cooperation, social dilemma, prisoner's dilemma, social value orientation, social support.*

# Social Psychology Alive: The Workbook

To apply what you've learned in this chapter to what happens in the real world, go to Chapter 12 of *Social Psychology Alive: The Workbook:*

- Can You Demonstrate the Social Norms of Casual Helping?
- Why Do People Donate Blood?
- Relief Cowboy: What Motivates Professional Relief Workers?
- Holocaust Rescuers and Bystanders
- Good Samaritan Laws

- Vacationing as a Volunteer
- Cooperation Versus Competition: Will You Choose to Compete?
- The Story of Kitty Genovese
- The Carnegie Hero Fund Commission: Heroes Do Exist!
- Thoughts on Helping by Authors, Philosophers, and Leaders
- How Can I Help?

# Social Psychology Alive: The Videos

To see video on the topics and experiments discussed in this chapter, you can go either to Social PsychologyNow or to the CD-ROM, if your instructor assigned either one, to the following section:

- Thanks for Nothing: Bystander Apathy
- Sick of Solitude: The Link Between Sociability and Health

# To Learn More

This list contains citations to books or articles that can help you learn more. These readings are good places to start if you want to gain a deeper understanding of the topics in this chapter.

- Schroeder, D. A., Penner, L. A., Dovidio, J. F., & Piliavin, J. A. (1995). *The psychology of helping and altruism: Problems and puzzles.* New York: McGraw-Hill.

- Schroeder, D. A. (1995). *Social dilemmas: Perspectives on individuals and groups.* Westport, CT: Praeger.
- Stroebe, W., & Stroebe, M. (1996). The social psychology of social support. In E. T. Higgins & A. W. Kruglanski (Eds.), *Social psychology: Handbook of basic principles* (pp. 597–621). New York: Guilford.

© Royalty-Free/CORBIS

# Liking, Loving, and Close Relationships

*Frank and Betty met during their first year in college. For Frank, it was love at first sight. "She was so beautiful," recalls Frank, "her smile just lit up the room. From the first time I met her, I knew that Betty and I were meant for each other." It took Betty a little longer to warm up to Frank. "He was nice enough, and very handsome. But it wasn't until our fourth or fifth date that I realized how much we had in common." Frank and Betty married soon after graduation. After 50 years of marriage, they are still very much in love. When Frank battled prostate cancer a few years ago, Betty never left his side. Frank credits his quick recovery and current good health to the love and support provided by Betty. "Of course I was there," replies Betty. "He has always been there for me."*

*Billy has followed a different path when it comes to romance. At age 38, none of his many relationships has lasted more than six months. "I guess I'm afraid of commitment," quips Billy. "I'm more the 'love 'em and leave 'em' kind of guy." Billy likes to "play the field," and bounces from one relationship to another.*

*More than any other topic in social psychology, research on close and intimate relationships highlights that we are, indeed, social beings. From our earliest moments as infants, and continuing through the oldest ages of adulthood, the close relationships and attachments we form with other people provide the basic foundations of social life. It is in the context of our intimate social relationships that we experience some of our most intense emotions—happiness, joy, love, desire, sorrow, despair, dejection, and heartache. The deep bonds we form with others provide a secure base from which we feel safe and empowered to explore and understand the world around us. And close social relationships afford an important degree of protection from many threats that await us.*

*Most close relationships begin with an initial attraction and sense of liking for another person, just as Frank and Betty described in their relationship. Why is it that we are attracted to some people, but not to others? On what basis do we develop a liking for one person, but not another? And is beauty in the eye of the beholder, or is it possible that some people are just more attractive than others? These questions are among those answered by research on liking and attraction. Some people are more attractive than others, with some interesting social consequences. But the affection that grows into a close relationship depends on many factors beyond those that simply meet the eye.*

*As we explore the nature and development of close interpersonal relationships, our focus will be on* **dyadic relationships**—*relationships that develop between two people. The very first close dyadic relationship is the one formed between an infant and a primary caregiver (usually the mother). The social world of the infant revolves around this relationship, and it can have a profound influence on social development later in life. Social life grows rapidly in childhood, and it is not long before children begin establishing close relationships with others—siblings, peers, and other adults. These relationships help to shape a child's social identity, and establish basic patterns of social interaction that carry into adulthood.*

**dyadic relationships**

*relationships that develop between two people*

*Starting in adolescence and early adulthood, people begin to establish intimate relationships. Romance and sex become an important part of social life. The rewards can be great—a sense of satisfaction, happiness, and even good health. But the costs can be great too. When a relationship ends or goes bad, the result can be loneliness, sadness, depression, and even poor health. Despite the downside, it seems that we are compelled to form close and intimate social relationships throughout the span of our lives. The ability to establish close relationships—to experience love and intimacy with another person—is a fundamental part of being human.*

## ● ● ● Attraction

Do you like everyone you meet? Probably not. Most of us take a liking to some people, but not to others. Why is this? What causes you to like one person, to be indifferent to another, and to dislike yet others? Your grandmother might tell you that opposites attract—that you like other people whose interests and backgrounds complement your own, and that you seek out the company of those who have different and unique perspectives. On the other hand, common folk wisdom has it that birds of a feather flock together—that it is similarity rather than difference that breeds liking and attraction for another. Which is it? Do opposites attract, or do we prefer those who are just like us?

Suppose that your friend is playing matchmaker and sets you up for a blind date. What's your first thought? You can admit it—you are probably wondering if this mystery date is good-looking. "Well," replies your friend, "beauty is more than skin deep. Looks aren't everything. Besides, he has a great personality." As you desperately look for a way out of this date, you begin to wonder why good looks and physical attraction are so important when it comes to potential romantic partners. "It really shouldn't matter," you tell yourself. But it does. Research on **interpersonal attraction** has shown that not only do birds of a feather flock together, but we also prefer the good-looking birds.

**interpersonal attraction**
*the study of attraction or liking between two or more people*

## Propinquity

Before two people can become lovers, or friends, or even mere acquaintances, they must first meet. The meeting can be face to face, it can be through the mail, or it can happen through the Internet. Regardless of the medium, a relationship cannot develop between two people until they meet. When Sam Cooke wrote a song about being alone on a Saturday night, he correctly identified the problem:

> If I could meet 'em I could get 'em
> but as yet I haven't met 'em
> that's how I'm in the state I'm in

This is why you go to parties and hang out in the common areas of the dorm— to meet people. When lonely hearts ask for advice, the columnists always suggest getting involved in activities with other people—at church, in a volunteer organization, wherever you can meet other people who share your interests. You may take this wisdom for granted, but the circumstances and causes of initial attraction often start with the boy or girl next door, simply because you are very likely to meet. The term **propinquity** captures this idea well—nearness or proximity in physical space,

**propinquity**
*nearness or proximity in physical space, which creates the opportunity to meet another person*

which creates the opportunity to meet another person. Despite the ready access to others provided by information technology (e-mail, instant messaging, and so on), physical proximity seems to play an important role in interpersonal communication and attraction (Burgoon, Bonito, Ramirez, Dunbar, Kam, & Fischer, 2002).

**The Likelihood of Meeting.** Whether you live in a dorm, in an apartment, or in a house, you probably live in the vicinity of other people. The typical apartment complex is a good example—hundreds of people living in close proximity. Out of all your neighbors, you are likely to run into some more than others. How often the paths of two neighbors cross will depend in large part on **spatial ecology**—the physical layout of the buildings and the distance separating apartments. Leon Festinger, Stanley Schachter, and Kurt Back (1950) took advantage of apartment life to study the effects of spatial ecology on the formation and development of friendships.

This classic study took place at two new housing projects—Westgate and Westgate West—which were built for married veteran students at the Massachusetts Institute of Technology in the mid-1940s. Because they were new developments, the students were assigned to houses or apartments based only on their order on a waiting list. This created an ideal opportunity to study the formation and development of friendships. The residents did not initially know one another, and they had no control over which particular house or apartment they were assigned. They were initially strangers, some of whom were destined to cross paths more often than others merely because of the physical arrangement of houses and apartments.

Consider the Westgate West apartments. These were former Navy barracks. Each had 10 apartments, with 5 to a floor. A schematic diagram of a Westgate West building is shown in Figure 13.1. The arrangement of the apartment units meant that the residents were likely to see some of their neighbors more than others. The residents of apartments 2 and 3 were next-door neighbors, whereas those in apartments 6 and 10 were separated by three other apartments. This difference in physical distance made it much more likely that the people in apartments 2 and 3 would bump into one another than would the people in apartments 6 and 10. But another kind of distance—**functional distance**—played an important role at Westgate West. Notice that two apartments—1 and 5—were located right in front of the stairs. This meant that the residents of those two first-floor apartments were more likely to see their upstairs neighbors than were the other first-floor residents. Physically, their apartments were farther apart, but functionally they were close together.

At one point in the study, the residents of Westgate and Westgate West were asked to name the three people they most often saw socially. The results showed a very clear effect of propinquity. The friends who were named most often were those who lived within closer physical *and* functional proximity. The lucky residents of the end apartments on the first floor (1 and 5) enjoyed a large number of

**spatial ecology**

*the physical layout of buildings and the distance separating different buildings, rooms, and other spaces*

**functional distance**

*compared to physical distance, the closeness between two places in terms of the opportunities for interaction*

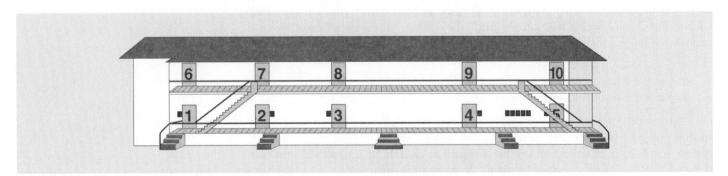

**FIGURE 13.1** Spatial arrangement of the apartments at Westgate West

From Festinger, Schachter, and Back, *Social Pressures in Informal Groups: A Study of Human Factors in Housing,* 1950. Reprinted by permission of HarperCollins Publishers, Inc.

friendships with the second-floor residents. The location at the foot of the stairs created a short functional distance to their second-floor neighbors. Indeed, this functional proximity was more important in determining mutual friendships than was physical proximity.

**Meeting Does Not Guarantee Liking.** Neighbors don't always get along. In fact, some neighbors hate one another. This suggests that living within close proximity of another is not a guarantee that you will become best friends. You could just as easily become bitter enemies. One reason is that your neighbors could do things that bother you—they may play the stereo too loud, fail to cut the grass, or constantly park their car in front of your house. In short, your neighbor can spoil the environment. Ebbe Ebbesen, Glenn Kjos, and Vladimir Konečni (1976) suggested that propinquity could just as easily produce disliking for your neighbor as it could a good friendship. To test this idea, they conducted a study very similar to the Westgate study, only this time it was done in an Irvine, California, housing development. The residents were asked to indicate three neighbors whom they liked

The simple fact that people live next door does not necessarily mean that they like each other.

*and* three neighbors whom they disliked. Just as Festinger, Schachter, and Back (1950) had found decades earlier, the liked neighbors were the ones who lived in closer proximity. And just as Ebbesen, Kjos, and Konečni suspected, the disliked neighbors were also the ones who lived within closer proximity. When an interviewer asked these residents why they disliked some of their close neighbors, it was most often because the neighbor did things to spoil their living environment. It seems that propinquity does not always lead to liking.

## Similarity

Why does propinquity matter? One reason is that it provides the opportunity and setting for the exchange of personal information (Brockner & Swap, 1976; Segal, 1974). Exchanging information—discovering what you have or don't have in common—is one of the principal ways in which people decide whether or not they like each other.

**Compatible Attitudes.** When you strike up a conversation with your neighbor, what do you talk about? Perhaps you comment on the weather or the latest sports scores, but that does not lay the foundation for a close and meaningful relationship. If you really want to establish some basis for a friendship, it is much more important to find out what the other person thinks and feels about current events, social and political issues, religion, morality, music, and literature. People find others more attractive and likable the more similar they are in their attitudes, beliefs, and preferences (Byrne, 1971; Klohnen & Luo, 2003). This is known as the **attitude-similarity effect**. For example, Donn Byrne and Gerald Clore (1966) had college students learn about a stranger's attitudes by either reading the stranger's responses to an attitude scale, listening to a tape recording of the stranger indicating his or her attitudes, or viewing a color movie of the stranger expressing his or her attitudes. Regardless of the medium of presentation, students found the stranger more attractive the more his or her attitudes were similar to their own. A number of studies indicate that we are more attracted to others who are similar to ourselves (Klohnen & Luo, 2003; Luo & Klohnen, 2005). Our attraction toward

**13.1**
ONLINE
LAB

**attitude-similarity effect**
*the idea that people find others more attractive and likable the more similar they are in their attitudes, beliefs, and preferences*

© Alex Wong/Getty Images

Not only are we attracted to similar others, but we are also repulsed by dissimilar others.

similar others need not be based on deep similarities, such as attitudes and values. John Jones and his colleagues (Jones, Pelham, Carvallo, & Mirenberg, 2004) found that people are more likely to marry someone whose first or last name is similar to their own!

The relationship between similarity and attraction can be viewed from another perspective, however. Milton Rosenbaum (1986) suggested that it is not so much that we are attracted to similar others, but rather that we are repulsed by dissimilar others. Here is the key to understanding this perspective: in the absence of any information about another person, we often tend to assume that we are similar in our attitudes and values. Adding information that tells us we are indeed similar should not cause a major change from our default assumption. However, learning that another person is actually quite different from ourselves should cause an adjustment—downward!—in our liking for that person. Rosenbaum calls this the **repulsion hypothesis,** and several studies show support for the idea (Chen & Kenrick, 2002; Rosenbaum, 1986).

**repulsion hypothesis**

*the idea that people find others less attractive and less likable if they differ substantially in their attitudes, beliefs, and preferences*

**self-disclosure**

*the process of people revealing to one another increasingly personal and intimate details about themselves*

**Self-Disclosure.** The development of a close dyadic relationship depends on both people revealing to one another increasingly personal and intimate details about themselves—a process known as **self-disclosure** (Derlega, Metts, Petronio, & Margulis, 1993; Reis, 2000). People who are willing to disclose intimate details about themselves are generally better liked than those who are less inclined to self-disclose. We also tend to reveal personal things about ourselves to others whom we initially like, and we tend to like others as a result of having disclosed personal information to them (Collins & Miller, 1994).

People do vary in their willingness or ability to engage in self-disclosure. Are you the type of person who is willing to completely and fully discuss with others your personal habits, deepest feelings, and worst fears? If so, then you are a high discloser. If you are the kind of person who is reluctant to discuss these things with others, then you are a low discloser. Not only do people differ in how much they self-disclose *to* others, but they also differ in how much they elicit disclosure *from* others (Miller, Berg, & Archer, 1983). Are you the type of person who can easily get people to open up, who enjoys listening to people, and who can keep other people talking about themselves? If so, then you are an opener—a person who is good at getting others to disclose intimate details about themselves.

Lynn Carol Miller, John Berg, and Richard Archer (1983) designed the Opener Scale to measure individual differences in people's ability to get other people to "open up" and to engage in intimate self-disclosure. Students at the University of Texas at Austin were classified as high or low disclosers, and as high or low openers. The students were then paired in all four combinations of discloser and opener status. One member in each pair was instructed to ask the other a series of questions in an effort to get acquainted. Some of the questions were fairly innocuous, such as "What do you dislike about your classes?" Other questions were more intimate, such as "What things in your past do you feel guilty about?" or "What attracts you to members of the opposite sex?" The high disclosers were willing to reveal intimate personal information to just about anyone, but the low disclosers were more comfortable revealing intimate personal details to partners who had good rather than poor opener abilities.

## Facial Beauty

Even before you strike up a conversation with a stranger, you have already taken in a great deal of information. One of the first things you notice when you meet another person face to face is his or her face. In the process of getting acquainted and deciding whether you like another person, do looks matter to you? If you are like most people, looks do matter (Hatfield & Sprecher, 1986). Most of us respond more favorably to, and show more interest in, attractive than unattractive people. It seems to start early in infancy: babies show a preference for attractive over unattractive faces, they show more positive responses to attractive than unattractive strangers, and they prefer attractive to unattractive dolls (Langlois, Roggman, & Rieser-Danner, 1990). As children grow older, physical attraction continues to play an important role in interpersonal relationships.

Perhaps infants don't know better, and we do often hear that children can be cruel. But as adults, have we not learned that beauty is in the eye of the beholder, that we should never judge a book by its cover, and that beauty is only skin deep? The answer to all three questions seems to be no. A review of the research on facial attractiveness shows that beauty is *not* in the eye of the beholder, that people *do* judge "books" by their "covers," and that beauty is *sometimes* more than skin deep (Langlois, Kalakanis, Rubenstein, Larson, Hallam, & Smoot, 2000).

**Shared Perceptions of Beauty.** A common assumption is that standards of beauty are culture-specific, and that children within a particular culture gradually learn what is and is not considered attractive. The research evidence, however, does not support this assumption. Even very young infants show a preference for faces that adults have judged as attractive (Langlois, Ritter, Roggman, & Vaughn, 1991; Ramsey, Langlois, Hoss, Rubenstein, & Griffin, 2004). When people are asked to rate the attractiveness of strangers' faces, they show remarkable agreement (Berscheid & Walster, 1974). The consistency even cuts across cultural boundaries (Bernstein, Lin, & McClellan, 1982; Cunningham, 1986). Asian, Hispanic, Black, and White students show very strong agreement in their judgments of the physical attractiveness of Asian, Hispanic, Black, and White photographed faces (Cunningham, Roberts, Barbee, Druen, & Wu, 1995). People of all ages and cultural backgrounds seem to share a common view of what is, and what is not, an attractive face. But what is it, exactly, that makes a face attractive?

**The Components of Facial Features.** One way to answer this question is to measure specific features of the face. Does facial attractiveness depend on the length of your nose, the shape of your eyes, the height of your cheekbones, the

© Larry Williams/CORBIS

People of all ages and cultural backgrounds seem to share a common view of what is, and what is not, considered an attractive face.

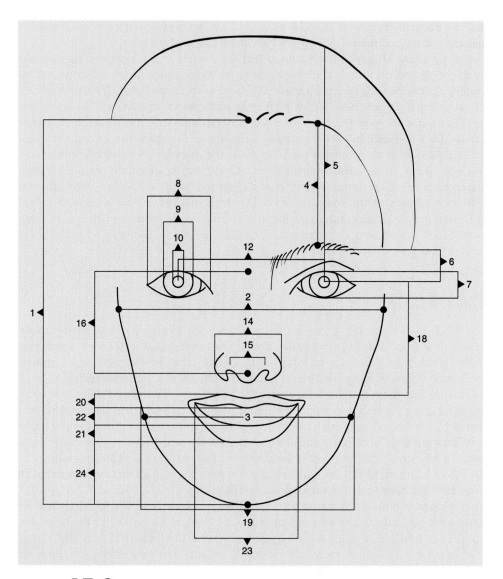

**FIGURE 13.2** Facialmetrics involves the measurement of different facial features, such as width of pupil (10), length of nose (16), and width of smile (23).

From Cunningham, "Measuring the physical in physical attractiveness: Quasi-experiments on the sociobiology of female facial beauty," *Journal of Personality and Social Psychology*, 50(5), 925–935. Copyright © 1986 by the American Psychological Association. Reprinted by permission.

fullness of your lips, the slant of your forehead, or the thickness of your eyebrows? Facialmetrics is one approach to studying facial beauty. As Figure 13.2 shows, facialmetrics involves the measurement of a large number of facial features, such as the size of a nose or the width of a smile. Using this approach, Michael Cunningham, Anita Barbee, and Carolyn Pike (1990) found that female college students rated male faces as more attractive when those faces featured prominent cheekbones, a large chin, and a wide smile. The women also showed a preference for male faces in which the height of the eyes did not deviate too far from average. In another study, Cunningham (1986) asked male college students to make similar ratings about female faces. The men indicated a preference for large eyes, a small nose and chin, prominent cheekbones, high eyebrows, large pupils, and a large smile.

**Average Faces Are Attractive Faces.** The facialmetric approach has shown that some facial features are related to attractiveness, but others are not.

And in some cases, such as height of the eyes, it is deviance from the average that makes a face less attractive. Yet this still does not answer the question of what particular combination of features makes one face more attractive than another. Nor does it explain the remarkable consistency across ages and cultures in what people consider attractive in a face. Rather than dissecting the face into hundreds of possible features, Judith Langlois and Lori Roggman (1990) approached the problem from a different angle. They noted two things. First, evolutionary pressures and natural selection generally favor average rather than extreme population features. Second, starting early in infancy, people routinely form prototypes or cognitive schemas that capture the central or average features of the many instances and exemplars of a particular category (see Chapters 3 and 4 on Social Cognition and Social Perception). Putting these two observations together, Langlois and her colleagues made a fascinating prediction: Faces will be judged as more attractive the closer they are to the average of the population of faces.

To test this prediction, pictures of faces were digitized into a standard 512 × 512 matrix. Composite faces were then created by calculating the arithmetic average across 2, 4, 8, 16, or 32 faces. Figure 13.3 illustrates the averaging process, and Figure 13.4 (p. 532) shows examples of what happens when you average across multiple digitized faces. Male and female college students were asked to rate the attractiveness of

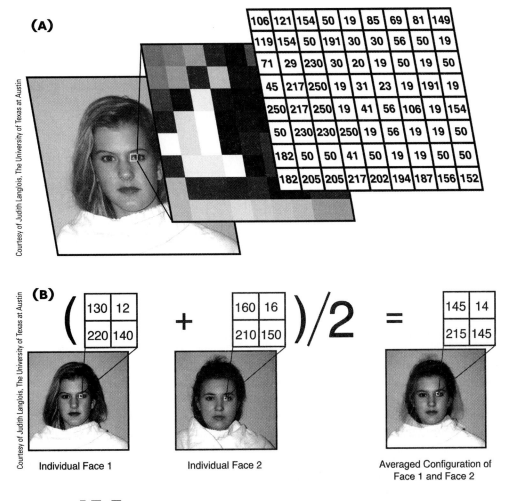

**FIGURE 13.3** Faces can be digitized (A) and then multiple faces can be averaged to create a composite (B).

From Langlois, Roggman, and Musselman, "What is average and what is not average about attractive faces?" *Psychological Science,* 5(4), 214–220, 1994. Reprinted by permission of Blackwell Publishing.

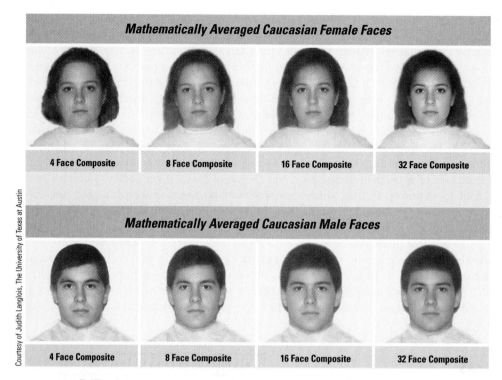

Courtesy of Judith Langlois, The University of Texas at Austin

**FIGURE 13.4** The effects of averaging across 4, 8, 16, or 32 faces. Faces are judged as more attractive the greater the number of faces contributing to the composite.

From website for Langlois, Roggman, and Musselman, "What is average and what is not average about attractive faces?" *Psychological Science*, 5(4), 214–220, 1994. Reprinted by permission of Blackwell Publishing.

both the individual and the various composite faces. The students showed a clear preference for the 16- and 32-face composites, rating them as more attractive than the individual faces that were used to create them. It seems that averaged faces are more appealing than individual instances. Does this imply that the best-looking faces are just average and undistinguished (Alley & Cunningham, 1991)? Not according to Langlois, Roggman, and Lisa Musselman (1994), who point out that averaged faces are anything but average. They simply represent the best example or prototype of what a face looks like. Perhaps because of their apparent familiarity, people find such prototypical faces very attractive (Berscheid & Reis, 1998).

## Bodily Features

Most of the research on physical attraction focuses on facial features (Berscheid & Reis, 1998). But the human body offers more than just the face as a basis for judging attractiveness. People differ in their height, weight, body shape, hair color, skin color, and odor. For these dimensions, a number of important consistencies have been found, but also some interesting cultural differences.

**Body Types.** People come in all different shapes and sizes. Some people are lean and muscular; others are softer and rounder. One aspect of body type that has shown a consistent relationship to rated attractiveness is the waist-to-hip ratio—the ratio of waist circumference to hip circumference. For most adult women, the waist is narrower than the hips and so the waist-to-hip ratio is less than 1.0. Of course women vary quite a bit, with some whose waist is much narrower than their hips, and others whose waist and hips are about the same. For most adult men, the waist

**FIGURE 13.5** Line drawings illustrate female waist-to-hip ratios of .7, .8, .9, and 1.0 (from left to right). Males judge females with lower waist-to-hip ratios as more attractive

From Singh, "Adaptive significance of female physical attractiveness: Role of waist-to-hip ratio," *Journal of Personality and Social Psychology*, 65(2), 293–307. Copyright © 1993 by the American Psychological Association. Reprinted by permission.

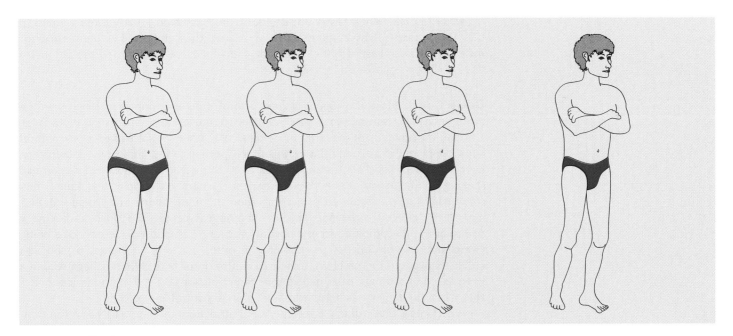

**FIGURE 13.6** Line drawings illustrate male waist-to-hip ratios of .7, .8, .9, and 1.0 (from left to right). Females judge males with higher waist-to-hip ratios as more attractive.

From Singh, "Female judgment of male attractiveness and desirability for relationships: Role of waist-to-hip ratio and financial status," *Journal of Personality and Social Psychology*, 69(6), 1089–1101. Copyright © 1995 by the American Psychological Association. Reprinted by permission.

and hips are nearly the same in circumference, and so the waist-to-hip ratio is much closer to 1.0. But men vary too, with some whose hips extend further around than their waists. Figures 13.5 and 13.6 show examples of male and female bodies that vary in their waist-to-hip ratios.

Judgments of body shape show that men prefer women whose waist is narrower than their hips, but women prefer men whose waist and hips are nearly the same in circumference.

Devendra Singh (1993) asked male college students to rate the attractiveness of female figures that varied in their waist-to-hip ratios. The men rated line drawings just like the ones in Figure 13.5. Results showed that the female figures were judged as more attractive when they exhibited a low rather than a high waist-to-hip ratio. In another study, Singh (1995) asked female college students to make similar ratings of male figures varying in waist-to-hip ratios. The women rated line drawings just like the ones in Figure 13.6. In contrast to the earlier study involving the ratings made by men of female figures, the women judged the male figures in this study as more attractive when they exhibited a waist-to-hip ratio closer to 1.0. It seems that men prefer women whose waist is narrower than their hips (see also Streeter and McBurney, 2003), whereas women prefer men who have a relatively tapered look with hips and waist approximately the same in circumference.

**Weight.** In some cultures, thinness is considered most attractive, but elsewhere the cultural ideal is a plump body (Symons, 1979). In North America, thin is in and there is a pervasive stigma attached to being overweight (Crandall, 1994; Crocker, Cornwell, & Major, 1993). But why should preferences for body weight differ across cultures? One explanation is that attitudes about weight are communicated through a culture's customs and media. If the culture equates thinness with beauty, then members of the culture will learn to prefer thin bodies. If the cultural tradition is to value plumpness, then members of the culture will learn to prefer heavier bodies.

**Height.** What's your preference in a date? Do you prefer someone who is taller than you, shorter than you, or about the same height? The apparent rule for heterosexual dating is that males should be taller (Berscheid & Walster, 1974). But perhaps not too tall. When Graziano, Brothen, and Berscheid (1978) asked women to rate the attractiveness of potential male dates, they indicated a preference for males of medium height (5'9"–5'11"). The short males (5'5"–5'7") and the tall males (6'2"–6'4") were judged as less attractive.

**Body Odor.** Most of us spend a good deal of time and money making ourselves smell good. We use underarm deodorant, brush our teeth with scented toothpaste, and dab ourselves with perfume or cologne. We assume that some of our natural body odors might be unattractive to others, perhaps even offensive. People who have a pleasant body odor *are* judged as more attractive than those who smell bad (Levine & McBurney, 1986). We are especially hard on people who know they smell bad and who could do something about it. John Levine and Donald McBurney (1977) created some portraits of hypothetical people described as having a severe body odor problem. In one portrait, the target person was described as being aware and able to control the problem. In other portraits, the target person was either unaware of the problem, unable to control it, or both. When college students were asked to evaluate each malodorous target person, they were much less favorable when the target was both aware and able to control the problem.

The factors that influence interpersonal attraction are summarized in the Concept Review on the next page.

## The Evolutionary Significance of Good Looks

Many of the results we just reviewed may make sense in terms of your own experience. But why should waist-to-hip ratios matter, and why the differences between genders? Why are people with a pleasant body odor judged as more attractive? Why does a person's weight matter when it comes to perceptions of attractiveness? Social psychologists often draw on evolutionary theory to explain these effects (Barrett, Dunbar, & Lycett, 2002).

© Randy Faris/CORBIS

## CONCEPT REVIEW
### *Interpersonal Attraction*

| Source of Information | Description | Effect | Example |
|---|---|---|---|
| Propinquity | Nearness or proximity in physical space, which creates the opportunity to meet another person. | Next-door neighbors are more likely to know one another. This can lead to either increased or decreased liking. | Residents of neighboring apartments are more likely to socialize and become friends. |
| Similarity | Sharing similar attitudes, values, and beliefs with another person. | The greater the similarity between two people, the greater the liking. | Learning that you and a stranger feel the same way about the major political parties will lead to increased liking. |
| Repulsion | People exhibit extremely dissimilar attitudes, values, and beliefs. | The greater the dissimilarity between two people, the less the liking. | You dislike another person when you discover major differences in your religious beliefs. |
| Self-disclosure | Disclosing intimate details about yourself to another person. | People who disclose intimate details about themselves are liked better. | Talking to another person about things that frighten you leads to increased attraction. |
| Facial features | Aspects of a person's face, such as size of a nose, width of a smile, slant of forehead, or thickness of eyebrows. | People are judged as more beautiful when their facial features are closest to the average. | A person with eyes very close together is judged as less attractive than others with more average spacing between their eyes. |
| Bodily features | Aspects of a person's body, such as body type, weight, height, or body odor. | For men, a waist-to-hip ratio close to 1 is judged as most attractive. For women, a waist-to-hip ratio less than 1 is judged as most attractive. | A pear-shaped man is judged as less attractive than a man with a tapered body type. |

For example, Singh (1993, 1995) draws on evolutionary theory to explain the effects of waist-to-hip ratios. Until boys and girls reach puberty, they have very similar waist-to-hip-ratios (both usually very close to 1.0). It all changes when females reach the age of menarche and become biologically capable of reproducing. This is when the hips of most young women become relatively larger than their waist. It is an outwardly visible signal to males that a female is capable of reproduction. As males mature, they tend to take on a more tapered look, but their hip-to-waist ratio stays roughly the same. This too is a signal of a male's reproductive ability: a waist-to-hip ratio closer to 1.0 is an outwardly visible signal to females that a male is in good health and capable of contributing his part to reproduction.

Accounting for the effects of body weight on attraction, an evolutionary view would emphasize that body weight serves as an outwardly visible signal of reproductive potential. Indeed, cultures that exhibit a preference for plump bodies are also ones where food resources are scarce. In that particular environmental context, greater body fat is a signal of greater reproductive potential (Symons, 1979). In North America, where food resources are not scarce, thinness may be a signal of relatively better reproductive health.

Other research shows that facial attractiveness is strongly related to the perceived health of the model's skin (B. C. Jones, Little, Burt, & Perrett, 2004; B. C.

Jones, Little, Feinberg, Penton-Voak, Tiddeman, & Perrett, 2004), and we seem to prefer faces that display symmetry—relative similarity of the left and right sides. The preference for symmetric faces appears to exist across cultures, and even young infants show the preference (Noor & Evans, 2003; Rhodes, Geddes, Jeffery, Dziurawiec, & Clark, 2002; Rhodes, Yoshikawa, Clark, Lee, McKay, & Akamatsu, 2001). Again drawing from an evolutionary explanation, it may be the case that nice skin and symmetrical faces communicate information about a person's overall state of health. To the extent that health is a sign of reproductive fitness, our species may be specially tuned to find these features attractive.

## The Social Benefits of Good Looks

The evidence is that some people are, indeed, better looking than others. But physical attractiveness is just a surface feature. What do good looks have to do with the more important internal qualities of a person—intelligence, character, personality, skills, or competence?

**What Is Beautiful Is Good.** We are frequently admonished to never judge a book by its cover, but when it comes to making judgments about other people, that's exactly what we do. People regularly make the inference that **what is beautiful is good**—that attractive people possess other desirable traits and abilities in addition to their good looks (Dion, Berscheid, & Walster, 1972). Based on nothing more than photographs, attractive babies were judged by adults as smarter, as easier to care for, and as causing parents fewer problems than unattractive babies (Stephan & Langlois, 1984). The same thing happened when kindergartners and fourth-graders were asked to consider photographs of second-graders. The attractive second-graders were judged as smarter, friendlier, and less mean than unattractive second-graders (Langlois & Stephan, 1977). In study after study, attractive people are judged as more socially competent and socially skilled than unattractive people (Eagly, Ashmore, Makhijani, & Longo, 1991; Feingold, 1992b).

The accompanying feature, Social Psychology in Your Life: Preparing for Your Day in Court, discusses how physical attractiveness may influence court decisions.

The *what is beautiful is good* stereotype does not apply to every personal quality. For example, attractive and unattractive people are judged as no different in their integrity or concern for others (Eagly et al., 1991). But keep in mind that most of the research has been conducted in North America, with North Americans judging other North Americans. Within this individualist cultural context, social competence and social skills are more highly valued than concern for others (Triandis, 1995). Now consider the very different context found in many Asian cultures, where concern for others and group allegiance are among the most highly prized personal qualities (Triandis, 1995). When students in Korea (a more collectivist culture) were asked to rate the photographs of other Korean students, the more attractive people were judged as higher in integrity and concern for others (Wheeler & Kim, 1997). Taking the cultural context into account, it would seem that what is beautiful is *culturally* good.

**The Real Benefits of Beauty.** Now we know that some people are better-looking than others and that it is common to make a variety of positive inferences about good-looking people. But does that mean that good-looking people actually do possess all of the desirable qualities and abilities that we assume they do? The answer is *sometimes yes* and *sometimes no* (Feingold, 1992b). Averaging over dozens of studies, it is true that physically attractive people are more popular, more socially skilled, and more sexually experienced than unattractive people. But attractive people are far from perfect, especially when you look beyond their social skills. For example, attractive and unattractive people do not differ in their intelli-

**what is beautiful is good**

*the inference that attractive people possess other desirable traits and abilities in addition to their good looks*

# Social Psychology in Your Life    *Preparing for Your Day in Court*

The benefits of being attractive extend well beyond the domain of liking and friendships. As we saw in Chapter 7, persuasive communications are more effective when they are attributed to an attractive rather than an unattractive source. Physical attractiveness can also be on your side when you find yourself in a court of law, whether you are there as a witness, as a plaintiff, as a defendant, or as an attorney. If you find yourself in one of these situations, you should attend to how you look.

During the 1950s, an ambitious program of research known as the Chicago Jury Project compared the decisions reached by actual juries with the decisions that would have been reached by judges. In about 3,500 cases in which they knew what the juries had decided, Kalven and Zeisel (1966) asked judges to render their own hypothetical verdicts. In about 14% of the cases, the judges said they would have convicted the defendant even though the jury had actually voted to acquit. Why did the jury let the defendant go in those cases? It may have been because the defendant was attractive or because the victim was unattractive (or both). In another 14% of the cases, the judges said they would have acquitted even though the jury had actually voted to convict the defendant. Why did the jury convict in those cases? Again, it was often because the defendant was unattractive or because the victim was attractive (or both). More recent studies in Canada have shown that physically unattractive defendants are more likely to be classified as Dangerous Offenders under the Canadian Criminal Code (Esses & Webster, 1988) and are more likely to receive severe sentences (Stewart, 1980).

This attractiveness bias has also been demonstrated in laboratory studies, in which mock or pretend jurors generally rate physically attractive defendants as less guilty and as deserving less punishment than unattractive defendants (Berg & Vidmar, 1975; Bray & Noble, 1987; Efran, 1974; Mitchell & Byrne, 1973; Reynolds & Sanders, 1975; Rumsey, 1976; Rumsey, Allgeier, & Castore, 1978; Vidmar & Crinklaw, 1974). But don't depend on your good looks to always get you off the hook. Laboratory studies have shown that being physically attractive can backfire on defendants who *use* their attractiveness to perpetrate a crime. Sigall and Ostrove (1975) found that attractive defendants who had been accused of burglary received shorter sentences than did unattractive defendants—just as the previous studies would have predicted. However, attractive defendants who were accused of swindling received longer sentences than did unattractive defendants. It seems that people take offense when criminals deliberately use their good looks to take advantage of others.

Does this evidence mean that attractiveness of trial participants controls the outcome in the majority of cases? Not at all. A defendant's (or plaintiff's) personal attributes, including attractiveness, are especially important when other information is lacking or extremely ambiguous. But usually, what determines the outcome of a case is the strength of the evidence.

gence or mental health. Still, attractive children and attractive adults do seem to possess better social skills than their unattractive counterparts.

   # Friendships

We have learned quite a lot about why people come to like one another, and about the physical features of other people that we find most and least attractive. But that's only the beginning when it comes to the close relationships we form with others. How does that initial sense of liking or attraction eventually grow into a deeper and closer relationship? Early in your life, you almost certainly developed very close relationships with the adults who cared for you—your mother, your father, and others. As you grew, friends became an increasingly important part of your life. Most adults can still name their best childhood friends, and you probably count a number of those people among your close friends today. Of course, you don't develop close friendships with everyone you meet, or even with everyone whom you like and find attractive. In this section, we will explore theories and research that help us to understand how and why we develop friendships with some people, but not with others.

You will notice that much of this section focuses on friendships among children. When it comes to adults, the research attention has been on romantic relationships rather than on friendships. Nevertheless, it is instructive to examine how children become friends. Much of what guides the formation of friendships in childhood also applies to the close relationships we form as adults.

## Friendships Among Children

In most settings, children spend much of their time in the company of other children—around the neighborhood, in school, and on sports teams (Ellis, Rogoff, & Cromer, 1981). As we discussed earlier, it is propinquity that provides the opportunity for children to develop close relationships with their peers.

Of the many possible dyads that can be formed, only a relatively few will result in close **friendships.** What distinguishes a friend from a mere acquaintance? The method most often used to establish that two people are friends is a **sociometric rating procedure.** Within a group of acquaintances, each person is asked to name everyone whom he or she considers a friend. Two peers within that social network are then considered to be friends if each one nominates the other as a friend.

Under what conditions does a mere acquaintanceship develop into a closer friendship? The strongest determinant is similarity: children are more likely to become friends when they are alike in age, sex, ethnicity, race, and interests (Hartup, 1989). Children quickly discover the dimensions along which they are similar. Kenneth Rubin and his colleagues (Rubin, Lynch, Coplan, Rose-Krasnor, & Booth, 1994) assembled four unfamiliar 7-year-olds together in a room and observed their social interactions and approaches to playing. When each child was then asked to indicate which of the other children was preferred as a playmate, they selected the one whose behavioral style was most similar to their own. In adolescence, as in adulthood, it is similarity in attitudes, life goals, and intelligence that helps to establish a friendship (Smollar & Youniss, 1982).

Some kinds of similarity are easy to recognize—the outwardly visible signs of age, sex, and race. But how do children learn about their similarities and differences when it comes to interests, preferences, attitudes, or goals in life? Just like adults, children rely on a process of self-disclosure—revealing to one another increasingly personal and intimate details. Children who are successful in communicating with another, and sharing information about themselves, are more likely to develop a close friendship (Gottman, 1983). The friendship will continue to grow as long as the children cooperate and reciprocate in their exchanges, and learn how to resolve their conflicts in a peaceful way (Hartup, 1989; Newcomb & Bagwell, 1995).

**Popularity.** Some children enjoy many friendships, while others seem to have few. What is it that distinguishes popular children from the unpopular ones? **Popular children** are the ones who are named frequently by others in a sociometric rating procedure. They are good at maintaining positive relationships with their peers, and tend to avoid drawing attention to themselves. They join in play with others without disrupting what the others are doing, they play constructively, they communicate clearly about their feelings and interests, and they are generally cooperative and sensitive to others' interests. Popular children can be aggressive in the sense of being assertive, but their aggression rarely disrupts the activi-

**friendships**

*dyadic relationships involving mutual liking*

**sociometric rating procedure**

*within a group of acquaintances, each person is asked to name everyone whom he or she considers a friend. Two peers within that social network are then considered to be friends if each nominates the other as a friend*

**popular children**

*children who are named frequently by others in a sociometric rating procedure*

Of the many possible dyads that can be formed, only a relatively few will result in close friendships. Children are more likely to become friends when they are alike in age, sex, ethnicity, race, and interests.

© Tom Stewart/CORBIS

ties of others (Newcomb, Bukowski, & Pattee, 1993). In addition to their social skills and competence, popular children also tend to be more physically attractive (Langlois, 1986).

**Unpopularity.** Some children are unpopular because they commonly engage in disruptive aggressive behaviors. These children are called **rejected-aggressive children.** They exhibit the opposite of the very same qualities that make children popular: They tend to brag about and call attention to themselves, are uncooperative in peer groups, and are relatively insensitive to others' interests and needs. They tend to be rejected by their peers because of their aggressiveness. Other children are spurned by their peers for a very different reason—because of their social awkwardness and immaturity. These are known as **rejected-withdrawn children.** They just never seem to "fit in," and over time they develop low self-esteem, avoid playing with others, and frequently become the victims of bullying attacks (Hodges, Malone, & Perry, 1997).

Most studies of popularity involve observation of peers who are already acquainted. To understand the origin of popularity, Kenneth Dodge (1983) observed the interactions in a group of initially unacquainted second-grade boys. Each group had eight boys, who were observed during a series of one-hour play sessions. The play sessions took place in a large room full of toys and furniture. The boys were free to play with the toys, climb on the furniture, engage in rough-and-tumble play, or to sit off by themselves if they wanted. After two weeks of these play sessions, some of the boys had emerged as popular within the group, while others were clearly suffering from peer rejection. What did these two groups of children do differently? For one thing, the rejected children were frequently aggressive; the popular children were not. The popular and rejected children engaged in about the same amount of social conversation with their peers during the first play session; but by the eighth play session, the popular children were engaging in social conversation twice as often as the rejected children. Similar to the findings of many other studies, among these second-grade boys, the popular children were more physically attractive than their rejected peers. In a similar study, John Coie and Janis Kupersmidt (1983) determined the popularity status within groups of fourth-grade boys who already knew each other. When the boys were then placed into new groups of unacquainted peers, they quickly reestablished their old social status: boys who were previously popular emerged as popular in the new group, and boys who were previously rejected found themselves rejected once again.

**How Peers Exert Their Influence.** It is a common observation that children and adolescents are influenced by their peers (Harris, 1995). Thomas Berndt (1979) asked groups of 3rd, 6th, 9th, and 11th–12th graders whether or not they would go along with the antisocial behavior of their peers. The antisocial behaviors included such things as cheating, stealing, and minor destruction of property. As an example, here is one of the scenarios described to the children:

> You are with a couple of your best friends on Halloween. They're going to soap windows, but you're not sure whether you should or not. Your friends all say you should, because there's no way you could get caught. What would you *really* do? (Berndt, 1979, p. 610)

The children were asked to indicate whether or not they would engage in the described behavior, and how certain they were about their choice. As you can see

Some children are rejected by their peers because of aggressive behavior. Others are rejected because of their social awkwardness and immaturity.

**rejected-aggressive children**
*children who are unpopular because they commonly engage in disruptive aggressive behaviors*

**rejected-withdrawn children**
*children who are spurned by their peers because of their social awkwardness and immaturity*

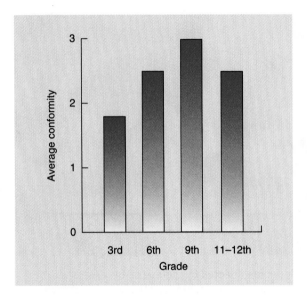

**FIGURE 13.7** Conformity with peers' antisocial behavior increases from 3rd to 9th grade, but then declines somewhat in 11th—12th grade.

Data from Berndt, 1979, "Developmental changes in conformity to peers and parents," Study 1. *Developmental Psychology*, 15(6), 608–616.

in Figure 13.7, peer conformity increased from the 3rd through the 9th grade, but then showed a reduction among 11th–12th graders. At least until early adolescence, children show increasing peer conformity. The reduction among 11th–12th graders, whose average age was 18, reflects a developmental trend toward greater autonomy in late adolescence and young adulthood.

Peer conformity is a classic example of normative social influence (Chapter 8). Remember that normative influence occurs because of social pressures, rewards, and norms. Fitting in with your peers, and fearing their rejection, brings heavy social pressure to conform. As children grow and develop during the grade school years, they become more sensitive to social norms, and their motivation to be accepted and liked by their peers increases.

## Friendships Among Adults

As we mentioned earlier, friendship formation among adults has received relatively little research attention (Derlega & Winstead, 1986). We know a fair amount about what adults find attractive in one another, the important role of attitude similarity as a determinant of liking, and the value that adults place in self-disclosure. Yet we don't know much about how adults move from initial attraction and sense of liking to a deeper, closer friendship. Nor do we know much about how adult friendships develop over time. Some initial insight, however, was provided in a study conducted by Robert Hays (1985).

At the very beginning of their first year in college, students were recruited for a 12-week longitudinal study of friendship development. At the outset, each student was asked to name two people of their same sex whom they did not know before school began but with whom they thought they might become friends. Then every three weeks the students completed a variety of questionnaires asking about their dyadic interactions with their budding friends.

Whatever led the students to initially nominate someone as a potential friend did not always result in a close friendship—about 63% of the potential friendships actually developed into close friendships by the end of the school term. One thing that did predict the success of a friendship was propinquity—a good friendship was more likely to develop between roommates or dorm-mates than between two students who lived in different buildings or in different parts of town. As the relationships developed over time, the students reported increasing levels of intimacy in their personal exchanges. At the outset, the would-be friends might discuss local, regional, or world events (a low level of intimacy). But as time went by, the friends were more likely to discuss things such as their current sexual activities (clearly a more intimate revelation). Indeed, self-disclosure of increasingly intimate details became a very important part of the growing friendships.

## Rejection

Nobody likes to feel rejected, yet social exclusion seems to start early in social life. Social relationships are so integral and important in our lives, and when others exclude or reject us it creates a feeling that can best be described as *painful.* Recent research suggests that the pain we feel may be deeply rooted in our brains. Naomi Eisenberger, Matthew Lieberman, and Kipling Williams (2003) engaged people in a simulated game of three-way catch. It became evident at some point that the participant was being excluded by the other two players. Here's the interesting feature of the study: the participants' brains were being scanned all the time using a method called functional magnetic resonance imaging (fMRI). The brain scans showed that social rejection in the three-way game of catch caused a response in the participants' brains that is very similar to the experience of physical pain. It is true that rejection hurts—quite literally!

 # Attachment

It may seem logical at this point to jump right into the topic of close and intimate relationships in adulthood. We will get to that topic soon. But first it is useful to step back and consider an integrative theoretical approach to understanding relationships—the theory of attachment. Rather than drawing a distinction between the relationships we form as children and the relationships we form as adults, attachment theory suggests that the same basic processes govern our close relationships throughout the span of our lives.

## Attachment Theory

Have you ever watched a litter of very young puppies? They spend most of their time playing, exploring the world, eating, and sleeping. They certainly seem to enjoy one another, and usually enjoy playing with people too. But what happens when a puppy is suddenly frightened, or finds that it has strayed too far from its familiar surroundings? Will the puppy take comfort if you hold it, pet it, and speak softly? Probably not. Most puppies will still show signs of distress—they whine, wiggle, and shake, frantically searching for their *mother*. Only the puppy's mother will do. Very early in life, those puppies become very *attached* to their mother. Indeed, we are always cautioned never to separate a puppy from its mother too early; we are often told that it can cause harm. People are not much different. Infants like to play and to explore, but they also become upset when they get separated from their mother or whomever else they are especially attached to. When babies become distressed, not just anyone is able to provide comfort and relief—only that special person will do, the one to whom the infant is closely attached.

John Bowlby (1969) used the concept of attachment to explain how and why people develop close relationships. Bowlby's **attachment theory** focused primarily on the infant and his or her caregiver, but the theory of attachment is also used to account for the relationships that develop between close friends and lovers throughout the life span (Colin, 1996). Bowlby emphasized an *ethological* approach, which focuses on innate behaviors that have been shaped during the course of evolution. Babies are cute—their faces, smiles, and body proportions seem to invite a positive response from adults. Positive attention from adults leads to a positive response from the infant, and before you know it a close relationship is developing. In Bowlby's view, both the infant and the adult come biologically prepared to develop attachments. The process is not instantaneous, however; it unfolds over time, and depends on each member of the dyad learning how to respond appropriately to the other.

**attachment theory**
*Bowlby's theory concerning the development and the effects of the emotional bond between an infant and its caregiver; also used to account for the relationships that develop between close friends and lovers throughout the life span*

## Infant Attachment

Most of attachment theory, and the research conducted to support the theory, has been developed in the context of infant–caregiver relationships. In this section,

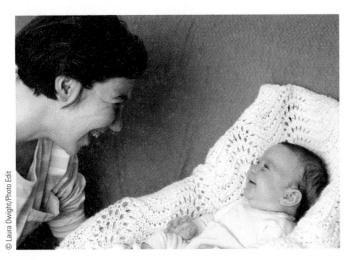

Social smiles between an infant and mother mark the beginning of a close emotional attachment.

**strange situation**

*developed by Mary Ainsworth, a procedure involving several brief episodes during which experimenters observe a baby's responses to strangers, separation from mother, and reunions with mother*

**secure attachment**

*the most common pattern seen in the strange situation procedure, in which the baby actively explores the room when left alone with mother, gets upset when mother leaves the room, is clearly happy when mother returns, and may seek close physical proximity with her in an effort to relieve distress; the baby uses its mother as a safe haven and a secure base from which it feels safe to explore a novel situation*

**insecure attachment**

*a pattern seen in the strange situation, in which the baby does not use its mother as a safe haven and secure base from which to explore a novel situation*

**resistant insecure attachment**

*a pattern seen in the strange situation, in which the baby prefers to stay close to mother rather than actively explore the room, becomes very upset when mother leaves the room, and appears to be upset or angry when mother returns, trying to remain near the mother but usually resisting any physical contact initiated by her; sometimes called ambivalent or anxious-ambivalent insecure attachment*

we will discuss some of that research. As you are reading about strange situations and forms of attachment, think about how these ideas might apply to the attachments and relationships we form as adults.

**The Strange Situation.** How do we take Bowlby's (1969) theory and test it in the laboratory? Mary Ainsworth and her colleagues (Ainsworth, Blehar, Waters, & Wall, 1978) created a situation involving several brief episodes during which the experimenters could observe the baby's responses to strangers, separation from mother, and reunions with mother. The procedure is known as the **strange situation.** The mother and baby are introduced to the experimental room, which contains a variety of toys and play objects. The mother and baby are left alone for a few minutes, and their behavior is observed and recorded through a one-way mirror. Then a stranger (the experimenter) enters the room, and soon begins conversing with the mother. The stranger then approaches the baby as the mother unobtrusively leaves the room. For the next few minutes, the stranger sits quietly in the room allowing the baby to explore and to play with toys. The mother then returns for a reunion with her baby. Another few minutes pass, then the mother says "bye bye" and leaves the baby alone in the room. Remember that the experimenters are observing and recording the baby's responses the whole time. After the baby has been left alone for a few minutes (less if severe signs of distress are observed), the stranger reenters the room, and offers comfort if the baby is clearly upset. The mother then returns for a final reunion.

What do babies actually do in the strange situation? Observation of 1-year-old infants usually shows the expected emotional responses: protest, despair, and detachment. But infants vary in their specific patterns of behavior. Not all infants display signs of distress, and not all show detachment. Generally, infants fall into one of three categories (Colin, 1996):

*Secure.* By far the most common pattern, **secure attachment** is seen when the baby actively explores the room when left alone with the mother, gets upset when the mother leaves the room, is clearly happy when the mother returns, and may even seek close physical proximity with her in an effort to relieve distress. This pattern is called *secure* attachment because the baby is clearly using its mother as a safe haven and a secure base from which it feels safe to explore a novel situation. Across many studies, about 62% of North American infants show the secure attachment pattern (Campos, Barrett, Lamb, Goldsmith, & Stenberg, 1983).

*Resistant.* One pattern of **insecure attachment** is seen among babies who prefer to stay close to the mother rather than actively exploring the room, who become very upset when the mother leaves the room, and who appear to be upset or angry when the mother returns. During the reunion episodes, these babies try to remain near their mothers, yet they usually resist any physical contact initiated by her. It seems that these infants want to cling to their mothers, but they clearly have become angry with her. This pattern is usually called **resistant insecure attachment.** Because of the vacillation between approach and avoidance, the pattern is sometimes called *ambivalent* or *anxious-ambivalent insecure attachment* (Cassidy & Berlin, 1994). About 15% of North American infants show this attachment pattern (Campos et al., 1983).

*Avoidant.* A second pattern of insecure attachment is seen among babies who basically ignore their mothers, and usually show no strong signs of disturbance when she leaves the room. These babies are often observed to avoid their

Different forms of attachment are expressed in distinct emotional expressions: (left) enjoying comfort and safety; (middle) being angry; and (right) being aloof and ignoring.

mothers during reunion episodes, or at least to greet her return rather casually. This is why the pattern is usually called **avoidant insecure attachment.** About 23% of North American infants show this pattern (Campos et al., 1983).

**Is It Universal?**  Attachment theory emphasizes the biological roots of emotional attachment, and draws upon evolutionary theory for support. It is therefore often assumed that attachment behaviors are universal—that North American infants behave the same way as do infants in Japan, Africa, or Europe. Indeed, infants from all around the world have been tested in the strange situation procedure—from Israeli kibbutzim to Japan, from Uganda to The Netherlands. In some cultures, the strange situation is very strange indeed. For example, Japanese infants rarely experience separation from their mothers. As a result, they show signs of extreme distress in the strange situation (Takahashi, 1990). Kibbutz-raised infants usually have

**avoidant insecure attachment**
*a pattern seen in the strange situation, in which the baby basically ignores the mother, usually shows no strong signs of disturbance when she leaves the room, and avoids the mother during reunion episodes or greets her return rather casually*

The development of close attachments is a universal experience.

multiple caregivers, but rarely do they come into contact with strangers (Sagi, 1990). When comparisons are made between two cultures (e.g., the United States versus Japan), large differences are often found in how much distress infants experience in the strange situation, and in the relative proportion of infants classified as secure, avoidant, or resistant. Despite these differences, greater variability in attachment-related behaviors is usually found within a single cultural setting than between cultural settings. Around the world, the secure pattern of attachment is clearly the most frequently observed pattern. The insecure patterns, however, are more culture-specific: the avoidant pattern occurs with greater frequency in Western European countries, whereas the resistant pattern is more common in Israel and Japan (van IJzendoorn & Kroonenberg, 1988).

**The Cultural Meaning of Insecurity.** There is a tendency to think of secure attachment as the ideal, and of insecure attachment as something less desirable. But cultural norms and practices may actually favor one form of insecure attachment over another. For example, the avoidant pattern may be found more frequently in Western European countries because of cultural preferences for children to become independent quickly. By comparison, the resistant pattern may be found more frequently in Japan because that culture emphasizes emotional dependence among family members. To test this idea, Robin Harwood and Joan Miller (1991) created three vignettes—one each for the kind of behavior you would expect of a secure, avoidant, or resistant toddler's behavior. Each vignette described a toddler's responses to separation and reunion in the unfamiliar setting of a dentist's waiting room. Mothers were asked to read each vignette, and to rate the desirability and typicality of the hypothetical toddlers' behavior. Some of the mothers were lower- to middle-class Anglo-Americans, and others were lower-class Puerto Rican Americans. All of the mothers agreed that the secure toddler was more desirable and typical. However, the Anglo and Puerto Rican mothers differed in how they assessed the resistant toddler: the Anglo mothers rated this hypothetical toddler as much less desirable and typical than did the Puerto Rican mothers. These results were complemented by the additional finding that the Anglo mothers placed greater value on independence and self-confidence, whereas the Puerto Rican mothers placed greater value on obedience and demeanor. Within the cultural milieu of the Puerto Rican mothers, it seems that the behavior of resistant infants is relatively more acceptable and typical.

**Learning About Relationships.** Those first early attachments provide the infant with a wealth of knowledge and experiences about close relationships. Over time, the infant begins to develop a mental representation, schema, or **working model of a close relationship**—the feelings, thoughts, beliefs, and expectations learned during the course of those first close relationships (Colin, 1996). For the securely attached infant, the working model or relationship schema indicates that other people can be trusted and relied upon to provide a safe haven, to be nurturing and supportive, and to provide a partnership in life. The securely attached infant also learns that he or she is a person who is worthy of trust, love, and support. But for insecurely attached infants, the world of close relationships must seem very different. These infants develop a working model that close relationships sometimes involve acceptance, but at other times rejection; that sometimes the other person is accessible, but at other times inaccessible; that the other person can be responsive and caring on some occasions, but unresponsive and uncaring on others. The insecurely attached infant learns that he or she may *not* be a person who is worthy of trust, love, and support. How does an infant or young child respond to such frustration and emotional pain? Avoidant infants respond by inhibiting or blocking thoughts and actions that make them aware of the other; resistant infants respond by expressing anger or ambivalence toward the other.

**working model of a close relationship**

*the feelings, thoughts, beliefs, and expectations learned during the course of an infant's first close relationships*

**Attachment Beyond Infancy.** The kind of attachment observed during infancy is usually stable over time and still evident in the early grade-school years. Mary Main and Jude Cassidy (1988) found that the attachment pattern observed when infants were 12 months old was still evident when the children were 6 years old. The attachment pattern is most stable over time when there has been little disruption or change in the child's life. Major disruptions—such as a parent's divorce or a dramatic change in socioeconomic circumstances—can produce more variability in attachment. This probably happens because of the effects a major disruption can have on a caregiver's ability to maintain a positive and supportive relationship (Ackerman, Izard, Schoff, Youngstrom, & Kogos, 1999; Conger et al., 1992). Suddenly finding yourself unemployed or a single parent can have a chilling effect—at least temporarily—on the relationship with your child. The other side to this is that a secure attachment can provide some protection or buffer against the harmful effects of an impoverished or disrupted social environment. Even in unfavorable environments, some children do manage to adapt effectively, developing competence in social and academic domains. Children who demonstrate this kind of resilience in the face of adversity are more likely to enjoy a close and positive relationship with their parents, to have good connections with members of an extended family, and to have developed relationships with supportive role models outside of the family (Masten & Coatsworth, 1998).

# Adult Attachment

When John Bowlby (1969) wrote about emotional attachments, he was focusing primarily on the emotional, behavioral, and cognitive responses of infants and young children—the positive and secure emotional bonds that typically develop between infant and primary caregiver, the distress and anxiety when they become separated, and the relief and comfort-seeking that usually occurs upon reunion. Until the 1980s, research on emotional attachment focused almost exclusively on the relationship between child and primary caregiver. Yet Bowlby thought of attachment as a lifelong quality of human relationships—as a process that begins during infancy, but one that continues to influence and guide all of the close relationships we form in adolescence and adulthood. Bowlby assumed that the mental representation—the working model—of close relationships formed during childhood persisted throughout adulthood.

**A Theory of Adult Attachment.** In 1987, Cindy Hazan and Phillip Shaver proposed that the concept of attachment could be used to describe and understand close relationships in adulthood. To develop a theory of **adult attachment**, they translated each of the three major patterns of attachment found among infants—secure, resistant (anxious/ambivalent), and avoidant—into their adult forms. The trick for doing this was to think about attachment in terms of an adult's close relationships with other adults rather than a child's relationship with his or her caregiver. To classify an adult into one of the three attachment patterns, Hazan and Shaver developed three brief descriptions. The one with which you agree most corresponds to your attachment pattern:

**adult attachment**
*the concept of attachment used to describe and understand close relationships in adulthood by translating each of the three major patterns of attachment found among infants—secure, anxious/ambivalent, and avoidant—into their adult forms*

> *Secure.* I find it relatively easy to get close to others and am comfortable depending on them. I don't often worry about being abandoned or about someone getting too close to me.

> *Anxious/Ambivalent.* I find that others are reluctant to get as close as I would like. I often worry that my partner doesn't really love me or won't want to stay with me. I want to get very close to my partner, and this sometimes scares people away.

*Avoidant.* I am somewhat uncomfortable being close to others; I find it difficult to trust them completely, difficult to allow myself to depend on them. I am nervous when anyone gets too close, and often, love partners want me to be more intimate than I feel comfortable being. (Shaver & Hazan, 1993, p. 35)

**Adults Are Not Children.** Shaver and Hazan (1993) acknowledge some important differences between attachment in early childhood compared to adulthood. For one thing, adult attachment relationships are far more reciprocal: adults are able to exchange roughly equivalent benefits, whereas children and their caregivers bring very different needs and contributions to the relationship. Attachment between children and adults typically involves a parent–child relationship, in which the ultimate goal is to raise healthy offspring. Attachment among adults typically involves a romantic relationship between peers in which the prominent elements are companionship, intimacy, and sex.

Despite these differences, the major functions of early attachment can also be found in adult attachment. Adults seek to maintain close proximity in an attachment relationship. Even as an adult, separation from your romantic partner can make you feel sad or lonely, and reunions can make you feel happy and warm. As an adult, you face threats and challenges in life, and a romantic partner can provide support, understanding, and a safe haven to help you through it. Adults do not pursue the same kinds of play and exploration as children, but they do rely on romantic attachments to provide a secure base for work and the adult forms of play.

One centerpiece of attachment theory is the concept of a working model—a person's mental representation of relationships. Kim Bartholomew and Leonard Horowitz (1991) made a distinction between two aspects of an adult's working model of attachment. One is the working model of other—your thoughts, beliefs, and judgments about whether or not the other person can be trusted and relied upon to provide support and protection. The other is the working model of self—perceptions of yourself as a person who is worthy of support and protection and to whom others are likely to respond in a positive and helpful way. A secure pattern of adult attachment occurs when both working models (of other and of self) are positive; an insecure pattern of attachment occurs when one or both working models are negative.

**How Do We Measure Adult Attachment?** To do research on early attachment, it was necessary to create a method for measuring attachment. That's why Mary Ainsworth invented the strange situation procedure. That method clearly won't do for adults. Instead, researchers rely on an adult's own description or rating of his or her attachment relationships. One approach, developed by Carol George, N. Kaplan, and Mary Main (1985), is called the Adult Attachment Interview (AAI). With the AAI, adults are asked in a variety of ways to describe their own attachment relationships during childhood—their own early experiences with their mother, father, or other primary caregiver. The AAI is designed to measure the quality of an adult's early attachment style, but it also provides a picture of how attachment continues to be experienced as an adult. A second approach to measuring adult attachment, developed by Nancy Collins and Stephen Read (1990), is the Adult Attachment Scale (AAS). The AAS consists of 18 questions designed to classify adults into one of the three attachment patterns. It differs from the AAI in that it focuses only on attachment relationships experienced as an adult with other adults. The complete set of scale items is shown in Know Yourself 13.1: The Adult Attachment Scale. Try the scale for yourself.

**Play and Work.** For infants and young children, differences in attachment style are related to differences in exploration and play (Ainsworth et al., 1978). Secure infants will readily explore new settings, try new toys, and generally go

# Know Yourself 13.1
## *The Adult Attachment Scale*

Rate the extent to which each statement below describes your feelings on a scale ranging from not at all characteristic (1) to very characteristic (5):

1. I find it difficult to allow myself to depend on others.

    | 1 | 2 | 3 | 4 | 5 |
    |---|---|---|---|---|
    | Not at all characteristic | | | | Very characteristic |

2. People are never there when you need them.

    | 1 | 2 | 3 | 4 | 5 |
    |---|---|---|---|---|
    | Not at all characteristic | | | | Very characteristic |

3. I am comfortable depending on others.

    | 1 | 2 | 3 | 4 | 5 |
    |---|---|---|---|---|
    | Not at all characteristic | | | | Very characteristic |

4. I know that others will be there when I need them.

    | 1 | 2 | 3 | 4 | 5 |
    |---|---|---|---|---|
    | Not at all characteristic | | | | Very characteristic |

5. I find it difficult to trust others completely.

    | 1 | 2 | 3 | 4 | 5 |
    |---|---|---|---|---|
    | Not at all characteristic | | | | Very characteristic |

6. I am not sure that I can always depend on others to be there when I need them.

    | 1 | 2 | 3 | 4 | 5 |
    |---|---|---|---|---|
    | Not at all characteristic | | | | Very characteristic |

7. I do not often worry about being abandoned.

    | 1 | 2 | 3 | 4 | 5 |
    |---|---|---|---|---|
    | Not at all characteristic | | | | Very characteristic |

8. I often worry that my partner does not really love me.

    | 1 | 2 | 3 | 4 | 5 |
    |---|---|---|---|---|
    | Not at all characteristic | | | | Very characteristic |

9. I find others are reluctant to get as close as I would like.

    | 1 | 2 | 3 | 4 | 5 |
    |---|---|---|---|---|
    | Not at all characteristic | | | | Very characteristic |

10. I often worry my partner will not want to stay with me.

    | 1 | 2 | 3 | 4 | 5 |
    |---|---|---|---|---|
    | Not at all characteristic | | | | Very characteristic |

11. I want to merge completely with another person.

    | 1 | 2 | 3 | 4 | 5 |
    |---|---|---|---|---|
    | Not at all characteristic | | | | Very characteristic |

12. My desire to merge sometimes scares people away.

    | 1 | 2 | 3 | 4 | 5 |
    |---|---|---|---|---|
    | Not at all characteristic | | | | Very characteristic |

*(continued on next page)*

13. I find it relatively easy to get close to others.

| 1 | 2 | 3 | 4 | 5 |
|---|---|---|---|---|
| Not at all characteristic | | | | Very characteristic |

14. I do not often worry about someone getting too close to me.

| 1 | 2 | 3 | 4 | 5 |
|---|---|---|---|---|
| Not at all characteristic | | | | Very characteristic |

15. I am somewhat uncomfortable being close to others.

| 1 | 2 | 3 | 4 | 5 |
|---|---|---|---|---|
| Not at all characteristic | | | | Very characteristic |

16. I am nervous when anyone gets too close.

| 1 | 2 | 3 | 4 | 5 |
|---|---|---|---|---|
| Not at all characteristic | | | | Very characteristic |

17. I am comfortable having others depend on me.

| 1 | 2 | 3 | 4 | 5 |
|---|---|---|---|---|
| Not at all characteristic | | | | Very characteristic |

18. Often, love partners want me to be more intimate than I feel comfortable being.

| 1 | 2 | 3 | 4 | 5 |
|---|---|---|---|---|
| Not at all characteristic | | | | Very characteristic |

**SCORING:** Items 3–4, 8–14, and 17 are scored as shown (1-2-3-4-5); items 1–2, 5–7, 15–16, and 18 are reverse-scored (5-4-3-2-1).

These items are grouped into three sets:

- Items 1–6 represent trust in others.
- Items 7–12 reflect anxiety in relationships.
- Items 13–18 relate to closeness and intimacy.

Each set has possible scores from 6 to 30, with higher scores reflecting more of the dimension.

From Collins and Read, "Adult attachment, working models, and relationship quality in dating couples," *Journal of Personality and Social Psychology*, 58(4), 644–663. Copyright © 1990 by the American Psychological Association. Reprinted by permission.

about mastering their environments. Resistant children are too worried about maintaining close proximity with their primary caregiver to engage in the sort of exploration that leads to mastery, but they may engage in exploratory activity in an effort to gain their caregiver's attention and approval. Avoidant children use exploration and play as a way of keeping busy, of distracting themselves from thoughts or awareness of their primary caregiver. How do these differences in play and exploration translate into adult attachment? Hazan and Shaver (1990) suggested that work represents the adult version of exploration and mastery. After classifying adults according to the three styles of attachment, they asked a variety of questions about work and relationships. Securely attached adults reported that they enjoy and value work, are not very concerned about failure, and do not let work interfere with their important personal relationships. Anxious/ambivalent adults seem to use work as a way to gain respect and approval from others, but sometimes loaf after receiving praise. Avoidant adults appear to use work as a way to avoid social interactions, and they are generally less satisfied with their jobs.

**Attachment and Daily Social Interactions.** You may have noticed a major difference between studies of infant/child attachment and studies of adult attachment. In the case of children, their behaviors, emotional responses, and social interactions are usually observed and recorded as they happen, by an outside observer. In contrast, adults are simply relied upon to provide their own reports of

```
                    ATTACHMENT AND SOCIAL INTERACTIONS

                              Social Security No. _____

Date: _____    Time: _____ a.m. or p.m.?    Length: _____ hrs. _____ min.

Who initiated the interaction? _____ I did. _____ Other did. _____ It was mutual.

Was this a phone call? _____ Yes _____ No

Initials of other(s): ____ ____ ____      If more than three others, number
Sex of other(s):      ____ ____ ____      of males _____  females _____

Intimacy ............................ superficial 1 2 3 4 5 6 7  meaningful
I disclosed.......................... very little 1 2 3 4 5 6 7  a great deal
Other disclosed ..................... very little 1 2 3 4 5 6 7  a great deal
Quality (How pleasant was it?) ....... unpleasant 1 2 3 4 5 6 7  very pleasant
I helped/supported other ............ very little 1 2 3 4 5 6 7  a great deal
Other helped/supported me ........... very little 1 2 3 4 5 6 7  a great deal
Degree of disagreement/conflict ..... very little 1 2 3 4 5 6 7  a great deal
Degree of closeness/camaraderie ..... very little 1 2 3 4 5 6 7  a great deal
Who mainly influenced or
     controlled the interaction? ......... I did 1 2 3 4 5 6 7  other did
My level of satisfaction ............ dissatisfied 1 2 3 4 5 6 7  very satisfied
I got from the interaction ..... less than expected/ 1 2 3 4 5 6 7  more than expected/
                                    hoped for                      hoped for

Nature of interaction:  Job  Task  Conversation  Leisure activity  Other: _____

Approximate content of the interaction (what you were doing and talking about): _____
_____
_____

During the interaction (or immediately after it), how much did you feel . . .

     happy/encouraged.................... not at all 1 2 3 4 5 6 7  a great deal
     sad/disappointed.................... not at all 1 2 3 4 5 6 7  a great deal
     frustrated/irritated ............... not at all 1 2 3 4 5 6 7  a great deal
     rejected/left out .................. not at all 1 2 3 4 5 6 7  a great deal
     comfortable/relaxed ................ not at all 1 2 3 4 5 6 7  a great deal
     needed/appreciated ................. not at all 1 2 3 4 5 6 7  a great deal
     bored/distant....................... not at all 1 2 3 4 5 6 7  a great deal
     caring/warm......................... not at all 1 2 3 4 5 6 7  a great deal
     hurt/treated badly ................. not at all 1 2 3 4 5 6 7  a great deal
     worried/anxious..................... not at all 1 2 3 4 5 6 7  a great deal
     stimulated/invigorated ............. not at all 1 2 3 4 5 6 7  a great deal
     tense/ill at ease .................. not at all 1 2 3 4 5 6 7  a great deal
     successful/productive .............. not at all 1 2 3 4 5 6 7  a great deal
     sexually interested/aroused ........ not at all 1 2 3 4 5 6 7  a great deal
     envious/jealous..................... not at all 1 2 3 4 5 6 7  a great deal
     accepted/like you belonged ......... not at all 1 2 3 4 5 6 7  a great deal
     embarrassed/self-conscious ......... not at all 1 2 3 4 5 6 7  a great deal
     disgusted/disapproving ............. not at all 1 2 3 4 5 6 7  a great deal
     ashamed/guilty...................... not at all 1 2 3 4 5 6 7  a great deal
     imposed upon/intruded upon ......... not at all 1 2 3 4 5 6 7  a great deal
     tired/low in energy ................ not at all 1 2 3 4 5 6 7  a great deal
```

**FIGURE 13.8** The social interaction diary. Research participants completed this form for every social interaction lasting more than 10 minutes.

From Reis and Wheeler, "Studying social interaction with the Rochester Interaction Record," in *Advances in Experimental Social Psychology*, ed. M. P. Zanna (vol. 24, pp. 269–318, 2004). Reprinted by permission of Elsevier.

past events. To remedy this, and to get a better idea of how adult attachment style might influence everyday interactions, Marie-Cecile Tidwell, Harry Reis, and Phillip Shaver (1996) used a method called **event sampling.** Students at the State University of New York at Buffalo were asked to keep a social interaction diary for one week. This involved filling out a standard diary form for every social interaction lasting more than 10 minutes. The standard diary form, shown in Figure 13.8, was to be completed as soon as possible after each interaction. In this way, the major social interaction events in each student's day were sampled and recorded.

**event sampling**

*a method used to study adult attachment that involves the recording of information about a person's social interactions over a period of time*

In addition to keeping their diaries for one week, the students were classified in terms of attachment style. Their photographs were also taken, and rated by others for physical attractiveness.

One thing was clear in this study: Students who were classified as avoidant experienced a variety of negative emotions in their daily social interactions with others. Compared to the other students, the interactions recorded in their diaries revealed more sadness, frustration, worry, tension, and embarrassment. Compared to the secure students, the avoidant students also spent less time and were less comfortable in their opposite-sex interactions. Physical attractiveness was not a major factor in this study. The students classified into the three attachment styles did not differ in their attractiveness (although the women were rated as more attractive than the men), nor did physical attractiveness account for any of the other results.

**The Adult Version of a Safe Haven.** Children and adults sometimes find themselves experiencing distress and anxiety. We know this happens for children in the strange situation procedure. In that setting, securely attached children will seek out their caregiver for comfort and relief—a safe haven. And the securely attached caregiver will provide it. This is clearly one of the benefits of a secure attachment relationship. The same benefit seems to apply for adults. Jeffry Simpson, William Rholes, and Julia Nelligan (1992) studied 83 dating couples at Texas A & M University. When each couple arrived at the laboratory, they were seated together and completed a series of questionnaires that included assessments of their attachment styles. The female partner was then escorted alone to another room, where she was told, "In the next few minutes, you are going to be exposed to a situation and set of experimental procedures that arouse considerable anxiety and distress in most people" (Simpson et al., 1992, p. 437). She was then shown a dark room containing some ominous psychophysiological recording equipment. The experimenter explained that the room was not quite ready yet, and led the woman back to the room where her male partner was waiting. It was during this waiting period that the experimenter was most interested in observing the interactions of the partners.

The procedure was designed to make the woman feel distressed and anxious. Nothing was said to her partner as the experimenter left the couple alone in the waiting room. What the unsuspecting couple didn't know was that their interactions for the next five minutes were recorded by a video camera hidden in the room. What would the women do? Would they seek comfort and relief from their partners? And what would the men do? Would they offer support and reassurance? Well, the securely attached women who had reported feeling very anxious were observed to seek out their partners during this waiting period for both emotional support and physical comfort. And the securely attached male partners responded by providing emotional support and by making reassuring comments. In contrast, when the avoidant women were feeling anxious, they were *less* likely to seek out support from their partner during the waiting period. The avoidant males were not very supportive: the more his partner experienced anxiety, the less emotional support or concern the avoidant male was likely to express for her well-being.

**Finding Satisfaction in Romance.** As you learned about the results from Simpson, Rholes, and Nelligan's (1992) study, what were you thinking? Did it occur to you that securely attached adults might enjoy more fulfilling and satisfying romantic relationships compared to their insecurely attached friends? It may be true, but the picture is not quite that simple. Lee Kirkpatrick and Keith Davis (1994) recruited 354 college-student couples who were involved "in steady or serious dating relationships" for a three-year longitudinal study of attachment style and stability in romantic relationships. Although many of the couples stayed together over the three-year period, many others broke up. Overall, most of the students—about 75%—showed the secure attachment pattern. As a result, the majority of dating couples involved a secure–secure pair. About 14% of the men and women showed the avoidant pattern, but they seemed to avoid one another: none of the dating couples involved an avoidant–avoidant pair! At the beginning of the study, the avoidant men reported the least satisfaction in their relationships; the secure and anxious men were happier. Yet, after three years, it was the anxious men who were more likely to have broken up. The pattern for women differed. It was the anxious women who were least satisfied at the outset, yet the avoidant women were more likely to break up during the ensuing three years.

# Close Relationships in Adulthood

The concept of attachment has been very useful in helping to understand the origin and nature of close relationships. Yet attachment theory is only one of many related perspectives on the formation and development of close relationships in adulthood. Adults relate to one another in a variety of ways; the closest relationships involve intimacy, love, and longtime partnerships. Some of our close relationships endure, maturing and growing deeper over time. Other close relationships weaken over time, occasionally ending in bitterness and hostility. Theory and research sheds light on when, how, and why our close relationships work this way.

## Dimensions of Adult Relationships

In 1959, John Thibaut and Harold Kelley wrote an influential book on the social psychology of groups—how two or more people interact and come to depend on one another. The simplest group is two people—a dyad. As a result, the theory developed by Thibaut and Kelley, and later expanded by Kelley (1979), has provided a foundation for understanding close personal dyadic relationships. Thibaut and Kelley observed that a close relationship between two people involves some degree of **interdependence**—a sharing of contributions and outcomes. The idea of a close, dyadic relationship is that two people see themselves as a unit—sharing in both the costs and the rewards of one another's outcomes. When your partner receives good news or a reward, it is just as though the good news or reward were for you—you enjoy the outcome as though it were your own. And when times are tough—when your partner is disappointed or hurt—you share the pain. One of the interesting consequences of interdependence is that people will often behave in ways that benefit their partner even if it is costly to themselves. In the long run, they will share in the benefit they provided to their partner.

**interdependence**
*a sharing of contributions and outcomes by two people*

**Closeness.** A really close relationship involves a high degree of interdependence. As Harold Kelley (1983) put it:

> A high degree of interdependence between two people is revealed in four properties of their interconnected activities: (1) the individuals have *frequent* impact on each other, (2) the degree of impact per each occurrence is *strong,* (3) the impact involves *diverse* kinds of activities for each person, and (4) all of these properties characterize the interconnected activity series for a relatively long *duration* of time. (p. 13)

Ellen Berscheid, Mark Snyder, and Allen Omoto (1989) followed up on this idea by developing a scale—the Relationship Closeness Inventory (RCI)—to assess the frequency, diversity, and strength of the interdependence between two people. Students at the University of Minnesota were asked to complete the RCI twice—once in reference to their closest, deepest, and most intimate relationship, and once in reference to a relationship that was considered to be not very close or intimate. As expected, the close relationships involved sharing in a greater number (diversity) of activities, and spending more time (frequency) with the close other in those activities. The strength of interdependence was assessed by asking the students to indicate the amount of influence the other person had on their thoughts, feelings, and behavior. Just as you would expect, the close other was rated as having more influence than the non-close other.

**Providing Benefits for the Other.** One of the ideas of interdependence is that the partners in a dyad provide benefits for one another. Margaret Clark and Judson Mills (1979) distinguished between two different ways in which benefits are provided in relationships. In some cases, the partners engage in an equal exchange of benefits—you scratch my back, and I'll scratch yours. When you are invited to a friend's house for dinner, you return the favor in kind; on holidays or birthdays, you exchange gifts of roughly equal value with your friends. These are examples of an **exchange relationship:** the partners tend to keep track of what they have given and what they have received, and they strive to keep the books balanced.

You can probably imagine a number of your relationships that are based on the rules of exchange. Yet other relationships—perhaps those you have with a romantic partner or a family member—seem to involve a different set of rules. In these relationships, you may find yourself providing or receiving benefits primarily when they are needed. In these cases, the rule is not to provide a benefit for a benefit, but rather to provide a benefit for a need. Clark and Mills refer to this as a **communal relationship:** the receipt of a benefit creates no specific obligation to return that benefit. Responding to the needs of your partner is the benefit in a communal relationship.

**Equity and Fairness.** Whether your relationship is exchange or communal, your satisfaction may depend on how fair you perceive it to be (Adams, 1965). For example, the rules that govern an exchange relationship create pressure to return one benefit with another of comparable value. Failing to return a benefit, or reciprocating with one of either lesser or greater value, creates an inequity in the relationship. Likewise, the rules that govern a communal relationship create pressure to provide benefits when needed, and to accept them when needed. Over time, it is the give and take in response to needs that keeps the communal relationship balanced. **Equity theory** was developed to help formalize the idea of perceived fairness or balance in interpersonal relationships (Walster, Walster, & Berscheid, 1978), including close dyadic relationships (Hatfield, Traupmann, Sprecher, Utne, & Hay, 1985). An equitable relationship is one in which both partners perceive that they are receiving relatively equal outcomes. When one partner contributes more to a relationship, that partner might expect relatively more in return. Equity is an interesting problem in communal relationships, because the benefits contributed by one partner may be very different from the benefits contributed by the other. It all depends on what each partner needs and what the other has to contribute.

How much do equity and social exchange really matter in close relationships? This is one of those cases in which it matters for most people some of the time, and for some people most of the time (Sprecher & Schwartz, 1994). For example, concerns about equity seem to make a difference during the initial stages of a developing romantic relationship. Elaine Walster, G. W. Walster, and Jane Traupmann (1978) contacted students at the University of Wisconsin who were in casual or steady dating relationships. The students were first asked a number of questions about how equitable or inequitable they perceived their dating relationships to be—how their own contributions and benefits to the relationship stacked up against their partner's. These questions were used to classify the students as being underbenefited (outcomes were less than they deserved), equitably treated (outcomes were fair compared to contributions), or overbenefited (outcomes were more than they deserved).

**exchange relationship**

*a relationship in which the partners tend to keep track of what they have given and what they have received, and strive to keep the books balanced*

**communal relationship**

*a relationship in which the receipt of a benefit creates no specific obligation to return that benefit; responding to the needs of your partner is the benefit*

**equity theory**

*the idea of perceived fairness or balance in interpersonal relationships, such that both partners perceive that they are receiving relatively equal outcomes*

The students also completed a survey about the intimacy of their sexual relationship. For example, they were asked how "far" they had gone with their partner (from kissing to intercourse and oral sex), how long they knew each other before they had sexual intercourse, and their reasons for having sex (they wanted it, their partner wanted it, or they both wanted it). Results showed that the students who described their relationships as relatively equitable were also more sexually intimate—not because one or the other partner wanted it, but because they both wanted it. Similar studies have found that dating men and women are more content, satisfied, and happy when they perceive themselves to be treated equitably in their relationship (Traupmann, Hatfield, & Wexler, 1983). Inequity in a relationship is associated with distress and unhappiness, but the distress is much greater when the inequity is in the form of being underbenefited rather than being overbenefited (Traupmann et al., 1983).

## Intimacy

At the center of a very close relationship is **intimacy**—an interactive process in which a person feels understood, validated, and cared for as a result of a partner's response (Reis & Patrick, 1996). It is intimacy that securely attached people often achieve in their close relationships, it is intimacy that avoidant people desperately seek to avoid, and it is intimacy that anxious/ambivalent people deeply desire but often fail to obtain. Intimacy is often achieved in a close relationship through a process of self-disclosure, during which partners become more understanding of and responsive to one another's needs.

**intimacy**
*an interactive process in which a person feels understood, validated, and cared for as a result of a partner's response*

**Self-Disclosure.** As we discussed earlier, people learn about each other by exchanging personal information. This is an important part of the process in establishing a friendship and, ultimately, an even closer relationship. When people are first getting to know one another, the reciprocal exchange of information is likely to focus on the facts—where did you grow up, what schools have you attended, what do you do for a living? As the relationship deepens, disclosure of feelings and emotions becomes much more important (Reis & Shaver, 1988). This is an essential part of developing an intimate understanding of a partner's needs.

**Responsiveness.** One of the hallmarks of a close relationship is that the exchange of information is reciprocal—you disclose something about yourself, and your partner discloses something back. But an intimate relationship involves more than just an equal exchange of information between partners. Intimacy depends on each partner's being responsive to what the other says, does, feels, and needs. The only way to know if you are really being understood is if your partner is appropriately responsive. This may involve simple forms of response, such as continuing a conversation on the same topic initiated by your partner, or granting a partner's direct request (D. Davis, 1982). But being responsive to a partner's emotions and needs may require less direct action, such as doing unasked favors when your partner has had a rough day. In a truly intimate relationship, this kind of responsiveness does not require an immediate repayment or reciprocation (Clark & Mills, 1993).

Fiugre 13.9 (page 554) illustrates the connections among self-disclosure, responsiveness, and intimacy.

**Understanding.** Self-disclosure and responsiveness are two important paths to achieving intimate understanding or empathy—a concept we defined in Chapter 12 as a person's

Close attachments and intimate self-disclosure are a part of social relationships throughout the span of life.

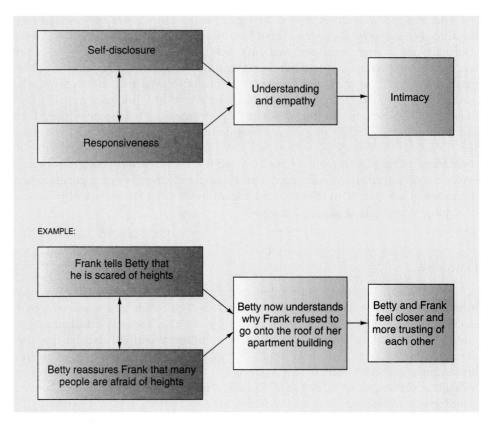

**FIGURE 13.9** Intimacy

ability to comprehend the experiences of another (Wispé, 1986). No matter how well-intentioned one is toward understanding another person's perspective (to empathize), true understanding cannot occur unless one is also accurate. This leads to an important distinction between empathy and **empathic accuracy,** which is a person's ability to be accurate in his or her understanding of another's experiences (Ickes, 1993, 1997, 2003). A person's empathic accuracy can usually be predicted by friends and acquaintances, but people are not very good at judging their own empathic accuracy (M. H. Davis & Kraus, 1997; Ickes, 1993). A common assumption is that women possess greater empathic accuracy than men. This turns out to be an overgeneralization. Women are better than men in understanding others' facial expressions, but they are no better at inferring others' thoughts or feelings (Graham & Ickes, 1997).

**Extreme Interdependence.** Very close relationships involve a high degree of interdependence, intimacy, and the sharing of benefits on a communal rather than an exchange basis. The achievement of intimacy depends on an ability to empathize accurately with your partner's thoughts, feelings, and needs. A very close relationship seems to involve the merging of two selves. Your partner becomes, in some sense, a part of you—and you become a part of your partner. The distinction between *you* and *me* becomes blurred, and you begin to think of yourselves as *we*.

Arthur and Elaine Aron expanded on this idea (Aron, Aron, Tudor, & Nelson, 1991), and even developed a method for measuring the extent to which a person perceives overlap between his or her own self and the other. Earlier, George Levinger (1988) suggested that a relationship between two people can be drawn as two overlapping circles—the more the overlap, the greater the intimacy. Aron, Aron, and Smollan (1992) used this idea to create the Inclusion of Other in the Self (IOS) scale. The scale, which is shown in Figure 13.10, is quite straightforward: you

**empathic accuracy**

*a person's ability to be accurate in his or her understanding of another's experiences*

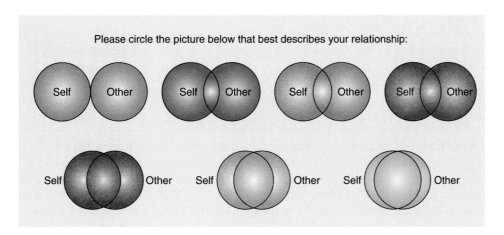

Please circle the picture below that best describes your relationship:

**FIGURE 13.10** Inclusion of Other in the Self scale

From Aron, Aron, and Smollen, "Inclusion of Other in the Self scale and the structure of interpersonal closeness," *Journal of Personality and Social Psychology*, 63(4), 596–612. Copyright © 1992 by the American Psychological Association. Reprinted by permission.

simply select the pair of circles that best describes your close relationship; the greater the overlap, the higher is your score on the IOS scale. Try it for yourself. Think about your closest romantic relationship, and choose the pair that best describes it. College students who score higher on the IOS scale also report greater intimacy and positive emotions about the other. Among people who are married, higher IOS scores go with perceptions of deeper commitment and greater marital satisfaction. Generally, people interpret the overlapping circles of the IOS as reflecting the degree of interconnectedness with a close other.

## Love

Our discussion of intimacy, attachment, closeness, and commitment all seems to be dancing around the idea of love. Poets and philosophers, musicians and writers, parents and advice columnists—all have their own definitions of love. The view emerging from social psychology is that love can be many different things, depending in large part on the nature of the relationship. The love you feel for your parents is different from the love you feel for your romantic partner. People profess love of their nation, love for apple pie, and brotherly love. All of these varieties of love differ, and probably none is the same as what you feel for your lover. Perhaps some closer scrutiny of the concept of love will help us to understand more about a very important and universal aspect of human experience.

**Passionate Love.** Sometimes we think of love as involving strong and intense feelings, infatuation, arousal, and a deep sense of passion. This is the kind of love that Elaine Hatfield and G. Walster (1978) called **passionate love.** Here is their definition:

> A state of intense longing for union with another. Reciprocated love (union with the other) is associated with fulfillment and ecstasy. Unrequited love (separation) with emptiness, anxiety, or despair. A state of profound physiological arousal. (p. 9)

Hatfield (1988) describes passionate love as a form of excitement involving a mixture of intense positive and negative emotions. It is euphoria, happiness, tranquillity,

**passionate love**

*The kind of love that involves strong and intense feelings, infatuation, arousal, and a deep sense of passion* anxiety, panic, and despair all wrapped up in the relationship we have—or might have—with another. Sometimes our passion for another is reciprocated, as when two people are *falling in love*. At other times, our passion is not reciprocated. We can still have fantasies about another, and this can be the source of great pleasure. But unrequited love is also associated with strong negative emotions—just think about those times in your life when you developed a deep crush on someone who hardly knew you existed.

**Companionate Love.** Passionate love is intense and exciting, and seems to be a very important part of being in love. But it is not the kind of love that sustains a long-term relationship or close attachment. Indeed, we can experience passionate love even in the absence of intimacy. In contrast, the kind of love that develops in a close and intimate relationship is **companionate love,** which Hatfield and Walster (1978) defined as "the affection we feel for those with whom our lives are deeply entwined" (p. 9). Certainly, passionate love is a part of those kinds of relationships, but intimacy and closeness only develop with companionate love.

**Styles of Love.** Some of us fall head-over-heels in love with every potential romantic partner we meet. Others are attracted only to a particular type. And some of us take a long time to warm up, preferring to ease slowly into romantic relationships. John Alan Lee (1988) elaborated on the idea that people might differ in their styles of love. Lee identified three primary **love styles,** but also recognized that people may change their preferred style over their lifetimes. Some people may even prefer more than one style at a time, blending two or three styles, or perhaps using different styles with different partners. The most recent studies show that the same primary love styles can be found among those who live in very different cultures (Kanemasa, Taniguchi, Daibo, & Ishimori, 2004).

Clyde and Susan Hendrick (1986) developed the Love Attitudes Scale as a way to measure the various styles of love. As we describe some of Lee's love styles, we will use items from the Love Attitudes Scale to illustrate them.

The three primary love styles are *eros, storge,* and *ludus.*

Some people know exactly what physical type turns them on, and become intensely excited when they meet a person who comes close to the ideal. *Eros*—named for the Greek god of love—is an erotic style of loving, which begins with a powerful physical attraction. Whether it is the color of another's hair, height, body type, or facial features, erotic lovers know what they want, and they experience love when they see it. In one study, Julie Fricker and Susan Moore (2002) found that people experience greater satisfaction in their romantic relationships the more they can be described by the eros love style. The intensity of eros may lessen over time, and ultimately develop into a more relaxed style. On the Love Attitudes Scale (Hendrick & Hendrick, 1986), eros is indicated by agreement with statements such as these:

> My lover and I have the right physical "chemistry" between us.
>
> Our lovemaking is very intense and satisfying.
>
> I feel that my lover and I were meant for each other.

In ancient Greek conceptions, *storge* (pronounced *store-gay*) referred to the kind of affection or love that develops between siblings or playmates. It is not the intense excitement or passion of eros. Rather, it is the kind of love that develops when people enjoy similar activities, start up a friendship, and then slowly build an affection and sense of commitment. Storgic lovers do not have a particular type

**companionate love**

*the kind of love that develops in a close and intimate relationship; the affection we feel for those with whom our lives are deeply entwined*

**love styles**

*the idea that people differ in their styles of love; the three primary styles are eros, storge, and ludus*

*"When I date someone, it doesn't take me long to figure out whether it's going to work or not. I get a sense right away if there's good chemistry between us. I think chemistry is the most important thing—it's how I know that I've found my 'one and only.'"*

in mind, and generally do not go looking for love. It is a much more sedate style of loving—one that is not typically accompanied by the kinds of things that erotic lovers do, such as staring into their lover's eyes and professing their love out loud. On the Love Attitudes Scale, storge is indicated by agreement with statements such as these:

> The best kind of love grows out of a long friendship.
>
> Love is really a deep friendship, not a mysterious, mystical emotion.
>
> Genuine love first requires caring for a while.

For some people, love is just a game. They bounce from lover to lover, preferring not to settle down in any single long-term close relationship. They are rovers. If they can't be with the one they love, then they love the one they are with. The term *ludus*—the Latin word for game or play—is a fitting description for this style of love. People who prefer this style appear to derive satisfaction from a life filled with numerous but shorter-lived love experiences. Yet those who clearly fall into the ludus category of love style seem to experience less satisfaction in their romantic relationships than do others, such as those who are better described by eros (Fricker & Moore, 2002). On the Love Attitudes Scale, ludus is indicated by agreement with statements such as these:

> I enjoy playing the "game of love" with a number of different partners.
>
> I try to keep my lover a little uncertain about my commitment to him/her.
>
> I have sometimes had to keep two of my lovers from finding out about each other.

Just as primary colors can be mixed to produce a large palette of hues, so can the primary love styles be blended to create many secondary styles of love. Among these, Lee (1988) identified three especially interesting ones, termed *mania, pragma,* and *agape.*

Some people are preoccupied with their lover. These lovers are very possessive and can become intensely jealous. At the same time, they are insecure and need repeated assurances that they are loved. What they fear most is unrequited love. It is almost as though a manic lover is in love with the idea of being in love, rather than being in love with a particular person. Lee (1988) describes the manic lover as having the ludus style, but without the confidence. On the Love Attitudes Scale, *mania* is indicated by agreement with statements such as these:

> When my lover doesn't pay attention to me, I feel sick all over.
>
> When I am in love, I have trouble concentrating on anything else.
>
> Sometimes I get so excited about being in love that I can't sleep.

The combination of ludus and storge produces *pragma*—from the Greek root for *pragmatic.* Some people keep an informal list of qualities they desire in a lover—the closer the match, the greater the love. Compatibility is the goal. On the Love Attitudes Scale, pragma is indicated by agreement with statements such as these:

> One consideration in choosing a partner is how he/she will reflect on my career.
>
> Before getting very involved with anyone, I try to figure out how compatible his/her hereditary background is with mine in case we ever have children.
>
> I try to plan my life carefully before choosing a lover.

The kind of love style that is so often preached and so rarely practiced is *agape*—selfless, giving, altruistic love. The agapic lover considers it a duty to love another who is in need of love, even in the absence of any sense of emotional attachment or eros. On the Love Attitudes Scale, agape is indicated by agreement with statements such as these:

I cannot be happy unless I place my lover's happiness before my own.

I would endure all things for the sake of my lover.

I would rather suffer myself than let my lover suffer.

**Three Components of Love.** In trying to make sense of all the different distinctions and styles of love, Robert Sternberg (1986) proposed that love can best be understood in terms of three basic components: intimacy, passion, and commitment. Intimacy is that sense of closeness or connectedness you experience when you feel understood and cared for by another. Passion is the intense physical and sexual attraction you may feel for another. Commitment in the short term is a decision to love someone, and in the long term a dedication to maintain that love. By placing each component at the three corners of a triangle, Sternberg suggests that a large variety of love experiences can be understood as combinations of the three components (see Figure 13.11). Indeed, almost all of the forms of liking and loving that we have discussed can be found in Sternberg's **triangular theory of love**.

Intimacy in the absence of passion and commitment is a deep friendship. Passion without intimacy and commitment is infatuated love. And commitment without intimacy and passion is empty love. By combining the three basic components, we get the many and varied forms of love. Companionate love is the combination of intimacy and commitment. With all three components present, we have complete or consummate love; in the absence of all three components, we are left with nonlove.

**Cultural Dimensions of Love.** They say that love makes the world go around. But is love experienced everywhere in the world in the ways we have discussed here? People in a wide variety of cultures do indeed show all the signs of experiencing one or more of the love styles reviewed above (Hatfield & Rapson, 1996). The companionate form of love, which is really an emotional attachment, seems especially prevalent. But some historians and anthropologists have suggested that passionate love is not such a universal experience. For them, romantic passion is a refinement of Western European culture and rarely found elsewhere in the world (Jankowiak, 1995). Yet when William Jankowiak and Edward Fischer (1992) looked at the evidence, it was clear that romance and passion was enjoyed from sub-Saharan Africa to East Asia, from the Pacific Islands to South America. Out of 166 different cultures, passionate love was documented in 147 of them. So, while it is true that romantic passion is not found *everywhere,* it is found in most places.

## Beyond Heterosexual Relationships

When it comes to research on close relationships in adulthood, it is almost always assumed that we are talking about heterosexual dyads—a man and a woman. Yet women fall in love with women, and men fall in love with men. Lesbians and gay men become closely attached, and they enjoy intimate and romantic relationships. What do we know about close relationships when the partners are of the same biological sex? For a long time, this question was simply ignored. It was not until the 1980s and 1990s that researchers started to pay serious attention to lesbian, gay, and bisexual close relationships (D'Augelli & Patterson, 1995).

Gay and lesbian couples do not differ from married heterosexual couples in the quality of their relationships. Lawrence Kurdek and J. Patrick Schmitt (1986) surveyed four groups of couples who were living together and considered their relationships to be monogamous. The four groups included 44 married heterosexual couples, 35 cohabiting heterosexual couples, 50 gay couples, and 56 lesbian couples. The married, gay, and lesbian couples did not differ in the quality of their relationships— all three groups reported the same degree of love and liking for their partners, and

**triangular theory of love**

*the idea that a wide variety of love experiences can be understood as combinations of three basic components: intimacy, passion, and commitment*

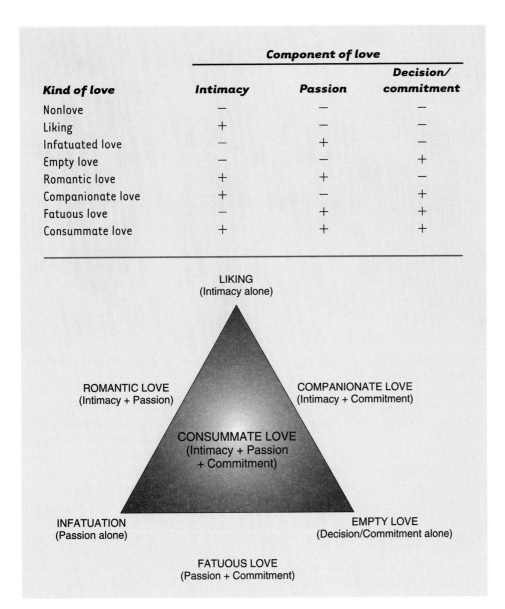

| Kind of love | Component of love | | |
|---|---|---|---|
| | Intimacy | Passion | Decision/commitment |
| Nonlove | − | − | − |
| Liking | + | − | − |
| Infatuated love | − | + | − |
| Empty love | − | − | + |
| Romantic love | + | + | − |
| Companionate love | + | − | + |
| Fatuous love | − | + | + |
| Consummate love | + | + | + |

LIKING
(Intimacy alone)

ROMANTIC LOVE
(Intimacy + Passion)

COMPANIONATE LOVE
(Intimacy + Commitment)

CONSUMMATE LOVE
(Intimacy + Passion
+ Commitment)

INFATUATION
(Passion alone)

EMPTY LOVE
(Decision/Commitment alone)

FATUOUS LOVE
(Passion + Commitment)

**FIGURE 13.11** A triangular theory of love

From Sternberg, "A triangular theory of love," *Psychological Review*, 93(2), 119–135. Copyright © 1986 by the American Psychological Association. Reprinted by permission.

satisfaction with the relationship. The cohabitating heterosexual couples experienced lower relationship quality—they reported less liking for their partner and lower relationship satisfaction. Within the context of their dyadic relationships, the gay and lesbian couples were just as happy as were the married heterosexual couples. However, the gay and lesbian couples perceived less social support from their families than did either of the heterosexual groups, emphasizing the stigma that is often associated with homosexuality.

The things that make heterosexual couples happy and satisfied in their relationships are basically the same things that make lesbian and gay couples happy in theirs (Kurdek, 1995). Satisfaction is greater when both partners feel that they share in decision making (Kurdek & Schmitt, 1986), when the perceived rewards of the relationship are greater than the perceived costs (Kurdek, 1991), and when the

Gay and lesbian couples do not differ from married heterosexual couples in the quality of their relationships.

couple engages in productive and positive methods for resolving their conflicts and problems (Kurdek, 1991). Shared decision making is one aspect of equality in a relationship, and the lesbian couples in Kurdek and Schmitt's (1986) survey reported more sharing in their decision making than did any of the other groups. This is consistent with earlier studies in which lesbian couples emphasized the importance of equality in their relationships (Blumstein & Schwartz, 1983).

## When Relationships End

Some romantic relationships are short-lived; others last a very long time. What is the difference between relationships that dissolve and those that are destined to endure? Most research on this question has focused on heterosexual marital relationships, and most approaches assume that relationship satisfaction is the critical determinant of stability (Berscheid & Reis, 1998).

Close relationships are like investments. You put a lot into them, and you expect something in return. As we learned in our discussion of interdependence and equity theory, people are happiest when their close relationship returns are in proportion to their investments. People are unhappy when they feel that they are underbenefiting—when their returns are perceived as low relative to their investments. Does this mean that close relationships end when one or both partners feel underbenefited? Not necessarily. Even when you sense the return on your investment is less than desired, you may be reluctant to abandon it. After all, you may already have put substantial personal resources into it, and to walk away would be giving up what you have already put in. You may decide to ride out the storm, just like a bad run in the stock market, in the hope that things will get better. Or you may decide to stick with the relationship because all of the alternatives look worse.

This analogy has been developed by Caryl Rusbult, who proposed an **investment model of close relationships.** According to this model, satisfaction and stability in a relationship depend on the degree to which its partners feel committed to the relationship (Rusbult, 1983). Commitment is determined by the balance or trade-off between the positive and negative aspects of the relationship (Kelley, 1983). For example, commitment will be strong if a relationship partner perceives

**investment model of close relationships**

*according to this model, satisfaction and stability in a relationship depend on the degree to which its partners feel committed to the relationship. Commitment is determined by the balance or trade-off between the positive and negative aspects of the relationship, with the idea that people compare the value of their current relationship with the value of available alternatives*

the costs of leaving as relatively high, and the value of the alternatives as relatively low. But commitment will be weak, and the relationship unstable, if a partner perceives low cost in leaving and high value in alternatives (Drigotas & Rusbult, 1992). An important part of the investment model is the idea that people compare the value of their current relationship with the value of available alternatives. In some cases, people may choose to stay in a bad relationship because the alternatives are no better, and may even be worse. This helps to explain why a person would stay in an abusive relationship. Along these lines, Rusbult and Martz (1995) interviewed women who had sought refuge at a shelter for battered women. Even though the women had good reason to leave their partners, many of them expressed a strong commitment to the relationship. Commitment was greater among those women who had no better alternatives—those with less education, poor financial resources, and no means of transportation.

When a close relationship ends, it is common for the partners to feel bad. Just how bad people feel depends, in part, on their degree of commitment to the relationship. Jeffry Simpson (1987) asked students at the University of Minnesota to complete a survey about their current or "most steady" dating partner. Three months later, the students were contacted again and asked if they were still dating the same person. If they were no longer in that relationship, they were also asked about the intensity of their emotional distress over the breakup. The students were more likely to still be together if, at the time of the initial interview, they had felt close to their partner, had dated that partner for a long time, and had engaged in sex with that partner. In other words, they were strongly committed to the relationship. But a deep sense of commitment had its downside: among the students who had broken up, emotional distress was greater the more they had felt a commitment to the relationship.

It sometimes happens that one partner feels less committed to the relationship than the other. What happens when one partner is relatively content, and the other is less content or even wants out? In these cases, stability of the relationship is determined mostly by the weak-link partner. Mark Attridge, Ellen Berscheid, and Jeffry Simpson (1995) interviewed dating couples at Texas A & M University. The couples were then contacted six months later and asked if they were still dating. As previous studies had found, the couples who had expressed greater commitment to the relationship were more likely to still be together. Whether or not the couple was still dating was determined mostly by the partner who felt less satisfied and less dependent on the relationship. The less commitment expressed by *that* partner, the more likely it was that the couple would separate.

# Chapter Summary

In this chapter, we reviewed the social psychology of close relationships—attraction, attachment, and close relationships from childhood through adulthood.

The study of **interpersonal attraction** starts with a consideration of **spatial ecology,** which calls our attention to close **functional distance** and **propinquity** that create the opportunity for exchanging personal information. We

discover information about others, and reveal information about ourselves, through a process called **self-disclosure.** This can lead to liking, or it can lead to disliking. We like others whose attitudes and values are similar to our own (the **attitude-similarity effect**) and dislike others whose attitudes and values are dissimilar to our own (the **repulsion hypothesis**). We also like others who are physically attractive. Faces are perceived as especially attractive when they are most like the average or prototypical face. Bodies are perceived as most attractive when they signal reproductive fitness. For example, women show a preference for male bodies in which the waist-to-hip ratio is close to 1.0. Men show a preference for female bodies in which the waist-to-hip ratio is substantially less than 1.0. Attractive people enjoy a number of social benefits—they are judged by others as more competent, and may be less likely to be convicted of a crime. At the root of these effects is the assumption that **what is beautiful is good.** Although attractive people do not enjoy all of the benefits attributed to them, it is sometimes the case that attractive people are more socially skilled than unattractive people.

Once two people decide they like one another, they may develop a deeper **friendship.** A **sociometric rating procedure** is commonly used to identify friendships within a group of acquaintances; two people are considered friends when each one nominates the other as a friend. Most research on friendships has been conducted with children, who establish their friendships on the basis of similarity, physical attraction, and self-disclosure. Some children enjoy many friendships, and tend to emerge as **popular children** even in new social groupings. Other children have very few friendships: **rejected–aggressive children** and **rejected–withdrawn children** tend to emerge as unpopular in new social groupings. Friendships among adults follow a developmental trajectory involving increasing levels of intimate self-disclosure.

John Bowlby's **attachment theory** provides a general framework for understanding the origin and maintenance of close relationships throughout the life span. Infants and their caregivers form emotional attachments, which provides the infant with a secure base and a safe haven for exploring the world. One hallmark of an emotional attachment is the occurrence of emotional distress upon separation. The **strange situation** procedure was designed to observe the response of infants when they become separated from their caregiver. Most infants show a **secure pattern of attachment,** but some show an **avoidant** or a **resistant** pattern of **insecure attachment.** Early attachment experiences form the basis for a person's **working model of a close relationship. Attachment theory** has been extended to the study of **adult attachment,** where forms of both the secure and insecure attachment patterns are found among adults in their close and romantic relationships. Because the **strange situation** procedure cannot be used to assess attachment in adults, researchers often use **event sampling** methods to have adults report on their close relationships.

Adult close relationships take many forms. A close relationship involves some degree of **interdependence. Exchange relationships** are based on the equal exchange of benefits, whereas **communal relationships** are based on provision of benefits when they are needed. **Equity theory** is used to explain how people keep track of, and are affected by, the equality of exchanges in close relationships. Very close relationships are indicated by a high degree of **intimacy,** which develops through **self-disclosure,** responsiveness, and **empathic accuracy** and understanding. Love is the emotional experience of a close relationship. **Passionate love** is an intense state of longing for union with another. **Companionate love** is more like an emotional attachment. People differ in their **love styles,** from the erotic passionate style of eros, to the practical and goal-oriented style of pragma. The **triangular theory of love** identifies intimacy, passion, and commitment as its three basic elements. Research in cultures around the world indicates that passionate love is a nearly universal experience.

An analogy can be drawn between close relationships and investments, which is the central idea underlying the **investment model of close relationships.** According to this model, satisfaction and stability in a relationship depend on the degree to which its partners feel committed to the relationship. The degree of partners' commitment and investment in a relationship is key to understanding whether or not the relationship is destined to last.

# Key Terms

adult attachment (545)
attachment theory (541)
attitude-similarity effect (527)
avoidant insecure attachment (543)
communal relationship (552)
companionate love (556)
dyadic relationships (524)
empathic accuracy (554)
equity theory (552)
event sampling (549)
exchange relationship (552)
friendships (538)

functional distance (526)
insecure attachment (542)
interdependence (551)
interpersonal attraction (525)
intimacy (553)
investment model of close relationships (560)
love styles (556)
passionate love (555)
popular children (538)
propinquity (525)
rejected-aggressive children (539)

rejected-withdrawn children (539)
repulsion hypothesis (528)
resistant insecure attachment (542)
secure attachment (542)
self-disclosure (528)
sociometric rating procedure (538)
spatial ecology (526)
strange situation (542)
triangular theory of love (558)
what is beautiful is good (536)
working model of a close relationship (544)

# Social Psychology Alive on the Web

## SOCIAL PSYCHOLOGY ALIVE: ONLINE LABS

To perform the following experiment and see how you compare to other students, go to Social Psychology Lab, which can be accessed through Social PsychologyNow.

- 13.1 Attitudes

## SOCIAL PSYCHOLOGY ALIVE: QUIZZING AND PRACTICE TESTS

You can access our website directly by going to http://psychology.wadsworth.com/breckler1e/ for online quizzes, flash cards, and Internet links.

## INFOTRAC® COLLEGE EDITION

For additional readings, explore InfoTrac College Edition, your online library of archived journal articles and periodicals dating back 22 years. If your instructor ordered InfoTrac College Edition with this book, you can access it from your CD-ROM, or go directly to www.infotrac-college.com/wadsworth and use the passcode from the InfoTrac College Edition card that came with your book. For this chapter, try these search terms: *propinquity, self-disclosure, interpersonal attraction, friendship, attachment, love.*

# Social Psychology Alive: The Workbook

To apply what you've learned in this chapter to the real world, go to Chapter 13 of *Social Psychology Alive: The Workbook*.

- Do the Westgate Findings Hold for Your Dorm or Apartment Building?
- Exploring Attitude Similarity and Liking
- What Determines Physical Attractiveness?

- Are You Headed for Court? What You Need to Know
- Does Your Attachment Style Affect Your Interactions With Other People?
- Can You Find True Love in Cyberspace?
- Do You Need an Excuse to Watch a Movie?
- Match That Tune!
- Dress for Success!

# Social Psychology Alive: The Videos

To see video on the topics and experiments discussed in this chapter, you can go either to Social PsychologyNow or to the CD-ROM, if your instructor assigned either one, to the following section:

- How Do I Love Thee? Expressions of Love Styles

# To Learn More

This list contains citations to books or articles that can help you learn more. These readings are good places to start if you want to gain a deeper understanding of the topics in this chapter.

- Sternberg, R. J., & Barnes, M. L. (1988). *The psychology of love.* New Haven, CT: Yale University Press.
- Reis, H. T., & Patrick, B. C. (1996). Attachment and intimacy: Component processes. In E. T. Higgins and A. W.

Kruglanski (Eds.), *Social psychology: Handbook of basic principles.* New York: Guilford Press, pp. 523–563.
- Berscheid, E., & Reis, H. T. (1998). Attraction and close relationships. In D. T. Gilbert, S. T. Fiske, & G. Lindzey (Eds.), *The handbook of social psychology* (4th ed., Vol. 2). Boston: McGraw-Hill, pp. 193–281.

© Franco Vogt/CORBIS

# Social Psychology in Your Life

Steve majored in psychology as an undergraduate and then spent four more years studying social psychology in graduate school. After another year working as a postdoctoral fellow in social psychology, Steve was hired as an assistant professor at a major university. His job was to teach and do research in his specialized field—social psychology. With a new job and exciting research to do, Steve was ready to finally join the ranks of professional social psychologists. The only thing he lacked was a car—he had no way to get to work.

On his first day in town, Steve headed to a local car dealership. He knew all the tricks of the trade. He was determined to get a good deal on a new car and not fall victim to the social influence tactics of a car salesperson. Steve figured that being a social psychologist made him immune to the tricks and techniques of the car dealer. "Low-balling won't work on me!" he thought confidently. Being forewarned is being forearmed, or so he thought.

It turns out that Steve got snookered. He paid way too much for a car he didn't really want to buy in the first place. The car he took for a test drive was a model with more options than Steve wanted. "Don't worry about it," remarked the salesman. "It'll only cost you a few dollars more each month. And just imagine yourself driving around town in this car." Back in the showroom, the salesman offered a good price for the car. "Just give me $5 and your driver's license, so I can go show the manager that you are serious," he explained. Returning with a sad look, he said that the dealer would be losing money at that price. For another $1,000, though, he could make a deal. Again, the salesperson urged Steve to "imagine yourself behind the wheel of that nice-looking car."

Steve could really see himself driving around in that car. He took the deal. And then came all the "necessary" extras—undercoating, extended warranty, floor mats, and on and on. By the time he finished, Steve had spent thousands of dollars

Purchasing a car highlights many aspects of social psychology.

© AP/Wide World Photos/Carlos Osorio

*more than he intended. As he drove off the lot, he realized that he had been taken. "How can I be so gullible?" he screamed to himself. Yet by the time he arrived at home, Steve was quite happy with the outcome. In the span of about an hour, he had convinced himself that he deserved the nicer car, and that the price he paid was fair. Besides, the poor car salesman had his own family to support and really needed the commission.*

*The true story of Steve's experience when buying a car highlights two important aspects of using social psychology in your own life. On the one hand, it reinforces the value of social psychological principles. Whether he knew it or not, the car salesman was relying on techniques of social influence, all of which we reviewed in Chapter 8.*

*On the other hand, Steve's story reminds us of the extraordinary difficulty in using the principles of social psychology to change our own behavior. In thinking about the applications of social psychology, it is tempting to seek practical advice on how to use social psychology to improve your own life. A number of books suggest a variety of such personal uses of social psychology (a good example is Lovaglia, 2000), dealing with problems such as depression, motivation, personal prejudices, and resisting influence. However, the truth is that knowing social psychology does not make you immune to social influence, stereotypes, prejudice, dissonance, obedience, groupthink, social loafing, or anything else you have learned about in this book. Social psychology may help you to better understand the real influences in your life, but translating that knowledge into practical action, especially applied to yourself, may be the most difficult challenge of all.*

*One way to appreciate the practical use of social psychology is by looking at how people use the principles and methods of social psychology in their jobs. As it turns out, social psychology has been put to good use in a variety of occupational settings. In this chapter, we provide a small sampling of careers in which knowledge of social psychology can be very useful. We also talk about career options for those who choose to make a career out of social psychology.*

*The future is quite bright for the maturing field of social psychology. New knowledge is accumulating rapidly, and thousands of social psychologists continue to work on refining and extending the theories and principles reviewed in this book. Later in this chapter, we will offer some modest speculation about exciting new directions for social psychology.*

## ● ● ●  Social Psychology and Your Career

Some people choose to make a career out of social psychology. All three authors of this book proudly identify themselves as social psychologists. Most of the authors who are cited throughout the book are social psychologists. Some focus their efforts in research, and others spend their time in the classroom. A career in research or in teaching social psychology can be rewarding and fulfilling.

Yet you do not need to make a career of social psychology to benefit from its insight. You will find that social psychology can be used to increase your success in almost any occupation. Perhaps you plan to go into business. Surely, this will involve the need to work in the context of an organization; it may lead to a career in marketing or advertising. If this sounds like you, your knowledge of social psychology will come in handy. Perhaps you want to enter the world of health care—to become a doctor, a physician's assistant, an emergency medical technician, a nutritionist, or a physical therapist. If this is your goal, social psychology will support you. Perhaps you aspire to be a teacher—as a K–12 educator or as a college professor. Your knowledge of social psychology will make you a better teacher.

In this section, we provide a few examples of how knowledge of social psychology can be put to use in your career. In some cases, we describe people who earned advanced degrees in social psychology. In other cases, we discuss how general knowledge of social psychology can be useful without the need for obtaining an advanced degree. Keep in mind that we barely scratch the surface of social psychology in this book. For every chapter, college-level courses drill down much deeper. If you think that social psychology will be relevant to your career aspirations, we urge you to learn more and enroll in specialized courses.

## Business and Organizations

Throughout this book, we have highlighted social psychological research of immense value to businesses and organizations. It should therefore come as no surprise that those who come armed with an understanding of social psychology can be of great value in these settings. People who work in direct sales can draw from a variety of social psychological principles, as illustrated in the opening to this chapter. In larger organizations, social psychology is used by those who work in human resources departments to help with hiring decisions, performance assessments, interpersonal conflicts, and other social dynamics in the workplace. Companies that develop and market products rely on social psychological insight from the initial design stages of a product, through product testing, to the marketing and advertising of the product.

If you are heading for business school, rest assured that more social psychology is in your future. You may want to hold onto your social psychology textbooks—you will need them! You will probably complete a course on consumer behavior, which includes a heavy dose of theory and research on attitudes (Chapter 6), persuasion (Chapter 7), and social influence (Chapter 8). In all likelihood, you will take a course on organizations, which will focus in part on such topics as group dynamics and leadership (Chapter 10). And most business schools require a course on research methods, which will be strongly oriented toward the research methods of social psychology (Chapter 2).

Most large companies operate their own research departments, and they employ a large staff of scientists. The process of developing and testing new products, and ultimately marketing them, relies on a team of people with expertise in such fields as engineering, chemistry, biology, economics, finance, and social psychology. The research methods used in such settings are fundamentally the same as those used in university settings. Yet the corporate research setting also differs substantially from the university research setting. The accompanying box, An Interesting Career: Social Psychology Meets Big Business, highlights the career of Richard Garfein, a social psychologist who pursued a career as a marketing researcher. As Garfein points out, research in a business setting differs from academic research in terms of the audience to which it is directed, the roles of individual scientists working in teams, and the final dissemination of results.

# An Interesting Career

## *Social Psychology Meets Big Business*

When Richard Garfein finished work on his PhD in the 1970s, he knew that a career in academic research was not for him (Garfein, 1997). He enjoyed research, but he did not have the same passion for teaching. While he was working on his doctoral dissertation, he took a part-time job at American Express, doing research in their human resources department. Garfein discovered that he liked the corporate environment, the excitement, the travel opportunities, and the pay. Once he finished graduate school, Garfein went back to American Express, where he worked as a marketing researcher for 18 years.

At the time Garfein entered the world of corporate research, it was not widely recognized that social psychologists commonly followed a career path in market research. As Garfein noted, however, "so many social psychologists have stumbled into market research . . . that it would have to be called a mainstream, alternative career path for social psychologists" (Garfein, 1997, p. 7). Indeed, many social psychologists have followed a similar path with companies such as IBM, AT&T, Procter & Gamble, and Quaker Oats.

Garfein highlights three important differences between doing research in a corporate setting and doing it in an academic setting. First, an academic researcher publishes articles in scientific journals with the goal of sharing that research with all who are interested. In the world of business research, most of the results stay within the company. When such research is shared, it is done much less formally than in scientific journals. Second, the audience for academic researchers is primarily other academic researchers within one's own area of specialization—the principal audience for social psychologists is other social psychologists. In the corporate world, the audiences for one's research are managers, colleagues who are not themselves social psychologists, and possibly business customers. These audiences require clear, friendly, and action-oriented presentations. Finally, corporate research environments tend to be organized around

Courtesy of Richard Garfein

**Richard Garfein pursued an interesting career as a market research consultant.**

teams of researchers, which requires the social psychologist to work hand in hand with researchers from different fields. It is a true multidisciplinary research environment.

Garfein's experience at American Express also highlights an important aspect of working in the business world—the opportunity it affords for advancement and new opportunities. By the late 1980s, Garfein had advanced to Vice President for International Market Research. When he left American Express in the 1990s to start his own international market research consulting practice, Garfein wrote, "I am excited about the prospects and feel that my social psychology doctoral training and 20 years of business experience have provided the ideal preparation."

In the business world, psychological research is valued because of the benefit it can provide in helping a company achieve its goals. Companies seek the scientific training and skills in research methodology that psychologists offer. As it turns out, training in social psychology is especially well suited for this purpose. Yet the research problems in which companies are interested are not typically focused on purely social psychological phenomena. Instead, they represent a blend of several areas of specialization, not only social psychology, but also human factors psychology, consumer psychology, and industrial/organizational psychology. In the business and corporate research worlds, the differences among these subareas of psychology are not as sharply delineated as they are in academic research settings.

## Government

In the United States and in Canada, the federal government includes a variety of agencies and institutions that rely on people with expertise in social psychology.

## TABLE 14.1
### A Sampling of Federal U.S. and Canadian Agencies in Which Social Psychology Makes a Contribution

| Research | Funding | Regulation |
| --- | --- | --- |
| National Institutes of Health | National Institutes of Health | Food and Drug Administration |
| Centers for Disease Control and Prevention | National Science Foundation | National Traffic Safety Board |
| National Institute for Occupational Safety and Health | Department of Defense | Department of Justice |
| Department of Defense | Department of Education | Federal Housing Administration |
| Federal Judicial Center | National Institute of Justice | Health Canada |
| Environmental Protection Agency | Centers for Disease Control | Transportation Safety Board of Canada |
| Census Bureau | Social Sciences and Humanities Research Council of Canada | Canadian Environmental Assessment Agency |
| Central Intelligence Agency | Canadian Institutes of Health Research | |
| National Aeronautics and Space Administration | Natural Sciences and Engineering Research Council of Canada | |
| Department of National Defense (Canada) | | |
| Correctional Services Canada | | |
| Sport Canada | | |

Some government organizations are in the business of doing research, others provide funding for research, and still others enact, monitor, and enforce government regulations. Table 14.1 provides a sampling of such agencies and offices within the U.S. and Canadian governments.

**Research.** The research staff of agencies such as the National Institutes of Health, the Department of Defense, or the Federal Judicial Center conduct studies and often contribute to the scientific literature, just as university-based academic researchers do. One major difference is that the research conducted in these agencies tends to be driven by the priorities of the government, rather than the priorities of the individual researchers. This is very similar to the situation we described earlier in businesses and corporations, where the research agenda is set by the company's priorities. The research conducted in government agencies is often connected very closely with national policy, addressing questions about the organization and functioning of government institutions (such as the federal courts or the military) and the implementation of federal regulations (in areas such as health, safety, or transportation). Because the research in government agencies is so closely connected with national policy, it can easily lead to implementation and broad impact. For example, one of the authors of this book (Elizabeth Wiggins) works as a senior researcher at the Federal Judicial Center, which conducts research to help improve the administration of federal courts in the United States.

Carolyn Cooper is a social psychologist who works as a social science analyst in the U.S. General Accounting Office. She nicely described the broad impact of a government agency:

> There are several differences between research conducted in an academic environment and that done in a nonacademic environment where the customers are policymakers. The critical aspect of working in a public-policy

environment is that many people can be directly affected by decisions over a very long period of time. Therefore, the research questions and hypotheses are often more complex, sensitive, and require much broader data collection efforts and greater coordination with staff from federal branch agencies and the private sector. (Cooper, 1997, p. 8)

**Funding.** Funding agencies of the federal government provide the money for doing research. Much of the social psychology research that we have discussed in this book was made possible through grants from the National Science Foundation or the National Institutes of Health. When researchers need money to conduct their research, they can apply for grants from these and other public and private sources. The funding agencies have developed very elaborate systems for reviewing grant proposals. Not only do they evaluate the scientific merit of the proposed research, they also take into account the relevance to society and the likelihood that the research will contribute to the solution of an important problem (e.g., curing a disease). Scientific experts work in the funding agencies to help manage the review and funding process.

Another of this book's authors (Steven Breckler) worked for nearly 10 years as a program officer at the National Science Foundation, where he had responsibility for the distribution of funding for social psychological research. Far from being government bureaucrats, program officers help agencies to set funding priorities, develop new funding opportunities for researchers in their fields, manage the review of proposals, and serve as the primary point of contact for researchers. This work can be extremely rewarding for scientists, who are among the first to get a preview of tomorrow's research.

**Regulation.** The regulatory agencies of the government are responsible for ensuring compliance with federal rules and laws. Social psychologists have advised the Federal Aviation Administration on airline cockpit and cabin safety, and the National Traffic Safety Board on matters having to with driving and traffic safety (recall our discussion of road rage in Chapter 11). One social psychologist (Nancy Ostrove) is a senior adviser for risk communications at the U.S. Food and Drug Administration. The areas of responsibility for these regulatory agencies bear directly on social behavior, dealing with issues of compliance, obedience, and social judgment.

## Law

We have already mentioned how social psychologists work in federal government agencies having to do with the law and judicial functioning. People who know social psychology are also in high demand in other ways that interact with the law and legal systems. For example, a large number of consulting companies employ social psychologists to help advise lawyers and their clients when it comes to jury selection and trial strategies. Social psychologists also provide guidance to police departments and law enforcement agencies to help improve their handling of criminal investigations. The multidisciplinary field of criminal justice draws from many facets of social psychology, including psychological theories of criminal behavior, policing strategies, courtroom process, racial profiling, gangs, drug crimes, and terrorism (Schmalleger, 2004; Wrobleski & Hess, 2006). Although lawyers do not typically obtain advanced training in social psychology, their work can often be improved by a fundamental understanding of social psychological principles.

The courtroom is a rich social environment.

# An Interesting Career

## *Social Psychologist as Trial Consultant*

Joy Stapp went to graduate school in social psychology. After spending several years working at the American Psychological Association, she took a job with a large trial consulting firm in Houston, Texas, marking the beginning of an interesting and successful career as a trial consultant. Stapp ultimately left the large firm to start her own company with partner Nancy Singleton. The firm of Stapp Singleton develops recommendations for trial strategy that are based on empirical research. "My background is in social psychology, and my partner, Nancy Singleton, has a doctorate in social anthropology. Our perspectives are quite different, but we share a belief in the experimental method and are sensitive to the biases that can skew our results. We are concerned with issues of reliability and

validity—concepts that are not always familiar to our attorney clients and their corporate clients" (Stapp, 1996, p. 12).

Stapp explains that some trial consultants focus most of their attention on jury selection. Others devote their energy to preparing witnesses and effective exhibits. Stapp Singleton works mainly on developing an effective trial strategy, one that "shapes juror perceptions during voir dire [jury selection] and opening statements, is supported by the presentations of the evidence through witnesses and exhibits, is reinforced in closing arguments, and leads to a favorable verdict

Courtesy of Joy Stapp

**Joy Stapp pursued an interesting career as a trial consultant.**

for our clients" (Stapp, 1996, p. 12). This approach clearly embraces more of the social psychological richness of a trial, and emphasizes the importance of skills in research methodology. Like most who work as trial consultants, Joy Stapp was not trained specifically for this kind of work. Her background in social psychology coupled with the opportunity to apply her research skills in a different area created the right mix to launch an interesting career.

Courtesy of Gary Wells

Research by Gary Wells has helped to provide guidelines for the collection of eyewitness information.

Over the past 25 years, a number of large consulting companies have been established to help attorneys and their clients prepare for their days in court (Kressel & Kressel, 2004). These companies conduct small experiments for their clients, often modeled very closely on social psychology experiments. A mock courtroom might be built, and actors hired to portray the roles of judge, attorneys, clients, and witnesses. Participants are then recruited from the community to play the role of jurors. In different experimental conditions, different lines of argument can be tried out or different approaches to structuring the trial can be tested. The pretend jurors are then sent to deliberate, and their discussions are carefully observed and noted. The results may provide good guidance for attorneys and their clients. These consulting companies are constantly hiring people who have varying degrees of knowledge about the theories and methods of social psychology. The accompanying box, An Interesting Career: Social Psychologist as Trial Consultant, describes the career of trial consultant Joy Stapp.

Social psychology has also been put to very productive use in advising police departments in their use of criminal lineups. Social psychologist Gary Wells and his colleagues helped to develop a guide for law enforcement agencies and their collection of eyewitness evidence. Some of the research that formed the basis for this guide was discussed in Chapter 3. The U.S. Department of Justice picked up on this work, and commissioned a special report (Technical Working Group for Eyewitness Evidence, 1999) for distribution to law enforcement agencies—a good example of social psychologists' reaching out to cops on the beat to help them better do their jobs. Time will tell whether local police departments utilize this work to improve the way they handle eyewitness evidence. If you happen to pursue a career in law enforcement, one of your contributions can be to recognize such applications and to draw upon them.

# An Interesting Career

## *A Social Psychologist Working to Prevent Disease*

Social psychologist Robert Croyle always had an interest in health-related behaviors. After earning his PhD at Princeton University, he followed a traditional academic career path, winding up as a professor at the University of Utah. Much of his research has focused on how people perceive and respond to threats to their health. For example, Croyle and his colleagues have studied the psychological responses of women who learn that they have inherited a gene mutation that makes them highly vulnerable to breast and ovarian cancer (Croyle, Smith, Botkin, Baty, & Nash, 1997). He has an ongoing interest in the psychological and social effects of screening for disease prevention and detection (Croyle, 1995). Croyle's research is a great example of how social psychology contributes to our understanding of the social and psychological underpinnings of disease and illness.

Croyle spent more than 10 years doing research in academic settings. Then, in 1998, he accepted a job at the National Cancer Institute—one of the funding agencies of the National Institutes of Health. For an academically trained researcher, this represented a big career change. He now has responsibility for allocating more than $400 million each year to fund research on cancer control. Croyle's career path could just as easily be highlighted in the previous section on careers in government agencies. It is important to recognize, however, that researchers can use their positions in federal granting agencies to continue advancing research.

Courtesy of National Cancer Institute, Division of Cancer Control and Population Sciences

**Robert Croyle now directs the Division of Cancer Control and Population Sciences at the National Cancer Institute.**

Croyle's research background and his job at the National Cancer Institute have helped him to realize how important it is for psychologists, including social psychologists, to join with colleagues in other fields. "I encourage colleagues to reach beyond their programs, engage colleagues in the biomedical and population sciences, and read one of the many recent reports from the National Academy of Sciences on the future of behavioral and biomedical research (http://www.nap.edu). The conceptual and methodological expertise of psychologists is needed now more than ever" (Croyle, 2004, p. 4).

A career as a lawyer is one that you may not immediately associate with expertise in social psychology. Yet consider the many different instances in which a lawyer could make good use of social psychology. As we just mentioned, the courtroom setting is one that is rich in social psychological phenomena: persuasion, social influence, and group (jury) decision making. Even outside the courtroom, lawyers get involved with interpersonal conflict, negotiation, and sometimes very emotional clients. In many respects, a career in law is a career in applied social psychology. Earlier, we advised students heading off to business school to hold onto their social psychology textbooks. The advice also applies if you plan to attend law school!

## Health and Medicine

Increasingly, social psychologists and those with some knowledge of social psychology are pursuing careers in health care settings. Health psychology itself is a multidisciplinary field, drawing from medicine, biology, psychology, and other social and behavioral sciences. Health psychologists work in a wide array of settings. Some conduct basic research in universities, especially in medical schools and schools of public health. Others work in government laboratories, such as the National Institutes of Health. The accompanying box, An Interesting Career: A Social Psychologist Working to Prevent Disease, describes the health-related career of Robert Croyle. Still others work in primary care, joining teams of health care professionals in hospitals, clinics, rehabilitation centers, and public health departments.

Social interaction is an important part of health care.

**biopsychosocial model**

*model that emphasizes that good health and illness are determined by a combination of biological, social, and psychological factors*

The guiding model in health psychology is known as the **biopsychosocial model,** which emphasizes that good health and illness are determined by a combination of biological, social, and psychological factors. Acceptance of the biopsychosocial model is growing within the medical community, and contributes to more effective and comprehensive health care. Indeed, throughout this book we introduced connections between social psychology and health. We hope you remember these selected examples (see Friedman & Silver, 2005, or Taylor, 2002, for more detailed treatments):

- Chapter 4 (Social Perception: Perceiving the Self and Others): In Higgins's *self-discrepancy theory,* perceived discrepancies between the actual self and either the ideal self or the ought self are hypothesized as being associated with specific kinds of emotions and behaviors. Higgins proposed that failure to reach our ideals can lead to depression, whereas failure to live up to our obligations can lead to anxiety. As it happens, the most common psychological complaints reported to clinical psychologists and psychiatrists are depression and anxiety. Higgins's work on self-discrepancy theory links a particular pattern of self-perceptions to each of these two states.

- Chapter 6 (Attitudes and Social Behavior): Following from the reasoned-action model of attitude–behavior relationships, we discussed the *IMB model of AIDS-preventive behavior* (Fisher & Fisher, 1992). The IMB (Information, Motivation, and Behavioral skills) model helps to identify the most important determinants of "safer sex behaviors," such as using a condom during intercourse and refusing to have unsafe sex. When a person makes decisions about engaging in risky sexual behaviors, it is important to know that those decisions are influenced by information the person possesses, the person's motivation to perform risky or safer behaviors, and the person's skill at performing preventive behaviors correctly.

- Chapter 7 (Attitude Change): We focused on the effectiveness of persuasive communications that arouse fear. Fear appeals are very common in health-related advertising campaigns. Good examples can be found in efforts to stop people from smoking or abusing drugs, or to encourage people to engage in safe sex (by emphasizing the negative consequences of not doing so). Although there is a limit on the effectiveness of fear appeals, the research shows that the arousal of fear *increases* the impact of messages on attitudes and behavioral intentions. The usual explanation of this finding is that fear is an aversive state, which people want to reduce; people accept the recommendations of the message because doing so reduces their fear.

- Chapter 12 (Helpful Social Behavior): The evidence is quite clear and consistent that perceiving a wide social support network has positive effects on health and well-being. For example, perceiving that a wide social support network is available if necessary has been shown to improve recovery from physical illness, to reduce the negative impact of stressful events, and to protect against depression. It is less clear whether the actual receipt of social support helps or hurts, suggesting that more research is needed to better understand the relationship between social support and health.

## Education

Good teachers possess a good sense of social behavior and interpersonal relationships. They understand how social processes bear on learning and education outcomes. If you plan to be a teacher—no matter what subject or grade level—the principles of social psychology will help you do a better job. Traditionally, most teachers in training complete a course in developmental psychology. This makes sense, because effective teaching depends on an understanding of how children grow and develop. Increasingly, teacher education programs are adding social psychological principles to the list of fundamental prerequisites for a career in education. This recognizes that the social context of learning is clearly important for teachers to understand.

A background in social psychology can be helpful in a variety of careers relating to education and learning. In addition to its value for teachers, social psychology is an important part of research in educational psychology. As in other fields we have touched upon, educational psychology is itself a blend of many distinct areas of psychology. It draws together the theory and research traditions of cognitive psychology, developmental psychology, social psychology, psychometrics, neuroscience, and other areas. Within the U.S. government, the Department of Education formulates education priorities for the country and allocates money for educational research. As in the other funding agencies, the Department of Education employs people with scientific backgrounds to help manage their programs.

Traditionally, research on education and learning has primarily drawn the attention of developmental and cognitive psychologists. Increasingly, social psychologists have been doing research on education and academic achievement. Good examples are found in a recent book edited by Joshua Aronson (2002b), who is a social psychologist doing research and teaching in the School of Education at New York University. In this book, a variety of social psychological perspectives is brought to bear on improving academic achievement. Just a few examples will give you a good sense of how social psychology can offer important insight:

- In the typical classroom, children are prodded and motivated by external rewards—gold stars, the honor roll, the teachers' praise. The carrot is always dangling just within reach. However, social psychology tells us that this may not be the best way to nurture long-term motivation and achievement. Instead, people tend to do better and to achieve more when they are motivated by internal goals—when they learn and achieve because they enjoy it, because it is fun, because it will help them achieve other goals. This is the difference between extrinsic motivation (direct rewards) and intrinsic motivation (being driven from within). Academic achievement is greater when learners are driven by intrinsic motivation (Deci & Ryan, 2002). Indeed, the most successful tutors are those who manage to engage students' intrinsic motivations (Lepper & Woolverton, 2002).

- One of the problems that poor-performing students face is the debilitating effects of failure. They blame themselves, and others go along by attributing their failure to stable, internal factors. As we often see with depression, academic failure can lead to a vicious self-fulfilling spiral of continued failure. A fascinating set of interventions, inspired by attribution theory, can help. In an early study (Miller, Brickman, & Bolen, 1975), one classroom of students was subjected to the classic scenario: the teacher persuaded and chided the students by explaining (quite rationally) why they needed to do well in math. In another classroom, the teacher used a little social psychology. The students in this class were simply told that they were good at math, that they were the high math performers. Whether it was true or not, the attribution of high math ability was attached to the students in this class. These students did better on a standard math test when compared to those who got the classic persuasion treatment. More recent research shows that a variety of attribution-inspired interventions succeed in motivating students to do well (Wilson, Damiani, & Shelton, 2002).

- Recall from Chapter 9, where we introduced the idea of *stereotype threat,* how awareness of one's membership in a stigmatized group can have negative consequences for high-stakes performance tests (J. Aronson, 2002a). In a recent study, Michael Johns, Toni Schmader, and Andy Martens (2005) showed that teaching women about stereotype threat is an effective way of reducing its detrimental effects on their math test performance. More generally, it is important for teachers to understand that a student's identity as a member of a socially stigmatized group can have an important bearing on academic success.

In summarizing the state of knowledge on learning and instruction, the American Psychological Association identified 14 learner-centered psychological principles. One of those principles focuses on social influences on learning:

Learning can be enhanced when the learner has an opportunity to interact and to collaborate with others on instructional tasks. Learning settings that allow for social interactions, and that respect diversity, encourage flexible thinking and social competence. In interactive and collaborative instructional contexts, individuals have an opportunity for perspective taking and reflective thinking that may lead to higher levels of cognitive, social, and moral development, as well as self-esteem. Quality personal relationships that provide stability, trust, and caring can increase learners' sense of belonging, self-respect and self-acceptance, and provide a positive climate for learning. Family influences, positive interpersonal support, and instruction in self-motivation strategies can offset factors that interfere with optimal learning such as negative beliefs about competence in a particular subject, high levels of test anxiety, negative sex role expectations, and undue pressure to perform well. Positive learning climates can also help to establish the context for healthier levels of thinking, feeling, and behaving. Such contexts help learners feel safe to share ideas, actively participate in the learning process, and create a learning community. (American Psychological Association, 1997)

Social psychology provides important insight into the social environment of the classroom.

# Basic Research

To this point, we have deliberately focused on career opportunities and areas of application that take social psychology and social psychologists far from the college-based research laboratory. We hope to have convinced you that social psychology is relevant in a variety of settings, and that an understanding of social psychology will be useful no matter where your career interests lie. For some, those career ambitions are to stay at a college or university and continue doing basic research in social psychology.

So what's it like to be a research social psychologist, and how do you get to be one? Most of us started right where you are today—completion of an introductory course and a burning desire to learn more. We took advanced courses in social psychology, and rounded out our education by taking courses in other subdisciplines of psychology. Many social psychologists got hooked by getting involved in research—first as a participant (a research subject), and then as a research assistant.

If you want to pursue a career in research following college, then graduate school is most likely the next step. Dozens of outstanding graduate training programs offer a PhD in social psychology. Graduate training averages four to five years, so prepare yourself for the continuing life of a student. Most programs involve another two years of coursework and the beginning of a research apprenticeship. You will learn how to plan and conduct a program of research, how to present your research to colleagues, and how to publish your research in scientific journals. You will focus your attention on a well-specified problem in social psychology, and you will master all there is to know about that problem. All of this hard work will culminate in a doctoral dissertation—your own contribution to science and a demonstration that you are finally ready to join the ranks of full-fledged social psychologists.

For those who pursue a university-based research career, one of the major obstacles is finding a job. Faculty positions in a specific area (such as social psychology) are not available every year at every school. You need to be prepared to hunt far and wide, and in all likelihood to move far away from where you live. It is an exciting time when you finally get to set up your own research laboratory, plan your own program of research, and help to train the next generation of social psychologists. Life as a college professor is great. The hours are flexible (but long!), the campus setting is familiar and comfortable, and you get to interact with students and other faculty. Even with all these benefits, it is not an easy job. Junior faculty are under constant pressure to publish their research, to obtain funding, and to otherwise contribute to the academic community.

# College Teaching

Many social psychologists find college teaching to be the most rewarding career choice. They like to spend their time with students, acquainting future generations with the principles of social psychology. This is also hard work. In addition to teaching their courses, faculty at teaching-oriented colleges are expected to supervise students' research projects and to keep abreast of the ever-growing literature in their field.

Graduate schools typically offer their students the opportunity to spend time in the classroom. Indeed, this is where many instructors initially learned the great joy and satisfaction of teaching. If you think this might be where your interest lies, we can offer a little advice: Most PhD programs devote little time to the training of future teachers. The emphasis tends to be on the training of future researchers. This means that you will need to devote special attention to acquiring and refining your own teaching skills. Don't be dissuaded—most colleges and universities offer resources for learning how to be an effective teacher. But you will probably need to look beyond your immediate training program.

# The Future of Social Psychology

One of the greatest joys of studying social psychology is that the science keeps evolving. The chapters of this book have been organized to reflect the major areas on which social psychology has focused, and will continue to focus. Every so often, new approaches and new problems gain the attention of social psychologists. Although we can't predict the future with great precision, we can see on the horizon at least two areas that promise to grab significant attention from social psychologists over the next decade. One is based on our growing ability to understand how the human brain supports cognition and emotion. The other relates to the emergence of new technologies that promise to transform science and society.

## Social Behavior and the Brain

Advances in cognitive science and neuroscience make it possible to look inside the brain as people engage in everyday perception and thought. To a large extent, technology has facilitated this progress. One method, functional magnetic resonance imaging (fMRI), helps us to identify areas of the brain that are involved in emotion and cognition. Much of the research in this area focuses on very fundamental cognitive processes, such as visual perception or the manipulation of numerical information. Recently, social psychologists have drawn on these methods to learn more about the connection between the brain and social behavior (Ochsner & Lieberman,

Magnetic resonance imaging (MRI) technology is used in social neuroscience research.

2001), and the specialty field of **social neuroscience** is beginning to take shape (Cacioppo, 2002; Cacioppo et al., 2002; Cacioppo, Berntson, Sheridan, & McClintock, 2000). Research in this area is focusing on such classic social psychology problems as social cognition (Mitchell, Heatherton, & Macrae, 2002), decision making (Camerer, 2003; Sanfey, Rilling, Aronson, Nystrom, & Cohen, 2003), and aggression (Davidson, Putnam, & Larson, 2000; Harmon-Jones & Sigelman, 2001).

**social neuroscience**

*an emerging area of research combining the perspectives of social psychology and neuroscience to understand the relationship between the brain and social behavior*

One very promising area of social neuroscience research focuses on people's perceptions, cognitions, and emotions concerning race. In earlier chapters (especially Chapter 9), we focused a lot of attention on the racial bases of stereotypes, prejudice, and discrimination. In the past few years, teams of social psychologists, cognitive psychologists, and neuroscientists have used the methods of neuroimaging to gain deeper insight into these phenomena (Eberhardt, 2005).

For example, research shows that overt and explicit expressions of racial prejudice have declined over the past few decades. However, as we discussed in Chapter 9, measures of racial prejudice that are disguised in their true intent continue to reveal that people harbor racial prejudice and negative stereotypes. The picture emerging from this research suggests that people can sometimes control their expressions of racial bias, but other times not. Indeed, the first and automatic response that many people show often indicates some degree of racial bias. Yet if you give the same people the opportunity to control their responses, then their overt expressions of such bias tend to go away.

It must take a fair degree of cognitive effort and control to suppress an initial, automatic bias. This is where brain imaging becomes a very useful and powerful tool. Research in neuroscience has helped to identify a specific region of the brain that is heavily involved in cognitive control, attention, judgment, and critical thinking. Collectively, these advanced cognitive processes are called **executive function.** The region of the brain associated with executive function is the prefrontal cortex, which is highlighted in Figure 14.1.

**executive function**

*the set of advanced cognitive processes involved in cognitive control, attention, judgment, and critical thinking*

Recent experiments have blended social psychology with neuroscience by looking at activity in the brain as participants are exposed to racial information. In a typical experiment, White participants might be shown pictures of both White and Black faces. In social psychology experiments, racial bias is often revealed by implicit measures over which participants have little control, but such bias is not usually evident on explicit measures over which participants can exercise their control. Until recently, of course, it was presumed or theorized that participants engaged in some form of cognitive control—executive function—when responding to explicit measures. With neuroimaging methods, we can now look more directly into the brains of participants to see if, indeed, they do engage in extra cognitive control in response to different race faces.

The accumulating evidence confirms that exposure to different race faces produces a significant activation in portions of the prefrontal cortex (Cunningham, Johnson, Raye, Gatenby, Gore, & Banaji, 2004; Richeson, Baird, Gordon, Heatherton, Wyland, Trawalter, et al., 2003). When racially biased White participants are exposed to Black faces, regions of the prefrontal cortex show a lot more activity than when they are exposed to White faces. It would seem that racially biased participants engage in a lot of cognitive effort to control their responses. The results of two such studies are shown in Figures 14.2 and 14.3 (p. 580).

Even without relying on high-tech brain imaging devices, cognitive neuroscientists have developed methods for understanding how brain processes might be involved in perception and cognition. One common approach is to study research participants who show brain-related cognitive disorders. If the main focus is on memory, then researchers might examine memory-related processes among people who suffer from amnesia or Alzheimer's disease. If the main focus is on motor behavior, then researchers might focus on people who suffer from Parkinson's disease. In both cases, the logic is that we can learn about the role of brain processes

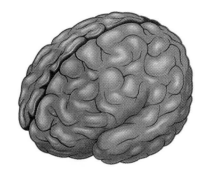

**FIGURE 14.1** The blue shaded region shows the location of the prefrontal cortex.

Adapted from *The Prefrontal Cortex* by J. M. Fuster, 1989.

a: Dorsolateral PFC    b: Anterior Cingulate    c: Ventrolateral PFC

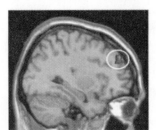 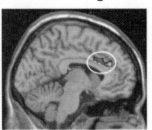 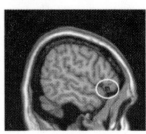

**FIGURE 14.2** Imaging results from Cunningham et al. (2004) show increased prefrontal cortex (PFC) activity in White participants' responses to Black versus White faces.

From Cunnigham, Johnson, Raye, Gatenby, Gore, Banaji, Separable Neural components in the processing of Black and White faces. *Psychological Science*, Vol. 15, Number 12. Copyright 2004, American Psychological Society.

by including in our studies people who suffer from brain disorders that are known to produce specific deficits.

How might this help in our effort to learn more about social behavior? Let's take a look at an experiment reported by Matthew Lieberman, Kevin Ochsner, Daniel Gilbert, and Daniel Schacter (2001). These researchers were interested in the cognitive underpinnings of attitude change produced by *cognitive dissonance*. In Chapter 7 we explained how the unpleasant feelings produced by dissonant cognitions motivate people to do something to change their state. One common way for people to reduce their dissonance is by changing their attitudes to make them more consonant with their behavior. What Lieberman and his colleagues wanted to know is whether people need to be explicitly aware of the discrepancy between their attitudes and behavior—whether people need to remember that they recently engaged in counterattitudinal behavior—in order for them to engage in dissonance-reducing attitude change.

To answer this question, the researchers compared unimpaired adults with patients who were suffering from anterograde amnesia—a form of memory loss in which people are unable to form new memories that can be recognized and retrieved. Using a standard *free-choice paradigm* (described in Chapter 7), Lieber-

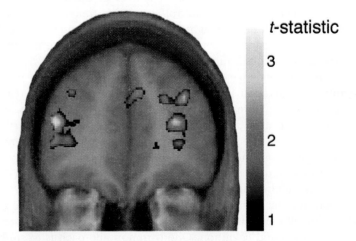

**FIGURE 14.3** Imaging results from Richeson et al. (2003) show increased prefrontal cortex (PFC) activity in White participants' responses to Black versus White faces.

From Cunnigham, Johnson, Raye, Gatenby, Gore, Banaji, Separable Neural components in the processing of Black and White faces. *Psychological Science*, Vol. 15, Number 12. Copyright 2004, American Psychological Society.

man et al. (2001) found that amnesics showed just as much attitude change as did the control participants. These results were used to support the view that people need not remember that they have engaged in attitude-discrepant behaviors to nevertheless engage in dissonance-reducing attitude change.

# Emerging Technologies

The emergence of new technologies, especially information technology, is starting to show an impact in social psychology. In Chapter 2, we talked about the Internet as providing an important new context for collecting data (Birnbaum, 2000, 2001). We also described how immersive virtual environments can be used to create social environments for research (Bailenson, Blascovich, Beall, & Loomis, 2003; Blascovich, Loomis, Beall, Swinth, Hoyt, & Bailenson, 2001).

**Immersive Environments.** Consider how immersive virtual environments might play an important role in the future of social psychology. Throughout this book, we have described examples of research involving the use of an experimenter's confederate—a person working for the experimenter who is trained to behave or respond in very specific ways. Research confederates were an important part of Asch's conformity experiments, Milgram's obedience experiments, Sherif's normative influence experiments, and Latané and Darley's emergency bystander experiments (to cite just a few examples).

The use of a live "plant" in social psychology experiments is often critical for setting the necessary social stage. Yet we also know that it introduces additional sources of variability into the experimental setting. Suppose the confederate behaves differently on different days, or at different times of the same day. What if the confederate's behavior interacts with characteristics of the real participants? Perhaps a confederate will respond differently to tall respondents than to short ones. All of these possibilities create important threats to the validity of an experiment. Social psychologists would place a high value on gaining additional control over these variables.

The technology of immersive virtual environments may offer the methodological solution. Although the technology is still in its infancy, it is easy to see how it affords a high degree of control. Everything about the "situation" presented to participants is constructed and controlled by a computer. A nice illustration is offered in a recent experiment by Jeremy Bailenson and Nick Yee (in press). These researchers were interested in a phenomenon that Tanya Chartrand and John Bargh had earlier called the *chameleon effect* (Chartrand & Bargh, 1999). Chartrand and Bargh found that participants automatically mimic the motor behaviors of a stranger, and that people generally like others who engage in such mimicry. Following the tradition of social psychological research, these experiments feature the use of a live confederate.

Bailenson and Yee wanted to know if the same effect would be observed under the more controlled conditions of an immersive virtual environment. To find out, they created a digital chameleon—a computer-controlled agent in immersive virtual reality. Figure 14.4 (p. 582) shows a participant in the experimental apparatus. Within this virtual environment, participants "interacted" with the virtual agent. The digital chameleon was programmed either to mimic the participant's head movements (with a 4-second delay) or to respond with the prerecorded movements of another participant. As the

© Andersen Ross/Photodisc Red/Getty Images

Social communication is often mediated by computers.

agent was moving its head, it verbally presented a persuasive argument. Results showed that the agent was more persuasive and better liked when it mimicked the participant's own head movements.

Another fascinating use of immersive virtual environments relates to the burgeoning fields of cognitive and social neuroscience. Research in these areas depends heavily on neuroimaging technology. The current state of that technology requires that research participants lie still in a very confined space. This creates a special challenge in presenting stimulus materials. It is relatively easy to show still photographs or computer-generated images as people's brains are being scanned. It is much harder to create immersive social situations for people when they are lying flat on their backs inside the tunnel of a magnetic resonance imaging device. The recent advances in immersive virtual environment technology may offer a solution (Tarr & Warren, 2002). An engaging virtual environment can be created for participants, even when they are in the confines of the imaging device.

**The Internet.**  Whenever new technology is introduced, people worry about its impact on society. This is especially true of communication technology, whose history includes the introduction of telephones and television. In both cases, the technology was greeted with a sort of ambivalence—excitement about its benefits, but apprehension about its consequences. Internet technology is today's center of attention. Internet technology goes well beyond its use as simply another method in the social psychologist's toolbox (Chapter 2). The Internet, instant messaging, and chat rooms have pervaded social life. The Internet has become one of the main ways in which people communicate, and it provides an important new medium for the delivery of persuasive messages. This makes Internet-mediated communication a social phenomenon in its own right (Kiesler, 1997).

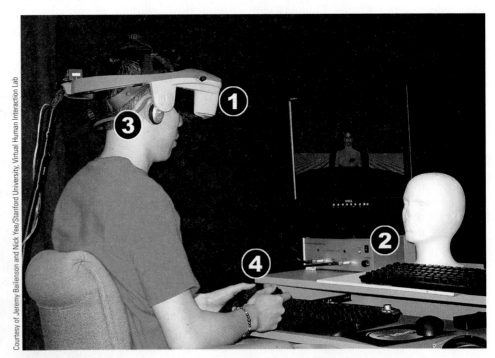

Courtesy of Jeremy Bailenson and Nick Yee/Stanford University, Virtual Human Interaction Lab

**FIGURE 14.4** A participant engaged in Bailenson and Yee's (in press) immersive virtual environment system. The components are: (1) orientation tracking sensor, (2) image generator, (3) head-mounted display, and (4) game pad input device.

Researchers are beginning to examine social behavior within this technological context (Calvert, 2002; Katz & Rice, 2002; Kiesler & Kraut, 1999; Kraut, Patterson, Lundmark, Kiesler, Mukophadhyay, & Scherlis, 1998), and we expect that this will become a booming area of research in the next decade. In some ways, the Internet is a sort of moving target for doing research, especially on social behavior. For example, in one major longitudinal study conducted in the late 1990s, Robert Kraut and his colleagues at Carnegie Mellon University (Kraut et al., 1998) followed people over a period of 1 to 2 years, just after Internet accessibility became available in their homes. Participants in this study made heavy use of the Internet, especially for communication with others. At that time, Internet use actually caused a decline of communication among family members within the households—they experienced declines in the sizes of their social circles, and increases in depression and loneliness. Yet in a more recent follow-up study of the same households (Kraut, Kiesler, Boneva, Cummings, Helgeson, & Crawford, 2002), those negative consequences had evaporated. Indeed, during the intervening years it appears that Internet use in this sample was associated with relatively positive outcomes.

The technology that allows electronic interpersonal communication also has a potential application in the field of social neuroscience. As we just discussed, one challenge of doing research with magnetic resonance imaging technology is that it constrains the social situation. Recently, researchers have been using Internet technology to allow for social interaction while two people are separately ensconced in the imaging equipment (Montague et al., 2002).

People are sometimes reluctant to accept the products of new technology.

**New Technologies.** It is fun to imagine what other new technologies might intersect the world of social psychology. An important way this will probably happen is the increasing need to understand the societal impact of new technologies. We saw this just above in the case of Internet technology. Indeed, it seems that people may be growing skeptical or even fearful of new technologies. A good example is in public resistance to the use of genetically modified foods. This may not be high on the list of North American concerns (Hallman, Hebden, Aquino, Cuite, & Lang, 2003), but across Europe people are reluctant to consume genetically modified foods, and often protest the development of such foods. The subject has become an important part of European thought, attitudes, and values (Cook, Kerr, & Moore, 2002; Koivisto Hursti & Magnusson, 2003; Laros & Steenkamp, 2004; Miles & Frewer, 2003). However, efforts to understand how people respond to the introduction of new technologies has not drawn much research attention yet from social psychologists.

Another interesting example is in the area of nanotechnology—technology that allows us to manipulate matter at the level of individual atoms or molecules. As with genetically modified foods, social psychologists may begin investigating the social consequences of this new technology, especially if people are reluctant to adopt nanotechnology because they fear negative and aversive results (Roco & Bainbridge, 2001). In the area of research methods, it may be that this technology will produce new tools that permit unprecedented opportunities for observing and recording affective, cognitive, and behavioral processes (Roco & Bainbridge, 2002). Whatever new technologies the future holds, it is likely that social psychologists will have a role to play in understanding them—both their social consequences and influences on social behavior, and the advances in research methods that they might allow.

Nanotechnology may someday be a big frontier for social and behavioral science.

# Chapter Summary

This is the end—the last summary of the last chapter. In this chapter, we highlighted the many interesting career possibilities that are enabled by a background in social psychology, including in business, government, law, health, education, research, and teaching. We also engaged in a little forecasting, suggesting that emerging frontiers in social psychology can be found at the intersections with neuroscience and with new technologies.

# Key Terms

**biopsychosocial model** (574)  **executive function** (579)  **social neuroscience** (579)

# Social Psychology Alive on the Web

## SOCIAL PSYCHOLOGY ALIVE: QUIZZING AND PRACTICE TESTS

You can access our website directly by going to http://psychology.wadsworth.com/breckler1e/ for online quizzes, flash cards, and Internet links.

##  INFOTRAC® COLLEGE EDITION

For additional readings, explore InfoTrac College Edition, your online library of archived journal articles and periodicals dating back 22 years. If your instructor ordered InfoTrac College Edition with this book, you can access it from your CD-ROM, or go directly to http://www.infotrac-college.com/wadsworth and use the passcode from the InfoTrac College Edition card that came with your book. For this chapter, try these search terms in combination with *social psychology: careers, consumer behavior, marketing, biopsychosocial model, education, teaching, social neuroscience, immersive virtual environments, Internet.*

# Social Psychology Alive: The Workbook

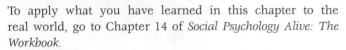

To apply what you have learned in this chapter to the real world, go to Chapter 14 of *Social Psychology Alive: The Workbook.*

- Name That Job

- Proverbs, Adages, and Platitudes: A Look Back at Chapter 1
- The Practical Relevance of Social Psychology

# Developing a Measure of a Social Psychological Construct

In the following paragraphs, we outline the basic steps involved in developing a measure of a social psychological construct. The construct might be a disposition (trait), attitude, set of beliefs, or other stable concept (see Chapter 6 for additional information specifically on developing measures of attitudes). We assume that the construct is not so simple or straightforward that it can be assessed with a single item (e.g., "Do you support or oppose the use of the death penalty?").

The steps we describe are those needed to produce a *self-report* measure, which means that respondents provide their answers directly and describe their own traits and behaviors. Self-report measures assume that respondents are able and willing to answer honestly. In Chapter 6, we discuss some of the limitations of self-report measures (see pages 209–210), so you might want to review these points before proceeding. In particular, self-report measures can be influenced by socially desirable responding, such that participants' answers are influenced by a desire to make themselves look good. Thus, if the construct is one on which there is a socially "good" or "correct" position (or, conversely, a negative or unpopular position), self-report measures can be problematic. We will assume that the construct to be measured lends itself to a self-report approach.

## Step 1: Get a Clear Idea of What the Construct Means

Before researchers can develop a measure of a construct, they must have a clear idea of what it means. They formulate an appropriate definition of the construct, as well as provide a detailed analysis of what it represents. What are the key elements in the construct? What behaviors reflect the construct? Does the construct have different facets/components, or is it a simple, one-dimensional concept? Are there synonyms for the construct (words that mean the same thing) that help to clarify its meaning?

For example, imagine that we want to measure the construct of *shyness*. The first step in designing a measure would be to define shyness and think about its key elements and behaviors. We might define shyness as *a tendency to feel discomfort and self-consciousness in the presence of other people.* This definition would mean that we should obtain self-reports of discomfort and self-consciousness in social settings rather than ratings of how people feel in private settings. Are there different components of shyness? We might say yes, shyness can involve physical symptoms like blushing, psychological symptoms like anxiety in public, and behavioral symptoms like avoiding social situations. We would therefore want to assess each of these components of shyness. We might also recognize that shyness can be evidenced in many different settings, including interactions with strangers, interactions with opposite-sex others, giving talks in front of a group, and other social situations. We would therefore try to ask about shyness behaviors and reactions in each of these possible settings; perhaps some people are shy with specific target groups but not others, whereas some people are shy in just about all social settings.

## Step 2: Develop Items for the Self-Report Measure

The second step in developing a self-report measure of a construct is to design or collect a reasonably large set of statements or questions that the researcher thinks reflect the construct. This step can be more challenging than expected: it is often easy to think of one or two items that clearly measure a construct but very difficult to think of many more. There is no "correct" number of questionnaire items to generate, but broad concepts like personality traits are best assessed by many items—10, 20, or even more. If the concept is relatively simple and unidimensional (e.g., attitudes toward a social issue, such as the importance of a strong military), then fewer items are needed—as few as 3 or 4 items may be enough.

The statements or questions developed for the scale should possess a number of characteristics, which are summarized below.

- *Aim for clear wording.* Each questionnaire item should be clear and unambiguous in its meaning. Words should be common ones that all respondents will understand. Sentences should be relatively short and simple in both grammar and meaning. Furthermore, unless the questionnaire is designed to be sex-specific, the items should apply to both men and women.

- *Aim for nonredundancy.* Questionnaire items should be distinct and different from one another in some way. Avoid the simple rephrasing of existing items. It is fine to have some similarly worded items (e.g., "Tests make me anxious" and "I get nervous before exams"), but if the construct is so simple that there are *only* two or three ways it can be described, then keep the measure short.

- *Aim for comprehensiveness.* Include questionnaire items that assess each facet or component of the construct. By including items that reflect the various elements, you help ensure that the measure is comprehensive and captures the construct's full range. At the same time, avoid items that reflect related but distinct constructs. For example, a measure of aggression should not have large numbers of items related to anger; otherwise your scale might be measuring some mix of the two constructs.

- *Aim for a balanced scale.* Include some items in which a response of "agree" reflects *more* of the construct and other items in which a response of "agree" reflects *less* of the construct. If all of the questionnaire items are phrased in the same direction (an unbalanced scale), then a general tendency to agree with statements will bias respondents' total scores on the scale. In other words, include different items on which the same response (e.g., "strongly agree") means contrasting things. For example, a measure of tidiness or neatness should *not* include only items like "I am a neat person," "I usually clean up after myself," and "Materials on my desk are always well organized," because these are all worded in the same direction: agreement reflects greater tidiness. It should also include some items on which *disagreement* reflects greater tidiness, such as "I often leave dirty dishes in the sink" and "People sometimes tell me I am a slob."

- *Avoid double negatives:* Do not include statements or items that are double negatives (e.g., "I never state that I do not support capital punishment"), because they are confusing and difficult to understand.

- *Avoid two-component items.* Do not use questionnaire items that include two separate points, because participants may agree with one part but not the other. For example, asking participants to rate agreement with the statement "Capital punishment should be abolished and death row inmates should be treated better" is problematic, because respondents may feel differently about the two components (abolishing capital punishment versus treating death row inmates better).

- *Avoid items that have a strong positive or negative connotation.* For instance, even the most authoritarian person may be unwilling to publicly endorse the statement "I believe the torture of war prisoners is warranted." Similarly, even the least helpful person might feel compelled to agree with an altruism item such as "It is only proper to help the sick and needy."

Each item in the measure must have a "response scale" on which participants circle a number, a word, or a phrase to indicate their answer. The most common response scales are agreement (e.g., "strongly disagree" to "strongly agree"), self-descriptiveness (e.g., "very untrue of me" to "very true of me"), and degree or strength (e.g., "not at all" to "extremely"). The answer scale for an item always includes several possible responses; the most common number of options is probably 7, but anywhere from 5-point to 11-point scales are common. Responses are generally scored from 1 to 7 (or 1 to 5, or 1 to 11, etc.) such that higher scores reflect *more* of the construct being measured. Thus, if the measure is intended to assess tidiness, high scores should reflect greater tidiness; if the measure is intended to assess support for capital punishment, high scores should reflect stronger support for capital punishment.

Let's continue our example of developing a measure of shyness. What are some questionnaire items that conform to these guidelines and that could be used to measure shyness? Ten sample items are listed below, with a one-sentence instruction explaining how responses should be made:

*Please indicate the extent to which you disagree or agree with each of the following statements by circling one of the numbers on the answer scale.*

1. I feel self-conscious when other people watch me entering a room.

|     1     |     2     |     3     |     4     |     5     |     6     |     7     |
|-----------|-----------|-----------|-----------|-----------|-----------|-----------|
| Strongly disagree | | | Neutral | | | Strongly agree |

2. My friends would describe me as outgoing.

|     1     |     2     |     3     |     4     |     5     |     6     |     7     |
|-----------|-----------|-----------|-----------|-----------|-----------|-----------|
| Strongly disagree | | | Neutral | | | Strongly agree |

3. I feel awkward interacting with members of the opposite sex.

|     1     |     2     |     3     |     4     |     5     |     6     |     7     |
|-----------|-----------|-----------|-----------|-----------|-----------|-----------|
| Strongly disagree | | | Neutral | | | Strongly agree |

4. Large parties are very enjoyable for me.

|     1     |     2     |     3     |     4     |     5     |     6     |     7     |
|-----------|-----------|-----------|-----------|-----------|-----------|-----------|
| Strongly disagree | | | Neutral | | | Strongly agree |

5. I feel comfortable introducing myself to other students in my classes.

|     1     |     2     |     3     |     4     |     5     |     6     |     7     |
|-----------|-----------|-----------|-----------|-----------|-----------|-----------|
| Strongly disagree | | | Neutral | | | Strongly agree |

6. Blushing is *not* a problem for me.

| 1 | 2 | 3 | 4 | 5 | 6 | 7 |
|---|---|---|---|---|---|---|
| Strongly disagree | | | Neutral | | | Strongly agree |

7. I dislike speaking in front of a group.

| 1 | 2 | 3 | 4 | 5 | 6 | 7 |
|---|---|---|---|---|---|---|
| Strongly disagree | | | Neutral | | | Strongly agree |

8. I am a shy person.

| 1 | 2 | 3 | 4 | 5 | 6 | 7 |
|---|---|---|---|---|---|---|
| Strongly disagree | | | Neutral | | | Strongly agree |

9. I enjoy meeting new people.

| 1 | 2 | 3 | 4 | 5 | 6 | 7 |
|---|---|---|---|---|---|---|
| Strongly disagree | | | Neutral | | | Strongly agree |

10. I often avoid social settings.

| 1 | 2 | 3 | 4 | 5 | 6 | 7 |
|---|---|---|---|---|---|---|
| Strongly disagree | | | Neutral | | | Strongly agree |

A total score on this scale would be calculated by adding up participants' responses across all items, with higher scores representing more shyness. Thus, all items that reflect more shyness when respondents *agree* with them (Items 1, 3, 7, 8, and 10) would be scored using the response scale exactly as it appears below the items—from 1 (strongly disagree) to 7 (strongly agree). However, all items that reflect more shyness when respondents *disagree* with them (Items 2, 4, 5, 6, and 9) would be scored by *reversing* the scale as it appears below the items: responses would be scored from 7 (strongly disagree) to 1 (strongly agree). For example, if respondents circled "2" on the answer scale, they would be assigned a score of 6, or if they circled "5" on the answer scale, they would be assigned a score of 3. Possible total scores on the 10 items would range from 10 (if a respondent answered every item by circling the least shy response and received a score of 1 on each of the 10 items) to 70 (if a respondent answered every item by circling the most shy response and received a score of 7 on each of the 10 items).

But these total scores would assume that all 10 items in the questionnaire are "good" or "effective" items. This assumption must actually be tested before the researcher's job is done. We describe how to assess the quality of the items in the next section.

## Step 3: Assess the Quality of the Items

After a researcher has come up with questionnaire items that seem to be worded clearly, are balanced, and reflect the breadth of the construct, the next step is to evaluate the quality of these items. Are they, in fact, all accurate reflections of the same underlying construct? Do they "hold together" as a scale? Are they unambiguous?

There are two very common ways to assess the quality of the items in a scale: examining the item–total correlations and conducting a factor analysis. We will explain the first procedure in some detail, but factor analysis is complex enough that we will only outline its purposes or goals. If you want to do a factor analysis (after understanding what it is intended to do), you can ask for assistance from someone who is relatively expert in statistics and computer analysis.

**Item—Total Correlations.** In any initial pool of statements designed by a researcher, there will probably be some items that are ambiguous, poorly phrased, or even unrelated to the construct being measured. These questionnaire items will not contribute meaningfully to respondents' scores and should be identified and removed from the questionnaire. For example, suppose that a researcher wanting to measure shyness included the following statement in the original set: "I occasionally wonder what people think of me." The researcher might have expected this item to reflect shyness, with shy people agreeing with the statement more than non-shy people. But perhaps *everyone* wonders occasionally what other people think of them, so this item might elicit high agreement from both shy and non-shy respondents. If this is the case, then the item does not reflect shyness and should be eliminated.

Item–total correlations help to identify such ineffective statements. To compute item–total correlations, we must first calculate respondents' total scores across all items. Although these total scores include the bad items as well as the good items, they provide an initial estimate of the construct for each person. Next, taking one item at a time, participants' responses on that item are correlated with their total scores. If scores on the item correlate significantly with the total scores (that is, people who score high on that one item also tend to score high on the total scores), then it is assumed to be an effective item. But if the item does *not* correlate significantly with the total scores, then it is assumed to be an ineffective item, because participants' answers do not appear to reflect the intended construct. That is, someone who agrees with that item is just as likely to be high on the construct as low. After all items have been tested in this manner, the ineffective items are dropped from the scale. The remaining items can then be included in a revised measure for future studies (or as a basis for recalculating the current participants' scores if the researcher wants to do so).

**Factor Analysis.** Factor analysis is a statistical procedure that shows which items in a scale tend to "go together" to form a *factor.* A factor can be thought of in this context as an underlying theme to the items. Factor analysis identifies how many factors or themes exist in the set of items and which items form each factor. The researcher can interpret what a factor means by looking at the specific items that form the factor. In many cases, the researcher expects or hopes that *all* of the items in a scale will form just one factor, because the construct is conceptualized as unidimensional (e.g., degree of liking for chocolate) and so the items should represent that one theme. But sometimes the construct may be expected to have two or even more factors, because it has different components or elements. Earlier, we explained the importance of getting a clear idea of what the construct means—Step 1 in the process of developing a measure. This understanding of the construct will presumably include the number of components that are expected. For example, it has been proposed that the construct of risk taking is made up of four distinct but related facets: physical risk taking, monetary risk taking, social risk taking, and ethical risk taking. A factor analysis would test whether this four-factor structure is, in fact, exhibited in a set of items on risk taking.

## Step 4: Assess the Validity of the Scale

Item–total correlations and factor analysis indicate whether your questionnaire's items are all measuring the same construct, but those methods do not tell you whether it is the construct you intended to measure. To be confident that scores on the new measure actually reflect what they are supposed to reflect (the *validity* of the measure; see page 39 in Chapter 2), the researcher should also collect data showing that the measure correlates with other, established measures of the construct (if they exist) or with appropriate, related constructs. That is, the researcher should document the validity of the scale by showing that it predicts other things that are conceptually related. These "other things" can include measures of behavior, personality traits, beliefs, or anything else that *should* correlate with the new measure.

For example, to establish the validity of a measure of shyness, a researcher might try to show that scores on the scale correlate significantly with other known measures of shyness. (You may be wondering why a researcher would develop a new measure of a construct if other measures already exist. The existing measures may not be appropriate for the researcher's goals for a variety of reasons. For example, existing measures may have been developed for use with a different population or may not capture all components of the construct.) Alternatively, the researcher can think about other constructs that are relevant to shyness. One such measure could be peer judgments of shyness—ratings of participants' shyness by their friends. If the new measure is valid, then people who score high in shyness on the new measure should be rated as more shy by their friends than people who score low in shyness. Other measures could consist of participants' self-reports of *behaviors* that presumably reflect shyness, such as the number of parties they have attended in the last month, or the number of new friends they have made while at university. Presumably, people who score high in shyness on the new measure will report having attended fewer parties and having made fewer new friends than people who score low in shyness.

Another way to demonstrate the validity of a measure of shyness could involve constructing controlled settings where participants' shyness could be observed and rated. For example, participants could be brought into the laboratory to interact for 10 minutes with one or two assistants of the experimenter. Scores on the new shyness measure should predict how much conversation participants initiate during the interaction, with shy participants initiating less conversation than non-shy participants. Participants could also be asked following the interaction to rate their feelings of discomfort; scores on the measure of shyness should predict ratings of discomfort during the interaction, with shy participants reporting more discomfort than non-shy participants.

## Conclusion

We have outlined four steps in the development of a self-report measure of a social psychological construct: (1) get a clear idea of what the construct means, (2) develop items for the measure, (3) assess the quality of the items, and (4) assess the validity of the scale. These steps are necessary no matter what construct is being measured—a personality trait or a more limited concept such as an attitude or a belief. This process of developing a measure represents the challenge of *operational definitions* discussed in Chapter 2 (see page 35). Theoretical ideas must be translated into testable questions, and psychological constructs must be translated into measurable responses before good empirical research can be conducted. By developing sound measures of social psychological constructs, researchers can collect the data necessary to evaluate important theories in psychology.

# Glossary

**accessibility** the ease with which a schema comes to awareness

**achievement motivation** a disposition that represents the extent to which people are positively or negatively aroused by performance settings

**actor-observer difference** a pattern of differences in attributions in which actors tend to make external attributions for their own behavior, whereas observers tend to make internal attributions for the same actions

**actual self** a conception of the self describing our perception of how we really are

**additive tasks** activities in which the group output reflects the total of all individual members' contributions

**adult attachment** concept used to describe and understand close relationships in adulthood by translating each of the three major patterns of attachment found among infants—secure, anxious/ambivalent, and avoidant—into their adult forms

**aggression** behavior that is intended to injure someone physically or psychologically

**aggression questionnaire (AQ)** a scale that measures individual differences in trait aggressiveness

**alcohol myopia** the tendency for intoxication to reduce cognitive capacity, which results in a narrowing of attention

**altruistic motivation** a motive for helping purely for the sake of providing benefit to another person

**ambivalent attitudes** evaluations of targets that include both positive and negative elements

**ambivalent sexism inventory** a measure of stereotyped attitudes toward women, which is composed of two dimensions, one positive and one negative: benevolent sexism and hostile sexism

**appearance self-esteem** an individual's satisfaction with his or her physical looks

**archival research** correlational investigations that are based on preexisting information obtained by researchers, such as historical records, newspaper articles, or other forms of public data

**associative network** a very large system of schemas that are linked together on the basis of shared meaning or shared experience; it is one way to conceptualize how information is organized in memory

**attachment theory** Bowlby's attachment theory concerns the development and effects of the emotional bond between an infant and its caregiver; the theory is also used to account for the relationships that develop between close friends and lovers throughout the span of their lives

**attitude** an individual's evaluation of a target along a good-bad dimension

**attitude-similarity effect** people find others more attractive and likeable the more similar they are in their attitudes, beliefs, and preferences

**attributions** causal judgments about why an event or behavior occurred

**augmentation principle** a rule of attribution that states that the perceived role of a cause will be augmented (increased) if other factors are present that would work against the behavior

**autobiographical memory** stored information about the self, such as goals, personality traits, past experience, and other qualities

**autokinetic effect** in a darkened room, a stationary point of light will appear to move periodically

**automatic process** a judgment or thought that we cannot control, which occurs without intention, very efficiently, and sometimes beneath our awareness

**availability heuristic** the tendency to base a judgment on how easily relevant examples can be thought of

**aversive racism** a "modern" kind of prejudice held by people who do not consider themselves prejudiced and who would find any accusation of being prejudiced aversive, but who nevertheless harbor some negative beliefs and hostile feelings toward members of minority groups

**avoidant insecure attachment** a pattern of insecure attachment seen among babies who basically ignore their mother, usually show no strong signs of disturbance when mother leaves the room, and avoid mother during reunion episodes

**behavioral intention** an individual's plan to perform or not perform an action

**behaviorism** an approach in psychology that assumes that behavior can be explained purely in terms of stimulus–response connections established through experience and reinforcement

**benevolent sexism** positive but paternalistic attitudes toward women

**bias blind spot** the tendency to think that biases and errors in judgments are more common in others than in ourselves

**biopsychosocial model** emphasizes that good health as well as illness is determined by a combination of biological, social, and psychological factors

**blank lineup** a group of individuals that does not include the suspect; everyone in the lineup is known to be innocent

**bystander effect** the likelihood that an individual will intervene in an emergency goes down as the number of bystanders increases

**categorization** the process of recognizing and identifying something

**catharsis** the idea that aggressive behavior releases people's pent-up frustration and reduces the likelihood of subsequent aggression

**central route to persuasion** persuasion that occurs when attitude change results from a careful analysis of the information in a persuasive communication

**chronic accessibility** the degree to which schemas are easily activated for an individual across time and situations

**cognitive dissonance theory** a model that states that awareness of consonant cognitions makes us feel good, whereas awareness of dissonant cognitions makes us feel bad; further, the unpleasant feelings produced by dissonant cognitions motivate us to do something to change our state

**cognitive miser model** a view of information processing that assumes people usually rely on heuristics to make judgments and will engage in careful, thoughtful processing only when necessary

**cognitive neoassociation model of aggression** a theory of harm-doing proposing that aversive events activate the schemas for *fight* and *flight*, which elicit the emotions of anger and fear; whether people respond with aggression or escape depends on the pattern of cues in the situation

**cognitive response theory** a model of persuasion that assumes that the impact of a message on attitudes depends on the thoughts evoked by the message

**cognitive restructuring** recognizing and modifying anger-related thoughts and attributions; it forms part of CRCS training

**cognitive-relaxation coping skills training (CRCS)** an intervention program designed to reduce anger, which involves teaching people a set of relaxation techniques and ways to modify their anger-related thoughts

**collectivist cultures** cultures in which people are seen as interdependent beings who should contribute to harmonious group functioning

**color-blind approach** the hypothesis that, to reduce prejudice, people should be encouraged to categorize other people as individual persons rather than as members of groups

**communal relationship** a relationship in which the receipt of a benefit creates no specific obligation to return that benefit

**companionate love** the kind of love that develops in a close and intimate relationship; the affection we feel for those with whom our lives are deeply entwined

**compatibility principle** a theory stating that a measure of attitudes will correlate highly with a measure of behavior only when the two measures are matched in terms of being general/broad or specific/narrow

**compliance** a change in behavior that is requested by another person or group

**conflictive ethos** an atmosphere of distrust and hatred that can develop in long-standing disputes

**conformity** any change in behavior caused by another person or group

**conjunctive tasks** activities in which the performance of the group depends on the least talented member

**consonant cognitions** beliefs that are consistent or compatible with one another

**contact hypothesis** the idea that exposure to members of an outgroup will produce more favorable attitudes toward that group

**contingency model of leadership effectiveness** a theory that predicts that task-oriented leaders will be more successful than relationship-oriented leaders in groups where the situation is either very favorable or very unfavorable for the leader, whereas relationship-oriented leaders will be more successful than task-oriented leaders in groups where the situation is mixed for the leader

**controlled process** a judgment or thought that we command, that is intentional, that requires significant cognitive resources, and that occurs within our awareness

**cooperation** collaborative behavior with other people that takes into account both one's own outcomes and the outcomes of the others

**correlational research** studies in which investigators measure two or more concepts and see whether the concepts are associated with one another

**correspondence bias** the tendency to assume that people's actions and words reflect their personality, their attitudes, or some other internal factor, rather than external or situational factors

**counterfactual thoughts** reflections on how past events might have turned out differently

**covariation model of attribution** an attribution theory proposing that we make causal judgments by determining whether a particular behavior correlated with a person, a situation, or some combination of persons and situations

**Crutchfield apparatus** a machine that consists of an electrical panel with several rows of lights; it allows the efficient study of conformity by simulating the responses of numerous hypothetical participants

**cultural truisms** attitudes and beliefs that are widely shared and rarely challenged in a society

**culture** the set of values, beliefs, and behaviors shared by a group of people and communicated from one generation to the next

**culture of honor** a social network in which men are taught from an early age to defend their reputation for strength by responding to insults or threats with aggression

**debriefing** a postexperimental procedure in which participants are given a full and complete description of the study's design, purpose, and expected results; if there has been any deception during the study, it must be identified and explained in the debriefing

**decision tree** a set of five steps that must be completed before an individual will intervene in an emergency situation

**defensive high self-esteem** a positive self-view that is fragile and vulnerable to threat

**degrading pornography** sexually explicit material that debases or dehumanizes people, usually women

**dehumanization** the process of perceiving members of a group as subhuman or inferior to members of one's own group; it allows people to inflict pain and suffering on the group without worrying about the morality of their behavior

**deindividuation** a psychological state in which people lose their sense of personal identity and feel immersed in a group

**demand characteristics** cues in a study that suggest to participants how they are supposed to respond

**dependent variable** a concept that is measured by the researcher after the manipulation(s) in an experiment; it is typically expected to be affected by the manipulation(s)

**destructive cult** a rigidly structured group, led by a charismatic leader, which recruits and retains members using manipulative, deceptive techniques

**discounting principle** a rule of attribution that states that the perceived role of a cause will be discounted (reduced) if other plausible causes are also present

**discrimination** negative, harmful behavior toward people based on their group membership

**disjunctive tasks** activities in which the performance of the group depends on the most talented member

**displaced aggression** harmdoing that is directed at someone or something that was not the actual source of frustration

**display rules** norms in a culture for how and when emotions should be expressed

**dispositional gratitude** an individual differences variable reflecting the extent to which people feel thankful for receiving help from others

**dispositional optimism** a disposition that represents the extent to which people have positive, confident expectations about their own future outcomes

**dispositions** individuals' consistencies across time and settings in a specific type of feeling, thought, and/or action, which make individuals different from other people

**dissonant cognitions** beliefs that are inconsistent or logically discrepant with one another

**dominant response** the action that is most likely to occur in a situation or on a task when the individual is alone

**door-in-the-face technique** a strategy to increase compliance, based on the fact that refusal of a large request increases the likelihood of agreement with a subsequent smaller request

**downward counterfactual thoughts** reflections on how past events might have turned out worse

**downward social comparison** social comparison with people who are worse off or less skilled than we are

**dyadic relationships** relationships that develop between two people

**effort justification paradigm** a research methodology used to test dissonance theory, which arouses dissonance by getting people to invest time or energy to achieve a goal that may not be worthwhile

**egoistic motivation** a motive for helping in order to obtain rewards or avoid punishments

**elaboration likelihood model** a theory of attitude change that specifies the conditions under which people will think carefully about the content of a persuasive message; it distinguishes between two types of processing—the central route to persuasion and the peripheral route to persuasion

**empathic accuracy** a person's ability to be accurate in his or her understanding of another's experiences

**empathy** the ability to comprehend how another person is experiencing a situation

**empathy–altruism hypothesis** the idea that feelings of empathy for a person can lead to behavior that is motivated solely by wanting to help that person

**encoding** the process of getting information into memory, including attention, comprehension, and storage

**equity theory** theory developed to help formalize the idea of perceived fairness or balance in interpersonal relationships; an equitable relationship is one in which both partners perceive that they are receiving relatively equal outcomes

**erotica** sexually explicit material that depicts nonviolent, consensual sexual activity

**ethos of peace** an atmosphere of acceptance and cooperation, which can facilitate the resolution of disputes

**evaluative conditioning** a process by which objects come to evoke positive or negative affect simply by their association with affect-inducing events

**event sampling** a method used to study adult attachment that involves the recording of information about a person's social interactions over a period of time

**exchange relationship** partners in an exchange relationship tend to keep track of what they have given and what they have received, and they strive to keep the books balanced

**excitation transfer** the idea that physiological arousal from sources other than frustration or anger can be linked to anger-related thoughts and cognitions, thereby increasing aggression

**executive function** the set of advanced cognitive processes involved in cognitive control, attention, judgment, and critical thinking

**experimental realism** the extent to which a study's setting feels realistic and involving to participants and elicits spontaneous behavior

**experimental research** investigations in which a researcher manipulates one concept (or more than one) and assesses the impact of the manipulation on one or more other concepts

**explicit attitudes** evaluations that people can report consciously

**external validity** the extent to which research results can be generalized beyond the current sample, setting, and other characteristics of the study

**extraneous variables** potential sources of error in the experiment that should be controlled; they encompass everything in the experiment except the independent and dependent variables

**facial electromyography (facial EMG)** a procedure for measuring muscle contractions in the face that may be sensitive to positive versus negative responses to a stimulus

**factorial design experiment** an experimental study that involves two or more independent variables

**false consensus effect** the tendency to assume that other people share our own attitudes and behaviors to a greater extent than is actually the case

**false hope syndrome** the tendency to try repeatedly but unsuccessfully to achieve a goal because of unrealistic expectations about the likelihood of success

**field experiment** an experimental study that is conducted in a setting outside the laboratory; it tends to produce high mundane realism and external validity

**foot-in-the-door technique** a strategy to increase compliance, based on the fact that agreement with a small request increases the likelihood of agreement with a subsequent larger request

**free choice paradigm** a research methodology used to test dissonance theory, which arouses dissonance by getting people to choose between two or more alternatives

**free-gift technique** a strategy to increase compliance, based on the fact that giving someone a small gift increases the likelihood of agreement with a subsequent request

**friendships** dyadic relationships involving mutual liking

**frustration–aggression hypothesis** the twin propositions that frustration always leads to some form of aggression and frustration is the only cause of aggression

**functional distance** compared to physical distance, the closeness between two places in terms of the opportunities for interaction

**general aggression model (GAM)** a broad theory that conceptualizes aggression as the result of a chain of psychological processes, including situational events, aggressive thoughts and feelings, and interpretations of the situation

**genocide** an attempt to systematically eliminate an ethnic group through banishment or murder

**Gestalt theory** an approach in psychology that assumes that people's subjective interpretations of objects are more important than the object's physical features, and that objects are perceived in their totality, as a unit, rather than in terms of their individual features

**Great Person theory** the hypothesis that exceptional leaders possess extraordinary qualities and skills—consistent with the trait approach to leadership

**group** two or more persons who are interacting with one another and/or influencing one another

**group cohesiveness** the combined strength of all forces acting on members of a group to remain in the group

**group dynamics** the social psychological study of groups and group processes

**group maintenance function** aspects of leadership that relate to morale in the group

**group polarization** the tendency for group discussion to strengthen the initial leanings of the members in a group

**groupthink** a way of thinking that can occur in decision-making groups when pressure to agree leads to inadequate appraisal of options and poor decisions

**hard sell** an advertising strategy that relies on presenting information about the positive features of a product

**helping** behavior that is intended to assist another person

**heuristic** an informal rule or shortcut that is used to make everyday judgments

**heuristic persuasion** attitude change resulting from cues that indicate that the position advocated in a message is valid

**heuristic processing** superficial analysis of a message that focuses on cues indicating the validity or invalidity of the advocated position

**hindsight bias** the tendency for people to overestimate the predictability of known outcomes

**hostile aggression** harmdoing that is borne out of negative emotions like anger, frustration, or hatred

**hostile media phenomenon** the tendency for people who feel strongly about an issue to believe that the media coverage of the issue is biased against their side

**hostile sexism** negative attitudes toward women who violate the traditional stereotype of women

**hypocrisy paradigm** a research methodology used to test dissonance theory, which arouses dissonance by having people publicly promote a socially desirable behavior and then be made aware that they have not always exhibited the behavior themselves in the past

**hypothesis** a specific prediction about what should occur if a theory is valid; it provides the means by which a theory can be tested

**ideal self** a conception of the self describing our perception of how we would ideally like to be

**identity** the characteristics that individuals think define them and make up their most important qualities

**illusion of control** the tendency to overestimate our control of situations and events

**illusory correlation** the belief that two variables are related to one another when, in fact, they are not

**IMB model of AIDS-preventive behavior** a theory postulating that information, motivation, and behavioral skills guide individuals' protective actions in the sexual domain

**Implicit Association Test (IAT)** a reaction time procedure that provides a measure of implicit attitudes; participants sort targets into a "good" category or a "bad" category, and the speed at which the sorting is completed is taken as a sign of one's implicit attitude toward the object

**implicit attitudes** automatic evaluative responses to a target, which may occur without awareness

**implicit intergroup bias** distorted judgments about members of a group based on a stereotype, which can occur without the person's awareness

**impression management** self-presentation

**impression management theory** an alternative to dissonance theory, which argues that participants in dissonance experiments want to appear consistent to the experimenter and therefore lie about their attitudes

**inclusive fitness** the principle that some social behaviors have been selected during the course of evolution because they increase the survival of our genes

**independent variable** a concept or factor that is manipulated by the researcher in an experiment; its causal impact on one or more other variables is assessed in the experiment

**individualist cultures** cultures in which people are seen as independent beings who possess stable abilities, traits, and attitudes

**induced compliance paradigm** a research methodology used to test dissonance theory, which arouses dissonance by getting people to engage in counterattitudinal behavior; participants are induced to comply with an experimenter's request that they behave in a way that is inconsistent with their attitudes

**informational influence** influence from other people that is motivated by a desire to be correct and to obtain accurate information

**informed consent** a procedure by which participants are told beforehand what to expect in the study and are reminded that they can withdraw at any time

**ingratiation** behavior designed to make someone like us

**inoculation theory** a model of building resistance to persuasion by exposing people to arguments against their attitude position and giving them counterarguments that refute the attack; it is based on the process of medical inoculation

**insecure attachment** a pattern seen in the strange situation; the baby does not use its mother as a safe haven and secure base from which to explore a novel situation

**Institutional Review Board (IRB)** a committee that must approve all studies before they can be started; it ensures that the procedures will not cause unacceptable harm to participants

**instrumental aggression** harmdoing that is motivated by goals other than hurting the target, such as obtaining something of value

**integrated threat theory** a theory proposing that prejudice results from four types of threats: realistic threats, symbolic threats, threats stemming from intergroup anxiety, and threats arising from negative stereotypes

**interaction** result showing that the effect of one experimental manipulation depends on the level of another experimental manipulation; it can only be observed in a factorial design experiment

**interactionist approach to leadership** the perspective that certain kinds of people are likely to emerge as leaders (or to be effective leaders) under one set of conditions, whereas other kinds of people are likely to emerge as leaders (or to be effective leaders) under a different set of conditions

**interdependence** a sharing of contributions and outcomes by two people

**internal validity** the extent to which research yields clear causal information; it tends to be low in correlational research and high in experimental research

**interpersonal attraction** the study of attraction or liking between two or more people

**Interpersonal Reactivity Index (IRI)** a disposition reflecting the extent to which people feel empathy in response to others' experiences

**intimacy** an interactive process in which a person feels understood, validated, and cared for as a result of a partner's response

**intuitive scientists** laypersons who, like untrained scientists, try to make causal judgments in a rational, scientific manner

**investment model of close relationships** the idea that satisfaction and stability in a relationship depend on the degree to which its partners feel committed to the relationship; commitment is determined by the balance or trade-off between the positive and negative aspects of the relationship

**jeer pressure** the conformity pressure that is produced by seeing someone ridiculed by another person

**jigsaw classroom** a method of teaching designed to foster positive interracial contact, which involves forming small, culturally diverse groups of students who are each given one part of the material to be learned

**just world theory** a model proposing that humans need to believe that the world is a fair place where people generally get what they deserve

**learned helplessness** a state of apathy in which we simply give up trying to achieve our goals

**Life Orientation Test (LOT)** a measure of dispositional optimism

**liking technique** a strategy to increase compliance, based on the fact that people are more likely to assist others they find appealing than others they do not find appealing

**Likert-type scale** an attitude measurement technique that requires respondents to indicate the extent of their agreement or disagreement with several statements on an issue

**looking glass self** the tendency to internalize other people's judgments about us into our self-concept

**love styles** the idea that people differ in their styles of love; the three primary styles are eros, storge, and ludus

**low-ball technique** a strategy to increase compliance, in which something is offered at a given price, but then, after agreement, the price is increased

**mere exposure effect** the tendency for repeated contact with an object, even without reinforcement, to increase liking for the object

**minimal group studies** experiments in which participants are divided into groups based on trivial features or information

**mob** a crowd acting under strong emotional conditions that often lead to violence or illegal acts

**mood-congruent recall** the idea that positive feelings will activate positive memories and negative feelings will activate negative memories

**multiculturalism** the hypothesis that, to reduce prejudice, different cultural groups within a society should each maintain their own identity while simultaneously respecting all other groups

**mundane realism** the extent to which the study's setting looks and feels like the outside world; it increases the external validity of research results

**narcissism** a disposition that represents the extent to which people have excessive love for themselves

**need for cognition** a disposition that represents how much people enjoy and engage in thinking

**nonverbal behavior** actions and cues that communicate meaning in ways other than by words

**norm of obedience** the principle that we should obey legitimate authorities

**norm of reciprocity** the principle that we should give back in return any favors that are done for us

**norm of social responsibility** the rule or guideline that we should help those who need help, if possible

**normative influence** influence from other people that is motivated by a desire to gain rewards or avoid punishment

**obedience** a change in behavior that is ordered by another person or group

**object appraisal function** a function of attitudes by which attitudes provide rapid evaluative judgments of targets, which facilitate approach or avoidance

**observational studies** correlational investigations in which researchers watch participants and code measures from the observed behavior, either "live" or from videotapes

**operational definition** a specific, observable response that is used to measure a concept

**optimal distinctiveness theory** a model hypothesizing that people want to maintain a balance between similarity to other people and individuality from other people

**ought self** a conception of ourselves describing our perception of how we think we should or ought to be

**outgroup homogeneity effect** the tendency for people to overestimate the similarity within groups to which they do not belong

**overjustification effect** an inference that we performed a potentially enjoyable activity for external reasons (e.g., for a reward) rather than because we enjoyed it

**parental investment hypothesis** the idea that having children is more costly for women than for men, which has led to the evolution of some differences between the sexes in the characteristics they seek in mates

**participant–observation research** a special type of observational study in which a researcher actually joins an ongoing group to observe the members' behavior

**passionate love** the kind of love that involves strong and intense feelings, infatuation, arousal, and a deep sense of passion

**payoff matrix** a table representing the outcomes for each player in a prisoner's dilemma game based on the players' combined choices

**peripheral cues** simple features or heuristics that are assumed to show that a message is valid

**peripheral route to persuasion** persuasion that occurs when attitude change results from noncognitive factors; it encompasses evaluative conditioning and mere exposure

**perseverance effect** the tendency for people to make self-evaluations that are consistent with information that has been discredited

**personal norms** guidelines that have been internalized to become expectations for oneself in particular situations

**personal–group discrimination discrepancy** the tendency for people to report that they as individuals have experienced less negative treatment based on their group membership than the average member of their group

**popular children** children who are named frequently by others in a sociometric rating procedure

**power distance** the extent to which a culture accepts an unequal distribution of influence within the society

**preference for consistency (PFC)** a disposition that represents the extent to which people desire predictability and compatibility within their own responses and within others' responses

**prejudice** a negative attitude toward members of a group, which is often very strongly held

**priming** the process by which the activation of a schema increases the likelihood that the schema will be activated again in the future

**prisoner's dilemma game** a simulated social dilemma that requires participants to make choices between acting selfishly and cooperatively when selfishness looks better initially but can damage long-term joint outcomes of the players

**propaganda** a persuasive attempt that is motivated by an ideology, or set of values, and that is deliberately biased in its presentation of information

**propinquity** nearness or proximity in physical space that creates the opportunity to meet another person

**prosocial behavior** any action that provides benefit to others

**protection motivation theory** a model that articulates how threatening messages can influence attitudes and behavior

**psychometrics** a subdiscipline within psychology that is devoted to understanding and refining methods for psychological measurement

**psychosocial law** a principle in social impact theory that specifies the nature of the relation between the size of a group and its social influence; the principle predicts that as the number of social forces increases, overall social influence also increases, but at a declining rate

**Racial Arguments Scale (RAS)** an indirect measure of prejudice in which respondents rate how well arguments support positive or negative conclusions about an outgroup

**random assignment** a procedure by which each participant in an experiment is equally likely to take part in any of the experimental conditions; it controls extraneous variable problems coming from characteristics of the participants

**random sampling** a recruitment process in which every person in a particular population has exactly the same probability of being in the study; it produces a representative sample

**reactance theory** a model of how people respond to threats on their freedoms

**realistic group conflict theory** a theory proposing that when groups in society are perceived to be competing with one another for resources, intergroup hostility can be aroused, which leads to prejudice

**reconstructive memory** the process of trying to rebuild the past based on cues and estimates

**reference group** a collection of people that serves as a standard of comparison for an individual, whether in terms of attitudes, values, or behavior

**refutational defense** exposing people to arguments against their attitudinal position along with counterarguments that refute the attack

**rejected-aggressive children** children who are unpopular because they commonly engage in disruptive aggressive behaviors

**rejected-withdrawn children** children who are spurned by their peers because of their social awkwardness and immaturity

**relational aggression** behavior that is intended to damage another person's peer relationships

**relative deprivation** a feeling of anger or resentment about one's own outcomes based on comparisons with better-off others

**reliability** the extent to which a measure is free of "random" fluctuations, both over time and across judges

**representative sample** a group of respondents that accurately reflects a larger population from which it was drawn and to which the researcher wants to generalize the results

**representativeness heuristic** the tendency to judge the likelihood that a target belongs to a category based on how similar the target is to the typical features of the category

**repulsion hypothesis** the idea that people find others less attractive and less likeable if they differ substantially in their attitudes, beliefs, and preferences

**resistant insecure attachment** in the strange situation procedure, babies with such an attachment prefer to stay close to mother rather than actively explore the room, become very upset when mother leaves the room, and appear to be upset or angry when mother returns

**retrieval** the process of getting information out of memory

**scapegoat theory** a theory proposing that prejudice occurs because members of dominant groups use discrimination against members of weak target groups to vent their frustration and disappointment

**scarcity technique** a strategy to increase the attractiveness of a product by making it appear rare or temporary

**schemas** mental representations of objects or categories, which contain the central features of the object or category as well as assumptions about how the object or category works

**secure attachment** the most common pattern seen in the strange situation procedure—the baby actively explores the room when left alone with mother, gets upset when mother leaves the room, is clearly happy when mother returns, and may even seek close physical proximity with her in an effort to relieve distress

**secure high self-esteem** a positive self-view that is confidently held

**self-affirmation theory** an alternative to dissonance theory, which argues that people are threatened by behavior that challenges their self-worth and can deal with this threat by reaffirming an important value

**self-concept** all information about the self in memory

**self-disclosure** the process of people in a relationship revealing to one another increasingly personal and intimate details about themselves

**self-discrepancy theory** a theory proposing that perceived differences between the actual self and the ideal self produce depression, and perceived differences between the actual self and the ought self produce anxiety

**self-efficacy** the belief that we are capable of performing a particular behavior that is required for a certain goal

**self-esteem** a disposition that represents people's judgments of their own worthiness

**self-fulfilling prophesy** a process in which a perceiver's expectancy about a target person influences the perceiver's behavior toward the target person in such a way as to elicit the expected actions from the target person

**self-handicapping** the tendency to seek, create, or claim inhibitory factors that interfere with performance and thus provide an explanation for potential failure

**self-handicapping scale** a scale that measures how often people engage in self-handicapping behavior

**self-monitoring** a disposition that represents the extent to which people rely on external or internal cues to guide their behavior

**self-perception theory** a theory proposing that we often judge our own internal states by reviewing our past behavior and inferring internal states consistent with our behavior unless there were clear external causes of our behavior

**self-presentation** the deliberate control of our public behavior to create a certain impression

**self-promotion** behavior designed to make someone respect us

**self-serving judgments** perceptions or comparisons that enhance the perceived worth of the self

**semantic differential scale** an attitude measurement technique that requires respondents to rate a target on several evaluative dimensions (such as good-bad and favorable-unfavorable)

**sequential lineup** the procedure of showing an eyewitness each individual in the group separately rather than together in a simultaneous line

**sexism** prejudice and discrimination directed against women because of their gender

**single-factor experiment** an experimental study that involves only one independent variable

**situational approach to leadership** the perspective that external, situational factors can influence who will become leader of a group, such as seating arrangements

**social cognition** the study of how information about people is processed and stored

**social comparison** the process of comparing ourselves to others in order to judge the self

**social comparison orientation** a disposition that represents how often people engage in social comparison

**social contract** the idea that human societies have developed basic rules of social and moral conduct, which members of the societies implicitly agree to follow

**social dilemma** a situation in which selfish choices produce better immediate outcomes for the individual than do cooperative choices, but long-term outcomes for everyone will suffer if everyone behaves selfishly

**social facilitation** the effects of the presence of other people on individual performance, which will usually be improved performance on simple tasks and impaired performance on complex tasks

**social identity theory** a model hypothesizing that people want to have positive appraisals of groups to which they belong

**social impact theory** a model that conceives of influence from other people as being the result of social forces acting on individuals, much like physical forces can affect an object

**social learning theory** an approach proposing that humans learn many kinds of responses, including aggressive ones, by observing others; observation shows people both how to perform a behavior and whether that behavior will be rewarded or punished

**social loafing** the reduction of effort that people often exhibit when working in a group where individual contributions are unidentifiable

**social neuroscience** an emerging new area of research, combining the perspectives of social psychology and neuroscience to understand the relationship between the brain and social behavior

**social norm** a rule or guideline in a group or culture about what behaviors are proper and improper

**social psychology** the scientific study of how individuals' thoughts, feelings, and behaviors are influenced by other people

**social support network** people who can be called upon for help and who will provide help when needed, such as family, friends, and neighbors

**social value orientation** a disposition that reflects individual differences in cooperativeness in social dilemmas; three orientations are typically distinguished: individualists, competitors, and prosocials

**socialization** the process by which infants are molded into acceptable members of their society

**socially desirable responding** a form of responding that involves giving answers that portray the respondent in a positive light

**socioemotional leader** an individual who takes charge of issues related to morale in a group

**sociometric rating procedure** within a group of acquaintances, each person is asked to name everyone whom he or she considers a friend; two peers within that social network are then considered to be friends if each nominates the other as a friend

**soft sell** an advertising strategy that relies on the use of images, emotions, symbols, or values to promote a product

**spatial ecology** the physical layout of buildings and the distance separating different buildings, rooms, and other spaces

**spontaneous self-concept** the aspects of identity that are in conscious awareness at a given point in time

**spreading activation** the process by which the use of one schema increases the likelihood that other, related schemas in memory will also be used

**stereotype** a set of characteristics that a perceiver associates with members of a group

**stereotype threat** the pressure experienced by individuals who fear that if they perform poorly on a task, their performance will appear to confirm an unfavorable belief about their group

**strange situation** a procedure involving several brief episodes during which experimenters observe a baby's responses to strangers, separation from mother, and reunions with mother

**subjective norm** an individual's feelings of social pressure to perform or not perform an action

**subliminal priming procedure** a method of activating a schema or stereotype by flashing words or pictures very briefly on a computer screen in front of a participant

**supportive defense** exposing people to arguments that are consistent with their attitude position

**survey** a correlational study in which the researcher asks questions to respondents, either in a printed questionnaire, on a computer, over the telephone, or during an interview

**systematic processing** careful, deliberative analysis of the arguments in a message

**systematic-heuristic model** a theory of attitude change that distinguishes between two types of processing that can occur in response to a persuasive message—systematic processing and heuristic processing

**task achievement function** aspects of leadership that relate to group productivity

**task leader** an individual who takes charge of issues related to productivity in a group

**terror management theory** a model hypothesizing that recognition of their own mortality raises anxiety in humans, which they can reduce by affirming and conforming to their cultural worldview

**terrorism** actual or threatened violence against civilians for alleged political purposes

**Thematic Apperception Test (TAT)** a procedure that involves showing participants drawings of ambiguous scenes and asking them to write stories about what is happening, which are then scored for the presence of particular themes

**theory** an explanation of why an event or outcome occurs; it identifies the underlying causes of an event or phenomenon

**theory of reasoned action** a model of behavior that views humans as rational decision makers who behave on the basis of logical beliefs

**threatened egotism** a hostile, aggressive response to criticism from others, which has been linked to narcissism

**Thurstone scale** an attitude measurement technique that requires respondents to place a check mark beside statements with which they agree

**tragedy of the commons** the depletion of a communal resource, such as a shared cow pasture for a group of farmers, because each individual pursues selfish interests

**trait aggressiveness** a disposition that represents how likely people are to respond to provocations with aggression

**trait approach to leadership** the perspective that people become leaders, or perform well as leaders, because of their individual characteristics, such as intelligence and charisma

**transformational leaders** individuals who produce fundamental changes in how members of a group view themselves and the group

**triangular theory of love** the idea that a wide variety of love experiences can be understood as combinations of three components—intimacy, passion, and commitment

**"Type A" coronary-prone behavior pattern** a constellation of characteristics, including impatience, anger, and hostility, which has been linked to heart disease

**uncertainty orientation** a disposition that represents the extent to which people want to learn new things about themselves and their environment

**unilateral conciliatory initiatives** actions to reduce conflict that one group takes without any request from the opponent and without any explicit demands for concessions from the opponent

**unobtrusive measures** assessments that are taken without the realization of participants, thereby minimizing socially desirable responding

**upward counterfactual thoughts** reflections on how past events might have turned out better

**upward social comparison** social comparison with people who are better off or more skilled than we are

**validity** the extent to which a measure really assesses what it is supposed to assess—whether scores on the measure actually reflect the assumed underlying concept

**value-expressive function** a function of attitudes by which attitudes can communicate individuals' identity and beliefs

**violence** aggression that is intended to cause extreme injury

**violent pornography** sexually explicit material that depicts aggressive, hostile sexual activity

**volunteerism** unpaid helping behavior that is given willingly to a worthwhile cause or organization

**what is beautiful is good** the belief that physically attractive people possess other desirable traits and abilities in addition to their good looks

**working model of a close relationship** from his or her early attachments, the infant develops a mental representation, schema, or working model of what a close relationship is all about—the feelings, thoughts, beliefs, and expectations learned during the course of his or her first close relationships

# References

Aaker, J. L., Benet-Martínez, V., & Garolera, J. (2001). Consumption symbols as carriers of culture: A study of Japanese and Spanish brand personality constructs. *Journal of Personality and Social Psychology, 81,* 492–508.

Abele, A. E. (2003). The dynamics of masculine-agentic and feminine-communal traits: Findings from a prospective study. *Journal of Personality and Social Psychology, 85,* 768–776.

Abend, T. A., & Williamson, G. M. (2002). Feeling attractive in the wake of breast cancer: Optimism matters, and so do interpersonal relationships. *Personality and Social Psychology Bulletin, 28,* 427–436.

Aberson, C. L., Healy, M., & Romero, V. (2000). Ingroup bias and self-esteem: A meta-analysis. *Personality and Social Psychology Review, 4,* 157–173.

Aboud, F. E., & Doyle, A. B. (1996). Parental and peer influences on children's racial attitudes. *International Journal of Intercultural Relations, 20,* 371–383.

Abrahamson, A. C., Baker, L. A., & Caspi, A. (2002). Rebellious teens? Genetic and environmental influences on the social attitudes of adolescents. *Journal of Personality and Social Psychology, 83,* 1392–1408.

Abramson, L. Y., Metalsky, G. I., & Alloy, L. B. (1989). Hopelessness depression: A theory-based subtype of depression. *Psychological Review, 96,* 358–372.

Ackerman, B. P., Izard, C. E., Schoff, K., Youngstrom, E. A., & Kogos, J. (1999). Contextual risk, caregiver emotionality, and the problem behaviors of six- and seven-year-old children from economically disadvantaged families. *Child Development, 70,* 1415–1427.

Adams, J. S. (1965). Inequity in social exchange. In L. Berkowitz (Ed.), *Advances in experimental social psychology* (Vol. 2, pp. 267–299). New York: Academic Press.

Adams, W. C., & Beatty, M. J. (1977). Dogmatism, need for social support, and resistance to persuasion. *Communication Monographs, 44,* 321–325.

Adelman, H. (2000). Rwanda revisited: In search for lessons. *Journal of Genocide Research, 2,* 431–44.

Adelman, H. (2004). The theory and history of genocide. *International History Review, 26,* 89–96.

Adorno, T. W., Frenkel-Brunswik, E., Levinson, D. J., & Sanford, R. N. (1950). *The authoritarian personality.* New York: Harper.

Ainsworth, M. D. S., Blehar, M. C., Waters, E., & Wall, S. (1978). *Patterns of attachment : A psychological study of the strange situation.* Hillsdale, NJ: Erlbaum.

Ajzen, I. (1985). From actions to intentions: A theory of planned behavior. In J. Kuhl & J. Beckman (Eds.), *Action control: From cognition to behavior* (pp. 11–39). New York: Springer-Verlag.

Ajzen, I. (1991). Theory of planned behavior. *Organizational Behavior and Human Decision Processes, 50,* 179–211.

Ajzen, I., & Fishbein, M. (1977). Attitude-behavior relations: A theoretical analysis and review of empirical research. *Psychological Bulletin, 84,* 888–918.

Ajzen, I., & Fishbein, M. (1980). *Understanding attitudes and predicting social behavior.* Englewood Cliffs, NJ: Prentice-Hall.

Albarracín, D., & Wyer, R. S., Jr. (2000). The cognitive impact of past behavior: Influences on beliefs, attitudes, and future behavioral decisions. *Journal of Personality and Social Psychology, 79,* 5–22.

Alicke, M. D. (1985). Global self-evaluation as determined by the desirability and controllability of trait adjectives. *Journal of Personality and Social Psychology, 3,* 1621–1630.

Alicke, M. D. (2000). Evaluating social comparison targets. In J. Suls & L. Wheeler (Eds.), *Handbook of social comparison: Theory and research* (pp. 271–293). New York: Kluwer Academic/Plenum.

Allen, B. P. (1995). Gender stereotypes are not accurate: A replication of Martin (1987) using diagnostic vs. self-report and behavioral criteria. *Sex Roles, 32,* 583–600.

Allen, M., D'Alessio, D., & Brezgel, K. (1995). A meta-analysis summarizing the effects of pornography: II. Aggression after exposure. *Human Communication Research, 22,* 258–283.

Allen, V. L. (1965). Situational factors in conformity. In L. Berkowitz (Ed.), *Advances in experimental social psychology* (Vol. 2, pp. 133–175). New York: Academic Press.

Allen, V. L. (1975). Social support for nonconformity. In L. Berkowitz (Ed.), *Advances in experimental social psychology* (Vol. 8, pp. 1–43). New York: Academic Press.

Alley, T. R., & Cunningham, M. R. (1991). Averaged faces are attractive, but very attractive faces are not average. *Psychological Science, 2,* 123–125.

Allison, S. T., Messick, D. M., & Goethals, G. R. (1989). On being better but not smarter than others: The Muhammad Ali effect. *Social Cognition, 7,* 275–296.

Allport, G. W. (1935). Attitudes. In C. Murchison (Ed.), *The handbook of social psychology* (pp. 798–844). Worcester, MA: Clark University Press.

Allport, G. W. (1954). *The nature of prejudice.* Reading, MA: Addison-Wesley.

Allport, G. W. (1985). The historical background of social psychology. In G. Lindzey & E. Aronson (Eds.), *The handbook of social psychology* (3rd ed., Vol. 1, pp. 1–46). New York: Random House.

Allport, G. W., & Kramer, B. M. (1946). Some roots of prejudice. *Journal of Psychology, 22,* 9–39.

Altemeyer, B. (1988). *Enemies of freedom: Understanding right-wing authoritarianism.* San Francisco, CA: Jossey-Bass.

Altemeyer, B. (1994). Reducing prejudice in right-wing authoritarians. In M. P. Zanna & J. M. Olson (Eds.), *The psychology of prejudice: The Ontario symposium* (Vol. 7, pp. 131–148). Mahwah, NJ: Erlbaum.

Alwin, D. F., Cohen, R. L., & Newcomb, T. M. (1991a). *Political attitudes over the life span: The Bennington women after fifty years.* Madison: University of Wisconsin Press.

Alwin, D. F., Cohen, R. L., & Newcomb, T. M. (1991b). *The women of Bennington: A study of political orientations over the life span.* Madison: University of Wisconsin Press.

Amato, P. R. (1983). Helping behavior in urban and rural environments: Field studies based on a taxonomic organization of helping episodes. *Journal of Personality and Social Psychology, 45,* 571–586.

American Automobile Association. (1997). *Aggressive driving: Three studies.* Washington, DC: American Automobile Association Foundation for Traffic Safety.

American Automobile Association. (1999). *Controlling road rage: A literature review and pilot study.* Washington, DC: American Automobile Association Foundation for Traffic Safety.

American Psychological Association (1997). Learner-centered psychological principles: A framework for school redesign and reform. Available from http://www.apa.org/ed/lcp.html

American Psychological Association. (2001). *Publication manual of the American Psychological Association* (5th ed.). Washington, DC: American Psychological Association.

Ames, D. R., Flynn, F. J., & Weber, E. U. (2004). It's the thought that counts: On perceiving how helpers decide to lend a hand. *Personality and Social Psychology Bulletin, 30,* 461–474.

Amir, Y. (1969). Contact hypothesis in ethnic relations. *Psychological Bulletin, 71,* 319–341.

Amodio, D. M., Harmon-Jones, E., & Devine, P. G. (2003). Individual differences in the activation and control of affective race bias as assessed by startle eyeblink response and self-report. *Journal of Personality and Social Psychology, 84,* 738–753.

Anderson, C. A. (1989). Temperature and aggression: Ubiquitous effects of heat on occurrence of human violence. *Psychological Bulletin, 106,* 74–96.

Anderson, C. A. (1997). Effects of violent movies and trait hostility on hostile feelings and aggressive thoughts. *Aggressive Behavior, 23,* 161–178.

Anderson, C. A., Berkowitz, L., Donnerstein, E., Huesmann, L., Johnson, J. D., Linz, D., et al. (2003). The influence of media violence on youth. *Psychological Science in the Public Interest, 4,* 81–110.

Anderson, C. A., & Bushman, B. J. (2001). Effects of violent video games on aggressive behavior, aggressive cognition, aggressive affect, physiological arousal, and prosocial behavior: A meta-analytic review of the scientific literature. *Psychological Science, 12,* 353–359.

Anderson, C. A., & Bushman, B. J. (2002a). Human aggression. *Annual Review of Psychology, 53,* 27–51.

Anderson, C. A., & Bushman, B. J. (2002b). Media violence and the American public revisited. *American Psychologist, 57,* 448–450.

Anderson, C. A., Bushman, B. J., & Groom, R. W. (1997). Hot years and serious and deadly assault: Empirical tests of the heat hypothesis. *Journal of Personality and Social Psychology, 73,* 1213–1223.

Anderson, C. A., Deuser, W. E., & DeNeve, K. M. (1995). Hot temperatures, hostile affect, hostile cognition, and arousal: Tests of a general model of affective aggression. *Personality and Social Psychology Bulletin, 21,* 434–448.

Anderson, C. A., Lepper, M. R., & Ross, L. (1980). Perseverance of social theories: The role of explanation in the persistence of discredited information. *Journal of Personality and Social Psychology, 39,* 1037–1049.

Anderson, C., John, O. O., Keltner, D., & Kring, A. M. (2001). Who attains social status? Effects of personality and physical attractiveness in social groups. *Journal of Personality and Social Psychology, 81,* 116–132.

Antonucci, T. C., & Jackson, J. S. (1990). The role of reciprocity in social support. In I. G. Sarason, B. R. Sarason & G. R. Pierce (Eds.), *Social support: An interactional view* (pp. 173–198). New York: Wiley.

Archer, D. (1997). Unspoken diversity: Cultural differences in gestures. *Qualitative Sociology, 20,* 79–105.

Archer, D.. & Akert, R. M. (1977). Words and everything else: Verbal and nonverbal cues in social interpretation. *Journal of Personality and Social Psychology, 35,* 443–449.

Archer, D., & Gartner, R. (1984). *Violence and crime in cross-national perspective.* New Haven, CT: Yale University Press.

Archer, J. (Ed.). (1994). *Male violence.* New York: Routledge.

Argyle, M., Alkema, F., & Gilmour, R. (1971). The communication of friendly and hostile attitudes by verbal and nonverbal signals. *European Journal of Social Psychology, 1,* 385–402.

Arkes, H. R., Wortmann, R. L., Saville, P. D., & Harkness, A. R. (1981). Hindsight bias among physicians weighing the likelihood of diagnoses. *Journal of Applied Psychology, 66,* 252–254.

Arkin, R. M., & Baumgardner, A. H. (1985). Self-handicapping. In J. H. Harvey & G. Weary (Eds.), *Attribution: Basic issues and applications* (pp. 169–202). New York: Academic Press.

Armitage, C. J., & Conner, M. (2000). Attitude ambivalence: A test of three key hypotheses. *Personality and Social Psychology Bulletin, 26,* 1421–1432.

Arndt, J., Schimel, J., Greenberg, J., & Pyszczynski, T. (2002). The intrinsic self and defensiveness: Evidence that activating the intrinsic self reduces self-handicapping and conformity. *Personality and Social Psychology Bulletin, 28,* 671–683.

Aron, A., Aron, E. N., & Smollan, D. (1992). Inclusion of other in the self scale and the structure of interpersonal closeness. *Journal of Personality and Social Psychology, 63,* 596–612.

Aron, A., Aron, E. N., Tudor, M., & Nelson, G. (1991). Close relationships as including other in the self. *Journal of Personality and Social Psychology, 60,* 241–253.

Aronson, E. (1968). Dissonance theory: Progress and problems. In E. Aronson, R. Abelson, W. McGuire, T. Newcomb, M. Rosenberg, & P. Tannenbaum (Eds.), *Theories of cognitive consistency: A sourcebook* (pp. 5–27). Chicago, IL: Rand McNally.

Aronson, E. (1990). Applying social psychology to desegregation and energy conservation. *Personality and Social Psychology Bulletin, 16,* 118–132.

Aronson, E. (2000). *Nobody left to hate: Teaching compassion after Columbine.* New York: Freeman.

Aronson, E., & Carlsmith, J. M. (1968). Experimentation in social psychology. In G. Lindzey & E. Aronson (Eds.), *The handbook of social psychology* (2nd ed., Vol. 2, pp. 1–79). Reading, MA: Addison-Wesley.

Aronson, E., Ellsworth, P. C., Carlsmith, J. M., & Gonzales, M. H. (1990). *Methods of research in social psychology* (2nd ed.). New York: McGraw-Hill.

Aronson, E., Fried, C. B., & Stone, J. (1991). Overcoming denial and increasing the use of condoms through the induction of hypocrisy. *American Journal of Public Health, 81,* 1636–1638.

Aronson, E., & Mills, J. (1959). The effect of severity of initiation on liking for a group. *Journal of Abnormal and Social Psychology, 59,* 177–181.

Aronson, E., Stephan, C., Sikes, J., Blaney, N., & Snapp, M. (1978). *The jigsaw classroom.* Beverly Hills, CA: Sage.

Aronson, J. (2002a). Stereotype threat: Contending and coping with unnerving expectations. In J. Aronson (Ed.), *Improving academic achievement: Impact of psychological factors on education* (pp. 279–301). New York: Academic Press.

Aronson, J. (Ed.) (2002b). *Improving academic achievement: Impact of psychological factors on education.* New York: Academic Press.

Aronson, J., Fried, C. B., & Good, C. (2002). Reducing the effects of stereotype threat on African American college students by shaping theories of intelligence. *Journal of Experimental Social Psychology, 38,* 113–125.

Aronson, J., Lustina, M. J., Good, C., Keough, K., Steele, C. M., & Brown, J. (1999). When White men can't do math: Necessary and sufficient factors in stereotype threat. *Journal of Experimental Social Psychology, 35,* 29–46.

Asch, S. E. (1951). Effects of group pressure upon the modification and distortion of judgments. In H. Guetzkow (Ed.), *Groups, leadership and men* (pp. 177–190). Pittsburgh, PA: Carnegie Press.

Asch, S. E. (1952). *Social psychology.* New York: Prentice-Hall.

Asch, S. E. (1956). Studies of independence and conformity: I. A minority of one against a unanimous majority. *Psychological Monographs: General and Applied, 70(9),* 1–70.

Ashmore, R. D., Deaux, K., & McLaughlin-Volpe, T. (2004). An organizing framework for collective identity: Articulation and significance of multidimensionality. *Psychological Bulletin, 130,* 80–114.

Aspinwall, L. G., Kemeny, M. E., Taylor, S. E., Schneider, S. G., & Dudley, J. P. (1991). Psychosocial predictors of gay men's AIDS risk-reduction behavior. *Health Psychology, 10,* 432–444.

Atkin, C., & Block, M. (1983). Effectiveness of celebrity endorsers. *Journal of Advertising Research, 23,* 57–61.

Atkinson, J. W. (1964). *An introduction to motivation.* Princeton, NJ: Van Nostrand.

Attridge, M., Berscheid, E., & Simpson, J. A. (1995). Predicting relationship stability from both partners versus one. *Journal of Personality and Social Psychology, 69,* 254–268.

Atwater, L. E., Carey, J. A., & Waldman, D. A. (2001). Gender and discipline in the workplace: Wait until your father gets home. *Journal of Management, 27,* 537–566.

Ausubel, D. P. (1955). Relationships between shame and guilt in the socializing process. *Psychological Review, 62,* 378–390.

Axelrod, R. (1986). Presidential election coalitions in 1984. *American Political Science Review, 80,* 281–284.

Axsom, D., & Cooper, J. (1985). Cognitive dissonance and psychotherapy: The role of effort justification in inducing weight loss. *Journal of Experimental Social Psychology, 21,* 149–160.

Axtell, R. (1991). *Gestures: The do's and taboos of body language around the world.* New York: Wiley.

Backer, T. E., Rogers, E. M., & Sopory, P. (1992). *Designing health communication campaigns: What works?* Newbury Park, CA: Sage.

Bailenson, J. N., Blascovich, J., Beall, A. C., & Loomis, J. M. (2003). Interpersonal distance in immersive virtual environments. *Personality and Social Psychology Bulletin, 29,* 819–833.

Bailenson, J. N., & Yee, N. (in press). Digital chameleons: Automatic assimilation of nonverbal gestures in immersive virtual environments. *Psychological Science.*

Baldwin, M. W., Fehr, B., Keedian, E., Seidel, M., & Thomson, D. W. (1993). An exploration of the relational schema underlying attachment styles: Self-report and the lexical decision approaches. *Personality and Social Psychology Bulletin, 19,* 746–754.

Bales, R. F., & Slater, P. (1955). Role differentiation in small decision-making groups. In T. Parsons & R. F. Bales (Eds.), *The family, socialization, and interaction processes* (pp. 259–306). Glencoe, IL: Free Press.

Banaji, M. R., & Greenwald, A. G. (1994). Implicit stereotypes and prejudice. In M. P. Zanna & J. M. Olson (Eds.), *The psychology of prejudice: The Ontario symposium* (pp. 55–76). Hillsdale, NJ: Erlbaum.

Bandura, A. (1973). *Aggression: A social learning analysis.* Englewood Cliffs, NJ: Prentice-Hall.

Bandura, A. (1977). Self-efficacy: Toward a unifying theory of behavior change. *Psychological Review, 84,* 191–215.

Bandura, A. (1986). *Social foundations of thought and action.* Englewood Cliffs, NJ: Prentice-Hall.

Bandura, A. (1991). Human agency in social cognitive theory. *American Psychologist, 44,* 1175–1184.

Bandura, A., Ross, D., & Ross, S. (1963). Imitation of film-mediated aggressive models. *Journal of Abnormal and Social Psychology, 66,* 3–11.

Bandura, A., & Walters, R. H. (1963). *Social learning and personality development.* New York: Holt, Rinehart, and Winston.

Barden, J., Maddux, W. W., Petty, R. E., & Brewer, M. B. (2004). Contextual moderation of racial bias: The impact of social roles on controlled and automatically activated attitudes. *Journal of Personality and Social Psychology, 87,* 5–22.

Barefoot, J. C. (1992). Developments in the measurement of hostility. In H. S. Friedman (Ed.), *Hostility, coping and health* (pp. 13–31). Washington, DC: American Psychological Association.

Bargh, J. A. (1994). The four horsemen of automaticity: Awareness, intention, efficiency, and control in social cognition. In R. S. Wyer, Jr., & T. K. Srull (Eds.), *Handbook of social cognition: Vol 1. Basic processes* (2nd ed., pp. 1–40). Hillsdale, NJ: Erlbaum.

Bargh, J. A., Bond, R. N., Lombardi, W. L., & Tota, M. E. (1986). The additive nature of chronic and temporary sources of construct accessibility. *Journal of Personality and Social Psychology, 50,* 869–879.

Bargh, J. A., & Pietromonaco, P. (1982). Automatic information processing and social perception: The influence of trait information presented outside of conscious awareness on impression formation. *Journal of Personality and Social Psychology, 43,* 437–449.

Bar-On, D. (2001). The bystander in relation to the victim and the perpetrator: Today and during the Holocaust. *Social Justice Research, 14,* 125–148.

Baron, R. A. (1979). Aggression and heat: The "long hot summer" revisited. In A. Baum, J. E. Singer, & S. Valins (Eds.), *Advances in environmental psychology* (pp. 57–84). Hillsdale, NJ: Erlbaum.

Baron, R. A., & Richardson, D. (1994). *Human aggression.* New York: Plenum Press.

Baron, R. S. (2000). Arousal, capacity, and intense indoctrination. *Personality and Social Psychology Review, 4,* 238–254.

Baron, R. S., Logan, H., Lilly, J., Inman, M., & Brennan, M. (1994). Negative emotion and message processing. *Journal of Experimental Social Psychology, 30,* 181–201.

Baron, R. S., Moore, D., & Sanders, G. S. (1978). Distraction as a source of drive in social facilitation research. *Journal of Personality and Social Psychology, 36,* 816–824.

Baron, R. S., Vandello, J. A., & Brunsman, B. (1996). The forgotten variable in conformity research: Impact of task importance on social influence. *Journal of Personality and Social Psychology, 71,* 915–927.

Barrera, M., Jr. (1981). Social support in the adjustment of pregnant adolescents: Assessment issues. In B. H. Gottlieb (Ed.), *Social networks and social support* (pp. 69–96). Beverly Hills, CA: Sage.

Barrera, M., Jr., Sandler, I. N., & Ramsay, T. B. (1981). Preliminary development of a scale of social support: Studies on college students. *American Journal of Community Psychology, 9,* 435–447.

Barrett, L., Dunbar, R., & Lycett, J. (2002). *Human evolutionary psychology.* Princeton, NJ: Princeton University Press.

Bar-Tal, D. (1990). Causes and consequences of delegitimization: Models of conflict and ethnocentrism. *Journal of Social Issues, 46*(1), 65–81.

Bar-Tal, D. (2000). From intractable conflict through conflict resolution to reconciliation: Psychological analysis. *Political Psychology, 21,* 351–365.

Bartholomew, K., & Horowitz, L. M. (1991). Attachment styles among young adults: A test of a four-category model. *Journal of Personality and Social Psychology, 61,* 226–244.

Bartholow, B. D., Anderson, C. A., Carnagey, N. L., & Benjamin, A. J., Jr. (2005). Interactive effects of life experience and situational cues on aggression: The weapons priming effect in hunters and nonhunters. *Journal of Experimental Social Psychology, 41,* 48–60.

Bass, B. M., & Avolio, B. J. (1993). Transformational leadership: A response to critiques. In M. M. Chemers & R. Ayman (Eds.), *Leadership theory and research: Perspectives and directions* (pp. 49–80). San Diego, CA: Academic Press.

Bassili, J. N. (1996). Meta-judgmental versus operative indexes of psychological attributes: The case of measures of attitude strength. *Journal of Personality and Social Psychology, 71,* 637–653.

Bassili, J. N. (2003). The minority slowness effect: Subtle inhibitions in the expression of views not shared by others. *Journal of Personality and Social Psychology, 84,* 261–276.

Bassili, J. N., & Smith, M. C. (1986). On the spontaneity of trait attribution: Converging evidence for the role of cognitive strategy. *Journal of Personality and Social Psychology, 50,* 239–245.

Batson, C. D. (1991). *The altruism question: Toward a social-psychological answer.* Hillsdale, NJ: Erlbaum.

Batson, C. D. (1998). Altruism and prosocial behavior. In D. T. Gilbert, S. T. Fiske, & G. Lindzey (Eds.), *The handbook of social psychology* (Vol. 2, 4th ed., pp. 317–356). Boston, MA: McGraw-Hill.

Batson, C. D., Chang, J., Orr, R., & Rowland, J. (2002). Empathy, attitudes, and action: Can feeling for a member of a stigmatized group motivate one to help the group? *Personality and Social Psychology Bulletin, 28,* 1656–1666.

Batson, C. D., Duncan, B. D., Ackerman, P., Buckley, T., & Birch, K. (1981). Is empathic emotion a source of altruistic motivation? *Journal of Personality and Social Psychology, 40,* 290–302.

Batson, C. D., Lishner, D. A., Carpenter, A., Dulin, L., Harjusola-Webb, S., Stocks, E. L., Gale, S., Hassan, O., & Sampat, B. (2003). ". . . As you would have them do unto you": Does imagining yourself in the other's place stimulate moral action? *Personality and Social Psychology Bulletin, 29,* 1190–1201.

Batson, C. D., O'Quin, K., Fultz, J., Vanderplas, M., & Isen, A. M. (1983). Influence of self-reported distress and empathy on egoistic versus altruistic motivation to help. *Journal of Personality and Social Psychology, 45,* 706–718.

Baumann, D. J., Cialdini, R. B., & Kenrick, D. T. (1981). Altruism as hedonism: Helping and self-gratification as equivalent responses. *Journal of Personality and Social Psychology, 40,* 1039–1046.

Baumeister, R. F. (1982). A self-presentational view of social phenomena. *Psychological Bulletin, 91,* 3–26.

Baumeister, R. F. (1997). *Evil: Inside human violence and cruelty.* New York: Freeman.

Baumeister, R. F. (1998). The self. In D. T. Gilbert, S. T. Fiske, & G. Lindzey (Eds.), *Handbook of social psychology* (4th ed., Vol. 1, pp. 680–740). New York: McGraw-Hill.

Baumeister, R. F., Bushman, B. J., & Campbell, W. K. (2000). Self-esteem, narcissism, and aggression: Does violence result from low self-esteem or from threatened egotism? *Current Directions in Psychological Science, 9,* 26–29.

Baumeister, R. F., & Leary, M. R. (1995). The need to belong: Desire for interpersonal attachments as a fundamental human motivation. *Psychological Bulletin, 117,* 497–529.

Baumeister, R. F., Smart, L., & Boden, J. M. (1996). Relation of threatened egotism to violence and aggression: The dark side of high self-esteem. *Psychological Review, 103,* 5–33.

Baumeister, R. F., & Twenge, J. M. (2003). The social self. In T. Millon & M. J. Lerner (Eds.), *Handbook of psychology: Personality and social psychology* (Vol. 5, pp. 327–352). Hoboken, NJ: Wiley.

Baumgardner, A. H. (1990). To know oneself is to like oneself: Self-certainty and self-affect. *Journal of Personality and Social Psychology, 58,* 1062–1072.

Baumrind, D. (1964). Some thoughts on the ethics of research: After reading Milgram's "Behavioral study of obedience." *American Psychologist, 19,* 421–423.

Beach, S. R. H., & Tesser, A. (2000). Self-evaluation maintenance and evolution. In J. M. Suls & L. Wheeler (Eds.) *Handbook of social comparison: Theory and research* (pp. 123–140). New York: Kluwer Academic/Plenum.

Beaman, A. L., Cole, C. M., Preston, M., Klentz, B., & Steblay, N. M. (1983). Fifteen years of foot-in-the-door research: A meta-analysis. *Personality and Social Psychology Bulletin, 9,* 181–196.

Becker, E. (1962). *The birth and death of meaning.* New York: Free Press.

Bem, D. J. (1967). Self-perception: An alternative interpretation of cognitive dissonance phenomena. *Psychological Review, 74,* 183–200.

Bem, D. J. (1972). Self-perception theory. In L. Berkowitz (Ed.), *Advances in experimental social psychology* (Vol. 6, pp. 1–62). New York: Academic Press.

Bem, S. L. (1981). *Bem Sex Role Inventory professional manual.* Stanford, CA: Consulting Psychologists Press.

Bem, S. L. (1984). Androgyny and gender schema theory: A conceptual and empirical integration. In T. B. Sonderegger (Ed.), *Nebraska symposium on motivation: Psychology and gender* (Vol. 32, pp. 179–226). Lincoln: University of Nebraska Press.

Benoit, W. L., & Strathman, A. (2004). Source credibility and the elaboration likelihood model. In J. S. Seiter & R. H. Gass (Eds.), *Perspectives on persuasion, social influence, and compliance gaining* (pp. 95–111). Boston, MA: Pearson Education.

Bensley, L., & Van Eenwyk, J. (2001). Video games and real-life violence: Review of the literature. *Journal of Adolescent Health, 29,* 244–257.

Berg, K. S., & Vidmar, N. (1975). Authoritarianism and recall of evidence about criminal behavior. *Journal of Research in Personality, 9,* 147–157.

Bergen, D. J., & Williams, J. E. (1991). Sex stereotypes in the United States revisited: 1972–1988. *Sex Roles, 24,* 413–423.

Berglas, S., & Jones, E. E. (1978). Drug choice as a self-handicapping strategy in response to non-contingent success. *Journal of Personality and Social Psychology, 36,* 405–417.

Berkman, L. F., & Syme, S. L. (1979). Social networks, host resistance, and mortality: A nine-year follow-up study of Alameda County residents. *American Journal of Epidemiology, 109,* 186–204.

Berkowitz, L. (1962). *Aggression: A social psychological analysis.* New York: McGraw-Hill.

Berkowitz, L. (1972). Social norms, feelings, and other factors affecting helping and altruism. In L. Berkowitz (Ed.), *Advances in experimental social psychology* (Vol. 6, pp. 63–108). New York: Academic Press.

Berkowitz, L. (1989). Frustration-aggression hypothesis: Examination and reformulation. *Psychological Bulletin, 106,* 59–73.

Berkowitz, L. (1990). On the formation and regulation of anger and aggression: A cognitive-neoassociationistic analysis. *American Psychologist, 45,* 494–503.

Berkowitz, L. (1993). *Aggression: Its causes, consequences, and control.* New York: McGraw-Hill.

Berkowitz, L., & Heimer, K. (1989). On the construction of the anger experience: Aversive events and negative priming in the formation of feelings. In L. Berkowitz (Ed.), *Advances in experimental psychology* (Vol. 22, pp. 1–37). San Diego, CA: Academic Press.

Berkowitz, L., & LePage, A. (1967). Weapons as Aggression-Eliciting Stimuli. *Journal of Personality and Social Psychology, 7,* 202–207.

Bernard, M. M., Maio, G. R., & Olson, J. M. (2003). The vulnerability of values to attack: Inoculation of values and value-relevant attitudes. *Personality and Social Psychology Bulletin, 29,* 63–75.

Berndt, T. J. (1979). Developmental changes in conformity to peers and parents. *Developmental Psychology, 15,* 608–616.

Bernstein, D. M., Atance, C., Loftus, G. R., & Meltzoff, A. (2004). We saw it all along: Visual hindsight bias in children and adults. *Psychological Science, 15,* 264–267.

Bernstein, I. H., Lin, T., & McClellan, P. (1982). Cross- vs. within-racial judgments of attractiveness. *Perception and Psychophysics, 32,* 495–503.

Berscheid, E., Graziano, W., Monson, T., & Dermer, M. (1976). Outcome dependency: Attention, attribution, and attraction. *Journal of Personality and Social Psychology, 34,* 978–989.

Berscheid, E., & Reis, H. T. (1998). Attraction and close relationships. In D. T. Gilbert, S. T. Fiske, & G. Lindzey (Eds.), *Handbook of social psychology* (4th ed., Vol. 2, pp. 193–281). New York: McGraw-Hill.

Berscheid, E., Snyder, M., & Omoto, A. (1989). The relationship closeness inventory: Assessing the closeness of interpersonal relationships. *Journal of Personality and Social Psychology, 57,* 792–807.

Berscheid, E., & Walster, E. (1974). Physical attractiveness. In L. Berkowitz (Ed.), *Advances in experimental social psychology* (Vol. 7, pp. 157–215). New York: Academic Press.

Bettencourt, B. A., Brewer, M. B., Croak, M. R., & Miller, N. (1992). Cooperation and the reduction of intergroup bias: The role of reward structure and social orientation. *Journal of Experimental Social Psychology, 28,* 301–319.

Bettencourt, B., & Kernahan, C. (1997). A meta-analysis of aggression in the presence of violent cues: Effects of gender differences and aversive provocation. *Aggressive Behavior, 23,* 447–456.

Bickman, L. (1974). The social power of a uniform. *Journal of Applied Social Psychology, 4,* 47–61.

Bierman, K. L., Smoot, D. L., & Aumiller, K. (1993). Characteristics of aggressive-rejected, aggressive (nonrejected), and rejected (nonaggressive) boys. *Child Development, 64,* 139–151.

Biernat, M., Vescio, T. K., & Green, M. L. (1996). Selective self-stereotyping. *Journal of Personality and Social Psychology, 71,* 1194–1209.

Birnbaum, M. H. (Ed.). (2000). *Psychological experiments on the Internet.* San Diego, CA: Academic Press.

Birnbaum, M. H. (2001). *Introduction to behavioral research on the Internet.* Upper Saddle River, NJ: Prentice Hall.

Bizer, G. Y., & Krosnick, J. A. (2001). Exploring the structure of strength-related features: The relation between attitude importance and attitude accessibility. *Journal of Personality and Social Psychology, 81,* 566–586.

Bjorkvist, K., Osterman, K., & Lagerspetz, K. M. J. (1994). Sex differences in covert aggression among adults. *Aggressive Behavior, 20,* 27–33.

Blaine, B., & Crocker, J. (1993). Self-esteem and self-serving biases in reactions to positive and negative events: An integrative review. In R. F. Baumeister (Ed.), *Self-esteem: The puzzle of low self-regard* (pp. 55–85). New York: Plenum.

Blair, I. V. (2001). Implicit stereotypes and prejudice. In G. B. Moskowitz (Ed.), *Cognitive social psychology: The Princeton Symposium on the legacy and future of social cognition* (pp. 359–374). Mahwah, NJ: Erlbaum.

Blair, I. V. (2002). The malleability of automatic stereotypes and prejudice. *Personality and Social Psychology Review, 6,* 242–261.

Blair, I. V., Ma, J. E., & Lenton, A. P. (2001). Imagining stereotypes away: The moderation of implicit stereotypes through mental imagery. *Journal of Personality and Social Psychology, 81,* 828–841.

Blair, M. E., & Shimp, T. A. (1992). Consequences of an unpleasant experience with music: A second-order negative conditioning perspective. *Journal of Advertising, 21,* 35–44.

Blanchard, F. A., Lilly, T., & Vaughn, L. A. (1991). Reducing the expression of racial prejudice. *Psychological Science, 2,* 101–105.

Blanton, H., Cooper, J., Skurnik, I., & Aronson, J. (1997). When bad things happen to good feedback: Exacerbating the need for self-justification with self-affirmations. *Personality and Social Psychology Bulletin, 23,* 684–692.

Blascovich, J., Ginsburg, G. P., & Veach, T. L. (1975). A pluralistic explanation of choice shifts on the risk dimension. *Journal of Personality and Social Psychology, 31,* 422–429.

Blascovich, J., Loomis, J., Beall, A. C., Swinth, K. R., Hoyt, C. L., & Bailenson, J. N. (2001). Immersive virtual environment technology as a methodological tool for social psychology. *Psychological Inquiry, 13,* 103–124.

Blascovich, J., Mendes, W. B., Hunter, S. B., & Salomon, K. (1999). Social "facilitation" as challenge and threat. *Journal of Personality and Social Psychology, 77,* 68–77.

Blass, T. (1991). Understanding behavior in the Milgram obedience experiment: The role of personality, situations, and their interactions. *Journal of Personality and Social Psychology, 60,* 398–413.

Bless, H. (2001). Mood and the use of general knowledge structures. In L. L. Martin & G. L. Clore (Eds.), *Theories of mood and cognition: A user's guidebook* (pp. 9–26). Mahwah, NJ: Erlbaum.

Blumstein, P., & Schwartz, P. (1983). *American couples.* New York: William Morrow.

Bochner, S., & Insko, C. A. (1966). Communicator discrepancy, source credibility, and attitude change. *Journal of Personality and Social Psychology, 4,* 614–621.

Bodenhausen, G. V. (1988). Stereotypic biases in social decision making and memory: Testing process models of stereotype use. *Journal of Personality and Social Psychology, 55,* 726–737.

Bodenhausen, G. V., Kramer, G. P., & Susser, K. (1994). Happiness and stereotypic thinking in social judgment. *Journal of Personality and Social Psychology, 66,* 621–632.

Bolger, N., Foster, M., Vinokur, A. D., & Ng, R. (1996). Close relationships and adjustments to a life crisis: The case of breast cancer. *Journal of Personality and Social Psychology, 70,* 283–294.

Bolger, N., Zuckerman, A., & Kessler, R. C. (2000). Invisible support and adjustment to stress. *Journal of Personality and Social Psychology, 79,* 953–961.

Bonanno, G. A., Field, N. P., Kovacevic, A., & Kaltman, S. (2002). Self-enhancement as a buffer against extreme adversity: Civil war in Bosnia and traumatic loss in the United States. *Personality and Social Psychology Bulletin, 28,* 184–196.

Bond, C. F., & Titus, L. J. (1983). Social faciliation: A meta-analysis of 241 studies. *Psychological Bulletin, 94,* 265–292.

Bond, R., & Smith, P. B. (1996). Culture and conformity: A meta-analysis of studies using Asch's (1952b, 1956) line judgment task. *Psychological Bulletin, 119,* 111–137.

Booth-Kewley, S., & Friedman, H. S. (1987). Psychological predictors of heart disease: A quantitative review. *Psychological Bulletin, 101,* 343–362.

Bornstein, R. F. (1989). Exposure and affect: Overview and meta-analysis of research, 1968–1987. *Psychological Bulletin, 106,* 265–289.

Bornstein, R. F., & D'Agostino, P. R. (1992). Stimulus recognition and the mere exposure effect. *Journal of Personality and Social Psychology, 63,* 545–552.

Bosson, J. K., Haymovitz, E. L., & Pinel, E. C. (2004). When saying and doing converge: The effects of stereotype threat on self-reported versus nonverbal anxiety. *Journal of Experimental Social Psychology, 40,* 247–255.

Bourhis, R. Y. (1994). Power, gender, and intergroup discrimination: Some minimal group experiments. In M. P. Zanna & J. M. Olson (Eds.), *The psychology of prejudice: The Ontario symposium* (Vol. 7, pp. 171–208). Hillsdale, NJ: Erlbaum.

Bower, G. H. (1981). Mood and memory. *American Psychologist, 36,* 129–148.

Bowers, K. S., & Farvolden, P. (1996). Revisiting a century-old Freudian slip: From suggestion disavowed to the truth repressed. *Psychological Bulletin, 119,* 355–380.

Bowlby, J. (1969). Attachment and loss. New York: Basic Books.

Brandon, R., & Davies, C. (1973). *Wrongful imprisonment.* London: Allen & Unwin.

Branscombe, N. R., Schmitt, M. T., & Harvey, R. D. (1999). Perceiving pervasive discrimination among African Americans: Implications for group identification and well-being. *Journal of Personality and Social Psychology, 77,* 135–149.

Brauer, M., Judd, C. M., & Gliner, M. D. (1995). The effects of repeated attitude expressions on attitude polarization during group discussions. *Journal of Personality and Social Psychology, 68,* 1014–1029.

Brauer, M., Judd, C. M., & Jacquelin, V. (2001). The communication of social stereotypes: The effects of group discussion and information distribution on stereotypic appraisals. *Journal of Personality and Social Psychology, 81,* 463–475.

Bray, R. M., & Noble, A. M. (1987). Authoritarianism and decisions of mock juries: Evidence of jury bias and group polarization. In L. S. Wrightsman, S. M. Kassin, & C. E. Willis (Eds.), *In the jury box: Controversies in the courtroom* (pp. 83–94). Thousand Oaks, CA: Sage.

Breckler, S. J. (1984). Empirical validation of affect, behavior, and cognition as distinct components of attitude. *Journal of Personality and Social Psychology, 47,* 1191–1205.

Breckler, S. J., & Wiggins, E. C. (1989). Affect versus evaluation in the structure of attitudes. *Journal of Experimental Social Psychology, 25,* 253–271.

Brehm, J. W. (1956). Post-decision changes in desirability of alternatives. *Journal of Abnormal and Social Psychology, 52,* 384–389.

Brehm, J. W. (1966). *A theory of psychological reactance.* New York: Academic Press.

Brehm, J. W. (1972). *Responses to loss of freedom: A theory of psychological reactance.* Morristown, NJ: General Learning Press.

Brendl, C. M., Markman, A. B., & Messner, C. (2001). How do indirect measures of evaluation work? Evaluating the inference of prejudice in the Implicit Association Test. *Journal of Personality and Social Psychology, 81,* 760–773.

Brescoll, V., & LaFrance, M. (2004). The correlates and consequences of newspaper reports of research on sex differences. *Psychological Science, 15,* 515–520.

Breuer, J., & Freud, S. (1957). *Studies on hysteria.* New York: Basic Books.

Brewer, M. B. (1991). The social self: On being the same and different at the same time. *Personality and Social Psychology Bulletin, 17,* 475–482.

Brewer, M. B. (1993). Social identity, distinctiveness, and in-group homogeneity. *Social Cognition, 11,* 150–164.

Brewer, M. B., & Brown, R. J. (1998). Intergroup relations. In D. T. Gilbert, S. T. Fiske, & G. Lindzey (Eds.), *Handbook of social psychology* (4th ed., Vol. 2, pp. 554–594). Boston, MA: McGraw-Hill.

Brewer, M. B., & Miller, N. (1984). Beyond the contact hypothesis: Theoretical perspectives on desegregation. In N. Miller & M. B. Brewer (Eds.), *Groups in contact: The psychology of desegregation* (pp. 281–302). New York: Academic Press.

Brickner, M. A., Harkins, S. G., & Ostrom, T. M. (1986). Effects of personal involvement: Thought-provoking implications for social loafing. *Journal of Personality and Social Psychology, 51,* 763–769.

Brigham, J. C. (1990). Target person distinctiveness and attractiveness as moderator variables in the confidence-accuracy relationship in eyewitness identifications. *Basic and Applied Social Psychology, 11,* 101–115.

Brindberg, D., & Durand, J. (1983). Eating at fast-food restaurants: An analysis using two behavioral intention models. *Journal of Applied Social Psychology, 13,* 459–472.

Brinthaupt, T. M., Moreland, R. L., & Levine, J. M. (1991). Sources of optimism among prospective group members. *Personality and Social Psychology Bulletin, 17,* 36–43.

Brockner, J., & Swap, W. C. (1976). Effects of repeated exposure and attitudinal similarity on self-disclosure and interpersonal attraction. *Journal of Personality and Social Psychology, 33,* 531–540.

Brosius, H., & Engel, D. (1996). The causes of third-person effects: Unrealistic optimism, impersonal contact, or generalized negative attitudes toward media influence? *International Journal of Public Opinion Research, 8,* 142–162.

Brown, B. R. (1968). The effects of need to maintain face on interpersonal bargaining. *Journal of Experimental Social Psychology, 4,* 107–122.

Brown, J. D. (1986). Evaluations of self and others: Self-enhancement biases in social judgments. *Social Cognition, 4,* 353–376.

Brown, L. S. (1997). The private practice of subversion: Psychology as tikkun olam. *American Psychologist, 52,* 449–462.

Brown, R. J. (1988). *Group processes: Dynamics within and between groups.* Oxford, UK: Blackwell.

Brown, R. P., & Pinel, E. C. (2003). Stigma on my mind: Individual differences in the experience of stereotype threat. *Journal of Experimental Social Psychology, 39,* 626–633.

Brownstein, R. J., & Katzev, R. D. (1985). The relative effectiveness of three compliance techniques in eliciting donations to a cultural organization. *Journal of Applied Social Psychology, 15,* 564–574.

Bruner, J. S. (1957). Going beyond the information given. In H. Gruber, G. Terrell, & M. Wertheimer (Eds.), *Contemporary approaches to cognition* (pp. 41–69). Cambridge, MA: Harvard University Press.

Bryan, J. H., & Test, M. A. (1967). Models and helping: Naturalistic studies in aiding behavior. *Journal of Personality and Social Psychology, 6,* 400–407.

Bryant, F. B., & Brockway, J. H. (1997). Hindsight bias in reaction to the verdict in the O. J. Simpson criminal trial. *Basic and Applied Social Psychology, 19,* 225–241.

Buckhout, R. (1974). Eyewitness testimony. *Scientific American, 231,* 23–31.

Burger, J. M. (1999). The foot-in-the-door compliance procedure: A multiple-process analysis and review. *Personality and Social Psychology Review, 3,* 303–325.

Burger, J. M., & Cornelius, T. (2003). Raising the price of agreement: Public commitment and the lowball compliance procedure. *Journal of Applied Social Psychology, 33,* 923–934.

Burger, J. M., Messian, N., Patel, S., del Prado, A., & Anderson, C. (2004). What a coincidence! The effects of incidental similarity on compliance. *Personality and Social Psychology Bulletin, 30,* 35–43.

Burger, J. M., Soroka. S., Gonzago, K., Murphy, E., & Somervell, E. (2001). The effect of fleeting attraction on compliance to requests. *Personality and Social Psychology Bulletin, 27,* 1578–1586.

Burgoon, J. K., Bonito, J. A., Ramirez, A., Dunbar, N. E., Kam, K., & Fischer, J. (2002). Testing the interactivity principle: Effects of mediation, propinquity, and verbal and nonverbal modalities in interpersonal interaction. *Journal of Communication, 52,* 657–677.

Burn, S. M. (2004). *Groups: Theory and practice.* Belmont, CA: Thomson/Wadsworth.

Burnstein, E., Crandall, C., & Kitayama, S. (1994). Some neo-Darwinian decision rules for altruism: Weighing cues for inclusive fitness as a function of the biological importance of the decision. *Journal of Personality and Social Psychology, 67,* 773–789.

Bushman, B. J. (1996). Individual differences in the extent and development of aggressive cognitive-associative networks. *Personality and Social Psychology Bulletin, 22,* 811–819.

Bushman, B. J. (2002). Does venting anger feed or extinguish the flame? Catharsis, rumination, distraction, anger and aggressive responding. *Personality and Social Psychology Bulletin, 28,* 724–731.

Bushman, B. J., & Anderson, C. A. (2001a). Is it time to pull the plug on the hostile versus instrumental aggression dichotomy? *Psychological Review, 108,* 273–279.

Bushman, B. J., & Anderson, C. A. (2001b). Media violence and the American public: Scientific facts versus media misinformation. *American Psychologist, 56,* 477–489.

Bushman, B. J., & Anderson, C. A. (2002). Violent video games and hostile expectations: A test of the general aggression model. *Personality and Social Psychology Bulletin, 28,* 1679–1686.

Bushman, B. J., & Baumeister, R. F. (1998). Threatened egotism, narcissism, self-esteem, and direct and displaced aggression: Does self-love or self-hate lead to violence? *Journal of Personality and Social Psychology, 75,* 219–229.

Bushman, B. J., Baumeister, R. F., & Stack, A. D. (1999). Catharsis, aggression, and persuasive influence: Self-fulfilling or self-defeating prophecies? *Journal of Personality and Social Psychology, 76,* 367–376.

Bushman, B. J., & Bonacci, A. M. (2004). You've got mail: Using e-mail to examine the effect of prejudiced attitudes on discrimination against Arabs. *Journal of Experimental Social Psychology, 40,* 753–759.

Bushman, B. J., & Cooper, H. M. (1990). Effects of alcohol on human aggression: An integrative research review. *Psychological Bulletin, 107,* 341–354.

Buss, A. H. (1961). *The psychology of aggression.* New York: Wiley.

Buss, A. H., & Perry, M. (1992). The aggression questionnaire. *Journal of Personality and Social Psychology, 63,* 452–459.

Buss, D. M. (1989). Sex differences in human mate preferences: Evolutionary hypotheses tested in 37 cultures. *Behavioral and Brain Sciences, 12,* 1–49.

Buss, D. M. (1996). The evolutionary psychology of human social strategies. In E. T. Higgins & A. W. Kruglanski (Eds.), *Social psychology: Handbook of basic principles* (pp. 3–38). New York: Guilford.

Buss, D. M. (1999). *Evolutionary psychology: The new science of the mind.* Boston, MA: Allyn & Bacon.

Buss, D. M., & Kenrick, D. T. (1998). Evolutionary social psychology. In D. T. Gilbert, S. T. Fiske, & G. Lindzey (Eds.), *The handbook of social psychology* (4th ed., Vol. 2, pp. 982–1026). Boston: McGraw-Hill.

Butler, R. (1989). On the psychological meaning of information about competence: A reply to Ryan and Deci's comment on Butler (1987). *Journal of Educational Psychology, 8,* 269–272.

Buunk, B. P. (1995). Comparison direction and comparison dimension among disabled individuals: Toward a refined conceptualization of social comparison under stress. *Personality and Social Psychology Bulletin, 21,* 316–330.

Buunk, B. P., Oldersma, F. L., & de Dreu, C. K. W. (2001). Enhancing satisfaction through downward comparison: The role of relational discontent and individual differences in social comparison orientation. *Journal of Experimental Social Psychology, 37,* 452–467.

Byrne, D. E. (1971). *The attraction paradigm.* New York: Academic Press.

Byrne, D. E., & Clore, G. L. (1966). Predicting interpersonal attraction toward strangers presented in three different stimulus modes. *Psychonomic Science, 4*(6), 239–240.

Cacioppo, J. T. (2002). Social neuroscience: Understanding the pieces fosters understanding the whole and vice versa. *American Psychologist, 57,* 819–831.

Cacioppo, J. T. (2004). Common sense, intuition, and theory in personality and social psychology. *Personality and Social Psychology Review, 8,* 114–122.

Cacioppo, J. T., Berntson, G. G., Adolphs, R., Carter, C. S., Davidson, R. J., McClintock, M., et al. (Eds.). (2002). *Foundations in social neuroscience.* Cambridge, MA: MIT Press.

Cacioppo, J. T., Berntson, G. G., Sheridan, J. F., & McClintock, M. (2000). Multilevel integrative analyses of human behavior: Social neuroscience and the complementing nature of social and biological approaches. *Psychological Bulletin, 126,* 829–843.

Cacioppo, J. T., Bush, L. K., & Tassinary, L. G. (1992). Microexpressive facial actions as a function of affective stimuli: Replication and extension. *Personality and Social Psychology Bulletin, 18,* 515–526.

Cacioppo, J. T., Marshall-Goodell, B. S., Tassinary, L. G., & Petty, R. E. (1992). Rudimentary determinants of attitudes: Classical conditioning is more effective when prior knowledge about the attitude stimulus is low rather than high. *Journal of Experimental Social Psychology, 28,* 207–233.

Cacioppo, J. T., Martzke, J. S., Petty, R. E., & Tassinary, L. G. (1988). Specific forms of facial EMG response index emotions during an interview: From Darwin to the continuous flow hypothesis of affect-laden information processing. *Journal of Personality and Social Psychology, 54,* 592–604.

Cacioppo, J. T., & Petty, R. E. (1982). The need for cognition. *Journal of Personality and Social Psychology, 42,* 116–131.

Cacioppo, J. T., & Petty, R. E. (1985). Central and peripheral routes to persuasion: The role of message repetition. In L. F. Alwitt & A. A. Mitchell (Eds.), *Psychological processes and advertising effects* (pp. 91–111). Hillsdale, NJ: Erlbaum.

Cacioppo, J. T., Petty, R. E., Feinstein, J., & Jarvis, B. (1996). Dispositional differences in cognitive motivation: The life and times of individuals varying in need for cognition. *Psychological Bulletin, 119,* 197–253.

Cacioppo, J. T., Petty, R. E., & Kao, C. F. (1984). The efficient assessment of need for cognition. *Journal of Personality Assessment, 48,* 306–307.

Cacioppo, J. T., Petty, R. E., Losch, M. E., & Kim, H. S. (1986). Electromyographic activity over facial muscle regions can differentiate the valence and intensity of affective reactions. *Journal of Personality and Social Psychology, 50,* 260–268.

Callaway, M. R., & Esser, J. K. (1984). Groupthink: Effects of cohesiveness and problem-solving procedures on group decision making. *Social Behavior and Personality, 12,* 157–164.

Calvert, S. L. (2002). The social impact of virtual environment technology. In K. M. Stanney (Ed.), *Handbook of virtual environments: Design, implementation, and applications.* (pp. 663–680). Mahwah, NJ: Erlbaum.

Camerer, C. F. (2003). Strategizing in the brain. *Science, 300,* 1673–1675.

Campbell, D. T. (1957). Factors relevant to validity of experiments in social settings. *Psychological Bulletin, 54,* 297–312.

Campbell, D. T. (1965). Ethnocentric and other altruistic motives. In D. Levine (Ed.), *Nebraska Symposium on Motivation* (Vol. 13, pp. 238–311). Lincoln: University of Nebraska Press.

Campbell, J. D. (1990). Self-esteem and clarity of self-concept. *Journal of Personality and Social Psychology, 59,* 538–549.

Campos, J. J., Barrett, K., Lamb, M. E., Goldsmith, H., & Stenberg, C. R. (1983). Socioemotional development. In M. M. Haith & J. J. Campos (Eds.), *Handbook of child psychology* (Vol. 2, pp. 783–915). New York: Wiley.

Cann, A., Sherman, S. J., & Elkes, R. (1975). Effects of initial request size and timing of a second request on compliance: The foot in the door and the door in the face. *Journal of Personality and Social Psychology, 32,* 774–782.

Cannon, W. B. (1932). *The wisdom of the body.* New York: Norton.

Caporael, L. R., & Brewer, M. B. (1995). Hierarchical evolutionary theory: There is an alternative and it's not creationism. *Psychological Inquiry, 6,* 31–80.

Cardeña, E., Butler, L. D., & Spiegel, D. (2003). Stress disorders. In I. B. Weiner (Series Ed.) & G. Stricker & T. A. Widiger (Vol. Eds.), *Handbook of psychology: Vol 8. Clinical psychology* (pp. 229–249). Hoboken, NJ: Wiley.

Carli, L. L. (2001). Gender and social influence. *Journal of Social Issues, 57,* 725–742.

Carlo, G., Eisenberg, N., Troyer, D., Switzer, G., & Speer, A. L. (1991). The altruistic personality: In what contexts is it apparent? *Journal of Personality and Social Psychology, 61,* 450–458.

Carlsmith, J. M., & Gross, A. E. (1969). Some effects of guilt on compliance. *Journal of Personality and Social Psychology, 11,* 232–239.

Carlson, M., Charlin, V., & Miller, N. (1988). Positive mood and helping behavior: A test of six hypotheses. *Journal of Personality and Social Psychology, 55,* 211–229.

Carlston, D. E., & Skowronski, J. J. (1994). Savings in the relearning of trait information as evidence for spontaneous trait generation. *Journal of Personality and Social Psychology, 66,* 840–856.

Carlston, D. E., & Smith, E. R. (1996). Principles of mental representation. In E. T. Higgins & A. Kruglanski (Eds.), *Social psychology: Handbook of basic principles* (pp.184–210). New York: Guilford Press.

Carnevale, P. J., & Leung, K. (2001). Cultural dimensions of negotiation. In M. A. Hogg & S. Tindale (Eds.), *Blackwell handbook of social psychology: Group processes* (pp. 482–496). Oxford, UK: Blackwell.

Cartwright, D. S., & Zander, A. (Eds.). (1968). *Group dynamics: Research and theory* (3rd ed.). New York: Harper & Row.

Carver, C. S., Coleman, A. E., & Glass, D. C. (1976). The coronary-prone behavior pattern and the suppression of fatigue on a treadmill test. *Journal of Personality and Social Psychology, 33,* 460–466.

Carver, C. S., Ganellen, R. J., Froming W. J., & Chambers, W. (1983). Modeling: An analysis in terms of category accessibility. *Journal of Experimental Social Psychology, 19,* 403–421.

Carver, C. S., Pozo, C., Harris, S. D., Noriega, V., Scheier, M. F., Robinson, D. S., Ketcham, A. S., Moffat, F. L., Jr., & Clark, K. C. (1993). How coping mediates the effects of optimism on stress: A study of women with early stage breast cancer. *Journal of Personality and Social Psychology, 65,* 375–391.

Cassidy, J., & Berlin, L. J. (1994). The insecure/ambivalent pattern of attachment: Theory and research. *Child Development, 65,* 971–991.

Chaiken, S. (1980). Heuristic versus systematic processing and the use of source versus message cues in persuasion. *Journal of Personality and Social Psychology, 39,* 752–766.

Chaiken, S. (1987). The heuristic model of persuasion. In M. P. Zanna, J. M. Olson, & C. P. Herman (Eds.), *Social inference: The Ontario symposium* (Vol. 5, pp. 3–39). Hillsdale, NJ: Erlbaum.

Chaiken, S., & Baldwin, M. W. (1981). Affective-cognitive consistency and the effect of salient behavioral information on the self-perception of attitudes. *Journal of Personality and Social Psychology, 41,* 1–12.

Chaiken, S., & Maheswaran, D. (1994). Heuristic processing can bias systematic processing: Effects of source credibility, argument ambiguity, and task importance on attitude judgment. *Journal of Personality and Social Psychology, 66,* 460–473.

Chang, E. C., & Asakawa, K. (2003). Cultural variations on optimistic and pessimistic bias for self versus a sibling: Is there evidence for self-enhancement in the West and for self-criticism in the East when the reference group is specified? *Journal of Personality and Social Psychology, 84,* 569–581.

Chang, E. C., Asakawa, K., & Sanna, L. J. (2001). Cultural variations in optimistic and pessimistic bias: Do Easterners really expect the worst and Westerners really expect the best when predicting future life events? *Journal of Personality and Social Psychology, 81,* 476–491.

Chapman, L. J. (1967). Illusory correlation in observational report. *Journal of Verbal Learning and Verbal Behavior, 6,* 151–155.

Chapman, L. J., & Chapman, J. P. (1967). Genesis of popular but erroneous diagnostic observations. *Journal of Abnormal Psychology, 72,*193–204.

Chapman, L. J., & Chapman J. P. (1969). Illusory correlation as an obstacle to the use of valid psycho-diagnostic signs. *Journal of Abnormal Psychology, 74,* 272–280.

Chartrand, T. L., & Bargh, J. A. (1999). The chameleon effect: The perception-behavior link and social interaction. *Journal of Personality and Social Psychology, 76,* 893–910.

Chassin, L., Presson, C. C., & Sherman, S. J. (1984). Cigarette smoking and adolescent psychosocial development. *Basic and Applied Social Psychology, 5,* 295–315.

Chemers, M. M. (2000). Leadership research and theory: A functional integration. *Group Dynamics: Theory, Research, and Practice, 4,* 27–43.

Chemers, M. M., & Ayman, R. (Eds.). (1993). *Leadership theory and research: Perspectives and directions.* San Diego, CA: Academic Press.

Chen, F. F., & Kenrick, D. T. (2002). Repulsion or attraction? Group membership and assumed attitude similarity. *Journal of Personality and Social Psychology, 83,* 111–125.

Chen, M., & Bargh, J. A. (1997). Nonconscious behavioral confirmation processes: The self-fulfilling consequences of automatic stereotype activation. *Journal of Experimental Social Psychology, 33,* 541–560.

Cheng, P. W., & Novick, L. R. (1992). Covariation in natural causal induction. *Psychological Review, 99,* 365–382.

Chesney, M. A., & Rosenman, R. H. (Eds.). (1985). *Anger and hostility in cardiovascular and behavioral disorders.* Washington, DC: Hemisphere.

Cho, H., & Witte, K. (2004). A review of fear-appeal effects. In J. S. Seiter & R. H. Gass (Eds.), *Perspectives on persuasion, social influence, and compliance gaining* (pp. 223–238). Boston, MA: Pearson Education.

Choi, I., & Nisbett, R. E. (1998). Situational salience and cultural differences in the correspondence bias and the actor-observer bias. *Personality and Social Psychology Bulletin, 24,* 949–960.

Christensen, P. N., Rothgerber, H., Wood, W., & Matz, D. C. (2004). Social norms and identity relevance: A motivational approach to normative behavior. *Personality and Social Psychology Bulletin, 30,* 1295–1309.

Cialdini, R. B. (2001). *Influence: Science and practice* (4th ed.). Boston, MA: Allyn & Bacon.

Cialdini, R. B., Borden, R., Thorne, A., Walker, M., Freeman, S., & Sloane, L. T. (1976). Basking in reflected glory: Three (football) field studies. *Journal of Personality and Social Psychology, 34,* 366–375.

Cialdini, R. B., Cacioppo, J. T., Bassett, R., & Miller, J. A. (1978). Low-ball procedure for producing compliance: Commitment then cost. *Journal of Personality and Social Psychology, 36,* 463–476.

Cialdini, R. B., & Goldstein, N. J. (2004). Social influence: Compliance and conformity. *Annual Review of Psychology, 55,* 591–621.

Cialdini, R. B., Schaller, M., Houlihan, D., Arps, K., Fultz, J., & Beaman, A. L. (1987). Empathy-based helping: Is it selflessly or selfishly motivated? *Journal of Personality and Social Psychology, 52,* 749–758.

Cialdini, R. B., & Trost, M. R. (1998). Social influence: Social norms, conformity, and compliance. In D. T. Gilbert, S. T. Fiske, & G. Lindzey (Eds.), *The handbook of social psychology* (3rd ed., Vol. 2, pp. 151–192). Boston, MA: McGraw-Hill.

Cialdini, R. B., Trost, M. R., & Newsom, J. T. (1995). Preference for consistency: The development of a valid measure and the discovery of surprising behavioral implications. *Journal of Personality and Social Psychology, 69,* 318–328.

Cialdini, R. B., Vincent, J. E., Lewis, S. K., Catalan, J., Wheeler, D., & Darby, B. L. (1975). Reciprocal concessions procedure for inducing compliance: The door-in-the-face technique. *Journal of Personality and Social Psychology, 31,* 206–215.

Clark, K. B., & Clark, M. P. (1947). Racial identification and preference in Negro children. In T. M. Newcomb & E. L. Hartley (Eds.), *Readings in social psychology* (pp. 169–178). New York: Holt, Rinehart, & Winston.

Clark, M. S., & Mills, J. (1979). Interpersonal attraction in exchange and communal relationships. *Journal of Personality and Social Psychology, 37,* 12–24.

Clark, M. S., & Mills, J. (1993). The difference between communal and exchange relationships: What it is and is not. *Personality and Social Psychology Bulletin, 19,* 684–691.

Clay, C. (1987). *No freedom for the mind: A study of the cult phenomenon from a Canadian perspective.* Burlington, ON: Trinity Press.

Clore, G. L., & Gormly, J. B. (1974). Knowing, feeling, and liking: A psychophysiological view. *Journal of Research in Personality, 8,* 218–230.

Clore, G. L., Schwarz, N., & Conway, M. (1994). Affective causes and consequences of social information processing. In R. S. Wyer, Jr., & T. K. Srull (Eds.), *Handbook of social cognition: Vol.1. Basic processes* (2nd ed., pp. 323–417). Hillsdale, NJ: Erlbaum.

Clore, G. L., Wyer, R. S., Jr., Dienes, B., Gasper, K., Gohm, C., & Isbell, L. M. (2001). Affective feelings as feedback: Some cognitive consequences. In L. L. Martin & G. L. Clore (Eds.), *Theories of mood and cognition: A user's guidebook* (pp. 27–62). Mahwah, NJ: Erlbaum.

Cohen, A. R. (1962). An experiment on small rewards for discrepant compliance and attitude change. In J. W. Brehm & A. R. Cohen (Eds.), *Explorations in cognitive dissonance* (pp. 73–79). New York: Wiley.

Cohen, C. E. (1981). Person categories and social perception: Testing some boundaries of the processing effects of prior knowledge. *Journal of Personality and Social Psychology, 40,* 441–452.

Cohen, D., & Hoshino-Browne, E. (2005). Insider and outsider perspectives on the self and social world. In R. M. Sorrentino, D. Cohen, J. M. Olson, & M. P. Zanna (Eds.), *Culture and social behavior: The Ontario symposium* (Vol. 10, pp. 49–76). Mahwah, NJ: Erlbaum.

Cohen, D., & Nisbett, R. E. (1997). Field experiments examining the culture of honor: The role of institutions in perpetuating norms about violence. *Personality and Social Psychology Bulletin, 23,* 1188–1199.

Cohen, D., Nisbett, R. E., Bowdle, B. F., & Schwarz, N. (1996). Insult, aggression, and the southern culture of honor: An "experimental ethnography." *Journal of Personality and Social Psychology, 70,* 945–960.

Cohen, E. S., & Fromme, K. (2002). Differential determinants of young adult substance use and high-risk sexual behavior. *Journal of Applied Social Psychology, 32,* 1124–1150.

Cohen, G. L., Aronson, J., & Steele, C. M. (2000). When beliefs yield to evidence: Reducing biased evaluation by affirming the self. *Personality and Social Psychology Bulletin, 26,* 1151–1164.

Cohen, S. (2004). Social relationships and health. *American Psychologist, 59,* 676–684.

Coie, J. D., & Dodge, K. A. (1998). Aggression and antisocial behavior. In N. Eisenberg (Ed.), *Social, emotional, and personality development* (5th ed., Vol. 4, pp. 779–862). New York: Wiley.

Coie, J. D., & Kupersmidt, J. B. (1983). A behavioral analysis of emerging social status in boys' groups. *Child Development, 54,* 1400–1416.

Colby, K. M. (1968). A programmable theory of cognition and affect in individual personal belief systems. In R. P. Abelson, E. Aronson, W. J. McGuire, T. M. Newcomb, M. J. Rosenberg, & P. H. Tannenbaum (Eds.) *Theories of cognitive consistency: A source book* (pp. 520–525). Chicago: Rand McNally.

Coleman, J. F., Blake, R. R., & Mouton, J. S. (1958). Task difficulty and conformity pressures. *Journal of Abnormal and Social Psychology, 57,* 120–122.

Colin, V. L. (1996). *Human attachment.* Philadelphia: Temple University Press.

Collins, N. L., & Miller, L. C. (1994). Self-disclosure and liking: A meta-analytic review. *Psychological Bulletin, 116,* 457–475.

Collins, N. L., & Read, S. J. (1990). Adult attachment, working models, and relationship quality in dating couples. *Journal of Personality and Social Psychology, 58,* 644–663.

Collins, R. L. (1996). For better or worse: The impact of upward social comparisons on self-evaluations. *Psychological Bulletin, 34,* 366–375.

Collins, R. L. (2000). Among the better ones: Upward assimilation in social comparison. In J. M. Suls & L. Wheeler (Eds.), *Handbook of social comparison: Theory and research* (pp. 159–171). New York: Kluwer Academic/Plenum.

Colman, A. M. (1991). Crowd psychology in South African murder trials. *American Psychologist, 46,* 1071–1079.

Colvin, C. R., & Block, J. (1994). Do positive illusions foster mental health? An examination of the Taylor and Brown formulation. *Psychological Bulletin, 116,* 3–20.

Colvin, C. R., Block, J., & Funder, D. C. (1995). Overly positive evaluations and personality: Negative implications for mental health. *Journal of Personality and Social Psychology, 68,* 1152–1162.

Conger, R. D., Conger, K. J., Elder, G. H., Lorenz, F. O., Simmons, R. L., & Whitebeck, L. B. (1992). A family process model of economic hardship and adjustment of early adolescent boys. *Child Development, 63,* 526–541.

Conway, M., & Ross, M. (1984). Getting what you want by revising what you had. *Journal of Personality and Social Psychology, 47,* 738–748.

Cook, A. J., Kerr, G. N., & Moore, K. (2002). Attitudes and intentions towards purchasing GM food. *Journal of Economic Psychology, 23,* 557–572.

Cook, S. W. (1969). Motives in a conceptual analysis of attitude-related behavior. In W. J. Arnold & D. Levine (Eds.), *Nebraska Symposium on Motivation* (Vol. 17, pp. 179–231). Lincoln: University of Nebraska Press.

Cook, S. W. (1990). Toward a psychology of improving justice: Research on extending the equality principle to victims of social injustice. *Journal of Social Issues, 46*(1), 147–161.

Cooley, C. H. (1902). *Human nature and the social order.* New York: Charles Scribner's Sons.

Cooper, C. (1997, March/April). An interesting career in psychology: Social science analyst in the public sector. *Psychological Science Agenda, 10*(2), 8.

Cooper, J. (1980). Reducing fears and increasing assertiveness: The role of dissonance reduction. *Journal of Experimental Social Psychology, 16,* 199–213.

Cooper, J. (1998). Unlearning cognitive dissonance: Toward an understanding of the development of dissonance. *Journal of Experimental Social Psychology, 34,* 562–575.

Cooper, J., Bennett, E. A., & Sukel, H. L. (1996). Complex scientific testimony: How do jurors make decisions? *Law and Human Behavior, 20,* 379–394.

Cooper, J., & Fazio, R. H. (1984). A new look at dissonance theory. In L. Berkowitz (Ed.), *Advances in experimental social psychology* (Vol. 17, pp. 229–264). New York: Academic Press.

Cooper, J., Zanna, M. P., & Taves, P. A. (1978). Arousal as a necessary condition for attitude change following induced compliance. *Journal of Personality and Social Psychology, 36,* 1101–1106.

Correll, J., Park, B., Judd, C. M., & Wittenbrink, B. (2002). The police officer's dilemma: Using ethnicity to disambiguate potentially threatening individuals. *Journal of Personality and Social Psychology, 83,* 1314–1329.

Cortina, L. M. (2004). Hispanic perspectives on sexual harassment and social support. *Personality and Social Psychology Bulletin, 30,* 570–584.

Cottrell, N. B., Wack, D. L., Sekerak, G. J., & Rittle, R. H. (1968). Social facilitation of dominant responses by the presence of an audience and the mere presence of others. *Journal of Personality and Social Psychology, 9,* 245–250.

Cousins, N. (1979). *Anatomy of an illness.* New York: Norton.

Cozzarelli, C. (1993). Personality and self-efficacy as predictors of coping with abortion. *Journal of Personality and Social Psychology, 65,* 1224–1236.

Crandall, C. S. (1994). Prejudice against fat people: Ideology and self-interest. *Journal of Personality and Social Psychology, 66,* 882–894.

Crandall, C. S. (1995). Do parents discriminate against their heavy-weight daughters? *Personality and Social Psychology Bulletin, 21,* 724–735.

Crandall, C. S., & Eshleman, A. (2003). A justification-suppression model of the expression and experience of prejudice. *Psychological Bulletin, 129,* 414–446.

Crano, W. D., & Brewer, M. B. (2002). *Principles and methods of social research* (2nd ed.). Mahwah, NJ: Erlbaum.

Crawford, M. T., & McCrea, S. M. (2004). When mutations meet motivations: Attitude biases in counterfactual thought. *Journal of Experimental Social Psychology, 40,* 65–74.

Crelia, R. A., & Tesser, A. (1996). Attitude heritability and attitude reinforcement: A replication. *Personality and Individual Differences, 21,* 803–808.

Crick, N. R. (1996). The role of overt aggression, relational aggression, and prosocial behavior in the prediction of children's future social adjustment. *Child Development, 67,* 2317–2327.

Crick, N. R., Casas, J. F., & Mosher, M. (1997). Relational and overt aggression in preschool. *Developmental Psychology, 33,* 579–588.

Crick, N. R., & Grotpeter, J. K. (1995). Relational aggression, gender, and social-psychological adjustment. *Child Development, 66,* 710–722.

Crites, S. L., Jr., Fabrigar, L. R., & Petty, R. E. (1994). Measuring the affective and cognitive properties of attitudes: Conceptual and methodological issues. *Personality and Social Psychology Bulletin, 20,* 619–634.

Crittenden, J. (1962). Aging and party affiliation. *Public Opinion Quarterly, 26,* 648–657.

Crocker, J. (1981). Judgment of covariation by social perceivers. *Psychology Bulletin, 90,* 272–292.

Crocker, J., Cornwell, B., & Major, B. (1993). The stigma of overweight: Affective consequences of attributional ambiguity. *Journal of Personality and Social Psychology, 64,* 60–70.

Crocker, J., & Park, L. E. (2004). The costly pursuit of self-esteem. *Psychological Bulletin, 130,* 392–414.

Crocker, J., Sommers, S. R., & Luhtanen, R. K. (2002). Hopes dashed and dreams fulfilled: Contingencies of self-worth and graduate school admissions. *Personality and Social Psychology Bulletin, 28,* 1275–1286.

Croizet, J.-C., & Claire, T. (1998). Extending the concept of stereotype threat to social class: The intellectual underperformance of students from low socioeconomic backgrounds. *Personality and Social Psychology Bulletin, 24,* 588–594.

Croizet, J.-C., Després, G., Gauzins, M.-E., Huguet, P., Leyens, J.-P., & Méot, A. (2004). Stereotype threat undermines intellectual performance by triggering a disruptive mental load. *Personality and Social Psychology Bulletin, 30,* 721–731.

Crosby, F. (1976). A model of egoistical relative deprivation. *Psychological Review, 83,* 85–113.

Crosby, F. (1984). The denial of personal discrimination. *American Behavioral Scientist, 27,* 371–386.

Cross, S. E., & Vick, N. V. (2001). The interdependent self-construal and social support: The case of persistence in engineering. *Personality and Social Psychology Bulletin, 27,* 820–832.

Croyle, R. T. (Ed.). (1995). *Psychosocial effects of screening for disease prevention and detection.* New York: Oxford University Press.

Croyle, R. T. (2004). Is psychology a player in big science? *Psychological Science Agenda, 18*(10), 4.

Croyle, R. T., & Cooper, J. (1982). Dissonance arousal: Physiological evidence. *Journal of Personality and Social Psychology, 45,* 782–791.

Croyle, R. T., Smith, K. R., Botkin, J. R., Baty, B., & Nash, J. (1997). Psychological responses to BRCA1 mutation testing: Preliminary findings. *Health Psychology, 16,* 63–72.

Crutchfield, R. S. (1955). Conformity and character. *American Psychologist, 10,* 191–198.

Cunningham, M. (2001). The influence of parental attitudes and behaviors on children's attitudes toward gender and household labor in early adulthood. *Journal of Marriage and the Family, 63,* 111–122.

Cunningham, M. R. (1986). Measuring the physical in physical attractiveness: Quasi-experiments on the sociobiology of female facial beauty. *Journal of Personality and Social Psychology, 50,* 925–935.

Cunningham, M. R., Barbee, A. P., & Pike, C. L. (1990). What do women want? Facialmetric assessment of multiple motives in the perception of male facial physical attractiveness. *Journal of Personality and Social Psychology, 59,* 61–72.

Cunningham, M. R., Roberts, A. R., Barbee, A. P., Druen, P. B., & Wu, C. (1995). "Their ideas of beauty are, on the whole, the same as ours": Consistency and variability in the cross-cultural perception of female physical attractiveness. *Journal of Personality and Social Psychology, 68,* 261–279.

Cunningham, M. R., Shaffer, D. R., Barbee, A. P., Wolff, P. L., & Kelly, D. J. (1990). Separate processes in the relation of elation and depression to helping: Social versus personal concerns. *Journal of Experimental Social Psychology, 26,* 13–33.

Cunningham, M. R., Steinberg, J., & Grev, R. (1980). Wanting to and having to help: Separate motivations for positive mood and guilt-induced helping. *Journal of Personality and Social Psychology, 38,* 181–192.

Cunningham, W. A., Johnson, M. K., Raye, C. L., Gatenby, J. C., Gore, J. C., & Banaji, M. R. (2004). Separable neural components in the processing of black and white faces. *Psychological Science, 15,* 806–813.

Cunningham, W. A., Nezlek, J. B., & Banaji, M. R. (2004). Implicit and explicit ethnocentrism: Revisiting the ideologies of prejudice. *Personality and Social Psychology Bulletin, 30,* 1332–1346.

Cunningham, W. A., Preacher, K. J., & Banaji, M. R. (2001). Implicit attitude measures: Consistency, stability, and convergent validity. *Psychological Science, 12,* 163–170.

Cutler, B. L., & Penrod, S. D. (1995). *Mistaken identification: The eyewitness, psychology and the law.* New York: Cambridge University Press.

Cutrona, C. E., & Troutman, B. R. (1986). Social support, infant temperament, and parenting self-efficacy: A mediational model of post-partum depression. *Child Development, 57,* 1507–1518.

Daly, M., & Wilson, M. (1988). *Homicide.* New York: Aldine deGruyter.

Darley, J. M., & Batson, C. D. (1973). "From Jerusalem to Jericho": A study of situational and dispositional variables in helping behavior. *Journal of Personality and Social Psychology, 27,* 100–108.

Darley, J. M., & Gross, P. H. (1983). A hypothesis-confirming bias in labelling effects. *Journal of Personality and Social Psychology, 24,* 20–33.

Darley, J. M., & Latané, B. (1968). Bystander intervention in emergencies: Diffusion of responsibility. *Journal of Personality and Social Psychology, 8,* 377–383.

Darwin, C. (1872). *The expression of the emotions in man and animals.* London: Murray.

Das, E. H. H. J., de Wit, J. B. F., & Stroebe, W. (2003). Fear appeals motivate acceptance of action recommendations: Evidence for a positive bias in the processing of persuasive messages. *Personality and Social Psychology Bulletin, 29,* 650–664.

Dasgupta, N., & Asgari, S. (2004). Seeing is believing: Exposure to counterstereotypic women leaders and its effect on the malleability of automatic gender stereotyping. *Journal of Experimental Social Psychology, 40,* 642–658.

Dasgupta, N., & Greenwald, A. G. (2001). On the malleability of automatic attitudes: Combating automatic prejudice with images of admired and disliked individuals. *Journal of Personality and Social Psychology, 81,* 800–814.

D'Augelli, A. R., & Patterson, C. J. (Eds.). (1995). *Lesbian, gay, and bisexual identities over the lifespan.* New York: Oxford University Press.

Davidson, R. J., Putnam, K. M., & Larson, C. L. (2000). Dysfunction in the neural circuitry of emotion regulation: A possible prelude to violence. *Science, 289,* 591–594.

Davis, C. G., Lehman, D. R., Wortman, C. B., Silver, R. C., & Thompson, S. C. (1995). The undoing of traumatic life events. *Personality and Social Psychology Bulletin, 21,* 109–124.

Davis, D. (1982). Determinants of responsiveness in dyadic interaction. In W. Ickes & E. S. Knowles (Eds.), *Personality, roles, and social behavior* (pp. 85–139). New York: Springer-Verlag.

Davis, J. H., Kerr, N. L., Atkin, R. S., Holt, R., & Meek, D. (1975). The decision processes of 6- and 12-person mock juries assigned unanimous and two-thirds majority rules. *Journal of Personality and Social Psychology, 32,* 1–14.

Davis, M. H. (1983). Measuring individual differences in empathy: Evidence for a multidimensional approach. *Journal of Personality and Social Psychology, 44,* 113–126.

Davis, M. H. (1996). *Empathy: A social psychological approach.* Boulder, CO: Westview.

Davis, M. H., Hall, J. A., & Meyer, M. (2003). The first year: Influences on the satisfaction, involvement, and persistence of new community volunteers. *Personality and Social Psychology Bulletin, 29,* 248–260.

Davis, M. H., & Kraus, L. A. (1997). Personality and empathic accuracy. In W. Ickes (Ed.), *Empathic accuracy.* New York: Guilford.

Dawes, R. (1989). Statistical criteria for establishing a truly false consensus effect. *Journal of Experimental Social Psychology, 25,* 1–17.

Dawes, R. M., McTavish, J., & Shaklee, H. (1977). Behavior, communication, and assumptions about other people's behavior in a commons dilemma situation. *Journal of Personality and Social Psychology, 35,* 1–11.

Dawkins, R. (1976). *The selfish gene.* New York: Oxford University Press.

De Cremer, D., & van Dijk, E. (2002). Reactions to group success and failure as a function of identification level: A test of the goal-transformation hypothesis in social dilemmas. *Journal of Experimental Social Psychology, 38,* 435–442.

De Dreu, C. K. W., Weingart, L. R., & Kwon, S. (2000). Influence of social motives on integrative orientation: A meta-analytic review and test of two theories. *Journal of Personality and Social Psychology, 78,* 889–905.

De Houwer, J., Thomas, S., & Baeyens, F. (2001). Associative learning of likes and dislikes: A review of 25 years of research on human evaluative conditioning. *Psychological Bulletin, 127,* 853–869.

de Rivera, J. (1997). Estimating the number of false memory syndrome cases. *American Psychologist, 52,* 996–997.

Deary, I. J., Whiteman, M. C., Starr, J. M., Whalley, L. J., & Fox, H. C. (2004). The impact of childhood intelligence on later life: Following up the Scottish mental surveys of 1932 and 1947. *Journal of Personality and Social Psychology, 86,* 130–147.

Deaux, K., & LaFrance, M. (1998). Gender. In D. T. Gilbert, S. T. Fiske, & G. Lindzey (Eds.), *The handbook of social psychology* (4th ed., Vol. 1, pp. 788–827). New York: McGraw-Hill.

DeBono, K. G., & Packer, M. (1991). The effects of advertising strategy on perceptions of product quality. *Personality and Social Psychology Bulletin, 17,* 194–200.

Deci, E. L., & Flaste, R. (1995). *Why we do what we do: The dynamics of personal autonomy.* New York: Putnam.

Deci, E. L., & Ryan, R. M. (1985). *Intrinsic motivation and self-determination in human behavior.* New York: Plenum.

Deci, E. L., & Ryan, R. M. (2002). The paradox of achievement: The harder you push, the worse it gets. In J. Aronson (Ed.), *Improving academic achievement: Impact of psychological factors on education* (pp. 61–87). New York: Academic Press.

Deffenbacher, J. L., Filetti, L. B., Richards, T. L., Lynch, R. S., & Oetting, E. R. (2003). Characteristics of two groups of angry drivers. *Journal of Counseling Psychology, 50*, 123–132.

Deffenbacher, J. L., Huff, M. E., Lynch, R. S., Oetting, E. R., & Salvatore, N. F. (2000). Characteristics and treatment of high-anger drivers. *Journal of Counseling Psychology, 47*, 5–17.

Deffenbacher, J. L., Lynch, R. S., Oetting, E. R., & Kemper, C. C. (1996). Anger reduction in early adolescents. *Journal of Counseling Psychology, 43*, 149–157.

Deffenbacher, J. L., Oetting, E. R., Huff, M. E., & Thwaites, G. A. (1995). Fifteen-month follow-up of social skills and cognitive-relaxation approaches to general anger reduction. *Journal of Counseling Psychology, 42*, 400–405.

Deffenbacher, J. L., Thwaites, G. A., Wallace, T. L., & Oetting, E. R. (1994). Social skills and cognitive-relaxation approaches to general anger reduction. *Journal of Counseling Psychology, 41*, 386–396.

DePaulo, B. M., & Friedman, H. S. (1998). Nonverbal communication. In D. Gilbert, S. T. Fiske, & G. Lindzey (Eds.), *The handbook of social psychology* (4th ed., Vol. 2 pp. 3–40). New York: McGraw-Hill.

DePaulo, B. M., Lindsay, J. J., Malone, B. E., Muhlenbruck, L., Charlton, K., & Cooper, H. (2003). Cues to deception. *Psychological Bulletin, 129*, 74–118.

Derlega, V. J., Metts, S., Petronio, S., & Margulis, S. T. (1993). *Self-disclosure.* Newbury Park, CA: Sage.

Derlega, V. J., & Winstead, B. A. (1986). *Friendship and social interaction.* New York: Springer-Verlag.

Desforges, D. M., Lord, C. G., Ramsey, S. L., Mason, J. A., Van Leeuwen, M. D., West, S. C., & Lepper, M. R. (1991). Effects of structured cooperative contact on changing negative attitudes toward stigmatized social groups. *Journal of Personality and Social Psychology, 60*, 531–544.

DeSteno, D., Dasgupta, N., Bartlett, M. Y., & Cajdric, A. (2004). Prejudice from thin air: The effect of emotion on automatic intergroup attitudes. *Psychological Science, 15*, 319–324.

DeSteno, D., Petty, R. E., Rucker, D.D., Wegener, D. T., & Braverman, J. (2004). Discrete emotions and persuasion: The role of emotion-induced expectancies. *Journal of Personality and Social Psychology, 86*, 43–56.

Deutsch, M. (1973). *The resolution of conflict.* New Haven, CT: Yale University Press.

Deutsch, M., & Coleman, P. T. (Eds.). (2000). *The handbook of conflict resolution.* San Francisco: Jossey-Bass.

Deutsch, M., & Gerard, H. B. (1955). A study of normative and informational social influences upon individual judgment. *Journal of Abnormal and Social Psychology, 51*, 629–636.

Deutsch, M., & Krauss, R. M. (1960). The effect of threat upon interpersonal bargaining. *Journal of Abnormal and Social Psychology, 61*, 181–189.

Deutsch, M., & Krauss, R. M. (1962). Studies of interpersonal bargaining. *Journal of Conflict Resolution, 6*, 52–76.

Devine, P. G., (1989). Stereotypes and prejudice: Their automatic and controlled components. *Journal of Personality and Social Psychology, 56*, 5–18.

Dickerson, C., Thibodeau, R., Aronson, E., & Miller, D. (1992). Using cognitive dissonance to encourage water conservation. *Journal of Applied Social Psychology, 22*, 841–854.

Diekman, A. B., & Eagly, A. H. (2000). Stereotypes as dynamic constructs: Women and men of the past, present, and future. *Personality and Social Psychology Bulletin, 26*, 1171–1188.

Diekman, A. B., Eagly, A. H., & Kulesa, P. (2002). Accuracy and bias in stereotypes about the social and political attitudes of women and men. *Journal of Experimental Social Psychology, 38*, 268–282.

Diener, E., Fraser, S. C., Beaman, A. L., & Kelem, R. T. (1976). Effects of deindividuation variables on stealing among Halloween trick-or-treaters. *Journal of Personality and Social Psychology, 33*, 178–183.

Dion, K., Berscheid, E., & Walster, E. (1972). What is beautiful is good. *Journal of Personality and Social Psychology, 24*, 285–290.

Dion, K. L., & Kawakami, K. (1996). Ethnicity and perceived discrimination in Toronto: Another perspective on the personal/group discrimination discrepancy. *Canadian Journal of Behavioural Science, 28*, 203–213.

Dodge, K. A. (1983). Behavioral antecedents of peer social status. *Child Development, 54*, 1386–1399.

Dolinski, D. (2000). On inferring one's beliefs from one's attempt and consequences for subsequent compliance. *Journal of Personality and Social Psychology, 78*, 260–272.

Dolinski, D., Nawrat, M., & Rudak, I. (2001). Dialogue involvement as a social influence technique. *Personality and Social Psychology Bulletin, 27*, 1395–1406.

Doll, J., & Ajzen, I. (1992). Accessibility and stability of predictors in the theory of planned behavior. *Journal of Personality and Social Psychology, 63*, 754–765.

Doll, J., & Orth, B. (1993). The Fishbein and Ajzen theory of reasoned action applied to contraceptive behavior: Model variants and meaningfulness. *Journal of Applied Social Psychology, 23*, 395–415.

Dollard, J., Miller, N. E., Doob, L. W., Mowrer, O. H., & Sears, R. R. (1939). *Frustration and aggression.* New Haven, CT: Yale University Press.

Donnerstein, E. (1980). Aggressive erotica and violence against women. *Journal of Personality and Social Psychology, 39*, 269–277.

Doob, A. N., & Wood, L. E. (1972). Catharsis and aggression: Effects of annoyance and retaliation on aggressive behavior. *Journal of Personality and Social Psychology, 22*, 156–162.

Dooley, D. (2001). *Social research methods* (4th ed.). Upper Saddle River, NJ: Prentice-Hall.

Dovidio, J. F., & Gaertner, S. L. (1998). On the nature of contemporary prejudice: The causes, consequences, and challenges of aversive racism. In J. Eberhardt & S. T. Fiske (Eds.), *Confronting racism: The problem and the response* (pp. 3–32). Newbury Park, CA: Sage.

Dovidio, J. F., & Gaertner, S. L. (2000). Aversive racism and selection decisions: 1989 and 1999. *Psychological Science, 11*, 315–319.

Dovidio, J. F., Kawakami, K., & Gaertner, S. L. (2002). Implicit and explicit prejudice and interracial interaction. *Journal of Personality and Social Psychology, 82*, 62–68.

Dovidio, J., Kawakami, K., Johnson, C., Johnson, B., & Howard, A. (1997). On the nature of prejudice: Automatic and controlled processes. *Journal of Experimental Social Psychology, 33*, 510–540.

Dovidio, J. F., ten Vergert, M., Stewart, T. L., Gaertner, S. L., Johnson, J. D., Esses, V. M., Riek, B. M., & Pearson, A. R. (2004). Perspective and prejudice: Antecedents and mediating mechanisms. *Personality and Social Psychology Bulletin, 30*, 1537–1549.

Downes, B. T. (1968). Social and political characteristics of riot cities: A comparative study. *Social Science Quarterly, 49*, 504–520.

Downey, G., Freitas, A. L., Michaelis, B., & Khouri, H. (1998). The self-fulfilling prophecy in close relationships: Rejection sensitivity and rejection by romantic partners. *Journal of Personality and Social Psychology, 75*, 545–560.

Drachman, D., DeCarufel, A., & Insko, C. A. (1978). The extra credit effect in interpersonal attraction. *Journal of Experimental Social Psychology, 14*, 458–465.

Drigotas, S. M., & Rusbult, C. E. (1992). Should I stay or should I go? A dependence model of breakups. *Journal of Personality and Social Psychology, 62*, 62–87.

Duck, J. M., Hogg, M. A., & Terry, D. J. (1998). Perceived self-other differences in persuasibility: The effects of interpersonal and group-based similarity. *European Journal of Social Psychology, 28*, 1–21.

Duff, S. J., & Hampson, E. (2000). A beneficial effect of estrogen on working memory in post-menopausal women taking hormone replacement therapy. *Hormones and Behavior, 38*, 262–276.

Duff, S. J., & Hampson, E. (2001). A sex difference on a novel spatial working memory task in humans. *Brain and Cognition, 47,* 470–493.

Duncan, B. L. (1976). Differential social perception and attribution of intergroup violence: Testing the lower limits of stereotyping of Blacks. *Journal of Personality and Social Psychology, 34,* 590–598.

Duncan, C. P., & Nelson, J. E. (1985). Effects of humor in a radio advertising experiment. *Journal of Advertising, 14*(2), 33–40.

Dunning, D. (1993). Words to live by: The self and definitions of social concepts and categories. In J. M. Suls (Ed.), *Psychological perspectives on the self* (Vol. 4, pp. 99–126). Hillsdale, NJ: Erlbaum.

Dunning, D., & Cohen, G. L. (1992). Egocentric definitions of traits and abilities in social judgment. *Journal of Personality and Social Psychology, 63,* 341–355.

Dunning, D., Meyerowitz, J. A., & Holzberg, A. (1989). Ambiguity and self-evaluation: The role of idiosyncratic trait definitions in self-serving assessments of ability. *Journal of Personality and Social Psychology, 57,* 1082–1090.

Dunning, D., Perie, M., & Story, A. L. (1991). Self-serving prototypes of social categories. *Journal of Personality and Social Psychology, 61,* 957–968.

Dunning, D., & Perretta, S. (2002). Automaticity and eyewitness accuracy: A 10- to 12-second rule for distinguishing accurate from inaccurate positive identifications. *Journal of Applied Psychology, 87,* 951–962.

Dweck, C. S. (1986). Motivational processes affecting learning. *American Psychologist, 41,* 1040–1048.

Dweck, C. S., Goetz, T. E., & Strauss, N. L. (1980). Sex differences in learned helplessness: IV. An experimental and naturalistic study of failure. *Journal of Personality and Social Psychology, 38,* 441–452.

Dweck, C. S. & Leggett, E. L. (1988). A social-cognitive approach to motivation and personality. *Psychological Review, 95,* 256–273.

Eagly, A. H. (1978). Sex differences in influenceability. *Psychological Bulletin, 85,* 86–116.

Eagly, A. H. (1987). *Sex differences in social behavior: A social-role interpretation.* Hillsdale, NJ: Erlbaum.

Eagly, A. H. (1995). The science and politics of comparing women and men. *American Psychologist, 50,* 145–158.

Eagly, A. H., Ashmore, R. D., Makhijani, M. G., & Longo, L. C. (1991). What is beautiful is good, but . . .: A meta-analytic review of research on the physical attractiveness stereotype. *Psychological Bulletin, 110,* 109–128.

Eagly, A. H., & Carli, L. L. (1981). Sex of researchers and sex-typed communications as determinants of sex differences in influenceability: A meta-analysis of social influence studies. *Psychological Bulletin, 90,* 1–20.

Eagly, A. H., & Chaiken, S. (1984). Cognitive theories of persuasion. In L. Berkowitz (Ed.), *Advances in experimental social psychology* (Vol. 17, pp. 267–359). New York: Academic Press.

Eagly, A. H., & Chaiken, S. (1993). *The psychology of attitudes.* Fort Worth, TX: Harcourt Brace Jovanovich.

Eagly, A. H., & Chaiken, S. (1998). Attitude structure and function. In D. Gilbert, S. Fiske, & G. Lindzey (Eds.), *The handbook of social psychology* (4th ed., Vol. 1, pp. 269–322). New York: McGraw-Hill.

Eagly, A. H., Chen, S., Chaiken, S., & Shaw-Barnes, K. (1999). The impact of attitudes on memory: An affair to remember. *Psychological Bulletin, 125,* 64–89.

Eagly, A. H., & Chrvala, C. (1986). Sex differences in conformity: Status and gender role interpretations. *Psychology of Women Quarterly, 10,* 203–220.

Eagly, A. H., & Johnson, B. T. (1990). Gender and leadership style: A meta-analysis. *Psychological Bulletin, 108,* 233–256.

Eagly, A. H., & Karau, S. J. (1991). Gender and the emergence of leaders: A meta-analysis. *Journal of Personality and Social Psychology, 60,* 685–710.

Eagly, A. H., & Karau, S. J. (2002). Role congruity theory of prejudice toward female leaders. *Psychological Review, 109,* 573–598.

Eagly, A. H., Karau, S. J., & Makhijani, M. G. (1995). Gender and the effectiveness of leaders: A meta-analysis. *Psychological Bulletin, 117,* 125–145.

Eagly, A. H., Makhijani, M. G., & Klonsky, B. G. (1992). Gender and the evaluation of leaders: A meta-analysis. *Psychological Bulletin, 111,* 3–22.

Eagly, A. H., & Wood W. (1999). The origins of sex differences in human behavior. *American Psychologist, 54,* 408–423.

Eagly, A. H., Wood, W., & Fishbaugh, L. (1981). Sex differences in conformity: Surveillance by the group as a determinant of male nonconformity. *Journal of Personality and Social Psychology, 40,* 384–394.

Eargle, A., Guerra, N., & Tolan, P. (1994). Preventing aggression in inner-city children: Small group training to change cognitions, social skills, and behavior. *Journal of Child and Adolescent Group Therapy, 4,* 229–242.

Earley, P. C. (1989). Social loafing and collectivism: A comparison of the United States and the People's Republic of China. *Administrative Science Quarterly, 34,* 565–581.

Easterbrook, J. A. (1959). The effects of emotion on cue utilization and the organization of behavior. *Psychological Review, 66,* 183–201.

Eaves, L. J., Eysenck, H. J., & Martin, N. G. (1989). *Genes, culture, and personality: An empirical approach.* London, UK: Academic Press.

Ebbesen, E. B., Kjos, G. L., & Konecni, V. J. (1976). Spatial ecology: Its effects on the choice of friends and enemies. *Journal of Experimental Social Psychology, 12,* 505–518.

Eberhardt, J. L. (2005). Imaging race. *American Psychologist, 60,* 181–190.

Edwards, K., & Smith, E. E. (1996). A disconfirmation bias in the evaluation of arguments. *Journal of Personality and Social Psychology, 71,* 5–24.

Efran, M. G. (1974). The effect of physical appearance on the judgment of guilt, interpersonal attraction, and severity of recommended punishment in a simulated jury task. *Journal of Research in Personality, 8,* 45–54.

Ehrensaft, M. K., Cohen, P., Brown, J., Smailes, E., Chen, H., & Johnson, J. G. (2003). Intergenerational transmission of partner violence: A 20-year prospective study. *Journal of Consulting and Clinical Psychology, 71,* 741–753.

Eisenberg, N., Cialdini, R. B., McCreath, H., & Shell, R. (1987). Consistency-based compliance: When and why do children become vulnerable? *Journal of Personality and Social Psychology, 52,* 1174–1181.

Eisenberg, N., Guthrie, I. K., Cumberland, A., Murphy, B. C., Shepard, S. A., Zhou, Q., & Carlo, G. (2002). Prosocial development in early adulthood: A longitudinal study. *Journal of Personality and Social Psychology, 82,* 993–1006.

Eisenberger, N. I., Lieberman, M. D., & Williams, K. D. (2003). Does rejection hurt? An fMRI study of social exclusion. *Science, 302,* 290–292.

Ekman, P., & Friesen, W. V. (1969a). Nonverbal leakage clues to deception. *Psychiatry, 32,* 88–106.

Ekman, P., & Friesen, W. V. (1969b). The repertoire of nonverbal behavior: Categories, origins, usage, and coding. *Semiotica, 1,* 49–98.

Ekman, P., Friesen, W. V., O'Sullivan, M., Chan, A., Diacoyanni-Tarlatzis, I., Heider, K., Krause, R., LeCompte, W. A., Pitcairn, T., Ricci-Bitti, P. E., Scherer, K., Tomita, M., & Tzavaras, A. (1987). Universals and cultural differences in the judgments of facial expressions of emotion. *Journal of Personality and Social Psychology, 53,* 712–717.

Ekman, P., & O'Sullivan, M. (1991). Who can catch a liar? *American Psychologist, 46*, 913–920.

Elfenbein, H. A., & Ambady, N. (2002). On the universality and cultural specificity of emotion recognition: A meta-analysis. *Psychological Bulletin, 128*, 203–235.

Elfenbein, H. A., & Ambady, N. (2003). Universals and cultural differences in recognizing emotions. *Current Directions in Psychological Science, 12*, 159–164.

Ellickson, P. L., & Bell, R. M. (1990). Drug prevention in junior high: A multisite longitudinal test. *Science, 247*, 1299–1305.

Ellickson, P. L., McCaffrey, D. F., Ghosh-Dastidar, B., & Longshore, D. L. (2003). New inroads in preventing adolescent drug use: Results from a large-scale trial of project ALERT in middle schools. *American Journal of Public Health, 93*, 1830–1836.

Ellis, S., Rogoff, B., & Cromer, C. C. (1981). Age segregation in children's social interactions. *Developmental Psychology, 17*, 399–407.

Epley, N., & Dunning, D. (2000). Feeling "holier than thou": Are self-serving assessments produced by errors in self- or social prediction? *Journal of Personality and Social Psychology, 79*, 861–875.

Esser, J. K. (1998). Alive and well after 25 years: A review of groupthink research. *Organizational Behavior and Human Decision Processes, 73*, 116–141.

Esses, V. M., & Dovidio, J. F. (2002). The role of emotions in determining willingness to engage in intergroup contact. *Personality and Social Psychology Bulletin, 28*, 1202–1214.

Esses, V. M., Dovidio, J. F., Jackson, L. M., & Armstrong, T. L. (2001). The immigration dilemma: The role of perceived group competition, ethnic prejudice, and national identity. *Journal of Social Issues, 57*, 389–412.

Esses, V. M., Haddock, G., & Zanna, M. P. (1994). The role of mood in the expression of intergroup stereotypes: In M. P. Zanna & J. M. Olson (Eds.) *The psychology of prejudice: The Ontario symposium* (pp. 77–101). Hillsdale, NJ: Erlbaum.

Esses, V. M., & Maio, G. R. (2002). Expanding the assessment of attitude components and structure: The benefits of open-ended measures. In W. Stroebe & M. Hewstone (Eds.), *European review of social psychology* (Vol. 12, pp. 71–102). Chichester, UK: Wiley.

Esses, V. M., & Webster, C. D. (1988). Physical attractiveness, dangerousness, and the Canadian Criminal Code. *Journal of Applied Social Psychology, 18*, 1017–1031.

Esses, V. M., & Zanna, M. P. (1995). Mood and the expression of ethnic stereotypes. *Journal of Personality and Social Psychology, 69*, 1052–1068.

Evans, R. (2001). Examining the informal sanctioning of deviance in a chat room culture. *Deviant Behavior, 22*, 195–210.

Fazio, R. H. (1990). Multiple processes by which attitudes guide behavior: The MODE model as an integrative framework. In M. P. Zanna (Ed.), *Advances in experimental social psychology* (Vol. 23, pp. 75–109). San Diego, CA: Academic Press.

Fazio, R. H. (2000). Accessible attitudes as tools for object appraisal: The costs and benefits. In G. R. Maio & J. M. Olson (Eds.), *Why we evaluate: Functions of attitudes* (pp. 1–36). Mahwah, NJ: Erlbaum.

Fazio, R. H., Jackson, J. R., Dunton, B. C., & Williams, C. J. (1995). Variability in automatic activation as an unobtrusive measure of racial attitudes: A bona fide pipeline? *Journal of Personality and Social Psychology, 69*, 1013–1027.

Fazio, R. H., & Williams. C. J. (1986). Attitude accessibility as a moderator of the attitude-perception and attitude-behavior relations: An investigation of the 1984 presidential election. *Journal of Personality and Social Psychology, 51*, 505–514.

Fazio, R. H., & Zanna, M. P. (1981). Direct experience and attitude-behavior consistency. In L. Berkowitz (Ed.), *Advances in experimental social psychology* (Vol. 14, pp. 161–202). San Diego, CA: Academic Press.

Fazio, R. H., Zanna, M. P., & Cooper, J. (1977). Dissonance and self-perception: An integrative view of each theory's proper domain of application. *Journal of Experimental Social Psychology, 13*, 464–479.

Feeney, B. C., & Collins, N. L. (2001). Predictors of caregiving in adult intimate relationships: An attachment theoretical perspective. *Journal of Personality and Social Psychology, 80*, 972–994.

Feeney, B. C., & Collins, N. L. (2003). Motivations for caregiving in adult intimate relationships: Influences on caregiving behavior and relationship functioning. *Personality and Social Psychology Bulletin, 29*, 950–968.

Fein, S., & Spencer, S. J. (1997). Prejudice as self-image maintenance: Affirming the self through derogating others. *Journal of Personality and Social Psychology, 73*, 31–44.

Feingold, A. (1992a). Gender differences in mate selection preferences: A test of the parental investment model. *Psychological Bulletin, 112*, 125–139.

Feingold, A. (1992b). Good-looking people are not what we think. *Psychological Bulletin, 111*, 304–341.

Feldman Barrett, L., & Barrett, D. J. (2001). An introduction to computerized experience sampling in psychology. *Social Science Computer Review, 19*, 175–185.

Ferraris, C., & Carveth, R. (2003). NASA and the *Columbia* disaster: Decision-making by groupthink? In L. Beamer & B. Shwom (Eds.), *Proceedings of the 68th annual convention of the Association for Business Communication* (pp. 1–13). Albuquerque, NM: Association for Business Communication.

Festinger, L. (1950). Informal social communication. *Psychological Review, 57*, 271–282.

Festinger, L. (1954). A theory of social comparison processes. *Human Relations, 7*, 117–140.

Festinger, L. (1957). *A theory of cognitive dissonance.* Stanford, CA: Stanford University Press.

Festinger, L., & Carlsmith, J. M. (1959). Cognitive consequences of forced compliance. *Journal of Abnormal and Social Psychology, 58*, 203–210.

Festinger, L., Pepitone, A., & Newcomb, T. (1952). Some consequences of de-individuation in a group. *Journal of Abnormal and Social Psychology, 47*, 382–389.

Festinger, L., Riecken, H. W., & Schachter, S. (1956). *When prophecy fails.* Minneapolis: University of Minnesota Press.

Festinger, L., Schachter, S., & Back, K. (1950). *Social pressures in informal groups: A study of human factors in housing.* New York: Harper & Row.

Fiedler, F. E. (1967). *A theory of leadership effectiveness.* New York: McGraw-Hill.

Fiedler, F. E. (1978). The contingency model and the dynamics of the leadership process. In L. Berkowitz (Ed.), *Advances in experimental social psychology* (Vol. 11, pp. 59–112). New York: Academic Press.

Fiedler, K., Nickel, S., Muehlfriedel, T., & Unkelbach, C. (2001). Is mood congruency an effect of genuine memory or response bias? *Journal of Experimental Social Psychology, 37*, 201–214.

Fincham, F. D., & Bradbury, T. N. (1993). Marital satisfaction, depression, and attributions: A longitudinal analysis. *Journal of Personality and Social Psychology, 64*, 442–452.

Finkelhor, D. (1997). The homicides of children and youth: A developmental perspective. In G. K. Kantor & J. L. Jasinski (Eds.), *Out of the darkness: Contemporary perspectives on family violence* (pp. 17–34). Thousand Oaks, CA: Sage.

Fischhoff, B. (1975). Hindsight≠Foresight: The effects of outcome knowledge on judgment under uncertainty. *Journal of Experimental Psychology: Human Perception and Performance, 3*, 288–299.

Fishbein, M., & Ajzen, I. (1975). *Belief, attitude, intention and behavior: An introduction to theory and research.* Reading, MA: Addison-Wesley.

Fisher, J. D., & Fisher, W. A. (1992). Changing AIDS risk behavior. *Psychological Bulletin, 111*, 455–474.

Fisher, J. D., Fisher, W. A., Misovich, S. J., Kimble, D. L., & Malloy, T. E. (1996). Changing AIDS risk behavior: Effects of an intervention emphasizing AIDS risk reduction information, motivation, and behavioral skills in a college student population. *Health Psychology, 15,* 238–250.

Fisher, J. D., Nadler, A., & Whitcher-Alagna, S. (1982). Recipient reactions to aid. *Psychological Bulletin, 91,* 27–54.

Fisher, W. A. (1986). A psychological approach to human sexuality: The Sexual Behavior Sequence. In D. Byrne & K. Kelley (Eds.), *Alternative approaches to the study of sexual behavior* (pp. 113–172). Hillsdale, NJ: Erlbaum.

Fisher, W. A., & Barak, A. (2001). Internet pornography: A social psychological perspective on Internet sexuality. *Journal of Sex Research, 38,* 312–323.

Fisher, W. A., Fisher, J. D., & Rye, B. J. (1995). Understanding and promoting AIDS-preventive behavior: Insights from the theory of reasoned action. *Health Psychology, 14,* 255–264.

Fisher, W. A., & Grenier, G. (1994). Violent pornography, antiwoman thoughts, and antiwoman acts: In search of reliable effects. *Journal of Sex Research, 31,* 23–38.

Fiske, A. P., Haslam, N., & Fiske, S. T. (1991). Confusing one person with another: What errors reveal about the elementary forms of social relations. *Journal of Personality and Social Psychology, 60,* 656–674.

Fiske, A. P., Kitayama, S., Markus, H. R., & Nisbett, R. E. (1998). The cultural matrix of social psychology. In D. T. Gilbert, S. T. Fiske, & G. Lindzey (Eds.), *The handbook of social psychology* (4th ed., Vol. 2, pp. 915–981). Boston, MA: McGraw-Hill.

Fiske, S. T. (1998). Stereotyping, prejudice, and discrimination. In D. T. Gilbert, S. T. Fiske, & G. Lindzey (Eds.), *The handbook of social psychology* (4th ed., Vol. 2, pp. 357–411). Boston, MA: McGraw-Hill.

Fiske, S. T. (2002). What we know now about bias and intergroup conflict, the problem of the century. *Current Directions in Psychological Science, 11,* 123–128.

Fiske, S. T. (2004). Mind the gap: In praise of informal sources of formal theory. *Personality and Social Psychology Review, 8,* 132–137.

Fiske, S. T., Cuddy, A. J. C., Glick, P., & Xu, J. (2002). A model of (often mixed) stereotype content: Competence and warmth respectively follow from perceived status and competition. *Journal of Personality and Social Psychology, 82,* 878–902.

Fiske, S. T., & Taylor, S. E. (1991). *Social cognition* (2nd ed.). New York: McGraw-Hill.

Flowers, M. L. (1977). A laboratory test of some implications of Janis' groupthink hypothesis. *Journal of Personality and Social Psychology, 35,* 888–896.

Foels, R., Driskell, J. E., Mullen, B., & Salas, E. (2000). The effects of democratic leadership on group member satisfaction: An integration. *Small Groups Research, 31,* 676–701.

Ford, T. E., Ferguson, M. A., Brooks, J. L., & Hagadone, K. M. (2004). Coping sense of humor reduces effects of stereotype threat on women's math performance. *Personality and Social Psychology Bulletin, 30,* 643–653.

Forgas, J. P. (1992). Affect and social perception: Research evidence and an integrative theory. In W. Stroebe & M. Hewstone (Eds.), *European review of social psychology* (Vol. 3, pp. 183–223). Chichester, England: Wiley.

Forgas, J. P., & Bond, M. H. (1985). Cultural influences on the perception of interaction episodes. *Personality and Social Psychology Bulletin, 11,* 75–88.

Forgas, J. P., Levinger, G., & Moylan, S. J. (1994). Feeling good and feeling close: Affective influences on the perception of intimate relationships. *Personal Relationships, 1,* 165–184.

Forsterling, F. (2001). *Attribution: An introduction to theories, research, and applications.* Philadelphia, PA: Taylor and Francis Group.

Forsyth, D. R. (1999). *Group dynamics* (3rd ed.). Pacific Grove, CA: Brooks/Cole.

Frank, M. G., & Ekman, P. (2004). Appearing truthful generalizes across different deception situations. *Journal of Personality and Social Psychology, 86,* 486–495.

Frazier, P. A., Tix, A. P., & Barnett, C. L. (2003). The relational context of social support: Relationship satisfaction moderates the relations between enacted support and distress. *Personality and Social Psychology Bulletin, 29,* 1133–1146.

Freedman, J. L., & Fraser, S. C. (1966). Compliance without pressure: The foot-in-the-door technique. *Journal of Personality and Social Psychology, 4,* 195–202.

Frey, D. (1986). Recent research on selective exposure to information. In L. Berkowitz (Ed.), *Advances in experimental social psychology* (Vol. 19, pp. 41–80). San Diego, CA: Academic Press.

Fricker, J., & Moore, S. (2002). Relationship satisfaction: The role of love styles and attachment styles. *Current Research in Social Psychology, 7*(11), 182–204.

Friedman, H. S. (Ed.). (1992). *Hostility, coping and health.* Washington, DC: American Psychological Association.

Friedman, H. S., & Schustack, M. W. (2003). *Personality: Classic theories and modern research.* Boston, MA: Allyn & Bacon.

Friedman, H. S., & Silver, R. C. (Eds.). (2005). *The Oxford handbook of health psychology.* New York: Oxford University Press.

Friedman, M., & Rosenman, R. H. (1974). *Type A behavior and your heart.* New York: Knopf.

Frith, U., & Frith, C. (2001). The biological basis of social interaction. *Current Directions in Psychological Science, 10,* 151–155.

Fu, G., Lee, K., Cameron, C. A., & Xu, F. (2001). Chinese and Canadian adults' categorization and evaluation of lie- and truth-telling about prosocial and antisocial behaviors. *Journal of Cross-Cultural Psychology, 32,* 720–727.

Gaertner, S. L., & Dovidio, J. F. (1986). The aversive form of racism. In J. F. Dovidio & S. L. Gaertner (Eds.), *Prejudice, discrimination, and racism* (pp. 61–89). Orlando, FL: Academic Press.

Gaertner, S. L., Dovidio, J. F., Anastasio, P. A., Bachman, B. A., & Rust, M. C. (1993). The common ingroup identity model: Recategorization and the reduction of intergroup bias. In W. Stroebe & M. Hewstone (Eds.), *European review of social psychology* (Vol. 4, pp. 1–26). New York: Wiley.

Galanter, H. (1989). *Cults: Faith, healing, and coercion.* New York: Oxford University Press.

Galen, B. R., & Underwood, M. K. (1997). A developmental investigation of social aggression among children. *Developmental Psychology, 33,* 589–600.

Galinsky, A. D., & Moskowitz, G. B. (2000). Perspective-taking: Decreasing stereotype expression, stereotype accessibility, and in-group favoritism. *Journal of Personality and Social Psychology, 78,* 708–724.

Gambaro, S., & Rabin, A. I. (1969). Diastolic blood pressure responses following direct and displaced aggression after anger arousal in high- and low-guilt subjects. *Journal of Personality and Social Psychology, 12,* 87–94.

Gangestad, S. W., & Simpson, J. A. (2000). The evolution of human mating: Trade-offs and strategic pluralism. *Behavioral and Brain Sciences, 23,* 573–587.

Gantner, A. B., & Taylor, S. P. (1992). Human physical aggression as a function of alcohol and threat of harm. *Aggressive Behavior, 18,* 29–36.

Garcia, S. M., Weaver, K., Moskowitz, G. B., & Darley, J. M. (2002). Crowded minds: The implicit bystander effect. *Journal of Personality and Social Psychology, 83,* 843–853.

Gardner, R. C. (1994). Stereotypes as consensual beliefs. In M. P. Zanna & J. M. Olson (Eds.), *The psychology of prejudice: The Ontario symposium* (pp. 1–31). Hillsdale, NJ: Erlbaum.

Gardner, W. L., Gabriel, S., & Hochschild, L. (2002). When you and I are "we," you are not threatening: The role of self-expansion in social comparison. *Journal of Personality and Social Psychology, 82,* 239–251.

Gardner, W. L., Gabriel, S., & Yee, A. Y. (1999). "I" value freedom, but "we" value relationships: Self-construal priming mirrors cultural differences in judgment. *Psychological Science, 10,* 321–326.

Garfein, R. (1997, May/June). An interesting career in psychology: International market research consultant. *Psychological Science Agenda, 10*(3), 7.

Gawronski, B., & Strack, F. (2004). On the propositional nature of cognitive consistency: Dissonance changes explicit, but not implicit attitudes. *Journal of Experimental Social Psychology, 40,* 535–542.

Geary, D. C. (1999). *Male, female: The evolution of human sex differences.* Washington, DC: American Psychological Association.

Geen, R. G. (1968). Effects of frustration, attack, and prior training in aggressiveness upon aggressive behavior. *Journal of Personality and Social Psychology, 9,* 316–321.

Geen, R. G. (1998). Aggression and antisocial behavior. In D. T. Gilbert, S. T. Fiske, & G. Lindzey (Eds.), *The handbook of social psychology* (4th ed., Vol. 2, pp. 317–356). Boston, MA: McGraw-Hill.

Geen, R. G., & Gange, J. J. (1977). Drive theory of social facilitation: Twelve years of theory and research. *Psychological Bulletin, 84,* 1267–1288.

Gelfand, M. J., Higgins, M., Nishii, L. H., Raver, J. L., Dominguez, A., Murakami, F., Yamaguchi, S., & Toyama, M. (2002). Culture and egocentric perceptions of fairness in conflict and negotiation. *Journal of Applied Psychology, 87,* 833–845.

George, C., Kaplan, N., & Main, M. (1985). *The adult attachment interview.* Unpublished manuscript, University of California, Berkeley.

Gerard, H. B., Wilhelmy, R. A., & Conolley, E. S. (1968). Conformity and group size. *Journal of Personality and Social Psychology, 8,* 79–82.

Gergen, K. J., Gergen, M. M., & Barton, W. H. (1973). Deviance in the dark. *Psychology Today, 7,* 129–130.

Gershoff, E. T. (2002). Corporal punishment by parents and associated child behaviors and experiences: A meta-analytic and theoretical review. *Psychological Bulletin, 128,* 539–579.

Gibbons, F. X., & Buunk, B. P. (1999). Individual differences in social comparisons: Development of a scale of social comparison orientation. *Journal of Personality and Social Psychology, 76,* 129–142.

Gibbons, F. X., Gerrard, M., Cleveland, M. J., Wills, T. A., & Brody, G. (2004). Perceived discrimination and substance use in African American parents and their children: A panel study. *Journal of Personality and Social Psychology, 86,* 517–529.

Gigone, D., & Hastie, R. (1997). Proper analysis of the accuracy of group judgments. *Psychological Bulletin, 121,* 149–167.

Gilbert, D. T. (1989). Thinking lightly about others: Automatic components of the social inference process. In J. A. Bargh &J. S. Uleman (Eds.), *Unintended thought* (pp. 189–211). New York: Guilford.

Gilbert, D. T., & Hixon, J. G. (1991). The trouble of thinking: Activation and application of stereotypic beliefs. *Journal of Personality and Social Psychology, 60,* 509–517.

Gilbert, D. T., & Malone, P. S. (1995). The correspondence bias. *Psychological Bulletin, 117,* 21–38.

Gilbert, D. T., Pelham, B. W., & Krull, D. S. (1988). On cognitive busyness: When person perceivers meet persons perceived. *Journal of Personality and Social Psychology, 54,* 733–740.

Gilovich, T. (1991). *How we know what isn't so: The fallibility of human reason in everyday life.* New York: Macmillan.

Gilovich, T., Griffin, D, & Kahneman, D. (Eds.). (2002). *Heuristics and biases: The psychology of intuitive judgment.* New York: Cambridge University Press.

Gilovich, T., Vallone, R., & Tversky, A. (1985). The hot hand in basketball: On the mis-perception of random sequences. *Cognitive Psychology, 17,* 295–314.

Giner-Sorolla, R., & Chaiken, S. (1994). The causes of hostile media judgments. *Journal of Experimental Social Psychology, 30,* 165–180.

Glass, D. C. (1977). *Behavioral patterns, stress, and coronary disease.* Hillsdale, NJ: Erlbaum.

Gleason, M. E. J., Iida, M., Bolger, N., & Shrout, P. E. (2003). Daily supportive equity in close relationships. *Personality and Social Psychology Bulletin, 29,* 1036–1045.

Gleicher, F., & Petty, R. E. (1992). Expectations of reassurance influence the nature of fear-stimulated attitude change. *Journal of Experimental Social Psychology, 28,* 86–100.

Glick, P., DeMorest, J. A., & Hotze, C. A. (1988). Self-monitoring and beliefs about partner compatibility in romantic relationships. *Personality and Social Psychology Bulletin, 14,* 485–494.

Glick, P., & Fiske, S. T. (1996). The ambivalent sexism inventory: Differentiating hostile and benevolent sexism. *Journal of Personality and Social Psychology, 70,* 491–512.

Glick, P., Fiske, S. T., Mladinic, A., Saiz, J. L., Abrams, D., Masser, B., et al. (2000). Beyond prejudice as simple antipathy: Hostile and benevolent sexism across cultures. *Journal of Personality and Social Psychology, 79,* 763–775.

Glick, P., Lameiras, M., Fiske, S. T., Eckes, T., Masser, B., Volpato, C., et al. (2004). Bad but bold: Ambivalent attitudes toward men predict gender inequality in 16 nations. *Journal of Personality and Social Psychology, 86,* 713–728.

Goethals, G. R. (1986a). Fabricating and ignoring social reality: Self-serving estimates of consensus. In J. M. Olson, C. P. Herman, & M. P. Zanna (Eds.), *Relative deprivation and social comparison: The Ontario symposium* (Vol. 4, pp. 135–157). Hillsdale, NJ: Lawrence-Erlbaum.

Goethals, G. R. (1986b). Social comparison theory: Psychology from the lost and found. *Personality and Social Psychology Bulletin, 12,* 261–278.

Goethals, G. R., & Darley, J. M. (1977). Social comparison theory: An attributional approach. In J. M. Suls & R. L. Miller (Eds.), *Social comparison processes: Theoretical and empirical perspectives* (pp. 259–278). Washington, DC: Hemisphere.

Goethals, G. R., & Klein, W. M. P. (2000). Interpreting and inventing social reality: Attributional and constructive elements in social comparison. In J. M. Suls & L. Wheeler (Eds.), *Handbook of social comparison: Theory and research* (pp. 23–44). New York: Kluwer Academic/Plenum.

Goethals, G. R., Messick, D. M., & Allison, S. T. (1991). The uniqueness bias: Studies of constructive social comparison. In J. M. Suls & T. A. Wills (Eds.), *Social comparison research: Contemporary theory and research* (pp. 149–176). Hillsdale, NJ: Erlbaum.

Goldstein, D. G., & Gigerenzer, G. (2002). Models of ecological rationality: The recognition heuristic. *Psychological Review, 109,* 75–90.

Gorassini, D. R., & Olson, J. M. (1995). Does self-perception change explain the foot-in-the-door effect? *Journal of Personality and Social Psychology, 69,* 91–105.

Gosling, S. D., Rentfrow, P. J., & Swann, W. B., Jr. (2003). A very brief measure of the Big-Five personality domains. *Journal of Research in Personality, 37,* 504–528.

Gottfredson, L. S., & Deary, I. J. (2004). Intelligence predicts health and longevity, but why? *Current Directions in Psychological Science, 13,* 1–4.

Gottman, J. M. (1983). How children become friends. With commentary by William G. Graziano. *Monographs of the Society for Research in Child Development, 38*(2, Serial No. 201).

Gouldner, A. W. (1960). The norm of reciprocity: A preliminary statement. *American Sociological Review, 25,* 161–178.

Govan, C. L., & Williams, K. D. (2004). Changing the affective valence of the stimulus items influences the IAT by re-defining the category labels. *Journal of Experimental Social Psychology, 40,* 357–365.

Graham, K. (1980). Theories of intoxicated aggression. *Canadian Journal of the Behavioral Sciences, 12,* 141–158.

Graham, T., & Ickes, W. (1997). When women's intuition isn't greater than men's. In W. Ickes (Ed.), *Empathic accuracy* (pp. 169–193). New York, NY: Guilford.

Graziano, W. G., Brothen, T., & Berscheid, E. (1978). Height and attraction: Do men and women see eye-to-eye? *Journal of Personality, 46,* 128–145.

Greenberg, J., Pyszczynski, T., Solomon, S., Rosenblatt, A., Veeder, M., Kirkland, S., & Lyon, D. (1990). Evidence for terror management theory II: The effects of mortality salience on reactions to those who threaten or bolster the cultural worldview. *Journal of Personality and Social Psychology, 58,* 308–318.

Greenberg, J., Pyszczynski, T., Solomon, S., Simon, L., & Breus, M. (1994). Role of consciousness and accessibility of death-related thoughts in mortality salience effects. *Journal of Personality and Social Psychology, 67,* 627–637.

Greenberg, J., Solomon, S., & Pyszczynski, T. (1997). Terror management theory of self-esteem and cultural worldviews: Empirical assessments and conceptual refinements. In M. P. Zanna (Ed.), *Advances in experimental social psychology* (Vol. 29, pp. 61–139). San Diego, CA: Academic Press.

Greenberg, M. S., & Shapiro, S. P. (1971). Indebtedness: An adverse aspect of asking for and receiving help. *Sociometry, 34,* 290–301.

Greenwald, A. G. (1968). Cognitive learning, cognitive response to persuasion, and attitude change. In A. G. Greenwald, T. C. Brock, & T. M. Ostrom (Eds.), *Psychological foundations of attitudes* (pp. 147–170). New York: Academic Press.

Greenwald, A. G., & Banaji, M. R. (1995). Implicit social cognition: Attitudes, self-esteem, and stereotypes. *Psychological Review, 102,* 4–27.

Greenwald, A. G., Banaji, M. R., Rudman, L. A., Farnham, S. D., Nosek, B. A., & Mellott, D. S. (2002). A unified theory of implicit attitudes, stereotypes, self-esteem, and self-concept. *Psychological Review, 109,* 3–25.

Greenwald, A. G., Carnot, C. G., Beach, R., & Young, B. (1987). Increasing voting behavior by asking people if they expect to vote. *Journal of Applied Psychology, 72,* 315–318.

Greenwald, A. G., McGhee, D. E., & Schwartz, J. L. K. (1998). Measuring individual differences in implicit cognition: The implicit association test. *Journal of Personality and Social Psychology, 74,* 1464–1480.

Greenwald, A. G., Oakes, M. A., & Hoffman, H. G. (2003). Targets of discrimination: Effects of race on responses to weapon holders. *Journal of Experimental Social Psychology, 39,* 399–405.

Griffin, E. (1997). *A first look at communication theory* (3rd ed.). New York: McGraw-Hill.

Griffiths, M. (1999). Violent video games and aggression: A review of the literature. *Aggression and Violent Behavior, 4,* 203–212.

Grotpeter, J. K., & Crick, N. R. (1996). Relational aggression, overt aggression, and friendship. *Child Development, 67,* 2328–2338.

Grube, J. A., & Piliavin, J. A. (2000). Role identity, organizational experiences, and volunteer performance. *Personality and Social Psychology Bulletin, 26,* 1108–1119.

Grusec, J. (1991). The socialization of altruism. In M. S. Clark (Ed.), *Prosocial behavior* (pp. 9–33). Newbury Park, CA: Sage.

Gruter, M., & Masters, R. D. (1986). Ostracism as a social and biological phenomenon: An introduction. *Ethology and Sociobiology, 7,* 149–158.

Guadagno, R. E., Asher, T., Demaine, L. J., & Cialdini, R. B. (2001). When saying yes leads to saying no: Preference for consistency and the reverse foot-in-the-door effect. *Personality and Social Psychology Bulletin, 27,* 859–867.

Guéguen, N., & Jacob, C. (2001). Fund-raising on the web: The effect of an electronic foot-in-the-door on donation. *CyberPsychology & Behavior, 4,* 705–709.

Guglielmi, R. S. (1999). Psychophysiological assessment of prejudice: Past research, current status, and future directions. *Personality and Social Psychology Review, 3,* 123–157.

Haddock, G., Rothman, A. J., Reber, R., & Schwarz, N. (1999). Forming judgments of attitude certainty, intensity, and importance: The role of subjective experiences. *Personality and Social Psychology Bulletin, 25,* 771–782.

Haddock, G., & Zanna, M. P. (1998). On the use of open-ended measures to assess attitudinal components. *British Journal of Social Psychology, 37,* 129–149.

Hafer, C. L. (2000). Do innocent victims threaten the belief in a just world? *Journal of Personality and Social Psychology, 79,* 165–173.

Hafer, C. L., & Bègue, L. (2005). Experimental research on just-world theory: Problems, developments, and future challenges. *Psychological Bulletin, 131,* 128–167.

Hafer, C. L., & Olson, J. M. (2003). An analysis of empirical research on the scope of justice. *Personality and Social Psychology Review, 7,* 311–323.

Hafer, C. L., Reynolds, K. L., & Obertynski, M. A. (1996). Message comprehensibility and persuasion: Effects of complex language in counterattitudinal appeals to laypeople. *Social Cognition, 14,* 317–337.

Hall, J. A. (1984). *Nonverbal sex differences: Communication accuracy and expressive style.* Baltimore: Johns Hopkins University Press.

Halladay, J., & Wolf, R. (2000, July 18). Indianapolis OKs restrictions on violent video game usage. *USA Today,* p. A5.

Hallman, W. K., Hebden, W. C., Aquino, H. L., Cuite, C. L., & Lang, J. T. (2003). *Public perceptions of genetically modified foods: A national study of American knowledge and opinion.* New Brunswick, NJ: Food Policy Institute, Cook College, The State University of New Jersey.

Halpern, D. F. (1992). *Sex differences in cognitive abilities* (2nd ed.). Hillsdale, NJ: Erlbaum.

Halpern, D. F. (2004). A cognitive-process taxonomy for sex differences in cognitive abilities. *Current Directions in Psychological Science, 13,* 135–139.

Hamilton, D. L., & Gifford, R. K. (1976). Illusory correlation in interpersonal perception: A cognitive basis of stereotypic judgments. *Journal of Experimental Social Psychology, 12,* 392–407.

Hamilton, D. L., & Sherman, J. W. (1994). Stereotypes. In R. S. Wyer, Jr., & T. K. Srull (Eds.), *Handbook of social cognition. Volume 2: Applications* (2nd ed., pp. 1–68). Hillsdale, NJ: Erlbaum.

Hamilton, W. D. (1964). The genetical evolution of social behavior. I and II. *Journal of Theoretical Biology, 7,* 1–52.

Hampson, E. (2002). Sex differences in human brain and cognition: The influence of sex steroids in early and adult life. In J. B. Becker, S. M. Breedlove, D. Crews, & M. McCarthy (Eds.), *Behavioral endocrinology* (2nd ed., pp. 579–628). Cambridge, MA: MIT Press.

Han, S., & Shavitt, S. (1994). Persuasion and culture: Advertising appeals in individualistic and collectivistic societies. *Journal of Experimental Social Psychology, 30,* 326–350.

Hans, V. P., & Vidmar, N. (1986). *Judging the jury.* New York: Plenum.

Hansen, R. D., & Hall, C. A. (1985). Discounting and augmenting facilitative and inhibitory forces: The winner takes almost all. *Journal of Personality and Social Psychology, 49,* 1482–1493.

Hansen, R. D., & Hansen, C. H. (1988). Repression of emotionally tagged memories: The architecture of less complex emotions. *Journal of Personality and Social Psychology, 55,* 147–169.

Harackiewicz, J. M., & Elliot, A. J. (1998). The joint effects of target and purpose goals on intrinsic motivation: A mediational analysis. *Personality and Social Psychology Bulletin, 24,* 675–689.

Hardin, G. (1968). The tragedy of the commons. *Science, 162,* 1243–1248.

Hardy, C., & Latané, B. (1988). Social loafing in cheerleaders: Effects of team membership and competition. *Journal of Sport and Exercise Psychology, 10,* 109–114.

Harmon-Jones, E., Brehm, J. W., Greenberg, J., Simon, L., & Nelson, D. E. (1996). Evidence that the production of aversive consequences is not necessary to create cognitive dissonance. *Journal of Personality and Social Psychology, 70,* 5–16.

Harmon-Jones, E., Greenberg, J., Solomon, S., & Simon, L. (1996). The effects of mortality salience on intergroup bias between minimal groups. *European Journal of Social Psychology, 26,* 677–681.

Harmon-Jones, E., & Harmon-Jones, C. (2002). Testing the action-based model of cognitive dissonance: The effect of action orientation on postdecisional attitudes. *Personality and Social Psychology Bulletin, 28,* 711–723.

Harmon-Jones, E., & Mills, J. (Eds.). (1999). *Cognitive dissonance: Progress on a pivotal theory in social psychology.* Washington, DC: American Psychological Association.

Harmon-Jones, E., & Sigelman, J. (2001). State anger and prefrontal brain activity: Evidence that insult-related relative left-prefrontal activation is associated with experienced anger and aggression. *Journal of Personality and Social Psychology, 80,* 797–803.

Harris, J. R. (1995). Where is the child's environment? A group socialization theory of development. *Psychological Review, 102,* 458–489.

Harris, J. R. (1998). *The nurture assumption: Why children turn out the way they do.* New York: Free Press.

Harris, M. B., Harris, R. J., & Bochner, S. (1982). Fat, four-eyed, and female: Stereotypes of obesity, glasses, and gender. *Journal of Applied Social Psychology, 12,* 503–516.

Harris, P. (1996). Sufficient grounds for optimism? The relationship between perceived controllability and optimistic bias. *Journal of Social and Clinical Psychology, 15,* 9–52.

Hartup, W. W. (1989). Social relationships and their developmental significance. *American Psychologist, 44,* 120–126.

Harwood, R. L., & Miller, J. G. (1991). Perceptions of attachment behavior: A comparison of Anglo and Puerto Rican mothers. *Merrill-Palmer Quarterly, 37,* 583–599.

Hassan, S. (1988). *Combatting cult mind control.* Rochester, VT: Park Street Press.

Hastie, R. (1981). Schematic principles in human memory. In E. T. Higgins, C. P. Herman, & M. P. Zanna (Eds.), *Social cognition: The Ontario symposium* (Vol. 1, pp. 39–88). Hillsdale, NJ: Erlbaum.

Hastie, R., Penrod, S. D., & Pennington, N. (1983). *Inside the jury.* Cambridge, MA: Harvard University Press.

Hatfield, E. (1988). Passionate and companionate love. In R. J. Sternberg & M. L. Barnes (Eds.), *The psychology of love* (pp. 191–217). New Haven, CT: Yale University Press.

Hatfield, E., & Rapson, R. L. (1996). *Love and sex: Cross-cultural perspectives.* Boston, MA: Allyn & Bacon.

Hatfield, E., & Sprecher, S. (1986). *Mirror, mirror: The importance of looks in everyday life.* Albany, NY: State University of New York Press.

Hatfield, E., Traupmann, J., Sprecher, S., Utne, M., & Hay, J. (1985). Equity in intimate relations: Recent research. In W. Ickes (Ed.), *Compatible and incompatible relationships* (pp. 91–117). New York: Springer.

Hatfield, E., & Walster, G. W. (1978). *A new look at love.* Reading, MA: Addison-Wesley.

Haugtvedt, C. P., & Petty, R. E. (1992). Personality and persuasion: Need for cognition moderates the persistence and resistance of attitude changes. *Journal of Personality and Social Psychology, 63,* 308–319.

Hausenblas, H. A., & Carron, A. V. (1999). Eating disorder indices and athletes: An integration. *Journal of Sport and Exercise Psychology, 21,* 230–256.

Hawkins, S. A., & Hastie, R. (1990). Hindsight: Biased judgments of past events after the outcomes are known. *Psychological Bulletin, 107,* 311–327.

Haynes, G. A., & Olson, J. M. (in press). Coping with threats to just world beliefs: Derogate, blame, or help? *Journal of Applied Social Psychology,*

Hays, R. B. (1985). A longitudinal study of friendship development. *Journal of Personality and Social Psychology, 48,* 909–924.

Hazan, C., & Shaver, P. R. (1987). Romantic love conceptualized as an attachment process. *Journal of Personality and Social Psychology, 52,* 511–524.

Hazan, C., & Shaver, P. R. (1990). Love and work: An attachment-theoretical perspective. *Journal of Personality and Social Psychology, 59,* 270–280.

Hazlewood, J. D., & Olson, J. M. (1986). Covariation information, causal questioning, and interpersonal behavior. *Journal of Experimental Social Psychology, 22,* 276–291.

Hebl, M. R., & Heatherton, T. F. (1997). The stigma of obesity: The differences are black and white. *Personality and Social Psychology Bulletin, 24,* 417–426.

Hebl, M. R., & Mannix, L. M. (2003). The weight of obesity in evaluating others: A mere proximity effect. *Personality and Social Psychology Bulletin, 29,* 28–38.

Heider, F. (1958). *The psychology of interpersonal relations.* New York: Wiley.

Heilman, M. E., Block, C. J., & Martell, R. F. (1995). Sex stereotypes: Do they influence perceptions of managers? *Journal of Social Behavior and Personality, 10,* 237–252.

Heine, S. J., & Lehman, D. R. (1995). Cultural variation in unrealistic optimism: Does the West feel more invulnerable than the East? *Journal of Personality and Social Psychology, 68,* 595–607.

Heine, S. J., & Lehman, D. R. (1997a). Culture, dissonance, and self-affirmation. *Personality and Social Psychology Bulletin, 23,* 389–400.

Heine, S. J., & Lehman, D. R. (1997b). The cultural construction of self-enhancement: An examination of group-serving biases. *Journal of Personality and Social Psychology, 72,* 1268–1283.

Helgeson, V. S., & Mickelson, K. (1995). Motives for social comparison. *Personality and Social Psychology Bulletin, 21,* 1200–1209.

Helgeson, V. S., & Taylor, S. E. (1993). Social comparisons and adjustment among cardiac patients. *Journal of Applied Social Psychology, 23,* 1171–1195.

Heller, J. F., Pallak, M. S., & Picek, J. M. (1973). The interactive effects of intent and threat on boomerang attitude change. *Journal of Personality and Social Psychology, 26,* 273–279.

Henderlong, J., & Lepper, M. R. (2002). The effects of praise on children's intrinsic motivation: A review and synthesis. *Psychological Bulletin, 128,* 774–795.

Hendrick, C., & Hendrick, S. (1986). A theory and method of love. *Journal of Personality and Social Psychology, 50,* 392–402.

Hendrick, S. S., Hendrick, C., & Adler, N. L. (1988). Romantic relationships: Love, satisfaction, and staying together. *Journal of Personality and Social Psychology, 54,* 980–988.

Herek, G. M. (1986). The instrumentality of attitudes: Toward a neofunctional theory. *Journal of Social Issues, 42*(2), 99–114.

Herek, G. M., & Capitanio, J. P. (1998). Symbolic prejudice or fear of infection? A functional analysis of AIDS-related stigma among heterosexual adults. *Basic and Applied Social Psychology, 20,* 230–241.

Hewstone, M., & Jaspars, J. (1983). A re-examination of the role of consensus, consistency and distinctiveness: Kelley's cube revisited. *British Journal of Social Psychology, 22,* 41–50.

Higgins, E. T. (1987). Self-discrepancy: A theory relating self and affect. *Psychological Review, 94,* 319–340.

Higgins, E. T. (1989). Knowledge accessibility and activation: Subjectivity and suffering from unconscious sources. In J. S. Uleman & J. A. Bargh (Eds.), *Unintended thought* (pp. 75–123). New York: Guilford Press.

Higgins, E. T. (1996). Knowledge activation: Accessibility, applicability, and salience. In E. T. Higgins & A. W. Kruglanski (Eds.), *Social psychology: Handbook of basic principles* (pp. 133–168). New York: Guilford Press.

Higgins, E. T. (2004). Making a theory useful: Lessons handed down. *Personality and Social Psychology Review, 8,* 138–145.

Higgins, E. T., Bond, R. N., Klein, R., & Strauman, T. (1986). Self-discrepancies and emotional vulnerability: How magnitude, accessibility, and type of discrepancy influence affect. *Journal of Personality and Social Psychology, 51,* 5–15.

Higgins, E. T., King, G. A., & Mavin, G. H. (1982). Individual construct accessibility and subjective impressions and recall. *Journal of Personality and Social Psychology, 43,* 35–47.

Higgins, E. T., Klein, R., & Strauman, T. (1985). Self-concept discrepancy theory: A psychological model for distinguishing among different aspects of depression and anxiety. *Social Cognition, 3,* 51–76.

Higgins, R. L., Snyder, C. R., & Berglas, S. (Eds.). (1990). *Self-handicapping: The paradox that isn't.* New York: Plenum.

Hilton, D. J., & Slugoski, B. R. (1986). Knowledge based causal attribution: The abnormal conditions focus model. *Psychological Review, 93,* 75–88.

Hilton, J. L., & Darley, J. M. (1991). The effects of interaction goals on person perception. In M. P. Zanna (Ed.) *Advances in experimental social psychology* (Vol. 24, pp. 235–267). San Diego, CA: Academic Press.

Hirt, E. R. (1990). Do I see only what I expect? Evidence for an expectancy-guided retrieval model. *Journal of Personality and Social Psychology, 58,* 937–951.

Hirt, E. R., Deppe, R. K., & Gordon, L. J. (1991). Self-reported versus behavioral self-handicapping: Empirical evidence for a theoretical distinction. *Journal of Personality and Social Psychology, 61,* 981–991.

Hirt, E. R., McCrea, S. M., & Kimble, C. E. (2000). Public self-focus and sex differences in behavioral self-handicapping: Does increasing self-threat still make it "just a man's game"? *Personality and Social Psychology Bulletin, 26,* 1131–1141.

Hirt, E. R., Zillman, D., Erickson, G. A., & Kennedy, C. (1992). Costs and benefits of allegiance: Changes in fans' self-ascribed competencies after team victory versus defeat. *Journal of Personality and Social Psychology, 63,* 724–738.

Hodges, E. V., Malone, M. J., & Perry, D. G. (1997). Individual risk and social risk as interacting determinants of victimization in the peer group. *Developmental Psychology, 33,* 1032–1039.

Hodson, G., & Esses, V. M. (2002). Distancing oneself from negative attributes and the personal/group discrimination discrepancy. *Journal of Experimental Social Psychology, 38,* 500–507.

Hodson, G., & Sorrentino, R. M. (1997). Groupthink and uncertainty orientation: Personality differences in reactivity to the group situation. *Group Dynamics: Theory, Research, and Practice, 1,* 144–155.

Hoffman, M. L. (1981). Is altruism part of human nature? *Journal of Personality and Social Psychology, 40,* 121–137.

Hofling, C. K., Brotzman, E., Dalrymple, S., Graves, N., & Pierce, C. (1966). An experimental study in nurse-physician relationships. *Journal of Nervous and Mental Disease, 143,* 171–180.

Hofstede, G. H. (1980). *Culture's consequences: International differences in work-related values.* Beverly Hills, CA: Sage.

Hofstede, G. H. (1991). *Cultures and organizations: Software of the mind.* London, UK: McGraw-Hill.

Hofstede, G. H. (2001). *Culture's consequences: Comparing values, behaviors, institutions, and organizations across nations* (2nd ed.). Thousand Oaks, CA: Sage.

Hokanson, J. E., & Shetler, S. (1961). The effect of overt aggression on physiological arousal level. *Journal of Abnormal and Social Psychology, 63,* 446–448.

Holland, R. W., Verplanken, B., & van Knippenberg, A. (2002). On the nature of attitude-behavior relations: The strong guide, the weak follow. *European Journal of Social Psychology, 32,* 869–876.

Hollander, E. P. (1985). Leadership and power. In G. Lindzey & E. Aronson (Eds.), *The handbook of social psychology* (3rd ed., Vol. 2, pp. 485–537). New York: Random House.

Holsti, O. R., & Rosenau, J. N. (1980). Does where you stand depend on when you were born? The impact of generation on post-Vietnam foreign policy beliefs. *Public Opinion Quarterly, 44,* 1–22.

Holtzworth-Munroe, A. (2000). A typology of men who are violent toward their female partners: Making sense of the heterogeneity in husband violence. *Current Directions in Psychological Science, 9,* 140–143.

Holtzworth-Munroe, A., & Stuart, G. L. (1994). Typologies of male batterers: Three subtypes and the differences among them. *Psychological Bulletin, 116,* 476–497.

Holtzworth-Munroe, A., Stuart, G. L., & Hutchinson, G. (1997). Violent versus nonviolent husbands: Differences in attachment patterns, dependency, and jealousy. *Journal of Family Psychology, 11,* 314–331.

Hoorens, V., & Nuttin, J. M. (1993). Overvaluation of own attributes: Mere ownership or subjective frequency? *Social Cognition, 11,* 177–200.

Hoorens, V., & Ruiter, S. (1996). The optimal impact phenomenon: Beyond the third person effect. *European Journal of Social Psychology, 26,* 599–610.

Hopper, J. R., & Nielsen, J. M. (1991). Recycling as altruistic behavior: Normative and behavioral strategies to expand participation in a community recycling program. *Environment and Behavior, 23,* 195–220.

Hornsey, M. J., & Jetten, J. (2004). The individual within the group: Balancing the need to belong with the need to be different. *Personality and Social Psychology Review, 8,* 248–264.

Hornstein, H. A., LaKind, E., Frankel, G., & Manne, S. (1975). Effects of knowledge about remote social events on prosocial behavior, social conception, and mood. *Journal of Personality and Social Psychology, 32,* 1038–1046.

Horvitz, T., & Pratkanis, A. R. (2002). A laboratory demonstration of the fraudulent telemarketers' 1-in-5 prize tactic. *Journal of Applied Social Psychology, 32,* 310–317.

Hoshino-Browne, E., Zanna, A. S., Spencer, S. J., & Zanna, M. P. (2004). Investigating attitudes cross-culturally: A case of cognitive dissonance among East Asians and North Americans. In G. Haddock & G. R. Maio (Eds.), *Contemporary perspectives on the psychology of attitudes* (pp. 375–397). London, UK: Psychology Press.

House, J. S., Landis, K. R., & Umberson, D. (1988). Social relationships and health. *Science, 241,* 540–545.

House, R. J., & Shamir, B. (1993). Toward the integration of transformational, charismatic, and visionary theories. In M. M. Chemers & R. Ayman (Eds.), *Leadership theory and research: Perspectives and directions* (pp. 81–107). San Diego, CA: Academic Press.

Houston, D. A., & Fazio, R. H. (1989). Biased processing as a function of attitude accessibility: Making objective judgments subjectively. *Social Cognition, 7,* 51–66.

Hovland, C. I., Janis, I. L., & Kelley, H. H. (1953). *Communication and persuasion.* New Haven, CT: Yale University Press.

Hovland, C. I, & Sears, R. (1940). Minor studies in aggression: VI. Correlation of lynchings with economic indices. *Journal of Psychology, 9,* 301–310.

Hovland, C. I., & Weiss, W. (1951). The influence of source credibility on communication effectiveness. *Public Opinion Quarterly, 15,* 635–650.

Howard, D. J., Gengler, C., & Jain, A. (1995). What's in a name? A complimentary means of persuasion. *Journal of Consumer Research, 22,* 200–211.

Howells, L. T., & Becker, S. W. (1962). Seating arrangement and leadership emergence. *Journal of Abnormal and Social Psychology, 64,* 148–150.

Hraba, J., & Grant, G. (1970). Black is beautiful: A reexamination of racial preference and identification. *Journal of Personality and Social Psychology, 16,* 398–402.

Huesmann, L. R., & Eron, L. D. (Eds.). (1986). *Television and the aggressive child: A cross-national comparison.* Hillsdale, NJ: Erlbaum.

Huesmann, L. R., Moise-Titus, J., Podolski, C.-L., & Eron, L. D. (2003). Longitudinal relations between children's exposure to TV violence and their aggressive and violent behavior in young adulthood: 1977–1992. *Developmental Psychology, 39,* 201–221.

Huff, R., Rattner, A., & Sagarin, E. (1986). Guilty until proven innocent. *Crime and Delinquency, 32,* 518–544.

Hugenberg, K., & Bodenhausen, G. V. (2003). Facing prejudice: Implicit prejudice and the perception of facial threat. *Psychological Science, 14,* 640–643.

Hugenberg, K., & Bodenhausen, G. V. (2004). Ambiguity in social categorization: The role of prejudice and facial affect in race categorization. *Psychological Science, 15,* 342–345.

Hui, C. H. (1988). Measurement of individualism-collectivism. *Journal of Research in Personality, 22*, 17–36.

Hull, J. G., & West, S. G. (1982). The discounting principle in attribution. *Personality and Social Psychology Bulletin, 8*, 208–213.

Hyde, C. R. (1999). *Pay it forward.* New York: Simon & Schuster.

Hyman, I. E., Jr., Husband, T. H., & Billings, F. J. (1995). False memories of childhood experiences. *Applied Cognitive Psychology, 9*, 181–197.

Ickes, W. (1993). Empathic accuracy. *Journal of Personality, 61*, 587–610.

Ickes, W. (Ed.). (1997). *Empathic accuracy.* New York: Guilford.

Ickes, W. (2003). *Everyday mind reading: Understanding what other people think and feel.* Amherst, NY: Prometheus Books.

Insko, C. A., & Schopler, J. (1998). Differential distrust of groups and individuals. In C. Sedikides, J. Schopler, & C. A. Insko (Eds.), *Intergroup cognition and intergroup behavior* (pp. 75–107). Mahwah, NJ: Erlbaum.

Insko, C. A., Schopler, J., Hoyle, R. H., Dardis, G. J., & Graetz, K. A. (1990). Individual-group discontinuity as a function of fear and greed. *Journal of Personality and Social Psychology, 58*, 68–79.

Insko, C. A., Thibaut, J. W., Moehle, D., Wilson, M., Diamond, W. D., Gilmore, R., Solomon, M. R., & Lipsitz, A. (1980). Social evolution and the emergence of leadership. *Journal of Personality and Social Psychology, 39*, 431–448.

Irwin, A. R., & Gross, A. M. (1995). Cognitive tempo, violent video games, and aggressive behavior in young boys. *Journal of Family Violence, 10*, 337–350.

Isbell, L. M. (2004). Not all happy people are lazy or stupid: Evidence of systematic processing in happy moods. *Journal of Experimental Social Psychology, 40*, 341–349.

Isen, A. M., Clark, M., & Schwartz, M. F. (1976). Duration of the effect of good mood on helping: "Footprints on the sands of time." *Journal of Personality and Social Psychology, 34*, 385–393.

Isen, A. M., & Levin, P. F. (1972). The effect of feeling good on helping: Cookies and kindness. *Journal of Personality and Social Psychology, 21*, 384–388.

Isen, A. M., Means, B., Patrick, R., & Nowicky, G. (1982). Some factors influencing decision making strategy and risk-taking. In M. S. Clark & S. T. Fiske (Eds.), *Affect and cognition: The 17th annual Carnegie Mellon symposium on cognition* (pp. 243–261). Hillsdale, NJ: Erlbaum.

Isen, A. M., Shalker, T. E., Clark, M., & Karp, L. (1978). Affect accessibility of material in memory, and behavior: A cognitive loop. *Journal of Personality and Social Psychology, 36*, 1–12.

Isenberg, D. J. (1986). Group polarization: A critical review and meta-analysis. *Journal of Personality and Social Psychology, 50*, 1141–1151.

Islam, M. R., & Hewstone, M. (1993). Dimensions of contact as predictors of intergroup anxiety, perceived out-group variability, and out-group attitude: An integrative model. *Personality and Social Psychology Bulletin, 19*, 700–710.

James, W. (1890/1948). *Psychology.* Cleveland, OH: World Publishing.

Jamieson, D. W., Lydon, J. E., & Zanna, M. P. (1987). Attitude and activity preference similarity: Differential bases of interpersonal attraction for low and high self-monitors. *Journal of Personality and Social Psychology, 53*, 1052–1060.

Janes, L. M. (2003). *The effects of goals on self-assessment versus self-protection.* Doctoral dissertation, University of Western Ontario, London, Ontario, Canada.

Janes, L. M., & Olson, J. M. (2000). Jeer pressure: The behavioral effects of observing ridicule of others. *Personality and Social Psychology Bulletin, 26*, 474–485.

Janis, I. L. (1972). *Victims of groupthink.* Boston, MA: Houghton Mifflin.

Janis, I. L. (1982). *Groupthink* (2nd ed.). Boston, MA: Houghton Mifflin.

Janis, I. L., & Feshbach, S. (1953). Effects of fear-arousing communications. *Journal of Abnormal and Social Psychology, 48*, 78–92.

Jankowiak, W. R. (1995). *Romantic passion: The universal experience?* New York: Columbia University Press.

Jankowiak, W. R., & Fischer, E. F. (1992). A cross-cultural perspective on romantic love. *Ethnology, 31*, 149–155.

Jemmott, J. B., Jemmott, L. S., & Fong, G. T. (1992). Reductions in HIV risk-associated sexual behaviors among Black male adolescents: Effects of an AIDS prevention intervention. *American Journal of Public Health, 82*, 372–377.

Jennings, M. K. (1987). Residues of a movement: The aging of the American protest movement. *American Political Science Review, 81*, 367–382.

Jessop, D. J. (1982). Topic variation in levels of agreement between parents and adolescents. *Public Opinion Quarterly, 46*, 538–559.

Johns, M., Schmader, T., & Martens, A. (2005). Knowing is half the battle: Teaching stereotype threat as a means of improving women's math performance. *Psychological Science, 16*, 175–179.

Johnson, D. J., & Rusbult, C. E. (1989). Resisting temptation: Devaluation of alternative partners as a means of maintaining commitment in close relationships. *Journal of Personality and Social Psychology, 57*, 967–980.

Johnson, J. G., Cohen, P., Smailes, E. M., Kasen, S., & Brook, J. S. (2002). Television viewing and aggressive behavior during adolescence and adulthood. *Science, 295*, 2468–2471.

Johnson, J. T., Boyd, K. R., & Magnani, P. S. (1994). Causal reasoning in the attribution of rare and common events. *Journal of Personality and Social Psychology, 66*, 229–242.

Johnson, R. D., & Downing, L. L. (1979). Deindividuation and valence of cues: Effects on prosocial and antisocial behavior. *Journal of Personality and Social Psychology, 37*, 1532–1538.

Jones, B. C., Little, A. C., Burt, D. M., & Perrett, D. I. (2004). When facial attractiveness is only skin deep. *Perception, 33*, 569–576.

Jones, B. C., Little, A. C., Feinberg, D. R., Penton-Voak, I. S., Tiddeman, B. P., & Perrett, D. I. (2004). The relationship between shape symmetry and perceived skin condition in male facial attractiveness. *Evolution and Human Behavior, 25*, 24–30.

Jones, E. E. (1979). The rocky road from acts to dispositions. *American Psychologist, 34*, 107–117.

Jones, E. E. (1990). *Interpersonal perception.* New York: Macmillan.

Jones, E. E., & Berglas, S. C. (1978). Control of attributions about the self through self-handicapping strategies: The appeal of alcohol and the role of underachievement. *Personality and Social Psychology Bulletin, 4*, 200–206.

Jones, E. E., & Harris, V. A. (1967). The attribution of attitudes. *Journal of Experimental Social Psychology, 3*, 1–24.

Jones, E. E., & Nisbett, R. E. (1972). The actor and the observer: Divergent perceptions of the causes of behavior. In E. E. Jones, D. E. Kanouse, H. H. Kelley, R. E. Nisbett, S. Valins, & B. Weiner (Eds.), *Attribution: Perceiving the causes of behavior* (pp. 79–94). Morristown, NJ: General Learning Press.

Jones, E. E., & Pittman, T. S. (1982). Toward a general theory of strategic self-presentation. In J. M. Suls (Ed.), *Psychological perspectives on the self* (Vol. 1, pp. 231–262). Hillsdale, NJ: Erlbaum.

Jones, E. E., & Rhodewalt, F. (1982). *Self-handicapping scale.* Unpublished scale, Department of Psychology, Princeton University, and Department of Psychology, University of Utah.

Jones, E. E., & Wortman, C. (1973). *Ingratiation: An attributional approach.* Morristown, NJ: General Learning Press.

Jones, J. M. (1997). *Prejudice and racism* (2nd ed.). New York: McGraw-Hill.

Jones, J. T., Pelham, B. W., Carvallo, M., & Mirenberg, M. C. (2004). How do I love thee? Let me count the Js: Implicit egotism and interpersonal attraction. *Journal of Personality and Social Psychology, 87*, 665–683.

Jones, J. T., Pelham, B. W., & Mirenberg, M. C. (2002). Name letter preferences are not merely mere exposure: Implicit egotism as self-regulation. *Journal of Experimental Social Psychology, 38*, 170–177.

Jordan, C. H., Spencer, S. J., & Zanna, M. P. (2003). "I love me . . . I love me not": Implicit self-esteem, explicit self-esteem, and defensiveness. In S. J. Spencer, S. Fein, M. P. Zanna, & J. M. Olson (Eds.), *Motivated social perception: The Ontario symposium* (Vol. 9, pp. 117–145). Mahwah, NJ: Erlbaum.

Jordan, C. H., Spencer, S. J., Zanna, M. P., Hoshino-Browne, E., & Correll, J. (2003). Secure and defensive high self-esteem. *Journal of Personality and Social Psychology, 85,* 969–978.

Joule, R. V. (1987). Tobacco deprivation: The foot-in-the-door technique versus the low-ball technique. *European Journal of Social Psychology, 17,* 361–365.

Judd, C. M., Blair, I. V., & Chapleau, K. M. (2004). Automatic stereotypes vs. automatic prejudice: Sorting out the possibilities in the Payne (2001) weapon paradigm. *Journal of Experimental Social Psychology, 40,* 75–81.

Judd, C. M., & Park, B. (1988). Out-group homogeneity: Judgments of variability at the individual and group levels. *Journal of Personality and Social Psychology, 54,* 778–788.

Judge, T. A., Bono, J. E., Ilies, R., & Gerhardt, M. W. (2002). Personality and leadership: A qualitative and quantitative review. *Journal of Applied Psychology, 87,* 765–780.

Judge, T. A., Erez, A., Bono, J. E., & Thorsen, C. J. (2002). Are measures of self-esteem, neuroticism, locus of control, and generalized self-efficacy indicators of a common core construct? *Journal of Personality and Social Psychology, 83,* 693–710.

Jussim, L. (1991). Social perception and social reality: A reflection-construction model. *Psychological Review, 98,* 54–73.

Jussim, L., Soffin, S., Brown, R., Ley, J., & Kohlhepp, K. (1992). Understanding reactions to feedback by integrating ideas from symbolic interactionism and cognitive evaluation theory. *Journal of Personality and Social Psychology, 62,* 402–421.

Kacmar, K. M., Delery, J. E., & Ferris, G. R. (1992). Differential effectiveness of applicant impression management tactics on employment interview decisions. *Journal of Applied Social Psychology, 16,* 1250–1272.

Kahn, M. (1966). The physiology of catharsis. *Journal of Personality and Social Psychology, 3,* 278–286.

Kahneman, D. (2003). A perspective on judgment and choice. *American Psychologist, 58,* 697–720.

Kahneman, D., & Frederick, S. (2002). Representativeness revisited: Attribute substitution in intuitive judgment. In T. Gilovich, D. Griffin, & D. Kahneman (Eds.), *Heuristics and biases: The psychology of intuitive judgment* (pp. 49–81). New York: Cambridge University Press.

Kahneman, D., & Miller, D. T. (1986). Norm theory: Comparing reality to its alternatives. *Psychological Review, 93,* 136–153.

Kahneman, D., & Tversky, A. (1973). On the psychology of prediction. *Psychological Review, 80,* 237–251.

Kaiser, C. R., Major, B., & McCoy, S. K. (2004). Expectations about the future and the emotional consequences of perceiving prejudice. *Personality and Social Psychology Bulletin, 30,* 173–184.

Kaiser, C. R., & Miller, C. T. (2001). Stop complaining! The social costs of making attributions to discrimination. *Personality and Social Psychology Bulletin, 27,* 254–263.

Kalven, H., & Zeisel, H. (1966). *The American jury.* Boston, MA: Little, Brown.

Kanemasa, Y., Taniguchi, J., Daibo, I., & Ishimori, M. (2004). Love styles and romantic love experiences in Japan. *Social Behavior and Personality, 32,* 265–282.

Kaplan, K. J. (1972). On the ambivalence-indifference problem in attitude theory and measurement: A suggested modification of the semantic differential technique. *Psychological Bulletin, 77,* 361–372.

Karabenick, S. A., & Youssef, Z. I. (1968). Performance as a function of achievement motive level and perceived difficulty. *Journal of Personality and Social Psychology, 10,* 414–419.

Karau, S. J., & Williams, K. (1993). Social loafing: A meta-analytic review and theoretical integration. *Journal of Personality and Social Psychology, 65,* 681–706.

Kardes, F. R., Sanbonmatsu, D. M., Voss, R. T., & Fazio, R. H. (1986). Self-monitoring and attitude accessibility. *Personality and Social Psychology Bulletin, 72,* 468–474.

Kashima, Y., Kokubo, T., Kashima, E. S., Boxall, D., Yamaguchi, S., & Macrae, K. (2004). Culture and self: Are there within-culture differences in self between metropolitan areas and regional cities? *Personality and Social Psychology Bulletin, 30,* 816–823.

Kashima, Y., Siegal, M., Tanaka, K., & Kashima, E. S. (1992). Do people believe behaviours are consistent with attitudes? Toward a cross-cultural psychology of attribution processes. *British Journal of Social Psychology, 31,* 111–124.

Kashima, Y., Yamaguchi, S., Kim, U., Choi, S.-C., Gelfand, M. J., & Yuki, M. (1995). Culture, gender, and self: A perspective from individualism-collectivism research. *Journal of Personality and Social Psychology, 69,* 925–937.

Kasser, T., Koestner, R., & Lekes, N. (2002). Early family experiences and adult values: A 26-year, prospective longitudinal study. *Personality and Social Psychology Bulletin, 28,* 826–835.

Kasser, T., Ryan, R. M., Zax, M., & Sameroff, A. J. (1995). The relations of maternal and social environments to late adolescents' materialistic and prosocial values. *Developmental Psychology, 31,* 907–914.

Katz, D. (1960). The functional approach to the study of attitudes. *Public Opinion Quarterly, 24,* 163–204.

Katz, I., & Hass, R. G. (1988). Racial ambivalence and American value conflict: Correlational and priming studies of dual cognitive structures. *Journal of Personality and Social Psychology, 55,* 893–905.

Katz, J., Monnier, J., Libet, J., Shaw, D., & Beach, S. R. H. (2000). Individual and crossover effects of stress on adjustment in medical student marriages. *Journal of Marital and Family Therapy, 26,* 341–351.

Katz, J. E., & Rice, R. E. (2002). *Social consequences of Internet use: Access, involvement, and interaction.* Cambridge, MA: MIT Press.

Kawakami, K., & Dovidio, J. (2001). The reliability of implicit stereotyping. *Personality and Social Psychology Bulletin, 27,* 212–225.

Kay, A. C., & Ross, L. (2003). The perceptual push: The interplay of implicit cues and explicit situational construals on behavioral intentions in the prisoner's dilemma. *Journal of Experimental Social Psychology, 39,* 634–643.

Kazdin, A. E., & Benjet, C. (2003). Spanking children: Evidence and issues. *Current Directions in Psychological Science, 12,* 99–103.

Keller, J., & Dauenheimer, D. (2003). Stereotype threat in the classroom: Dejection mediates the disrupting threat effect on women's math performance. *Personality and Social Psychology Bulletin, 29,* 371–381.

Kelley, H. H. (1967). Attribution theory in social psychology. In D. Levine (Ed.), *Nebraska Symposium on Motivation* (Vol. 15, pp. 192–238). Lincoln: University of Nebraska Press.

Kelley, H. H. (1973). The process of causal attribution. *American Psychologist, 28,* 107–128.

Kelley, H. H. (1979). *Personal relationships: Their structures and processes.* Hillsdale, NJ: Erlbaum.

Kelley, H. H. (1983). *Close relationships.* New York: W. H. Freeman.

Kelly, C., & Breinlinger, S. (1995). Attitudes, intentions, and behavior: A study of women's participation in collective action. *Journal of Applied Social Psychology, 25,* 1430–1445.

Kelman, H. C. (1967). Human use of human subjects: The problem of deception in social psychological experiments. *Psychological Bulletin, 67,* 1–11.

Kelman, H. C., & Hamilton, V. L. (1989). *Crimes of obedience: Toward a social psychology of authority and responsibility.* New Haven, CT: Yale University Press.

Kemmelmeier, M., & Winter, D. G. (2000). Putting threat into perspective: Experimental studies on perceptual distortion in international conflict. *Personality and Social Psychology Bulletin, 26,* 796–809.

Kennamer, J. D. (1990). Self-serving biases in perceiving the opinions of others. *Communication Research, 17,* 393–404.

Kenrick, D., Ackerman, J., & Ledlow, S. (2003). Evolutionary social psychology: Adaptive predispositions and human culture. In J. Delamater (Ed.), *Handbook of social psychology* (pp. 103–122). New York: Kluwer/Plenum.

Kenrick, D. T., Li, N. P., & Butner, J. (2003). Dynamical evolutionary psychology: Individual decision rules and emergent social norms. *Psychological Review, 110,* 3–28.

Kernis, M. H. (1984). Need for uniqueness, self-schemas, and thought as moderators of the false-consensus effect. *Journal of Personality and Social Psychology, 35,* 381–391.

Kernis, M. H., & Paradise, A. W. (2002). Distinguishing between secure and fragile forms of high self-esteem. In E. L. Deci & R. M. Ryan (Eds.), *Handbook of self-determination research* (pp. 339–360). Rochester, NY: University of Rochester Press.

Kernis, M. H., & Waschull, S. B. (1995). The interactive roles of stability and level of self-esteem: Research and theory. In M. P. Zanna (Ed.), *Advances in experimental social psychology* (Vol. 27, pp. 93–141). San Diego, CA: Academic Press.

Kerr, N. L., Aronoff, J., & Messe, L. A. (2000). Methods of small group research. In H. T. Reis & C. M. Judd (Eds.), *Handbook of research methods in social psychology* (pp. 160–189). Cambridge, UK: Cambridge University Press.

Kerr, N. L., & Kaufman-Gilliland, C. M. (1994). Communication, commitment, and cooperation in social dilemmas. *Journal of Personality and Social Psychology, 66,* 513–529.

Kiesler, S. (1997). *Culture of the Internet.* Mahwah, NJ: Erlbaum.

Kiesler, S., & Kraut, R. (1999). Internet use and ties that bind. *American Psychologist, 54,* 783–784.

Kihlstrom, J. F. (1994). Hypnosis, delayed recall, and the principles of memory. *International Journal of Clinical and Experimental Hypnosis, 42,* 337–345.

Kim, M., & Hunter, J. E. (1993). Attitude-behavior relations: A meta-analysis of attitudinal relevance and topic. *Journal of Communication, 43,* 101–142.

Kinder, D. R. (1998). Opinion and action in the realm of politics. In D. T. Gilbert, S. T. Fiske, & G. Lindzey (Eds.), *The handbook of social psychology* (4th ed., Vol. 2, pp. 778–867). New York: McGraw-Hill.

King, K. B., Reis, H. T., Porter, L. A., & Norsen, L. H. (1993). Social support and long-term recovery from coronary artery surgery: Effects on patients and spouses. *Health Psychology, 12,* 56–63.

Kirk, R. E. (2003). Experimental design. In J. A. Schinka & W. F. Velicer (Eds.), *Handbook of psychology: Volume 2. Research methods in psychology* (pp. 3–32). Hoboken, NJ: Wiley.

Kirkpatrick, L. A., & Davis, K. E. (1994). Attachment style, gender, and relationship stability: A longitudinal analysis. *Journal of Personality and Social Psychology, 66,* 502–512.

Kitayama, S., & Markus, H. R. (Eds.). (1994). *Emotion and culture: Empirical studies of mutual influence.* Washington, DC: American Psychological Association.

Kitayama, S., Snibbe, A. C., Markus, H. R., & Suzuki, T. (2004). Is there any "free" choice? Self and dissonance in two cultures. *Psychological Science, 15,* 527–533.

Kitayama, S., & Uchida, Y. (2003). Explicit self-criticism and implicit self-regard: Evaluating self and friend in two cultures. *Journal of Experimental Social Psychology, 39,* 476–482.

Kitzmann, K. M., Gaylord, N. K., Holt, A. R., & Kenny, E. D. (2003). Child witnesses to domestic violence: A meta-analytic review. *Journal of Consulting and Clinical Psychology, 71,* 339–352.

Kiviniemi, M. T., Snyder, M., & Omoto, A. M. (2002). Too many of a good thing? The effects of multiple motivations on stress, cost, fulfillment, and satisfaction. *Personality and Social Psychology Bulletin, 28,* 732–743.

Kling, K. C., Ryff, C. D., Love, G., & Essex, M. (2003). Exploring the influence of personality on depressive symptoms and self-esteem across a significant life transition. *Journal of Personality and Social Psychology, 85,* 922–932.

Klohnen, E. C., & Luo, S. (2003). Interpersonal attraction and personality: What is attractive—self similarity, ideal similarity, complementarity or attachment security? *Journal of Personality and Social Psychology, 85,* 709–722.

Knight, G. P., Fabes, R. A., & Higgins, D. A. (1996). Concerns about drawing causal inferences from meta-analyses: An example in the study of gender differences in aggression. *Psychological Bulletin, 119,* 410–421.

Knox, R. E., & Safford, R. K. (1976). Group caution at the racetrack. *Journal of Experimental Social Psychology, 12,* 317–324.

Koivisto Hursti, U.-K., & Magnusson, M. K. (2003). Consumer perceptions of genetically modified and organic foods. What kind of knowledge matters? *Appetite, 41,* 207–209.

Konečni, V. J. (1972a). Some effects of guilt on compliance: A field replication. *Journal of Personality and Social Psychology, 23,* 30–32.

Konečni, V. J. (1972b). Some effects of guilt on compliance: A field replication. *Journal of Personality and Social Psychology, 23,* 30–32.

Konečni, V. J. (1975a). Annoyance, type and duration of postannoyance activity, and aggression: The "cathartic effect." *Journal of Experimental Psychology: General, 104,* 76–102.

Konečni, V. J. (1975b). The mediation of aggressive behavior: Arousal level versus anger and cognitive labeling. *Journal of Personality and Social Psychology, 32,* 706–712.

Koss, M. P., Goodman, L. A., Browne, A., Fitzgerald, L. F., Keita, G. P., & Russo, N. F. (1994). *No safe haven: Male violence against women at home, at work, and in the community.* Washington, DC: American Psychological Association.

Krackow, A., & Blass, T. (1995). When nurses obey or defy inappropriate physician orders: Attributional differences. *Journal of Social Behavior and Personality, 10,* 585–594.

Kramer, R. (1999). Trust and distrust in organizations: Emerging perspectives, enduring questions. *Annual Review of Psychology, 50,* 569–598.

Kramer, R. M., & Brewer, M. B. (1984). Effects of group identity on resource use in a simulated commons dilemma. *Journal of Personality and Social Psychology, 46,* 1044–1057.

Kramer, R. M., McClintock, C. G., & Messick, D. M. (1986). Social values and cooperative response to a simulated resource conservation crisis. *Journal of Personality, 54,* 576–592.

Krantz, D. S., Glass, D. C., & Snyder, M. L. (1974). Helplessness, stress level, and the coronary-prone behavior pattern. *Journal of Experimental Social Psychology, 10,* 284–300.

Kraus, S. J. (1995). Attitudes and the prediction of behavior: A meta-analysis of the empirical literature. *Personality and Social Psychology Bulletin, 21,* 58–75.

Krauss, R. M., & Deutsch, M. (1966). Communication in interpersonal bargaining. *Journal of Personality and Social Psychology, 4,* 572–577.

Kraut, R., Kiesler, S., Boneva, B., Cummings, J. N., Helgeson, V., & Crawford, A. M. (2002). Internet paradox revisited. *Journal of Social Issues, 58*(1), 49–74.

Kraut, R., Patterson, M., Lundmark, V., Kiesler, S., Mukophadhyay, T., & Scherlis, W. (1998). Internet paradox: A social technology that reduces social involvement and psychological well-being? *American Psychologist, 53,* 1017–1031.

Kressel, N. J., & Kressel, D. F. (2004). *Stack and sway: The new science of jury consulting.* Boulder, CO: Westview Press.

Kreuger, J. (1988). On the perception of social consensus. In M. P. Zanna (Ed.), *Advances in experimental social psychology* (Vol. 30, pp. 164–240). New York: Academic Press.

Kreuger, J. (1998). Enhancement bias in descriptions of self and others. *Personality and Social Psychology Bulletin, 24,* 505–516.

Krosnick, J. A., & Alwin, D. F. (1989). Aging and susceptibility to attitude change. *Journal of Personality and Social Psychology, 57,* 416–425.

Kruger, J., & Burrus, J. (2004). Egocentrism and focalism in unrealistic optimism (and pessimism). *Journal of Experimental Social Psychology, 40,* 332–340.

Kruglanski, A. W. (1996). Motivated social cognition: Principles of the interface. In E. T. Higgins & A. W. Kruglanski (Eds.), *Social psychology: Handbook of basic principles* (pp. 493–520). New York: Guilford Press.

Kruglanski, A. W., & Higgins, E. T. (Eds.). (2004). Special Issue: Theory construction in social personality psychology: Personal experiences and lessons learned. *Personality and Social Psychology Review, 8*(2).

Krull, D. S., Loy, M. H., Lin, J., Wang, C., Chen, S., & Zhao, X. (1999). The fundamental fundamental attribution error: Correspondence bias in individualist and collectivist cultures. *Personality and Social Psychology Bulletin, 25,* 1208–1219.

Kuhn, M. H., & McPartland, T. S. (1954). An empirical investigation of self-attitudes. *American Sociological Review, 19,* 68–76.

Kumkale, G. T., & Albarracín, D. (2004). The sleeper effect in persuasion: A meta-analytic review. *Psychological Bulletin, 130,* 143–172.

Kunda, Z. (1990). The case for motivated reasoning. *Psychological Bulletin, 108,* 480–498.

Kunda, Z. (1999). *Social cognition: Making sense of people.* Cambridge, MA: MIT Press.

Kunda, Z., & Nisbett, R. E. (1986). The psychometrics of everyday life. *Cognitive Psychology, 18,* 195–224.

Kunda, Z., & Oleson, K. (1997). When exceptions prove the rule: How extremity of deviance determines deviants' impact on stereotypes. *Journal of Personality and Social Psychology, 72,* 965–979.

Kunda, Z., & Thagard, P. (1996). Forming impressions from stereotypes, traits and behaviors: Parallel constraint satisfaction theory. *Psychological Review, 103,* 284–308.

Kurdek, L. A. (1991). Correlates of relationship satisfaction in cohabiting gay and lesbian couples: Integration of contextual, investment, and problem-solving models. *Journal of Personality and Social Psychology, 61,* 910–922.

Kurdek, L. A. (1995). Lesbian and gay couples. In A. R. D'Augelli & C. J. Patterson (Eds.), *Lesbian, gay, and bisexual identities over the lifespan* (pp. 243–261). New York: Oxford University Press.

Kurdek, L. A., & Schmitt, J. P. (1986). Relationship quality of partners in heterosexual married, heterosexual cohabiting, and gay lesbian relationships. *Journal of Personality and Social Psychology, 51,* 711–720.

Kurman, J. (2001). Self-enhancement: Is it restricted to individualistic cultures? *Personality and Social Psychology Bulletin, 27,* 1705–1716.

Kwong, M. J., Bartholomew, K., Henderson, A. J. Z., & Trinke, S. J. (2003). The intergenerational transmission of relationship violence. *Journal of Family Psychology, 17,* 288–301.

LaFrance, M., Hecht, M. A., & Paluck, E. L. (2003). The contingent smile: A meta-analysis of sex differences in smiling. *Psychological Bulletin, 129,* 305–334.

Lakey, B., Adams, K., Neely, L., Rhodes, G., Lutz, C. J., & Sielky, K. (2002). Perceived support and low emotional distress: The role of enacted support, dyad similarity and provider personality. *Personality and Social Psychology Bulletin, 28,* 1546–1555.

Lancelotta, G. X., & Vaughn, S. (1989). Relation between types of aggression and sociometric status: Peer and teaching perceptions. *Journal of Educational Psychology, 81,* 86–90.

Landau, M. J., Solomon, S., Greenberg, J., Cohen, F., Pyszczynski, T., Arndt, J., Miller, C. H., Ogilvie, D. M., & Cook, A. (2004). Deliver us from evil: The effects of mortality salience and reminders of 9/11 on support for President George W. Bush. *Personality and Social Psychology Bulletin, 30,* 1136–1150.

Langer, E. J. (1975). The illusion of control. *Journal of Personality and Social Psychology, 32,* 311–328.

Langlois, J. H. (1986). From the eye of the beholder to behavioral reality: Development of social behaviors and social relations as a function of physical attractiveness. In C. P. Herman, M. P. Zanna, & E. T. Higgins (Eds.), *Physical appearance, stigma, and social behavior: The Ontario symposium* (Vol. 3, pp. 23–51). Hillsdale, NJ: Erlbaum.

Langlois, J. H., Kalakanis, L., Rubenstein, A. J., Larson, A., Hallam, M., & Smoot, M. (2000). Maxims or myths of beauty? A meta-analytic and theoretical review. *Psychological Bulletin, 126,* 390–423.

Langlois, J. H., Ritter, J. M., Roggman, L. A., & Vaughn, L. S. (1991). Facial diversity and infant preferences for attractive faces. *Developmental Psychology, 27,* 79–84.

Langlois, J. H., & Roggman, L. A. (1990). Attractive faces are only average. *Psychological Science, 1,* 115–121.

Langlois, J. H., Roggman, L. A., & Musselman, L. (1994). What is average and what is not average about attractive faces? *Psychological Science, 5,* 214–220.

Langlois, J. H., Roggman, L. A., & Rieser-Danner, L. A. (1990). Infants' differential social responses to attractive and unattractive faces. *Developmental Psychology, 26,* 153–159.

Langlois, J. H., & Stephan, C. W. (1977). The effects of physical attractiveness and ethnicity on children's behavioral attributions and peer preferences. *Child Development, 48,* 1694–1698.

LaPiere, R. T. (1934). Attitudes vs. actions. *Social Forces, 13,* 230–237.

Laros, F. J. M., & Steenkamp, J.-B. E. M. (2004). Importance of fear in the case of genetically modified food. *Psychology and Marketing, 21,* 889–908.

Larsen, J. T., McGraw, A. P., Mellers, B. A., & Cacioppo, J. T. (2004). The agony of victory and the thrill of defeat: Mixed emotional reactions to disappointing wins and relieving losses. *Psychological Science, 15,* 325–330.

Lassiter, G. D., Geers, A. L., Munhall, P. J., Ploutz-Snyder, R. J., & Breitenbecher, D. L. (2002). Illusory causation: Why it occurs. *Psychological Science, 13,* 299–305.

Latané, B. (1981). The psychology of social impact. *American Psychologist, 36,* 343–356.

Latané, B., & Darley, J. M. (1968). Group inhibition of bystander intervention in emergencies. *Journal of Personality and Social Psychology, 10,* 215–221.

Latané, B., & Darley, J. M. (1970). *The unresponsive bystander: Why doesn't he help?* New York: Appleton-Century-Crofts.

Latané, B., & Rodin, J. (1969). A lady in distress: Inhibiting effects of friends and strangers on bystander intervention. *Journal of Experimental Social Psychology, 5,* 189–202.

Latané, B., Williams, K. P., & Harkins, S. G. (1979). Many hands make light the work: The causes and consequences of social loafing. *Journal of Personality and Social Psychology, 37,* 822–832.

Lavine, H., Thomsen, C. J., Zanna, M. P., & Borgida, E. (1998). On the primacy of affect in the determination of attitudes and behavior: The moderating role of affective-cognitive ambivalence. *Journal of Experimental Social Psychology, 34,* 398–421.

Leana, C. R. (1985). A partial test of Janis' groupthink model: Effects of group cohesiveness and leader behavior on defective decision making. *Journal of Management, 11,* 5–17.

Leary, M. R. (1990). Responses to social exclusion: Social anxiety, jealousy, loneliness, depression, and low self-esteem. *Journal of Social and Clinical Psychology, 9,* 221–229.

Leary, M. R. (1995). *Self-presentation: Impression management and interpersonal behavior.* Madison, WI: Brown & Benchmark.

Leary, M. R., & Baumeister, R. F. (2000). The nature and function of self-esteem: Sociometer theory. In M. P. Zanna (Ed.), *Advances in experimental social psychology* (Vol. 32, pp. 1–62). San Diego, CA: Academic Press.

Leary, M. R., & Kowalski, R. (1995). *Social anxiety.* New York: Guilford.

Leary, M. R., & Shepperd, J. A. (1986). Behavioral self-handicaps versus self-reported self-handicaps: A conceptual note. *Journal of Personality and Social Psychology, 51,* 1265–1268.

Leathers, D. G. (1997). *Successful nonverbal communication: Principles and applications.* Boston: Allyn & Bacon.

Lee, F., Hallahan, M., & Herzog, T. (1996). Explaining real life events: How culture and domain shape attributions. *Personality and Social Psychology Bulletin, 22,* 732–741.

Lee, J. A. (1988). Love-styles. In R. J. Sternberg & M. L. Barnes (Eds.), *The psychology of love* (pp. 38–67). New Haven, CT: Yale University Press.

Leippe, M. R., & Eisenstadt, D. (1994). Generalization of dissonance reduction: Decreasing prejudice through induced compliance. *Journal of Personality and Social Psychology, 67*, 395–413.

Lepore, L., & Brown, R. (1997). Category and stereotype activation: Is prejudice inevitable? *Journal of Personality and Social Psychology, 72*, 275–287.

Lepper, M. R., & Greene, D. (Eds.). (1978). *The hidden costs of reward.* Hillsdale, NJ: Erlbaum.

Lepper, M. R., Greene, D., & Nisbett, R. E. (1973). Undermining children's interest with extrinsic rewards: A test of the "overjustification effect." *Journal of Personality and Social Psychology, 28*, 129–137.

Lepper, M. R., & Woolverton, M. (2002). The wisdom of practice: Lessons learned from the study of highly effective tutors. In J. Aronson (Ed.), *Improving academic achievement: Impact of psychological factors on education* (pp. 135–158). New York: Academic Press.

Lerner, M. J. (1977). The justice motive in social behavior: Some hypotheses as to its origins and forms. *Journal of Personality, 45*, 1–52.

Lerner, M. J. (1980). *The belief in a just world: A fundamental delusion.* New York: Plenum Press.

Lerner, M. J., & Simmons, C. H. (1966). The observer's reaction to the "innocent victim": Compassion or rejection? *Journal of Personality and Social Psychology, 4*, 203–210.

Leventhal, H., & Cameron, L. (1994). Persuasion and health attitudes. In S. Shavitt & T. C. Brock (Eds.), *Persuasion: Psychological insights and perspectives* (pp. 219–249). Boston, MA: Allyn & Bacon.

Levine, J. M. (1989). Reaction to opinion deviance in small groups. In P. Paulus (Ed.), *Psychology of group influence* (2nd ed., pp. 187–231). Hillsdale, NJ: Erlbaum.

Levine, J. M., & McBurney, D. H. (1977). Causes and consequences of effluvia: Body odor awareness and controllability as determinants of interpersonal evaluation. *Personality and Social Psychology Bulletin, 3*, 442–445.

Levine, J. M., & McBurney, D. H. (1986). The role of olfaction in social perception and behavior. In C. P. Herman, M. P. Zanna, & E. T. Higgins (Eds.), *Physical appearance, stigma, and social behavior: The Ontario symposium* (Vol. 3, pp. 179–217). Hillsdale, NJ: Erlbaum.

Levine, J. M., & Moreland, R. L. (1994). Group socialization: Theory and research. In W. Stroebe & M. Hewstone (Eds.), *European review of social psychology* (Vol. 5, pp. 305–336). Chichester, UK: Wiley.

Levine, J. M., & Moreland, R. L. (1998). Small groups. In D. T. Gilbert, S. T. Fiske, & G. Lindzey (Eds.), *Handbook of social psychology* (4th ed., Vol. 2, pp. 415–469). Boston, MA: McGraw-Hill.

Levine, J. M., & Moreland, R. L. (2004). Collaboration: The social context of theory development. *Personality and Social Psychology Review, 8*, 164–172.

Levine, R. (2003). *The power of persuasion: How we are bought and sold.* Hoboken, NJ: Wiley.

Levine, R. V., Martinez, T. S., Brase, G., & Sorenson, K. (1994). Helping in 36 U.S. cities. *Journal of Personality and Social Psychology, 67*, 69–82.

Levinger, G. (1988). Can we picture "love"? In R. J. Sternberg & M. L. Barnes (Eds.), *The psychology of love* (pp. 139–158). New Haven, CT: Yale University Press.

Levy, B. (1996). Improving memory in old age through implicit self-stereotyping. *Journal of Personality and Social Psychology, 71*, 1092–1107.

Levy, S. R., Freitas, A. L., & Salovey, P. (2002). Construing action abstractly and blurring social distinctions: Implications for perceiving homogeneity among, but also empathizing with and helping, others. *Journal of Personality and Social Psychology, 83*, 1224–1238.

Lewin, K. (1951). *Field theory in social science* (D. Cartwright, Ed.). New York: Harper.

Leyens, J.-P., & Parke, R. D. (1975). Aggressive slides can induce a weapons effect. *European Journal of Social Psychology, 5*, 229–236.

Liberman, V., Samuels, S. M., & Ross, L. (2004). The name of the game: Predictive power of reputations versus situational labels in determining prisoner's dilemma game moves. *Personality and Social Psychology Bulletin, 30*, 1175–1185.

Lieberman, M. D., Ochsner, K. N., Gilbert, D. T., & Schacter, D. L. (2001). Do amnesics exhibit cognitive dissonance reduction? The role of explicit memory and attention in attitude change. *Psychological Science, 12*, 135–140.

Liebrand, W. B., Jansen, R. W., Rijken, V. M., & Suhre, C. J. (1986). Might over morality: Social values and the perception of other players in experimental games. *Journal of Experimental Social Psychology, 22*, 203–215.

Lifton, R. J. (1961). *Thought reform and the psychology of totalism: A study of "brainwashing" in China.* New York: Norton.

Likert, R. (1932). A technique for the measurement of attitudes. *Archives of Psychology, 140*, 5–53.

Linder, D. E., Cooper, J., & Jones, E. E. (1967). Decision freedom as a determinant of the role of incentive magnitude in attitude change. *Journal of Personality and Social Psychology, 6*, 245–254.

Lindorff, M. (2000). Is it better to perceive than receive? Social support, stress and strain for managers. *Psychology, Health, and Medicine, 5*, 271–286.

Lindsay, D. S., Hagen, L., Read, J. D., Wade, K. A., & Garry, M. (2004). True photographs and false memories. *Psychological Science, 15*, 149–154.

Lindsay, J. J., & Anderson, C. A. (2000). From antecedent conditions to violent actions: A general affective aggression model. *Personality and Social Psychology Bulletin, 26*, 533–547.

Lindskold, S., & Aronoff, J. (1980). Conciliatory strategies and relative power. *Journal of Experimental Social Psychology, 16*, 187–196.

Litt, M. D., Tennen, H., Affleck, G., & Klock, S. (1992). Coping and cognitive factors in adaptation to in vitro fertilization failure. *Journal of Behavioral Medicine, 15*, 351–369.

Lockwood, P., & Kunda, Z. (1997). Superstars and me: Predicting the impact of role models on the self. *Journal of Personality and Social Psychology, 73*, 91–103.

Loftus, E. F. (1979). *Eyewitness testimony.* Cambridge, MA: Harvard University Press.

Loftus, E. F. (2004). Memories of things unseen. *Current Directions in Psychological Science, 13*, 145–147.

Loftus, E. F., & Ketcham, K. (1994). *The myth of repressed memory: False memories and allegations of sexual abuse.* New York: St. Martin's Press.

Loftus, E. F., Miller, D. G., & Burns, H. J. (1978). Semantic integration of verbal information into a visual memory. *Journal of Experimental Psychology: Human Learning and Memory, 4*, 19–31.

Loftus, E. F., & Palmer, J. C. (1974). Reconstruction of automobile destruction: An example of the interaction between language and memory. *Journal of Verbal Learning and Verbal Behavior, 13*, 585–589.

Loomis, J. M., Blascovich, J., & Beall, A. C. (1999). Immersive virtual environment technology as a basic research tool in psychology. *Behavior Research Methods, Instruments, & Computers, 31*, 557–564.

Lord, C. G., Desforges, D. M., Chacon, S., Pere, G., & Clubb, R. (1992). Reflections on reputation in the process of self-evaluation. *Social Cognition, 10*, 2–29.

Lord, C. G., Lepper, M. R., & Preston, E. (1984). Considering the opposite: A corrective strategy for social judgment. *Journal of Personality and Social Psychology, 47*, 1231–1243.

Lord, C. G., Ross, L., & Lepper, M. R. (1979). Biased assimilation and attitude polarization: The effects of prior theories on subsequently considered evidence. *Journal of Personality and Social Psychology, 37*, 2098–2109.

Lord, R. G., DeVader, & Alliger, G. M. (1986). A meta-analysis of the relation between personality traits and leadership perceptions: An application of validity generalization procedures. *Journal of Applied Psychology, 71,* 402–410.

Losier, G. F., & Koestner, R. (1999). Intrinsic versus identified regulation in distinct political campaigns: The consequences of following politics for pleasure versus personal meaningfulness. *Personality and Social Psychology Bulletin, 25,* 287–298.

Lovaglia, M. J. (2000). *Knowing people: The personal use of social psychology.* Boston, MA: McGraw-Hill.

Lowery, B. S., Hardin, C. D., & Sinclair, S. (2001). Social influence effects on automatic racial prejudice. *Journal of Personality and Social Psychology, 81,* 842–855.

Luce, R. D., & Raiffa, H. (1957). *Games and decisions: Introduction and critical survey.* New York: Wiley.

Luginbuhl, J., & Palmer, R. (1991). Impression management aspects of self-handicapping: Positive and negative effects. *Personality and Social Psychology Bulletin, 17,* 655–662.

Luo, S., & Klohnen, E. C. (2005). Assortative mating and marital quality in newlyweds: A couple-centered approach. *Journal of Personality and Social Psychology, 88,* 304–326.

Lutz, C. J., & Lakey, B. (2001). How people make support judgments: Individual differences in the traits used to infer supportiveness in others. *Personality and Social Psychology Bulletin, 81,* 1070–1079.

MacCoun, R. J., & Kerr, N. L. (1988). Asymmetric influence in mock jury deliberation: Jurors' bias for leniency. *Journal of Personality and Social Psychology, 54,* 21–33.

MacDonald, T. K., & Ross, M. (1999). Assessing the accuracy of predictions about dating relationships: How and why do lovers' predictions differ from those made by observers? *Personality and Social Psychology Bulletin, 25,* 1417–1429.

MacDonald, T. K., Zanna, M. P., & Fong, G. T. (1995). Decision making in altered states: Effects of alcohol on attitudes toward drinking and driving. *Journal of Personality and Social Psychology, 68,* 973–985.

MacDonald, T. K., Zanna, M. P., & Fong, G. T. (1996). Why common sense goes out the window: Effects of alcohol on intentions to use condoms. *Personality and Social Psychology Bulletin, 22,* 763–775.

MacHovec, F. J. (1989). *Cults and personality.* Springfield, IL: Charles C. Thomas.

MacLeod, C., & Campbell, L. (1992). Memory accessibility and probability judgments: An experimental evaluation of the availability heuristic. *Journal of Personality and Social Psychology, 63,* 1890–902.

MacLin, O. H., MacLin, M. K., & Malpass, R. S. (2001). Race, arousal, attention, exposure, and delay: An examination of factors moderating face recognition. *Psychology, Public Policy, and Law, 7,* 134–152.

MacNeil, M. K., & Sherif, M. (1976). Norm change over subject generations as a function of arbitrariness of prescribed norms. *Journal of Personality and Social Psychology, 34,* 762–773.

Maddux, J. E., & Rogers, R. W. (1983). Protection motivation and self-efficacy: A revised theory of fear appeals and attitude change. *Journal of Experimental Social Psychology, 19,* 469–479.

Maddux, W. W., Barden, J., Brewer, M. B., & Petty, R. E. (2004). Saying no to negativity: The effects of context and motivation to control prejudice on automatic evaluative responses. *Journal of Experimental Social Psychology, 41,* 19–35.

Madsen, D. B. (1978). Issue importance and choice shifts: A persuasive arguments approach. *Journal of Personality and Social Psychology, 36,* 1118–1127.

Main, M., & Cassidy, J. (1988). Categories of response to reunion with the parent at age 6: Predictable from infant attachment classifications and stable over a 1-month period. *Developmental Psychology, 24,* 415–426.

Maio, G. R., Esses, V. M., & Bell, D. W. (2000). Examining conflict between components of attitudes: Ambivalence and inconsistency are distinct constructs. *Canadian Journal of Behavioural Science, 32,* 58–70.

Maio, G. R., & Olson, J. M. (1998). Values as truisms: Evidence and implications. *Journal of Personality and Social Psychology, 74,* 294–311.

Maio, G. R., & Olson, J. M. (Eds.). (2000a). *Why we evaluate: Functions of attitudes.* Mahwah, NJ: Erlbaum.

Maio, G. R., & Olson, J. M. (2000b). What *is* a value-expressive attitude? In G. R. Maio & J. M. Olson (Eds.), *Why we evaluate: Functions of attitudes* (pp. 249–269). Mahwah, NJ: Erlbaum.

Maio, G. R., Olson, J. M., Allen, L., & Bernard, M. M. (2001). Addressing discrepancies between values and behavior: The motivating effects of reasons. *Journal of Experimental Social Psychology, 37,* 104–117.

Major, B., Cozzarrelli, C., Sciacchitano, A. M., Cooper, M. L., Testa, M., & Mueller, P. M. (1990). Perceived social support, self-efficacy, and adjustment to abortion. *Journal of Personality and Social Psychology, 59,* 452–463.

Malamuth, N. M., Addison, T., & Koss, M. (2000). Pornography and sexual aggression: Are there reliable effects and can we understand them? *Annual Review of Sex Research, 11,* 26–91.

Maner, J. K., Luce, C. L., Neuberg, S. L., Cialdini, R. B., Brown, S., & Sagarin, B. J. (2002). The effects of perspective taking on motivations for helping: Still no evidence for altruism. *Personality and Social Psychology Bulletin, 28,* 1601–1610.

Marcus-Newhall, A., Pedersen, W. C., Carlson, M., & Miller, N. (2000). Displaced aggression is alive and well: A meta-analytic review. *Journal of Personality and Social Psychology, 78,* 670–689.

Marin, G. (1984). Stereotyping Hispanics: The differential effect of research method, label, and degree of contact. *International Journal of Intercultural Relations, 8,* 17–27.

Markman, K. D., Gavanski, I., Sherman, S. J., & McMullen, M. N. (1993). The mental simulation of better and worse possible worlds. *Journal of Experimental Social Psychology, 29,* 87–109.

Marks, G., & Miller N. (1987). Ten years of research on the false-consensus effect: An empirical and theoretical review. *Psychological Bulletin, 102,* 72–90.

Markus, H. R., & Kitayama, S. (1991). Culture and the self: Implications for cognition, emotion, and motivation. *Psychological Review, 98,* 224–253.

Markus, H. R., Kitayama, S., & Heiman, R. J. (1996). Culture and "basic" psychological principles. In E. T. Higgins & A. W. Kruglanski (Eds.), *Social psychology: Handbook of basic principles* (pp. 857–913). New York: Guilford Press.

Markus, H. R., & Kunda, Z. (1986). Stability and malleability of the self-concept. *Journal of Personality and Social Psychology, 51,* 858–866.

Martin, C. L. (1987). A ratio measure of sex stereotyping. *Journal of Personality and Social Psychology, 52,* 489–499.

Martin, C. L., Ruble, D. N., & Szkrybalo, J. (2002). Cognitive theories of early gender development. *Psychological Bulletin, 128,* 903–933.

Martin, L. L., Seta, J. J., & Crelia, R. A. (1990). Assimilation and contrast as a function of people's willingness and ability to expend effort in forming an impression. *Journal of Personality and Social Psychology, 59,* 38–49.

Martin, R. A. (2001). Humor, laughter, and physical health: Methodological issues and research findings. *Psychological Bulletin, 127,* 504–519.

Martin, R., Hewstone, M., & Martin, P. Y. (2003). Resistance to persuasive messages as a function of majority and minority status. *Journal of Experimental Social Psychology, 39,* 585–593.

Marx, D. M., & Roman, J. S. (2002). Female role models: Protecting women's math test performance. *Personality and Social Psychology Bulletin, 28,* 1183–1193.

Masten, A. S., & Coatsworth, J. D. (1998). The development of competence in favorable and unfavorable environments. *American Psychologist, 53,* 205–220.

Masuda, T., & Kitayama, S. (2004). Perceiver-induced constraint and attitude attribution in Japan and the US: A case for the cultural dependence of the correspondence bias. *Journal of Experimental Social Psychology, 40,* 409–416.

Matheson, K., & Dursun, S. (2001). Social identity precursors to the hostile media phenomenon: Partisan perceptions of coverage of the Bosnian conflict. *Group Processes and Intergroup Relations, 4,* 116–125.

Matsumoto, D. (1996). *Culture and psychology.* Pacific Grove, CA: Brooks/Cole.

Matthews, K. A. (1982). Psychological perspectives on the Type A behavior pattern. *Psychological Bulletin, 91,* 293–323.

Matthews, K. A. (1988). Coronary heart disease and Type A behaviors: Update on and alternative to the Booth-Kewley and Friedman (1987) quantitative review. *Psychological Bulletin, 104,* 373–380.

Mayer, B. (2000). *The dynamics of conflict resolution: A practitioner's guide.* San Francisco: Jossey-Bass.

Mayo, C., & Henley, N. M. (Eds.). (1981). *Gender and nonverbal behavior.* New York: Springer-Verlag.

McArthur, L. Z. (1972). The how and what of why: Some determinants and consequences of causal attribution. *Journal of Personality and Social Psychology, 18,* 195–224.

McCann, S. J. H. (1992). Alternative formulas to predict the greatness of U.S. presidents: Personological, situational, and zeitgeist factors. *Journal of Personality and Social Psychology, 62,* 469–479.

McCaskill, J. W., & Lakey, B. (2000). Perceived support, social undermining, and emotion: Idiosyncratic and shared perspectives of adolescents and their families. *Personality and Social Psychology Bulletin, 26,* 820–832.

McCaul, K. D., O'Neill, H. K., & Glasgow, R. E. (1988). Predicting the performance of dental hygiene behaviors: An examination of the Fishbein and Ajzen model and self-efficacy expectations. *Journal of Applied Social Psychology, 18,* 114–128.

McCauley, C. R., & Segal, M. E. (1987). Social psychology of terrorist groups. In C. Hendrick (Ed.), *Group processes and intergroup relations: Review of personality and social psychology* (Vol. 9, pp. 231–256). Thousand Oaks, CA: Sage.

McClelland, D. C., Atkinson, J. W., Clark, R. A., & Lowell, E. L. (1953). *The achievement motive.* New York: Appleton-Century-Crofts.

McConahay, J. B. (1986). Modern racism, ambivalence, and the modern racism scale. In J. F. Dovidio & S. L. Gaertner (Eds.), *Prejudice, discrimination, and racism* (pp. 91–125). Orlando, FL: Academic Press.

McConnell, A. R., & Leibold, J. M. (2001). Relations among the Implicit Association Test, discriminatory behavior, and explicit measures of racist attitudes. *Journal of Experimental Social Psychology, 37,* 435–442.

McCullough, M. E., Emmons, R. A., & Tsang, J.-A. (2002). The grateful disposition: A conceptual and empirical topography. *Journal of Personality and Social Psychology, 82,* 112–127.

McCullough, M. E., Kilpatrick, S. D., Emmons, R. A., & Larson, D. B. (2001). Is gratitude a moral affect? *Psychological Bulletin, 127,* 249–266.

McDougall, W. (1908). *An introduction to social psychology.* London, UK: Methuen.

McFarland, C., & Ross, M. (1987). The relationship between current impressions and memories of self and dating partners. *Personality and Social Psychology Bulletin, 13,* 228–238.

McGuire, A. M. (1994). Helping behaviors in the natural environment: Dimensions and correlates of helping. *Personality and Social Psychology Bulletin, 20,* 45–56.

McGuire, W. J. (1964). Inducing resistance to persuasion: Some contemporary approaches. In L. Berkowitz (Ed.), *Advances in experimental social psychology* (Vol. 1, pp. 191–229). New York: Academic Press.

McGuire, W. J. (1969). The nature of attitudes and attitude change. In G. Lindzey & E. Aronson (Eds.), *Handbook of social psychology* (2nd ed., Vol. 3, pp. 136–314). Reading, MA: Addison-Wesley.

McGuire, W. J. (1972). Attitude change: The information-processing paradigm. In C. G. MClintock (Ed.), *Experimental social psychology* (pp. 108–141). New York: Holt, Rinehart, and Winston.

McGuire, W. J., McGuire, C. V., & Winton W. (1979). Effects of household sex composition on the salience of one's gender in the spontaneous self-concept. *Journal of Experimental Social Psychology, 15,* 77–90.

McGuire, W. J., & Padawer-Singer, A. (1976). Trait salience in the spontaneous self-concept. *Journal of Personality and Social Psychology, 33,* 743–754.

McGuire, W. J., & Papageorgis, D. (1961). The relative efficacy of various types of prior belief defense in producing immunity against persuasion. *Journal of Abnormal and Social Psychology, 62,* 327–337.

McIntyre, R. B., Paulson, R. M., & Lord, C. G. (2003). Alleviating women's mathematics stereotype threat through salience of group achievements. *Journal of Experimental Social Psychology, 39,* 83–90.

Medin, D. L. (1989). Concepts and conceptual structure. *American Psychologist, 44,*1469–1481.

Medvec, V., H., Madey, S. F., & Gilovich, T. (1995). When less is more: Counterfactual thinking and satisfaction among Olympic medalists. *Journal of Personality and Social Psychology, 69,* 603–610.

Meeus, W. H. J., & Raaijmakers, Q. A. W. (1995). Obedience in modern society: The Utrecht studies. *Journal of Social Issues, 51,* 155–176.

Mehrabian, A. (1968). Relationship of attitudes to seated posture, orientation, and distance. *Journal of Personality and Social Psychology, 10,* 26–30.

Mehrabian, A. (1972) *Nonverbal communication.* Chicago: Aldine-Atherton.

Meissner, C. A., & Brigham, J. C. (2001). Thirty years of investigating the own-race bias in memory for faces: A meta-analytic review. *Psychology, Public Policy, and Law, 7,* 3–35.

Mellor, D. (2003). Contemporary racism in Australia: The experiences of Aborigines. *Personality and Social Psychology Bulletin, 29,* 474–486.

Mendelsohn, H. (1973). Some reasons why information campaigns can succeed. *Public Opinion Quarterly, 37,* 50–61.

Meyer, J. R., Nash, J. D., McAlister, A. L., Maccoby, N., & Farquhar, J. W. (1980). Skills training in a cardiovascular health education campaign. *Journal of Consulting and Clinical Psychology, 48,* 129–142.

Mezulis, A. H., Abramson, L. Y., Hyde, J. S., & Hankin, B. L. (2004). Is there a universal positivity bias in attributions? A meta-analytic review of individual, developmental, and cultural differences in the self-serving attributional bias. *Psychological Bulletin, 130,* 711–747.

Michener, H. A., DeLamater, J. D., & Myers, D. G. (2003). *Social psychology* (5th ed.). Belmont, CA: Wadsworth.

Miles, S., & Frewer, L. J. (2003). Public perception of scientific uncertainty in relation to food hazards. *Journal of Risk Research, 6,* 267–283.

Milgram, S. (1963). Behavioral study of obedience. *Journal of Abnormal and Social Psychology, 67,* 371–378.

Milgram, S. (1964). Issues in the study of obedience: A reply to Baumrind. *American Psychologist, 19,* 848–852.

Milgram, S. (1970). The experience of living in cities. *Science, 167,* 1461–1468.

Milgram, S. (1974). *Obedience to authority: An experimental view.* New York: Harper & Row.

Milgram, S., Bickman, L., & Berkowitz, L. (1969). Note on the drawing power of crowds of different size. *Journal of Personality and Social Psychology, 13,* 79–82.

Miller, A. G. (1986). *The obedience experiments: A case study of controversy in social science.* New York: Praeger.

Miller, C. T., & Downey, K. T. (1999). A meta-analysis of heavyweight and self-esteem. *Personality and Social Psychology Review, 3,* 68–84.

Miller, D. T., & Turnbull, W. (1986). Expectancies and interpersonal processes. *Annual Review of Psychology, 37,* 233–256.

Miller, D. T., Turnbull, W., & McFarland, C. (1990). Counterfactual thinking and social perception: Thinking about what might have been. In M. P. Zanna (Ed.), *Advances in experimental social psychology* (Vol. 23, pp. 305–331). New York: Academic Press.

Miller, J. G. (1984). Culture and the development of everyday social explanation. *Journal of Personality and Social Psychology, 46,* 961–978.

Miller, J. G., Bersoff, D. M., & Harwood, R. L. (1990). Perceptions of social responsibilities in India and in the United States: Moral imperatives or personal decisions? *Journal of Personality and Social Psychology, 58,* 33–47.

Miller, L. C., Berg, J. H., & Archer, R. L. (1983). Openers: Individuals who elicit intimate self-disclosure. *Journal of Personality and Social Psychology, 44,* 1234–1244.

Miller, L. C., Cooke, L. L., Tsang, J., & Morgan, F. (1992). Should I brag? Nature and impact of positive and boastful disclosures for women and men. *Human Communication Research, 18,* 364–399.

Miller, N., Pedersen, W. C., Earleywine, M., & Pollock, V. E. (2003). A theoretical model of triggered displaced aggression. *Personality and Social Psychology Review, 7,* 75–97.

Miller, R. L., Brickman, P., & Bolen, D. (1975). Attribution versus persuasion as a means for modifying behavior. *Journal of Personality and Social Psychology, 31,* 430–441.

Mills, J., & Jellison, J. M. (1967). Effect on opinion change of how desirable the communication is to the audience the communicator addressed. *Journal of Personality and Social Psychology, 56,* 82–92.

Mills, J. S., Polivy, J., Herman, C. P., & Tiggemann, M. (2002). Effects of exposure to thin media images: Evidence of self-enhancement among restrained eaters. *Personality and Social Psychology Bulletin, 28,* 1687–1699.

Mischel, W., Cantor, N., & Feldman, S. (1996). Principles of self-regulation: The nature of willpower and self-control. In E. T. Higgins & A. W. Kruglanski (Eds.), *Social psychology: Handbook of basic principles* (pp. 329–360). New York: Guilford Press.

Mitchell, H. E., & Byrne, D. (1973). The defendant's dilemma: Effects of jurors' attitudes and authoritarianism on judicial decisions. *Journal of Personality and Social Psychology, 25,* 123–129.

Mitchell, J. P., Heatherton, T. F., & Macrae, C. N. (2002). Distinct neural systems subserve person and object knowledge. *Proceedings of the National Academy of Sciences, 99,* 15238–15243.

Miyamoto, Y., & Kitayama, S. (2002). Cultural variation in correspondence bias: The critical role of attitude diagnosticity of socially constrained behavior. *Journal of Personality and Social Psychology, 83,* 1239–1248.

Moghaddam, F. M. (2005). The staircase to terrorism: A psychological exploration. *American Psychologist, 60,* 161–169.

Moghaddam, F. M., Taylor, D. M., & Wright, S. C. (1993). *Social psychology in cross-cultural perspective.* New York: Freeman.

Montada, L., & Lerner, M. J. (Eds.). (1998). *Responses to victimizations and belief in a just world.* New York: Plenum Press.

Montague, P. R., Berns, G. S., Cohen, J. D., McClure, S. M., Pagnoni, G., Dhamala, M., et al. (2002). Hyperscanning: Simultaneous fMRI during linked social interactions. *Neuroimage, 16,* 1159–1164.

Monteith, M. J. (1993). Self-regulation of prejudiced responses: Implications for progress in prejudice reduction efforts. *Journal of Personality and Social Psychology, 65,* 469–485.

Monteith, M. J. (1996). Affective reactions to prejudice-related discrepant responses: The impact of standard salience. *Personality and Social Psychology Bulletin, 22,* 48–59.

Moorhead, G., & Montanari, J. R. (1986). An empirical investigation of the groupthink phenomenon. *Human Relations, 39,* 399–410.

Moreland, R. L., & Beach, S. R. (1992). Exposure effects in the classroom: The development of affinity among students. *Journal of Experimental Social Psychology, 28,* 255–276.

Morf, C. C., & Rhodewalt, F. (1993). Narcissism and self-evaluation maintenance: Explorations in object relations. *Personality and Social Psychology Bulletin, 19,* 668–676.

Morgan, M. Y. (1987). The impact of religion on gender-role attitudes. *Psychology of Women Quarterly, 11,* 301–310.

Morris, M. W., & Larrick, R. P. (1995). When one cause casts doubt on another: A normative analysis of discounting in causal attribution. *Psychological Review, 102,* 331–355.

Morris, M. W., & Peng, K. (1994). Culture and cause: American and Chinese attributions for social and physical events. *Journal of Personality and Social Psychology, 67,* 949–971.

Morris, M. W., Podolny, J. M., & Ariel, S. (2000). Missing relations: Incorporating relational constructs into models of culture. In P. C. Earley & H. Singh (Eds.), *Innovations in international and cross-cultural management* (pp. 52–90). Thousand Oaks, CA: Sage.

Morton, J. B., & Trehub, S. E. (2001). Children's understanding of emotion in speech. *Child Development, 72,* 834–843.

Moscovici, S. (1980). Toward a theory of conversion behavior. In L. Berkowitz (Ed.), *Advances in experimental social psychology* (Vol. 13, pp. 209–239). New York: Academic Press.

Moscovici, S., & Doise, W. (1994). *Conflict and consensus.* London, UK: Sage.

Mueller, C. M., & Dweck, C. S. (1998). Praise for intelligence can undermine children's motivation and performance. *Journal of Personality and Social Psychology, 75,* 33–52.

Mullen, B. (1986). Atrocity as a function of lynch mob composition: A self-attention perspective. *Personality and Social Psychology Bulletin, 12,* 187–197.

Mullen, B., Anthony, T., Salas, E., & Driskell, J. E. (1994). Group cohesiveness and quality of decision making: An integration of tests of the groupthink hypothesis. *Small Group Research, 25,* 189–204.

Mullen, B., & Cooper, C. (1994). The relation between group cohesiveness and performance: An integration. *Psychological Bulletin, 115,* 210–227.

Mullen, B., Migdal, M. J., & Rozell, D. (2003). Self-awareness, deindividuation, and social identity: Unraveling theoretical paradoxes by filling empirical lacunae. *Personality and Social Psychology Bulletin, 29,* 1071–1081.

Mullen, B., Salas, E., & Driskell, J. E. (1989). Salience, motivation, and artifact as contributions to the relation between participation rate and leadership. *Journal of Experimental Social Psychology, 25,* 545–559.

Murphy, C. M., & O'Leary, K. D. (1989). Psychological aggression predicts physical aggression in early marriage. *Journal of Consulting and Clinical Psychology, 57,* 579–582.

Murphy, S. T., Monahan, J. L., & Zajonc, R. B. (1995). Additivity of nonconscious affect: Combined effects of priming and exposure. *Journal of Personality and Social Psychology, 69,* 589–602.

Murray, H. A. (1943). *Thematic apperception test.* Cambridge, MA: Harvard University Press.

Murray, S. L., Haddock, G., & Zanna, M. P. (1996). On creating value-expressive attitudes: An experimental approach. In C. Seligman, J. M. Olson, & M. P. Zanna (Eds.), *The psychology of values: The Ontario symposium* (Vol. 8, pp. 107–133). Mahwah, NJ: Erlbaum.

Murray, S. L., & Holmes, J. G. (1997). A leap of faith? Positive illusions in romantic relationships. *Personality and Social Psychology Bulletin, 23,* 586–604.

Murray, S. L., Holmes, J. G., & Griffin, D. W. (1996a). The benefits of positive illusions: Idealization and the construction of satisfaction in close relationships. *Journal of Personality and Social Psychology, 70,* 79–98.

Murray, S. L., Holmes, J. G., & Griffin, D. W. (1996b). The self-fulfilling nature of positive illusions in romantic relationships: Love is not blind, but prescient. *Journal of Personality and Social Psychology, 71,* 1155–1180.

Murray, S. L., Holmes, J. G., MacDonald, G., & Ellsworth, P. C. (1998). Through the looking glass darkly? When self-doubts turn into relationship insecurities. *Journal of Personality and Social Psychology, 75*, 1459–1480.

Mussen, P., & Eisenberg-Berg, N. (1977). *Roots of caring, sharing, and helping.* San Francisco: W. H. Freeman.

Mussweiler, T. (2003). Comparison processes in social judgment: Mechanisms and consequences. *Psychological Review, 110*, 472–489.

Mussweiler, T., Rüter, K., & Epstude, K. (2004). The man who wasn't there: Subliminal social comparison standards influence self-evaluation. *Journal of Experimental Social Psychology, 40*, 689–696.

Mussweiler, T., & Strack, F. (2000). Consequences of social comparison: Selective accessibility, assimilation, and contrast. In J. M. Suls & L. Wheeler (Eds.), *Handbook of social comparison: Theory and research* (pp. 253–270). New York: Kluwer Academic/Plenum.

Myers, D. G., & Bishop, G. D. (1970). Discussion effects on racial attitudes. *Science, 169*, 778–789.

Myers, D. G., & Lamm, H. (1976). The group polarization phenomenon. *Psychological Bulletin, 83*, 602–627.

Nadler, A., & Fisher, J. D. (1986). The role of threat to self-esteem and perceived control in recipient reaction to help: Theory development and empirical validation. In L. Berkowitz (Ed.), *Advances in experimental social psychology* (Vol. 19, pp. 81–122). New York: Academic Press.

Nadler, A., Fisher, J. D., & Streufert, S. (1976). When helping hurts: The effects of donor-recipient similarity and recipient self-esteem on reactions to aid. *Journal of Personality, 44*, 392–409.

Nail, P. R., MacDonald, G., & Levy, D. A. (2000). Proposal of a four-dimensional model of social response. *Psychological Bulletin, 126*, 454–470.

Nasco, S. A., & Marsh, K. L. (1999). Gaining control through counterfactual thinking. *Personality and Social Psychology Bulletin, 25*, 556–568.

National Research Council. (2003). *Protecting participants and facilitating social and behavioral sciences research.* Washington, DC: National Academic Press.

Neff, L. A., & Karney, B. R. (2005). Gender differences in social support: A question of skill or responsiveness? *Journal of Personality and Social Psychology, 88*, 79–90.

Nelson, T. D. (2002). *The psychology of prejudice.* Boston, MA: Allyn & Bacon.

Nemeth, C. J. (1987). Influence processes, problem solving and creativity. In M. P. Zanna, J. M. Olson, & C. P. Herman (Eds.), *Social influence: The Ontario symposium* (Vol. 5, pp. 237–246). Hillsdale, NJ: Erlbaum.

Nemeth, C. J., & Chiles, C. (1988). Modelling courage: The role of dissent in fostering independence. *European Journal of Social Psychology, 18*, 275–280.

Neuberg, S. L. (1994). Expectancy-conformation processes in stereotype-tinged social encounters: The moderating role of social goals. In M. P. Zanna & J. M. Olson (Eds.), *The psychology of prejudice: The Ontario symposium* (Vol 7, pp. 103–130). Hillsdale, NJ: Erlbaum.

Neuling, S. J., & Winefield, H. R. (1988). Social support and recovery after surgery for breast cancer: Frequency and correlates of supportive behaviors by family, friends and surgeon. *Social Science and Medicine, 27*, 385–392.

Neumann, R., Hülsenbeck, K., & Seibt, B. (2004). Attitudes toward people with AIDS and avoidance behavior: Automatic and reflective bases of behavior. *Journal of Experimental Social Psychology, 40*, 543–550.

Newcomb, A. F., & Bagwell, C. L. (1995). Children's friendship relations: A meta-analytic review. *Psychological Bulletin, 117*, 306–347.

Newcomb, A. F., Bukowski, W. M., & Pattee, L. (1993). Children's peer relations: A meta-analytic review of popular, rejected, neglected, controversial, and average sociometric status. *Psychological Bulletin, 113*, 99–128.

Newcomb, T. M. (1943). *Personality and social change.* New York: Dryden.

Newcomb, T. M. (1963). Persistence and regression of changed attitudes: Long-range studies. *Journal of Social Issues, 19*, 3–14.

Newcomb, T. M., Koeing, K. E., Flacks, R., & Warwick, D. P. (1967). *Persistence and change: Bennington College and its students after 25 years.* New York: Wiley.

Newman, L. S. (1991). Why are traits inferred spontaneously? A developmental approach. *Social Cognition, 9*, 221–253.

Neyer, F. J., & Lang, F. R. (2003). Blood is thicker than water: Kinship orientation across adulthood. *Journal of Personality and Social Psychology, 84*, 310–321.

Nickerson, R. S. (2001). The projective way of knowing: A useful heuristic that sometimes misleads. *Current Directions in Psychological Science, 10*, 168–172.

Nisbett, R. E., & Cohen, D. (1996). *Culture of honor: The psychology of violence in the south.* Boulder, CO: Westview Press.

Nisbett, R. E., & Wilson, T. D. (1977). Telling more than we can know: Verbal reports on mental processes. *Psychological Review, 84*, 231–259.

Noor, F., & Evans, D. C. (2003). The effect of facial symmetry on perceptions of personality and attractiveness. *Journal of Research in Personality, 37*, 339–347.

Norenzayan, A., Choi, I., & Nisbett, R. E. (2002). Cultural similarities and differences in social inference: Evidence from behavioral predictions and lay theories of behavior. *Personality and Social Psychology Bulletin, 28*, 109–120.

Northouse, P. G. (1997). *Leadership: Theory and practice.* Thousand Oaks, CA: Sage.

Novaco, R. W. (1975). *Anger control.* Lexington, MA: Lexington Books.

Nuttin, J. M. (1987). Affective consequences of mere ownership: The name-letter effect in twelve European languages. *European Journal of Social Psychology, 17*, 381–402.

O'Brien, L. T., & Crandall, C. S. (2003). Stereotype threat and arousal: Effects on women's math performance. *Personality and Social Psychology Bulletin, 29*, 782–789.

Ochsner, K. N., & Lieberman, M. D. (2001). The emergence of social cognitive neuroscience. *American Psychologist, 56*, 717–734.

Oettingen, G., & Mayer, D. (2002). The motivating function of thinking about the future: Expectations versus fantasies. *Journal of Personality and Social Psychology, 83*, 1198–1212.

O'Keefe, G. J. (1985). "Taking a bite out of crime": The impact of a public information campaign. *Communication Research, 12*, 147–178.

Oliner, S. P., & Oliner, P. M. (1988). *The altruistic personality.* New York: Free Press.

Olson, J. M. (1992). Self-perception of humor: Evidence for discounting and augmentation effects. *Journal of Personality and Social Psychology, 62*, 369–377.

Olson, J. M., Buhrmann, O., & Roese, N. J. (2000). Comparing comparisons: An integrative perspective on social comparison and counterfactual thinking. In J. M. Suls & L. Wheeler (Eds.), *Handbook of social comparison: Theory and research* (pp. 379–398). New York: Kluwer Academic/Plenum.

Olson, J. M., & Hafer, C. L. (1996). Affect, motivation, and cognition in relative deprivation research. In R. M. Sorrentino & E. T. Higgins (Eds.), *Handbook of motivation and cognition* (Vol. 3, pp. 85–117). New York: Guilford.

Olson, J. M., Hafer, C. L., Couzens, A., & Kramins, I. (2000). You're OK, I'm OK: The self-presentation of affective reactions to deprivation. *Social Justice Research, 13*, 359–371.

Olson, J. M., Roese, N. J., Meen, J., & Robertson, D. J. (1995). The preconditions and consequences of relative deprivation: Two field studies. *Journal of Applied Social Psychology, 25,* 944–964.

Olson, J. M., Roese, N. J., & Zanna, M. P. (1996). Expectancies. In E. T. Higgins & A. W. Kruglanski (Eds.), *Social psychology: Handbook of basic principles* (pp. 211–238). New York: Guilford Press.

Olson, J. M., & Stone, J. (in press). The influence of behavior on attitudes. In D. Albarracín, B. T. Johnson, & M. P. Zanna (Eds.), *Handbook of attitudes and attitude change.* Mahwah, NJ: Erlbaum.

Olson, J. M., Vernon, P. A., Harris, J. A., & Jang, K. L. (2001). The heritability of attitudes: A study of twins. *Journal of Personality and Social Psychology, 80,* 845–860.

Olson, J. M., & Zanna, M. P. (1987). Understanding and promoting exercise: A social psychological perspective. *Canadian Journal of Public Health, 78,* S1–S7.

Olson, M. A., & Fazio, R. H. (2004). Reducing the influence of extrapersonal associations on the Implicit Association Task: Personalizing the IAT. *Journal of Personality and Social Psychology, 86,* 653–667.

Omoto, A. M., & Snyder, M. (1995). Sustained helping without obligation: Motivation, longevity of service, and perceived attitude change among AIDS workers. *Journal of Personality and Social Psychology, 68,* 671–686.

Opotow, S. (1994). Predicting protection: Scope of justice and the natural world. *Journal of Social Issues, 50* (3), 49–63.

Opotow, S. (2001). Reconciliation in times of impunity: Challenges for social justice. *Social Justice Research, 14,* 149–170.

Opotow, S., & Weiss, L. (2000). Denial and the process of moral exclusion in environmental conflict. *Journal of Social Issues, 56,* 475–490.

Orbell, J. M., van de Kragt, A. J. C., & Dawes, R. M. (1988). Explaining discussion-induced cooperation. *Journal of Personality and Social Psychology, 54,* 811–819.

Orne, M. T. (1962). On the social psychology of the psychological experiment: With particular reference to demand characteristics and their implications. *American Psychologist, 17,* 776–783.

Osgood, C. E. (1962). *An alternative to war or surrender.* Urbana: University of Illinois Press.

Osgood, C. E., Suci, G. J., & Tannenbaum, P. H. (1957). *The measurement of meaning.* Urbana: University of Illinois Press.

Osherow, N. (1999). Making sense of the nonsensical: An analysis of Jonestown. In E. Aronson (Ed.), *Readings about the social animal* (8th ed., pp. 71–88). New York: Worth.

Oskamp, S. (1991). *Attitudes and opinions* (2nd ed.). Englewood Cliffs, NJ: Prentice Hall.

Ottati, V. C., Tindale, R. S., Edwards, J., Bryant, F. B., Heath, L., O'Connell, D. C., et al. (Eds.). (2002). *The social psychology of politics.* New York: Plenum.

Oyserman, D., Coon, H. M., & Kemmelmeier, M. (2002). Rethinking individualism and collectivism: Evaluation of theoretical assumptions and meta-analyses. *Psychological Bulletin, 128,* 3–72.

Page, M. M., & Scheidt, R. J. (1971). The elusive weapons effect: Demand awareness, evaluation apprehension, and slightly sophisticated subjects. *Journal of Personality and Social Psychology, 20,* 304–318.

Paik, H., & Comstock, G. (1994). The effects of television violence on antisocial behavior: A meta-analysis. *Communication Research, 21,* 516–546.

Pan, H. S., Neidig, P. H., & O'Leary, K. D. (1994). Predicting mild and severe husband-to-wife physical aggression. *Journal of Consulting and Clinical Psychology, 62,* 975–981.

Paolini, S., Hewstone, M., Cairns, E., & Voci, A. (2004). Effects of direct and indirect cross-group friendships on judgments of Catholics and Protestants in Northern Ireland: The mediating role of an anxiety-reduction mechanism. *Personality and Social Psychology Bulletin, 30,* 770–786.

Papastamou, S., & Mugny, G. (1990). Synchronic consistency and psychologization in minority influence. *European Journal of Social Psychology, 20,* 85–98.

Park, B. (1986). A method for studying the development of impressions of real people. *Journal of Personality and Social Psychology, 51,* 907–917.

Park, W. (1990). A review of research on groupthink. *Journal of Behavioral Decision Making, 3,* 229–245.

Parks, C. D., & Rumble, A. C. (2001). Elements of reciprocity and social value orientation. *Personality and Social Psychology Bulletin, 27,* 1301–1309.

Parks, C. D., Sanna, L. J., & Berel, S. R. (2001). Actions of similar others as inducements to cooperate in social dilemmas. *Personality and Social Psychology Bulletin, 27,* 345–354.

Parks, C. D., Sanna, L. J., & Posey, D. C. (2003). Retrospection in social dilemmas: Thinking about the past affects future cooperation. *Journal of Personality and Social Psychology, 84,* 988–996.

Pasupathi, M. (1999). Age differences in response to conformity pressure for emotional and nonemotional material. *Psychology and Aging, 14,* 170–174.

Paulhus, D. L. (1998). Interpersonal and intrapsychic adaptiveness of trait self-enhancement: A mixed blessing? *Journal of Personality and Social Psychology, 74,* 1197–1208.

Pavlov, I. P. (1927). *Conditional reflexes.* London, UK: Oxford University Press.

Payne, B. K. (2001). Prejudice and perception: The role of automatic and controlled processes in misperceiving a weapon. *Journal of Personality and Social Psychology, 81,* 181–192.

Payne, B. K., Lambert, A. J., & Jacoby, L. L. (2002). Best laid plans: Effects of goals on accessibility bias and cognitive control in race-based misperceptions of weapons. *Journal of Experimental Social Psychology, 38,* 384–396.

Pearce, P. L., & Amato, P. R. (1980). A taxonomy of helping: A multidimensional scaling analysis. *Social Psychology Quarterly, 43,* 363–371.

Pedersen, W. C., Gonzales, C., & Miller, N. (2000). The moderating effect of trivial triggering provocation on displaced aggression. *Journal of Personality and Social Psychology, 78,* 913–927.

Pelham, B. W. (1999). *Conducting experiments in psychology: Measuring the weight of smoke.* Pacific Grove, CA: Brooks/Cole.

Pelham, B. W., Koole, S. L., Hardin, C. D., Hetts, J. J., Seah, E., & DeHart, T. (2005). Gender moderates the relation between implicit and explicit self-esteem. *Journal of Experimental Social Psychology, 41,* 84–89.

Pelham, B. W., Mirenberg, M. C., & Jones, J. T. (2002). Why Susie sells seashells by the seashore: Implicit egotism and major life decisions. *Journal of Personality and Social Psychology, 82,* 469–487.

Peng, K., & Knowles, E. D. (2003). Culture, education, and the attribution of physical causality. *Personality and Social Psychology Bulletin, 29,* 1272–1284.

Penner, L. A., & Finkelstein, M. A. (1998). Dispositional and structural determinants of volunteerism. *Journal of Personality and Social Psychology, 74,* 525–537.

Pennington, J., & Schlenker, B. R. (1999). Accountability for consequential decisions: Justifying ethical judgments to audiences. *Personality and Social Psychology Bulletin, 25,* 1067–1081.

Perloff, L. S. (1983). Perceptions of vulnerability to victimization. *Journal of Social Issues, 39,* 41–61.

Perloff, R. M. (1989). Ego-involvement and the third person effect of televised news coverage. *Communication Research, 16,* 236–262.

Perloff, R. M. (2003). *The dynamics of persuasion: Communication and attitudes in the 21st century* (2nd ed.). Mahwah, NJ: Erlbaum.

Perry, D. G., Williard, J. C., & Perry, L. C. (1990). Peers' perceptions of the consequences that victimized children provide aggressors. *Child Development, 61,* 1310–1325.

Pessin, J. (1933). The comparative effects of social and mechanical stimulation on memorizing. *American Journal of Psychology, 45,* 263–270.

Peters, L. H., Hartke, D. D., & Pohlmann, J. T. (1985). Fiedler's contingency theory of leadership: An application of the meta-analysis procedures of Schmidt and Hunter. *Psychological Bulletin, 97,* 274–285.

Petersen, L.-E., & Dietz, J. (2000). Social discrimination in a personnel selection context: The effects of an authority's instruction to discriminate and followers' authoritarianism. *Journal of Applied Social Psychology, 31,* 206–220.

Peterson, R. S. (1997). A directive leadership style in group decision making can be both virtue and vice: Evidence from elite and experimental groups. *Journal of Personality and Social Psychology, 72,* 1107–1121.

Pettigrew, T. F. (1978). Three issues in ethnicity: Boundaries, deprivations, and perceptions. In J. M. Yinger & S. J. Cutler (Eds.), *Major social issues: A multidisciplinary view* (pp. 25–49). New York: Free Press.

Pettigrew, T. F. (1986). The intergroup contact hypothesis reconsidered. In M. Hewstone & R. Brown (Eds.), *Contact and conflict in intergroup encounters* (pp. 169–195). New York: Basil Blackwell.

Pettigrew, T. F. (1998). Intergroup contact theory. *Annual Review of Psychology, 49,* 65–85.

Pettigrew, T. F., & Tropp, L. R. (2000). Does intergroup contact reduce prejudice? Recent meta-analytic findings. In S. Oskamp (Ed.), *Reducing prejudice and discrimination* (pp. 93–114). Mahwah, NJ: Erlbaum.

Petty, R. E., & Cacioppo, J. T. (1981). *Attitudes and persuasion: Classic and contemporary approaches.* Dubuque, IA: Brown.

Petty, R. E., & Cacioppo, J. T. (1983). Source factors and the elaboration likelihood model of persuasion. *Advances in Consumer Research, 11,* 668–682.

Petty, R. E., & Cacioppo, J. T. (1986). The elaboration likelihood model of persuasion. In L. Berkowitz (Ed.), *Advances in experimental social psychology* (Vol. 19, pp. 123–205). New York: Academic Press.

Petty, R. E., Cacioppo, J. T., & Goldman, R. (1981). Personal involvement as a determinant of argument-based persuasion. *Journal of Personality and Social Psychology, 41,* 847–855.

Petty, R. E., Cacioppo, J. T., & Schumann, D. (1983). Central and peripheral routes to advertising effectiveness: The moderating role of involvement. *Journal of Consumer Research, 10,* 134–148.

Petty, R. E., & Krosnick, J. A. (1995). *Attitude strength: Antecedents and consequences.* Mahwah, NJ: Erlbaum.

Petty, R. E., Rucker, D. D., Bizer, G. Y., & Cacioppo, J. T. (2004). The elaboration likelihood model of persuasion. In J. S. Seiter & R. H. Gass (Eds.), *Perspectives on persuasion, social influence, and compliance gaining* (pp. 65–89). Boston, MA: Pearson Education.

Petty, R. E., Wells, G. L., & Brock, T. C. (1976). Distraction can enhance or reduce yielding to propaganda: Thought disruption versus effort justification. *Journal of Personality and Social Psychology, 34,* 874–888.

Pfau, M., & Szabo, E. A. (2004). Inoculation and resistance to persuasion. In J. S. Seiter & R. H. Gass (Eds.), *Perspectives on persuasion, social influence, and compliance gaining* (pp. 265–286). Boston, MA: Pearson Education.

Pfau, M., Tusing, K. J., Koerner, A. F., Lee, W., Godbold, L. C., Penaloza, L. J., Shu-Huei Yang, V., & Hong, Y. (1997). Enriching the inoculation construct: The role of critical components in the process of resistance. *Human Communication Research, 24,* 187–215.

Phillips, D. P. (1977). Motor vehicle fatalities increase just after publicized suicide stories. *Science, 196,* 1464–1465.

Pickett, C. L., Gardner, W. L., & Knowles, M. (2004). Getting a cue: The need to belong and enhanced sensitivity to social cues. *Personality and Social Psychology Bulletin, 30,* 1095–1107.

Plaks, J. E., Stroessner, S. J., Dweck, C. S., & Sherman, J. W. (2001). Person theories and attention allocation: Preferences for stereotypic versus counterstereotypic information. *Journal of Personality and Social Psychology, 80,* 876–893.

Plant, E. A. (2004). Responses to interracial interactions over time. *Personality and Social Psychology Bulletin, 30,* 1458–1471.

Plant, E. A., & Devine, P. G. (2003). The antecedents and implications of interracial anxiety. *Personality and Social Psychology Bulletin, 29,* 790–801.

Pliner, P., Chaiken, S., & Flett, G. (1990). Gender differences in concern with body weight and physical appearance over the lifespan. *Personality and Social Psychology Bulletin, 16,* 263–273.

Plous, S. L., & Zimbardo, P. G. (2004). How social science can reduce terrorism. *The Chronicle of Higher Education,* September 10, 2004, B9–B10.

Polivy, J., & Herman, C. P. (2002). If at first you don't succeed: False hopes of self-change. *American Psychologist, 57,* 677–689.

Pomerantz, E. M., Ruble, D. N., Frey, K. S., & Greulich, F. (1995). Meeting goals and confronting conflict: Children's changing perceptions of social comparison. *Child Development, 66,* 723–738.

Pope, K. S. (1996). Memory, abuse, and science: Questioning claims about the false memory syndrome epidemic. *American Psychologist, 51,* 957–974.

Postmes, T., & Spears, R. (1998). Deindividuation and antinormative behavior: A meta-analysis. *Psychological Bulletin, 123,* 238–259.

Postmes, T., Spears, R., & Cihangir, S. (2001). Quality of decision making and group norms. *Journal of Personality and Social Psychology, 80,* 918–930.

Postmes, T., Spears, R., Sakhel, K., & de Groot, D. (2001). Social influence in computer-mediated communication: The effects of anonymity on group behavior. *Personality and Social Psychology Bulletin, 27,* 1243–1254.

Pratkanis, A., & Aronson, E. (2000). *Age of propaganda: The everyday use and abuse of persuasion* (Rev. ed.). New York: Freeman.

Pratto, F., & Bargh, J. A. (1991). Stereotyping based on apparently individuating information: Trait and global components of sex stereotypes under attention overload. *Journal of Experimental Social Psychology, 27,* 26–47.

Prentice-Dunn, S., & Rogers, R. W. (1980). Effects of deindividuating situational cues and aggressive models on subjective deindividuation and aggression. *Journal of Personality and Social Psychology, 39,* 104–113.

Prentice-Dunn, S., & Rogers, R. W. (1989). Deindividuation and the self-regulation of behavior. In P. B. Paulus (Ed.), *The psychology of group influence* (2nd ed., pp. 86–109). Hillsdale, NJ: Erlbaum.

Price, P. C., Pentecost, H. C., & Voth, R. D. (2002). Perceived event frequency and the optimistic bias: Evidence for a two-process model of personal risk judgments. *Journal of Experimental Social Psychology, 38,* 242–252.

Priester, J. R., & Petty, R. E. (1996). The gradual threshold model of ambivalence: Relating the positive and negative bases of attitudes to subjective ambivalence. *Journal of Personality and Social Psychology, 71,* 431–449.

Prochaska, J. O., DiClemente, C. C., & Norcross, J. C. (1992). In search of how people change: Applications to addictive behaviors. *American Psychologist, 47,* 1102–1114.

Pronin, E., Lin, D. Y., & Ross, L. (2002). The bias blind spot: Perceptions of bias in self versus others. *Personality and Social Psychology Bulletin, 28,* 369–381.

Pruitt, D. G. (1998). Social conflict. In D. T. Gilbert, S. T. Fiske, & G. Lindzey (Eds.), *Handbook of social psychology* (4th ed., Vol. 2, pp. 470–503). Boston, MA: McGraw-Hill.

Prunier, G. (1995). *The Rwanda crisis: History of a genocide.* New York: Columbia University Press.

Pyszczynski, T., LaPrelle, J., & Greenberg, J. (1987). Encoding and retrieval effects of general person characterizations on memory for incongruent and congruent information. *Personality and Social Psychology Bulletin, 13,* 556–567.

Quinn, A., & Schlenker, B. R. (2002). Can accountability produce independence? Goals as determinants of the impact of accountability on conformity. *Personality and Social Psychology Bulletin, 28,* 772–783.

Quinn, K. A., & Olson, J. M. (2003). Framing social judgment: Self-ingroup comparison and perceived discrimination. *Personality and Social Psychology Bulletin, 29,* 228–236.

Radcliffe, N. M., & Klein, W. M. P. (2002). Dispositional, unrealistic, and comparative optimism: Differential relations with the knowledge and processing of risk information and beliefs about personal risk. *Personality and Social Psychology Bulletin, 28,* 836–846.

Ramirez, J. M. (1993). Acceptability of aggression in four Spanish regions and a comparison with other European countries. *Aggressive Behavior, 19,* 185–197.

Ramsey, J. L., Langlois, J. H., Hoss, R. A., Rubenstein, A. J., & Griffin, A. M. (2004). Origins of a stereotype: Categorization of facial attractiveness by 6-month-old infants. *Developmental Science, 7,* 201–211.

Rankin, R. F., & Campbell, D. T. (1955). Galvanic skin response to Negro and White experimenters. *Journal of Abnormal and Social Psychology, 51,* 30–33.

Rapoport, A., & Chammah, A. M. (1965). *Prisoner's dilemma: A study in conflict and cooperation.* Ann Arbor: University of Michigan Press.

Raskin, R., & Hall, C. S. (1979). A narcissistic personality inventory. *Psychological Reports, 45,* 590.

Raskin, R., & Terry, H. (1988). A principal-components analysis of the Narcissistic Personality Inventory and further evidence of its construct validation. *Journal of Personality and Social Psychology, 54,* 890–902.

Regan, D. T. (1971). Effects of a favor and liking on compliance. *Journal of Experimental Social Psychology, 7,* 627–639.

Regan, P. C., Snyder, M., & Kassin, S. M. (1995). Unrealistic optimism: Self-enhancement or person positivity? *Personality and Social Psychology Bulletin, 21,* 1073–1082.

Reis, H. T. (2000). Self-disclosure. In A. E. Kazdin (Ed.), *Encyclopedia of psychology* (Vol. 17, pp. 210–212). Washington, DC: American Psychological Association.

Reis, H. T., & Patrick, B. C. (1996). Attachment and intimacy: Component processes. In E. T. Higgins & A. W. Kruglanski (Eds.), *Social psychology: Handbook of basic principles* (pp. 523–563). New York: Guilford.

Reis, H. T., & Shaver, P. (1988). Intimacy as an interpersonal process. In S. W. Duck (Ed.), *Handbook of personal relationships* (pp. 367–389). Chichester, UK: Wiley.

Reynolds, D. E., & Sanders, M. S. (1975). Effect of defendant attractiveness, age, and injury on severity of sentence given by simulated jurors. *Journal of Social Psychology, 96,* 149–150.

Rhodes, G., Geddes, K., Jeffery, L., Dziurawiec, S., & Clark, A. (2002). Are average and symmetric faces attractive to infants? Discrimination and looking preferences. *Perception, 31,* 315–321.

Rhodes, G., Yoshikawa, S., Clark, A., Lee, K., McKay, R., & Akamatsu, S. (2001). Attractiveness of facial averageness and symmetry in non-Western cultures: In search of biologically based standards of beauty. *Perception, 30,* 611–625.

Rhodewalt, F. (1990). Self-handicappers: Individual differences in the preference for anticipatory, self-protective acts. In R. L. Higgins, C. R. Snyder, & S. Berglas (Eds.), *Self-handicapping: The paradox that isn't* (pp. 69–106). New York: Plenum.

Rhodewalt, F., & Fairfield, M. (1991). Claimed self-handicaps and self-handicappers: The relation of reductions in intended effort to performance. *Basic and Applied Social Psychology, 16,* 397–416.

Rhodewalt, F., Sanbonmatsu, D. M., Tschanz, B., Feick, D. L., & Waller, A. (1995). Self-handicapping and interpersonal trade-offs: The effects of claimed self-handicaps on observers' performance evaluations and feedback. *Personality and Social Psychology Bulletin, 21,* 1042–1050.

Richardson, D., Hammock, G., Smith, S., & Gardner, W. (1994). Empathy as a cognitive inhibitor of interpersonal aggression. *Aggressive Behavior, 20,* 275–289.

Richeson, J. A., Baird, A. A., Gordon, H. L., Heatherton, T. F., Wyland, C. L., Trawalter, S., et al. (2003). An fMRI investigation of the impact of interracial contact on executive function. *Nature Neuroscience, 6,* 1323–1328.

Richeson, J. A., & Nussbaum, R. J. (2004). The impact of multiculturalism versus color-blindness on racial bias. *Journal of Experimental Social Psychology, 40,* 417–423.

Ridgeway, C. L. (2001). Gender, status, and leadership. *Journal of Social Issues, 57,* 637–656.

Robins, R. W., Hendin, H. M., & Trzesniewski, K. H. (2001). Measuring global self-esteem: Construct validation of a single-item measure and the Rosenberg Self-Esteem Scale. *Personality and Social Psychology Bulletin, 27,* 151–161.

Roccas, S., Sagiv, L., Schwartz, S. H., & Knafo, A. (2002). The big five personality factors and personal values. *Personality and Social Psychology Bulletin, 28,* 789–801.

Roch, S. G., & Samuelson, C. D. (1997). Effects of environmental uncertainty and social value orientation in resource dilemmas. *Organizational Behavior and Human Decision Processes, 70,* 221–235.

Roco, M. C., & Bainbridge, W. S. (2001). *Societal implications of nanoscience and nanotechnology.* Arlington, VA: National Science Foundation.

Roco, M. C., & Bainbridge, W. S. (2002). *Converging technologies for improving human performance: Nanotechnology, biotechnology, information technology and cognitive science.* Arlington, VA: National Science Foundation.

Roehling, M. (1999). Weight-based discrimination in employment: Psychological and legal aspects. *Personnel Psychology, 52,* 969–1016.

Roese, N. J. (1994). The functional basis of counterfactual thinking. *Journal of Personality and Social Psychology, 66,* 805–818.

Roese, N. J. (1997). Counterfactual thinking. *Psychological Bulletin, 121,* 133–148.

Roese, N. J. (2005). *If only: How to turn regret into opportunity.* New York: Broadway Books.

Roese, N. J., & Olson, J. M. (1995). Counterfactual thinking: A critical overview. In N. J. Roese & J. M. Olson (Eds.), *What might have been: The social psychology of counterfactual thinking* (pp. 1–55). Mahwah, NJ: Erlbaum.

Roese, N. J., & Olson, J. M. (1997). Counterfactual thinking: The intersection of affect and function. In M. P. Zanna (Ed.), *Advances in experimental social psychology* (Vol. 29, pp. 1–59). San Diego, CA: Academic Press.

Rogers, C. R. (1961). *On becoming a person.* Boston: Houghton Mifflin.

Rogers, R. W. (1983). Cognitive and physiological processes in fear appeals and attitude change: A revised theory of protection motivation. In J. T. Cacioppo & R. E. Petty (Eds.), *Social psychophysiology: A sourcebook* (pp. 153–176). New York: Guilford.

Rogers, R. W., & Mewborn, C. R. (1976). Fear appeals and attitude change: Effects of a threat's noxiousness, probability of occurrence, and the efficacy of coping responses. *Journal of Personality and Social Psychology, 34,* 54–61.

Rogers, R. W., & Prentice-Dunn, S. (1981). Deindividuation and anger-mediated interracial aggression: Unmasking regressive racism. *Journal of Personality and Social Psychology, 41,* 63–73.

Rogge, R. D., & Bradbury, T. N. (1999). Till violence does us part: The differing roles of communication and aggression in predicting adverse marital outcomes. *Journal of Consulting and Clinical Psychology, 67,* 340–351.

Rohan, M. J., & Zanna, M. P. (1996). Value transmission in families. In C. Seligman, J. M. Olson, & M. P. Zanna (Eds.), *The psychology of values: The Ontario symposium* (Vol. 8, pp. 233–276). Mahwah, NJ: Erlbaum.

Rose, A. J., Swenson, L. P., & Waller, E. M. (2004). Overt and relational aggression and perceived popularity: Developmental differences in concurrent and prospective relations. *Developmental Psychology, 40,* 378–387.

Rosenbaum, M. E. (1986). The repulsion hypothesis: On the nondevelopment of relationships. *Journal of Personality and Social Psychology, 51,* 1156–1166.

Rosenberg, M. (1979). *Conceiving the self.* New York: Basic Books.

Rosenberg, M. J., & Hovland, C. I. (1960). Cognitive, affective, and behavioral components of attitudes. In C. I. Hovland & M. J. Rosenberg (Eds.), *Attitude organization and change* (pp. 1–14). New Haven, CT: Yale University Press.

Rosenthal, R. (2003). Covert communication in laboratories, classrooms, and the truly real world. *Current Directions in Psychological Science, 12,* 151–154.

Ross, E. A. (1908). *Social psychology.* New York: Macmillan.

Ross, L. (1977). The intuitive psychologist and his shortcomings. In L. Berkowitz (Ed.), *Advances in experimental social psychology* (Vol. 10, pp. 173–220). San Diego, CA: Academic Press.

Ross, L., Amabile, T. M., & Steinmetz, J. L. (1977). Social roles, social control, and biases in social-perception processes. *Journal of Personality and Social Psychology, 35,* 485–494.

Ross, L., Greene, D., & House, P. (1977). The "false consensus effect": An egocentric bias in social perception and attribution processes. *Journal of Experimental Social Psychology, 13,* 279–301.

Ross, L., Lepper, M. R., & Hubbard, M. (1975). Perseverance in self-perception and social perception: Biased attributional processes in the debriefing paradigm. *Journal of Personality and Social Psychology, 32,* 880–892.

Ross, L., & Nisbett, R. E. (1991). *The person and the situation: Perspectives of social psychology.* New York: McGraw-Hill.

Ross, M. (1989). Relation of implicit theories to the construction of personal histories. *Psychological Review, 96,* 341–357.

Ross, M., & Wilson, A. E. (2002). It feels like yesterday: Self-esteem, valence of personal past experiences, and judgments of subjective distance. *Journal of Personality and Social Psychology, 82,* 792–803.

Ross, S. M., & Offermann, L. R. (1997). Transformational leaders: Measurement of personality attributes and work group performance. *Personality and Social Psychology Bulletin, 23,* 1078–1086.

Rothbart, M., Evans, M., & Fulero, S. (1979). Recall for confirming events: Memory processes and the maintenance of social stereotypes. *Journal of Experimental Social Psychology, 15,* 343–355.

Rozin, P., Lowery, L., Imada, S., & Haidt, J. (1999). The CAD triad hypothesis: A mapping between three moral emotions (contempt, anger, disgust) and three moral codes (community, autonomy, divinity). *Journal of Personality and Social Psychology, 76,* 674–686.

Ruback, R. B., & Juieng, D. (1997). Territorial defense in parking lots: Retaliation against waiting drivers. *Journal of Applied Social Psychology, 27,* 821–834.

Rubin, K. H., Lynch, D., Coplan, R., Rose-Krasnor, L., & Booth, C. L. (1994). "Birds of a feather...": Behavioral concordances and preferential personal attraction in children. *Child Development, 65,* 1778–1785.

Rubin, M., & Hewstone, M. (1998). Social identity theory's self-esteem hypothesis: A review and some suggestions for clarification. *Personality and Social Psychology Review, 2,* 40–62.

Ruble, D. N., & Frey, K. S. (1991). Changing patterns of behavior as skills are acquired: A functional model of self-evaluation. In J. M. Suls & T. A. Wills (Eds.), *Social comparison: Contemporary theory and research* (pp. 79–113). Hillsdale, NJ: Erlbaum.

Ruble, D. N., & Goodnow, J. J. (1998). Social development in childhood and adulthood. In D. T. Gilbert, S. T. Fiske, & G. Lindzey (Eds.), *The handbook of social psychology* (4th ed., Vol. 1, pp. 741–787). New York: McGraw-Hill.

Rudman, L. A. (1998). Self-promotion as a risk factor for women: The costs and benefits of counterstereotypical impression management. *Journal of Personality and Social Psychology, 74,* 629–645.

Rudman, L. A., Ashmore, R. D., & Gary, M. L. (2001). "Unlearning" automatic biases: The malleability of implicit prejudice and stereotypes. *Journal of Personality and Social Psychology, 81,* 856–868.

Rudman, L. A., & Fairchild, K. (2004). Reactions to counterstereotypic behavior: The role of backlash in cultural stereotype maintenance. *Journal of Personality and Social Psychology, 87,* 157–176.

Rudman, L. A., & Glick, P. (2001). Prescriptive gender stereotypes and backlash toward agentic women. *Journal of Social Issues, 57,* 743–762.

Rudman, L. A., & Kilianski, S. E. (2000). Implicit and explicit attitudes toward female authority. *Personality and Social Psychology Bulletin, 26,* 1315–1328.

Rumsey, M. G. (1976). Effects of defendant background and remorse on sentencing judgments. *Journal of Applied Social Psychology, 6,* 64–68.

Rumsey, M. G., Allgeier, E. R., & Castore, C. H. (1978). Group discussion, sentencing judgments, and the leniency shift. *Journal of Social Psychology, 105,* 249–257.

Rusbult, C. E. (1983). A longitudinal test of the investment model: The development (and deterioration) of satisfaction and commitment in heterosexual involvements. *Journal of Personality and Social Psychology, 45,* 101–117.

Rusbult, C. E., & Martz, J. M. (1995). Remaining in an abusive relationship: An investment model analysis of nonvoluntary dependence. *Personality and Social Psychology Bulletin, 21,* 558–571.

Russell, J. A. (1994). Is there universal recognition of emotion from facial expression? A review of the cross-cultural studies. *Psychological Review, 115,* 102–141.

Sagar, H. A., & Schofield, J. W. (1980). Racial and behavioral cues in Black and White children's perceptions of ambiguously aggressive acts. *Journal of Personality and Social Psychology, 39,* 590–598.

Sagarin, B. J., Cialdini, R. B., Rice, W. E., & Serna, S. B. (2002). Dispelling the illusion of invulnerability: The motivations and mechanisms of resistance to persuasion. *Journal of Personality and Social Psychology, 83,* 526–541.

Sagi, A. (1990). Attachment theory and research from a cross-cultural perspective. *Human Development, 33,* 10–22.

Salovey, P., Rothman, A. J., & Rodin, J. (1998). Health behavior. In D. T. Gilbert, S. T. Fiske, & G. Lindzey (Eds.), *The handbook of social psychology* (4th ed., Vol. 2, pp. 633–683). New York: McGraw-Hill.

Salovey, P., & Wegener, D. T. (2002). Communicating about health: Message framing, persuasion, and health behavior. In J. Suls & K. Wallston (Eds.), *Social psychological foundations of health and illness.* Oxford: Blackwell.

Sande, G. N., Goethals, G. R., & Radloff, C. E. (1988). Perceiving one's own traits and others': The multifaceted self. *Journal of Personality and Social Psychology, 54,* 13–20.

Sanders, G. S., & Baron, R. S. (1977). Is social comparison irrelevant for producing choice shifts? *Journal of Experimental Social Psychology, 13,* 303–314.

Sanfey, A. G., Rilling, J. K., Aronson, J. A., Nystrom, L. E., & Cohen, J. D. (2003). The neural basis of economic decision-making in the ultimatum game. *Science, 300,* 1755–1758.

Sanitioso, R. B., & Wlodarski, R. (2004). In search of information that confirms a desired self-perception: Motivated processing of social feedback and choice of social interactions. *Personality and Social Psychology Bulletin, 30,* 412–422.

Sanna, L. J. (1992). Self-efficacy theory: Implications for social facilitation and social loafing. *Journal of Personality and Social Psychology, 62,* 774–786.

Sanna, L. J., & Turley, K. J. (1996). Antecedents to spontaneous counterfactual thinking: Effects of expectancy violation and outcome valence. *Personality and Social Psychology Bulletin, 22,* 906–919.

Santee, R. T., & Maslach, C. (1982). To agree or not to agree: Personal dissent amid social pressure to conform. *Journal of Personality and Social Psychology, 42,* 690–700.

Sarason, I. G., Levine, H. M., Basham, R. B., & Sarason, B. R. (1983). Assessing social support: The social support questionnaire. *Journal of Personality and Social Psychology, 44,* 127–139.

Sarason, I. G., Sarason, B. R., Pierce, G. R., Shearin, E. N., & Sayers, M. H. (1991). A social learning approach to increasing blood donations. *Journal of Applied Social Psychology, 21,* 896–918.

Satow, K. (1975). Social approval and helping. *Journal of Experimental Social Psychology, 11,* 501–509.

Saucier, D. A., & Miller, C. T. (2003). The persuasiveness of racial arguments as a subtle measure of racism. *Personality and Social Psychology Bulletin, 29,* 1303–1315.

Schachter, S. (1951). Deviation, rejection, and communication. *Journal of Abnormal and Social Psychology, 46,* 190–207.

Schachter, S., & Singer, J. E. (1962). Cognitive, social, and physiological determinants of emotional state. *Psychological Review, 69,* 379–399.

Schacter, D. L. (1996). *Searching for memory: The brain, the mind, and the past.* New York: Basic Books.

Schaefer, C., Coyne, J. C., & Lazarus, R. S. (1981). The health-related functions of social support. *Journal of Behavioral Medicine, 4,* 381–406.

Schafer, R. (1967). Ideals, the ego ideal, and the ideal self. In R. R. Holt (Ed.), *Motives and thought: Psychoanalytic essays in honor of David Rapaport* [Special Issue], *Psychological Issues, 5,* 131–174.

Scheier, M. F., & Carver, C. S. (1985). Optimism, coping and health: Assessment and implications of generalized outcome expectancies, *Health Psychology, 4,* 219–247.

Scheier, M. F., Matthews, K. A., Owens, J., Magovern, G. J., Sr., Lefebvre, R. C., Abbott, R. A., & Carver, C. S. (1989). Dispositional optimism and recovery from coronary artery bypass surgery: The beneficial effects on physical and psychological well-being. *Journal of Personality and Social Psychology, 57,* 1024–1040.

Schiaffino, K. M., & Revenson, T. A. (1992). The role of perceived self-efficacy, perceived control, and causal attributions in adaptation to rheumatoid arthritis: Distinguishing mediator from moderator effects. *Personality and Social Psychology Bulletin, 18,* 709–718.

Schlenker, B. R. (1980). *Impression management: The self-concept, social identity, and interpersonal relations.* Monteray, CA: Brooks/Cole.

Schlenker, B. R., & Britt, T. W. (2001). Strategically controlling information to help friends: Effects of empathy and friendship strength on beneficial impression management. *Journal of Experimental Social Psychology, 37,* 357–372.

Schmader, T. (2002). Gender identification moderates stereotype threat effects on women's math performanace. *Journal of Experimental Social Psychology, 38,* 194–201.

Schmader, T., & Johns, M. (2003). Converging evidence that stereotype threat reduces working memory capacity. *Journal of Personality and Social Psychology, 83,* 440–452.

Schmalleger, F. (2004). *Criminal justice today: An introductory text for the 21st century* (8th ed.). Upper Saddle River, NJ: Prentice Hall.

Schmidt, F. L., & Hunter, J. E. (2003). Meta-analysis. In J. A. Schinka & W. F. Velicer (Eds.), *Handbook of psychology: Vol. 2. Research methods in psychology* (pp. 533–554). Hoboken, NJ: Wiley.

Schmidt, G., & Weiner, B. (1988). An attribution-affect-action theory of behavior: Replications of judgments of help-giving. *Personality and Social Psychology Bulletin, 14,* 610–621.

Schopler, J., Insko, C. A., Graetz, K. A., Drigotas, S., Smith, V. A., & Dahl, K. (1993). Individual-group discontinuity: Further evidence for mediation by fear and greed. *Personality and Social Psychology Bulletin, 19,* 419–431.

Schroeder, D. A. (Ed.). (1995). *Social dilemmas: Perspectives on individuals and groups.* Westport, CT: Praeger.

Schroeder, D. A., Penner, L. A., Dovidio, J. F., & Piliavin, J. A. (1995). *The psychology of helping and altruism: Problems and puzzles.* New York: McGraw-Hill.

Schroeder, D. A., Steel, J. E., Woodell, A. J., & Bembenek, A. F. (2003). Justice within social dilemmas. *Personality and Social Psychology Review, 7,* 374–387.

Schuette, R. A., & Fazio, R. H. (1995). Attitude accessibility and motivation as determinants of biased processing: A test of the MODE model. *Personality and Social Psychology Bulletin, 21,* 704–710.

Schuman, H., & Rieger, C. (1992). Historical analogies, generational effects, and attitudes toward war. *American Sociological Review, 57,* 315–326.

Schuman, H., Steeh, C., Bobo, L., & Krysan, M. (1997). *Racial attitudes in America* (2nd ed.). Cambridge, MA: Harvard University Press.

Schwartz, S. H. (1977). Normative influences on altruism. In L. Berkowitz (Ed.), *Advances in experimental social psychology* (Vol. 10, pp. 221–279). New York: Academic Press.

Schwartz, S. H. (1992). Universals in the content and structure of values: Theoretical advances and empirical tests in 20 countries. In M. P. Zanna (Ed.), *Advances in experimental social psychology* (Vol. 25, pp. 1–65). San Diego, CA: Academic Press.

Schwartz, S. H. (1996). Value priorities and behavior: Applying the theory of integrated value systems. In C. Seligman, J. M. Olson, & M. P. Zanna (Eds.), *Values: The Ontario symposium* (Vol. 8, pp. 1–24). Mahwah, NJ: Erlbaum.

Schwartz, S. H., & Bardi, A. (1997). Influences of adaptation to communist rule on value priorities in Eastern Europe. *Political Psychology, 18,* 385–410.

Schwartz, S. H., & Sagiv, L. (1995). Identifying culture-specifics in the content and structure of values. *Journal of Cross-Cultural Psychology, 26,* 92–116.

Schwarz, N. (1990). Feelings as information: Informational and motivational functions of affective states. In E. T. Higgins & R. M. Sorrentino (Eds.), *Handbook of motivation and cognition: Foundations of social behavior* (Vol. 2, pp. 527–561). New York: Guilford Press.

Schwarz, N., Bless, H., Strack, F., Klumpp, G., Rittenauer-Schatka, H., & Simons, A. (1991). Ease of retrieval of information: Another look at the availability heuristic. *Journal of Personality and Social Psychology, 61,* 195–202.

Schwarz, N., & Clore, G. L. (1983). Mood, misattribution, and judgments of well-being: Informative and directive functions of affective states. *Journal of Personality and Social Psychology, 45,* 513–523.

Schwarz, N., & Clore, G. L. (1996). Feelings and phenomenal experience. In E. T. Higgins and A. W. Kruglanski (Eds.), *Social psychology: Handbook of basic principles* (pp. 433–465). New York: Guilford Press.

Schwarz, N., & Vaughn, L. A. (2002). The availability heuristic revisited: Ease of recall and content of recall as distinct sources of information. In T. Gilovich, D. Griffin, & D. Kahneman (Eds.), *Heuristics and biases: The psychology of intuitive judgment* (pp. 103–119). New York: Cambridge University Press.

Schwarzwald, J., Raz, M., & Zvibel, M. (1979). The application of the door-in-the-face technique when established behavioral customs exist. *Journal of Applied Social Psychology, 9,* 576–586.

Sczesny, S., & Kuhnen, U. (2004). Meta-cognition about biological sex and gender-stereotypic physical appearance: Consequences for the assessment of leadership competence. *Personality and Social Psychology Bulletin, 30,* 13–21.

Sears, D. O. (1981). Life stage effects on attitude change, especially among the elderly. In S. B. Kiesler, J. N. Morgan, & V. K. Oppenheimer (Eds.), *Aging: Social change* (pp. 183–204). New York: Academic Press.

Sears, D. O., & Henry, P. J. (2003). The origins of symbolic racism. *Journal of Personality and Social Psychology, 85,* 259–275.

Sechrist, G. B., Swim, J. K., & Stangor, C. (2004). When do the stigmatized make attributions to discrimination occurring to the self and others? The roles of self-presentation and need for control. *Journal of Personality and Social Psychology, 87,* 111–122.

Sedikides, C. (1990). Effects of fortuitously activated constructs versus activated communication goals on person impressions. *Journal of Personality and Social Psychology, 58,* 397–408.

Sedikides, C., Gaertner, L., & Toguchi, Y. (2003). Pancultural self-enhancement. *Journal of Personality and Social Psychology, 84,* 60–79.

Sedikides, C., Rudich, E. A., Gregg, A. P., Kumashiro, M., & Rusbult, C. (2004). Are normal narcissists psychologically healthy? Self-esteem matters. *Journal of Personality and Social Psychology, 87,* 400–416.

Sedikides, C., & Strube, M. (1997). Self-evaluation: To thine own self be good, to thine own self be sure, to thine own self be true, and to thine own self be better. In M. P. Zanna (Ed.), *Advances in experimental social psychology* (Vol. 29, pp. 209–269). San Diego, CA: Academic Press.

Segal, M. W. (1974). Alphabet and attraction: An unobtrusive measure of the effect of propinquity in a field setting. *Journal of Personality and Social Psychology, 30,* 654–657.

Seiter, J. S., & Gass, R. H. (2004). *Perspectives on persuasion, social influence, and compliance gaining.* Boston, MA: Pearson Education.

Sekaquaptewa, D., & Espinoza, P. (2004). Biased processing of stereotype-incongruency is greater for low than high status groups. *Journal of Experimental Social Psychology, 40,* 128–135.

Sekaquaptewa, D., & Thompson, M. (2003). Solo status, stereotype threat, and performance expectancies: Their effects on women's performance. *Journal of Experimental Social Psychology, 39,* 68–74.

Seligman, M. E. P. (1975). *Helplessness: On depression, development, and death.* San Francisco: Freeman.

Sensenig, J., & Brehm, J. W. (1968). Attitude change from an implied threat to attitudinal freedom. *Journal of Personality and Social Psychology, 8,* 324–330.

Seto, M. C., Maric, A., & Barbaree, H. E. (2001). The role of pornography in the etiology of sexual aggression. *Aggression and Violent Behavior, 6,* 35–53.

Shapiro, J. P., Baumeister, R. F., & Kessler, J. W. (1991). A three-component model of children's teasing: Aggression, humor, and ambiguity. *Journal of Social and Clinical Psychology, 10,* 459–472.

Sharkey, W. F. (1992). Use of and responses to intentional embarrassment. *Communication Studies, 43,* 257–275.

Sharp, M. J., & Getz, J. G. (1996). Substance use as impression management. *Personality and Social Psychology Bulletin, 22,* 60–67.

Shaver, P., & Hazan, C. (1993). Adult romantic attachment: Theory and evidence. In D. Perlman & W. H. Jones (Eds.), *Advances in personal relationships* (Vol. 4, pp. 29–70). Philadelphia, PA: Jessica Kingsley.

Shavitt, S. (1990). The role of attitude objects in attitude functions. *Journal of Experimental Social Psychology, 26,* 124–148.

Shavitt, S., Swan, S., Lowery, T. M., & Wanke, M. (1994). The interaction of endorser attractiveness and involvement in persuasion depends on the goal that guides message processing. *Journal of Consumer Research, 3,* 137–162.

Shaw, M. E. (1976). *Group dynamics: The psychology of small group behavior* (2nd ed.). New York: McGraw-Hill.

Sheldon, K. M., Elliot, A. J., Kim, Y., & Kasser, T. (2001). What's satisfying about satisfying events? Testing 10 candidate psychological needs. *Journal of Personality and Social Psychology, 80,* 325–339.

Sheppard, B. H., Hartwick. J., & Warshaw, P. R. (1988). The theory of reasoned action: A meta-analysis of past research with recommendations for modifications and future research. *Journal of Consumer Research, 15,* 325–343.

Shepperd, J. A., & McNulty, J. K. (2002). The affective consequences of expected and unexpected outcomes. *Psychological Science, 13,* 85–88.

Shepperd, J. A., Maroto, J. J., & Pbert, L. A. (1996). Dispositional optimism as a predictor or health changes among cardiac patients. *Journal of Research in Personality, 30,* 517–534.

Sherif, M. (1935). A study of some social factors in perception. *Archives of Psychology, 27*(187), 1–60.

Sherif, M. (1936). *The psychology of social norms.* Oxford, UK: Harper.

Sherif, M. (1937). An experimental approach to the study of attitudes. *Sociometry, 1,* 90–98.

Sherif, M., Harvey, O., White, B., Hood, W., & Sherif, C. (1961). *Intergroup conflict and cooperation: The Robber's Cave experiment.* Norman: University of Oklahoma, Institute of Group Relations.

Sherman, D. K., & Cohen, G. L. (2002). Accepting threatening information: Self-affirmation and the reduction of defensive biases. *Current Directions in Psychological Science, 11,* 119–123.

Sherman, D. K., Nelson, L. D., & Steele, C. M. (2000). Do messages about health risks threaten the self? Increasing the acceptance of threatening health messages via self-affirmation. *Personality and Social Psychology Bulletin, 26,* 1046–1058.

Sherman, S. J., Presson, C. C., & Chassin, L. (1984). Mechanisms underlying the false consensus effect: The special role of threat to the self. *Personality and Social Psychology Bulletin, 10,* 127–138.

Sherry, J. L. (2001). The effects of violent video games on aggression: A meta-analysis. *Human Communication Research, 27,* 409–431.

Shultz, T. R., & Lepper, M. R. (1996). Cognitive dissonance reduction as constraint satisfaction. *Psychological Review, 103,* 219–240.

Shultz, T. R., Leveille, E., & Lepper, M. R. (1999). Free choice and cognitive dissonance revisited: Choosing "lesser evils" versus "greater goods." *Personality and Social Psychology Bulletin, 25,* 40–48.

Sigall, H., & Ostrove, N. (1975). Beautiful but dangerous: Effects of offender attractiveness and nature of the crime on juridic judgment. *Journal of Personality and Social Psychology, 31,* 410–414.

Silke, A. (2003a). Deindividuation, anonymity, and violence: Findings from Northern Ireland. *Journal of Social Psychology, 143,* 493–499.

Silke, A. (Ed.). (2003b). *Terrorists, victims, and society: Psychological perspectives on terrorism and its consequences.* Chichester, UK: Wiley.

Silverman, I., Choi, J., Mackewn, A., Fisher, M., Moro, J., & Olshansky, E. (2000). Evolved mechanisms underlying wayfinding: Further studies on the hunter-gatherer theory of spatial sex differences. *Evolution and Human Behavior, 21,* 201–213.

Simon, B., Stürmer, S., & Steffens, K. (2000). Helping individuals or group members? The role of individual and collective identification in AIDS volunteerism. *Personality and Social Psychology Bulletin, 26,* 497–506.

Simonton, D. K. (1987). *Why presidents succeed: A political psychology of leadership.* New Haven, CT: Yale University Press.

Simpson, J. A. (1987). The dissolution of romantic relationships: Factors involved in relationship stability and emotional distress. *Journal of Personality and Social Psychology, 53,* 683–692.

Simpson, J. A., Rholes, W. S., & Nelligan, J. S. (1992). Support seeking and support giving within couples in an anxiety-provoking situation: The role of attachment styles. *Journal of Personality and Social Psychology, 62,* 434–446.

Simpson, J. A., Rholes, W. S., Oriña, M. M., & Grich, J. (2002). Working models of attachment, support giving, and support seeking in a stressful situation. *Personality and Social Psychology Bulletin, 28,* 598–608.

Sinclair, L., & Kunda, Z. (1999). Reactions to a Black professional: Motivated inhibition and activation of conflicting stereotypes. *Journal of Personality and Social Psychology, 77,* 885–904.

Sinclair, L., & Kunda, Z. (2000). Motivated stereotyping of women: She's fine if she praised me but incompetent if she criticized me. *Personality and Social Psychology Bulletin, 26,* 1329–1342.

Sinclair, R. C. (1988). Mood, categorization breadth, and performance appraisal: The effects of order of information acquisition and affective state on halo, accuracy, information retrieval, and evaluations. *Organizational Behavior and Human Decision Processes, 42,* 22–46.

Singelis, T. M. (1994). The measurement of independent and interdependent self-construals. *Personality and Social Psychology Bulletin, 20,* 580–591.

Singer, E., & Levine, F. J. (2003). Protection of human subjects of research: Recent developments and future prospects for the social sciences. *Public Opinion Quarterly, 67,* 148–164.

Singh, D. (1993). Adaptive significance of female physical attractiveness: Role of waist-to-hip ratio. *Journal of Personality and Social Psychology, 65,* 293–307.

Singh, D. (1995). Female judgment of male attractiveness and desirability for relationships: Role of waist-to-hip ratio and financial status. *Journal of Personality and Social Psychology, 69,* 1089–1101.

Singh, U. P., & Prasad, T. (1973). Self-esteem, social-esteem, and conformity behaviour. *Psychologia: An International Journal of Psychology in the Orient, 16,* 61–68.

Sistrunk, F., & McDavid, J. W. (1971). Sex variable in conformity behavior. *Journal of Personality and Social Psychology, 17,* 200–207.

Skowronski, J. J., Carlston, D. E., & Isham, J. T. (1993). Implicit versus explicit impression formation: The differing effects of overt labeling and covert priming on memory and impressions. *Journal of Experimental Social Psychology, 29,* 17–41.

Smeesters, D., Warlop, L., Van Avermaet, E., Corneille, O., & Yzerbyt, V. (2003). Do not prime hawks with doves: The interplay of construct activation and consistency of social value orientation on cooperative behavior. *Journal of Personality and Social Psychology, 84,* 972–987.

Smith, C. P. (Ed.). (1992). *Motivation and personality: Handbook of thematic content analysis.* New York: Cambridge University Press.

Smith, E. R. (1994). Social cognition contributions to attribution theory. In P. G. Devine, D. L. Hamilton, & T. M. Ostrom (Eds.), *Social cognition: Impact on social psychology* (pp. 77–108). San Diego, CA: Academic Press.

Smith, E. R. (1998). Mental representations and memory. In D. Gilbert, S. T. Fisk & G. Lindzey (Eds.), *Handbook of social psychology* (4th ed., Vol. 1, pp. 391–445). Boston, MA: McGraw-Hill.

Smith, E. R., & DeCoster, J. (2000). Dual process models in social and cognitive psychology: Conceptual integration and links to underlying memory systems. *Personality and Social Psychology Review, 4,* 108–131.

Smith, M. B., Bruner, J. S., & White, R. W. (1956). *Opinions and personality.* New York: Wiley.

Smith, P. B., & Bond, M. H. (1994). *Social psychology across cultures: Analysis and perspectives.* Boston: Allyn & Bacon.

Smith, R. H. (2000). Assimilative and contrastive emotional reactions to upward and downward social comparisons. In J. M. Suls & L. Wheeler (Eds.), *Handbook of social comparison: Theory and research* (pp. 173–200). New York: Kluwer Academic/Plenum.

Smith, S. M., Lindsay, R. C. L., Pryke, S., & Dysart, J. E. (2001). Postdictors of eyewitness errors: Can false identifications be diagnosed in the cross-race situation? *Psychology, Public Policy, and Law, 7,* 153–169.

Smith, T. W., Snyder, C. R., & Perkins, S. (1983). On the self-serving function of hypochondriacal complaints: Physical symptoms as self-handicapping strategies. *Journal of Personality and Social Psychology, 44,* 787–797.

Smith, W. P., & Arnkelsson, G. R. (2000). Stability of related attributes and the inference of ability through social comparison. In J. M. Suls & L. Wheeler (Eds.), *Handbook of social comparison: Theory and research* (pp. 45–66). New York: Kluwer Academic/Plenum.

Smollar, J., & Youniss, J. (1982). Social development through friendship. In K. H. Rubin & H. S. Ross (Eds.), *Peer relationships and social skills in childhood* (pp. 279–298). New York: Springer-Verlag.

Snyder, M. (1974). Self-monitoring of expressive behavior. *Journal of Personality and Social Psychology, 30,* 526–537.

Snyder, M. (1987). *Public appearances, private realities: The psychology of self-monitoring.* New York: Freeman.

Snyder, M., Berscheid, E., & Glick, P. (1985). Focusing on the exterior and the interior: Two investigations of the initiation of personal relationships. *Journal of Personality and Social Psychology, 48,* 1427–1439.

Snyder, M., & Cantor, N. (1998). Understanding personality and social behavior: A functionalist strategy. In D. T. Gilbert, S. T. Fiske, & G. Lindzey (Eds.), *The handbook of social psychology* (4th ed., Vol. 1., pp. 635–679). Boston, MA: McGraw-Hill.

Snyder, M. L., & Fromkin, H. L. (1980). *Uniqueness: The human pursuit of difference.* New York: Plenum.

Snyder, M., & Gangestad, S. (1986). On the nature of self-monitoring: Matters of assessment, matters of validity. *Journal of Personality and Social Psychology, 51,* 125–139.

Snyder, M., & Haugen, J. A. (1995). Why does behavioral confirmation occur? A functional perspective on the role of the target. *Personality and Social Psychology Bulletin, 21,* 963–974.

Snyder, M., & Jones, E. E. (1974). Attitude attribution when behavior is constrained. *Journal of Experimental and Social Psychology, 10,* 585–600.

Snyder, M., & Swann, W. B., Jr. (1976). When actions reflect attitudes: The politics of impression management. *Journal of Personality and Social Psychology, 34,* 1034–1042.

Snyder, M., & Uranowitz, S. W. (1978). Reconstructing the past: Some cognitive consequences of person perception. *Journal of Personality and Social Psychology, 36,* 941–950.

Solomon, S., Greenberg, J., & Pyszczynski, T. (1991). A terror management theory of social behavior: The psychological functions of self-esteem and cultural worldviews. In M. P. Zanna (Ed.), *Advances in experimental social psychology* (Vol. 24, pp. 91–159). San Diego, CA: Academic Press.

Solso, R. L., & MacLin, M. K. (2002). *Experimental psychology: A case approach* (7th ed.). Boston, MA: Allyn & Bacon.

Sommer, K. L., Williams, K. D., Ciarocco, N. J., & Baumeister, R. F. (2001). When silence speaks louder than words: Explorations into the intrapsychic and interpersonal consequences of social ostracism. *Basic and Applied Social Psychology, 23,* 225–243.

Son Hing, L. S., Li, W., & Zanna, M. P. (2002). Inducing hypocrisy to reduce prejudicial responses among aversive racists. *Journal of Experimental Social Psychology, 38,* 71–78.

Sorrentino, R. M., & Boutillier, R. G. (1975). The effect of quantity and quality of verbal interaction on ratings of leadership ability. *Journal of Experimental Social Psychology, 11,* 403–411.

Sorrentino, R. M., Cohen, D., Olson, J. M., & Zanna, M. P. (Eds.). (2005). *Culture and social behavior: The Ontario symposium* (Vol. 10). Mahwah, NJ: Erlbaum.

Sorrentino, R. M., & Field, N. (1986). Emergent leadership over time: The functional value of positive motivation. *Journal of Personality and Social Psychology, 50,* 1091–1099.

Sorrentino, R. M., & Hewitt, E. (1984). Uncertainty-related properties of achievement tasks revisited. *Journal of Personality and Social Psychology, 4,* 884–899.

Sorrentino, R. M., & Higgins, E. T. (1986). Motivation and cognition: Warming up to synergism. In R. M. Sorrentino & E. T. Higgins (Eds.), *Handbook of motivation and cognition* (pp. 3–19). New York: Guilford Press.

Sorrentino, R. M., & Roney, C. J. R. (2000). *The uncertain mind: Individual differences in facing the unknown.* Philadelphia, PA: Psychology Press.

Sorrentino, R. M., Short, J. C., & Raynor, J. O. (1984). Uncertainty orientation: Implications for affective and cognitive views of achievement behavior. *Journal of Personality and Social Psychology, 46,* 189–206.

Spears, R., Lea, M., Corneliussen, R. A., Postmes, T., & ter Haar, W. (2002). Computer-mediated communication as a channel for social resistance: The strategic side of SIDE. *Small Group Research, 33,* 555–574.

Spence, J. T. (1993). Gender-related traits and gender ideology: Evidence for a multifactorial theory. *Journal of Personality and Social Psychology, 64,* 624–635.

Spencer, S. J., Steele, C. M., & Quinn, D. M. (1999). Stereotype threat and women's math performance. *Journal of Experimental Social Psychology, 35,* 4–28.

Sporer, S. L. (1993). Eyewitness identification accuracy, confidence, and decision times in simultaneous and sequential lineups. *Journal of Applied Psychology, 78,* 22–33.

Sporer, S. L. (2001). The cross-race effect: Beyond recognition of faces in the laboratory. *Psychology, Public Policy, and Law, 7,* 170–200.

Sporer, S. L., Penrod, S. D., Read, J. D., & Cutler, B. L. (1995). Choosing, confidence, and accuracy: A meta-analysis of the confidence-accuracy relation in eyewitness identification studies. *Psychological Bulletin, 118,* 315–327.

Sprecher, S., & Schwartz, P. (1994). Equity and balance in the exchange of contributions in close relationships. In M. J. Lerner & G. Mikula (Eds.), *Entitlement and the affectional bond* (pp. 11–41). New York: Plenum.

Srull, T. K., & Wyer, R. S., Jr. (1980). Category accessibility and social perception: Some implications for the study of person memory and interpersonal judgments. *Journal of Personality and Social Psychology, 38,* 841–856.

Stang, D. J. (1972). Conformity, ability, and self-esteem. *Representative Research in Social Psychology, 3,* 97–103.

Stangor, C., Lynch, L., Duan, C., & Glass, B. (1992). Categorization of individuals on the basis of multiple social features. *Journal of Personality and Social Psychology, 62,* 207–218.

Stangor, C., & McMillan, D. (1992). Memory for expectancy-congruent and expectancy-incongruent information: A review of the social and social developmental literatures. *Psychological Bulletin, 111,* 42–61.

Stapp, J. (1996, January/February). An interesting career in psychology: Trial consultant. *Psychological Science Agenda, 9,* 12.

Stark, R. (1972). *Police riots, collective violence and law enforcement.* Belmont, CA: Wadsworth.

Staub, E. (1989). *The roots of evil: The origins of genocide and other group violence.* New York: Cambridge University Press.

Staub, E. (1999). The origins and prevention of genocide, mass killing and other collective violence. *Peace and Conflict: Journal of Peace Psychology, 5,* 303–337.

Staub, E., Pearlman, L. A., & Miller, V. (2003). Healing the roots of genocide in Rwanda. *Peace Review, 15,* 287–294.

Staub, E., & Rosenthal, L. H. (1994). Mob violence: Cultural-societal sources, instigators, group processes, and participants. In L. D. Eron, J. H. Gentry, & P. Schlegel (Eds.), *Reason to hope: A psychosocial perspective on youth and violence* (pp. 281–313). Washington, DC: American Psychological Association.

Steblay, N. M. (1987). Helping behavior in rural and urban environments: A meta-analysis. *Psychological Bulletin, 102,* 346–356.

Steele, C. M. (1988). The psychology of self-affirmation: Sustaining the integrity of the self. In L. Berkowitz (Ed.), *Advances in experimental social psychology* (Vol. 21, pp. 261–302). New York: Academic Press.

Steele, C. M., & Aronson, J. (1995). Contending with a stereotype: African-American intellectual test performance and stereotype threat. *Journal of Personality and Social Psychology, 69,* 797–811.

Steele, C. M., & Josephs, R. A. (1990). Alcohol myopia: Its prized and dangerous effects. *American Psychologist, 45,* 921–933.

Steele, C. M., & Liu, T. J. (1981). Making the dissonance act unreflective of self: Dissonance avoidance and the expectancy of a value-affirming response. *Personality and Social Psychology Bulletin, 7,* 393–397.

Steele, C. M., & Liu, T. J. (1983). Dissonance processes as self-affirmation. *Journal of Personality and Social Psychology, 45,* 5–19.

Steele, C. M., Southwick, L. L., & Critchlow, B. (1981). Dissonance and alcohol: Drinking your troubles away. *Journal of Personality and Social Psychology, 41,* 831–846.

Steele, C. M., Spencer, S. J., & Lynch, M. (1993). Dissonance and affirmational responses: Resilience against self-image threats. *Journal of Personality and Social Psychology, 64,* 885–896.

Steinel, W., & De Dreu, C. K. W. (2004). Social motives and strategic misrepresentation in social decision making. *Journal of Personality and Social Psychology, 86,* 419–434.

Steiner, I. D. (1972). *Group process and productivity.* New York: Academic Press.

Stenberg, C., & Campos, J. (1990). The development of anger expressions in infancy. In N. Stein, T. Trabasso, & B. Leventhal (Eds.), *Concepts in emotion.* Hillsdale, NJ: Erlbaum.

Stephan, C. W., & Langlois, J. H. (1984). Baby beautiful: Adult attributions of infant competence as a function of infant attractiveness. *Child Development, 55,* 576–585.

Stephan, W. G. (1986). Effects of school desegregation: An evaluation 30 years after *Brown.* In L. Saxe & M. Saks (Eds.), *Advances in applied social psychology* (Vol. 4, pp. 181–286). New York: Academic Press.

Stephan, W. G., Boniecki, K. A., Ybarra, O., Bettencourt, A., Ervin, K. S., Jackson, L. A., McNatt, P. S., & Renfro, C. L. (2002). The role of threats in the racial attitudes of Blacks and Whites. *Personality and Social Psychology Bulletin, 28,* 1242–1254.

Stephan, W. G., & Stephan, C. W. (1985). Intergroup anxiety. *Journal of Social Issues, 41*(3), 157–175.

Stephan, W. G., & Stephan, C. W. (1989). Antecedents of intergroup anxiety in Asian-Americans and Hispanic-Americans. *International Journal of Intercultural Relations, 13,* 203–219.

Stephan, W. G., & Stephan, C. W. (2000). An integrated threat theory of prejudice. In S. Oskamp (Ed.), *Reducing prejudice and discrimination* (pp. 23–46). Mahwah, NJ: Erlbaum.

Sternberg, R. J. (1986). A triangular theory of love. *Psychological Review, 93,* 119–135.

Sternberg, R. J., & Kolligan, J. (Eds.). (1990). *Competence considered.* New Haven, CT: Yale University Press.

Stevens, C. K., & Kristof, A. L. (1995). Making the right impression: A field study of applicant impression management during job interviews. *Journal of Applied Psychology, 80,* 587–606.

Stewart, J. E. (1980). Defendant's attractiveness as a factor in the outcome of criminal trials: An observational study. *Journal of Applied Social Psychology, 10,* 348–361.

Stice, E., & Shaw, H. E. (1994). Adverse effects of the media portrayed thin-ideal on women and linkages to bulimic symptomatology. *Journal of Social and Clinical Psychology, 13,* 288–308.

Stodgill, R. M. (1974). *Handbook of leadership.* New York: Free Press.

Stone, J. (1999). What exactly have I done? The role of self-attribute accessibility in dissonance. In E. Harmon-Jones & J. Mills (Eds.), *Cognitive dissonance: Progress on a pivotal theory in social psychology* (pp. 175–200). Washington, DC: American Psychological Association.

Stone, J. (2001). Behavioral discrepancies and the role of construal processes in cognitive dissonance. In G. B. Moskowitz (Ed.), *Cognitive social psychology: The Princeton symposium on the legacy and future of social cognition* (pp. 41–58). Mahwah, NJ: Erlbaum.

Stone, J. (2002). Battling doubt by avoiding practice: The effects of stereotype threat on self-handicapping in White athletes. *Personality and Social Psychology Bulletin, 28,* 1667–1678.

Stone, J. (2003). Self-consistency for low self-esteem in dissonance processes: The role of self-standards. *Personality and Social Psychology Bulletin, 29,* 846–858.

Stone, J., Aronson, E., Crain, A. L., Winslow, M. P., & Fried, C. B. (1994). Inducing hypocrisy as a means of encouraging young adults to use condoms. *Personality and Social Psychology Bulletin, 20,* 116–128.

Stone, J., & Cooper, J. (2001). A self-standards model of cognitive dissonance. *Journal of Experimental Social Psychology, 37,* 228–243.

Stone, J., & Cooper, J. (2003). The effect of self-attribute relevance on how self-esteem moderates dissonance processes. *Journal of Experimental Social Psychology, 39,* 508–515.

Stone, J., Lynch, C. I., Sjomeling, M., & Darley, J. M. (1999). Stereotype threat effects on Black and White athletic performance. *Journal of Personality and Social Psychology, 77,* 1213–1227.

Stone, J., Wiegand, A. W., Cooper, J., & Aronson, E. (1997). When exemplification fails: Hypocrisy and the motive for self-integrity. *Journal of Personality and Social Psychology, 72,* 54–65.

Stoner, J. A. F. (1968). Risky and cautious shifts in group decisions: The influence of widely held values. *Journal of Experimental Social Psychology, 4,* 442–459.

Strack, F., & Deutsch, R. F. (2004). Reflective and impulsive determinants of social behavior. *Personality and Social Psychology Bulletin, 8,* 220–247.

Strack, F., Schwarz, N., Bless, H., Kubler, A., & Wanke, M. (1993). Awareness of the influence as a determinant of assimilation versus contrast. *European Journal of Social Psychology, 23,* 53–62.

Straus, M. A. (1994). *Beating the devil out of them: Corporal punishment in American families.* New York: Lexington Books.

Straus, M. A., & Gelles, R. J. (1990). *Physical violence in American families: Risk factors and adaptation to violence in 8,145 families.* New Brunswick, NJ: Transaction.

Streeter, S. A., & McBurney, D. H. (2003). Waist-hip ratio and attractiveness: New evidence and a critique of a "critical test." *Evolution and Human Behavior, 24*(2), 88–98.

Strickland, B. R., & Crowne, D. P. (1962). Conformity under conditions of simulated group pressure as a function of the need for social approval. *Journal of Social Psychology, 58,* 171–181.

Stroebe, W., & Stroebe, M. (1996). The social psychology of social support. In E. T. Higgins & A. W. Kruglanski (Eds.), *Social psychology: Handbook of basic principles* (pp. 597–621). New York: Guilford Press.

Stroessner, S. J. & Plaks, J. E. (2001). Illusory correlation and stereotype formation: Tracing the arc of research over a quarter century. In G. Moskovitz (Ed.), *Cognitive social psychology: The Princeton symposium on the legacy and future of social cognition.* Mahwah, NJ: Erlbaum.

Strube, M., & Garcia, J. (1981). A meta-analysis investigation of Fiedler's contingency model of leadership effectiveness. *Psychological Bulletin, 90,* 307–321.

Stukas, A. A., Jr., & Snyder, M. (2002). Targets' awareness of expectations and behavioral confirmation in ongoing interactions. *Journal of Experimental Social Psychology, 38,* 31–40.

Sturges, J. W., & Rogers, R. W. (1996). Preventive health psychology from a developmental perspective: An extension of protection motivation theory. *Health Psychology, 15,* 158–166.

Stürmer, S., & Simon, B. (2004). The role of collective identification in social movement participation: A panel study in the context of the German gay movement. *Personality and Social Psychology Bulletin, 30,* 263–277.

Suh, E. M. (2002). Culture, identity consistency, and subjective well-being. *Journal of Personality and Social Psychology, 83,* 1378–1391.

Suls, J. M. (1986). Comparison processes in relative deprivation: A life-span analysis. In J. M. Olson, C. P. Herman, & M. P. Zanna (Eds.), *Relative deprivation and social comparison: The Ontario symposium* (Vol. 4, pp. 95–116). Hillsdale, NJ: Erlbaum.

Suls, J. M., Martin, R., & Wheeler, L. (2002). Social comparison: Why, with whom, and with what effect? *Current Directions in Psychological Science, 11,* 159–163.

Swenson, O. (1987). *The perilous path of cultism.* Caronport, SK: Briercrest Books.

Swim, J. K. (1994). Perceived versus meta-analytic effect sizes: An assessment of the accuracy of gender stereotypes. *Journal of Personality and Social Psychology, 66,* 21–36.

Swim, J. K., Aikin, K. J., Hall, W. S., & Hunter, B. A. (1995). Sexism and racism: Old-fashioned and modern prejudices. *Journal of Personality and Social Psychology, 68,* 199–214.

Swim, J. K., & Stangor, C. S. (Eds.). (1998). *Prejudice: The target's perspective.* New York: Academic Press.

Symons, D. (1979). *The evolution of human sexuality.* New York: Oxford University Press.

Syzbillo, G. J., & Heslin, R. (1973). Resistance to persuasion: Inoculation theory in a marketing context. *Journal of Marketing Research, 10,* 396–403.

Tajfel, H. (1970). Experiments in intergroup discrimination. *Scientific American, 223*(2), 96–102.

Tajfel, H. (Ed.). (1978). *Differentiation between social groups: Studies in the social psychology of intergroup relations.* London, UK: Academic Press.

Tajfel, H., & Turner, J. C. (1986). The social identity theory of intergroup behavior. In S. Worchel & W. G. Austin (Eds.), *The psychology of intergroup relations* (2nd ed., pp. 7–24). Chicago: Nelson-Hall.

Takahashi, K. (1990). Are the key assumptions of the "strange situation" procedure universal? A view from Japanese research. *Human Development, 33,* 23–30.

Tanford, S., & Penrod, S. (1984). Social influence model: A formal integration of research on majority and minority influence processes. *Psychological Bulletin, 95,* 189–225.

Tang, S, & Hall, V. C. (1995). The overjustification effect: A meta-analysis. *Applied Cognitive Psychology, 9,* 365–404.

Tarr, M. J., & Warren, W. H. (2002). Virtual reality in behavioral neuoscience and beyond. *Nature Neuroscience, 5* (Supplement), 1089–1092.

Taylor, D. M., & Moghaddam, F. M. (1994). *Theories of intergroup relations: International social psychological perspectives* (2nd ed.). Westport, CT: Praeger.

Taylor, D. M., Wright, S. C., Moghaddam, F. M., & Lalonde, R. N. (1990). The personal/group discrimination discrepancy: Perceiving my group, but not myself, to be a target for discrimination. *Personality and Social Psychology Bulletin, 16,* 254–262.

Taylor, D. M., Wright, S. C., & Porter, L. E. (1993). Dimensions of perceived discrimination: The personal/group discrimination discrepancy. In M. P. Zanna & J. M. Olson (Eds.), *The psychology of prejudice: The Ontario symposium* (Vol. 7, pp. 233–255). Hillsdale, NJ: Erlbaum.

Taylor, S. E. (2002). *Health psychology* (5th ed.). New York: McGraw-Hill.

Taylor, S. E., & Brown, J. D. (1988). Illusion and well-being: A social psychological perspective on mental health. *Psychological Bulletin, 103,* 193–210.

Taylor, S. E., & Brown, J. D. (1994). Positive illusions and well-being revisited: Separating fact from fiction. *Psychological Bulletin, 116,* 21–27.

Taylor, S. E., Kemeny, M. E., Reed, G. M., Bower, J. E., & Gruenewald, T. L. (2000). Psychological resources, positive illusions, and health. *American Psychologist, 55,* 99–109.

Taylor, S. E., Klein, L. C., Lewis, B. P., Gruenewald, T. L., Gurung, R. A. R., & Updegraff, J. A. (2000). Biobehavioral responses to stress in females: Tend-and-befriend, not fight-or-flight. *Psychological Review, 107,* 411–429.

Taylor, S. E., Lerner, J. S., Sherman, D. K., Sage, R. M., & McDowell, N. K. (2003a). Portrait of the self-enhancer: Well adjusted and well liked or maladjusted and friendless? *Journal of Personality and Social Psychology, 84,* 165–176.

Taylor, S. E., Lerner, J. S., Sherman, D. K., Sage, R. M., & McDowell, N. K. (2003b). Are self-enhancing cognitions associated with healthy or unhealthy biological profiles? *Journal of Personality and Social Psychology, 85,* 605–615.

Taylor, S. E., & Lobel, M. (1989). Social comparison activity under threat: Downward evaluation and upward contacts. *Psychological Bulletin, 96,* 569–575.

Taylor, S. E., Sherman, D. K., Kim, H. S., Jarcho, J., Takagi, K., & Dunagan, M. S. (2004). Culture and social support: Who seeks it and why? *Journal of Personality and Social Psychology, 87,* 354–362.

Taylor, S. E., Wayment, H. A., & Carillo, M. (1996). Social comparison, self-regulation, and motivation. In R. M. Sorrentino & E. T. Higgins (Eds.), *Handbook of motivation and cognition: The interpersonal context* (Vol. 3, pp. 3–27). New York: Guilford.

Taylor, S. P. (1967). Aggressive behavior and physiological arousal as a function of provocation and the tendency to inhibit aggression. *Journal of Personality, 35,* 297–310.

Tazelaar, M. J. A., Van Lange, P. A. M., & Ouwerkerk, J. W. (2004). How to cope with "noise" in social dilemmas: The benefits of communication. *Journal of Personality and Social Psychology, 87,* 845–859.

Technical Working Group for Eyewitness Evidence. (1999). *Eyewitness evidence: A guide for law enforcement.* Washington, DC: U.S. Department of Justice.

Tedeschi, J. T., Schlenker, B. R., & Bonoma, T. V. (1971). Cognitive dissonance: Private ratiocination or public spectacle? *American Psychologist, 26,* 685–695.

Tennen, H., & Affleck, G. (1987). The costs and benefits of optimistic explanations and dispositional optimism. *Journal of Personality, 55,* 377–393.

Tennen, H., & Affleck, G. (1993). The puzzles of self-esteem: A clinical perspective. In R. F. Baumeister (Ed.), *Self-esteem: The puzzle of low self-regard* (pp. 241–262). New York: Plenum.

Tesser, A. (1988). Toward a self-evaluation maintenance model of social behavior. In L. Berkowitz (Ed.), *Advances in experimental social psychology* (Vol. 21, pp. 181–227). New York: Academic Press.

Tesser, A. (1993). The importance of heritability in psychological research: The case of attitudes. *Psychological Review, 100,* 129–142.

Tesser, A. (2000). On the confluence of self-esteem maintenance mechanisms. *Personality and Social Psychology Review, 4,* 290–299.

Tesser, A., Millar, M., & Moore, J. (1988). Some affective consequences of social comparison and reflection processes: The pain and pleasure of being close. *Journal of Personality and Social Psychology, 54,* 49–61.

Thibaut, J. W., & Kelley, H. H. (1959). *The social psychology of groups.* New York: Wiley.

Thompson, M. M., Zanna, M. P., & Griffin, D. W. (1995). Let's not be indifferent about (attitudinal) ambivalence. In R. E. Petty & J. A. Krosnick (Eds.), *Attitude strength: Antecedents and consequences* (pp. 361–386). Mahwah, NJ: Erlbaum.

Thornton, B., & Moore, S. (1993). Physical attractiveness contrast effect: Implications for self-esteem and evaluations of the social self. *Personality and Social Psychology Bulletin, 19,* 474–480.

Thurstone, L. L. (1928). Attitudes can be measured. *American Journal of Sociology, 33,* 529–554.

Tice, D. M., & Baumeister, R. F. (1990). Self-esteem, self-handicapping, and self-presentation: The strategy of inadequate practice. *Journal of Personality, 58,* 443–464.

Tidwell, M.-C. O., Reis, H. T., & Shaver, P. R. (1996). Attachment, attractiveness, and social interaction: A diary study. *Journal of Personality and Social Psychology, 71,* 729–745.

Tormala, Z. L., & Petty, R. E. (2002). What doesn't kill me makes me stronger: The effects of resisting persuasion on attitude certainty. *Journal of Personality and Social Psychology, 83,* 1298–1313.

Towles-Schwen, T., & Fazio. R. H. (2001). On the origins of racial attitudes: Correlates of childhood experiences. *Personality and Social Psychology Bulletin, 27,* 162–175.

Townsend, J. M., & Wasserman, T. (1998). Sexual attractiveness: Sex differences in assessment and criteria. *Evolution and Human Behavior, 14,* 171–191.

Trafimow, D., & Sheeran, P. (1998). Some tests of the distinction between cognitive and affective beliefs. *Journal of Experimental Social Psychology, 34,* 378–397.

Traupmann, J., Hatfield, E., & Wexler, P. (1983). Equity and sexual satisfaction in dating couples. *British Journal of Social Psychology, 22,* 33–40.

Travis, L. E. (1925). The effect of a small audience upon eye-hand coordination. *Journal of Abnormal and Social Psychology, 20,* 142–146.

Triandis, H. C. (1989). The self and social behavior in differing cultural contexts. *Psychological Review, 96,* 506–520.

Triandis, H. C. (1994). *Culture and social behavior.* New York: McGraw-Hill.

Triandis, H. C. (1995). *Individualism and collectivism.* Boulder, CO: Westview Press.

Triandis, H. C., McCusker, C., & Hui, C. H. (1990). Multimethod probes of individualism and collectivism. *Journal of Personality and Social Psychology, 59,* 1006–1020.

Triplett, N. (1898). The dynamogenic factors in pacemaking and competition. *American Journal of Psychology, 9,* 507–533.

Trivers, R. L. (1972). Parental investment and sexual selection. In B. Campbell (Ed.), *Sexual selection and the descent of man* (pp. 136–179). Chicago: Aldine.

Trope, Y. (1986). Identification and inferential processes in dispositional attribution. *Psychological Review, 93,* 239–257.

Trope, Y., Cohen, O., & Maoz, Y. (1988). The perceptual and inferential effects of situational inducements on dispositional attribution. *Journal of Personality and Social Psychology, 55,* 165–177.

Tschanz, B. T., & Rhodewalt, F. (2001). Autobiography, reputation, and the self: On the role of evaluative valence and self-consistency of the self-relevant information. *Journal of Experimental Social Psychology, 37,* 32–48.

Turner, C. W., Layton, J. F., & Simons, L. S. (1975). Naturalistic studies of aggressive behavior: Aggressive stimuli, victim visibility, and horn honking. *Journal of Personality and Social Psychology, 31,* 1098–1107.

Turner, M. E., Pratkanis, A. R., Probasco, P., & Leve, C. (1992). Threat, cohesion, and group effectiveness: Testing a social identity maintenance perspective on groupthink. *Journal of Personality and Social Psychology, 63,* 781–796.

Tversky, A., & Kahneman, D. (1973). Availability: A heuristic for judging frequency and probability. *Cognitive Psychology, 5,* 207–232.

Twenge, J. M., & Campbell, W. K. (2003). "Isn't it fun to get the respect that we're going to deserve?" Narcissism, social rejection, and aggression. *Personality and Social Psychology Bulletin, 29,* 261–272.

Tyler, T. R., & Blader, S. L. (2000). *Cooperation in groups: Procedural justice, social identity, and behavioral engagement.* Philadelphia: Psychology Press.

Tyler, T. R., & Schuller, R. A. (1991). Aging and attitude change. *Journal of Personality and Social Psychology, 61,* 689–697.

Uleman, J. S., Newman, L. S., & Moskowitz, G. B. (1996). People as flexible interpreters: Evidence and issues from spontaneous trait inference. In M. P. Zanna (Ed.), *Advances in experimental social psychology* (Vol. 28, pp. 211–279). San Diego, CA: Academic Press.

Underwood, M. K. (2003). *Social aggression among girls.* New York: Guilford Press.

Utz, S. (2004). Self-activation is a two-edged sword: The effects of I primes on cooperation. *Journal of Experimental Social Psychology, 40,* 769–776.

Vallerand, R. J. (1997). Toward a hierarchical model of intrinsic and extrinsic motivation. In M. P. Zanna (Ed.), *Advances in experimental social psychology* (Vol. 29, pp. 271–360). San Diego, CA: Academic Press.

Vallone, R. P., Ross, L., & Lepper, M. R. (1985). The hostile media phenomenon: Biased perception and perceptions of media bias in coverage of the Beirut massacre. *Journal of Personality and Social Psychology, 49,* 577–585.

van der Velde, F. W., & van der Pligt, J. (1991). AIDS-related health behavior: Coping, protection motivation, and previous behavior. *Journal of Behavioral Medicine, 14*, 429–451.

van Dick, R., Wagner, U., Pettigrew, T. F., Christ, O., Wolf, C., Petzel, T., Castro, V. S., & Jackson, J. S. (2004). Role of perceived importance in intergroup contact. *Journal of Personality and Social Psychology, 87*, 211–227.

van IJzendoorn, M. H., & Kroonenberg, P. M. (1988). Cross-cultural patterns of attachment: A meta-analysis of the strange situation. *Child Development, 59*, 147–156.

Van Lange, P. A. M., & Kuhlman, D. M. (1994). Social value orientations and impressions of partner's honesty and intelligence: A test of the might versus morality effect. *Journal of Personality and Social Psychology, 67*, 126–141.

Van Lange, P. A. M., & Sedikides, C. (1998). Being more honest but not necessarily more intelligent than others: Generality and explanations for the Muhammad Ali Effect. *European Journal of Social Psychology, 28*, 675–680.

Vanman, E. J., Saltz, J. L., Nathan, L. R., & Warren, J. A. (2004). Racial discrimination by low-prejudiced Whites: Facial movements as implicit measures of attitudes related to behavior. *Psychological Science, 15*, 711–714.

Van Overwalle, F., & Jordens, K. (2002). An adaptive connectionist model of cognitive dissonance. *Personality and Social Psychology Review, 6*, 204–231.

Van Reekum, C. M., Van den Berg, H., & Frijda, N. H. (1999). Cross-modal preference acquisition: Evaluative conditioning of pictures by affective olfactory and auditory cues. *Cognition and Emotion, 13*, 831–836.

Van Vugt, M., & Hart, C. M. (2004). Social identity as social glue: The origins of group loyalty. *Journal of Personality and Social Psychology, 86*, 585–598.

Van Vugt, M., Jepson, S. F., Hart, C. M., & De Cremer, D. (2004). Autocratic leadership in social dilemmas: A threat to group stability. *Journal of Experimental Social Psychology, 40*, 1–13.

Vargas, P. T., von Hippel, W., & Petty, R. E. (2004). Using partially structured attitude measures to enhance the attitude-behavior relationship. *Personality and Social Psychology Bulletin, 30*, 197–211.

Vasquez, E. A., Denson, T. F., Pedersen, W. C., Stenstrom, D. M., & Miller, N. (2005). The moderating effect of trigger intensity on triggered displaced aggression. *Journal of Experimental Social Psychology, 41*, 61–67.

Verkuyten, M. (2004). Emotional reactions to and support for immigrant policies: Attributed responsibilities to categories of asylum seekers. *Social Justice Research, 17*, 293–314.

Vidmar, N., & Crinklaw, L. D. (1974). Attributing responsibility for an accident: A methodological and conceptual critique. *Canadian Journal of Behavioural Science, 6*, 112–130.

Vignoles, V. L., Chryssochoou, X., & Breakwell, G. M. (2000). The distinctiveness principle: Identity, meaning, and the boundary of cultural relativity. *Personality and Social Psychology Review, 4*, 337–354.

Vinokur, A., & Burnstein, E. (1974). Effects of partially-shared persuasive arguments on group-induced shifts: A group-problem-solving approach. *Journal of Personality and Social Psychology, 29*, 305–315.

Visser, P. S., & Krosnick, J. A. (1998). Development of attitude strength over the life cycle: Surge and decline. *Journal of Personality and Social Psychology, 75*, 1389–1410.

Visser, P. S., & Mirabile, R. R. (2004). Attitudes in the social context: The impact of social network composition on individual-level attitude strength. *Journal of Personality and Social Psychology, 87*, 779–795.

Vonk, R. (2002). Self-serving interpretations of flattery: Why ingratiation works. *Journal of Personality and Social Psychology, 82*, 515–526.

Vroom, V. H., & Yetton, P. W. (1973). *Leadership and decision-making*. Pittsburg, PA: University of Pittsburg Press.

Wade-Benzoni, K. A., Okumura, T., Brett, J. M., Moore, D. A., Tenbrunsel, A. E., & Bazerman, M. H. (2002). Cognitions and behavior in asymmetric social dilemmas: A comparison of two cultures. *Journal of Applied Psychology, 87*, 87–95.

Walker, I., & Smith, H. J. (Eds.). (2002). *Relative deprivation: Specification, development, and integration*. Cambridge, UK: Cambridge University Press.

Wallach, M., Kogan, N., & Bem, D. J. (1962). Group influence on individual risk taking. *Journal of Abnormal and Social Psychology, 65*, 75–86.

Waller, J. (2002). *Becoming evil: How ordinary people commit genocide and mass murder*. New York: Oxford University Press.

Waller, N. G., Kojetin, B. A., Bouchard, T. J., Jr., Lykken, D. T., & Tellegen, A. (1990). Genetic and environmental influences on religious interests, attitudes, and values: A study of twins reared apart and together. *Psychological Science, 1*, 138–142.

Walster, E., Walster, G. W., & Berscheid, E. (1978). *Equity: Theory and research*. Boston, MA: Allyn & Bacon.

Walster, E., Walster, G. W., & Traupmann, J. (1978). Equity and premarital sex. *Journal of Personality and Social Psychology, 36*, 82–92.

Walther, E. (2002). Guilty by mere association: Evaluative conditioning and the spreading attitude effect. *Journal of Personality and Social Psychology, 82*, 919–934.

Waltz, J., Babcock, J. C., Jacobson, N. S., & Gottman, J. M. (2000). Testing a typology of batterers. *Journal of Consulting and Clinical Psychology, 68*, 658–669.

Webb, W., & Worchel, S. (1986). Trust and distrust. In S. Worchel & W. G. Austin (Eds.), *The psychology of intergroup relations* (2nd ed.). Chicago: Nelson-Hall.

Weber, J. M., Kopelman, S., & Messick, D. M. (2004). A conceptual review of decision making in social dilemmas: Applying a logic of appropriateness. *Personality and Social Psychology Review, 8*, 281–307.

Webster, G. D. (2003). Prosocial behavior in families: Moderators of resource sharing. *Journal of Experimental Social Psychology, 39*, 644–652.

Wegener, D. T., & Petty, R. E. (1997). The flexible correction model: The role of naive theories in bias correction. In M. P. Zanna (Ed.), *Advances in experimental social psychology* (Vol. 29, pp. 141–208). San Diego, CA: Academic Press.

Weigel, R. H., & Newman, L. S. (1976). Increasing attitude-behavior consistency by broadening the scope of the behavioral measure. *Journal of Personality and Social Psychology, 33*, 793–802.

Weinstein, N. D. (1980). Unrealistic optimism about future life events. *Journal of Personality and Social Psychology, 39*, 806–820.

Weinstein, N. D. (1984). Why it won't happen to me: Perceptions of risk factors and susceptibility. *Health Psychology, 3*, 431–457.

Weinstein, N. D., & Klein, W. M. (1996). Unrealistic optimism: Present and future. *Journal of Social and Clinical Psychology, 15*, 1–8.

Weiss, E. M., Kemmier, G., Deisenhammer, E. A., Fleischhacker, W. W., & Delazer, M. (2003). Sex differences in cognitive function. *Personality and Individual Differences, 35*, 863–875.

Welch, D. (1983). *Nazi propaganda*. Beckenham, UK: Croom Helm.

Wells, G. L. (1993). What do we know about eyewitness identification? *American Psychologist, 48*, 553–571.

Wells, G. L., & Olson, E. A. (2001). The other-race effect in eyewitness identification: What do we do about it? *Psychology, Public Policy, and Law, 7*, 230–246.

Wells, G. L., Olson, E. A., & Charman, S. D. (2002). The confidence of eyewitnesses in their identifications from lineups. *Current Directions in Psychological Science, 11*, 151–154.

Werner, N. E., & Crick, N. R. (1999). Relational aggression and social-psychological adjustment in a college sample. *Journal of Abnormal Psychology, 108*, 615–623.

Werth, L., Strack, F., & Forster, J. (2002). Certainty and uncertainty: The two faces of the hindsight bias. *Organizational Behavior and Human Decision Processes, 87*, 323–341.

Wethington, E., & Kessler, R. C. (1986). Perceived support, received support, and adjustment to stressful life events. *Journal of Health and Social Behavior, 27*(March), 78–89.

Whalley, L. J., & Deary, I. J. (2001). Longitudinal cohort study of childhood IQ and survival up to age 76. *British Medical Journal, 322,* 1–5.

Wheeler, L., & Kim, Y. (1997). What is beautiful is culturally good: The physical attractiveness stereotype has different content in collectivistic cultures. *Personality and Social Psychology Bulletin, 23,* 795–800.

Wheeler, L., Martin, R., & Suls, J. M. (1997). The proxy model of social comparison for self-assessment of ability. *Personality and Social Psychology Review, 1,* 54–61.

Wheeler, S. C., & Petty, R. E. (2001). The effects of stereotype activation on behavior: A review of possible mechanisms. *Psychological Bulletin, 127,* 797–826.

White, J. R. (2003). Sex differences in personality in the United States and the Philippines: An investigation of cross-cultural universality. *Dissertation Abstracts International: Section B. The Sciences and Engineering, 63,* 3507.

Whitely, B. E., Jr. (1990). The relationship of heterosexuals' attributions for the causes of homosexuality to attitudes toward lesbians and gay men. *Personality and Social Psychology Bulletin, 16,* 369–377.

Whiting, B. B., Whiting, J. W. M., & Longabaugh, R. (1975). *Children of six cultures: A psycho-cultural analysis.* Cambridge, MA: Harvard University Press.

Whyte, G. (1993). Escalating commitment in individual and group decision making: A prospect theory approach. *Organizational Behavior and Human Decision Processes, 54,* 430–455.

Wicker, A. W. (1969). Attitude versus actions: The relationship of verbal and overt behavioral responses to attitude objects. *Journal of Social Issues, 25*(4), 41–78.

Wiggins, E. C. (2000). Federal regulation. In A. E. Kazdin (Ed.), *Encyclopedia of psychology* (Vol. 4, pp. 1–2). Washington, DC: American Psychological Association.

Wilcox, G. B., Murphy, J. H., & Sheldon, P. S. (1985). Effects of attractiveness of the endorser on the performance of testimonial ads. *Journalism Quarterly, 62,* 548–552.

Wildschut, T., Pinter, B., Vevea, J. L., Insko, C. A., & Schopler, J. (2003). Beyond the group mind: A quantitative review of the interindividual-intergroup discontinuity effect. *Psychological Bulletin, 129,* 698–722.

Williams, D. R., & Williams-Morris, R. (2000). Racism and mental health: The African American experience. *Ethnicity and Health, 5,* 243–268.

Williams, G. C., Cox, E. M., Hedberg, V. A., & Deci, E. L. (2000). Extrinsic life goals and health-risk behaviors in adolescents. *Journal of Applied Social Psychology, 30,* 1756–1771.

Williams, K. D., Cheung, C. K. T., & Choi, W. (2000). Cyberostracism: Effects of being ignored over the internet. *Journal of Personality and Social Psychology, 79,* 748–762.

Williams, K. D., Harkins, S. G., & Latane, B. (1981). Identifiability as a deterrent to social loafing: Two cheering experiments. *Journal of Personality and Social Psychology, 40,* 303–311.

Williams, R. B., Barefoot, J. C., Califf, R. M., Haney, T. L., Saunders, W. B., Pryor, D. B., et al. (1992). Prognostic importance of social and economic resources among medically treated patients with angiographically documented coronary artery disease. *Journal of the American Medical Association, 267,* 520–524.

Wills, T. A. (1981). Downward comparison principles in social psychology. *Psychological Bulletin, 90,* 245–291.

Wills, T. A. (1991). Social support and interpersonal relationships. In M. Clark (Ed.), *Prosocial behavior* (pp. 265–289). Newbury Park, CA: Sage.

Wilson, A. E., & Ross, M. (2000). The frequency of temporal-self and social comparisons in people's personal appraisals. *Journal of Personality and Social Psychology, 5,* 928–942.

Wilson, A. E., & Ross, M. (2001). From chump to champ: People's appraisals of their earlier and present selves. *Journal of Personality and Social Psychology, 80,* 572–584.

Wilson, T. D., Damiani, M., & Shelton, J. N. (2002). Improving the academic performance of college students with brief attributional interventions. In J. Aronson (Ed.), *Improving academic achievement: Impact of psychological factors on education* (pp. 89–108). New York: Academic Press.

Wilson, T. D., Lindsey, S., & Schooler, T. Y. (2000). A model of dual attitudes. *Psychological Review, 107,* 101–126.

Wilson, T. D., Wheatley, T. P., Kurtz, J. L., Dunn, E. W., & Gilbert, D. T. (2004). When to fire: Anticipatory versus postevent reconstrual of uncontrollable events. *Personality and Social Psychology Bulletin, 30,* 340–351.

Winquist, J. R., & Larson, J. R., Jr. (2004). Sources of the discontinuity effect: Playing against a group versus being in a group. *Journal of Experimental Social Psychology, 40,* 675–682.

Winter, L., & Uleman, J. S. (1984). When are social judgments made? Evidence for the spontaneousness of trait inferences. *Journal of Personality and Social Psychology, 47,* 237–252.

Wispé, L. (1986). The distinction between sympathy and empathy: To call forth a concept, a word is needed. *Journal of Personality and Social Psychology, 50*(2), 314–321.

Wit, A. P., & Kerr, N. L. (2002). "Me versus just us versus us all" categorization and cooperation in nested social dilemmas. *Journal of Personality and Social Psychology, 83,* 616–637.

Witte, K., & Allen, M. (2000). A meta-analysis of fear appeals: Implications for effective public health campaigns. *Health Education and Behavior, 27,* 591–615.

Witte, K., Meyer, G., & Martell, D. (2001). *Effective health risk messages: A step-by-step guide.* Thousand Oaks, CA: Sage.

Wittenbrink, B., Judd, C. M., & Park, B. (1997). Evidence for racial prejudice at the implicit level and its relationship with questionnaire measures. *Journal of Personality and Social Psychology, 72,* 262–274.

Wittenbrink, B., Judd, C. M., & Park, B. (2001). Spontaneous prejudice in context: Variability in automatically activated attitudes. *Journal of Personality and Social Psychology, 81,* 815–827.

Wolf, S. (1987). Majority and minority influence: A social impact analysis. In M. P. Zanna, J. M. Olson, & C. P. Herman (Eds.), *Social influence: The Ontario symposium* (Vol. 5, pp. 207–235). Hillsdale, NJ: Erlbaum.

Wolfe, D. A. (1999). *Child abuse: Implications for child development and psychopathology.* Thousand Oaks, CA: Sage.

Wolsko, C., Park, B., Judd, C. M., & Wittenbrink, B. (2000). Framing interethnic ideology: Effects of multicultural and color-blind perspectives on judgments of groups and individuals. *Journal of Personality and Social Psychology, 78,* 635–654.

Wood, J. V. (1989). Theory and research concerning social comparisons of personal attributes. *Psychological Bulletin, 106,* 231–248.

Wood, J. V., Michela, J. L., & Giordano, C. (2000). Downward comparison in everyday life: Reconciling self-enhancement models with the mood-cognition priming model. *Journal of Personality and Social Psychology, 79,* 565–579.

Wood, J. V., & Van der Zee, K. (1997). Social comparisons among cancer patients: Under what conditions are comparisons upward and downward? In B. P. Buunk & F. X. Gibbons (Eds.), *Health, coping, and well-being* (pp. 299–328). Mahwah, NJ: Erlbaum.

Wood, W. (2000). Attitude change: Persuasion and social influence. *Annual Review of Psychology, 50,* 539–570.

Wood, W., & Eagly, A. H. (2002). A cross-cultural analysis of the behavior of women and men: Implications for the origins of sex differences. *Psychological Bulletin, 128,* 699–727.

Wood, W., & Kallgren, C. A. (1988). Communicator attributes and persuasion: Recipients' access to attitude-relevant information in memory. *Personality and Social Psychology Bulletin, 14,* 172–182.

Wood, W., Wong, F. Y., & Chachere, G. (1991). Effects of media violence on viewers' aggression in unconstrained social interaction. *Psychological Bulletin, 109,* 371–383.

Worchel, S. (1992). Beyond a commodity theory analysis of censorship: When abundance and personalism enhance scarcity effects. *Basic and Applied Social Psychology, 13,* 79–92.

Worchel, S., Andreoli, V., & Folger, R. (1977). Intergroup cooperation and intergroup attraction: The effect of previous interaction and outcome of combined effort. *Journal of Experimental Social Psychology, 13,* 131–140.

Worchel, S., & Arnold, S. E. (1973). The effects of censorship and attractiveness of the censor on attitude change. *Journal of Experimental Social Psychology, 9,* 365–377.

Worchel, S., & Austin, W. G. (Eds.). (1986). *The social psychology of intergroup relations* (2nd ed.). Chicago: Nelson-Hall.

Worchel, S., & Brehm, J. W. (1970). Effect of threats to attitudinal freedom as a function of agreement with the communicator. *Journal of Personality and Social Psychology, 14,* 18–22.

Worchel, S., Lee, J., & Adewole, A. (1975). Effects of supply and demand on ratings of object value. *Journal of Personality and Social Psychology, 32,* 906–914.

Word, C. H., Zanna, M. P., & Cooper, J. (1974). The nonverbal mediation of self-fulfilling prophecies in interracial interaction. *Journal of Experimental Social Psychology, 10,* 109–120.

Wrightsman, L. S. (1991). *Psychology and the legal system* (2nd ed.). Pacific Groves, CA: Brooks/Cole.

Wrobleski, H. M., & Hess, K. M. (2006). *Introduction to law enforcement and criminal justice* (8th ed.). Belmont, CA: Wadsworth.

Wyer, N. A. (2004). Not all stereotypic biases are created equal: Evidence for a stereotype-disconfirming bias. *Personality and Social Psychology Bulletin, 30,* 706–720.

Yaniv, I. (2004). The benefit of additional opinions. *Current Directions in Psychological Science, 13,* 75–78.

Zaheer, A., McEvily, B., & Perrone, V. (1998). Does trust matter? Exploring the effects of interorganizational and interpersonal trust on performance. *Organizational Science, 9,* 141–159.

Zajonc, R. B. (1965). Social facilitation. *Science, 149,* 269–274.

Zajonc, R. B. (1968). Attitudinal effects of mere exposure. *Journal of Personality and Social Psychology, 9* (Monograph suppl., No. 2, Pt. 2), 1–27.

Zanna, M. P. (2004). The naive epistemology of a working social psychologist (or the working epistemology of a naive social psychologist): The value of taking "temporary givens" seriously. *Personality and Social Psychology Review, 8,* 210–218.

Zanna, M. P., & Cooper, J. (1974). Dissonance and the pill: An attribution approach to studying the arousal properties of dissonance. *Journal of Personality and Social Psychology, 29,* 703–709.

Zanna, M. P., Detweiler, R. A., & Olson, J. M. (1984). Physiological mediation of attitude maintenance, formation, and change. In W. M. Waid (Ed.), *Sociophysiology* (pp. 163–195). New York: Springer-Verlag.

Zanna, M. P., Kiesler, C. A., & Pilkonis, P. A. (1970). Positive and negative attitudinal affect established by classical conditioning. *Journal of Personality and Social Psychology, 38,* 432–440.

Zanna, M. P., & Olson, J. M. (Eds.). (1994). *The psychology of prejudice: The Ontario symposium* (Vol. 7). Mahwah, NJ: Erlbaum.

Zanna, M. P., & Rempel, J. K. (1988). Attitudes: A new look at an old concept. In D. Bar-Tal & A. W. Kruglanski (Eds.), *The social psychology of knowledge* (pp. 315–334). Cambridge, UK: Cambridge University Press.

Zanna, M. P., & Sande, G. N. (1987). The effect of collective actions on the attitudes of individual group members: A dissonance analysis. In M. P. Zanna, J. M. Olson, & C. P. Herman (Eds.), *Social influence: The Ontario symposium* (Vol. 5, pp. 151–163). Hillsdale, NJ: Erlbaum.

Zárate, M. A., Garcia, B., Garza, A. A., & Hitlan, R. T. (2004). Cultural threat and perceived realisitic group conflict as dual predictors of prejudice. *Journal of Experimental Social Psychology, 40,* 99–105.

Zawadzki, B. (1948). Limitations on the scapegoat theory of prejudice. *Journal of Abnormal and Social Psychology, 43,* 127–141.

Zillmann, D., & Bryant, J. (1974). Effect of residual excitation on the emotional response to provocation and delayed aggressive behavior. *Journal of Personality and Social Psychology, 30,* 782–791.

Zillmann, D., Katcher, A. H., & Milavsky, B. (1972). Excitation transfer from physical exercise to subsequent aggressive behavior. *Journal of Experimental Social Psychology, 8,* 247–259.

Zimbardo, P. G. (1969). The human choice: Individuation, reason, and order vs. deindividuation, impulse, and chaos. In W. J. Arnold & D. Levine (Eds.), *Nebraska Symposium on Motivation* (Vol. 17, pp. 237–307). Lincoln: University of Nebraska Press.

Zimbardo, P. G. (1972). *The Stanford prison experiment.* Slide show produced by Philip G. Zimbardo, Inc.

Zimbardo, P. G., Weisenberg, M., & Firestone, I. (1965). Communication effectiveness in producing public conformity and private attitude change. *Journal of Personality, 33,* 233–255.

Zuckerman, M. (1995). Good and bad humors: Biochemical bases of personality and its disorders. *Psychological Science, 6,* 325–332.

Zuckerman, M., DePaulo, B. M., & Rosenthal, R. (1981). Verbal and nonverbal communication of deception. In L. Berkowitz (Ed.), *Advances in experimental social psychology* (Vol. 14, pp. 1–59). New York: Academic Press.

Zuckerman, M., Koestner, R., & Alton, A. O. (1984). Learning to detect deception. *Journal of Personality and Social Psychology, 46,* 519–528.

# Author Index

# Subject Index